The Oxford Encyclopedia of

ISLAM AND WOMEN

The Oxford Encyclopedia of Islam and Women

Natana J. DeLong-Bas
EDITOR IN CHIEF

VOLUME 1
Ābīsh Khātūn bint Saʿd II –Mutʿah

OXFORD
UNIVERSITY PRESS

OXFORD
UNIVERSITY PRESS

Oxford University Press is a department of the University of Oxford.
It furthers the University's objective of excellence in research,
scholarship, and education by publishing worldwide.

Oxford New York
Auckland Cape Town Dar es Salaam Hong Kong Karachi
Kuala Lumpur Madrid Melbourne Mexico City Nairobi
New Delhi Shanghai Taipei Toronto

With offices in
Argentina Austria Brazil Chile Czech Republic France Greece
Guatemala Hungary Italy Japan Poland Portugal Singapore
South Korea Switzerland Thailand Turkey Ukraine Vietnam

Oxford is a registered trademark of Oxford University Press in the UK and certain other countries.

Published by Oxford University Press, Inc.
198 Madison Avenue, New York, NY 10016
www.oup.com

Library of Congress Cataloging-in-Publication Data
The Oxford encyclopedia of Islam and women / Natana J. DeLong-Bas, editor in chief.
p. cm.
Includes bibliographical references and index.
ISBN 978-0-19-976446-4—ISBN 978-0-19-999803-6—ISBN 978-0-19-999804-3
1. Women in Islam—Encyclopedias. I. DeLong-Bas, Natana J.
BP173.4.O94 2013
297.082'03—dc23
2012050203

Printed in the United States of America
on acid-free paper

This work is dedicated to Muslim women of every time and place whose courage, spirit, and determination to make their voices, presence, and contributions known made this project possible.

❖

May you live in health, in safety, and in a world that recognizes and appreciates your achievements and encourages you to continue to dream, to dare, and to inspire.

❖

And to my husband, Christophe, who exemplifies the true meaning of zawj *– spouse, partner, and soulmate without whom I could never be complete.*

EDITORIAL AND PRODUCTION STAFF

Acquiring Editor
Damon Zucca

Development Editor
Anne Whittaker

Editorial Assistant
Lauren Konopko

Production Editor
Claudia Dukeshire

Copyeditors
Johanna Baboukis
Dorothy Bauhoff
Michele Bowman
Patti Brecht
Mary Flower
Mary Funchion
Kristen Holt-Browning
Richard Isomaki
Theresa V. Kornak
Jan A. Maas
Benjamin Sadock
Alan Thwaits

Proofreaders
Alan H. Hartley
Heather Dubnick
Carol Holmes

Indexer
Katharyn Dunham

Compositor
SPi

Manufacturing Controller
Genieve Shaw

Cover Design
Brady McNamara

Managing Editor
Mary Araneo

Production Manager
David Ford

Senior Editor, Development
Alixandra Gould

Publisher
Damon Zucca

Contents

The Oxford Encyclopedia of Islam and Women

List of Articles

Introduction to the Series

The **Oxford Islamic World Encyclopedia Series** is a series of four authoritative reference works, two volumes each, within a major subfield of Islamic studies: *Islam and Women*; *Islam and Politics*; *Islam and Law*; and *Philosophy, Science, and Technology in Islam*. Each multivolume set has its own editor in chief and editorial board.

Although the *Oxford Encyclopedia of the Islamic World* offers a comprehensive foundation of information, the four two-volume sets form an eight-volume series that provides far more detailed study of many aspects of the Islamic world. The Islamic World Encyclopedia Series has been designed to be a primary reference not only for scholars and students of religion, history, and the social sciences but also for government, media and corporate analysts, as well as interfaith organizations, which will find a reliable source of information for many topics and issues not covered by existing reference works and coverage in emerging areas.

Each multivolume set includes general overview articles from the *Oxford Encyclopedia of the Islamic World* as a foundation, drawing on its extensive coverage of Islam and Muslim societies and communities going back to the beginnings of Islam. However, the majority of articles are newly commissioned in-depth entries written by leading experts. Upon completion, the four sets will form an eight-volume series that taken together will provide an in-depth, comprehensive, and detailed study of key aspects of the Islamic world.

Each encyclopedia is offered in print and e-book format. Customers interested in a complete reference library in Islamic studies will be able to purchase the series. Because of the interdisciplinary nature of the research, we are also offering each set individually. All of the newly commissioned material will be included in the *Oxford Islamic Studies Online* website (http://www.oxfordislamicstudies.com), where it can be accessed in one place.

The Oxford Encyclopedia of Islam and Women
Editor in Chief
Natana J. DeLong-Bas
Boston College

Scholarship on Islam and women has expanded exponentially over the past twenty years, with increasing specialization within the field as well as cross-pollination between other fields and disciplines. Recent scholarship has tended to focus on expanding both historical and contemporary case studies relative to countries and regions through both archival and theoretical studies, as well as mapping out transnational trends and the reinterpretation of ideas and disciplines by Muslim women throughout the world.

With this surge in interest, a genuine need has developed for a systematic reference work to provide balanced comprehensive coverage of the field. An up-to-date, carefully organized reference source is urgently needed to help scholars assess the progress that has been made and to chart the path for future research. *The Oxford Encyclopedia of Islam and Women* is designed to meet this need by providing clear, current, comprehensive information on the major topics of scholarly interest within the study of women and Islam.

The Oxford Encyclopedia of Islam and Politics
Editor in Chief
Emad El-Din Shahin
The American University in Cairo

The Oxford Encyclopedia of Islam and Politics provides in-depth coverage of the political dimensions of Islam and the Muslim world. At no time has the understanding of the nature, political dimensions, and implications of these developments been more needed. Developments in Muslim societies in the nineteenth and twentieth centuries have highlighted the need for a major reference work focusing primarily on the political dimensions of Islam.

The recognition of internal decay and relentless quest for reform; the collapse of the Islamic caliphate; the fall of most parts of the Muslim world under Western colonialism; the emergence of nation-states; the dominance of secular ideologies; the rise of Islamic revivalist movements and faith-based political, economic, and social alternatives; and the confrontation between Islamic movements and secular-inspired regimes have constituted major turning points in the contemporary history of Muslim societies. *The Oxford Encyclopedia of Islam and Politics* seeks to target specialized users, scholars, students, experts, policy makers, and media specialists and offer them accurate and balanced scholarship on Islam and politics.

The Oxford Encyclopedia of Islam and Law
Editor in Chief
Jonathan AC Brown
Georgetown University

Recent years have witnessed an increase in scholarly publications on the subject of Islamic law, and the topic has received growing attention in the popular press. *The Oxford Encyclopedia of Islam and Law* is intended to be the primary reference source for questions of Islamic law. It is conceived to help scholars assess the progress that has been made and chart the path for future developments in this flourishing area of research.

The *Oxford Encyclopedia of Islam and Law* is designed to meet this need by providing clear, current, comprehensive information on the major topics of scholarly interest within the study of Islam and the law. It is intended to be the main reference source for questions of Islamic law among engaged readers in the West, and academics in general and legal researchers in particular. This encyclopedia contains conceptual entries that help readers from a Western legal background understand Islamic law, and offers an extensive listing of Islamic legal technical terms, with an emphasis on discussing how Islamic law influences or exists in modern nation-states.

The Oxford Encyclopedia of Philosophy, Science, and Technology in Islam
Editor in Chief
Ibrahim Kalin
Georgetown University

Philosophy and science in the Islamic tradition have not yet been covered systematically in a single, authoritative reference work. *The Oxford Encyclopedia of Philosophy, Science, and Techno-*

logy in Islam builds on the subjects of philosophy, science, and technology presented in *The Oxford Encyclopedia of the Islamic World,* expanding them to provide comprehensive and in-depth coverage of the achievements of classical Islam as well as a detailed survey of the main features of philosophy, science, medicine, and technology in the Muslim world.

Like other major religious traditions before the modern period, the Islamic tradition treated philosophy, science, and technology as part of a single quest to understand the reality of things. Nature was studied and researched as a subject matter for both philosophy and science. The methodology and subject matter of the classical sciences allowed philosophy and the natural sciences to interact with one another in complementary ways. Technology, a field in which the Muslim world produced an immense body of work, from astrolabes to watermills, developed as an extension of both philosophy and science. Advanced techniques and technological devices quickly became a feature of urban life in the vast Muslim world stretching over the middle belt of the globe. Royal patronage was an important catalyst for the development of scientific institutions, including hospitals, libraries, and observatories.

This encyclopedia also covers the modern period during which interaction with modern (Western) philosophy and science as well as the transfer of modern technology into Muslim countries has led to the rise of new schools of thought and generated heated debates about Islam, tradition, and modernity up to the present time.

John L. Esposito
Georgetown University

Preface

The motivation behind *The Oxford Encyclopedia of Islam and Women* was to provide a supplemental volume to *The Oxford Encyclopedia of the Islamic World* that would focus more deeply on a particular theme, in this case, women and gender. Although there were some conceptual concerns about splitting off this topic—thus running the risk of giving the false impression that women's issues are somehow separate from the major issues facing and being addressed in the Islamic world—we decided to take this as an opportunity to showcase the myriad ways in which women, both past and present, have played a vital role at all levels of family and society. We also sought to avoid the dual pitfall of focusing so exclusively on women's herstory that men ended up being written out of history altogether. Our hope was to provide a more balanced approach—their story—in order to show interconnectedness. With this goal in mind, the encyclopedia was organized around ten themes that the editors believed would initiate new conversations and ways of thinking about what often seem to be standard issues.

Of particular concern in the selection of themes and entries was the shared goal of challenging stereotypes of women as passive recipients, whether of political policies or charity, in favor of restoring their contributions as active agents, including in politics and philanthropy, such as is highlighted in *Politics and Polity*, and *Wealth, Welfare, and Labor*. By choosing the theme of *Self and Body*, we sought to examine how women's bodies are used and controlled not only by authorities and religions, but also, more importantly, by women themselves. Similarly, *Community and Society* was selected because it offers the opportunity to demonstrate women's integral roles within their communities and societies and connecting them to the same, rather than sidelining them to exclusively female issues. This encyclopedia splits topics typically brought together under "religion" into two independent sections: *Religion, Theory, Practice, and Interpretation*, and *Sharīʿah, Fiqh, Philosophy, and Reason*, to highlight the varying levels at which religion is used and has an impact on both private and public life, and to assert the important differences between theory and practice and levels of authority. This distinction also shows how women are increasingly part of the conversation, rather than simply subjects of discussion.

The inclusion of *Science, Medicine, and Education* challenges the predominant stereotype that these endeavors have been historically male-dominated, while also demonstrating that women have made some of their most remarkable contributions to these fields in recent decades. Education has particularly opened many doors for women who are entering the workforce and professional careers in ever-larger numbers, changing both social and family dynamics. This section addresses the often overlooked historical contributions of women and attempts to challenge the assumption that there is an institutional monopoly on work in these fields by highlighting women's work in informal settings. *Culture and Expression* encompasses a variety of fields, including literature, cinema, and contemporary means of expression, such as television, the Internet, social media, and blogs, bringing attention to the variety of media women use to express themselves, often to different audiences and with particular goals, rather than simply focusing on the medium itself.

Issues related to *Immigration and Minorities* appear frequently in headline news, although "immigrants" and "minorities" are typically presented as monolithic entities. The articles on these topics seek to introduce more complex ways of analyzing what these labels mean based on who assigns them, and to explore different constructs of these terms. Because so much theoretical literature related to women, gender, and feminism has appeared since the 1970s, these topics are given their own theme—*Scholarly Approaches and Theoretical Constructs*—to give a sense of their historical development with respect to, about, and, especially, by Muslim women.

The editors of this volume believed it was important to encourage cross-conversation between disciplines and approaches. We challenged authors to make connections between the specific topics and broader methodologies, such as feminist theory, postcolonial thought, and world history. Our goal was to highlight the cross-pollination of ideas and experiences, as well as the interconnectedness of historical development. The resulting compilation of 451 entries by 267 contributors representing 38 countries reflects this global, interdisciplinary vision.

We decided to include a significant number of biographies in this collection, not to subscribe to the "great woman in history" approach, but to restore these voices in history and to draw attention to new voices as they make history. In each case, care has been taken to demonstrate how the individual represents broader trends or concerns without asserting that she worked alone or in a vacuum. The inclusion of these biographies is intended to serve as a response to claims by various parties that women have never served in a particular capacity before, thus purportedly justifying ongoing refusal to allow them to do so now. The provision of a variety of examples is intended to challenge this status quo and to create space for new conversation.

Many international flashpoints occurred during the course of this project, not the least of which were the Arab Spring and its resulting questions about the "appropriate" role of women in the new governments and societies and who was to determine what such a role would be, various laws in different European countries and even FIFA banning certain types of clothing typically associated with Muslim women, and periodic reports of Muslim women being charged with adultery in the aftermath of rape and being stoned or lashed to death, as sadly occurred in Pakistan and Bangladesh. Yet, even in the midst of such contention, some victories were also achieved: women played a prominent role in the events of the Arab Spring, as leaders, organizers, and participants, and a number of Muslim women were appointed to different positions for the first time; Saudi women received the right to vote and serve as full members of the Shura Council; three Bahraini women were appointed as *muezzins* (callers to prayer); and Malaysia appointed its first female judge and launched a TV show *Solehah* to seek the best female preachers. All these issues directly relate to issues we sought to address in the encyclopedia—women's agency, the increasing insertion of women's voices into even the most traditionally male aspects of religious interpretation in public ways, the creation of new public spaces for women's voices and contributions, and the very real need to continue to raise awareness of the ways in which religion has been and continues to be misused and misinterpreted to commit injustice against women, as well as some of the creative and insightful ways women are fighting back against such abuse by reasserting and reinterpreting their religion themselves.

Using the Encyclopedia

Entries in the encyclopedia are arranged alphabetically for ease of access and a table of contents appears at its beginning. A topical outline listing all the entries is included for each theme in alphabetical order at the end of the encyclopedia, along with a list of contributors and a full index. There are also overview articles for each theme in the main body of the encyclopedia, written by the responsible area editor, explaining the theoretical approaches undertaken in organizing and analyzing the theme. Cross-references are provided at the end of each article in order to guide readers to other related topics that may be of interest. "Blind entries" are also included to direct readers to the main entry terms from alternate titles.

This volume contains a variety of linguistic origins, mainly Arabic, Farsi, and Turkish, but Urdu, Bahasa Malaysia, Bahasa Indonesia as well, in addition to some African dialects, among others. Anglicized versions of words have been standardized. Diacritical marks have been used to indicate long vowels and non-English characters. In a few cases, such as "hijab" and "jihad," the words appear without diacritical marks because they have passed into common English usage. Finally, we have elected to use the word "God," rather than "Allah," throughout in order to make clear the connection between the Abrahamic faith traditions.

Acknowledgments

The board of area editors for this volume was selected with the goal of combining expertise in different disciplines, geographic regions, and time periods. In working on this encyclopedia, we were sure to reflect the goal of not just talking *about*, but talking *with*, Muslim women from the very beginning, as well as to provide personal connection to and experience with different geographic regions and the interpretations of Islam particular to them, as shown through our collective connections to Bangladesh, Egypt, the Gulf, Sudan, and the United States.

It has been a delight to work with a talented board whose collective vision and dedication made this volume what it is. Asma Afsaruddin often led the way with timely submissions and revisions, and a positive outlook and energy to keep us all moving forward. Hibba Abugideiri juggled her responsibilities for the encyclopedia in the midst of welcoming a new baby into the world while also caring for a toddler and teaching full-time. Heba Raouf provided the intellectual vision at the beginning by challenging the board to break out of past standard themes and create our own framework. Her voice from inside Tahrir Square in Cairo during the uprisings that led to the fall of the Mubarak regime and ongoing work within the movement for democracy in Egypt has kept us all mindful of the importance of completing this work at this moment in time. To Asma, Hibba, and Heba, "alf mabruk" for a job well done and many thanks for bringing this project to fruition.

In addition to the editorial board, it took a team of dedicated people to bring this project to light, from its conception through its birth.

Many thanks are due, especially, to our hard-working contributors who took seriously their commitment to write substantive pieces connecting their topics to broader issues, responded graciously to our queries and requests for revisions, and, in many cases, pushed us further in our own thinking about the issues, opening our eyes to different ways of conceiving topics and adding a wealth of new information and resources in the process. It has been an honor to have the voices of senior scholars included in this volume and we are delighted to include some exciting new young scholars as well.

Thanks are due to Damon Zucca, acquiring editor, who began the conversation about the project in October 2009 and shepherded it through the construction process, offering valuable feedback with respect to how it fit into the bigger picture of *Oxford Islamic Studies Online*, as well as narrowing the considerable number of proposed entries.

Our deepest appreciation goes to Mary Funchion, former development editor, who cheerfully and confidently steered the project forward and took over portions of its administration, contacting and following up with authors and keeping the project on track. Her departure in May 2012 for other responsibilities was a loss to the project that could have proven disastrous, but we were fortunate to have two capable and committed interim support team members: editorial assistant Lauren Konopko and senior editor Alixandra Gould. Then, in June 2012, Anne Whittaker came on board as our new development editor and brought the project home. Anne enthusiastically jumped into the encyclopedia and doggedly pursued both articles and authors. She has been my right arm in the final stages of this project, providing a needed sense of humor, energy, and encouragement. We simply could not have completed it on time without her.

John Esposito, as series editor, has provided guidance, feedback, and support throughout, always believing in the importance of this project and quickly responding to any questions and concerns despite his own pressing schedule. He truly exemplifies and sets the gold standard for a mentor and deeply valued colleague and friend.

As often happens with projects of this scope and length, we were deeply saddened by the deaths of a few contributors, while others had to drop out because of extensive commitments or due to family challenges. We also had the joy of sharing in the welcoming of new lives as babies were born and new married couples as they came into existence.

Finally, we must extend a heartfelt thank-you to the husbands, fathers, and extended families and friends who took seriously the commitments of partnership, family, and community, especially by sharing child-care and household responsibilities and providing mutual support in career-building with us so that we could dedicate a portion of our time and attention to bringing this project to fruition, while remaining connected to our families.

Natana J. DeLong-Bas

Common Abbreviations Used in This Work

AD	*anno Domini,* in the year of the Lord
AH	*Anno Hijra,* in the year of migration from Meccato to Medina
b.	Born
BCE	before the common era (= bc)
c.	*circa,* about, approximately
CE	common era (= ad)
cf.	*confer,* compare
d.	Died
diss.	Dissertation
ed.	editor (pl., eds), edition
f.	and following (pl., ff.)
fl.	*floruit,* flourished
l.	line (pl., ll.)
n.	Note
n.d.	no date
no.	Number
n.p.	no place
n.s.	new series
p.	page (pl., pp.)
pt.	Part
rev.	Revised
ser.	Series
supp.	Supplement
vol.	volume (pl., vols.)

THE OXFORD ENCYCLOPEDIA OF ISLAM AND WOMEN

A

Ābish Khātūn bint Saʿd II. c. 1260–86/7 CE (r. 1265–1285) Ruler of Fārs Province, wife of Mongol prince Tash-Möngke bin Hülegü Khan. A daughter of the Salghurid dynasty whose grandfather, Abū Bakr Qutlugh Khan (r. 1226–60) in 1258 had marched with Hülegü Khan on Baghdad, Abīsh Khātūn was first appointed ruler of the province in 1263–64 while still a child. After a forced exile, she returned to her capital in Shiraz, where—despite a highly questionable record—she was given a rapturous welcome by the citizenry.

In contrast with the situation in Kermān, especially under Terkān Khātūn, a pervasive culture of corruption and financial chaos defined the province of Fārs, which strove to keep its distance, politically and financially, from the Ilkhans and their capital Tabrīz. Not only did the people of Shīrāz resist outside interference, but, highly unusually, one of their Salghurid monarchs, Seljuk Shāh, in 1263–64, actually led a short-lived rebellion against the Mongol Ilkhans. The ill-fated uprising, which resulted in Seljuk Shāh's execution, led to the enthronement of the four-year-old Abīsh on the Salghurid throne. Abīsh and her sister Salgham were the only remaining direct heirs to the Salghurid throne.

In 1273–4 a deterioration of the situation in Shīrāz and the involvement in corruption of some advisers close to Abīsh resulted in her removal from the city and the consummation of her marriage to Prince Tash-Möngke, a union arranged many years previously by her ambitious mother. Though she eventually became his chief wife, there is evidence that not all was well within the marriage and while Tash-Möngke saw to affairs in Shīrāz his wife remained behind with Öljei Khātūn, her husband's mother, and intrigued among the courts in Azerbaijan. Tash-Möngke returned from Shīrāz in 1283–84 and on the Ilkhan Ahmad Tegudar's (r. 1282–84) directive, Abīsh was appointed governor in his place. It is said that though their paths crossed as they travelled to take up their new posts, Tash-Möngke declined to meet or speak with his wife as their caravans passed each other. The historian, Waṣṣāf, dismisses Tash-Möngke as being extremely stupid and proud.

Upon entering Shīrāz, Abīsh was lavishly welcomed by the citizens, but the fervor was undeserved and soon forgotten. Abīsh Khātūn was very capable, confident, and resourceful but interested only in amassing personal wealth.

With her two royal daughters, Kürdüjin and Alghanchi, under her protection, she felt her position was unassailable and her person untouchable. Her greed and arrogance knew no bounds and little of the revenue that she milked from the province found its way back to the state coffers of Tabrīz.

However, Ahmad Tegudar's successor, Arghūn Khan (r. 1284–90), had little sympathy with Abīsh's excesses and he angrily demanded her appearance at court while at the same time appointing a certain ʿImād al-Dīn Alavī to replace her as governor of the province. She refused to move and immediately began undermining Arghūn Khan's new governor. Her intrigues led to a confrontation between her supporters and ʿImād al-Dīn, which resulted in the governor's death during a brawl and the murder of his nephew shortly afterward, both deaths blamed directly on Abīsh Khātūn. Her removal to Arghūn Khan's ordu to face a *yarghu* (Mongol court) was now inevitable and Shīrāz passed to direct rule from the Ilkhanid capital.

As a concession in recognition of her royal status Abīsh Khātūn was allowed to appoint a representative to appear in court on her behalf, an indulgence that saved her life. The chief nāʾib of her *dīwān*, Jamāl al-Dīn, was subjected to vigorous interrogation by the *yarghuchi* and after three strikes of the bastinado he admitted his and Abīsh's guilt and for this he was cut in two, a not uncommon form of Mongol execution. Abīsh herself was forced to pay compensation to the families of ʿImād al-Dīn and his nephew and she was forced to remain at the ordu where in 1286–87 she died.

Though a Muslim, she did not follow Islamic custom in disposing of her considerable estate, and her two daughters, Kürdüjin and Alghanchi, received a half of her wealth while Taichu, her son with Tash-Möngke, was awarded a quarter, and the final quarter was divided among her household slaves. Mongol practice rather than Islamic custom was also followed for her funeral service and burial and her body was accompanied by gold and silver vessels of wine for her final journey.

Like some other Muslim Khwātin (pl. Khatun) in Ilkhanid Iran (1258–1335), Abīsh maintained an ambiguous relationship with her professed religion, Islam. Her daughter, Kürdüjin, was far more devout and observant than she and Kürdüjin did not marry out of the faith, a practice forbidden for Muslim women but contravened among others, by Abīsh and Pādeshāh Khātūn, the daughter of Qutlugh Terkān of Kermān. Like other women from Iran's ruling houses, Abīsh used her family's Turkic ethnicity to exploit her connections to the ruling Ilkhans in Tabrīz. Though many generations away from the steppe and out of the saddle such brave women as Abīsh Khātūn provided aspirational role models for many of the women of her time.

[*See also* Baghdād Khātūn *and* Qutlugh Terkān Khātūn.]

BIBLIOGRAPHY

Shabānkārāʾī Moḥammed b. ʿAlī b. Moḥammed, *Majmaʾ-ʿAnsāb*, Tehran, 1984 [1363].

Ibn Zarkūb Shīrāzī, (ed.) Ismāʾīl Wāʾiẓ Javādī, *Shīrāznāma*, Inteshārāt Baniyād Farhang, Tehran, 1971 [1350].

Wassāf, Shihab al-Dīn ʿAbdallah Sharaf Shīrāzī, (ed.) M. M. Isfahānī, *Tārīkh-i-Wassāf*, Tehran, 1959/1338.

Howorth, Henry Hoyle, *History of the Mongols: The Mongols of Persia*, Lightning Source U.K.: Milton Keynes, 2011

Lambton, A. K. S. *Continuity and Change in Medieval Persia: Aspects of Administrative, Economic, Social History in 11th–14th Century Persia*. London: I. B. Taurus, 1988.

Lane, George, *Early Mongol Rule in Thirteenth Century Iran*. London: RoutledgeCurzon, 2003.

Lane, George, *Daily Life in the Mongol Empire*. Westport, Conn.: Greenwood Press, 2006.
Spuler, B., "ĀBEŠ ḴĀTŪN," *Encyclopaedia Iranica*, vol. I, 1985.

George Lane

ABLUTIONS. The state of ritual purity (*ṭahārah*) that is an essential condition for the fulfillment of many religious practices in Islam is attained through ablutions, washing or alternative actions. Ritual purity is a prerequisite for the performance of such major acts of worship as the ritual prayer and the pilgrimage, and, according to some schools of legal thought, for other religious performances such as reciting the Qurʾān or even for teaching. The absence of the state of purity makes such acts invalid though not necessarily forbidden: a person in a state of impurity may recite the Qurʾān for comfort or protection. Ablutions are normally performed at least five times a day by a practicing Muslim and may be performed more frequently, either as a preliminary to acts such as reciting the Qurʾān or because the Muslim in question follows the practice of remaining in a state of ritual purity at all times, which many more pious Muslims regard as desirable though not obligatory. Ablutions are thus a major part of the daily life of the practicing adult Muslim.

Historically, concepts of purity and impurity and thus of ablutions are common in the religious context of the Semitic world, practiced by Jews and Samaritans, although through different procedures. The presence of purifying rites based on ablution is evident as well in epigraphic documentation of pre-Islamic South Arabian cultures.

A distinction is made between minor ablutions (*wuḍūʾ*) and major ablutions or bathing (*ghusl*), depending on the level of impurity. Minor ablutions are necessary to remove minor impurities (*al-ḥadath al-aṣghar*) produced, for example, as a result of physiological functions such as passing urine, excrement, gas, blood, or vomit; as a result of loss of consciousness through deep sleep or fainting; or—according to some—as a result of touching one's own genitals or a person of the opposite sex, or by certain other forms of contact. Major ablutions are necessary to remove major impurities (*al-ḥadath al-akbar*; also *janābah*) produced by sexual intercourse, ejaculation, the menstrual period, and childbirth. It should be noted that, among the causes of impurity, only the menstrual period and childbirth are specific to women, whereas only ejaculation is specific to men. These specificities vanish, however, under the general principle that impurity is produced by the emission of any liquid whatsoever, other than tears, from a fixed position in the body (with sweat not falling under this category).

As well as being necessary to remove major impurities, major ablutions are also recommended before the Friday prayer and on certain other major ritual occasions such as beginning the pilgrimage. Furthermore, they are required while preparing the corpse of a deceased Muslim for the funeral prayer and subsequent burial. This form of major ablution—the washing of the corpse—is not required for the burial of martyrs, who are buried as they were when they died.

The basic procedure for minor ablutions consists of washing the hands, rinsing the mouth and nose, washing the face, washing the forearms up to the elbows, rubbing the head with the damp hand, washing the ears, and washing the feet up to the ankles. Each part of this procedure, save the rubbing of the head and the washing of the ears, is performed three times. The procedure for major ablutions consists of washing every part of the body, including hair and the scalp. In both types of ablution, priority is always given to the right side of the body.

The washing must be done with a purifying liquid. Rainwater is regarded as the perfect purifying element. Water may lose its ability to purify or even become impure itself as a result of the addition of other substances, however. Coca-cola, for example, is not purifying. Water containing urine is not only not purifying, it is also not pure: contact with it produces impurity. In exceptional cases, such as either the total unavailability of water or the unavailability of water at a reasonable price—circumstances that may arise in desert conditions even in the twenty-first century—a type of dry ablution (*tayammun*) using sand or another solid material, such as dust or stone, is permitted.

As for other religious practices, there are differences within and between the major Sunnī schools of legal thought, as well as between Sunnīs and Shīʿīs. Many of these concern which varieties of water are pure and/or purifying, or which elements in the basic procedure for ablutions described above may or may not be omitted without invalidating the ablutions and thus also the act of worship performed after them. There is general agreement that the water in a muddy puddle is not purifying, for example, and that the water in a broad and fast-flowing stream is purifying, but much discussion has arisen over types of water in between these extremes, such as what minimum volume of non-running water may be assumed to be purifying. In practice, it is nowadays generally assumed that water produced by a faucet or tap is purifying, but issues surrounding the purity of water can still arise in areas lacking the reliable provision of piped water.

Significant differences also exist with regard to what produces ritual impurity in the first place. As is often the case, there is general agreement on the basic points given above, but disagreement on some details. Within Sunnī Islam, for example, all save the Mālikīs consider ablutions necessary after contact with a dog. Differences also abound regarding contact between the sexes. The Shāfiʿīs hold ablutions to be necessary after any kind of contact, even a handshake, whereas the Ḥanafīs believe ablutions are not needed unless the contact was accompanied by lustful desires.

BIBLIOGRAPHY

Badawi, Jamal A. *Aṭ-ṭahārah: Purity and State of Undefilement.* Plainfield, Ind.: Islamic Teaching Center, 1979.

Burton, John. "The Qur'ān and the Islamic Practice of *wuḍū'*." In *The Koran: Critical Concepts in Islamic Studies*, edited by Colin Turner, pp. 111–159. Vol. 2: *Themes and Doctrines*. London: RoutledgeCurzon, 2004.

Jazīrī, ʿAbd al-Raḥmān al-. *Kitāb al-fiqh ʿalá al-madhāhib al-arbaʿah*. Beirut: Dār Ibn Ḥazm, 2012.

Katz, Marion H. "The Study of Islamic Ritual and the Meaning of *wuḍū'*." *Der Islam* 82 (2005): 106–145.

Kuşçular, Remzi. *Cleanliness in Islam: A Comprehensive Guide to Tahara*. Somerset, N.J.: The Light, 2007.

Sābiq, Sayyid. *Fiqh us-sunnah: At-tahara and as-salah*. Indianapolis, IN: American Trust Publications, 1991.

Subḥānī, Ayatollah Jaʿfar. *Doctrines of Shīʿī Islam: A Compendium of Imami Beliefs and Practices*. Translated and edited by Reza Shah-Kazemi. London: I. B. Tauris, 2001. See especially pp. 185–187.

Gabriele Tecchiato
Updated by Mark Sedgwick

Abortion. In the medical sense, abortion is the termination of pregnancy before the fetus is viable and is capable of survival outside the uterus. In legal terms, regardless of the religious and/or cultural context in which abortion takes place, the definition is predicated on the idea that abortion is a deliberate expulsion of the fetus from the womb prematurely and artificially without the presence of any need for such an action. Hence, the link between medicine and legal opinions is largely centered on the question of whether a need for an abortion exists.

Although Muslim, Christian, and Jewish conceptions of abortion differ in their constructions, they all share a fundamental trait in terms of content: abortion is framed in terms of unplanned and unwanted pregnancies. While in canon Christian texts, abortion is discussed within the context of morality, it is not mentioned at all in the Qurʾān. It is, however, referred to implicitly in the *sunnah*. In Judaism, abortion is invoked explicitly in relation to the state of the health of the mother (Mishna Oholoth 7:6). Much of the time, the circumstances that call for such a change involve a pregnancy that is either the result of a rape or endangers the mother's health. Unlike in Christianity, which considers abortion to be one of the gravest transgressions, Islam and Judaism do not view it as a murder or a crime, but, rather, as an inevitable scourge that one may have to endure in order to avoid an even greater evil. Traditional Muslim (and Jewish) views on abortion are more permissive than classical Christian views. Anti-abortion positions and opinions exist in both Islam and Judaism, but they are not categorical, as is the case with orthodox Christianity.

While Muslims encountered other cultures between the eighth and twelfth centuries as they spread their faith throughout the territory between Spain and Afghanistan, Muslim canon texts, like Muslims themselves, adapted to local customary laws and traditions. This explains why many societies that had tolerated abortion prior to Islamization continued to do so after the advent of Islam.

Although there is no textual evidence from the Qurʾān or *sunnah* regarding the prohibition of abortion, Muslim jurists (*fuqahāʾ*) have attempted to determine the legal implications of abortion, engaging in what is termed *ijtihād* (intellectual deliberation or reinterpretation) in order to deduce laws from the broad teachings of the Qurʾān and the *ḥadīth*. Thus, most legal opinions derived from either the four legal schools (*madhāhib al-Arbaʿa*) or *fatāwā* (legal opinions) have based their deductions on the interpretation (*taʾwīl*) of some verses of the Qurʾān and/or the *ḥadīth* where there is a high premium placed on life and its preservation. Examples include verses 4:93 and 17:31.

Medical science and Muslim law have recognized that life begins as soon as the ovum is fertilized (combines with sperm). Modern Islamic jurisprudence, in general, rejects the notion that, before a certain period of time, it is merely a "lump of flesh," one devoid of life. From Islamic scriptural sources, however, Muslim jurists have also deduced the sanctity of human life and unanimously held abortion to be blameworthy. They then faced the problem of determining the gravity of the crime and the appropriate punishment. Their deliberations on this matter revolved around the quality of personhood endowed in the fetus. On the other hand, the fact that there was no franc banning (*tahrim sarih*) either in the Qurʾān or in the *sunnah* rendered the gates of *ijtihād* wide open in this instance.

The word *janīn* (fetus; pl. *ajinnah*) literally means "that which is veiled or covered." The Qurʾān refers to *janīn* as the procreated being inside a woman's body, irrespective of the stage of its development (53:32). However, commentators on the Qurʾān (*mufassirūn*) have held that the expression *khalqan ākhar* (another act of creation), which appears in 23:13, signifies the ensoulment of the fetus. The *ḥadīth* contain at least two critical references related to the fetus. In one, it is stated that organ differentiation occurs forty nights after fertilization. In another, ensoulment of the fetus is said to occur 120 days after conception. Thus, Muslim scholars differ in their definition of the fetus. Some maintain simply that the fetus stands for that which is in the womb. Others, including the Islamic jurist al-Shāfiʿī, hold that the fetus is initiated after the stages of *al-mudghah* (the chewed lump) and *al-ʿalaqah* (something that clings) have been completed; only then can a human possessing differentiated characteristics, such as fingers, nails, or eyes, be clearly identified. A third group uses the word *janīn* to mean that which exists in the womb after the ensoulment has taken place. However, despite these differences in interpretation, there is consensus among scholars that, after the ensoulment of the fetus, abortion constitutes homicide and is thus liable to penalty.

The Legal Rights of the Fetus. The schools of Islamic jurisprudence allot certain rights to the fetus. First, the fetus is accorded the right to life, that is, the right to be born and to live as long as God permits. Thus, in the event of the death penalty being passed on a pregnant woman, the sentence may only be carried out after delivery and provisions have been made for the child to be suckled by a wet nurse. The Shāfiʿī school provides that the belly of a pregnant woman who has died be cut open in order to give the fetus a chance to survive.

Second, the fetus has a right to inheritance. The fetus cannot, according to the *Sharīʿah*, inherit while still in the womb, but the law provides that the inheritance be kept in abeyance for various practical reasons until birth occurs. In the case of a stillborn fetus, there is no question of existence. Shares of the inheritance are determined after birth, on the basis of the infant's sex.

Third, the *Sharīʿah* provides that a stillborn baby or miscarried fetus has the right to a burial. Babies who die before uttering any sound should be given the ceremonial bath (*al-ghusl*) and a name, placed in a white cloth (*kafan*), and then buried. These provisions apply to both formed and unformed fetuses. The only difference between the burial of a human being and that of a stillborn or miscarried fetus is that no prayer is said for the latter.

Concept of "Therapeutic Abortion." Ḥanafī jurists render abortion permissible up to 120 days after conception and only for a juridically valid reason. "Therapeutic abortion" before the fourth month of pregnancy may be sanctioned in the following cases: (1) if the doctors fear that the pregnant mother's life is in danger; (2) if the pregnancy may cause a disease in the mother; and (3) if a second pregnancy severely reduces the mother's ability to lactate while her infant is completely dependent on her milk for survival.

Muslim scholars are not unanimous about the prohibition of abortion before the animation of the fetus. Views range between permissibility, discouragement, and prohibition. Ḥanafīs, Zaydīs, and some Shāfiʿīs rule that abortion is permitted before animation in an unqualified manner without the need for an excuse. A second opinion from some Hanafīs and Shāfiʿīs is that pre-animation abortion is permitted if there is an excuse, and if there is no excuse, it is a discouraged act. The third opinion comes from the Mālikīs, who opined that it is discouraged in all cases, regardless of the existence of an excuse. The last opinion is also the authoritative view of the Ẓāhirīs, who in addition state that abortion before 120 days is prohibited.

Abortion after animation is prohibited in Islam. However, certain circumstances are classified as a *ḍarūrah* (necessity), which can be accepted as a valid reason for abortion after animation. As stated earlier, "necessity" includes a case in which the mother's life is in danger or the pregnancy will cause a fatal disease to the mother. Muslim scholars do not recognize the risk of bearing disfigured babies, or a baby having a fatal defect or disease, as excuses for abortion. This ruling is based on the reason that the life of the fetus should not be disposed of when uncertainty exists over its inevitable death by a disease. However, some Muslim councils, such as the High Council for Islamic Legal Opinion in Kuwait and Majmaʿ al-Fiqh al-Islāmī, permit termination of a pregnancy before 120 days for malformation of the fetus. The ruling is the same for abortion in cases of rape or adultery. The strict rule of this prohibition after the fourth month is based on a *ḥadīth* of the Prophet regarding a woman who conceived adulterously; he ordered the punishment to be postponed until she had delivered. However, some *ʿulamāʾ* have proposed that pregnancies resulting from adultery or rape can be aborted before animation, as giving birth to these babies could be extremely distressing, especially for rape victims. This ruling is also based on the earlier view of some Hanafīs and Shāfiʿīs who permit abortion even without a valid reason before the lapse of 120 days.

Another issue regarding abortion, apart from rape, is the question of whether or not the victim can use the morning after pill. Contemporary Muslim scholars have distinguished between the use of these pills and abortion, as the pills only expel the semen before it establishes itself in the womb, and the woman has the right to expel the semen before it reaches her womb. Moreover, these attempts to reduce the extent of any legal transgression in terminating a pregnancy before 120 days (either by using morning after pills or by other means) rely on an analogy between early-stage pregnancy and coitus interruptus.

Throughout the Arab-Muslim world, abortion for medical reasons, aiming to preserve maternal health or to prevent the birth of handicapped children, is the only legal form of abortion. In most Muslim countries, the penal codes condemn abortions that do not meet at least one of these two criteria. For this reason, in Morocco, for instance, between 600 and 800 abortions are conducted clandestinely every day.

In the wake of the Arab Spring (2011–2012), many NGOs and feminist associations in the Middle East and Arab North Africa and Muslim feminist associations in Europe have increasingly demanded the abolition of the articles in the penal codes of these states that confine the legal justification of abortion to medical reasons alone. Studies on abortion in the context of contemporary Muslim societies must take into consideration the technological shift (in both communications and medical sciences), which has been accompanied by a spirit of liberalism that resulted from the Arab Spring. In the wake of the Arab Spring, many feminist voices (and women in general) are trying to influence the process of constitutional (re)writing in order to introduce, among other things, pro-choice articles that grant them legal jurisdiction over their own bodies.

[*See also* Family Law; Family Planning; *and* Surrogate Motherhood.]

BIBLIOGRAPHY

Alami, M. H., N. Pirou, R. Bezad, and M. T. Alaoui. "Therapeutic Abortion: Critical Study of 22 Cases." *Contraception, Fertilité, Sexualité* 26 (1998): 225–228.

Atighetchi, Darius. *Islamic Bioethics: Problems and Perspectives.* Dordrecht, Netherlands: Springer, 2007. See especially pp. 7–8.

Belhous, A., F. Ait Boughima, H. Benyaich, and N. Samouth. "Les aspects médicolégaux de l'avortement au Maroc [Aspects of Forensic Medicine of Abortion in Morocco]." *La Revue de Médecine Légale* 2 (2011): 170–173.

Boucherit, Farida. *L'enfant endormi dans le ventre de sa mère: représentation et réalité d'une croyance.* Paris: Sorbonne, 2005.

Bowen, Donna Lee. "Abortion, Islam and the 1994 Cairo Population Conference." *International Journal of Middle East Studies* 29 (1997): 161–184.

Brockopp, J. E., ed. *Islamic Ethics of Life: Abortion, War, and Euthanasia.* Columbia: University of South Carolina, 2003.

Dabash, Rasha, and Farzaneh Roudi-Fahimi. *Abortion in the Middle East and North Africa.* Washington, DC: Population Reference Bureau, Gynuity Health Project, 2008. http://www.prb.org/pdf08/MENA abortion.pdf.

Ebrāhīm, Abul Fa ḍl Moḥsin. *Abortion, Birth Control, and Surrogate Parenting: An Islamic Perspective.* Indianapolis, Ind.: American Trust, 1989.

International Planned Parenthood Federation, Middle East and North Africa Region. *Islam & Family Planning.* Beirut: International Planned Parenthood

Federation, Middle East and North Africa Region, 1974.
"Islam Science, Environment, and Technology." http://www.islamset.com.
"Islamic Medical Association of North America." http://www.imana.org.
"IslamiCity." http://www.islamicity.com.
Musallam, Basim F. *Sex and Society in Islam*. New York and Cambridge, U.K.: Cambridge University Press, 1983.
Naciri, Mohamed Mekki. "A Survey of Family Planning in Islamic Legislation." In *Muslim Attitudes toward Family Planning*, edited by Olivia Schieffelin, pp. 129–145. New York: Population Council, 1973.
al-Qaraḍāwī, Yūsuf. *The Lawful and the Prohibited in Islam*. Indianapolis, Ind.: American Trust, 1980(?).
Serour, Gamal I. "Islamic Views." In *Proceedings of the First International Conference on Bioethics in Human Reproduction Research in the Muslim World, December 1991*, edited by Gamal I. Serour, 234–242. Cairo: International Center for Population Studies and Research, Al-Azhar University, 1992.
Yacoub, Abdel Aziz. *The Fiqh of Medicine-Responses in Islamic Jurisprudence to Developments in Medical Science*. London: Ta-Ha Publishers, 2001.

Abul Fadl Mohsin Ebrahim
Updated by Yasmin Safian,
Robert Gleave,
and Samir Ben-Layashi

Adivar, Halide Edip. (1884–1964), Turkish nationalist, novelist, reformer, and activist.

Halide Edip (sometimes spelled Edib) was a well-rounded intellectual, reformer, and activist working in male-dominated circles, a somewhat unusual experience for an early-twentieth-century woman. She developed close relationships with the politicians and pashas of her day, including Talat and Ahmed Cemal Pasha of the Union and Progress Party and Mustafa Kemal Pasha (Atatürk) of the Nationalist Revolution. She also participated in heated debates with ideologues like Ziya Gökalp, Yusuf Akçura, and Ahmet Ağaoğlu.

Halide Edip utilized the privileges of being born to a progressive and intellectual upper-class family, mediating it with the advantages of growing up in a traditional extended Ottoman family and a multi-ethnic Ottoman neighborhood Beşiktaş. She thus stayed away from elitist intellectualism and ethnocentric nationalism. Combining her competitive nature and artistic talent with given opportunities, such as easy access to intellectual circles and the print world, Halide Edip went from being "entirely unknown" to a distinguished columnist and novelist. Meanwhile, she assumed dynamic roles in educational, national, and women's (not necessarily feminist, as she did not count herself as one) projects.

She wrote for the major sociopolitical periodicals like *Tanin* and *Türk Yurdu* from the early days of the Second Constitution (1908). During her marriage to Salih Zeki (1901–1910), she signed her articles as Halide Salih. She retained her maiden name even after divorcing Salih Zeki and marrying Dr. Adnan Adıvar in 1917, and the couple received the surname "Adıvar" after the surname law was issued in 1934.

Exclusively in terms of her fiction and two-volume memoir in English, Halide Edip may be regarded as an ardent Turkish nationalist, novelist, and feminist. After her political split from Mustafa Kemal (Atatürk) in 1924, some Kemalists accused her of being Atatürk's rival. In fact, a comprehensive reading of her day-to-day intellectual development and life circumstances, as reflected in her periodical articles (1908–1964), provides a more complex and accurate picture that challenges those ready-made assumptions about Halide Edip.

During the sociopolitical turbulence of the Constitutional regime, Balkan Wars (1912–1913), and Occupation Years (1918–1922), she voted for collaboration and the common good of society and ran numerous relief campaigns with other women, improved public and, especially, girls' education through school inspections and curriculum reports, and inspired thousands to participate in mass demonstrations to protest the occupations of Izmir and Istanbul. Furthermore, she took part in underground activities to organize a national resistance in Istanbul and defended the country as a colonel when she moved to Ankara in World War I. Because of her disputes with Mustafa Kemal Atatürk over the newly founded Turkish Republic's reformation project, she went into voluntary exile in 1924.

During her stay in Europe and the United States, Halide Edip maintained a politically silent but intellectually productive life. She wrote her two-volume memoir in English and publicized her account as an alternative to the official narrative of the independence struggle. She delivered university and public lectures in the United States and India and, consequently, was transformed into an internationally renowned figure. After her return to Turkey in 1939, she headed the Department of English Literature at Istanbul University, actively participated in politics as the MP of Izmir for one term (1950–1954), and spent the rest of her life writing.

In addition to her memoirs, Halide Edip is renowned for her novels, including *The Shirt of Flame* (1923) and *The Clown and His Daughter* (1936). She also published short stories, plays, and non-fiction books.

Bibliography

Adıvar, Halide Edib. *Memoirs of Halide Edib.* Piscataway, N.J.: Gorgias Press, 2005. A facsimile reprint of the original edition first published 1926 by Century Co.

Adıvar, Halide Edib. *The Turkish Ordeal: Being the Further Memoirs of Halide Edib.* Westport, Conn.: Hyperion Press, 1981.

Enginün, İnci. *Halide Edib Adıvar'ın Eserlerinde Doğu ve Batı Meselesi.* 3rd ed. İstanbul: Dergah yay., 2007. A uniquely comprehensive work analyzing the concepts of East and West in Halide Edip's works with a primary focus on her fiction.

Iner, Derya. "Halide Edib Adıvar's Role as Social Reformer and Contributor to Public Debate on Constitutionalism, Status of Women, Educational Reform, Ottoman Minorities, and Nationalism during the Young Turk Era (1908–1918)." Ph.D. diss., University of Wisconsin-Madison, 2011. Establishes a more balanced and comprehensive understanding of Halide Edip's role in Turkish intellectual history and social activism. It casts light on not only Halide Edip's thoughts and experiences but also the historical, social, and intellectual life of the transformation era in Turkish history (1908–1919).

Derya Iner

Afghanistan. Afghanistan's history demonstrates how gender relations in that nation have been affected by ethnic conflict, state formation, state-society relations, and imperial domination. In Afghanistan, as in Muslim-majority societies in general, the interaction of Islamic culture and religion with secularism, nationalism, ethnicity, and other important historical, social, and economic mechanisms structures the lives of women and men. Afghan women's struggle against local male domination and imperial hegemony is thus a central theme in Afghanistan's history and development.

Historical Background. Afghan history is peppered with strong and heroic women. In the tenth century, Rabia Balkhi was, as far as is known, the first woman to write love poetry in the Persian language. She died after her brother slashed her wrists because of her sexual relationship with a slave; she is reputed to have written her last poem in her own blood as she lay dying. In 1880, at the Battle of Maiwand, a Pashtun woman named Malalai led the Pashtun army against the British, who were attempting to colonize the area and annex it with what was then British India. When the army was losing morale, Malalai raised the Afghan flag and encouraged the troops to fight. She was killed in the battle, but her words and actions helped bring about the Afghan victory. There are schools, hospitals, and other institutions named after her in Afghanistan.

In this period, the British Empire was threatened by the expansion of the Russian Empire into the Afghan region. The British, therefore, attempted to conquer Afghanistan through the manipulation of different ethnic groups. Afghanistan became a buffer state between these two empires, and successive Afghan monarchs ruled with no legitimacy, as they subjugated the interests of the people to those of the foreign powers.

After World War I, however, resistance to British interference grew. In 1919, independence was declared and successive monarchs introduced a limited degree of reforms in areas including property, trade, tax collection, health care, education, and women's rights. However, these weak rentier administrations (reliant on foreign loans) remained unpopular with the majority of the people. Under pressure from conservative religious forces, Afghan monarchs often consolidated their rule by making concessions, which often included omitting women's rights reforms. Many failed attempts at modernization based on Western models led to a return to religious conservatism. This pattern was repeated by successive kings until 1973, when the monarchy was dissolved. However, post-monarchy leaders also failed to build institutions to meet the needs of Afghanistan's diverse society. In 1978, the pro-Soviet People's Democratic Party of Afghanistan was established. The pro-Soviet faction attempted a number of reforms, including those related to women's rights issues. But reform in this period was not much different than that initiated since the late nineteenth century, as it continued to be formulated by the male Afghan elite, who followed Western models, and none of the reforms resolved the harsh reality faced by the majority of the people.

This failure to adequately address development and women's rights issues was not simply the result of tensions between modernity and tradition; it was also the result of the widening gap between the urban elite and the urban and rural majority. As this gap grew, leaders lost respect and credibility. In the absence of socioeconomic development and state-building, ethnic conflicts escalated. In 1979, Soviet troops invaded Afghanistan, the Cold War intensified, and the Afghan *mujāhidīn* emerged as the US-backed anti-Soviet force.

The support of the U.S. for the *mujāhidīn* led to a brutal civil war (1992–1996) in which 1.5 million Afghans died, 7 million took refuge in neighboring countries (Iran and Pakistan), and the country was devastated. While the U.S. saw the collapse of the Soviet Union as the failure of the communist regime, many Muslims in the region and beyond saw it as a victory for Islam. The Taliban grew out of the discontent of many of the younger generation of *mujāhidīn*, who felt that their older leadership had failed, as people were suffering from death and destruction and women, particularly, were suffering, as sexual violence escalated to an unprecedented level and many were murdered and raped by the *mujāhidīn*. The Taliban disarmed the warlords and brutally enforced their own model of law and order. They imposed the *chador* or burqa on women and punished those women who did not obey its law. Throughout the periods of civil war (1992–1996) and Taliban rule (1996–2001), Washington ignored the situation in Afghanistan, until the events of September 11, 2001.

Women's activism in twentieth-century Afghanistan was diverse. Under the pro-Soviet government, Anahita Ratib became the Minister of Social Affairs in 1977; in 1994, Fatima Gailani was a member of the guerrilla army of the Afghan resistance against the Soviets. The Revolutionary Association of the Women of Afghanistan (RAWA) was established in 1977 to agitate for democracy and women's rights. Although ethnic conflict was at its highest level during the rule of the *mujāhidīn* and, later, the Taliban, women of diverse groups (Shīʿah, Sunnī, Pashtun, Tajik, Uzbek) worked together on food distribution projects which were agreed between the UN and the Taliban. These women bravely and imaginatively used these projects to organize secret organizations to support women. They generated networks, norms, and trust in their communities, helping each other and the most vulnerable women through their secret schools.

Afghanistan under Invasion: 2001–2012. In October 2001, the U.S. and the U.K. led a bombing campaign against the Taliban government and invaded Afghanistan. The war against the Taliban was justified as self-defense in response to terrorist acts in the U.S. The invaders used the discourses of capacity building, women's empowerment, and the universality of democracy to justify the invasion of Afghanistan. With the fall of the Taliban, Afghan women believed that, in their own way and according to their own culture, they could change their communities to accept women's participation in the economy and society and find legitimate roles for women in the process of reconstruction. However, under NATO rule, the change in their material conditions that would prefigure such social transformation was absent. Afghanistan has been left shattered and fragmented. The brutal rule of the Taliban has been replaced by the brutal rule of warlords and, since 2010, the U.S. and other Western governments have been negotiating with the Taliban.

The US-led invasion of Afghanistan was not about peace, security and development, or women's liberation and democracy. Facing the rise of China and India as economic powers, the Western hegemonic alliance rationalized the war on Afghanistan to facilitate the West's desire to control the energy resources of Central Asia and the Middle East. The events of 9/11 simply speeded up this process. Afghan women have contested the Western imperial account of their oppression—that is, the portrayal of Afghan women as passive and victimized to be liberated by the West. Nevertheless, the rhetoric of women's rights has played a particularly important role in the past and at present in determining the national and international power relations and denying the West's imperial domination of the region.

Through pressure from women activists, as well as support and pressure from the international community and organizations, women hold 25 percent of the seats in the Afghan parliament. However, those women's rights activists who stand up to protest and defend women's rights often face intimidation and violence. In 2008 Malalai Joya, representing Farah Province, was kicked out of the Parliament for courageously speaking out and calling for an end to the invasion of Afghanistan when her province was bombed, resulting in the deaths of many civilians. She argued that only 5 percent of school-age girls pursue their education in Afghanistan. In addition, 25 to 31 percent of women suffer physical, sexual, and psychological violence, 57 percent of women are married before the age of sixteen, and between 70 and 80 percent of women endure forced marriages. Girls as young as nine are sold as "opium brides" to pay off the family's debts. Most sex workers are widows with children, who often feel suicide (self-immolation) is their only alternative. Another female MP, Azita Rafat, argues that many women prisoners are being punished for "moral crimes" such as running away from home, because they have been kidnapped, raped, and forced into drug trafficking.

Afghanistan is a product of the dark side of globalization, as it is a center of the drug trade, and its economy relies on international aid and drugs. Annually, the equivalent of billions of dollars of opium revenue is poured into the pockets of warlords and traffickers. Investment in the agricultural sector could have become a viable alternative. However, international organizations and Western governments have failed to invest in agriculture, industry, or services. The majority of the population suffers from high food prices, but are unable to access food through their own production.

Nation-building from outside and above has excluded the majority of the population and has exacerbated ethnic, religious, class, and gender conflicts, and the prospect of a local democracy has been undermined. A rentier state has been propped up by foreign aid and opium revenue. The majority of the population lives in absolute poverty and despair, while watching a tiny minority grow wealthy with the help of international financial organizations.

As is argued by Chishti and Farhoumand-Sims (2011), transnational feminism is entangled with international aid and military apparatuses. Hence, the gender agenda in Afghanistan is based on neo-imperial power relations: the interactions between the outsider "givers" and the insider "receivers" of aid. In this context, Western feminists' campaign to liberate Afghan women is little more than thinly disguised Orientalism intended to advance a neo-imperialist agenda. The transnational feminists' work with a small group of Afghan women oversimplifies the complexities of the religion, culture, and history of the Afghans. This has created tensions between a minority and the majority of Afghan women and men. It is, therefore, crucial that transnational feminists become aware of the needs of the majority of Afghans and their objection to the invaders' gender programs.

Historically, feminism in Muslim-majority societies has been diverse. Critical tensions have existed within feminist discourse, ranging from affiliation to Westernizing and secularizing tendencies to voices searching for a way to articulate women's rights and gender equality within an indigenous discourse, including Islamic discourse. The dominant tendency suggests a critical consciousness of the politics of local male domination, and a feminist contestation of the cultural practices sanctioning injustices to women within the Islamic context, without abandoning that Islamic heritage.

Despite many obstacles on their path, women's-rights activists find a space to exercise autonomy and agency in their own way and according to their own culture. Local NGOs, such as Afghan Women Council, Afghan Women Network, and Humanitarian Assistance for the Women and Children of Afghanistan, help women's education and health initiatives and provide limited resources to poorer women. There are also women's councils that are engaged in planning, budgeting, and participating in decision-making about the welfare of the whole community. Women have also shown their capacity for social action and empowerment by creating commonalities between ethnic, religious, linguistic, and cultural diversities through literature, music, and art.

Conclusion. Afghan women's perceptions of women's liberation is a world apart from those of the invading forces. Historically, foreign domination and invasion have had a negative impact on Afghan women's struggle for rights and equality. Today the domination and oppression of women is as much imperial as it is patriarchal. In the view of Afghan women, socioeconomic development, coupled with the engagement of all ethnic groups and religions in the process, is the only way to achieve peace, security, and development, and only this can pave the way for real, lasting change in gender relations.

BIBLIOGRAPHY

Ahmed, Leila. *A Quiet Revolution: The Veil's Resurgence from the Middle East to America*. New Haven, Conn.: Yale University Press, 2011.

Ahmed, Leila. *Women and Gender in Islam: Historical Roots of a Modern Debate*. New Haven, Conn.: Yale University Press, 1992.

Barakat, Sultan, and Gareth Wardell. "Capitalizing on Capacities of Afghan Women: Women's Role in Afghanistan's Reconstruction and Development." *InFocus Programme on Crisis Response and Reconstruction*, Working Paper 4, 2001. http://www.ilo.int/wcmsp5/groups/public/---ed_emp/---emp_ent/---ifp_crisis/documents/publication/wcms_116393.pdf.

Chishti, Maliha, and Cheshmak Farhoumand-Sims. "Transnational Feminism and the Women's Rights Agenda in Afghanistan." In *Globalising Afghanistan: Terrorism, War, and the Rhetoric of Nation Building*, edited by Zubeda Jalalzai & David Jefferess, pp. 117–144. Durham, N.C.: Duke University Press, 2011.

Dupree, Nancy. "Revolutionary Rhetoric and Afghan Women in Afghanistan." In *Revolution and Rebellion in Afghanistan: Anthropological Perspectives*, edited by M. Nazif Mohib Shahrani and Robert Canfield. Berkeley: Institute of International Studies, University of California, 1984.

Gibson, Nigel C. "It's the Opium, Stupid." In *Globalising Afghanistan: Terrorism, War, and the Rhetoric of Nation Building*, edited by Zubeda Jalalzai and David Jefferess, pp. 31–50. Durham, N.C.: Duke University Press, 2011.

Hassan, Riffat. "Muslim Women's Rights: A Contemporary Debate." In *Women for Afghan Women: Shattering Myths and Claiming the Future*, edited by Sunita Mehta, pp. 137–144. New York: Palgrave Macmillan, 2002.

Jalal, Massouda, Malalai Joya, Fawzia Koofi, and Azita Rafat. "Voices of Parliamentarians: Four Women MPs Share Their Thoughts." In *Land of the Unconquerable: The Lives of Contemporary Afghan Women*, edited by Jennifer Heath and Ashraf Zahedi, pp. 128–139. Berkeley: University of California Press, 2011.

Johnson, Chris, and Jolyon Leslie. *Afghanistan: The Mirage of Peace*. London: Zed Books, 2004.

Mills, Margaret A. "Between Covered and Covert: Traditions, Stereotypes, and Afghan Women's Agency." In *Land of the Unconquerable: The Lives of Contemporary Afghan Women*, edited by Jennifer Heath and Ashraf Zahedi, pp. 60–73. Berkeley: University of California Press, 2011.

Oates, Lauryn. "Painting Their Way into the Public World: Women and the Visual Arts." In *Land of the Unconquerable: The Lives of Contemporary Afghan Women*, edited by Jennifer Heath and Ashraf Zahedi, pp. 333–341. Berkeley: University of California Press, 2011.

Olszewska, Zuzanna. "A Hidden Discourse: Afghanistan's Women Poets." In *Land of the Unconquerable: The Lives of Contemporary Afghan Women*, edited by Jennifer Heath and Ashraf Zahedi, pp. 342–356. Berkeley: University of California Press, 2011.

Poya, Maryam. *Iran's Influence: A Religious-Political State and Society in Its Region*. London: Zed Books, 2010.

Rostami-Povey, Elaheh. *Afghan Women: Identity and Invasion*. London: Zed Books, 2007.

Young, Iris Marion. "The Logic of Masculinist Protection: Reflections on the Current Security State." *Signs: Journal of Women in Culture and Society* 29 (2003): http://www.politicas.unam.mx/razoncinica/site-papime-tendenciascp/sitio/Iris_Marion_Young/texto.pdf.

Elaheh Rostami-Povey

African Languages and Literature.

[*This entry includes two subentries:*

East Africa *and*
West Africa.]

East Africa

The study of languages and literatures in East Africa demonstrates the complexity of the different forms of texts, as well as the relationship between literacy and orality in the region (Barnes and Carmichael, 2006). Oral forms of language and literature have been at the heart of rich linguistic, historical, anthropological, and ethnomusicological studies for decades, whereas Islamic literate culture has only recently received greater scholarly attention. The study of both literary and oral texts and their interdependence has particularly been the focus of interdisciplinary scholarship, with special attention given to the contexts, circumstances, tools, and meanings of textual production, as well as to the ways they could be interpreted as means of self-expression.

Ethiopia is remarkable among sub-Saharan African societies for its ancient indigenous literacy that generated its own script. Because "literacy was power" there, it was instrumental in "mystifying the power of the state, ruling class and church vis à vis the overwhelming mass of illiterate subjects" (Crummey, 2006, p. 10). However, the region in general is animated by rich oral cultures that are expressed particularly in poetry, a literary genre produced for performance. This is the case of Somali language and literature (in Somalia, Djibouti, the northeastern region of Kenya, and the Somali regions of Ethiopia), wherein a writing system based on Latin script was not introduced until 1972. Despite the introduction of written orthography, Somali literature is still predominantly orally composed, memorized, and recited among its largely nomadic pastoralist people. Furthermore, scholars have noted that literacy has had little effect on the practice and performance of oral poetry in Somalia, although it has changed the ways that poems are memorized and diffused among broader audiences. According to Jonhson, the written word comprises just one tool—not unlike cassette tapes and other new media—for circulating this genre of literature both nationally and internationally.

Somali "classical poems" are divided into four main styles: *gabay*, *geeraar*, *jiifto*, and *buraambur*, with the latter being considered the female genre. According to Zainab, the style adopted by a poet or a poetess currently depends on that particular artist, although regional influences on the artist's style are present. Zainab further argues that poetry by women concerning political matters is not in wide circulation because the role of professional memorizer has traditionally been reserved for men. Besides, audiotape, radio transmission, and public performances to large audiences (such as that performed by a group of women called Allah-Amin) have permitted the circulation of women's poetry, bypassing the restrictions socially imposed by male memorizers. Through radio broadcasting, poetesses' compositions have fulfilled the dual purposes of entertainment and political consciousness-raising. For example, during the Siad Barre regime, the compositions of Halimo Ali Kurtin and Hawa Aaje Mohamed were transmitted by Radio Mogadishu, while political opposition songs by Maryam Haji Hassan were broadcast by a clandestine radio station in Addis Ababa. From the 1940s to 1950s, a group of poetesses who were also members of the Somali Youth League (such as Halimo Godane, Halimo Shiil, Barni Warsame, and Timiro Ukash) were active in the nationalist struggle.

Scholars have paid special attention to the oral performance of Muslim prayer, a well-established genre of orality in the region. Among Muslim communities in Ethiopia, Islamic panegyrics are popular, particularly songs of praise called *dhikr* or *menzuma*. Even women and children used to perform *menzuma* repertoires in Harar, one of the main centers of Islamic learning in the Horn. Unfortunately, studies on Muslim women's literary production in Ethiopia are still almost absent. Exceptions are represented by the studies of Muna and Sartori.

Some Muslim prayers are characterized by being performed only by women. In Somalia and Djibouti, *sittat*, also known as *Nebi-Ammaan*, *Hawa iyo Faadumo*, and *Abbey Sittidey*, are exclusively feminine rituals where songs of verses about religious themes embedded in *dhikr*'s melodies and rhythms are performed. In *dhikr* sessions, popular poems can be incorporated, such as those of Dada Masiti (1804–1921), a prominent poet, scholar, and mystic. Her poetry is memorized, transmitted, and quoted by Bravanese people, particularly women, in Somalia and in the diaspora.

The didactic function of poetry is often remarkable. This is certainly the case of the *utendi wa Mwana Kupona*, a famous and unique classical Swahili epic composed by a woman and translated into English by Hichens and Werner in 1934. The author, Mwana Kupona of Mombasa (c. 1810–1860), addressed the poem to her daughter, to provide advice, mainly on the wife–husband relationship. The advice is given within the ethical framework of Islam as perceived by the author (Topan, 2004).

According to Mbele, Swahili women in their poetry "have been inclined to advocate social cohesion and harmony as opposed to the destructive values of war, revenge, and aggressiveness that one encounters in Swahili heroic poetry" (Mbele, 1996, p. 80).

Women's participation has also been noticed in a particular style of Swahili music characterized by its distinctive sound and poetry, the so-called *tarabu*. The latter was the most popular musical entertainment in early twentieth century Zanzibar.

Throughout the twentieth century in East Africa, one can notice a cultural hybridity, influenced by media, films, songs, fashion, tourism, and migration, that impacted contemporary literatures. Special attention is also needed for postcolonial and migration literatures, well expressed by famous Italian women writers of Somali origin, such as Igiaba Scego (b. 1974, Rome), Cristina Ali Farah (b. 1973, Verona), and Shirin Ramzanali Fazel (b. 1959, Mogadishu). Leading women's voices in contemporary Kiswahili literature include Penina Mlama (b. 1949, Tanzania), Amandina Lihamba (Tanzania), Angelina Chogo Wapakabulo (Tanzania/Uganda), Elvinia Namukwaya Zirimu (Uganda), Ari Katini Mwachofi (Kenya), and Sheila Ali Ryanga (Kenya).

BIBLIOGRAPHY

Barnes, Cedric, and Tim Carmichael. "Language, Power and Society: Orality and Literacy in the Horn of Africa." *Journal of African Cultural Studies* 18.1 (June 2006): 1–8.

Crummey, D. "Literacy in an Oral Society: The Case of Ethiopian Land Records." *Journal of African Cultural Studies* 18.1 (June 2006): 9–22.

Declich, F. "Sufi Experience in Rural Somali: A Focus on Women." *Social Anthropology* 8.3 (2000): 295–318.

Ishiara, Minako. "Beyond Authenticity: Diverse Images of Muslim Awliya in Ethiopia." *African Study Monographs*, Suppl. 41 (March 2010): 81–89.

Kapteijins, Lidwien. "Sittat: Somali Women's Songs for the Mothers of Believers." In *The Marabout and the Muse: New Approaches to Islam in African Literature*, edited by Ken Harrow, pp. 124–141. Portsmouth, N.H.: Heinemann, 1996.

Kapteijins, Lidwien, with Maryam Omar Ali. *Women's Voices in a Man's World: Women and the Pastoral Tradition in Northern Somali Orature, c. 1899–1980*. Portsmouth, N.H.: Heinemann, 1999.

Kassim, M. "Dhikr Will Echo from All Corners: Dada Masiti and the Transmission of Islamic Knowledge." *Bildhaan: An International Journal of Somali Studies* 2 (2002): 104–119.

Mbele, Joseph L. "Wimbo wa Miti: An Example of Swahili Women's Poetry." *African Languages and Cultures* 9.1 (1996): 71–82.

Sartori, Ilaria. "Cultural Identity, Islamic Revivalism and Women's New-found Role in Preserving and Transmitting Musical Traditions." [http://is4mwmd.yolasite.com/writings.php]. In Conference on Music in the World of Islam, Assilah, 2007.

Topan, Farouk. "From Mwana Kupona to Mwamvita: Female Representations in Swahili Literature." In *Swahili Modernities*, edited by Pat Caplan and Farouk Topan, pp. 213–227. Trenton, N.J.: Africa World Press, 2004.

Zainab, Mohamed Jama. "Fighting to Be Heard: Somali Women's Poetry." *African Languages and Cultures* 1.1 (1991): 43–53.

Zainab, Mohamed Jama. "Silent Voices: The Role of Somali Women's Poetry in Social and Political Life." *Oral Tradition* 9.1 (1994): 185–202.

Silvia Bruzzi

West Africa

There are two levels of Islamic literature in West Africa, as Knappert points out. First is the scholarly level of the learned *ʿulamāʾ*, fully literate in classical Arabic, who composed original works in classical Arabic to interpret the Sharīʿah in light of African conditions and to explain Islamic theology against a background of prevailing animism. Typical of such endeavors in West Africa were the Arabic works of the nineteenth-century Fulani Islamic reformers of the Hausa states. Local historical chronicles in classical Arabic were also written by West African *ʿulamāʾ* from the sixteenth century onward.

In addition to this endogenous classical Arabic literature—and no doubt arising out of it—there also developed in Hausa, Fulani, Wolof, Mandinka, and other languages of Islamized groups in West Africa—what may be considered a vernacular tradition of African Islamic literature. Although the literature deals primarily with Islamic themes, its functions gradually expanded to encompass secular themes and to serve as a written means of communication. This literature, which was initially meant to be recited, is written in vernacular languages using a modified form of the Arabic script known as *ajami* or *aʿjami* (from the Arabic root *ʿ-j-m*, "foreign").

The writing systems are not standardized, and various diacritical marks were added to the classical Arabic script (for modifications to Arabic script to write Hausa see Hiskett, 1975; for Wolof, see Ngom, 2010.

Although religious leaders produce most of the *ʿajami* literature, and an important part of the literature deals with religious issues, *ʿajami* is by no means confined to the religious sphere. In Senegambia, for example, Cisse notes that some colonial treaties established between the French and Wolof kingdoms were written in Wolofal. Yet *ʿajami* continues to serve as one of the major means of written communication in many rural areas in Muslim communities in West Africa, where Qurʾānic schools are the primary educational institutions.

It is uncertain when *ʿajami* scripts and the literatures they record first emerged, but there is evidence that suggests that Kanuri, spoken just north of Lake Chad, was one of the first to be written in Arabic script, then Fulani, and later Hausa, Wolof, and Yoruba. A written literature with Islamic themes in Fulfulde probably emerged somewhat later, in the eighteenth century. Hausa written literature is believed to have arisen later still, during the nineteenth century, as the Hausa peasantry was drawn more closely into Islam; it gathered force after the successful *jihad* in the Hausa states in the early nineteenth century. The continuing discovery of *ʿajami* documents in various parts of Sudanic Africa indicates that the literary tradition of *ʿajami* in the region is less understood, more widespread, and more diverse than is commonly assumed. Special attention is deserved by unwritten vernacular Islamic literatures in Fulfulde and particularly in Hausa, including stories commonly known as "Hausa novels," an inappropriate term that disguises their ancient Islamic folkloric origin.

In the late eighteenth and early nineteenth centuries, within the sub-Saharan Qādirīyah community, there was an intensification of literary production. Poetry, treatises, rhetoric, prayer, and praise of the Prophet were newly popular modes of communication for the spread of Sufism. The overall aim of this activity was the elevation of Islamic consciousness throughout society, regardless of the general level of literacy.

Scholarship available on Muslim women's literary production in West Africa is rare and fragmentary. A noteworthy exception is given by that available on Nana Asmaʾu (1793–1864), daughter of Uthman ʿdan Fodiyo, the leader of jihads in Sokoto. Nana Asmaʾu devoted her life to the promotion of Islam in the Sokoto Caliphate, founded by her father in 1808. She assumed a leading role in politics, education, and social reforms and was a prolific scribe, scholar, and teacher. Author of a rich collection of poems in Fulfulbe and in Hausa, she is a well-documented case available of a Muslim woman writer. Her writings belong to several Arabic literary genres, whereas her Hausa verses were mostly oral texts mnemonically transmitted from one generation to another and later transcribed literarily. Apart from teaching students in her communities, she created a network of itinerary female teachers (*'yan taru*) whom she herself educated with the aim of broadly spreading her Islamic teachings, including to women living in the countryside and in more distant regions. These itinerant teachers used Asmaʾu's literary productions and mnemonic texts as classes to teach at other women's houses. Her verses describe Muslim practices to observe (such as in dressing and praying), but also the religious obligations of the Islamic pillars and Ṣūfī practices. Her aim was to teach orthodox Islam and Sufism to Muslim families, devoting special attention to women's education. Her Hausa didactic verses were addressed to concubines, servants, and illiterate women from the countryside with the goal of teaching them Islam. Asmaʾu is an emblematic example of an outstanding Muslim woman who assumed a scholarly, yet purposeful, role within the nineteenth century Islamic renewal movement in sub-Saharan Africa.

More recently, around 1930, women religious leaders emerged within the Tijaniyya Islamic brotherhood in Kano. Of particular noteworthiness is the role of the *mullābājī*—female Islamic teacher in the Hausa language—in promoting women's education. Notwithstanding these available case studies, scholarship on Muslim women's literary production is still rare and in need of more in-depth analysis.

BIBLIOGRAPHY

Boyd, Jean. "Distance Learning from Purdah in Nineteenth-Century Northern Nigeria: The Work of Asma'u Fodiyo." *Journal of African Cultural Studies* 14.1 (2001): 7–22.

Camara, Sana. "Ajami Literature in Senegal: The Example of Sëriñ Muusaa Ka, Poet and Biographer." *Research in African Literatures* 28.3 (1997): 163–182.

Cisse, Mamadou. "Écrits et écriture en Afrique de l'ouest." *Sud Langues* 6 (2006): 63–88.

Gutelius, David. "Newly Discovered 10th/16th C. Ajami Manuscript in Niger and Kel Tamachek History." *Saharan Studies Newsletter* 8.1–2 (2000): 1–6.

Haafkens, J. *Chants musulmans en Peul.* Leiden, The Netherlands: E. J. Brill, 1983. Study of the Fulfulde written vernacular tradition.

Hiskett, Mervyn. *A History of Hausa Islamic Verse.* London: School of African and Oriental Studies, University of London, 1975. Detailed account of the Hausa written vernacular tradition.

Hunwick, John. *West Africa, Islam, and the Arab World.* Princeton, N.J.: Marcus Wiener, 2006.

Hutson, Alaine. "African Sufi Women and Ritual Change." *Journal of Ritual Studies* 18.2 (2004): 61–73.

Kane, Ousmane. *Intellectuels non-europhones.* Dakar, Senegal: Council for the Development of Social Science Research in Africa, 2003.

Knappert, Jan. "The Islamic Poetry of Africa." *Journal for Islamic Studies* 10 (1990): 91–140.

Mack, Beverly B., and Jean Boyd. *One Woman's Jihad: Nana Asmaʿu, Scholar and Scribe.* Bloomington: Indiana University Press, 2000.

Ngom, Fallou. "Ajami Scripts in the Senegalese Speech Community." *Journal of Arabic and Islamic Studies*, 2010.

Qadhi, Abu Ammaar Yasir. *An Introduction to the Sciences of the Qurʿān.* Birmingham, U.K.: Al-Hidaayah Publishing, 1999.

MERVYN HISKETT
Updated by FALLOU NGOM
and SILVIA BRUZZI

AFTERLIFE. The three Abrahamic religions—Judaism, Christianity, and Islam—share the concept of an afterlife, albeit in different forms. The concept of the afterlife in the Abrahamic religions differs from the concept of reincarnation in religions such as Hinduism. Afterlife is considered to be the fate of the human being and humankind in general after death and the disappearance of This World, which is its contrast or binary opposite, although they make up an inseparable whole. Even though the afterlife is the ultimate goal and final destination of every human being (in the view of the Abrahamic religions), its shape completely depends on the actions and deeds committed in This World.

In Islam, This World is called *Dunyā*, and The Next World is called *ʾĀḫirah*. The afterlife from this worldly perspective represents the *ghayb*, or the unknown/unseen. Thus, human beings cannot with certainty tell what their fate in *ʾĀḫirah* would look like.

Afterlife in Islam includes several phases, of which the first is death. Humankind will be born again on the Day of Resurrection (*Yawm al-qiyāmah*) or the Day of Judgment (*Yawm al-dīn* or *Al-yawm al-ʿāḫir*). The belief in *Al-yawm al-ʿāḫir* represents one of the six main tenets of faith, apart from believing in God, angels, holy books, prophets, and God's will and predestination. The Day of Judgment decides where the human beings will finally continue with their eternal life.

As is obvious from various Qurʾānic depictions of the afterlife, there are two distinctive afterlife abodes that are the final destinations of every human being, and they are named *Jannah* (Paradise) and *Jahannam* (Hell). The Qurʾān frequently mentions these two words and gives depictions of them that are interpreted by some exegetes as symbolic. *Jannah* is the rewarding abode of the righteous, while *Jahannam* presents the punishing place of the unbelievers and sinners. The Qurʾān also mentions *Barzaḫ*, which cannot strictly be considered Purgatory in the Christian sense of the word, but rather the abode of human souls from the time of their death to the day of resurrection. However, this is not the exclusive use of the word, since *Barzaḫ* in the Qurʾān also corresponds not only to the borderline or barrier between two opposites, but also to the pre-existent time of souls (from their creation to the time of their birth).

Numerous verses (*ayats*) from the Qurʾān point out that the human beings are solely responsible for their fate in the afterlife, which depends on *ʾimān* (belief) and the good deeds one has committed during one's life. The Qurʾān emphasizes that men and women are equal in this respect, as seen from the following verses, among others: "Whoever works righteousness, man or woman, and has Faith, verily, to him will We give a new Life, a life that is good and pure and We will bestow on such their reward according to the best of their actions" (16:97), and "(Being) those who have believed in Our Signs and bowed (their wills to Ours) in Islam. Enter ye the Garden, ye and your wives, in (beauty and) rejoicing" (43:69–70).

The concept of afterlife in Islam, apart from confirmation of the belief in God, also emphasizes justice and equality, as stated in the Qurʾānic words: "But never will they fail to receive justice in the least little thing" (4:49). Equality is not reserved for humankind only, but to the ultimate equality of the two worlds: *Dunyā* and *ʾĀḫirah*. Muslims consider that both worlds are important, since their creator is One Lord, and if they enjoy a pious life in This World, that is the beginning of their afterlife.

Bibliography

Nasr, Seyyed Hossein, ed. *Islamic Spirituality* (I-Foundations, II-Manifestations). New York: Crossroad, 1987.

Rahman, Fazlur. *Major Themes of the Qurʾan*. Minneapolis: Bibliotheca Islamica, 1980.

Smith, Jane, and Yvonne Haddad. *The Islamic Understanding of Death and Resurrection*. Albany: State University of New York Press, 1981.

Dženita Karić

Aga Khan Foundation. The Aga Khan Foundation (AKF) is a private, nondenominational, philanthropic institution that was established in 1967 by Aga Khan IV, the Ismaili Imam, as part of a larger umbrella organization, the Aga Khan Development Network. The Foundation was conceived as an outreach to the developing world and as a way of linking Islam's humanitarian philosophy to issues of modern development. The ideals and ethics of Islam act as a springboard for the Foundation to address economic and social needs in an integrated manner for the benefit of Muslims and non-Muslims alike. As Aga Khan IV himself articulates: "The engagement of the Imamat in development is guided by the ethics of Islam that bridge faith and society, a premise on which I established [the AKDN]. Its cultural, social and economic development agencies seek to improve opportunities and living conditions of the weakest in society, without regard to their origin, gender or faith" (Khan, 2008, p. 58).

Since its inception, the AKF, headquartered in Geneva, Switzerland, has become a recognized international development agency with programs in Africa, Asia, Europe, and North America. Although it is a funding agency, the AKF also involves itself in the formation and development of projects, enabling local populations to create and manage sustainable institutions that are sensitive to cultural values, as well as development needs. The AKF country units develop projects according to the needs of the local communities, but pursue common objectives under the guidance of a board of directors chaired by the Aga Khan. The Foundation concentrates its attentions on four major thematic concerns: health care, education, rural development, and financial services, specifically microfinance.

One of the AKF's foremost goals is to build what Aga Khan IV has called "an enabling environment," in which individual volunteers, as well as the private and public sectors, contribute jointly to create favorable conditions for building permanent capacities in developing societies. In order to realize its goals, the Foundation has identified several "cross-cutting concerns" that are found across all the programming of the organization, among which is "Gender and Development." The Foundation hopes to both raise women's confidence and competence while expanding traditional male thinking about women in the societies in which it works, based on research and experience that have shown that including gender considerations in economic and social planning greatly increases the likelihood of success.

Aside from a general commitment to promoting the role of women in development, the AKF also runs several initiatives specifically directed at women's issues. In Afghanistan, the Foundation works closely with NGOs to expand access to education for girls. In several countries, including Afghanistan and Pakistan, the AKF has assisted in the development of community councils to facilitate greater engagement of women in local politics. The AKF promotes initiatives in several countries to expand access to sanitation and health care for women, particularly in rural communities. The Foundation also supports programs such as village credit schemes and training in crop and livestock management, accounting, and marketing skills for women. Through these endeavors, the Foundation hopes to affect the long-term process of cultural and attitudinal changes toward women in the areas in which it works.

BIBLIOGRAPHY

Aga Khan. *Where Hope Takes Root: Democracy and Pluralism in an Interdependent World.* Vancouver, British Columbia: Douglas & McIntyre, 2008.

The Aga Khan Development Network. www.akdn.org.

Aga Khan Foundation Afghanistan. "Annual Report 2010." http://www.akdn.org/publications/2010_akf_afghanistan_annual_report.pdf.
Aga Khan Foundation U.S.A. "Annual Report 2011." http://www.akdn.org/publications/2011_akf_usa_annual_report.pdf.

AZIM A. NANJI
Updated by MARYANNE RHETT
Updated by ZOHRA ISMAIL-BEBEN

AHL AL-BAYT. Literally "the people of the house," over time, the term *ahl al-bayt* has come to mean, more specifically, "the household of the Prophet," and particularly five members of that household: the Prophet Muḥammad, his daughter Fāṭimah, Fāṭimah's husband (and Muḥammad's cousin) ʿAlī, and their two sons, al-Ḥasan and al-Ḥusayn. Opinions have varied over the centuries as to who is included in the *ahl al-bayt*. It was first applied to the families of the caliphs, with growing Shīʿī sentiment supporting the inclusion of ʿAlī and the family of Muḥammad.

The interpretation of the concept has played a key role within the larger question of leadership and legitimacy after Muḥammad's death. The term appears in the Qurʾān several times, with meanings ranging from Abraham's family (11:71–74) to the Prophet's wives, or more generally Muḥammad's family, which would be the Banū Hāshim and his two uncles (Abū Ṭālib [d. 619 CE] and al-ʿAbbās [d. 653 CE]), or a subset limited to the five members listed above (33:33; 42:23 cf. 33:6). Thus, the ʿAbbāsid Empire claimed legitimacy for their rule in part due to their blood relations with Muḥammad. Indeed, the Qurʾān accords the *ahl al-bayt* of Muḥammad an elevated status above the rest of the faithful (33:6). However, many commentators, such as al-Haytamī (d. 974 CE) interpreted this verse as referring to ʿAlī, Fāṭimah, Ḥasan, and Ḥusayn. In addition, Shīʿī traditions, such as *ḥadīth al-kisāʾ* ("Tradition of the Cloak"), support this limited definition of the Prophet's household, in support of which it is said that Muḥammad gathered the four and proclaimed: "O God, these are my family (*ahl baytī*) whom I have chosen; take the pollution from them and purify them thoroughly," and, "He who oppresses my *ahl bayt* or fights against them or attacks them or curses them, God forbids him from entering paradise" (Sharon, 1986, p. 172).

For Shīʿī Muslims, given their interpretation that the rightful and designated successor to Muḥammad was the Imām ʿAlī and his male descendants, the *ahl al-bayt* became the model family to emulate. With this acceptance of the sanctity of the Prophet's family and the unique hereditary aspects of his progeny, religious symbolism developed that assigned to them various characteristics. Muḥammad, as the recipient of the revelation and thus the direct link with God, is only approachable through his family members. ʿAlī represents the intellectual, esoteric, and legal aspects of religion, providing both the true meaning of revelation and complete knowledge of religious law. Ḥasan typifies wisdom through quietism with his withdrawal from political activities, despite remaining an imam. Ḥusayn came to represent atonement and martyrdom due to his noble death. Fāṭimah, who retains the singular honour of being the only woman among the Holy Five, as well as a member of the Twelver Shīʿī's Fourteen Pure Souls (Muḥammad, Fāṭimah and the Twelve Imāms), is the model and ideal of womanhood; this ideal often takes the form of the mother-creator, often in relation to the image of Mary, Jesus's mother.

While Sunnī Islam respects and honors the family of the Prophet, Shīʿī Islam focuses on the *ahl al-bayt* as one of the distinguishing features of Shiism, with its emphasis on the hereditary nature of the leadership of the community. This elevation and veneration has led to the most common definition of the term: the five members of the family of Muḥammad.

BIBLIOGRAPHY

Daftary, Farhad. *The Ismāʿīlīs: Their History and Doctrines.* 2d ed. Cambridge: Cambridge University Press, 2007. Provides a short discussion of the Ismāʿīlī Shīʿī viewpoint.

Madelung, Wilferd. *The Succession to Muḥammad: A Study of the Early Caliphate.* Cambridge, U.K.: Cambridge University Press, 1997. Clarifies the context of the early development of the questions surrounding the issue of succession to Muḥammad.

Momen, Moojan. *An Introduction to Shiʿi Islam: The History and Doctrines of Twelver Shiʿism.* New Haven, Conn.: Yale University Press, 1985. Traces Imāmi Shīʿite perspectives.

Sharon, Moshe. "Ahl al-Bayt–People of the House." *Jerusalem Studies in Arabic and Islam* 8 (1986): 167–184. A comprehensive study of the concept.

CHARLES FLETCHER

AHMED, LEILA. (b. 1940), Egyptian-American feminist writer and intellectual. Born in Cairo to a professional middle-class father and a mother of Turkish upper-class origin, Ahmed received her basic education in Cairo before she moved to England for her higher education. She studied English literature at the University of Cambridge in the 1960s and graduated with a Ph.D.

Her first appointment was in Abu Dhabi, where she worked on national school curriculum reform and taught at Abu Dhabi University. She moved to the United States in 1979 and was appointed professor in women's studies and Near Eastern studies at the University of Massachusetts at Amherst in 1981. While there she served as director of the Near Eastern studies program from 1991 to 1992 and director of the women's studies program from 1992 to 1995. In 1999 she became the first professor of women's studies in religion at Harvard Divinity School.

During her stay in Abu Dhabi, Ahmed increasingly came to situate her work within a feminist conceptual framework and to focus on issues related to women's roles in and perceptions of Islam—themes central to her work. In 1992 she published *Women and Gender in Islam*, a book that soon became a classic. The book constituted the first comprehensive compilation of historical information about Arab Middle Eastern women's living conditions, with a key focus on the wide range of religious discourses on women and gender that have set the coordinates for women's lives in this region historically and into the twenty-first century.

The rich variety of religious interpretations and practices that exist within lived Islam, and the compassion and generosity that distinguishes many of these religious expressions from the more learned versions that tend to be perceived as "accurate" Islam by their proponents as well as by Western observers, is another recurring topic in Ahmed's writings. In her 1999 autobiography, *A Border Passage*, this topic is vividly presented in her descriptions of the religious perceptions and practices she grew up with. She also deals with a closely related topic, the modern constructions of the pan-Arab and -Islamic identities and their delegitimizing effect on lived local cultural and religious expressions in the Arab world.

Ahmed's later work increasingly concentrates on expressions of Islam in the Western world, in particular the United States, and the interplay between Muslim and Western values and perspectives. Her 2011 book, *A Quiet Revolution*, is a milestone in this respect. In this book, Ahmed traces the reasons for the ebbs and flows of the use of veils in the Arab world over the previous hundred years, highlighting the role of Western (colonial) powers in both the unveiling and re-veiling of Arab women. Ahmed also follows this symbol of Muslim faith into post-9/11 American society and explores how religiously based activism in fact creates an important arena for Muslim women's feminist reinterpretations of their religion and renegotiations of their gendered living conditions.

Leila Ahmed has become one of the most authoritative voices on modern Islam in the United States and on Islamic feminism.

BIBLIOGRAPHY

Abdelrazek, Amal Talaat. *Contemporary Arab American Women Writers: Hyphenated Identities and Border Crossings*. Youngstown, N.Y.: Cambria Press, 2007.

Ahmed, Leila. *A Border Passage: From Cairo to America—A Woman's Journey*. New York: Penguin Books, 1999.

Ahmed, Leila. *A Quiet Revolution: The Veil's Resurgence, from the Middle East to America*. New Haven, Conn.: Yale University Press, 2011.

Ahmed, Leila. *Women and Gender in Islam: Historical Roots of a Modern Debate*. New Haven, Conn.: Yale University Press, 1992.

"Leila Ahmed." http://www.hds.harvard.edu/people/faculty/leila-ahmed. Ahmed's profile at Harvard Divinity School.

MARIT TJOMSLAND

ʿĀʾISHA BINT SAʿD BINT B. ABI WAQQAS. (d. 735), *ḥadīth* transmitter. ʿĀʾisha bint Saʿd bint b. Abi Waqqas al-Zuhriyya al-Madaniyya was the daughter of a well-known Companion. Classical ḥadīth scholars differed as to whether she herself was a Companion (of the Prophet) or a Successor (of the generation of Companions). Ibn Hibban (d. 965) includes a brief biographical entry for her among the female Successors in his *Kitab al-Thiqat*. In his *Kitab Tadhkirat al-huffaz, al-Dhahabi* (d. 1348) lists her among the scholarly Successors (*ulamaʾ al-tabiʿin*). However, in his *Isaba*, Ibn Hajar al-Asqalani (d. 1449) notes the existence of a well-known *ḥadīth* in which Saʿd tells Muhammad that he only has one daughter. If this daughter was ʿĀʾisha, then she would be a Companion. Ibn Hajar's "solution" is that Saʿd had two daughters named ʿĀʾisha—one a Companion, and the other a Successor.

Ibn Saʿd (d. 845) states that ʿĀʾisha had met six wives of the Prophet; she related *ḥadīth* from several of them, as well as from her father Saʿd—and "people" passed on *ḥadīth* from her. Classical sources give divergent assessments of her as a *ḥadīth* transmitter. Al-Khatib al-Baghdadi (d. 1071) recounts traditions asserting that Imam Malik (d. 796) did not relate *ḥadīth* from ʿĀʾisha bt. Saʿd, because he regarded her as a weak transmitter. However, al-Mizzi (d. 1341) includes Malik in his list of those who received *ḥadīth* from her; he also states that al-Bukhari, Abu Dawud, al-Tirmidhi, and al-Nasaʾi recount *ḥadīth* on her authority. In his *Siyar*, al-Dhahabi includes ʿĀʾisha among those from whom Malik related traditions with incomplete chains of transmission. The development of more stringent standards in *ḥadīth* transmission appears to have affected perceptions of her reliability.

Topics dealt with in *ḥadīth* transmitted from ʿĀʾisha include bequests, the issue of drinking while standing, and the merits of the Prophet's mosque in Medina.

Memorialized chiefly as a *ḥadīth* transmitter, she reportedly died at the age of eighty-four.

BIBLIOGRAPHY

Al-Bukhari, Muhammad b. Ismaʿil b. al-Mughira. *Sahih al-Bukhari*. Translated by Muhammad Muhsin Khan. *K. al-Jihad*, vol. 4. Medina, Saudi Arabia: Dar al-Fikr, 1979.

Al-Dhahabi, Shams al-Muhammad. *Kitab Tadhkirat al-huffaz*. Edited by Zakariyya Umayrat. Beirut, Lebanon: Dar al-Kutub al-Ilmiyya, 1998.

Al-Dhahabi, Shams al-Muhammad. *Siyar aʿlam al-nubalaʾ*. Edited by Shuʿayb Arnaʾut. Beirut, Lebanon: Muʾassasat al-Risala, 1981.

Al-Dhahabi, Shams al-Muhammad. *Taʾrikh al-Islam wa-wafayat al-mashahir l-aʿlam*. Edited by Umar Abd al-Salam Tadmuri. Beirut, Lebanon: Dar al-Kutub al-Arabi, 1997.

Al-Khatib al-Baghdadi, Abi Bakr Ahmad b. Ali. *Kitab al-Kifaya fi ilm al-riwaya* Hyderabad, India: Osmania Oriental Publications, 1970.

Al-Mizzi, Jamal al-Din. *Tahdhib al-kamal fi asma' al-rijal*. Edited by Bashshar Awwad Ma'ruf. Beirut, Lebanon: Mu'assasat al-Risala, 1992.

Al-Tabarani, Abu al-Qasim Sulayman b. Ahmad. *Al-Mu'jam al-Kabir*. Edited by Abu Muhammad al-Asyuti. Beirut, Lebanon: Dar al-Kutub al-Ilmiyya, 2007.

Ibn Hajar al-Asqalani. *Al-Isaba fi tamyiz al-sahaba*. Edited by Hasan 'Abd al-Mannan. Riyadh, Saudi Arabia: Afkar, 2004.

Ibn Hibban, Abu Hatim Muhammad. *Kitab al-Thiqat*. Edited by Ibrahim Shams al-Din and Turki Farhan al-Mustafa. Beirut, Lebanon: Dar al-Kutub al-Ilmiyya, 1998.

Ibn Sa'd, Muhammad. *Al-Tabaqat al-kubra*. Edited by Hamza al-Nashrati et al. Cairo, Egypt: al-Maktaba al-Qayyima, n.d.

AISHA GEISSINGER

'Ā'ISHA BINT TALHA. (d. c. 728), Successor and transmitter of *ḥadīth*. 'Ā'isha bint Talha was the daughter of a well-known Companion, Talha b. Ubaydallah al-Taymi. Her mother, Umm Kulthum, was a daughter of Abu Bakr. 'Ā'isha bt. Talha's first marriage was to her cousin, Abdallah b. Abd al-Rahman b. Abi Bakr. Following his death, she married Mus'ab b. al-Zubayr b. al-Awwam, the amir of Iraq. After Mus'ab was killed, she married Umar b. Ubaydallah al-Taymi. She died in or around the year 728.

'Ā'isha is presented in varying ways in the classical sources. Ibn Sa'd's (d. 845) very short biographical note for her simply gives her lineage, names her husbands, and states that she related *ḥadīth* from A'isha bt. Abi Bakr.

Some classical biographers focus on her lively social life as an elite wealthy woman and her marriages. Al-Dhahabi (d. 1348) notes her beauty and social prominence, as well as the large sums of money that she famously received as *mahr* from her second and third husbands. Al-Safadi (d. 1363) describes her beauty in detail and provides a number of colorful anecdotes about her conflicts with Mus'ab. She is said to have adamantly refused to veil her face.

Some sources discuss her primarily as a Successor who reliably transmitted *ḥadīth* from her famous aunt, 'Ā'isha bt. Abi Bakr. Ibn Hibban (d. 965) includes a brief passage on her among the female Successors in his *Kitab al-ThiqÁt*, stating that she transmitted *ḥadīth* from 'Ā'isha bt. Abi Bakr, and that the people of Medina related *ḥadīth* from her. Al-Mizzi (d. 1341) notes that the well-known *ḥadīth* critic, Yahya b. Ma'in (d. 848), characterized her as a reliable transmitter (*thiqah*), but that Abu Zur'a al-Dimashqi (d. 815) stated that people related *ḥadīths* from her due to her merits and refinement (*li-fada'iliha wa-adabiha*)—that is, because of her social prominence, rather than her reputation as a transmitter.

'Ā'isha bt. Talha appears in the chains of transmission (*isnāds*) of a small number of *ḥadīth* found in major Sunni collections. These *ḥadīth* address topics including fasting, destiny (*qadr*), and the best *jihad* for women to undertake—which is said to be performing the *hajj*.

BIBLIOGRAPHY

Al-Bukhari, Muhammad b. Isma'il b. al-Mughira. *Sahih al-Bukhari*. Translated by Muhammad Muhsin Khan. *K. al-Jihad*, vol. 4. Medina, Saudi Arabia: Dar al-Fikr, 1979.

Al-Dhahabi, Muhammad b. Ahmad. *Siyar a'lam al-nubala'*. Edited by Shu'ayb Arna'ut. Beirut, Lebanon: Mu'assasat al-Risala, 1981.

Ibn Hibban, Abu Hatim Muhammad. *Kitab al-Thiqat*. Edited by Ibrahim Shams al-Din and Turki Farhan al-Mustafa. Beirut, Lebanon: Dar al-Kutub al-'Ilmiyya, 1998.

Ibn Sa'd, Muhammad. *Al-Tabaqat al-kubra*. Edited by Hamza al-Nashrati et al. Cairo, Egypt: al-Maktaba al-Qayyima, n.d.

Al-Mizzi, Jamal al-Din. *Tahdhib al-kamal fi asma' al-rijal*. Edited by Bashshar 'Awwad Ma'ruf. Beirut, Lebanon: Mu'assasat al-Risala, 1992.

Muslim b. al-Hajjaj al-Qushayri. *Sahih Muslim*. Beirut, Lebanon: Dar Ihya' al-Turath al-'Arabi, 2000.

Roded, Ruth. *Women in Islamic Biographical Collections: From Ibn Sa'd to Who's Who*. Boulder, Colo.: L. Rienner, 1994.

Al-Safadi, Salah al-Din b. Aybak. *Kitab al-Wafi bi-l-Wafayat*. Edited by Widad al-Qadi. Wiesbaden, Germany: Franz Steiner Verlag, 1982.

AISHA GEISSINGER

ʿĀʾISHAH. ʿĀʾishah (lit., "the one who lives") al-Ṣiddīq (the true friend), daughter of Muḥammad's closest companion Abū Bakr, is central to Muslim salvation history. At the age of six she was engaged to the fifty-year-old Muḥammad and in 623 CE, at the age of nine, she became one of his wives. In 627, at the age of fourteen, she was accused of adultery and then absolved of the charge by divine revelation. (Qurʾān 24:23, a general verse on the subject of accusing innocent women, is understood to refer to her). In 632, at the age of eighteen, she was widowed when Muḥammad died in her lap; he was buried in her chamber. She was the only wife of Muḥammad who was a virgin at the time of marriage, and this, along with her beauty and intelligence, was part of her sensual appeal to him. She was also the only wife in whose company, while sharing the same blanket, the Prophet received revelation. She was the most beloved wife with the exception of Khadīja, the Prophet's first wife, during whose lifetime he did not marry another woman.

As a widow of the Prophet, the young, beautiful, and childless ʿĀʾishah, *umm al-muʾminīn* (mother of the faithful), was forbidden to remarry (33:53). Based on her status through birth and marriage, she continued to play a leading role in the life of the community, which was torn apart over the issue of rightful succession after the Prophet. In 656 her opposition to ʿAlī, the fourth caliph, led to the first civil war. (For the men who shaped her narrative, her action set a negative precedent that justifies denying women access to public life and leadership.) After withdrawing from political life, ʿĀʾishah devoted herself to the education of the community, since her proximity to the Prophet and her presence while he performed ritual acts gave her a religious knowledge that the community needed. ʿĀʾishah died in 678 at the age of sixty-six, having survived the Prophet by forty-eight years. Two-thirds of the Sunnī *ḥadīth* are reported on the authority of ʿĀʾishah.

In Shīʿī sources, ʿĀʾishah is cast as a negative figure who opposed the first Shīʿī imam, ʿAlī, and was a rival for the Prophet's affection for Fāṭimah, his daughter (by Khadīja) and ʿAlī's wife. For Sunnī Muslims of all persuasions, the *ḥabībah* (beloved) ʿĀʾishah retains her appeal. While the traditionalists continue to present her as a role model for Muslim women, others, in their efforts to promote gender equity, continue to reflect on and re-imagine the narrative of ʿĀʾishah. For example, some raise her age at marriage from nine to between fourteen and nineteen years. And some, instead of condemning her political involvement, seek lessons from the legacy of ʿĀʾishah to promote autonomy in their own lives.

[*See also* Companions of the Prophet; Fāṭimah; Ḥadīth, *subentry on* Transmission; Khadīja bint Khuwaylid; Religious Biography and Hagiography; Wives of the Prophet; *and* Women of the Prophet's Household: Interpretation.]

BIBLIOGRAPHY

Ahmed, Leila. "Women and the Advent of Islam." *Signs* 11, no. 4 (Summer 1986): 665–691. Ahmed names ʿĀʾishah, rather than Khadīja, the first woman of Islam. She contrasts the differences in their lives as an illustration of how the advent of Islam circumscribed the freedom and rights of women. She takes a critical feminist approach to early Islamic history, while treating the medieval sources as historical rather than literary sources.

Elsadda, Hoda. "Discourses on Women's Biographies and Cultural Identity: Twentieth-Century Representations of the Life of ʿĀʾishah Bint Abi Bakr." *Feminist Studies* 27, no. 1 (Spring 2001): 37–64. The article discusses six modern biographies of ʿĀʾishah with the aim of demonstrating how construction of biographies is used to create representations of cultural identity and disseminate political ideology.

Spellberg, Denise A. *Politics, Gender, and the Islamic Past: The Legacy of ʿĀʾishah bint Abi Bakr*. New York: Columbia University Press, 1994. Spellberg presents a strong case that the persona of ʿĀʾishah should be seen as a creation of medieval men to serve their sociopolitical and sectarian purposes.

Ghazala Anwar

Aisyiyah, Nasyiatul. Nasyiatul Aisyiyah, usually shortened as Nasyiah and popularly abbreviated as NA, is one of the largest and longest-standing mass organizations in Indonesia established by and for young Muslim women. It currently claims membership of two million young women, with hundreds of local branches spread all over the country's provinces. Nasyiah's development reflects the struggles of young Muslim women for public recognition and participation alongside the development of the Indonesian nationhood, feminist and women's, and Islamic movements. Currently, Nasyiah members are between sixteen and thirty-five years old, reside in urban areas, and come from relatively well-educated family backgrounds.

Before it reached its current organizational structure and culture, Nasyiah was structured as an extracurricular activity within Muhammadiyah's girls' schools—then called Siswa Praja Wanita (SPW, Respectable School for Girls)—which were founded in 1917 in the Javanese town of Yogyakarta. The Muslim girls attending schools and participating in SPW were aged between seven and fourteen years old. In order to reach wider girl audiences outside the town of Yogyakarta, in 1924, SPW was incorporated with another Muhammadiyah women's wing organization called Aisyiyah, and became the latter's section for young girls. SPW spread quickly to other islands of the archipelago, along with Muhammadiyah and Aisyiyah development. As a consequence, members from outside Java demanded that the name of the organization be changed to avoid the "Java-centric" SPW. Thus, in 1931, SPW was changed to Nasyiatul Aisyiyah, which means "the young generation of Aisyiyah." The name "Aisyiyah" was taken from the name of the Prophet Muhammad's wife ʿĀʾishah, who was recognized as a loving and caring, smart, knowledgeable, and independent woman. The figure of ʿĀʾishah provided the theological, historical, and political inspiration of both organizations: Aisyiyah for adult women, and Nasyiah for young women.

The social and discursive space for young womanhood created and maintained by Nasyiah throughout its history—from colonial times up through the present day—is significant for a number of reasons. The concept of youth within Nasyiah is not static; on the contrary, it is a dynamic notion relevant to its respective development within the history of gender politics in Indonesia. During Dutch colonial rule, all common people in general, including, especially, girls, were denied access to school, and early marriage was a very common practice. Once a girl was married, she would suddenly be counted as an adult woman, regardless of her age. Thus, marriage became a significant rite of passage whereby a girl was transformed into an adult woman and deemed no longer suitable to stay at school and within the Nasyiah organization. Parents married daughters off early because marriage was regarded as the most important ritual by which a

Javanese woman might attain higher social status, especially if she was desired by a man of higher standing, or simply by any man at an early age. It was considered shameful to have unmarried fourteen-year-old girls in the home, as these girls were stigmatized as "unwanted old virgins." Another reason for early marriage was to prevent girls from being polluted by illegitimate sexual relations with boys. Given this cultural construction of young womanhood, Nasyiah defines youth to include girls aged from seven to eighteen years old. Together with its maternal organization, Aisyiyah, Nasyiah focuses on improving the access to and participation of Muslim girls in education, including religious learning, life skills, and general literacy, so that they can challenge traditional cultural norms. Nasyiah provides space and respect for girls older than fourteen who are seeking knowledge, skills, and a meaningful life outside of the context of marriage.

After the end of the country's war for independence in the early 1950s (the proclamation of independence itself was made in 1945), discrimination in the area of basic education against girls and the general indigenous population was officially lifted. Girls' access to education improved gradually, opening up new opportunities for them to stay in school longer and gain formal employment in offices and firms afterward—options that they had not enjoyed before. The Nasyiah membership grew and evolved alongside such social changes. As more Nasyiah girls stayed in school, attended college, and gained new experiences, they brought new ideas back to the organization and proposed changes accordingly.

In the 1960s, Nasyiah members increasingly felt dissatisfied with the program for young women assigned by Aisyiyah, its maternal organization, and sought approval from Muhammadiyah to be an autonomous organization for young women, separate from Aisyiyah. The demand for autonomy was granted in 1964 during a Muhammadiyah and Aisyiyah national congress. Upon gaining autonomy, Nasyiah strengthened its commitment to supporting young, Indonesian, Muslim women. These triple loyalties—young women, Indonesian, Muslim—also undergirded its organizational identity.

The defining issues focused on by Nasyiah, however, have changed significantly over the course of its history. The maximum membership age of Nasyiah was raised from eighteen to thirty-five years old, and marriage was no longer counted as a defining factor in membership. Programs that advance young women's literacy, leadership capacity, economic independence, and political awareness have been the highlights of Nasyiah since the 1970s, when the New Order regime under President Suharto silenced all women's and students' organizations with overt political motives. In return, the government sponsored and established a number of women' organizations that promote submissive, apolitical, married womanhood, and provide no social space, respect, or policy for women who delay marriage or opt not to marry at all.

During the 1990s, when the New Order regime allowed some differing opinions to emerge, and international donors arrived with funding to enhance their agenda interests in Indonesia, the nation witnessed the establishment of various non-governmental organizations (NGOs). The most apparent have been working to promote feminist ideas and practices. Others call for religious observance, and still others focus on current political issues. Nasyiah has been an active player in such feminist discourse, participating in shaping it. While many newly formed feminist NGOs were initially founded through grants from foreign foundations operating in the country, Nasyiah preferred to maintain its independence by limiting access to foreign funding, yet without denying cooperation and network-building.

In the twenty-first century, Nasyiah continued to strengthen its position as a learning center for young women in a broader sense, from promoting Qurʾānic literacy to feminist issues, from training in microfinance enterprises to voter education. Nasyiah is committed to continuing to provide support for young Muslim women not only in their practical gender interests, but also in advancing their strategic gender-based interests.

BIBLIOGRAPHY

Baried, Baroroh. "Islam and the Modernization of Indonesian Women." In *Islam and Society in Southeast Asia*, edited by Taufik Abdullah and Sharon Siddique, pp. 139–154. Singapore: Institute of Southeast Asian Studies, 1986.

Marcoes-Natsir, Lies M., and Johan H. Meuleman, eds. *Wanita Islam ndonesia dalam kajian Tekstual dan Kontekstual*. Jakarta, Indonesia: INIS, 1993.

Nakamura, Mitsuo. 1993. *The Crescent Arises over the Banyan Tree: A Study of the Muhammadiyah Movement in a Central Javanese Town*. Yogyakarta, Indonesia: Gadjah Mada University Press, 1993.

Pimpinan Pusat Nasyiatul Aisyiyah, ed. *Riwayat Singkat, Khittah Perjuangan, Kepribadian NA*. Yogyakarta, Indonesia: Departemen Dokin, PP NA, 1999.

Syamsiyatun, Siti. *Serving Young Indonesian Muslim Women: The Dynamic of the Gender Discourse in Nasyiatul Aisyiyah, 1965–2005*. Germany: Lambert Academic Publishing, 2010.

Van Doorn-Harder, Pieternella. *Women Shaping Islam: Indonesian Women Reading the* Qurʾān. Urbana: University of Illinois Press, 2006.

White, Sally Jane. 2004. "Reformist Islam, Gender and Marriage in Late Colonial Dutch East Indies, 1900–1942." Ph.D. diss., Australian National University, 2004.

SITI SYAMSIYATUN

AKHLĀQ. The Islamic concept of *akhlāq*, or ethics, is derived from a vast body of literature. It includes the Qurʾān, *ḥadīth*, commentaries on the Qurʾān, and the works of theologians, philosophers, mystics, historians, political thinkers, and other writers. Grounded in the religious worldview of Islam with influences from Greek philosophy, Islamic ethics extends to theology, spirituality, eschatology, social ethics, and the political order.

"Akhlāq" is the plural of "khulq", meaning character, nature, or disposition. While the word "akhlāq" is not found in the Qurʾān, "khulq" is used twice in the sense of character and disposition (26:137 and 68:4). Ethical qualities are discussed throughout the Qurʾān to emphasize the significance of faith and leading a virtuous life. Stories of previous prophets and nations are narrated to underline the central place of ethical norms in human history. In some stories, immoral acts, such as sodomy and oppression, are presented as destroying the moral integrity of society.

According to the Qurʾān, humans are endowed with reason and free will to make moral choices between good and evil (91:9–10). They have been created in the "best manner" (95:4); God has "breathed into them from His spirit" (15:29) and placed them on earth as "God's vicegerent" (2:30). This has led to an extensive body of literature about the ontological status and origin of moral values, and the extent to which humans can know good and evil through both reason and revelation.

A major difference between Islamic and pre-Islamic Arabic conceptions of ethics is Islam's emphasis on the oneness of God on the one hand, and the afterlife on the other. While the social function of ethical norms in this world is acknowledged, the divine reward and punishment in the afterlife forms a strong component of ethical behavior. The ultimate goal of behaving morally, however, is to gain "God's favor" (see 11:112, 42:15, and 76:8–9), which is the sine qua non of virtue in this world and eternal bliss and happiness in heaven. Muslim thinkers have generally rejected utilitarian ethics, and instead emphasize the intrinsic value of virtues and ethical norms.

According to a tradition, the Prophet Muḥammad "has been sent to complete the refinement of good character" (*makārim al-akhlāq*). When asked about the Prophet Muḥammad's "ethics," his wife ʿĀʾishah is reported to have said that "his was the ethics of the Qurʾān." The Qurʾān presents the Prophet Muḥammad as the "best example" (33:21) for moral behavior; this example of right ethical conduct is meant for everyone and goes beyond the philosophical elitism of the Greeks, which the Muslim Peripatetic school largely adopted. Later *ḥadīth* collections and the commonly referred to book of the "forty *ḥadīth*" bring together those sayings of Prophet Muḥammad that emphasize virtues and ethical norms.

Among the classics of Islamic ethics, one can mention al-Māwardī's *Adāb al-dunyā wa al-dīn* ("The Book of Good Manners for the World and Religion"), Ibn Ḥazm's *al-Akhlāq wa al-sīr* ("Ethics and Life"), Abū Naṣr al-Ṭabarsī's *Makārim al-akhlāq* ("Ethical Refinement"), Ibn Miskawayh's *Tahdhīb al-akhlāq* ("Refinement of Ethics"), Naṣīr al-Dīn al-Ṭūsī's *Akhlāq-i Naṣīrī* ("The Nasirian Ethics"), Jalāl al-Dīn Dawwani's *Akhlāq-i Jalālī* ("The Jalalian Ethics"), and Kinalizade Ali Efendi's *Akhlāq-i ʿAlaʾi* ("The Alaian Ethics"). While these are devoted exclusively to ethics, they also deal with other issues that have, traditionally, been part of the Islamic ethical tradition, for example household management, city life, politics, and governance. One should also mention such independent works as al-Ghazālī's *Iḥyāʾ ʿulūm al-dīn* ("The Revival of Religious Sciences"), which takes up ethical issues from a primarily spiritual point of view. Such literary works as *Kalilah wa Dimna*, an Indian book of fables or tales of wisdom translated into Arabic by Ibn al-Muqaffaʿ, have also served as popular books of ethics.

In the ethico-philosophical tradition, ethics is usually categorized under "practical wisdom" (*al-hikmat al-ʾamaliyyah*), which consists of three subdivisions: *akhlāq* (ethics), *tadbīr al-manzil* (household management), and *al-siyasat al-madaniyyah* (politics or city management). The first concerns the person him- or herself; the second his or her family and relatives; and the third the city, for example the sociopolitical body in which he or she lives. These three areas cover basic human relations and are addressed to both men and women. In his *Risalah fi al-siyasat al-manziliyyah* ("Concerning Household Management"), Ibn Sina discusses spousal relations within the household and describes the woman as an equal partner in possessing property with her husband and protecting their shared estate. She shares the burdens of the household and bears the responsibility for raising children. According to Ibn Sina, the ideal woman is smart, religious, productive, loyal, trustworthy, polite, and serious in her demeanor. As for the husband, he should protect his wife, respect her, provide for her and the house, and be fair toward family members. In the legal tradition, women have been given full rights for economic transactions (buying, selling, and trading) as well as for establishing nonprofit foundations and organizations.

All of the major schools and figures of the Islamic intellectual tradition have dealt with ethics. The *Mutakallimūn* (theologians) discussed the ontological status of ethical norms and the epistemic ways of knowing them. The Muʿtazilah defended the thesis that God, being omniscient and just, always acts in the interest of His servants. As a result, He is bound to do what is rationally true and morally perfect. This is complemented by man's God-given free will to choose between good and evil. Without free will, there would be no meaning for God's "reward" (*al-waʿd*) and "punishment" (*al-wʿīd*). Furthermore, if man is free to make moral choices, then he must be able to use his reason to distinguish right from wrong. In contrast to the Muʿtazilites, the Ashʿarī theologians explain moral values in terms of God's will. Giving man only a limited free will, the Ashʿarīs deny human agents the ability to judge if something is good, bad, or reprehensible unless it is clarified by revelation. Moral values are ontologically grounded in God's will, which in Ashʿarī theology takes precedence over other models of explanation.

The Muslim Peripatetic philosophers expanded the field of ethics to include psychology and the sociopolitical order. Adopting the Greek notions of rational ethics, they defined "happiness" (*saʿādah*) as the ultimate goal of ethical behavior. In tandem with the Platonic worldview, bodily pleasures cannot bring true happiness because they are partial, transitory, and defined by their opposites. True happiness is attained through intellectual contemplation, and this is possible only when the accomplished philosopher reaches "conjunction" (*ittiṣāl*) with the Active Intellect, which is the depository of all intelligible forms and perfect universal values. Since only a few can attain such a union with the universal truth, the vast majority of ordinary people fall short of reaching true happiness. This leads to a tension between the social and spiritual egalitarianism of Islam on the one hand, and the elitist and aristocratic ethics of the Greeks on the other.

Plato's *Republic* and Aristotle's *Nicomachean Ethics* were translated into Arabic early on and received significant attention from Muslim philosophers. Al-Fārābī's *Taḥṣīl al-saʿādah* ("The Attainment of Happiness") and *al-Madīnat al-fāḍilah* ("The Virtuous City"), *inter alia*, are woven around the three areas of Islamic ethics: ethics or virtues (*akhlāq*), household management (*tadbīr al-manzil*), and the virtuous city, or city governance (*siyasat al-mudun*). Abū al-ḥasan al-Āmirī's *Kitāb al-saʿādah wa al-isʿâd* ("The Book of Happiness and its Attainment") is designed like an encyclopedia of the philosophy and ethics of happiness. Given that ethics is also an elaborate discipline for the refinement of character, it has sometimes been called "spiritual medicine" (*al-ṭibb al-rūḥānī*). Abū Bakr Zakarīyā al-Rāzī's *al-Ṭibb al-rūḥānī* ("The Spiritual Medicine") combines ethics with traditional psychology and cosmology.

The Ṣūfīs have written extensively on both practical and spiritual ethics. The propensity of early Ṣūfīs toward simple devotion and asceticism (*zuhd*) has been complemented by more elaborate teachings of ethics in later centuries. Some Ṣūfīs defined *taṣawwuf* simply as ethics or "good character" (*ḥusn al-khulq*) and focused on the virtues. In the Ṣūfī tradition, morality is to appropriate the virtues, and the virtues are ways of participating in the universal truth. In a related sense, ethics is freedom from the bonds of the self. It is spiritual disengagement from what is transitory and illusionary.

In contrast to theologians and philosophers, the Ṣūfīs explained practical ethics through stories, manuals, parables, and other literary means. Abū Ṭālib al-Makkī's *Qūt al-qulūb* ("The Food of the Heart") is one of the earliest classics of Sufism and can also be read as a book of spiritual and practical ethics. Abū Bakr al-Sarrāj's *al-Lumʿa* ("The Reflecting Light"), al-Hujwīrī's *Kashf al-maḥjūb* ("Unveiling the Veiled"), Qushayrī's *Risālah*, and Suhrawardī's *ʿAwārif al-maʿārif* ("The Book of Guidance for Essential Knowledge") analyze the various aspects of the ethics of virtues as the basis of "spiritual wayfaring" (*sayr al-sulūk*). Ibn al-ʿArabī's *al-Futūḥāt al-makkīyah* ("The Meccan Revelations") and Jalāl al-Dīn Rūmī's *Mathnawi*, *Diwan-i Kabīr*, and *Fīhi ma fīh* are also among the main sources of Ṣūfī and popular Islamic ethics.

These major ethical themes have been addressed to all members of society, but their religious and social function has been emphasized especially in regard to women as founders of the household and those in charge of raising children. The Ṣūfī tradition has especially addressed women more directly through sermons, stories, parables, poems, and other scholarly and literary forms. Rūmi's *Mathnawi* and *Fihi ma fih*, for instance, contain numerous references to women as lovers and seducers but also as spouses, soul mates, spiritual partners, manifestations of divine beauty, and epitomes of ethical behavior, devotion, and God-consciousness (*taqwā*).

In contemporary scholarship, Islamic ethics have been discussed in relation to politics, law, business, leadership, intercommunal relations, war, science, sexuality, medical ethics, cloning, organ transplant, abortion, and the treatment of the sick. Contemporary Muslim scholars who have written about the various aspects of ethics and ethical issues include Ahmad Amin, Nurettin Topcu, Said Nursi, Abdallah Draz, Muhammad Arkoun, Murtaza Mutahhari, Seyyed Hossein Nasr, Tariq Ramadan, Ebrahim Moosa, and others. These authors have sought to address modern ethical challenges from an Islamic point of view by going back to the Qur'ān and the Islamic ethical tradition.

BIBLIOGRAPHY

Anees, Munawar A. *Islam and Biological Futures: Ethics, Gender, and Technology*. London: Mansell, 1989.

Brockopp, Jonathan E., ed. *Islamic Ethics of Life: Abortion, War, and Euthanasia*. Columbia: University of South Carolina Press, 2003.

Butterworth, Charles E. "Ethical and Political Philosophy." In *The Cambridge Companion to Arabic Philosophy*, edited by Peter Adamson and Richard C. Taylor. pp. 266–286. Cambridge, U.K.: Cambridge University Press, 2005.

Cagrici, Mustafa. "Ahlak." In *TDV Islam Ansiklopedisi*, vol. 2, pp. 1–14. Istanbul, Turkey: ISAM Yayinlari, 1989.

Fakhry, Majid. *Ethical Theories in Islam*. Leiden, Netherlands: E. J. Brill, 1991.

Frank, Daniel H. "Ethics." In *History of Islamic Philosophy*, edited by Seyyed Hossein Nasr and Oliver Leaman, pp. 959–968. London: Routledge, 1996.

Hashmi, Sohail H., and Jack Miles, eds. *Islamic Political Ethics: Civil Society, Pluralism, and Conflict*. Princeton, N.J.: Princeton University Press, 2002.

Hourani, George F. *Reason and Tradition in Islamic Ethics*. Cambridge, U.K.: Cambridge University Press, 2007.

Izutsu, Toshihiko. *Ethico-Religious Concepts in the Qur'ān*. Montreal: McGill University Press, 1966.

IBRAHIM KALIN

ALBANIA. Prior to the existence of Albania as a sovereign nation, the land was part of the Illyrian kingdom under Queen Teuta (r. 230–228 BCE), a great strategist and leader, and later the Roman and Ottoman Empires. Albania's borders were defined in 1912, after the fall of the Ottoman Empire, at which time half of the ethnic Albanians of the region were left just outside those borders in the neighboring countries of Montenegro, Kosovo, the former Yugoslav Republic of Macedonia, and Greece. Two important women during this period were Shote Galica (Kosovo Muslim, 1895–1927) and Sado Koshena (1855–1955). Galica fought with her husband, Azem Galica, against Austro-Hungarian and Bulgarian troops and Serb forces, not only in Kosovo but also in Albania. (Her grave is in Albania, in Fushë Kruja.) She was posthumously rewarded the title of "Hero of the People" and was also called the Albanian Zhan D'Ark (Joan of Arc). Koshena also earned the "Hero of the People" title for fighting with armies against Turkish (1907), Greek (1912), and Italian forces (1920).

Although the writer Pashko Vasa penned the oft-quoted phrase "The religion of the Albanians is Albanianism," it was language that defined Albanian nationalism at the beginning of the twentieth century. By the early twenty-first century, religion remained secondary to nationality for the majority of the population. The proportion of Albania's approximately 3.5 million inhabitants was roughly unchanged from a century ago when the population was only one-third of that figure: 70 percent Muslim, 20 percent Orthodox (in southern Albania), and 10 percent Catholic (in northern Albania). The country was known for its religious tolerance, and people of all faiths hid and protected Jews during World War II, including many who fled there from adjoining countries. In the period 1967–1991, under the strict Communist government (1945–1991), Albania was declared an atheist state and all manner of religious observance was forbidden. During this time, 2,169 religious institutions were either destroyed or turned over to secular uses. Until the 1920s, most Muslim women in Albania wore the veil. Under King Zog (r. 1928–1939), laws passed forbidding the practice were assisted by women's protest parades favoring the new laws. However, it was not until after World War II that Muslim women could participate equally with others in sports, theater, and dance.

While communism encouraged women to participate in the workplace, that did not release them from their traditional full domestic lives. Even in the early twenty-first century, while townswomen were more independent, life for women in remote rural areas was little changed. Migration to cities and abroad, especially by men, left the countryside sparsely inhabited and very poorly supplied with medical and educational needs. Patriarchal attitudes persist, especially in northern Albania. While the tradition of arranged marriage has decreased, especially among the educated, the only honorable mode of refusal for a betrothed girl is to become a "sworn virgin" and live her life as a celibate woman. Concern that a bride should be a virgin is most strongly felt by the Muslim community. Premarital or extramarital sex is always seen as the woman's fault, bringing shame not only to her family but also to her whole community. Gay relationships receive intense discrimination, leading to physically aggressive disapproval, especially from Muslim male family members.

Under Ottoman rule, it was forbidden to teach in the Albanian language; education was in Turkish or, in the south, Greek. Prior to World War II, 85 percent of the population was illiterate, but under communism this was reversed so that, by 1945, 85 percent were literate. By then it was no longer prohibited for Muslim women to participate in social and political life. The (Orthodox) sisters Sevasti and Parashqevi Qiriazi were the first to provide education for women (of all faiths) in Albania: their school opened in Korçë in 1891.

Basha Xhanfize Frasheri from Permet may have been the first Muslim woman from Albania to graduate in medicine (from the Women's Medical College of Pennsylvania, Philadelphia) in 1937; she returned to work as a fully qualified pediatrician in Tiranë. In the same year Ikbale Çika, a Muslim teacher and Albania's first woman journalist, became owner of *Java* (the *Week*) newspaper, writing particularly on women's emancipation. Drita Kajtazi contributed in the field of critical thinking with literary criticism for Albanian authors. The writer Musine Kokalari was the first Muslim woman to take an active role in opposing the Communist regime of the Albanian leader Enver Hoxha (r. 1945–1985). She founded the Social Democratic Party in 1943 and edited the newspaper *Zëri i lirisë* (the Voice of Freedom) in 1944, for which she was subsequently imprisoned for eighteen years. Naxhije Dume (b. 1921) was the first female education minister in Albania in 1948. She later suffered political persecution in internal exile, returning to Tiranë in 1996. Modern writers include Mimoza Ahmeti (b. 1963) and Flutura Açka (b. 1966), editor of Skanderbeg Books.

In 1945 women were given the vote in Albania. Under communism women made up 33 percent of members of parliament. Four of the top women under that regime were Muslim:

1. Liri Belishova, revered for her role during World War II in opposing Italian and German fascism, was a member of the Politburo. She was persecuted for thirty-one years once Albania's relations with the Soviet Union were cut (1961) and was freed in 1991.
2. Mine Guri was vice president of the Presidium of the People's Assembly.
3. Nexhmije Hoxha was the wife of Enver Hoxha.
4. Fiqirete Shehu, wife of Prime Minister Mehmet Shehu, was persecuted after his death in 1981.

As of 2012, parliament was only 15 percent women members; of these, approximately 25 percent were probably Muslim. The situation was very different in neighboring Kosovo (with a population 95 percent Albanian), where about 90 percent of women members are Muslim, and the president of the republic is a Muslim woman, Atifete Jahjaga.

BIBLIOGRAPHY

Academy of Sciences R. P. S. of Albania. *Fjalori Enciklopedik Shqiptar* (Albanian Encyclopedic Dictionary). Tiranë, Albania, 1985; repr. 2008.

Academy of Sciences R. P. S. of Albania. *Ilirët dhe Iliria : te autorët antikë* (*Illyrians and Illyria of the Ancient Authors*). Prepared by Selim Islami, Frano Prendi, Hasan Ceka, and Skënder Anamali, Tiranë, Albania: Toena, 2002.

Dibra, Zenepe, *Fjalor Enciklopedik I Gruas Shqiptare* (Encyclopedia of Albanian Women). Camaj-Pipa: Shkodër, 2009.

Elsie, Robert. *Historical Dictionary of Albania*, 2d ed. Historical Dictionaries of Europe, no. 75. Lanham, Md.: Scarecrow Press, 2010.

Stipčević, Aleksandar, and Nazmi Prahmani. *Ilirët: Historia, Jeta, Kultura, Simbolet e kultit.* Tiranë, Albania: Toena, 2002

Young, Antonia. *Women Who Become Men: Albanian Sworn Virgins*. Oxford and New York: Berg, 2000, repr. 2001.

ANTONIA YOUNG AND ZENEPE DIBRA

ALGERIA. Algeria's power structure prior to the French colonial era is typically described as three concentric zones: the central power (*makhzan*); the subject tribes under the central authority's control and subject to heavy taxation; and the largest, peripheral circle consisting of the majority of tribes seeking to remain autonomous and self-sufficient while avoiding taxes.

Kinship groups, often referred to as tribes, were responsible for social and behavioral control, explaining the centrality of family law in Algerian history. Any attempt by a centralized ruling power to control family law threatened the autonomy and authority of the kinship group. Complicating social dynamics was the existence of multiple, often competing, legal systems. Prior to French colonization, both Islamic law (predominantly the Mālikī school) and customary law, based on Berber traditions and culture, coexisted, with customary law overriding Islamic law among Berber minorities. There were three clearly identifiable codes of Berber customary law—Kabyle, Aures, and Touareg, with Kabyle constituting the majority and, thus, most frequently referenced customary law.

Although records are sparse prior to the French colonial era (1830–1962), there are glimpses of precolonial Algerian women in court records, travel accounts, records from *zawāyā* (Ṣūfī lodges), and economic transactions. Much of women's precolonial economic contributions occurred informally through unpaid agricultural labor. They were also known for their production of textiles, the most important handicraft in Algeria until the nineteenth century influx of European factory-produced goods.

Precolonial and colonial Algerian women expressed consistent agency and presence through their practice, membership, and even leadership in Ṣūfī religious orders (*ṭarīqah*). The Raḥmānīyah order permitted women to have their own female circle leaders (*muqaddamāt*) whenever their numbers were sufficient. Some records indicate that as many as 27,000 Algerian women were affiliated with Ṣūfī orders at the end of the nineteenth century.

The French colonial regime (1830–1962) tended to view much of their project through the lens of gender. Although Islam was obsessively characterized as active, masculine, and seditious and thus to be fought on the battlefield, women were viewed through the lens of their sexuality, femininity, and procreative powers. Thus it was believed that both Algerian men and women needed to be subjugated, as controlling the family was expected to lead to controlling the population.

Male colonial authorities were the first to raise the question of women's status in Algerian society. Some observers reported an "insurmountable cultural chasm" separating the French and the Arabs. Because the French believed they were engaged in a *mission civilisatrice*, colonial administrators questioned whether they had an obligation to protect Arab women from practices that they considered to be representative of deviant Arab Muslim sexuality, such as child marriage. The French colonial administration therefore became entangled in debates about family law. By 1944, there were three types of judicial institutions: tribal councils applying customary laws, Islamic judges applying Islamic law, and French courts applying French law, Islamic law, and, in some cases, customary law.

Family law remained central to the burgeoning sense of Algerian national identity during the War for Independence (1954–1962), a conflict that killed between 1 and 1.5 million Algerians out of a total population of 9 million. Marriage constituted the heart of French efforts at reform.

Added to the powerful symbolism of French colonial overtaking of family law was French opposition to the veil. French colonial officials denounced the veil as oppressive to women and forced many women to unveil publicly, an act of symbolic public rape in the eyes of many Algerians. Although some calls for women's emancipation and some discussion of issues related to family law, such as denunciation of compulsory and child marriages, began among Algerians at this time, the quest for national independence took center stage, calling upon all Algerians to participate in the liberation process.

Nothing spoke more powerfully with respect to women's status than the actions of women themselves. Building on historical precedents of participation in tribal rebellions against the French, women played active roles in the struggle for independence. Some, such as Djamila Bouhired, became icons of that struggle, particularly in the Western press. Peasant women were reported to have served as guides, particularly through the mountains. Women from all backgrounds bought weapons, carried arms and messages, gathered intelligence, fed other fighters, and recovered arms from killed fighters. They also supervised hiding places, collected food, medicine, and ammunition, worked as liaisons or guides, provided nursing services, removed the wounded from the streets, cared for the families of guerrilla fighters, cooked, washed, tailored, participated in terrorist activities, and did secretarial work.

Altogether, 10,949 women are registered with the Ministry of Veterans for their participation in the war for independence. Eighty-one percent worked for the Civil Organization of the National Liberation Front (OCFLN), supporting guerrilla and urban fighters. Seventy-eight percent of them worked in the countryside and 20 percent in the cities. During the conflict, one out of every five women from all age groups was jailed, tortured, or murdered. Yet there are disconnects between the state's lip service to women's glorious service and the difficulties women veterans faced in trying to register their service with the state. Only 3.25 percent of those registered are women—a statistic that does not reflect the actual rate of their participation. Despite their active role in the resistance, women were notably absent from Front de Libération Nationale (FLN, National Liberation Front) leadership positions, suggesting that women's participation was permitted only when it did not threaten male authority.

Having won independence in 1962, the new state's first task was to build national cohesion. Women's rights were not directly discussed. Women were not perceived as a specific, oppressed group during the 1960s and 1970s. The pressing concerns of national cohesion and "social problems" pushed women's emancipation to the side as an issue to be addressed "later."

Women were further encouraged to use their reproductive capacities in service of the state, engaging in patriotic motherhood to replace the many men killed during the war for independence. The result was a birthrate of 7.9 children per woman, one of the highest fertility rates in the world.

Despite their sacrifices and dedication, the new state remained ambiguous toward women. Although the new Code of Algerian Citizenship, adopted in March 1963, affirmed equal rights for men and women (Article 12), prohibited discrimination on the basis of gender (Article 29), required the state to work to include women in the governance and development of the country (Article 31), and guaranteed equal access to public positions and employment (Article 51), it nevertheless made agnatic relations and patrilineal kinship central to citizenship. This measure was followed in April 1963 with a directive requiring that consent to marriage be provided by a woman's marriage guardian and nullifying any marriage between an Algerian Muslim woman and a non-Muslim man. Civil registration was required for a marriage to be legally recognized.

Family law thus became the last major battleground in the unification process. Progressives sought to transform the definition of the family to give greater autonomy to the individual, couple, and nuclear family, while conservatives fought to retain traditional roles for the family and women. Many believed that unifying and codifying family law was symbolic of unifying the new nation. However, all attempts at codification between 1963 and 1984 were aborted because no single group had a strong enough power base to take a firm stand on the issue. By 1980, faced with high unemployment rates, youth unrest, and mass migration from rural to urban areas (about 1.3 million people between 1967 and 1978), the state formed an alliance with the Islamists, the most broad-based group across Algeria, accepting their conservative interpretation of Islamic law for the sake of national unity.

A new, conservative draft for family law reform was introduced in 1981, proposing the same support for agnatic relations and patrilineal kinship central to citizenship. However, a group of university women secretly obtained a draft and, along with veteran women from the war of independence, including Djamila Bouhired, Meriem Enmihoub, and Zoha Drif, organized public demonstrations in Algiers to oppose it. These demonstrations, which occurred between October 1981 and January 1982, marked not only the first grassroots protest involving women professionals, but also the first public demonstrations against the independent Algerian state. In addition to the protests, a petition demanding amendments to the proposed Family Code, including equality in inheritance rights, identification of divorce conditions, and monogamy, garnered ten thousand signatures.

Although the demonstrations were easily disrupted by the police and many activists were arrested, the bill was temporarily withdrawn from the assembly—the first time this had happened under the independent state. After two years of inaction on family law, the National Assembly suddenly passed a new Family Code on June 9, 1984, that was similar in content to the 1981 draft. Small women's associations formed about a year later in opposition, but the law became the unified national law of Algeria. Under the new Code, a woman's marriage guardian was required to give consent to the marriage and polygyny remained legal, although co-wives had to be informed. The husband also retained the right of repudiation at will, although it had to be registered with a judge.

Even with the new Constitution and Family Code, enforcement did not always take place. Women were still forced into unwanted marriages and abused and secluded by male relatives without recourse. The law made education compulsory for girls, but there were not enough schools to serve them. Women's employment was legal, but this did not make jobs available for them. Although women had the legal right to walk in the streets, men and police harassed and sometimes beat them. The Islamists, known as the Front Islamique du Salut (FIS, Islamic Salvation Front), stated that they did not object to women voting. However, they opposed women's employment outside the home. Although the objection was often framed in moral or religious terms, their opposition was likely also related to the high rates of unemployment for men. It was also during this time that many Algerian nationalists began to equate national and cultural integrity with women's behavior and dress.

When the ruling FLN cancelled 1991 election results that would have brought the FIS to power, a bloody civil war broke out, ultimately claiming more than 100,000 casualties and thousands more "disappeared." Several factions associated with violent Islamist extremist movements, including the Armed Islamic Group (Groupe Islamique Armé [GIA]), Armed Islamic Movement (Mouvement Islamique Algérien [MIA]), and the Army of Islamic Salvation (Armée Islamique du Salut [AIS]), appear to have been involved in the violence that specifically targeted civilian women for daily kidnapping, torture, rape, and murder. In some cases, women were targeted because they were deemed to be working in "inappropriate" jobs. In others, their behavior was targeted. Men were also targeted for execution for the political views and activities of their wives. Pressure to veil in public reached its height in March 1994 when the GIA issued a statement classifying all unveiled women appearing in public as potential military targets. Although the majority of women in Algiers remained unveiled, women and young girls in the rural areas and small towns largely gave in to the pressure to veil as a matter of personal security.

Women's activities, dress, and behavior became central to the Islamist movement's vision of the new idealized society. Women were banned from cultural centers and other public spaces. Sports and technical training for women were banned in schools. Yet, even after leading feminist activist, Nadia Djahnine, was killed in February 1995, some women continued to assert their right to go to work and school, refused to wear *hijab*, and continued to write and publish.

International pressure on Algeria escalated during and after the civil war, with particular attention focusing on the status of women. Algeria was pressed to become a signatory of the Convention on the Elimination of All Forms of Discrimination Against Women (CEDAW) in 1996. In 2005, the CEDAW Committee expressed concern at the ongoing weak representation of women in decision-making positions. The CEDAW Committee further underscored the inadequacy of the state's response to the violence perpetrated against women during the 1990s, civil war. The Committee also noted the lack of sufficient victim support services.

In 2011, the UN Special Rapporteur on violence against women called on the government to create an independent commission to investigate all forms of violence committed against women during the 1990s, civil war, although, as of 2012, this recommendation still has not been implemented. As recently as 2010, the Global Gender Gap report ranked Algeria 121 out of 134 countries for the most prevalent discrimination against women.

Despite these challenges, some progress has been made. The fertility rate, according to the Arab Human Development Report of 2010, has dropped to 2.2. Important amendments to the Family Code were won in 2005. The Code no longer requires women to obey their husbands and women have gained some rights in divorce. The Nationality Code was also amended to give women the right to pass their nationality on to their children. In addition, the penal code criminalizes rape and sexual harassment, although not domestic violence.

A marriage guardian is still required for women, although reforms from 2005 require the consent of both spouses. Women are required to prove strict conditions before the court for *ṭalāq* divorce, although they can initiate a no-fault divorce via *khulʿ*. After divorce or being widowed, a woman is required to observe a waiting period, during which time she cannot remarry and must respect specific rules, including not leaving the family home (Articles 30, 58–61). A man can be punished for adultery only if he knew the woman was married, but this condition does not apply to women (Article 339) ("Algeria").

On January 21, 2011, various civil society groups established the National Coalition for Change and Democracy (NCCD), calling for social and political reforms. They organized a series of small-scale protests in which men and women participated and in which women were included as leaders.

Although President Bouteflika promised certain concessions, such as constitutional reforms and draft laws to increase women's participation in government, few reforms were introduced. Women remain underrepresented in government, holding only 3 out of 38 positions as of 2012, although they won 143 out of 462 seats (31 percent) in the 2012 legislative elections and currently represent about one-third of judges. At the same time, new restrictions on freedoms of expression, assembly, and peaceful protest were implemented in January 2012.

[*See also* Bouhired, Djamila.]

BIBLIOGRAPHY

"Algeria." [arabwomenspring.fidh.net/index=php?title=Algeria].

An-Na'im, Abdullahi A., ed. *Islamic Family Law in a Changing World: A Global Resource Book*. London: Zed Books, 2002.

Bennoune, Karima. "S.O.S. Algeria: Women's Human Rights Under Siege." In *Faith and Freedom: Women's Human Rights in the Muslim World*, edited by Mahnaz Afkhami. Syracuse, N.Y.: Syracuse University Press, 1995, pp. 184–208.

Charrad, Mounira M. *States and Women's Rights: The Making of Postcolonial Tunisia, Algeria, and Morocco*. Berkeley: University of California Press, 2001.

Clancy-Smith, Julia. "La Femme Arabe: Women and Sexuality in France's North African Empire." In *Women, the Family, and Divorce Laws in Islamic History*, edited by Amira El Azhary Sonbol. Syracuse, N.Y.: Syracuse University Press, 1996, pp. 52–63.

Clancy-Smith, Julia. "The House of Zainab: Female Authority and Saintly Succession." In *Women in Middle Eastern History: Shifting Boundaries in Sex and Gender*, edited by Nikki R. Keddie and Beth Baron. New Haven, Conn.: Yale University Press, 1991.

Clancy-Smith, Julia A. *Rebel and Saint: Muslim Notables, Populist Protest, Colonial Encounters (Algeria and Tunisia, 1800–1904)*. Berkeley: University of California Press, 1994.

Graham-Brown, Sarah. "Women's Activism in the Middle East: A Historical Perspective." In *Women and Power in the Middle East*, edited by Suad Joseph and Susan Slyomovics. Philadelphia: University of Pennsylvania Press, 2001.

Guechi, Fatima Zohra. "Mahkama Records as a Source for Women's History: The Case of Constantine." In *Beyond the Exotic: Women's Histories in Islamic Societies*, edited by Amira El-Azhary Sonbol. Syracuse, N.Y.: Syracuse University Press, 2005.

Hammond, Andrew. *Popular Culture in the Arab World: Arts, Politics and the Media*. Cairo: The American University in Cairo Press, 2007.

Helie-Lucas, Marie-Aimee. "Women, Nationalism and Religion in the Algerian Liberation Struggle." In *Opening the Gates: A Century of Arab Feminist Writing*, edited by Margot Badran and miriam cooke. Bloomington: Indiana University Press, 1990, pp. 104–114.

Hoffman, Valerie. "Oral Traditions as a Source for the Study of Muslim Women: Women in the Sufi Orders." In *Beyond the Exotic: Women's Histories in Islamic Societies*, edited by Amira El-Azhary Sonbol. Syracuse, N.Y.: Syracuse University Press, 2005, pp. 365–380.

Noueided, Lin, and Alex Warren. *The Battle for the Arab Spring: Revolution, Counter-Revolution and the Making of a New Era*. New Haven, Conn.: Yale University Press, 2012.

"Report of the Special Rapporteur on Violence against Women, Its Causes and Consequences, Ms. Rashida Manjoo, Mission in Algeria, May 2011." [http://www.ohchr.org/EN/countries/MENARegion/Pages/DZIndex.aspx].

NATANA J. DELONG-BAS

AMĪN, NOṢRAT. (1886–1983), Iranian *mojtaheda*. Hajiyyeh Khānom Noṣrat Amīn Begum, was the most outstanding female *mojtahed* (Islamic jurist) of twentieth-century Iranian Shiism. She published more than nine major works in Arabic and Persian on *ḥadīth* (sayings, traditions, and customs derived from the Prophet Muḥammad), *akhlāq* (moral philosophy), and *kalām* (theology), among them a *tafsīr* (Qurʾānic exegesis) in fifteen volumes.

Amīn was born into an Esfahani merchant family and was most likely drawn toward religious study by the example of her paternal aunt, a *mojtaheda* in her own right. Amīn studied and spent most of her life in Esfahan, where she opened an all-girls Qurʾān school in the 1960s as well as an introductory Islamic seminary exclusively for women, called Maktab-e Fāṭemah.

After publishing her first two works in Arabic, Amīn received several *ejāzehs* (permissions) of *ejtehād* (independent reasoning), among them from Ayatollah Moḥammad Kazem Ḥosayni Shīrāzī (1873–1947) and Grand Ayatollah Abdolkarīm Ha'erī Yazdī (1859–1937), the founder of the Qom seminaries (*ḥawzahhā-ye ʿelmīyeh-ye Qom*). Grand Ayatollah Sayyed Ḥosayn Borujerdī (1875–1961), the leading Shīʿī *marjaʿ* (source of emulation) of the time, held her in highest regard and considered her on par with the leading Shīʿī scholars of her time. Ayatollah Yusuf Saneʿī (b. 1937) goes so far as to rank Amīn as one of the most accomplished Shīʿī scholars of the twentieth century.

Amīn herself granted *ejāzehs* to her male and female contemporaries, including to Ayatollah Sayyed Shahāb al-Dīn Marʿashī-Najafī (d. 1990), and to Zīnah al-Sādāt Homāyūnī (b. 1917), her most prominent female student, who translated her first Arabic work (*Arbaʿīn al-Hāshimīyah*) into Persian, and who directed the *maktab* (women's seminary).

Noṣrat Amīn's Writings. Amīn's first work was *al-Arbaʿīn al-Hāshimīyah*, a collection of legal rules and commentaries on forty *ḥadīth*, which she completed in the 1930s. A second work published in Arabic was *Jāmiʿ al-shatāt* (Collection of Small Pieces), a compilation of her responses to jurisprudential inquiries posed to her by scholars of the *ḥawzah* (Shīʿī seminaries). It was on the basis of these two works that Amīn received her first *ejāzehs* of *ejtehād* in 1935.

The first volume of Amīn's principles of *tafsīr*, '*Makhzan al-ʿirfān dar ʿolūm-e Qurʾān*' (Source of Knowledge: Interpretations of the Qurʾān) appeared in 1956, with fourteen additional volumes following over the next fifteen years. Before the 1979 revolution, the *tafsīr* was used as a key text in an introductory course on rules of conduct and Islamic law in the Islamic Studies Program at the University of Tehran.

Notable also is her Persian translation of Aḥmad ibn Muḥammad ibn Miskawayh's (d. 1030) *Tahdhīb al-Akhlāq* (The Refinement of Character) from Arabic. It was first published in 1949 under the title *Akhlāq wa rāhī sa'ādāt: Iqtibās az ṭahārat al-Irāqī Ibn Maskuyih/Miskawayh*, and was used in courses on moral philosophy in many universities and *ḥawzah* until a new Persian translation was published in 2003.

Amīn's early works in Arabic are considered to be of greatest importance from the viewpoint of Islamic jurisprudence, whereas her later Persian publications are predominantly concerned with *akhlāq* (morals) and *'irfān* (Islamic mysticism). In her books addressed to a more general audience, such as *Ravesh-e Khoshbakhtī* (Ways to Happiness), Amīn lays out the characteristics of a pious life for women, emphasizing the necessity of resisting the temptations of vanity and materialism. Her views on gender are defined by the axiom of domesticity: women are responsible for the home and the education of children. Yet, the fact that Amīn opened a girl's Islamic seminary in a clerical environment that did not offer a *ḥawzah* education to women, and in a political environment that sought to eliminate altogether any religious learning that was not under state oversight, indicates that she hardly lived by the axiom of domesticity herself. Instead, her works reveal a highly independent spirit deeply concerned with the moral constitution of the society she lived in.

BIBLIOGRAPHY

Amīn, Noṣrat. *Al-Arba'īn al-Hāshimīyah fi sharḥ jumlah min al-aḥādīth al-wāridah fi al-'ulūm al-dīnīyah*. Iran: al-'Alawīyah al-Amnīyah, 1379 [1959 or 1960] and Damascus: Dār al-Fikr, 1978.

Amīn, Noṣrat. *Jāmi' al-shatāt*. Iṣfahan, Iran: al-Maṭba'ah al-Muḥammadīyah, 1965.

Amīn, Noṣrat. *Akhlāq wa rāhī sa'ādāt: Iqtibās az ṭahārat al-Irāqī Ibn Maskuyih/Miskawayh*. Isfahan, Iran: Thaqafī, 1949.

Amīn, Noṣrat. *Makhzan al-'irfān dar 'olūm-e Qur'ān*. Isfahan, Iran: Chāp-e Moḥammadī, 1956.

Amīn, Noṣrat. *Ravesh-e Khoshbakhtī wa Tawṣīyah beh Khwāharān-e Imānī*. Iṣfahan, Iran: Thaqafī, 1961.

'Amū Khalīlī, Marjān. *Kawkab-i durrī: [sharḥ-i ahvāl-i bānū-ye mujtahidah Amīn]*. Tehran, Iran: Payām-e 'Adālat, 2000.

Badry, Roswitha. "Zum Profil weiblicher 'Ulama' in Iran: Neue Rollenmodelle für 'islamische Feministinnen'?" *Die Welt des Islams* 60.1 (March 2000): 7–40.

Künkler, Mirjam, and Roja Fazaeli. "The Life of Two *Mujtahidahs*: Female Religious Authority in Twentieth-Century Iran." In *Women, Leadership and Mosques: Changes in Contemporary Islamic Authority*, edited by Masooda Bano and Hilary Kalmbach, pp. 127–160. Leiden, Netherlands: Brill, 2012.

Tayyibī, Nāhīd. *Zindagānī-yi Bānū-yi Īrānī: Bānū-yi Mujtahidah Nuṣrat al-Sādāt Amīn*. Qom, Iran: Sābiqūn Publishers, 2001.

Yādnāmah-i bānū-yi mujtahidah Nuṣrat al-Sādāt Amīn: mashhūr bih Bānū-yi Īrāni. Iṣfahan, Iran: Vizārat-i Farhang wa Irshād-i Islāmī; Markaz-i Muṭāla'āt-i wa Tahqīqāt-i Farhangī, 1992.

MIRJAM KÜNKLER

ANDALUS, AL-. The parts of the Iberian peninsula (modern Spain and Portugal) inhabited by a Muslim-majority population from the 7th to the end of the 15th centuries were called al-Andalus by its inhabitants and in Arabic sources. Although the lives of women are not frequently addressed in these sources, contemporary research has still been able to use them to draw an approximative picture of gender relations in al-Andalus, and of the place of women in this society.

As in all medieval (Muslim or Christian) societies, women held a secondary position in the social hierarchy. They were subjected first to their fathers' authority and second to their husbands'. Marriage and motherhood were the destiny of women, and, at least among the higher strata of society, marriages were arranged by the families of the spouses. Most important for the married life of a wife was the marriage contract, which established her duties and rights, as well as the amount of dowry to be paid directly to her in case of widowhood or divorce. A characteristic of the marriage contract in al-Andalus was a clause preventing the husband from taking another lawful wife while married to the woman in question. Polygyny, in fact, was only practiced by the higher aristocracy and sovereign families. Interreligious marriages (Christian women married to Muslim men) have been attested mainly in the early periods of al-Andalus' history.

Under Islamic law, women are economically independent from their male relatives and are able to administer their patrimony by themselves. Andalusi legal sources provide a wealth of information on this topic, showing, for instance, how well-off families distributed their assets, through inheritances and other procedures, keeping land ownership in the hands of males, while giving women jewels, textiles, and cash. In the lower strata of society, women practiced different trades, the income for which belonged exclusively to them. Arabic sources refer to women working in agriculture and in the urban context, where they could be servants, cooks, spinners, wet nurses, midwives, teachers (for girls), merchants and commission merchants, washerwomen, seamstresses, hairdressers, singers, dancing girls, prostitutes, and so on. Reference is also made to women as medical doctors, working especially with girls and women. All these activities placed working Andalusi women in the public sphere, in which they circulated more freely than well-to-do women, who were subjected to more strict seclusion in their family homes.

Certain Andalusi women had access to the world of learning dominated by male scholars. Up to 116 women scholars have been traced in Arabic sources for the whole period of Andalusi history. Many of them were daughters or wives of scholars and could therefore study in their home with masters from their own family. They specialized mainly in caligraphy and the study of the prophetic tradition, but mention is also made of women religious preachers who traveled throughout al-Andalus to speak before female audiences. On the secular side of culture, al-Andalus produced a fair number of female poets, part of whose legacy of work has been preserved, such as Wallādah bint al-Mustakfī and Hafsa bint al-Hajj al-Rakuni. Although women's contribution to the intellectual and cultural life of al-Andalus was secondary to that life's main currents, it is nevertheless important to see how the field was open to their presence.

This was also the case for the political arena, where women of ruling families could and did play a role, significantly when male authority was weak. As mothers of heirs apparent or of infant rulers, women such as Subh (mother of Umayyad Caliph Hishām II, tenth century) exercised de facto power for a long period, only to be ultimately expulsed from it by a more powerful male in the palatial context.

BIBLIOGRAPHY

Ávila, María Luisa. "Las 'mujeres sabias' en al-Andalus." In *La mujer en al-Andalus: Reflejos históricos de su actividad y categorías sociales*, edited by María Jesús Viguera Molins, pp. 139–184. Madrid: Seminario de Estudios de la Mujer, 1989.

Ávila, María Luisa. "Women in Andalusi Biographical Sources." In *Writing the Feminine: Women in Arab Sources*, edited by Manuela Marín and Randi Deguilhem, pp. 149–163. London and New York: I. B. Tauris, 2002.

Garulo, Teresa. *Diwan de las poetisas de al-Andalus*. Madrid: Hiperion, 1986.

Marín, Manuela. "Marriage and Sexuality in al-Andalus." In *Marriage and Sexuality in Medieval and Early Modern Iberia*, edited by Eukene Lacarra Lanz, pp. 3–20. New York: Routledge, 2002.

Marín, Manuela. *Mujeres en al-Andalus*. Madrid: CSIC, 2000.

Viguera, María Jesús. "A Borrowed Space: Andalusi and Maghribi Women in Chronicles." In *Writing the Feminine: Women in Arab Sources*, edited by Manuela Marín and Randi Deguilhem, pp. 165–180. London and New York: I. B. Tauris, 2002.

Manuela Marín

Anwar, Zainah. (b. 1954), Malaysian political and women's rights activist. Zainah Anwar was born on 6 April 1954, in the state of Johor. Her father, politician Tan Sri Haji Anwar bin Abdul Malik (1898–1998), worked to unite different Malay nationalist groups in the United Malays National Organization, and her mother, Saodah bt. Abdullah, was a housewife. She grew up in a Muslim Malay society, but with a multicultural heritage, including an Ethiopian great-grandmother, an Arab great-grandfather, and a Javanese grandmother.

Anwar attended the Sultan Ibrahim Girls' School in Johor Bahru, where she studied the English language and English literature. She proceeded to the Mara Institute of Technology at Shah Alam (now the Universiti Teknologu Mara). Her initial exposure to journalism there led to her working as a journalist for the *New Straits Times*. Anwar then moved to the United States, where she completed her master's degree at Boston University in 1978. She also holds a degree in International Law and Diplomacy from the Fletcher School of Diplomacy at Tufts University.

Following her studies, Anwar returned to Kuala Lumpur, Malaysia, where she worked at the Institute of Strategic and International Studies from 1986 until 1991 and again from 1994 to 1996. She also worked as the chief programme officer at the Political Affairs division of the Commonwealth Secretariat in London.

In 1987, Anwar and a group of women lawyers and journalists founded Sisters in Islam, an NGO dedicated to articulating women's rights in Islam, particularly with respect to Islamic law and women's status in the Sharīʿah courts. Over time, the organization also addressed human rights, democracy, and constitutionalism more broadly. Anwar served as its executive director for more than two decades.

Sisters in Islam produced a series of pamphlet-style publications to raise public awareness about issues related to women's rights and status, particularly with respect to domestic violence, polygyny, and men's and women's equality in Islam, by turning directly to the Qurʾān and reinterpreting it in a way that liberates and empowers women. These easy-to-read, accessible, short policy statements were intended to have an impact at both the institutional and personal levels. Although many have welcomed the organization's work, both Anwar and Sisters-in-Islam have been criticized by some Islamic groups for their lack of formal Islamic credentials, although some *muftis* have participated in their conferences. There has even been a legal challenge against the use of "Islam" in the title of the organization.

Anwar is a member of WISE Muslim Women (Women's Islamic Initiative in Spirituality and Equality), a global social network and grassroots social justice movement led by and for Muslim women seeking greater levels of participation by women at all levels of society. Anwar also founded the organization Musawah in 2009 to work for reforms to family law, in particular, as a means of creating equality and justice for Muslim women.

Anwar is a prolific writer. Her book *Islamic Revivalism in Malaysia: Dakwah among the Students* has become a standard reference for those studying Islam in Malaysia. She is a well-known speaker globally and has served as member of Malaysia's Human Rights Commission.

BIBLIOGRAPHY

Anwar, Zainah. *Islamic Revivalism in Malaysia: Dakwah among the Students*. Petaling Jaya, Selangor, Malaysia: Pelanduk Publications, 1987.

Anwar, Zainah. *Kebangkitan Islam di Kalangan Pelajar*. Petaling Jaya, Selangor, Malaysia: IBS Buku, 1990.

Anwar, Zainah. *Legacy of Honour*. Kuala Lumpur, Malaysia: Yayasan Mohamed Noah, 2011.

Anwar, Zainah. "What Islam, Whose Islam? Sisters in Islam and the Struggle for Women's Rights." In *The Politics of Multiculturalism: Pluralism and Citizenship in Malaysia, Singapore, and Indonesia*, edited by Robert W. Hefner, pp. 227–252. Honolulu: University of Hawai'i Press, 2001.

Anwar, Zainah, and Ulil Abshar-Abdalla. *Political and Security Outlook 2003: Islam: The Challenge from Extremist Interpretations*. Singapore: Institute of Southeast Asian Studies, 2003.

Sisters in Islam: Empowering Voices for Change. http://www.sistersinislam.org.my.

Justin J. Corfield
and Natana J. DeLong-Bas

Arabic Literature. [*This entry contains two subentries,*

Overview *and*
Gender in Arabic Literature.]

Overview

Although women have been actively involved in the evolution of Arabic literature from the very beginnings of Arabic literary culture, their visibility has fluctuated over the centuries. This article traces some of women writers' most outstanding contributions to Arabic literary history at this tradition's most pivotal moments and across multiple genres.

Lyric Genres. Among the many genres of classical Arabic literature that are associated with women's writing, the mourning poem (*rithā'*) recurs most frequently in the classical Arabic literary tradition. As a genre, the *rithā'* idealizes the past and commemorates the deceased. Specific instances of this paradigmatic women's genre are known as *marāthī* (sing. *marthiya*). The best known early *rithā'* improviser is al-Khansā' ("Snub Nosed"), a seventh century Bedouin poetess who lamented the death of her brothers Mu'āwiyah and her half-brother Ṣakhr. Confounding expectations of female passivity, al-Khansā also called for her brother's deaths to be avenged in her poetry.

In the medieval period, the most significant exponent of the *rithā'* genre is a woman from Andalusian Spain named Laylā al-Akhyaliyya. Whereas al-Khansā lamented the loss of her brothers, Laylā al-Akhyaliyya *laments* the loss of her would-be lover Tawba ibn al-Ḥumayyir. Concomitantly with a tendency to idealize those she has lost, Laylā's predilection for genre-crossing made a lasting impacting on Arabic literary forms. Rejecting the "gender-prescribed literary norms" that presumed that women writers could produce only mourning odes, Laylā al-Akhyaliyya composed satires (*hajw*) and panegyric odes (*qaṣīdas*) in addition to *marāthī*.

The *marāthī* of al-Khansā and Laylā al-Akhyaliyya dominate the pre-Islamic and medieval periods, respectively. The genre was revived by the Palestinian poet Fadwā al-Ṭūqān (1917–2003) in a famous lament on the death of her brother. The consistent deployment of the mourning poem by Arab women writers across the centuries attests to both the cross-generational solidarity that women writers have been able to forge with each other as well as to the ability of this genre to transmit creatively the experience of bereavement to multiple audiences.

When they were not composing *rithā'*, premodern women poets worked in other short genres such as the *ghazal* (love lyric) and the *qita'* (fragment). Supplementing the *marāthī* repertoire that was one of the few literary genres permanently available to female poets, the eleventh-century Andalusian poetess Wāllada (994–1091) composed love poetry for Ibn Zaydun, as well as invective (*hajw*) against this same lover. In her capacity as hostess for a literary salon in Cordoba, Wāllada also set the tone for literary culture in eleventh-century Andalusia.

In the medieval period, women's writing functioned as a repository for traditional literary values. But with the passage of time and the increasing sophistication of this body of work, women writers facilitated the revival of past forms of knowledge by way of formal experimentation. To take just one example, the introduction of free verse (*al-shi'r al-ḥurr*) to Arabic literature by the Iraqi poet Nazik al-Mala'ika (1923–2007), which radically departs from traditional poetics through its orientation to syllabic progressions and intonations rather than rhyme or meter, permanently changed the literary scene.

Prose. Even as Arab women continued to produce traditional belles-lettres, above all in poetry, beginning in the nineteenth century, they also assumed new roles as social reformers and campaigners for women's equality. One of the best known such women authors who contributed to the emergent Arab public sphere, Malak Ḥifnī Nāṣṣif (1886–1918), did so under the pseudonym Bāḥithat al-Bādiyah ("Seeker in the Desert"). Nāṣṣif polemicized directly against Qāsim Amīn's influential *The Liberation of Women* (*Taḥrīr al-mar'a*, 1899) and *The New Woman* (*Al-mar'a al-jadīda*, 1900), two acclaimed treatises that sought to replace the veiling of women with a conception of gender relations based on Victorian moral norms. In her polemics, which were published serially and collected only posthumously in book form, Nāṣṣif deftly shows how Amīn reinforces patriarchal norms under the guise of reformist values. Even as they cultivated distinctive literary voices that transformed a primarily masculine public sphere, Arab women writers such as May Ziadeh followed the example of the Andalusian poetess Wāllada by regularly hosting salons where the literary community gathered to debate the burning issues of the day.

In *A Difficult, Mountainous Journey* (*Riḥlah jabalīyah, riḥlah ṣa'bah*, 1985), arguably the most accomplished twentieth century Islamic autobiography, Fadwā Ṭūqān (who first made her mark as poet by reviving the pre-Islamic mourning elegy) memorably portrays Palestinian society's encounter with modernity through the lens of a young girl coming of age in British mandate Nablus. Ṭūqān journeys to Oxford and later returns to her homeland with a renewed commitment to the Palestinian cause.

In narrating the emergence of her literary voice and the historically induced politicization of her poetics, Ṭūqān powerfully encapsulates within a single text the experience of being an Arab woman and a dispossessed Palestinian—two experiences that are not frequently brought together in the masculinist discourse of national liberation. By bringing the distinct facets of gender and political dispossession in modern Arab history together into the same text, Ṭūqān gestures toward the many ways in which Arab women's writing sheds light on the core of the modern Arab experience.

While women's contributions to Arabic literature were overwhelmingly in poetic genres before modernity, modern women authors such as Ghāda al-Sammān and Ulfat Idilbī of Syria, Saḥar Khalīfah and Lina Badr of Palestine, Leila Aboulela of Sudan, and Hanan al-Shaykh of Lebanon have more recently made substantial contributions to the development of Arabic prose genres. The novel, autobiography (*al-sīra al-dhatiyya*), and other forms of nonfictional literary reflection are the three most notable areas of achievement by Arab women writers. Although some contemporary women writers, such as Ghāda al-Sammān and Ulfat Idilbī, do not wish to apply the label "woman writer" to themselves and prefer to see their works as addressed to a nongendered general public, these writers too are embedded in a community of female readers that is becoming increasingly skilled at finding linkages between past and present forms of women's writing.

BIBLIOGRAPHY

cooke, miriam. "No Such Thing as Women's Literature." *Journal of Middle East Women's Studies* 1.2 (2005): 25–54.

cooke, miriam, and Badran, Margot. *Opening the Gates: An Anthology of Arab Feminist Writing*. Bloomington: Indiana University Press, 2004.

De Young, Terri. "Love, Death, and the Ghost of al-Khansa': The Modern Female Poetic Voice in Fadwa Ṭūqān's Elegies for her Brother Ibrahim." In *Issa Boullatta Festschrift: Tradition, Modernity, and Postmodernity in Arabic Literature: Essays in Honor of Professor Issa J. Boullata*, edited by Kamal Abdel-Malek and Wael Hallaq, pp. 44–75. Leiden: Brill, 2000.

Hammond, Marlé. *Beyond Elegy: Classical Arab Women's Poetry in Context*. Oxford: Oxford University Press, 2010.

Sajdi, Dina. "Trespassing the Male Domain: The Qasidah of Layla al-Akhyaliyyah." *Journal of Arabic Literature* 31.2 (2000): 121–146.

Ṭūqān, Fadwa. *A Mountainous Journey*. Translated by Olive Kenney. London: Women's Press, 1990.

Women's Autobiography in Islamic Societies. http://www.waiis.org.

Zeidan, Joseph T. *Arab Women Novelists: The Formative Years and Beyond*. Albany SUNY Press, 1995.

Fedwa Malti-Douglas
Updated by Devin J. Stewart
Updated by Rebecca Gould

Gender in Arabic Literature

Most twentieth-century Arabic fiction is *informed* by an Islamicate consciousness, even if relatively few authors have chosen specifically Islamic themes. Many writers question the place of tradition in a rapidly modernizing world, but few examine religion as a social, symbolic system. Those novels and poems that have dealt with Islam specifically have three foci: criticism of the institutions of orthodox Islam, the spiritual role of Islam and of the prophet Muḥammad as a counter-project to Westernization, and Islamist activism. Such texts tend to exaggerate traditional conceptions of gender roles and behaviors. Gender is here used to refer to the images, values, interests, and activities held to be important to the realization of men's and women's anatomical destiny. As women have added their voices to the corpus of literature on Islam, so have the understandings of gender changed.

Muslim intellectuals began to write fiction that reflected political and socioreligious concerns in the first quarter of the twentieth century. Members of the Egyptian Madrasah Ḥadīthah exposed the oppressive treatment of women and the unchallenged power of religious authorities. Maḥmūd Ṭāhir Lāshīn's 1929 short story, *Bayt al-ṭā'ah* (House of Obedience), criticizes men who use what they consider to be an Islamic institution to crush women's will; the "house of obedience" authorizes the husband of a woman who wants a divorce to become his wife's jailer. One of the earliest Arabic novels is Ṭāhā Ḥusayn's autobiographical *Al-ayyām* (The Days, published serially in 1926–1927 and as a book in 1929). In this Bildungsroman that traces the triumphs of Egypt's blind doyen of letters, the pro-Western Ṭāhā Ḥusayn criticizes the all-male, tradition-bound al-Azhar system and its hypocritical *'ulamā'* (religious authorities). He constructs himself as a strong man in defiance of social expectations that blind men should be as marginal to society as are women.

While some intellectuals were attacking the corrupt institutions and agents of modern Islam, others were invoking the power at the core of a well-understood, timeless faith. The neoclassical court poet Aḥmad Shawqī was one of the first to write long poems on Muḥammad; his *Al-hamzīyah al-nabawīyah* (The Hamzīyah Poem in Praīse of the Prophet) and *Nahj al-burdah* (Trail of the Cape) inspired others to write about Islamic history and the life of the Prophet. The 1930s in Egypt saw the publication of fiction and drama by leading modernist writers lauding the Islamic exemplar and showing that Islam is no obstacle to progress, for example, Tawfīq al-Ḥakīm's unwieldy play *Muḥammad* (1936), Muḥammad Ḥusayn Haykal's *Ḥayāt Muḥammad* (The Life of Muḥammad), and Ṭāhā Ḥusayn's *ʿAlā hāmish al-sīrah* (On the Margin of the Prophet's Life, 1937–1943). During the post-Revolution period, two more important works focusing primarily on Muḥammad were published. In 1959, the Egyptian Nobel laureate Najīb Maḥfūz (Naguib Mahfouz) published *Awlād ḥāratina* (Children of the Alley), an allegory based on the lives of several Islamic prophets that was considered blasphemous and was censored. Qāsim-Muḥammad is the revolutionary with the widest vision, the toughest foe whom the unruly gangs of the alley had yet confronted; yet he, like his predecessors, was doomed to find his revolution coopted. ʿAbd al-Raḥmān al-Sharqāwī's Marxist study, *Muḥammad rasūl al-ḥurrīyah* (Muhammad the Messenger of Freedom, 1962), presents the prophetic mission as an exploitative obsession. Each Muḥammad is at once an ordinary man and a driven reformer. The women characters in the Prophet's life are presented as, at best, foils to his greatness.

One of the first attempts to consider Islam in tandem rather than in mutually exclusive competition with modernity was *Qindīl Umm Hāshim* (The Lamp of Umm Hashim, 1944) by the Egyptian *adīb* (man of letters) Yaḥyā Ḥaqqī. It tells the paradigmatic tale of the rejection of Islam in favor of Western science, the failure of this science, and the recognition of the need to meld the spiritual and the material. Women act as vehicles of each culture's values; at times, they shake Ismail's convictions and masculinity, but they also finally shape his decisions.

During the globally troubled decade of the 1960s, Arab men and women began to question the role of religion in the rapidly changing life of the modern individual. While Saudis such as 'Abd al-Raḥmān Ṣāliḥ al-ʿAshmāwī and Ṭāhir Zamakhsharī were writing pious poetry, Egyptian secularists were targeting religion. Najīb Maḥfūz laments the transformation of Islam into an ideology and the concomitant loss of soul in society. Several characters search in vain for an absent father-figure, a transparent symbol for God. These desperate quests involve Ṣūfī masters and chaste prostitutes, the latter often providing greater solace than the former. With time, however, the sympathetic women of the earlier fiction disappear. The Sudanese al-Ṭayyib Ṣāliḥ seems less pessimistic: in *Urs al-Zayn* (Zayn's Wedding, 1966), Zayn, the saintly fool, wins the love of the village beauty and assumes his real persona when he becomes united with her. Both writers create women who merely facilitate a man's access to the spiritual realm.

While some women were writing overtly feminist texts, others turned to Islam to find a legitimate space for women as active agents. In 1966, the leader of the Egyptian Association of Muslim Ladies, Zaynab al-Ghazālī, published *Ayyām min ḥayātī* (Days from My Life), her memoir of six years in prison under Nasser. In a remarkable gender reversal, she projects herself as much stronger than her male co-inmates. She describes torture so great that only she, and not the men, could bear it. Her purpose in citing men is to demonstrate her spiritual superiority. At about the same time in Iraq, another pious woman was producing religiously didactic, yet also arguably feminist, literature. In the 1960s and 1970s, Amīnah Ṣadr, also known as Bint al-Hudā, participated in the Islamist revivalism in Najaf; in 1980, the Baʿth regime executed her. She wrote several novels (notably *Liqāʾfī al-mustashfā* [Meeting at the Hospital], c. 1970), short stories, and poems in which she created models of ideal behavior for Muslim women. These women embrace domesticity and advocate the veil, yet they are not subservient to men.

With the rise of Islamist movements during the 1970s and 1980s, a few women chose to devote their literary talents to Islam. These women do not try to support or oppose gender bias in Islam or its texts. They see rather the hand of patriarchy at work in the misappropriation of scripture to oppress women. The prolific Egyptian feminist novelist Nawāl al-Saʿdāwī wrote two novels that concentrate on Islam. The heroine of *Suqūṭ al-Imām* (*The Fall of the Imam*, 1987, trans. 2002) is called Bint Allah, or Daughter of God; not only is her name a blasphemy, but she also has dreams of being raped by God. *Jannāt wa-Iblīs* (*The Innocence of the Devil*, 1992; trans. 1994) delves into the psyche of the Islamist movement to expose men's expedient uses of religion. When God declares Satan to be innocent, the binary of good and evil is undermined. Saʿdāwī's fearless condemnations of those who abuse religious privilege earned her a place on the death list of a powerful fundamentalist group. Another Egyptian to write about women's role in Islam is Salwā Bakr. Her 1986 novella *Maqām ʿAṭīyah* (Atiya's Shrine) explores the relationship between Islamic sensibilities and the pharaonic heritage. Should the shrine of Lady ʿAṭīyah be removed to give access to archaeological remains that hold a secret that will transform modern Egypt? Her next novel, *Al-ʿarabah al-dhahabīyah lā taṣ ʿadu ilā al-samāʿ* (The Golden Chariot Does Not Rise to Heaven, 1991), takes place in the women's prison, by now a familiar place for readers of Egyptian women's writings, where a "mad woman" assesses her companions' eligibility to join her in the golden chariot that will whisk them all off to heaven.

The 1970s also saw the rise of Arab women's novels that explore gender roles in the context of war. Palestinian Saḥar Khalīfeh's 1976 novel *al-Ṣubbār* (*Wild Thorns*; trans. 1991) deals with the post-1967 Israeli occupation of the West Bank, the effect of occupation on individual psyches, and changing gender roles. Although primary characters are male, female characters serve to critique women's role in reproducing oppressive patriarchal institutions (Usāma's mother), and they also illustrate the potentially slow process by which women may come to terms with their own passivity (Nuwār). The almost absent character Līna represents women's emerging agency in society and politics, as she serves in the Palestinian Resistance. In 1980, Lebanese novelist and short story writer Ḥanān al-Shaykh published *Ḥikayat Zahra* (*The Story of Zahra*; trans. 1986). Set during the Lebanese civil war, the novel explores the effects of sexism and emotional and sexual abuse on the female psyche. The novel's literary significance lies in its fine interweaving of nationalist and feminist causes, as the author creates parallels between the disturbed mentality of the protagonist, Zahra, and the chaotic state of her homeland.

During the 1990s, more Arab women turned to a study of Islam and the Prophet. The Algerian Assia Djebar's *Loin de Médine* (Far from Medina, 1991) provides pen portraits of the many strong women who both supported and opposed Muḥammad during his life. A story about Fāṭimah's rebellion against the Companions' misogyny reveals the forthrightness of seventh-century women in Arabia. The Saudi Arabian Rajaʿal-ʿAlim has written several novels about women struggling to assert themselves against social expectations in Mecca, often using a magical realist approach to her topic.

Women of the new avant-garde in Egypt built on innovations of their predecessors in the 1970s and 1980s, particularly as the latter developed literary styles that involve experimentation with language to express women's experience of their bodies, sexuality, and emotions. Novelist May Telmissany's *Dunyāzād* (*Dunyazad*, 1997; trans. 2000) intimately explores the physical and emotional experience of a woman who has lost her child. Mīrāl al-Ṭaḥāwy takes this experimentation into a new subcultural context as she explores the complex family relationships in Bedouin society and the impact of conservative mores on the female psyche in *al-Khibā'* (*The Tent*, 1996; trans. 1998).

The events of September 11, 2001 produced an alarmist trend: several Muslim women published auto-ethnographies in which they exposed and expanded on their view of the misogyny of Islam. Their sensationalist insider stories have been snatched up by European and American presses and promoted by neoconservative interest groups in the West who use these exposés to bolster their claims of Islam's inherent barbarism.

Over the past hundred years, men and women have both extolled and criticized Islamic texts and institutions. Men have depicted the Prophet as the perfect man (*al-insān al-kāmil*) who might serve as a model for all, and women have looked to the founding moments of Islam and into the scriptures for right guidance in their search for power and position in society. Whereas the pioneers of modern Arabic literature, educated in Enlightenment values and norms, eschewed religious topics, early twenty-first century littérateurs are finding inspiration for new engagement with Islam. Of note is the Egyptian 'Alā' al-Aswāny's best-selling novel *'Imārat Ya'qūbyān* (*The Yacoubian Building*, 2002; trans. 2004), which provides a sweeping critique of Islamic fundamentalism and corruption at several levels of Egyptian society. Sometimes described as pulp fiction in part for its treatment of homosexuality, the novel takes on issues of gender and sexuality as it condemns social mores that provide a double standard of sexual behavior for men and women.

[*See also* Ghazālī, Zaynab al-.]

BIBLIOGRAPHY

Al-Aswāny, 'Alā'. *The Yacoubian Building*. Translated by Humphrey Davies. Cairo, Egypt: American University in Cairo Press, 2004. English translation of *'Imārat Ya'qūbyān*, originally published in 2002.

Bakr, Salwā. *Maqām 'Aṭīyah: riwāyah wa-qiṣaṣ qaṣīrah* (Atiya's Shrine). Cairo, Egypt and Paris: Dār al-Fikr lil-Dirāsāt wa-al-Nashr wa-al-Tawzī', 1986.

Bakr, Salwā. *Al-'arabah al-dhahabīyah lā taṣ'adu il' al-samā'* (The Golden Chariot Does Not Rise to Heaven). Cairo, Egypt: Sīnā lil-Nashr, 1991.

Bint al-Hudā. *Liqā' fī al-mustashfā* (Meeting at the Hospital). Beirut, Lebanon: Dār al-Ta'ārif lil-Maṭbū'āt, c. 1970.

cooke, miriam. *Women Claim Islam: Creating Islamic Feminism through Literature* New York: Routledge, 2001.

Ghazālī, Zaynab al-. *Ayyām min ḥayātī* (Days from My Life). Cairo, Egypt: Dār al-Shurūq, 1978.

Ḥakīm, Tawfīq al-. *Muḥammad*. Cairo, Egypt: Maktabat al-Ādāb, 1936.

Ḥaqqī, Yaḥyā. *The Lamp of Umm Hashim and Other Stories*. Translated from the Arabic *Qindīl Umm Hāshim* by Denys Johnson-Davies. Cairo, Egypt: American University in Cairo Press, 2004.

Haykal, Muḥammad Ḥusayn. *Ḥayāt Muḥammad* (The Life of Muhammad). Cairo, Egypt: Dār al-Ma'ārif, 1969.

Husain, Sarah, ed. *Voices of Resistance: Muslim Women on War, Faith, and Sexuality*. Emeryville, Calif.: Seal Press, 2006.

Ḥusayn, Ṭāhā. *'Alā hāmish al-sīrah* (On the Margin of the Prophet's Life). Cairo, Egypt: Dār al-Ma'ārif, 1966.

Ḥusayn, Ṭāhā. *The Days*. Translated from the Arabic *Al-ayyām* by E. H. Paxton et al. Cairo, Egypt: American University of Cairo Press, 1997.

Khalīfeh, Saḥar. *Wild Thorns*. Translated by Elizabeth Fernea and Trevor Legassick. Northampton, Mass.:

Interlink Publishing 1991. English translation of *al-Ṣabbār*, first published in 1976.
Lāshīn, Maḥmūd Ṭāhir. *Bayt al-ṭaʿah*. Cairo, Egypt, 1929.
Maḥfūz, Najīb (Mahfouz, Naguib). *Children of the Alley*. Translated from the Arabic *Awlād ḥāratinā* by Peter Theroux. New York: Doubleday, 1996.
Mernissi, Fatima. *The Veil and the Male Elite*. Reading, Mass: Addison Wesley, 1991.
Religion and Literature 20.1 (Spring 1988). Special issue devoted to Middle Eastern literature, with an Islamic focus.
Saʿdāwī, Nawāl al-. *The Innocence of the Devil*. Translated from the Arabic *Jannāt wa-Iblīs* by Sherif Hetata. Berkeley: University of California Press, 1994.
Saʿdāwī, Nawāl al-. *The Fall of the Imam*. Translated from the Arabic *Suqūṭ al-Imām* by Sherif Hetata. London: Saqi, 2002.
Ṣāliḥ, Al-Ṭayyib. *ʿUrs al-Zayn* (Zayn's Wedding). Beirut, Lebanon: Dār al-ʿAwdah, 1969.
Sharqāwī, ʿAbd al-Raḥmān al-. *Muḥammad rasūl al-ḥurrīyah*. (Muhammad the Messenger of Freedom) Cairo, Egypt: Dār al-Hilāl, 1965.
Shaykh, Ḥanān al-. *The Story of Zahra*. Translated by Peter Ford. New York: Anchor Books, 1986. English translation of *Ḥikāyat Zahra*, originally published in 1980.
Ṭahāwy, Mīrāl al-. *The Tent*. Translated by Anthony Calderbank. Cairo, Egypt: American University in Cairo Press, 1998. English translation of *al-Khibāʾ*, originally published in 1996.
Telmissany, May. *Dunyazad*. Translated by Roger Allen. London: Saqi Books, 2000. English translation of *Dunyāzād*, originally published in 1997.
Whitlock, Gillian. *Soft Weapons: Autobiography in Transit*. Chicago: University of Chicago Press, 2007.
Zeidan, Joseph. *Arab Women Novelists: The Formative Years and Beyond*. Albany, N.Y.: SUNY Press, 1995.

Miriam Cooke
Updated by Caroline Seymour-Jorn

Arab Spring. The new Arab revolutions would be unimaginable without women. The terrain for their participation had been prepared long in advance, particularly through the demographic revolution that has changed the landscape of most Arab countries in terms of the size of the family, the rate of birth, and the nature of anthropological relations within it. While the annual growth rate during the second half of the twentieth century was around 2.7 percent, causing the population to nearly quadruple in half a century, it is predicted that over the next half century the population will barely double. Women are visibly present in higher education in the Arab world, enjoying a literacy rate in the Middle East of between 58 percent (Egypt) and 91 percent (United Arab Emirates), with the exception of Yemen (43 percent).

Women as Social Agents in the First Revolutionary Period. Women served as full-fledged social actors in the Arab revolutions in a variety of ways. In countries like Yemen they were nearly invisible before the revolution, but came to the fore during the revolutions, as was seen in the street demonstrations in Tunisia, Egypt, Yemen, Syria, and Morocco and through their cultural activities as official or self-proclaimed journalists, sending e-mails, twitters, or Facebook messages to the international media or Al Jazeera, thus building up a virtual public sphere. They also engaged in artistic expressions to promote the revolution or protest movement, such as through hip-hop, heavy metal, and the art of graffiti. Some became famous as leaders of the street movement, such as Asma Mahfouz in Egypt and Tawakkul Karman in Yemen, while others, such as in Tunisia, Syria, and Morocco, have been prominent nationally without being well known to the international media.

Yet women's participation did not come out of a vacuum. They had previously taken strong roles in, for example, the Algerian war for independence (1954–1962), in which official estimates put them at around 3 percent (about eleven thousand) of the total number of fighters. Some women fighters like Djamila Bouhired achieved international fame, but women did not serve as leaders, even at the local level; instead, they were mainly foot soldiers or grassroots activists. This situation changed with the new Arab revolutions, in which some women achieved the status of local or even national leaders.

Women as Victims in the Second Period of the Arab Revolutions? In the first period of the Arab revolutions, up to the overthrow of the autocratic governments, women were dedicated agents, recognized as almost equal with men in their fight against oppressive regimes. This period was characterized by the "Tahrir youth" type of revolutionary, whose main features were egalitarianism, secularity, and tolerance. The second period, beginning after the overthrow of the authoritarian governments, witnessed a dramatic change: the advent of the Salafis as political forces, seriously threatening the emancipation of women. The latter's number in the parliament dwindled in Egypt to less than 2 percent in the November 2011 parliamentary elections, and in Tunisia, in the Constituent Assembly elections in October 2011, women represented slightly more than 26 percent of its members, two-thirds of them being from the Ennahda Party.

The first period witnessed the advent of democratic actors who put general citizenship and the dignity of the citizen (*karamah*) at the top of their agenda, inclusive of all religious minorities, and promoting gender equality as the consequence of citizen's rights, irrespective of their gender, or ethnic or religious origins. The second phase, largely after the overthrow of the authoritarian regimes, witnessed the domination of the political institutions by the Islamists (mainly Muslim Brotherhood), and, on the street, the disruptive influence of the Salafis, who asked for application of the traditional Sharīʿah, instead of the modern democratic laws. The gap between the two periods and the marginalization of most of the revolutionary actors in the ensuing political process has induced the disarray of the Tahrir-youth type of agents, including women.

In Tunisia the frequent attacks by the Salafis against unveiled women and in universities and the quest to impose Sharīʿah by minority Salafi students and activists induced a malaise among the secular groups who had not foreseen this turn in the Arab revolutions. The marginalization of the revolutionary youth seems to be translating into an overshadowing of recognition of women's rights as full-fledged citizens.

After the overthrow of the despotic regimes in Tunisia, Egypt, and Libya, women became, at least partially, targets of the conservative forces unleashed by the revolutions. The latter had not been visible during the first revolutionary period, in which the Muslim Brotherhood played a prominent role, yet was not the instigator of the revolutions. In fact the Muslim Brotherhood was careful in the early period to abide by the secular nature of the revolution, whether in Egypt or Tunisia. In the face of such forces, an alliance of secular men and women has appeared on the social and political scenes, particularly in Tunisia, in order to counter the attacks against them and the encroachments upon the equal rights of women in politics.

Tentative Explanation of the Two Disjointed Periods of the Arab Revolutions. The question remains as to why there was no push to oppose women's agency from the beginning and how the structure of human agency changed to render women targets of conservative attacks. One explanation is that women in the Muslim world, particularly the Arab world, are becoming more conscious of their equality with men as individuals, yet have not, as yet, been able to translate this individual feeling of equality into collective political action. Many young women in Egypt, Tunisia, and even less developed countries like Yemen share this feeling of equality with men in social terms, but they do not easily join together to defend their rights in groups. Repression of group activities, and the fact that women were mainly assisted and given gender rights by modernizing, authoritarian, secular governments, like the Tunisian and, to a lesser extent, Egyptian ones, made their case ambivalent.

The very structure of the revolutions also contributed to this situation. They began with secularized youth who intended to shake off the nondemocratic, patriarchal structure of society. But when it came to the polls they lost their advantage and were marginalized by the new Islamist actors. In the authoritarian regimes women without proper organization were cajoled by the governments (in Tunisia, the notorious wife of President Zine Ben Ali, Leila Trabelsi, was the president of the Arab Woman Organization), but were not allowed to have independent institutions. In Egypt the former first lady Suzanne Mubarak was supposed to embody women's claims, yet again she did not allow autonomous action on their part in favor of emancipation. In other words the authoritarian period witnessed women's rights offered to them rather than won over by them in their struggle for equality and freedom. This resulted in women being suspected of "collaborating" with the unpopular Tunisian, and Egyptian regimes. Furthermore the lack of organization of the Tahrir-Youth type revolutionary pushed women toward the sidelines after the ousting of the former regimes, as the more organized and deeply rooted Salafi and Muslim Brotherhood actors had stronger showings at the polls. The scattered votes of the secular and progressive revolutionaries and their inability to voice their views in a unified manner through new political parties made them vulnerable. They were also inclined to reject politics as dirty, preferring moral attitudes to political ones. Revolutionary women shared these characteristics to an even higher degree, resulting in the marginalization of revolutionary men and, a fortiori, women, in the second period of the Arab revolutions.

Another major problem that looms in regard to women is the overwhelming influence of the still highly patriarchal family that imposes certain norms of behavior, justifying them as "Islamic." Islamist groups mobilize their women who reject gender equality in the name of the complementary status of women and act under the protective umbrella of these organizations, whereas women activists who struggle for the equality of rights are devoid of institutions and organizations and have not been successful in building them up in the short term.

Secular authoritarian governments in the region had introduced legal norms that assured women less inequality in family matters, particularly inheritance, divorce, and making polygyny either illegal or difficult. Interestingly, although women took an active part in the Arab revolutions, they did not put their emancipation at the top of the priorities, as their major concern was the overthrow of the autocratic regimes, rather than promoting their equal status as women. Since the new revolutionary actors (among them women) did not wield any organization (political parties, associations) with widespread influence and deep-rooted ties in the society, Islamist parties (Muslim Brotherhood and their homologues like the Ennahda in Tunisia) easily gained the upper hand. But this situation could probably not last forever. Some analysts expect that over time the Islamists will prove incapable of delivering on their political promises and that the progressive awareness of women as to their rights will bring the gender question to the forefront in the future.

Women's Quasi Equality with Men. Many young women, were drawn into the struggle against authoritarianism based on their feeling of quasi equality with men. The feeling of sameness between men and women is increasingly embedded in the educational achievements of women who earn the same university degrees as men and gradually join the job market, despite the social prejudices against them. Yet employment has not kept pace with educational equality. Many obstacles to employment, including social prejudice and a patriarchal interpretation of Islam, block women's access to the job market, outside of some feminine jobs, particularly nursing and education.

On the personal level a sense of individuality is burgeoning among younger generation women that gradually puts into question the dissymmetrical behavior pattern in gender relations at the micro-level. There is a subjective sense of receding inequality that emerges out of the daily relationships between men and women, particularly as women have become better educated and are having fewer children. The result is a sense of shared responsibility with men in terms of intimacy with children and men's involvement in helping to raise their offspring. In other words the two gender worlds in which men and women evolved and lived in two distinct universes is receding. The best sign of this silent revolution in the Muslim world is the active presence of women in the first period of the Arab revolutions. This is in sharp contrast to the few women leaders in the Muslim world in the past who were accepted as quasi men in a patriarchal environment that they did not challenge, such as the former Pakistani prime minister Benazir Bhutto. Young women such as Tawakkul Karman in Yemen became leaders of the new Arab revolutions, not by belonging to powerful ruling families such as the Gandhi family in India or the Buttho family in Pakistan, but as part of the new generation of middle-class women, daring to mingle with men. Their failure to remain in the center of the debates is tied to the failure in general of secular activists to remain organized and united while building up new political entities and structures. The incapacity to transform from revolutionary actors to political actors, particularly by unifying with other political groups sharing the same ideals, and the failure to accept politics as such with its rules and restrictions, led to the weakening of women's position in the second phase of the Arab revolutions.

The division between "Islamist feminists" and "secular feminists" is also detrimental to their cause as the Islamist governments use this dissension to weaken women's action: when secular women ask for equal rights, the Islamists assert the complementary gender rights that are, in many cases, a disguised form of inequality. But Islamist women argue that the complementary issue makes change less brutal and men are thus less afraid since it is expressed through an Islamic idiom. Nevertheless the Iranian case, as well as many Arab ones, such as in Saudi Arabia, show the limits of Islamic feminism. When used by governments this type of feminism becomes instrumental in eroding gender equality.

Conclusion. In summary the Arab revolutions opened provisional vistas for women, but in order to become permanent, gender equality has to find institutional, legal, and political expressions. Women thus need to act collectively through political parties and trade unions that are congenial to their cause and to the creation of which they might actively contribute.

BIBLIOGRAPHY

Bar'el, Zvi. "For Egypt's women, the Arab Spring does not spell freedom http://www.haaretz.com/news/features/for-egypt-s-women-the-arab-spring-does-not-spell-freedom-1.424962

Clawson, Patrick. "Demography in the Middle East: Population Growth, Women's Situation Unresolved." *Meria Journal* 13, no. 1 (March 2009). www.gloria-center.org/2009/03/clawson-2009-03-04/.

Coleman, Isobel. "Is the Arab Spring Bad for Women?" *Foreign Policy*, December 20, 2011.

Global Education Digest 2010, UNESCO Institute for Statistics. "Comparing Education Statistics Across the World." http://unesdoc.unesco.org/images/0018/001894/189433e.pdf.

Sweis, Rana F. "Arab Spring Fails to Allay Women's Anxieties." *New York Times*, March 7, 2012. http://www.nytimes.com/2012/03/08/world/middleeast/arab-spring-fails-to-allay-womens-anxieties.html?pagewanted=all&_r=0.

Turshen, Meredeth. "Algerian Women in the Liberation Struggle and the Civil War: From Active Participants to Passive Victims?" *Social Research*, Fall 2002. http://www.jstor.org/discover/10.2307/40971577?uid=3738016&uid=2129&uid=2&uid=70&uid=4&sid=21101710583051.

"Women and the Arab Awakening: Now Is the Time." *The Economist*, October 15, 2011 http://www.economist.com/node/21532256/print/.

FARHAD KHOSROKHAVAR

ARCHITECTURE AND WOMEN.

[*This entry includes four subentries:*

India
Iran
Middle East and North Africa *and*
Turkey.]

INDIA

To assess the role of women in the architecture of Islamic India (tenth through the eighteenth centuries) is not easy. The chronicles, documents, orders, and inscriptions of the period deal overwhelmingly with the activities of men, and the evidence for the participation of women is scattered and piecemeal. Moreover, since the buildings that have survived are sturdy and expensive, their patrons must have been wealthy and privileged. Nevertheless, from the evidence (however fragmentary) that is available, it is possible to suggest something about the identities of the women involved and the varieties of buildings they erected, suggestions that are probably representative of the larger, mostly unknown, reality of the time.

Islam entered India in the early eighth century as a result of the eastward expansion of the Umayyad armies, and, in later years, victorious generals established empires—the Sultanate (c. 1290–1526) and the Mughal (1526–1739)—that ruled the subcontinent until the gradual conquest of the British began in the mid-eighteenth century. In the greater medieval and early modern Eurasian world, India was one of the largest and richest states. Two extensive river systems (the Indus and the Ganges) and the annual monsoon sustained an agricultural economy of two harvests a year. A long history of manufacture and trade also contributed to the wealth and prosperity of the subcontinent. As a result, the women of Islamic India had access to both the resources and the expertise (architects and artisans) necessary to erect a variety of buildings.

Any discussion of women and architecture in Islamic India inevitably brings to mind the Taj Mahal—the magnificent garden tomb erected by the Mughal Emperor Shahjahan (r. 1628–1658) for his beloved wife, Mumtaz Mahal. And although Mumtaz was the inspiration rather than a patron, it is in the reign of her husband that we find the majority of the evidence for the architectural activities of women. Shahjahan was the great builder of the dynasty—besides the Taj, he renovated the imperial palace-fortresses in Agra and Lahore, erected the Pearl Mosque and other buildings in Agra, and laid out garden retreats throughout Kashmir. But the capstone of his architectural passion was the new capital city of Shahjahanabad, erected in the Delhi area between 1639 and 1649.

The women who participated in the construction of the new capital were, for the most part, members of the imperial household. Although the emperor himself was responsible for the palace-fortress and the basic infrastructure, his daughters and wives contributed crucial elements to the final cityscape. Jahanara Begum, Shahjahan's unmarried daughter, was the most important of the group. With a substantial income and a keen interest in architecture and design, she underwrote the construction of Chandni Chawk, the great central bazaar of the new capital (containing 1,560 shops). At its western end, she erected a large caravanserai (90 rooms) and a bathhouse. Nearby, her builders laid out the Sahibabad garden. In the women's area of the imperial palace-fortress she erected a beautiful mansion for herself. Jahanara's sister, Raushan Ara Begum, laid out a large garden tomb just outside the city walls.

Whereas Shahjahan's daughters devoted themselves to secular architecture, Shahjahan's wives had more traditional interests—constructing three of the largest congregational mosques in the city. Akbarabadi Begum erected her mosque near the southern gate of the palace-fortress. It was flanked by a caravanserai and bathhouse. Like Jahanara, she also underwrote the construction of a commercial hub. Fazi Bazaar, 1,050 yards long and 30 wide, was bisected by a canal and flanked on both sides by 888 shops. Fathpuri Begum erected a congregational mosque and a caravanserai at the western end of Chandni Chawk, and Sirhindi Begum built her mosque just outside the western gate to the city. Nearby she laid out a garden tomb.

Two women from the household of Shahjahan's successor, the emperor Aurangzeb (r. 1658–1707), constructed congregational mosques in the new capital. Aurangabadi Begum, Aurangzeb's wife, erected a large mosque near the western wall of the city, while Zinat al-Begum, his daughter, was responsible for the mosque near the eastern wall. Zinat also laid out a garden tomb just beyond the western wall.

In addition to the information about members of the imperial household, there are scattered bits of evidence concerning the architectural activities of other women as well. In the first quarter of the eighteenth century Fakr al-Nisa Begum, wife of a ranking nobleman, erected a congregational mosque near the northern gate of the city. A short time later, Nur Bai, a famous singer, built a large mansion within the city walls.

What does all of this say about women and architecture in Islamic India? Given the lack of an overall, comprehensive accounting of building activity—numbers, styles, and patrons—it is impossible to arrive at any definite conclusions about the roles of women. Most of the information that is available suggests (not unsurprisingly) that it was men who predominated—as patrons, architects, artists, artisans, and laborers. Nevertheless, from the scanty details that have appeared, a few tentative conclusions can be drawn. First, although it is certainly possible that some architects, calligraphers, stone masons, painters, or tile workers were female, there is no evidence of them in the sources. The primary architectural role of women in Islamic India seems to have been as patron. Second, and as a result, the minority who did commission buildings were members of wealthy, usually elite, households. Because of the state of the sources, the women who have entered the spotlight of history have usually been members of imperial or noble households. However, given the agricultural and commercial wealth of the subcontinent, the daughters and wives of merchant and landowning families may well have funded buildings of various kinds. Finally, the kinds of structures underwritten—bazaars, caravanserais, bathhouses, and gardens as well as mosques and tombs—suggest that, in the architectural sphere, the women of Islamic India had interests far beyond the domestic and the religious.

Bibliography

Asher, Catherine B. *Architecture of Mughal India*. Cambridge, U.K.: Cambridge University Press, 1991.

Blake, Stephen P. "Contributors to the Urban Landscape: Women Builders in Safavid Isfahan and Mughal Shahjahanabad." In *Women in the Medieval Islamic World*, edited by Gavin R. G. Hambly, pp. 407–428. New York: Macmillan, 1998.

Blake, Stephen P. *Shahjahanabad: The Sovereign City in Mughal India, 1639–1739*. Cambridge, U.K.: Cambridge University Press, 1991.

Richards, John. *The Mughal Empire*. Cambridge, U.K.: Cambridge University Press, 1993.

STEPHEN P. BLAKE

IRAN

Although the stereotype of Islamic women as veiled and hidden, their activities confined to family and household, has been exploded, it is still quite difficult to find evidence of their public activities—especially in the medieval and early modern periods (ninth through the eighteenth centuries). This generalization is as true for Iran as it is for the other Islamic civilizations of the period.

After the death of the prophet Muḥammad, Iran was one of the first countries to experience the onslaught of the Bedouin armies. Under the leadership of Umar (r. 634–644), the second of the four rightly guided caliphs, Yazdigird III (r. 632–651), the last Sassanid Emperor, was defeated in 637. Over the centuries, a variety of Islamic ruling groups extended their sway over greater Iran—from the Umayyads (661–750) who were suspicious of all non-Arabs, to the Abbasids (750–1258) who moved their capital to Baghdad and championed the disenfranchised Iranians, to the Mongol Ilkhanids (1256–1335). The last dynasty before the modern period, the Safavid (1501–1722), was founded by Shah Ismail (r. 1501–1524), the charismatic leader of the Safaviyya Ṣūfī order who introduced Shiism to the country at large. It was, however, Shah Abbas I (r. 1587–1629) who created the mature state, reorganizing its military, administrative, and economic foundations and building the new capital city of Isfahan. Because of the ten-volume work of the French jeweler Jean Chardin (1643–1713) we know more about the building activities of women under the Safavids than during any other period of Iranian history.

During most of Islamic history the dominant architectural role of women was philanthropic: they were patrons of religious or charitable buildings. During the early centuries, elite women built aqueducts, wells, caravanserais, mosques, mausoleums, hospitals, and Ṣūfī retreats, establishing charitable endowments for their upkeep. The elder sister of the great Central Asian conqueror Timur (1370–1405), for example, erected a large tomb for herself in Samarqand and madrasas, retreats, and shrines for the public at large. Timur's principal wife, Saray Mulk Khanum, built a magnificent madrasa and tomb opposite the central mosque of the city.

When we come to Isfahan, the new capital of the Safavid dynasty, however, a somewhat different pattern emerges. From the available evidence, it appears that women were not major participants during the initial decades of construction—c. 1590–1630. Rather, they seemed to have concentrated their building activities during the later period of consolidation and expansion—from the mid-seventeenth to the early eighteenth centuries.

In Isfahan, as in the other towns and cities of medieval and early modern Islam, most of the women who patronized architects and funded buildings were wealthy members of ruling or imperial families. Dalaram Khanum, mother of Shah Safi (r. 1629–1642) and grandmother of Abbas I, was the most active of the imperial women, funding two caravanserais and two madrasas. The larger serai, known as the Grandmother's Serai, contained forty rooms and housed Indian cloth merchants, selling the rich and prized fabrics of the subcontinent. Her madrasas were smaller, their construction supervised by Vali Agha, the architect/engineer of her household. Dilaram Khanum also established charitable endowments to cover the expenses of teachers and students at both institutions. Maryam Begum, daughter of Shah Safi, erected a mansion, mosque, and madrasa. The endowment document for her madrasa contained considerable detail: the students must be industrious, pious, abstinent, and chaste and must finish their studies within five years. The mother of Abbas II (r. 1642–1666) erected a congregational mosque and a madrasa in the suburb of Abbasabad, and the sister of Shah Sultan Husain (r. 1694–1722) constructed a madrasa and a bathhouse, the revenues from the latter supporting the former.

In Isfahan, as in the other parts of the Islamic world, there was much less evidence for the activities of women from non-ruling families. A large mansion near the old fortress constructed by a rich courtesan was popularly dubbed "the mansion of the twelve tumans," after the price for her services. In the late seventeenth century, Sahiba Sultan Begum, daughter of a prominent physician and ambassador, built a small mosque in honor of her father. After hiring the son of a famous architect to design the building, she ordered Khwajah Saadat, a eunuch of her household, to oversee its construction. Zinat Begum, wife of the physician Hakim al-Mulk, built a beautifully tiled madrasa in the imperial bazaar. Her husband had been richly rewarded for successfully treating the sister of the Mughal Emperor Aurangzeb (r. 1658–1707), and the two of them funded an endowment for the college. In the late eighteenth century, Izzat Nissa Khanum, daughter of a merchant from Qum, built a madrasa in honor of her father and established an endowment for its expenses.

What does this brief survey suggest about women and architecture in Islamic Iran? The first and most obvious point is that the activities of women (in architecture as in other areas) are underreported and underrepresented. The sources deal primarily with men, and the women who do appear are, for the most part, from imperial or ruling families. Nevertheless, the Isfahan evidence, however scanty, does hint at a larger, mostly unknown, reality. We encounter wealthy women from non-elite families—courtesans and wives and daughters of merchants and physicians—subsidizing the construction and maintenance of a variety of buildings, attesting to the presence and participation of a group that rarely appears in the conventional sources. We also catch a glimpse into the mechanism of patronage, how wealthy women translated their interest in architecture into actual buildings on the ground. Like other patrons of the period, these women maintained large households—soldiers, administrators, accountants, physicians, astrologers, musicians, poets, cooks, and servants—a small community to manage the varied activities of a wealthy individual. For the woman who was interested in architecture, an engineer/architect, a construction manager, and a collection of skilled artisans—tile workers, calligraphers, painters, and stone masons—likely constituted an important part of her establishment.

Bibliography

Blake, Stephen P. "Contributors to the Urban Landscape: Women Builders in Safavid Isfahan and Mughal Shahjahanabad." In *Women in the Medieval Islamic World*, edited by Gavin R. G. Hambly, pp. 407–428. New York: St. Martin's Press, 1998.

Blake, Stephen P. *Half the World: The Social Architecture of Safavid Isfahan, 1590–1722*. Costa Mesa, Calif: Mazda, 1999.

Hillenbrand, Robert, "Safavid Architecture." In *The Cambridge History of Iran.*, Vol. 6: *The Timurid and Safavid Periods*, edited by Peter Jackson and Laurence Lockhart, pp. 759–842. Cambridge, U.K.: Cambridge University Press, 1986.

Newman, Andrew. *Safavid Iran: Rebirth of a Persian Empire*. London: I. B. Tauris, 2008.

Stephen P. Blake

Middle East and North Africa

Gender, the socially constructed set of differences between men and women at given historical periods, is a foundational feature of Islamic societies. Gender roles for women as well as men inform the production and the use of architecture in Islamic societies. In addition to gender, attributes such as social status, age, religion, and wealth determine spatial practices. Consequently, societies in which Muslims form majorities or where Islam is a dominant influence feature certain common spatial patterns that correlate with gender norms. The best known examples are the gendered regulation of access to public space and ideals of feminine behavior that privilege seclusion, limiting physical and visual access to women of high status. This article considers the sources available for the study of women and architecture in Islamic societies, women as users of architecture, and women as makers of architecture, and highlights examples of research that place gender questions at the center of studies of architecture.

Sources. It is commonly asserted that the intersection of gender and architecture in the Islamic world is little explored because very few primary sources address these issues. However, as few systematic investigations of the sources available for the study of gender and visual culture have actually been conducted, it is difficult to be certain that they do not exist. In addition to locating "new" primary material, however, much can be learned from reading the available sources critically, and from reading them for gender. The nature of the sources and their investigation by scholars differ according to geographic and temporal context, making for significant asymmetries in the literature.

The sources for the modern and contemporary period differ greatly from those for the premodern and early modern period. Today the institutional settings of the production and the practice of architecture allow the emergence of major women architects (Zaha Hadid). In addition to studying exceptional persons, one can also conduct fieldwork and oral history to document the lives and works of poor women in so-called traditional crafts such as nomadic architecture. Work of the latter kind has provided new ways of thinking about gender and labor, the meaning and value of architecture, and the commodification of "tradition." It is also possible today to interview individuals about their uses of space: anthropologist Susan Slyomovics's work on women and public space in 1990s Algeria relies on ethnography in addition to textual research to map the behavior of women and men in public space.

The nineteenth and early twentieth centuries have left behind a wealth of written sources, due in part to the advent of the printing press, the emergence of modern writing about the self, and the higher survival rate of visual materials. Zeynep Çelik focused on urban renewal projects in Algiers under French colonial rule by examining the gendered terms of architectural discourse on the colony, as well as the interplay among urbanism, French scholarship on the "indigenous" architecture of North Africa, and the perceptions of the social roles of Algerian women in public space.

By contrast, the challenge of doing research on women in the premodern period lies in creatively outfoxing the limitations imposed by both the small volume and the nature of the surviving sources and works of art. The visual productions of the poor and the less powerful rarely survive; consequently they are usually excluded from discussion. Any investigation into the intersection of gender and sexuality and visual culture must begin with a systematic interrogation of conventionally used sources. This type of research requires one to use the analytical tools and methods provided by theory and to commit to rethinking many of the accepted conventions and methods of art and architectural history. For example, endowment deeds (*waqfiyyas*), one of the most important documents on Islamic architecture, are rich in information but present some challenges. Leslie Peirce detected unusual or telling aspects of endowment deeds that she correlated with the gender of the patron and the resultant social expectations.

Women as Users of Architecture. Two main issues concern women as users of architecture: spaces meant specifically for women and the regulation of women's use of public spaces. The space most commonly associated with women in Islamic societies is the harem. The word "harem" may refer to the female members of a household or to their designated living space. In a general sense, the Arabic root h-r-m and its derivatives (including *ḥarīm*, harem in English) designate a thing or space that is considered forbidden, and inviolable or sacred. Spatially, such terms can designate sacred precincts, such as the Sacred Mosque of Mecca. In the domestic sphere, the harem designates those quarters and persons, including the female members of the household, that are forbidden to all but the lawful owner. Residences with separate quarters for women, and the spatial seclusion of women have historically been a social ideal attainable only by the wealthy and powerful. The best known architectural harems are also the most exceptional because of their royal or imperial status. The first royal harems appeared in the Umayyad period, and by the Abbásid period they had become part of a repertoire of prestigious spaces associated with the powerful. Recent studies have examined the notion of the harem in Islamic law and practice, historical examples of harems, the architectural features of known historical harems, and the representation of the harem. The dominant impression is one of tremendous variability across time and space. The architectural layout of the imperial harem at Topkapi Palace in Istanbul (fifteenth to eighteenth centuries) used carefully guarded passages, thresholds, and enclosed spaces in order to enforce the seclusion of the Ottoman sovereign and the female members of his household from the outside world, to stage hierarchies within the household, and to enable or prevent certain kinds of movements between subdivided areas.

The regulation of women's use of public spaces is a loaded issue. A traditional perception associated public space with men and the private sphere with women. This dichotomy is no longer widely accepted as research has shown the complex processes through which space is gendered in all societies. In Islamic societies the accessibility or inaccessibility of public space was regulated on the basis of the user's gender in addition to other social indicators such as age, social status, and religion. Certain public institutions such as mosques and baths included special sections reserved for women (such as elevated galleries, separate rooms, screened windows), or special times set aside for exclusive use by women. For example, the *ḥammām* (public bath) is a space at the intersection of the private and the public. Elyse Semerdjian investigated the social anxieties that prompted ongoing struggles over access to and appropriate behavior in the *ḥammām* that sought to maintain social hierarchies and divisions.

Among such public spaces, saints' shrines were often a focus for women's piety. Throughout Islamic history, certain exceptional women were revered and their tombs became sites of visitation (*ziyārah*) and sources for blessing (*barakah*). Women saints' tombs have not been well studied despite their architectural, social, and economic importance. These saints include widely revered female members of the family of the Prophet and the Imams, as in the case of the shrine of Sayyida Zaynab bint 'Ali ibn Abi Talib in Damascus. By contrast, certain shrines to women Ṣūfīs attract mostly local devotees, like the shrine of Setti

Fatma in the Ourika Valley of Morocco, studied by Michelle Rein.

Women as Makers of Architecture. Many women in the Islamic world were makers of architecture through their role as patrons. Indeed, women's patronage is the best studied aspect of the relationship of architecture to women and gender in the Islamic world. Patronage is an appealing subject, as there appears to be precious little evidence of female practitioners of architecture for the premodern period. A pioneering work in this vein was the 1993 special issue of *Asian Art*, devoted to "Patronage by Women in Islamic Art," as well as the essays in *Women, Patronage, and Self-Representation in Islamic Societies*. Most of the studies focus on the patronage of wealthy and powerful women in a variety of geographical and chronological contexts. They are therefore as much about status and wealth as they are about gender or sexuality in a given society. In some fields, such as Ottoman history, research by many scholars has allowed the emergence of a solid body of knowledge and of innovative theoretical insights. Ülkü Bates's work on the architectural patronage of Ottoman women was followed by Tülay Artan's work, which used archival research to investigate the intersection between material culture, wealth, and power among Ottoman princesses in eighteenth-century Istanbul. Leslie Peirce, through systematic examination of the patronage of urban institutional complexes by high-ranking female members of the Ottoman royal household, charted the expectations of patronage by women by tracking the shifts in the type of buildings commissioned and through a study of responses to such commissions. Lucienne Thys-Senocak analyzed mosque complexes commissioned by women of the Ottoman dynasty in seventeenth-century Istanbul in terms of their gendered use and their manipulation of the gaze. The restrictions on the movement and visibility of women of rank prompted specific solutions: female patrons mandated the creation of sight lines to enable them to look out from certain privileged viewpoints without being visible to the public. The Yeni Valide mosque complex in Eminönü, Istanbul (1597–1665) included a pavilion whose windows afforded the patron, royal mother Hatice Turhan, commanding views of the surrounding urban spaces and the harbor of the Golden Horn. Thys-Senocak thus highlighted how vision staged relations of power and how it related to gender. The manipulation of space and the staging of privileged viewpoints were part of the established Ottoman imperial repertoire of architecture and were adapted by powerful women to suit their social roles.

In general, less effort has been spent investigating vernacular architecture or the building practices of women of low socioeconomic status. One of the Aga Khan Awards for Architecture of 1989 was presented to the Grameen Bank Housing Project, which enables poor and rural women to build their own housing based on a standard module and materials provided by Grameen Bank in Bangladesh.

In the contemporary period, women have also been makers of architecture by entering the profession themselves. The late Selma al-Radi's activities were directed toward the preservation of historical architecture. To restore the Amiriyya Madrasa in Yemen, al-Radi and her colleagues reinvigorated local building crafts on a large scale, an achievement acknowledged by an Aga Khan Award for Architecture in 2007. Zaha Hadid is the Iraqi-British creator of contemporary architecture's most intriguing and celebrated designs, and the first female recipient of the Pritzker Architecture Prize in 2004, among many other distinctions. Through her London-based practice Hadid has constructed buildings mostly in the West and proposed highly influential theoretical designs. Her career and work also exemplify the condition of the Muslim diaspora in Europe in the late twentieth and twenty-first centuries.

Gender at the Center of Studies of Islamic Architecture. The architecture and the practice of space in Islamic societies as they intersect with gender provide opportunities to theorize issues of visibility and invisibility. Although the public invisibility of women in Islamic society is often attributed to disempowerment, this correlation is far from being clear-cut or simple. Indeed, the seclusion of women and notions of privacy were often ideal practices restricted to the wealthy and powerful. Recent studies of women's spaces and sociability in nineteenth-century Tunis by Julia Clancy-Smith and Istanbul by Nancy Micklewright explore the spaces and activities of elite women in two modernizing cities. As Marilyn Booth has shown, modern writers in the Islamic world, both male and female, frequently depicted the spaces and activities of respectable, as well as "fallen" women. These textual depictions of women's spaces evince a strong preoccupation with issues of class. As Heghnar Watenpaugh demonstrates, an analysis that places gender at the center focuses on Syrian texts written in the 1990s and discerns that their discussion of domestic feminine space paradoxically obscures and displaces the creative contribution of women to public life.

Another productive direction for feminist research in the field of architectural studies in the Islamic world must interrogate the categories used for the built environment, especially the binary opposition of public as masculine space and private or domestic as feminine space. Furthermore, studying a work of art or architecture includes not only the context of production of the work (the artist, architect, patron, the process of making or building), but also the context of its reception and consumption. What is the role of audiences, viewers, users of public spaces, such as worshippers in the women's section at the mosque? Those who use works of art and architecture and those who interpret them participate in creating their meaning, which is constantly negotiated. Art historian Carel Bertram investigated how the meaning of domestic architecture was created by its users through analyzing the image of the home in the construction of the self for mid-twentieth-century Turkish women. Normative gender roles as well as the subversion of such roles frequently feature key spaces and their normative or subversive use. Heghnar Watenpaugh studied an antinomian saint in sixteenth-century Aleppo who challenged gender roles, referring to himself in the feminine grammatical gender, just as he challenged normative social behavior in urban spaces by staging inversions of domestic and religious practices. Recent work on the social roles and spaces of eunuchs expands and refines the notion of gender in specific historical contexts. These and many other important problems at the intersection of gender and architecture in Islamic societies still await systematic investigation.

BIBLIOGRAPHY

Artan, Tülay. "Eighteenth-Century Ottoman Princesses as Collectors: From Chinese to European Porcelain." *Ars Orientalis* 39 (2010): 113–146.

Bertram, Carel. *Imagining the Turkish House: Collective Visions of Home*. Austin: University of Texas Press, 2008.

Booth, Marilyn, ed. *Harem Histories: Lived Spaces and Envisioned Places*. Durham, N.C., and London: Duke University Press, 2010.

Çelik, Zeynep. "Gendered Spaces in Colonial Algiers." In *The Sex of Architecture*, edited by Diana Agrest, Patricia Conway, and Leslie Kanes Weisman. New York: Harry N. Abrams, 1996. 127–40.

Clancy-Smith, Julia. "Where Elites Meet: Harem Visits, Sea Bathing, and Sociabilities in Precolonial Tunisia, c. 1800–1881." In *Harem Histories: Lived Spaces and Envisioned Places*, edited by Marilyn Booth. Durham, N.C., and London: Duke University Press, 2010. 177–210.

Hadid, Zaha, and Aaron Betsky. *The Complete Zaha Hadid*. Rev. and expanded ed. London: Thames and Hudson, 2009.

Lad, Jateen. "Panoptic Bodies: Black Eunuchs as Guardians of the Topkapı Harem." In *Harem Histories: Lived Spaces and Envisioned Places*, edited by Marilyn Booth. Durham, N.C. and London: Duke University Press, 2010: 136–176.

Micklewright, Nancy. "Harem/House/Set: Domestic Interiors in Photography from the Late Ottoman World." In *Harem Histories: Lived Spaces and Envisioned Places*, edited by Marilyn Booth. Durham, N.C. and London: Duke University Press, 2010: 239–260.

Peirce, Leslie. "Gender and Sexual Propriety in Ottoman Royal Women's Patronage." In *Women, Patronage, and Self-Representation in Islamic Societies*, edited by D. Fairchild Ruggles. Albany: State University of New York Press, 2000: 53–68.

Al-Radi, Selma. "Grameen Bank Housing Programme." In *Architecture for Islamic Societies Today*, edited by James Steele. London: Academy Editions, 1994: 60–71.

Al-Radi, Selma, et al. *The Amiriya in Rada: The History and Restoration of a Sixteenth-Century Madrasa in the Yemen*. Oxford: Oxford University Press, 1997.

Rein, Michelle A. "Islam: Saints and Sacred Geographies: North Africa." In *Encyclopedia of Women and Islamic Cultures*, Volume V: Practices, Interpretations and Representations. Leiden, The Netherlands: E. J. Brill: 225–227.

Ruggles, D. Fairchild, ed. *Women, Patronage, and Self-Representation in Islamic Societies*. Albany: State University of New York Press, 2000.

Semerdjian, Elyse. "Naked Anxiety: Bathhouses, Nudity, and the *Dhimmi* Woman in Eighteenth-Century Aleppo." *International Journal of Middle East Studies*, Forthcoming.

Slyomovics, Susan. "Hassiba Ben Bouali, If You Could See Our Algeria: Women and Public Space in Algeria." *Middle East Report* 192 (January–February 1995): 8–13.

Thys-Senocak, Lucienne. "Gender and Vision in Ottoman Architecture." In *Women, Patronage, and Self-Representation in Islamic Societies*, edited by D. Fairchild Ruggles. Albany: State University of New York Press, 2000: 69–89.

Thys-Senocak, Lucienne. *Ottoman Women Builders: The Architectural Patronage of Hatice Turhan Sultan*. Burlington, Vt.: Ashgate, 2006.

Watenpaugh, Heghnar Zeitlian. "Deviant Dervishes: Space, Gender and the Construction of Antinomian Piety in Ottoman Aleppo." *International Journal of Middle East Studies* 37:4 (2005): 535–565.

Watenpaugh, Heghnar Zeitlian. "The Harem as Biography: Domestic Architecture, Gender and Nostalgia in Modern Syria." In *Harem Histories: Lived Spaces and Envisioned Places*, edited by Marilyn Booth. Durham, N.C. and London: Duke University Press, 2010: 211–236.

HEGHNAR ZEITLIAN WATENPAUGH

TURKEY

In the region that comprises present-day Turkey, women have played an important role in shaping many aspects of the built environment for centuries. Although there have been several architectural projects in Turkey that have been funded by women prior to the founding of the Ottoman Empire, the contribution of women to architecture in Turkey is particularly important from the sixteenth through the eighteenth centuries, an era traditionally referred to as the "Sultanate of the Women." During this time, royal women of the Ottoman harem—the daughters, sisters, wives, and mothers of the sultan—along with women who served in the harem, became active patrons of pious endowments, particularly of architectural foundations, in the Ottoman capital of Istanbul and played more visible roles in royal ceremonial. The imperial women who became patrons of architecture in Turkey during these three centuries were often faced with decisions similar to those of their male counterparts; on occasion their responses as female patrons did differ because of their gender. Among the challenges male and female patrons faced were the expropriation of property, financing of building activities, selecting the building type and location, and choosing the epigraphic program and architectural style for their projects. Undertaking the patronage of monumental buildings required both Ottoman women and men to consider the opportunities and constraints of their particular social status, life stage, wealth, and ceremonial needs. Postmodern approaches to the study of women and architecture in Turkey have helped to bring a more nuanced understanding of the contributions made by patrons of both genders who influenced this region of the world through architecture. Recent research about architectural projects undertaken by both male and female patrons, such as the prolific builder of the eighteenth century, the Chief Black Eunuch Haci Besir Ağa, or of nonmonumental architectural spaces such as the coffee house, the early modern Ottoman home, and the urban neighborhood argue against a Habermasian conceptualization of public space as male space and promote a reconceptualization of building sites as locations where the identity of a place, along with its patrons and users, are continually shifting, redefined, and regendered. Rather than assess the role of women in architecture in Turkey through essentialized categories of male and female and employ a framework that neatly divides and dichotomizes public and private space, architectural historians are now analyzing Ottoman architectural projects of the early modern era using the concepts of a "gender continuum" and "decorum," the latter defined by Gülrü Necipoğlu in the *Age of Sinan: Architectural Culture in the Ottoman Empire*.

Seljuk Women, Ottoman Women: Historical Background. The pious endowment, or *waqf*, was one of the important Islamic institutions that allowed women to sponsor architectural projects. While the origins of the *waqf* pre-date the Seljuks of Rum (Anatolia), a Turkic dynasty that controlled most of Anatolia during the twelfth and thirteenth centuries, several notable Seljuk imperial women established *awqāf* to facilitate the creation and operation of socioreligious complexes, referred to as *külliye*, in later literature. As an example, Mahperi Hatun, the wife of Sultan Alaeddin Keykubad I (r. 1219–1237), stands out as a particularly active Seljuk patron of architecture, having built several caravanserais throughout Anatolia and a *külliye* in the central Anatolian town of Kayseri in 1238. The sisters, daughters, and wives of the Seljuk sultans of Anatolia chose a range of different building types to endow, including hospitals, monumental tombs, dervish lodges, mosques, and theological schools called madāris. While advertising their personal piety and largess through architecture, these women used their wealth and status to contribute to the power, legitimacy, and sovereignty of their families and the empire.

Imperial Ottoman women also undertook numerous architectural projects and frequently sought legitimacy and prestige for their architectural foundations by linking these to works undertaken by notable women from earlier Islamic empires, particularly the famous wives and female relatives of the Prophet Muḥammad. The Ottoman Sultan Süleyman's consort, then wife, Haseki Hürrem (d. 1558 CE), was referred to in her foundation deed for the *'imaret*, or hospice, she constructed in Jerusalem as Khadīja, ʿĀʾishah, and Fāṭimah, the Prophet's first wife, favorite wife, and daughter, respectively. The name of Zubayda (d. 831 CE), the wife of the Abbasid Caliph Harun al-Rashid and a celebrated patron of mosques, fortresses, hospices, fountains, aqueducts, and wells along the pilgrimage route to Mecca, was also frequently invoked in the epigraphic programs and official titulature used by imperial Ottoman women patrons of architecture. Ottoman women patrons occasionally undertook architectural projects in the same locations where renowned women patrons of an earlier era had erected buildings. For her Jerusalem *'imaret* Haseki Hürrem selected a building site where Helen, the mother of Emperor Constantine (r. 306–337 CE), was alleged to have built a church, and subsequently where the tomb of a fourteenth-century Mamluk woman, al-Sitt

Tunshuq, is reported to have been located. Hadice Turhan Sultan (d. 1683 CE), the mother of the Ottoman sultan Mehmed IV (r. 1648–1687 CE), resumed and followed to completion from 1661 to 1665 the Yeni Valide Mosque complex of Eminönü, Istanbul, a large *külliye* comprising a mosque, tomb, market, primary school, fountain, and school for the instruction of the Qurʾān, which had been initiated in 1598 by Safiye Sultan, the mother of Sultan Mehmed III (r. 1595–1603 CE) but abandoned in 1603 after the sultan died.

Principles of Decorum. Although some of the decisions surrounding the location, typology, and iconography of the architectural projects undertaken by imperial Ottoman women may be attributed to the connections, real or invented, that dynastic women wished to create with their ancestral consoeurs, both male and female patrons of architecture in the Ottoman Empire had to adhere to the principles of decorum that governed patronage and the displays of wealth, status, and piety that accompanied public and private building projects. Although these principles of decorum for architecture were not communicated via written documents or official regulations, they were part of a wider set of symbols and behavioral expectations linked to the social order and hierarchy of Ottoman elites. Among these were codes of dress, the quality and amount of household furnishings in one's possession, and the number of servants in one's household.' Principles of decorum had shaped the relationship between the architect, patron, and the public as early as Roman times as evidenced in the *De architectura*, Vitruvius's architectural treatise from 15 BCE This treatise, a copy of which was in the Topkapı Palace Library, specified the form, size, and several other rules concerning the architecture to be produced so that the patron's final product would be commensurate with his or her social position.

Ottoman architects and their patrons of both genders had to negotiate the principles of decorum of their times when deciding on the presence, absence, or size of architectural features of mosque complexes such as courtyards, domes, minarets, and minaret galleries. Age, gender, social status, and the blood ties to the House of Osman all dictated what could and could not be built. Princess Mihrümah (1522–1578 CE), the daughter of Süleyman the Magnificent (r. 1520–1566), was allowed two minarets for her Üsküdar mosque because of her direct dynastic link to the reigning sultan; Hadice Turhan Sultan, the mother of Mehmed IV, advertised her status as mother to the reigning sultan by adding two minarets to her Eminönü foundation. However, Haseki Hürrem, as the wife of the sultan, was permitted only a single minaret for her mosque complex in Avratpazarı, a poignant reminder that she was connected to the ruling family through marriage and had not reached the rank of *valide* or queen mother.

The Power of the Royal Gaze. Imperial Ottoman women who did undertake major building projects, such as the Friday mosques in the empire's capital, understood the potential of architecture to function as synecdoche, and to create, in lieu of their persons, a concrete and highly visible physical presence that could effectively advertise power, piety, and legitimacy to their Ottoman subjects. Contrary to the traditional view that royal women in the Ottoman Empire were powerless, or at best, invisible backstage manipulators of power because of the contemporary social norms and cultural practices that limited their physical access to the public arena and prohibited the display of their persons, recent scholarship has demonstrated that imperial Ottoman women undertook ambitious and highly visible building projects and actively engaged in the ceremonial and theater surrounding the architecture they endowed. Imperial Ottoman women patrons of architecture also learned how to exercise control over different spaces, urban and administrative, by exploiting and exercising the privileges of the imperial gaze. Changes in the Ottoman succession policies during the mid-sixteenth century, and the sedentarization of the sultanate that accompanied those changes, brought royal Ottoman women into closer contact with the Divan, the administrative chamber of Topkapı Palace. The Ottoman *valides*, in particular, began to understand how to utilize the complex dynamics of the royal gaze that had previously been the purview of the male sultan alone. The panoptic qualities of Hadice Turhan sultan's royal pavilion, which is appended to her mosque in Eminönü, and the role that the formidable covered access ramp, the *taht-i-revan yolu*, could have played in the ceremonial and theater surrounding the *valide*'s entrances and exits to the pavilion, suggest that Ottoman women patrons of architecture were aware of the ways in which the royal gaze could be optimized to gain access, acquire information, and create spectacle.

The Role of Women Patrons in the Design Process. To what extent were Ottoman royal women patrons of architecture involved in the actual design process of the buildings they founded? When answering this question concerning the patron's intention and the degree of involvement, particularly when the patron was female, it is important to define what constitutes the engagement of architectural patrons of any gender in the Ottoman Empire at this time. Archival sources reveal very limited evidence for regular on-site supervision of architectural works by patrons, male or female. Süleyman the Magnificent's repeated visits to the construction site of the Süleymaniye were an exception rather than a rule, and Ottoman chroniclers record that patrons usually came only to the groundbreaking and inaugural ceremonies. In the interim phases of construction, letters, official decrees, models, and some form of plans and/or drawings were the most frequent ways in which patrons were apprised of developments related to their building projects. Contemporary social norms did restrict public activities of Ottoman women more than Ottoman men, and it was customary at this time for women to pray at home rather than at the mosque. But negative evidence of the female patron's participation in decisions concerning her building projects should not lead to the conclusion that she was any more or less involved than her male counterparts. Male and female agents carried the patron's wishes to the court architects, tile makers, and epigrapher. Building supplies were ordered by patrons, regardless of gender; foundation charters from the sixteenth and seventeenth centuries that specified the wages and daily operations of pious endowments reveal that women patrons were as interested as male patrons in who benefited from their largess.

In the Ottoman era, as in Turkey today, patronage could also be a family affair, with both husband and wife, and occasionally children or siblings, partaking in the financial support and design decisions required for a building project to be realized. Although popular opinion today attributes the elaborate interior decoration of the Rüstem Pasha mosque in the Tahtakale district of Istanbul to the wealthy vizier (d. 1561 CE), it is clear from his widow Mihrümah's orders to the Venetian Senate for building materials, sent in 1562, a year after her husband's death, and the *waqf* itself, that Princess Mihrümah was closely supervising the project as a way to promote both her husband and herself. Other royal couples, such as the Princess İsmihan Sultan (1544–1585 CE), the daughter of Nurbanu Sultan (d. 1583 CE), and Selim II (r. 1566–1574 CE), and her husband, the vizier Sokollu Mehmed Pasha (d. 1579 CE), jointly commissioned a mosque complex in Istanbul from Mimar Sinan near the port of Kadirga and a funerary complex in Eyüp. Although numerous archival records show that both husband and wife were involved in these projects, in the foundation inscription of the Kadirga mosque, and in the autobiographical records left by Sinan, only Sokollu Mehmed Pasha is credited with its patronage. As a result, İsmihan's role as female co-patron has largely been forgotten today, as has Mihrümah's contribution to the Rüstem Pasha Mosque.

Women Patrons of the Ottoman Eighteenth and Early Nineteenth Centuries: Fountains and Palaces. During the eighteenth and early nineteenth centuries, Ottoman royal women, elite women, and occasionally women who had served in the harem continued activities as patrons of architecture. As Shirine Hamadeh has observed, the greater public presence of royal women during the eighteenth century resulted in an increase in women's charitable endowments; during the reign of Sultan Ahmed III alone, women's endowments comprised 27 percent of all new pious foundations. The eighteenth century also witnessed both a shift in the locus of royal women's patronage and the types of architecture that women chose to build. Whereas Üsküdar, on the Asian side of the Bosphorus, had been a popular location for the socioreligious foundations of imperial Ottoman women patrons of the sixteenth, seventeenth, and early eighteenth century centuries such as Mihrümah, Nurbanu, and Emetullah Gülnüş Sultan (d. 1715 CE) and the *valide* of sultans Mustafa II (r. 1695–1703 CE) and Ahmed III (r. 1703–1730 CE), the Ottoman princesses of the late eighteenth century and early nineteenth centuries, such as the daughter of Sultan Mustafa III (r. 1757–1774 CE), Hatice Sultan (d. 1821), and Princess Esma Sultan (d. 1848), the daughter of Sultan Abdülhamid I (r. 1774–1789 CE), chose to erect palaces along the shores of the Golden Horn or farther up the Bosphorus in waterfront villages such as Kürüçeşme and Ortaköy. According to Tulay Artan, by locating their royal residences in this area of Istanbul, these princesses contributed to the development of the straits as a new ceremonial axis of the city. Imperial architectural projects of the eighteenth and early nineteenth centuries were not of the grand scale as those from the preceding centuries, yet the class base of patronage expanded significantly in these later centuries to include men and women from the central administration, the palace household, as well as the *ulema* and merchants. The development of new water networks in the city of Istanbul in the eighteenth century also led to an increase in the patronage of architecture associated with water distribution, such as the fountain. In 1728, forty-eight fountains were built throughout the city of Istanbul, and several of these were situated along the shores of the Bosphorus. Fountains were a popular building type selected by women patrons; some of these were freestanding, such as Saliha Sultan's fountain at Azapkapı built in 1732, and all were elaborately decorated, as evidenced by the 1795 fountain of Mihrişah Sultan at Eyup. By participating in the building of palaces, smaller scale waterworks, and other kinds of architecture, Ottoman women of the eighteenth and early nineteenth centuries helped to shape a culture that now included promenades, picnics, and outdoor excursions as social activities, and that continued to promote their beneficence and their important role as patrons of architecture.

BIBLIOGRAPHY

Artan, Tulay. "Noble Women Who Changed the Face of the Bosphorus and the Palaces of the Sultanas." *Biannual Istanbul* I (January 1993): 87–97.

Faroqhi, Suraiya. *Stories of Ottoman Men and Women: Establishing Status, Establishing Control.* Istanbul: Eren 2002.

Hamadeh, Shirine. *The City's Pleasures: Istanbul in the Eighteenth Century.* Seattle: University of Washington Press, 2007.

Mikhail, Alan. "The Heart's Desire: Gender, Urban Space and the Ottoman Coffee House." In *Ottoman Tulips, Ottoman Coffee: Leisure and Lifestyle in the Eighteenth Century*, edited by Dana Sajdi, pp. 133–170. London: Tauris Academic Studies 2007.

Necipoğlu, Gülrü. *The Age of Sinan: Architectural Culture in the Ottoman Empire*. London: Reaktion Books, 2005.

Peirce, Leslie. *The Imperial Harem: Women and Sovereignty in the Ottoman Empire*. New York: Oxford University Press, 1993.

Singer, Amy. *Constructing Ottoman Beneficence: An Imperial Soup Kitchen in Jerusalem*, Albany: State University of New York Press, 2003.

Thys-Şenocak, Lucienne. *Ottoman Women Builders: The Architectural Patronage of Hadice Turhan Sultan*. Aldershot, U.K., and Burlington, Vt.: Ashgate, 2006.

Zilfi, Madeline C. "Muslim Women in the Early Modern Era." In *The Cambridge History of Turkey*, Vol. 3, *The Later Ottoman Empire, 1603–1839*, edited by Suraiya Faroqhi, pp. 226–255. Cambridge, U.K.: Cambridge University Press, 2006.

Lucienne Thys-Şenocak

Art, Women in Islamic. Any discussion of women in Islamic art is dependent upon a network of interrelated and oftentimes amorphous concepts, from the tenuous relationship between figural art and Islamic theology to the historical problematic of defining the role of women in Islamic culture. Images are neither benign expressions nor neutral objects; they are, rather, the visual recognition of cultural perceptions of gender, power, and religion. As critical vehicles of cultural and religious histories, images are central to the socialization process as societal constructs of masculine and feminine. The patriarchal attitude of a society results in the diminution, if not total elimination, of the iconography of women, especially in motifs of power and authority. The documentation and narrative of women's history, especially of artworks as central to understanding women's roles both within specific societies and the larger world, is a late-twentieth-century phenomenon. A further complication is the incalculable loss of many artworks through wars, religious iconoclasm, and natural disasters.

Art delineates the tenets and perceptions that form local identity, whether related to nation, religion, or class, with relation to regional and global politics and economics. With the nineteenth-century transformation in attitude toward the Middle Eastern, the borders of the discussion of "women in Islamic art" expanded, given the introduction of modern art from the West, the retrieval of earlier Pharaonic and Islamic art, and the influence of traditional folk arts and crafts on "modern" Islamic art. Both the analysis and presentation of women in Islamic art is complicated by (European) Orientalist painting, which has been criticized for stereotypical portrayals of women. Artworks communicate the common human experience through the implementation of gestures, postures, costumes, attributes, and signs. Just as the popular practice of religion reveals the religious experience(s) of the nonelite—including women—for whom daily experiences from domestic activities to childbirth and -rearing are central to religiosity, so too do the images projected beyond fine arts, including popular culture and crafts.

Given its geographic and societal breadth, there are difficulties in defining Islamic art, especially as reflective of a religious or cultural identity. Further complications are the traditional modes of identification by theme or motif, place, or function, as well as the religious affiliation of artist, patron, and consumer. Typically, religious art is understood to fulfill certain functions from pedagogy to spiritual encouragement, and ritual or devotional substantiation. Religious art is classified as iconic or representative of sacred figures or ideas; aniconic or symbolic of sacral figures or ideas; and iconoclastic, that is, denying or destroying images. Representational art, identified as *taṣwīr*, inhabits a debatable place in Islamic culture, especially with the inherited suspicion of idolatry and the tradition that figural representation in art is sinful. However, the visual arts contribute to the cultural and political processes of the contemporary Islamic world, and the evolution of *taṣwīr* from questionable to trustworthy characterizes the popular and pervasive figures in television, cinema, and advertising. Perhaps not surprisingly, then, the televised, filmed, and photographed images of women involved in the events of the "Arab Spring" provided visual forums for both the universal engagement of all citizens and the public acceptance of the authenticity of the visual.

Women's Participation in the Arts. The role of women in Islamic art extends beyond the category of "woman as subject" to include their little-acknowledged standing as artists, patrons, curators, critics, and consumers. Even before the advent of the modern Islamic world, whenever women were politically vested, they acknowledged that public image signified power and authority, so they commissioned artworks. During the periods of cultural domesticity, women's art flourished through embroidery, tapestry, crafts, and ultimately calligraphy. The cultural fusion of Islamic Spain afforded women greater freedom, as female calligraphers were praised for the beauty of their writing. Nevertheless women's participation in Islamic art prior to the Iranian Revolution is "missing history," which requires study premised on a reinterpretation of traditional history.

Woman as Subject. Whether defined by religious or cultural attitudes, the fundamental image of women in Islamic art is described as one of passivity. Such a characterization is more likely than not incomplete, and initially the result of a series of misleading stereotypes that are equally applicable to the depiction of women in Western art. Without doubt, the iconography of women is coordinated with cultural, societal, and religious orientations. The initial response is that Islamic art is aniconic and thereby contains no figures. If there is a "secular" Islamic art, then the figure is allowed but represented either ambiguously or overtly modest, so that the female figure is covered in loose, flowing garments with a veil, even unto the covering of her entire face.

However the cultural diversity of the Islamic world as it spanned the Mediterranean basin and the Arabian Peninsula into Asia and Africa included acceptance of the human figure, especially in Persian, Mughal, and Ottoman art. As with other early Mediterranean cultures, women's images originated in fertility figures, and fulfilled the sanctioned female phases of virgin, bride/wife, mother, and widow. From the earliest presentations of Islamic art, then, women are depicted in various modalities, including elements of the life cycle (wife, mother, lover), occupations (milkmaids, spinners, lacemakers, calligraphers, musicians, acrobats, dancers), and personifications of beauty (courtesans, princesses, angels) or of vice and virtue (sorceresses, fairies, angels). Whether the subject or minor players in the artworks, these women were typified by their activities, especially through gestures, postures, and costumes.

Portrayals of specific women, including historical figures such as Fāṭimah, biblical figures like Mary, and literary figures including Layla, were found in Islamic art, especially in manuscript illuminations. These women were presented as moral exemplars or personifications of feminine values. The advent of European colonialism, with few exceptions, presented the female figure in Orientalist art in unfavorable stereotypes. The connection between art and politics was never clearer as the female figure and her domestic environment heightened political, societal, and religious associations from the Western fantasy of the harem to colonial postcards. Although the topoi could be defined as Islamic, the artists, patrons, and audience were not, so the question arises: Is this Islamic art?

Contemporary Islamic Art, Feminism, and the "Arab Spring." The international exhibition, Dialogue of the Present: The Work of Eighteen Arab Women Artists, illustrates the dramatic transformations in the status and consideration of the role of women in Islamic art. This exhibition and its companion catalogue evidence not simply "a first" in the presentation of Arab women artists, it highlights the almost simultaneous effects of the retrieval of nationalistic artistic patrimony throughout the Arab world and the growth of capitalism and globalization. For example, the Iranian Muslim photographer Shirin Nehsat (b. 1957) replaces Orientalist stereotypes with proud militant women, while the French Algerian photographer Zineb Sedira (b. 1963) investigates the imagery of the veil.

As a philosophic and political stance, feminism has contributed to the critique of patriarchal culture, especially in terms of capitalism, cultural integrity, violence, and the commoditization of women within both the Islamic world and the larger global context. The role of Islamic women artists in the initiation and endurance of the "Arab Spring" is yet to be evaluated, but the seeds of their artistic future have been sown.

[*See also* Iconography]

BIBLIOGRAPHY

Resources on the topic of women and the arts are predominantly surveys or monographs on the history of women artists in Western culture; few specialized sources exist for the study of non-Western cultures.

Denny, Walter. "Art." Updated by Jennifer Winegar. In *Encyclopedia of the Modern Middle East and North Africa*, edited by Philip Mattar. 4 vols., 2nd ed. Vol. 1, pp. 309–314. Detroit: Macmillan Reference, 2004.

Denny, Walter. "Women and Islamic Art." In *Women, Religion, and Social Change*, edited by Yvonne Yazbeck Haddad and Ellison Banks Findly, pp. 147–180. Albany: State University of New York Press, 1985.

Keelan, Siumee H., curator, and Fran Lloyd, ed. *Contemporary Arab Women's Art: Dialogues of the Present*. London: WAL, 1999. See especially Tina Sherwell, Chapter 3: "Bodies in Representation: Contemporary Arab Women's Art," pp. 58–69. Exhibition catalogue.

Malt, Carol. "Women, Museums, and the Public Sphere." Special Issue: "Women's Activism and the Public Sphere, *Journal of Middle East Women's Studies* 2, no. 2 (2006): 115–136.

Walther, Wiebke. *Women in Islam*. Rev. ed. Princeton, N.J., 2009. English translation of *Die Frau im Islam*, first published in 1980. See especially "Women in Islamic Culture," pp. 143–154.

Diane Apostolos-Cappadona

Asmāʾ al-Husna, al-.

Asmāʾ al-Husna, al-. The term *al-asmāʾ al-ḥusna* (the Beautiful Names [of God]) is mentioned several times in the Qurʾān: "to him belong the beautiful names so call him by these names" (Qurʾān 7:180, also 17:110, 20:8, and 59:22–24). The most used names for God in the Qurʾān are al-Raḥman (The Compassionate) and al-Raḥīm (The Merciful).

Al-asmāʾ al-ḥusna is foundational to Islamic theology and mysticism (*taṣawwuf*). In Qurʾān 2:30–33, God teaches Adam "all the names" of which the angels have no knowledge. It is this knowledge that makes Adam (and humanity) superior to angels. In the exegetical tradition these names are identified with the *al-asmāʾ ul-ḥusna*. The *ḥadīth* (saying of the Prophet): "there are ninety-nine names of God… whoever memorizes [or recites] them enters Paradise" (al-Kabbani, 2002, p. 683), has led to the *al-asmāʾ al-ḥusna* being referred to as the ninety-nine names of God. In the mystical tradition, the divine names are the essence of the Qurʾān sufficient to guide one to the divine presence. Some Ṣūfīs (mystics) maintain that the names/attributes of God are God and others say that they are neither God nor other than God.

While the name Allāh is understood to refer to divine essence, the rest of the names are understood to refer to divine attributes, which are further divided into attributes of divine essence and attributes of divine acts. For example, al-Baṣīr (The Seer), al-Samīʿ (The Hearer), al-ʿAlīm (The Knower), and al-Hayy (The Living) are attributes of divine essence, and the opposites of such names, then, are not attributable to God. Al-Rāfiʿ (The Exalter) and al Muhyī (The Giver of Life) are attributes of divine acts and the opposites of such names, for example, (the Abaser) and al-Mumīt (The Giver of Death) are also attributable to God. Names of divine acts that describe His severity refer to God's response to the wrongdoers. The Qurʾānic command to call on God by *al-asmāʾ ul-ḥusna* is understood to preclude the divine names that describe God's severity, as humans would not be able to bear the divine response to such a name.

The oft-quoted *ḥadīth qudsī* (in which Muḥammad quotes God) "I was a hidden treasure and I created the world because I wanted to be known" (Chittick, 1983, pp. 47–48) gives the knowledge of God as the reason for creation. The way to this knowledge is through the contemplation of and constant remembrance of *al-asmāʾ al-ḥusna*. This remembrance of God, *dhikrullāh*, brings solace to the heart (*ʿala bīdhzikrillāhī la tatmaʾin al-qulūb*, Qurʾān 13:28) and is the central activity in Ṣūfī circles and in popular piety.

The *al-asmāʾ al-ḥusna* serve as a model for human character as expressed in the *ḥadīth* assume the virtues of God (*takhāllaqū bī khalqillāh,*). Contemplating or calling on God by a certain name is expected to manifest that divine attribute in a person's character and life. Thus, those in need of safety would call on God by reciting "*Ya ḥafīz* (O Protector)." The *asmāʾ-al ḥusna* are also often used as part of personal names.

An abundance of popular literature on the *al-asmāʾ al-ḥusna* and the ninety-nine names of God continues to be published through the print and electronic media as grassroots theology that supports faith and practice.

Bibliography

Arberry, A. J. *The Doctrine of the Ṣūfīs: A Translation of Abū Bakr al-Kalabadhī's Kitāb al-Taʿarrūf li madhhāb ahl-al-taṣawwūf.* Lahore: Suhail Academy, 2001. The fourth-century CE classic on Sufism is the earliest extant work on the subject. It does not contain much on *al-asmāʾ al-ḥusna* beyond what has been mentioned in the article above.

Burrel, David B., and Nazih Daher, translators. *Al-Ghazālī: The Ninety-nine Beautiful Names of God.* Cambridge, U.K.: The Islamic Texts Society, 1992. A sixth-century CE classic on the subject.

Chittick, William C. *The Sufi Path of Love: The Spiritual Teachings of Rumi.* Albany: State University of New York Press, 1983. Contains a short and helpful section on Divine Names and Attributes, pp. 42–49.

Al-Kabbani, Muhammad Hisham. *Classical Islam and the Naqshbandi Sufi Order.* Islamic Supreme Council of America, 2002. One of the first comprehensive manuals of Ṣūfī practice in English, representing the Naqshbandī Ṣūfī order. Mentions *al-asmāʾ al-ḥusna* and the individual divine names within a discussion on the related topic of *dhikr* (remembrance of God) and prescriptions for the practice of *dhikr*. A list of the ninety-nine beautiful names is given on pp. 771–773.

Ghazala Anwar

Astronomy and Astrology. Arabs have consistently taken a keen interest in the study of stars and constellations. This could be attributed to two main reasons: the belief that celestial bodies had an influence upon terrestrial and human affairs and the reliance upon constellations for guidance during night journeys. Arabs in the pre-Islamic period followed a primitive system of *anwāʿ* (kinds) that divided the year into precise periods of time based on the acronychal (occurring at nightfall) setting and helical rising of stars or constellations. They learned from the Indians to distinguish the stations or "mansions" (*manāzil*, sing. *manzil*) of the moon, numbering twenty-eight, which they combined with the *anwāʿ* to divide the solar zodiac into twenty-eight equal parts. Accordingly the term *ʿilm al-nujūm* was used to refer to both astronomy and astrology. Soon after, however, astronomy was unambiguously differentiated from astrology, and a clear terminological and conceptual distinction was made between the two sciences. The titles *ʿilm al-falak* (the science of the celestial orb) and *ʿilm al-hayʾa* (the science of the configuration of heavens) were used to refer to astronomy, while *ʿilm aḥkam al-nujūm* (judicial astrology), or simply *ʿilm al-nujūm* (the science of the stars), referred exclusively to astrology.

With the advent of Islam in the seventh century a distinctly Islamic character was added to Arabic folk astronomy. Astronomical observations were now used to define the times of Muslim prayer, to determine the visibility of the lunar crescent at the beginning of each Muslim month, and to find the direction of Mecca (the *qiblah*). This religious impetus for the study of the stars shaped the literary and observational activities of Muslim astronomers and gave it a unique position within the Islamic sciences.

According to the original sources available, we can distinguish four periods in the development of Islamic astronomy and astrology. The first period (c. 700–c. 825) is marked by the incorporation of pre-Islamic folk astronomy with mathematical astronomy from Greece, the Sassanid Empire, and India. These disparate elements were subsequently amalgamated to create a science that was essentially Islamic. The earliest extant astronomical texts translated into Arabic in the eighth century were of Indian and Persian origin. A number of *zījs*, astronomical handbooks with calculations of the positions of celestial bodies, were compiled in India and Afghanistan. Hellenistic astronomical texts were also translated into Arabic, the most important being the *Almagest* of Ptolemy (second century CE), of which different translations were made from both Syriac and Greek in the ninth century. Muḥammad al-Fazārī (c. 806), a prominent astronomer from this period, translated scientific works into Arabic and Persian, and is credited for building the first astrolabe in the Muslim world.

Astrological writings also entered the Muslim world during this period from the aforementioned regions. Astrological doctrines such as the government of individual horoscopes, the properties of the zodiacal signs, and the planets and their influences were inherited from Aristotelian philosophy and Hellenistic astrological doctrines; while others, like the cyclical government of universal world events, came from eastern Persian and Indian sources. The most influential of the sources to enter the Islamic lands was the *Tetrabiblos* of Ptolemy, a companion volume of the *Almagest* that deals with the philosophy and practice of astrology.

A second period of vigorous investigation (c. 825–c. 1025) followed thereafter in which the superiority of Ptolemaic astronomy, as incorporated in the *Almagest*, was accepted and exercised enormous authority in the Islamic world. The first Arabic translations of the *Almagest* were prepared while original works of Arabic astronomy were produced simultaneously. Thus original astronomical research went hand in hand with translation and Arabic astronomy attempted to revise, refine, and complement Ptolemaic astronomy, rather than simply reproduce it. Among the most prominent astronomers of this period, Muḥammad ibn Mūsā al-Khwārizmī (d. 850), wrote an essential work, *Zīj al-Sindhind* (Astronomical Tables of Sind and Hind) in which he used Indian astronomical methods to construct tables for the movements of the sun, the moon, and the five planets known at the time.

Astrology was influential and widespread in this period, although translations in the field of astronomy were far more industrious than in that of astrology. The most impressive astrologer during this period was Abu Maʿshar al-Balkhī (d. 886). Considered the greatest astrologer of the ʿAbbāsid court in Baghdad, he formulated the standard expression of Islamic astrological doctrines, and wrote influential works on historical astrology and genethlialogy, the science of casting. One of his known works, *Kitāb al-madkhal al-kabīr* (The Great Introduction to Astrology), is of particular importance since it was translated into Latin and had a great influence in Europe in later years.

During this period also the ʿAbbāsid caliph al-Maʾmūn (d. 833) built the famous library and translation institute *Bayt al-Ḥikmah* (House of Wisdom) in Baghdad. Its observatory housed prominent astronomers like Ḥabash al-Ḥāsib (d. 869), Banū Mūsā (a.k.a. the "sons of Mūsā ibn Shākir"), and al-Khwārizmī.

Another well-known figure from this period is the astronomer and astrologer Muḥammad ibn Jābir al-Battānī, known as Albategnius (d. 929). He is known for making important corrections to Ptolemy's measurements of planetary motion, discovering the movement of the sun's apogee, and calculating the values for the precession of the equinoxes and the obliquity of the ecliptic. His work is considered instrumental in the development of astronomy in the West, and was quoted frequently by Copernicus, Tycho Brahe, and Johannes Kepler, among others. As for astrology, after the ninth century few astrological treatises were written, and they were either elementary handbooks or large compendia based upon the work of earlier authorities, although the polymath Abū ar-Rayḥān al-Bīrūnī (d. 1048) wrote many treatises dealing with specific points of astrology.

It is very rare that we would encounter any mention of women involved in the medieval sciences. For various reasons the cultural and religious climate did not permit any apparent or widespread practice of astronomy or astrology by women. In that regard records reveal the names of only two Muslim women. The first one was an astrologer called Bawrān, the daughter of an astrologer and the wife of the caliph al-Maʾmūn. It is reported of her that she used the astrolabe to look at the horoscope of the caliph al-Muʿtasim (d. 842), al-Maʾmūn's younger brother and successor. The other woman was an astrolabe maker, known by the name of al-ʿIjlīya (fl. c. 960), daughter of al-ʿIjlī al-Asṭurlābī, an astrolabe maker in his own right.

In the third period (c. 1025–c. 1450) a distinctly Islamic astronomy flourished and continued to progress, but with decreasing vigor. It made its first impact through the work of Arab astronomers in Spain, such as al-Zarqālī, known as Arzachel (d. 1087), who corrected geographical calculations from Ptolemy and al-Khwārizmī, perfected astrolabes and equatoria and edited the Toledan Tables, astronomical tables used to predict the movements of the sun, moon, and planets relative to distant stars. Naṣīr al-Dīn al-Ṭūsī (d. 1274) is considered the most prominent astronomer of this period. Working in the prestigious Maragheh observatory built by Hülegü Khan in 1259, he made accurate astronomical tables for better astrological predictions. He also wrote *Zij-i Ilkhani,* which included an advanced model for the planetary system with accurate astronomical tables that calculate the positions of stars and planets. The most famous of his works, *Al-Tadhkirah fī ʿilm al-Hayʾah* (Memoir on Astronomy), set forward a comprehensive structure of the universe and was highly regarded in the Middle Ages. Al-Ṭūsī also invented a mathematical method called "Tusi couple" which enabled astronomers to explain observed planetary motions without violating the principle of uniform circular motion, as Ptolemy had done in his problematic equant.

A timekeeper of the Umayyad mosque in Damascus, Ibn al-Shaṭir (d. 1375), refined al-Ṭūsī's innovations further and developed models for the moon and Mercury, which reappeared in the works of Copernicus two centuries later. The last of the astronomers of this period was the Timurid sultan Ulugh Beg (d. 1449) who built an enormous observatory in Samarkand and compiled *Zij-i Sultani*, a great star catalog with their names. He is further noted for making accurate calculations of the length of the sidereal year and determining the earth's axial tilt, which remained the most accurate measurements for a long time.

Attacks against astrology intensified during this period as can be seen in the writings of Muslim theologians and philosophers like Ibn Sīnā, known as Avicenna (d. 1037), Abū Ḥāmid al-Ghazālī (d. 1111), Ibn Rushd (d. 1198), and Ibn Qayyim al-Jawzīyah (d. 1350). It was associated with the schismatic Shīʿī and Bāṭinīyah, or with the suspicious foreign sciences, or with outright atheism. It was also attacked on religious grounds for being closely aligned with divination and for denying divine intervention and free will. While its appeal to Muslim intellectuals declined rapidly after the Mongol invasions in the thirteenth century, astrological practice was widespread in Muslim lands, and its influence had already been transmitted to India, the Latin West, and Byzantium.

The death of Ulugh Beg marked the beginning of the last period (c. 1450–c. 1900). Marked by stagnation, traditional Islamic astronomy continued to be practiced during this time, yet without any significant scientific innovation. On the other hand further development and progress in astronomy shifted to western Europe with the scientific revolution and the contributions to astronomy made by Copernicus, Brahe, Kepler, Galileo, and Newton.

Nonetheless, as just illustrated, the influence of Islamic astronomy upon Europe is undeniable and, indeed, very considerable. This is further indicated by the preponderance of words of Arabic origin used in the technical vocabulary of modern astronomy, such as the azimuth (*al-sumūt*, "the direction of the paths"); the zenith (*samt ar-raʾs*, "the direction of the head"); and nadir (*naẓīr al-samt*, "the opposite of the direction"). This influence is also reflected in the names by which some of the more prominent stars are still popularly known. Among these are Betelgeuse (*bayt al-jawzāʾ*, "armpit of the center") and Rigel (*al-rijl*, "the foot") in the constellation Orion; Vega (*an-nasr al-wāqiʿ*, "the stooping eagle") in Lyra; Aldebaran (*al-dabarān*, "the follower") in Taurus; Algol (*al-ghūl*, "the ghoul") in Perseus; and Deneb (*al-dhanab al-dajāja*, "the tail") in Cygnus and so forth.

BIBLIOGRAPHY

Hill, Donald R. *Islamic Science and Engineering*. Edinburgh: Edinburgh University Press, 1993.

Saliba, George. *A History of Arabic Astronomy: Planetary Theories During the Golden Age of Islam*. New York: New York University Press, 1994.

Saliba, George. "The Role of the Astrologer in Medieval Islamic Society." *Bulletin des Etudes Orientales* 44 (1992): 45–68.

Saliba, George. "A Sixteenth Century Drawing of an Astrolabe Made by Khafif Ghulam ʿAli b. ʿIsa (c. 850 A.D.)." *Nuncius, Annali di Storia della Scienza* 6 (1991): 109–119.

Schacht, Joseph, with C. E. Bosworth, eds. *The Legacy of Islam*. 2d ed. Oxford: Clarendon Press, 1974.

Daniel Bannoura

AYATOLLAH. The term "ayatollah" literally means "a sign of God." It is a hierarchical honorific title designated to distinguish Iranian *Ithna Ashari* (Twelver) Shīʿī *mujtahids* who possess outstanding religious knowledge and authority. Historically, the office of ayatollah has been male-dominated and highly political. These hierarchies, based among the highest ranks of mudjtahids, and the political theories attached to them, began to form during the Ṣafavid dynasty, when Shiism became the state religion of Iran in 1501, and have evolved ever since.

Prior to the Iranian Constitutional Revolution (1905–1911), *mujtahids* were given the title "Hojatalislam" (proof of Islam). However, in early twenty-first century Iran, the title "Hojatalislam" is given to mid-level *mujtahids*, or used indiscriminately to refer to clergy. The title "ayatollah" was introduced during the Constitutional Revolution to honor those clerical leaders who were signatories to the new constitution. Following this event, the title began to be used occasionally in reference to a *marjaʿ al-taqlīd* (a Shīʿī religious authority deserving of emulation), and later to convey respect for other significant religious leaders as well. For this reason, the term "*ayatollah al-ʿuẓmā*" (literally, grand sign of God, translated as "Grand Ayatollah") has come to be used to distinguish a *marjaʿ al-taqlīd* from other high-ranking clerics.

Historically, and in contemporary Iran as well, women have also been *mujtahidas*. For example, *Mujtahidat* Nusrat Amin Esfahani (1886–1983) and Zohreh Ṣefātī (b. 1948) were each granted an *al-ijāzah* (certificate or diploma) of *ijtihād* (independent judgment in a legal or theological question) by their male ʿulamā peers. "No woman since Amin has published so prolifically in the realms of *fiqh*, *falsafah* and *akhlāq*, received as many endorsements by senior colleagues," or granted and received *al-ijāzahs* to and from male ʿulamā of such high authority" (Künkler and Fazaeli, 2011, p. 154). Yet, of the two *mujtahidas*, Ṣefātī is the one who has been referred to by some official Web sites, such as Ostandari Markazi, or English language Web sites, such as Islamic Insight, as a female ayatollah, in spite of the fact that Amin possessed a higher level of religious authority.

Ṣefātī designation is perhaps the first time that the title "ayatollah" has been applied to a woman, albeit in an honorific and unofficial manner (she is mainly referred to as *faqīh-e mutjahid* or *Banoo-e mujtahid* [female *mujtahid*]). This could be due to the fact that Ṣefātī lives in a time when the title "ayatollah" has been used more loosely to designate a high-level *mujtahid*, rather than a *marjaʿ al-taqlīd*. There are no prohibitions in the Qurʾān or the *sunnah* against a woman becoming a *marjaʿ*. There are varying views among the Shīʿī ʿulamā on this point, however. A number of Shīʿī ʿulamā, including Ayatollah al-Ozma Khoei, are opposed to the idea of a woman being a *marjaʿ*. However, Ayatollah al-Ozma Yosuf Saneʾi, as well as Zohreh Ṣefātī herself, both hold the opinion that women as well as men can become *marjaʿ al-taqlīds*. Amin not only received the *al-ijāzahs* of *ijtihād* and *ravāyat* from her contemporaries, including Ayatollah Mohammad Kazem Hosseini Shirazi (1873–1947) and the Ayatollah al-Ozma Abdolkarim Haʾeri Yazdi (1859–1937), but she also bestowed *ijtihād* and *ravāyat* to her peers, including Ayatollah Sayyid Shahab ad-Din Marʾashi-Najafi (d. 1990), and her female student Zinat al-Sadat Homayouni (b. 1917), attesting to the acceptance of her authority by the male ʿulamā. Likewise, Ṣefātī received *ravāyat* from Ayatollahs Agha Asli Ali Yari Gharani Tabrizi and Mohammad Fazel Lankarani (1931–2007). She claims that Ayatollah Lotfollah Safi Golpayegani (1919–2010) granted her *ravāyat* and *ijtihād* after he read her book *Ziyarat dar Partoye Velayat*. Ṣefātī attests to having given *ijāzas* of *ravāyat* to more than forty contemporary ʿulamā.

BIBLIOGRAPHY

Abdi, Zahara. "Exemplary Shia Women: Madam Zohreh Sefati." *Islamic Insight* (March 9, 2008). http://islamicinsights.com/religion/religion/exemplary-shia-women-madam-zohreh-sefati.html.

AhleBait Organisation. http://ahlebaitorg.blogspot.ie/2011/05/list-of-ayathollah-in-world.html.

Badiī, Muhammad. "Guftigu ba Faqih Pajuhandeh Bānū Zuhrah Ṣifātī (Interview with the Researcher Jurist, Lady Zuhrah Sifātī)." *Keyhan Farhangī* 199 (April 2003). http://www.noormags.com/view/fa/articlepage/19531?sta=%u0632%u0647%u0631%u0647+%u0635%u0641%u0627%u062a%u06cc.

Esposito, John L. *The Oxford Dictionary of Islam*. New York: Oxford University Press, 2003.

Fischer, Michael, M. J. "Becoming Mollah: Reflections on Iranian Clerics in a Revolutionary Age." *Iranian Studies* 13 (1980): 83–177.

Künkler, Mirjam, and Roja Fazaeli. "The Life of Two *Mujtahidahs*: Female Religious Authority in Twentieth-Century Iran." In *Women, Leadership and Mosques: Changes in Contemporary Islamic Authority*, edited by Masooda Bano and Hilary Kalmbach, pp. 127–161. Leiden, Netherlands: Brill, 2011.

Moin, Baqer. *Khomeini: Life of the Ayatollah*. New York: Thomas Dunne Books, 2000.

"Ostandari Markazi." http://www.ostan-mr.ir/akhbar/khabar/1403.

Saiedzadeh, Mohsen (writing as Mina Yadegar Azadi). "Ijtihad va Marja'iyate Zanan. (Ijtihad and Marja'iyat of Women)." *Zanan Magazine* 8 (1992): 24.

ROJA FAZAELI

B

Badawi, Jamal. (b. 1939), Egyptian-born Canadian Muslim preacher, author, academic, activist, and speaker. Dr. Jamal Badawi is Professor Emeritus at Saint Mary's University in Canada and recipient of an honorary doctorate from the same institution. He earned his undergraduate degree from Ain Shams University in Cairo, Egypt, and completed his Ph.D. in Business Administration at Indiana University. Badawi spent his teaching career at St. Mary's; he was formally appointed to the Department of Management, but also taught courses on Islam for the Department of Religious Studies. The central themes of his work have been interfaith dialogue and Islam as a complete way of life, all of which has helped to debunk popular stereotypes about Islam among non-Muslims and to refocus the Muslim community on more thorough readings and understandings of Islam's primary sources. He is married, with five children and twenty grandchildren.

Badawi is viewed as an authority on Islam, having written many books, booklets, and articles and produced a television series on the subject that aired over 350 episodes on many local public service TV stations in Canada, the United States, and other countries. He has written extensively on many topics related to Islam, including Islam's political, social, and economic systems, and relations between Muslims and non-Muslims. His writings show how the media often perpetuate misunderstandings of Islamic teachings and effectively craft the stereotype of "Islamic terrorism," which is assumed to encapsulate all or most Muslims, and render Islam as a violent religion in the eyes of the American public, in particular.

Some of Badawi's most controversial work within the Muslim community has addressed women, most notably his article, "The Status of Woman in Islam." This article focuses on women's dignity and equality with men, based on the primary sources of Islam. Badawi took a firm stance against any form of abuse or violence when dealing with women, particularly taking on interpretations of Qurʾānic verses 4:34 that he considers erroneous. Because this verse has been used by some to justify domestic violence, Badawi argued for placing the verse in the broader context of the Qurʾān, *sunnah*, and *fiqh* literature, highlighting the fact that the Prophet himself never resorted to violence or abusive measures with any of his wives. His examination of the meaning and context of the term *idhribuhun*, often translated as "strike," determined that "gentle tap" was a more contextually appropriate interpretation, making it clear that domestic violence is unacceptable in Islam. His book *Gender Equity in Islam: Basic Principles* (1995) also distinguishes between the Qurʾān's assertions versus scholars' interpretations and the varied cultural practices that are upheld by some Muslims. He strives to make it known that the oppressive nature and established system of inequity that exist in some areas of the Muslim world are un-Islamic, contradicting the principles prescribed by the Qurʾān and *ḥadīth*.

Jamal Badawi is a member of or on the executive board of several national and international organizations, including the Islamic Society of North America (ISNA), the Shura (Consultative) Council of the Islamic Society of North America, and the International Union of Muslim Scholars, among others.

BIBLIOGRAPHY

Badawi, Jamal A. *Gender Equity in Islam: Basic Principles*. Plainfield, Ind.: American Trust Publications, 1995.

Badawi, Jamal. Interview with the author, July 21, 2012.

Badawi, Jamal." The Status of Women in Islam." *Al-Ittihad*, 8.2 (1971). http://www.islamicweb.com/beliefs/women/status.htm.

"Dr. Jamal Badawi." http://jamalbadawi.org.

O'Keefe, Mark. "Expert Warns Against Making Islam Scapegoat: An Authority on Muslim-Christian Relations Fears Islam Will Be Blamed for Abuses Against Christians by Some Muslims." *The Oregonian*, November 24, 1998, p. B1.

Silas. "A Rebuttal to Jamal Badawi's 'Wife Beating,'" *Journal of Biblical Apologetics* 8 (2003): 104–110.

EREN TATARI

BADRAN, MARGOT. An accomplished and prolific scholar of Middle Eastern and Islamic history focusing on gender issues, Margot Badran is a Senior Scholar at the Woodrow Wilson International Center for Scholars and a Senior Fellow at the Prince Alwaleed Bin Talal Center for Muslim-Christian Understanding at Georgetown University.

She holds a D.Phil. from Oxford University, M.A.s from Harvard and Syracuse Universities, and a B.A. from Trinity College. She also holds a diploma from al-Azhar University in Arabic and Islamic Studies. Badran has been a visiting professor at numerous research institutions across the globe and has received a number of fellowships, awards, and honors. While she is mainly based in the U.S., she is a global bridge-builder and has her second home in Cairo.

Badran is the author of a long list of books and articles on gender issues in the Middle East with a special focus on developments in Egypt. Among her books are *Feminism in Islam: Secular and Religious Convergences* (2009), *Feminism beyond East and West: New Gender Talk and Practice in Global Islam* (2006), and *Feminists, Islam, and Nation: Gender and the Making of Modern Egypt* (1995).

In recent years, Badran has been an influential scholar of the controversial subject of "Islamic feminism." In a much-quoted 2002 article in the Egyptian *Al Ahram Weekly*, she defined this as "a feminist discourse and practice articulated within an Islamic paradigm. Islamic feminism, which derives its understanding and mandate from the Qurʾan, seeks rights and justice for women, and for men, in the totality of their existence" (Badran, 2002).

One of Badran's great strengths is her ability to draw on an extensive knowledge of both "secular" and "Islamic" expressions of feminism in Egypt and in the wider Islamic world. This gives her a unique vantage point for understanding the differences, respective changes, and interconnections between different expressions of feminism.

According to Badran, secular and Islamic feminisms have never been hermetically isolated entities—and we are currently witnessing an increasing convergence between them. Hence, rather than seeing secular and Islamic feminisms as oppositional forces (as they are indeed often presented), she suggests that it might be better to perceive them as engaging in what she refers to as a "constructive conversation" (Badran, 2009, p. 6). She also sees Islamic feminism as far more radical than secular feminism, in particular its Egyptian version and in diaspora societies (Badran, 1999, p. 164). Whereas the latter historically accepted differences between the public and private spheres, Islamic feminism eliminates this distinction due to its insistence on fundamental human equality (Badran, 2009, p. 3).

Badran has caused some controversy in some of her most recent work, where she explores the trajectory from secular to Islamic to what she refers to as a new "Muslim holistic feminism." She warns against the latter and suggests that the privileging of Muslim women's rights currently occurring at the global level and being exported to local terrains can be divisive and may threaten national unity (Badran, 2011).

BIBLIOGRAPHY

Badran, Margot. *Feminism beyond East and West: New Gender Talk and Practice in Global Islam*. New Delhi: Global Media Productions, 2006.

Badran, Margot. *Feminism in Islam: Secular and Religious Convergences*. Oxford: Oneworld Press, 2009.

Badran, Margot. *Feminists, Islam, and Nation: Gender and the Making of Modern Egypt*. Princeton, N.J.: Princeton University Press, 1995.

Badran, Margot. "From Islamic Feminism to a Muslim Holistic Feminism." *IDS Bulletin* 42 (2011): 78–87.

Badran, Margot. "Islamic Feminism: What's in a Name?" *Al Ahram Weekly* 569, January 17–23, 2002.

Badran, Margot. "Toward Islamic Feminisms: A Look at the Middle East." In *Hermeneutics and Honor: Negotiating Female "Public" Space in Islamic/ate Societies*, edited by Asma Afsaruddin, pp. 159–188. Cambridge, Mass.: Harvard University Press, 1999.

DR. JULIE PRUZAN-JØRGENSEN

BAGHDĀD KHĀTŪN. (d. 1335, r. 1323–1335), a Chobanid princess who, through marriage to Abū Saʿīd Bahārdar, the last Ilkhan of Iran, exerted great influence over political events in the state. Baghdād Khātūn was born into the Chopan family, a powerful political and military Turco-Mongol dynasty that wielded great influence throughout much of the fourteenth century in Mongol-dominated western Asia. She was the daughter of Amir Chopan (murdered in 1327) of the prestigious Soldus tribe who as chief minister to the newly appointed eleven-year-old sultan, Abū Saʿīd, effectively ran the state for many years until the young king felt confident enough to challenge his authority. An early example of Abū Saʿīd exercising his authority concerned Chopan's daughter, Baghdād Khātūn. The young king, beguiled by her legendary beauty and charms demanded Baghdād Khātūn's hand in marriage even though she was already married to another powerful prince, Hasan-i-Bozorg (Big Hasan). This was an outrageous demand to make of her father and his principal minister, the Amir Chopan, a highly respected figure and also a devout Muslim. Though being a Muslim himself, the Ilkhan Abū Saʿīd invoked the *yasa* (traditional Mongol law) and Mongol tradition, which gave the ruler automatic rights to any of his subjects' women as justification for his demands.

Baghdād Khātūn created controversy and intrigue throughout her life; she typified a generation nurtured in the Ilkhanate, a unique polity that grew out of the cultural meshing and mutual integration of the Turanian steppe and the Iranian sown, both steeped in Chinese tradition. She retained the fiery, independent nature of the Turkic steppe women, who were used to power and undaunted by the arrogance of warrior menfolk, while at the same time she appreciated the restraints of Islam and the limitations of the patriarchal Persian court, where the seductive wiles and ways of the smiling temptress were essential armor for a woman's survival and advancement. Baghdād Khātūn was a product of her time and elements of her story can be found reflected in those of other Ilkhanid Khwātīn (sing. Khātūn, lady), such as Pādeshāh Khātūn, Terkān Khātūn of Kermān, Abīsh Khātūn, Doḳūz Khātūn, and the redoubtable Soghaghtani Beki.

On her marriage to Ilkhan Abū Sa'īd in 1325, after the political demise of her father and brother, it was said of her, "The famous Chopans now served [the king] in another way" (Ward, p. 666). The story of her tempestuous marriage with the Ilkhan after he had destroyed her father and brother, of the intrigues and plots against the king, of the conspiracy with her former husband, Big Hasan, to whom she was married from 1323 to 1325, of her (rumored) secret dealings with one of the country's chief enemies, Özbek Khan of Turkestan, and of the death of Abū Sa'īd from poisoning are all tales endlessly recounted in the histories and chronicles of the time. It is said that it was the jealousy felt toward her young niece, Delshād Khātūn, Lady Happy Heart, who had captured her husband's heart and occupied her place in the marriage bed, which drove her to regicide. Others claim she had never ceased to love her first husband, Big Hasan (Hasan-i-bozorg), and that she had never forgiven Abū Sa'īd for the murder of her father and brother. She was instrumental in having her father's body returned home from Herāt and given a proper Muslim burial in the sacred lands of the Hejaz. Her influence was great and her political and financial machinations countered the power of the Mongol amirs and the Persian elite and even earned her the title of Khodāvandagār, "great lord" (*Ta'rīkh-i Shaikh Uwais*, 79 alef; tr. p. 57, text p. 156).

Anecdotes attesting to her wily and determined nature crop up in obscure histories and in all the main chronicles of the time including lesser-known works such as the Kurdish Shabānkārah'ī's history of Iran. In this account Baghdād Khātūn is credited with occupying the political vacuum created by the murder of her father and brother. It claims that her word was binding and her decisions were observed throughout the country. In Ibn Bazzāz's hagiography of the Ṣūfī shaykh Ṣafī al-Dīn of Ardabīl, two anecdotes recount her efforts to command the respect and direct recognition from the Ṣūfī shaykh or at least to be granted equal status with his male supplicants. Though the worthy shaykh could not be induced to look upon her famous face, the clout she commanded elsewhere attested to the great respect that others granted her.

On 16 November 1335 Abū Sa'īd Bahārdar's successor, Arpa Ka'un (*mong.* Prince), in a move designed to establish his rule and quash any opposition, ordered Baghdād Khātūn's immediate execution on charges of sedition and the murder of her husband. She was beaten to death in her bath. Her ignoble death, however, stands as testament to the power and influence that she was perceived as wielding and which her second husband's successor saw as a great and immediate threat.

Baghdād Khātūn achieved a position of power and influence in an increasingly patriarchal society using whatever gifts she possessed. Her political instinct, determination, intelligence, and feminine charm all played their own part in Baghdād Khātūn's tale, which was also the story of women's ascendancy in the patriarchy of medieval Iran.

[*See also* Ābish Khātūn bint Sa'd II; Qutlugh Terkān Khātūn; *and* Soghaghtani Beki.]

BIBLIOGRAPHY

Primary Sources

Abrū, Ḥafiẓ. *Dheil-i-Jāma' al-tavārīkh Rashīdī*. Edited by Khānbābā Biyānī. Tehran: n.p., 1350/1971.

Ahrī, Abū Bakr al-Qutbī. *Ta'rīkh-i Shaikh Uwais. History of Shaikh Uwais; an Important Source for the History of Adharbaijan in the Fourteenth Century*. Edited and translated by Johannes Baptist van Loon. 's Gravenhage: Mouton, 1954.

Khwāndamīr, Ghiyath al-Dīn ibn Humām al-Dīn. *Habib's-Siyar; The Reign of the Mongol and the Turk*, vol. 3. Translated by W. M. Thackston. Cambridge, Mass.: Harvard University, Department of Near Eastern Languages, 1994.

Mustawfī Qazvīnī, Hamdullāh. "Żafarnāma." Tehran: Iran University Press, 1377/1999.

Ward, L. J., tr. "The *Zafarnamah* of Mustawfi." Ph.D. diss., Manchester University, 1983

Waṣṣāf, Shihāb al-Dīn 'Abd Allāh. *Tārīkh-i-Wassāf*. Tehran: Ibn-e Sīnā, 1338/1959.

Secondary Sources

Howorth, Henry Hoyle. *History of the Mongols from the 9th to the 19th Century: The Mongols of Persia*. Vol. 3. Milton Keynes, UK: Lightning Source UK, 2011.

Lane, George. *Daily Life in the Mongol Empire*. Westport, Conn.: Greenwood Press, 2006.

Lane, George. *Early Mongol Rule in Thirteenth Century Iran: A Persian Renaissance*. New York and London: RoutledgeCurzon, 2003.

Melville, Charles. "The Chobanids." In *Encyclopaedia Iranica*, edited by Ehsan Yarshater. Vol. 5. London: Routledge and Kegan Paul, 1992.

Melville, Charles P. *The Fall of Amir Chupan and the Decline of the Ilkhanate, 1327–37: A Decade of Discord in Mongol Iran*. Bloomington: Research Institute for Inner Asian Studies, Indiana University, 1999.

GEORGE LANE

BAHRAIN. Bahrain is a small island archipelago with about 1.25 million inhabitants, out of which an estimated 54 percent are non-Bahraini residents. The main cities, the capital, Manama, and Muharraq and Rifa, are interlinked with an elaborate road system and bridges, facilitating communication and exchange of news and ideas. The country is also connected by a causeway to the Eastern Province of Saudi Arabia. Within the Gulf region Bahraini society has been renowned for its forward and outstanding women pioneers in education, social consciousness, and activism, famous today for their professional and personal achievements. Even before the discovery of oil (1932) and sudden wealth and before independence from the British (1971), Bahraini women were active participants in the development and sustenance of their society. At each historical juncture, in spite of societal constraints and religious and cultural conservatism, women in Bahrain pushed their way into the public scene by struggling to gain an education, to serve their society, to acquire paid employment, and still aspire for political empowerment. To the outside world Bahraini women from all walks of life project a role of achievement and challenge. Although symbolism and agency have been attached to this role, nevertheless these achievements have been hard won, accumulative, and remain a cause of challenge.

This role and status did not pop up out of nowhere; it implied the existence of a process going back for almost two generations of women that has produced a profuse number of capable, educated, and socially conscious women. It is recorded that the first Bahraini woman activist, Shahla Khalfan, joined the earliest street demonstrations in 1956, unveiled in public, protesting against British colonial rule and in support of Arab nationalism. The activists of the early twenty-first century are the granddaughters of this earliest generation who have had the benefits of developed education, economy, and society.

Education, as the base of this transformation started earlier in Bahrain than in the other Gulf states, with the first boys' public school in 1919 and the first girls' school in 1928. By the 1950s a process had been in place when women, particularly from the urban centers, educated, members of the elites, and the emergent middle classes initiated the first three women's societies, which aimed to tackle illiteracy and social charity services to less fortunate women. Some of these were the Jamiʿyat Nahdat Fatat al-Bahrain (1955) led by Aisha Yateem; Jamiʿyat Al-Riʿaya wal Tufula wal Umuma (1960) led by Sheikha Lulwa bint Muhammad Al-Khalifa (a member of the ruling family); and followed a few years later by the Awal Women's Society (1969), linked to such prominent Bahraini women as Sabika Al-Najjar, Salha Eisan, and later Aisha Mattar.

The period of the 1950s, 1960s, and early 1970s was a time of intense political activities, encouraged and promoted by the opening of the Gulf region onto the Arab world with its anticolonial and Arab nationalist movements (from Nasserism to Baʿthism and later by the Dhofar Rebellion, in which the Bahraini women Leila and Butheina Fakhro were prominent participants). The repatriation of the first crop of university graduates (males and females) coming from Lebanon, Egypt, Iraq, and Kuwait during the 1980s, as well as a new crop of graduates from England and the United States, in addition, also contributed to political activities. These new generations politicized the charitable women's associations and formed new ones such as Jamiʿyat Fatat al-Reef, which, although active among rural women, was not officially licensed by the government for operation.

The history of events resulting from these changes translated into political ferment and eruptions in which women participated. Bahrainis had common causes in the nationalist movements with their precedents in the attempts at democratization in the 1940s or those of the later decades, demanding constitutional rights and reforms and explaining the continuous currents of protests. However it was in the 1950s that women began to openly support the male-led demands for reform with respect to political and social issues in the nation. Whether the reactions involving women were spontaneous street demonstrations or the growth of underground political organizations or the emergence of civil servants with heightened sociopolitical consciousness, society changed in unprecedented ways. The unrest culminated in the popular movement for a parliament and political participation when women's rights were being considered. However women were disappointed when they were excluded from the short-lived liberal experiment due to the persistent traditional tribal orientation and lack of support by radical and liberalized men. Authoritarian politics was the victor and the whole experiment failed in 1975. Many active women paid the price of exile and enforced acquiescence.

The three decades following this, stretching to the late 1990s, were crucial in setting the stage for substantial achievements for women due to social reforms. A first step was the incorporation of village women (mostly Shīʿī) in the overall development and this resulted in the spread of education and public employment to a much larger number of women. While women in the 1950s had *organized* charitable societies, since the early 1970s many voluntary women's societies sprang up with political orientations representing all sociopolitical currents. Women of the growing middle class and a few from the working class had benefited from the developing education system, from the large numbers of schools, universities (government and Gulf Cooperation Council [GCC]-sponsored and private ones) and technical institutions, as well as from government-sponsored scholarships to universities in the Arab countries and abroad, and the growing need for Bahrainis in the job market, both public and private. By the end of this period the literacy rate among women had been raised to 83 percent and women university students made up almost 59 percent of the total. Furthermore women students constantly excelled over males in their performance. At this stage most employment for women was in the public sectors of education, health, and government administration, though it remained low, estimated at 19 percent. Additionally the number of women medical professionals, whether doctors, specialists, or nurses, surged, building a strong constituency of dedicated professionals. Such names as Najah al-Zayyani and Rula Al-Saffar are only samples in this field.

However it was at the turn of the new century that Bahraini women reached the zenith of their achievements. Since the assumption of King Hamad Al-Khalifa, the reign of rule following his father's death in 1999, he amended the 1975 constitution and provided a stipulation for equal political rights for women within the framework of promises for reform policies. Since then Bahrain has projected a modernized gender discourse, reflected in providing women with openings to prominent positions. This explains the number of remarkable women who have floated to the international, as well as the local, public sphere—particularly high-profile women, most often women endorsed by the ruling institution. A first such achievement by a Bahraini woman was Haya Rashid Al-Khalifa, the president of the UN General Assembly for 2006. Furthermore as a clear political stance using women to project modernity and diversity, Bahrain has appointed three women ambassadors to its foremost portfolios: Houda Nonoo, a Jew, as ambassador to the U.S.; Alice Samaan, a Christian, as ambassador to the U.K.; and Bibi Al-Alawi, a Shīʿī, as ambassador to China. During this same period, the local political scene has also become replete with women holding positions in the appointed ministerial cabinets, such as Mai Mohammad Al-Khalifa, who has served as both minister of culture and minister of information, bringing fame and international renown to the country's cultural and archaeological legacy. Other women ministers, Sunnī as well as Shīʿī, served sensitive positions, as minister of health (Nada Al-Haffad, 2004), social development and human rights (Fatima Al-Buloshi, 2005), and minister of state for information affairs (Samira Rajab, 2012). The Majlis Shura, the consultative council to Parliament, has had women appointed by royal decree, six members in 2002, raised to eleven in 2006. A most significant achievement in the process of establishing women rights and empowerment has been the contentious elections to the Representative Council of the Parliament. In the 2006 and 2010 campaigns women ran representing the spectrum of political alliances and affiliations. Although the progressive candidate, Munira Fakhro, lost in both due to deliberate manipulation, nevertheless the campaign itself brought out women's demands for rights and empowerment and exposed the public to them. The female winner was government supported and ran uncontested. Bahrain is also the first in the GCC to appoint women for the sensitive positions of women judges.

This atmosphere implies a political and a sociocultural climate that accepts this change, though gradually and in stages. But it gave women a chance to share in the social and political changes that society was undergoing. Other than the formal and official appointments, women were also recognized in most other professions, such as law (Jalila Al-Sayyid), banking (Sabah Al-Moayed), and the entrepreneurial private sectors (Elham Hassan, Fatima Akbar Ameena Janahi, to name a few). Furthermore a few women managed to break the glass ceiling and reached high-level positions that were for years restricted for men, such as Khawla Mattar who became the first female editor in chief when she took her position in 2006 as the editor of *Al-Waqt*, Bahrain's daily newspaper, and who was director of the UN Information Center in Cairo as of 2013.

In spite of these many achievements, Bahraini women still lack personal and civil rights. The maximum that women acquired was to establish their right to free education, limited participation in the job market, and they are still engaged in an uphill fight for personal status legislated rights and political empowerment. These concerns took second place in light of the latest uprisings when the political scene took precedence.

On 14 February 2011 women joined the popular movement of street demonstrations in Bahrain, demanding realization of promised reforms for democratic rights, economic transparency, and reversal of discriminatory policies, demands that were in tandem with similar calls in the Arab Spring already under way in Tunisia and Egypt. The movement in Bahrain was duplicated by similar, though milder, stirrings in other Gulf states; however in Bahrain, with an already tense and complex strife-laden history, the government claimed the events to be motivated by Iranian/Shīʿī irredentism, viewed as an extreme danger to the survival of the ruling institution and thus deserving the intense crackdown that followed. This has brought to the surface historically simmering political, economic, and social discontents and concretized polarizations. The results are deep political and sectarian/ethnic rifts, retrenched obduracy on all sides, and an impasse that seems difficult to resolve and in which Bahraini women are intrinsically anchored.

In Bahrain the immediate consequences were to bring in harsh, draconian policies of arrests, torture, and reinstating of the dreaded State Security Law. It also called in foreign aid in the form of GCC-Saudi help. Bahraini women representing most levels and professions, including the medical profession, were active participants in activities related to the uprising as they were also subjected to the same policies used to suppress it; an official punitive campaign was mounted against all those who participated in the events and women had their share. The Shīʿī community and its women, claiming a government historically programmed policy of discrimination and marginalization, bore the brunt of this policy and were thus subjected to police brutality on the street and in prisons, as well as being subjected to job dismissal and mistreatment. In spite of this situation, it should be noted that Bahraini women representing all backgrounds (ethnic, tribal, and social class, as well as from all spectrums of political currents and hues), both Shīʿī (who make up the majority of the Bahraini population, 60–65 percent) and Sunnī, went out together in the initial demonstrations with unified demands. Furthermore the coverage of these events has indicated the level and range of women's social and political consciousness, their achievements and sophisticated perception of their roles and societal commitments at periods of crisis. Unfortunately for Bahraini women, however, they find themselves sequestered into the narrow camps of "for" and "against" the government and the official orchestrated policy of Shīʿī versus Sunnī. This has confirmed and reasserted the politicization and polarization of the Bahraini scene where women, their rights and achievements become tools in the overall struggle and are often projected through the prism of contentious politics. Such an intense political atmosphere has masked, stunted, and delayed the path of struggle that Bahraini women as a whole had been on toward achieving more personal, educational, and professional goals and inching toward political rights, particularly since the 1990s.

Bibliography

'Abbas Fadhl', Mona. "Bahraini Women and Their Position in the Reform Process." *Arab Reform Initiative*, October 22, 2008.

Abdul-Rahman Al-Baker. *From Bahrain to Exile* (Mina al-Bahrain ila almanfa - Sant Hilana-). 2d ed. Beirut: Dar Al-Kunooz al-Adabiya, 2002.

Bahrain Independent Commission of Inquiry (BICI). http://www.bici.org.bh/.

CIA World Factbook. https://www.cia.gov/library/publications/the-world-factbook/fields/print_2119.html

Fakhro, Munira. *Women at Work in the Gulf: A Case Study of Bahrain*. New York: Kegan Paul International, 1990.

Freedom House Reports. http://www.freedomhouse.org/reports/.

Gharaibeh, Fakir Al. "Women's Empowerment in Bahrain." *Journal of International Women's Studies* 12, no. 3 (March 2011).

Khalaf, Abdul Hadi. "Qam'i Al-Nisaa bil-Nisaa" [Dual Attempts Confine Women's Activism]. *Assafir Al Arabi*, Beirut, October 11, 2012. http://arabi.assafir.com (site is in Arabic).

Khuri, Fuad. *Tribe and State in Bahrain: The Transformation of Political Authority in an Arab State*. Chicago: University of Chicago Press, 1980.

Ministry of Health, Singapore. Bahrain Statistics of population for 2011. http://www.moh.gov.bh/PDF/Publications/Statistics/hs2000/introduction.pdf

Najjar, Bāqir al-. *al-Dīmugrātīyah al-ʿasīyah fī al-Khalīj alʿArabī* [Elusive Democracy in the Arabian Gulf]. Beirut: Dar al-Saqi, 2008.

Najjar, Bāqir al-. *al-Marʾah fī al-Khalīj al-ʿArabī wa-tahawwulāt al-hadāthah al-ʿasrīyah* [Women in the Arabian Gulf and the Difficult Transitions to Modernity]. Beirut: Arab Cultural Center, 2000.

Seikaly, May. "Women and Religion in Bahrain: An Emerging Identity." In *Islam, Gender and Social Change*, edited by John L. Esposito and Yvonne Yazbeck Haddad. New York: Oxford University Press, 1997.

MAY SEIKALY

BAKHTIAR, LALEH. (b. 1938), Iranian-American Muslim author, translator, and clinical psychologist.

Laleh Bakhtiar, one of seven children, was born in New York City and raised as a Catholic by her American mother and Iranian father. Married with children, she moved to Iran when she was twenty-four, knowing nothing about Islam, or how to speak Farsi. She began studying Islam and Qurʾānic Arabic at Tehran University with Seyyed Hossein Nasr. She earned a B.A. in history from Chatham College in Pennsylvania, as well as M.A.s in philosophy and counseling psychology, and a Ph.D. in educational psychology from the University of New Mexico. Dr. Bakhtiar's central works as an author are those concerning Islamic unity, psychology, and psycho-ethics. They have also been translated into English, and she has written over twenty books on topics related to Islam and Islamic beliefs. She has presented and lectured extensively in both academic and religious arenas and is regarded as an essential figure within the Muslim community. She currently lives in Chicago and works as the president of the Institute of Traditional Psychology. She is also one of Kazi Publications' Scholars-in-Residence. She has been practicing Islam for over thirty years as mentored and taught by Seyyed Hossein Nasr.

Bakhtiar is identified as one of the leading scholars on the psychology of spiritual chivalry. Of her translated works, the one that has received the most attention and is viewed as the most controversial is *The Sublime Quran* (2007), the first and only English translation of the Qurʾān by an American woman. *The Sublime Quran* garnered both attention and international criticism in part due to Dr. Bakhtiar's mixed parentage, having been born in New York City and not being a native Arabic speaker. However, most of the criticism stems from the new word she used in Qurʾānic 4:34 regarding the punishment men may use against rebellious wives. For several centuries, the verse has typically been translated as giving the husband permission to "admonish, abandon in bed and ultimately 'beat' a wife who will not obey her husband." However, after years of research in preparation for the translation,

Bakhtiar interpreted the final punishment of the Arabic as "to walk away from" or "to leave," rather than "to beat." Her decision to use this particular translation is based, in fact, on Islamic tradition, as the Prophet Muḥammad never beat his wives when they were rebellious, choosing to instead leave them. *The Sublime Quran*, while receiving its share of notoriety (for example, Moḥammad Ashraf, secretary of the Islamic Society of North America, considered banning it from the organization's bookstore), the publication has received equal, if not greater, amounts of support and positive recognition.

Bakhtiar's main influence appears to be Seyyed Hossein Nasr who instructed and counseled her when she was converting to Islam. His teachings, like the topics of her works, range from studies of traditional Islam, Ṣūfism, and comparative religion, to spirituality as it is represented in the modern world. Bakhtiar also regards herself as a spiritual advocate when it comes to the Muslim form of feminism.

BIBLIOGRAPHY

Bakhtiar, Laleh. *God's Will Be Done*. 3 vols. Chicago: Kazi, 1995.

Bakhtiar, Laleh. *Sufi: Expressions of the Mystic Quest*. London: Thames & Hudson, 1979.

Bakhtiar, Laleh, trans. *The Sublime Quran*. Chicago: Kazi, 2007.

"Biography of Laleh Bakhtiar." Sufi Enneagram. http://www.sufienneagram.com/bio.html.

Colson, John. "Symposium Focuses on Muslim Women." *The Aspen Times*, August 15, 2007. http://www.aspentimes.com/article/20070815/NEWS/108150041.

"Human Rights and Women's Rights in Islam: A Keynote Address by Shirin Ebadi." Naropa University, Boulder, Colo., October 9, 2009. http://www.naropa.edu/academics/snss/ug/pei.

Scrivener, Leslie. "Furor over a Five-Letter Word." *Toronto Star*, October 21, 2007.

EREN TATARI

BALKAN STATES. The Balkans (or South Eastern Europe) include Bulgaria, Romania, Greece, Croatia, Albania, Montenegro, Bosnia and Herzegovina, Serbia, Kosovo, and the former Yugoslav Republic of Macedonia. The Balkans have a total population of about 25 million inhabitants. Some general characteristics of the Balkan countries are their common Communist past (without Greece), their geographical location at the semi-periphery of Europe, their similar economic and social transitions, and their patriarchal heritage still today felt in all segments of these societies. Also, some Balkan countries have recently contained a striking number of latent conflicts (genocide of Bosnian Muslims, ethnic tensions within Bosnia and Herzegovina, the conflict around Kosovo's independence, Macedonia's name dispute with Greece).

Islam in the Balkans. The Balkans' religious landscape is quite complex and multi-faceted. Christians represent the most prominent religious group (Orthodox Christians and Catholics). Islam came to the Balkans with the Ottoman conquest. Approximately 9 to 11 million Muslims live in the Balkans (making up 8 to 10 percent of the population). They consist of distinct ethnic groups (Albanians, Slavs, Turks, Pomaks, Torbesh, and Roma), and they adhere to different theological traditions (mainstream Sunnī Islam, Bektashism in Albania and Macedonia, and Alevi communities in Bulgaria). Most Balkan Muslims live in Albania, Bosnia and Herzegovina, and Kosovo (approx. 9–10 million). Balkan Muslims are hierarchically organized under the official Institution of the Islamic Community, representing Islam in each respective country and headed by a Mufti or Grand Mufti (e.g., *Bashkesie Islam* in Kosovo or *Bulgaristan* in Bulgaria).

Women's Movement and Status in the Balkans. The historical data on the status of women under the Ottomans is not abundant; but *sicils* (court records) and *defters* (lists, records) uncover some facts. Women under the Ottomans generally owned property even after marriage and were fully fledged subjects of the empire, which gave them at least the possibility of directly addressing the imperial court—although they were in an unfavorable social position compared to men. Because of this, we also find women who have been founders of pious endowments (*waqf*), independently or within other endowments. In terms of marriage, polygamy was highly uncommon. Divorce was a common occurrence and although men generally had a unilateral right to divorce, there are records of marriages being dissolved upon the request of a woman. Almost all urban women (notwithstanding their religion) wore *ferege* and *zar*, a full body covering including the face veil, although non-Muslim women often left their face uncovered. The lives of the urban women were primarily connected to their homes and the private sphere, and rural women were more likely to work on the land together with men. Still, there are records of urban women working and earning from their home or sometimes also outside of it.

In the period following Ottoman withdrawal toward the end of the nineteenth century, we find women writing articles, poems, and books—protesting their status and requiring that their voices be heard. Also at this time, as throughout Europe, the first women's organizations began to appear in the Balkan countries, including Serbian Women's Union, Bulgarian Women's Union, Socialist Women International, and a regional organization, Women's Little Entente. After World War II, we find the Communist Party's official women's organizations in many of these countries. Communism addressed the women's question from a "top-down" perspective and viewed women's unequal status in society as part of the class issue. Women therefore gained equality before the law, the right to vote and work, and many other rights, although their implementation faced resistance stemming from traditionally defined gender roles. The feminist movement also started being more active around the 1970s, appearing in its most prominent form in Yugoslavia, which had more open borders compared to other countries in the Communist bloc. The feminist approach was attacked for being bourgeois and it was claimed that the socialist emancipation of women only scratched the surface of gender relations, especially within the private sphere.

The change in political regimes from 1989 onward led to changes throughout these societies. In the early twenty-first century, all of these countries are beginning or ending the process of harmonization of their legislation with the EU legislative framework. They are all signatories of the Convention on the Elimination of All Forms of Discrimination against Women (CEDAW); in addition, all have constitutions and laws requiring gender equality and nondiscrimination, as well as gender mechanisms to monitor the proper implementation of these rules. Women's civil society organizations are quite present and active, with the quality of their work depending on their stable financing, expertise, and/or relations to other stakeholders, like governmental sectors or policy makers. The main women's issues are the rate of political participation, which ranges from 15 to 30 percent, domestic violence, unpaid work, and gender aspects of the economy.

Muslim Women in the Balkans. Along with other Balkan women, Muslim women started voicing their problems and establishing their own organizations—mostly of a humanitarian or ethnic character (Muslim Women's Club, Charitable Union of Muslim Women)—at the beginning of the twentieth century. Their focus, in terms of women's issues, was mostly on education of Muslim women and, later, their work. A Congress of Russian Muslim women in 1917 in Kazan voiced demands for equal rights, abolition of polygamy, and obligatory primary education. These ideas influenced some Muslim women (and men) of the Balkans. During Communism, the pressure on Muslim women to denounce the covering of the face (and head) was so strong that these practices (along with other practices related to religion) were almost abolished from the public scene in the Balkans.

In the early twenty-first century, Muslim women living in the patriarchal, transitional societies of the Balkans face the same problems as other women in such situations. They struggle with their minority status in the Balkan countries, as well as with issues related to the place of religion in secular societies. The specific problems they face are at least twofold.

On one side, they are struggling with the prejudice and anti-Muslim sentiments in their societies (especially if they wear the headscarf). In most Balkan societies, Muslim women wearing the headscarf can attend educational institutions (although Albania and Kosovo are highly problematic in this regard), but they face discrimination in the labor market. Since public expression of religion, especially Islam, is generally still not very socially desirable in all of these countries, there is frequent debate about religious teaching in schools or the wearing of the headscarf. For all that however, following the global trend of revival of religion, and especially Islam, young Muslim women, like their counterparts worldwide, are re-embracing the practice of head covering, giving it new and fresh meanings, including piety, female autonomy, and defiance of materialism.

On the other hand, they are struggling within their own communities in terms of understanding the place and role of women in Islam. Muslim women are not actively involved in the work of official Islamic institutions, or any of their bodies, although they are not officially prohibited from doing so. They are usually organized in formal and informal organizations and groups, but still quite distanced from secular organizations in their societies. The main focus of their work is on informal education, empowerment of women, and improvement of Islamic knowledge. There are some positive trends, such as the existence of some successful Muslim women's organizations (Edu Nisa in Macedonia, Shoqata Kulturore Gruaja in Albania, or Nahla in Bosnia and Herzegovina) or like the female quota introduced on the Fatwa council of the Islamic Community of Bosnia and Herzegovina (two of seven members must be women). These women, as indigenous European Muslims, are living in a framework guaranteeing them gender equality. At the same time, they are re-examining and reinterpreting the position of women in Islam, proving that civic and religious identities are not mutually exclusive, but complementary.

Bibliography

Blagojević, Marina. *Položajžena u zemljamaBalkana: Komparativnipregled* (Position of Women in the Balkans: A Comparative Overview), 2003: http://www.vladars.net/sr-SP-Cyrl/Vlada/centri/gendercentarrs/AKTI/Documents/Polozaj%20zena%20u%20zemljama%20Balkana.pdf (Accessed on 8 July 2012).

The British Academy project: *Contemporary Islam in the Balkans*: http://www.balkanmuslims.com (Accessed on 8 July 2012).

Buturović, Amila, and Irvin Cemil Schick, eds. *Women in the Ottoman Balkans: Gender, Culture, and History.* London: Tauris, 2007.

Faroqhi, Suraiya. *Subjects of the Sultan: Culture and Daily Life in the Ottoman Empire.* London: Tauris, 2005.

Gallup Balkan Monitor. *Insights and perceptions: Voices of the Balkans—2010 Summary of Findings.* http://www.balkan-monitor.eu/ (Accessed on 8 July 2012).

Ramet, Sabrina P., ed. *Gender Politics in the Western Balkans. Women and Society in Yugoslavia and the Yugoslav Successor States.* University Park: Pennsylvania State University Press, 1999.

Đermana Šeta

Bangladesh. Bangladesh is one of the most transnationalized places in the world, with more than 4 million women in its garment manufacturing industry and more than 20 million women in its microcredit sector, which was made famous by the 2006 Nobel Peace Prize winner, the Grameen Bank of Bangladesh. Bangladesh's entry into the world economy in 1971 coincided with three pivotal events that had begun to transform the global environment. The 1970s saw the beginning of the dismantling of the welfare state that soon led to the proliferation of neoliberal development policies worldwide. Simultaneously, there was a rise of the petro dollar economies of the Middle East that sought new labor from countries like Bangladesh and began to play a more visible role in shaping Muslim societies. Finally, there was recognition by the United Nations that women's issues were integral to development, leading to the declaration of the Decade for Women in 1975. These events shaped the landscape of the newly independent Bangladesh. This article explores Bangladeshi women's roles in three areas: law and politics, economy, and arts and literature. The article begins with a brief overview of the history of Bangladesh that set into motion the present conditions.

Bangladesh's population is ethnically Bengali, with less than 2 percent belonging to ethnic minorities. The country is 90 percent Muslim, with the remaining population made up of Hindus, Christians, and Buddhists. It is largely rural, and the primary source of employment is agriculture. It has a high population density of 160 million in a landmass of 56,000 square miles, and a ranking of 146 of all countries on the United Nations Human Development Index.

In 1947, when the British divided India, East Bengal (now Bangladesh) became East Pakistan. It was separated from its western wing (West Pakistan, now Pakistan) by 1,200 miles of Indian territory. As early as 1952, the fractures of this postcolonial nation-making became visible as Bengalis took to the streets to oppose Pakistani domination in what is known as the Language Movement. Bengalis who made up 60 percent of the population opposed the Pakistani government's imposition of Urdu as the state language. This movement for cultural, political, and economic autonomy eventually culminated in the freedom struggle in 1971. After a nine-month-long war for liberation, Bangladesh became independent from Pakistani rule on December 16, 1971. Bangladesh was conceived on four principles: secularism, nationalism, socialism, and democracy. Within three years of civilian government, the military came to power in a bloody coup and shifted the country toward Islamization. By 1988, the military dictatorship was able to institute Islam as the state religion, although religious freedom was granted to all minorities. The transnational movement of labor from Bangladesh to the Middle East brought Bangladeshi migrant men in contact with the Saudi Arabian form of Wahhābī Islam, a more rigid interpretation of Islam at odds with the syncretic Islam of Bangladesh. This contact as well as the sponsorship of the military dictatorship resulted in the rise of Islamic political parties and an unregulated growth of Islamic seminaries (madāris) funded by private funds. Historically, both the military and the democratic governments have all brokered deals with the various Islamic political elements to stay in power. Although it is unclear to what extent Western-style secularism would have taken root in Bangladesh, it is evident that a transnational Islam substantially displaced the syncretic form of Ṣūfī Islam in existence in Bangladesh, a move that was embraced by the majority of the population as an affirmation of their religious identity.

Women, Law, and Politics. In analyzing women's contributions in Bangladesh, the urban/rural divide is an important distinction. Bangladesh has a small and vibrant feminist movement, with women drawn largely from the urban, elite, and educated circles. Urban women are represented in all aspects of government, education, medicine, and engineering, including the police and military. The Bangladesh government has a Ministry of Women's Affairs that is responsible for women's education, employment, and gender-related issues. There are numerous women's and human rights advocacy groups in the country, with the majority of them located in the urban center, Dhaka. These include Mahila Parishad, Sammilito Nari Samaj, Ain-o-Salish Kendra (ASK), Bangladesh Legal Aid (BLAST), Nari Pokkho, and Women for Women, among others.

Since the transition to democracy in the 1990s, both elected heads of state—the current Prime Minister Sheikh Hasina and the former Prime Minister Begum Khaleda Zia—have been women. Women have 19 percent representation in the parliament, although it is largely facilitated through seats reserved for female candidates. Bangladesh, a signatory to the Beijing conference (1994), agreed to set aside one-third of all seats on all local governing bodies for female candidates. Since the mid-1990s, rural women have successfully competed for these seats. Women's participation in local elections has also resulted in a backlash as women have moved into traditional spheres of rural men's authority and power. In a 2012 study that compared levels of education, empowerment, and economic activities for women, Bangladesh was ranked higher, at 55 points to India's 37 points and Pakistan's 29 points. This improvement in women's welfare resulted from a combination of factors that included the increased number of factory women in the garment manufacturing industry, the ongoing grassroots work of Bangladeshi nongovernmental organizations (NGOs) that target women as clients, and the government's role in offering stipends to girls to stay in school.

However, the ongoing work in these areas is often hamstrung by weak governance and ineffectual policy implementation. Violence against women continues to be a serious issue in Bangladesh. Although many cases go unreported, the legal advocacy group Ain-o-Salish Kendro (ASK) has documented 330 cases of beatings, lashings, and public humiliations of women since the 1990s. Feminist groups have effectively lobbied for the passage of the Women and Child Repression Act (Nari o Shishu Nirjaton Domon Act, 2000), which grants legal protections to women. Such measures have also met with official resistance. For example, the Supreme Court (2012) issued a statement that no physical punishment can be issued in the name of *fatāwā* (religious edicts), but it did not uphold the lower court's opinion that all *fatāwā* were "extrajudicial and unconstitutional."

One area of critical importance is family laws that are governed by religious laws. Thus, for Muslim women, issues pertaining to marriage, divorce, infidelity, alimony, inheritance, child custody, etc., all fall under Sharīʿah (Islamic) laws. Similarly, Hindu, Christian, and Buddhist women are subject to the family laws of their religions. Feminist legal scholars have been at the forefront in trying to implement a universal civil code for women regardless of their religion. Owing to entrenched religious attitudes, they have not made much headway in this area.

In the political domain, Islamic groups have made gains since 1990s. There is a notable increase in educated young women joining Islamic movements. Many female college students have joined the Jamaat-i-Islami, and they participate in public demonstrations for a larger role for Islam in society. Similarly, many educated, middle-class women have turned to Islamic movements such as Tablighi Jamaʿat, a pietist movement begun in India in 1926 to return wayward Muslims to the fold and to construct a society on Islamic principles. Women from all social backgrounds belong to these new trends. It should be emphasized that the majority of women do not see Islam as oppressive to women. Instead, Islam is understood as a religion of social justice and egalitarianism, as long as it is properly interpreted and followed.

Women and Economics. Bangladeshi women have always participated in the informal labor market, performing work as domestics and in agriculture within the homestead that has been overlooked by macroeconomic studies. In recent years, there has been a sharp increase in women's participation in the labor market (1995–2003). Although it still remains low at 26 percent, it is higher than neighboring West Bengal (India), where it is flat at 17 to 18 percent. The highest increase in labor participation is among younger women. Several factors have contributed to women's increased participation in the labor market. These include gradual attitudinal changes toward women's work from long-term work by NGOs in rural society and the government's stipends to families to enroll their daughters in school, both of which have helped to educate more young women for entry into the formal labor market.

Bangladesh is also home to the largest garment industry in the world after China. It is a $19 billion industry that employs more than 4 million women. Garment exports make up 80 percent of the country's annual exports. The low wages paid to female labor have brought companies like Walmart, JC Penny, Carrefour, Tesco, and Marks and Spencer to Bangladesh. Women in the garment sector are unionized, and they often agitate for better wages and working conditions. However, average pay remains at an abysmal $30 a month, and work conditions are horrific. In November 2012, workers were trapped inside a locked factory when a fire broke out. As a result, 112 workers died and many were injured. Women's factory work has resulted in some positive social impacts. The majority of these women have moved from rural to urban areas in search of work. Compared to their rural counterparts, these women have a degree of physical mobility and exercise control over their income. Garment factory women workers usually meet their husbands at work and tend to have love marriages. Love marriages eliminate the demand for dowries that grooms make on their in-laws in arranged marriages.

Poor women who work as domestic workers in middle-class homes in Bangladesh, and as migrant domestic workers overseas, especially in the Middle East, fall into a black hole. These domestic labor conditions continue to be extremely abusive and seriously underpaid, but these women exist outside of any kind of regulatory oversight. This is an area under scrutiny by feminist human rights groups in Bangladesh.

Bangladesh is famous for the work of rural women in the microcredit sector. More than 20 million women are affiliated with microcredit loan programs. The largest microcredit institutions are the Grameen Bank, BRAC, ASA, and Proshika. Although the story of micro loans has been largely praised in the development literature, the reality is far more complex. Very few women have become entrepreneurs through these loan programs. The majority of the women are the carriers of loans for their husbands. Women who can use these loans successfully tend to have some marketable skills, or are widows or divorced; that is, they do not have a male relative who can lay claim to their money. But they form a small number within the large group of borrowers. The majority of the women depend on their husbands to invest the loans productively in order to repay them. It is important to note that the heavy presence of NGOs in rural areas has helped to shape social attitudes toward women's public roles. It is common to see women in the public sphere in rural Bangladesh. But, as noted earlier, visibility must not be misrecognized as the social acceptance of women's status and public roles. Most importantly, poor women continue to face severe punishments for transgressing socially sanctioned roles by patriarchal institutions.

Women in Arts and Literature. Bengali Muslim women have a long tradition of activism in the arts and literature that owes its origins to the Brahmo Samaj Reform Movement in colonial India.

For the Bengali Muslim feminists of the nineteenth and early twentieth centuries, writing and activism were entwined and focused on middle-class female aspirations of education and the arts. The earliest Muslim feminist in Bengal, Nawab Faizunnessa Chaudhurani, wrote *Rupjalal* in 1876, a counter-masculinist discourse about the social oppression of women. The best-known feminist writer of this period is Begum Rokeya Sakhwat Hossain for her acerbic articles decrying patriarchy. She is best known for her feminist science fiction, *Sultana's Dream* (1905). With the publication of the Muslim weekly *Saogat* in 1918 in undivided Bengal, more educated Muslim women found a space for literary expression.

With the creation of Pakistan in 1947, women took on prominent roles as musicians, painters, artists, and writers in the new state formed for India's Muslims. Women wrote poetry, plays, and essays that focused on women's right to education, equality in marriage, and employment as citizens of the new state. Prominent female figures include Nilima Ibrahim and Sufia Kamal (writers), Ferdousi Rahman and Firoza Begum (singers), and Novera Ahmed (sculptor), among others. In this discourse, modernity and Islam were not oppositional elements in society; rather, this period was the awakening of a nationalist spirit that transcended religious boundaries and sought to cultivate a distinctive Bengali identity and culture.

In the post-1971 era of nation building in Bangladesh, resource-rich Western development organizations came into rural areas to rebuild a war-torn nation. The incursion of NGOs, Western ideas of women's empowerment, and NGOs led by local feminists (e.g., Nijera Kori) into rural areas began to shift this discourse toward leveling social disparities between urban and rural women. This new movement began to challenge rural patriarchy and brought women's issues into the public domain. The challenges facing women in Bangladesh are enormous, but its local human rights and feminist groups remain vibrant and are strongly poised to address these issues through advocacy, at both national and transnational levels. Ultimately, it is the responsibility of the government of Bangladesh to safeguard the rights of its female citizens.

BIBLIOGRAPHY

Amin, Sonia N. *The World of Muslim Women in Colonial Bengal, 1876–1939*. Leiden, The Netherlands: E. J. Brill, 1994.

Chowdhury, Elora. *Transnationalism Reversed: Women Organizing Against Gendered Violence in Bangladesh*. Albany: State University of New York Press, 2011.

Eaton, Richard. *The Rise of Islam and the Bengal Frontier, 1204–1760*. Berkeley: University of California Press, 1996.

Hashmi, Taj. *Women and Islam in Bangladesh: Beyond Subjection and Tyranny*. Basingstoke, U.K.: Palgrave Macmillan, 2000.

Human Rights Watch. "Bangladesh: Protect Women Against 'Fatwa' Violence." http://www.hrw.org/news/2011/07/06/bangladesh-protect-women-against-fatwa-violence.

Kabeer, Naila. "The Quest for National Identity: Women and Islam in Bangladesh." *Feminist Review* 37 (Spring 1991): 38–58.

Karim, Lamia. *Development and Its Discontents: Women in Debt in Bangladesh*. Minneapolis: University of Minnesota Press, 2011.

Quadir, Serajul, and Ruma Paul. "Unrest Threatens Bangladesh's $19-Billion Clothing Industry." *Globe and Mail* (September 7, 2012).

Rahman, Aminur. *Women and Micro-credit in Rural Bangladesh: An Anthropological Study of Grameen*

Bank Lending. Boulder, Colo.: Westview Press, 2001.

Sarkar, Mahua. *Visible Histories, Disappearing Women*. Durham, N.C.: Duke University, 2008.

Shehabuddin, Elora. *Reshaping the Holy: Democracy, Development and Muslim Women in Bangladesh*. New York: Columbia University Press, 2008.

Social Watch. "Gender Equality in Bangladesh Is Above South Asia's Average." http://www.socialwatch.org/node/14589. *Social Watch*, March 15, 2012.

UNDP. "Bangladesh." http://hdrstats.undp.org/images/explanations/BGD.pdf. *Human Development Report*, United Nations Development Program.

World Bank. "Women's Employment in Bangladesh; Conundrums Amidst Progress." http://siteresources.worldbank.org/SOUTHASIAEXT/Resources/Publications/448813-1185396961095/4030558-1205418213360/ch4bdgender2008.pdf. Chapter IV, South Asia Resources Publications, World Bank.

LAMIA KARIM

BARAKAH. The concept of *barakah* is invested with a multitude of implicit or explicit religio-cultural meanings depending on historical and social context. It encapsulates Islamic spirituality and spiritual sensibilities, particularly in relation to mysticism, sainthood, holy persons and spaces, and, in some cases, the local popular understanding of Islam. Thus *barakah*'s diverse connotations are at once an expression of universal Islam and a manifestation of Islamic particularism. The word *barakah* is derived from the Arabic root b-r-k and is found in the Qurʾān, though only in the plural (*barakāt*). Its most fundamental meaning is "blessing," "beneficent force," or "supernatural power," conferred by God upon humankind.

Uncommonly pious individuals—prophets and especially Muḥammad and his house, both males and females—are privileged with *barakah*, as is the Qurʾān, God's word. In turn, those blessed with *barakah*, either living or dead, can transmit it to ordinary mortals who thereby benefit in both material fortune and spiritual rewards. As Islam spread and evolved, *barakah* came to play a significant role in the social construction of holy persons, both males and females, whether saints or mystics, and sacred places, and entered the practices of pilgrimage (*ziyārah*) and the veneration of saints. For the *awliyāʾ* (those close to God), *barakah* represented a sort of badge of saintly status. In this context, *barakah* signified an ineffable supernatural substance—grace, blessings, superabundance, purity, and piety—communicated from God to the believers via those who, in this life and the next, were endowed with heroic *iḥsān* (virtue). Yet mere possession of *barakah* was not sufficient to enter the ranks of holy persons: the possessor had to be able to convey it to others. In short, *barakah* helped to create the saint or mystic because it confirmed his or her privileged relation to God and thus conferred a special niche within the socio-religious order. Communal recognition of an individual's (or group's) access to *barakah* created a spiritual clientele that sought those individuals' favor as mediators, patrons, and intermediaries. One of the most visible, singular manifestations of *barakah* was the ability to perform miracles (*karāmāt*), signaling a temporary suspension of the natural order through divine intervention. Thus the social recognition of *barakah* and its unequal distribution were fundamental in the elaboration of saints, saint cults, and sainthood.

In the Maghrib and elsewhere from the fifteenth century onward, *barakah* came to be viewed as hereditary and could be transmitted to and through both males and females. Certain lineages, invariably of Sharīfī origins (descended from the prophet Muḥammad), claimed to be repositories of divine powers passed on through especially worthy individuals. In Morocco, *barakah* became conflated in the popular mind with extraordinary political wisdom and the ʿAlawī dynasty, with the sultan seen as a *barakah*-endowed figure.

Barakah was associated not only with beings but also with specific places, things, and acts, such as certain foods, animals, plants, events, words, and gestures. *Barakah*'s mysterious, wonder-working qualities were often concretized in charms, amulets, and other means of protection from evil spirits. Folk medicine and healing were also connected with *barakah*, which in the hands of extraordinary individuals was believed to cure illness, bestow fertility, and ward off harm. In this way *barakah*, as an ideology, as well as a set of diverse cultural practices spanned the fluid, uneasy boundaries between scripturalist, mosque-centered Islam and the more popular or local Islamic beliefs, offering authority and religious status to women in times and places where they tended to be shut out of such positions in more orthodox environments.

[*See also* Sainthood *and* Ziyārah.]

BIBLIOGRAPHY

Babou, Cheikh Anta. *Fighting the Greater Jihad: Amadu Bamba and the Founding of the Muridiyya of Senegal, 1853–1913*. Athens: Ohio University Press, 2007.

Coulon, Christian. "Women, Islam, and Baraka." In *Charisma and Brotherhood in African Islam*, edited by Donal B. Cruise O'Brien and Christian Coulon, pp. 113–133. Oxford: Clarendon Press, 1988.

Eickelman, Dale F. *Moroccan Islam: Tradition and Society in a Pilgrimage Center*. Austin: University of Texas Press, 1976.

Helminski, Camille Adams. *Women of Sufism: A Hidden Treasure: Writings and Stories of Mystic Poets, Scholars and Saints*. Boston: Shambhala, 2003.

Michon, Jean-Louis, and Roger Gaetani, eds. *Sufism: Love & Wisdom*. Bloomington, Ind.: World Wisdom, 2006.

Safi, Omid. *The Politics of Knowledge in Premodern Islam: Negotiating Ideology and Religious Inquiry*. Chapel Hill: University of North Carolina Press, 2006.

Trimingham, J. Spencer. *The Sufi Orders in Islam*. Oxford: Clarendon Press, 1971.

Westermarck, Edward A. *Ritual and Belief in Morocco*. 2 vols. London: Macmillan, 1926.

JULIA CLANCY-SMITH
Updated by NATANA J. DELONG-BAS

BARAZANGI, NIMAT HAFEZ. (b. 1943), Nimat Hafez Barazangi is a Syrian-American scholar, educator, and Muslim women's rights advocate.

The daughter of a lawyer and a school principal, Barazangi grew up concerned with the ethical, not just ritual, aspects of Islam. This focus led her to study philosophy and sociology at Damascus University, Syria. She completed her M.A. in educational and developmental psychology at Columbia University and Ph.D. in curriculum and instruction, Islamic and Arabic studies, and adult and community education at Cornell University, where she has been a research fellow since 1991. Through philosophy she tried to find answers in the Qurʾān directly; hence her focus on social issues based on what the Qurʾān teaches, not how it is interpreted. Her work emphasizes the importance of rethinking Islam as the only means to effect social change through self-identity and self-assessment.

Barazangi is one of several prominent female Muslim scholars and authors in the field of Qurʾānic hermeneutics and the study of women and gender from within Islam. She sees personal engagement with the Qurʾān as primary to her work, critiquing other scholars who yield to the "interpretation of complementarities," which she believes reflects their "unwillingness to question the prevailing social structure, or their inability to self-identify with the Qurʾan in a pedagogical sense" (Barazangi, p. 78). She also notes a lack of leadership initiative in the affirmation of woman's "autonomous religio-morality," arguing that this contributes to separating the formative and the perceptive. She contends that the self- realization of Muslim women may not take place unless they identify themselves with the Qur'ān. Because historically not many Muslim women have related Islamic knowledge to the public sphere, they have not been able to change perceptions of and attitudes toward their own reality, given their exclusion from participating in text interpretation, policymaking, and leadership positions.

The importance of Barazangi's work is her emphasis on and urgent call for Muslim women to reinterpret the Qur'ān and be present in shaping and developing Islamic thought. She argues that Muslim women embrace the Islamic worldview as just, yet the social realities under which these women live greatly contradict Islam's ideals. Questioning why the interpretation of religious texts has been exclusive to the male elite throughout history, she argues that "nothing will change in Muslim societies, unless women are considered equal partners with authority to interpret the Qur'an" (Barazangi, p. 113). She calls for a pedagogical reading of the Qur'ān and the development of a theory of educating Muslim women beyond the patriarchal discourse "that views woman as the passive depositor of culture." She discusses the importance of recognizing the positive contributions made by self-identified Muslim women as leading not only toward comprehensive change within the social fabric of Muslim societies, but also toward participatory policymaking based on a new inclusive understanding of the Qur'ānic principle of justice, including gender justice, in which women are recognized as autonomous human beings with a primary and direct relationship with God. She calls on women to engage the Qur'ānic text in accordance with its expectations, instead of strictly relying on interpretations that can contain human error. She proposes self-learning of Islam as a curricular framework and a means of self-realization and self-identity with the Qur'ān, as opposed to apologetic approaches to reading the Qur'ān. She also insists that Muslim women not only recapture their own agency in the textual interpretation process, but also move one step further by actually participating in social and judicial change, as well as policymaking. All of this is designed to restore women's human dignity, which she perceives to be the essential message of the Qur'ān.

Since 1982 Barazangi has contributed over a hundred lectures and presentations throughout the world on women and gender in Islam, curriculum development and evaluation, and policymaking. She has been a recipient of several awards, including Senior Fulbright scholarships and United Nations Development Program fellowships.

BIBLIOGRAPHY

Ali, Souad T. Phone Interview with Nimat Barazangi, November 30, 2011.

Ali, Souad T. Review of Nimat Hafez Barazangi's *Woman's Identity and the Qur'an: A New Reading. Anthropology & Education Quarterly* 36, no. 3 (2005).

Barazangi, Nimat Hafez. *Woman's Identity and the Qur'an: A New Reading*. Gainesville: University of Florida Press, 2004.

Hammer, Juliane. "Identity, Authority, and Activism: American Muslim Women Approach the Quran." *The Muslim World* 98, no. 4 (October 2008): 443–464.

SOUAD T. ALI

BARLAS, ASMA. (b. 1950), Pakistani-American academic and scholar of Qur'ānic hermeneutics and women's rights in Islam. The daughter of a Pakistani military officer, Barlas was born in Lahore, Pakistan. She has been Director of the Center for the Study of Culture, Race, and Ethnicity at Ithaca College, New York, since 2006, and is a professor in the Department of Politics. She holds a Ph.D. in International Studies from the University of Denver, as well as two M.A. degrees from universities in the U.S. and

Pakistan. She was previously a diplomat in the Pakistani Ministry of Foreign Affairs.

Barlas is one of several prominent female Muslim scholars and authors in the fields of Qurʾānic hermeneutics and the study of women and gender in Islam. The general focus of her work is "the ideologies, epistemologies, and practices of violence" (Barlas, 2005), as addressed in her analysis of the legacy of British colonial rule in contemporary South Asian politics, particularly military rule in Pakistan and electoral democracy in India (Barlas, 1995). Other major works critique Muslims for reading sexual inequality and oppression into the Qurʾān, and "the West" for failing to develop morally relevant ways of speaking about Islam and Muslims.

Barlas's landmark book, *"Believing Women" in Islam: Unreading Patriarchal Interpretations of the Qurʾān*, addresses Qurʾānic hermeneutics and women's rights in Islam. She asserts a need for reinterpretation of the Qurʾānic text, arguing that "the Qurʾān challenges the constitutive myths of patriarchy" and "does not inherently or symbolically privilege males or masculinity biologically or culturally" (Barlas, 2002, p. 93). Instead, she argues, the Qurʾān supports an egalitarian and anti-patriarchal understanding, opposing patriarchal constructs that cast the male gender as a "constituting Cartesian subject" (p. 129) and woman as his Other, and that fulfill the purpose of men "arrogating to themselves rights that belong only to God" (p. 127). While she asserts the absence of binary thinking in the Qurʾān that casts men and women as opposites, she does not argue for "sameness." Instead, she examines aspects of the Qurʾān that are "conducive to theorizing equality" (pp. 132–133) and calls for redefining the Qurʾān to reflect its values of social justice and gender equality.

Barlas posits that Islam is a "sex-positive" religion and that the Qurʾān "does not ascribe a particular type of sexual identity, drive or proclivity for certain types of behavior to either sex," promoting instead "an undifferentiated view of sexuality" (2002, p. 152) that acknowledges the natural role of sexuality in human life and provides a framework for its moral expression. On issues of modesty and lust, referring to verse 30:21, Barlas maintains that the Qurʾān provides a framework in which sexual expression in the context of marriage strengthens and affirms *sukun*, or tranquility.

The central question of *"Believing Women" in Islam* is whether the Qurʾān is a patriarchal text. Barlas argues that patriarchy, broadly conceived, is based on an ideology that ascribes social and sexual inequalities to biology. She believes that a fair reading of the Qurʾān must reflect God's justness. Any failure to generate an anti-patriarchal reading of the Qurʾān is both a theological and a hermeneutical problem. Epistemologically, she draws guidance for her reading of the Qurʾān from the Qurʾān itself. Methodologically, she ascribes intention/ality to the text, recognizing masculine references to God as a "bad linguistic convention" (2002, p. 22). She argues against de-historicized and decontextualized interpretations of the Qurʾān in favor of ongoing interpretation that allows the Qurʾān to maintain its universality through the capability of believers to constantly derive new meaning. Thus, she rejects "interpretive reductionism," which reduces the Qurʾān to a single strict reading or interpretation, in favor of a polysemic approach, which allows for multiple modes, like other texts. She also recognizes the Qurʾān's textual and thematic holism, noting that *tafasīr* (commentaries on the Qurʾān) have superseded the Qurʾānic text in most Muslim societies as a source of influence. Accordingly, she calls for and encourages an examination of the distinction between Islam's actuality and its transcendent truth (p. 60). Barlas's work has been credited with both challenging and supporting a range of scholarly and religious interpretations, placing her at the center of one of the early twenty-first century's most pressing debates within Islam.

A prolific writer and global lecturer, Barlas is the recipient of several awards and fellowships including an Oxford Fellowship, a United Nations Fellowship, and a Ford Foundation Grant. *"Believing Women" in Islam*, was nominated for the Grawemeyer Award in Religion in 2005.

BIBLIOGRAPHY

"Asma Barlas." http://www.asmabarlas.com.

Barlas, Asma. *"Believing Women" in Islam: Unreading Patriarchal Interpretations of the Qur'ān*. Austin: University of Texas Press, 2002.

Barlas, Asma. *Democracy, Nationalism and Communalism: The Colonial Legacy in South Asia*. Boulder, Colo.: Westview Press, 1995.

Barlas, Asma. Interview by Souad T. Ali, October 11, 2011.

Hammer, Juliane. "Identity, Authority, and Activism: American Muslim Women Approach the Qur'ān." *Muslim World* 98.4 (2008): 443–464.

Simone, Fera, ed., "Globalizing Equality: Muslim Women, Theology, and Feminisms," in *On Shifting Ground: Muslim Women in the Global Era*. New York Feminist Press, 2005.

Souad T. Ali

Bazaar. "Bazaar" is Persian for marketplace. The term is also used in Turkish and Urdu and has spread to many modern European languages, connoting a crowded, colorful, often Oriental place for buying and selling. Like the Arabic term "suq", bazaar is both the concrete place of trade and the more abstract notion of buying and selling. A bazaar/suq can refer to a range of economic and architectural forms from covered markets, to periodic rural markets and small neighborhood strips of shops in alleys. A bazaar is typically associated with covered markets in city centers where goods and merchandise are sold or produced in close proximity to each other. Large bazaars are complex occupational structures with not only shopkeepers, but also commission agents, jobbers, hawkers, peddlers, wholesalers, long-distance merchants, brokers, money-changers, craftsmen, and shop assistants. In many cities in the Muslim world, the bazaar encompasses a rich system of social and religious institutions. In addition to providing venues for especially male socializing, these institutions have contributed to the bazaar's effectiveness in political mobilization.

There are many descriptive accounts of particular bazaars from the suqs of North Africa to the Hindu-influenced bazaars of India and beyond, as well as excellent historical studies of bazaars or trade. There are also important detailed descriptions by geographers and historians of cities with bazaars, maps, and, sometimes, statistical information on the numbers and kinds of shops. The social history of especially the Ottoman world has been greatly enhanced by the use of court material, not least from urban and trading environments. Nelly Hanna (1998) and Margaret L Meriwether (1999) show that women in trading families were actively using their capital for investment by using court material from Cairo in the seventeenth century and from Aleppo between 1770 and 1840 respectively.

In the late 1960s Clifford Geertz collected material for an anthropological study on the bazaar economy in Sefrou, a small town in Morocco with about six hundred shops. This study (1979), and a short article (1978) have greatly influenced non-regional specialists in their perception of "the bazaar." Geertz stated that bazaars are found in many parts of the world as economic and social institutions, but each bazaar has a particular cultural expression. He saw the bazaar/suq as a leading institution in the Arab world, where goods of varied quality are sold under seemingly chaotic circumstances and asserted that the Sefrou market illustrated "what is

Moroccan about Moroccan commerce." He focused on negotiations and encounters between sellers and their customers, the general impression being that the bazaar has features which are little changed by time. He analyzed it as a communication system, where men compete with other men and women are largely absent.

The importance of the bazaar as a concrete place for trade, social interaction, and political mobilization has been particularly stressed in research on Iran. Arang Keshavarzian divides the bulk of research on Iranian bazaars into two categories. The bazaar may be viewed as a symbol of tradition and a market that operates not only in economic terms, but also as part of the class system, where the bazaaris can be classified as part of the petit bourgeoisie. Proponents of the first view often underline the importance of the close ties between the bazaaris and the Iranian clergy. They also, rather tautologically, claim that the bazaar has resisted modernization because it is traditional. The class background of the bazaaris is used to explain the underdevelopment of Iran and the position of the country in a global capitalist system. Although the bazaar is invariably seen as important, it does not, according to Keshavarzian, always receive critical reflection.

The bazaar-as-tradition view is found in popular writings for Western audiences. Walter Weiss claims that the bazaar is not only a marketplace, but also "a city within a city, with its own economy and way of life and a spiritual background," now threatened by "Western industry and technology" (Weiss, 1998, p. 7).

Contemporary social science research and writings on bazaars is quite varied in terms of theoretical and methodological complexity. For some, the main interest and focus is on social and economic relations in a particular market. For others a particular bazaar is used also as an entry to analyses of, for example, state policies or globalization processes. Today new shopping malls are just as interesting for researchers as are "classical" covered markets. Focusing on customer behavior, especially in retail trade, has also brought women into research of the bazaar.

Women are economically important in most parts of the Islamic world and often have legal rights as independent economic actors. Furthermore women may trade on a small scale to support their families. Apart from Muslim West Africa, women are typically not large scale traders or physically present in the bazaar, except as customers. Female wholesale traders from the former Soviet republics were exceptions in, for example, Aleppo and Istanbul in the 1980s and 1990s. Annika Rabo (2005) discusses how poorer Aleppo women earn small sums of money by working on commission for male traders. They sell clothes or fripperies in their own homes or in the homes of other women. Others earn small sums of money by selling clothing accessories, perfume, and makeup that they—or others—have bought in Lebanon or in the oil-rich countries in the Gulf. In the late 1990s women were also active in smuggling clothes from Turkey and reselling them in their homes or in semi-secret shops in residential quarters. Although earnings could be considerable in these economic ventures, they were not regarded as "real" traders by men in the bazaar or by themselves. A real trader—a *taajer*—needs to be publicly connected to the market in general and to the bazaar in particular, and recognized as a "real" trader by other men.

The relationships between women and men within bazaar families are central to the reputation of traders and, although wives and daughters are seldom physically present in the suq, they are very much present in everyday suq life. They discuss with husbands and fathers family plans for evenings and exchange advice on everything from shopping and cooking to family disputes. Women are also "present" in the bazaar as links between men since bazaaris often marry the sisters or daughters of other bazaaris. Such marriage links may strengthen the cooperative bonds between men, but may also cause conflicts if the fathers and brothers of the brides do not think they are treated and appreciated in a suitable manner. Fathers express that, although sons are important for the continuation of the family name and the family business, they are more concerned about their daughters. Fathers in the Aleppo bazaar also express that they are socially conservative and want their children to marry early and with individuals from families with good reputations. Women and men actively try to find suitable spouses for the young. Sons are helped by their fathers to raise money for the *mahr* and mothers are frequent supporters of their sons' ambitions in affairs of the heart as well as in affairs of the market. Thus the values, aspirations, and destinies of women are usually as closely, if not more closely, tied to the suq as those of their menfolk.

BIBLIOGRAPHY

Abu-Lughod, Janet L. "The Islamic City—Historic Myth, Islamic Essence, and Contemporary Relevance." *International Journal of Middle East Studies* 19, no. 2 (May 1987): 155–176.

Hanna, Nelly. *Making Big Money in 1600. The Life and Times of Isma'il Abu Taqiyya, Egyptian Merchant*. Cairo: The American University in Cairo Press, 1998.

Keshavarzian, Arang. *Bazaar and State in Iran: The Politics of the Tehran Marketplace*. Cambridge, U.K., and New York: Cambridge University Press, 2007.

Keshavarzian, Arang. *A Bazaar and Two Regimes: Governance and Mobilization in the Tehran Marketplace (b. 1963)*. Ph.D. diss. Princeton University, 2003.

Le Renard, Amélie. "Pratiques du shopping mall par les jeunes Saoudiennes: sociabilité et consumérisme à Riyad." In *Mondes et places du marché en Méditerranée: formes sociales et spatiales de l'échange*, edited by Franck Mermier and Michel Peraldi, pp. 187–213. Paris: Éditions Karthala, 2010.

Meriwether, Margaret L. *The Kin Who Count: Family and Society in Ottoman Aleppo 1770–1840*. Austin: University of Texas Press, 1999.

Rabo, Annika. *A Shop of One's Own: Independence and Reputation among Traders in Aleppo*. London and New York: I. B Tauris, 2005.

Troin, Jean-François. "Des souks ruraux marocains aux shopping centers du Golfe. Liex de commerce et mutations des societies." In *Mondes et places du marché en Méditerranée: formes sociales et spatiales de l'échange*, edited by Franck Mermier and Michel Peraldi, pp. 57–78. Paris: Éditions Karthala, 2011.

Vignal, Leïla. "Beyrouth, de la boutique au shopping mall: dynamiques métropolitaines et nouvel géo-économie au Moyen-Orient." In *Mondes et places du marché en Méditerranée: formes sociales et spatiales de l'échange*, edited by Franck Mermier and Michel Peraldi, pp. 279–302. Paris: Éditions Karthala, 2011.

Weiss, Walter M., and Kurt-Michael Westermann. *The Bazaar: Markets and Merchants of the Islamic World*. London: Thames and Hudson, 1998.

MICHAEL M. J. FISCHER
Updated by ALYSSA GABBAY
Updated by ANNIKA RABO

BHUTTO, BENAZIR. (1953–2007) was born in the port city of Karachi, Pakistan. She received her early education at elite English-language Pakistani schools. From 1969 to 1973 she attended Radcliffe College in Cambridge, Massachusetts, then went on to Harvard University, where she obtained a degree in comparative government. From 1973 to 1977 she studied philosophy, politics, and economics at Lady Margaret Hall, Oxford, where she was elected president of the Oxford Union. When her father, Zulfiqar ʿAli Bhutto, became president of Pakistan, Benazir returned to the country and began assisting her father on foreign policy issues. She accompanied him to India in 1972 when he signed the Simla Agreement with Indira Gandhi, the prime minister of India. She also hosted a current affairs program, *Encounter*, on state-controlled Pakistan Television.

Following the execution of her father in April 1979 by the military regime of General Zia ul-Haq, Benazir Bhutto entered the political arena by assuming the leadership of the Pakistan People's Party (PPP) founded by her father in 1968. After spending many years in detention and living in exile, she returned to Pakistan in 1986. In 1987 she married Asif Ali Zardari, a wealthy fellow Sindhi with a dubious reputation for honesty. On 2 December 1988 she was sworn in as prime minister of Pakistan and became the first woman to head the government of an Islamic state.

In her first address to the nation, Benazir pledged to work for a progressive and democratic Pakistan, one guided by Islamic principles of brotherhood, equality, and tolerance. She invoked the Quaid-i-Azam vision for a Pakistan that would grow as a modern state. Benazir promised to strengthen relations with the United States, the Soviet Union, and China, protect minority rights, improve education, introduce a comprehensive national health policy, and enhance rights for women. Her tenure as prime minister ended on 6 August 1990 when her government was dismissed on charges of corruption. Benazir called her dismissal "illegal," "unconstitutional," and "arbitrary." Her party lost in the elections of October 1990 and went into opposition in the National Assembly.

She became prime minister again in 1993 when her party won a plurality—eighty-six seats—and was able to form a coalition government by courting small regional parties and independent members of the National Assembly. Her party lost power in 1996 when President Farooq Leghari dismissed her government on charges of corruption.

After living in exile for over a decade, Benazir returned to Pakistan in October 2007. Her homecoming rally in Karachi was marred by a suicide bomb attack that killed 150 people belonging to her party. She herself was assassinated on 27 December 2007 after leaving a PPP election rally in Rawalpindi. She is survived by her son Bilawal and two daughters, Bakhtawar and Aseefa. Benazir Bhutto received the Bruno Kerensky Award for Human Rights in 1988 and Honorary Beta Kappa Award from Radcliffe in 1989.

[*See also* Pakistan.]

BIBLIOGRAPHY

Akhund, Iqbal. *Trial and Error: The Advent and Eclipse of Benazir Bhutto*. Oxford: Oxford University Press, 2000.

Bennett Jones, Owen. *Pakistan: Eye of the Storm*. New Haven, Conn.: Yale University Press, 2002.

Bhutto, Benazir. *Daughter of Destiny*. New York: Simon and Schuster, 1989.

Bhutto, Benazir. "Labels, Discrimination and Intolerance as Betrayers of Islam." In *Women at the Podium: Memorable Speeches in History*, edited by S. Michele Nix. New York: HarperCollins, 2000.

Bhutto, Benazir. *Reconciliation: Islam, Democracy, and the West*. New York: HarperCollins, 2008.

Padrino, Mercedes. *Benazir Bhutto*. New York: Chelsea House Publishers, 2004.

Panhwar, Sani Hussain, ed. *Benazir Bhutto: Selected Speeches from 1989–2007*. Hyderabad, India: M. H. Panhwar Trust, 2009.

Shaikh, Muhammed Ali. *Benazir Bhutto: A Political Biography*. Karachi: Orient Books Publishing House, 2000.

Syed, Anwar H. *The Discourse and Politics of Zulfikar Ali Bhutto*. New York: St. Martin's Press, 1992.

Weaver, Mary Anne. *Pakistan: In the Shadow of Jihad and Afghanistan*. New York: Farrar, Straus and Giroux, 2002.

SYED RIFAAT HUSSAIN

BLACK WIDOWS. The term, which translates from the Russian as "Black Widows," was used for the first time by Russian journalists to refer to Chechen women terrorists who committed themselves to martyrdom, thereby becoming *shakhidki* (Russian pl. based on the Arabic term *shahīd*, pl. *shuhadā'*). The choice of the word

"Black Widow" suggests two obvious symbols. The first is actual widowhood after loss of husbands as victims in the escalating Russo-Chechen violence since the 1990s. A second, completely symbolic, idea invites comparison of the *shakhidki* with the notorious poisonous black widow spider.

Although cases of women involved alongside men in Chechen armed resistance against Russian "occupiers" occurred as early as 1994, the first documented incident of terrorism involving Chechen women *shakhidki* came in 2000 when two women, aged sixteen and seventeen, detonated a truck filled with explosives at the gates of the Russian military quarters at Alkhan-Yurt near Grozny. Russian intelligence claimed the women were recruited and trained by the Reconnaissance and Sabotage Battalion of Chechen Martyrs, led by the thirty-five-year-old field commander Shamil Basayev (killed in 2006). Graphic handbills and a videoclip made of the two suicide bombers spread the word, in essence inviting other women to commit themselves to the cause of Chechen terrorism.

Numerous subsequent incidents between 2000 and 2010 drew worldwide attention to the mysterious identity of other Black Widows. Perhaps the most spectacular was the siege by Chechen terrorists of the Dubrovka theater in a suburban neighborhood in Moscow in October 2002. More than forty terrorists (again presumed to have followed Shamil Basayev's orders)—about half of them women—held more than seven hundred hostages until Russian forces used gas to subdue the attackers. Almost all the terrorists, as well as more than a hundred hostages, were killed in the final assault.

During the even more deadly (North Ossetia) Beslan school tragedy in September 2004, several Black Widows were present; all died when Russian forces stormed the site, resulting in the death of nearly four hundred, almost half innocent school children.

Details gleaned following other terrorist acts involving Black Widows over the next few years suggested that, in most cases, two factors influenced Chechen women who were willing to martyr themselves. In almost all cases *shakhidki* had been exposed to intensive indoctrination under the auspices of radical Islamic clerics. Often such indoctrination reflected the influence of a network of underground *djamaat* (inspired by militant resistance groups founded in Dagestan in the 1990s labeling themselves Wahhābīyah, in opposition to groups attached to Ṣūfī leaders active in Chechnya. Some religiously based recruiters were linked to military units led by particularly well-known field commanders such as Shamil Basayev or Salman Raduyev (the latter died in a Russian prison in 2002). By the end of the 1990s there is also evidence that Chechen women were being recruited for training at Islamic study centers, some of which openly declared commitment to Wahhābīyah (again anti-Ṣūfī) teachings. One of the most important of these was headed by one Samir bin Salekh al Suweilen, an Arab veteran of the struggle against the Soviets in Afghanistan.

Such devotion to the possibility of religious martyrdom was in some cases linked to a desire for revenge against Russian perpetrators of violence against the Chechen people in general or members of their families specifically. Beyond their ultimate commitment to lethal terrorist acts, it is impossible to generalize concerning personal characteristics shared by Chechen *shakhidki*.

Information gleaned from the biographies of several martyred Black Widows suggests considerable diversity in their age ranges and personal backgrounds. A twenty-seven-year-old (killed at the Beslan school tragedy in 2004) participated in major terrorist acts already at the age of sixteen. Twenty-three-year-old Zarema Muzhikhoyeva (born an ethnic Ingush in the village of Assinovskaya), whose husband and father were killed fighting the Russians, was the first Black Widow captured alive after a failed suicide bombing in Moscow in 2003. Her account of her recruitment provided profiles of other anonymous *shakhidki*. Many, she said, were committed to a middle-aged organizer of attacks in the Russian capital known only by her code name Lyuba. Such otherwise miscellaneous information suggests the possibility of a number of such underground operatives, both in Chechnya and in Russia itself.

BIBLIOGRAPHY

Murphy, Paul J. *Allah's Angels: Chechen Women in War*. Annapolis, Md.: Naval Institute Press, 2010.

Sjoberg, Laura, and Caron Gentry. *Mothers, Monsters, Whores*. London and New York: Zed Books, 2007.

Struckman, Sara." 'Black Widows' in the *New York Times*: Images of Chechen Women Rebels." In *Muslim Women in War and Crisis*, edited by Faegheh Shirazi, pp. 92–106. Austin: University of Texas Press, 2010.

Byron Cannon

Borrowing and Credit, Women's: Contemporary and Historical Practice. This article discusses women's access to borrowing and credit in the Middle East and North Africa (MENA region) and central and Southeast Asia, with special reference to Egypt, Iran, Saudi Arabia, Lebanon, Iraq, Syria, Afghanistan, and Bangladesh. Women's access to these resources is directly related to women's access to paid and unpaid work, their reproductive role within the family and the household, and their contribution to the production of goods and services in the wider society. Women's access to these resources also differ across classes and from urban to rural contexts. Patriarchal gender relations and poverty have created great barriers on the path of women to access these resources. However women have imaginatively found ways of obtaining and providing credit and borrowing and have made great contributions to their communities, particularly by creating networks of trust and reciprocity to generate income.

Historical Background. A brief history of these regions suggests that male dominance and female subordination can be traced back to pre-Islamic civilizations when male dominance and the patriarchal family were entrenched through the rise of urban class societies and increasing military competition. Islam inherited and reconstituted the social organization of gender in pre-Islamic civilization. In many pre-Islamic societies, in particular in the MENA region, women owned property. They were engaged in business, had access to credit and borrowing, entered into contracts, and gave loans. In many tribes, such as Quraysh, women delegated their financial matters to men. For example Muḥammad was the delegate of Khadījah before she proposed to him for marriage through a woman social mediator. After the rise of Islam in these regions, Islamic law entitled women to inherit and own property, but they inherited a smaller portion of an inheritance than men. Evidence for Turkey, Syria, and Egypt suggests that, since the sixteenth century, wealthy women were engaged in selling and buying real estate, invested in the spice and slave trades, and provided credit and loans with interest to others. In Syria and Turkey between the sixteenth and eighteenth centuries, for example, 40 percent of all buying and selling of commercial and residential properties were performed by women. Women sold more than they bought properties, indicating their desire to access credit. Although women's access to resources was limited, they nevertheless vigorously pursued their economic interests and legal rights.

Throughout history and in different parts of these regions, women's access to borrowing, credit, and paid and unpaid work was interpreted and reinterpreted by different schools of Islamic thought. Historically the tradition of seeing compatibility between Islam and modernism, including women's rights issues, has, of course, been a constant in Sunnism, Shīʿism, and Sufism. Jamāl al-Dīn al-Afghānī (1837–1897), who was born in Iran and received a Shīʿī education, was a pioneer of Islamic modernism, transforming Islam from a merely religious faith into a religio-political ideology, with an emphasis against Western domination. Muḥammad ʿAbduh (1849–1905) and Muḥammad Rashīd Riḍā (1865–1935), who were influenced by Afghānī, pioneered an Islamic modernist school of thought, which became prominent from the late nineteenth century. These Islamist modernists, in different ways, asserted the compatibility of Islam with modernism, including the acquisition of modern science, gender equality, and women's education. Ḥassan al-Bannā, the leader of the Muslim Brotherhood, and Sayyid Quṭb, an influential ideologue of the Muslim Brotherhood in Egypt, were also followers of Afghānī and ʿAbduh, and both played important roles against British colonialism in Egypt.

These modernist Islamists' view of women enabled women to resist male domination. Hence women have interpreted and reinterpreted patriarchal ideology in order to struggle for their rights. With industrialization and economic development in the early to mid-twentieth century, women's access to credit, borrowing, and formal employment increased. However, since the 1980s and the rise of neoliberalism and globalization, women's access to these resources has been reduced, especially in the Middle East and North Africa.

Women's Strategies in Obtaining and Providing Credit and Borrowing. Women have sought out alternative ways of formulating their objectives within the context of restricted resources and cultural practices. In these societies the communal identity is strong and has an enormous impact on gender relations. Women see themselves as an integral part of the family unit. The concept of family and the relationship of the members of the family are shaped by historical, economic, and cultural forces. The boundaries of the public and private spheres of life are permeable. In this context family ties can be empowering as women use these ties as an asset in terms of borrowing and generating money.

Since the late nineteenth century women, especially in the MENA region, have sought to extend their rights outside of the family through negotiations with their male kin and through the institutions of *zakāt* (religious taxes) and *awqāf* (endowments). Their engagement with these institutions is more than fulfilment of their religious duties. They include social relations, community service, and participation in the public sphere of life. These women locate the roots of community service and participation in the public sphere of life in a long-standing Islamic moral discourse and connect their contemporary activism to the historical and religious past by arguing that they are the embodiment of women of early Islam who played important roles in these Islamic institutions. Many charity organizations are dedicated by middle- and upper-class women for women. These organizations exist in the arena of the community (civil society) and provide resources for poorer women to satisfy their basic needs, as well as providing poorer women with social and economic capital to participate in the public arena.

Poorer women have sought to pool their financial resources as a hedge against insecurity in different ways. These poorer women have relied on "private credit" or "informal credit" systems, available to them within their family and community. In some cases women pooling their resources in "saving clubs" has served to provide a rotating basis for access to credit. These informal sources of credit and borrowing (outside of the formal banking and financial institutions) are considered by some to be exploitative and not oriented toward development.

In this context, since the 1990s, micro-enterprise credit has become a popular tool of poverty alleviation and women's empowerment. The Grameen Bank model is a good example of micro-credit programs targeted at poor households, especially women. It is popular with donors, project designers, and implementers as an approach to facilitate women's productive economic activities. This approach, associated with the Women in Development (WID) position, has been criticized for ignoring gender relations, increasing women's hours of work, increasing conflict within the household, and increasing women's dependence on men for additional debts and repayment burdens.

The institution of the Al-Qard Al-Hassan Association (good gift or good loan without interest) in Lebanon has been a more popular and successful formal institution with the poor communities. It is a micro-credit banking scheme that gives loans/gifts to people who need them. The loan is given to anyone who is eligible. To be eligible women and men have to convince this formal banking system that they will use the gift/loan to improve their life.

However, for many poorer women the informal system assures their basic survival and allows them to have a degree of flexibility and risk, which is a necessary step toward approaching institutional or formal credit offered by financial institutions. Different examples here demonstrate women's management of both informal and formal credit.

In Afghanistan women have been mostly active in managing informal credit. Considering the level of poverty and female exclusion, women have sought to obtain credit not for productive investment, but simply as a means for consumption and provision of food. They have created favorable circumstances for availability of informal credit through building social relations. The construction of strong social relations has led to the formation of a culture within the family and neighborhood that allows the provision of interest-free credit and borrowing to the poor. Many poorer women prefer this system to the government and the Western NGOs' imposition of micro-credit systems for productive investment, as they object to development programs imposed from above and outside.

In contrast in Saudi Arabia, upper- and middle-class women who have access to money but have been excluded from formal institutions, through collective action have established women's banks that allow them to have access to formal borrowing and credit without reliance on their male kin. Some are active members of the chamber of commerce and make use of the services it provides. They have been challenging the patriarchal rules in their own way and according to their own culture. They have pushed for the reform of policies in relation to women's economic activities. As a result since 2005 women have the right to vote and run for office on the board of directors of these institutions and several women have been elected in Jeddah. Since 2011 they have gained the right to vote in political elections. As a result, women are now offered relatively favourable borrowing facilities and financial incentives for their businesses.

In Iran there are forty-five hundred women traders who work in the formal sector of the economy. They obtain and provide credit and borrowing facilities to many other women traders who work in the informal sector. Only three of these women are members of the Iran Traders Representatives, which shows the unequal representation of women in the economy of Iran.

Nevertheless these women constantly challenge patriarchal gender relations. In 2007 they established the Council of Women Traders. The aim of this council is to raise women's profile in international trade and cooperate with women traders in other Muslim majority societies. It is the largest women's council whose members are engaged in different economic fields, especially the provision of credit and borrowing to women.

Furthermore there are many local women's NGOs in Iran, Iraq, Palestine, Lebanon, Egypt, and Afghanistan. Many do not rely on foreign aid; instead they rely on public and religious institutions for funding. They identify the needs of the poorest and most vulnerable women, providing borrowing and credit facilities to them and creating opportunities for them to be involved in local community projects. These projects focus on provision of health and education, as well as cooperative productive activities, such as production and sale of food and local crafts in rural and urban areas. Poorer women identify with these projects and prefer these to the projects funded by governments and international NGOs and other financial institutions, which, in their view, are insensitive to the wishes of local people and more concerned with implementing the mandates of governments and foreign NGOs.

Conclusion. The financial institutions in the MENA region and central and South Asia are explicitly and implicitly embedded in structures and hierarchies that exclude women. However, evidently, women have been devising strategies to challenge the high barriers and have positively changed the borrowing and credit systems in favor of women.

BIBLIOGRAPHY

Ahmed, Leila. *Women and Gender in Islam: Historical Roots of a Modern Debate*. New Haven, Conn.: Yale University Press, 1992.

Altorki, Soraya. "The Concept and Practice of Citizenship in Saudi Arabia." In *Gender and Citizenship in the Middle East*, edited by Suad Joseph. Syracuse, N.Y.: Syracuse University Press, 2000.

Bayat, Asef. *Making Islam Democratic: Social Movements and the Post-Islamist Turn*. Stanford, Calif.: Stanford University Press, 2005.

Deeb, Lara. *An Enchanted Modern: Gender and Public Piety in Shi'i Lebanon*. Princeton, N.J.: Princeton University Press, 2006

Goetz, A. M., and R. S. Gupta. "Who Takes the Credit? Gender, Power and Control over Loan Use in Rural Credit Programmes in Bangladesh." *World Development* 24, no. 1 (1996): 45–63.

Grace, Jo, and Adam Pain. "Rural Women's Livelihood: Their Position in the Agrarian Economy." In *Land of the Unconquerable: The Lives of Contemporary Afghan Women*, edited by Jennifer Heath and Ashraf Zahedi. Berkeley: University of California Press, 2011.

Hourani, Albert. *Arabic Thought in the Liberal Age, 1798–1939*. Oxford: Oxford University Press, 1962.

Kabeer, Naila. "Money Can't Buy Me Love: Re-evaluation of Gender, Credit and Empowerment in Rural Bangladesh." IDS Discussion Papers 363. Brighton, U.K: University of Sussex Institute of Development Studies, 1998.

Mosse, David. "'People's Knowledge,' Participation and Patronage: Operations and Representations in Rural Development." In *Participation: The New Tyranny?*, edited by Bill Cooke and Uma Kothari. London and New York: Zed Books, 2001.

Nejadbahram, Zahra. "Women and Employment." In *Women, Power and Politics in 21st Century Iran*, edited by Tara Povey and Elaheh Rostami-Povey. Farnham, U.K., and Burlington, Vt.: Ashgate, 2012.

Poya, Maryam. *Women, Work and Islamism: Ideology and Resistance in Iran*. London and New York: Zed Books, 1999.

Riyadh Chamber of Commerce & Industry. "Expectations Low as Businesswomen Ready for RCCI Vote." http://www.riyadhchamber.com/newsdisplay.php?id=717.

Rostami-Povey, Elaheh. *Iran's Influence: A Religious-Political State and Society in Its Region*. London and New York: Zed Books, 2010.

Rostami-Povey, Elaheh. "Trade Unions and Women's NGOs, Diverse Civil Society Organisations in Iran." In *Development NGOs and Labour Unions: Terms of*

Engagement, edited by Deborah Eade and Alan Leather. Bloomfield, Conn.: Kumarian Press, 2005.
Singerman, Diane, *Avenues of Participation: Family, Politics and Networks in Urban Quarters of Cairo*. Princeton, N.J.: Princeton University Press, 1995.

Elaheh Rostami-Povey

Bosnia and Herzegovina. With the rise of medieval Bosnian kingdoms, the sources mention the names of women, rulers or members of royal families, as well. These are some of the earliest references to women in Bosnia and Herzegovina. The stories and legends about Bosnian queens were revived after the Bosnian War (1992–1995) in an attempt to present the often tragic Bosnian fate in keeping its independence among neighboring powers. Since there are not many confirmed and reliable data, it is very hard to discern the true historical facts on these rulers and members of the royal elite and the myths that arose for various purposes during the modern times.

The arrival of the Ottoman Empire in Bosnia and Herzegovina (in 1463) resulted in significant changes in social and religious structure. The Ottomans brought not only a new faith, Islam, but also a new legal system that regulated gender and family affairs as well. The evidence for participation of women in Ottoman Bosnia can be traced through various *defters* (tax registers), *sijils* (court records), and *vakufnamas*, which were the registers of the pious endowments. These *vakufnamas* showed that women held a certain amount of economical and social power, which they used to enact larger pious endowments and also when it came to smaller donations or supporting *vakfs*. In these and similar cases, women often financially supported *vakfs* or even enacted those together with men. Although the number of women endowers is smaller than the number of men, the average amount of money given to *vakfs* was comparatively similar (Filan, p. 109). It is also worth noting that financial strength was not always the crucial factor, since less-wealthy women also established pious endowments. The establishment of *vakfs* was not the only action women dealt with in this manner; they were also supervisors or administrators. Apart from the *vakf* system, women appeared in other documents as wealthy, middle-income, or poor brides; heiresses or testators: respondents or plaintiffs. It is also important to point out how Christian and Jewish women appear regularly in *defters* and *sijils* in all the mentioned roles, which also included cases of divorces. However, the written records in other spheres of women's lives are relatively poor. Still, Bosnian historiography lists two poetesses living in Ottoman Bosnia: Habiba Stočević Rizvanbegović and Umihana Čuvidina, whose poetics are entirely different: one belonged to the classical Ottoman poetical canon and the other to folk poetry. There are indications of widespread literacy among Bosnian Muslim women; however, literacy was expressed largely in knowing the *arebica* script (that used Arabic letters for Bosnian language). The widespread literacy solely in *arebica* meant that when the newly formed Austro-Hungarian Empire came to Bosnia and Herzegovina, the majority of the population was suddenly left illiterate, since it did not use the Latin or Cyrillic script, which eventually became the primary scripts for communication in Bosnia and Herzegovina.

The Austro-Hungarian Empire brought about tremendous changes in Bosnian society. Traditional Islamic society was threatened by Western modernization that often seemed to be extremely hostile to the established mores of Bosniak family. Bosniaks reacted to this new age in three different ways: by refusing to accept the change of times; by total assimilation and adaptation to the new circumstances; and by a moderate but uneasily attainable approach to the traditional heritage of Muslim family and to the challenging times that arrived. Bosnian Muslims particularly coped with two social aspects when it came to the question of women: the dress code and education. Their relation to these issues defined the overall relationship of Bosniaks to Western modernity.

The period after 1878 (the year of the Austro-Hungarian conquest of Bosnia and Herzegovina) was marked by numerous treatises, debates, and written arguments on the issue of female education and dress (the question of veiling was among the most prominent ones). The more aggressive debates were initiated by the 1911 polemics between the Muslim politician Hamdija Karamehmedović, who opted for female education, and Sofija Pletikosić ("Safija-hanuma"), who romanticized the status of the Muslim woman in Bosnia and Herzegovina (Karčić, pp. 202–203). Although the Austro-Hungarian Empire opened several schools for girls that were attended by the Catholic, Orthodox, and Jewish populations, Bosnian Muslims largely felt a strong repulsion to what they considered to be (not without any grounds) proselytistic and anti-Islamic school programs. In that same year, Muslim representatives in Bosnian Sabor (*Bosanski sabor*) voted against the obligatory schooling for Muslim girls and in that way impaired the prospective for future development of women's education and employment in Bosnia and Herzegovina. Still, the numerous debates concerning the "female question" brought significant changes. One of them is the fact that women could express themselves more often in the public sphere, especially in the domain of literary creativity. The name of Nafija Sarajlić stands to the front of all the early Bosnian women authors (together with several other Christian and Jewish female authors, such as Staka Skenderova, Laura Papo-Bohoreta, Anka Topić) since she was the first female short-story writer in Bosnia and Herzegovina. However, Bosnian women writers rose to prominence only in the second half of the twentieth century, with the names of Jasmina Musabegović, Ferida Duraković, Bisera Alikadić, and others.

During the period of the Kingdom of Yugoslavia, the name of the raisu-l-ulama Džemaludin Čaušević should be particularly noted, as he tried to apply the reformist ideas (inspired by the Egyptian thinker Muhammad Abduhu) to Bosnian society, which included the improvement of the state of Muslim women based on the rethinking of Islamic tradition.

The period of the Socialist Federal Republic of Yugoslavia brought effective changes for Bosnian Muslim women. Primary education was made obligatory for all, and this decision caused the wide entrance of women to the working and educational scene. However, religious rights and activities were largely suppressed and confined to the tiny private sphere. Here again arose the question of veiling, which was abruptly brought to an end with the 1950 law on the prohibition of wearing the veil, enacted by the National Assembly of the People's Republic of Bosnia and Herzegovina.

By the end of the 1980s, more religious freedom was given in the educational and cultural sphere. Girls' madrassa were reopened in 1978 (after almost thirty years of pause) and there were wider possibilities for women to be active in the scene of religious education.

All the discussions on the role of Bosnian Muslim women in the post-socialist society abruptly ended with the break of war in 1992. The debates on modernism, traditionalism, and secularism could not even foresee one of the greatest crimes committed against Bosnian Muslim women in this aggression—namely the systemized rape by the members of Serb army. Raping of Bosnian women was used as one of the war strategies against both men and women, since the raped women could not integrate into their own society afterward.

The postwar period in Bosnia and Herzegovina has brought many challenges to all peoples living in it. The principal obstacles for women are still the economic and nationalistic issues, wartime residues, and unresolved conflicts that prevent the society in its wholeness to ensure the fulfillment of universal rights to all its citizens.

[*See also* Ottoman Empire; Rape as War Tool; *and* Veiling.]

BIBLIOGRAPHY

Bećirević, Edina. *Na Drini Genocid* (Genocide on the River Drina). Sarajevo: Buybook, 2009.

Filan, Kerima. "Women Founders of Pious Endowments." In *Women in the Ottoman Balkans: Gender, Culture and History*, edited by Amila Buturović and Irvin Cemil Schick. London and New York: I. B. Tauris, 2007.

Hadžijahić, Muhamed, Mahmud Traljić, and Nijaz Šukrić. *Islam i Muslimani u Bosni i Hercegovini*. Sarajevo: Starješinstvo Islamske zajednice u SR Bosni i Hercegovini, 1977.

Karčić, Fikret. *Društveno-pravni aspekt islamskog reformizma: pokret za reformu šerijatskog prava i njegov odjek u Jugoslaviji u prvoj polovini XX vijeka*. Sarajevo: Islamski Teološki Fakultet, 1990.

Malcolm, Noel. *Bosnia: A Short History*. New York: New York University Press, 1994.

Spahić-Šiljak, Zilka. *Žene, religija i politika: analiza utjecaja interpretativnog religijskog naslijeđa judaizma, kršćanstva i islama na angažman žene u javnom životu i politici u BiH*. Sarajevo: Internacionalni Multureligijski i Interkulturni Centar IMIC Zajedno, 2007.

DŽENITA KARIĆ

BOUHIRED, DJAMILA. (b. 1937), icon of Algerian national resistance to French colonial rule and the struggle for women's rights. Popularly known as the "Arab Joan of Arc," Djamila Bouhired (or Jamilah Burayd), the daughter of a businessman and a seamstress, became involved in the Algerian quest for independence following a massacre by French forces in which both of her parents and one of her uncles were killed. She was further propelled to action by the death of one of her friends, Aminah, who committed suicide by ingesting poison after being arrested by the French police for carrying a bomb in her handbag.

Bouhired was recruited by Saadi Yacef, the FLN (Front de Liberation National) commander of the Algiers Qasbah. Young Algerian women who could pass as Europeans when dressed in Western clothing were needed by the FLN to plant bombs in cafés and other gathering places frequented by the French, as heavy surveillance of young males made it difficult for males to execute attacks. The devastating bombings, which began in September 1956, sparked a concerted effort by the French army to round up FLN activists in Algiers. In April 1957, Bouhired was arrested and savagely tortured by French soldiers, but refused to divulge information about FLN leaders. Her refusal to name her comrades even under torture made her an international symbol of resistance to French colonial rule, highlighting at the same time the pivotal role played by Algerian women in the struggle for independence.

At her military trial in July 1957, Bouhired acknowledged belonging to the FLN, but denied participating in the fatal bombing with which she was charged. In a trial marred by irregularities, Jacques Vergès, her French communist attorney, was denied access to essential documents and prohibited from making a final plea in her defense. The most incriminating testimony came from a woman accused of planting bombs with Bouhired. Despite the fact that the witness showed clear signs of mental instability, Bouhired was found guilty and sentenced to death. Yacef ordered a new round of bombings and threatened to engulf the city in violence if the sentence was carried out, but the French had been systematically uncovering FLN cells in Algiers, and he was captured in August 1957.

Outraged by both the conduct of the trial and the increasingly commonplace resort to torture by the authorities, Vergès and fellow communist Georges Arnaud published a pamphlet entitled "Pour Djamila Bouhired" ("For Djamila Bouhired"). Her case became a cause célèbre as French leftists and many others distressed by the dehumanizing aspects of the Algerian conflict organized rallies on her behalf, as did FLN sympathizers elsewhere in Europe. Bouhired's story was also widely publicized throughout the Arab world, where she was portrayed as a heroine of the revolution and a symbol of the strength of Algerian women.

The demonstrations reached a crescendo in March 1958, with the termination of Bouhired's appeals process. Under considerable international pressure, and with the FLN threatening to reopen its bombing campaign if Bouhired were executed, French President René Coty commuted her sentence to life imprisonment. She was transferred to France and remained incarcerated until the war's end.

Bouhired returned to Algeria upon its independence in 1962 and ran unsuccessfully for a seat in Algeria's first National Assembly. She married Vergès and worked with him and Zohra Drif (another of Yacef's former agents) in editing the left-wing Algerian political journal, *Révolution africaine*, until a purge of communists forced them from their positions in 1963. She subsequently divorced Vergès and pursued an entrepreneurial venture in Algiers, but did not return to public life. Instead, she dedicated her time to improving social conditions at the neighborhood level, fighting poverty, and working to protect orphans and war widows.

Because Algerian independence could not have been won without women's participation, many, including Bouhired, expected that Algerian women would be included in the postindependence work of constructing the welfare and future of Algeria, particularly through reforms to family law and the expansion of women's rights. However, there was little change to the status of Algerian women after independence, in part because most women activists did not press forward with gender issues, believing that the work of nation-building and the construction of a new Algerian identity were more immediate tasks.

Frustrated by the subsequent marginalization of women, Bouhired returned to public attention in 1981 with her open letter to then-president Chedli Benjedid, "No to the Betrayal of the Ideals of November 1, 1954." Bouhired then began leading women to demonstrate against the government, marking the first public confrontation of the state in the postindependence era. In the 1990s, Bouhired worked with the Algerian feminist movement to demand that women's civil rights be respected. In 2011, in the midst of the uprisings of the Arab Spring, Bouhired and other women who were active in the struggle for independence spoke out publicly against the Algerian government for its planned destruction of the Bois des Pins, a small forest of eucalyptus trees that had become a symbol of national resistance during the War for Independence. Accusing the government of arbitrary and violent actions against its own people reminiscent of the French attacks in 1957, they demanded that attention be paid to the social, economic, and ecological needs of Algerian citizens.

[*See also* Algeria.]

BIBLIOGRAPHY

Charrad, Mounira M. *States and Women's Rights: The Making of Postcolonial Tunisia, Algeria, and Morocco.* Berkeley: University of California Press, 2001.

DeLong-Bas, Natana J. "Bouhired, Djamila." In *Notable Muslims: Muslim Builders of World Civilization and Culture*, pp. 54–56. Oxford: OneWorld, 2006.

Fernea, Elizabeth Warnock, and Basima Qattan Bezirgan, eds. "Jamilah Buhrayd." In *Middle Eastern Muslim Women Speak*, pp. 251–262. Austin: University of Texas Press, 1977. Two interviews with Bouhired conducted by Lebanese journalists in 1971.

Horne, Alistair. *A Savage War of Peace: Algeria, 1954–1962*. New York: New York Review Books, 2002. The best account in English of the Algerian War, with several pages devoted to Bouhired.

Moghadam, Valentine M., ed. *Gender and National Identity: Women and Politics in Muslim Societies*. London: Zed Books, 1994.

Kenneth J. Perkins
Updated by Natana J. DeLong-Bas

Business Ownership and Women: Historical and Contemporary Practice. The literature on women in the Muslim world is rich and voluminous, and it tends to focus on cultural factors. Overrepresentation of certain cultural aspects of women in the Muslim world has a tendency to produce a type of literature that feeds upon stereotypical assumptions. These assumptions separate Islam from its socioeconomic and political context and view it as frozen in time and as an ahistorical phenomenon. Such assumptions can feed into a simplistic and universalistic understanding of Islam, which, at best, may be misleading and, at worst, erroneous. This type of analysis is applied especially to how Islam and its rules are encoded in the Sharīʿah law. This has been challenged by leading scholars on Islamic discourse such as Leila Ahmed (1992), John Esposito and Yvonne Haddad (1998), and Margot Badran (1995). The issue has also been taken up with scholars who specialize on women in the Third World countries, such as those whose approach falls into postcolonial feminist theory.

Stereotypical assumptions about Islam and gender/women in the Muslim world are mentioned throughout this encyclopedia. The focus here is on issues related to women's economic status. When reviewing women's economic role in the Muslim world, there are two complications. First, as postcolonial feminist theory argues, there is no one single category of Muslim women. Women are divided by class, race, and geographical location, to name but a few. Second, when we examine the Muslim world, it is extremely difficult, if not impossible, to lump more than a billion people (half of them women), who live in many parts of the world into yet another single category. There are fifty-one Muslim majority countries stretching from Southeast Asia to the Middle East and North Africa, African sub-Sahara, and Eastern Europe, in addition to huge Muslim minority communities within non-Muslim countries such as India and, more contemporarily, increasingly, many Muslims live in Western countries. This fact alone makes it impossible to write something inclusive and comprehensive about Muslim women's business ownership.

If one wishes to create such a general category of women in the Muslim world in order to examine their business ownership, the starting point might be their legal status, which is related to Sharīʿah law. There are many different interpretations of this law. There are two major schools of thought: Shīʿī and Sunnī; the latter has many official groups, such as Shāfiʿī, Safiʾi Zaidi, Ḥanbalī, Ḥanafī, Ḥanafī ʿAlawī , and Mālikī, and unofficial ones, such as Kharaji, all of which have their own interpretations. This does not mean that the two major schools do not mix; they do, as in the case of the ʿAlawīs. This has been evolving over a long historical process. But there are more recent movements and more contemporary groups, which makes matters more complicated. An example is Wahhābīyah, which has posited a more conservative interpretation in general since the nineteenth century, especially with regard to women in the Arabian Peninsula.

To make the picture even more complex, in the contemporary Muslim world, the state legal system may or may not officially adhere to Sharīʿah. In some countries, the state is officially secular, such as Syria, Senegal, and Turkmenistan, which might imply that laws that govern women's business ownership and state policy to promote women's economic role is secular, suggesting that it will be in line with the Western way of promoting women's role in the economy (which is yet another trajectory that is beyond the scope of this article). Some other countries call themselves "Islamic states," raising the question of whether we can assume that those who live under a secular state are different from those who live under an Islamic state. The answer would create more questions. In fact, if one takes three cases that call themselves an Islamic state, namely, Iran, Saudi Arabia, and Afghanistan, a very diverse set of practices can be observed with regard to women's economic status. In the case of Iran, women are highly educated, and their role as entrepreneurs is increasing (although severely hampered by sanctions on Iran). In Saudi Arabia, women are highly segregated and are not allowed to drive cars, though many of them are venturing into businesses, while in Afghanistan, women cannot even have easy access to education. All three follow different policies regarding the promotion of women's role in the economy.

There are indeed several layers to the issue of women's business ownership at the macro-historical, as well as at the micro level. At a more micro level, the complexities are even more numerous. To give an example, there are other legal systems parallel to the statutory law and that of the Sharīʿah: they are customary laws. In the case of Indonesia, for instance, there is a wide range of customary legal system/institutions called *Adat*, which govern the everyday lives of many Indonesians, who live predominantly in the countryside and mainly outside of the mainstream business world of a now booming economy in Southeast Asia. These customary legal entities govern a whole array of community lives, including women's economic rights.

The vast array of complexities and variety of contexts raises the question of whether the topic of women and the economy should be abandoned altogether. At the same time, it also raises the question of whether "Islam" is at the heart of the issue. In fact, women's access to economic resources, both historically as well as in more contemporary practices, seems to be more a function of factors other than Islamic religions and includes issues related to socioeconomic and political circumstances, as well as local cultural values, including those preexisting in Islam. As an example of the latter, matrilinearity and matrilocality are common in certain parts of Indonesia—in Western Sumatra, women inherit land from their grandmothers and, on marriage, men move to live with their wives. The Minangkabau people have had a long tradition of matrilinearity and matrilocality, predating Islam. This is clearly against what is commonly practiced among Muslims, or any other religious society and in developing countries for that matter. But the example shows how religion becomes part of a preexisting culture. I use this case because it not only contradicts what is common in the Muslim world, but it is also uncommon in the world in general and is a practice against the historical global pattern.

Another important point, again drawn from Indonesia, the largest Muslim country in the world (its population is more than that of the entire Middle East), is that the general pattern of female ownership follows what is common to that of women in Southeast Asia. Major indicators of economic status, such as level of employment, are in line with those of women in Southeast Asia and are relatively high.

This can be argued to be true of other countries; namely, women's access to economic resources, such as employment, follows a more regional pattern. Just to give another example, this time from sub-Saharan African countries, the general tendency suggests a regional picture highly elaborated within women and the development literature. African women's economic status, similar to those in other parts of the world, has been dictated according to patriarchal relations, which undermine women's right to ownership in general. But there is an important trajectory, whereby, by and large, when ownership is communal, women tend to have more control over resources and enjoy better terms when it comes to economic transactions (though not necessarily monetary types, including barter). Moreover, the rise of the modern economy and economic development has further deprived women of their access to means of economic resources (as has been true globally). (For a more elaborate discussion of property rights, customary laws, impact of colonialism, and development efforts and women's right, see Joireman, 2007.) Some have argued that, in the initial stage of development, women's access to means of production and their economic status declines, but it rises as development prospers the country (U-shape theory). But it is unlikely that many parts of the world will increase their share of wealth, and it is not quite clear if women have, in fact, benefited from the increase in wealth and income, not to mention the fact that, although some women in some countries may in fact increase their share of economic resources, this may or may not be the case for all of them.

Thus, we are again back to where we started, namely, that women's access to business ownership is more a function of other factors related to socioeconomic and political factors, which is why regional patterns can bring more insight into the topic than Islam. Elsewhere, I have discussed women's entrepreneurship in the Middle East and North Africa Region MENA and one can make some general arguments and give some general overviews.

First, it is highly problematic to write about the state of women's business ownership in the Muslim world. In an ironic way, Islam is part of the culture and cultural factors do play a role in women's access to ownership. Especially now with cultural globalization, ideas about cultural specificities feed into a global picture. In other words, what used to be local cultural practices now feed into a global picture that feeds back to local cultural characteristics, and this can work against women's rights, as well as for women's rights, depending on who is representing what Islamic culture is and how it is presented and to whom.

Generally and historically, infant girls were a source of shame among the Quraysh tribe and were buried alive at their birth. But it is interesting to note that, with the advent of Islam, women became equal in the eyes of God regarding ownership, and the practice of infanticide of girls was prohibited by the Qur'ān itself.

Here going back to the point about the relationship between the decline of communal ownership and that of women's access to economic resources, when private ownership rises, there is a tendency toward increases in men's ownership of economic resources. And throughout history, with the decline of communal ownership, men have come to own the means of production. In this general historical process, religion has come to be dominated by men and become part of the entrenched patriarchal arrangements. This is incidentally true of Islam, with the exception of the time it was born. After the death of the Prophet, especially with the rise of the Umayyad Caliphate (661–750), women's role and their access to economic resources was curtailed and fell back into preexisting cultural practices.

A review of the mainstream interpretation of Islamic Sharīʿah can give some insight into how women's economic equality and ownership rights have been curtailed in the way the Sharīʿah law has been encoded.

Yet, interestingly, in the Qurʾān, which is the main source of Sharīʿah, there is no differentiation between men and women regarding ownership, commercial transactions, and economic rights. What has been a source of impediment to women's business ownership stems from inheritance laws and those that govern family law.

Historical records show that one can find many examples wherein women have exercised more control over economic resources in some periods, and even the general point about the rise of communal property and private ownership has its own nuances. For instance, women (bearing in mind that we are talking about elite women) during the Ottoman era were in charge of *awqāf* (Islamic charitable foundations), and there are court records that indicate how women exercised ownership over them, in this case, not for profit. There are other examples from Syria and Egypt.

Interestingly, Muslim women were allowed to have property ownership in their name and keep it on their marriage at the time Egypt was under the British Mandate and in a state of colonial British presence. Ironically, whereas British women would lose their ownership entitlement and their name to their husband on marriage, Muslim women in Egypt and India would keep their property ownership and businesses.

In a postcolonial world and with a failed modernization attempt and development initiative in many parts of the Muslim world, women's economic status has not kept pace with that of the rich countries. Thus, it is really problematic to try to explain women's business ownership through Islamic religion.

It is useful to return to the point of how women's economic role is defined in the Muslim world, or rather how women can be defined and portrayed in ways that can empower rather than hinder their access to business ownership. It is possible to pave the way to a new way of thinking about religious discourses and religious debates vis-à-vis the role of women and their economic rights that can strengthen their role. Just as increasingly educated women are challenging patriarchal interpretations of Islam, one can argue that the development discourse needs to bring in new ideas as to how Islam as a religion can be a vehicle of social change in favor of women's economic rights.

Here it is worth reminding policymakers that it is not necessary to discard local cultural beliefs to bring about economic change and social transformation. On the contrary, it may be extremely effective and efficient as part of a bottom-up approach to development to use existing cultural norms and practices in ways that enhance women's socioeconomic rights. To give an example, women in Iran managed to win a battle that feminists in the West have not. They argued that based on Islamic jurisprudence, women are not obliged to work at home; in other words, women are not forced to give their reproductive labor (unpaid women's work at home). If they do, they can claim a wage. This forced the Iranian government to pass a law in 1993 that gives women the right to claim wages for housework (although, in practice, the implementation of the law leaves a great deal to be desired, to say the least). Nonetheless, this was an ingenious idea and had it been picked up by international organizations and disseminated throughout the Muslim world as an example of how religious discourses can be used to empower women's economic role, it might have had an important impact. But because there is little will to see that religion and, especially, Islamic religion, can be interpreted in ways that empower women, no international development effort embarked to take up this approach. To elaborate more on this type of idea and how religion can be used to improve economic conditions and to promote development, the Berkeley Center for Religion and the work of Katharine Marshal illustrated how religion and development can come together. The Centre has dedicated its work to documentation of how this can be done. There is much work to be done on this and more discussion to be conducted. But this is a way of turning the table in ways that do not antagonize the Muslim community, but bring it on board for changes that can be of benefit to the population as a whole.

To give another example, perhaps it is no accident that the most successful microcredit model developed started in a Muslim country—Bangladesh—through the Grameen Bank, a model that has now become a panacea for development assistance to alleviate poverty for women. Some Muslims have challenged this model because it charges interest, so it is interesting to consider what might happen if interest-free microcredit was advocated. For example, in field work in Indonesia, South Lebanon, and Iran, I have found numerous rotating savings and credit associations, ROCAs (also found in other parts of the world). This is a mode through which a group of women come together and contribute to a fund, which is then lent to each member of the group based on a rotating system and through mechanisms such as a lottery. They can be a model for Islamic credit/microcredit because there no interest is charged and, more importantly, they are indigenous to the local culture. These savings do not turn into credit, but are channelled into consumer goods or emergency expenditure and are typically not used for income-generating activities. If policymakers were open to such existing indigenous practices, these associations could be turned into a development model that would not have to rely on outside funding or charge an 18 to 24 percent interest rate, as is the case for the Grameen model.

As, too often, promotion of any kind of women's rights, including their socioeconomic rights, can instigate certain hostility and resistance and could be labeled as imperialism. It is important to recall that existing norms and indigenous cultural practices are part and parcel of development initiatives regarding women's economic role. Within this framework, they have a better chance of being welcomed and are prone to easier implementation.

BIBLIOGRAPHY

Abu-Lughod, L. "Oriental and Middle East Feminist Studies." *Feminist Studies* 1 (2001): 101–114.

Agnes, F. "Patriarchy, Sexuality and Property: The Impact of Colonial States Policies on Gender Relations in India." In *Family, Gender, and Law in a Globalizing Middle East and South Asia*, edited by K. M. Cuno. Syracuse, N.Y.: Syracuse University Press, 2009.

Ahmed, L. *Women and Gender in Islam: Historical Roots of a Modern Debate*. New Haven, Conn.: Yale University Press, 1992.

Armstrong, K. *Islam: A Short History*. New York: Modern Library, 2000.

Badran, M. *Feminists, Islam, and Nation: Gender and the Making of Modern Egypt*. Princeton, N.J.: Princeton University Press, 1995.

Bahramitash, R., and H. S. Esfahani "Modernization, Revolution and Islamism: Political Economy of Women's Employment." In *Veiled Employment: Islamism and the Political Economy of Women's Employment*, edited by R. Bahramitash and H. S. Esfahani. Syracuse, N.Y.: Syracuse University Press, 2011.

Bahramitash, R., and S. Kazemipour "Veiled Economy: Gender and the Informal Sector." In (Eds.), *Veiled Employment: Islamism the Political Economy of Women's Employment in Iran*, edited by R. Bahramitash and H. S. Esfahani. Syracuse, N.Y.: Syracuse University Press, 2011.

Bahramitash, R., J. C. Olmsted, and F. F. Farahani (forthcoming). "Choice, Constraint and Power: An Examination of Women's Informal Sector Employment in Iran." Washington, D.C.: World Bank, 2012, forthcoming.

Haddad, Y. Y., and J. L. Esposito, eds. *Islam, Gender and Social Change*. New York: Oxford University Press, 1998.

Hasso, F. S. "Problems and Promise in Middle East and North Africa Gender Research." *Feminist Studies* 31.3 (2005): 653–679.

Joireman, S. F. "The Mystery of Capital Formation in sub-Saharan Africa: Women, Property Rights and Customary Law." *World Development*, 36.7 (2007).

Moallam, M. *Between Warrior Brother and Veiled Sister: Islamic Fundamentalism and the Politics of Patriarchy*. Berkeley: University of California Press, 2005.

Mohanty, Chantra. "Under the Western Eyes in Signs" *Journal of Women in Culture and Society*, 28.2 (2002),

Olmsted, J. C. "Is Paid Work the (Only) Answer? Women's Well-being, Neoliberalism and the Social Contract in Southwest Asia and North Africa." *Journal of Middle East Women's Studies* 2.1 (2005): 112–139.

ROKSANA BAHRAMITASH

C

Calligraphy and Epigraphy. Given the extraordinary importance of the word in Islam, it is no surprise that women were both practitioners and patrons of this quintessential form of Islamic art, albeit on a much more limited scale than their male counterparts. Our earliest evidence for female calligraphers is textual, and the sources collected by Ṣalāḥ al-Dīn al-Munajjid show that from the tenth century a few women practiced and taught calligraphy. Women also patronized fine calligraphy, as attested by the large and distinctive "Nurse's Qur'ān" prepared under the supervision of the female secretary (*al-kātiba*) Durra and endowed to the Great Mosque of Qayrawan/Kairouan in Tunisia in January 1020 CE by Fāṭimah, the former nurse (*al-ḥāḍina*) of the Zīrid prince al-Muʿizz ibn Badis (Blair, fig. 5.5). These women were closely connected with court circles. Similarly, the earliest surviving calligraphy by a woman from the Islamic lands is a thirty-volume Qur'ān manuscript transcribed by Zumurrud Khatun ("Emerald Lady") bint Maḥmūd ibn Muḥammad ibn Malikshah and endowed by her to the shrine at Mashhad in Iran in August–September 1145 CE A notable patron of the arts who also donated an extensive revetment of inscribed luster tiles to the shrine at Mashhad, she can be identified as the daughter of the nephew of the Seljuk sultan Sanjar, the Qarākhānid prince Maḥmūd ibn Muḥammad, who succeeded his uncle as Seljuk ruler in 1157 CE.

By the age of empires in the sixteenth century, women were more common as calligraphers as well as patrons and collectors of calligraphy. Many of the most famous were connected with the Ṣafavid, Qājār, Ottoman, and Mughal royal families. Around the year 1669–1670 CE, for example, Zinat al-Nisā', the pious daughter of the Mughal emperor Awrangzīb, copied a small personal copy of the Qur'ān (London, Khalili Collection, QUR417) in a fine *naskh* hand with extensive decoration in gold, blue, and carmine red. Many women at the Mughal court appreciated fine calligraphy. A magnificent Qur'ān manuscript made for the Ṣafavids, perhaps even for Shah Ṭahmāsp himself (London, Khalili Collection, QUR729) and then presented to the Mughal emperor Shah Jahān, who inscribed the first page, contains the seals of several Mughal court officials bearing the title *khwājah*, probably referring to the eunuchs of the women's quarters (*zanāna*); one official named Muḥammad Khan may even be the eunuch of

Zinat al-Nisā'. Her elder sister Zīb al-Nisā', who is said to have memorized the Qur'ān, collected not only books but also their authors, such as the theologian Mulla Safi al-Din Ardabīlī whose Persian translation of the Qur'ānic commentary came to be known as *Zīb al-tafsīr* ("The Ornament of Commentaries") after his patron.

With increasing literacy and growing demand for calligraphy in pre-modern and modern times, the social base of female calligraphers broadened. Some came from clerical families. Emine Servet Hanım, for example, was the youngest daughter of the Shaykh al-Islām, Sayyid Ḥasan Hayrallah; she married a bathhouse owner but separated from him and went to live in Madina with her grandfather. Childless, she regarded her nine *ḥilyas* (calligraphic compositions describing the Prophet) as her offspring. The best known of these compositions is the one that she penned for her calligraphic license issued in 1874–1875 CE and certified by the major Ottoman calligraphers of the day, including the master Qāḍī-'askar Muṣṭafā 'Izzet Efendi. This tradition continues in such modern masters as Hilal Kazan (Simonowitz).

Women today play an important role in maintaining and developing many forms of calligraphic art. In countries such as Iran and Turkey, there are enough female practitioners to hold exhibitions of traditional calligraphy solely by women. Female artists are also part of the trend to expand traditional types of calligraphy in new directions and into new media. Iranian-born Jila Peacock (b. 1948), for example, adapts traditional zoomorphic calligraphy, penning the poems of the Persian classical poet Ḥāfiẓ in the shapes of animals and birds mentioned in the verses (Porter, no. 22). The Lebanese-born poet and painter Etel Adnan (b. 1925) makes "artist's books" by folding rolls of Japanese paper like an accordion and decorating the pages with words and poems in Arabic script combined with watercolor paintings (Porter, no. 25; Blair, fig. 13.12). Many female artists incorporate writing in their works. Jordanian-born Wijdan Ali (b. 1939) inscribes single letters and verses from poems on her oil paintings and watercolors to evoke the memory of the past (Porter, nos. 25 and 63). Iraqi-born Suad al-Attar (b. 1942) expands the feminist literary canon by including snippets from a poem by the early Arab poetess Layla bint Lukayz on the base of her etching (Porter, no. 16). Probably the most famous of these multi-media artists is Iranian-born Shirin Neshat (b. 1957), whose early work includes photographs highlighted with Persian poetry in ink (Porter, no. 24). The point in most of these works is not to read the words, but to recognize that the works contain writing, a theme that adds historical resonance and sometimes reverence to the art. Often the writing is deliberately rough and non-calligraphic. Widjan Ali coined the term "calligraffiti" for this script written without the rules of proportion and with shapes that are close to scribbling. It is deliberately intended to juxtapose the smooth, regular, and seemingly effortless forms of classical Islamic calligraphy. Many of these artists developed their styles outside the lands in which they were born, but the reverence for the word means that their work is increasingly appreciated in their homelands as well.

[*See also* Art, Women in Islamic.]

BIBLIOGRAPHY

Ali, Wijdan. *Modern Islamic Art: Development and Continuity*. Gainesville: University Press of Florida, 1997. Survey of modern Islamic art with several chapters on calligraphy and brief biographies of some of the major practitioners.

Blair, Sheila S. *Islamic Calligraphy*. Edinburgh: Edinburgh University Press, 2006. Survey of the history of calligraphy throughout the Islamic lands.

al-Munajjid, Ṣalāh al-Dīn. "Women's Roles in the Art of Arabic Calligraphy." In *The Book in the Islamic World: The Written Word and Communication in the*

Middle East, edited by George N. Atiyeh, pp. 141–148. Albany: State University of New York Press, 1995. Article citing many textual sources for female calligraphers in the early period.

Porter, Venetia. *Word into Art: Artists of the Modern Middle East.* London: British Museum Press, 2006. Catalog of a landmark exhibition of modern calligraphy, including nineteen works by women.

Simonowitz, David. "A Modern Master of Islamic Calligraphy and Her Peers." *Journal of Middle East Women's Studies* 6.1 (Winter 2010): 75–102. Study of a modern master, with extensive bibliography.

SHEILA S. BLAIR

CAMBODIA. Until the arrival in Cambodia of the Cham from Champa Kingdom (present-day central and southern Vietnam) and the Chvea-Malay (Javanese descendants) from Malaysia and Indonesia around the seventeenth century, there was no evidence of Islam in Cambodia. Long before their migration, the Cham were influenced by Indian culture, which had spread along the maritime trade routes of Southeast Asia in the early centuries CE Islam was probably introduced to the kingdom through Arab traders around the thirteenth century, after which it soon began to override the existing Indian influences.

Other scholars suggest that the Chvea-Malay migrated from Minangkabau, West Sumatra, Java Islands, and other parts of Malaysia such as Kelantan and Kedah, to Cambodia (see Center for Advanced Study, 2009, and Nik Hassan Shuhaimi Nik Abd and Muhamad Zain Musa, 2006). Although the Cham and Chvea did not communicate with each other well, the Chvea-Malays, who were already Muslims, nevertheless are believed to have converted more of the Cham to Islam. The Cham accused the Chvea-Malay of persecuting Cham people in the aftermath of the Vietnamese incursion. However, they later both embraced Islam strictly and cooperated with one another, with the exception of a small group of Cham called Cham Jahed, which still practices syncretic Islam in the Champa tradition, and remains faithful to non-mainstream practices such as praying once a week instead of five times daily.

Because both ethnic groups have adopted Sunnī Islam, including its protocol and dress, it has become difficult to distinguish the Cham and the Chvea-Malay physically. However, the Cham speak the Cham language, whereas Chvea speak mostly Khmer with a little *bahasa* (Malay). Osborne (2004) estimates the Chvea-Malay population at 15 percent of Cambodia's Muslims. Combined with their local beliefs and traditions (non-Islamic practice), Cham and Chvea-Malay (thereafter, Cham Muslims) are making efforts to modernize and adapt to the new transnational Islam. Even so, the local practices influenced by Khmer culture are also still upheld by many Cham Muslims, including visitations to ancestor's tombs and using the lunar calendar to match a couple or decide on a couple's marriage.

During the colonial period (1863–1954), Sangkum Reastr Niyum (1955–1970) period, led by the late King Sihanouk, and Lon Nol period (1970–1975) led by then Marshal Lon Nol, Islam was tolerated, but there was some discrimination regarding its practice, norms, and beliefs. The discriminatory behavior and attitudes arose from a general lack of understanding, misconceptions about Islam, and ethnic jokes about the Cham. This was reduced gradually through social integration and public awareness about both Islam and the Cham. In an effort to integrate Cham Muslims fully, Prince Norodom Sihanouk gave Cham Muslims the title "Khmer Islam" in the 1960s. Socially, this move yielded an enormously positive outcome. Ethnically, it seems to have put their identity at risk, because they are now called Khmer Islam instead of Cham or Chvea.

In recent history, the Democratic Kampuchea (DK), better known as the Khmer Rouge (KR) regime, which was headed by a group of Cambodian communists (1975–1979), forbade Islam and its ritual practices. Religious leaders like the Grand *Mufti* (Highest Council of Islamic Religious Affairs in Cambodia) were targeted for execution. Islamic schooling was prohibited, Qur'ānic schools were closed down, and mosques were desecrated. In the aftermath of the genocide, Islam, like Buddhism, had to be essentially recreated from the ground up. The regimes following the fall of the Democratic Kampuchea (1979 to the early twenty-first century) have been sympathetic toward Islam and its people, as the entire population, across religious and ethnic lines, experienced the same horrific events. The Cambodian government has issued a directive allowing Cham Muslim women to wear Muslim attire and headscarves in school and has allowed more religious freedom. Buddhist-Muslim relations have also proved to be amicable.

Muslim Women. Cham Muslims make up approximately 6 percent of the total population of 14 million in Cambodia. Cham Muslim women make up over half the Cham Muslim population, according to a survey by the Grand *Mufti*, the Highest Council of Islamic Religious Affairs in Cambodia. After the fall of the Khmer Rouge, women accounted for about 65 percent of all survivors and became the driving force in restoring the communities and the country because so many men had died. They worked to reconstruct their society and reformulate ethnic, religious, and social identities at both the personal and community levels by helping to rebuild mosques, provide moral and spiritual supports to strengthen Islam, and contribute personal stories to the collective memory, transmitting Cham traditions and culture to the new generation.

However, women's efforts in producing a new generation and reconstructing the community have not improved their social status. In the official religious structure, no woman is present, and no women have been reported as assistants to any religious figures. A lack of skills and education, and the limits on women imposed by traditional cultural practices, cause women to lag behind men. Even though a new generation of women is rising up to demand education and a presence in the public sphere, if there is no empowerment and recognition, they will end up as marginalized as past generations.

The Impact of Globalization and Transnational Influences. Globalization and transnational influences have both positive and negative impacts. The flow of goods, people, and information across the globe all create new opportunities and challenges for Muslims in Cambodia. However, the integration of global and regional forces with local processes has been perceived as both a threat to Muslim identities, and as beneficial to the development of a new transnational Islam. For example, some Cham Muslim women are affected by the harsh response of some orthodox Muslim men to materialism and transnational influences, who see Western ideology as corrupting and weakening religious beliefs.

Gender Relations. Marriage is a central element of Muslim communities. Premarital sex is prohibited and polygamy is not common among Cham Muslim people. In a Cham family, men dominate decision-making processes, while women are responsible for household chores and childrearing. The husband teaches his wife, while the wife teaches her children. Men administer religious affairs and security, as well as any kind of conflict resolution. Nevertheless, moderate factions in society maintain that economic factors give a person the right to make decisions, which means that, regardless of gender, whoever financially supports the family has the right to make decisions, which then determine their status. Since women have the minority voice and lower position, they have little power to make decisions. Women have little role in community conflict transformation, as only men are included in the public religious structure.

As in many of the world's major religions, power distribution in Islamic religious affairs is not equal. While *amīrs* (leaders, always male) give sermons to both male and female followers, female group leaders read texts on *hukum* (norm), *faḍīlah* (morality), and punishment excerpted from the Qurʾān and *ḥadīth* to their female companions. In addition, women are told to completely cover their body from head to toe to protect themselves from male harassment. These exclusionary practices limit their leadership roles and participation in society. Although some religious teachers are women, still they have little voice.

Issues, Challenges, and Achievements. The issues and challenges that face women and shape women's present and future include religious issues, lack of education, and socioeconomic and sociopolitical issues. First, the complexity of interpretation of religious texts regarding women's code of conduct and roles in society affects their participation in society. While Seth Muhammad Sis, of the Ministry of Education, Youth, and Sports believes that veiling (covering the whole body and head except the eyes) can conflict with women's role in society and limits their relations with other people outside their communities, the majority of moderate Cham Muslims believe that women should be covered from head to toe, leaving only the face and hands exposed. At the extreme, the minority or Dakwah Tablighi (minority religious sect), demands that women veil themselves completely and not leave the house or go anywhere without permission from their husband.

Regarding secular education, few women went to public school during the reign of King Sihanouk (1953–1969) because of Cham traditions, which held that women should focus solely on household chores. Some women did attend public school during the Lon Nol regime (1970–1975), but then stopped due to fighting between the Khmer Rouge guerrillas and Lon Nol forces. Under these two regimes, no Cham Muslim woman was reported to be a prominent figure. Under the Democratic Kampuchea communist regime (1975–1979), which banned religion, women were forced to cut their hair short, remove their headscarves, and downplay their traditional roles as mothers and wives. Instead, they had to do hard labor and obey the Khmer Rouge leadership.

In the early twenty-first century, several obstacles hinder women from obtaining education. Women had not been allowed to wear headscarves in class since roughly the turn of the century, but this issue was addressed in 2008, when the government's directive allowing headscarves in public schools was circulated and implemented. However, the practice of arranged marriage remains common in some villages. While many parents encourage their daughters to go to school, some other women are encouraged to get married when they are still very young. Once they get married, there is no chance for them to go back to school. In addition, a lack of economic support discourages women from further studies.

As far as sociopolitical and socioeconomic issues are concerned, women's representation in politics is relatively low in Cambodia, and this is even more pronounced in Muslim communities, due to lack of education, lack of empowerment, and the pressure of tradition. This limits their leadership positions in economic issues, despite the fact that many women are involved in the economic sphere. Although there are more than three dozen Cham Muslim male leaders in government offices, only two women hold prominent government positions at the time of this writing: Kop Mariah, Under Secretary of the Ministry of Women's Affairs and Veterans, and Math Mara, Under Secretary of the Ministry of

Rural Development. About a dozen women have become department heads and deputy heads in government offices.

Women's Organizations, Institutions, and Movements. Cambodia has the smallest number of Muslim women's organizations, compared to other countries in Southeast Asia. The Cambodian Islamic Women's Development Association (CIWDA), founded in 1997 by Othsman Hassan, is the sole women's organization. Headed by Kop Mariah, it works to promote women's well-being through vocational training and scholarships to young students. The association imparts English-language and computer skills to unemployed youth and provides sewing machines and training to unemployed women. Another women's association was created in 2010 by Aseah Hamzah, of the Ministry of Cults and Religion, to offer sewing classes and material support to widows and orphans.

There are a few Islamic organizations working on gender issues. The Islamic Local Development Organization (ILDO) works on human rights, women's health issues, and education. The Cambodian Islamic Youth Association (CIYA) works on education. The Cambodia Muslim Student Association (CAMSA) provides dorms for female Muslim students from the provinces to stay in during their studies in the city.

Recommendations. Despite these issues and challenges, Cham Muslim women continue to strive to be active leaders and activists in their communities, and to raise children for the new generation. Their achievements can be seen through education, integration in the larger community, the number of women enrolled in universities, changing attitudes toward women and gender equality, and women's confidence in working in their community and with other people. The trend of women asserting themselves in public is an improvement when compared against the situation in the latter half of the twentieth century. For the community to continue to develop and prosper, it must provide opportunities for women, who contribute half of its human resources, and commit to adopting progressive attitudes toward women and to approving a more moderate interpretation of Islam.

BIBLIOGRAPHY

Blengsli, Bjørn Atle. "Muslim Metamorphosis: Islamic Education and Politics in Contemporary Cambodia." In *Making Modern Muslims: The Politics of Islamic Education in Southeast Asia*, edited by Robert W. Hefner, pp. 172–204. Honolulu: University of Hawaii Press, 2009.

Brown, Daniel W. *A New Introduction to Islam*. 2d ed. Chichester, U.K.: Wiley-Blackwell, 2009.

Center for Advanced Study. *Ethnic Groups in Cambodia*. Phnom Penh, Cambodia: Center for Advanced Study, 2009.

Kiernan, Ben. *The Pol Pot Regime: Race, Power, and Genocide in Cambodia under the Khmer Rouge, 1975–1979*. New Haven, Conn.: Yale University Press, 1996.

National Council of the United Front of Kampuchea. *Islam in Kampuchea*. National Council of the United Front of Kampuchea for the Building and Defense of the Homeland, 1987.

Nik Abd, Nik Hassan Shuhaimi, and Muhamad Zain Musa. *The Cham Community Through the Ages*. Universiti Kebangsaan Malaysia (National University of Malaysia), 2006.

Osborne, Milton. "The 'Khmer Islam' Community in Cambodia and Its Foreign Patrons." *Lowy Institute for International Policy* Issues Brief (November 2004). http://lowyinstitute.cachefly.net/files/pubfiles/Osborne%2C_The_Khmer_Islam_community_v4.pdf.

Schleifer, Aliah. *Motherhood in Islam*. Cambridge, U.K.: Islamic Academy, 1996.

So, Farina. "Cham Muslim Community: Inevitable Trends of Change." *Searching for the Truth*, Special English Edition, First Quarter (2009): 45–47.

So, Farina. *The Hijab of Cambodia: Memories of Cham Muslim Women after the Khmer Rouge*. Phnom Penh, Cambodia: Documentation Center of Cambodia, 2011.

So, Farina. "The Study of the Qur'ān versus Modern Education in Cambodia." Presented at the Short Course of Islam, Gender, and Reproductive Rights in Southeast Asia, 4–25 June 2005, Indonesia. http://www.d.dccam.org/Projects/Public_Info/Cham%20Muslim%20Leaders/Cham_Muslim_Leaders.htm.

Wadud, Amina. *Qur'ān and Woman: Rereading the Sacred Text from a Woman's Perspective.* New York: Oxford University Press, 1999.

Wagner, Carol. *Soul Survivors: The Stories of Women and Children in Cambodia.* Berkeley, Calif.: Creative Arts Book Company, 2002.

FARINA SO

CANADA. Although research on early Muslims' lives is scant, it is known that Muslims have been immigrating to Canada since the 1840s. Hamdani (2008) concludes that Canada's first Muslims, arriving from Scotland, found it difficult to keep their Islamic faith, so that by 1871 none identified as Muslim. But early records show that, as the Muslim community grew larger, it became easier to create "community," and pass faith and customs on to the next generation. The first mosque was built in Edmonton, Alberta, in 1938. Muslim women were key members of community-building efforts from this time, particularly by helping new immigrants start over and by organizing dinners at the mosque. Interfaith harmony was also aimed for by inviting neighbors and coworkers, whether Muslims, Christians, or Jews, to join them. This crucial role of informal settlement assistance continues to be played predominantly by women to this day. Although intangible, this contribution to community building should not be underestimated, particularly because homesickness can be debilitating. To the extent that Muslim women's efforts to create bonds of "family" and community across ethnic, tribal, sectarian, and familial differences has assisted in alleviating loneliness, they should be recognized as a vital contribution to community sustainability and development.

The early mosques gave women leadership and networking opportunities: serving on an executive board; running the weekend Islamic school or the mosque newsletter; or speaking at community events. Some of the founding members of the Canadian Council of Muslim Women (CCMW), Canada's first and only national Muslim women's organization (founded in 1982), had worked together in such activities in Toronto's first mosque.

Like other immigrant women, Muslim women have volunteered in both Muslim and non-Muslim grassroots organizations. In addition to CCMW, there are many regional Muslim women's organizations, such as the Amal Women's Center in Montreal, the Federation of Muslim Women in the Greater Toronto Area, the Coalition of Muslim Women of Kitchener-Waterloo, and the Ottawa Muslim Women's Organization. Typically these organizations focus on issues to do with women and Islam both within the community, such as domestic violence, and outside the community, such as the representation of Muslim women in the media, and interfaith relations.

Some Canadian Muslim women have come to prominence in national Muslim organizations, including offshoots of organizations founded in the U.S.: Khadija Haffajee became the first female member of the *majlis-as-shura* (executive board) of the Islamic Society of North America (ISNA) in 1997. In 2006, the Canadian convert Dr. Ingrid Mattson became ISNA's first female president. Dr. Sheema Khan founded the Canadian Council on American-Islamic Relations (CAIR-CAN) in 2000. Shahina Siddiqui is, as of 2013, the executive director of the first national social services organization, the Islamic Social Services Association, which she cofounded in 1999. In 2006, Farzana Hassan was elected president of the Muslim Canadian Congress, which was founded in 2001. In 2009, Wahida Valiante became the first woman elected to the presidency of the Canadian Islamic Congress. Two women, Dalia Abdellatif and Rania Lawendy, as of 2013, are on the national board of directors for the Muslim Association of Canada. Muslim women, especially the younger generation, are increasingly active in every kind of local, regional, and national organization.

Community-based activism is often a precursor to involvement in the formal political process. Dr. Lila Fahlman, a cofounder of CCMW, was the first Muslim woman to run for office, pursuing the New Democratic Party's (NDP) Winnipeg nomination for the 1971 federal election. This trend has continued, with a handful of Muslim women, including Monia Mazigh and Shaila Kibria, moving from community activists to running as NDP candidates.

Canadian Muslim women represent different modalities of living Islam in Canada, reflecting larger global debates about women's position and role in Islam. Mazigh and Kibria competed in the elections while wearing *hijab*. The first Muslim woman senator, Mobin Jaffer, is Ismaili, as is Yasmin Ratansi, who was the first Muslim (Ismaili) woman elected to federal Parliament (2004–2011). The first Muslim woman elected to the Quebec legislature, Fatima Houda-Pepin (1994), spoke out against an Ontario faith-based arbitration initiative that would have allowed reference to Islamic law. Pakistani scholar Farhat Hashmi runs a successful branch of her conservative, worldwide Al Huda Institute in Mississauga, while in 2005 Raheel Raza led Toronto's first woman-led *jumʿah* (Friday prayer) for the Muslim Canadian Congress.

Male-female dynamics in Muslim organizations in Canada remain understudied. But it is fair to conclude that the early patterns set by the first immigrant women have held: (i) many women working behind the scenes in more traditional female roles (cooking, cleaning, and fundraising through dinners; offering room and board to new community members; bonding the community by maintaining social relations; focusing on children's needs such as weekend Islamic schooling, Eid parties and the like); (ii) a smaller number in official positions in community-based (coed) organizations; and (iii) working with other Muslim women in women-only Muslim organizations. They also continue their volunteer work with non-Muslim nonprofit organizations. "Sister" wings of large national Muslim organizations, such as the Islamic Circle of North America (ICNA), albeit subordinate to the main (male) executive, have nevertheless allowed for autonomous space for female leadership, organization, planning, and management.

Anecdotal research suggests that immigrants to Canada predating the global rise of political Islam in the 1980s were more open to folkloric practices, and few of the women wore *hijab*. Post-1980s, immigrants arrived with different understandings of practicing Islam. The splits that occurred in early Muslim communities do not seem to have turned on women's issues—rather, they reflected personal conflicts and ethnic and broader ideological differences.

Over the 170 years since Muslim women have immigrated to Canada, a summary of their challenges would best be divided into two parts: challenges from without, some of which are common to all immigrants (language/jobs/housing), some common to all immigrant women (childcare/jobs/racism), and some specific to being Muslim (anti-Muslim racism); and challenges from within, again, some of which are common to all women (domestic violence); or some specific to Muslims' culturally based biases against Muslim women taking public roles outside the confines of their motherly/wifely duties in the home.

BIBLIOGRAPHY

Abu-Laban, Y. "Challenging the Gendered Vertical Mosaic: Immigrants, Ethnic Minorities, Gender and

Political Participation." In *Citizen Politics: Research and Theory in Canadian Political Behaviour*, edited by Joanna Marie Everitt and Brenda Lee O'Neill, pp. 268–282. Don Mills, Ont., Canada: Oxford University Press, 2002.

Ali, S. "Building a Women's Movement." *Islamic Horizons* (May–June 2003): 16–24.

Bullock, Katherine. "Toward A Framework for Investigating Muslim Women and Political Engagement in Canada." In *Islam in the Hinterlands: A Canadian Muslim Studies Anthology*, edited by Jasmin Zine, pp. 92–114. Vancouver, Canada: University of British Columbia Press, 2012.

Bullock, Katherine. "Women, Gender and Political Participation and Political Parties: Canada." In *Encyclopedia of Women and Islamic Cultures*, vol. 2, edited by S. Joseph, pp. 268–282. Leiden, Netherlands: Brill, 2004.

Bullock, Katherine, ed. *Muslim Women Activists in North America: Speaking For Ourselves*. Austin: University of Texas Press, 2005.

Fahlman, L. "Lila." In *At My Mother's Feet: Stories of Muslim Women*, edited by Sadia Zaman, pp. 51–70. Kingston, Ont., Canada: Quarry Press, 1999.

Hamdani, Daood. "Muslim History of Canada: Pre-Confederation to the First World War," Lecture, The Tessellate Institute, April 27, 2008. http://www.tessellateinstitute.com/wp-content/uploads/2009/07/Hamdani-Muslim-History-of-Canada.TTI.pdf.

Milo, Michael. *A New Life in a New Land: The Muslim Experience in Canada*. DVD. Part One, "The Mosaic," 2004.

"Mosque One: Oral Histories of Toronto's First Mosque." http://www.mosqueone.com.

Katherine Bullock

CEMETERIES. For many centuries, cemeteries (*maqābir*) have often been placed outside villages, towns, or cities in the Muslim world. They contain tombs (*qubūr*), the form of which varies considerably from region to region and period to period. A tomb may be unmarked; marked by an upright stone slab, grand building, or even a mosque; or constructed in the form of a house. Mosques are generally built only around the tombs of major religious figures or sometimes rulers. A grand tomb or a mosque-tomb may be in a town or city, rather than in a cemetery, or a town or city quarter may grow up around it.

Visits (*ziyārāt*) to tombs and cemeteries by women are both frequent and controversial. Women may visit tombs of family members, as often happens in many countries on public holidays and festivals, especially the *ʿīd al-fiṭr* at the end of Ramadan. On these occasions, visits to living family members are also exchanged, and families of the middle and lower classes often gather at the tombs of deceased relations to eat and socialize, sometimes even spending the night there. In addition, women may participate in the general practice of visiting the tombs of members of the family of the Prophet (*ahl al-bayt*), or the "friends of God" or saints (*awliyāʾ*), or (in the case of the Shīʿa) the imams. What is specific to women in the case of the family of the Prophet and the friends of God is that certain tombs are visited especially by women, such as the tomb of Zaynab and the tomb of Nafīsa in Cairo. Both are located in major mosques, and both are tombs of women, the former being the granddaughter of the Prophet and the latter being an Arab woman known for her piety and scholarship who died in 824 CE.

It has been plausibly argued that visits to tombs have been especially important in the lives of Muslim women because the religious space of the mosque has often been closed to them. This explanation relates to one of the two reasons for visits to tombs being controversial, namely, the desire to prevent the temptation and disorder (*fitnah*) thought to attend the mixing of men and women in public spaces, which some seek to avoid by forbidding visits to tombs and cemeteries by women. The other reason why visits to tombs by women have been subject to controversy is that all varieties of visits to the tombs of the family of the Prophet and of the friends of

God, by women or by men, have been controversial, because of concern that such visits might amount to the worshipping of the tombs or their inhabitants, and thus to associating others with God (*shirk*). Those opposing visits to tombs for this reason may have exaggerated reports of the disorder and immoral behavior associated with women's presence in cemeteries.

This controversy has been ongoing, especially among Sunnī scholars, for many centuries, facilitated by the existence of a number of statements by the Prophet (*ḥadīth*) on the question. One of these clearly forbids the visiting of tombs by women, while another repeals an earlier general prohibition on the visiting of tombs by men or women, replacing it with a general encouragement of such visits. The question, then, is whether the repeal of the earlier prohibition applied to both women and men, or only to men. Scholars following the school (*madhhab*) of Aḥmad ibn Ḥanbal, and notably scholars in modern Saudi Arabia, have been especially vehement in attempting to prohibit visits to tombs by women.

BIBLIOGRAPHY

Beranek, Ondrej, and Pavel Tupek. "From Visiting Graves to Their Destruction: The Question of Ziyara through the Eyes of Salafis." Crown Center for Middle East Studies, Brandeis University, Waltham, MA, July 2009. Available at http://www.brandeis.edu/crown/publications/cp/CP2.pdf. Accessed 12 January 2013.

Diem, Werner, and Marco Schöller. *The Living and the Dead in Islam: Studies in Arabic Epitaphs*. Wiesbaden, Germany: Harrassowitz, 2004.

MARK SEDGWICK

CENTRAL ASIA AND THE CAUCASUS.

[*This entry includes two subentries:*

Kazakhstan and Kyrgyzstan *and*
Tajikistan, Turkmenistan, and Uzbekistan]

KAZAKHSTAN AND KYRGYZSTAN

The neighboring countries of Kazakhstan (population 16.9 million) and Kyrgyzstan (population 5.7 million) share a common border and have strong historical, cultural, and linguistic ties. Kazakhstan is surrounded by Russia, China, Uzbekistan, and Turkmenistan. Kyrgyzstan borders Uzbekistan, Tajikistan, and China. Islam is the dominant religion in multiethnic Kazakhstan and Kyrgyzstan. In addition to the Turkic-speaking Kazakh and Kyrgyz people, there are dozens of ethnic minorities in both countries, some of them deported during World War II. Russians (who predominantly adhere to Orthodox Christianity) constitute the largest ethnic minority in Kazakhstan, and Uzbeks make up a sizeable diaspora in Kyrgyzstan. The diverse community of Muslims in Kazakhstan and Kyrgyzstan includes the ethnic groups of Uzbeks, Tartars, Uighurs, Dungans (Hui, Chinese Muslims), and other peoples from the former Soviet Union. Both nations pursue the policy of ethnic and religious tolerance and multiculturalism.

The process of Islamization in Kazakhstan and Kyrgyzstan began in the eighth century. Muslims in both countries belong to the Hanafi *madhhab* (legal school) of Sunnī Islam. It is widely believed that Abu Nasr al-Farabi, known as the "Second Master" (after Aristotle), was born in Farab (Otrar, Kazakhstan) in 872 CE. The region is home to famous Islamic architecture such as the Uzgen mausoleums and minaret (eleventh and twelfth centuries), the mausoleum of Shah-Fazil (eleventh century) in Kyrgyzstan, and the Aisha Bibi mausoleum (eleventh and twelfth centuries) and the mausoleum of Ṣūfī mystic Khoja Ahmad al-Yasavī (fourteenth century) in Kazakhstan.

Historically, the status of women in the nomadic and seminomadic societies of Kazakhstan and Kyrgyzstan was relatively higher than in adjacent sedentary societies. Pastoral women did not cover their faces and wear the *paranja*, although covering the head with a headscarf or a head wrap was a compulsory element of traditional clothing of married women. Kazakh and Kyrgyz women frequently participated in public discussions, and some of them were accepted as rulers or military leaders. For example, after the death of her husband Alymbek-datka, Kurmanjan-datka (1811–1907) was recognized as a leader of south Kyrgyzstan (Alay Queen) by the khans of Bukhara and Khoqand and, later, the Russian tsarist administration. The Kyrgyz epic heroine Janyl Myrza, a young woman often compared to Joan of Arc, led her troops to liberate the homeland.

The Russian Empire colonized the Kazakh and Kyrgyz peoples in the eighteenth and nineteenth centuries. The tsarist administration refrained from challenging the Muslim identity of the Kazakh and Kyrgyz peoples. During the Soviet era (1917–1991), the Communist Party pursued a policy of aggressive state atheism and rapid female emancipation as a part of the de-Islamization of Central Asia. Under state atheism, a number of mosques and churches were demolished and religious leaders were harassed and executed. To facilitate control over Muslims, the Kremlin established the Spiritual Administration of Muslims of Central Asia and Kazakhstan in Tashkent (Uzbekistan) in 1943, which supervised the official institutions for almost fifty years. Muslims were discouraged from learning and using Arabic; instead, Russian was imposed as the *lingua franca* in all Soviet republics. Despite the Communist policy of creating a new community of Soviet people, intermarriages between Muslims and non-Muslims remained rare.

In the process of the forced and unforced emancipation of women, Communist decision-makers encouraged education for women and their participation in public life. Soviet laws granted women the right to vote and provided special medical and workplace protection. The Communist authorities motivated women to work outside the home and offered financial assistance, such as maternity leave, childcare allowance, low-cost kindergarten, to support motherhood. By the end of Soviet rule, women constituted roughly half of the labor force. However, women have been considered as passive beneficiaries of Communist policy in building a new Soviet community and family.

During World War II, women, together with men, fought against Nazi Germany on the front lines. The Soviet government posthumously granted the title Hero of the Soviet Union (the highest award of the state) to two Kazakh women: machine-gunner Manshuk Mametova (1922–1943) and sniper Alia Moldagulova (1925–1944). A number of talented female artists became famous in the Soviet Union and the Central Asian region. Among them were the national artists of the USSR: a Kyrgyz ballerina, Bibisara Beishenalieva (1926–1973), and a Kazakh singer, Roza Rymbaeva (born in 1957).

Mikhail Gorbachev's *glasnost* (openness) policy in the mid-1980s, and the fall of the Soviet Union in 1991, brought significant changes in both countries. It was a turning point away from the policies of state atheism and restriction of religious freedom. Men and women freely expressed their cultural, ethnic, and religious identities. Most people from traditionally Muslim ethnic groups identify themselves as Muslims, despite seventy years of the ruthless policy of de-Islamization. The role of religion has remarkably increased. Almost every community has built or restored its own place of worship. Thousands of mosques have been erected since 1991.

Numerous foreign missionaries poured in to facilitate the conversion of post-Soviet citizens to Islam, Christianity, and other religions. The funding for new mosques came from generous donations from foreign countries, organizations, and private sponsors. The restoration of a traditional gender-discriminative interpretation of the Qur'ān and ethnic traditions by some local leaders inspired a part of the population to draw closer to other non-Muslim denominations. A number of women and men from originally Muslim families have converted to Protestantism and other denominations and faiths. This trend has led to some tension between new non-Muslim converts and Muslims.

Ideas central to political Islam spread in some peripheral areas where clandestine cells effectively substituted for political parties. The pan-Islamic movement, Hizbut-Tahrir (Party of Liberation) claims to express the interests of all Muslims regardless of their national identity and to educate post-Soviet Muslims. The group's anti-government agenda and criticism of corruption and inequality have been supported by some people, especially in areas where the influence of political parties remains weak.

Islamic beliefs in Kazakhstan and Kyrgyzstan include sustainable elements of pre-Islamic religions, such as ancestor worship and Tengriism, the ancient beliefs of the Turks and Mongols. The veneration of numerous holy places (mazars), including Islamic tombs and objects of nature (stones, trees, caves, springs, waterfalls, etc.) has continued to rise since the end of state atheism. Traditional pilgrimages to holy shrines remain popular partly because of the de-Sovietization process, restoration of religious and cultural identity, and decline of public health care.

In both countries, the erosion of the social safety net and health care has negatively affected women and children, especially in the countryside. Kazakhstan, the most economically developed of the Central Asian countries, has considerable carbon-mineral resources and foreign private investments. Compared to oil- and gas-rich Kazakhstan, Kyrgyzstan faces more economic challenges related to social and political security, poverty, and, as a result, significant outmigration of men and women. Hundreds of thousands of Kyrgyzstani guest workers have migrated to Russia and Kazakhstan to support their families.

According to post-Soviet laws, women and men have roughly equal rights. However, in practice, gender discrimination is thriving. The rule of customary law has been steadily strengthening in various communities since the collapse of Soviet law and Communist party control of everyday life. A flipside of the market economy is increasing gender inequality, as customary law welcomes inheritance of land and other assets by male relatives. The rights of women and children in polygamous families and unregistered marriages are not protected by post-Soviet legislation. Economic hardship, social inequalities, and traditional patriarchal beliefs reinforce gender-discriminatory practices such as underage marriage, polygamy, bride kidnapping, prostitution, trafficking, and gender segregation. Multiple marriages reemerged as a sign of social and economic status for men in the post-Soviet societies. A weakening of the status of women contributed to the spread, in various forms, of gender-based violence and harassment.

Rigid traditions of age and gender discrimination complicate liberalization of women in the transitional societies. In Kazakhstan and Kyrgyzstan, some families still accept bride kidnapping as the customary practice. In the pre-Soviet societies a strong social hierarchy encouraged disapproval of bride kidnapping, and later, under Soviet rule, the practice was also discouraged. The Soviet egalitarian ideology gradually eradicated a system of social ranking in traditional society that might have had an impact on an increasing number of nonconsensual kidnappings of young women when Moscow's rule ended.

Despite the numerous challenges people faced after the demise of the command economy and social protection system, many women and men found ways to survive and prosper. A number of them opened new businesses and integrated into the market economy. In post-independence Kazakhstan and Kyrgyzstan, both women and men have high levels of literacy and enjoy a relatively high Internet usage, compared to other Central Asian states. Hundreds of non-governmental organizations (NGOs) and movements in both countries promote women's rights, human rights, social justice, and participatory democracy. Numerous women play an increasingly important role in public life as active agents of political and social change. NGOs supported by the international donor community and, to a certain extent, by national governments advocate empowerment of women and sensitize the public at large to problems of gender inequality and discrimination. Both countries significantly strengthen national mechanisms for the advancement of women and strategies for gender equality. The Eastern Europe and Central Asia Sub-Regional Office of UN Women CIS (is located in Almaty (Kazakhstan).

Contemporary Kyrgyzstan and Kazakhstan are regarded as more liberal states in Central Asia when compared to their neighboring countries. Kyrgyzstan liberalized its economy faster than other neighboring states and emerged, in 1998, as the first country in Central Asia and the CIS to join the World Trade Organization. In 2010, Kazakhstan became the first Central Asian and CIS country to chair the Organization for Security and Co-operation in Europe (OSCE). Yet, succession mechanisms have not been established in the latter: Kazakhstan has been ruled by a single leader, Nursultan Nazarbayev for over two decades, whereas in Kyrgyzstan, united opposition forces ousted the first two unpopular presidents, in 2005 and 2010. As a result of political upheavals in Kyrgyzstan, an opposing politician, Roza Otunbaeva (b. 1950), was chosen as an interim head of state in 2010 and became the first female president elected in Central Asia and CIS. Under her rule, a precedent of a peaceful and constitutional transfer of executive power in Central Asia has been established.

Strategically located between Russia and China, Kazakhstan and Kyrgyzstan are part of Eurasian security organizations: the Russia-centered CIS Collective Security Treaty Organization (CSTO), and the China-centered Shanghai Cooperation Organization (SCO). The latter includes other Central Asian and Eurasian states: Uzbekistan, Tajikistan, Russia, and China. Kyrgyzstan hosts Russian and U.S. military airbases, which are located around the capital Bishkek. The Transit Center at Manas (the U.S. airbase) in Kyrgyzstan has served as a logistical hub for the international effort in Afghanistan.

BIBLIOGRAPHY

Kandiyoti, Deniz. "The Politics of Gender and the Soviet Paradox: Neither Colonized, nor Modern?" *Central Asian Survey* 26.4 (2007): 601–623.

Olcott, Martha Brill. "Women and Society in Central Asia." In *Soviet Central Asia: The Failed Transformation*, edited by William Fierman, pp. 235–254. Boulder, Colo.: Westview Press, 1991.

Tabyshalieva, Anara. "Revival of Traditions in Post-Soviet Central Asia." In *Making the Transition Work for Women in Europe and Central Asia*, edited by Marnia Lazreg, pp. 51–57. Washington, D.C.: World Bank, 2000.

Tabyshalieva, Anara. "Women of Central Asia and the Fertility Cult." *Anthropology and Archeology of Eurasia* 36.2 (1997): 45–62.

Anara Tabyshalieva

Tajikistan, Turkmenistan, and Uzbekistan

Tajikistan, Turkmenistan, and Uzbekistan were delineated as republics within the Soviet Union in 1924, and became independent in 1991. Politically, these areas were largely under the rule of the Bukhara Emirate in the early modern period, and then were conquered by the Russian Empire in the late nineteenth century. These Central Asian lands are ethnically diverse. Traditionally, Turkmens and a minority of Uzbeks were nomadic or seminomadic herders, while Tajiks and a majority of Uzbeks were sedentary farmers or urban merchants and artisans.

Women's livelihoods and opportunities varied accordingly. Turkmen women often earned money through carpet-weaving; carpets, sold under the name "Turkmen" or "Bukhara," became a national symbol and an important export. Uzbek and Tajik women traditionally contributed to the household economy, and often produced embroidered work for sale, such as gold-thread embroidery (*zarduzi*) and wall hangings (*suzani*). From the early modern period, some women earned fame as wives of rulers, or as poets. The poet Nodira Begim (d. 1842), wife of Umar Khan, ruled the Kokand khanate as regent for her son Madali Khan in the 1820s.

Following the Russian conquest, many changes came to Central Asian societies. Railroads helped to establish cotton as the most important crop, which in turn promoted expansion of canals and irrigated lands, growth of cities, sedentarization of nomads, and an influx of Russians and other non-Central Asians. Central Asian reformers, known as *jadīds*, responded to the changes brought by Russian rule by drawing on modernist movements from Egypt, the Ottoman Empire, and Russia. The *jadīds* began publishing newspapers that called for embracing new forms of education, and for expanding girls' education, arguing that modern education would enable girls to become educated mothers, which was necessary to national revival—an argument similar to that of reformers in the Arab world during the same period. In the early twentieth century, a Central Asian girl who lived in a city might gain a traditional Islamic education from a woman teacher (*otin*); she might attend a *jadīd* school for girls, or, rarely, she might attend a Russian school. In rural areas, traditional Islamic education was the only possibility; women's literacy rates were far lower than men's rates.

The Bolshevik Revolution (October 1917) brought Communist rule to Central Asia. The Communist Party forcefully transformed Central Asian economies, societies, and cultures by introducing new laws, nationalizing land and industries, and carrying out campaigns against Islam and Central Asian customs and traditions. Each of the newly formed republics—Tajikistan, Turkmenistan, and Uzbekistan—led by its Communist Party, enacted laws that raised the minimum age of marriage for girls to sixteen and for boys to eighteen; forbade, or at least gave no legal recognition to, polygynous marriages; stated women's right to vote and to be elected to office; and established equality before the law for women and men. The Communist Party's stance on women's issues was complicated by conflicting ideologies and commitments: Russia's Communists opposed feminism, which they viewed as a bourgeois women's movement obsessed with suffrage. Bolshevik Communists argued that women's rights should not be addressed separately; they should develop with the rights of the working class. However, Communist women activists regarded women's issues as demanding specific attention.

Through its Women's Division, the Party focused on changing women's opportunities and bringing women into active participation in socialist society. The Communist Party sent activists from Russia and other republics of the Soviet Union to Turkmenistan, Uzbekistan, and Tajikistan; these activists tried to educate Central Asian women about Soviet laws. Throughout the three republics, the Women's Division sought to recruit women of Central Asian nationalities to become activists. This effort was most successful in Uzbekistan, where women who had attended *jadīd* schools, like the Uzbek educator Robiya Nosirova, became involved with the Women's Division. In Turkmenistan and Tajikistan, the Women's Division was dominated by outsiders, and the agenda for all of Central Asia was set by the Party's Central Asia Bureau Women's Division leader, the dynamic Russian activist Serafima Liubimova.

The Party promoted its version of women's emancipation not only by encouraging women to attend schools, participate in Women's Division activities, and work outside the home, but also by pressuring men to accept changing roles for women. In 1927, the Party launched the *hujum* (attack) campaign. In Uzbekistan and Tajikistan, the campaign focused on convincing women to unveil, and forcing men to make women unveil. Many men rejected these changes violently, attacking and, in some cases, murdering unveiled women. In Turkmenistan, Party attempts at changing Turkmen gender relations focused on criminalizing the payment of bride wealth and promoting women's right to initiate divorce. Many Turkmens found ways to continue bride wealth payment in new forms, and argued that Turkmen women, who did not veil in public, were already men's equals. Eventually, Party attention shifted away from the *hujum*, but legal changes and state efforts to bring women into the paid workforce changed daily life measurably.

From the 1930s through the 1980s, women's rates of literacy and higher education rose rapidly in Uzbekistan, Tajikistan, and Turkmenistan, although in all three republics, Central Asian families tended to encourage higher education for sons much more than for daughters. Women's rate of participation in the paid labor force also rose rapidly: socialist agriculture programs on collective farms pressured women to join in farm labor. In cities and towns, some women went to work in factories, usually in light industry, and many became teachers, office workers, and professionals. While women's rates of official, paid labor participation were lower in the Central Asian Soviet Socialist Republics than in Russia, they were much higher than in Western Europe or in the Middle East. Central Asian women participated in the Communist Party at much lower rates than men, but some reached high levels of political influence, such as Yadgar Nasriddinova, who became president of the Supreme Soviet of Uzbekistan. The Communist Party was the only political party, and the Party shaped discourse and action concerning women's issues. In its final decades, the Soviet Union presented Central Asian Muslim women's accomplishments as examples in its Middle Eastern and Third World diplomacy.

The Soviet system repressed religious practice and gave no role to Islamic law. Central Asian families continued to carry out prayers, and to teach children about Islam and about their religious and cultural traditions. Islam and tradition continued to shape the ways that Central Asians thought about, and practiced, gender relations. Men continue to be seen as head of the family; women's chastity remains a cornerstone of gender relations; polygyny is accepted in practice, although it is not legally recognized; and parents are heavily involved in arranging marriages for their children, who are expected to start married life in a patrilocal household. Turkmen customs forbidding daughters-in-law to speak to fathers-in-law remain strong, as do Tajik traditions of cousin marriage.

With the collapse of the Soviet Union in 1991, Tajikistan, Turkmenistan, and Uzbekistan became independent republics. Communists no longer monopolized politics; instead, while the socialist economy crumbled, international Islamist trends, neoliberal economic policies, and non-governmental organizations (NGOs) proposed new possibilities for women.

Turkmenistan maintained much of its socialist framework, and a centralized dictatorship continues to control politics and to prevent citizens' self-organization. The Turkmen government signed the United Nations Convention on the Elimination of All Forms of Discrimination against Women (CEDAW), but there is no independent reporting concerning women's rights in independent Turkmenistan. The state, which has grown rich on gas export revenues, officially follows the teachings of its late president, Saparmurat Niyazov, on gender: a Turkmen man should be the leader of his family, and a Turkmen woman should wear a long Turkmen dress and be chaste, should not cover her face, and should participate actively in society

Following independence, Tajikistan experienced civil war (1992–1997), which exacerbated the decay of the country's post-socialist economic system, and created refugees and harmed the educational opportunities of a generation. The government of Tajikistan includes ex-communists and Islamists, and it permits some diversity of political thought. Women's NGOs emerged to advocate for women's economic opportunities, to address domestic violence, and to spread new Islamist thought among women. The state officially supports women's legal equality with men, but also has passed laws forbidding women to attend prayers in mosques, claiming that Muslim women should pray at home (see Turajonzoda, 2011, pp. 201–204, for details). Extremely high levels of male labor migration, coupled with a low rate of women's higher education, pose difficulties for women's livelihoods and their empowerment, though both Tajikistan and Uzbekistan have made efforts to strengthen rural girls' access to higher education.

Uzbekistan's government, dominated by its president, Islam Karimov, allowed NGOs to exist until 2005, when most were shut down, and the government of Uzbekistan represses Islamist movements. Women NGO activists in Uzbekistan, such as Marfua Tokhtakhodjaeva, focused on empowering women and combating de facto discrimination. As in Tajikistan, new modes of piety emerged, and many women symbolized their commitment to Islam by adopting styles of veiling that reflect international trends—a tendency that the government suppresses by denying veiled women admission to state-supported higher education. As with Turkmenistan, a dearth of independent reporting and the relative absence of citizens' self-organization means that Uzbekistan's official compliance with CEDAW benchmarks has to be viewed with skepticism.

Women in Tajikistan see their opportunities limited more by poverty than by politics, while women in Uzbekistan and Turkmenistan face political obstacles that deter the development of women's organizations, independent voices, and social movements.

BIBLIOGRAPHY

Aminova, Rakhima. *The October Revolution and Women's Liberation in Uzbekistan*. Translated by B. M. Meierovitch. Moscow, Russia: Nauka Publishing House, 1977.

Edgar, Adrienne Lynn. *Tribal Nation: The Making of Soviet Turkmenistan*. Princeton, N.J.: Princeton University Press, 2004.

Kamp, Marianne. *The New Woman in Uzbekistan: Islam, Modernity, and Unveiling under Communism*. Seattle: University of Washington Press, 2006.

Massell, Gregory J. *The Surrogate Proletariat: Moslem Women and Revolutionary Strategies in Soviet Central Asia, 191–1929*. Princeton, N.J.: Princeton University Press, 1974.

Nabieva, Rohat. *Zhenshchiny Tadzhikistana v bor'bezasotsializm* [Women of Tajikistan in the Struggle for Socialism]. Dushanbe, Tajikistan: Izdatel'stvo Irfon, 1973.

Niyazov, Saparmurat. *Rukhnama* [The Book of the Soul]. Official translation.

Pal'vanova, Bibi. *Emantsipatsiia Musul'manki: opyt raskreposhcheniia zhenshchiny sovetskogo vostoka*

[Emancipation of the Muslim Woman: The Experience of Liberation of the Woman of the Soviet East]. Moscow, Russia: Izdatel'stvo Nauka, 1982.

Tokhtakhodjaeva, Marfua. *Between the Slogans of Communism and the Laws of Islam*. Translated by Sufian Aslan. Lahore, Pakistan: Shirkat Gah Women's Resource Center, 1994.

Turajonzoda, Hoji Akbar. *Joygohi zan dar Islom* [The Place of Woman in Islam]. Dushanbe, Tajikistan: Shujoiyon, 2011.

Marianne R. Kamp

Central Asian Literatures. Nomadic culture among certain Turkic tribes is credited with providing higher status, self-expression, and freedom for women. The nomadic economy was dependent on women's participation in the workforce through animal husbandry, carpet weaving, etc. In general the nomadic groups are viewed as less Islamized than the sedentary communities in Central Asia; however it should be noted that nomads much more easily adopted Islam and meshed it with their customs and traditions. Therefore many practices attributed to Islam in Central Asia can be traced back to the pre-Islamic culture of Central Asian societies.

Central Asian Islam is typically characterized by Sufism. In this context Muslim women mostly acted within the Ṣūfi sisterhood networks. *Otines*, Central Asian Muslim women teachers, played a major role as transmitters of religious knowledge to youth. Muslim women were also actively involved in organizing Islamic social activities, such as *mawlud* (a set of rituals that celebrates the birth of Prophet Muḥammad), for every major occasion and rite of passage, such as birth or death.

In the late nineteenth and early twentieth century the discussion of women and Islam in Central Asia was mostly an outcome of the debate between the *Jadīd* (Muslim reformers) and the traditional *ʿulamāʾ* (scholars). *Jadīdī* were a rising reform-minded young generation of Turkic intellectuals in the Russian Empire, who centered their activities on reforming the traditional Islamic educational institutions and publication of newspapers and journals, as well as new textbooks, in the vernacular. Regarding Muslim women, leading *jadīd* intellectuals, such as Ismail Bey Gasprinskii (Ismail Gaspıralï), argued for the education of women, more public visibility for them, and recognizing their equal rights with an emphasis on reinterpretation of the original sources of Islam. These arguments indirectly reflected the Muslim intellectuals' encounter with western modes of progress either in the Ottoman, Russian, or Western European context, but were mostly engrained in a deeply Islamic methodology of *ijtihād*. The *jadīdī* provided a discursive avenue for reforming the Muslim Central Asian societies and steadily gained popular support, which enabled them to expand and diversify their resources and fields of activism. *Jadīdī* reformist discourse was reflected in practice through schools for girls, publications for women (*Alem-i-Nisvan* (Bakhchesarai, 1906–1910), *Suyum Bike* (Kazan, 1913–1917), *Ishiq* (Baku, 1911–1912), and articles and books published by Muslim women (major authors include Shefika Hanim [Ismail Gasprinskii's daughter], Sona Akhundova, Mehbüpcemal Akçurina, and Khadija Alibeyova). Although under Soviet rule this reformist movement soon faded away, its argument for women's liberation became a precursor for certain Soviet policies of education and equality of women, and their participation in the workforce.

The Soviet regime paid special attention to the status of Muslim women in Central Asia. Traditions based on Islam were viewed as the source of oppression, subordination, and inequality of women. On the other hand, in the eyes of the Bolsheviks, the liberation of women was one of the indispensable tenets of the Marxist ideology. This obviously led to conflict between local practices and the ideals of Bolshevik rule in Central Asia. Soviets viewed liberation of women as a way to transform Central Asian society into a socialist one. They viewed women as an alternate to the proletariat, which did not exist in Central Asia. However, the *hujum* (assault) in Central Asia, specifically in Uzbekistan, led by the Central Asian Bureau of the Communist Party and the Women's Branch, *Zhenotdel*, to unveil Muslim women gave way to a strengthening of local reaction against the socialist campaign for women's liberation. Religious traditions and local practices acquired an additional dimension of national and religious identity as instruments of passive resistance. Thus many religious practices were preserved through the Soviet regime not as a result of strong dedication to religion, but as traditional national markers of identity.

The Soviet rule of Central Asia is often depicted as one of a colonizing empire. At the same time it is viewed as a means of introducing modern Western values into Central Asia through the Russian model. The Soviet system had its limits in terms of women's liberation. Although the modernization perspective and the Bolshevik propaganda practices treated Muslim women as the prime target for social revolution, the Soviet system prioritized certain kinds of professions as more suitable to women as mothers. Thus there was an extensive emphasis on women as nurses and teachers. Rearing children was also valued and publicly praised. The Soviets provided extensive opportunities and support for childcare. These practices gave way to high birthing rates and participation in the workforce simultaneously among Muslim women. High rates of education played a crucial role in enabling Central Asian women to participate in the workforce, both in rural and urban settings. As explained by authors such as Gail W. Lapidus and Thomas G. Schrand, by rearing more children and actively participating in the Soviet workforce, Central Asian women too faced the double burden parallel to women in the West, specifically the United States.

In post-Soviet Central Asia women's role was presented in the context of nation-state building. Each one of the Central Asian republics conducted the writing of a unique national history and a return to traditional national values, which most of the time implicated a reaction against the Russian, especially Soviet, imposition of foreign cultural values. Despite the implications of such a return to traditional values and the emergence of various Islamic movements, some of which emphasized a more conservative vision for women, the post-Soviet leaders of Central Asia, although at varying degrees, adopted an assertive secular model in which the state actively reduced religious practice to the private sphere. Although the new national leaders were mostly secular, a return back to the traditional patriarchal structure and at times the revival of tribal identity were visible. While patriarchy was viewed as the natural course of events after a break by the Russian/Soviet, unnatural, a search for national identity in the pre-Soviet times also gave way to a realization and reexploration of *jadīdī* and rearticulation of a progressive discourse within the Islamic, traditional, and national framework.

Post-Soviet Central Asia also witnessed an influx of Western influence through economic and political interactions. While this engagement opened up space for women's rights organizations devised in the Western liberal model, it also caused a backlash by the supporters of the new nation-state building process on the basis of national values and traditions. Islam has also been utilized as a discursive tool by various movements and organizations, foreign or domestic, to support arguments ranging from defending women's rights to reviving traditional patriarchal mores. Leading women literary figures in contemporary Central Asian republics include Umit Tazhikenova, Svetlana Nazarova, and Liliya Kalaus of Kazakhstan; Mehriban Vezir, Afag Masud, and Sara Nazirova of Azerbaijan; Sona Yazova and Gözel Şaguliyeva of Turkmenistan; Zulfiya Isroilova, Oydin Hojiyeva, and Halima Hudoybardieva of Uzbekistan; Inoyat Hojieva and Golrokhsar Safi of Tajikistan; and Fatima Abdalova of Kyrgyzstan.

BIBLIOGRAPHY

Kamp, Marianne. *The New Woman in Uzbekistan: Islam, Modernity, and Unveiling Under Communism*. Seattle: University of Washington Press, 2006.

Kandiyoti, Deniz. "The Politics of Gender or the Soviet Paradox: Neither Colonized, nor Modern?" *Central Asian Survey* 26, no. 4 (December 2007): 601–623. Includes a comprehensive literature review of women in Soviet Central Asia.

Khalid, Adeeb. *The Politics of Muslim Cultural Reform: Jadidism in Central Asia*. Berkeley: University of California Press, 1998. An excellent in-depth study of Jadid movement also addressing its approach on women.

Northrop, Douglas Taylor. *Veiled Empire: Gender & Power in Stalinist Central Asia*. Ithaca, N.Y.: Cornell University Press, 2004.

Mustafa Gökçek

Ceramics, Women's Representation in.

Glazed ceramics and tiles produced in the Islamic lands are distinguished by their rich decoration. Much of it is vegetal, geometric, or epigraphic; some is figural, and a small part of that represents women. Distinguishing characteristics such as beard, mustache, and turban identify men, but traits such as long hair, earrings, and robes were not exclusive to women, who are often identified only by the lack of male features. Many figures are androgynous and may represent youths or simply generic "people" of indeterminate sex. Such ambiguity was probably intentional, as second- and third-person pronouns in Persian do not distinguish gender, and the "beloved" can be male or female.

A few women are depicted on lusterwares made during the period of Fatimid rule in Egypt (969–1171). A good example is a large dish in the Freer Gallery of Art (46.30) that shows a figure with bent knees, long scarves, and swinging arms who is flanked by two large jars. She is thought to represent a dancing girl.

Figural decoration in general, and of women in particular, is much more prevalent in the arts produced in Iran, undoubtedly because of the strong figural tradition that has existed there since pre-Islamic times. Women are depicted occasionally on slipwares made in eastern Iran in the ninth and tenth centuries. The finest is a unique fragment of a bowl, reportedly from Maimana in Afghanistan, that shows a figure seated on a platform throne, playing a lute, and flanked by a ewer (Dar al-Athar al-Islamiyya, Kuwait, LNS 791C). The extra-long tresses and hennaed hands lend weight to the identification of the musician as female.

Figural depiction proliferated on ceramics made in Iran from the late twelfth century, especially with the development of new techniques such as underglaze painting and overglaze luster and enameling (Persian *mīnaʾī*) that allowed more painterly decoration. Women are depicted on these medieval Iranian ceramics in several roles. Some figures come from narratives. The most famous is Bahrām Gūr's slave girl, known in Firdawsī's *Shāhnāmah* as Āzāda ("Freedom") and in Niẓāmī's *Khamsa* as Fitna ("Sedition"), who is shown holding her lute, seated behind the king on a camel, and sometimes being trampled beneath it as well (e.g., two enameled bowls in the Metropolitan Museum of Art, 57.36.2 and 57.36.13; and luster tiles such as V&A 1841–1876, probably from the Mongol palace at Takht-i Sulaymān). Other scenes, such as the veiled woman in a howdah on elephant-back on a footed bowl, part of a hoard found in Gurgān in eastern Iran (Museum of Islamic Art, Doha, PO285), may be part of a narrative that we so far fail to recognize.

A second role for women on medieval Iranian ceramics is as one figure of a princely couple. Often the couple is shown together seated next to one another on the same bowl, as on an enameled example in the Freer Gallery (38.12) or a luster one made by the potter Abu Zayd in 1204 (David Collection, Copenhagen, 2001). Sometimes, the couple is shown individually, presumably as part of a set, as on a rare surviving example of matched underglaze-painted bowls in the Freer Gallery (67.24 and 67.25).

Women are commonly depicted again on ceramics made during the period of Ṣafavid rule (1501–1722). They are often seen on the polychrome tile ensembles made in the *cuerda seca* (Pers. *haft-rang*, "seven color") technique to decorate mansions in Shah ʿAbbās's new capital at Isfahan (e.g., Metropolitan Museum 03.9a and 03.9c; V&A 139:1 to 4-1891). Typically shown against a yellow ground sniffing a flower or in a garden setting, sometimes with foreigners, these women may represent courtesans. Similar women are found on both vessels (e.g., Metropolitan Museum 14.40-733 and 17.120.56) and tiles (British Museum OA+.10819, OA+.10824, and 1895,0603.123) made in the provincial "Kubachi" style, named for the village in the Caucasus where many were found.

Many of these types were revived in the nineteenth century under Qājār rule. The scenes on some tiles may represent episodes from romantic literature such as the story of the lovers Khusraw and Shīrīn, but others are more generic, as on a tile (V&A 230-1887) that depicts a group of men and women dressed in late Ṣafavid costume, with Armenian churches in the background. Women also appear on a few vessels in overglaze enamel that copy contemporary Chinese export wares of the *famille-rose* style, such as a bowl made by ʿAlī Akbar Shīrāzī in 1846 (V&A 632-1878), with scenes of Persian men and women framed in a pastoral landscape.

Bibliography

Porter, Venetia. *Islamic Tiles*. London: British Museum, 1995.

Watson, Oliver. *Ceramics from Islamic Lands*. London: Thames & Hudson, 2004.

Sheila S. Blair

Cerić, Mustapha. Mustafa Cerić (b. 1952, Visoko) is *rais al-ulama* (or the head of the Islamic Community) of Bosnia and Herzegovina, which is a title often translated into English as "Grand Mufti." After graduation from Gazi Husrev-bey's madrasa in Sarajevo, Mustafa Cerić spent several years studying at the University of al-Azhar in Cairo. In 1981, he was appointed Imam at the Islamic Cultural Center of Greater Chicago (ICC) in Northbrook, Illinois. (The members of one local Islamic community here are of Bosnian descent.) In 1986, he completed his Ph.D. in Islamic Studies at the University of Chicago, with a doctoral thesis titled, *A Study of the Theology of Abu Mansur Al-Maturidi*, under the advisorship of professor Fazlur Rahman. He also lectured at the American Islamic College in Chicago. However, in 1987, he was appointed as Imam of the Islamic Centre in Zagreb, Republic of Croatia. He held this position until 1991, when he became a visiting professor at the Institute for Islamic Thought and Civilization (ISTAC) in Kuala Lumpur, Malaysia. He held this post until the spring of 1993, when he was appointed as *naib al-rais al-ulama* (deputy-chief of the Islamic community) in war time Bosnia and Herzegovina. In 1998, he was reappointed as the *rais al-ulama* of Bosnia-Herzegovina, a post he still holds as of this writing.

Cerić has published several books and numerous articles, including *Roots of Synthetic Theology in Islam: A Study of the Theology of Abu Mansur Al-Maturidi (d. 944)* and *Vjera, narod, jdomovina* (Faith, people, homeland).

Since the 1990s, Cerić has become a prominent public figure and has won several international awards, including UNESCO's Felix Houphouet Boigny peace prize. In the earlier part of his career (before his appointment as *naib al-rais*), he wrote articles on the issues of prenatal medicine, abortion, human life, and the rights of the unborn child. Since the 1990s, he has addressed the themes of religious rights, secularism and faith, education (with the accent on religious education), politics and its relationship to religion, religious identity in the modern world, multiculturalism and plurality, as well as the relationship between the West and the Islamic world.

Despite receiving international acclaim, Cerić has not escaped criticism during his tenure as *rais al-ulama*. First, he acted during difficult war times, when, according to the International Criminal Tribunal for the former Yugoslavia (ICTY) verdict, a genocide against Muslims was committed. Second, his numerous critics in Bosnia and Herzegovina and abroad claim that, as a religious leader, he did not abstain from entering into political matters because he attempted to take part in political arbitration in Bosnia and Herzegovina. Third, there are others who have alleged that he committed himself more to the "foreign policy" of the Islamic community with his journeys abroad, and paid less attention to the internal advancement of the Islamic community in Bosnia and Herzegovina.

Despite these criticisms, Cerić has left controversial trace in his actions and influence on religious life in Bosnia and Herzegovina, and he has continued to assert his voice in calling for tolerance, peaceful coexistence, and interreligious cooperation.

BIBLIOGRAPHY

Cerić, Mustafa. *Vjera, narod i domovina: hutbe, govori i intervjui*. Udruženje ilmijje Islamske zajednice, Sarajevo, 2002.

DeLong-Bas, Natana J. "Mustafa Ceric," in *Notable Muslims: Muslim Builders of World Civilization and Culture*. Oxford: OneWorld Publications, 2006.

Islamic Community in Bosnia and Herzegovina, official Web page. http://www.rijaset.ba/index.php?option=com_content&task=view&id=67

Moe, Christian. "A Sultan in Brussels? European Hopes and Fears of Bosnian Muslims." *Südosteuropa*, 55:4 (2007): 374–394

Dženita Karić

Chastity (*ʿIffa*). *ʿIffa* in the Arabic language means to abstain from what is forbidden and sinful desires or shameful acts. Two forms of its root are mentioned in the Qurʾān: *yastaʿfif* in 18:33 and 18:60 relates to guarding one's chastity and checking oneself against temptations if the person (male or female) cannot marry lawfully. In another context, *yastaʿfif* in Qurʾān 4:6 and *taʿaffuf* in 2:273 relate to exercising self-discipline toward worldly pleasures. In Ṣūfism, *ʿiffa* means disciplining the power of lust through reason and *sharʿ* (divine law). In social contexts, *ʿiffa* is a virtue that entails restraining the self from worldly desires by seeking moderation (neither overindulgence nor deficiency). In this way, the human being avoids being enslaved by his or her desires.

Although Islamic textual sources address the chastity and modesty of men and women equally, social practices differ considerably in this regard. There is more emphasis on the chastity of women as reflected in the socialization process by which girls are raised, taught appropriate behaviors, and scolded for immodest acts. In tribal or rural communities across the Muslim world, chastity of women is directly related to the honor of their families, which in turn govern social relations in kinship-based communities. According to some anthropologists, the social role of maintaining ideal chaste behavior for women is a way of preserving patrilineal kin groups, as well as patriarchal control, which propagate gender hierarchies. For example, "honor killings" are still practiced in some cultural contexts whereby a woman is killed by a male family member if she engaged in or is even suspected of illicit sexual behavior. Honor killings disseminate the idea that women solely carry the burden of protecting men's honor or bringing disgrace to their families. Despite the fact that Islamic law is adamant about the equal *ḥadd* (punishment) imposed on men and woman if proven guilty of *zinah* (illicit sexual behavior), social customs mostly result in women being accused of the offense, while disregarding the man's role.

With the Islamic revival witnessed in the last decades of the twentieth century, women's chastity assumed religious, rather than cultural, meanings. Chastity and upholding modest behavior is deemed a religious virtue and essential for a woman to be close to God. Women strive to uphold modest behavior and take on the veil as a reflection of their piety and chastity. Thus, instead of being associated with family honor and preserving social customs, chastity became a personal endeavor undertaken by religious and pious women.

The visible form of upholding women's chastity, such as veiling, has been appropriated or exploited by political actors in modern nation-states in the Muslim world. In order to legitimize a political order, some political movements have used women's veiling as a symbol of its Islamic authenticity and the preservation of moral values. In some cases, such as under the Taliban regime in Afghanistan, women have been subjected to cruel treatment and oppression under the cover of religion. In other cases, women's chastity and veiling became a symbol of resistance against Western capitalist penetration and exploitation. The Iranian intellectual ʿAlī Sharīʿatī criticized the sexual exploitation of women in Western consumerism, thereby warning women against becoming a weak link in capitalist infiltration.

BIBLIOGRAPHY

Badawi, El Said, and Muhammad Abdel Haleem. *Arabic-English Dictionary of Qur'anic Usage*. Leiden, Netherlands, and Boston: Brill, 2008.

Jihāmī, Jīrār, and Samīḥ Daghīm. *Al-Mawsūʿa al-Jāmiʿa li-Muṣṭalaḥāt al-Fikr al-ʾArabī wal-ʿIslāmī*. Vol. 16. Beirut: Maktabat Lubnān Nāshirūn, 2006.

Joseph, Suad, Afsaneh Najmabadi, et al., eds. *Encyclopedia of Women and Islamic Cultures*. Vols. 2 and 3. Leiden, Netherlands: Brill, 2007.

Nadvi, Mohammad Zafeeruddin. *Modesty and Chastity in Islam*. Translated by Sharif Ahmad Khan. Kuwait: Islamic Book Publishers, 1982.

KATRIN JOMAA

CHECHNYA. Because of Chechnya's geographical isolation and largely mountainous topography, many secular and religious features of Chechen society differ from those of other areas of the Islamic world—as well as from those of the republic's immediate ethnic neighbors (notably the Ingush, who are both closest physically to Chechnya and have at times been under the same administration). This observation applies to both longer-term historical factors and to the situation of Chechnya in the years following the collapse of the Soviet Union in the 1990s—an era characterized by almost constant political violence.

Several dividing lines in history have inevitably worked important influences on the lives of Chechen women and traditional patterns in their relations with Chechen men. Such turning points came in stages during the nineteenth century, as czarist Russia expanded its control into the northern Caucasus between 1817 and 1864. Although reliable sources for generalists studying

Chechen society in this earlier period are sparse, at least two historical trends affecting the status of Chechen women would come forward into contemporary times: regional resistance to Russian domination reflected in anti-Russian (i.e., "nationalist") and Islamic religious dimensions.

An important historical landmark and symbol suggesting linkages between these two trends was the major rebellion led by Naqshabandi Imam Shamil, which spanned several decades ending in 1859. Although Imam Shamil's attempts to use Ṣūfi Islam as means to unite broad areas of the Caucasus (not just Chechnya) against Russia were unsuccessful, the combined effect of widespread armed mobilization of his male supporters (bringing inevitable destabilization of family organization) and increased emphasis on necessary defense of Islamic values to hold society together in difficult times was bound to affect Chechen women's sense of their identity and responsibilities.

There is little doubt that Chechnya's historical experience of forceful control by czarist Russian, and Soviet governmental regimes had an important impact on Chechnyan family life generally, and on Chechnyan women in particular in their roles as wives and mothers.

On one hand, the advent of the Russian Revolution and the beginning of a Soviet provincial rule dominated by Communist ideology served to bolster secular (indeed anti-religious) foundations in regional and local government institutions; on the other, Soviet theories of egalitarianism may have provided increased independence for Chechen women. To the degree that Soviet ideology sought to challenge traditional perceptions of the role of women in Chechen society, conditions between the two world wars may have encouraged women, particularly those who gained access to state-controlled education and state-run administrative posts, to expect wider recognition of their roles as equals in certain spheres. Such expectations, however, took on different forms according to geographical localities (e.g., urban or semi-urban vs. rural, mountain villages, or more accessible plains) and/or degrees of identification with tribal and local clan origins.

Where individual Islamic religious identity was at issue, however, a substantial number of Chechen women resisted in private what was imposed in public during the Communist atheist regime: carrying out prayer rituals at home, for example, and following the essential dress codes of Islamic law.

The fact that Chechen society has always been associated with tribal and local clan values has helped sustain traditional definitions of the status of women according to culture-specific secular terms alongside more general Islamic mores. A notable example of the former was embodied in local groups' selection of a "state daughter" (*mekhk yo'*)—a woman whose leadership abilities qualified her to make pronouncements vital for safeguarding cultural traditions. Divisions of economic roles similar to other traditional societies also helped secure mutual respect for the respective contributions of both men and women.

In their search for identity as part of the emergent republic, Chechen women are confronted, as are male members of the population, with the challenge of either defending or overcoming the influence of diverse ethnic lines of descent that, depending on the circumstances, might affect their position in the broader polity. This is most apparent in the sphere of marriage, where historically distant inter-clan relations can potentially affect contacts not only at the easily cited (e.g., Ingush-Chechen) level, but—for "purists" who have not lost sight of other distant ethnically based origins—as guidelines for acceptable intergroup relations.

To these traditional guidelines should be added "mixed" Islamic and clan specific practices for protecting the honor of Chechen women—practices that also can be found in a number of traditional societies around the world: for example, removal (by recourse to violence if necessary) of any possible doubt concerning unacceptable acts of intimacy between the sexes, and appropriate arrangements for marriage. Equally important among men is the custom of showing full respect for one's mother and her immediate relatives. Chechen marriage patterns are also guided by traditions that mix Islamic and unwritten customary laws. Traditionally endogamy was an assumed requirement within the *tukhum*, or broad tribal entity, but marriage partners were necessarily selected (usually through family channels) beyond closely related members of the clan (*taip*). Rules in these domains were to be observed even in cases where individuals resided in distant areas or had chosen to adopt an urban lifestyle.

In-field interviews of Chechen girls regarding attitudes toward marriage (Procházková, 2005) reveal persisting recognition of traditional mores despite drastically changed circumstances brought about by post-1990 violence associated with resistance to continued Russian domination of Chechnya. For example, acceptance of early age marriage (beginning in the mid-teens) remains widespread; particularly when both families agree most girls assume their role is to obey. In cases where respected clan elders insist on raising questions concerning the appropriateness of a match (based on the relative status of two families) "drastic" action (i.e., elopement) is sometimes the only recourse, accompanied by the risk of ostracism launched by one or both clans involved.

An entire generation of Chechen women, whether steeped in tradition or tending toward secularist values inculcated by Soviet ideology, suffered a wrenching experience when, in 1944, the Soviets used forced exile of Chechen (and other "suspect" ethnic populations of the Caucasus zone and Crimean Tatars) to Central Asia and Siberia, ostensibly as a wartime security measure. Twelve years would pass before Premier Khrushchev announced that the Chechens and other ethnic exiles would be allowed to return. During this period deportees were forced to reside in NKVD-run "special settlements" organized as collective and state farms. Under such conditions, totally unfamiliar demands for what amounted to forced labor on both genders undoubtedly added to tensions for Chechen women seeking to fulfill their traditional roles as mothers, wives, and keepers of households.

Chechens would feel another impact of the years in exile as they faced the challenge of maintaining their ethnic identity and family traditions while surrounded by an essentially foreign "host" population (many, for example, were deported to Kazakhstan), and as they encountered groups from other areas of the Caucasus, some of whom, despite ethnic and religious differences, had had comparable experiences of Soviet oppression.

Instead of resolving such tensions, Khrushchev's decision to allow Chechens to return to their homelands after 1956 merely added a new chapter to deteriorating conditions for the descendants of the generation of forced exile. For example, not all families or not all individual members of families opted to return to the restored (but demographically altered) Chechen-Ingush ASSR.

Therefore a certain number of mothers, wives, or sisters separated from male members of families that had shared a common experience of exile had to reestablish themselves in a "home" environment that was destined to make stronger and stronger demands on both genders as resistance to Russian dominance took on increased Chechen nationalist (indeed revolutionary) dimensions.

The ensuing thirty years of unsettled political, economic, and social conditions that accompanied the Cold War would be followed by even greater challenges for Chechen women as, with the dissolution of the Soviet Union, Moscow's attempts to maintain firm control over the former Ingush-Chechen ASSR brought open armed conflicts in the first and second Russo-Chechen Wars of 1994–1996 and 1999–2000. Disastrous direct military conflict, plus prolonged tensions resulting from Chechnya's still unresolved political status vis-à-vis Moscow have left their mark on the role of women in Chechen society. Effects range from increased economic responsibilities for women whose husbands or fathers fell as victims of war or face threats of imprisonment, to actual involvement by women (the most notorious labeled the "Black Widows") in anti-Russian terrorist acts—in Chechnya as well as on Russian soil.

More and more responsibility for providing minimal income for basic family needs, beginning with food and shelter, fell upon Chechen women's shoulders from the mid-1990s forward. In situations that more or less fit within traditional gender roles, such as expanding ways for women to gain income from market-related dealings, no additional onus might appear on the surface. In more extreme situations, however, various levels of psychological alienation have emerged.

Although less immediately visible than physical damage associated with the Russo-Chechen conflict, many "after shocks" still affect family life and gender relations in Chechnya. Some evolutionary changes may stem from demographic factors that might have occurred with or without the crisis conditions that began in the 1990s. These can result from almost universal trends, such as rural to urban migration, particularly for work opportunities (creating gender imbalances in both settings) or, as some sociological studies suggest, as a consequence of educational advances among key segments of the female population. Members of the emerging younger generation of Chechen women, while adhering to traditional values in most spheres, increasingly expect wider degrees of independence in areas where secular legislation can affect their status (notably in higher education and in court disputes over property, contracts, etc.).

Such changing attitudes among a minority of Chechen women may be a reaction to their awareness of pressing needs to take on diverse non-traditional roles as material providers for family basics. There appears to be a rising level of emotional alienation in which Chechen women risk losing hope for improved conditions—both material and in their perceptions of marriage and the family—in the future.

Indirectly implied in such views is an increasing disappointment in what Chechen women traditionally assumed should be men's sense of dignity deriving from fulfillment of their role—as a provider and as a defender of family honor.

International journalists who have observed living conditions and attitudes of Chechen women during recent decades (Procházková) record a number of recurring and disturbing themes. Mainly these revolve around family relationships that have been affected by war conditions starting in the 1990s. Some women seem to have reached such stages of despair that—despite their determination to remained married—scarcely speak to husbands who don't even resemble their former selves.

Numerous recorded interviews with Chechen women who experienced the first and second Russo-Chechen conflicts (Procházková) suggest widespread psychological damage affecting relations between Chechen men and women. Many women feel that men are no longer certain of the role they should or can play in an environment of daily tension, in part due to repeated humiliation when police authorities subject them to various levels of surveillance—often intruding into their homes.

The same observers have noted that material insecurity and the lack of viable employment options for male members of their families have forced Chechen women to take on "untraditional" ways of earning money. Some, given the presence of Russian soldiers in or near their towns and villages, have fallen victim to the inevitable shame of prostitution. Others resort to scavenging for any sellable scraps, particularly metal left behind after the destruction of battles and shellings.

The separatist Chechen regime that gained control in mid-1996 introduced, under the label "Pure Islam," Sharīʿah -based laws that included recognition of polygamy and a variety of controls over (women). Reactions to this presumed "return" to Islamic ways were mixed. In some cases, communities most affected by the experience of Communist secularism were resistant to any rising influence of Islam, not only in the status of women in general, but also in relations between the sexes.

More isolated village communities expressed identification with former traditional guidelines for women among themselves or in social contacts with men—traditions that were more familiar to them than religious precepts of the Sharīʿah.

BIBLIOGRAPHY

Hughes, James. *Chechnya: From Nationalism to Jihad.* Philadelphia: University of Pennsylvania Press, 2007.

Jaimoukha, Amjad. *The Chechens: A Handbook.* London and New York: RoutledgeCurzon, 2005.

Murphy, Paul J. *Allah's Angels: Chechen Women in War.* Annapolis, Md.: Naval Institute Press, 2010

Procházková, Petra *La guerre russo-tchétchène: Parole des femmes.* Translated by Barbora Faure. Monaco: Editions du Rocher/Le Serpent à Plumes, 2005

Shirazi, Faegheh, editor. *Muslim Women in War and Crisis: Representation and Reality.* Austin: University of Texas Press, 2010.

BYRON CANNON

CHILD ABUSE.

Islamic Substantive Law, the body of laws governing Islam known as Sharīʿah , are primarily founded on the principles of the Qurʾān and the Sunnah (practices and sayings of the Prophet Mohammed). Guiding the analysis and interpretation (*ijtihad*) of the primary sources is consensus of the scholars or the community (*ijmaʿ*), analogical reasoning as a tool of interpretation (*qiyas*), and finally predominant customs (*urf*) and concerns for the public interest (*maslaha*), among other more specialized and sophisticated juristic tools. Generally, the rules and principles governing the protection of the child from abuse in the Sharīʿah is rooted both in the primary sources, as well as in the progressive efforts of the jurists and law makers in interpreting the sources according to inevitable changes in consciousness.

Protection from Child Abuse and the Primary Sources. Islam protects the right to life. Historically, Islam brought a major improvement to the protections afforded to children in the pre-Islamic Arabian Peninsula by putting an end to a number of traditions and customs prevalent at the time, such as female infanticide carried out by the regional tribes, prompted mainly by the fear of famine and the perceived economic burden of women (Smith, 1979). With the advent of Islam, the killing of infant girls by their families was equated to the gravest of sins by the Qurʾān (17:31).

Further, Islam and the teachings of the Prophet Muḥammad sought to protect children from harm or abuse in a vast array of circumstances (Sait, 2000, p. 43). On physical abuse, children were excluded from war campaigns during the era of Prophet Muḥammad. Similarly, on protecting children during armed conflict, the Prophet Muḥammad prohibited the execution of children and women during war (Abiad and Zia Mansoor, 2010, pp. 45–47). Some Islamic principles offer full protection against child labor, since this is detrimental and dangerous and can adversely affect the physical and mental health and overall development of children, including their education (Abiad and Zia Mansoor, pp. 45–47). Indeed, there are a number of examples that demonstrate the leniency of the Prophet with respect to dealing with the inappropriate behavior of children or the children's wrongdoing (Al Bukhari, book 83, ḥadīth 46) For example, on emotional abuse, in answer to a father who was saying that he has never kissed his children, it is provided in the Sunnah that those who show no mercy on children will be shown no mercy in return (Hadith, Sahih Al Bukhari, book 73, ḥadīth 26–).

Finally, Islam also imposed a religious obligation on parents and society to protect and fulfill the basic needs of children, including spending toward the child's needs of food, clothing, housing, education, culture, and guidance toward a suitable profession. It also imposes a general principle of justice toward children and a principle of care and education.

a. Exceptions Made for Children: Corporal Abuse and Crime and Punishment in Sharīʿah. The controversial punishments laid down in the Islamic criminal laws, known as *Hudood* and *Qisas*, do not apply to children. There is clear evidence in the Sunnah that children are exempted from criminal liability for their acts not only because of their lack of puberty but also because of their lack of understanding and maturity.

b. Islamic Principle of the "Best Interest of the Child"—Past and Present. The Qurʾān acknowledges, while dealing with matters related to orphans, that their best interests have to be kept in mind (Surah Al-Baqarah, verse 220). However, this essential principle with regard to the guardianship of property (*al wilayatu alal mal*) might be used in different cases affecting children, particularly with regard to education. With regard to custody for example, Sunnī Sharīʿah courts in Lebanon adopt the "best interest of the child" approach as the main criterion in deciding guardianship (*hadana*) cases (Highest Assembly, Sunnī Courts in Lebanon, Decision of 4 February 1987).

The development by Islamic jurists (*fuqaha*) of the principle of "best interest of the child," and its integration into domestic and regional instruments, as well as its implementation before the courts (secular and religious courts within the Islamic states) not only echo the protections enshrined in the UN Convention on the Rights of the Child (UNCRC, Art. 3), but also have the potential to create within the framework of the Sharīʿah a comprehensive mechanism for the protection of the child.

The Present: The Challenges of Modernity. While the advent of Islam articulated new and specific rights and protections for children, modern norms, specifically as enshrined in international legal instruments, pose a challenge. Indeed, the very definition of "child" in Sharīʿah varies among communities and scholars and, now, among nation states where Islam is a source of law. The definition of a child in Sharīʿah can range from age 7 and below, to "puberty" and below. Meanwhile, the Convention on the Rights of the Child defines a child as "every human being below the age of 18 years" (UNCRC, Art. 1). In view of this, it is important to reflect on the tension between Sharīʿah and international modern norms on children, as the ripple effects can be extensive. For example, the marrying age in most Sharīʿah schools of thought, which is puberty, is irreconcilable with provisions of international human rights law on children. In the former, the concerned human being is a fully fledged adult whereas in the latter, the concerned human being is a child who is at grave risk of abuse. It is interesting to note that governments throughout the Muslim countries have regularly interfered to amend Islamic family norms such as those pertaining to the age of marriage. For example a minimum age for marriage is set at 15 for girls and 18 for boys in Morocco; 16 for females and 18 for males in Pakistan, and 17 for females and 18 for males in Syria. This also applies within conservative Islamic frameworks, including the Islamic Republic of Iran, where the government, as mentioned by the Iranian delegation to the Committee of the Rights of the Child, reconsidered in 2005 the relevant Sharīʿah provisions in light of the need for children to have attained a certain level of maturity before entering into marriage (U.N. Doc. CRC/C/SR.1016 (28 Jan. 2005).

The Present: Islam, Regional Mechanisms and Child Abuse. Muslim states have further developed the mechanisms pertaining to the protection of children as afforded by Islam. These protections have largely developed through purposeful juristic efforts. The Organization of Islamic Cooperation (OIC) adopted in 2004 the Covenant on the Rights of the Child in Islam, which represents a legally binding document aimed at affirming the rights of the child as defined in the Islamic Sharīʿah. The Islamic Covenant provides a comprehensive protection to the child including its health, education, social and criminal matters. Further, it protects children from all forms of torture or inhumane or humiliating treatment in all circumstances and conditions. The Covenant explicitly provides that it is the responsibility of the state parties to take necessary measures to ensure that children are protected from "all forms of abuse" and particularly "sexual abuse" (Article 17–4). The Arab Declaration on Human Rights adopted by the Arab League affirms that the death penalty is not inflicted on persons less than eighteen years old.

It is therefore evident that despite certain tensions between Sharīʿah and modern norms on the protection of children from abuse, Muslim states and communities are adapting to the modern consciousness and aim to do so within the boundaries of the Sharīʿah.

Finally, it is interesting to reflect on the role of the media in raising awareness about child abuse throughout the Muslim world. The media coverage of the tumultuous developments in Egypt, Libya, and Syria, or also in the Israel-Palestinian conflict, emphasizes the extent to which children are caught in the crossfire, often arrested, tortured, and killed.

Bibliography

Nisrine, Abiad, Farkhanda Zia Mansoor, and Robert McCorquodale. *Criminal Law and the Rights of the Child in Muslim States: A Comparative and Analytical Perspective.* London: British Institute of International and Comparative Law, 2010.

Saouda Mohammad El-Khatib. *Oussous houkouk el Insan fi Altachrii eldinny wal douwali, Manchourat al-halabi alhoukoukiyya.* Beirut, 2010.

Sait, Siraj. "Islamic Perspectives on the Right of the Child." In *Revisiting Children's Rights*, edited by Deirdre Fottrell. The Hague: Kluwer Law International, 2000.

"Smith, Jane I."Women in Islam: Equity, Equality, and the Search for the Natural Order." *Journal of the American Academy of Religion* 47:4 (1979): 517–537.

Nisrine Abiad

Child-Rearing Practices. In the course of its historic expansion from the seventh to the twentieth centuries, Islam encountered thousands of societies with their respective systems of kinship, marriage, gender, and family relations. Although the Arabian heartland during Muḥammad's time is thought to have had patrilineal lineages characterized by a patrilateral emphasis, others among the diverse societies that converted to Islam, such as those found in parts of sub-Saharan Africa as well as mainland and insular Southeast Asia, had kinship systems of a cognatic or even matrilineal nature. In these societies the public role of women is pronounced and the socialization of children makes extensive accommodations to girls and women. In the face of this diversity of kinship, marriage, and family systems, any generalizations about child-rearing practices in the Muslim world must be made with caution.

Notwithstanding this diversity of custom, since at least the third century of the Muslim era Muslim societies have had legal and educational institutions at their hearts that have generated normative pressures for the reform of kinship, marriage, and socialization practices to more closely reflect the model offered by the Qurʾān and traditions of the Prophet (*Sunnah*). The Qurʾān and the *Sunnah* do not contain a comprehensive blueprint for every aspect of these social forms, but they can be interpreted in a manner that has important, if still diverse, implications for family relations and child-rearing practices, not least of all with regard to gender and sexuality.

The Blessing of Children. Within Islam marriage on the model of the Prophet is considered a duty and children are considered a blessing from God. Even in societies that lack the patrilineal emphases of the Arab heartlands, reproduction is identified as central to definitions of womanhood throughout the Muslim world and as a primary role of wives. Conversely infertility may be considered a personal and moral failing—most often blamed on the woman no matter what its cause and made more difficult by the Muslim prohibition on adoption in its legal sense. Although in some Muslim societies the birth of a son is considered a greater cause for celebration than that of a daughter, this more commonly reflects local cultural biases rather than tradition-grounded religious understanding. More generally across the Muslim world, the birth of a child, particularly a first child, is always a joyous event.

Mothers are considered the major caretakers and socializers of their young children. The importance placed on the role of the mother and her relationship to her offspring is expressed in the saying attributed to the Prophet that "Paradise is found at the feet of one's mother." Children are said to owe a debt of gratitude to their parents, but particularly their mothers, for giving birth to them, nurturing, and supporting them. According to the *Sunnah* mothers are enjoined to breastfeed their infants for a period of two years and, at least according to legal discourse, have the right to be paid for this service. Breastfeeding is not only important for the health of the infant, but is also understood to underscore the relation of *maḥram* between mother and child; that is, it reinforces a relationship of intimacy without taboo. Fathers may be quite affectionate with their sons and daughters but typically leave the daily caretaking to their wives. In some Muslim societies the more distant role of the father is viewed as critical to the child's development of a culturally valued attitude of patriarchal deference and respect.

The moral education of children begins as early as age three with parents assuming an important role as religious teachers and moral models for their offspring. Very young children are encouraged to imitate their parents in ritual ablutions and in daily prayers and are praised for their efforts. In many Muslim societies, by the age of seven or eight, boys and girls join their peers at the neighborhood mosque or prayer house for religious lessons and may attempt to follow the Ramadan fast. By the age of ten, according to the scriptures, children may be disciplined if they neglect their devotions.

It is around this same time or soon after that many Muslim boys are circumcised. Male circumcision on the model of the Prophet is enjoined in virtually all Muslim societies and indeed is conceived as an introduction of the young boy into the community of believers (*ummah*). As such, male circumcision is typically an occasion of great celebration, not uncommonly involving elaborate feasting and entertainment. Female circumcision is less consistently performed and takes more varied and culturally inflected forms. The relevant scriptures have been interpreted in different manners in different Muslim societies and eras. The majority of Muslim societies recognize female circumcision as permissible but not required. Those societies that follow the practice do so in ways that range from significant genital cutting to symbolic cleansing of the labia.

Young boys are generally afforded greater freedom to roam their neighborhoods and explore while young girls are expected to stay closer to home. Boys similarly are given fewer chores and those that involve working outside or at a distance from home, while girls help their mothers with domestic chores like cooking and cleaning. In modern times, of course, there is considerable variation in the number and type of chores expected of boys and girls by class and in rural versus urban areas, with children devoting considerably more time to school and homework in urban areas and among the new middle classes. Nonetheless greater expectations with regard to helping around the house are typically placed on girls than on boys as these skills are viewed as critical to the girl's eventual roles as wife and mother.

Puberty. Societal and family expectations intensify as children approach the age of puberty (*bāligh*) because, according to the scriptures, from the time of puberty, one's sins will be counted (and punished) by God. In the case of young boys, puberty is associated with the experience of wet dreams or nocturnal emissions. In the case of young girls, it is indicated by menarche or *haidh*. For pubescent girls—who have been taught modesty and restraint from a young age—puberty involves an intensification of such concerns particularly in interactions with nonrelated (non-*maḥram*) men. While there is considerable variation by class and region, in many Muslim societies adolescent females are required to curtail their public activities. They must ask permission to go out and in order to guard family honor and their reputations must always be accompanied by a family member. In modern times, and especially since the 1960s, the movement of young women into secondary and tertiary education has complicated this pattern considerably.

Similar concerns underlie the phenomenon of veiling. While the Qur'ān and *Sunnah* make clear that modesty and restraint should extend to both males and females, it is the demeanor of females that is of most systematic parental concern. Both males and females are enjoined to cover their *awrat* or "shameful parts of the body." For young men this is understood to refer to that portion of the body between the waist and knees and is easily accomplished by the wearing of trousers or a sarong; for young women it refers to the whole body, excluding the palms of the hands and the face. The precise manner and extent of female covering however vary enormously from society to society and from era to era. In premodern times, for example, it was rare that female slaves wore headscarves (*hijab*). And even in the early decades of the twentieth century, Muslim women in some countries interpreted the injunction of modesty as not requiring that they cover their heads. However, in the aftermath of the great Islamic resurgence that took place in the final decades of the twentieth century, growing numbers of Muslim parents have concluded that the demands of modesty require that they teach their daughters not only to wear the headscarf, but more enveloping clothing styles as well. Here again, however, the pattern has been greatly complicated by mass education, urbanization, and economic and cultural globalization, all of which have inflected the practices of modesty and sexual restraint in class- and region-specific ways.

The emphasis placed on modesty and self-control in Muslim societies extends to the parental concern with chastity. According to the scriptures, premarital sex is a serious sin and is considered a particular source of shame for the young woman and a dishonor to her family. In those portions of the Muslim world with tribal and extended family groupings (not least patrilineages), the culture and practices of family honor typically weigh especially heavily on girls and women. In countries such as Pakistan, Iraq, Turkey, and Afghanistan the perceived dishonorable acts of daughters may result in severe punishment, even death, at the hands of male family members. In general, however, the separation of the sexes has become increasingly difficult in the face of the massive social changes and increased communications that have swept the Muslim world in the past several decades. New and expanded educational opportunities in many Muslim countries have resulted in the prolongation of the period of youthful autonomy and social exploration and have posed challenges to traditional patterns of parenting and child socialization. New opportunities for unchaperoned interactions between young men and women have triggered repeated moral panics and continuing debates over the proper interpretation of gender roles within Islam. Never unitary nor uniquely determined by scripture, the practices of child-rearing and socialization in the late-modern Muslim world vary enormously, but everywhere remain the focus of intense public attention.

BIBLIOGRAPHY

Abu-Lughod, Lila. *Veiled Sentiments: Honor and Poetry in a Bedouin Society*. Updated ed. Berkeley: University of California Press, 1999. Classic ethnography on Egyptian Bedouin family life.

Ali, Kecia. *Sexual Ethics and Islam: Feminist Reflections on Qur'an, Hadith, and Jurisprudence*. Oxford: Oneworld Press, 2006.

Davis, Susan Schaefer, and Douglas A. Davis. *Adolescence in a Moroccan Town: Making Social Sense*. New Brunswick, N.J.: Rutgers University Press, 1989. A description of Moroccan family life and social relations.

Fernea, Elizabeth Warnock. *Guests of the Sheik: An Ethnography of an Iraqi Village*. Garden City, N.Y.: Anchor Books, 1965. A classic work on family and gender roles in Iraq.

Herrera, Linda, and Asef Bayat, eds. *Being Young and Muslim: New Cultural Politics in the Global South and North*. Oxford: Oxford University Press, 2010. A collection of articles on Muslim youth from a variety of Muslim countries; it takes up issues of identity, gender, politics, and youth culture.

Mernissi, Fatima. *Dreams of Trespass: Tales of a Harem Girlhood*. Reading, Mass.: Addison-Wesley, 1994. A personal reflection on growing up in a harem in Fez, Morocco.

Starrett, Gregory. *Putting Islam to Work: Education, Politics, and Religious Transformation in Egypt*. Berkeley: University of California Press, 1998.

Tucker, Judith E. *Women, Family, and Gender in Islamic Law*. Cambridge, U.K.: Cambridge University Press, 2008. Islamic law as it relates to women and family relations.

NANCY J. SMITH-HEFNER

CHINA. In the early twenty-first century China's Muslim population is estimated to be between 20 and 35 million, spread throughout the country. Of China's fifty-five officially recognized ethnic minority groups, ten are predominantly Muslim. The largest of these groups are the Uighur and the Hui, each having a population of approximately 10 million. The Uighur live primarily in Xinjiang Province, in northwest China, and are a Turkic-speaking people who settled in that region over a thousand years ago. The Hui live in every region of the country and are the descendants of the hundreds of thousands of Muslims from the Middle East and Central Asia who settled in China during the Mongol Yuan dynasty (1260–1368). These early settlers were either recruited or forcibly relocated by the Mongols who needed their assistance in establishing their empire and rule of China. They included craftsmen, astronomers, architects, medical doctors, hydraulic engineers, military technicians, artists, bureaucrats, linguists, and more. Primarily male, some were allowed to bring their families with them, but most settled down and married Chinese women. Children born to Muslim fathers were raised as Muslims, and daughters were expected to marry other Muslims. In addition, Muslim families would often adopt children abandoned by Han Chinese families during periods of famine or hardship.

Over the centuries, Muslim communities in China both flourished and experienced periods of state-sponsored persecution. During much of their history, Chinese Muslims were also cut off from the rest of the Islamic world. As a result, a very strong tradition of Islamic education developed in China. Women played a very active role in ensuring that Islamic knowledge was maintained over the generations. In the mid-nineteenth century in central China, an Islamic school for women was established in Kaifeng, Henan Province, to meet the growing demand for advanced religious studies for women. The school later developed into a women's mosque and became a model that was followed throughout much of central China and into Beijing as well.

In recent decades, with the revival of Islamic education in the aftermath of the Cultural Revolution (1966–1976), Islamic schools have been set up throughout the country (except Xinjiang). Classes are offered in pre-schools, during the summer for schoolchildren, during the day for the elderly and retired, and in the evenings and weekends for working adults. Independent Islamic colleges have also been established that train teachers and translators. Many of the young women graduates volunteer to help set up schools for girls in China's more remote and impoverished regions. Since the early 1990s, young people, both men and women, pursued more advanced studies at international centers of Islamic learning around the world, including Syria, Pakistan, Egypt, Iran, Malaysia, Indonesia, and for men only in Saudi Arabia. Upon their return from studies overseas, most women graduates become teachers at Islamic schools. Many of these private schools are based in mosques, and many of them also offer charitable activities run by women.

Unfortunately, research on Muslim women in China is quite limited. However, to shed light on how one Muslim woman made a huge difference in the lives of countless deaf and blind students and their teachers in Yunnan Province, one should consider the case of Ma Qiongxuan. In 1993 Chinese sign language was being taught at the Kunming School for the Deaf and Blind with an extraordinarily positive attitude by all of the teachers at that institution. The enthusiasm and dedication of the teachers were remarkable. At the time in China, all college students received government scholarships and upon graduation were assigned jobs anywhere in the country where their skills were needed. Refusing to accept a job placement was not a possibility. Teachers at the Kunming school were recruited from the local teachers' college; however, Principal Ma had negotiated an arrangement with local education officials guaranteeing that any graduating student who did not want to teach at the school would be given another assignment without any negative consequences. In addition, after completing one year of teaching at the school, all new teachers were asked if they wished to continue at Kunming or be reassigned. Ma had taken an extraordinary and unprecedented initiative to ensure that her teachers were dedicated to the school's children, children who needed more care. That she was able to convince local government officials to go along with her policy reflects both her determination to ensure that the blind and deaf students received the best education possible from teachers committed to their education, and the respect she must have engendered in the community.

It is estimated that by 2020 there will be 40 million fewer women than men in China and thus 40 million men with no hope of ever marrying. This social demographic catastrophe is the result of female infanticide, selective abortions, and the preferential treatment of boys. In addition, trafficking in women for forced sex work and forced marriage is a major problem throughout the country, and China also has the highest rate of female suicide in the world, and is the only place where female suicides outnumber male suicides.

In the early twenty-first century Muslim women in China appear to be less vulnerable to these forms of abuse than other Chinese women. To begin with, female infanticide is an anathema to most Muslim societies. As a result, Muslim communities do not suffer from the severe shortages that face most of the rest of the society. In addition, when Chinese Muslim women leave their villages to find work in the cities, they are able to use the networks linking Chinese Muslims throughout the country, and are thus less vulnerable to the traffickers who prey on young women arriving in cities.

However, this is not to suggest that Muslim women in China are not susceptible to regional cultural values regarding women and gender roles. Gender relations among the many different Muslim ethnic groups in China vary widely depending on both the region and the dominant local culture. In most of China, Muslims live near Han Chinese. Northwest China is known for being extremely patriarchal, with men wielding a large amount of power within households. Muslims from other parts of China are often shocked at how women are treated in that area.

For example, women are often forbidden from entering mosques in much of northwest China. In southwest China, however, almost all mosques include a section for women in the main prayer hall right next to the men (there is usually a half-curtain dividing the room). In central China, women have their own mosques. Recently, the practice of women imams (known as *nu ahong* in Chinese) and women's mosques in China have gained increasing amounts of attention within the nation as well as worldwide. Young women from areas where women's mosques are common have moved to other regions of China and set up women's mosques there. In addition, Chinese Muslim women from other regions of China have traveled to central China and become familiar with this practice. According to Islamic legal scholar Khaled Abou El Fadl, the practice of women's mosques and women *ahong* in China may represent a rare surviving example of a practice that might have been common in the early years of Islam. One Chinese Muslim leader even went so far as to say the rest of the Muslim world may have something important to learn from this Chinese Muslim tradition.

BIBLIOGRAPHY

Allès, Elisabeth. "Chinese Muslim Women: From Autonomy to Dependence." In *Devout Societies vs. Impious States? Transmitting Islamic Learning in Russia, Central Asia and China, through the Twentieth Century*, edited by Stephane Dudoignon, pp. 91–103. Berlin: Klaus Schwarz Verlag, 2004.

Armijo, Jacqueline. "Narratives Engendering Survival: How the Muslims of Southwest China Remember the Massacres of 1873." *Traces: An International Journal of Comparative Cultural Theory* 2 (2001): 293–329.

Armijo, Jacqueline. "A Unique Heritage of Leadership: Muslim Women in China." *Special 10th Anniversary Edition: Women in Power. Georgetown Journal of International Affairs* 10, no. 1 (Winter/Spring 2009): 37–45.

Jaschok, Maria, and Hau Ming Vicky Chan. "Education, Gender and Islam in China: The Place of Religious Education in Challenging and Sustaining 'Undisputed' Traditions among Chinese Muslim

Women." *International Journal of Educational Development* 29 (2009): 487–494.
Jaschok, Maria, and Shui Jingjun. *The History of Women's Mosques in Chinese Islam: A Mosque of Their Own.* Richmond, UK: Curzon, 2000.

Jacqueline Armijo

Cinema.

[*This entry includes four subentries:*

Arab Women's Contributions
Iranian Women's Contributions
North African Women's Contributions, *and*
Turkish Women's Contributions.]

Arab Women's Contributions

At the advent of cinema in Europe in 1895, control over the Arab world was divided between France and Britain. Two different approaches to colonial occupation resulted in diverse cinematic developments. While England's colonial policy did not pay attention to cinema, France's legacy is one of cultural development. The Arab world is vast, with an array of traditions, languages, religions, and cultures, where diverse political philosophies determine governments' cultural policies. While it is acknowledged that censorship rules Arab media, it is not widely known that there is a vibrant cinema culture where internationally renowned filmmakers contribute to the area's identity formation and its growing transnational reputation. From cinema's very beginnings in the Arab world, women have made their mark and have helped to define it, in different ways.

In the 1890s the French Lumière brothers went to the Maghrib to record exotic landscapes. As early as 1896, screenings of their films were organized in *cinematographs* in North African cities. As in all colonial cinemas, visual exploitation lead to a simplification of culture, divided into blunt opposites. The contrasts between colonizer and colonized, men and women, exotic and norm, were part of European stories that took shape in the colonial space. Arabs in general were irrelevant, either absent or integral to the décor. Women remained an unidentifiable mass.

Indigenous Cinema. The Tunisian Albert Chikly, who had organized a few Lumière screenings, shot his own two films in the early 1920s. The short *Zohra* (1922) and feature-length *The Girl of Carthage* (1924) were both written by his daughter, Haydée, who took the main roles. The films intimately dealt with women's issues, such as forced marriage. As these are now accepted as the first Arab films, it is important to note that, from the very first films made in North Africa, women took center stage.

The first feature film produced entirely by a woman, the Egyptian Aziza Amir, was the 1927 film *Layla. Layla* showed that women's issues and organizations were increasingly important in Egyptian society by focusing on class problems while dealing with love and arranged marriage. *Layla* became the prototype of Egyptian melodrama.

While a limited number of silent films were made in the 1920s, Cairo's film industry became a regional force with the coming of sound in the 1930s. Singers and belly dancers became the stars of Egyptian musicals. Melodramas have dominated the Middle Eastern film industry ever since, with Cairo being named Hollywood on the Nile.

Women dominated the formative period of cinema as writers, producers, and actresses. The actresses Laila Mourad, Hind Rostom, and Umm Kulthūm ruled screens, while the producers Aziza Amir and Mary Queeny were active behind the scenes. However women's roles lost prominence due to increased social pressures based on Islam's mores. Melodramas turned a carefully constructed middle-class Arab identity into stock characters. In this construct women were confined to the house. Women involved in the film industry from the 1940s until the 1960s were actresses typecast in stereotypical roles.

As was the case around the globe, the 1960s were crucial years in Arab cinema. The tendency to minimize women's contributions to mainstream cinema was compensated by a strong sense of emancipation and anti-establishment movements in art house cinema. In 1968 two vital manifestos crossed paths in Arab cinema: Third Cinema and New Arab Cinema. Both movements intended to liberate cinema from the domination of the mainstream. Third Cinema reacted against the constraints of Hollywood, but failed to liberate women. New Arab Cinema succeeded in its goal of setting Middle Eastern cinema free from patriarchal melodrama.

Maghrib. In the context of Third Cinema, Algerian revolutionary cinema ruled productivity during and after the War for Independence in the 1960s. Women hardly had any presence. This was and still is due to the exceptionally violent circumstances in the country, where cinema is defined by war and trauma. The War for Independence lasted until the mid-1960s, and in the 1990s there was a resurgence of violence. A few notable women made films, such as Assia Djebbar's *The Nouba of the Women of Mount Chenoua* (1979), acclaimed as a feminist masterpiece. However, since Djebbar, barely any women have made their mark on Algerian cinema, apart from Djamila Sahraoui's *Barakat!* (*Enough!*, 2006) and Yamina Bachir Chouikh's *Rachida* (2002).

From the 1980s onward it was Tunisia that dominated Maghrib cinema. Tunisia's golden age of filmmaking, according to Férid Boughédir (one of the most popular filmmakers from Tunisia), lasted until 1996. He defines Tunisian cinema as *cinéma au féminin*. In his documentary *Caméra Arabe* (1987) he shows how he sees feminist themes running through it in female figures defined by absent fathers or husbands, orphaned heroes, domineering mothers, hysterical women, and the Oedipus complex. This is a male-centered definition of female cinema. Also in *Caméra Arabe* Naéjia Ben Mabrouk disagrees with him, and she states that men's viewpoints on women needed to be readdressed in New Arab Cinema. According to Mabrouk it is not enough for women to get a central role in films—women also need to narrate their own stories as directors. It took until 1978 before a woman, Selma Baccar, made a feature-length film, *Fatma 75*.

While Boughédir claims that the golden age ended in 1996, for women it continued. Films such as Moufida Tlatli's *Season of Men* (2000), Nadia El Fani's *Bedwin Hacker* (2003), Selma Baccar's *Flower of Oblivion* (2006), and Raja Amari's *Red Satin* (2002) and *Anonymes* (*Buried Secrets*, 2009), are ground breaking, not only because of the female directors, but because of the unusual trajectory of the women in the films, their performative personalities, and their refusal to be oppressed by men.

Morocco's cinema suffered from years of oppression under King Ḥassan II. When Muḥammad VI succeeded his father in the 1990s, the hope was that his modern approach to the monarchy would stimulate cultural growth. This process has been slow, but Morocco is now the main producer of films in the Maghrib.

Before 2003 Farida Benlyazid and Iza Génini were the only women making films in Morocco. Benlyazid's first feature, *Bab al-Sama Maftuh* (*A Door to the Sky*, 1989) is recognized as a masterpiece about a modern woman's struggles with societal and religious pressures. A younger generation of women is returning to Morocco, and exploring their heritage. Yasmine Kassari, Narjiss Nejjar, Leila Kilani, and Laila Marrakchi tackle issues pertinent to the fluctuations in women's personal status laws and the perils of emigration to Europe.

Egypt. In the Arab world Egypt has often functioned as a hinge between North Africa and the Middle East. It was in Egypt that New Arab

Cinema influenced one of the most interesting female documentary makers of the Arab world, Ateyyat El Abnoudy. Her many documentaries have courted controversy nationally and attracted attention abroad. She was the first woman to focus on documentary, and is still acknowledged as the mother of Arab documentary.

Middle East. There are a few countries in the Middle East where it is almost impossible to find a filmmaker, let alone a female one. However in the United Arab Emirates (UAE) there is a wave of underground filmmaking at universities. Many of these "Emerging Emiratis" are young women. The UAE are primarily known for their lavish film festivals in Abu Dhabi and in Dubai. Prosperous Gulf states, including Qatar and Bahrain, are investing in the film industry, purpose-building studios and developing their attractiveness for international coproductions. Neighboring Saudi Arabia has an active ban on cinemas as public spaces, although a budding audiovisual industry and the largely adolescent population are challenging this. The first Saudi film made by a Saudi woman, Haifa Al-Mansour, featuring a ten-year-old Saudi girl, and filmed in Saudi Arabia—*Wadjda*—was released in fall 2012 to critical international acclaim.

The development of Lebanese and Syrian cinema has been stalled by war and one-party systems. Since the 1960s Syria has been dominated by the Baʿth, who control the National Film Organization (NFO). In spite of this, film production is critically acclaimed abroad and women are the most politically engaged filmmakers. Halla Alabdallah (*As if We Were Catching a Cobra* [2012], *I Am the One Who Brings Flowers to Her Grave* [2006], *Hey! Don't Forget the Cumin* [2011]), Soudade Kaadan (*Damascus Roof and Tales of Paradise* [2010]), Reem Ali (*Zabad* [2011]), and Sulafa Hijazi (animation films) are only four women working across different genres with varying degrees of dissent.

In Lebanon there is no such censorship body, but due to the occupation of the country by Syria and the twenty-five-year-long civil war between Lebanon and Israel, the film industry suffered, as filmmakers exiled themselves in Europe. Nevertheless since the earliest developments of Arab cinema, Lebanese women have had a major presence. Like many actresses, Assia Dagher and Mary Queeny, two film producers in Egypt, were originally from Lebanon. Jocelyne Saab and Mai Masri were among the women who refused to be silenced by the war. Saab's films *Lebanon in a Whirlwind* (1975) *Once Upon a Time in Beirut* (1995), and *What's Going On* (2009) explicitly refer to the war. This continues in award-winning Nadine Labaki's films *Caramel* (2007) and *Where Do We Go Now?* (2011), which are redefining Lebanese cinema through women's stories.

Iraqi cinema has been dependent on drastic political shifts since the 1920s. Insurgencies, war, and dictatorship have defined an Iraqi mythology and drained national resources. Since the end of the Baʿth era slow democratization of Iraq has revealed a new generation of filmmakers. A film school was set up in Baghdad by the female filmmaker Maysoon Pachachi. Together with women such as Khairiya Al Mansour, Radhia Al Timimi, and Khadija Mandil, she is giving Iraqi cinema a new lease on life.

Looking Forward. Arab cinema's future is undoubtedly affected by the Arab revolutions of 2011–2012. While it initially instigated hope for women's liberties and opportunities for cultural expression, there is a living fear that Islamism will determine increasing prohibitions. One woman suffering persecution is the Tunisian Nadia El Fani, whose *Laïcité, Inch'Allah!* (2011) is a daring exploration of the hypocrisies of a society in transition, the hopes and fears for the future, and women's roles in the new constitution. This threat of exile is present all over the Arab world of film. Defiance of censorship has always been central in

Arab women's films, and has become more overt. What is uncertain, however, is whether political upheaval will liberate Arab filmmakers from censorship, and whether it will further propel women into the public sphere. It is hoped that the near future will bring opportunities for filmmakers, both male and female, to express themselves freely and independently once again.

Bibliography

Armes, Roy. *African Filmmaking North and South of the Sahara*. Edinburgh: Edinburgh University Press, 2006. Together with Armes's earlier book, *Postcolonial Images: Studies in North African Film* (Bloomington: Indiana University Press, 2005), the best thematically structured work on North African cinema in English.

Hillauer, Rebecca. *Encyclopedia of Arab Women Filmmakers*. Cairo and New York: American University of Cairo Press, 2005. One of the most complete annotated bibliographies of Arab women filmmakers, but due to rapid recent developments, slightly outdated.

Shafik, Viola. *Arab Cinema: History and Cultural Identity*. 2d ed. Cairo: American University in Cairo Press, 2005. Defining theorization of cinema and its heritage in the Arab world.

Shafik, Viola. *Popular Egyptian Cinema. Gender, Class and Nation*. Cairo: American University in Cairo Press, 2007. Best scholarly work on popular Egyptian cinema that refrains from a dismissive tone about melodrama and musical.

Stefanie Van de Peer

Iranian Women's Contributions

In the years directly before and after the Iranian Revolution of 1979 (often referred to as the Islamic Revolution), film culture in Iran experienced a short period of transition before the emergence of what is now commonly known as the post-revolutionary Iranian cinema. During this transition cinema as a whole was rejected for constituting a crucial apparatus in the Pahlavi monarchy's efforts to westernize Iran. One of the anti-Shah protests in the early days of the Revolution was the 1978 burning of the Cinema Rex in the city of Abadan. This event inspired the destruction of 180 cinemas and cemented the view that cinema, as an institution, was a key player in cultural colonization. As the film historian Hamid Naficy has argued, the years immediately following the revolution involved a "purification process" that significantly diminished opportunities to both produce and exhibit domestic films, as well as to import and exhibit foreign films.

In these early years of post-revolutionary Iran, it might have appeared as though cinema would never again emerge as a major cultural force. Yet just as the trajectory of the Islamic Republic was unclear in this period, so too was the form of Iranian cinema to come. Following the establishment of the Islamic Republic of Iran (1979), the New Iranian Cinema experienced a period of creative productivity hitherto unparalleled in the nation's history. Indeed the only era that is comparable to this period in terms of the consolidation of cinema as a key cultural institution is the time following the Constitutional Revolution of 1905–1911. Before engaging with exactly how Iranian cinema changed with the New Iranian Cinema, it is necessary to examine the history of women's contributions to cinema prior to 1979.

Women in Iranian Cinema, 1897–1979. Prior to the revolution of 1979 Iranian women made up very little of the production side of the domestic film industry. While histories of Iranian culture are increasingly moving away from the notion that 1979 presents an absolute rupture in Iranian history, in the case of women's participation in cinema, most of the fundamental changes did occur after this date. Before the revolution women were rarely represented in films. This scarcity was due to cultural and religious conventions prohibiting public performances by women. The modesty that was typical in the early years of Iranian cinema also had to do with reactionary notions of cinema as a cheap and morally corrupt form of entertainment, rather than an art. While the shock of the novelty of the new medium of the moving image was ubiquitous across global sites of early cinema, it is likely that the first Iranian filmmakers attempted to temper this shock by controlling the audacity of the represented content, that is, not filming women.

The first Iranian sound film, *Dokhtare Lor* (*The Lor Girl*, 1932, directed by Abdolhossein Sepanta and Ardeshir Irani), was filmed in India. This choice of locale was a way to avoid the difficulties posed by conservative authorities. *The Lor Girl* was also the first Iranian film to feature a Muslim Iranian actress, Rouhangiz Saminejad (1916–1997). Until this point Armenian and/or Christian women performed in the few instances where women were represented on screen. Although *The Lor Girl* is a key film that exhibits anxieties about women, the nation, and gender relations at a crucial point in Iranian history, Saminejad faced a great deal of rejection and public humiliation for participating in the film. At the time Sepanta (1907–1969) also worked with Fakhrol-Zaman Jabar-Vaziri, an actress who had studied briefly in Paris and was the lead in all of Sepanta's films after *The Lor Girl*, most notably in *Shirin and Farhad* (1934), *Black Eyes* (1936), and *Leyli and Majnun* (1937). Many historians of Iranian cinema consider her, rather than Saminejad, to be Iran's first film actress.

In the mid-twentieth century the commercial cinema (often referred to as *filmfarsi*, or films made in the Persian [*Farsi*] language), gave rise to a star system that featured women in a set of representations that became the dominant norm. In *filmfarsi*, which relied on the formal and narrative structures of melodrama and simplistic renderings of good versus evil, representations of women reflect a synthesis of imported ideology and domestic cultural modes. Women appeared in the form of stock characters with little nuance or complexity, and were often portrayed as singers and dancers in cafés and restaurants. These performances were filmed from a heterosexual male point of view and strived to imitate the gaze of Hollywood cinema. Women's bodies were often fragmented in close-up shots of individual body parts that separated the representation of women from the development of the narrative. Naficy has argued that the increased fame of the actresses, along with their appearances in advertisements, consolidated an integrated entertainment industry in which cinema was linked to pop culture and consumer goods. The sexual objectification of women in the commercial cinema, particularly because of its perceived link with "modernity," helped to facilitate this culture. The exception to the norm of *filmfarsi* was the representation of women in documentary cinema and in the art cinema, known as the New Wave (*Mowj-e No*). Some of the actresses in the commercial cinema star system, such as Susan Taslimi (whose career continued successfully following the revolution, most notably in Bahram Beizai's *Bashu Gharib-e Khuchak* [*Bashu, the Little Stranger*, 1986], were also employed by the directors of art cinema films and worked in theatrical productions. These venues provided a stark contrast to the roles offered in *filmfarsi* and added to the actresses' fame and recognition. However, as Naficy has argued, the ability to act in films and theater productions did not give women the opportunity to exert influence on the film industry at large. Toward the end of the 1970s, as the resistance to and rejection of the Pahlavi monarchy's vision of modernity increased, the entertainment industry—and particularly its performers—would be rejected and, in many cases, banned, precisely because of what was perceived as a gratuitous public display of sexuality.

Forough Farrokhzad and the Iranian New Wave. Given that, in the early 1960s, film was a medium that had thus far been largely limited to commercial cinema and state-funded documentary film, it continued to hold unrealized creative potential for becoming an "Iranian" art. By this time the Iranian literary scene had already experienced its own reinvention with New Poetry (*Shehr-e No*), which broke from traditional verse and used everyday, colloquial language to experiment with rhyme and develop the individual voice as its mode of expression. One of the foremost poets of the twentieth century was Forough Farrokhzad (1935–1967), who brought into the sphere of poetry questions of gender, the body, sexuality, and subjectivity. Farrokhzad is widely recognized as one of the most important cultural figures in the modern history of Iran. Although Farrokhzad is known primarily for her poetry, she single-handedly changed the landscape of film culture in Iran with her 1962 experimental documentary *Khaneh Siah Ast* (*The House Is Black*). To this point there had only been one female director in Iranian cinema, Shahla Riahi (b. 1926), an actress who directed, produced, and starred in the feature film *Marjan* in 1956. In fact, after Farrokhzad, there would only be two other female filmmakers in the period prior to the Revolution: Marva Nabili, who directed the New Wave film *Khake Sar beh Morh (The Sealed Soil)* in 1977 and Kobra Saidi, director of *Maryam va Mani* (*Maryam and Mani*, 1979).

Farrokhzad did not arrive at filmmaking via an acting career, as Riahi did, but rather because of her involvement with the Golestan Film Workshop (GFW), a small, semi-independent studio run by the controversial writer, intellectual, and filmmaker Ebrahim Golestan (b. 1922), with whom she was romantically involved. In 1958 Farrokhzad was hired as the in-house film editor for the studio. The employment of a poet as a film editor is indicative of the collaborative and interdisciplinary culture of the GFW, which employed artists working across diverse media. The GFW provided funds for Farrokhzad to attend film school in the United Kingdom. Upon her return, she worked as the main editor on Golestan's short film *Yek Atash* (*A Fire*, 1961), which won the Bronze prize at the Venice Film Festival the same year. Farrokhzad worked on a number of other film projects before making *The House Is Black*. In 1959 she made the "Heat" section of the film *Water and Heat*, which she co-directed with Golestan. She also acted in front of the camera, playing minor roles in some of Golestan's films such as *Khesht va Ayneh* (The Brick and the Mirror, 1965) and *Why Was the Sea Stormy?*, an unfinished film based on a story by the surrealist writer Sadegh Hedayat (1903–1951). Farrokhzad's accomplishments also brought international attention to the intermedial arts scene in 1960s Iran. In 1965 two films were made about Farrokhzad. The first was a thirty-minute documentary about her life made by UNESCO. The second was a fifteen-minute film made by the Italian filmmaker Bernardo Bertolucci (b. 1940).

The House Is Black heralded the beginning of the New Wave cinema and anticipated many of what would become the main features of the New Iranian Cinema after 1979. Although film critics such as Hamid Dabashi cite Dariush Mehrjui's *Gav* (*The Cow*, 1969) as the first film of the New Wave and indicative of a new style of cinema, Farrokhzad's film precedes it by several years and was the first Iranian film to use aspects of formal film technique that were already prevalent in global art cinema, particularly in French poetic realism of the 1930s and Italian neorealism of the 1940s and 1950s. However *The House Is Black* was not derivative of these movements; the film has a uniquely Iranian sensibility. Shot in a state-funded leper colony, the film experiments with the generic conventions of documentary by combining voiceovers of Farrokhzad reading her own poetry and passages from the Qur'ān and the Hebrew Bible, alternating with a male voiceover (spoken by Golestan) discussing leprosy in medical terms. The film exhibits an astute awareness of the gaze of ethnography by exploring the positions of subject and object. Decades later directors of the New Iranian Cinema such as Abbas Kiarostami, Bahman Ghobadi, and Samira Makhmalbaf picked up Farrokhzad's interrogation of visuality, her use of non-actors, and her disruption of the boundaries between fiction and nonfiction.

Cinema in Iran after 1979. Following the ousting of Muhammad Reza Shah Pahlavi (1919–1980) in 1979 and the revolution's complete disruption of domestic film production, the future of Iranian cinema looked bleak. The religious authority of the newly formed Islamic state, Ayatollah Ruhollah Khomeini (1902–1989), declared that the revolution was in support of cinema, albeit a cinema in stark opposition to the obscene cinema of the West. The film scholar Negar Mottahedeh has argued that Khomeini saw a new national cinema as a way for the nation to recover from its self-estrangement. In his *Last Will and Testament* (1989) Khomeini stated that this estrangement resulted from the nation's alienation from its collective sense perceptions. Mottahedeh argues that for Khomeini, sense perception was configured by the senses' attachment to film technologies. Given that film technology was precisely the means through which westernization was brought to the national body during the Pahlavi era, this relationship to technology had to be reconfigured in Islamist terms. Khomeini did not reject cinema and its various technologies wholesale, but instead insisted that cinema was in need of "cleansing." Like many other newly formed states in world history—particularly those working in an anti-imperial or decolonized context, such as the USSR, Cuba, and Senegal—the newly formed government of Iran recognized cinema's power to corral a reimagined and reconstructed nation. By creating a new kind of spectator, the newly formed Islamic Republic of Iran sought, in effect, to create a new citizen.

The new government's investment in cinema created productive new possibilities for women filmmakers while at the same time strictly limiting the content and structure of their representation. Although the guidelines for filmmaking were focused on a film text's adherence to Islamic moral values, as the film critic Gönül Dönmez-Colin has argued, censorship laws centered on the representation of female characters. Women characters with whom the audience could identify had to be written as chaste and traditional; nontraditional women were often cast as *bad jens*, or disreputable and promiscuous, in the new commercial cinema. One of the effects of the censorship laws was that women were now in full hijab on screen, even when the diegesis, or story of the film, depicted an interior, private space, or an all-female space. In *Displaced Allegories* Mottahedeh has persuasively argued that the censorship guidelines take the ideal (imagined) spectator to be a heterosexual male, but that the auteurs of the New Iranian Cinema, such as Kiarostami and Beizai, have worked around these rules to create, ironically, a "women's cinema."

In addition to limiting the ways in which women were represented on screen, the new guidelines for film and television also restricted the depiction of romantic and sexual relations; the laws prohibited physical contact between individuals of the opposite sex. Women were to be the objects of a newly defined "sisterly look," as opposed to the former sexualized male gaze. Many film critics have argued that the dominance of storylines built around children in post-revolutionary Iranian cinema is precisely due to the stifling censorship laws. Instead of trying to work around the guidelines, filmmakers avoided anything that could get cut or edited out by the censors. In addition to making films centered on child characters, many directors worked with screenplays that completely excluded either men or women. For example, Rakhshan Bani-Etemad's *Banu-ye ordibehesht* (The May Lady, 1999) is an epistolary romance in which the male love interest is not physically present. Until 2002's *Ten* the films of Abbas Kiarostami avoided an explicit treatment of women by not representing them or writing films centered on male-female relationships. Since *Ten*, which was his first film to focus exclusively on a woman (Mania Akbari as an unnamed woman driving around Tehran), Kiarostami has made another female-centric film with *Shirin* (2008). In *Shirin* a group of women are sitting in a theater watching a film adaptation of the twelfth-century poet Niẓāmī's epic poem, *Khosrow and Shirin*. Seemingly in spite of the censors Kiarostami makes every single shot of the film a close-up on each female spectator, all of whom are famous Iranian actresses playing themselves (in addition to the French actress Juliette Binoche). We see the story of the famous love triangle between Shirin, Khosrow, and Farhad through the women's point of view; Kiarostami even writes the men out of the title.

A Woman's Cinema. While the early years of the Islamic Republic saw the establishment of strict guidelines for filmmaking, after the 1997 election of President Muḥammad Khātamī (b. 1943), these guidelines were somewhat loosened, although they still required the mandatory hijab and no physical contact between the sexes. Several projects that were rejected under the first republic, such as feminist filmmaker Tahmineh Milani's *Do zan* (*Two Women*, 1999), were produced during the Khātamī era (1997–2005). The Ministry of Culture and Islamic Guidance during Khātamī's presidency worked closely with the film industry, however, and it is arguable that, at this point, the moral regulations created a productive limit for filmmakers. In the late 1980s and throughout the 1990s Iranian cinema flourished after a period of stagnation and enjoyed international recognition at film festivals and in emerging film criticism and scholarship on the post-revolutionary films. Whereas in the 1960s and early 1970s art cinema constituted a small portion of films being made in Iran, the period after 1979 saw a collective shift in film style and language with an emphasis on films informed by both European modernist and neorealist techniques and Iranian iconography and narrative structures. As the American film critic Godfrey Cheshire has argued, the fusion of aesthetic styles from both the East and West resulted in a highly original, nonderivative, and often difficult style. Women filmmakers as diverse as Tahmineh Milani, Rakhshan Bani-Etemad, Marzieh Meshkini, Niki Karimi, and Samira Makhmalbaf, among many others, emerged in a creative atmosphere that, despite its restrictions, had no precedents in the history of Iranian cinema.

The two most prominent women filmmakers following the revolution, Rakhshan Bani-Etemad (b. 1954) and Tahmineh Milani (b. 1960) explicitly address women's issues in their films. They also happen to be two of the most widely acclaimed filmmakers in Iran, regardless of gender. Bani-Etemad's film *Nargess* won first prize at Iran's Fajr Film Festival in 1992, marking the first time a woman had won this prize. Bani-Etemad's films have tended to address class issues among women and suggest that for "women's cinema" in Iran, class and gender are understood to be interlocking in terms of their force and articulation. Milani has also been vocal about the need for a cinema that reflected women's experiences. The fact remained that, although after the revolution, more women were involved on the production side of filmmaking, the content of films continued to confine women to stock character roles. Once again, they were either *bad jens*, or disreputable, or exceedingly "good" model mothers and citizens. As Gönül Dönmez-Colin discusses, Milani and Bani-Etemad are the two women directors who have broached taboo subjects relating to women's lives in their work and have therefore changed the landscape of filmmaking. Milani's stance—as well as the tone of her films—is generally bolder and more direct than that of Bani-Etemad, and as a result she has had to deal with countless rejections, delays, and intervention from the government while making her films. The international film community has recognized both filmmakers for their work.

Other women filmmakers working in Iran have critiqued the state and social life after the revolution without necessarily identifying their work as belonging to something like "women's cinema." One of the most provocative films of the post-revolutionary era was Samira Makhmalbaf's documentary-cum-feature film *Sib* (*The Apple*, 1998). The film portrayed the life of two young girls whose parents had kept them in isolation in their home since their birth. Like Kiarostami in 1990's *Nema-ye nazdik* (*Close-Up*), Makhmalbaf (b. 1980) enlisted the actual family to play themselves in the documentary about their lives. The film's stance on the self, isolation, and society is a fresh, youthful take on a subject that has appeared across a variety of modern Iranian texts, including *The Blind Owl* and *The House Is Black*, among others. Marzieh Meshkini's *Roozi ke zan shodam* (The Day I Became a Woman, 2000) is a film that experiments with narrative structure in order to think about time, motion, and the process of "becoming woman." As such the film scholar Michelle Langford has argued that the film mounts a significant challenge to the censorship regulations of the Islamic Republic. Not only do the female characters of Meshkini's film drive the entire narrative—a rarity in commercial Iranian cinema—but their intense physical activities, such as cycling, directly challenge the regime of looking, which prohibits the exhibition of women's bodies exerting themselves with energy, or in a highly physical manner.

The question of a "women's cinema" has varied across critiques and scholarly analyses of Iranian cinema. While some scholars, such as Mottahedeh, have argued that the restructuring of the filmic gaze makes the post-revolutionary cinema a women's cinema, it is not evident that male filmmakers have provided radical interrogations around the question of "woman" in cinema. The censorship laws are one reason why this has been the case. Other readings of Iranian cinema address work that has been identified as militantly feminist by the directors themselves. For example, the postcolonial scholar Nima Naghibi has argued that a feature evident across women's cinema after the revolution is the emphasis on female bonding and homo-social spaces that contest traditional cultural prejudices against women, as well as contemporary legislative measures that discriminate against women. Naghibi's reading thus works to align films by filmmakers like Milani and Bani-Etemad with feminist work from across global sites of Islam that also contest notions of female solidarity that rely on western feminist discourses of sisterhood. The films of Milani in particular demonstrate that these discourses of sisterhood rely on structural inequalities between culture, class, race, and religion. Placing her argument within the context of a larger discourse on veiling and the representation of women, Naghibi argues that the post-revolutionary women's cinema configures an entirely new Iranian women: veiled, but neither modest nor unchaste.

Iranian Women Filmmakers in the Diaspora. One of the long-term social effects of the 1979 revolution has been the massive and ongoing emigration of Iranians, and especially of artists and intellectuals. To speak today of an Iranian cinema is also to speak of the variety of filmmakers who live beyond Iran's borders but continue, in their work, to engage either explicitly or implicitly with questions of the nation. By beginning to think about the concept of national cinema in a transnational world, the contributions of Iranian women filmmakers multiply greatly. One of the most renowned diasporic filmmakers is Ziba Mir-Hosseini whose 1997 documentary, *Divorce Iranian Style* (made in collaboration with Kim Longinotto), has been influential to global feminist activists and scholars. The Iranian-French graphic artist Marjane Satrapi (b. 1969) achieved international recognition with her graphic novel series *Persepolis*, the film adaptation of which she then co-directed with Vincent Paronnaud. Satrapi's most recent work *Poulet aux prunes* (*Chicken with Plums*) is a live-action adaptation of her graphic novel of the same name. Both these works deal with questions of memory, belonging, and the estrangement of the exilic condition. The video artist Shirin Neshat's adaptation of Shahrnush Parsipur's 1990 novella *Zanan-e bedun-e mardan* (*Women without Men*) won the Silver Lion for best directing at the Venice Film Festival in 2009. Until the release of *Women without Men*, Neshat (b. 1957), who has been living in exile since the late 1970s, was known for her short, provocative videos, such as 1998's two-screen installation *Turbulent*, which looks at the question of "voice" and gender relations in Iran. The attention brought to Iranian cinema with the worldwide success of *Women without Men* coincided with two important events: the massive protests in Tehran against the 2009 presidential election results and the imprisonment of the filmmaker Jafar Panahi.

BIBLIOGRAPHY

Cheshire, Godfrey. "How to Read Kiarostami." *Cineaste* 25, no. 4 (2000).

Dabashi, Hamid. *Close Up: Iranian Cinema, Past, Present, and Future*. London: Verso, 2001.

Dönmez-Colin, Gönül. *Women, Islam and Cinema*. London: Reaktion Books, 2004.

Issari, M. Ali. *Cinema in Iran, 1900–1979*. Metuchen, N.J.: Scarecrow Press, 1989.

Langford, Michelle. "Allegory and the Aesthetics of Becoming-Woman in Marziyeh Meshkini's *The Day I Became a Woman*." *Camera Obscura* 64, no. 22 (2007): 1–41.

Mottahedeh, Negar. *Displaced Allegories: Post-Revolutionary Iranian Cinema*. Durham, N.C.: Duke University Press, 2008.

Naficy, Hamid. *A Social History of Iranian Cinema*. 4 vols. Vol. 1: *The Artisanal Era, 1897–1941* and vol. 2: *The Industrializing Years, 1941–1978*. Durham, N.C.: Duke University Press, 2011.

Naficy, Hamid. "Veiled Visions/Powerful Presences: Women in Post-revolutionary Iranian Cinema." In *Life and Art: The New Iranian Cinema*, edited by Rose Issa and Sheila Whitaker, pp. 44–65. London: National Film Theatre, 1999.

Naghibi, Nima. *Rethinking Global Sisterhood: Western Feminism and Iran*. Minneapolis: University of Minnesota Press, 2007.

SARA SALJOUGHI

NORTH AFRICAN WOMEN'S CONTRIBUTIONS

The history of Maghribī women's cinema started with the French colonial encounter and the Lumière Brothers. Despite a few differences related to each country's historical specificity and nationalist politics, whether in Tunisia, Algeria, or Morocco, women's cinema is a latecomer in relation to that of men. It also has the particularity of being at the same time anti-imperial and anti-nationalist with one foot home and the other in Europe.

Tunisia. The seventh art was introduced to Tunisia fourteen years after the establishment of the French Protectorate (1881–1956). In 1895 the Lumière Brothers shot eleven one-minute silent films in Tunisia, each of which showed an aspect of native daily life in the colony. In these first ethnic films native women moved about like ghosts in sharp contrast with French women who wore makeup and sophisticated dresses. Native women had no role in colonial cinema other than enhancing the local flavor of the film and serving the colonial rescue fantasy of saving native women from native men. As the film critic Abdelkrim Gabous put it, colonial cinema represented native women in a "simplistic" and stereotypical fashion as harem creatures draped in muslin; baby-making "machines"; brides on a "palanquin"; or in the kitchen making "couscous" (Gabous, 1998, p. 17).

Colonial cinema did not break away from, but rather reproduced the stereotypical image of Oriental women in French Orientalist literature, paintings, and photography. Luitz-Morat's silent movie *Five Accursed Gentlemen* (1920), the first feature-length movie to be filmed in Tunisia, included trance dances, veils and exotic native women luring and inviting French men. Similarly Charles-Roger Dessort's *Marouf* (1921) and Viktor Tourjansky's *The Tales of the One Thousand and One Nights* (1921) portrayed native women as sensual and voluptuous creatures. In colonial cinema it was customary to have native women's roles played by French or African American actresses such as Huguette Duflos's role in André Hugon's film *Yasmina* (1926), or Josephine Baker's role as Alwina in Edmond T. Gréville's *Princess Tam Tam* (1935). The roles of native men were also played by French actors in Arab drag as exemplified in Georges Péclet's role as Al Dar and Jean Galland as the Maharajah of Datane in Gréville's film.

Native women did not enter the cinema until the Tunisian Jewish filmmaker Albert Samama Chikly made his cinematographic debut with *Zohra* (1922) and then *Aïn al Ghazal* (*The Girl from Carthage*) (1923–1924). In both films he gave the leading role to his daughter Hayde Chikly who also happened to write the script for his first film. It was not until Abdelaziz Ben Hassine's *Tergui* (1935) that Tunisia had its first Muslim movie star (Hassiba Rochdi). The absence of Tunisian women filmmakers before independence is due to the segregationist nature of French colonial society and local patriarchal attitudes, which prevented women not only from acting in or making movies, but also from watching them. Neither cinema, opera, theater, or *le café chantant* was deemed a decent profession or a suitable space for a virtuous woman. Contrary to the national celebration of the first woman doctor from the Paris School of Medicine (Wahida Ben Esheikh) in 1936, the social stigma attached to the artistic milieu and female moviegoers explains why Tunisian women filmmakers did not emerge until the late 1960s and 1970s.

In 1927 Tunis Film, the first Tunisian film company, was created. It was replaced in 1957 by the Socièté Anonyme Tunisienne de Production et d'Expansion Cinématographique (SATPEC), which held the monopoly of the production, imports, exports, and distribution of Tunisian films. SATPEC slowly lost its monopoly over the film industry to the benefit of the private sector. With privatization and the return of younger Tunisian filmmakers from abroad in the 1980s, Tunisian cinema has witnessed a boost in terms of the quality and quantity of its production. Some women filmmakers even managed to beat the odds and create their own production companies such as Selma Baccar's Inter-Media Prod and Najia Ben Mabrouk's No Money Company. The dissolution of SATPEC in 1992 paved the way for the emergence in 2004 of the first school of Tunisian cinema, the Gammarth Higher Institute of Film and Audiovisual Studies (ESAC). It was followed by El Omrane School of Arts and Cinema (EDAC), a private film institute founded in 2010 by the choreographer Sihem Belkhodja.

Because Tunisia did not have its own cinema schools in the first decades of independence, like their male counterparts the first generation of Tunisian women filmmakers pursued their film studies abroad in Switzerland, France, and Belgium. Most of them come from the Tunisian urban bourgeoisie and developed a taste for cinema through local film associations and festivals like the Hammam Lif Cinema Amateur Club, the Tunisian Federation of Amateurs Filmmakers, the International Carthage Film Festival (JCC) founded in 1966 by the film director Tahar Cheria, and the International Amateur Film Festival of Kelibia. Almost all Tunisian women filmmakers worked their way up to make a name for themselves. Before they could make movies of their own, Salma Baccar, Moufida Ttatli, Kalthoum Bornaz, Nadia El Fani, and Mounira B'Har had to work as technicians, script writers, or assistants for male directors such as Sadok Ben Aïcha, Nouri Bouzid, Moncef Dhouib, Nacer Khemir, and Férid Boughedir (Tunisia); Ali Ghanem, Mohammed Lakhdar-Hamina, and Merzak Allouache (Algeria); and Claude Chabrol, Franco Zeffirelli, and Roman Polanski (Europe).

The work of Tunisian women filmmakers can be divided into three categories: documentary, TV film production through the Agence Nationale de Promotion de l'Audiovisuel (ANPA), and short or feature-length film. To start with the first the anthropologist Sophie El Goulli Ferchiou entered the world of filmmaking through her work at the National Center for Scientific Research and the Ethnographic Film Committee at the Museum of Man in France. Her first documentary *Chéchia* (1970), had for a subject ethnic artisanal work, namely, the traditional Tunisian wool hat woven by women but worn by men. With the next generation of filmmakers, the female documentary evolved from the ethnic to the green or ecological type, as illustrated in Khalthoum Bornaz's *El Medfun Forest* (1998), a documentary about the degradation of Tunisia's forests and fauna. Although in the form of a Brechtian fable, Mounira B'Har's film *The Treasure* (1993) is also a call for the conservation of the medina and the protection of Tunisia's national heritage.

In the second category Fatma Skandrani is the only woman of her generation who avoided gender ghettoization and directed films for Tunisia National Television right at the beginning of her career. Because her interest in children's education did not clash with the state's vision of women's role in postcolonial Tunisia as mothers, educators, and nurses, she had the privilege of producing pedagogic youth programs, such as *Ashraf's Dreams* (1967), *The Island of Dreams* (1983) adapted from Hans Christian Andersen's *The Little Match Girl*, and Antoine Saint-Exupéry's *The Little Prince*; and the famous 1971 TV series *Kammoucha* (*The Miser*), which brought to fame the nascent theater star Jalila Baccar.

The third category comprises more internationally known feminist filmmakers like Salma Baccar, the first Tunisian woman to make a feature film (*Fatma*, 1975); Moufida Tlatli whose two works, *The Silences of the Palace* (1994) and *Season of Men* (2000), brought Tunisian cinema to the international stage; Raja Amari (*Red Satin*, 2002); and Nadia El Fani, director of the *Bedouin Hacker* (2003), the first Arab feminist sci-fi film with a lesbian and anti-imperialist theme.

While in the male cinema of Nouri Bouzid or Férid Boughedir Tunisian women appear in the patriarchal roles of mothers, wives, prostitutes, or symbols of the nation, with the first and second generation of women filmmakers, female protagonists emerge as individual and complex characters rather than symbols. Just as Baccar's *Fatma* traces the history of three generations of Tunisian women, Tlatli's masterpiece *The Silences of the Palace* is a post–third-world feminist cinema that is, at the same time, anti-imperialist and anti-nationalist. Through her judicious play of past and present, as well as national and personal stories, Tlatli shows not only the social, economic, and external forces that prevented Tunisian women's emancipation before and after independence, but also the prisons from within, that is, the values of gender subordination that Tunisian women internalized and passed on unaware to the next generations. Even though she does not identify herself as a feminist per se because she finds this label reductive of her work as a filmmaker, Bornaz's film *The Other Half of the Sky* (2007) tackles the issue of gender inequity in Tunisia's inheritance laws. These filmmakers face not only issues related to their gender, but also lack of funding, access to equipment, and, especially, the Orientalist bias of Western distributors who market only works on oppressed Muslim women. Bornaz was once disinvited by a French film festival when they discovered that her film *Trois personnages en quête d'un théâtre* (*Three Characters in Search of a Theater*) (1988) was a documentary on the preservation of the Municipal Theater of Tunis. Another feature of Tunisian women's cinema is that it is more known to European and North American academics than to the Tunisian public, who rarely get the opportunity to see the films because of the complex problems of distribution.

Before the 14 January 2011 revolution it was very common for Tunisian women filmmakers to resort to self-censorship or, at best, the allegorical mode, to ensure the release of their films. This placed Tunisian women filmmakers in a vulnerable position: If they got state funding, they became the mascots of the state feminism of Zine El Abidine Ben Ali, then Tunisia's leader. Were they to rely on foreign investors and appeal to Western markets through stereotypical scenes of harem life and *ḥammāms*, they would be guilty of cultural treason and self-Orientalism. Because for years the Ben Ali regime used the rhetoric of state feminism to conceal from his Western audience his poor record on human rights, Tunisian feminist activists, including filmmakers, actresses, lawyers, and writers, found themselves, after the revolution, accused of complicity with the Ben Ali regime. The memory of the actress Raja Ben Ammar being insulted, beaten, and dragged by the hair by the Ben Ali police during the 11 January 2011 artists' protest against government brutality was quickly buried.

After the downfall of Ben Ali, Moufida Tlatli was nominated minister of culture in the provisional government of Mohamed Ghannouchi. Many voices in the social media (including academics) opposed her nomination because of her alleged ties with Ben Ali and the issues she raised in her films such as rape, female sexuality, and the status of single mothers. In spring 2011 another controversy arose when Salafis smashed the windows of Cinéma Africa in Tunis to protest the projection of Nadia El Fani's *Neither God, nor Master* (*Ni Allah, Ni Maïtre*), a documentary shot during Ramadan 2010 in defense of secularism. Because the title led people to believe the film was an attack on Islam, El Fani had to change her title to *Laïcité, Inch'Allah!* (*Secularism, God Willing!*). For more than a year the ruling Ennahda Party banned *Tunisian Stories* (2011) by the young director Nada Mezni Hafaiedh for breaking the silence over male homosexuality among married men. In her film *It Was Better Tomorrow* (2012), the Tunisian director Hinde Boujemaa tells of the Tunisian revolution from the point of view of an uneducated woman for whom nothing has changed. In light of the ongoing battle between the religious right and the secular left over Tunisia's national identity, it is feared that films which do not fit into the political ideology of the ruling party will lose state funding because of being deemed either trivial or offensive to the sacred beliefs of Muslims. The battle for Tunisian women filmmakers is not lost yet. One of the most interesting outcomes of the Tunisian revolution is the election of the film director Salma Baccar as an MP to the 23 October 2011 National Constituent Assembly (NCA). Denouncing the 18 October 2012 political assassinations in Tataouine, she invited the Assembly to observe two minutes of silence in honor of the late Khaled Nagdh and, bringing the artistic to the political, she closed her intervention with: "*Silence! On réfléchit*" ("Silence! We are thinking").

Algeria. Unlike in Tunisia and Morocco the history of women's cinema in Algeria has been shaped by France's colonial policy of assimilation and the country's national struggle for liberation. Because l'Algérie Française was seen a territory of France rather than a protectorate like its neighbors, Algeria did not develop a national cinema per se until the first decade of independence. Out of the two hundred French films produced in

Algeria during the colonial period, only eleven were by native directors and not a single one of them was shot in Algeria. As early as 1911 the colonial government built movie houses to spread documentary propaganda films. In 1962 Boujmaa Karèche created La Cinémathèque Algérienne, which received modest subventions from the state. In 1964 the Algerian government founded L'Office National pour le Commerce et l'Industrie Cinématique (ONCIC). After a long dispute with American film distributors, in 1974 the ONCIC destroyed the U.S. monopoly by supplying Algerian cinemas with films acquired from eastern European countries.

The first Algerian feature film, *The Winds of the Aures* (1967) directed by Mohammad Lakhdar-Hamina, was a nationalist film about the tribulations of an Algerian mother who goes from one French camp to another in search of her maquisard son. The socialist agricultural reforms of 1971 inaugurated the second wave of Algerian cinema called *sinima al tajdid* (new cinema), which addressed social and economic issues like immigration, urbanization, women's liberation, unemployment, housing projects, etc. Years before the rise of the Islamic Salvation Front (FIS) Islamist threat, the government passed the Family Code of 1984, which conferred on Algerian women the legal status of a minor who is dependent on the tutelage of male relatives. Dozens of feminist organizations were created between 1989 and 1992 to protest these discriminatory laws, as well as the rising Islamist threat of FIS. It is within this context that Algerian women's cinema was born in the 1980s.

As in Morocco and Tunisia almost all Algerian women filmmakers pursued their cinema studies in Europe and North America and started their careers as film editors or assistant managers before producing their first feature-length film (Yamina Bachir Chouikh, Amal Bejaoui, and Nadia Cherabi). Films by Algerian women could be classified into four broad categories: the documentary genre produced in Algeria; *cinéma beur*; the Civil War film; and Algerian Jewish cinema. Assia Djebbar's film *The Nouba of the Women of Mount Chenoua* (1979) about the memoirs of illiterate Algerian women peasants who participated in the war of liberation falls within this first category. An important theme in this pioneer work is women's right to occupy private and public space. In her second film, *Zerda or the Songs of Forgetting* (1983), Djebbar examines over 131,000 feet (40,000 m) of French colonial newsreel to retrieve Algerian collective memory thought hitherto to have been lost. Nadia Cherabi's film *Fatima Amaria* (1993), about a black Algerian woman singer, and Naima Lefkir's *Iraq, the Second War* (1992) and *Those from the Casbah* (1993) fall within the categories of the ethnic and political documentary respectively.

The *cinéma beur* of French-born daughters of Algerian immigrants examines the immigrant memories and musical heritage of their parents such as Benguigui's film series *Women of Islam* (1994), *Immigrant Memories* (1997), or *Inch'Allah Sunday* (2001). It also delves into the epistemic violence against Muslim women writers and filmmakers who are manipulated by the French media "to stoke the fear of Islam" in France (Hillauer, 2005, p. 314). The third category is best illustrated in Chouikh's film *Rachida* (2002), which focuses on terrorism and the violence against women in the Algerian Civil War. Contrary to the first generation of Jewish women filmmakers who focused on the theme of exile from the Algerian homeland, such as Sarah Taouss-Matton's semiautobiographical film *The Journey Continues* (1981), the second generation of Algerian women Jewish filmmakers define themselves through tropes that are central to European Jewishness. Karin Albou's *Little Jerusalem* (2004) about Algerian Jewish emigrants in Paris cannot be understood outside the debate on citizenship and secularism in

France. Similarly her film *Wedding Song* (2008), about Jewish women during the Nazi occupation of North Africa has less to do with Vichy colonial politics in Africa or the Palestinian-Israeli conflict as some would argue than the reinscription of Sephardic Jewry into the history of the Holocaust, which became essential to the self-definition of European Jews in post–World War II Europe.

Morocco. *Mektoub* (*Destiny*, 1919) was the first colonial film to be shot in the protectorate of Morocco, which the French added to their empire in 1912. The birth of Le Centre Cinématographique Marocain (CCM) in 1944 marked the beginning of an independent Moroccan cinema, which came under the aegis of the state in the postcolonial era. The CCM became responsible for sponsorship, censorship, and the importation and distribution of foreign films, including the control of foreign film production on Moroccan soil. Even though the natural landscape of Morocco was used as a "backdrop" for American western movies, no major world film distributors showed interest in "Moroccan productions." It was not until late 1968 that a national Moroccan cinema was born with two first feature films—*Conquer to Live* by Mohammed B. A. Tazi and Ahmed Mesnaoui and *When the Dates Ripen* (1968) by Abdelaziz Ramdani and Larbi Bennani. Because Morocco did not have a school of cinema, all Moroccan film directors, including women, studied in France and the former Soviet Union. It was also common to hire women technicians from Tunisia and Europe to fill in the lack of skilled staff.

While the number of movie theaters in Morocco dropped as they did in Tunisia and Algeria because of the introduction of satellite dishes and video stores, Moroccan cinema is the only cinema of the Maghrib that saw a boost in film production since the early 2000s despite state censorship and the growing influence of Islamists who accuse liberal filmmakers like Nabil Ayouch or Laila Marrakchi of immorality. In 2004 the government passed the Mudawana or Personal Status Code, which improved Moroccan women's lives by raising the legal age of marriage to eighteen, and gave them joint family responsibility and rights in marriage and divorce. Polygamy is now acceptable only with the permission of the first wife and a judge. Because of these important social changes, today Morocco is the only country of the Maghrib to have an annual women's film festival, as seen in the Women's International Festival of Salé.

Two generations of women filmmakers had their imprint on Moroccan cinema. In the first generation of the 1980s, Farida Benlyazid stands out among both Western and Arab film critics. In her film *A Door to the Sky* (1989) about female spirituality in Islam, Benlyazid grounds female self-realization in the Islamic tradition of female maraboutism and the history of Muslim scholar Fāṭimah al-Fihri, not the discourse of Western modernity. She also wrote several screenplays for male directors such as Tazi's 1994 *Looking for My Husband's Wife*, a satirical comedy about polygamy in Morocco. Also included in this generation is the Jewish director Izza Genini who directed the film *Aita* (1987) on the music of *chikhat* or female troubadours and the documentary *Embroidered Canticles* (1991) on the Arabic and Hebrew musical heritage of Morocco. Fatima Jebli Ouazzani's educational film *In My Father's House* (1997) about the taboo of virginity in Morocco illustrates how Moroccan women directors use cinema as a medium of female empowerment and liberation. In this provocative autobiographical journey, Ouazzini enters a difficult dialogue with her grandfather who often compared a "deflowered woman" to "yesterday's couscous" (Hillauer, 2005, p. 353). The second generation of Moroccan women filmmakers consists of young filmmakers like the beurette Yasmine Kassari, director of *The Sleeping Child* (2004), which addresses the topic of immigration from the point of view of the Maghribī female imaginary, or Laila Marrakchi, whose film *Marock* (2005) featuring a love story between a Muslim girl and a Jewish boy created a stir in Morocco because such a liaison is prohibited by the Islamic legalistic patriarchy which forbids the marriage of a Muslim woman to Christian or Jewish man, but allows marital unions between a Muslim male and Women of the Book. The impact of the victory of the Islamist group, Party of Justice and Development (PJD), in the November 2011 parliamentary elections on Moroccan women's cinema remains to be seen.

BIBLIOGRAPHY

Alloula, Malek. *Le harem colonial: Images d'un sous-érotisme*. Paris: Garance, 1981.

Carroll, Jill. "Scarce at Home, the Movies of Tunisia's Female Filmmakers Draw World Acclaim." *The Christian Science Monitor*, October 4, 2007. http://www.csmonitor.com/2007/1004/p05s01-wome.html/.

Carter, Sandra Gayle. *What Moroccan Cinema? A Historical and Critical Study 1956–2006*. Lanham, Md.: Lexington Books, 2009.

Faaiek, Ahmed. "Fears of 'Enhanced' Censorship in the Wake of the Arab Spring." *Variety Arabia*, June 11, 2012. http://varietyarabia.com/Docs.Viewer/99a0d09a-431c-42f0-93b8-5eac751df1bc/default.aspx/.

Gabous, Abdelkrim. *Silence, elles tournent: Les femmes et le cinéma en Tunisie*. Tunis: Cérès Editions, 1998.

Hillauer, Rebecca. *Encyclopedia of Arab Women Filmmakers*. Translated by Allison Brown, Deborah Cohen, and Nancy Joyce. Rev. and updated ed. Cairo and New York: American University in Cairo Press, 2005.

Machta, Insaf. "Le Film et les malentendus de la révolution: L'affaire Nadia Al Fani et *Persepolis*." *Nawaat*, May 30, 2012. http://nawaat.org/portail/2012/05/30/le-film-et-les-malentendus-de-la-revolution-laffaire-nadia-al-fani-et-persepolis/.

Shohat, Ella Habiba. "Framing Post-Third-Worldist Culture: Gender and Nation in Middle Eastern/North African Film and Video." *Jouvert: A Journal of Postcolonial Studies*, 1997. http://english.chass.ncsu.edu/jouvert/v1i1/SHOHAT.HTM/.

Slimani, Leila. "Les artistes tunisiens disent: 'Vive la révolution!'" *Jeune Afrique*, March 2, 2011. http://www.jeuneafrique.com/Article/ARTJAJA2612p082085.xml0/actualite-afriqueles-artistes-tunisiens-disent-vive-la-revolution.html/.

Young, Deborah. "It Was Better Tomorrow (*Ya man Aach*): Venice Review." *The Hollywood Reporter*, September 7, 2012. http://www.hollywoodreporter.com/review/was-better-tomorrow-ya-man-aach-review-venice-368843/.

Zayzafoon, Lamia Ben Youssef. "Memory as Allegory: The Specter of Incest and the (Re)naming of the Father in Moufida Tlatli's *The Silences of the Palace* (1994)." *Critical Arts* 21, no. 1 (2007): 47–67.

Lamia Ben Youssef

Turkish Women's Contributions

Until 1923, when Muhsin Ertuğrul decided to adapt Halide Edip Adıvar's novel *Ateşten Gömlek* (The Shirt of Fire), which told the story of a young woman who works for the liberation of her country, Turkish women were not allowed to act either in theater plays or in films due to religious and patriarchal constraints. When female characters were needed in films, they were chosen from those living in Turkey who were not Muslims, including Greek, Armenian, and Russian women. The first film that had a female character central to its narrative was the 1917 adaptation of Mehmet Rauf's theater play by Sedat Simavi, *Pençe* (The Claw), which focused on marriage and its constraints. The film offered a representation of women's place in society at the time, underpinning the idea that marriage was a necessity for women. *Mürebbiye* (*The Governess*; Ahmet Fehim, 1919) followed *Pençe* with a female protagonist being central to the narrative. Madam Kalitea, a Greek actress, starred as the heroine of the film, and she is regarded as the first vamp character in Turkish cinema. Released in the context of the occupation of Istanbul by the Allied forces, the film tells the story of a French woman who seduces the members of a snobbish family for whom she works, focusing on the corrupt French tutor who represented the Western woman. The negative connotations assigned to the tutor act as a token expression of resistance against foreign forces in, and the occupation of, the country. It was banned by the Allied forces on the same grounds.

The first film that assigned a female protagonist and a distinct description of that female character in its narrative is *Bataklı damın kızı, Aysel* (The Girl from the Marsh Croft; Muhsin Ertuğrul, 1934). It is the first film in Turkish cinema dealing with the issue of rape, albeit by offering marriage to women as a fitting end to the rape. In the films of the 1950s female characters were gifted with marriage unless they resisted. Women were portrayed as a source of discontent and trouble for men. During the 1960s there were a significant number of films focusing on women's place in society. Female characters were stereotypically either good and virtuous or bad and dishonorable and lacking in depth. In the 1970s sex films and social realist films coexisted as the prominent trends in cinema. It is interesting to note that Turkish actresses who took part in the sex films (where the sole purpose of the woman's presence was sexual or erotic) changed their names in order to continue with their real lives. Some married, used their husbands' surnames, and never worked for the film industry again. Actors in these films, by contrast, were able to continue their careers in cinema and theater because, as men, their dignity was not perceived as sullied.

The military intervention of 12 September 1980 repressed all political activities and attempted a systematic depoliticization of the masses. The 1980s women's movement in Turkey was the first social and political movement that emerged in a period of depoliticization. Women were, for the first time, raising their own independent voices through campaigns, festivals, demonstrations, publication of journals, and the formation of consciousness-raising groups. Profoundly affected by the social and political milieu, Turkish cinema went through a period of change as overtly political or social realist films were censored, banned, or destroyed as a result of forcible depoliticization. In their attempt to avoid the political, filmmakers chose to focus on women, and this occurred in parallel to the emergence of the women's movement. The entrance of sophisticated characters and a focus on the individual informed the shift in representations of women in cinema. This shift was from one-dimensional to multidimensional characters. Prominent among the film trends of the 1980s were films dealing with the coup's psychological effects on individuals and women's films (in parallel with the rise of feminism in Turkey) with their depictions of female characters engaged in a search for identity and independence. Since the 1990s there has been an increase in the number of films that attempt to critique the concept of honor, a recurring motif in Turkish films. There are countless narratives that treat the concept as an integral part of representing womanhood.

Contemporary women filmmakers in Turkey tend to focus on a range of issues around political, cultural, and ethnic identity, as well as memory. Tomris Giritlioğlu's *Salkım hanımin taneleri* (Mrs. Salkım's Diamonds, 1999) has received a number of awards nationally for its treatment of the controversial topic of the non-Muslim population in Turkey in the 1940s. At the heart of Yeşim Ustaoğlu's *Bulutları beklerken* (Waiting for the Clouds, 2003) are Greek and Turkish identities presented through the stories of women in northern Turkey. In *Güneşe Yolculuk/Journey to the Sun* (1999), it is the Kurdish identity that is the center of the narrative. *Sırtlarındaki hayat* (*Life on Their Shoulders*, 2004) is Ustaoğlu's only documentary to date. The film documents the difficult working conditions for women in northern Turkey, in the Black Sea region. It also sheds light on a number of problems including child brides, health issues, and illiteracy. Handan İpekçi's successful film, *Büyük adam, küçük aşk* (*Big Man, Little Love*, 2001), is about the relationship between a Kurdish child and a Turkish pensioner.

Women of Turkey have been the theme of several documentaries made by women directors who live outside Turkey. These films tend to focus on the relationship between religion and women's place in Turkey. Olga Nakkas's 2006 film, *Women of Turkey: Between Islam and Secularism*, for instance, draws on interviews with women and examines the individual and political resonance of the headscarf and veiling. Binnur Karaevli's 2009 film, *Voices Unveiled: Turkish Women Who Dare*, provides a critique of the ban on wearing headscarves at the same time as touching upon issues including female officers in mosques, violence in the name of Islam, lack of education and the economic dependence of women, women and Turkey's EU candidacy, and the tensions inherent between Muslim and Western cultures.

Bibliography

Abisel, Nilgün. *Türk sineması üzerine yazılar*. Ankara: İmage Kitabevi, 1994.

Atakav, Eylem. *Women and Turkish Cinema: Gender Politics, Cultural Identity and Representation*. London and New York: Routledge, 2012.

Özgüç, Agah. *Türk sinemasında cinselliğin arihi*. İstanbul: Broy Yayınları, 1988.

Scognamillo, Giovanni. *Türk sinema tarihi, 1896–1997*. İstanbul: Kabalcı Yayınevi, 1998.

Eylem Atakav

Citizenship. Citizenship is defined, following the legacy of the English sociologist T. H. Marshall (1950), as a bundle of rights and duties that define an individual's identity and status within a political community, typically a nation state. Marshall identified three types of citizenship rights, namely the juridical (such as habeas corpus), the political (the right to vote and form political parties), and the social rights associated with the welfare state. The forms of citizenship obviously vary between societies depending on whether social security is a top-down state strategy or the outcome of bottom-up struggles for the redistribution of resources (Turner, 1990). Social rights are said to mitigate negative market forces by providing some minimal protection from accidents, unemployment, poor health, and old age through collectivized social security. In a capitalist society, citizenship is often contrasted with social class, because the entitlements associated with citizenship modify the full impact of class inequality. While critical sociologists have been sceptical of the claim that citizenship can significantly modify the capitalist logic of economic exploitation, citizenship is seen to be a fundamental basis of modern democracies.

The original notion of citizenship has nevertheless been subject to constant revision, mainly to accommodate changes brought about by the growing cultural diversity associated with multiculturalism, labor migration (both legal and illegal), and refugees and asylum seekers associated with globalization. To rethink citizenship in relation to changing state borders, sociologists have invented new concepts such as "flexible citizenship" or "semi-citizenship" to capture situations where "guest workers" can acquire partial rights, such as the right to vote in local but not national elections.

Despite significant growth in sociological research into the social and cultural foundations of citizenship, the gender dimension of social rights has yet to be adequately conceptualized. Feminist critics of the legacy of Marshall's theory argued that the persistence of gender inequality in industrial societies (with respect to employment, wages, child support and social mobility) indicates the limitations of the liberal model of citizenship. The effects of the glass ceiling on the social and economic advancement of women have demonstrated the limitations of liberal contract theory and the Marshallian theory of citizenship, wherein the consequences of the public/private divide have been systematically ignored (Pateman, 1988). While demanding the full range of rights of secular citizenship (including the right to vote and to participate fully in the public domain), advocates of the rights of women have focused on issues relating to sexuality, reproduction, marriage, and divorce.

The notion of sexual citizenship raises interesting criticisms of the traditional divisions between the public and private. Feminists argue that heterosexuality and domesticity have been constructed as necessary conditions of citizenship. For example, the Marshallian model of citizenship and the welfare state presupposed the presence of a stable nuclear family, a working husband and a reproductive wife. In this combination of a Fordist economy, based on mechanized mass-production manufacturing, liberal citizenship, and the nuclear family, women are exposed to exploitation at work where their wages are lower than their male colleagues', and in the home where their role was to provide unpaid services to their husbands. According to these criticisms, citizenship has been closely connected with the hegemonic form of heterosexuality, especially in the institutions of inheritance, marriage, divorce, and adoption.

Early feminist criticisms of traditional notions of citizenship have now been extended to consider the rights of gay and lesbian individuals. The relationship between entitlement and gender can be viewed as an important aspect of the emergence of sexual citizenship. Through the influence of the French philosopher Michel Foucault (1926–1984), modern theories of citizenship regard identity, subjectivity, and gender position as more salient in modern societies than traditional debates about social class, income equality, and employment opportunities. Gay and lesbian movements have claimed that sexual liberation, especially the right of individuals to decide on their own sexual orientation, is a necessary entitlement of autonomous individuals in a democratic society. These arguments have promoted claims for enhanced sexual rights under the umbrella of "intimate citizenship" or the right to sexual pleasure without state interference. Critics of these developments such as the Cambridge philosopher Onora O'Neill (b. 1941) note that the modern emphasis on entitlement is taking place without corresponding notions of duty and responsibility.

We may divide these new perspectives into two categories. Firstly, there are rights to reproduction: with whom may one reproduce, and under what social and legal conditions? The second perspective concerns the rights of sexual consumption: with whom may one enjoy sexual intimacy, and under what conditions? Reproductive rights are closely connected with the so-called capabilities approach to human development of the American philosopher Martha Nussbaum (b. 1947), in which the education of women and the achievement of literacy are necessary stages toward achieving personal health, including reproductive health. Expanding the capabilities of women is important in giving them control over their own fertility. The second form of sexual citizenship promoting the idea of sexual intimacy as a right makes no assumptions about reproduction and is more concerned about promoting the idea of freedom of sexual expression, experience, and association.

In the West, the emergence of citizenship was closely associated with the rise of the bourgeoisie and the concepts of citizenship and civil society in European languages reflect this class origin. Whereas a citizen is basically a member of a state, the traditional idea of civil society also included notions about civility, civic duty, and a code of moral behavior. In the Middle East by contrast, rentier states do not generate a middle class but rather foster elites based on rent from oil production. Historically, state building occurred through the collapse of empires and hence it assumed a top-down character. However, today, Western notions of citizenship are now being tested and criticized in a broad comparative and historical framework embracing Asia, Africa, and the Middle East.

For example, Selma Botman's study of Egypt (1999) provides a pioneering account of the vicissitudes of the status of women in the public realm under liberal, nationalist, and fundamentalist forces. In 1922, when Britain granted Egypt partial independence, the constitutional arrangements made no provision for women's political equality and women who had been politically active were expected to return to their domestic duties. Nevertheless, women came to play a significant part in the development of Egyptian nationalism. World War II radicalized political consciousness in Egyptian society and the Egyptian Feminist Party was formed in 1944 with a political platform for social reform, birth control, and abortion. Active in the rise of Egyptian nationalism through the Women's Committee for Popular Resistance in 1951, women supported the struggle against the British in the Suez crisis. They enjoyed support from the Islamic modernists who argued that the Qurʾān gave women equal social and political rights. The nationalist government of Gamal Abdel Nasser (1918–1970) introduced a range of social reforms that enhanced women's status in post-colonial Egyptian society. While Nasser's "state feminism" undermined the power of husbands and fathers, it made women dependent on the state, giving rise to state patriarchy. In more recent times, Anwar Sadat (1918–1981) and Hosni Mubarak (b. 1928) achieved political continuity by forging an alliance between fundamentalists, state officials, and middle-class allies. In the 1980s, many of the social advances of women were challenged by the politics of "Islamism" that attempted to reestablish traditional values. Among conservative clerics, the "politics of reversal" sought to enforce the *hijab* (curtain) as a potent symbol of the (re)domestication of women.

Western critics have often regarded Islamic tradition as a major hurdle in the growth of citizenship for women outside the liberal democratic societies of the West. Veiling, female circumcision, and polygamy are often cited as key disadvantages confronting the enjoyment of equal rights of citizenship for women in Muslim communities. These traditional patriarchal structures severely limit the life chances of Muslim women to adequate education, social mobility, and control over their own sexuality. Although there have been many voices of opposition against the West demanding change within the Islamic Middle East, Iran, India, and Pakistan—Muhammad Iqbal (1877–1938), Sayyid Abul ʿAla Maududi (1903–1979), Sayyid Qutb (1906–1966), Mehdi Haeri Yazd (1923–1999), Mohammad Khatami (b. 1943), and Seyyed Hossein Nasr (b. 1933)—and calling for a spiritual renewal, their pleas for Islamic modernization did not include the modernization of the family, the status of women, or the rights of gays and lesbians. Recognizing such rights remains one of the most contentious and unresolved issues in contemporary Islam.

One important exception to religious conservatism was the Algerian philosopher Mohammad Arkoun (1928–2010) who obtained his Ph.D. from the Sorbonne and became an influential writer on the need for a critical reading and demystification of the Qurʾān and ḥadīth. Arkoun

(2002), *The Unthought in Contemporary Islamic Thought*, argued that Islamic thought had to break out of its "dogmatic enclosure" and that Muslims needed to rethink gender relations, because, in Islam, only men had full legal status as persons and citizens. While early Islam had broken the tribal structures of traditional societies creating a community based on faith, socially conservative practices around women, marriage, and the family had acquired sacred status. While the revealed Word of God had opened up the thinkable, socially conservative values had produced the unthinkable.

The influential work of Suad Joseph (2000) on Lebanon provides an important insight into how tribal and familial structures underlying patriarchy have blocked the growth of secular citizenship and the social rights of women. Religion has played a major role in defining citizenship in the Middle East, especially its gendered nature. Religion is a necessary component of the patriarchal structures that underpin the power of men within the family, tribe, and state. More importantly, citizenship as a legal entity has in the Middle East often been constituted through membership of a religious community and hence the distribution of rights and resources is organized on the basis of membership of religious sects. What follows is that the nation is imagined as an assembly of subcommunities that are in turn defined by religion. Political conflicts between and within the nation-state assume the form of religious conflicts, and establishing peaceful relations between different religious communities is a difficult and protracted process.

One further consequence is that civil society is not understood as an arena of secular negotiation and compromise, but rather a sphere in which absolute religious claims to truth cannot be subject to debate and compromise. Where Islam is the dominant religion, the only contractual relations are with God and hence the conventional political processes of debate, contest, and compromise are regarded as inadmissible. However, in recent years, a flourishing opposition to patriarchy by Muslim women through the agency of voluntary associations and the Arab Spring of 2011 has created opportunities for Islamic organizations such as the Muslim Brotherhood in Egypt to enter legally into democratic politics. Sherine Hafez (2011) in *An Islam of Her Own* has shown through a study of women's voluntary associations how women become empowered as citizens through local activism.

In Indonesia during the presidencies of both Sukarno (1901–1970) and Suharto (1921–2008), "rights" smacked of western liberalism and were declared to be "un-Indonesian." However, Susan Blackburn in *Women and the State in Modern Indonesia* (2000), and Kathryn Robinson (2009) in *Gender, Islam and Democracy in Indonesia* have shown how women's organizations played a major role in the downfall of the authoritarian New Order regime (1965–1998) of Suharto who ruled over Indonesia from 1967 to 1998. Women's associations have also emerged as important in the Reform period after 1998. In their confrontation with the government, women activists led public campaigns condemning the systematic rape of women in Aceh and East Timor as state-sponsored attacks on women, thereby establishing rights associated with sexual citizenship. Their prominence in the growth of democracy is important, since Indonesia is the largest Muslim society with a population of 217 million of whom 80 percent are Muslim. Criticism of polygamy and female circumcision became widespread in the Nahdlatul Ulama, the largest Islamic organization, under the leadership of Abdurrachman Wahid (1940–2009). The election of women to high office in predominantly Muslim societies, such as President Megawati (2001–2004) in Indonesia and President Benazir Bhutto (1988–1990, and

1993–1996) in Pakistan, is evidence of the growth of the political rights of citizenship.

Across the Islamic world, as women acquire entry to secondary and higher education, and control over their own fertility through access to contraception, their voices are no longer silenced by traditional values and patriarchal structures. The global growth of women's organizations is indicative of an emerging civil society and patterns of active citizenship that are the foundation of popular demands for rights and the end of authoritarianism across the Arab world.

BIBLIOGRAPHY

Arkoun, Mohammed. *The Unthought in Contemporary Islamic Thought*. London: Saqi, 2002. A controversial plea for an open and creative rereading of the authoritative sources of Islamic orthodoxy in the Qur'ān and ḥadīth or traditions associated with the Prophet.

Blackburn, Susan. *Women and the State in Modern Indonesia*. Cambridge, U.K.: Cambridge University Press, 2000. Considers the complex evolution of women's rights to education, voting, and reproduction from Dutch colonialism, independence, and beyond.

Bodman, Herbert, and Tohidi, Nayereh, eds. *Women in Muslim Societies. Diversity within Unity*. Boulder, Colo.: Rienner, 1998. A useful reminder of the great diversity of the status of women within Muslim societies.

Botman, Selma. *Engendering Citizenship in Egypt*. New York: Columbia University Press, 1999. An early and classic study of the growth of women's rights in Nasserite Egypt.

Hafez, Sherine. *An Islam of Her Own: Reconsidering Religion and Secularism in Women's Islamic Movements*. New York and London: New York University Press, 2011. Employing ideas from Michel Foucault, the book explores women's subjectivities and examines the importance of women's organizations as vehicles of active citizenship.

Joseph, Suad, ed. *Gender and Citizenship in the Middle East*. Syracuse, N. Y.: Syracuse University Press, 2000. The standard and authoritative work on citizenship in various Middle East societies from secular states such as Turkey to conservative societies such as Saudi Arabia.

Marshall, Thomas H. *Citizenship and Social Class, and Other Essays*. Cambridge, U.K.: Cambridge University Press, 1951. The publication that launched the contemporary debate about citizenship in western sociology.

Pateman, Carole. *The Sexual Contract*. Stanford, Calif.: Stanford University Press, 1988. A basic and original feminist criticism of the liberal traditions that separated the private and the public realm, allocating women to the former as exclusively concerned with raising children.

Robinson, Kathryn. *Gender, Islam, and Democracy in Indonesia*. London and New York: Routledge, 2009. Describes the role of women's organizations in the growth of reformism and the fall of New Order authoritarian rule.

Turner, Bryan S. "Outline of a theory of citizenship." *Sociology* 24 (2) (1990): 189–217. Offers a general analysis of four types of citizenship in terms of passive and active forms, and the public/private split.

BRYAN S. TURNER

CLITORIDECTOMY. Clitoridectomy, commonly known as female circumcision, has historically been practiced in some areas of the Islamic world. The practice is pre-Islamic in origin and its distribution should be attributed to indigenous cultural norms rather than specifically religious requirements. It is known primarily in a number of African societies, Islamic and non-Islamic, in the area extending eastward from Senegal to the Horn of Africa. The operations referred to collectively as clitoridectomy range from excising only the tip of the clitoris to total excision of the clitoris and labia, and total excision with infibulation. This most severe form of the practice, total excision with infibulation, is referred to commonly as either "pharaonic" or "Sudanese" circumcision and is attested primarily in Sudan, Somalia, Djibouti, and parts of Ethiopia. In those areas where it is practiced, clitoridectomy is not limited to Muslims. In Egypt, for example, clitoridectomy has a long history among the Coptic population. On the other hand, it is relatively unknown among non-Muslims in Sudan. It is not practiced in Saudi Arabia, Tunisia, Iran, or Turkey, and it is practiced unevenly in Java.

The Arabic terminology used to refer to the practice is *khafd* or *khitān*, the latter term being used also to refer to male circumcision. There is no mention of it in the Qurʾān, although there is evidence of its existence in the traditions of the Prophet, who condemned the severe forms of the operation as being harmful to women's sexual health and recommended the minor form of the operation (excising only the tip of the clitoris) if it were to be performed. Generally, the schools of Islamic law regard it as a recommended, but not obligatory, practice. Although explicitly religious justifications may be invoked, the rationales given for continuing the practice are generally not expressed in religious terms. The most common justification is that it is "the custom"; however, numerous other reasons are also given, for example, the control of female sexuality and the preservation of virginity. Failure to perform clitoridectomy is believed by some cultures to result not only in promiscuity and adultery, but also in infant mortality, infertility, and poor general health. In addition, in the cultures where it is practiced, uncircumcised female genitalia are considered to be ugly, and uncircumcised women are considered, for diverse reasons, to be unmarriageable. The practitioners of clitoridectomy are ordinarily women, many of whom are also midwives. Because clitoridectomy is often performed under septic conditions and is associated with a variety of medical complications, better educated parents, especially in urban areas, may seek medical professionals to perform the operation on their daughters under sterile conditions. In some countries where clitoridectomy was widespread, it has been prohibited by law for a number of years (e.g., Egypt and Sudan). In recent decades, clitoridectomy has become a highly politicized issue in the context of human rights and women's rights campaigns dedicated to eradicating genital mutilation.

BIBLIOGRAPHY

Bell, Heather. "Midwifery Training and Female Circumcision in the Inter-War Anglo-Egyptian Sudan." *Journal of African History* 39.2 (1998): 293–312.

Braddy, Cathleen M., and Julia A. Files. "Female Genital Mutilation: Cultural Awareness and Clinical Considerations." *Journal of Midwifery and Women's Health* 52.2 (March–April 2007): 158–163.

Giorgis, Belkis Wolde. *Female Circumcision in Africa.* Addis Ababa: United Nations Economic Commission for Africa, 1981. U.N. publication with an extensive annotated bibliography.

"Khafḍ or Khifāḍ." In *Encyclopaedia of Islam*, edited by P. Bearman, Th. Bianquis, C. E. Bosworth, E. van Donzel, and W. P. Heinrichs. Leiden, The Netherlands: E.J. Brill, 2008.

Saadawi, Nawal El. *The Hidden Face of Eve.* Translated by Sherif Hetata. London: Zed Books, 1980. Considered a classic statement on clitoridectomy by an Arab feminist.

Wensinck, A. J."Khitān." In *Encyclopaedia of Islam*, edited by P. Bearman, Th. Bianquis, C. E. Bosworth, E. van Donzel, and W. P. Heinrichs. Leiden, The Netherlands: E.J. Brill, 2008.

PAULA SANDERS

COMMISSION ON INTERNATIONAL RELIGIOUS FREEDOM. The United States Commission on International Religious Freedom (USCIRF) is an independent bipartisan federal government agency created by the passage of the International Religious Freedom Act of 1998 (IRFA). The commission's mandate requires it to monitor the status of religious freedom throughout the world and to provide policy recommendations on religious freedom to the president of the United States, secretary of state, and both houses of Congress. In addition to one nonvoting ambassador-at-large for International Religious Freedom, the Commission is composed of nine volunteer commissioners, whose main role is to vote on and report policy recommendations through the USCIRF Annual Reports. Past and current Muslim commissioners include Laila al-Marayati (1999–2001), Shirin R. Tahir-Kheli (2001–2003), Leila Nadya Sadat (2001–2003), Khaled Abou El Fadl (2003–2007), Azizah al-Hibri (2011–present), and M. Zuhdi Jasser (2012–present).

The USCIRF Annual Reports profile various foreign countries and monitor, on an ongoing basis, religious freedom violations (e.g., the status of Ṣūfīs and Bahāʾi in Iran, or Ahmadis and Hindus in Pakistan). In addition, these reports recommend to the United States president those countries that should be designated a country of particular concern (CPC) or those that should be placed on a watch list for their violations of religious freedom. CPC's are those countries that commit ongoing and egregious violations of religious freedom, while those countries placed on the watch list tolerate or commit religious freedom violations, but do not reach the mandate threshold for CPC status. Countries designated a CPC by the U.S. government may be subject to specific government action, including economic sanctions. Many of those identified as countries of particular concern by the USCIRF Reports have Muslim-majority populations.

In each annual report, specific violations and religious freedom abridgements are detailed by country, and each commissioner's approval or dissent of each identified country's CPC status is noted. In 2012, the commission recommended Turkey as a CPC, which met with great controversy and commissioner dissent. In the same report, violations of women's rights were detailed for Iran, citing polygamy, unequal legal status, and required dress codes as affecting the human rights of women in the state. Additionally, Saudi Arabia is frequently recommended as a CPC, particularly for the state's control of religious interpretation and the detention of Shīʿah Muslim dissidents.

In addition to publishing the USCIRF Annual Reports, USCIRF commissioners testify before Congress, participate in multilateral meetings at the United Nations, and produce policy reports on a variety of subjects pertaining to the commission's work. In 2005, USCIRF staff published *The Religion-State Relationship and the Right to Freedom of Belief: A Comparative Textual Analysis of the Constitutions of Predominantly Muslim Countries*, which comprehensively reviews the constitutions of Muslim-majority countries and endeavors to understand how these constitutions can accommodate religious freedom and other international human rights norms. The report claims that, unlike in secular countries, making citizen equality subject to Islamic principles may expose women to discriminatory treatment in both law and practice, particularly in regard to personal-status issues.

Controversy surrounding the commission has focused on the Christian lobbying for the IRFA, the Egyptian Coptic community protest of a 2001 USCIRF country visit, and the public criticism of the commission by former Ambassador-at-Large for International Religious Freedom, Robert Seiple, for focusing on religious persecutions in foreign countries rather than recognizing country efforts in advancing religious freedom. Additionally, throughout USCIRF's history, major civil society groups have expressed concern over which countries the commissioners recommend as CPC's, suggesting ideological bias and partisanship as major determining factors, resulting in many countries being overlooked despite continued religious freedom violations.

BIBLIOGRAPHY

Stahnke, Tad, and Robert C. Blitt. *The Religion-State Relationship and the Right to Freedom of Religion or Belief: A Comparative Textual Analysis of the Constitutions of Predominantly Muslim Countries.* Washington, D.C.: United States Commission on International Religious Freedom, 2005.

United States Commission on International Religious Freedom. "Annual Report 2012." http://www.uscirf.gov/images/Annual%20Report%20of%20USCIRF%202012(2).pdf.

Dominic T. Bocci

Communications Media. Inherent in the Islamic teachings are basic rights of communication, including the rights to know, read, write, and speak. The notion of *ʿilm* (knowledge) prevails throughout the Qurʾān as the basic tenet of all communication in Islam. The word *iqrāʾ* (read) is important in the Qurʾān and conveys the idea of acquiring knowledge and communicating it with the Muslim community, which is why *tablīgh* (propagation and dissemination of Islamic beliefs and practices) is considered a duty for those capable of it.

The process of communication between Muslims was made easier as the majority of the Islamic world spoke a unified language, Arabic, hence unifying Muslims in the larger Islamic community, the *ummah,* especially in the decades following Muḥammad's death.

Communication has been an integral tool to preserve and spread Islamic teachings around the world and pass them on over the centuries. In turn Islamic civilization has played an integral role in the development of different forms of communication to ensure accurate transmission of the teachings and values of Islam after Prophet Muḥammad and his Companions passed away. As the religion became widespread across the world, it was crucial to develop a system to document the Qurʾān, the *sunnah* (practices of the Prophet), and the *ḥadīth* (a record of the Prophet's sayings and practices) to ensure accuracy of the relayed word.

From Oral to Written Communication. The need for documenting and disseminating the Qurʾān, *sunnah,* and *ḥadīth* led to the development of both oral and written communications. During his lifetime the Prophet ensured that many of his Companions memorized and recited the Qurʾān. Verses were also written down haphazardly on scattered leather pieces and parchments.

It was only after Muḥammad's death in 632 that his Companion and first caliph, Abū Bakr, ordered gathering the Qurʾān into one book, forming the first ever *maṣḥaf* (holy book). Although Abū Bakr was hesitant at first, after many of the Prophet's Companions and Qurʾān reciters died in the battle of Yamama, Companion ʿUmar ibn al-Khaṭṭāb urged Abū Bakr to gather the Qurʾān quickly into one book in fear of it vanishing with the death of its reciters, or getting inaccurately transmitted through time. Zayd ibn Thabit was ordered to gather the scattered verses of the Qurʾān. The final book was kept with Abū Bakr, followed by ʿUmar ibn al-Khaṭṭāb and then his daughter, Hafsa. It was the third caliph, ʿUthman ibn Affān, who ordered the making of multiple copies of the Qurʾān held by Hafsa bint ʿUmar to ensure accuracy and unity of the holy book. He then ordered that all other versions be destroyed, hence ensuring that there is only one accurate and verified version of the Qurʾān, which is the same one known today.

The *sunnah* and *ḥadīth,* however, were not written down and were still transmitted orally. Although there had been scattered individual efforts to document the *ḥadīth,* it wasn't until almost two hundred years after the Prophet's death that a collective effort was made to institutionalize and formalize the collection and documentation of the *ḥadīth.* The documentation of *ḥadīth* and *sunnah*, however, have always followed strict rules of *isnād* (validation) to ensure that only those teachings or sayings relayed by an unbroken series of reliable authorities are documented.

Even though written communication had developed, oral communication remained an important mode in the Islamic world. Memorization of the Qurʾān in Arabic is still common practice among Muslims and practiced widely across the Muslim world serving as an inextricable link between the oral and written modes. Mosques, followed by religious centers, have remained throughout history the center of communication, especially during the daily and Friday congregations. The mosque served not only for daily prayers, but also for spreading news and opinions and as a forum for political decision-making and discussions between people as well as with *ʿulamāʾ* (religious scholars). This form of communication, including the formal address or sermon (*khuṭbah*), was largely based on the Islamic tradition of combining political and religious discourses.

Cultural Renaissance. The expansion of Islamic states in Asia, Africa, and the Iberian Peninsula, coupled with the introduction of new means of communication, accelerated the process of scientific, commercial, and artistic communication.

Medieval Islamic culture with its scholarly interest in the entire universe provided an intellectual environment that advanced studies in such fields as astronomy, chemistry, geography, history, mathematics, medicine, and philosophy. These studies in turn stimulated a respect for information and knowledge that directed both the domestic and international relations of the Islamic community. The interconnected Islamic civilization also took advantage of its pivotal geopolitical position by developing navigation science and communication, not only for commerce and trade, but also for distributing scholarly and practical knowledge. Written manuscripts and books permeated Islamic society and inspired profound cultural developments.

A group of efficient and intellectual scribes, the *warrāqīn*, served the Islamic community by commenting on and copying manuscripts, often completing more than a hundred pages a day. Under the supervision of the *warrāqīn*, writers and their publishers established an effective system of cooperation within the publication industry. The high demand for books led to the building of numerous private and public libraries.

Between the thirteenth century and the modern era, however, the Islamic world fell short in adopting new communication technologies because of political, economic, and social factors, both internal and external. The European invention of the printing press in the mid-fifteenth century heralded the birth of the print culture and a tremendous quantitative jump in the output of information. In the Islamic societies, however, one mode of communication did not supersede another; rather, oral and written communication both continued to develop and came to complement technological forms of communication in the modern era. Hence the growth of communication in the Islamic world was characterized by qualitative progress rather than quantitative jumps.

From the sixteenth to the early nineteenth century, when more or less formalized councils of ministers came into being in Islamic countries such as Iran and Turkey, the official government news writer occupied an important place. Occasionally the government news was also read to the public from the stairs of mosques. The official governmental report functioned as a successful medium for disseminating news until the introduction of modern journalism.

Printing presses were introduced into Islamic countries such as Egypt, India, Iran, and Turkey as early as the seventeenth century. During the late eighteenth century and the first half of the nineteenth, the printing press facilitated the establishment of newspapers throughout the Islamic world. This early period of the press was responsible for the importation of modern nationalism and secularism from Europe. It also played an important role in the spread of the nineteenth-century Islamic reform movement as well as the campaign against European colonialism.

The early growth of the modern mass media in the Islamic world was associated first with state intervention in the production and distribution of the press, and second with the influence of both secular and religious leaders who sought to use the press for sociopolitical reforms. Thus, during the last two decades of the nineteenth century, two types of publications emerged in the Islamic world: liberal and religious press. The Western-trained journalistic establishment that was led by the educated elite promoted European ideas of secularism, liberalism, and modern nationalism. The religious establishments, on the other hand, were led by Islamic reformists such as Sayyid Jamāl al-Dīn al-Afghānī, who was campaigning for a unified Islamic community throughout the Middle East, Asia, and North Africa. By the turn of the century the new tool of journalism was in widespread use in the Islamic world from Indonesia to North Africa.

With the revolt of the Young Turks against the sultan in 1908, there came a sudden upsurge in the number of newspapers being published in the Arabic-speaking provinces of the Ottoman Empire. Anticolonial movements and the struggle for independence in India, Indonesia, Morocco, and Algeria led to the growth of the press, political parties, and a number of ideological movements ranging from Islamic radicalism to communist socialism.

Modern-day Communication. The twentieth century thus marked the rise of modern mass communication in the Islamic world. The process of decolonization in a number of Islamic countries in Asia and Africa, coupled with the delineation of economic classes and the recognition of the nation-state system, elevated the communications media to new prominence in which the state played a major role. In the Central Asian republics where Soviet models of media became dominant, Islamic institutions of communication such as mosques and *madāris* remained under the control and supervision of the state. In North and West Africa the communications media of the newly established independent states were developed along the lines of French and English models.

A characteristic of the mass media in the contemporary Islamic world has been the multiplicity of press agencies as well as broadcasting, telecommunications, and cultural industries, which has largely reflected the diversity of ethnic, linguistic, and geographical groups. As a whole the media in the Islamic world, particularly television, have been strongly influenced by their counterparts in the West. In contrast to the press, which has had a fairly independent, private status, radio and television have been typically operated by centralized, government-supervised institutions.

Until the last decade of the twentieth century, because of the lack of production facilities in some Muslim countries and the generally low level of the economy, the media had to import much of their equipment. At the same time the lack of sufficient telecommunications and transportation infrastructure made distribution both costly and haphazard. For these reasons the media often relied heavily on outside sources for news and programming. Frequent charges that the media were influenced and even controlled by international agencies, postcolonial ties, and government organizations stemmed largely from this imbalance in the financing of indigenous news agencies, as well as from a lack of comprehensive national communications policies.

The contemporary Islamic media are special products of their social milieu. Certain traits are peculiar to each Islamic region's social and cultural structure. The Middle East and South Asia have the most developed mass communication systems, whereas the regions of Africa and Central and East Asia require more investment in their systems. However most Islamic countries fall short in the average number of modern media outlets when compared to the industrialized countries of Europe and North America.

Before widespread access to the Internet, in the mid- and late 1990s, cassette tapes were an important source for religious communications. Having been an important tool to communicate between Egyptians abroad, mainly in the Gulf, and their families back home who were often illiterate, cassettes were always a popular means of communication and alternative to mail or books, especially in lower classes. Many used cassettes to listen to the Qurʾān, but, during the 1990s the phenomenon of religious preaching through cassettes became widespread. The greatest influence was seen by the contemporary preacher Amr Khaled's tape on the veil, which became an instant hit among young girls. The widespread presence of hijab in younger generations was attributed to Amr Khaled's recorded preaching.

After the late 1990s, and especially with the rapid transformation of satellite television pioneered by Al Jazeera's phenomenal growth, Arab media sources distinguished themselves from their international counterparts. While mimicking the latter's technical and professional capabilities, Arab television programs presented genuine alternatives, often to articulate what was taboo in the West. For example, coverage of the Arab-Israeli conflict, the 2006 Israel-Hizbullāh war in Lebanon, the post-9/11 "war on terrorism," and various religious questions were all presented with far less bias than before the 1990s, when Western news outlets enjoyed a near monopoly. This phenomenon was duplicated throughout Asia, where coverage of domestic concerns in Indonesia and Malaysia in particular received preferential coverage on the BBC and CNN. In fact several new satellite networks, including Al-Arabiya, Al-Hurra, Middle East Broadcasting Corporation (MBC), and Lebanese Broadcasting Corporation (LBC), among others, all increased their own reporting to present the Arab and Muslim points of view. Sophisticated religious programs, which brought pulpits into living rooms, proved contagious.

The growth of satellite television has increased the freedom of expression on both ends of the spectrum: liberal as well as radical Islamic speech. State censorship imposed on television and newspapers made satellite channels and electronic media a freer alternative that tackled issues the state media couldn't. This resulted in controversy around freedom of speech versus racism, extremism, and creating strife.

The other remarkable development of the past few decades was the epochal growth of the Internet as a unique communication medium. Muslim leaders, as well as state religious institutions, Islamist groups, and violent groups took to the Internet with ease. Thousands of new sites emerged within a very short period of time, often characterized by extraordinary adaptability to change, and even to the utility of the medium as a communication channel—both for good and malevolence. The Internet helped Islam to grow and gave millions of Muslims unfettered access to primary texts and new perspectives, nurturing healthy online debates on arcane religious topics. It allowed believers to interact with religious scholars, to seek advice and solicit *fatāwā* as needed. It even provided a mechanism to express views that could only be protected by the medium's anonymity.

Even if traditional media outlets lost their monopolies, what also was sacrificed in this rush was the measured reflections made by well-read authors who relied on their own, as well as their institutional, memories. Cyber muftis issued *fatāwā* that were not always popular or within traditional norms. Thus the Web created confusion, stirring a volatile mix of competing opinions—including serious divisions over who speaks for Islam—that sidelined local imams. Young and more educated Muslims flocked to the Internet for a variety of sermons by Muslim authorities living in faraway lands, but who appealed to the tech savvy through modernizing additions.

The Internet also provided a platform for shunned opposition voices, like the Muslim Brotherhood, to find alternative platforms for communication. Across the Arab world the Muslim Brotherhood formed a strong presence in the blogosphere and dominated most of the English- and Arabic-language blogospheres. The strongest network of blogs and the most prominent blogs were dominated by Muslim Brotherhood bloggers. It also became a medium to defend freedoms and attract Western media attention to issues mainstream media ignored. Calls for freeing detained bloggers and journalists, for instance, became prominent online, attracting the attention of Western audiences and forming pressures on the government. Activists also started using the Internet to post videos documenting issues shunned from mainstream media, like police brutality or sexual harassment. All this led governments to crack down on several prominent bloggers across the Muslim world, which in turn led to even more viral campaigns promoting freedom of expression and human rights.

The Arab Spring. The Arab Spring highlighted the importance of the Internet, as well as the traditional modes of communication. In Egypt it was the calls of bloggers and social media makers that triggered the 25 January uprising, but the masses gathered only when protesters walked the streets, calling for people in their homes to come down and join them. Across the Arab world the use of the Internet and the oral forms of communication gathered the masses that toppled the regimes.

The Arab Spring marked a turning point in communications; after many lost their faith in state media for their massively biased reporting during the earlier days of the uprisings, satellite channels, social media, and blogs became trusted news and opinion sources on current affairs.

Along with this came a change in the status of bloggers and social media makers, ultimately moving from underground opposition to journalists with national prominence who are mainstreamed into the media, the economic sector and the public sphere. Internet penetration surged in the aftermath of the Arab Spring, penetration rate in Egypt increased from 24.5 percent in December 2010, to 30 percent a year later. Facebook and Twitter became primary media for online activists to communicate with each other, the media, the public and even the government during the days of the protests and the aftermath. Facebook penetration growth rate in Egypt has gone from 12 percent in the period from 25 January to 5 April 2010, or the period immediately following the protests, to 29 percent in the same period the following year (2011). Facebook users in Egypt grew from 4.7 million in December 2010 (Arab Social Media Report, 2011) to 9,391,580 in January 2012 (Socialbakers, 2012), up by around 100 percent in just one year; compared to an average annual growth rate of 76 percent throughout 2010. Twitter users had reached 130,000 in 2011 to send over 35,000 tweets on 11 February, the day Mubarak stepped down, up from an average of under 15,000 daily tweets before the protests.

Media organizations that once had no presence on social media websites started creating Twitter and Facebook accounts to try and recapture some of their lost audience. Popular broadcast channels and newspapers started hosting and quoting prominent bloggers and online activists—apparently attempting to gain trust and validity through the bloggers. The private sector also took notice and reacted widely, not only through strengthening their online presence, but also through directly targeting social media makers. Companies like Nokia started holding press conferences exclusively for bloggers to launch their products and began looking for coverage by bloggers and Tweeps rather than conventional media. The governments, for the first time, created Facebook and Twitter accounts to communicate to the public in general and online activists in specific.

The Arab Spring also noted a decrease in media censorship, leading to a trend almost similar to the surge of the Internet. More extreme preaching and radical Islamist thought found its way in not only satellite channels, but also mainstream media after several former regimes had banned such speech from state as well as private channels, which risked having their licenses revoked if they didn't follow the state's broad guidelines. For instance, a religious satellite channel called Myriam was launched to feature only face-veiled anchors and crew. Preachers like shaykh Yusuf al-Qaradawi, who had a strong online following, but was banned from television prior to the Arab Spring, were now allowed on satellite channels and sometimes on state television across the Muslim world.

The Internet: An Alternative Platform for Female Voices. Muslim women played a prominent role in the media, participating in movies, press, and broadcast. There had been an unspoken code, however, banning veiled women's participation in mass media, specifically in movies and broadcast media. Veiled women weren't hired as presenters on channels and found very few roles in the movie industry. The ban on veiled anchors on Egyptian television, however, was lifted after the 25 January uprising.

The social restrictions that women suffer from are also present in their participation in the communications sector. Actresses who act explicit scenes, for instance, or dress provocatively are largely frowned upon and a certain stigma plagues actresses in general. Women who discuss taboo issues are also considered too outspoken by the conservative sector and blamed for opening up the minds of innocent girls to what they consider obscene and indecent topics.

Female journalists who were once expected to tackle only certain issues, like social issues, or the arts, however, have found new freedom in the past few years. Talk show hostesses like Mona el-Shazly and Lamis el Hadidi have become household names equal to prominent male talk show hosts. Their popularity also increased after the Arab Spring, as they became more and more engaged in political issues that concerned males and females equally. The photography sector that was once dominated by males has also grown to include females who are found on the ground of hotspots, shooting the live clashes and events, especially after the Arab Spring.

While the media, including cinema, often discussed women rights' issues and presented taboo issues like sexual harassment, the space women's issues and voices took in the mainstream media wasn't nearly enough to discuss more sensitive issues in depth. The media did, for instance, lead to discussions on the right to get a divorce and ultimately presenting women with the right of *khulʿ* (to file for a compulsory divorce). However issues like marital rape, social stigmas, and others of interest to women remained underpresented on mainstream media. In the early twenty-first century, however, a strong wave of female bloggers found sanctuary in the anonymity of the Internet to discuss issues they wouldn't otherwise discuss. Saudi female writers, for instance, have a prominent presence in the blogosphere, one they can't enjoy in the mainstream media that doesn't allow for serious female participation or for discussing sensitive issues. Enjoying very few freedoms elsewhere, the Internet provided Saudi women, along with many other Muslim women, an alternative to voice their concerns. Muslim females soon took to the Internet to discuss issues like male oppression, patriarchal attitudes of their societies, sexual harassment, sexual issues, virginity, unequal participation in the workforce, and even marital rape. Many of the issues those writers discussed online, like marital rape, they couldn't discuss even in their private lives among their friends.

Ultimately many of those female bloggers who were once concerned only with social issues started getting engaged in political and social discourse. So while many of them gave up their anonymity and started engaging in mainstream public spheres and mass media, taking their outspoken attitudes and newly found freedoms with them, others who discussed more sensitive issues couldn't follow suit. Many online writers still prefer to remain anonymous bloggers using pseudonyms, be it because they fear prosecution from their society at large, or because their families, parents, or husbands wouldn't approve of their writings or engagement in the public sphere.

BIBLIOGRAPHY

Abdallah, Nagwa. "The Role of the Media in the Democratic Transition in Egypt: A Case Study of the January 2011 Revolution." Reuters Institute, 2011. http://reutersinstitute.politics.ox.ac.uk/about/news/item/article/the-role-of-the-media-in-the-democr.html.

Allagui, I., and J. Kuebler. "The Arab Spring and the Role of ICTs: Editorial Introduction." *International Journal of Communication* 5 (2011): 1435–1442.

Aouragh, M., and A. Alexander. "The Egyptian Experience: Sense and Nonsense of the Internet Revolution." *International Journal of Communication* 5 (2011): 1344–1358.

Arab Social Media Report. May 2011. Dubai School of Government. http://www.dsg.ae/en/asmr3/.

Eickelman, Dale F., and Jon W. Anderson, eds. *New Media in the Muslim World: The Emerging Public Sphere*. Indianapolis: Indiana University Press, 2003. Covers aspects of modern media that, in common, challenge notions of gender, authority, justice, and politics.

El-Nawawy, Mohammed, and Adel Iskandar. *Al-Jazeera: How the Free Arab News Network Scooped the World and Changed the Middle East*. Cambridge, Mass.: Westview, 2002.

Emirates Center for Strategic Studies and Research. *Arab Media in the Information Age*. Abu Dhabi: ECSSR, 2006. First comprehensive assessment of Arab satellite stations, websites, and transnational newspapers and magazines.

Ghazaly, B. *The Holy Qur'an in the Orientalists Studies: A Study in the History of Quraan*. Amman, Jordan: Dar Alnafa'es for Printing and Distribution, 2008.

Kamalipour, Yahya, and Hamid Mowlana, eds. *Mass Media in the Middle East: A Comprehensive Handbook*. Westport, Conn.: Greenwood, 1994.

Kilany, M. *Tadwin Al Hadith*. Casablanca, Morocco: Dar Al Maghreb Al Islamy, 2004.

Miles, Hugh. *Al-Jazeera: The Inside Story of the Arab News Channel that Is Challenging the West*. New York: Grove Press, 2005.

Poole, Elizabeth, and John E. Richardson, eds. *Muslims and the News Media*. London and New York: I. B. Tauris, 2006. A comprehensive examination of the links between context, content, production, and audiences of news about Islam and Muslims for both Muslim and non-Muslim consumers.

Rugh, William A. *Arab Mass Media: Newspapers, Radio, and Television in Arab Politics*. Westport, Conn.: Praeger, 2004. An outstanding resource by a former American diplomat with rare insights.

Said, Edward W. *Covering Islam: How the Media and the Experts Determine How We See the Rest of the World*. Rev. ed. New York: Vintage, 1997. A classic academic effort that depicts stereotypes and prejudices in the reporting about Muslims.

Zayani, Mohamed, ed. *The Al Jazeera Phenomenon: Critical Perspectives on New Arab Media*. Boulder, Colo.: Paradigm, 2005.

HAMID MOWLANA
Updated by JOSEPH KÉCHICHIAN
Updated by NADINE EL SAYED

Community and Society (Theoretical Overview). The theme "community and society" was chosen to highlight the integral roles that women have played in the more informal settings of community and society. When juxtaposed to the theme "politics and polity," we found women's contributions to communal life to be as impactful as those made to politics. Read together these two themes in particular challenge the intellectual privileging of "hard power," associated with high politics and official decision-making, over the "soft power" of less formal spaces where cultural relations and cooperative ties between group members are cultivated. Community and society, then, similarly argues that through participation, here in the form of traditional roles within rituals, customs, and traditions and modern ones related to female social advancement, women also enjoyed key opportunities to shape the identities and development of their societies, as they gave voice to their own.

Women have always played a role in their communities and societies. Muslim women are no exception. Islam has often been blamed for relegating women to their homes and isolating, if not prohibiting, them from societal participation altogether. The goal of this theme was to uncover, rediscover, and update how we have understood the nature and scope of Muslim women's agency within community and society and how various institutions—Islamic and otherwise—have influenced, and been influenced by, women's participatory power.

What we discovered in other themes equally applies to community and society: what we know about women's agency is largely driven by available sources and how those sources are interpreted. Most of the articles here frame female agency as deriving from women's more traditional roles as social mediators. That is, their primary function within communal life has been to create, deepen, and extend relational ties, starting with the family, but extending beyond. For instance, as mothers, Muslim women have assumed the responsibility of imparting Islamic identity, not only to their children, as seen in shared childrearing customs, but also to their communities. Their role as spiritual guides and *shaikhas* (heads of Ṣūfī orders) gives some indication of how women envisioned themselves as models of piety outside the home, as they sought to contribute to the moral instruction, and thus cohesion, of society. Standard entries like family, tribal societies and women, midwifery, childrearing, hospitality, marriage, *mahr*, and divorce showcase women's many and varied roles and functions in creating, sustaining, and strengthening Muslim communal identity.

However to broaden the scope of the theme and capture when, how, and why women's societal participation has expanded, constricted, or how it has been reshaped by the exigencies of modern life and new technologies, we also added some unexpected entries like surrogate motherhood, suicide, and youth culture. As a result, we uncovered some inspiring markers of female social advancement, like higher rates of female employment as a result of young women delaying marriage, but also more depressing indices, like women's suicidality. Such findings provide some indication of how Muslim women globally have been able to overcome, or not, the mounting pressure of fulfilling traditional roles while dealing with lifestyle challenges linked to economic development.

As the articles make clear, generalizations about Islam's role in determining women's ability to participate in their communities and societies, historically and today, are difficult. The role of religion in any society is always complex, variegated, and ever changing, ultimately rendering it context-specific. However there are discernable patterns across Muslim societies that demonstrate Islam's indelible imprint on women's roles in the community and society. In some instances

Islam helped shape the content of communal rites and rituals that have historically applied to females and males alike. Birth rites, including the *adhān* being whispered in the child's right ear, a community celebration (*aqiqah*), naming ceremonies, and death rites of washing and wrapping the body, praying over it, and burying it facing Mecca, are noteworthy examples.

In other instances Islam provided women with opportune moments to shape communal identity, especially within the family, as they crafted their own. Most striking here are those Islamic legal rites, like marriage and divorce, that offered women room to exercise their agency by asserting their legal, thus social, identity as wives and mothers. The articles on marriage and divorce especially illustrate the rich complexities behind Muslim women's rights, including, among others, the right of marital consent, contract stipulations as a safeguard against polygamy, *mahr*, guardianship, annulment, arbitrated divorce, and maintenance. Collectively, they illustrate the many ways that women were guaranteed input about the type of marital arrangement, and therefore the type of family they wanted for themselves. This point, however, should not be overstated. As many of the articles attest, there have certainly been marital abuses of the law that were either legalized or have gone unpunished (e.g., forced and arranged marriages, *misyar*, and *urfi* marriages), which reveal the problematic ways that Islam has also challenged female agency. Modern campaigns to reform family law, and therefore women's legal rights, across the Muslim world have signaled hopeful signs of more equitable change.

In yet other cases, women's social activity was not linked to Islamic orthodoxy at all, but rather to extracanonical rituals that were often performed in female groups. For instance, Sunnī and Shīʿī mothers-to-be visited holy shrines to make offerings to saints as a way of guaranteeing a healthy birth. Muslim women have also practiced a healing ritual, the *zār*, found predominantly in North African societies. Such moments offer intimate sketches of female solidarity and women's collective expression of their gender identity.

Finally, the role of the West, often starting with European colonialism, has been transformative across the Muslim world, for better or for worse. Whether at the broader level of institutions, like the family, or more specific social customs, like the naming of a child, these effects have in turn impacted women's societal participation. For example, as colonial discourse targeted the Muslim family as proof of Islam's antiquated legal system, Muslims increasingly saw it as a sanctuary where Islamic religious values were honored in their resistance to European cultural imperialism. Consequently women's customs, like the hijab, have been subject to intense scrutiny and more conservative articulations of modesty. Other challenges presented by modernizing influences associated with the West include new scientific technologies that have offered women new options for reproduction, yet have been constrained by Islamic debates about reproductive rights; naming practices where Muslims in western societies have increasingly chosen less traditional names or immigrant Muslim women have encountered challenges as a result of keeping their maiden names; unchaperoned interactions between men and women, especially with the advent of the Internet; debates about who should dispense sexual education to Muslim youth; and tourist industries in Muslim states that have altered where and how hospitality rituals, some of which were traditionally performed by women, have been performed.

Whether focused on traditional or modern roles, in the past or the present, all the articles offer vibrant glimpses, if not colorful portraits, of women acting on their own behalves as they advanced their societies. The "soft power" found in the intimate settings of family, community, and society, then, offered women a rich site of diverse female expression, and, as a result, opportunities to cultivate and deepen social relations and affect social change.

HIBBA ABUGIDEIRI

COMPANIONS OF THE PROPHET.

Among majoritarian Sunnī Muslims, the collective moral excellence of the Companions (al-Ṣaḥābah) inheres in their status as contemporaries of the Prophet Muḥammad and on any measure of proximity or access to him. Thus "companionship" (Ar. *suhbah*) could be ascribed to someone who had known the Prophet intimately and interacted with him on a regular basis, as well as to someone who had met him only once. The Companions, along with the next two generations of Muslims, are part of "the Pious Forbears" (al-Salaf al-Ṣāliḥ). This high status is encoded in a well-known ḥadīth in which the Prophet states, "The best of people are from my generation; then from the second [generation], then from the third. Then will come a group of people in whom there will be no good."

In contradistinction to the Sunnīs, the Shīʿah, it should be noted, would progress from an early neutral and ambivalent stance toward the Ṣaḥābah to condemnation of the majority of the Companions. This later negative attitude results from their belief that, except for a handful of Companions, the rest had withheld from ʿAlī ibn Abī Tālib what they assumed to be his preordained right to become the *imām* (caliph) after the Prophet's death.

In the third century of Islam (ninth century of the common era), the famous biographer Ibn Saʿd (d. 845) would eulogize the Companions of the Prophet as a collectivity in the following manner, reflecting a consensus that had emerged among the Sunnī majority by this time:

> All the Companions of the Messenger of God, peace and blessings be upon him, were models to be emulated, whose actions are remembered, whose opinions were consulted, and who voiced their opinions. Those who were the most prominent among the Companions of the Messenger of God, peace and blessings be upon him, listened to *ḥadīths* and transmitted them. (Ibn Saʿd, *Kitāb al-ṭabaqāt al-kubra*, 2:376)

As this statement points out, particularly significant is the role of the best known Companions in the preservation of the memory of the Prophet, his actions and particularly his speech—that is to say, their role in the formation of the *sunnah*, the second most important source of law after the Qurʾān, of which the primary component is Muḥammad's recorded speech known as ḥadīth.

On account of the importance of ḥadīth transmission in the development of the religious sciences after the Qurʾān and the indispensable role of the Companions in this activity, interest in recording the details of the lives of the Companions emerged fairly early. Biographical works written specifically for the assessment of the reliability of ḥadīth transmitters are termed *rijāl* (men). This term is something of a misnomer since the *rijāl* literature contains entries on many women transmitters as well, typically set apart as a special section.

Early biographical and ḥadīth works are also distinctive in depicting many women Companions (Ṣaḥābiyyat) as deeply involved in community affairs and assuming prominent roles in defending the community against its enemies, in carrying out humanitarian activities, and in educating and counseling men and women. Compared with some late biographical works, the biographical work of Ibn Saʿd mentioned above and known as *Kitāb al-ṭabaqāt al-kubra* (The Book of the Great Generations) provides fulsome and laudatory descriptions of many of the women Companions' achievements. As conceptions of women's public roles changed over time, so did the portrayals of the women Companions' lives to a certain extent in later works. Thus ʿA'isha's very public and almost embarrassingly aggressive persona by later standards had to be explained away or ameliorated by later male biographers in an attempt to preserve her role as a female paragon of virtue from the first generation of Muslims. To this day, biographical works remain an essential source for reconstructing the lives and contributions of many of these prominent women Companions besides the wives of the Prophet, such as Umm Waraqa.

BIBLIOGRAPHY

Afsaruddin, Asma. *Excellence and Precedence: Medieval Islamic Discourse on Legitimate Leadership*. Leiden, Netherlands: Brill, 2002.

Ibn Saʿd, Muḥammad. *Al-Tabaqat al-kubra*. Ed. Muhammad ʿAbd al-Qadir ʿAta'. Lebanon: Dar Sadir, 1997.

Jabali, Fu'ad. *The Companions of the Prophet: A Study of Geographical Distribution and Political Alignments*. Leiden, Netherlands: Brill, 2003.

Lucas, Scott C. *Constructive Critics*, Hadith *Literature, and the Construction of Sunni Islam*. Leiden, Netherlands: Brill, 2004.

Spellberg, Denise. *Politics, Gender, and the Islamic Past: The Legacy of ʿA'isha bint Abi Bakr*. New York: Columbia University Press, 1994.

Asma Afsaruddin

Concubinage. Concubine (*surriyya*) refers to the slave-woman (*jāriya*)—Muslim or non-Muslim—with whom the master engages in sexual intercourse. The word *surriyya* is not mentioned in the Qur'ān. However, the expression "that which your right hands own," which occurs fifteen times in the sacred book, refers to slaves and therefore, though not necessarily, to concubines. Concubinage was a pre-Islamic custom that was allowed to be practiced under Islam. The Prophet Muḥammad had a concubine, Mārya the Copt (d. 637 C.E.), a slave-girl who had been given to him as a diplomatic gift. According to some sources, Muḥammad set her free when she bore him a child who died in infancy.

Islamic jurisprudence sets limits on the master's right to sexual intercourse with his female slave. A man's ownership of his unmarried slave-girl gave him an exclusive right to have sex with her that he could not sell to others. A man could own a limitless number of concubines, but could not have access to the slave-girls owned by his wife. Marriage between the master and his concubine was only possible if she was granted free status first. On occasions, manumission constituted the bridal dowry (*mahr*). The master had the right to practice *coitus interruptus* without the slave's permission, to avoid pregnancy. The birth of progeny would change the legal status of the concubine to that of *umm al-walad* (mother of the child). As mother of the master's offspring, the concubine could not be sold. She would automatically acquire free status at the death of her master and her children would be considered freeborn and legitimate.

The expansion of the Islamic Empire meant that a growing number of concubines came to be acquired as booty, captives of wars, gifts, and through purchase into all royal, princely and well-to-do households. As was true of other empires, ownership of a large number of concubines became a symbol of dynastic power and prestige. An eleventh-century prince of medium importance could count some five hundred concubines in his harem. The ʿAbbasids (r. 750–1258) were the first dynasty to raise the status of the concubine as a means of royal reproduction. On many occasions it was the children of concubines who came to succeed their fathers as caliphs and rulers, at the expense of sons born within marriage. The Ottomans (r. c. 1299–1922) stand out as the rulers who, more than others, championed dynastic succession through concubinage. By the mid fifteenth century, Ottoman royal heirs came to be exclusively chosen from among the sons of concubines who, in turn, were not allowed to give birth to more than one male child. Across the dynasties, many royal concubines came to exercise considerable influence in most areas of court life. In sixteenth-century West Africa, the royal concubines in Kano's palace were in charge of collecting grain as a form of taxation, the proceeds of which they then managed and marketed. The implementation of the abolition of slavery in the ninteenth century marked the beginning of the decline of concubinage, which was to come to an end as part of a slow process.

BIBLIOGRAPHY

Kecia, Ali. *Marriage and Slavery in Early Islam*. Cambridge, Mass.: Harvard University Press, 2010.

Nast, Heidi J. *Concubines and Power: Five Hundred Years in a Northern Nigerian Palace*. Minneapolis: University of Minnesota Press, 2005.

Peirce, Leslie P. *The Imperial Harem: Women and Sovereignty in the Ottoman Empire*. New York: Oxford University Press, 1993.

DELIA CORTESE

CONVENTION ON THE ELIMINATION OF ALL FORMS OF DISCRIMINATION AGAINST WOMEN (CEDAW).

The Convention on the Elimination of All Forms of Discrimination against Women (CEDAW or the Convention) was adopted by the General Assembly of the United Nations in 1979 (CEDAW 1981). However, the Convention did not come into force until 1981 after its twentieth ratification. One hundred and eighty-seven countries had ratified CEDAW as of October 2011.

CEDAW "is the most prominent international normative instrument" to address the special concerns of women (Charlesworth, Chinkin, and Wright, 1991, p. 631). The Convention moves from a sex neutral norm to one of equality between men and women. Many critics believe this is a male-based model of equality and thus fails to address the real problems and injustices women face as women (Charlesworth, 1994, p. 64).

CEDAW is nonetheless the first UN convention to break the barriers of rights hierarchy. It guarantees enjoyment of equality in civil and political as well as economic, social, and cultural contexts. The Convention also "imposes explicit obligations on state parties in respect of discrimination by *private* parties, not just by the state or public officials." (Byrnes, 2002, p. 120). Furthermore, CEDAW "progresses beyond the earlier human rights conventions by addressing the pervasive and systematic nature of discrimination against women, and identifies the need to confront the social causes of women's inequality by addressing "all forms" of discrimination that women suffer. (Cook, 1993, p. 233).

Critiques of CEDAW. The Convention has faced an array of criticism. In the early 1990s, Charlesworth et al. asked whether the terms of the Convention, and the manner in which member states accepted it, "prompt us to ask whether it offers a real or chimerical possibility of change" (Charlesworth, Chinkin, and Wright, p. 631).

The Convention does not explicitly cover discrimination on the basis of sexuality or sexual orientation (Byrnes, p. 124.). However, the Convention allows for a wide scope of interpretation. While specifically naming the "political, economic, social, cultural and civil" fields, it goes further by adding "or any other field" (CEDAW, article 1). This wide scope of interpretation leads to an increase in the number of reservations, a considerable number of which are entered on ratification by Muslim-majority countries.

Compared to other International Conventions, especially the International Convention on Elimination of All Forms of Racial Discrimination and the International Covenant on Civil and Political Rights (ICCPR), the Women's Convention has a much weaker implementation procedure. Because of the specialized nature of CEDAW, "mainstream" human rights bodies sometimes ignore or minimize women's perspectives. Since the CEDAW Committee is the body to deal with these specific gender issues, other bodies are relieved of this task (Charlesworth, Chinkin, and Wright, p. 632). However, the Committee's move to Geneva in 2008 has assisted a more consolidated working relationship between the CEDAW Committee and other UN human rights treaty bodies. Like the other nine treaty bodies, the CEDAW Committee is "now fully serviced by the Office of the High Commissioner for Human Rights (OHCHR) in Geneva" (http://www.ohchr.org/EN/NewsEvents/Pages/Cedaw.aspx).

CEDAW Committee and the Optional Protocol. The Committee on the Elimination of All Forms of Discrimination against Women (hereafter the Committee or the CEDAW Committee) is the supervisory mechanism established by CEDAW. The Committee was established under article 17 of the Convention for "the purpose of considering the progress made in the implementation for the Convention," with the main part of the task being the examination of the reports submitted by state parties in accordance with article 18 of the Convention (CEDAW, article 17). CEDAW provides for the establishment of a Committee of twenty-three experts who are elected by the state parties to serve in their personal capacity. Like other UN treaty bodies, the Committee has limited power to compel states to comply.

In addition to considering reports, the Committee has developed twenty-eight general recommendations. These recommendations have been a significant contribution "to a conceptual expansion of the understanding of human rights violations suffered primarily or even solely by women, such as domestic violence, and including female genital mutilation, discrimination against women in the family, discrimination in civil and political life and discrimination against women in the areas of maternal and general health" (Schöpp-Schilling, 2007, p. 217).

Since the Optional Protocol to the Convention came into force on 22 December 2000, the Committee has been able to consider communications submitted by individuals or groups of individuals. The Optional Protocol also entitles the Committee to inquire into grave or systematic violations of the Convention by states parties that have accepted this procedure (Optional Protocol 2000).

CEDAW and "Islamic" Reservations. To date, all members of the Organisation of Islamic Cooperation (OIC), apart from Iran, Sudan, and Somalia, have ratified CEDAW.

CEDAW "has been subject to more substantive reservations than any other major human rights treaty" (U.N. Doc. E/CN.4/Sub.2/1996/20, 11 June 1996). Many of the reservations to CEDAW are based on conflict with religious laws, which is especially true in the case of the Muslim-majority countries discussed below. While some of these reservations are narrow in scope, others are wide-ranging and have the potential to limit the obligations undertaken by the reserving states significantly (U.N. Doc. E/CN.4/Sub.2/1996/20, 11 June 1996). The first part of Saudi Arabia's reservation, for example, states: "In case of contradiction between any term of the Convention and the norms of Islamic law, the Kingdom is not under obligation to observe the contradictory terms of the Convention" (http://treaties.un.org/pages/ViewDetails.aspx?src=TREATY&mtdsg_no=IV-8&chapter=4&lang=en).

Articles 2, 9, 16, 15, and 29 of CEDAW have been subject to the largest number of reservations by Muslim-majority countries, although some have since withdrawn their reservations to specific articles. For example, in June 2007 the Syrian Arab Republic made a decision to remove reservations to articles 2, 15(4), 16(1)(g) and 16(2) (U.N. Doc. CEDAW/C/SYR/CO/1, 11 June 2007).

Algeria, Bahrain, Bangladesh, Egypt, Libyan Arab Jamhiriya, Morocco, Niger, and the Syrian Arab Republic have all entered reservations or declarations to article 2, which obliges "States Parties condemn discrimination against women in all its forms." Iraq entered a reservation to article 2(f) and (g), the United Arab Emirates has also made a reservation to article 2(f). Most reservations are entered in the name of Islamic Shariʿa. Bahrain's reservations to article 2, for example, have been explained as ensuring "its implementation within the bounds of the provisions of the Islamic Shariah." Apart from Bangladesh, which explains that Shariʿa law is based on the Qurʾan and Sunna, others use the term "Islamic *Shariʿa*" loosely without providing any definition (http://treaties.un.org/pages/ViewDetails.aspx?src=TREATY&mtdsg_no=IV-8&chapter=4&lang=en).

Article 9(1), asks state parties to grant women and men equal rights in acquiring nationality. Paragraph 2 of the same article deals with the nationality of children, asking state parties "to grant women equal rights as men with respect to the nationality of their children" (CEDAW, article 9). Iraq and the United Arab Emirates have made reservations to 9(1) and Turkey a declaration to article 9(1). Algeria, Bahrain, Jordan, Kuwait, Lebanon, Malaysia, Oman, Saudi Arabia, Syrian Republic, and Tunisia have all entered reservations to article 9(2). Apart from Malaysia, which mentions Sharīʿah as one of the conflicting factors for its reservation, the other states do not mention incompatibility with Sharīʿah. Rather they regard article 9(2) to be in conflict with the states' Nationality Acts.

The United Arab Emirates made a reservation to article 15(2), which demands of state parties to grant women "in civil matters, a legal capacity identical to that of men and the same opportunities to exercise that capacity." Algeria, Bahrain, Jordan, Morocco, Niger, Oman, and Syria have all made reservations to article 15(4), which states "States Parties shall accord to men and women the same rights with regard to the law relating to the movement of persons and the freedom to choose their residence and domicile." Turkey has entered reservations to article 15(2) and (4).

Bahrain, Jordan, Niger, Oman, and Syria give no or very vague reasons for not complying with article 15(4). These reservations restrict women's rights to free movement and choice of residence. In the cases of Algeria and Morocco, article 15(4), is said to be in conflict with the Algerian Family Code and the Moroccan Code of Personal Status respectively. In most of these countries, a woman's movement is contingent on the permission of her husband, where she is married, or a male family member, if she is unmarried. A married woman in many cases needs the written permission of her husband to attain a passport. Such practices clearly discriminate against women and violate principles of non-discrimination and equality.

Algeria, Bahrain, Egypt, Iraq, Jordan, Kuwait, Lebanon, Malaysia, Maldives, Niger, Oman, the Syrian Arab Republic, Tunisia, and the United Arab Emirates have all filed reservations exempting themselves from implementing all or parts of article 16 on the basis of it being in conflict, prejudiced, or incompatible with the provisions of Islamic Sharīʿah. At its crux, article 16 asserts state parties shall "take all appropriate measures to eliminate discrimination against women in all matters relating to marriage and family relations and in particular shall ensure, on a basis of equality of men and women" (CEDAW, article 16).

Although the main justification for reservations to article 16 has been that all or part of the article is incompatible with Islamic Sharīʿah, nonetheless each state has chosen to interpret what is and is not in conflict with Islamic Sharīʿah. No state has taken upon itself to explain the meaning of Islamic Sharīʿah or what incompatibility with Shariʿa entails.

These reservations are considered incompatible with the "object and purpose" of the Convention. As early as 1987, the CEDAW committee adopted a decision regarding *Shariʿa*-based reservations, asking the United Nations and the specialized agencies to "promote or undertake studies on the status of women under Islamic laws and customs and in particular on the status and equality of women in the family, on issues such as marriage, divorce, custody and property rights and their participation in public life of the society, taking into consideration the principle of El-Ijtihad in Islam" (General Recommendation, 4 and Charlesworth, Chinkin, and Wright, p. 636).

Muslim-majority states' reservations to CEDAW, although entered in the name of Islam, are not absolute and can be withdrawn at any time. For example, some reservations to specific articles were withdrawn by Bangladesh and Malaysia in 1997 and 1998 respectively, by Egypt in 2008, and Morocco in 2011. No specific reasons have been given by those state parties for the withdrawal of their reservations. This shows how "evolving political contingencies, not Islamic beliefs, turn out to be determinative factors." (Mayer, 2005, p. 2). It is therefore important not to confuse reservations entered by the Muslim-majority countries with their exercise of religious freedom. Few of the state-interpreted Islam or, so-called, "Islamic reservations" are a direct consequence of belief. Rather, they are more likely the result of male dominated power politics (Mayer, p. 2).

Bibliography

Byrnes, Andrew. "The Convention on the Elimination of All Forms of Discrimination Against Women." In *Human Rights of Women, International Instruments and African Experiences*, edited by Wolfgang Benedek, Esther M. Kisaakye, and Gerd Oberleitner. London: Zed, 2002, pp. 119–173.

Charlesworth, Hilary, Christine Chinkin, and Shelley Wright. "Feminist Approaches to International Law." *American Journal of International Law*, 85:4, (October 1991): 613–645.

Charlesworth, Hilary. "What Women's International Rights Are Women's International Human Rights?" In *Human Rights of Women: National and International Perspectives*, edited by Rebecca Cook. Philadelphia: University of Pennsylvania Press, 1994, pp. 58–85.

Cook, Rebecca. "Women's International Human Rights Law: The Way Forward." *Human Rights Quarterly* vol. 15, (1993): 233.

Mayer, Ann Elizabeth. "The Convention on the Elimination of All Forms of Discrimination against Women. The Political Nature of "Religious" Reservations." March 2005. Accessible online http://lgstdept.wharton.upenn.edu/mayera/documents/frankfurt-mayo3edit.pdf

Rosenbloom, Rachel, ed. *Unspoken Rules: Sexual Orientation and Women's Human Rights*. London: Cassell, 1996, pp. ix, xiv–xxi.

Schöpp-Schilling, Hanna Beate. "Reservations to the Convention on the Elimination of All Forms of Discrimination against Women: An Unresolved Issue or (No) New Development?" In *Reservations to Human Rights Treaties and the Vienna Convention Regime, Conflict, Harmony or Reconciliation*, edited by Ineta Ziemele. Leiden: Nijhoff, 2004, pp. 3–41.

Schöpp-Schilling, Hanna Beate. "Treaty Body Reform: The Case of the Committee on the Elimination of Discrimination Against Women." *Human Rights Law Review*, 7:1 (2007): 217.

UN Documents

A full list of the CEDAW committee's general recommendations are available at the website of the High Commissioner for Human Rights at: http://www2.ohchr.org/english/bodies/cedaw/comments.htm.

A List of state parties reservations and declarations are available at the website of the High Commissioner for Human Rights at: http://treaties.un.org/Pages/ViewDetails.aspx?src=TREATY&mtdsg_no=IV-8&chapter=4&lang=en.

Concluding Comments of the Committee on the Elimination of Discrimination against Women: Syrian Arab Republic, U.N. Doc. CEDAW/C/SYR/CO/1, 11 June 2007, at paragraph 6.

Convention on the Elimination of All Forms of Discrimination against Women, G.A. res. 34/180, 34 U.N. GAOR Supp. (No. 46) at 193, U.N. Doc. A/34/46, entered into force Sept. 3, 1981 (CEDAW).

General Recommendation No. 4, Report of the Committee on the Elimination of Discrimination against Women, Sixth Session, 42 UN GAOR Supp. (No. 38), para. 579, U.N. Doc. A/42/38 (1987).

The Implementation of the Human Rights of Women, Note by the Secretary-General, Distr. GENERAL U.N. Doc. E/CN.4/Sub.2/1996/20, 11 June 1996

Optional Protocol to the Convention on the Elimination of Discrimination against Women, G.A. res. 54/4, annex, 54 U.N. GAOR Sup. (No. 49) at 5, U.N. Doc. A/54/49 (Vol.1) (2000), entered into force Dec. 22, 2000.

Roja Fazaeli

Cosmetics. Muslim women have adorned, inscribed, and purified their bodies with cosmetics since the beginning of Islam, high standards of cleanliness and beauty being upheld in the Qurʾān. Women continued many of the same cosmetic preparations developed as early as the Bronze Age, adapting more as materials and technologies became available. Henna was used to stain skin, particularly hands, feet, and nails. Kohl was used to rim the eyes. Henna, indigo, katam, and seder were used to dye and clean hair. Miswak sticks from *Salvadora persica* cleaned the mouth and teeth. *Swak*, walnut root, darkened the lips. Women used simple cosmetics for daily upkeep, and more costly materials and more meticulous cosmetic applications for Eid and other celebrations. The bride had the most complex cosmetic work, to create a ritually pure virginal body, to inscribe her with auspicious markings, and to prepare her for presentation to her husband

Women gendered their bodies with cosmetics, negotiated position among co-wives and concubines, created ritual fitness, and marked their bodies as belonging to one particular group, distinct from another. Some women created their own cosmetics from guarded and complex personal recipes; others preferred prestigious, expensive, novel imports. Cosmetics usually managed private beauty, for private viewing in personal relationships, though cosmetics have also spoken in public, such as hennaed political slogans on hands held up to cameras in political demonstrations

Henna was considered a particularly suitable cosmetic in Islam, because the stain was not considered to be a barrier to ritual cleanliness. Paints had to be removed for ablution before prayer, and tattoos were interpreted to be an obstruction to prayerful purity

Henna, *Lawsonia inermis*, is a small tree indigenous to semi-arid tropical zones. The henna-growing zone coincides with most culturally Arab, Maghribī, Western India, and Persian regions, from the Atlantic coast of North Africa to western India. Henna leaves contain lawsone, 2-hydroxy-1,4-naphthoquinone, an orange dye that readily stains keratin. Henna paste made of pulverized fresh or dried leaves and a mildly acidic liquid can be used to stain skin, nails, and hair a color in the range of orange, red, brown, and to near black under some conditions. Ornamental stains can be drawn on skin with sieved paste. Palms and soles take up the most dye because that skin is thick and dry, giving the darkest, longest-lasting stains. Facial and torso skin take up the least dye because that skin is thinner and oilier, giving in those places a lighter-colored stain that disappears quickly

When henna paste is applied to the skin, the lawsone molecules migrate into and stain skin, nails, or hair. Left in place for several hours, the keratin becomes thoroughly saturated with dye and is stained red-orange. When the henna paste is removed, the stain remains in the skin, darkening to deep reddish brown over forty-eight hours. This stain exfoliates from skin in one to four weeks, but is permanent in hair and fingernails

Henna was believed to be beneficial, or to have *barakah*, blessedness. For auspicious occasions, henna's beneficence was inscribed onto the body by drawing culturally significant patterns, such as patterns to avert the Evil Eye, onto the skin

For daily wellness, women stained their soles with henna to prevent cracking, discomfort, and fungal infections. When women stained their fingertips and palms, henna strengthened the skin, fingertips, and fingernails, preventing calluses and split cuticles. Henna was applied to soothe the pubic area after depilation

Henna gendered the female body. Because it is difficult to henna both of one's own hands, henna was usually done socially rather than privately. Friends and family applied henna at home; specialists applied henna in the *ḥammām*. Adult females received more henna patterns than children. Male bodies were sometimes marked with henna as an auspicious blessing for ceremonial occasions, such as circumcision and marriage, but less so than the female body. Henna was applied for wellness regardless of age or gender, for fungal infections, skin irritations, dandruff, head lice, to heal burns, and to cure migraines

Women hennaed their hair to cover gray, to make it thick and glossy, and to eliminate dandruff and head lice. Henna dyes gray hair red or auburn. Henna mixed with buxus dioica or vashma indigo dyes hair brown, creating the appearance of youthful dark hair. Women dyed their hair black by first applying henna, rinsing, and then applying indigo

Indigo was used less commonly than henna, though in similar ways. The liquid from an indigo dye vat, if locally available, could be painted on skin to create blue patterns and to stain the eyelids blue. In Persia, women extended their eyebrows with indigo, in an arc across their forehead. Eyebrow extension and enhancement with indigo and black cosmetics was popular in many regions

Kohl was a fine carbon-based powder used to accentuate eyes and preserve visual wellness throughout Arab, North African, Turkish, and Persian cultures. Women could prepare kohl with the simplest materials, or with rare and costly materials such as amber, antimony, frankincense, and burnt almond shells. The simplest kohl was lampblack collected over a fire, applied with a feather or pic drawn between nearly closed eyelashes. Lampblack was the most common source of pigment, though galena (lead sulfide) and stibnite (an antimony compound) were also used to manufacture kohl. These metals were toxic to bacteria carried by flies and contaminated water, so they provided some protection from conjunctivitis and trachoma. The irritation from having kohl particles in one's eyes caused tearing, which kept the eyes washed clean of contaminants, grit, and bacteria. Blue and green eye paints were made with copper, malachite, and indigo

For special occasions such as a wedding or the visit of a prestigious guest, a woman's face might be enhanced with red, yellow, blue, and white paints, harquus (black paint made from carbonized nut shells), spangles, gold leaf, and artificial moles, in addition to her usual cosmetics. Greater adornment and greater beauty were appropriate to greater value in Muslim culture

[*See also* Ablutions; Ḥammām; *and* Hygiene]

REFERENCES

Field, Henry. *Body Marking in Southwestern Asia.* Papers of the Peabody Museum of Archaeology and Ethnology, Harvard University, vol. 45, no. 1. Cambridge, Mass.: Peabody Museum, 1958.

The Henna Page. http://www.hennapage.com/.

Al-Jawziyya, Ibn Qayyim. *The Medicine of the Prophet* Translated by Penelope Johnstone. Cambridge, U.K.: Islamic Texts Society, 1998.

Mernissi, Fatima. *Dreams of Trespass*. Boston: Addison-Wesley, 1994.

TapDancing Lizard. http://www.tapdancinglizard.com/.

Westermark, Edward. *Ritual and Belief in Morocco*. 2 vols. London: Macmillan, 1926.

Catherine Cartwright-Jones

Cultural Activities, Women's Historical. As the historical textual sources of the Muslim world evince, Muslim women were active in several cultural fields, most notably poetry and music. This article focuses, however, exclusively on their role in the Islamic visual arts and crafts. The area suffers a dearth of scholarship compared with the now substantial literature successfully reassessing the role of women in Islamic social, economic, and political history or with feminist European, East Asian, and, perhaps to a lesser degree, African art historical writing. That the contribution of women to Islamic visual culture remains little explored is usually ascribed to the lack of material and textual evidence. Craftswomen were in the majority involved in fiber-based arts, which do not withstand the effects of time as do other artistic media such as clay, glass, or metal. However, while Islamic art historians all face the challenge that no need was felt in the Muslim world to develop a textual tradition specifically dedicated to art and aesthetics, a variety of sources, particularly biographical dictionaries, but also historical treatises, *waqfiyya*, or *hisba* manuals, provide insight into women's relationship with and practice of the arts. Their glossing over by Western scholars confirms the idea that primary sources are not yet sufficiently used in Islamic studies generally and, more significantly, the reality that Orientalist views of Muslim women and patriarchy continue to inform the writing of art history. Research addressing women's role in Islamic art has effectively been impeded by the tendency to accept rather than question the established norms of the field. From the inception of Islamic art history in nineteenth-century Europe, art historians have applied the definitions, concepts, and methods used in the study of post-medieval European art to that of Islamic art, regardless of the tremendous differences between the two traditions. The former can be broadly characterized by mimesis, narrative, and the notions of individual genius and the masterpiece, while the latter privileges analogy, abstraction, collective authorship, anonymity, and functionality. Islamic arts, with few exceptions, were decorative, rather than fine, arts. The lack of distinction seems only to have consolidated the class-based taxonomy inherent to art history. Luxury commodity artifacts and monumental architecture came to be categorized as art while artistic productions catering to the general population of urban centers or those made in rural and tribal contexts in which Muslim craftswomen were especially prominent were excluded. The omission of women has equally been aggravated by the fact that, although textiles are central to Islamic art, textile, and carpet studies have developed as a somewhat separate field of inquiry in which questions of gender are also rarely highlighted and when they are it has not informed Islamic art historical scholarship.

The study of the role of women in Islamic art has concentrated on the representation of women in Islamic art and female architectural patronage with some innovative research having also been undertaken on the relationship between gender and urban or architectural space. The assumption of the absence of female artists, however, mirrors that of both art history and Orientalism. How else to explain that feminist Islamic art historians, with the exception of Walter Denny, overlook the reality that women were also makers of art and have not, echoing feminist Western art historians, stretched the definition of art to include the textile arts, especially in light of their aesthetic, cultural, and economic importance throughout Islamic history?

Representation and Patronage. Denny's pioneering essay on the image of women in Islamic art remains relevant today in its identification of four main representational themes: women as pleasure, lover, moral example, and hero. Similar studies only appeared well over a decade later (Najmabadi; Diba) although many important questions deserve further exploration. For example, while art historians have observed that gender in Persianate painting is conveyed through clothing and adornment rather than physiognomy and anatomy, only one text thus far attempts to unravel the meaning of marking gender through social rather than biological signs. If iconographic studies highlight the diversity of ways in which women were imagined and depicted, the examination of male-produced images of women does not provide insight on self-representation.

Scholarship on female patronage emerged as part of the larger project of deconstructing the notion of Muslim women's invisibility but became the central pillar of feminist Islamic art historical scholarship positing that women patrons exercised artistic agency. As no surviving texts articulate the nature of the patron-architect relationship, the evidence put forth consists of stylistic and comparative analyses. Ülkü Bates proposes, for example, that the buildings commissioned by Turkish royal women, when compared to those financed by their male counterparts, display more inventive plans and decorative programs. Lucienne Thys-Şenocak pushes the idea further in an article devoted to the Yeni Valide Mosque. Coining the expression "optical politics," she concludes that the complex was consciously designed to ensure "visual access to the various components of the complex for a royal female patron whose actual physical access was restricted" (Thys-Şenocak, p. 81), thus allowing the powerful *valide sultan* to appropriate the sultan's omniscient gaze.

Calligraphy ***Calligraphy.*** Because of the cultural norm of gender non-mixity, Muslim women, like European women, did not have access to the necessary technical education to practice a variety of crafts from architecture to metalsmithing until the modern era. However a significant number of women are recorded as master calligraphers from the earliest period of Islamic history. Those trained in *khaṭṭ* encompass women from ruling, wealthy, or pious families, those employed as court secretaries, or still yet the large number of women copyists working for Islamic schools or on the public book market of medieval Córdoba. Two articles in European languages (al-Munajjid; Masala) and, more recently, a much-needed book (Kazan) have appeared on the topic, all drawing upon biographical dictionaries. The exclusion of women calligraphers from Western Islamic art historical scholarship is surprising not only because calligraphy is considered the highest art form in Islam and that, like patronage, it is associated with social privilege, but also because women calligraphers sometimes formed part of the chains of transmission. For example, Shuhda al-Kātiba (d. 1178 CE) known as *Fakhr al-Nisā'* (Glory of Women) constitutes the link between the two most famous medieval calligraphers, Ibn al-Bawwāb (d. 1032) and Yāqūt al-Musta'ṣimī (d. 1298). The challenge for historians is that, while sources provide the names and usually minimal information about women scribes, extremely few surviving examples of their work predate the late Ottoman period. Nonetheless the very fact that women calligraphers were awarded diplomas (*'ijāza*) and reaped social and economic benefits from their art is in itself historically noteworthy.

Textile Arts. Textiles formed the economic backbone of the Muslim world up until the modern period and women were involved in their production in massive numbers whether for domestic consumption or trade. Women were engaged in felting, carding, spinning, dyeing, embroidery, weaving, and brocade and carpet making. It is effectively impossible to overestimate the role women played in the textile arts; the irony of its non-acknowledgment is aptly noted by Denny who, referring to carpets, writes that if "these forms have been neglected by traditionally trained historians of Islamic art, there can be no question that in the West today the most popular works of art from the Islamic world are products of women artists" (Denny, p. 177). Women carpet makers were particularly recognized for both the economic benefits and artistic merits of their work, although so far no evidence would suggest that Muslim women, like European ones, belonged to guilds. Women-produced textiles were not only domestic arts, but also desired and treasured objects of public consumption that possessed public visibility in all three social contexts: urban, rural, and tribal.

While Islamic art history focuses on the luxury textiles produced in male-manned ateliers, integrating the study of the myriad textile traditions produced by women would afford a clearer understanding of both Islamic art and Muslim women. Women-crafted textiles are related to numerous wider issues: the provision of shelter (e.g., fabrication of tents or yurts), the production of gender (e.g., dowry textiles) and distinctive group identity (e.g., Amazigh weaving, Kyrghiz shyrdak), the marking of lifecycles (e.g., textiles relating to marriage or death), traditional piety (e.g., rugs offered to a mosque for a prayer answered), female-specific forms of piety (e.g., the taboo on men approaching looms in some North African contexts), artistic genealogies (e.g., transmission of motifs), politics (e.g., Uzbek khans offering suzanis as diplomatic gifts to visiting dignitaries), and, of course, female economic empowerment. More appreciably, while there are recognizable stylistic and iconographic differences between women's textiles, particularly tribal and village ones, and those produced in urban, particularly court, workshops, both prefer stylized, often abstract, forms and bright colors and emerge from regimes of representation not based on the division between the subject and object of the gaze and hence on the gendered implications such a division carries in European art. Because one can posit fewer differences between male- and female-fashioned artifacts than in other traditions, women's textiles in the Muslim world only further demonstrate the necessity to address the critical question of interpretation in Islamic art. The acknowledgment and articulation of the meaning of its aniconism has been inhibited by Eurocentric norms and definitions of art, especially problematic in the case of female art traditions that, often transmitted from generation to generation, evoke the contemporary concept of *écriture feminine* referring to a psychic space that, because outside the symbolic order of language, is unhindered by patriarchy.

Future Directions. The project of rewriting women into Islamic art history is in its infancy. Its success requires redefining the concept to include artifacts made by women in all social contexts as well as in additional Muslim-majority geographical regions. Islamic art refers only to the art of the Muslim Middle East, North Africa, and South Asia; integrating Southeast Asia, East Asia, and sub-Saharan Africa into the discussion would draw awareness not only to other fiber-based arts practiced by Muslim women but also to other media such as pottery making, which has a long history as a woman's art in West Africa. The recovery project effectively involves widening the definition of art to acknowledge the various traditions of Muslim women's artistic practice whether textiles, basketry, leatherwork, or wall painting, and thereby disputing allegedly normative definitions of art that in large part effectively account for the systemic omission of women. In the particular case of Islamic art, it also means recognizing that pre-modern non-narrative largely abstract art traditions also constitute systems of meaning. If Islamic art history is to take part in the nascent ambitious comparative endeavor known as global or world art studies, a situated approach toward Islamic art and an understanding of its visual vocabularies are essential.

BIBLIOGRAPHY

Bates, Ülkü Ü. "Women as Patrons of Architecture in Turkey." In *Women in the Muslim World*, edited by Lois Beck and Nikki Keddie, pp. 245–260. Cambridge, Mass.: Harvard University Press, 1978.

Denny, Walter B. "Women and Islamic Art." In *Women, Religion, and Social Change*, edited by Yvonne Yazbeck Haddad and Ellison Banks Findly, pp. 147–180. Albany: State University of New York Press, 1985.

Diba, Layla S. "Lifting the Veil from the Face of Depiction: The Representation of Women in Persian Painting." In *Women in Iran from the Rise of Islam to 1800*, edited by Guity Nashat and Lois Beck, pp. 206–236. Urbana and Chicago: University of Illinois Press, 2003.

Kazan, Hilal. *Female Calligraphers Past and Present.* Istanbul: Kültür A.Ş., 2010.

Masala, Ana. "Maestre ottoman di calligrafia." *Islàm: Storia e civilità* 7, no. 3 (1988): 199–208.

Munajjid, Salah al-Din al-. "Women's Roles in the Art of Arabic Calligraphy." In *The Book in the Islamic World: The Written Word and Communication in the Middle East*, edited by George N. Atiyeh, pp. 141–148. Albany: State University of New York Press, 1995.

Najmabadi, Afsaneh. "Reading for Gender through Qajar Painting." In *Royal Persian Paintings: The Qajar Epoch, 1785–1925*, edited by Layla S. Diba and Maryam Ekhtiar, pp. 76–89. London: I. B. Tauris Publishers in association with the Brooklyn Museum of Arts, 1998.

Pirouz Moussavi, Farzaneh. "Ambiguïté des genres dans les peintures des manuscrits arabes et persans." In *L'Orient des femmes*, edited by Marie-Élise Palmier-Chatelain and Pauline Lavagne d'Ortigue, pp. 35–46. Lyon, France: ENS Éditions, 2002.

Schimmel, Annemarie. *Calligraphy and Islamic Culture.* New York: New York University Press, 1984.

Thys-Şenocak, Lucienne. "The Yeni Valide Mosque Complex of Eminönü, Istanbul (1597–1665): Gender and Vision in Ottoman Architecture." In *Women, Patronage, and Self-representation in Islamic Societies*, edited by D. Fairchild Ruggles, pp. 37–73. New York: State University of New York Press, 2000.

Watenpaugh, Heghnar Zeitlian. "Art and Architecture." In Vol 1 of *Encyclopedia of Women and Islamic Cultures*, Suad Joseph, general editor. 6 vols. Leiden, Netherlands, and Boston: Brill, 2003–2007, 315–320.

Valérie Behiery

Culture and Expression (Theoretical Overview). Because women are the culture bearers of a society and because much of what is expressed about Islam in the public sphere revolves around representations of and conversations about Muslim women, it is fitting that one of the themes around which this project was organized is "culture and expression." Our particular concern was to distinguish between women's bodies, which are often the subjects and objects of patriarchy, and women's voices, which remain theirs alone to articulate.

Topics pertaining to questions of women's bodies and literary and artistic production are often lumped together in reference works in a category such as "culture and society," removing these discussions from the more important power topics of politics and economics and suggesting that women are peripheral members of society, much as art and literature are often considered to be elite pastimes that become possible to address only when the more critical issues of authority, leadership, and security have been satisfied. Such a construct also perpetuates the notion that women's issues are simply a cultural question or a matter of social concern, rather than a central and vibrant aspect of how a society operates.

By splitting the questions of self and body from culture and expression, we sought to challenge this construct. Culture and expression particularly challenges stereotypes of Muslim women as passive and voiceless in favor of focusing on Muslim women's agency in the creation of culture and modes of expression, whether oral, written, or visual. We aim to demonstrate the vast array of women's voices and the multitude of ways in which they are expressed by including articles on literature, both fiction, such as poetry, novels, and short stories, and non-fiction, such as biographies, hagiographies, pamphlets, and Islamic literature; artistic expressions and representations, such as found in calligraphy, epigraphy, and painting; cinema production, including women as directors and producers, as well as representations of women in film; communications media, including both print and visual journalism, television, and social media; and other cultural expressions, such as physical expression through dance and vocal expression through music, in addition to expression through the Internet, whether through websites, blogs, or social networking sites. The purpose is to demonstrate the myriad of creative and dynamic ways in which women have taken agency in expressing their voices, ideas, and opinions to reach ever vaster audiences.

The Internet has offered a particularly important venue for women who might otherwise not have a public voice, due to social constraints in some places on women's access to the public sphere. The Internet provides women with a venue for writing articles, stories, and blogs, and taking and sending photographs and videos, from the privacy of their own homes, allowing them to push the boundaries of seclusion and the separation of private and public by using their private space to communicate their message of choice into the very public arena of cyberspace. Such use of the Internet not only permits greater—and instantaneous—global distribution of women's expression, but also provides opportunities for women to communicate and share ideas across what might otherwise be impassable boundaries, challenging the meaning of seclusion, offering agency even within the parameters of physical confinement, and suggesting that the private-public dichotomy itself is no longer a useful analytical construct—if it ever was.

Literature is a vast topic of expression and culture, as there are many different styles and types of literature, specific to location and time period, each of which reflects a particular interest and targets a different audience. Devotional poetry, for example, combines the rich heritage of poetic expression with a religious dimension, while Islamic biographies focus on important personalities across time and space with respect to the heritage and interpretation of Islam as a faith tradition, sometimes suggesting the need to imitate or adhere to the past in order to remain faithful to history, however imagined, and at others, particularly where women are concerned, suggesting the need to recover the past in order to change the present. Within literature we consider both oral and written literary expression, reflecting the heritage of oral culture in poetry not only in the Middle Eastern context, but also throughout Africa. We examine literature as a product for both expression and consumption, as well as a venue for socializing, such as in the case of literary salons.

Cinema has become another important means for women to claim a voice in public debates and conversations because it offers the unique opportunity to speak indirectly through representation, rather than the often more confrontational direct approach of speech in the public arena. Through cinematic representation, women from throughout the Muslim world have not only expressed their artistic voices, but have also carved a new space for themselves to offer their thoughts and critiques on the status of women, politics, society, culture, and beyond, as directors, producers, and even actresses.

In some cases we have included architectural masterpieces because they express collective memories, such as the Taj Mahal's evocation of the death of a ruler's beloved wife, making it a monument to lost love, or permit the construction of ceremonies enabling expressions of power that are visible only to a select audience, such as in Topkapi Saray. Architecture uniquely offers the opportunity for large-scale displays of wealth and power, while creating space with both private and public purposes, again blurring the dichotomous construct and suggesting multiple modes of expression and performance.

By presenting so many modes of expression and how culture is cultivated, constructed, refined, and reinterpreted, we hope to expand the definition of "women's voices" in order to more fully appreciate what they communicate—about their societies, as well as themselves—as well as how such expression occurs.

Natana J. DeLong-Bas

D

Dance. There has never been any tradition of "Islamic dance" or "Muslim dance" per se but Muslim dance cultures are recognizable though stylized artistic manifestations of abstractions. The Islamic ideal of beauty rejects the representation of living forms—either animal or human—and is instead stylized and depersonalized to negate any impression of naturalism. Thus, dance in Islamic culture has tended to comprise a series of movement motifs that are individually pleasing and satisfying. The movement motifs are self-contained parts that are harmoniously arranged to form a larger design in the form of dance phrases—that is, a culturally grammatical choreographic unit made up of a constellation of motifs that occur simultaneously and sequentially, satisfying and exuberant in form. The structural characteristic of stylized dance gestures and the symmetrical repetition of dance motifs within a prescribed spatial plan invoke the elaboration of a never-ending pattern of the arabesque or curvilinear designs peculiar to Muslim societies.

Dances by women in Muslim societies manifest the notion of abstractions through many of their dance cultures, which include traditional styles evolving around solo improvisational repertoires, such as the *raqṣ baladī* (dance of the people, the traditional form of women's solo dance) and the *raqṣ sharqī* (dance of the east); dances of specific gender groups performed in circular or linear chain formations, such as the *raqṣ al-hawānim* (dance of the women); and the dances of *dhikr* sessions such as the *rateeb meuseukat* (a seated linear dance performed by Acehnese women).

The solo dances (and to some extent the group dances) feature improvisational creativity: dance steps or even spatial plans are invented by combining and truncating dance motifs and sequences for the pleasure of individual or communal self-expression. Female solo dances are performed only in the home among women as a social pastime or in the presence of the women's male *maḥram*. In such intimate social occasions, the audience becomes spontaneous performers when the *zagharīt*, an ululation or cry of encouragement, is echoed by the spectators; this may also urge participants to prolong the dance.

Gender-specific group dances are performed by Muslim women in the form of chain dances, cluster dances, and linear seated dances. In some of these dances, performers hold one another's hands or waists, while some are performed separately in unison. Rhythmical stamping of feet and clapping of hands by rows of dancers who sing repetitive refrains, often repeated to the same melody, characterize gender-specific group dances. Physical contact between male and female dancers is almost nonexistent. In the chain dances, performers advance and retreat from one section of the dance floor in unison to a specific tune or rhythm. Participants are allowed to join or leave the ensemble when a new tune or refrain is introduced. Improvisation in group dances is allowed within the context of the genre being performed; individual performers may deviate a little from the repetitive dance motifs to execute an outburst of improvised solo dance movements before returning to the conventional movements of the group dance. Voluntary and spontaneous substitution of performers may alter or lengthen group dances.

BIBLIOGRAPHY

Buonaventura, Wendy. *Serpent of the Nile: Women and Dance in the Arab World*. New York: Interlink Books, 1990.

Faruqi, Lois Ibsen al-. "Dance as an Expression of Islamic Culture." *Dance Research Journal* 10, no. 2 (1978): 6–13.

Faruqi, Lois Ibsen al-. "Dances of the Muslim Peoples." *Dance Scope* 11, no. 1 (1976): 43–51.

Faruqi, Lois Ibsen al-. *Islam and Art*. Islamabad: National Hijra Council, 1985.

Mohd Anis Md Nor. "Arabesques and Curvilinear Perimeters in the Aesthetics of Maritime-Malay Dances." In *2003 Yearbook for Traditional Music*. International Council for Traditional Music, vol. 35, pp. 179–181. New York: International Council for Traditional Music, 2003.

Mohd Anis Md Nor. "Dance." In *The Oxford Encyclopedia of the Modern Islamic World*, edited by John L. Esposito, pp. 335–336. New York: Oxford University Press, 1995.

Mohd Anis Md Nor. "Dancing Divine Iconography in Southeast Asia." In *Dance, Transcending Borders*, edited by Urmimala Sarkar Munsi, pp. 19–34. New Delhi: Tulika Books, 2008.

Mohd Anis Md Nor. "Structural Constructs in Indigenous Dances in Malaysia." In *Dance Structures: Perspectives on the Analysis of Human Movement*, edited by Adrienne L. Kaeppler and Elsie Ivancich Dunin, pp. 357–362. Budapest: Akadémiai Kiadó, 2007.

Mohd Anis Md Nor. *Zapin: Folk Dance of the Malay World*. Oxford, Singapore and New York: Oxford University Press, 1993.

Nasr, Seyyed Hossein. *Islamic Art and Spirituality*. Albany: State University of New York Press, 1987.

MOHD ANIS MD NOR

DASHTI, ROLA. (b. 1964), Kuwaiti women's rights activist, economist, and former member of parliament. Dr. Rola Dashti obtained a Bachelor of Science degree in agricultural business from California State University, Chico in 1984 and then her PhD in population economics from Johns Hopkins University in 1993. Upon her return to Kuwait in 1992, she worked in the field of research and development to modernize Kuwait's economy at the Kuwait Institute for Scientific Research. She then worked as a senior economist at the National Bank and as a consultant to the World Bank. She currently heads an international consultancy firm that focuses on small and medium enterprise development. She is also one of the leading women's rights activists in Kuwait, focusing on obtaining political rights for women, and thus an important player in the women's movement that began in the 1960s. She has been an involved member of the prominent women's organization Nadi al-Fatat (Girls Club), which has been campaigning for women's political rights since its founding in 1974 by merchant-class women. After repeated unsuccessful attempts to lobby the National Assembly (Parliament) to grant women political rights, Dr. Dashti and two other women convinced the Constitutional Court to hear their cases in 2000–2001, arguing that the law forbidding women's suffrage and from running for political office was unconstitutional. Unfortunately, the courts refused to hear the cases and they were dismissed. Since 2004, Dr. Dashti has held the post of Chair of the Kuwait Economist Society, becoming the first woman to head a mixed-sex organization in Kuwait and the first Shīʿī Muslim (a minority in Kuwait) to chair the society. Through her position at the Economist Society and as a feminist, she continued alliances with other mixed-sexed organizations and prominent women's organizations, such as Nadi al-Fatat and the Women's Cultural and Social Society, to lobby Parliament to finally pass the bill that granted women full political rights in May 2005. It came as no surprise that she was the first woman to file her papers at the elections department to run for the National Assembly when the *amīr* dissolved the National Assembly and called for elections in 2006. Unfortunately she lost in her first run at office, after a difficult campaign where she was accused of being a foreign agent because of her Lebanese accent (her mother is Lebanese) and of accepting American support. However, in 2009, Dr. Dashti succeeded her father, Abdullah Aly Dashti, in winning a seat in the National Assembly with three other women. Dr. Dashti praised the performance of the first female MPs in 2010: "Women members also have brought discipline to the parliamentary system itself. We attend committee meetings and do our homework, which embarrasses some of the male members who do not attend." Finally, she has received several awards, including the King Hussein Humanitarian Award in 2005 and the Council of Europe's North South Prize with Mr. Mikhail Gorbachev in 2010. She was listed as one of the one hundred most influential Arabs in the world in 2007 and 2008.

[*See also* Kuwait *and* Political Activism, Women's, *subentry* Contemporary Discourse.]

BIBLIOGRAPHY

al-Mughni, Haya. *Women in Kuwait: The Politics of Gender*. 2nd ed. London: Saqi Books, 2001.

Rizzo, Helen Mary. *Islam, Democracy, and the Status of Women: The Case of Kuwait*. New York: Routledge, 2005.

Shultziner, Doron, and Mary Ann Tétreault. "Paradoxes of Democratic Progress in Kuwait: The Case of the Kuwaiti Women's Rights Movement." *Muslim World Journal of Human Rights* 7, no. 2 (2011): 1–25.

Tétreault, Mary Ann, Katherine Meyer, and Helen Rizzo. 2009. "Women's Rights in the Middle East: A Longitudinal Study of Kuwait." *International Political Sociology* 3, no. 2 (2009): 218–237.

DINA EL-SHARNOUBY AND HELEN MARY RIZZO

DA'WAH, WOMEN'S ACTIVITIES IN.

According to the *Oxford Dictionary of Islam*, the word *da'wah* means "call" and is associated with "God's way of bringing believers to faith and the means by which prophets call individuals and communities back to God." In contemporary usage, the word *da'wah* is used to refer to activities of individuals and organizations who appropriate this responsibility of calling people and communities "back to God." A woman who undertakes acts of invitation is called a *da'iyah* (masculine: *da'i*; plural: *du'at*); her work is similar to that of a missionary in Christian contexts. A *da'iyah* might encourage Muslims to improve their faith practice; in such cases, rather than proselytizing, this work may be perceived as *iṣlāḥ*, or reform. Such proselytizing, often aimed at Muslims who practice their faith infrequently or Muslims from denomination groups different than those of the *du'at*, are based on the premise that "historical misunderstandings and misinterpretations have distorted the original meanings of texts, introducing harmful practices and that therefore reform consists of a return to Islam's original message" (Esposito, 2003, p. 143). *Da'wah* may also refer to evangelical activities aimed at converting non-Muslims to Islam, although, according to some scholars, this type of *da'wah* activity is less dominant in contemporary contexts.

Women and *Da'wah*. Women involved in *da'wah* activities draw inspiration from general Qur'ānic injunctions regarding *da'wah* that address all of humankind: for example, to call upon all people to enjoin good and forbid evil (3:104); to invite others to the way of your Lord with wisdom and good instruction (16:125); and the injunction stating that *du'at* are better in speech because they call to the way of God (41:33). Women may also draw inspiration from verses that address them directly, such as verse 9:72, according to which "believing men and believing women are allies of one another," and they must enjoin what is right and forbid what is wrong. There are other verses of the Qur'ān which specifically address women and urge them to undertake *da'wah* activities—for example, verse 33:32 exhorts the wives of the Prophet and, by extrapolation, all Muslim women, to "say that which is good." These verses, by addressing both sexes, offer a mandate to both men and women to participate in *da'wah* activities. Muslim theologians agree that this is a religious duty that is incumbent on all believers, including women.

However, in many Muslim communities, female participation in *da'wah* is influenced by societal and religious understandings of issues such as segregation of the sexes, modesty, and whether a woman's proper place is the domestic sphere. Patriarchal interpretations of such issues limit women's social roles, including in *da'wah* activities. In extreme cases, a few religious leaders insist that although *da'wah* is an important religious duty, women may not leave their homes to participate in it, or may only travel in groups to attend study circles in the homes of other women. Other scholars suggest that in order to preserve their modesty, women may only address groups of women, with no men present. Such rulings have meant that women's roles are often limited to the private domain. Although female scholars and *da'iyah* may be actively involved in *da'wah*, their work usually remains unnoticed beyond their communities. Some female scholars and activists (and a few men) criticize current *da'wah* programs which, due to the dominance of male voices and standpoints, are not equipped to be accessible to women or to address their needs.

Da'wah is a religious duty that many pious Muslim women consider an important aspect of their religious practice, and they therefore have found means to circumvent limiting cultural norms around gender roles. Furthermore, in pluralist contexts, religious Muslim women are visible due to faith practices (including, but not limited to, their *hijab* or headscarves), which can vest in them the opportunity to be representatives of their faith, allowing them to engage in wider religious discussion (Contractor 2012). Women's *da'wah* activities usually encompass the wider meaning of the word and extend beyond proselytizing and can include community work, education, writing, and interfaith dialogue work. 'Ā'ishah, the wife of the prophet, set a precedent with her well-known contributions as a scholar, for her work in recording and transmitting *ḥadīth* (sayings of the Prophet), issuing *fatwās* (legal rulings), and teaching (she is claimed to have taught over two thousand male and female students during her lifetime).

Women and Da'wah Activities. In their da'wah activities, women continue to follow 'Ā'ishah's example and that of other *ṣaḥābah* (female companions of the Prophet) and key historical female personalities. They have made considerable contributions to the collation and dissemination of Islamic knowledge, first as students and then as teachers of male and female students, both in formal contexts (in *madāris* (religious schools)) and informal ones (in each other's homes and in study circles).

This has led to the development of women's *da'wah* organizations, and women's wings of traditionally male-dominated *da'wah* organizations, that specialize in working with and addressing women. For example, Zaynab al-Ghazālī' (1917–2005) founded the Muslim Women's Association (*Jama'at al-Sayyidaat al-Muslimaat*) in Egypt, which, among other services, offered Islamic education to women. Zaynab al-Ghazālī' was also socially and politically visible and made significant contributions to Islamic feminism. Pakistani scholar Farhat Hashmi's organization for women, Al-Huda International, established in 1994, similarly aims to teach Muslim women about their religion. In contemporary contexts there is increased realization in some Muslim communities (particularly those living in pluralist contexts in the West) of the need for women to address male and female audiences in all *da'wah* work, and to take the lead in discussing women and gender issues in public forums. This is demonstrated in Bt Ariffin's (2004) research on women's contribution to Islamic *da'wah* in Malaysia. She reports that these activities include religious talks, seminars, television programs, Islamic counselling programs, and religious education for families. Such activities can have social impacts that range beyond the religious and into social and economic realms, as reported by Mohamed (2006) in his commentary on Muslim women's *da'wah* activities in South Africa. There is an increase in Muslim women authors writing about *da'wah* subjects, such as discussions about the Islamic faith, Islam and gender roles, and how to challenge perceived misconceptions about Islam and Muslims. The rise of social media, and the opportunities it provides to anonymously share opinions, has opened up further avenues for Muslim women to participate in *da'wah* work by writing online articles and blogs, and participating in online forums.

BIBLIOGRAPHY

Bewley, Aisha Abdurrahman. *Islam: The Empowering of Women*. London: Ta-Ha Publishers, 1999.

Bt Ariffin, Mimi Hasliza. "Women's Contribution toward Islamic Da'wah at Kuala Lumpur." PhD diss., Kolej Universiti Islam, Kuala Lumpur, Malaysia, 2004.

Contractor, Sariya. *Muslim Women in Britain: De-mystifying the Muslimah*. New York: Routledge, 2012.

Esposito, John L., ed. *The Oxford Dictionary of Islam*. New York: Oxford University Press, 2003.

Khan, Kamillah. *Niqaab: A Seal on the Debate*. Kuala Lumpur, Malaysia: Da Al Wahi Publication, 2008.

Khattab, Huda. *Bent Rib: A Journey through Women's Issues in Islam*. 2d ed. Riyadh, Saudi Arabia: International Islamic Publishing House, 2007.

Mahmood, Saba. *Politics of Piety: The Islamic Revival and the Feminist Subject*. Princeton, N.J.: Princeton University Press, 200.

Mohamed, Sayed Iqbal. "Da'wah: Muslim Women's Contributions to the Reconstruction of the South African Society through Entrepreneurial and Religious Efforts." PhD thesis, University of KwaZulu-Natal, South Africa. 2006.

Uthman, Ibrahim Olatunde. "Rereading Zaynab Al-Ghazālī's Representations of Muslim Women and Islamic Feminism in the 21st Century." *The Islamic Quarterly* 55.3 (2011): 215–221.

Sariya Cheruvallil-Contractor

Delhi Sultanate. The thirteenth to sixteenth centuries in Indian history, broadly referred to as the sultanate period, cover an enormous range of human experience. It would be unfair to generalize from incidences in the lives of a few individual elite women who do find mention in the available historical records the conditions of millions of others, with total disregard of vastly divergent social, ethnic, or geographical variances. Equally problematic is the very category of "woman" in the Indo-Persian chronicles that comprise the bulk of the sources for modern historiography. In the works of historians ranging from Fakhr-i Mudabbir and Sayyid Sharīf Juzjānī in the thirteenth century to Shaykh Rizqullāh Mushtāqī in the sixteenth, gendered categories within a particular narrative serve specific political and "ideological" purposes that, socially relevant though they are, will certainly not reflect historical reality in a straightforward way. It is indispensable, therefore, to an investigation of the history of women during the sultanate to take into consideration both the authorial intent of the relevant source material as well as its factual content.

The importance of the best-represented women in the Indo-Persian documents, queens, for example, has to be understood within specific historical contexts both politically and based on narrative. The reign of the fourth Delhi sultan, for instance, that of Raḍiyya (r. 1236–1240), reflects the struggle between the throne and the powerful military elite that served it. According to Juzjānī, Shamsuddīn Iltutmish chose his capable daughter to be his heir over his profligate sons in the face of opposition from some of his commanders. The main point was that the sultan could chose whomever he wanted, *even* a woman, to succeed him, and that powerful commanders were obligated to show obedience to whoever occupied the throne, again *even* a woman. The historical fact, however, is that Raḍiyya did rule successfully for four years, and thus a kingship that transcended gender norms did find acceptance for a significant part of the population. Nor was she the only such example. Modern historiography credits Radiyya's rule to the relative lack of restrictions on women in the Central Asian culture of the elite group to which she belonged. Nevertheless, we do find brief mentions of more such royal figures in the sources who have no Turco-Mongol connections at all. For instance, Ibn Baṭṭūṭah mentions a Sultana Khadīja, daughter of Sultan Jalāl al-Dīn, in the Maldives who had the sermon read in her name. There were also queens who ruled smaller domains, as in the case of Rani Durgauti in fourteenth-century Deccan. Unfortunately, we know little of these histories, but they belie the historiographical tradition that sees the example of Raḍiyya as a foreign exception to an otherwise male-dominated medieval monarchy. Overall, as many or more women occupied royal positions in medieval India as in other areas such as medieval Anatolia, Iran, Central Asia, or the Arab lands.

Moving on to the end of the period, when Mushtaqi describes Bībī Mastū Lodī leading the defenses of Delhi by ordering Afghan women to dress in armor and protect the ramparts against the invading armies of the Sharqī sultanate—one must understand the episode in the context of female honor and its association with the inner core of the fortress that informs many similar narratives in the text. Generally, stories about the fall of a fortified area would end in the capture of elite women who resided there. Yet, one cannot but accept women fighters as a historical fact as so many other sources from different periods document their activities. Raḍiyya is again the best-known example of such individuals, but there is the equally famous Chand Bībī, the queen of Bijapur and Ahmednagar, who led Deccani resistance against the Mughals in the sixteenth century. Moreover, we find even ordinary, albeit anonymous, women fighters in early texts such as Fakhr-i Mudabbir's thirteenth-century manual of warfare. In it, the author states that Muslim women should be conscripted along with men to defend their land in the face of attack by a large *kāfir* army.

Looking southward, this time at the Bahmanid court, Persian historians such as Firishtah, who depict the pattern of politics as a long struggle between Perso-Arab immigrants and locals, write approvingly about two successive queen mothers (Makhdūmah-i Jahān) who sided with prominent immigrants to place their sons on the throne. The extent of their power far outshone that of their counterparts in, for instance, the Ottoman Empire, where the *valide sultan* engaged in politics through a powerful network of allies. According to Firishtah, for example, the mother of the young monarch Niẓām Shāh Bahmanī, along with the great merchant statesmen from the Persian Gulf region, Hasan Baṣrī and Maḥmūd Gāwān, led their army in a surprise attack against the "ray of Orissa" and the "zamindars of Talang." Bībī Makhdūmah-i Jahān ruled along with the famous Iranian statesman Maḥmūd Gāwān as regent during the reign of her son Sultan Muḥammad III (r. 1463–1482). According to the historian Rafī' al-Dīn Shīrāzī, she helped organize the state, established justice, and even led her army on a very profitable holy war (*ghazā*). As a result of her collaboration with Maḥmūd Gāwān, we are told, the Bahmanī state expanded further, while Persian cultural influences also increased in the Deccani kingdom. Although as characters, these queens serve a particular function in Shīrāzī and Firishtah's histories, the fact of their power and influence is incontrovertible. Also, as in the other examples cited here, there are so many other illustrations of such roles played by women at court, that one must abandon the notion of a male-dominated political sphere with women excluded behind purdah. To do so, one must necessarily misunderstand the nature of government during the period. Shāh Terken, Iltutmish's wife, patronized artists, men of letters, and scholars. She protected her son against his rivals. Malikah-i Jahān Khaljī personally undertook diplomacy that her husband Sultan Jalāl al-Dīn did not feel at ease to pursue. Shams Khātūn and Bībī Ambha Lodī actively promoted war or determined the course of dynastic succession. The former disrupted a truce between Sultan Bahlūl Lodī and Sultan Muḥammad Sharqī by urging Bahlūl to continue the war until the release of her brother, Quṭb Khān Lodī, who had been imprisoned in Jaunpur. Bībī Ambha helped inform her son and heir to the throne, Prince Niẓam (Sikandar Lodī), of a conspiracy against him by a number of Lodī emirs who preferred another son of Sultan Bahlūl Lodī for the succession.

Where they did not engage directly in politics, elite women still exerted great social influence through their wealth. The main historical evidence for this comes not from narrative sources but from inscriptions. Examples of such powers are inferential, although they do find parallels in other Islamic societies, such as Mamluk Egypt or the later Ottoman Empire. We know, for instance, that prominent wealthy women often subsidized the construction of buildings with religious or charitable functions. To cite a few examples, Makhdūmah-i Jahān Tughluq commissioned caravanserais (inns) for travelers. Bībī Rājī Sharqī paid for mosques and madrasas to be built in and around Jaunpur. Sittī Maghūla Lodī funded at least several mosques, one in Delhi and the other in eastern Punjab, where presumably her family had originated. Such activity did not only bring prestige to the noblewoman involved, it also placed her in the powerful role of patron for those who used such structures—merchants and the Muslim jurists/scholars or *'ulamā'*. Although the male Muslim religious elite is generally viewed today as hostile to the social influence and power of women, its relationship to its female patrons would have had to be of a different kind in the past.

Less is known about other socially prominent women. Ṣūfī hagiographies occasionally refer to important figures, though usually because of their direct relationship to a famous male saint. Some recent scholarship also focuses on women as entertainers or prostitutes, but these roles were not specific to women and would have been shared at times by men as well. While this brief survey has outlined some patterns in which women are represented at the highest level of society, a more detailed and nuanced study is needed not simply for analyzing the representation, but also for recovering the voice of "subaltern" women in Delhi Sultanate sources.

One can nevertheless state that, compared with their counterparts in other parts of the Islamic world during this period, elite women in both the Delhi Sultanate and the Deccan enjoyed a great degree of political power that extended to diplomacy, management of state affairs, and even participation in wars. Further scholarship should not only analyze this pattern against the background of the structures of politics as a whole, but also look beyond the sixteenth century to trace the changes that resulted from the establishment of Mughal rule.

Bibliography

Aftab, Tahera. *Inscribing South Asian Muslim Women: An Annotated Bibliography & Research Guide*. Leiden, Netherlands, and Boston: Brill, 2008.

Hambly, Gavin R. G., ed. *Women in the Medieval Islamic World*. New York: St. Martin's, 1998.

Kausar, Zinat. *Muslim Women in Medieval India*. Patna, India: Janaki Prakashan, 1992.

Nand, Lokesh Chandra. *Women in Delhi Sultanate*. Allahabad, India: Vohra, 1989.

Nasiri, Muhammad Riza, ed. *Tarikh-Firishtah*. 2 vols. Tehran: Anjuman-i Asar va Mafakhir-i Farhangi, 2009.

Parihar, Subhash. "A Lodi Inscription from Eastern Panjab." *Iran* 35 (1997): 79–81.

Sahu, Kishori Prasad. *Some Aspects of North Indian Social Life, 1000–1526 AD* Calcutta: Punthi Pustak, 1973.

Shirazi, Rafiʿ al-Din. *Tazkirat al-Muluk*. British Library mss., add. 23883.

Siddiqi, Iqtidar Husain, and W. H. Siddiqi, eds. *Vaqiʿat-i Mushtaqi*. Rampur, India: Rampur Raza Library, 2002.

Ali Anooshahr

Devotional Poetry. Devotional poetry is a subgenre of wider religious poetry, although it can be claimed that devotional poetry sometimes uses not only standard recognizable religious vocabulary, but also more profane forms to express its content. Devotional poetry is often composed for purposes of supplication, intercession, admiration, pleas for forgiveness, or even personal encounters with God, and, in a more pragmatic sense, it is used as an accompaniment to religious rituals or performances. Devotional poetry has to be separated from the notion of didactic poetry, although both forms can share similarities (for example, in the domain of religious symbols and vocabulary). It is composed and used in both private and public spheres, by men and women alike.

Devotional poetry throughout history came in various forms and was intended for different types of readers and listeners. However, the perennial question with regard to tracing down examples of devotional poetry is linked to the priority of religious content over poetic expression, which enables us to recognize its form in text of predominantly religious content. Thus, as is the case with other forms of devotional art, the question of what comes first, the form or the content, has often been posed. However, it may be firmly claimed that devotional poetry stems from the content of a particular religion, although it can deviate in certain alternative directions as well.

The development of devotional poetry is peculiar to the tradition and culture of every religion, both monotheistic and polytheistic. Examples of devotional poetry abound in many religious traditions, from Hinduistic devotional poetry (closely connected to two music traditions in that country, the Carnatic and Hindustani) to Jewish devotional poetry (as in the example of poems by Solomon ibn Gabirol). In this respect, it might be suggested that one of the early prominent examples of devotional poetry may be found in the Biblical psalms, which later influenced Christian devotional poetry. Christian religious tradition in

England influenced the group of poets assembled under the label "metaphysical poets" in the seventeenth century, including Richard Crashaw, John Donne, George Herbert, Andrew Marvell, and others, but it could also be said that their innovativeness (in usage of wit and conceit) expressed the religious devotional thematic in a new and possibly original way. The devotional imprint in poetry may be traced to Blake and later to Christina Georgina Rossetti in the nineteenth century. However, Christian and Islamic devotional poetry have been expressed not only in refined artistic form, but also more commonly in the folk oral poetry of various nations. In addition, other religious traditions developed devotional poetry of their own, as is the case with Hinduism and the famous Bhakti movement. Modern devotional Hindu poets include Tagore, and Hinduistic tradition is also deeply influenced by one of the most famous women poets in the field of religious poetry from the sixteenth century, Mirabai.

When it comes to the Islamic tradition of devotional poetry, scholars often primarily mention the Qurʾānic stand on poetry. Although Qurʾānic *āyāt*s on poetry (XXVI, 224–227) have been sometimes interpreted as a complete or partial ban on poetry, Islamic tradition has recognized and promoted poetry as an artistic tool for expressing and conveying the religious message (in this respect, with didactic poetry). Therefore, in the centuries following the death of the Prophet and consequent rise of Islamic empires, poetry witnessed a great shift in themes and topics, which gave rise to poetry written in the praise of God (*hamd*), but also poetry written to praise the Prophet Muḥammad or for his intercession (*naʿt*), and to praise important religious personages (*manqabat*).

Poetry written in the praise of God has been connected to mystical experiences since the early ages of Islam. One of the first names encountered in this respect is Rābiʿah al-ʿAdawīyah, a mystical Ṣūfī saint and poet from the eighth century from Basra. This name stands at the fore of not only women mystical poets in general, but also Ṣūfī poets who came after her, such as Farīd al-Dīn ʿAṭṭār, Jalāl al-Dīn Rūmī, Maḥmūd Shabistarī, or ʿUmar Ibn al-Fāriḍ. Rābiʿah not only lived an unusual life for a woman of that historical period (she never married and she was a Ṣūfī teacher of men) but also enlivened Ṣūfī thought, as is largely reflected in her poetry. And although her emergence as a poet and a Ṣūfī in this period seemed groundbreaking, it should be noted that Ṣūfīsm itself has been seen as fertile ground for women seekers on the Ṣūfī path, as both mystics and poets. In her poems, Rābiʿah addresses God in direct terms, just as numerous Ṣūfī poets did after her. These devotional poets that followed Rābiʿah often described a perilous Ṣūfī path, a journey to the *ḥajj*, impostors encountered on the path, the emotional and spiritual states and stations of the seeker; sometimes, the poets even used songs of formally profane expression (chronicling an encounter with a woman) to describe the ultimate meeting with the Divine Essence.

The type of poetry that praises the Prophet (*madīḥ nabawī*) flourished in both folk and high artistic form from the thirteenth century onward, and has also been used in both the private and public spheres. Publicly, *madīḥ nabawī* was recited on various social and religious occasions, but especially during the celebration of the Prophet's birthday (*mawlīd nabawī*, but at times named simply *mawlid*, or *mevlid*, *mevlit*, *milād*). These occasions (with particular emphasis on *mawlīd*) preserved, and still preserve, a cohesive force in many traditionally Islamic countries, owing to a great degree to the force of the poetic text of *madīḥ nabawī*, since it presented not only the praise poem for the Prophet, but also a narrative of the history of Islam including events concerning the Prophet's Companions (*al-aṣḥāb*).

The important part of *mawlīd nabawī* has usually been the story of *miʿrāj* or the Prophet's ascension, often described in elaborate details evoking the author's imagination. Portions of *mawlīd nabawī* were dedicated to the women in the Prophet's life, such as his mother Amina (whose delivery of Muḥammad was described in emotionally moving terms). In some countries (for example, countries with strong communist and socialist backgrounds, such as the former Yugoslav republics), *mawlīd nabawī* was often the only way to orally transmit religious narratives and thus to ensure their place in the memory of the community. It should also be noted that *mawlīd nabawī* was often performed in several languages, of which Arabic, Turkish, Persian, or Urdu were deemed to be the languages of the lettered, although local languages of the Islamic world were also abundantly used. Modern times have witnessed the emergence of *mawlīd nabawī* written in some Western languages (such as English), combined with Arabic verses, which speaks of the peculiar flexible nature of this poetic form, adjustable to changing times and circumstances. One of the most famous *mawlīd nabawī* poems is *Süleyman Çelebi*, in Turkish. The strong echoes of *mawlīd nabawī* through their Turkish mediator found their way into the languages of the Balkans. It might be suggested that, in modern times, *mawlīd nabawī* became part of a religious subculture in these areas, one that is not always directly connected to the Ṣūfī *ṭarīqats*.

Praise poems of the Prophet (*madīḥ nabawī*) date back to the Prophet's own time, from Kaʿb ibn Zuhayr's famous *qasida Bānat Suʿād*, to a *qasida* by Hasan ibn Thābit, both of which later received various interpretations. Of these, the most famous interpretation appeared to be Sharaf al-Dīn al-Būṣīrī's *Qaṣīdat al-Burda*, which was translated into many languages of the Islamic world. Some of the translations gained even more fame in certain parts of the Islamic world, such as the Persian translation by ʿAbd al-Raḥmān Jāmī and the anonymous Malaysian translation of this influential song. Numerous interpretations of the poem must be noted, with ʿĀʾishah bint Yusuf al-Baʿuniyya from Damascus (d. 1517) named as one of the corresponding women poets, as well as the commentaries and reworkings made to the core text of the poem. The pragmatic use of the *madīḥ nabawī*, reflected in the plea for intercession (*shafāʿah*), also found its way into praise and elegical poems of the Shīʾah provenance, as well as Ṣūfī devotional poems up to this day. It is worth mentioning that *mawlīd nabawī* itself emerged with the flourishing of Ṣūfī *ṭarīqats* in the thirteenth century, which therefore makes these two phenomena closely related. Shīʾah devotional poems in many cases developed into elegies to the members of Ali's family (the Prophet's grandsons Hasan and Husayn), and in the case of Ṣūfī devotional poems, they often developed into praise of Ṣūfī shaykhs or other prominent Ṣūfī personages, who could, according to some beliefs, intercede for them for forgiveness, blessings, or an interest of this world such as health. Because of the nature of these poems, they have been received frequently with displeasure by more legalistic and literalistic community members, who believed that seeking such intercession is a turn away from the attention to God and thus presents an unwelcome change in religious tradition (*bidʿah*). Such criticism misses the often stated point of love toward the Prophet stemming from love toward God. At this point, it must be clearly stated that *madīḥ nabawī* and *mawlīd nabawī* became a very successful middle ground between official theology and folk beliefs already existing before the arrival of Islam in any particular region.

In close connection to Ṣūfī devotional practice is *qawwālī* devotional poetry, usually associated with the Ṣūfī tradition of South Asia (India and Pakistan) and particularly with the Chishti order and shrines of Ṣūfī shaikhs. This devotional poetry, sung by professional singers named *qawwāls*, is a part of *samā*ʿ (listening to the music), and thus deemed an important part of a religious ritual that also includes *zikr* or the remembrance of God. With the rise of mass media, *qawwālī* gained prominence and started to appeal to Ṣūfī and non-Ṣūfī audiences alike, and even brought fame to some women *qawwālī* performers, such as Abida Parveen. The influence of *qawwālī* devotional poetry influenced the poetic *ghazal* writing of one of the most prolific authors and thinkers of the twentieth century—Allama Muhammad Iqbal.

Devotional poetry of all religious traditions was notable for its more relaxed approach to religious issues and for a certain creative and artistic freedom in expression. This is evidenced by usage of local languages, elaborate imagery, and a special poetical relationship to God, Prophet, or a prominent Ṣūfī personage in the case of Muslim devotional poetry. In many instances, devotional poetry adopted poetic expressions and symbols from the surrounding (non-Muslim) environment, as is the case with mutual influences in the devotional poetry of South Asia, for instance. The most striking example of the shifting paradigms is the usage of poetic terms that relate to God or the Prophet as the Beloved, thus placing the standard believer-Lord or believer-Prophet relationship outside the established norms of common piety. However, the usage of terms such as the one mentioned above has to be understood in its metaphorical sense: thus, the form of profane love (*ʾishq majazi*), as it appears on the surface of many poems, is only a reflection of true love (*ʾishq haqiqi*). Since such stylistic choices appeal to the emotions of believers, Islamic devotional poetry has gained a great number of lovers and followers across diverse nations and religious factions, and within the wide spectrum of Islamic societies.

BIBLIOGRAPHY

Abbas, Shemeem Burney. *The Female Voice in Sufi Ritual: Devotional Practices of Pakistan and India*. Austin: University of Texas Press, 2002.

Būṣīrī-al, Sharaf al-Dīn Muḥammad ibn Saʿid. *The Mantle Adorned: Imam al-Busiri's Burda*. Translated by Abdal Hakim Murad. London: Quilliam Press, 2009.

Ernst, Carl W., and Bruce B. Lawrence. *Sufi Martyrs of Love: The Chishti Order in South Asia and Beyond*. London: Palgrave Macmillan, 2002.

Lings, Martin. *A Sufi Saint of the Twentieth Century: Shaikh Aḥmad al-Alawī—His Spiritual Heritage and Legacy*. Cambridge, UK: Islamic Texts Society, 1993.

Metcalf, Barbara Daly. *Islam in South Asia in Practice*. Princeton, NJ: Princeton University Press, 2009.

Schimmel, Annemarie. *My Soul Is a Woman: The Feminine in Islam*. Translated from German by Susan H. Ray. New York: Continuum, 2003. Originally published in 1997.

Smith, Margaret. *Rabiʿa the Mystic and Her Fellow-Saints in Islam*. Cambridge, UK: Cambridge University Press, 2010. First edition published in 1928.

Stetkevych, Suzanne Pinckney. *The Mantle Odes: Arabic Praise Poems to the Prophet Muḥammad*. Bloomington: Indiana University Press, 2010.

Dženita Karić

Dhimmī. In Islamic law, a non-Muslim who is under a covenant of protection (*dhimmah*) with the local Muslim authority is considered *dhimmī*. In principle, the covenant could be made between a Muslim government and non-Muslims within a Muslim territory, including populations of non-Muslim areas conquered by Muslim forces. However, in the traditional meaning and practice, the covenant was made only with *ahl al-kitāb* (people of the book). Besides Jews, Christians, and Sabaeans, the category of *ahl al-kitāb* was often extended to cover Zoroastrians and sometimes members of other faiths, such as Hindus.

Originally, adult male *dhimmī* of sound mind were required to pay the special *jizyah* (poll tax) on their incomes as well as the *kharāj* (land tax).

In later centuries, the *kharāj* was exacted less and ultimately disappeared. Restrictions and regulations in dress, occupation, and residence were often placed upon *dhimmī*, although such regulations were applied to other segments of the population, as well, such as under the Ottoman Empire, so that a person's status was easily and publicly visible. The legal status of *dhimmī* was in many aspects unequal to that of Muslims. *Dhimmī* were obliged to comport themselves in a self-effacing and inoffensive manner and were not permitted to publicize or proselytize for their faiths, although they were permitted to practice their faiths, including abiding by their religious laws. In return for compliance with the stipulations of the *dhimmah* covenant, Muslim rulers offered them security of life and property, defense against enemies, communal self-government, and freedom of religious practice. The *dhimmah* regulations were applied with varying degrees of rigor in different times and places.

In the modern period, the *dhimmī* status has in practice become quite meaningless in most Muslim countries. This is a result of the creation of nation-states throughout the Islamic world and the consequent adoption of Western and quasi-Western legal and political systems. Although Islamic law in most instances played some role in the formation of the new sociopolitical order, the *dhimmah* in a traditional sense was usually not represented. This is because former *dhimmī* became citizens of modern states, in which modern conceptions and institutions of nationality and citizenship were more relevant to the nation-state than religious affiliation. In the case of the Jews, large numbers emigrated from the Arab states and North Africa as a result of the creation of the new Jewish state of Israel in 1948, while some communities remained elsewhere, particularly in Turkey and Iran.

Nonetheless, the concept of *dhimmī* has remained in force intellectually and psychologically in intercommunal relations, though in weakened form. With regard to the Palestine conflict, it has figured prominently in some of the main Arab nationalist and Islamic thought on the subject. In both strains of thought, the pre-Zionist history of Arab-Jewish (or Muslim-Jewish) relations was often portrayed as a positive experience, in contrast with the post-Zionist conflict. Many writers called for a return to the *dhimmah* or some modern version thereof as a solution to the conflict. For most conservative Muslim thinkers in the modern period, the *dhimmah* has been an integral part of their version of a reconstituted Islamic society and polity, although mainstream Muslims reject this concept as incompatible with contemporary understandings of citizenship.

BIBLIOGRAPHY

Courbage, Youssef, and Philippe Fargues. *Christians and Jews under Islam*. Translated by Judy Mabro. London: Tauris, 1997 Particularly good on demographic information.

Haddad, Yvonne Yazbeck, and Wadi Z. Haddad, eds. Christian-Muslim Encounters. Gainesville: University Press of Florida, 1995. Good survey of the subject.

Masters, Bruce Alan. *Christians and Jews in the Ottoman Arab World: The Roots of Sectarianism*. New York: Cambridge University Press, 2001. The only general book in English providing information on the treatment of *dhimmī* in the Ottoman Arab lands.

Nielsen, Jørgen S., ed. *The Christian-Muslim Frontier: Chaos, Clash, or Dialogue?* London: I. B. Tauris, 1998. Deals with contemporary Muslim attitudes toward Christians.

Stillman, Norman A. *The Jews of Arab Lands in Modern Times*. Philadelphia: Jewish Publication Society, 1991. Although mainly about the Jews, gives a good survey of the *dhimmī* situation in the modern period.

Tritton, A. S. *The Caliphs and Their Non-Muslim Subjects: A Critical Study of the Covenant of ʿUmar.* London: F. Cass, 1970. Originally published in 1930, this is a standard work on the subject, though somewhat dated.

RONALD L. NETTLER
Updated by NATANA J. DELONG-BAS

DIVORCE. [*This entry includes three subentries:* Historical Practice, Modern Practice, *and* Legal Foundations.]

HISTORICAL PRACTICE

"Divorce" can be defined as the dissolution of the marital bond through a process other than death. This article describes divorce law in the Muslim world in the period between the consolidation of Islamic legal doctrine (tenth century) until the time when the various states started to codify family law. It distinguishes between the formal rules on the one hand and practice on the other. Formal Islamic norms in the field of divorce are important until this day, as most family law codifications are based on (or at least presented as being based on) the classical norms. [*See* Divorce: Modern Practice.] However, it is necessary to look at the practices too, as several studies show that often, legal practices differed from the *Sharīʿah*.

The Law. Islamic law, or *Sharīʿah*, is a general term for the norms that were derived by legal scholars (*fuqahāʾ*) from the Qurʾān and *ḥadīth* during the first centuries of Islam (seventh to tenth centuries). As the Qurʾān and *ḥadīth* are often open to interpretation, different interpretations were possible and thus, within this large body of law called *Sharīʿah*, there are various schools of thought. This variety resulted in a situation in which the norms concerning divorce differed from one geographical area to another, depending on the dominant legal school in that particular region. A relatively large part of Islamic law, or *Sharīʿah*, pertains to marriage and divorce, and the norms with respect to divorce may vary widely from one school to another (Vikør, 2005).

The four major Sunnī law schools (Mālikī, Ḥanafī, Ḥanbalī, and Shāfiʿī), as well as the Jaʿfarī Shīʿī school of law, recognize four types of divorce: (1) divorce pronounced by the husband (*ṭalāq*), (2) divorce by mutual consent (*khulʿ*), (3) judicial divorce (*taṭlīq/tafrīq/faskh*), and (4) the husband's oath. The specific norms pertaining to these divorce types differ significantly from one school to another.

Ṭalāq. *Ṭalāq*, often translated as "repudiation" but literally meaning "divorce," is the term that is used to denote the right of the husband to divorce his wife. In Islamic law, this right is discretionary, requiring neither a justification nor the consent of the wife or a *qāḍī* (Linant de Bellefonds, 1965, p. 315). The husband simply needs to declare "I divorce you," a declaration typically pronounced out of court, meaning that no judicial interference is required. The presence of the wife is not necessary either, nor will she need to be informed of the divorce; the only obligation is that the husband has the intention to repudiate, and that he be a lucid adult. The Shīʿī norms differ somewhat, requiring the presence of witnesses when the husband pronounces the divorce, and also that the marriage has been consummated, that the *ṭalāq* is pronounced during an intermenstrual period, and that the spouses have not had sexual relations since the wife's last menstruation. A divorce that conforms to these conditions is the *ṭalāq sunnī*, as opposed to the *ṭalāqbidʿī*.

The discretionary right of the man to divorce stands in clear contrast with women's access to divorce, as a woman is dependent on her husband's consent (*khulʿ*), or on the *qāḍī* (*taṭlīq/faskh*). The explanation for this discrepancy may be explained by the norm that marriage in Islamic law imposes financial obligations only on the husband. Besides, gendered access to divorce has often been explained as coming from the opinion of the *fuqahāʾ* that: "The female nature is wanting in rationality and self-control". As a result, Rapoport described *ṭalāq* as: "A symbol of patriarchal authority," which the author puts on a par with other male privileges, such as polygamy, concubinage, and the right of physical chastisement (Rapoport, 2005, p. 69). It should be underlined, however, that even Islam itself considers *ṭalāq* reprehensible, even if it is a valid means of divorce.

The Islamic norms of *ṭalāq* are the result of reform of the norms existing in pre-Islamic times (the *jāhilīyah*): it has been argued that Islam tried to make divorce less accessible to men and less frequent (Esposito with DeLong-Bas, 2001, p. 27). In Arabia, before the advent of Islam, men kept their wife in a state of "limbo" (Peters, 2006, p. 7) by continuously repudiating them and taking them back at their will. The Qur'ān put an end to this: 2:230 delimits the number of repudiations that a man may pronounce against his wife to three, after which she becomes unlawful for him, meaning that he cannot take her back. This can be remedied only by an intermediate marriage. The Qur'ān also introduced the "waiting period" (*'idda*), which commences as soon as the husband pronounces the divorce (2:228; 2:234; 33:49, and 65:4), and allows the husband to revoke the divorce if he has regrets; after this period has ended, the man cannot take the wife back unless they remarry.

Besides the "normal" *ṭalāq*, there are some specific forms of unilateral divorce. For example, the husband can delegate his right to *ṭalāq* to the wife, or he can appoint her as his agent. In these cases, she can pronounce the *ṭalāq* herself. Agency and delegation can be restricted to specific conditions. For example, the couple can include in the marriage contract that the husband delegates his right to divorce to his wife if he marries a second wife, meaning that the wife can repudiate herself if the condition is fulfilled. Another special form of *ṭalāq* is the triple one, meaning that the husband repudiates his wife three times at once, or three times during the same waiting period to ensure that he does not take her back during the waiting period; there is a difference of opinion between the legal scholars who developed Islamic law as to whether this is allowed.

***Khul'*.** Unlike the man, the woman can divorce only with the consent of her husband (*khul'*) or the approval of the *qāḍī* (*taṭlīq/faskh*). The *khul'* also takes place out of court, although the Shī'īs require the presence of witnesses. In general, it is the wife who proposes the divorce, and the husband who either consents or refuses, but if he accepts the offer to divorce, he can demand financial compensation. This may consist of paying the husband money, or waiving outstanding financial rights, such as the remaining part of her dower (*mahr mu'akhir*) or maintenance during the waiting period (*nafaqat al-'idda*). In this way, the husband benefits from a *khul'* divorce financially. Only the Ḥanafī and Mālikī schools do not require that the wife pay compensation. The *khul'* is an irrevocable divorce, meaning that the husband cannot take the wife back during the waiting period. Nevertheless, the waiting period does apply for other purposes, and the husband is obligated to continue to pay maintenance during this term unless this is waived by the wife as part of her compensation. Like *ṭalāq*, divorce by mutual consent predates the coming of Islam. As marriage was a sale contract between the groom and the bride's father, the groom paid the dower to the latter or the entire clan. In the event of *khul'*, it was the bride's clan who compensated the husband (Layish, 1988, p. 428). The Qur'ān affirmed the possibility of *khul'* (2:229), stipulating that, if the spouses fear breaking the limits set by God, the husband should release his wife in exchange for compensation. However, as in Islamic law, the *mahr* is paid to the wife herself, it is the wife who should compensate the husband.

Judicial divorce (taṭlīq or tafrīq and faskh). If the husband refuses to divorce, the wife can seek recourse in court. The *qāḍī* can pronounce the divorce, but only on specific grounds, which differ from one school to another.

In Ḥanafī and Shī'ī law, the wife can obtain a judicial divorce only if the husband is not able to have intercourse and if she was not aware of this when contracting the marriage and has not accepted it afterwards. These schools further provide that the woman can have the marriage nullified (*faskh*) by a judge if it was contracted during the woman's minority through force by a marriage guardian other than her father or grandfather. Also, the woman and her marriage guardian can have it nullified if there is moral or social incompatibility (lack of *kafā'a*), or if the husband fails to pay the immediate part of the dower (*mahr mu'akhir*).

The Shāfi'ī and Ḥanbalī schools recognize wider access to judicial divorce. Besides impotence, other physical defects are accepted as grounds for judicial divorce, if they make sexual intercourse impossible, and this applies to both husband and wife. The physical grounds for divorce can be expanded by the future spouses with stipulations in the marriage contract, such as that the other spouse be free of specific physical defects (*sharṭ al-salāma*). The husband can also stipulate that his wife possess certain qualities, such as virginity; if the contract is breached, the husband can have the marriage nullified without having to turn to *ṭalāq*.

The Shāfi'ī and Ḥanbalī schools grant the wife more grounds for divorce. Both schools recognize the husband's failure to pay maintenance as acceptable grounds for divorce. The Ḥanbalīs allow this even if the wife knew that she married a poor man. The Ḥanbalī school is also the only school that allows the wife to stipulate in her marriage contract that her husband shall not marry another woman, and that she obtains a divorce if he breaches the contract. Also in Ḥanbalī law, a wife may obtain a divorce if her husband is absent for more than six months. By contrast, Ḥanafī law requires the husband's absence for 99 years in order to assure that he is deceased.

Mālikī law is the most generous in granting the wife the possibility to have her marriage annulled by the *qāḍī*. With regard to physical defects, nonpayment of maintenance, and abandonment, the Mālikīs share the same rules as the Ḥanbalī school, although the Mālikīs do not accept nonpayment of maintenance as grounds for divorce if the wife knew beforehand that her future husband was poor. In case of nonpayment of maintenance, the husband is granted a delay of three months and the husband can revoke the divorce by paying the due amount during the waiting period. The husband's absence justifies divorce after one year. But a ground that is very specific for the Mālikī school is divorce for "harm" (*ḍarar*), a notion that offers significant discretion to the *qāḍī*, who determines what acts are qualified as "harm." Mālikī doctrine provides that severe and unjustified domestic violence is qualified as such, but if the wife cannot prove her complaint, two arbiters are appointed to reconcile the couple. If they fail, they establish who is to blame; if it is the husband, the judge can pronounce *ṭalāq* on his behalf. If the wife is responsible, the judge can either leave the marriage intact or pronounce divorce by obliging her to pay compensation.

The oath. The husband can end marriage through three types of oaths: the oath of continence (*īlā'* and *izhar*), the denial of paternity (*li'an*), and the oath of divorce. The first two are a continuation of pre-Islamic practices, confirmed by the Qur'ān (*'īlā'*: 2:226–227, *izhar*: 58:2–4), although it is made clear in this same source that *izhar*, if valid, is nevertheless reprehensible.

The doctrine of *īlā'* (turning away) provides that if a man swears that he shall not approach his wife sexually for four months, and he does not break this oath by resuming intercourse with her, the wife can obtain divorce through the *qāḍī*, or, according to the Ḥanafī school, is *ipso facto* divorced after the four months have come to an end. *Ẓihār* is the oath sworn by the husband comparing the wife to a body part of a woman who is prohibited to him in marriage, thus indicating that his wife is no longer attractive to him (e.g.: "My wife is like my mother's back," hence the term *ẓihār*). Mālikī law gives the wife the right to obtain a divorce through the *qāḍī*. If the husband swears that the child born to his wife is not his (*liʿān*), the wife is *ipso facto* divorced and the couple can never remarry.

Another oath of divorce is called the "conditional *ṭalāq*." This takes place when the husband declares that if his wife performs a certain act, she shall be divorced, or that she will be divorced if *he* performs a certain act, such as marrying a second wife. In the first example, the conditional *ṭalāq* is a threat, whereas in the second case, it provides security to the wife. All schools accept the conditional divorce, except the Shīʿīs (Nasir, 1990, p. 117).

Consequences of divorce. During the waiting period (*ʿidda*), the wife cannot remarry, but she does (in principle) receive maintenance. After the end of the waiting period, the wife does not receive any maintenance for herself. However, if she has custody of her children, the latter might receive maintenance, depending on their own means. The wife receives the remaining part of the dower (*mahr muʾakhir*). As Islamic law does not recognize the concept of the community of goods, the goods acquired before and during marriage are not common property, and, so, there is no division of common goods upon divorce. Instead, there is an attribution of the goods that belong to either spouse, and possible disagreements over the property of certain goods (e.g., furniture) shall be taken care of by means of taking an oath.

In principle, the wife obtains custody of the children, while the father retains guardianship, that is, the authority to take important decisions involving them. This means that the children live with their mother until custody ends, or until someone else obtains custody for some reason. The father can visit the children. The age at which custody ends differs per school: for the Mālikīs, custody ends at puberty for boys and at marriage for girls; for Ḥanafīs, it ends at age seven for boys and at puberty for girls; the Shāfiʿīs determine that custody lasts until the children have reached the age of discretion (*rushd*); for the Ḥanbalīs, custody ends at seven, and for the Shīʿīs, custody ends at two years for boys and at seven years for girls. In all schools, the rule is that when custody has ended, meaning that the children have reached the aforementioned ages, the children shall live with their father. If the woman remarries before the children have reached the aforementioned ages, custody rights transfer to her mother, or another female relative, such as the father's mother. For Ḥanafīs, apostasy is also a reason to lose custody, whereas Shāfiʿīs and Shīʿīs deny custody to the mother who is not a *kitābiyya* (Muslim, Christian, or Jew), even if the father is Muslim.

Practice. Law in practice did not always correspond, at least not completely, with the precepts of the dominant school in a certain geographical area: the "law in action" differed from "the law on the books." Schacht writes that: "Even in the field of [...] divorce [...], actual practice has been strong enough to prevail over the spirit, and in certain cases over the letter, of religious law, either depressing the position of women or raising it" (Schacht, 1964, pp. 76–77). The following two case studies demonstrate how legal practice sometimes deviated from *fiqh*: the Mamluks (Egypt, fourteenth and fifteenth centuries) and the Ottomans in Syria, Palestine, Egypt, and the Balkans (sixteenth to nineteenth centuries). In both empires, the Ḥanafī doctrine was dominant, yet practice did not always coincide with what was stipulated within Ḥanafī doctrine.

Ṭalāq. In Ottoman Syria and Palestine, neither the muftis nor the *qāḍīs* questioned the male prerogative of *ṭalāq* found in Ḥanafī doctrine (Tucker, 1998, p. 95). Nevertheless, women had means to render a *ṭalāq* invalid, namely by stating that the husband had shown signs of "diminished rationality" when pronouncing the divorce (Tucker, 1998, pp. 88, 89). If this was proven, the wife remained married and continued to have a right to maintenance.

There were also means for women to divorce by means of *ṭalāq*. Again in Ottoman Syria and Palestine, a woman could use her husband's declaration of *ṭalāq*, even if it was made without the intention to divorce, against him: if the husband had pronounced a *ṭalāq* without taking it back, the wife could address a *mufti* or a judge to have her divorce confirmed, if she could prove it. This practice provided "one way for a woman to choose divorce" (Tucker, 1998, p. 92).

In sixteenth century Ottoman Egypt, it was common to include conditions in the marriage contract, providing that, in case of violation of such conditions, the wife would automatically be divorced. As this would then be a conditional *ṭalāq*, the wife was not obliged to pay the compensation due in the case of a *khulʿ* divorce (Abdal Rahman, 1996, p. 103). Such conditions made divorce possible in cases of nonpayment of maintenance, but also in the event that the husband married a second wife, grounds that Ḥanafī law does not recognize for divorce. This was true even if Ḥanafī law does not allow such stipulations.

Among the Mamluks in the Middle Ages, *ṭalāq* was not the principal means of divorce. Since the unilateral divorce was generally considered a disaster for women, depriving them of financial support and protection and preventing them from remarriage because they would lose child custody, pronouncing the *ṭalāq* without a good reason was not considered "proper behavior." Moreover, men were deterred by the financial consequences of *ṭalāq*, which in practice consisted not only of the deferred dower and maintenance during the waiting period, but also of an additional compensation (*mutʿa*) (Rapoport, 2005, pp. 70–71).

***Khulʿ*.** Among the Mamluks, *khulʿ*, rather than *ṭalāq*, was the principal means of divorce. The same was true in the Ottoman Balkans in the seventeenth and eighteenth centuries (Ivanova, 1996, p. 118). And, although, formally, women were dependent on their husbands' consent to obtain a divorce through *khulʿ*, Mamluk women employed various strategies to force their husbands to agree. For example, a woman would forfeit her marital duties, such as housekeeping or maintaining sexual relations with her husband, thus making marital life impossible for the husband and pushing him to agree to a divorce. Another means would be to claim the remaining part of the dower, knowing that the husband was unable to pay; in such cases, the husband agreed to a divorce because otherwise, he would go to prison for violation of the contract (Rapoport, 2005, pp. 72–73).

Compensations offered by women to obtain a *khulʿ* divorce often consisted of more than what was initially required by Ḥanafī law: women would not only waive outstanding financial rights (the remainder of the dower and maintenance during the waiting period), but would also take the duty of child maintenance upon them. On the other hand, if no compensation was agreed upon, the *khulʿ* was nevertheless valid, as is prescribed in Ḥanafī doctrine.

Ottoman muftis in seventeenth and eighteenth century Palestine and Syria would ensure that women did not unjustifiably compensate the husband: if the wife contracted *khulʿ*, the *mufti* would call witnesses to establish if the divorce had not actually been a *ṭalāq*, in the sense that the husband had proposed to divorce his wife if she compensated him. In such cases, *mufti*s would tell the woman that she was not obliged to pay anything, and that she could even claim her deferred dower (Tucker, 1998, pp. 96–97). Women could also take advantage of this by asking a *mufti* to force the husband to pay the financial duties of a *ṭalāq*, arguing that the *khulʿ* agreement had actually been a *ṭalāq*. In such cases, witnesses would be called as well (Tucker, 1998, p. 99).

Ṭatliq and faskh. In the Mamluk period, it was hardly possible for women to obtain divorce other than through *khulʿ*, except if they had included conditions in their marriage contract (Rapoport, 2005, p. 69). The same was true in Ottoman Egypt (Sonbol, 1996, p. 281), but there were nevertheless a number of ways in which this rigidity was softened, by opening up the way of judicial divorce.

In Ḥanafī law, judicial divorce is allowed only in the case in which the husband cannot have intercourse. The Ḥanafī muftis in Ottoman Palestine and Syria, however, would allow women to have their marriage nullified for other defects as well, recognizing that serious contagious diseases and mental illnesses could make sexual life impossible, too (Tucker, 1998, 81).

One main problem for women under Ḥanafī law, however, was abandonment: as Ḥanafī law does not recognize this as grounds for divorce, women who were abandoned by their husbands could not divorce, and thus they could not remarry either. Abandonment was quite a recurrent phenomenon: in the Ottoman Balkans, many men preferred to abandon their wives instead of divorce them (Ivanova, 1996, p. 122). A solution for this problem could be offered by the husbands themselves: among the Mamluks, it was common that, if the husband was going to travel, he gave his wife a letter allowing her to pronounce the *ṭalāq* in his name after a specific period of time (Rapoport, 2005, pp. 76–77). But in case the husband did not offer his wife this possibility, *qāḍīs* and *muftis* could help out: in Ottoman Syria and Palestine, Ḥanafī *qāḍīs* invited a Shāfiʿī or Ḥanbalīi colleague to pronounce the divorce, as in these schools, abandonment is a ground for divorce (Tucker, 1998, 83–85). The Ottoman courts of Jaffa and Haifa went even further, including "unacceptable distance" within the grounds for (a Ḥanafī) divorce (Agmon, 1996, p. 137). Another possibility was for the women themselves to address a Ḥanbalī or Mālikī *qāḍī* instead of a Ḥanafī one—a type of "forum shopping" that was allowed in seventeenth century Cairo (Hanna, 1996, p. 146).

Another problem for women was nonsupport, as Ḥanafī law did not recognize this as a cause for divorce. But here, again, muftis and *qāḍīs* could offer a helping hand, inviting representatives from other schools to pronounce the divorce (Tucker, 1998, 83).

In the Ottoman Balkans, women could even file for divorce with the *qāḍī* on the grounds that the husband was not a good Muslim: cursing and blasphemy were accepted as valid grounds for divorce initiated by the wife (Ivanova, 1996, p. 119).

The oath. The studies of Mamluk and Ottoman practices do not make mention of the oaths of abstinence or of *liʿān*, suggesting that these were not widely practiced. Nevertheless, the oath of divorce seems to have played an important role in these empires, in the sense that men pledged a conditional oath of divorce, swearing that if this did or did not happen, the wife would be divorced.

Both among the Mamluks, and in Ottoman Syria and Palestine, the conditional *ṭalāq* could be pronounced to *threaten* the wife. By swearing that, "If you do/do not do this, you shall be divorced," men controlled their wife's behavior, as "society expected men to supervise the womenfolk of their household, and neglect of this duty could affect their social standing" (Rapoport, 2005, pp. 69–72). In this way, *ṭalāq* became a "weapon of domination" (Tucker, 1998, pp. 101–102).

But the conditional *ṭalāq* could also be a means to make a *promise* to the wife; for example, the husband would swear that if he did not pay maintenance, his wife would be divorced. This practice, observed in seventeenth and eighteenth century Ottoman Syria and Palestine, offered the woman a weapon in case of nonpayment of maintenance, for which Ḥanafī law, not recognizing nonpayment of maintenance as grounds for divorce, does not provide.

The consequences of divorce. With regard to child custody, Tucker observed that practice was in accordance with Ḥanafī *fiqh:* if a woman was divorced, she could keep her children unless she remarried and her ex-husband claimed custody, in which case the children were kept by her female family members (Tucker, 1998, p. 125). Otherwise, the children stayed with her until they reached a certain age: for boys, this was the moment that they could get dressed by themselves, and for girls when they reached puberty, at which point they went to stay with their father (Tucker, 1998, pp. 117–118). In sixteenth century Ottoman Egypt, however, it was common for children to stay with their mothers beyond this age (Abdal Rahman, 1996, p. 108). Among the Mamluks, women could waive the right to child maintenance in order to obtain child custody (Rapoport, 2005).

BIBLIOGRAPHY

Abdal Rahman Abdal-Rehim, Abdal Rehim. "The Family and Gender Laws in Egypt during the Ottoman Period." In *Women, the Family, and Divorce Laws in Islamic History*, edited by Amira Sonbol, pp. 96–111. New York: Syracuse University Press, 1996.

Agmon, Iris. "Muslim Women in Court According to the *Sijill* of Late Ottoman Jaffa and Haifa." In *Women, the Family, and Divorce Laws in Islamic History*, edited by Amira Sonbol, pp. 126–142. New York: Syracuse University Press, 1996.

Ahmed, Leila. *Women and Gender in Islam. Historical Roots of a Modern Debate*. New Haven, Conn.: Yale University Press, 1992.

Ali, Kecia. *Marriage and Slavery in Early Islam*. Cambridge, Mass.: Harvard University Press, 2010.

Bousquet, G. H. "Islamic Law and Customary Law in French North Africa." *Journal of Comparative Legislation and International Law* (1950): 57–65.

Bousquet, G. H., and L. Bercher. *Le statut personnel en droit musulman Hanéfite: Texte et traduction annotés du Mukhtasar d'al-Quduri*. Tunis: Institut des Hautes Etudes de Tunis, s.d.

Coulson, Nigel J. *A History of Islamic Law*. Edinburgh: Edinburgh University Press, 1964.

Esposito, John L. with Natana J. DeLong-Bas. *Women in Muslim Family Law*. 2d ed. Syracuse, N.Y.: Syracuse University Press, 2001.

Gerber, Haim. "Social and Economic Position of Women in an Ottoman City, Bursa 1600–1700." *IJMES* no. 12 (1980): 231–244.

Hallaq, Wael Ibn. "Was the gate of ijtihad closed?" *International Journal of Middle East Studies* 16.I (1984): 3–41.

Hanna, Nelly. "Marriage among Merchant Families in Seventeenth Century Cairo." In *Women, the Family, and Divorce Laws in Islamic History*, edited by Amira Sonbol, pp. 143–154. Syracuse, N.Y.: Syracuse University Press, 1996.

Ivanova, Svetlana. "The Divorce between Zubaida Hatun and Esseid Osman Aga: Women in the 18th Century Sharia Court in Rumelia. In *Women, the Family, and Divorce Laws in Islamic History*, edited by Amira Sonbol, pp. 112–125. Syracuse, N.Y.: Syracuse University Press, 1996.

Jennings, Ronald. "Women in Early Seventeenth Century Ottoman Judicial Records—the Sharia Court of Anatolian Kayseri." *Journal of the Economic and Social History of the Orient* no. 18 (1975): 53–114.

Layish, Aharon. *Women and Islamic Law in a Non-Muslim State: A Study Based on the Decisions of the Sharia Courts in Israel*. New York and Jerusalem: John Wiley & Sons, 1975.

Layish, Aharon. "Customary *khul'* as Reflected in the *Sijill* of the Libyan *Sharia* Courts." *Bulletin of the School of Oriental and African Studies* 51.3 (1988): 428–439.

Layish, Aharon. *Divorce in the Libyan Family: A Study Based on the Sijills of the Sharia Courts of Ajdabiyya and Kufra*. New York: New York University Press, 1991.

Linant de Bellefonds, Y. *Traité de droit musulman comparé*. Paris: Mouton, 1965.

Masud, Muhammad Khalil, David S. Powers, and Ruud Peters, eds. *Dispensing Justice in Islam: Qadis and Their Judgments*. Leiden, The Netherlands: E.J. Brill, 2006.

Nasir, Jamal J. *The Islamic Law of Personal Status*. 2d ed. London: Graham and Trotman, 1990.

Rapoport, Yossef. *Marriage, Money and Divorce in Medieval Islamic Society*. Cambridge, U.K.: Cambridge University Press, 2005.

Schacht, Joseph. *An Introduction to Islamic Law.* Oxford: Clarendon Press, 1964.
Sonbol, Amira el-Azhari. "Law and Gender Violence in Ottoman and Modern Egypt. In *Women, the Family, and Divorce Laws in Islamic History*, edited by Amira Sonbol, pp. 277–289. Syracuse, N.Y.: Syracuse University Press, 1996.
Spectorsky, Susan A. *Chapters on Marriage and Divorce: Responses of Ibn Hanbal and Ibn Rahwayh.* Austin, Tex.: University of Texas Press, 1993.
Stern Gertrude. *Marriage in Early Islam.* London: Royal Asiatic Society, 1939.
Tucker, Judith E. *Women in Nineteenth Century Egypt.* Cambridge, U.K.: Cambridge University Press, 1985.
Tucker, Judith E. "Marriage and Family in Nablus, 1720-1856: Towards a History of Arab Muslim Marriage." *Journal of Family History* no. 13 (1988): 165–179.
Tucker, Judith E. *In the House of the Law. Gender and Islamic Law in Ottoman Syria and Palestine.* Berkeley: University of California Press, 1998.
Tucker, Judith E. *Women, Family, and Gender in Islamic Law.* Themes in Islamic Law 3, Cambridge, U.K.: Cambridge University Press, 2008.
Vikør, Knut. *Between God and the Sultan: A History of Islamic Law.* New York: Oxford University Press, 2005.

Maaike Voorhoeve

Modern Practice

"Divorce," or the dissolution of the marital bond through processes other than death, is organized by norms that change along with time and space, depending on formal rules and practice. Traditionally, divorce in the Muslim world was organized by *fiqh*. [*See* Divorce, Historical Practice.] In the twentieth century, an important change took place, as personal status law was codified. As a consequence, the decision of what norms organized divorce shifted from the *fuqahā*ʾ to the state. These codes generally remained "within the orbit of Islamic law" (Peters, 2005, pp. 107–134) because of the "divine character" of personal status law. As it is generally considered that the prescriptions on family law are more detailed in the Qurʾān and *ḥadīth* than in other domains (penal and civil law), Anderson, Coulson and others have argued that it is complicated for believers to deviate from these rules (Anderson, 1976, p. 17 and Coulson, 1996, p. 161). Nevertheless, states grasped this opportunity to reform divorce law, in order to enhance women's rights, but also to increase state control over family matters and reduce divorce rates. Reforms were effectuated by selecting those rules from *fiqh* that answered to the state's wishes (*takhayyur*, selection) and by imposing procedures, for example the registration of *ṭalāq*.

The first reform in the field of divorce law originated in the Ottoman Empire in 1915. Muslims from all parts of the Islamic world visited Istanbul, married local women, and lived with them for the duration of their stay, only to leave them behind without divorcing them. As Ḥanafī law has limited possibilities for women to file for divorce, women called for reform (Anderson, 1976, p. 39). The Sultan issued two decrees providing that, in cases of divorce, *qāḍī*s should apply the Mālikī and Ḥanbalī rules that allow judicial divorce in case of abandonment. In other personal status matters, the *qāḍī*s continued to apply Ḥanafī *fiqh*, until a more comprehensive code followed two years later: the Ottoman Law of Family Rights (OLFR). This code remained in force in the Ottoman Empire until 1919, and after the fall of the Ottoman Empire, the newly established state of Turkey introduced the Swiss Civil Code. Nevertheless, the importance of the OLFR can hardly be overestimated: not only did it remain in force in some of the mandate states for the decades to follow (Syria, Jordan, Lebanon, and Israel), but it also paved the way for reforms in almost the entire Muslim world (Anderson, 1976, p. 40). In 1920 and 1939, respectively, the next steps were taken in Egypt and the Indian subcontinent, where laws extended the grounds on which women could apply for judicial divorce.

It is not a coincidence that the first reforms took place in areas where the Ḥanafī doctrine was dominant, as this *maḍhhab* is the most restrictive in granting women the right to divorce. But, in the 1950s, some Mālikī countries followed, issuing relatively elaborate family codes. These codes were comprehensive codifications of personal status law as a whole, instead of piecemeal laws. While the Moroccan *mudawwanah* (1957) remained close to the Mālikī *fiqh*, Tunisia issued a Personal Status Code that until today, is considered the most "progressive" in the Arab Muslim world, introducing equal divorce rights for men and women by providing that both spouses can file for divorce with mutual consent, for harm, and without grounds (Article 31 of the Tunisian Personal Status Code). In the decades that followed, other Muslim majority countries issued personal status codes. Most codifications extended the grounds for women to obtain judicial divorce and curtailed the husband's access to *ṭalāq*, albeit in a restrictive way. But the codes were not finalized achievements. In a situation in which "conservatives" and "progressives" continuously struggle over the degree to which codification should or should not remain within the orbit of Islamic law, most codes have been amended or replaced. Some changes resulted in the enhancement of women's rights in the field of divorce, for example, in Morocco in 2004 and Egypt in 2000. But sometimes the changes resulted in their deterioration, for example, in Libya, where the law of 1984 restricted women's access to divorce through *khulʿ*, as the provision that the judge replaces the husband's consent was abolished. Also, many amendments were stalled by heated public debates, particularly in Iran, Syria, Senegal, Indonesia, and Sudan. These debates reintensified in some countries after the "Arab Spring."

Codifications. Reforms have been effected in terms of both the mechanisms of divorce and its implications in many countries.

Ṭalāq. Hardly any code curtails the husband's *right* to divorce his wife: men retained their discretionary right to divorce, regardless of the agreement of the wife or a third party (the judge). The Iranian family Code of 1975 was revolutionary in the respect, allowing both spouses to obtain divorce, but only if they proved the existence of one of the prescribed grounds. This law was revoked after the Islamic Revolution of 1979.

Provisions may, however, make *ṭalāq* more complicated by adding procedures or imposing additional financial duties. For example, many codes require that a *ṭalāq* pronounced out of court be registered with the authorities, that it be pronounced in front of a judge, or even that a reconciliation procedure is undertaken by the court. The consequences of violation of such a rule range from incompetence of the court in claims concerning the *ṭalāq* to a penal sanction or straightforward invalidity of the divorce. The obligation to pay compensation (*mutʿa* or *gharāma*), introduced in some codes, may constitute a financial impediment to pronouncing the *ṭalāq*, as it is added to the remaining part of the dower and maintenance during the waiting period that the husband is obligated to pay.

Taṭlīq. Reforms of judicial divorce consist of the extension of the grounds for women to obtain such a divorce to making this divorce type available to men, too. This demonstrates that reforms are directed not only at the enhancement of women's rights.

The extension of the grounds of *taṭlīq* may consist of copying the Mālikī grounds of nonpayment of maintenance, absence, and harm in countries where the Mālikī doctrine is not dominant (Hosseini, 2007). Also, other grounds may be added, such as the husband's polygamous marriage, AIDS, and infertility. Some countries introduced marital discord (*nizāʿ wa shiqāq*) as grounds for divorce. However, even if the grounds for judicial divorce are extended, women *do* need a reason for divorce, except in case of delegation of the right of *ṭalāq* (*tamlīk*). This is different only in Tunisia, where the wife can obtain divorce without any grounds whatsoever.

Making judicial divorce available to men seems contradictory in a situation in which men have absolute access to divorce through repudiation. But according to Mayer, its justification is found in the consideration that, if the wife is responsible for the marital breakdown, the husband should not carry the financial burden of a *ṭalāq* (Mayer, 1978, p. 36). Thus, some countries made judicial divorce available to men in cases such as harm (Tunisia) and marital discord (Morocco, Syria).

Khulʿ. Reforms of *khulʿ* range from judicial intervention to measures to prevent abuse by the husband or even to the abolition of the requirement of the husband's consent.

As in the case of *ṭalāq*, some codes make the validity of *khulʿ* dependent on its being registered with the authorities, or require that such a divorce take place in court, or that a reconciliation procedure is undertaken. These are procedural obstacles to contract *khulʿ*, which have a possible deterring function; in this way, they serve to bring about a decrease in divorce rates, but court interference may also deter women who wish to keep their marital problems private (Welchman, 2007, p. 121). An example of provisions that protect the wife against specific agreements is the Kuwaiti interdiction to give up child custody by means of compensation. Some countries abolished the duty to pay compensation, making *khulʿ* more accessible to women. For example, Article 114 of the Moroccan *mudawwanah* of 2004, allows *khulʿ* with and without compensation.

In Pakistan, Egypt, and Algeria, courts can enforce a *khulʿ* upon a husband who is unwilling to agree to a divorce. This means that a woman can obtain a divorce regardless of her husband's consent.

The consequences of divorce. Some codes provide that children stay longer in their mother's custody after divorce than in *fiqh*, even in the case of the mother's remarriage. Also, codes may require the husband to pay damages (*mutʿ a* or *gharāma*) after *ṭalāq*. In India, Muslim women have a right to maintenance until they remarry or can take care of themselves. Some codes, such as Articles 56 and 56 bis of the Tunisian Personal Status Code, provide that the woman may get to stay in the former marital home if she has custody.

Practice. Law in practice does not always correspond with the law on the books. As legal-anthropological literature shows, litigants' strategies and judicial practices can significantly influence access to and consequences of divorce. The following examples from Syria, Egypt, Morocco, Iran, Yemen, the West Bank, Gaza, and Tunisia illustrate where, sometimes, practice deviates from legislation.

Ṭalāq. In many countries, couples stipulate in their marriage contracts that a small part of the dower is paid upon marriage, while payment of the outstanding dower is postponed until, for example, *ṭalāq*. These deferred dowers can be significant, and in this way, they not only function as financial security for the wife in the absence of maintenance after divorce, but the deferred dower also is a deterrent for the husband to pronounce the *ṭalāq*.

Taṭlīq. Judicial interpretation is crucial when it concerns *taṭlīq* on the grounds of "harm," "hardship," or "antipathy," or judicial divorce for irretrievable breakdown (*shiqāq*), as these terms are very vague. In Iran, some judges interpreted "hardship" in such a restrictive manner that they refused any divorce on these grounds if the husband opposed it (Hosseini, 2007, p. 199), a situation that may have changed since the legislature intervened in 2002 by defining "hardship" more clearly in 2002. In Yemen, whether or not a certain act is qualified as "antipathy" depends on the social class of the woman, since lower-class women are supposed to endure more from their husbands than uppe;r-class women in case of divorce on the grounds of "antipathy" (Würth, 2000). In Tunisia, the wife's petition for divorce for nonpayment of maintenance is rejected if she abandoned the marital home without a valid reason, as she is then considered to have lost her right to maintenance (Voorhoeve, 2013). Also, judges may apply strict evidence requirements with regard to the grounds for *taṭlīq*; for example, in Morocco and Tunisia, judges require a penal conviction as evidence of domestic violence in order to obtain divorce for harm (*ḍarar*).

These judicial practices influence litigants' practices. For example, women in Morocco and Syria turn to divorce for discord (*nizāʿ wa shiqāq*) instead of *taṭlīq*, even in cases of domestic violence. This is true despite the fact that they would receive money in case of *taṭlīq*, while, in a *shiqāq* procedure, they risk carrying a large financial burden, namely if the arbiters in the *shiqāq* procedure decide that she is responsible for the marital breakdown (Carlisle, 2007). The cause of this practice is that in these countries, *shiqāq* is generally granted, whereas *taṭlīq* is not (Carlisle, 2007). This situation is opposite to the one in Iran (Hosseini, 2007). Welchman has further observed in the Palestinian West Bank that the wife should prove discord, while the husband's petition of divorce for discord and strife is accepted if he insists (Welchman, 2000, p. 290).

Women may also seek a *khulʿ* divorce, in which case they carry the financial burden, but they may also simply abandon the marital home instead of filing for divorce, as was observed in Tunisia (Voorhoeve, 2013). These choices are caused not only by restrictive access to *taṭlīq*: with regard to the West Bank, Welchman connects the lack of judicial divorces to the shame attached to disclosing the intimacies of a failing marriage in court (Welchman, 2000, p. 248).

Not only women, but men also employ strategies with regard to judicial divorce. In countries where this divorce type is also available to men, some men prefer judicial divorce, as it relieves them from the financial burden of *ṭalāq*. Judges may encourage this practice by interpreting terms such as "harm" extensively when the husband files for *taṭlīq*. For example, in Tunisia, judges qualify as "harm" the wife's abandonment of the marital home without a valid reason, and the wife's flirting by texting or chatting on the internet. They may even qualify the fact that the wife has a job outside of the home as "rebellion" (*nushūz*), justifying divorce (Voorhoeve, 2013).

***Khulʿ*.** Women may employ strategies to force the husband into a divorce. For example, in Iran, women pressure their husbands by claiming their deferred dower. As future spouses agree on high amounts of *mahr* that the wife may claim at any given moment, women who claim their *mahr* can cause their husband's imprisonment. What follows is a negotiation in which the wife proposes to drop (part of) her claim in exchange for a divorce (Osanloo, 2006). In Morocco, the wife's abandonment of the marital home is the impetus for divorce negotiations between the wife's family and the husband (Maher, 1974).

Practical access to *khulʿ* also depends on the (financial) consequences for the wife. In Tunisia, judges protect women, as they prohibit waiving child support (Voorhoeve, 2013). In Egypt, on the other hand, Sonneveld observed that judges oblige women to pay large amounts of money, in this way restricting women's access to divorce (Sonneveld, 2012).

Although *khulʿ* is generally presented as divorce on the woman's demand, some men employ strategies to force their wife into *khulʿ*, as this is more financially beneficial for them than *ṭalāq* (Welchman, 2000, p. 280).

Consequences of divorce. With regard to the damages that the husband should pay upon divorce, it has been observed that in practice, men do not comply as they are not forced to do so. For this reason, the Moroccan legislature provided that the divorce can be pronounced only when the husband has deposited the money he is due to pay at the court (Article 86 Moroccan *mudawwanah* of 2004). The same is true with regard to the marital home: in countries where the woman is allowed to stay in the home after divorce, there are no measures to force the husband to move out, leading to a situation in which, finally, the woman moves back in with her family (Voorhoeve, 2013).

With regard to custody, it has been observed that in Gaza, regardless of statute law providing that children stay with their mother until they have reached ten and twelve years respectively, practice depends largely on the relationship between the mother and the father's family, and on the mother's financial means; if the mother's financial situation or her relation with her former family-in-law is bad, the father's family might claim the children before they reach this age (Shehada, 2004, p. 106).

These examples show that, besides statute law, other elements in society may influence divorce in practice, such as the financial consequences (Welchman, 2000, p. 251). Also, it has been argued repeatedly that social stigma imposes an extra-legal restriction on divorce for women (Welchman, 2000, pp. 250–251). The lack of the use of *tamlīk* because of its social unacceptability is one telling example of this (An-Na'im, 2002, p. 100). But, although social stigma may indeed influence women's (and men's) access to divorce, it should be pointed out that, for example, in the Libyan desert in the 1970s, women remarried twice or even three times, which challenges the idea that divorced women are taboo (Layish, 1991).

Bibliography

El Alami, Daoud Sudqi, and Doreen Hinchcliffe. *Islamic Marriage and Divorce Laws of the Arab World.* London: Kluwer Law International, 1996.

An-Na'im, Abdullah A., ed. *Islamic Family Law in a Changing World. A Global Resource Book.* London: Zed Books, 2002.

Anderson, J. N. D. "Reforms in the Law of Divorce in the Muslim World. *Studia Islamica* 31 (1970): 41–52.

Anderson, J. N. D. *Law Reform in the Muslim World.* London: Athlone Press, 1976.

Coulson, Nigel J. *A History of Islamic Law.* Edinburgh: Edinburgh University Press, 1964.

Esposito, John L., and Natana DeLong-Bas. *Women and Muslim Family Law.* 2d ed. Syracuse, N.Y.: Syracuse Press, 2001.

Hosseini, Ziba Mir. "When a Woman's Hurt Becomes an Injury: "Hardship" as Grounds for Divorce in Iran." *Hawwa* 5.I (2007): 111–126.

Moors, Annelies. "'Public Debates on Family Law Reform: Participants, Positions, and Styles of Argumentation in the 1990s." *Islamic Law & Society* 10, i (2003): 1–11.

Welchman, Lynn. *Beyond the Code: Muslim Family Law and the Shari'a Judiciary in the Palestinian West Bank,* p. 290. The Hague, The Netherlands: Kluwer Law International, 2000.

Welchman, Lynn. *Women and Muslim Family Laws in Arab States. A Comparative Overview of Textual Development and Advocacy.* Amsterdam: Amsterdam University Press, 2007.

Wurth, Anna. *Ash-shari'a fi bab al-yaman.* Berlin: Duncker & Humblot, 2000.

Egypt

Bernard-Maugiron, Nathalie. "Divorce and Remarriage of Orthodox Copts in Egypt: The 2008 State Council Ruling and the Amendment of the 1938 Personal Status Regulations." *Islamic Law & Society* 18 (2011): 356–386.

Bernard-Maugiron, Nathalie, and Baudouin Dupret. "Breaking Up the Family: Divorce in Egyptian Law and Practice." *Hawwa* 6.i (2006): 52–74.

Al-Sharmani, Mulki. "Egyptian Family Courts: A Pathway of Women's empowerment?" *Hawwa* 7 (2009): 89–110.

Al-Sharmani, Mulki. *Khul' Divorce in Egypt. Public Debates, Judicial Practices, and Everyday Life,* Cairo: The American University in Cairo Press, 2012.

Sonneveld, Nadia. "Khul' Divorce in Egypt: How Family Courts Are Providing a "Dialogue" between Husband and Wife. *Anthropology of the Middle East* 5.ii (2010): 100–120.

Al-Sharmani, Mulki. *Khulʿ Divorce in Egypt*. Cairo: AUC Press, 2011.

Southeast Asia

Angeles, Vivienne S. M. "Philippine Muslim Women: Tradition and Change." In *Islam, Gender and Social Change*, edited by Yvonne Yazbeck Haddad and John L. Esposito, pp. 209–234. New York and Oxford: Oxford University Press, 1998.

Bedner, Adriaan, and Stijn van Huis. "Plurality of Marriage Law and Marriage Registration for Muslims in Indonesia: A Plea for Pragmatism." *Utrecht Law Review* 6.ii (2010): 175–191.

Bowen, John R. *Islam, Law and Equality in Indonesia. An Anthropology of Public Reasoning*. Cambridge, U.K.: Cambridge University Press, 2003.

Cammack, M. et al., "Islamic Divorce Law and Practice in Indonesia." In *Islamic Law in Contemporary Indonesia: Ideas and Institutions*, edited by M. Cammack and R. Feener, pp. 99–127. Cambridge Mass.: Harvard University Press, 2007.

Utriza, Ayang. « La transformation du droit musulman en droit positif de l'État indonésien." In *La charia dans le monde d'aujourd'hui*, edited by B. Dupret, pp. 199–208. Paris: La Découverte, 2011.

Iran

Haeri, Shahla. "Divorce in Contemporary Iran: A Male Prerogative in Self-Will. In *Islamic Family Law*, edited by C. Mallat and J. Connors, pp. 55–70. London: Graham and Trotman, 1993.

Mir-Hosseini, Ziba. *Marriage on Trial: A Study of Islamic Family Law, Iran and Morocco Compared*. London: I.B. Tauris, 1993.

Mir-Hosseini, Ziba. "When a Woman's Hurt Becomes an Injury: 'Hardship' as Grounds for Divorce in Iran." *Hawwa* 5.i (2007): 111–126.

Osanloo, Arzoo. "Islamico-civil 'Rightstalk': Women, Subjectivity, and Law in Iranian Family Court." *American Ethnologist* 33.ii (2006): 190–209.

Osanloo, Arzoo. "What a Focus on 'Family' Means in the Islamic Republic of Iran." In *Family Law in Islam: Divorce, Marriage and Women in the Muslim World*, edited by M. Voorhoeve, pp. 51–76. London/New York: IB Tauris, 2012.

Iraq

Anderson, Norman. "A Law of Personal Status for Iraq." *International and comparative Law Quarterly* (1960): 542–564.

Anderson, Norman. "Changes in the Law of Personal Status in Iraq." *International and Comparative Law Quarterly* (1963): 1026–1031.

Anderson, Norman. *Law Reform in the Muslim World*. London: Athlone Press, 1976.

Efrati, Noga. "Negotiating Rights in Iraq: Women and the Personal Status Law." *The Middle East Journal* 59.iv (2005): 577–595.

Linant de Bellefonds, Y. "Le Code du Statut Personnel Irakien du 30 décembre 1959." *Studia Islamica* xiii (1960): 79–135.

Mallat, Chibli. "Shi'ism and Sunnism in Iraq: Revisiting the Codes." In *Islamic Family Law*, edited by Chibli Mallat and Jane Connors, pp. 71–92. London: Graham and Trotman, 1993.

Israel, West Bank, Gaza, Lebanon

Abou Ramadan, Moussa. "Divorce Reform in the Sharia Court of Appeals in Israel (1992–2003)." *Islamic Law & Society* 13.ii (2006): 242–274.

Di Ricco, Massimo. "Reclaiming Changes within the Community Public Sphere: Druze Women's Activism, Personal Status Law and the Quest for Lebanese Multiple Citizenship." In *Family Law in Islam: Divorce, Marriage and Women in the Muslim World*, edited by M. Voorhoeve, pp. 31–50. London and New York: I.B. Tauris, 2012.

Jacobsen, Heather. "The Marriage Dower: Essential Guarantor of Women's Rights in the West Bank and Gaza Strip." *Michigan Journal of Gender and Law* 10 (2003): 143–167.

Moors, Annelies. *Women, Property and Islam. Palestinian Experiences 1920–1990* Cambridge, U.K.: Cambridge University Press, 1995.

Reiter, Yithzak. "*Qadis* and the Implementation of Islamic Law in Present Day Israel." In *Islamic Law. Theory and Practice*, edited by Robert Gleave and Eugenia Kermeli, pp. 205–231. London: I.B. Tauris, 1997.

Shehada, Nahda. "Uncodified Justice: Women Negotiating Family Law and Customary Practice in Palestine." *Development Journal* 47.i (2004): 103–108.

Shehada, Nahda. "Women's Experience in the *Shari'a* Court of Gaza City: The Multiple Meanings of Maintenance." *Review of Women's Studies* 2 (2004): 57–71.

Shehada, Nahda. "House of Obedience: Social Norms, Individual Agency and Historical Contingency." *Journal of Middle Eastern Women's Studies* 5.x (2009): 24–49.

Welchman, Lynn. *Beyond the Code: Muslim Family Law and the Shar'i Judiciary in the Palestinian West Bank*. The Hague, The Netherlands: Kluwer Law International, 2000.

Welchman, Lynn. "In the Interim: Civil Society, the Shar'i Judiciary and Palestinian Personal Status Law in the Transitional Period." *Islamic Law & Society* 10.i (2003): 34–69.

The Maghreb and Libya

Ben Jemia, Monia. "Le juge tunisien et la légitimation de l'ordre juridique positif par la charia." In *La charia aujourd'hui*, edited by B. Dupret pp. 153–170. Paris: La Découverte, 2012.

Buskens, Léon P. H. M. *Islamitisch recht en familiebetrekkingen in Marokko*. Amsterdam: Bulaaq, 1999.

Buskens, Léon P. H. M. "Recent Debates on Family Law Reform in Morocco: Islamic Law as Politics in an Emerging Public Sphere." *Islamic Law and Society* 10.i (2003): 70–131.

Carlisle, Jessica. "Moroccan Divorce Law, Family Court Judges and Spouses' Claims: Who Pays the Cost When a Marriage Is Over?" In *Legal Reform and Feminist Activism: Comparative Perspectives*, edited by Mulki Shamani (forthcoming).

Jansen, Willy. *Women Without Men: Gender and Marginality in an Algerian Town*. Leiden, The Netherlands: E.J. Brill, 1987.

Khalidi, M.S. "Divorce in Libya: A Critical Commentary." *Journal of Comparative Family Studies* 20.i (1989): 118–126.

Layish, Aharon. *Divorce in the Libyan Family: A Study Based on the Sijills of the Sharia Courts of Ajdabiya and Kufra*. New York: New York University Press, 1991.

Maher, Vanessa. "Divorce and Property in the Middle Atlas of Morocco. *Man* 9.i (1974): 103–122.

Mayer, Ann Elizabeth. "Developments in the Law of Marriage and Divorce in Libya since the 1969 Revolution." *Journal of African Law* 22.i (1978): 30–49.

Mitchell, Ruth. "Family Law in Algeria before and after the 1404/1984 Family Code." In *Islamic Law. Theory and Practice*, edited by Robert Gleave and Eugenia Kermeli, pp. 194–204. London: I.B. Tauris, 1997.

Vincent-Grosso, Sarah. "Maktoub: An Ethnography of Evidence in a Tunisian Divorce Court." In *Family Law in Islam: Divorce, Marriage and Women in the Muslim World*, edited by M. Voorhoeve, pp. 171–198. London and New York: IB Tauris, 2012.

Voorhoeve, M. "The interaction between codified law and divine law: The Case of Divorce for Disobedience in Tunisia." *Revue IBLA* 204 (2009): 267–286.

Voorhoeve, M. *Gender and Divorce in North Africa: Sharia, Custom and Personal Status Law in Tunisia*. London and New York: IB Tauris (2013).

Pakistan, India, Bangladesh

Carroll, Lucy "Qur'ān' 2:229: 'A charter granted to the wife?' Judicial *khul'* in Pakistan." *Islamic Law & Society* 3.i (1996): 91–126.

Gilani, Riazul Hasan. "A Note on Islamic Family Law and Islamisation in Pakistan." In *Islamic Family Law*, edited by Chibli Mallat and Jane Connors, pp. 339–348. London: Graham and Trotman, 1993.

Imtiaz, Ahmad, ed. *Divorce and Remarriage among Muslims in India*. New Delhi: Manohar, 2003.

Mahmood, Tahir. "Islamic Family Law: Latest Developments in India." In *Islamic Family Law*, edited by Chibli Mallat and Jane Connors, pp. 295–320. London: Graham and Trotman, 1993.

Masud, Muhammad Khalid. "Définir la normativité de la charia au Pakistan." In *La charia aujourd'hui*, edited by B. Dupret, pp. 185–198. Paris: La Découverte, 2012.

Menski, Werner F. "The Reform of Islamic Family Law and a Uniform Civil Code for India." In *Islamic Family Law*, edited by Chibli Mallat and Jane Connors, pp. 254–294. London: Graham and Trotman, 1993.

Pearl, David "Three Decades of Executive, Legislative and Judicial Amendments to Islamic Family Law in Pakistan. In *Islamic Family Law*, edited by Chibli Mallat and Jane Connors, pp. 321–338. London: Graham and Trotman, 1993.

Sub-Saharan Africa

Jeppie, Shamil, Ebrahim Moosa, and Richard Roberts, eds. *Muslim Family Law in Sub-Saharan Africa: Colonial Legacies and Post-Colonial Challenges*. Amsterdam: Amsterdam University Press, 2010.

N'Diaye, Marième. "Ambiguïtés de la laïcité sénégalaise: La référence au droit islamique." In *La charia aujourd'hui*, edited by B. Dupret, pp. 209–226. Paris: La Découverte, 2012.

Peters, Ruud. "The Enforcement of God's Law, The *Shari'ah* in the Present World of Islam." In *Comparative Perspectives on Sharī'ah in Nigeria*, edited by Ph. Ostien, Jamila M. Nasir, and F. Kogelmann, pp. 107–134. Ibadan, Nigeria: Spectrum Books, 2005.

Schulz, Dorothea E. "Political Factions, Ideological Fictions: The Controversy over Family Law Reform in Democratic Mali." *Islamic Law & Society* 10.i (2003): 132–164.

Stiles, Erin E. *An Islamic Court in Context: An Ethnographic Study of Judicial Reasoning* Basingstoke, U.K.: Palgrave Macmillan, 2009.

Tønessen, Liv. "Gendered Citizenship in Sudan: Competing Debates on Family Laws among Northern and Southern Elites in Khartoum." *The Journal of North African Studies* 13.iv (2008): 455–469.

Syria

Carlisle, Jessica. "'Asbab l'il-darb ktir basita': The legality of claims of violence during judicial divorce cases in Damascus." *Hawwa* 5.ii (2007): 239–261.

Carlisle, Jessica. "Telling Tales: Arbitration of Judicial Divorce Claims in Damascus." In *La Syrie au présent: Reflets d'une société*, edited by Baudouin Dupret, pp. 661–670. Paris: Sindbad, 2007.

Carlisle, Jessica. "Mother Love: A Forced Divorce in Damascus." *Anthropology of the Middle East* 2.i (2007): 89–102.

Eijk, Esther van. "Divorce Practices in Muslim and Christian Courts in Syria." In *Family Law in Islam: Marriage, Divorce and Women in the Muslim World*, edited by M. Voorhoeve, pp. 147–170. London and New York: IB Tauris, 2012.

Turkey

Örücü, Esin. "Judicial Navigation as Official Law Meets Culture in Turkey." *International Journal of Law in Context* 4 (2008): 35–61.

Starr, June. "The Role of Turkish Secular Law in Changing the Lives of Rural Muslim Women." *Law and Society Review* 23.iii (1989): 497–523.

Yemen

Dahlgren, Susanne. "Women's *adah* versus 'Women's Law': The Contesting Issue of *mahr* in Aden, Yemen." *Egypte Monde Arabe* 3.1 (2005): 125–144.

Dahlgren, Susanne. "'She Brings Up Healthy Children for the Homeland'": Morality Discourses in Yemini Legal debates." In *Family Law in Islam: Marriage, Divorce and Women in the Muslim World*, edited by M. Voorhoeve, pp. 13–30. London and New York: IB Tauris, 2012.

Würth, Anna. "A Sana'a Court: The Family and the Ability to Negotiate." *Islamic Law & Society* 2.iii (1995): 320–340.

Würth, Anna. *Ash-shari'a fi bab al-yaman: Recht, Richter und Rechtspraxis an der familienrechtlicher Kammer des Gerichts Süd-Sanaa, Republik Jemen (1983–1995)*. Berlin: Duncker & Humblot, 2000.

Würth, Anna. "Stalled Reform: Family Law in Post-unification Yemen." *Islamic Law & Society* 10.i (2003): 12–33.

Würth, Anna. "Mobilizing Islam and Custom against Statutory Reform: *bayt al-ta'a* in Yemen." *Egypte/Monde Arabe* 3.i (2005): 277–298.

MAAIKE VOORHOEVE

LEGAL FOUNDATIONS

Unlike in Catholicism and Hinduism, Islam permits the dissolution or termination of a marriage, albeit with reluctance. The Prophet Muḥammad is believed to have said that the throne of the Divine shakes when a marriage is dissolved. He is also reported to have said that God's most hated lawful conduct is the dissolution of a marriage. Not surprisingly, the majority of jurists held that a divorce without a compelling reason was reprehensible (*makrūh*), to be exercised sparingly and avoided if possible.

Indeed, the fundamental public policy objectives (*maqāṣid*) of *Sharīʿah* are to protect and preserve life, religion, property, intellect, and lineage. Just as marriage in Islam serves as a means to promote and preserve the *maqāṣid* maxims, the law of divorce seeks that both spouses and children exit a marriage with due regard for the preservation of the maxims, as well. Reserved to both husband and wife are certain protections—albeit not perfect—to prevent destitution; to ensure the fair devolution of wealth; to ensure the ability remarry and thus fulfill a religious rite; and to ensure the protection of children, materially and physically. All of these practical considerations touch upon one of the five maxims in one way, shape, or form.

As it did with marriage, in divorce, the Qurʾān substantially revamped and to a large extent abrogated the systemic discrimination and gender inequity toward women in pre-Islamic Arabia, although some remnants of patriarchy survived and others thrived after the death of the Prophet Muḥammad. Among the many positive examples of the Qurʾānic egalitarian overhaul of gender relations in divorce are that the both husband and wife have the right to initiate divorce, the husband's claim to his wife's property was abrogated; inheritance to males was changed to require females to inherit pending a divorce; unlimited utterances of divorce were now limited to three and divorce without compelling reason was reprehensible; financial responsibilities of a husband toward his wife during marriage and post marriage were instituted; allegations of a wife's infidelity (*liʿan*) without absolute proofs subjected the husband to criminal prosecution; and custody and support of children of divorce was legally formalized.

The dissolution or termination of a marriage in Islam is very different from divorce in the Western sense. A marriage is dissolved, annulled, or terminated according to several methods. A husband's unilateral and exclusive right to dissolve the marriage is called *ṭalāq*. The Arabic word *ṭalāq* is routinely translated into English as divorce. Such translation is misleading and inaccurate. *Ṭalāq* is more appropriately translated as repudiation (hereinafter repudiation or divorce or *ṭalāq*). The other methods of terminating or dissolving a marriage are *tafriq* (judicial divorce based on various grounds), *khulʿ* (mutual divorce), and *faskh* (annulment).

The foundation for the law on dissolution of marriage in Islam resides in the Qurʾān. The subject is addressed in no less than four chapters in the Qurʾān, specifically chapters 2, 4, 33, and 65. The Qurʾānic framework for divorce can be simply summarized in God's directive: "If you divorce women, and they reach their appointed term, hold them back in amity or let them go in amity. Do not hold them back out of malice, to be vindictive. Whoso does this does himself injustice" (2:231).

Types of Divorce. *Ṭalāq* is the husband's exclusive unilateral right to dissolve the marriage by simply announcing to his wife that he repudiates her. The formal validity of the divorce, according to the jurists, depended on the form of the language (*sigha*) utilized, the sound state of mind of the exercising husband, and whether the wife is in a state of purity, that is, not menstruating at the time of the repudiation. The majority of the jurists required that the husband's choice of words must be unambiguous and clear. This meant that using the verbal form of *ṭalāq* was sufficient: "I repudiate you"; "You are repudiated." Linguistic clarity is required because of the serious consequences—economic, social, and moral—of the dissolution of a marriage. There should be no room for interpretation or the need to probe the intent of the utterer; hence ambiguous language has no legal effect.

Furthermore, at the moment of uttering the words of divorce, the husband must be of the age of majority, must be of sound mind and doing the same voluntarily, without duress or undue pressure or mistake. A husband's repudiation is invalid if he was insane, a minor, coerced or intoxicated (some schools including the Ḥanafī and Mālikī schools held intoxicated repudiation as valid).

The jurists also required that the repudiation take place when the wife is in a state of purity, that is, not menstruating and where no sexual intercourse took place since the menstrual cycle ended. The valid and proper repudiation, therefore, is when a husband uses the words—"I divorce you" while in possession of his sound mental free will when his wife is not menstruating and they did not have sexual relations since the end of her menstrual cycle. This is called *ṭalāq al sunnah* or sound *sunnah* divorce.

The majority of jurists consider a husband's repudiation during his wife's menstrual cycle or after having sexual relations as effective but discouraged. This is called *ṭalāq al bidʿah*, innovation divorce. Such repudiation is ineffective according to the Ḥanbalī school.

As a unilateral exclusive right of the husband, the husband can assign or transfer such right to repudiate the marriage to his wife. Many Muslim women included such a contractual term to repudiate the marriage in their marriage contracts. This is called *ṭalāq al-tafawud*, a contractual right to dissolve the marriage, thereby leveling the gender repudiation rights. This right for the wife to repudiate the marriage could be available even if not included in the marriage contract. This is called *tamlik*, in which a husband informs his wife during their marriage that he assigns to her the right to repudiate if she so desires.

The initial repudiation of a marriage does not have the immediate legal effect of dissolving or terminating the marriage. That is why it is described as a revocable repudiation—*ṭalāq rajʿah*. The husband has the right to revoke or retract his repudiation any time before the wife completes three menstrual cycles. If the repudiation took place during the wife's menstrual cycle, the three-menstrual-cycle period commences after another menstrual cycle concludes. If the repudiation took place after the parties had sexual intercourse and before the wife's menstrual cycle started, the three-menstrual-cycle period commences after the completion of a menstrual cycle following the sexual relations.

The three-menstrual-cycle period is called the *ʿiddah*, or waiting period, which the Qurʾān defines specifically as three successive menstrual cycles (2:228). Scholars agree that the *ʿiddah* is intended as a cooling off period during which the husband may retract his repudiation, thus reconciling with his wife. The reconciliation could be mutual or one sought unilaterally by the husband. A resumption of sexual relations automatically retracts the husband's repudiation. A reconciliation in all of its forms can be exercised only during the *ʿiddah* because, after the *ʿiddah* expires, the repudiation becomes final and irrevocable. If the husband repudiates the marriage before consummation, the *ʿiddah* waiting period does not apply, that is, the repudiation is effective, immediately terminating the marriage.

The *ʿiddah* also has the more practical effect of assuring that the wife is not pregnant. This is a concern because of the obligations that the husband would have to the wife and to the child. Neither party may remarry during the *ʿiddah*. All rights remain intact during the *ʿiddah*, including the wife's right to inherit from the husband.

Under the majority of classical Sunnī schools of law, a husband's repudiation is valid if uttered orally and without any witnesses. As noted earlier, the method of dissolution is the exclusive right of the husband without any control or interference from the wife. Responding to the social and moral problems surrounding women being divorced without their knowledge, the trend in modern Sunnī jurisprudence today requires witnesses in order for a divorce to be valid. Relying on the Qurʾān, specifically, 65:2, the Jaʿfarī school requires two witnesses to the pronouncement.

Because a husband is limited to three repudiations, a final irrevocable divorce is either (1) *bayn baynuna sughra*, a minor final irrevocable divorce; or (2) *bayn baynuna kubra*, a major final irrevocable divorce. In a minor final divorce, a husband repudiates his marriage and the *ʿiddah* period has expired; thus the marriage was effectively dissolved. If this was the first dissolution initiated by the husband, the husband and the wife are free to remarry under a new marriage contract. If the husband repudiates his wife for a second time and the *ʿiddah* period has expired, they are permitted to remarry again under a new marriage contract. If the husband now repudiates his wife for a third time, the marriage is irrevocably dissolved with no right to remarry or reconcile available until the wife marries a third party, consummates said marriage, and then divorces her husband. Only then can she remarry her original husband. This irrevocable final divorce is called *bayn baynuna kubra* or major final divorce. This is also the case if the husband repudiates the first time but retracts/reconciles before the waiting period has expired, and then a second time but retracts/reconciles before the waiting period has expired; the third time he repudiates is irrevocable major divorce—*bayn baynuna kubra*.

There are two positions regarding whether a major divorce—*bayn baynuna kubra*—occurs if a husband at the same time repudiates his wife by uttering the words "You are divorced" thrice, known as a triple *ṭalāq*. Some schools held that such clear intent to divorce three times in a single meeting is tantamount to a major divorce. Others held that such thrice announcement has the effect of one repudiation and constitutes a minor divorce in which retraction is not available. In other words, the husband would have to remarry under a new contract without the marriage to a third person.

Judicial Divorce. Another method to terminate or dissolve a marriage according to Islamic law is through a judicial divorce called *tafriq*. While either spouse can seek such divorce, they must have fault or grounds sufficiently compelling to the court to dissolve the marriage. The first step in the process of a judicial divorce is the appointment of an arbiter from each family to mediate the spousal disagreements with the objective of saving their marriage (4:35). If the mediation and/or reconciliation fail, the court is required to adjudicate the matter by rendering a decision in connection with assigning or apportioning fault for the breakdown of the marriage with the associated financial consequences. Examples of fault are cruelty; lack of maintenance by failing to provide food, clothing, or shelter, desertion; disease or other ailment; or imprisonment harmful to the marriage. Furthermore, women have the right to seek divorce based on violation of contractual terms included in their marriage contracts, such as if the husband married a second wife, triggering her right to a divorce. The schools of law accepted some of these grounds but not others. For example, the husband has only one ground for judicial divorce in the Ḥanafī school, that is, his wife's infidelity; but the Ḥanafī school permits the wife to seek a judicial divorce for infidelity alleged by the husband, the husband's impotence, or his misrepresentation at the time of entering into the marriage. The Mālikī school is the most liberal because it accepts a wide variety of grounds to permit a judicial divorce.

When a husband accuses his wife of committing adultery, this is called *li'an*. In the *li'an* context, the wife is then offered the option of taking an oath denying it. If she denies and the husband insists, the court will judicially dissolve their marriage. Some schools of law do not consider this a traditional divorce, but rather *fasikh* or an annulment. When *li'an* concludes, the couple is prohibited from ever remarrying.

'Ila' is another ground to dissolve the marriage, in which a husband takes an oath that he shall refrain from having sexual relations with his wife for more than four months. When four months pass without sexual intercourse, the marriage is dissolved. If the husband resumes sexual intercourse before the expiration of four months, the oath is retracted and the marriage subsists. The husband is required to make expiation for his oath by, for example, feeding the poor or fasting for an extended period of time. Another similar type of grounds for dissolution of marriage is where a husband takes an oath stating that his wife is prohibited sexually to him as his mother is prohibited. This is called *dhihar*. In this case, the husband is able to resume sexual relations and retract his oath by expiation such as by fasting or feeding the poor.

Khulʿ/Mutual Divorce. Another method to terminate or dissolve a marriage according to Islamic law is through the wife's exclusive right for *khulʿ*. *Khulʿ* literally means to remove something or pull it off or break it off, that is, remove or pull yourself out of your marriage. *Khulʿ* is a contractual type of dissolution, exclusively reserved for women. The authority for *khulʿ* is found in verse 2:228: "It is not licit for you to take back anything you have given them unless the two of them fear that they cannot conform to the bounds of God, no blame attaches to them both. If the woman gives back that with which she sets herself free. These are the bounds set by God; do not transgress them."

The *aḥādīth* relate the following:

> The wife of Thabit bin Qais came to the Prophet and said, "O God's Apostle! I do not blame Thabit for defects in his character or his religion, but I, being a Muslim, dislike to behave in un-Islamic manner (if I remain with him)." On that God's Apostle said (to her), "Will you give back the garden which your husband has given you (as Mahr)?" She said, "Yes." Then the Prophet said to Thabit, "O Thabit! Accept your garden, and divorce her once."

A *khulʿ* dissolution is concluded when a wife offers to divorce her husband in exchange for paying him monetary compensation—generally waiver of part or all of the deferred *mahr*. The Qurʾān makes it clear that the financial compensation cannot exceed the *mahr* amount. If the husband accepts the offer, a valid contract irrevocably dissolving their marriage is concluded.

The divorce becomes effective immediately at the moment the contract is concluded, regardless of whether the wife is menstruating. The divorce is final and irrevocable. There is no retraction or revocation period. Such divorce is considered a minor divorce, *bayn baynuna sughra*. Remarriage must be mutual under a new contract. A *khulʿ* dissolution is considered one divorce out of the three available before the dissolution would constitute a final major irrevocable divorce, *bayn baynuna kubra*.

Like in a regular divorce, the wife must seek the *khulʿ* divorce voluntarily without coercion or threat. A husband who refuses to divorce his wife and creates a hostile, vindictive environment with the objective of pressuring his wife to seek a *khulʿ* in order to extract financial gain from her or avoid his financial responsibilities renders the *khulʿ* invalid. Such behavior would be directly at odds with numerous Qurʾānic directives, including: "Do not hold them back out of malice, to be vindictive" (2:231). The majority of the schools of Islamic jurisprudence recognize the *khulʿ* except for the Jaʿfarī school.

Annulment/*Fasikh*. Another method to dissolve the marital relationship is *fasikh*, which is an annulment of a marriage contract necessitated due to defects in the contract. For example, a marriage without the proper witnesses, a marriage to a person among the forbidden affinity degrees (such as marrying one's aunt or niece), a marriage in which a party renounces Islam, a female Muslim marrying a non-Muslim, and other defects.

Fasikh does not reduce the three available repudiations before the dissolution becomes a major irrevocable divorce. In other words, if after the annulment occurred because of a defect, the parties cured the defect, they would be free to marry with the availability of the three repudiations.

Material Rights in Divorce and after Divorce. The Qurʾān stresses that a divorce may not leave the wife without any financial means. Broadly, 2:241 states, "For divorced women, maintenance is decreed, fair, and affable. This is an obligation upon the pious."

The financial rights of the parties in a divorce depend on the type of dissolution.

In a *ṭalāq* initiated by a husband, the majority of the schools agree that the wife cannot be expelled from the marital residence during the divorce: "Allow them to reside where you reside, according to your means, and do not pester them in order to constrict their lives. If pregnant, you are to pay their expenses until they deliver" (65:6).

Upon *ṭalāq*, the wife is entitled to the full payment of her *mahr* if it has not already been paid. The Qur'ān even provides for the wife to keep one half of her *mahr* if she is divorced before the marriage is consummated (2:237). The husband's obligation for financial support continues until conclusion of the waiting period or the delivery of her child, if the wife is pregnant. In addition, the wife has a claim for past due maintenance and child support.

In the case where a wife secured the dissolution of her marriage through *khul*ʿ, she is forfeiting or returning all or part of her *mahr* to the husband for his consent to the divorce. In the case of *faskh* before consummation, the wife would not be entitled to any *mahr*. In the case of consummation, she is entitled to the entire *mahr*. In the case of judicial divorce, the financial rights of the parties would depend on the allocation of fault causing the dissolution.

Although premodern Islamic law does not support a marital assets regime, there is sufficient basis to establish a marital asset regime consistent with Islamic law in light of the political-social-economic transformations in modern nation-states.

In the premodern period, at the time of divorce, the parties divided any property jointly titled in their names, but each kept any property titled in their individual names.

Conclusion. The Islamic law of divorce is complex and multifaceted, anchored in the social and economic circumstances of the premodern period. The classical law of divorce is still relevant today. The modern manifestations of *Sharīʿah* are either a source of legislation or actual nation-state law in many Muslim countries, comprising more than forty countries with an estimated 1.2 billion adherents. Islamic law is a primary source of the family law codes in the majority of Muslim countries and, in some instances, the supreme law of the land. The premodern *Sharīʿah* governing divorce, therefore, continues to be relevant in the evolving laws governing divorce in Muslim majority countries.

BIBLIOGRAPHY

Averroes, Ibn Rushd, and Imran Ahsan Khan Nyazee. *The Distinguished Jurist's Primer: A Translation of Bidayat al-Mujtahid*. Ithaca, N.Y.: Cornell University Press, 1995.

Bakhtiar, Laleh, and Kevin Reinhart. *Encyclopedia of Islamic Law: A Compendium of the Major Schools*. Chicago: Kazi Publications, 1996.

Browning, Don S., M. Christian Green, and John Witte, Jr., eds. *Sex, Marriage, and Family in World Religions*. New York: Columbia University Press, 2006. The Islamic section is co-edited by Azizah al-Hibri.

Esposito, John L., and Natana J. Delong-Bas, *Women in Muslim Family Law*. Syracuse, N.Y.: Syracuse University Press, 2002.

Hallaq, Wael B. *Sharīʿah: Theory, Practice, Transformations*. Cambridge, U.K.: Cambridge University Press, 2009.

Hibri, Azizah Y. al-. "Muslim Women's Rights in the Global Village: Opportunities and Challenges." *The Journal of Law and Religion* 15 (Fall 2001): 29–81.

Hibri, Azizah Y. al-. "The Nature of the Islamic Marriage: Sacramental, Covenantal, or Contractual." In *Covenant Marriage in Comparative Perspective*, edited by John Witte, Jr. and Eliza Ellison. Grand Rapids, Mich.: Wm. B. Eerdmans, 2005.

Kamali, Muhammad Hashim. *Principles of Islamic Jurisprudence*. Cambridge, U.K.: Islamic Texts Society, 2006.

Khalidi, Tarif. *The Qur'an, A New Translation*. New York: Viking, 2008.

Nasir, Jamal J. *The Islamic Law of Personal Status*. New York: Springer, 2009.

Rapoport, Yossef. *Marriage, Monday and Divorce in Medieval Islamic Society*. Cambridge, U.K.: Cambridge University Press, 2005.

Sonbol, Amira El-Azhary, ed. *Women, the Family, and Divorce Laws in Islamic History*. Syracuse, N.Y.: Syracuse University Press, 1996.

Wadud, Amina. *Quran and Woman: Rereading the Sacred Text from a Woman's Perspective*. New York: Oxford University Press, 1999.

Welchman, Lynn. *Women and Muslim Family Laws in Arab States: A Comparative Overview of Textual Development and Advocacy* Amsterdam: Amsterdam University Press, 2007.

Zaidan, Abdul Hakim. *Al-Mufassal fi Ahkam al-Marʿah wa al-Bait al-Muslim* (*Detailed Account of Rules Relating to Women and the Muslim Household*). 2d ed., 10 vols. Beirut, 1994.

ABED AWAD *and* HANY MAWLA

DOMESTIC VIOLENCE. Emotional, verbal, spiritual, financial, physical, and sexual abuse have existed in various forms in every society throughout recorded history. Yet it was not until the nineteenth century that domestic violence (DV) became a social issue in the United States. Once considered one of the most underreported crimes in the U.S., DV made its way onto the national stage as a major social ill during the 1980s and 1990s. The public soon realized that no religious or ethnic community could be considered immune, and as a result, faith-based anti-DV advocacy has become an integral part of the DV movement over the last twenty years (Fortune, Abugideiri, and Dratch, 2010). According to a study conducted in 1998 by Sharifa Alkhateeb, as president of the North American Council for Muslim Women (NACMW), physical violence occurs in about 10 percent of Muslim marriages in the U.S. The rates of emotional and verbal abuse are estimated to be as high as 50 percent, based upon international studies and preliminary research in the U.S (http://www.peacefulfamilies.org/aboutdv.html).

Definition. Domestic violence is an umbrella term that usually refers to violence or abusive behaviors that occur within a domestic setting, where one family member asserts control over one or more family members (Hegarty, Hindmarsh, and Gilles, 2000). This may include verbal abuse, financial abuse, emotional, sexual, and physical abuse. DV includes acts of violence perpetrated by husbands against wives, wives against husbands, parents against children (child abuse), children against parents, siblings against siblings, and abuse of the elderly (Hegarty et al., 2000). The United Nations estimated that at least one-third of women around the world are victims of physical or sexual violence (United Nations Development Fund for Women UNIFEM, 2007).

The body of existing research has indicated that DV is not confined to any particular age, social status, culture, religious, socioeconomic, or ethnic group (Vandello and Cohen, 2008). The causes of DV also vary, and researchers continue to explore how race, class, religion, and culture, as well as psychological variables such as low self-esteem and abusive childhood, affect one's experiences with violence. As research becomes more interdisciplinary it will reveal a more clear understanding of the intricacies of DV.

Although the specific term "Domestic Violence" has not been used traditionally in Muslim cultures, and while there has been some denial historically that domestic violence is a phenomenon that exists in Muslim communities, the Qurʾān identifies the behaviors consistent with domestic violence under the umbrella of oppression. Oppression is a broad category that includes any type of injustice against another person and is clearly prohibited in Islam. The concept in the Qurʾān that "believers, men and women, are protectors of one another" (Qurʾān 9:71 Muhammad Asad) establishes the nature of relationships between men and women at the societal level, and is meant to be applied at the family level as well.

Within the family, oppression is defined as any act that violates the specific boundaries delineated by God (see 2:227–237) to protect spousal and children's rights. The general categories of domestic oppression mentioned in the Qur'ān include aggression, wrongdoing, harsh treatment, and inflicting harm or injury (the Arabic terms used in the Qur'ān for these categories are: *'udwaan, 'adhl,* and *darar.*). Actions that fall into any of these categories are in violation of the Islamic values of justice, equality, freedom, mercy and forgiveness.

Islam and Domestic Violence. Prophetic precedent *(sunnah),* a secondary source of Islamic law, establishes that Prophet Muḥammad never hit his wives and severely reprimanded those who hit their wives. While the Qur'ān describes the marital relationship as premised on mercy and love, one verse in the Qur'ān, however, has been interpreted by some exegetes to suggest that the Qur'ān permits men to physically discipline their wives *if* they are guilty of *nushuz.* There is no consensus regarding the exact meaning of *nushuz.* Most classical commentators of the Qur'ān interpreted women's *nushuz* as their disobedience or rebelliousness towards their husbands (Ali Sexual Ethics in Islam). In some versions of the Prophet's farewell sermon, he identifies *nushuz* as "clear lewdness" (most of the versions of the Prophet last sermon in Arabic clearly mentioned misconduct [*fahisha*]; however, it is not mentioned in the English version). Accordingly, some Qur'ānic commentators interpret *nushuz* as a wife's sexual deviation or misconduct (*fahisha*). In his prominent English translation of the Qur'ān, Muhammad Asad translated *nushuz* as "ill-will" and elaborated that it is the "deliberate, persistent breach of her marital obligations" (Asad, p. 109, footnote #44). Interestingly, verse 128 in the same Qur'ānic chapter refers to men's *nushuz.* However, most Qur'ānic exegetes make no correlation between men and women's *nushuz;* moreover, they define both types of *nushuz* differently. Men's *nushuz* is defined as their ill-treatment or cruelty towards their wives, whereas women's *nushuz* is their disobedience towards their husbands. On the other hand, the contemporary researchers tend to read only 4:34 and ignore 4:35, where the Qur'ān stresses the importance of arbitration between conflicting spouses.

> "*And as for those women whose ill-will (nushuz) you have reason to fear, admonish them [first]; then leave them alone in bed; then hit them (lightly) [daraba]; and if thereupon they pay you heed,* (translation is "if they return to obedience." It should be noted that obedience here is in the context of obedience to God. The husband, as head of the family, is responsible for encouraging his family to be obedient to God, as he himself must be obedient to God.) *do not seek to harm them. Behold, God is indeed most high, great! And if you have reason to fear that a breach might occur between a [married] couple, appoint an arbiter from among his people and an arbiter from among her people; if they both want to set things right, God may bring about their reconciliation. Behold, God is indeed all-knowing, aware*" (4:34–35; Translation from Asad, Muhammad. The Message of the Qur'an, 1980).

Therefore, the Qur'ān outlines steps to remedy this problem of *nushuz*: 1) advise them (those women guilty of *nushuz*), 2) abandon them in bed (do not have sexual intercourse with them); 3) "lightly beat them," hitting should be *ghayr mubarrih,* according to the most predominant classical interpretation of the Qur'ānic term "*wadribuhunna*" (however, like the term *nushuz,* there is almost no consensus as to the exact meaning of this term); 4) if a couple cannot resolve these issues on their own, each spouse is advised to bring a trusted person to represent him/her for arbitration, as stipulated in the verses above. Any available resource that might help in solving the problem should be explored. In the event that all efforts fail to resolve the problem, divorce can be considered as an option.

In fact, the implications of this verse, 4:34, has been subject to intense debate and disagreement since early Islamic history. Aspects of this verse have been subject to a great deal of controversy among Muslims, as well as different interpretations by Muslim scholars depending on the historical and cultural context in which they lived. As Ayesha Chaudhry demonstrates in her extensive Ph.D. dissertation on this topic, classical scholars in the three fields of Qur'ānic exegesis, *ḥadīth*, and jurisprudence all employed certain tools, such as historical precedent and philology, to expand husbands' disciplinary power over wives. She writes, "scholars in all three fields ubiquitously qualified the prescription to hit wives instead of leaving it unqualified.... This qualification was based largely on prophetic reports, although Q. 4:34 itself did not figure prominently in *ḥadīth* literature" (Chaudhry, p. 6).

Even among Muslim scholars who interpret 4:34 to literally mean hitting one's wife, they all restrict its severity by interpreting it as symbolic hitting, using nothing harder than the equivalent of a paper tissue. There is consensus that leaving any marks or injury to any degree is unacceptable. They further restrict the use of this verse by noting that the Prophet Muḥammad never hit a woman, and that he, "stipulated that beating should be resorted to only if the wife has become guilty, in an obvious manner, of immoral conduct, and that it should be done in such a way as not to cause pain" (Asad, p. 110, footnote #45, views of various scholars are compared).

Another significant strain of interpretation among contemporary scholars is to interpret this verse in a way to mean something other than *hit*. One contemporary scholar, Abdul-Hamid Abu Sulayman, analyzed this verse within the overall framework of the Qur'ān and concluded that in this context, the Arabic word "*daraba*" does not mean "beat," but rather the temporary separation of a husband from his wife (for the complete analysis and discussion, see Abu Sulayman).

Western academic scholars of the Qur'ān such as Amina Wadud and Asma Barlas argue that this verse serves as a restriction against wife-beating, not a license to wife-beating. Based on a linguistic analysis of the Arabic word *daraba*, Wadud concludes that there is more than one meaning to this term, including "to set an example." Wadud writes in *Quran and Women: Rereading the Sacred Text from a Women's Perspective*, "In light of the excessive violence towards women indicated in the biographies of the Companions and by practices condemned in the Qur'ān (female infanticide), this verse should be taken as prohibiting unchecked violence against females. Thus, this is not permission, but a severe restriction of existing practices" (p. 76). By examining the historical context of this verse, Asma Barlas, like Wadud, concludes that the Qur'ān uses the term *daraba* in a restrictive rather than prescriptive sense. She writes, "at a time when men did not need permission to abuse women, this Ayah [verse] simply could not have functioned as a license; in such a context, it could only have been a restriction insofar as the Qur'ān made *daraba* the measure of last, not the first or even second, resort" (p. 188).

Some scholars argue that it is important to read this verse in the context provided by the Qur'ān in its entirety, as well as by the example of the Prophet Muḥammad. A leading contemporary Muslim jurist, Dr. Taha Jabir Al-alwani, explained that jurists consider the purposes of marriage when deriving rulings from these verses. The general purposes of marriage include fulfilling the conditions needed for living in tranquility and harmony, building family relationships and networks, and procreation. Application of teachings from the Qur'ān must not undermine these goals. Sometimes, jurists apply the literal meaning of a verse when that meaning will achieve these goals; other times they apply the spirit of a verse if the literal meaning hinders the achievement of these goals (Abugideiri and Alwani, 2003).

Given the cultural context at the time the Qur'ān was revealed, this verse introduced reforms to protect women by introducing less destructive ways to address the problem. As Badawi points out, this verse puts a limit on the maximum severity of intervention, thereby preventing people from excessive or abusive behavior that may occur if the steps were not restricted.

Dr. Al-alwani suggests that in today's societies, the third step in the process described in 4:34 ("hitting" the wife), might not be applicable. He bases his opinion on the legislative rulings of the companions of the Prophet Muḥammad and other jurists in this matter as well as other areas of Islamic law where rulings take into consideration the specific circumstances and elements of any given issue (Personal Communication, Taha Jabir Al-alwani, President of the Graduate School of Islamic Social Sciences, Leesburg, Virginia. See: What Islam says about Domestic Violence, p. 31). Emphasis is placed on the spirit of the verse, which is the protection of the family unit from a real threat to its survival. In today's world, beating one's wife would surely lead to the very destruction of the family unit that this verse seeks to preserve.

Most of the traditional and contemporary scholars look at the life of the Prophet Muḥammad (peace be upon him) as an example of how these serious problems can be addressed. As noted above, he was known for never hitting a woman or a child and for being strongly against the use of any type of violence. In reference to men who use violence at home, the Prophet said, "Could any of you beat his wife as he would beat a slave, and then lie with her in the evening?" (narrated in the *ḥadīth* collections of Bukhārī and Muslim). He also said, "Never beat God's handmaidens (female believers)" (cited by *Asad*, p. 110). The Prophet himself was put in several situations where he could have beaten his wives had he chosen to apply the verses with the literal interpretation. His wives sometimes caused him a lot of trouble; once, his wife ʿĀ'ishah was even accused of adultery by some members of the community. (Adultery is a serious offense in the Islamic context. A claim of adultery is grounds for a legal proceeding.) In none of these situations did he ever raise a hand or even his voice. He gave his wives options when they complained, and allowed ʿĀ'ishah to stay at her father's house for a month at her request, until her innocence was established.

Divorce and Domestic Violence. Today, there is another issue that relates to domestic violence among Muslims, which is divorce. Divorce is mentioned multiple times throughout the Qur'ān and the *sunnah*; indeed, the Qur'ān devotes an entire chapter to the details of divorce (chapter 65, entitled "The Divorce."). In these primary sources of religious law, divorce is allowed, but is in some respects discouraged. Men are explicitly commanded in many passages (e.g., Qur'ān 2:226 and 4:20) to either retain their wife in honor or release her from the marital bonds without taking back the marriage gift, or *mahr*, property, or symbolic asset given or promised by the husband to the wife the time of marriage. Women also are permitted to seek a termination of the marriage contract through *khul*ʿ (lit. "pulling out" or "getting rid"), and does so without blame and by arranging to return a portion of the marriage gift to ease the separation (Qur'ān 2:229). Today, this form of divorce typically requires the intervention of a judge. It is frequently subject to lengthy processing delays and involves financial negations, particularly if the husband resists the arrangement. Another form of divorce is judicial rescission, which may be initiated by the wife (or the husband) on the grounds that the spouse has violated an essential aspect of the marriage agreement. Recognized reasons for such terminations have varied historically and across schools of legal thought, however rationale may include injury or discord, prolonged absence on the part of the husband without due cause, his imprisonment, his failure to maintain the wife financially, or a breach of a given stipulation written into the couple's individual marriage contract. Although emphasis is placed on ensuring spousal and children's rights, these rights are often abused. Despite the permissibility of divorce, in many cultures that are predominantly Muslim, divorced women may be stigmatized even if they have been mistreated by their husbands. These women may also experience difficulty obtaining a divorce from the court. Women may struggle a great deal when trying to decide whether to leave an abusive home or remain. In these situations, it is important to understand the cultural impact on the victim's decision-making process while reminding her of the religious permissibility of ending the marriage.

The Muslim Response to Domestic Violence. In the past ten years, the Muslim community has made much progress in acknowledging the existence of DV among Muslims and in creating initiatives to fight this problem. Though advocacy began with isolated Muslim voices speaking out against this issue, today there are examples all across the world of mobilizing resources to understand the problem and to work towards prevention and solutions.

In the Washington, D.C., metropolitan area, with the efforts of the Peaceful Families Project, a group of imams representing communities throughout the country signed a proclamation in 2010 to publicly state their unified position against domestic violence. In other parts of the United States, domestic violence task forces are being established, Muslim shelters and social service agencies are being created, and national organizations such as the Peaceful Families Project, the Islamic Society of North America, and the Islamic Social Services Association are training Muslim leaders and advocating against domestic violence.

[*See also* Divorce *and* Marriage.]

BIBLIOGRAPHY

Abusulayman, Abdulhamid A. *Marital Discord: Recapturing the Full Islamic Spirit of Human Dignity.* Occasional Papers Series II. London: The International Institute of Islamic Thought, 2003.

Abugideiri, S., and Z. Alwani. What Islam Says about Domestic Violence, Herndon, VA.: FAITH, 2003.

Ali, Abdullah Yusuf. *The Meaning of the Holy Qur'an.* 10th Edition. Brentville, Md.: Amana Publications, 1999.

Ali, Kecia. *Sexual Ethics in Islam.* (See p. 120.)

Asad, Muhammad. *The Message of the Qur'an.* Gibraltar: Dar al-Andalus, 1980.

Badawi, Jamal. *Gender Equity in Islam: Basic Principles.* Plainfield, Ind.: American Trust Publications, 1995.

Barlas, Asma. *"Believing Women" in Islam: Unreading Patiarchal Interpretations of the Qur'an.* Austin: University of Texas Press, 2002.

Chaudhry, Ayesha. *Wife-Beating in the Pre-Modern Islamic Tradition: An Inter-Disciplinary Study of Ḥadīth, Qur'anic Exegesis and Islamic Jurisprudence.* Ph.D. diss. Sept. 2009, New York University, p. 6.

Esposito, John L. with Natana J. Delong-Bas. *Women in Muslim Family Law.* 2d ed., Syracuse, N.Y.: Syracuse University Press, 2001. 1st ed., 1982.

Fortune, Marie M., Salma Abugideiri and Mark Dratch. "A Commentary on Religion and Domestic Violence," 2010. http://www.faithtrustinstitute.org/resources/articles/Commentary.pdf

Hegarty, K., Hindmarsh E. D., and Gilles, M. T. Domestic "Violence in Australia: Definition, Prevalence, and Nature of Presentation in Clinical Practice," *Medical Journal of Australia* 173 (2000): 363–367. Public/issues/173-07-021000/hegarty/hegarty.html#refbody4.

Ibrahim, Nada., M. Abdalla. *A Critical Examination of Qur'an 4:34 and its Relevance to Intimate Partner*

Violence in Muslim Families. Journal of Muslim Mental Health 5, no. 3, (2010): 327–349.

Miller, Kathleen Portuan. "Who Says Muslim Women Can't Divorce? A Comparison of Divorce Under Islamic and Anglo-American Law," *New York International Law Review* 22, no. 1 (Winter 2009): 201–248.

Sonbol, Amira El Azhary, ed. *Women, the Family, and Divorce Law in Islamic History.* Syracuse, N.Y.: Syracuse University Press, 1996.

Tucker, Judith E. *Women, Family, and Gender in Islamic Law.* Cambridge, U.K.; New York: Cambridge University Press, 2008.

Vandello, J.A., and Cohen, D. "Culture, Gender, and Men's Intimate Partner Violence." *Social and Personality Psychology Compass* 2, no. 2 (2008): 652–667.

Wadud, Amina. *Quran and Women: Rereading the Sacred Text from a Women's Perspective.* New York: Oxford University Press, 1999.

Zainab Alwani

Dorai, Fawzieh al-. (b. 1954), (also spelled Fawzeyah Al-Durai), Kuwaiti psychologist, sex therapist, and television talk show host. Dr. Fawzieh al-Dorai earned a bachelor's degree in psychology from Kuwait University, a master's degree in sex education from Pacific Lutheran University in the US, and, in 1987, a PhD in psychology with a specialization in sex education from the University of York in England. She is the first Kuwaiti woman to obtain a PhD with an emphasis in sex education. Because of her marriage to the Iraqi physics professor Dr. Farag Yousef, they had to leave Kuwait during the 1990–1991 Iraqi occupation. During that time they went to England, where Dr. al-Dorai continued her studies in behavioral and alternative therapies, including music therapy.

Since the 1980s, she has been an advocate for better sex education in Kuwait through her work as a clinical psychologist specializing in sexual problems. More specifically, she has been lobbying the Ministry of Education to include sex education in the school curriculum. She also writes articles for local and regional newspapers and magazines, and has written over fifteen books dealing with issues and problems related to love, marriage, and sex. She also hosts a weekly television program called *Seerat El Hob* (The Love Story) that focuses on relationship problems. With millions of viewers from across the region, the most popular and controversial segment of the show occurs when she answers callers' questions about sex, which has resulted in several lawsuits. Despite her notoriety, Dr. al-Dorai's private practice continues to thrive, with new patients waiting months to receive an appointment.

Because of the success of her show, she was named by Arabian Business.com as one of the 100 most powerful Arab women of 2009, 2010, and 2011. Arabian Business also described her as the Middle Eastern Oprah Winfrey. Dr. al-Dorai is part of a growing movement in the Arab world encouraging more open discussion of sex. This movement is being led by women, particularly therapists. In addition to Dr. al-Dorai, Dr. Wedad Lootah and Dr. Heba Kotb also believe that sex should be enjoyable for married couples, and sexual problems should be discussed and solved openly. All three women have faced controversy and condemnation, but have been able to maintain their legitimacy by grounding their advice in religious teachings and through their conservative dress (Dr. al-Dorai and Dr. Kotb wear the *hijab*, while Dr. Lootah is completely covered, which includes wearing the *niqāb*). They are also challenging the dominant viewpoints of sexuality in the region, which have been particularly harmful for women. Traditional, conservative Islamic interpretations argue that women's sexuality needs to be tightly controlled. Islamic law is portrayed as monolithic and unchanging, while the reality of everyday life is ignored. Islamists often justify such control by arguing that women's sexuality is dangerous, and would result in chaos for the Islamic community if left unchecked. While

Dr. al-Dorai and her colleagues do not condone expressions of sexuality outside of heterosexual marriage, they have broken the taboo against discussing sexuality publicly. Through sex education and therapy, they aim to help women and men enjoy their sexuality within their marriages.

BIBLIOGRAPHY

ArabianBusiness.com. "100 Most Powerful Arab Women 2011: 17: Dr. Fawzieh Al Dorai." http://www.arabianbusiness.com/100-most-powerful-arab-women-2011-384182.html?view=profile&itemid=383781.

al-Dorai, Fawzieh. *Alta'am We Aljinsljns.* - Cologne, Germany: 2007,

al-Dorai, Fawzieh. *Mlyoun Sou'al Fi Aljns - Aljz' Althani.* Cologne, Germany: 2006,

Eltahawy, Mona. "The Arab World Would Benefit from Talking Openly About Sex." *Mona Eltahawy: An Egyptian from the Inside and Outside.* 2009. http://www.monaeltahawy.com/blog/?p=150.

Semerdjian, Elyse. "Rewriting the History of Sexuality in the Islamic World." *Hawwa* 4 (2006): 119–130.

DINA EL-SHARNOUBY AND HELEN MARY RIZZO

DRESS.

[*This entry includes two subentries:* Contemporary *and* Historical.]

CONTEMPORARY

Islam has spread to virtually all corners of the earth since its establishment in seventh-century Arabia. Historically, new converts retained their traditional dress provided it was appropriately modest, while the conquering Muslims inevitably adopted the dress of the local populace. Thus, regional dress survived with relatively few modifications through the centuries. Then, as now, dress expresses identity, taste, income, regional patterns of trade, and the religiosity of its wearers. Dress and its use vary with regard to gender, age, marital status, geographic origin, occupation, wealth, and even political sentiment. Although the term "Islamic dress" has taken on new meanings in the contemporary period, the dress of Muslims, or the significance of dress in Muslim life, extends beyond the indicators of an Islamist or non-Islamist orientation.

Islamic dress began to change significantly at the beginning of the twentieth century when Egyptian women discarded their face veils. This act was greatly supported and encouraged by the ruling British elite based on their belief that the face veil was a symbol of oppression of women and evidence of the backwardness of Islamic societies. Shortly thereafter, Mustafa Kemal Atatürk, the father of modern Turkey, embarked on a campaign to modernize Turkey and separate government from its religious past. His secular government required the abolition of the fez for men and traditional coverings for women, and forced the adoption of contemporary Euro-American dress. Reza Shah Pahlavi of Iran followed suit in the 1920s and 1930s and implemented official reform programs for modernization. These included dress regulations, which required men to wear a Western style suit of coat, jacket, and trousers and a leather belt and shoes. As in Turkey, women were forbidden to veil and veiled women were refused entry to public facilities and ran the risk of having any non-Western headgear forcibly removed in public. Ironically, a few short decades later, covered dress would not only again become the norm, but also be required by the government.

Egypt, Turkey, and Iran were not alone in abandoning traditional dress in favor of Euro-American attire. The Arabian Gulf states gained enormous wealth from oil during the mid-twentieth century and Saudi Arabia, in particular, encouraged Western dress for men. The Saud family, who had gathered independent tribally governed city-states under their rule in the 1930s, sought to diminish tribal affiliations in the Peninsula, which were easily identifiable by dress. Adopting Western dress served the dual purpose of breaking down tribal loyalties and simultaneously expressing newly found prosperity and modernity. By the 1980s Kuwait, Qatar, Bahrain, and the United Arab Emirates had almost entirely discarded local dress and were following Euro-American fashion.

While covering dress was being rejected in the Arabian Gulf, it was re-adopted in Egypt. Young female university students began to wear headscarves and long concealing coats as a sign of their piety and commitment to political Islam. This conservative move was aligned with a growing attitude in the Muslim world that it was possible to be modern without adopting secular Western traditions. Pride in tradition and declaration of religious affiliation resulted in the return to covered dress by the late 1980s in many countries. This took numerous forms for women, from a small headscarf to a fully concealing garment, covering hands, face, and feet. The term "hijab," literally "to screen," generally refers to covering the head and neck.

As covered dress once again became pervasive in the Middle East and Muslims in European countries adopted it, debates started to occur. These debates seem to have two separate bases. In European countries, the issue appears to be about differentiation and deliberate separation from non-Muslims. This self-identity created ongoing controversy in France where, finally, law 2004-228 was enacted in 2004, banning students from wearing any conspicuous religious symbols in primary or secondary public schools. In countries previously under Islamic religious rule, the use of covered dress is either discouraged or outright forbidden. Turkey, in particular, is adamant that the government remain officially secular and therefore banned covered women from working in the public sector. This became a political flashpoint in 1999, when Merve Kavakçi won election to the parliament and attempted to take her oath wearing a headscarf. She was booed out of the parliament and ultimately stripped of her elected position and even Turkish citizenship for her illegal action. The headscarf has remained a matter of intense public debate. The ban was lifted in February 2008, and then the lifting of the ban was annulled four months later. This applies to anyone working on state property and includes government offices, hospitals, schools, and institutions of higher education. Although headscarves are officially banned at universities, the ban has not been widely enforced since 2010.

Various forms of regional covered dress survive, although their use is diminishing. In Afghanistan, the "burqa" is a tentlike garment with a fitted cap and a cloth mesh screen for vision. It completely covers the wearer and is usually blue, although it may be other colors. The *chador* is the traditional cloak in Iran. It is a large semi-circle worn atop the head and wrapped around the body, leaving the face exposed, but covering its wearer to the ankle.

The most recognizable and possibly most used modern Islamic dress for women is the *shayla*, a large rectangular scarf wrapped around the head and neck, and the *ʿabāya*, a loose, silky outer robe worn over another complete set of clothing. The garment is always black and the intent is to identify the wearer as an observant and conservative Muslim. Occasionally, the *khimār*, a waist-length hoodlike garment, replaces the *shayla*. The *shayla* and *ʿabāya* may be worn with a variety of face covers, such as the *lithām*, a cloth tied across the lower part of the face, or the *niqāb*, a wide band around the forehead with cloth covering the face below the eyes. The *niqāb* is frequently constructed of two layers: a solid layer exposing only the eyes and a sheer top layer that, when worn down, completely covers the face. A variety of masks such as the *batula* may still be found among very conservative, older women but they are seldom seen on younger or even middle-aged women.

Women wear an enormous range of clothing under the *ʿabāya*, from Euro-American jeans and T-shirts to international haute couture, to regional folk dress. There is an unspoken agreement that an *ʿabāya*-clad woman is to be respected and simultaneously ignored. Men are thought to have weak self-control, so by concealing her body, a woman protects both herself and male strangers from indecent thoughts, *fitnah*, or social chaos.

Despite the intent of anonymity, *shayla*s and *ʿabāya*s have become increasingly decorative, featuring all manner of embellishment. Many of them are so decorative as to attract attention, rather than deflecting it. Both regional designers and international haute couturiers have taken notice of the decorative *ʿabāya* trend and now offer a wide range of extremely expensive *ʿabāya*s, meant to be replaced regularly. *ʿAbāya*s have thus evolved from a utilitarian garment to a fashion item with seasonal offerings and ever-changing styles.

There is no single type of dress that can be identified as Islamic dress. In Turkey, pious women wear a headscarf; in the Arabian Gulf, the same woman who wears a *shayla* and *ʿabāya* may well appear in fashionable Western dress when in Europe or America. Iranian women wear a headscarf and long coat, while Yemeni women wear a variety of styles depending on their age and station in life. Muslim women in Africa often wear brightly colored tops and skirts. The single consistent aspect of Muslim dress is that it be modest and not reveal the body with plunging necklines, short skirts, or overly sheer or tight garments.

BIBLIOGRAPHY

Ahmed, Leila. *Women, Gender and Islam*. New Haven, Conn.: Yale University Press, 1992.

Akou, Heather Marie. "Building a New 'World Fashion': Islamic Dress in the Twenty-First Century." *Fashion Theory* 11, no. 4 (2007): 403–422.

Baker, Patricia L. "Politics of Dress: The Dress Reform Laws of 1920s/30s Iran." In *The Language of Dress in the Middle East*, edited by Nancy Lindesfarne-Tapper and Bruce Ingham Bruce, pp. 178–192. Surrey, U.K.: Curzon, 1997.

Doumato, Eleanor A. "Gender, Monarchy, and National Identity in Saudi Arabia." *British Journal of Middle Eastern Studies* 19, no. 1 (1992): 31–47.

Gökarıksel, Banu, and Anna Secor. "Islamic-Ness in the Life of a Commodity: Veiling-Fashion in Turkey." *Transactions of the Institute of British Geographers* 35 (2010): 313–333.

El-Guindi, Fadwa. *Veil: Modesty, Privacy and Resistance*. Oxford, U.K.: Berg, 1999.

Karimi, Sawsan Ghuloom. *Dress and Identity: Culture and Modernity in Bahrain*. London: University of London, 2003.

Keddie, Nikki R. *Women in the Middle East, Past and Present*. Princeton, N.J.: Princeton University Press, 2006.

Kelly, Marjorie. "Clothes, Culture and Context: Female Dress in Kuwait." *Fashion Theory* 14, no. 2 (2010): 215–236.

Lindesfarne-Tapper, Nancy, and Bruce Ingham Bruce, eds. *The Language of Dress in the Middle East*. Surrey, U.K.: Curzon, 1997.

Osella, Caroline, and Filippo Osella. "Muslim Style in South India." *Fashion Theory* 11, no. 2/3 (2007): 233–252.

Sandikci, Ozlem, and Guliz Ger. "Aesthetics, Ethics and Politics of the Turkish Headscarf." In *Clothing as Material Culture*, edited by Susanne Küchler and Daniel Miller. Oxford, U.K.: Berg, 2005.

Scarce, Jennifer. *Women's Costume of the Near and Middle East*. London: Unwin Hyman, 1987.

Shirazi, Faegheh. *The Veil Unveiled: The Hijab in Modern Culture*. Tallahassee, Fla.: University of Florida Press, 2001.

Stillman, Yedida Kalfon. *Arab Dress: A Short History*. Themes in Islamic Studies. Leiden, Netherlands, and Boston: Brill, 2000.

Tarlo, Emma. *Visibly Muslim*. Oxford, U.K.: Berg, 2010.

Vogelsand-Eastwood, Gillian, and Willem Vogelsand. *Covering the Moon*. Leuven, Belgium: Peeters, 2008.

al-Wahabi, Najla Ismail al-Izzi. *Qatari Costume*. London: Islamic Art Society, 2003.

SHERIFA ZUHUR
Updated by CHRISTINA LINDHOLM

Historical

Ancient dress is difficult to describe with any certainty as few actual garments survive. The most fragile of all material cultural objects, clothing was often worn until no longer usable, handed down, or remade. Useful items were seldom merely discarded. Any special garments that were saved likely deteriorated over time. Historians rely on descriptions from travelers, artistic representations in drawings, paintings, statuary, and various written texts. The shortcoming with this method is that descriptions and depictions are viewed through the lens of the artist, traveler, or writer. Women were seldom the travelers and their interaction with male strangers was extremely limited in the early years of Islam.

Dress at the dawn of Islam, believed to be between 610 and 632 CE, was representative of what all people wore in the Arabian Peninsula. Traditional dress included an undergarment such as a loincloth, the *izar*, or loose trousers, *sirwāl*, an undershirt, and a tunic or dress over the top. Cloth was laboriously handwoven on narrow looms and therefore not as likely to be cut and sewn into elaborate shapes that generated wasted fabric, but rather constructed of geometric shapes that used the entire loomed width. Gussets, neck slits, and insets were used to accommodate fit and allow physical movement. Although trade brought a variety of goods to Arabia, the Prophet Muḥammad rejected luxurious fabrics, so it was likely that he and his followers used locally produced wool for garments. A cloak or wrap called an *ʿabāya* or *bisht* was worn as outerwear and both men and women wore some sort of headcover and probably a type of sandal on the feet. How many pieces a person wore was dependent on a number of issues, including status, rank, and wealth. The extreme heat of the Arabian Peninsula demanded garments that were loose and flowing, yet covering the body for protection from the sun.

People who embraced Islam adhered to the Prophet's directive for men and women to dress modestly. The body was concealed to various degrees, depending on whether one was alone, or with a spouse, among friends or relatives of the same sex, or in a mixed setting. Specific areas of the body were regarded as virtues to be protected, or as sexual in nature and thus to be kept strictly private. Men were required to cover from the waist to the knee at a minimum, to cover their heads, and to wear appropriate outerwear in public. Women were expected to draw their veils over their bosom and not display their beauty (24:31). Further, the Qurʾān instructed the Prophet's wives, daughters, and "believing women" to allow their garments to "hang low" when outside the home in order to identify them as Muslims and thus avoid harassment (33:59). The intent of covering the body is to make clear the virtuous character of a woman who otherwise might attract male attention. Thus, a historical aim of Muslim dress has been to identify observant and respectable women and delineate acceptable degrees of modesty. Men were considered to lack self-control and to be easily stimulated visually, so impeding their view of women's bodies could possibly discourage illicit advances toward women, which would lead to *fitnah* or social chaos.

Traditional clothing was also designed to cover a woman's hair and neck. Many women additionally donned a face cover when in public and it is these items, more than any others, that have caused controversy and debate for more than 150 years. The practice is associated with Islam, although face coverings were in place for hundreds of years before Islam. Women in ancient Mesopotamia wore facial veils as a sign of marriage and respectability and the punishment for wearing a face veil if one was not entitled to do so was flogging, pouring boiled pitch over the offender's head, or cutting off her ears. Muslim women adopted the facial veil in the earliest years of Islam as a means of announcing their religiosity and a way to create privacy and anonymity, thus protecting them from non-believers. Face veils have a wide variety of styles and ancient examples have been discovered at the Quseir al-Qadim archeological site dating from 1169–1252 CE Examples found are the burqa, two rectangles of cloth that join at each side of the forehead and at the bridge of the nose, leaving a wide slit for vision, and the *niqāb*, a single piece of cloth with holes or a slit for the eyes.

Under the Umayyad caliphate (661–750 CE), the second of four major ruling Islamic dynasties, Arab armies spread throughout the region and established the Domain of Islam. By the mid-eighth century, they had conquered the entire Middle East, Syria, Palestine and Egypt, Iraq and Iran, as well as the Iberian Peninsula and Irano-Turkic Central Asia. Each of these areas had specific dress traditions. In Arabia, people wore loose, flowing robes, while in the Mediterranean region, women and men wore tunics and wraps. Tailored clothing of a far more fitted style, such as coats, jackets, and trousers, was typical of the Irano-Turkic area. Each style of dress evolved from available materials, social conventions, and climatic requirements.

Initially, the conquerors retained their traditional loose robe of humble cloth. However, the combination of highly sophisticated existing textile industries in Egypt, Syria, Iraq, and Iran, and the religious conversion of local peoples to Islam contributed to an evolution of styles that took advantage of beautiful and luxurious textiles. In the centuries after the Prophet's death, silks, brocades, and richly embroidered garments became the norm for the ruling Muslim class. Styles were adopted from Persian attire and, during Umayyad rule, dress became elaborate coats over *sirwāl* trousers. Women's dress during the Umayyad reign is depicted in a mural in the desert castle Qusayr Amra, located in present-day eastern Jordan. Several female figures wear sleeveless ankle-length dresses and shoulder-length head veils. Two significant features of Islamic dress developed during the Umayyad period. The first was the enactment of a sumptuary law requiring differentiated clothing for Muslims and non-Muslims. This law prohibited conquered people from adopting Islamic dress. This ruling indicated who was Muslim, and therefore not likely to be a military or security threat and thus entitled to privileged treatment; it also helped to establish a social hierarchy and prevent assimilation.

The second event was the production of lavishly embroidered cloth, *ṭirāz*, especially for clothing. These rich garments were worn by rulers and could be awarded as tokens of royal favor. People wearing this cloth could be safely assumed to be of high rank and to enjoy the protection of the ruling class.

The Umayyads were overthrown by the Abbasids in 750 CE The Abbasids moved the center of the Islamic world to their headquarters in Baghdad and retained power until they were overthrown by the Mongols in 1258 CE Abbasid Muslims established a cultured and refined fashion practice. Men and women did not dress very differently, with the exception of their outer dress. Wide sleeves and a drawstring in the neckline were recommended for women and white was to be avoided as it was considered a masculine color.

After the fall of Baghdad, the Turkish Ottomans expanded their empire and claimed rule of the Muslim world in 1299 CE The center of Islam was then moved to Istanbul, where leadership of the Muslim world resided until the early twentieth century. A wealth of information about dress may be found in Turkish costume albums illustrated from the sixteenth century through the end of the Ottoman Empire. British Orientalist

Edward William Lane (1801–1876), in particular, carefully described dress and drew accurate depictions. As in previous centuries, the shapes were basic, using as much of the cloth as possible and modestly all-covering.

Dress silhouettes remained relatively unchanged over the centuries, with regional distinctions in color and embellishment emerging. These could identify membership in a particular tribe or residency in a particular village or district. Palestinian women, for example, became well known for their vibrant cross-stitch embroidery primarily in red, while *zari* embroidery found in India and the Arabian Gulf depicted geometric designs in gold wrapped thread. Trade and migration introduced new materials and impacted construction techniques, as well as costs, and these items allowed for small variations in traditional dress. Some parts of the Muslim world interacted closely with the West and, in many instances, Muslim women in international urban areas completely adopted Western dress. Other areas, notably, the Arabian Gulf countries, retained their traditional dress far into the twentieth century.

Bibliography

Ahmed, Leila. *Women, Gender and Islam*. New Haven, Conn.: Yale University Press, 1992.

Graham, Helga. *Arabian Time Machine*. London: Heinemann, 1978.

Graham-Brown, Sarah. *Images of Women: The Portrayal of Women in the Photography of the Middle East, 1860–1950*. London: Quartet, 1988.

El-Guindi, Fadwa. *Veil: Modesty, Privacy and Resistance*. Oxford, U.K.: Berg, 1999.

Keddie, Nikki R., and Beth Baron, eds. *Women in Middle Eastern History*. New Haven, Conn.: Yale University Press, 1991.

Ross, Heather Colyer. *The Art of the Arabian Costume: A Saudi Arabian Profile*. Studio City, Calif.: Players Press, 1994.

Scarce, Jennifer. *Women's Costume of the Near and Middle East*. London: Unwin Hyman, 1987.

Stillman, Yedida Kalfon. *Arab Dress: A Short History*. Themes in Islamic Studies. Leiden, Netherlands, and Boston: Brill, 2000.

Vogelsang-Eastwood, Gillian and Willem Vogelsang. *Covering the Moon: An Introduction to Middle Eastern Face Veils*. Leuven, Belgium: Peeters, 2008.

Sherifa Zuhur
Updated by Christina Lindholm

E

EBADI, SHIRIN. Shirin Ebadi was born on 22 June 1947 in Hamadan, Iran. She was educated in Tehran, beginning her law degree in 1965 and completing it within three years. In 1970, after a period of internship, she became one of the first female judges in Iran. She progressed through the ranks and was appointed as chief magistrate of the twenty-sixth Divisional Court in Tehran in 1975, making her the youngest and first female for the post. Ebadi married Javad Tavassoli in 1975. They have two daughters, Negar Tavassoli and Nargess Tavassoli.

In 1979, immediately after the Islamic Revolution in Iran, all female judges were dismissed, as the revolutionaries believed that women were forbidden from passing judgment. Ebadi was demoted to the post of a magistrate's clerk in the very same court over which she once presided. Soon after she opted for early retirement.

In 1992 Ebadi set up a private practice handling contentious cases. She was the defense lawyer for many controversial political and human rights cases in Iran, including Zahra Kazemi (a journalist killed in Evin prison), Parvaneh and Dariush Foroohar (well-known political activists, killed by security forces), Ezat Ebrahim Nejad (killed in the dormitory of Tehran University, 1999), and Zahra Bani Yaghoob (a young doctor, killed in detention). She also took on the case of the seven leaders of the Bahāʾī faith in Iran. All these activities led to her incarceration on charges of spreading and publishing lies against the Islamic Republic in 1999. She spent twenty-five days in solitary confinement. The first court convicted her to one and a half years' imprisonment and barred her from practicing law for five years. In the appeal process and due to international pressure, her sentence was reduced to a fine.

Ebadi received the Nobel Prize for Peace in 2003, becoming the first Muslim woman and the first Iranian Nobel laureate. She received this prize for her brave, persistent, and nonviolent struggle for defending human rights (especially of children and women) and representing many risky cases of political prisoners as their defense lawyer. She used some of the prize money to support the families of political prisoners and to set up an office for the Center for Defenders of Human Rights (CDHR), which she had founded in 2001. This center became a prominent human rights organization, honored by the National Human Rights of France in 2003. In 2008 the center was closed down by security forces.

Ebadi left Iran shortly before the June 2009 presidential election to participate in a conference in Spain. She did not return due to the severe restrictions imposed on human rights activists and upon receiving news of her colleagues' arrests and many killings. She continued her activities in de facto exile. The Iranian government, disapproving of her actions, filed a case against her in the revolutionary court. The government confiscated her properties, including the office of the CDHR that had been closed down earlier, on the pretext of unpaid taxes. Moreover, to blackmail and silence Dr. Ebadi, security forces arrested her sister and husband.

As a secular yet devout Muslim, Ebadi believes the misuse of religion and lack of an independent judiciary system are the most important barriers to human rights and democracy in Iran. Her writings have been critical of the Sharīʿah-based law. She has challenged the religious authorities' interpretation of Islam, especially the discriminatory nature of laws against women, non-Muslims, and non-Shīʿī religious minorities.

Ebadi has taught law and human rights at various universities on a part-time basis and has authored twelve books, some of which have been translated into several languages. She has founded several national and international nongovernmental organizations, including the Society for Protecting the Rights of the Child in 1995, the Center for Defenders of Human Rights (CDHR) in 2001, and the Nobel Women Initiative in 2006 in collaboration with six other women peace-prize laureates. She has also played an active role in the leadership of several campaigns, including the One Million Signatures Campaign to Change Discriminatory Laws Against Women (2006) and the Mourning Mothers of Laleh Park (2009). She has received honorary doctorate degrees from twenty-three universities and more than forty awards from various foundations and organizations in various countries.

BIBLIOGRAPHY

Primary Works

The Golden Cage: Three Brothers, Three Choices, One Destiny. Carlsbad, Calif.: Kales Press, 2011.

Ghavānin-e Keyfari ba hamkāri-ye Abdolhossein Ali Abadi [Criminal Law in collaboration with Professor Abdolhossein Aliabadi]. Tehran: Enteshārāt-e Amirkabir, 1973.

History and Documentation of Human Rights in Iran (1994). Translated by Nazila Fathi. New York: Bibliotheca Persica Press, 2000.

Hoghogh-e Adabi va Farhangi [Literary and Artistic Rights]. Tehran: Nashre- Cheshmeh, 1990.

Hoghogh-e Pezeshki [Medical Rights]. Tehran: Enteshārāt-e Ganje Danesh, 1989.

Hoghogh-e Tatbighi-ye Koodak [Comparative Rights of the Child]. Tehran: Enteshārāt-e Roshangarān va Motāleāt-e Zanān, 1997.

Hoghogh-e Zan dar Ghavānin-e Jomhuri-ye Islami-ye Iran [Women's Rights in the laws of the Islamic Republic of Iran]. Tehran: Ganj-e Dānesh (2002–2003).

Iran Awakening: One Woman's Journey to Reclaim her Life and Country. New York: Random House, 2007.

The Rights of the Child: A Study on Legal Aspects of Children's Rights in Iran (1988). Translated by M. Zaimaran. Tehran: UNICEF, 1994.

Refugee Rights in Iran (1994). Translated by Banafsheh Keynoush. London: Saqi in association with UNHCR, 2008.

Sonat va Tajadod dar System-e Hoghoghi-ye Iran [Tradition and Modernity in the Iranian Legal System]. Tehran: Ganj-e Dānesh, 1996.

Kārgarān-e Khordsāl [The Underaged Workers]. Tehran: Enteshārāt-e Roshangarān va Motāleāt-e Zanān, 1990.

Hoghogh-e Me'māri va Shahrsāzi [Architectural Rights]. Tehran: Enteshārāt-e Roshangarān va Motāleāt-e Zanān, 1992.

Secondary Works

"Ebadi, Shirin." In *Biographical Encyclopedia of the Modern Middle East*, edited by Michael R. Fishbach. Farmington Hills, Mich.: Thomson Gale, 2007.

"Ebadi, Shirin." In *Iran Today: Encyclopedia of Life in the Islamic Republic*, edited by Mehran Kamrava and Manochehr Dorraj. 2 vols., vol. 1, pp. 131–141. Westport, Conn.: Greenwood Publishers, 2008.

Nayereh Tohidi

Economics and Finance. The paucity of research and the lack of a significant female presence in the high echelons of global economics and finance do not reflect women's involvement in and contribution to the global economy over the last fifty years. Although not until after the Second World War was a female minister of finance appointed anywhere outside of the Soviet Union and not until 1988 did Benazir Bhutto become the first Muslim woman to serve as a nation's prime minister, the twenty-first century has witnessed a noticeable shift in such trends. Since 2001 Muslim women have been appointed minister of finance in nine Muslim states: Turkmenistan, United Arab Emirates, Kuwait, Jordan, Indonesia, Kazakhstan, Kyrgyzstan, Lebanon, and Syria. Four Muslim women appear on *Forbes Magazine*'s "world's 100 most powerful women" listing, all of them from the Middle East, whereas the magazine *CEO Middle East*'s listing of the "100 most powerful Arab women" of 2012 reveals the diversity of women's working roles, with 45 percent assuming CEO or principal directorial roles in traditional "male" sectors of the economy, including banking and finance, transport, construction and industry, IT and science, with banking and finance and construction and industry each accounting for 13 percent of the total. The rising profile of women of the Arab world in national and global economic decision making stands in direct contradistinction to the fact that the region has the world's lowest female participation rates in the registered labor force.

Ethno-cultural influences define the nature and extent of women's engagement in the political economy of Muslim states. Principally, the fact that Islam is not simply a religion but a way of life defines a particular set of rights and obligations for both men and women. Moreover, Islam permits both individual and collective interpretations of the Qurʾān and, as such, constructs multi-contextual understandings and practices within *ʿādah* (customary law) that differ substantially both in and between families, communities, and societies. This impacts not only on the "rules of engagement" for women in all areas of their life but also, most especially, on the range of possibilities for women wishing to participate in the labor force or engage in income-generating activities.

Islam and the Political Economy of Gender Relations. In all societies, gender stereotypes underpin the dynamics of gender relations. Depending on the cultural mores of specific societies, these are more likely to be negotiated in private among individuals, between families and family members. Sociocultural change in inter- and intra-familial gender relations is dealt with more expeditiously than in public life. Gender relations in the public sphere are affected/shaped by *ʿādah*, religious law, and/or civil law that impacts on government policy and, in any society, is extremely slow in keeping up with public opinion and practice. Thus, it is the dynamics of gender relations in the private sphere that are often the more accurate indicator of socioeconomic change.

In Muslim society, family is considered the most critical societal microcosm. Marriage within this cultural context has frequently been referred to as "business," involving a social and economic contract agreed upon by two families whose "alliance" takes precedence over that of the bride and groom. Marriages can be arranged or "guided" but, in all Muslim societies, they rarely occur between people of a different social status or class without the consent and/or blessing of the immediate or extended family. The marriage settlement in the form of dowry (bride to groom) or dower (groom to bride) may be a payment exclusive to one family or both. While culturally complex, marital customs, expectations, and economic obligations have been subject to modification since the early 1990s. For example, within the course of economic development, the expansion of free trade zones across Asia and the oil economy in the Middle East has increased employment and income-generating opportunities for women. This, in turn, has led to delayed marriage, inflated marriage settlements, and changes to women's social and legal status.

In 2005 a UNDP report revealed that, between 1990 and 2003, while the increase in women's economic participation globally was 3 percent, that for Arab women was 19 percent. Although the Arab region still has one of the lowest rates of registered economic participation (33.3 percent), some of the most conservative countries in the Middle East—Saudi Arabia, Jordan, and Oman—experienced a 50 percent increase during the same period. Even if one considers the higher rate of Muslim women's labor market participation in the Asia-Pacific region, the statistics only account for economic activities that appear in those statistics, rather than hidden economic activities, such as family labor, self-employment, and entrepreneurial activities.

The expansion of opportunities in both education and employment/economic engagement is reflected in the changing socioeconomic indicators with respect to marriage and family. Delayed marriage is a phenomenon that has occurred across Muslim societies in both Asia and the Middle East, not simply among the middle and upper classes or the principally urban population. As women gain a certain level of independence, economically if not socially, they prolong it by delaying marriage in most cases until after the age of 22, while, in some Arab states, the number of never married women between the ages of 35–39 ranges from 15 to 21 percent of the population. Moreover, among the oil states of the Arab region, the bride price has increased exponentially. To facilitate endogamous marriage and stem the tide of male nationals marrying women outside of their own culture, the United Arab Emirates, Bahrain, Saudi Arabia, and Qatar have introduced marriage funds. These funds have been crucial to those males with lower earnings faced with a bride price that might take them and their families up to ten years to save. As such, men can apply to the fund for a marriage grant. Although it is far more common in both Asia and the Middle East for women to make more of a contribution to the costs of marriage, the groom and his family often still bear the brunt of the cost.

Among the present generation of young men and women, the changes since the 1990s are apparent. Both sexes are more educated than any generation before them; women are more likely to work outside the home; and marriage has, for most men and women, become more of a shared, respectful relationship. Nevertheless, change in the public sphere has been slower. Men generally have been able to maintain their economic dominance due to the consistent wage disparity between men and women. Above all, the maintenance of what Valentine Moghadam (2005) calls the "patriarchal gender contract" ensures male privilege in both public and private realms, especially in the Middle East, but also in the Muslim countries of South and Southeast Asia. Regardless of what women do outside of the home, they are expected to prioritize the care of the family. Coupled with this is the continued need for women to seek male consent to work, travel, take out loans, and stand for political office. This expectation is imposed to varying degrees in most Muslim countries, irrespective of whether women are still legally required to do so. The following case studies offer some insight into women's pathways to economic empowerment and independence and the ways in which the political economy of gender relations has changed.

Bangladesh—Microfinance as a Global Pivotal Development Practice. One of the most notable examples of action research is that of the Grameen Bank, an academic project developed by Professor Muhammad Yunus in the mid-1970s that became a national phenomenon in Bangladesh. By 2008 it had 7.5 million borrowers, 97 percent of them women, and was a presence in 82,000 rural villages. This experiment in economic development aimed to engage women of the rural poor in interdependent self-help strategies linked to a system of graduated loans. With an estimated repayment rate between 95–98% and loans funded through member savings, the bank's apparently successful template of self-help development took banking directly to the poor. This not only attracted a stream of development funding to Bangladesh; the viability of "banking" the income-generating activities of women of the rural poor with demonstrably positive outcomes also had a global impact. Microfinance became a pivotal international development practice for poverty alleviation, and, most importantly, within the remit of gender-specific development projects aimed at empowering women, it provided a seemingly simple solution in the intransigent cultural complexity of gender relations in the developing world.

The Grameen Bank "enterprise" resolved ambiguities in the lives of rural families, satisfying the need for increased income on the one hand, while maintaining the restrictions of the family. This model was expected to result in positive outcomes for Muslim women. Yunus believed that economically empowering women would lead to the transformation of the sociocultural mores that shaped gender relations in the highly conservative rural village communities.

Studies undertaken since 2004 have focused on the gender question, the impact of loans, and the effect of women's self-employment on gender relations within the family. When addressing the question of who actually uses or benefits from the loan taken out by the women, the response is complex. The percentage of loans going directly to men can be anywhere from 39 to 70 percent. In terms of what the loans are used for, one large study found that 85 percent were used for agricultural purposes and, when used in this way, women were able to exercise greater control over the loan (Kelkar et al., 2004). Loans used directly by women were invested in expanding their stock of small animals and their vegetable and fruit growing. Women as the principal food producers were able to extend subsistence agriculture to engage in production for the market. The expansion of their unpaid agricultural activities into self-employment or income-generating activities allowed women to increase their skills and status without dishonoring the family.

Women who have neither the skills nor opportunity to engage in income-generating activities for the market have entered the field of traditional moneylending. They offer flexible loans at the traditional 120 percent interest rate to assist women who are unable to make their loan payments on time or are in need of emergency cash. By turning to loans, women are able to conduct business from their homes, rather than in public offices or markets where women are usually barred from entering or trading in public. Moreover, this service has become increasingly important because, in Bangladeshi culture, women only borrow from women.

Women's role in family decision making is enhanced as they gain a voice with respect to how loans or income are spent. Traditionally, the marketplace is taboo for women; even basic shopping is undertaken by the husband. In some areas, women now accompany their husband to the markets to select and purchase goods. In one study, it was found that women, in order to maintain control over their income, would sooner sell to intermediaries than give goods to their husband to sell at the market (Kelkar et al., 2004). For women of the rural poor, establishing good credit and savings became possible only with the advent of microfinance. Under the Grameen model, a woman's account could not be accessed by her husband, unlike the practice in other financial institutions. Consequently, women who were able to accumulate a small amount of capital could make further loans to spend on their children's education, undertake home improvements, or build a dowry for a "good" marriage for their daughters.

Nevertheless, microfinance has also drawn women of the rural poor into the world of global capital and debt. The flexibility of traditional moneylending has been transformed into the rigidity of regular repayment and self-help. One family emergency can throw even the best financial calculations off course; while the traditional moneylender will wait, NGO institutions will not. As a member of a "savings and loan group," the failure of one woman to make a timely payment impacts on the entire group, meaning that no one will receive credit until such an individual's debt is paid. "Shaming," a practice well known to Muslim women, involves acts of retribution meted out by women on women. This may range from verbal and physical abuse to the seizure of property.

In Bangladesh, the lives of Muslim women of the rural poor follow a precarious socioeconomic path wherein the balance of rural subsistence often rolls from one harvest to the next. In the cash-poor reality of rural existence, the strict regimen of microfinance and credit to the poor is, for many, untenable and, as such, it has reinforced the position of the traditional moneylender in an externally driven cycle of credit and debt. The capacity for change within the private and public world of gender relations tends to depend on the former, rather than the latter. Even those women who have successfully navigated microfinance rely on a certain level of tolerance and support from their husbands and/or family. Thus, for men for whom "losing face" equates with loss of honor, the option is to demand that their wives withdraw from the system, a request to which even women who have acquired considerable status, skills, and economic independence may accede.

Saudi Arabia—Unexpected Leadership and Path-Breaking Subversions. It is now recognized that women own one-third of all businesses in developing countries. In 2007 almost twenty thousand companies were owned by Saudi businesswomen. The twenty largest companies owned or controlled by Saudi women range from traditional fields, such as fashion, eyewear, interior design, cosmetics, and event management, to more typically male-dominated sectors, including audiovisual production, industrial processing, architecture, and public relations. The largest woman-owned Saudi business operates in the field of metal-processing and salvage operation—Al Sale Eastern Company in Al Khobar—with an annual revenue of $176.5 million. Saudi women accounted for 21 percent of private sector investment. Moreover, the National Commercial Bank reported that "Saudi women owned 40 per cent of the Kingdom's real estate assets, 20 per cent of stocks and over 18 per cent of current bank accounts" (Ahmad, 2011, p. 127). Thus, Saudi women controlled a total of over $US16 billion in bank accounts and "untapped" assets.

One powerful woman in the field of economics and finance is Lubna Olayan, CEO of Olayan Financing. The second most powerful woman in the Arab world, she appears on a list of the fifty most powerful women in the world outside of the

United States. In 2004 she was the first female keynote speaker at the Jeddah Economic Forum, where she advocated for Saudi women and against gender discrimination.

The discovery of oil in Saudi Arabia underwrote a succession of five-year economic plans that focused on socioeconomic development to the universal benefit of Saudi citizens. Education and employment became the foundation of these development plans, with a special focus on the education of women to increase their involvement in economic development. Saudi elites led the way in prioritizing their daughters' education, setting an example followed by the majority of the population when rates of urbanization increased and education became a prerequisite for employment. Since the 1990s, the number of women in the formal labor force has tripled, although, in total, it remains one of the lowest in the world, at 17 percent.

In Saudi Arabia, women have the right to work but the areas in which they might seek employment have been, until recently, circumscribed, as women were not permitted to study and/or work in specific areas, such as architecture, engineering, and the law. Moreover, over 90 percent of women in the registered labor force have a university degree, yet most work in "feminized" areas of the public sector, such as teaching, nursing, and public administration. For the majority of women outside of the privileged classes, the universal free education in Saudi Arabia does not adequately equip them with the skills required by the labor market. These women constitute the majority of the visible unemployed and the invisible employed. Women's participation in the economy is, for the most part, occulted not only because they form the majority of family workers in small enterprise, of one form or another, but also because much of their income-generating activities occur on the cusp of the private/public sphere and, by a deft sleight of hand, become statistically invisible.

Wahhābīyah, the form of Islam practiced in Saudi Arabia, follows a highly conservative interpretation of the Qur'ān that determines and defines gender relations in both public and private spaces. Men and women occupy and use separate public spaces and this creates barriers to women's terms of engagement in the economy, despite Islam's clear support for women's rights to own property and engage in business transactions, even with unrelated males. Until 2004 women required a husband's consent to work, travel, apply for an ID card, and borrow from a financial institution. Until 2008 travel outside of a woman's immediate locality required that she be accompanied by a *maḥram*, although some changes have been introduced, such as permitting a woman traveling alone to stay in a hotel, largely fueled by the need for mobility when engaging in business. Until 2005 all public dealings with institutions, such as applying for a commercial licence, paying bills, or engaging in commercial activities, were mediated by a *wakīl* (legal intermediary). Women who were self-employed or owned a business that required them to engage with a mixed public environment were expected to hire a male manager who would engage with non-*maḥram* males on their behalf. Only in 2006 did Saudi women gain the right to obtain business licenses without a male partner.

Most of the restrictions on women in public, except for the driving ban, which is strictly enforced, are often ignored. The political economy of gender relations, however, is changing, driven by Saudi women's need for independence. Confronted by the complexity of a counterintuitive separation of genders in public places, Saudi women and their families have been "creative" in their subversion of the "rules" in order to facilitate their access to economic opportunities.

In 2005 there were approximately twenty-three thousand registered businesswomen. Including unregistered women, that figure is estimated to be closer to forty thousand. Most of these businesses have been started from home and operate outside the male-only public places in what are termed the "family only" zones. Women themselves fund their businesses; under Sharīʿah law, women retain the rights to and control of their assets; neither their husband nor children may make any claim, and, under *ʿādah* law, the marriage settlement is paid to women. For middle- and upper-class women, the oil economy has significantly increased the bride price and, as such, women have sufficient assets to invest in independent entrepreneurial initiatives. Operating in a parallel public space that non-*maḥram* men cannot enter, women cater to other women in areas such as tailoring, childcare centers, beauty parlors, women's fitness, catering, and light manufacturing. What is distinctive in Saudi Arabia is that, of all of women's small and medium enterprises, over 72 percent operate outside of the home and 92 percent have paid employees.

Until recently, some of the difficulties in business regulation and the existence of bureaucratic rules antagonistic to women engaging in commercial activity meant that women became adept in sidelining. A woman may not register a business, at least not initially, that could be conducted from her home, and when a suitable commercial category does not exist, she will register her business under an existing category. To avoid the often illogical red tape surrounding health and safety regulations, for example, a health and fitness establishment would be registered as a beauty parlor. Women socialize with women, and through their family, friendships, and community networks, their businesses are supported, facilitating the development of a clientele despite the restrictions on women selling goods in the broader public sphere. The Internet and cell phones have further simplified the process and created avenues for women to successfully conduct a wide range of business ventures without contravening Sharīʿah law.

The changing socioeconomic terrain has created a slow but relevant response to the expansion of women's initiatives in private sector employment and women's demand for employment opportunities. The development of women's business associations and the election of two prominent businesswomen, Lama Al-Sulaiman and Nashwa Taher, to the board of the male-dominated Jeddah Chamber of Commerce and Industry in 2005 signaled a major turning point. Under the most recent development plan, women were given maternity benefits, the right to deal with public institutions without intermediaries, and encouragement to undertake paid work, albeit part-time. Moreover, the private sector has also responded to the rising profile of women in the economic development of the Kingdom, creating more women-only spaces. For example, the Kingdom's National Commercial Bank now has forty-six women-only branches, which transcend traditional banking services into the area of wealth investment.

For women entering the professions, there are fields in which women now work in a mixed environment, such as medicine, teaching, and banking and finance. The male domination of retail is also being eroded, with the 2011 enforcement of a 2006 labor law requiring that lingerie and cosmetics be sold only by female salespersons—the result of a two-year campaign, orchestrated by women, using mainstream and social media, including Facebook, who considered the previous practice of hiring exclusively male salespersons disingenuous and embarrassing. This change could create up to forty thousand jobs for Saudi women in the retail sector alone. By all accounts, this is expected to be only the beginning.

The call for the expansion of women-only public spaces, including women's shopping malls, by women has been acceded to, in part. In 2013 work will start on a new city with separate work environments and public spaces for men and women in retail and manufacturing to expand job opportunities for women while adhering to the public gender segregation decreed by Sharīʿah law.

These developments have begun to affect marriage trends, as Saudi girls are marrying later in their twenties in order to complete their educations and establish themselves in the workforce. In many instances, a single income is no longer sufficient to meet household expenses, rendering an employed female a preferred bride. Women's expectations of marriage are also changing, as access to education and the possibility of a paid career are for many attractive alternatives to full-time motherhood. Nevertheless, many Saudi women enter the workforce with the expectation of working only until they have children, at which time they expect to become full-time mothers and housewives.

Summary. In the Muslim world, women's engagement in economics and finance is a long-standing, but growing, field of operation. The number of studies on the topic continues to increase, but the low visibility of women's activities in economic development in many Muslim societies limits our knowledge and understanding of the phenomenon. In a public world dominated by men, women still enter and engage only with the support and approval of their husbands and/or family. Nevertheless, in the world of economics and finance, women demonstrate optimism, personal investment in a better future, and the ingenuity to overcome the many obstacles they face.

BIBLIOGRAPHY

Ahmad, Syed Zamberi. "Evidence of the Characteristics of Women Entrepreneurs in the Kingdom of Saudi Arabia." *International Journal of Gender and Entrepreneurship* 3, no. 2 (2011): 123–143.

Ahmed, Fauzia Erfan. "Microcredit, Men and Masculinity." *Feminist Formations* 20, no. 2 (2008): 122–155.

Al-Munajjed, Mona. *Women's Employment in Saudi Arabia: A Major Challenge.* Dubai, UAE: Ideation Center Insight, 2010. A twenty-four-page report, available at http://www.ideationcenter.com/home/ideation.

Alturki, Naura, and Rebekah Braswell. *Businesswomen in Saudi Arabia: Characteristics, Challenges and Aspirations in a Regional Context.* Riyadh, Saudi Arabia: Monitor Group, 2010. See especially pp. 1–70.

Cons, Jason, and Kasia Paprocki. "Contested Credit Landscapes: Microcredit, Self-Help and Self-Determination in Rural Bangladesh." *Third World Quarterly* 31, no. 4 (2010): 637–654.

Doumaro, Eleanor Abdella. "Saudi Arabia." In *Women's Rights in the Middle East and North Africa: Citizenship and Justice*, edited by Sameena Nasir and Leigh Tomppert, pp. 257–270. Lanham, Md.: Rowman & Littlefield, 2005.

Gray, Kenneth R., and Joycelyn Finley-Hervey. "Women and Entrepreneurship in Morocco: Debunking Myths and Discerning Strategies." *International Entrepreneurship and Management Journal* 1 (2005): 203–217.

Heath, Jennifer, and Ashraf Zahedi, eds. *Land of the Unconquerable: The Lives of Contemporary Afghan Women.* Los Angeles: University of California Press, 2011.

Heyat, Farideh. *Azeri Women in Transition: Women in Soviet & Post-Soviet Azerbaijan.* London: Routledge, 2002.

Karim, Lamia. "Demystifying Micro-Credit: The Grameen Bank, NGOs, and Neoliberalism in Bangladesh." *Cultural Dynamics* 20, no. 1 (2008): 5–29.

Kelkar, Govind, Dev Nathan, and Rownok Jahan. *We Were in Fire, Now We Are in Water: Microcredit and Gender Relations in Rural Bangladesh.* New Delhi: IFAD-UNIFEM, Gender Mainstreaming Programme in Asia, 2004. See especially pp. 1–47.

Khateeb, Salwa Abdel Hameed al-. "Women, Family and the Discovery of Oil in Saudi Arabia." *Marriage and Family Review* 27, no. 1–2 (1998): 167–189.

Kocaoglu, Timur. "The Past as Prologue? Challenging the Myth of the Subordinated, Docile Woman in

Muslim Central Eurasia." In *Gender Politics in Post-Communist Eurasia*, edited by Linda Raccioppi and Katherine Sullivan, pp. 169–205. East Lansing: Michigan State University Press, 2009.

Lippman, Thomas W. *Saudi Arabia on the Edge: The Uncertain Future of an American Ally*. Washington, DC: Potomac Books, 2012.

Metcalfe, Beverley Dawn. "Women, Management and Globalisation in the Middle East." *Journal of Business Ethics* 83 (2008): 85–100.

Moghadam, Valentine M. "Women's Economic Participation in the Middle East: What Difference Has the Neo-Liberal Policy Turn Made?" *Journal of Middle East Women Studies* 1, no. 1 (2005): 110–140.

Rao, Nitya. "Breadwinners and Homemakers: Migration and Changing Conjugal Expectations in Rural Bangladesh." *Journal of Development Studies* 48, no. 1 (2012): 26–40.

Ross, Michael L. "Oil, Islam and Women." *American Political Science Review* 102, no. 1 (2008): 107–185.

Sadi, Muhammad Asad, and Basheer Muhammad al-Ghazali. "Doing Business with Impudence: A Focus on Women Entrepreneurship in Saudi Arabia." *African Journal of Business Management* 4, no. 1 (2010): 1–11

Shane, Daniel. "Revealed: 100 Most Powerful Arab Women 2012." http://www.arabianbusiness.com/revealed-100-most-powerful-arab-women-2012-448409.html.

UNDP. "Towards the Rise of Women in the Arab World." Arab Human Development Report, 2005. http://www.arab-hdr.org/contents/index.aspx?rid=4.

Weeks, Julie R. "Women Business Owners in the Middle East and North Africa: A Five Country Research Study." *International Journal of Gender and Entrepreneurship* 1, no. 1 (2008): 77–85.

"Worldwide Guide to Women in Leadership." http://www.guide2womenleaders.com.

YVONNE CORCORAN-NANTES

EDUCATION AND WOMEN.

[*This entry contains four subentries:*

Historical Discourse
Contemporary Discourse
Educational Reform *and*
Women's Religious Education.]

HISTORICAL DISCOURSE

For the purposes of this article, women's education in Islam refers to the rights and responsibilities of women to formalized instruction by authoritative teachers, in contrast to the rights and responsibilities of men to such formalized instruction, as well as the reasons for any differences based on gender. As with other domains, scholars of women's education arrive at many different conclusions from the same basic, foundational Islamic sources, such as Qur'ānic verses, the sunnah (path or behavior) of Muḥammad and his female family members, and *ḥadīth* (sayings of Muḥammad). The historical debates about the role of women's education in Islam revolve around both specific practices at educational institutions and general understandings of the duties of Muslim women. The key contemporary debates about Muslim women's education include gender segregation, women's activity outside the home during adolescence and after marriage, and content and quality of women's education.

Islamic Sources. The foundational Islamic sources have been the primary reference for historical debates about the role of women's education in Islam. Across the Islamic world and throughout Islamic history, most Muslim scholars have argued that Islam encourages religious literacy and education in general, noting that the first word from God to Muḥammad was *iqrā'* ("read, recite"). However, verses in the Qur'ān seem contradictory regarding Muslim women's education. Some verses (4:34; 24:31; 2:228–229) enjoin women to be separate from men, be covered or veiled, be submissive to men, and stay in the home. Other verses (33:35; 3:195; 16:97; 4:124; 16:58–59; 4:1) affirm the equality of men and women and their pursuit of knowledge. There are also *ḥadīth* that provide seemingly contradictory exhortations on the subject of Muslim women's education. The behavior of Muḥammad and his Companions, wives, and daughters also provide sources of reference for proper Muslim womanhood and include stories of his first wife Khadījah, a successful businesswoman, and ʿĀʾishah, a *ḥadīth* scholar and military leader. The overwhelming scholarly consensus is that Muḥammad and foundational Islamic sources in historical context greatly expanded women's rights to life, property ownership, inheritance, education, and divorce.

Acceptable practices and discourses of Muslim women's education became codified through the development of Islamic law and the Sunnī and Shīʿī *madhāhib* (legal schools). The different legal schools gave varying levels of priority to the foundational Islamic texts, legal precedence, accepted cultural practices, consensus of jurists, and a jurist's independent interpretation. This atmosphere provided a certain level of ambiguity, so that many women attended formal instruction and became recognized scholars on topics including *ḥadīth* and *fiqh* (jurisprudence). Yet many scholars also argued against women receiving formal instruction. Higher education for women was most common in the families of highly educated men, as male scholars were more likely to encourage education for their wives and daughters. Arguments against women's education generally cited prohibitions against gender mixing, women's speech in public, or women's activity outside the family home. Although there were no legal restrictions on female education in premodern Islamic history, James Lindsay found complaints by those who did not approve of the presence of women in male-dominated educational settings.

Women's Education in Islamic History. Muḥammad's wives and his daughter Fāṭimah are significant role models and historical precedents for learned Muslim women. Within decades of the origin of Islam, there are records of Umm al-Darda, who debated with male scholars, lectured on *ḥadīth* and *fiqh* in women's and men's sections of the mosque, taught the caliph of Damascus, and issued *fatāwā* (fatwas) on *ḥajj* rituals, commerce, and allowing women to pray in the same position as men. From Afghanistan and Iran to Damascus and Fez, noblewomen were active donors and patrons of educational institutions from primary to higher levels, mosques, and charitable establishments. As an exemplar, the well-educated daughter of a wealthy merchant, Fāṭimah al-Fihri, used her inheritance to found the mosque school in 859 that soon became the University of Karaouine, one of the oldest universities in the world. Women's attendance at formal and informal classes was noted by the twelfth-century Fāṭimid scholars Ibn al-Tuwayr and al-Musabbihi and in fifteenth-century Iran in Ismāʿīli gatherings held by the imam.

The percentage of Islamic scholars who were women rose from 1 percent in the twelfth century to 15 percent in the fifteenth century, as estimated by Ignaz Goldziher. There are many records of notable female scholars in all subjects as jurists, scholars, and teachers. Ibn ʿAsākir, a twelfth-century Sunnī scholar, wrote that he studied with eighty different female teachers. Ruth Roded (1994) noted that the proportion of female lecturers in many classic Islamic colleges was higher than in modern Western universities, and Mohammad Akram Nadwi (2007) compiled forty volumes with at least eight thousand female scholars of *ḥadīth*. In the sixteenth and seventeenth centuries barriers grew against female scholarship as education became more formalized, gender-segregated, and oriented toward careers in the courts and mosques.

As was common around the world for most of history, premodern formal education for Muslim women was limited to the political and economic elite or members of their family, including highly educated female slaves serving noble families.

Generally, women received basic education in literacy and religion, either with family at home, with private tutors, or at mosque schools. Formal education and religious education were closely tied, as schools were generally associated with a mosque and both run by *waqf*s (religious endowments). Female relatives of male scholars sometimes achieved formal degrees at higher levels in *madāris* (schools). Scholars have noted a wealth of biographical information on female scholars in Islamic history, contrasted with an absence of such recordings in other parts of the world. However, little detail is known about the content and structures of most Muslim women's education.

Modern Developments. The massive political restructuring of the nineteenth and twentieth centuries through colonialism, world wars, and the globalization of the nation-state model have changed both formal educational systems in general and the debates about women's education in Islam in particular. The introduction of colonial institutions such as Christian missionary schools and military colleges resulted in the standardization of formal schooling along European models across Africa, the Middle East, and Asia. For example, Syrian Protestant College, founded by Daniel Bliss, precursor to the American University in Beirut, started a nursing program for women in 1905 and accepted women in the College of Arts and Sciences in 1924.

Many prominent reformists and scholars contributed to new conversations about the form and content of proper education for men and women, the need for mass literacy and civil society, and the implementation of a "modern" curriculum, which included the study of religion as one subject among many others of greater priority. Along with institutional change came discourses of ethnic nationalism, secularism, progressivism, and modernization. These voices include those of the modernist Muḥammad ʿAbduh and his student Rashīd Riḍā in Egypt, as well as the revivalist Ḥasan al-Bannā, founder of the Muslim Brotherhood in Egypt. They argued that, because the original social and cultural contexts of Qurʾānic instructions had changed, the understanding of the proper place of women in society who were now independent citizen-subjects also needed to be changed.

From Africa to Southeast Asia, women participated in reforming practices and discourses about their role in Muslim societies and new nation-states. In nineteenth-century West Africa, Nana Asmaʾu taught women's religious education, trained a sisterhood of women teachers, and wrote more than sixty works of poetry and scholarship. Many women participated in nationalist movements and organized women for political and literary activity. Women such as Aisha Taymour, Malak Hifnī Nāṣif, Nabawīyya Mūsā, ʿĀʾishah ʿAbd al- Rahman, Zaynab al-Ghazālī, and Rokeya Sakhawat Hossain advocated for women's emancipation and education, supported by male nationalist intellectuals like Qāsim Amīn, in his pivotal work *Taḥrīr al-marʾah*. European-style socialist nationalism heavily influenced many policy makers, activists, and ladies' associations, though they were usually based on anticolonial and nationalist reform platforms. In Egypt, Hudā Shaʿrāwī, founder of the Egyptian Feminist Union and representative at the International Women's Alliance, was one of many women activists involved in intellectual and political circles. Women's organizations, such as Aisyiyah in Indonesia, focused on mass literacy, gender segregation, the veil and Islamic dress, polygyny, inheritance, and the protection of widows and orphans.

Turn of the Twenty-First Century. With the late twentieth-century independence movements, these reformist programs began to be framed in the context of international law and human rights. Dozens of independent Muslim-majority nation-states provided mass education based on globalized concepts of national citizenship and governmental systems (legal, economic, financial, educational, military, etc.) based on European models. Many male and female scholars, including those who later became government ministers or heads of state, traveled abroad for Western higher education and returned to their home countries determined to integrate or adopt certain ideas or practices. As one example, Princess Basma bint Talal of Jordan was educated in England at Oxford University and in 1998 established the Women's Studies Center at the University of Jordan as one of the first institutions to grant graduate degrees in women's studies in the Arab Middle East.

Both private and national Islamic organizations arose to provide religiously based discourses and reform programs as alternatives to Anglo-European models. Many Islamic scholars criticized the role of governmental and nongovernmental organizations from former colonial powers and the United Nations, claiming they pressured Muslim-majority countries to adopt neocolonial discourses and practices. The largest women-only Islamic movement in the world is the Qubaysiat of Syria, directing almost one hundred Islamic schools for girls. The founder of the movement, Munira al-Qubaysi, was considered the world's most influential Muslim woman according to the Royal Islamic Strategic Studies Centre in 2011. The Qubaysiat encourages women to bring their society closer to authentic Islamic values and practices and away from foreign values.

With the 1979 Islamic Revolution in Iran and the spread of political Islam throughout governments in Saudi Arabia, Afghanistan, Pakistan, Sudan, and elsewhere, different interpretations of the proper role for women in society (including women's education) were codified in a variety of national laws and practices and were justified based on Islamic sources and traditions. Some states and non-state groups that identify as Islamist or Islamic fundamentalist, such as the Taliban in Afghanistan, justify some acts of violence against women according to the un-Islamic *bidʿah* (innovation) of women's attendance at public schools. Yet there is great diversity and political complexity in these programs that defy easy generalizations, as the strict gender segregation in Iran resulted in high educational achievement for women in all fields, and Saudi Arabia has had public, compulsory schooling for girls since 1962. In Saudi Arabia in 2009 King Abdullah appointed Norah al-Fayes as the first female deputy minister (for women's education) and opened King Abdullah University of Science and Technology as the first coeducational university campus.

The international establishment of United Nations-associated programs and organizations, Anglo-European countries and associated international aid organizations, and, especially, English-language scholarship, frames the gender discourse in terms of development goals and human rights conventions. Many attempts to accommodate these discourses, of a right to mass public education, within local traditions and Islamic gender discourse, have resulted in gender-segregated schools such as the women's college of al-Azhar University in Egypt, the women's Islamic education center, al-Huda Institute of Pakistan, and the world's largest women's college, Princess Nora bint Abdul Rahman University in Saudi Arabia.

Contemporary Debates. The main issues in contemporary debates are the functionalization of Islam by the state, global standardization or essentialization of Islam, neocolonialism, Islamophobia, and democratization of authority in Islam. The "functionalization of Islam by the state" is Gregory Starrett's (1998) term for the governmental takeover of authority to judge what practices are "Islamic." The global standardization of Islam is the sense that there should be a universal agreement as to what constitutes Islam and Islamic behavior. "Neocolonialism" is a term for the continued practice of foreign governments of putting undue pressure on local governments in order to benefit the foreign governments instead of locals, for example, when foreign development aid must be spent on products from the donor country. Islamophobia is expressed in hate speech, violence or hate crimes, and discrimination against Muslims or those associated with Muslims. The democratization of authority in Islam with mass literacy, immigration, and communication technology like the Internet, has popularized the authority to speak for Islam. These issues are related to the major debates about appropriate roles for women in society, gender segregation, the role of the state, and new communication technologies. The debates about education of women in Islam generally fall into three major groups: modernism/progressivism, Muslim feminism, Islamic fundamentalism.

The modernist/progressivist discourse tends to favor progress toward a universal ideal of human rights and equality, and often argues that Islamic sources must be reinterpreted for a new social context or that traditions in Muslim-majority countries are not truly Islamic and should be discarded. Some who argue from a modernist/progressive approach promote secularism or secular feminism and do not engage with Islamic sources. Male and female intellectuals (from Mohammad Ali Jinnah and Ḥasan Turābī to Muhammad Tahir-ul-Qadri and Samana Siddiqi) have claimed that equality is a core Islamic principle and the disempowerment and illiteracy of women is not in accordance with Islam.

The "Muslim feminist" or "Islamic feminist" approach emerged in the 1980s and tends to argue that the principles of international human rights are not at odds with the principles of equality in Islam, but Muslim women should be free to live devout lives as wives and mothers and wear the veil. This approach sometimes seeks to redefine the term "feminism" from an Islamic perspective of complementarity instead of sameness and can be equally critical of both hyper-patriarchal Islam and the colonial West.

The Islamic fundamentalist approach tends to conclude that the concepts and practices of international human rights are foreign to Islam and that abiding by the directives in the foundational Islamic sources and following original Muslim practices are the only ways for Muslims to live properly. This is separated from Islamic feminism by its extremist and literalist operations that restrict and ban women's education and public activity in ways that are disavowed by most Islamic scholars.

Women's Contribution. With massive expansion of information and communication technologies and compulsory public schooling across the globe, more and more women have access to information and avenues for contribution to the debates. Scholars and activists such as Leila Ahmed, Fatima Mernissi, Amina Wadud, Margot Badran, miriam cooke, Ziba Mir-Hosseini, Lara Deeb, Saba Mahmood, Fida Adely, Kecia Ali, and Heba Ra'uf are furthering research, analysis, ethnography, and community organizing on Muslim women's education. One aspect of educational demography that may be relevant to future discussion on this topic is that much of Muslim women's education in the modern world is in the field of education itself. In Saudi Arabia 93 percent of all female university degrees were in education or social sciences. In Jordan most students seeking education degrees are women and education is one of the primary sectors of women's employment.

BIBLIOGRAPHY

Ahmed, Leila. *Women and Gender in Islam: Historical Roots of a Modern Debate.* New Haven, Conn.: Yale University Press, 1992.

Badran, Margot, and miriam cooke, eds. *Opening the Gates: A Century of Arab Feminist Writing.* Bloomington: Indiana University Press, 1990.

Jawad, Haifaa. *The Education of Women in Islam.* London: Gulf Center for Strategic Studies, 1991.

Keddie, Nikki R. *Women in the Middle East: Past and Present.* Princeton: Princeton University Press, 2007.

Lindsay, James E. *Daily Life in the Medieval Islamic World.* Westport, Conn.: Greenwood Press, 2005.

Mack, Beverly B., and Jean Boyd. *One Woman's Jihad: Nana Asma'u, Scholar and Scribe.* Bloomington: Indiana University Press, 2000.

Nadwi, Mohammad Akram. *Al-Muhaddithāt: The Women Scholars in Islam.* Oxford: Interface Publications, 2007. The most exhaustive compilation of female scholars in Islamic history in biographical dictionary format.

Rhouni, Raja. *Secular and Islamic Feminist Critiques in the Work of Fatima Mernissi.* Leiden, Netherlands, and New York: Brill, 2010.

Roded, Ruth. *Women in Islamic Biographical Collections: From Ibn Sa'd to Who's Who.* Boulder, Colo.: Lynne Rienner Publishers, 1994. An excellent collection of female scholars from biographical collections throughout Islamic history and a productive companion to Nadwi.

Starrett, Gregory. *Putting Islam to Work: Education, Politics, and the Religious Transformation in Egypt.* Berkeley: University of California Press, 1998.

Virani, Shafique N. *The Ismailis in the Middle Ages: A History of Survival, A Search for Salvation.* Oxford and New York: Oxford University Press, 2007.

Wadud, Amina. *Qur'an and Woman: Rereading the Sacred Text from a Woman's Perspective.* New York: Oxford University Press, 1999.

REBECCA MCLAIN HODGES

CONTEMPORARY DISCOURSE

Education is highly valued in the scriptural sources of Islam. In fact, education is not only a universal right granted to all members of a Muslim community; it is also viewed as a strict obligation. The education of women is therefore viewed as an analogous right to that of men. The Islamic understanding of education in all its forms is built upon an essentially democratic principle of education for all.

The Islamic theory of education is derived from the Qur'ān and sunnah of the Prophet Muḥammad. Muslim scholars have interpreted the first Qur'ānic verses revealed to Muḥammad as evidence of Islam's respect for knowledge. The first revelation begins with the words: "Read in the name of your Lord who created everything" (96:1). The importance and pursuit of knowledge is highlighted both directly and indirectly in more than five hundred verses in the Qur'ān. It commands all Muslims to advance their knowledge irrespective of their sex. It repeatedly encourages Muslims to read, think, contemplate, and learn: "Are the wise and the ignorant equal? Truly, none will take heed but men of understanding" (39:9). The concept of knowledge in Islam, moreover, is not restricted to the traditional religious sciences but covers a broad spectrum of subjects, both religious and secular, that men and women are invited to learn.

The first message that Muḥammad preached was to "read." One of his famous traditions encourages Muslims "to search for knowledge, even as far as China," which, for seventh-century Arabians, represented the outermost reaches of the world. Muslim scholars proudly point out that Islam granted women respect and honor, in stark contrast to their pre-Islamic status in Arabia. Against the backdrop of the misogynist practices of pre-Islamic Arabia, such as infanticide, the Prophet encouraged the fair treatment of women, the least of which included educating them. Those who fulfilled the obligation of raising and educating their daughters were promised Paradise, according to *ḥadīth*. The Prophet made clear that seeking knowledge is a matter of religious duty binding upon every Muslim man and woman.

The Qur'ān encourages women to speak their minds and not be silent, because their personal growth could not be achieved otherwise. In early Islamic history women used to discuss and debate with Muḥammad; he listened to their opinions and gave them opportunities to develop their own individuality, independence, and talents. The

Prophet encouraged women to develop a sense of inquisitiveness and curiosity. He used to receive delegations of women who presented their cases to him. Some women asked the Prophet to teach them just as he taught the men. He responded by appointing a day for their religious instruction.

As a result of their religious knowledge, women have participated in building up Islamic societies. During the early years of Islam, Muslim women made their contributions to various fields of knowledge, including religious studies, literature, Sufism, medicine, history, jurisprudence, arts and artistic crafts, and other fields. For example, during the early days of Islam there were many women scholars who played significant roles in the formulation of Islam. ʿĀ'ishah, one of the Prophet's wives, was one of the most famous Muslim scholars and was considered one of the most important transmitters of *ḥadīth*. By the time the Prophet died she was accepted by men and woman as a religious authority, and she became a great scholar and religious judge.

Because education was not restricted to scholarly and religious matters (as seen in the case of Prophet's wife ʿĀʾishah), the Prophet's other wives contributed in various practical fields—Khadījah was an excellent manager and trader; Sawdah developed her skill in fine leather; Zaynab was active in charitable works; Umm Salamah, bright and clever, acted as a political adviser to the Prophet. Hafsa, the daughter of the second caliph, ʿUmar, was also active in public affairs. That education mattered outside the confines of the home is seen, for example, when, during the reign of ʿUmar, a woman (al-Shafa) was appointed as a market inspector in Medina, thus applying her skills in the public space.

The above analysis of the Qurʾānic and sunnah concept of education shows the importance of women's education and their capacity to educate others in the main tenets of Islamic religion. However, even though the Qurʾān introduced substantial reforms regarding women's education, providing new regulations, and even though women had access to education and were encouraged to pursue it during the Prophet's era, they were later quickly pushed to the margins of social life, thereby reducing their opportunities for education.

With the death of Muḥammad and the transformation of the early Islamic community into an empire, women's rights were steadily taken away. A patriarchal system of values as a norm in which the most desirable place for women was the family environment and studying the Qurʾān and *ḥadīth* in the privacy of the woman's own home was gradually emerging in Muslim societies from the early ages of Islam. The cultural climate of the seventh and eighth centuries was strongly patriarchal, so the academic Muslim elite interpreted the Qurʾān in the spirit of cultural and civilization heritage, creating a dichotomy between male and female spheres of activity. Although historical sources give only sparse information on women's activities in both private and public spheres, it can be supposed that women's initial education was obtained within the family, because they were considered the primary would-be caretakers of children who had to be raised in Islam, according to the prevalent norms in Muslim societies. The pursuit of scholarship was evidently the prerogative of elite women. The fact is that women from higher social classes were privileged in comparison to other women by being able to have private tutors or to become teachers—not only to women, but also to men. Some famous Islamic scholars such as Ibn al-ʿArabī, Ibn Ḥazm, and Ibn ʿAsākir reported that, apart from male teachers, they were also receiving education from female teachers. Despite that fact, women were not involved as professors at public educational institutions, but more likely acted as private teachers. The role of women in education was not socially recognized, which resulted in an increased reduction in their participation in education and public life in general.

Women's contributions to education, as far we can tell from the existing historical sources, was an exception to the general rule of women being largely excluded from contributing to the science. Women did not contribute to the central narratives of Islam, they were not among the founders of the Islamic law schools or theological schools of thought, nor were they interpreters of the Qur'ān, except for Bint al-Shati (in the twentieth century), who wrote a commentary on some chapters of the Qur'ān, but even that fact is little known in the wider academic public. Therefore a universal message and principle from the first words of revelation, "Read in the name of your Lord...," turned into a privilege of men who ruled the intellectual scene, in sharp contrast to the Prophet's lifetime, when women were considered equal intellectual partners.

Even today when scholars speak about the "Golden Age" of Islam, or the age of the ʿAbbāsid caliphate, the question of female education is most often missed. Researchers point out how, in ʿAbbāsid society, women were conspicuous for their absence from all arenas of the community's central affairs. In the records related to this period, they are not described as active participants in cultural life. As far as it is known, women were not enrolled in the first university, al-Azhar in Cairo, in the tenth century, nor in the first major school, Niẓāmīyah in Baghdad, in the eleventh century, and they were not involved in many other academic institutions in the Muslim world.

There are numerous explanations of the gradual decline of women's education (and rights) in the Muslim world. An interesting interpretation of the erosion of women's rights, and, therefore, educational rights, has been given by a prominent Bosnian Islamic scholar, Enes Karić. Karić believes that women were deprived of their rights when Muslims deviated from the idea of true Islam and attached themselves to *taqlīd,* or blind imitation of old and ineffective models of thought. When Muslim men were directing their actions and behavior according to the Prophet's example, they had a positive attitude toward women. However, when they stepped away from that ideal, their attitude toward women became negative. Historically, adherence to *taqlīd* has meant the silencing of the possiblities of *ijtihād* (independent reasoning). Other explanations for negative attitudes toward women might include the subjection of religion to the traditions and cultures of the conquered territories and the patriarchal nature of most of these societies. Such policies and conservative interpretations resulted in high rates of illiteracy among women historically.

Apart from these internal factors, there are external factors that contributed to massive exclusion of women from education. The main external factor that acted in further detriment of women's rights in the Muslim world is colonialism. This widespread phenomenon had different consequences in various Muslim countries, from Algiers to India, with a unique imprint on the state of women's rights. It either strengthened the already existing patriarchal structures or imposed First World models on differing traditions and cultures. In the first case, European colonialism furthered the marginalization of women from the public sphere, and thus women in many Islamic societies were deprived of educational opportunities. The effects of European colonial policies in general were highly negative regarding the education of women, because these policies were primarily built on the notion of the superiority of Western "enlightened" values in comparison to the values of the native cultures. Education that promoted such an attitude provoked a sharp reaction on the other side. The ignorant or hostile attitude toward some Muslim practices, such as veiling, often resulted in middle- and lower-class Muslim families keeping their daughters out of state-sponsored educational institutions. On the other hand, the openness toward women studying

European educational subjects was reflected in the practices of some members of the upper classes, who experienced benefits from the economic and political presence of the West, and therefore usually accepted colonial policies. Upper-class families also employed European educators for their daughters to teach them privately, because the majority of Muslim parents (regardless of class) were still reluctant to entrust their daughters to missionary schools which were, among other things, established for the purpose of converting pupils to Christianity.

In the discourse on women in the Islamic world under colonial domination, modernist Islamic scholars (*ʿulamāʾ*) played an important rule in advocating women's education, particularly because they saw the impending need for activation of this question. Among the most influential were Jamāl al-Dīn al-Afghānī and Muḥammad ʿAbduh in Egypt. Both drew attention to the importance of education for both sexes. Many schools for girls were established throughout the country under their initiatives. ʿAbduh's revivalist ideas about restoring an "original" Islam and authentic "indigenous" culture, the aquisition of modern sciences, adaptation to the modern world, and revival of the early Islamic tradition of education for both sexes had an enormous influence in Egypt, Iran, and Turkey, as well as in other parts of the Islamic world. Apart from the Islamic world, ʿAbduh's influence at the beginning of the twentieth century was felt even in countries which were farther from the main Islamic centers and closer to the capital cities of European political power, such as Bosnia. The Bosnian Islamic community chief and scholar Džemaludin Čaušević, echoing some of ʿAbduh's major ideas, advocated educational reforms and stressed the importance of women's education. He managed to implement reforms which are still felt today, including in modernized *madrasah* curricula, prestigious higher Islamic educational institutions, and the significant rate of female enrollment in Islamic educational institutions at all levels.

Apart from the combined efforts of modernist *ʿulamāʾ*, liberal intellectuals, and certain goverment policies in social and political developments, feminist discourses and movements contributed to fundamental changes in many Arab countries, improving women's intellectual and social life in colonized Muslim countries. Hudā Shaʿrāwī, the most famous Arab feminist, started her movement in Egypt in 1919, impacting other Arab countries in the 1930s and 1940s in terms of spreading feminist networks. This legacy is kept alive today by feminists such as Fatima Mernissi, Leila Ahmed, Alya Baffoun, Riffat Hassan, and many others.

When it comes to modern religious discourse, Muḥammad al-Ghazālī was probably the most revolutionary in addressing women's concerns. His ideas are shared by other contemporary influential *ʿulamāʾ*, including Yūsuf al-Qaraḍāwī, Ḥasan al-Turābī, and others. While the *ʿulamāʾ* can sometimes include prominent women thinkers, common and current practice shows that the vast majority of the *ʿulamāʾ* are still males.

Even after the collapse of the colonialist project, the question of women's education remained in the political movements and relations after World War II. State policies of some countries (e.g., Turkey) emphasized women's education as part of a greater secularist project. State ideologies dictated the course of women's education in many countries of the Middle East. Still, it remains to be seen how women's education is going to be developed in these countries after the Arab Spring.

Significant developments in the Muslim world concerning women's education were affected by other factors as well, such as international discourses on women, particularly those coming from activities of the United Nations. In the contemporary era the effects of globalization, religious reformations, secularization, and mass communication have resulted in the emergence of many Muslim women possessing both Eastern and Western education establishing themselves as scholars of Islam. They are making critical contributions toward a new legacy of quality scholarship that is rethinking the intricate relationships of Islam, women, and education.

The most dramatic increase in women's participation in education occured in higher education but is still concentrated in fields such as literature, the humanities, and the social sciences. For instance, in universities in Saudi Arabia, female students account for more than half the total student population, while at universities in the United Arab Emirates the female population is approaching 80 percent. Certain Arab women have achieved outstanding results in the fields of engineering and science, including, in October 2012, the Saudi scholar Dr. Hayat al-Sindi, who was appointed as a goodwill ambassador for UNESCO because of her contribution to the development of science, technology, and engineering in the Middle East.

Despite these efforts in the contemporary Muslim world, Arab Human Development Reports indicate that the Arab region still has one of the highest rates of female illiteracy (as much as one-half, compared to only one-third among males). In some countries Muslim women face restrictions in accessing education, although these restrictions differ greatly from one region to another. Arabic-speaking countries also generally have the highest percentage of primary-age girls who are not enrolled in schools when compared to global statistics. Girls are less likely to have access to education than boys, rural children have fewer chances to be educated than those living in urban areas, and class divisions are still influential factors in obtaining education. It also needs to be borne in mind that persisting wars and Western imperialistic ambitions in the Middle East directly and indirectly negatively affect sustainable efforts in developing women's education. Any reasonable initiative toward improvement of women's education in very diverse Muslim societies must therefore be aware of the deep political and social factors behind it, and not just the religious ones.

BIBLIOGRAPHY

Ahmed, Leila. *Women and Gender in Islam: Historical Roots of a Modern Debate.* New Haven, Conn.: Yale University Press, 1992.

"Arab Knowledge Report 2009." http://www.mbrfoundation.ae/English/Documents/AKR-2009-En/AKR-English.pdf.

Hawwal, Sawsan Fahd al-. *The Woman in Islam.* Translated by Ibrahim Abu Shakra. Beirut: Dār al-ʿUlūm al-ʿArabīyah, 2006.

Hefner, Robert W., and Muhammad Qasim Zaman. *Schooling Islam: The Culture and Politics of Modern Muslim Education.* Princeton, N.J.: Princeton University Press, 2007.

Jawad, Haifaa A. *The Rights of Women in Islam: An Authentic Approach.* New York: St. Martin's Press, 1998.

Karić, Enes. "Muslim Women Enslaved by Muslim Men!" *The New Teacher* (*Novi Muallim*) 48 (2011).

Marzouqi, Ibrahim Abdulla al-. *Human Rights in Islamic Law.* Abu Dhabi: no publisher, 2001.

Osman, Fathi. *Muslim Women in the Family and the Society.* Kuala Lumpur, Malaysia: SIS Forum Berhad, 1996.

Schimmel, Annemarie. *My Soul Is a Woman: The Feminine in Islam.* Translated by Susan H. Ray. New York: Continuum, 1997.

Šiljak, Zilka. *Women, Religion and Politics: Impact Analysis of Interpretative Religious Heritage of Judaism, Christianity and Islam on the Engagement of Women in Public Life and Politics in Bosnia and Herzegovina.* Translated by Đermana Šeta and Aida Spahić. Sarajevo: International Multireligous Intercultural Centre IMIC Zajedno, 2010.

"The Arab Human Development Report 2005: Towards the Rise of Women in the Arab World." http://www.arab-hdr.org/publications/other/ahdr/ahdr2005e.pdf.

Zaman, Muhammad Qasim. *The Ulama in Contemporary Islam: Custodians of Change*. Princeton, N.J.: Princeton University Press, 2002.

Zilfi, Madeline C. *Women in the Ottoman Empire: Middle Eastern Women in the Early Modern Era*. Leiden, Netherlands, and New York: E. J. Brill, 1997.

Dina Sijamhodžić-Nadarević

Educational Reform

As the world's Muslim population is expected to increase by about thirty-five percent by 2030, there is a growing demand for a more transparent interpretation of Islam's views on various issues, including education and women. Prior to the rise of Islam in seventh-century Arabia, the people of that region lived in a patriarchal society. Islam improved the status of women predominantly by emphasizing education. In Arabic the word for education is encapsulated in the three terms *ta'līm* (to know, be aware, perceive, learn), *tarbiyah* (to increase, grow, rear), and *ta'dīb* (to be cultured, refined, well-mannered). The importance of education has been highlighted numerous times in the Qur'ān; those verses that deal with education and knowledge are consistently gender-neutral. In the Qur'ān, the Prophet Muḥammad's first interaction with the divine world is seen as a declaration against illiteracy: "Read in the name of your Lord Who created. He created man from a clot. Read and your Lord is Most Honorable, Who taught (to write) with the pen, Taught man what he knew not (96:1–5).

In addition to the Qur'ān, the Prophet Muḥammad stated that seeking knowledge is an absolute requirement for every Muslim. One of Muḥammad's more famous quotes states that one must acquire knowledge even if it means traveling to China, which was considered the farthest country at the time. Muḥammad urged his followers to seek knowledge from the cradle to the grave, which would later constitute the basis of Islamic epistemology that focused on knowledge, reason, and enquiry. Muḥammad's son-in-law and cousin, 'Alī bin Abī Ṭalīb—considered to be the first imam among Shī'ī Muslims—maintained that knowledge resuscitates the soul, clarifies the mind, and is fatal for ignorance.

Educational Institutions. Muslim communities have experienced different educational institutions' including the *maktab* (writing school), the *halgha* (circle school), the *masjid* (mosque school), and the *madrasah* (school of public instruction, pl. *madāris*). From the onset of Islam the *masjid* (mosque) has taken center stage in educational activities. It was around the eleventh century that a new institution of higher learning known as the *madrasah* emerged. Before this the *masjid-khān*, a mosque with an inn, was a popular institution for education in Baghdad. The establishment of more than three thousand of these complexes by the tenth-century Baghdad governor and philanthropist Badr ibn Ḥasanawayh al-Kurdī helped with the expansion of education in the Muslim world. This was while the Iranian scholar and vizier of the Seljuq Empire Niẓām al-Mulk, often thought of as the father of the Islamic public education system, successfully established a vast network of *madāris* more than nine hundred years ago.

While for centuries Islamic universities were ahead of Western educational institutions, European imperialism had a detrimental impact on Islamic education. The new wave of colonialism introduced a modern system of education that aspired to replace the role of Muslim educational institutions. The new schools introduced by the Europeans educated only the elite by means of secular methods, while the poor were either left to their own devices or driven toward religious education.

Education, Islam, and Women. Muslim women's education before the pre-modern era is either defined by the Qur'ān and the examples set by the Prophet Muḥammad and his companions, or social histories which provide evidence from chronicles and biographical dictionaries that reconstruct the role played by women in various educational realms. For instance Muḥammad referred to education as the best "ornament of a woman" and encouraged women to be present in the mosque alongside the men. The knowledge and social responsibilities of the Prophet's wife Khadījah and his daughter Fāṭimah can also be perceived as sources of inspiration for Muslim women. Khadījah was an affluent businesswoman, while Fāṭimah's extensive knowledge, which was evident in her sermons, prompted some Muslims to turn to her for answers on religious issues.

Throughout Islamic history Muslim women also played a significant role in the foundation of countless educational institutions. In the twelfth and thirteenth centuries, for example, 26 of the 160 mosques and schools (*madāris*) in Damascus alone were founded by women. The acquisition of academic qualifications as scholars and teachers by women was not unheard of either. By the end of the Mamlūk period in the fourteenth century, it was hard to find a woman who did not have a teaching license.

Aisha Bewley offers historical sources indicating that, up until three hundred years ago, Muslim women were active in various aspects of life. Throughout Islamic history Muslim women established themselves as scholars, politicians, businesswomen, jurists, and doctors. Examples of Muslim women's success stories include Fāṭimah al-Firhi, who founded the first university in 859 in Morocco; Radiyya bint Iltutmish, who ruled the Delhi Sultanate in India in 1236; and Umm Darda, a Syrian scholar who taught imams and jurists along with the fifth Umayyad caliph, who ruled from Spain to India. In Muslim historical texts the names of some eight thousand women scholars have been documented as jurists, intellectuals, artists, and philosophers.

Bewley blames colonialism as the main reason behind the decline in women's rights, including education, in the Muslim world. European imperialists' presumed monopoly on civilization led to their justification of colonial conquests in the name of defending women's rights. Edward Said maintains that the plea of emancipating Muslim women from Muslim patriarchy had a deeper political motive, like occupying distant lands. Consequently, state-run schools became proxies for the implementation of colonial policy. In her book, *Women and Gender in Islam*, Leila Ahmed argues that, despite the growth in enrollment, girls were denied places in classrooms. The placement of tuition in secondary schools also proved to be a hindrance to girls' education in Muslim-majority states.

While the educational gender gap in Islamic countries has been mostly associated with colonialism, a different factor contributing to this issue can be attributed to Muslim rulers who created new armies and schools in the hope of warding off Western colonialism. This gave rise to anticolonialist and nationalist movements that reversed some of the advances made in women's rights, including education. With the rise of nation-states in the Muslim world and the reemergence of questions relating to women's role in society, educational changes brought on by colonialists that were of a vocational and instrumentalist nature engaged in a head-on collision with Islamic education that focused on altruism and character development. This tension allowed breathing room for postcolonialist secular and socialist governments to centralize education. State-run schools, embodying a chaotic amalgamation of different educational philosophies, came to breed a contemporary form of patriarchy in Muslim countries.

In an effort to reclaim their voice, the world has witnessed the reemergence of educated Muslim women who promote Islamic feminism and support women's rights through Islamic discourse and persuasively repudiate sexist interpretations of the Qur'ān and Islamic law. In her book, *Paradise Beneath Her Feet*, Isobel Coleman journeys through the greater Middle East to reveal how Muslim activists are pushing for reform and working within Islamic principles to create economic, political, and educational opportunities for women.

BIBLIOGRAPHY

Abbasi-Shavazi, Mohammad Jalal, and Fatemeh Torabi. "Women's Education and Fertility in Islamic Countries." In *Population Dynamics in Muslim Countries: Assembling the Jigsaw*, edited by Hans Groth and Alfonso Sousa-Poza, pp. 43–62. Heidelberg, Germany, and New York: Springer, 2012. http://www.springerlink.com/content/v1w424t0816l9152/abstract/.

Ahmad, Leila. *Women and Gender in Islam: Historical Roots of a Modern Debate*. New Haven, Conn.: Yale University Press, 1992.

Alkanderi, Letafeh. "Exploring Education in Islam: Al-Ghazali's Model of the Master-Pupil Relationship Applied to Educational Relationships Within The Islamic Family." Unpublished doctoral thesis. Pennsylvania State University, 2001.

Anzar, Uzma. "Islamic Education: A Brief History of Madrassas with Comments on Curricula and Current Pedagogical Practices." Paper presented at the International Conference on Curricula, Textbooks, and Pedagogical Practice, and the Promotion of Peace and Respect for Diversity. Washington, D.C.: The World Bank, 2006.

Bewley, Aisha Abdurrahman. *Islam: The Empowering of Women*. 2d ed. London: Ta-Ha Publishers, 1999.

Coleman, Isobel. *Paradise Beneath Her Feet: How Women Are Transforming the Middle East*. New York: Random House, 2010.

Hafez, Rania. "Islamic Principles of Education." University of East London, 2011. http://www.philosophy-of-education.org/uploads/papers2011/Hafez.pdf.

Halstead, J. Mark. "An Islamic Concept of Education." *Comparative Education* 40, no. 4 (2004): 517–529.

Hasan, M. M. "The Orientalization of Gender." *The American Journal of Islamic Social Sciences* 22, no. 4 (2005): 26–56.

Khamis, Muhamad Hafiz, and Mohamad Johdi Salleh. "The Philosophy and Objectives of Education in Islam," February 12, 2012. http://irep.iium.edu.my/11677/.

Makdisi, George. *Rise of Colleges: Institutions of Learning in Islam and the West*. Edinburgh: Edinburgh University Press, 1981.

Said, Edward. *Culture and Imperialism*. New York: Alfred A. Knopf, 1993.

Salleh, Mohamad Johdi. "The Integrated Islamic Education: Principles and Needs for Thematic Approaches," November 2009. http://irep.iium.edu.my/11676/.

Salleh, Mohamad Johdi. "The Principles of Education in Islam." Paper presented at the International Seminar on Philosophy of Education and Islamic Civilisation, Institute of Education. International Islamic University Malaysia (IIUM), 2008.

Sayeed, Asma. "Muslim Women's Religious Education in Early and Classical Islam." *Religion Compass* 5, no. 3 (March 1, 2011): 94–103.

Shakir, M. H., trans. *The Qur'an in Translation*. 10th ed. New York: Tahrike Tarsile Qur'an, 1999.

SOUDEH OLADI

WOMEN'S RELIGIOUS EDUCATION

Historically, women in Muslim-majority countries have had limited access to religious education in comparison to their male counterparts. Nonetheless, women religious scholars have emerged through private religious education and, more recently, through state-sponsored programs.

Mohammad Akram Nadwi, in his study of women *ḥadīth* scholars, *Al-Muḥaddithāt*, observes that during Islam's formative period "women scholars are not only great in number but also great in prominence, great in their authority. Men go to them to learn, and doing so is normal" (Nadwi, 2007). Nadwi records eight thousand *muḥaddithāt* from the first to fifteenth centuries of Islam. In addition to women *muḥaddithāt*, female mystics, such as Rābiʿa al-ʿAdawīyah (d. c. 801) and Fāṭima of Nīshāpūr (d. 849), hold notable places in the history of women's religious education. Rābiʿa is said to have had male disciples such as jurist Sufyān al-Thawrī (d. 777) and Fāṭima was revered by Dhū l-Nūn l-Miṣrī, who regarded her as his teacher and a saint. Among modern Ṣūfī scholars, teachers, and leaders, Celmanur Sergut (b. 1952) of Turkey is a noteworthy figure who has many male and female students and followers both inside and outside of Turkey

Discrete periods and places are also marked by the prominence of women in religious education. These include the Sokoto Caliphate in eighteenth-century northern Nigeria, where family context and connection helped to shape women's religious education. The Caliphate, founded by Usman dan Fodio (1754–1817), boasted a number of female scholars, educators, and leaders, of which Nana Asmaʾu (1793–1864) is the best known. As an educator and scholar she "was put in charge of the educational system with significant consequences for the institutions of religious learning for women" (Fazaeli and Künkler, 3). Asmaʾu's method of educating rural women of different ages through memorization of her composed verses was groundbreaking in terms of a new educational system. Asmaʾu was also a writer who left behind sixty written works in three different languages.

The educational reforms undertaken by the Hui Muslim population of central China in the sixteenth and seventeenth centuries "offered opportunities for women to gain more religious knowledge and also to become educators themselves." Cultural and religious segregation meant that educated and devout women "were called upon to take the place of men as teachers of girls and women" (Jaschok, 2012, p. 41). Women *ahong*s emerged as educated and ordained religious leaders who reside in mosques and "are in charge of religious affairs, education, the training of *hailifan* (studying to become *ahong*), and of general guidance of women in their "*fang*" (Jaschok, 2012, p. 42).

Women's religious education in Iran has also had a long history. According to Rostami-Kolayi (60–61), royal women were privately trained in Qurʾānic studies, reading, writing, calligraphy, and Persian grammar. One prominent example was the Safavid princess Pari Khan Khanum, the daughter of Shah Tahmasp, who was reported to have mastered Islamic law, jurisprudence, and writing poetry, in addition to being a patron to poets. The women of the Qajar dynasty (1796–1925) were also privately educated. For example, in the 1850s, Shukuh Sultaneh, the mother of Muzaffar al-Din Shah (r. 1896–1907), hired a *mullābājī* (female religious instructor) named Khadijeh to instruct her daughters.

In more recent history, women in Muslim-majority countries have had limited access to religious education. Consequently, few women in contemporary Muslim-majority contexts have reached a level of religious authority on a par with that of their male counterparts. However, this near monopoly of male religious leadership has been shifting gradually in the last thirty years to include women religious leaders who work as preachers, judges, teachers, and *mujtahid*s. This shift is, in large part, due to state-funded programs designed to improve women's access to religious education and training in religious authority as a way of meeting societal demands.

On 10 June 2008, the Grand Mufti of Syria, Shaykh Ahmed Hassoun, stated that *shuyūkh* who held teacher positions were to be prepared to become *muftī*s with the authority to issue Islamic legal and religious opinions and rulings, a role previously generally monopolized by men. Dilek Zaptcioglu has found that three women were certified as *muftī*s (or *muftīyahs)* at the local Islamic faculty in Hyderabad, to form the first Indian all-female *dār al-iftāʾ* (*fatwā* council). Zaptcioglu also notes the certification of women in Turkey by the Diyanet as assistant *muftis*. In a project run by the Moroccan Ministry of Habous (Religious Endowments), a number of women received training to be female religious counsellors (*mourchidat*) who were to be assigned to mosques around the country to respond to religious enquiries. The Iranian *mujtahida* Noṣrat Amīn (1886–1983) founded an all-girls Islamic high school (Dabirestan-e Dokhtaran-e Amin), and one of the first all-female seminaries in the Shīʿī world, called Maktabe Fatimah, in 1965 in Isfahan. Zohreh Ṣefātī (b. 1953), another leading *mujtahida*, co-founded Maktab-e Tawhid, an all-female seminary, in Qom, Iran in 1971. Maktab-e Tawhid was refashioned in the mid-1980s into Jamaʾat al-Zahra, a state-funded women's seminary that boasts more than sixteen thousand female students.

Not all recent advancements in female religious education are a result of state programs. On the Island of Java, for instance, a strong tradition of women preachers has emerged without state aid. They direct prayer circles, write *tafsīrs* (Qurʾānic commentaries), and are leading the campaign to reform *pesantren* (Islamic boarding schools) curriculum for a more egalitarian reading of the religious texts. Women on Java have served as judges in Islamic family courts since 1977.

Despite these various advances, contemporary sociolegal and political barriers continue to stunt and prohibit the growth of women's religious education in Muslim majority countries. The promise of women's religious education observed in early forms of Muslim community threatens to remain unfulfilled because of the influence of highly conservative regimes, such as the Taliban, whose interpretations of the faith, unmoored from text and history, mistakenly invoke cultural norms to justify withholding the right to education to which all Muslim women are both legally and religiously entitled.

BIBLIOGRAPHY

Boyd, Jean. "Jihad: Sub-Saharan Africa: West Africa." In *Encyclopedia of Women & Islamic Cultures: Family, Law and Politics*, Vol. II, edited by Joseph Suad and Afsaneh Najmabadi, pp. 327–330. Leiden, Netherlands: E. J. Brill, 2005.

Fazaeli, Roja, and Mirjam Künkler. *Of alimat, vaizes and mujtahidas. Forgotten Histories and New State Initiatives*, n.p.

Fazaeli, Roja, and Mirjam Künkler. "Training Female ulama in Jama'at al-Zahra: New Opportunities for Old Role Models?" In *Knowledge and Authority within the Hawza*, edited by Robert Gleave. Forthcoming.

Hermansen, Marcia. "Sufi Orders and Movements: Turkey, South Asia, Central Asia, Afghanistan, Iran, the Caucasus, the Arab East." In *Encyclopedia of Women & Islamic Cultures: Family, Law and Politics*, Vol. II, edited by Joseph Suad and Afsaneh Najmabadi, pp. 766–770. Leiden, Netherlands: E. J. Brill, 2005.

ICIP (International Center for Islam and Pluralism). *The Perception of* Pesantren *Communities in West Java. Towards Secularism, Pluralism and Liberalism*. A Research Report. September 2005–October 2005.

Jaschok, Maria. "Female *Ahong* and Women's Mosques in China." In *Women, Leadership and Mosques*, edited by in Masooda Bano and Hilary Kalmbach, pp. 37–51. Leiden: Netherlands: E. J. Brill, 2012.

Kalmbach, Hilary. "Introduction: Islamic Authority and the Study of Female Religious Leaders." In *Women, Leadership and Mosques*, edited by Masooda Bano and Hilary Kalmbach, pp. 1–31. Leiden, Netherlands: E. J. Brill, 2012.

Khatib, Line. *Islamic Revivalism in Syria: the Rise and Fall of Ba'thist Secularism*. Abingdon, U.K.: Routledge, 2011.

Künkler, Mirjam, and Roja Fazaeli. "Women, Leadership and Mosques: Changes in Contemporary Islamic Authority." In *Women, Leadership and Mosques: Changes in Contemporary Islamic Identity*, edited by Masooda Bano and Hilary Kalmbach, pp. 127–161. Leiden, Netherlands: E. J. Brill, 2012.

Lancaster, John. "In India, Ruling for Women, by Women, Muslims Turn to Female Scholars on Varied Matters of Faith and Femininity." *Washington Post Foreign Service* (5 October 2003): A28. [http://www.onlinewomeninpolitics.org/archives/03_1005_in_wid.htm].

Nadwi, Mohammad Akram. *Al-Muhaddithat: The Women Scholars in Islam*. Oxford/London: Interface Publications, 2007.

Nadwi, Mohammad Akram. "*al-Muhaddithat:* Notes for a talk on the women scholars of *ḥadīth*." [http://www.interfacepublications.com/images/pdf/AKRAM_Article2.pdf].

Rostami-Kolayi, Jasamin. "Origins of Iran's Modern Girls' Schools: From Private/National to Public/State." *Journal of Middle East Women's Studies* 4, no. 3 (Fall 2008): 60–61.

Sargut, Cemalnor. [http://www.cemalnur.org/contents/detail/cemalnur-sargut-biography/736].

van Doorn-Harder, Pieternella. *Women Shaping Islam: Indonesian Women Reading the Qur'an*. Champaign, IL: University of Illinois Press, 2006.

Zaptcioglu, Dilek. "Women Issuing Fatwas." [http://www.qantara.de/webcom/show_article.php/_c-478/_nr-138/i.html].

ROJA FAZAELI

EGYPT. Women have contributed to Egyptian history over the centuries, serving, among other things, as leaders, scholars, merchants, literary figures, educators, and labor organizers. In the modern era, women have been important to Egyptian history in two critical ways. Debates about women have shaped both secular and Islamic narratives about the origins of the Egyptian people, the roots of their history, and their place in the modern world. Women have also actively participated in creating the institutions and organizations through which the modern nation-state emerged and on which it continues to depend

The Nineteenth-Century Turn. State-sponsored and private educational projects inaugurated across the nineteenth century produced a class of literate, elite Egyptians for whom "the woman question" and the modern experience were almost synonymous. The elite women who graduated from khedival schools ca. 1900 slowly joined the debate, and they translated their exposure to both traditional and Western educational curricula into employment in Egypt's emerging educational system. Nabawīyya Mūsā (1886–1951) and Malik Hifnī Nassif (1886–1918), also known by her pseudonym Bahithat al-Badiyya, are both examples of women who used the schoolroom to advocate for continued education for women and to break free from traditional gender expectations. Some educated, elite women founded journals targeted at women like them. A nascent women's press addressed topics such as the domestic sciences, history, and literature, while advancing causes such as the importance of women's education and women's right to companionate marriage. Women also used their journals to circulate stories about praiseworthy women from the past. Biographies of great women from Islamic as well as European history provided object lessons in morals and behavior, while at the same time discussing the relationship of Egypt's present to its history.

Elite women in turn-of-the-twentieth-century Egypt were typically also members of a burgeoning civil society, participating in an increasing number of associations designed to better the lot of the emerging Egyptian nation. The Society of Compassion for Children (1908), the Mohammed ʿAli Dispensary (1909), and the Society for Women's Education (1910) are just a few of the societies opened by elite women and aimed at the betterment of women of all classes.

In such capacities, elite women joined ranks with male Egyptian intellectuals for whom "the woman question" was part and parcel of state building and anticolonial projects. After the British occupation in 1882, an active and growing press took up the discussion of topics related to women as a means of responding to British critiques of Egyptian society. In debates among themselves and in conversation with women, men were thus participants in the same kinds of conversations that elite women were undertaking. The most famous of these ranks was the lawyer and intellectual Qāsim Amīn (1865–1908). His many journal articles and his two published books, *Tahrīr al-mar'ah* (The Liberation of Women, 1899) and *al-Mar'a al-jadidah* (The New Woman, 1901) inaugurated a series of debates that harnessed women to the nationalist project. Amin argued that Egypt would neither modernize nor be free of the British until women were liberated from traditional customs such as face veiling and seclusion. The best known of Amin's critics, Mohammed Tala'at Harb (1867–1941), while agreeing that the reform of Egyptian society would hasten the end of the occupation, parted ways with Amin over the reforms best suited to Egypt and over the models that women should emulate. Harb encouraged an emulation of the Islamic past, and argued that modeling the behavior of women from early Islamic history would steer Egyptians back to their roots.

A crucial by-product of these debates was the emergence over the first decade of the twentieth century of the idea that the emerging Egyptian nation-state was an entity that was best embodied in female form. "Lady Egypt," or "Mother Egypt" as she was sometimes called, represented ongoing debates about Egyptian womanhood. Egypt in feminine guise was a rallying symbol for the aspirations a growing number of male and female nationalists who sought to liberate Egypt from the British. The most high-profile and enduring representation from the revolutionary era was the statue of "Nahdet Misr" or "The Egyptian Renaissance" (1920) by Mahmud Mokhtar, featuring a peasant woman standing proudly next to the Sphinx.

Independence: 1919. Nationalist aspirations were put to work in the spring of 1919, by men and women alike. By mid-March of that year, shortly after the Wafd—a delegation of male politicians—had been exiled by the British for their demands to represent themselves at the post–World War I peace conferences, upper-class Cairene women organized and led what are referred to as the "ladies' demonstrations." Hundreds of women took to the streets, demanding independence. Two of the most distinguished and beloved figures of that revolution, Hoda Sha'arawi (1879–1947) and Safiyya Zaghlul (1876–1946), wife of the Wafd's leader Sa'ad Zaghlul, were instrumental in organizing and facilitating women's participation in the demonstrations. In June, 1920, elite and middle-class women created the Wafdist Women's Central Committee (WFCC). When male Wafdists were in exile, the WFCC worked behind the scenes and expanded the Wafd's power base. In the provinces, women of the traditional classes played central roles in boycotts on British-produced goods, and helped provide food and assistance to local militants engaged in sabotage against the British infrastructure.

After the Revolution ended, Egyptian men and women were split over the role that women would play in independent Egypt's body politic. During the demonstrations, elite women presented themselves both as kin to the male, nationalist leadership, and as members of the Egyptian nation itself. For some women, participation in the Revolution portended actual, political enfranchisement. Male Egyptian politicians were grateful for women's participation in the Revolution, but they did not enfranchise women in the constitution that was promulgated in 1923. The political aspirations of real women seemed to clash with the symbolism of "Lady Egypt," who was a stand-in both for the nation and for the idea that women best contributed to that nation from the home.

The Emergence of an Egyptian Women's Liberation Movement. In March, 1923, a handful of WFCC members translated their exclusion from the political realm into the creation of a new entity, the Egyptian Feminist Union (EFU). The EFU represented the continuity of women's political activism and aspirations. The EFU's continued affiliation with the International Alliance of Women (IAW) and participation in its international conferences illustrates their commitment to changing women's position in Egyptian society (as did their symbolic removal of their face veils in the spring of 1923). The EFU's distancing of itself from its seminal alliance with the Wafd signaled its determination to gain women political rights. Over the course of the 1920s and 1930s, the EFU built a philanthropic network that was wholly independent of men, using their "House of the Woman" as a center from which to provide educational, medical, and vocational services. The EFU's philanthropic commitment did not mean an end to its determination to secure political participation for women. In addition to campaigning for suffrage, the EFU worked to hold the Egyptian state accountable to its commitments to universal education, economic development, and the expansion of social services. The EFU also worked to make marriage and divorce laws more equitable for both sexes. Regional issues were also on the Congress' agenda, in particular the struggle for Palestine. In 1944, Hoda Shaʿrawi hosted the Arab Women's Congress, the focus of which was women's suffrage.

Members of the EFU used magazines and participation in philanthropic organizations to popularize their missions. By shifting the language of some of their periodicals from French to Arabic, by opening a branch of the society explicitly for younger and more middle-class women, and by opening increasing numbers of vocational workshops aimed at women of the urban and rural working poor, the organization expanded its base.

During the 1930s and the 1940s the EFU's efforts were joined by several new organizations, some with complementary agendas and others with divergent ones. Zaynab al-Ghazālī (1917–2005) left the EFU in 1935 to establish the Muslim Women's Society (MWS). Whereas the MWS occasionally cooperated with the EFU, al-Ghazali's new association was founded to protest what its leader saw as the EFU's efforts to establish the culture and civilization of Western women in the Arab and Islamic worlds. Al-Ghazali understood Islam to call for relative equality between men and women, and therefore sought to promote women's rights within the framework of religion. Whereas the EFU struggled for women's greater access to the public realm, the MWS extolled women's duties to their families. At the same time, however, the MWS promoted the training of women in the art of preaching (daʿwa) and founded "The Center for Preaching and Advice," which was linked with al-Azhar University.

Between the founding of the MWS and al-Ghazali's decision to link the organization with the Muslim Brotherhood in 1948 (henceforth the group was known as the Muslim Sisters), the group engaged in philanthropic activities that were not unlike those of the EFU. The EFU and the WMS were also united in their determination to expel British forces from Palestine. Although the two organizations parted ways over the frameworks in which they contextualized the feminist agenda, both groups worked to better the Egyptian social order.

The EFU also saw secular offshoots. In 1944, journalist Fatima Niʿmat Rashid opened the National Women's Party (NWP), the aim of which was the greater inclusion of Egypt's middle class. In 1945, Inji Aflatun (1924–1989) opened the left-leaning League of University and Institutes' Young Women, which linked women's issues to imperialism and decolonization. Durrīyah Shafiq (1908–1975) established the Bint al-Nil (Daughter of the Nile) Union (DNU) in 1948 to popularize women's rights and to include the Egyptian working and middle classes in its activities.

Like the EFU, each of these new secular organizations promoted a Western feminist agenda. Unlike the EFU, however, the new groups sought to expedite suffrage. Shafik and her fellow DNU members engaged in increasingly radical confrontations with the state. In 1951, Shafik organized a sit-in for women's suffrage. She organized women's participation in the demonstrations that led to the July Revolution of 1952. That year, Shafik also delivered her White Paper on the Rights of Egyptian Women to Parliament, insisting that the new military regime extend suffrage to all Egyptian citizens.

Women and the State: Nasser. After Gamal abdul Nasser (r. 1954–1970) consolidated his rule over Egypt, Shafik and several of her contemporaries waged a hunger strike for women's suffrage. The Nasser regime gave women the right to vote and to run for political office in 1956 and extended education and health-care services to an increasingly large number of Egyptians. Egypt (and the larger Arab world) had its first female parliamentarian, Rawya Attiya (1926–1997) in 1957.

Yet, just as the Nasser regime granted suffrage, it sought to curtail a growing movement in favor of women's rights by dismantling the EFU in 1956. Subsequently, that organization was renamed the Hoda Shaʿarawi Association, and its activities were redirected toward philanthropy. The Muslim Sisters were similarly banned in 1964. Nasser had al-Ghazali imprisoned in 1965 in a wave of arrests of the Muslim Brotherhood. Attempts by several female activists to create a national union were blocked by the state, and women's agendas that did not adhere to Nasser's brand of socialism therefore went underground. Some Egyptian women retained international ties, however, and remained active in global feminist organizations. Others such as Amina al- Saʿid (1914–1995) worked with the Nasser regime to promote women's education and employment. Al-Said also used the press to promote a brand of emancipatory discourse that was similar to Nasser's vision for the state. Women's literacy rates and employment percentages continued to increase over the course of the Nasser years, and Nasser linked the visibility of women in the schoolroom and the workplace with Egypt's postcolonial success.

Women and the State: Sadat Era. Anwar al-Sadat's administration (r. 1970–1981) allowed for the reemergence of women's demands and expanded once again the parameters for public discourse about women's issues. The Sadat years also witnessed the full fruition of Nasser's educational projects in the emergence of a new rank of well educated, professional women with new agendas for women's rights. Nawāl al-Saʿadāwī (b. 1931), a medical doctor, addressed Egyptian women's health needs, and turned her attention full force to the problems attendant to female genital cutting (FGC). She would also use her pen to address the victimization of women within the Egyptian social and familial orders. Al-Saʿdāwī began writing during the Nasser era and was a frequent critic of both the Sadat regime and that of his successor, Husni Mubarak (r. 1981–2011). Although heralded as a feminist in the West, she was often marginalized at home because of her taboo-breaking discussions of women's sexuality.

Journalist Safinaz Kazim (b. 1937) joined ranks with al-Ghazali who, after her release from prison in 1971, once again took up the training of female preachers and continued to call for the establishment of an Islamic state in Egypt. Kazim promoted the idea that women had the right to work, both in and outside the home, suggesting that it is the West, and not Islam, that promotes the idea that the home is women's proper place.

The Sadat administration made women's issues high-profile. The president's wife, Jehan al-Sadat (b. 1933), was an advocate of women's issues, including literacy and economic self-sufficiency. President Sadat promulgated a constitution guaranteeing a balance between women's private and public roles and duties. He set up a quota system whereby women would be guaranteed seats in Egypt's legislature. Sadat revised Egypt's personal status law in 1979 (known as Jehan's laws because of his wife's role in promoting them), giving women greater divorce and custody rights.

Sadat's administration also produced a host of conditions that would bring women back into the spotlight as objects of heated debate. The flooding of the public realm with professional women, increased crowding in urban areas, the increasingly high cost of living, and an emerging cultural conservatism combined to bring traditional forms of dress back in vogue. As the hijab became increasingly popular, debates about idealized womanhood intensified. Sadat's reinclusion of Islamists into acceptable public discourse and his increased attempts to appease their determination to include Islam in politics elevated "the woman question" to a position reminiscent that of the early twentieth century, and seemingly divided Egyptians over the relationship between women's clothing, public activities, and the state of the body politic.

Women and the State: Mubarak. The Mubarak regime saw the reemergence of organized women's movements. The Arab Women's Solidarity Movement (AWSA) emerged in 1985, headed by Nawāl al-Saʿadāwī. Though rooted in a leftist nationalist discourse, the movement shifted to a global feminist discourse in 1985 as the result of the Nairobi international Conference for Women. The organization worked for women's full participation in and integration into the political, economic, cultural, and social arenas of Arab society. AWSA members were critical both of the Mubarak regime and the increasingly conservative Islamist positions on women's issues. That year also saw the appearance of the Committee for the Defense of the Rights of Women and the Family, which succeeded, in limited measure, in challenging Mubarak's rescinding of Sadat's reformed personal-status laws. The 1980s also saw the establishment of the New Woman Group, an informal study group which, like the AWSA, insisted upon men and women's shared contributions to Arab society. Like earlier generations of women activists, the group worked to meet the health and educational needs of ordinary Egyptian women.

Mubarak's neo-liberal economic practices produced a growing gap between the rich and the poor and witnessed the inability of the state to keep up with the needs of its citizens. As nongovernmental organizations (NGOs) and nonprofit organizations (NPOs) and welfare societies of many sorts worked to fill in the gaps, women gained valuable experience organizing and facilitating a wide variety of services, building on the professional capacities in which they had served since the Nasser years. Under Mubarak, women remained active in labor unions and professional syndicates, where they gained important organizational skills. With the rise of independent dissent circles beginning at the turn of the twenty-first century, women's activities in such organizations were translated into foundational roles in the 6th of April Youth movement (2008), which supported strikes among industrial workers, and the January 25th movement of 2011, which brought the Mubarak regime to an end.

Under the Mubarak administration, the "revival phenomenon," which sought to bring Islam back into a central place in Egypt's public realm, witnessed the rise of a strong Islamic women's movement, known equally as the piety movement and the mosque movement. The movement encourages women to meet in mosques to study, listen, and train to be teachers and preachers to other women (*daʿwa*). The movement promotes the idea that women's strength is achieved through the cultivation of personal piety and not through activism or activities in the public realm. As in an earlier generation, the goals of the Islamic women's movement are seen as clashing with those of women who draw on Western models. In reality, both movements work for the empowerment of women, despite their different contexts and frames of reference.

The January 25, 2011 Revolution. In the eighteen days that witnessed uprisings against the Mubarak regime and in the aftermath of the revolution, during which Egyptians continue to work to forge a new body politic, women have emerged both as heroes of the revolution and as symbols of the nation's future. Asma'a Mahfouz (b. 1985) posted the video blog in support of the January 25, 2011 protests that are credited with bringing youth to the streets. Millions of unnamed young men and women from across Egypt's spectrum of political orientations and social classes took to the streets. Samira Ibrahim (b. 1987) squared off against the Supreme Council of Armed Forces (SCAF), which controlled Egypt until the presidential elections in June 2012, to challenge and condemn the military's use of virginity tests on the women it arrested during the 2011 uprisings. In the months following Mubarak's resignation, women were critical in organizing the strikes that pressured the SCAF to allow for elections and to oversee Egypt's full transition to democratic rule. But the small number of seats (8 out of 508, or 2%) women took in the new parliament has sadly led observers both in and outside of Egypt to draw parallels between Egyptian women's experience in 2011 and that of 1919. Also reminiscent of 1919 is the use of women as symbols of the Egyptian nation's essence, as well as its political struggles. A caricature from the Egyptian press from March, 2011, for example, has two women struggling to kill a serpent, the head of which is Husni Mubarak's. Each woman wears a national flag. One is unveiled and wearing trousers. The other sports a *galabiyya* and a hijab. The caricature seems to herald an enduring link between the triumph of the nation, Egypt's identity, and women's continued struggle to secure a place for themselves in a fully democratic body politic. Although the parliament was suspended over legal disputes that are currently being addressed by the constitutional court, the new president, Mohammed Mursi, decided to appoint a woman, Pakinam El-Sharkawi (professor of comparative politics at Cairo University) to be one of four assistants in his office. A few women also sit in the assembly that is currently drafting the constitution, on a board of advisors to the president, and on another advisory committee to the constitutional assembly. Such token representation does not send reassuring signals to the majority of women's organizations, so women's aspirations continue to motivate millions of Egyptian women to keep a close eye on the unfolding transitional political scene.

BIBLIOGRAPHY

Ahmed, Leila. *A Border Passage: From Cairo to America: A Woman's Journey* (New York: Penguin: 1999 and 2012). This is an autobiographical account of the author's experiences with the changes in Egypt over the course of the twentieth century. Ahmed pays particular attention to changes in women's position in Egyptian society and to the role of women in shaping public discourse about the nation.

Badran, Margot. *Feminists, Islam and Nation: Gender and the Making of Modern Egypt* (Princeton, N.J.: Princeton University Press, 1995). Badran's text represents a pioneering history of the Egyptian feminist movement through the 1940s. The text is based on a rich variety of Arabic, French, and English sources.

Badran, Margot. *Feminism in Islam: Secular and Religious Convergences* (Oxford: Oneworld Publications, 2009). *Feminism in Islam* is a collection of Badran's articles and lectures. The book covers Egyptian feminism from the turn of the twentieth century through the Mubarak regime and covers both Western and Islamic feminism.

Baron, Beth. *The Women's Awakening in Egypt: Culture, Society and the Press* (New Haven, Conn.: Yale University Press, 1994). Baron provides an historical account of women's journalistic, philanthropic, and organizational activities in the early decades of the twentieth century.

Baron, Beth. *Egypt as a Woman: Nationalism, Gender and Politics* (Berkeley and Los Angeles: University of California Press, 2005). Baron examines women's dual experiences as historical subjects and objects of debate in the years leading up to and immediately following the Egyptian Revolution of 1919.

Bier, Laura. *Revolutionary Womanhood: Feminisms, Modernity and the State in Nasser's Egypt* (Stanford, Calif.: Stanford University Press, 2011). This text is a pioneering account of women under Gamal Abdel Nasser's regime. Bier accounts for women's lived experiences under Nasser and for Nasser's spin on "the woman question."

Booth, Marilyn. *May Her Likes Be Multiplied: Biography and Gender Politics in Egypt* (Berkeley and Los Angeles: University of California Press, 2001). Booth provides an historical and literary account of male and female biographers of women in the early twentieth century.

Elsadda, Hoda, ed. *Women Pioneers in the 20th Century: Figures and Issues* (Cairo: Women and Memory Forum, 2000). Historical accounts of women in twentieth-century Egypt and of debates surrounding women's activities, edited by a founding member of the Cairo-based Women and Memory Forum.

Mahmoud, Saba. *Politics of Piety: The Islamic Revival and the Feminist Subject* (Princeton, N.J.: Princeton University Press, 2005). This text is an ethnographic account of the woman's mosque movement in 1990s Egypt.

Russell, Mona. *Creating the New Egyptian Woman: Consumerism, Education and National Identity, 1863–1922* (New York: Palgrave Macmillan, 2004). An historical account of the rise of women's education in nineteenth-century Egypt and the role of education in producing new generations of female nationalists and consumers.

Lisa Pollard

Environmental Activism. Unquestionably, activism among Muslim women in the twentieth and twenty-first centuries has centered on gender relations and women's rights. Yet a ten-year follow-up in 2005 to the women and environment section of the 1995 Beijing Platform of Action of the United Nations Conference on Women has shown that women all over the world still face a lack of decision-making power, little to no input on environmental policies and programs, and limited access to natural resources. Muslim women are particularly central stakeholders in the environment, as they manage scarce resources and their families suffer from environmental health problems due to, among other factors, lack of infrastructure, air and water pollution, ill-managed natural-resource extraction (oil in Nigeria, rock quarries in Palestine), and even the legacy of nuclear testing in Central Asia by the former Soviet Union.

Broadly conceived, environmental activism includes conscious lifestyle changes aimed at improving environmental conditions, raising public awareness of environmental issues through a variety of media, and forming grassroots, nongovernmental, and community-based organizations that can respond directly to local environmental crises. As with women's lives in historical texts, women's creative and subtle responses to ecological crises have gone largely unnoticed and undocumented. Despite these constraints, Muslim women at all levels of society have contributed to and developed theoretical, practical, and policy solutions to environmental issues.

Theological and Theoretical Support. Whether the prevailing Islamic worldview emphasizes God's transcendence or immanence, individuals are instructed to act moderately, justly, thankfully, and in good measure (*mīzān*) (Qurʾān 6:141, 7:31, 36:73, 38:26, 54:28, 55:8). In light of a perceived global environmental crisis, Muslim women have turned to their holy book and the traditions (*aḥādīth*) of the Prophet Muḥammad to inform, guide, and support their environmental activism. Muslim scholars were a vital part of the religion-and-ecology movement that began to develop in the 1980s and 1990s. They brought gender and human rights to the forefront of discussions on environmental issues, contributing to broader issues of ecological justice.

Nawal Ammar, whose recent work focuses on domestic violence in Muslim communities, contributed to early theological discussions of religion and ecology by calling for a retrieval of Islamic fundamentals before formulating a new theology. She, along with a number of other Muslim scholars, including Seyyed Hossein Nasr and Mawal Izzi Dien, outlined Islamic approaches to the ecological crisis by drawing on Qur'ānic notions of stewardship (*khalīfa*), trust (*amanah*), and oneness of God (*tawḥīd*), as well as on established legal regulations (*fiqh*, *sharīʿa*) regarding waste reduction, overconsumption, and equal exchange. Central to her argument that the oneness of God can be the basis of a "deep relational perspective on natural and social ecology" is that Muslims too must claim a share of responsibility for the current environmental crisis, address issues of disempowerment in their respective sociopolitical contexts, and reassess the ideological need to protect their culture from Western encroachment. Interested in an "action-oriented ethic toward the environment," Ammar calls attention to and encourages the practice of *ḥayā'*, or dignified reserve, a neglected economic and political principle that she sees as largely responsible for the gender disparity in the distribution of resources at the root of the ecological crisis.

The Pakistani ecofeminist Tahera Aftab has also turned her attention more recently toward broader issues of gender and policy development after writing specifically on women and ecology in the 1990s. With a clear link to ecofeminist conceptions of a strong relationship between women and the environment, Aftab outlines the intimate connection of degradation of gender and ecology in indigenous Muslim contexts. Yet Aftab avoids the theoretical problem of equating women with nature (and hence men with culture) by pointing to the concrete connection between policies that oppress women and subsequently destroy the environment. Drawing on historical South Asian sources from the twelfth to the eighteenth centuries, she finds Muslim women publically engaged with the local environment and its preservation. Aftab points directly to policies restricting women from actively participating in community life as the major factor in the environmental destruction of the following centuries.

Policy. As individuals, Muslim women have been professionally engaged with environmental issues since the 1960s and 1970s. However, it was not until the 1990s and the turn of the twenty-first century that a more persistent, organized environmental activism took hold. Environmentally active Muslim women are meeting some of the same challenges as such women all over the world. The following are examples of women who illustrate trends of combining professional disciplines with policy formation, community activism, and data collection of women's "gendered knowledge" of local environments.

Azizan Baharuddin approaches sustainable development, a term heavily laden with Western assumptions, as a path to de-imperialize colonialist legacies in Muslim lands and thought. As a professor at the University of Malaysia and a fellow at the Institute for Policy Research in Malaysia, Baharuddin sees one aspect of this legacy in the strict academic separation of the humanities, especially religion, from science. She exposes how both areas have suffered from this divide first by pointing to the disregard of Islamic principles and ideas in science, which renders it complicit in environmental degradation, and then by criticizing how religion is still primarily taught by *taqlīd* (imitation), which produces a quiescent fraction of its dynamic potential if coupled with other fields of knowledge. She determines that environmentally sound policy will emerge from truly interdisciplinary collaboration and scholarship.

The Hisaar Foundation in Pakistan is dedicated to providing water, food, and security and was cofounded by Simi Kamal, a Cambridge University–trained geographer. Kamal describes the Pakistani ethos as consisting of a weak sense of civic responsibility and a strong hands-off notion of philanthropy. Coupled with an attitude that environmental concerns are "technical" or "political" issues that are out of citizens' hands, this ethos has made organizing grass-roots activism a challenge. In response, the Hisaar Foundation directly engages women through its sponsorship of the Women and Water Network, which introduces the concept of gender and integrated water-resources management to both men and women in chapters throughout Pakistan. The Women and Water Network has, since 2010, networked with the Women's Parliamentary Caucus in hopes of ensuring better representation at the provincial and national levels.

One of the first in a burgeoning number of nongovernmental organizations in Iran, the Women's Society against Environmental Pollution, founded by Victoria Jamali and Mahlagha Mallah in 1995, has branches throughout the country educating political officials and women of all backgrounds about pollution and related issues of water and land conservation. Iranian women too face the global divide separating women's voices from government support and equitable policy. Massoumeh Ebtekar is perhaps the closest link to parliamentary support in Iran. A former head of Iran's Environmental Protection Organization (and a former vice president of the Republic of Iran), she is currently the president of the Center for Peace and the Environment, a nongovernmental organization focusing on the connections of war and peace, the environment, and spirituality.

Women's involvement in environmental nongovernmental organizations has been boosted by targeted funding from international organizations. In 2006 the Africa Muslim Environment Network was founded by the Alliance of Religions and Conservation with funding aid from the World Bank. Maimuna Mwidau was named secretary general to the Africa Muslim Environment Network, to lead in the organization's main objective of confronting poverty and environmental degradation in Muslim Africa by implementing projects with a commitment to *Sharīʿah* law, balancing women's and men's contributions to the projects, and promoting bottom-up resource allocation. Mwidau admits to varying opinions within the network, and its progress to date is unclear—an indication of the cultural complexities of their international backing, goals, and objectives.

Practical Activism. In many regions, women, as household managers, have inadvertently become activists by managing scarce and polluted resources. At this time, such online resources as Muslim environmentalist blogs are the best for learning about this type of local activism. Where lack of technology and limited literacy inhibit online access, the twofold result is resounding silence by these hidden activists and a lack of exchange of pertinent environmental and grassroots information. Green Prophet (http://greenprophet.com) is one important online resource reporting on environmental activism in the Middle East and North Africa region. Their writers repeatedly make connections between gender equity, human rights, and the environment, and give voice to otherwise silent stories. One such story highlights two Jordanian Bedouin women chosen by their community to attend a six-month course at Barefoot College in India to be trained in solar-energy technology in order to reduce a village's reliance on kerosene. Education has been a critical component in mobilizing action and transforming Muslim organizations.

Saudi Arabia has several examples of women leading environmental activism. Fatin Bundagji, a member of the Jeddah Chamber of Commerce and a former director of Women's Empowerment and Research, founded the environmental advocacy group Muwatana as a result of an initiative dedicated to restoring and protecting a beloved stretch of Jeddah coastline. Naqa'a Environmental Enterprise was founded by a team of young university women consciously fulfilling their Islamic duty to preserve the environment. They provide environmental-impact assessments and sustainability programs promoting green practices in business.

Environmental activism in the Muslim diaspora historically has been associated with community or religious institutions. In recent years, leading up to 2012, Muslim environmental organizations have proliferated in the United States and Europe, including, among others, the DC Green Muslims in Washington, D.C.; the Minnesota Ecological and Environmental Muslims; and Wisdom in Nature, located in London and Brighton. Similar Egyptian youth-led environmental organizations have focused on permaculture and urban agriculture, recycling, bicycle use over the use of automobiles, antinuclear campaigns, climate workshops, and sustainable green architecture. Though these groups maintain a high level of women's participation and leadership, gender is not their focus. Nonetheless, online blogs consolidating information on green Muslims worldwide effectively make the connection (see the blog "A World of Green Muslims").

Radio broadcasts, because they are technologically widely accessible and offer a format for limited literacy, are a popular medium in Muslim communities. Daniel Nilsson DeHanas's examination of the "Women's Hour" broadcast on London's Muslim Community Radio aims to show the sociological relationship between "religiously conservative Muslim women" and environmental advocacy. By using Islamic terminology and linking to Islamic practice such behavior changes as conserving energy, minimizing waste, and supporting ecologically friendly, fair-trade products, these women become agents of change through what DeHanas calls the "sacralization of environmental discourse" (p. 149). Although DeHanas observes that the Muslim environmental agenda is partially motivated as a diplomatic entry to broader cultural conversations, environmental agendas worldwide have shown that issues on these agendas are integrally connected to a host of other social and political concerns.

Considerations for the Future. DeHanas points out the "distinctly gendered" environmental message emerging from a framework of complementary gender roles. While obliged at times to make bargains with the patriarchy, Muslim women activists have added the environment to an already full agenda addressing gender disparities in education, civil rights, law, and physical and structural violence. They are challenging patriarchal interpretations of the Qur'ān that read women out of their roles as stewards (*khalīfa*) of the earth. And they have a multifarious approach to activism that draws theoretical support from Islam and ecofeminism, develops policy with scientific tools, and directly responds to water shortages or illnesses due to pollution with local and culturally specific knowledge. The overall consensus is that there continues to be a great need for strong leadership and access to information and training in order to increase women's participation in environmental advocacy, especially among rural, illiterate women, who are often the critical stakeholders in ecological degradation.

BIBLIOGRAPHY

Aftab, Tahera. "Text and Practice: Women and Nature in Islam." In *Women as Sacred Custodians of the Earth? Women, Spirituality, and the Environment*, edited by Alaine Low and Soraya Tremayne, pp. 141–158. Oxford: Berghahn Books, 2002.

Ammar, Nawal. "Ecofeminism in the Egyptian Context." *Civil Society* 20, no. 4 (Winter 2000): 1–7.

Ammar, Nawal. "An Islamic Response to the Manifest Ecological Crisis: Issues of Justice." In *Visions of New Earth: Religious Perspectives on Population, Consumption, and Ecology*, edited by Harold G. Coward and Daniel C. Maquire, pp. 131–146. Albany: State University of New York Press, 2000.

Coleman, Isabel. *Paradise beneath Her Feet: How Muslim Women Are Transforming the Middle East.* New York: Random House, 2010.

DeHanas, Daniel Nilsson. "Broadcasting Green: Grassroots Environmentalism on Muslim Women's Radio." *Sociological Review* 57, no. 2 (October 2009): 141–155.

Foltz, Richard, Fredrik Denny, and Azizan Baharuddin, eds. *Islam and Ecology: A Bestowed Trust.* Cambridge, Mass.: Center for the Study of World Religions, 2003.

Kassam, Zayn R., ed. *Women and Islam*. Santa Barbara, Calif.: Praeger, 2010. This book focuses generally on Muslim women's activism in social and national contexts, many of which intersect with environmental issues. One chapter addresses gendered epistemologies among Muslim women in Ethiopia and ecospirituality.

"A World of Green Muslims." http://aworldofgreenmuslims.wordpress.com.

MELINDA KROKUS

ESACK, FARID. (b. 1959), South African Muslim scholar, professor, author, and antiapartheid activist.

Professor Farid Esack is a South African Muslim and Islamic scholar who especially focuses on social justice issues. The experiences of growing up in a single-parent household and watching his mother struggle as she worked at a steam laundry to raise him and his five brothers would influence and form the social activism and liberal politics that he is known for today, the hallmarks of which are gender and racial equality. His stance against apartheid comes from his own background of having been relocated to a different neighborhood under the Group Areas Act (acts under the parliament of South Africa that assigned racial groups to separate residential and business sectors). His activism also led to the establishment of Positive Muslims, an organization that works with HIV positive Muslims in South Africa.

His scholarly talent was recognized from a young age. He joined the Tablīghī Jamāʿat—a staunchly pious international brotherhood—when he was nine years old. A year later he was teaching at a local Islamic school. The year he turned fifteen he received a scholarship to go to school in Karachi, Pakistan. He spent nine years in Karachi, becoming a certified Muslim cleric, earning a degree in Islamic theology and sociology, completing the Dārs-i-Niẓāmī (traditional Islamic studies program). He would leave South Africa again in 1990 for an additional five years to pursue his doctorate degree, earning his PhD at the University of Birmingham in Britain and conducting post-doctoral work at the Philosophisch-Theologische Hochschule Sankt Georgen, in Frankfurt am Main. He is currently a professor in the Study of Islam at the University of Johannesburg in Guateng, South Africa.

Esack's works focus on topics such as Islam, interfaith relations, gender, religion as it pertains to one's identity, and Qurʾānic hermeneutics. He has authored and published several journal articles and books, some of the most important of which are *On Being a Muslim: Finding a Religious Path in the World Today* and *The Qurʾan: A Short Introduction*. His current work is focused on Islam and AIDS, and he has produced a series of publications in this field.

Esack previously held office as a National Commissioner on Gender Equality, appointed by President Nelson Mandela. Esack's comprehensive approach to social justice led him to push for an end to all types of discrimination during South Africa's constitutional discussions, including against homosexuals. He has garnered recognition throughout the scholastic arena. He has held teaching positions at the University of the Western Cape, Gadjah Mada University, and Union Theological Seminary in New York. He was once a Distinguished Mason Fellow at the College of William & Mary. At Ohio's Xavier University he was recognized as the Best Professor in Ethics, Religion, and Society.

BIBLIOGRAPHY

Primary Works

On Being a Muslim: Finding a Religious Path in the World Today. Oxford: Oneworld, 1999.

The Qur'an: A Short Introduction. Oxford: Oneworld. 2002.

Secondary Works

Helen Suzman Foundation. "Profile of Farid Esack." http://www.hsf.org.za/resource-centre/focus/issues-11-20/issue-17-first-quarter-2000/profile-of-farid-esack/.

University of Johannesburg. Faculty profile of Farid Esack. http://www.uj.ac.za/EN/Faculties/humanities/researchcentres/cod/aboutus/Staff/Associates/Pages/ProfFaridEsack.aspx/.

EREN TATARI

ETHNICITY. The Qur'ān states that humankind has been separated into nations and tribes to "know one another" (49:13) and to "compete in goodness" (5:48). Muslims insist that commitment to Islam supplants ties of ethnicity, that is, the ways in which individuals and groups characterize themselves on the basis of shared language, culture, descent, place of origin, history—and today many would add gender. Yet from the first Muslim conquests in seventh-century Arabia, as Muslim armies spread out from the Arabian Peninsula to encounter peoples who neither spoke Arabic nor could claim Arab descent, ethnic concerns frequently surfaced.

Notions of ethnicity are cultural constructions. Arab identity, for example, suggests how historically and contextually diverse ethnic claims can be. Many Arabs assert that they are a "race," although for centuries populations have mixed and intermarried throughout the Arab world and beyond. The stylistic conventions of Muslim historiography often make it difficult to appreciate fully the implications of intermarriage for the crossing of ethnic boundaries. Thus, the famous Tangier-born traveler Ibn Baṭṭūṭah (1304–c. 1368) married and divorced repeatedly during his travels through North Africa, Andalusia, the Middle East, East Africa, Anatolia, Central Asia, South Asia, and China. Yet for the purposes of his writings and those of others, marriage was considered intensely private. His relationships with women, both wives and concubines, receive scant mention in his writings, and often only through reference to his children. Many of the marriages were evidently strategies to gain access to elite circles. Thus, in the past as the present, ethnic boundaries were permeable and situational and not part of a fixed hierarchy of ethnic distinctions.

The spread of mass higher education throughout the region since the mid-twentieth century contributed to widening opportunities for women as well as men. The greater access of women to education at all levels since the mid-twentieth century has significantly increased their public roles, sometimes accentuating and sometimes attenuating ethnic distinctions. The Sultanate of Oman and the neighboring United Arab Emirates offer examples of women "taking charge" by attenuating distinctions of ethnicity and origin. Throughout the 1980s, women's clothing in these countries indicated tribe and region. Since then, the black *'abāya* has erased such distinctions. This trend toward common dress in public is an aggregate of individual decisions, not an administrative directive or royal decree.

In North Africa, on the other hand, women's clothing—again an individual choice—was often used in the early twenty-first century to assert pride of origin. Some peoples of the region claim identity as Berbers or Arabs or both—claims based on linguistic and cultural characteristics. In Morocco, nearly half of the population speaks one of several related Berber languages, known collectively as Amāzaghiya. Most adult men, however, speak Arabic as a second language, although the spread of education is narrowing the linguistic gender gap. Since the mid-1990s, the three major Berber languages have been used on television in Morocco, and since 2005, a unified Berber language has been introduced in schools in Berber-speaking regions and on state television.

In the Berber highlands of Morocco and in Morocco's southern oases, women play an important role in preserving distinctly Berber notions of home and homeland. This is expressed through distinctive tattoos, textile motifs, clothing, pottery designs, poetry, and rites of passage such as birth, marriage, and death. Women play similar roles in sustaining ethnic identity elsewhere in Muslim-majority societies—for example in visits to shrines linked to particular ethnic groups.

Assertion of an ethnic identity often has significant political implications, and modern notions of ethnicity emphasize how such distinctions are generated, produced, and maintained. As late as the 1970s, the argument could be made for immigrant families in Europe that women were more likely to sustain ethnic distinctions because they were less likely to be multilingual and schooled. Higher levels of education have tended to make women as likely as men to think and act beyond their ethnic boundaries of origin and to attenuate such identities.

Contemporary ethnic and religious identities in the new states of Central Asia, the Balkans, and the Caucasus highlight the volatile political dimensions of ethnic identity—distinctions that had an equal impact on women and men. In the early decades of the Soviet era (1917–1990), Stalin created ethnic identities—"national" identities in the political language of the former Soviet Union—to weaken the possibility of resistance to Soviet domination. Subsequently, those speaking Turkic languages, including the Turkmen, Kazakh, and Kyrgyz (whose traditional lifestyles involved pastoralism), and the Uzbeks (primarily agricultural and urban), were considered separate for administrative purposes, as were the Persian-speaking Tajiks. The demise of the Soviet Union has led to a growth in ethnic consciousness and ethnic conflicts linked to competing claims over land, water, and other national resources. Because the various ethnic populations often live side by side—many Tajiks, for example, live in Uzbekistan, and many Uzbeks live in the neighboring republics—the possibilities for conflict are enormous. Marriages between ethnic groups have been common, but, in times of conflict, inter-group marriages have done little to mitigate the risks of ethnic and sectarian violence.

Ethnic identity is increasingly transregional and transnational. As women share with men higher levels of education, women play increasingly important roles in sustaining transnational ties and representing ethnic groups to a wider public, whether in a post-Soviet "folklore" presentation in Almaty, Kazakhstan, or a festival of Muslim arts and music in Brooklyn, New York. A Yemeni grocer in Brooklyn might serve as a link for others from his tribe and village in Yemen, and the Turkish factory worker in Germany might facilitate the adjustment for others from his home region or country in adjusting to life in a foreign land. In the early twenty-first century, the bilingual Yemeni grocer's daughter might also work alongside her father in the convenience store, and only their accent, the choice of foods, and customers—and possibly a bilingual sign—suggest their ethnicity of origin.

Understanding claims to ethnic identity entails attention both to constructed collective meanings and to the economic and political contexts in which such identities are created and sustained. Ethnic distinctions, like those of region, sect, gender, language, and even tribe, are not being erased by modern conditions, as was once assumed, but these distinctions provide the base from which newer social distinctions are created and sustained. Slowest to change are life milestone rituals, including those surrounding birth, marriage, and death. In these rituals, women have always played an important, although unremarked, role. In modern conditions, the performance of such rituals, including visits to shrines, acquires a heightened significance. Shared notions of community by ethnic group and region continue to provide the basis of trust and solidarity necessary for the effective functioning of and participation in modern society. Unfortunately, they can also be used to intimidate and to destroy.

BIBLIOGRAPHY

Becker, Cynthia J. *Amazigh Arts in Morocco: Women Shaping Berber Identity*. Austin: University of Texas Press, 2006. An evocative account of what it means to be "Berber" in contemporary Morocco.

Dunn, Ross E. *The Adventures of Ibn Battuta: A Muslim Traveler of the 14th Century*. 2d ed. Berkeley: University of California Press, 2005. Offers fascinating clues to the role of women in strategic alliances.

Eickelman, Dale F. *The Middle East and Central Asia: An Anthropological Approach*. 4th ed. Upper Saddle River, N.J.: Prentice Hall, 2002. Discusses factors contributing to social and cultural identity throughout the region, including gender and ethnicity (pp. 176–92, 192–214).

Kaiser, Robert John. *The Geography of Nationalism in Russia and the USSR*. Princeton, N.J.: Princeton University Press, 1994. A brilliant historical geography of the creation of ethnic and national distinctions in the USSR that continue to shape ethnic tensions in Russia today.

Stewart, Pamela J., and Andrew Strathern, eds. *Contesting Rituals: Islam and Practices of Identity-Making*. Durham, N.C.: Carolina Academic Press, 2005. Includes important chapters on the role of women in sustaining ethnic identity through ritual.

Tapper, Richard. "Ethnicity, Order, and Meaning in the Anthropology of Iran and Afghanistan." In *Le fait ethnique en Iran et en Afghanistan*, edited by Jean-Pierre Digard, pp. 21–31. Paris: Éditions du Centre national de la recherche scientifique, 1988. One of the clearest discussions of ethnicity available for these two countries.

DALE F. EICKELMAN

EUROPE. Muslim women in Europe stem from a mix of longstanding populations (for instance, in the Baltics and the Balkans), more recent immigration to Western, Northern, and, increasingly, Southern European countries, and by conversion. Their situation is commonly characterized by the minority context in which they live; however, a crucial difference exists between the established—even if in some cases challenged—institutions of long-standing Muslim communities and the low degree of institutionalization and/or acknowledgment by society and administration of younger communities. Within the rising geopolitical and national debates about the presence of Islam and Muslims in Europe, Muslim women appear to be positioned at the verge of religious and national, as well as racialized and ethnicized, identities. In these often gendered debates, Muslim women are caught between exclusion and belonging, having to face marginalization within both larger societies and Muslim communities. Furthermore, in the minority situation, women find themselves frequently in the role of (often visible) representatives of Muslim communities, while, simultaneously, their legitimacy to speak for Islam and Muslims tends to be questioned, by both Muslim and non-Muslim actors.

Muslims in Europe are both facing and contributing to religious plurality in society. Moreover, internally they are characterized by a high level of diversity concerning national and linguistic backgrounds, religious orientation, social stratification, and mobility and lifestyles, as well as concepts of gender relations, to mention just a few features of inner-Muslim plurality. Gender and Islam and, thereby, the situation of Muslim women, have become central issues in European and national-identity politics. Islam, Muslim families, and Muslim communities are often understood and presented as counterparts to the European self and especially to liberal values and civic virtues, among which gender equality thereby becomes pivotal. Debates on religious clothing, forced marriages, and so-called honor killings have turned the bodies of Muslim women into, as some writings coined it, "emblematic symbols in the representation of Islam" (Fadil, 2011, p. 84).

Islam in Europe: Spread and Recent History. Muslims in Europe are a minority at the junction between religious and ethnic belonging and freedom of religious practice. The presence of Muslims in Europe is first made up of longstanding populations in the Balkans, the European part of Turkey, Greece, Crete and Cyprus, the Baltic countries, Poland, Finland, and parts of Russia. Here, being Muslim has often been perceived as equal to belonging to an ethnic community, like the Turks or Tatars. In the post–World War II era, immigration to Western European countries took place, which caused a wave of conversion, as well as factors of globalization. The presence of Muslims in Western European countries before World War II had mostly the character of temporary settlement of male students, activists, soldiers, and workers and only in rare cases by Muslim families or, in exceptions, single women travelers. This presence was especially strong in Western European capitals such as Paris, London, Berlin, and Vienna, but also in harbor cities such as Liverpool, Hamburg, and Marseille. Whereas Muslims have come to Western Europe in larger numbers since the 1960s as workers and later on in the context of family reunion or as refugees and students, Scandinavian countries experienced a later arrival of workers and refugees. Since the 1990s, the southern parts of Europe have received immigrants from Africa and Asia.

As a result of a shortage in the workforce, France and the United Kingdom invited labor, especially from their former colonies, or, in the case of as the Netherlands and Germany, from Southern European and Mediterranean countries, leading to different textures of the Muslim populations in different national contexts. The background of most Muslims in France is therefore North African (Algerian, Tunisian, and Moroccan); in the United Kingdom it is South Asia (Pakistani and Indian); and in the Netherlands, as well as in Germany, it is Turkish and Moroccan. Refugees are contributing to the further diversification of Muslim populations, with Palestinians arriving in the late 1980s, Bosniaks in the mid-1990s, and Somalis in the 2000s. Muslim women immigrated to Europe in smaller numbers than men as workers and mainly subsequently in the course of family reunions and as refugees.

Even though the academic and political focus on Muslims in Europe tends to be on immigrant Muslims, a growing number are born there as descendants of converts or offspring of immigrants. Meanwhile research on longstanding populations throughout Europe is gaining momentum, and the concentration on Muslim immigrants has received some criticism as a feature of a limited understanding of Europe as only Western Europe.

Structures and Strategies of Women's Organizations. Ongoing negotiations over Islam's status as the religion of a minority and the institutionalization of Islam characterize the current challenge faced by younger Muslim communities in Europe that were established by immigrants and converts as well as their descendants. Muslims in Western European countries are—in contrast to those in countries with established majority Islamic institutions—mainly struggling not to change structures of Islamic authority but to come up with basic institutional frames. The absence of historically grown institutions presents itself as an ambivalent condition. On the one hand, knowledge production and diffusion are rather underdeveloped and largely influenced by transnational actors, often foreign governmental bodies of religious affairs. On the other hand, there are sometimes no established or outdated structures to be reformed or overcome. This enables women to take an active role in shaping the Islamic religious sphere in these evolving communities.

Three different structural approaches to achieving women's objectives can be found in the European context: (1) gender-segregated spaces and structures in mixed-gender organizations; (2) participation in mixed-gender organizations, including access to resources and decision making by both men and women; and (3) exclusive organizations for Muslim women with structure, space, and decision making in their own hands. Whereas in many South Asian communities neither women's visits to mosques nor attendance at communal prayers are common practices, Turkish organizations routinely established parallel structures and spaces for men and women. In several Arab, Tatar, and ethnically mixed communities, female members have access to leadership positions, associational boards, and religious spaces even if this access can only in rare cases be described as equal. It is worth mentioning that the Islamic Council Norway (Islamsk Råd Norge [IRN]), a national umbrella organization, had a female president from 2000 to 2003; the Young Muslims of Sweden (Sveriges Unga Muslimer [SUM]) were led by a woman from 2004 to 2008; and the national umbrella organization Muslim Council of Sweden (Sveriges Muslim Skaråd [SMR]) has been headed by a woman since 2004. In several European countries, female Muslims formed separate organizations to meet the needs of Muslim women that they felt were not met by mainstream public services or Muslim communities and to represent their interests vis-à-vis the state, media, and male-dominated Islamic organizations. Out of the large number of women's organizations, a few examples are given here: since 2002, the AMINA Muslim Women's Resource Centre has offered counseling in Glasgow and Dundee (U.K.) and, since 1996, the Muslim Women´s Centre for Encounter and Further Education (Begegnungs-und Fortbildungszentrum muslimischer Frauen, BFmF) in Cologne has provided education, counseling, and childcare (Germany). Apart from local initiatives, others concentrate on the representation at the national and transnational level such as Al Nisa, founded in 1982 in the Netherlands; the Union of Muslim Women of Spain (Unión de Mujeres Musulmanas de España [UMME]); the Coalition of Muslim Women in Germany (Aktionsbündnismuslimischer Frauen in Deutschland [AMF]), founded in 2009; and The European Forum of Muslim Women (EFOMW), founded in 2006 that claims to represent female Muslims in Europe. Transnational networks within Europe and beyond seem to be an important resource, especially for those marginalized in their local and national communities.

Individual Muslim women have established themselves as successful exponents in various professions, such as medicine, law, and research. In several European countries, Muslim women are members of national parliaments and governments. Worth mentioning are women of Muslim immigrant background who take a critical position toward Islam or Islamic organizations and, through creating controversy, obtain special prominence in media and public discourse.

Religious Practice and Living Conditions. Researchers have been trying to measure and compare the practice of Muslim women with the practice of Muslim men as well as non-Muslim women. However, the particularities of women's practice of Islam have still not been captured adequately, especially in quantitative works presented so far. Qualitative descriptions of Muslim women's engagement in Islamic communities stress the central role of mosques and religious spaces in Europe compared to Muslim majority countries. Female presidents of Tatar religious communities in Poland and Latvia and the existence of women's spaces in mosques since the sixteenth century have been highlighted (Nalborczyk, 2009). However, the struggle for access to the main prayer room and the main entrance of mosques has also been described (Karlsson Minganti, 2012). Current research documents the growing number of women interested and engaged in the study of Islamic thought and religious-knowledge acquisition as a technique of the self. Several studies focus on religiosity among young Muslim women, who are often characterized as second-generation immigrants. Some of them understand Muslim women's appropriation of religiosity as a means to bridge their origin and European lifestyles. Others describe ambiguities between the affirmation of gender boundaries and segregation on the one side and simultaneous growing relevance off male religious authority on the other (Jouili and Amir-Moazami, 2006). This goes hand in hand with women addressing what they perceive as tensions between patriarchal and ideal Islam. Hence, an increasing figuration of the inner-Muslim discourse is to separate Islamic practices from cultural traditions and the misuse of the divine law in combination with structural positions of power by men (Kuppinger, 2012).

Although in the public discourse requests for the right of women to become imams have gained some momentum, existing female authorities or women of influence within and beyond Muslim (women's) communities seem to be neglected. However, within the European context, women do perform the role of gendered authorities, for instance in Turkish communities in the function of the *hoca* (under the same name as male prayer and community leaders); in North African communities one can find female *mukadma*; and in Ṣūfī communities female leaders are serving under the names "Shaikha" or, in a few cases, "Imama."

Headscarf debates led to the production of a vast body of academic literature thereby reflecting the public attention to this debate. In contrast, less literature has been published on living situations and experiences of Muslim women, for instance, based on the analysis of statistical data. Increasingly however, researchers are investigating the application of Muslim family law within European legal systems, as well as experiences and strategies of female Muslims in matters of marriage and divorce.

Women's Bodies as a Battlefield for Piety and Secularity. Muslim women are facing various challenges within European societies, as well as in their communities and families. Besides minarets, religious clothing of women became a main issue in realizing and discussing the presence of Islam in (especially Western) Europe. Focal points of these debates tended to be visible symbols of religious piety or belonging that culminated in bans of the headscarf and/or other religious symbols in parts of the public sphere in several European countries, especially the educational sector. Possibilities of banning the wearing of headscarves and, to a lesser extent, face veils have been discussed in all Western European countries, with different intensity and subtexts but always reflecting on integration, the role and visibility of religion—especially Islam—in the public sphere, national identity and the situation of Muslim women. Debates in the 1990s and the early 2000s led to the prohibition of students attending public schools with a headscarf in France and, in Germany, for teachers to wear a headscarf in public schools. Other countries found ways of accommodating religious clothing, not only in the educational sector for pupils and teachers but even in other public services, such as in the police attire (e.g., Sweden and the United Kingdom). The most recent debates addressed the face veil discussed under the misleading term *burqa*. The majority of women wearing face coverage dress in what in Arabic is called *niqāb*, a piece of fabric with elastic ties that is worn around the face together with a one-piece over-garment, usually black, over the clothing. The introduction of laws banning the face veil in the public sphere has been debated most heatedly in Belgium, Denmark, France, the Netherlands, Norway, and Spain. In 2010 Belgium and in 2011 France introduced legislation banning face veils outside private spaces; these are mostly referred to as *burqa* bans. The banning of both the headscarf and the face veil have been legitimized as support for the freedom and integrity of Muslim women vis-à-vis their husbands and families. Another strand of the public discourse, however, highlights the discriminating and excluding effects of such legislation toward Muslim women, whether or not they wear religious clothing.

Simultaneously the oppression of Muslim women, especially in the form of domestic and honor-related violence, became a key issue in integration and immigration debates. In several European countries, public debates about forced marriages and honor killings led to the introduction of legislation that targets gender specific and culture- or religion-based violence and coercion. In a comparison of media debates and legal policies in four national contexts, Gökçe Yurdakul and Anne Korteweg contend that discussions of honor-related violence that stigmatize certain immigrant communities are more likely to lead to general anti-immigrant policies or policies that impede settlement, whereas debates that frame honor-related violence as a variant of the generally widespread problem of domestic violence, including violence against women, are more likely to lead to policies that directly target these forms of violence. In the first case, women are not supported, while immigration is further restricted, which politicians present as an instrument to fight violence against women. In the second case, victims of violence are directly and indirectly supported.

The figure of the oppressed Muslim woman in public debates itself is increasingly addressed in research on Muslims in Europe, which understands the reference to oppressive Muslim communities and families as part of European narratives of itself as liberal and characterized by the achievement of gender equality. At the same time several European states in their policies related to Islam adopt the role of the flagship of women's liberation, teaching Muslims to treat their women adequately, while emancipation is presented as a condition for belonging. Even though gender equality is thereby established as a core liberal value, these narratives are in turn criticized as a strategy to avoid the discussion of still-existing gender inequalities in Europe and, respectively, in national contexts, especially on the structural level. Hence, debates about oppression of women in minority groups seem to serve particular purposes: to describe the self as gender equal in opposition to the backward other and meanwhile refute discussions about one's own deficits.

BIBLIOGRAPHY

Adamak, Elzbieta, Malgorzata Chrzastowska, and Sonia Sobowiak, eds. *Gender and Religion in Central and Eastern Europe*, Poznan University, 2009.

Al-Ali, Nadje, Schirin Amir-Moazami, Christine M. Jacobsen, and Maleiha Malik, eds. *Feminist Review:*

Islam in Europe, p. 98. Basingstoke, U.K.: Palgrave Macmillan, 2011.

Bano, Masooda, and Hilary Kalmbach, eds. *Women Leadership, and Mosques: Changes in Contemporary Islamic Authority*. Leiden, Netherlands: E. J. Brill, 2012.

Berghahn, Sabine, and Petra Rostock, eds. *Der Stoff, aus dem Konflikte sind. Debatten um das Kopftuch in Deutschland, Österreich und der Schweiz*. Bielefeld, Germany: Transcript, 2009.

Blagojević, Marina. *Women's Situation in the Balkan Countries: Comparative Perspective*. Luxembourg. 2003. http://www.europarl.europa.eu/RegData/etudes/etudes/femm/2003/335149/DG-4-FEMM_ET%282003%29335149_XL.pdf.

Fadil, Nadia. "Not Unveiling as an Ethical Practice. *Feminist Review* 97 (2011): 83–109.

Howard, Erica. *Law and the Wearing of Religious Symbols: European Bans on the Wearing of Religious Symbols in Education*. London: Routledge, 2012.

Jouili, Jeannette, and Schirin Amir-Moazami. "Knowledge, Empowerment and Religious Authority among Pious Muslim Women in France and Germany." *Muslim World* 97, no. 4 (2006): 615–640.

Karlsson Minganti, Pia. "Challenging from Within: Youth Associations and Female Leadership in Swedish Moques." In *Women Leadership, and Mosques: Changes in Contemporary Islamic Authority*, edited by Masooda Bano and Hilary Kalmbach, pp. 371–391., Leiden, Netherlands: E. J. Brill, 2012.

Kuppinger, Petra. "Women, Leadership, and Participation in Mosques and Beyond: Notes from Stuttgart, Germany." In *Women Leadership, and Mosques: Changes in Contemporary Islamic Authority*, edited by Masooda Bano, and Hilary Kalmbach, 323–344. Leiden, Netherlands: E. J. Brill, 2012.

Mansson McGinty, Anna. *Becoming Muslim, Western Women's Conversions to Islam*. Basingstoke, U.K.: Palgrave Macmillan, 2006.

Mehdi, Rubya, and Jørgen S. Nielsen. *Embedding Mahr (Islamic Dower) in the European Legal System*. Copenhagen, Denmark: DJØF, 2011.

Nalborczyk, Agata S. "Muslim Women in Poland and Lithuania: Tatar Tradition, Religious Practice, Hijab and Marriage." In *Gender and Religion in Central and Eastern Europe*, edited by Elzbieta Adamak, Malgorzata Chrzastowska, and Sonia Sobowiak, pp. 53–69. Poznan, Poland: Uniw. im. Adama Mickiewicza, Wydzial Teologiczny, 2009.

Nielsen, Jørgen S., Samim Akgönül, Ahmet Alibašić, Brigitte Maréchal, and Christian Moe, eds. *Yearbook of Muslims in Europe*. Leiden, Netherlands: E. J. Brill, 2009, 2010 and 2011.

Nieuwkerk, Karin van, ed. *Women Embracing Islam: Gender and Conversion in the West*. Austin, Tex.: University of Texas Press, 2006.

Open Society Foundation. *Unveiling the Truth: Why 32 Muslim Women Wear the Full-Face Veil in France*. Budapest: Open Society Foundation, 2011.

Roald, Anne Sofie. *Women in Islam:, The Western Experience*. London: Routledge, 2002.

Silvestri, Sara. *Europe's Muslim Women: Potential, Aspirations and Challenges*. Brussels, Belgium, 2008. http://www.kingbaudouinfoundation.org/uploadedFiles/KBS-FRB/3%29_Publications/PUB_1846_MuslimWomen_03.pdf.

Spahić-Šiljak, Zilka, ed. "Contesting Female, Feminist and Muslim Identities: Post-Socialist Contexts of Bosnia and Herzegovina and Kosovo." Sarajevo, 2012. http://www.rrpp-westernbalkans.net/en/News/BiH-Book-Promotion-Post-Feminism-.html.

Yurdakul, Gökçe, and Anne Korteweg. *Religion, Culture and the Politicization of Honour-Related Violence: A Critical Analysis of Media and Policy Debates in Western Europe and North America*. Geneva, Switzerland: United Nations Research Institute for Social Development, 2010. http://www.unrisd.org/80256B3C005BCCF9/httpNetITFramePDF?ReadForm&parentunid=E61F80827BF3409FC1257744004DC465&parentdoctype=paper&netitpath=80256B3C005BCCF9/%28httpAuxPages%29/E61F80827BF3409FC1257744004DC465/$file/KortewegYurdaku.pdf.

RIEM SPIELHAUS

EZZAT, HEBA RAOUF. (b. 1965) is a political scientist by training and well-known in Egypt for her views on gender and women's equality within the Islamic context. She was educated at Cairo University, where she earned her BA (1987), MA (1995), and PhD (2007), all in political science. She became a lecturer in the faculty of economics and political sciences at Cairo University, where she has taught political theory since 1987. She has also taught at the American University in Cairo since 2006, and has been a visiting researcher at the Centre for the Study of Democracy (CSD) at the University of Westminster (1995–1996) and associate researcher at the Oxford Centre for Islamic Studies (1998), both in the United Kingdom.

Ezzat is well-known for her social and political activism, particularly on gender issues. Her mentors have included the Egyptian activists Zaynab al-Ghazālī, founder of the Muslim Women's Association, and Safinaz Kazem, a prominent journalist and writer. Like many Muslim feminists (a term she does not have a particular affinity for), she argues for gender reform and for women's rights from within the Islamic tradition, citing textual evidence and historical precedent to make the case that women can serve as leaders in public life as long as they have the proper Islamic credentials. She wrote a weekly column, "Women's Voice," for *al-Sha'b* ("The People"), a publication of the Egyptian Labor Party, between 1992 and 1997, in which she expressed many of these convictions. Raouf continues to write extensively for the mass media and participates in online debates on critical political and contemporary topics. She serves as adviser to the English section of IslamOnline.net.

Ezzat has further worked with a variety of civil society groups, including the Egyptian Federation for Youth Associations and Transparency International in Egypt. As an individual and academic of faith, she has taken part in a number of interfaith dialogues, such as the Muslim-Christian Common Word initiative launched in 2007, making her one of the few Muslim women to be formally included in such dialogue. She has joined the Building Global Democracy Programme, an initiative of the Centre for Globalisation and Regionalisation at the University of Warwick in the United Kingdom, which was launched in 2008, in an effort to promote the concepts of global citizenship, democratization, and multiculturalism.

Ezzat's publications in Arabic include: *Women and Politics: An Islamic Perspective* and "The Political Imagination of Islamists: A Conceptual Analysis." She has also edited two volumes on Egyptian citizenship published by the Centre for Political Research and Studies at Cairo University, as well as *Globalization: New Visions for a Changing World*. Her writings in English include chapters contributed to a number of edited volumes on issues ranging from Islam and secularism to gender and minority rights in the Middle East. She was chosen by the World Economic Forum as a Young Global Leader in 2005.

Bibliography

Primary Works

Women and Politics: An Islamic Perspective. Washington, D.C.: IIIT, 1995.

Globalization: New Visions for a Changing World. Cairo: Department of Political Science, Cairo University, 2002.

"The Political Imagination of Islamists: A Conceptual Analysis." In *Islamists and Democrats*. Cairo: Al-Ahram Center for Strategic Studies, 2004.

"Women and the Interpretation of Islamic Sources." *Islam 21*, September 4, 2007.

Secondary Works

El-Gawhary, Karim. "An Interview with Heba Ra'uf Ezzat." *Middle East Report* 191 (November–December 1994): 26–27.

Karam, Azza. *Women, Islamisms and the State: Contemporary Feminisms in Egypt*. London: Macmillan, 1998.

Asma Afsaruddin

F

FAMILY. The basic social unit of Islamic society, as in many other societies, is the family. If Islam can be described as the soul of Islamic society, then the family might be seen metaphorically as its body. For centuries the family has been the principal focus of people's emotional, economic, and political identity. Social changes in the twentieth and twenty-first centuries placed great strains on the unit, and especially on the patriarchal, extended family unit. Yet the family, together with the Islamic faith, retains a central place in the lives of people in every social class, in both rural and urban contexts, and in every Muslim-majority country.

Family means different things in different societies and contexts. In the Western world of the twenty-first century, family now includes the traditional nuclear family, the blended or step family resulting from divorces, the single-parent family, and the same-sex family unit. The Arabic word for family, *ahl* or *ahila*, is a more comprehensive term and may include grandparents, uncles, aunts, and cousins on both sides of the marital connection. In its broadest sense, the family might be perceived as an even larger unit, equal to the *ummah*, or the community of believers in Islam. Nevertheless the family unit in many parts of the Islamic world has experienced nuclearization, the result of modernization, urbanization, and women's educational attainment.

Pre-Islamic Family. As early as 3000 BC in ancient Sumer, the site of contemporary Iraq, evidence is found of a social unit similar to the contemporary Islamic family. This early manifestation, recorded in tablets and on monumental steles, was also a precursor to the family structure of Judaism and Christianity, the other two great monotheistic religions that originated in the Middle East. Christians and Jews are known in Islam as "people of the book" or *dhimmī*, those related to Islam through holy scripture and toward whom a Muslim must be tolerant.

This early form of the family was patrilineal, a form of social organization found in perhaps 80 to 90 percent of all human societies. In a patrilineal society the name of the child and the inheritance pass through the male line; children therefore are known by the names of their fathers. Although not all patrilineal families are equally patriarchal, the primacy attached to the male line reflects male dominance, both legal and informal, in the family and society. The use of the term "patriarch" to refer to the prophets of Judaism and Christianity is an indication of this tendency.

Family in the Qurʾān. The advent of Islam in the seventh century CE brought changes to the structure of the Arabian family. Although the basic outline of patrilineality was retained, some modifications came about with respect to women, girls, and orphans. The Qurʾān prohibited infanticide, a practice that is said to have reached scandalous proportions in pre-Islamic Arabia, particularly in the case of infant girls. Orphans were to be protected and treated with kindness. The Qurʾān also recognized women as having legal status as persons with rights and responsibilities. Women have the same religious duties as men, though they may be excused from fasting during Ramadan if, for example, they are pregnant or nursing. (Such latitude is meant to protect not only the health of the individual woman, but that of the child, either unborn or newly born, and by extension the health of the family unit itself.) The Qurʾān also gives women the right to accept or reject a marriage partner and the right to divorce in certain cases (desertion, impotence, or insanity of the husband are most often cited). However only men can divorce without cause, and they may have up to four wives at any one time. Patrilineality is retained, and sons inherit twice as much as daughters.

Traditional Function of the Family. In the past, and to a great extent today, the family provided economic and emotional support to its members. An individual, as Halim Barakat points out, "inherited" his or her religious, class, and cultural identity, which was reinforced by the customs and mores of the group. In exchange for the allegiance of its members, the family group served as a kind of employment bureau, insurance agency, child- and family-counseling service, old people's home, bank, school, home for the handicapped (including the mentally ill), and hostel in time of economic need. Men and women both remained members of their birth families for all of their lives, even after marriage. A divorced woman returned to her birth family, which was responsible for her support until remarriage. A divorced man returned to his birth family, and his parents cared for his children. In exchange for these services, the individual members were expected to place the group's survival above their personal desires, especially at the time of marriage, and to uphold the reputation of the family by behaving properly and "maintaining the family honor." This system largely describes patrilineal systems, say, in the Middle East. Whether or not this describes tribal Muslim societies in Africa, where there is evidence of matriarchal societies where gender norms operated differently, is an open question (see, e.g., Ibn Baṭṭūṭah's fourteenth-century description of the kingdom of Mali and his critique of gender norms and familial structures). What this suggests is perhaps more diversity in family structures in Muslim societies than the broad outline described here.

This outline of the "Islamic family," of course, was the ideal. In everyday life ideals are not always realized. Some members have always rebelled and refused to marry the person chosen for them by their family. Some groups did not take in divorced members, sometimes because of poverty, sometimes out of spite. Vengeful fathers did not always pass on to their sons, at the time of maturity, authority over land or shops. Maintaining the family honor sometimes resulted in tragedy. The care of handicapped and elderly members often put an undue stress upon the younger members of the family. And not all women welcomed a co-wife or a divorce. Yet the institution of the Islamic family unit persisted because it met real needs, especially in the absence of other social institutions.

Western Influence. In the West, socioeconomic and political changes led to a transformation of the family, from extended to nuclear, from patriarchal to egalitarian, and from the male breadwinner/female homemaker model to a dual income-earning model. Such a shift may be observed in the Muslim world, though not to the same extent.

The family unit in Muslim societies came under new pressures with the beginning of Western colonial rule in the late eighteenth and early nineteenth centuries. From Egypt to India, Morocco to Indonesia, European immigrants, soldiers, and administrators assumed political control. The family unit became first a religious, cultural, and social refuge from colonial domination, and eventually the site of political resistance. This action was strengthened by Western colonial policy, which, in most areas, left local control intact only in religious affairs and, by inference, Islamic family law, including inheritance. This was crucial for the continuation and support of the family, which, in response to the presence of strangers, turned in upon itself. Men found their families a sanctuary, a representation of Islamic religious values wherein they were honored. Protection of Muslim women from strangers became more important as well. For example, the all-enveloping *jallābīyah*, with hood and face veil, found in Morocco today, dates only from about 1912, when the French conquered Morocco. Before that time women as well as men in Morocco wore the *ḥāʾik*, a length of cloth wrapped about the body in various ways. The Qurʾānic school increased in importance as a source of religious instruction (though largely for boys) even as colonial governments were attempting to limit its influence and elites were attending the secular schools of Christian missionaries.

As organized anticolonial resistance became more serious and militant, the family became the focus and locus of resistance. Such resistance was often framed in terms of the protection of Islam and the family in the face of a common enemy—Western political and economic power, with its perceived secularist and anti-Islamic aims. A consequence was that women came to be locked into a patriarchal family unit, and a large proportion were denied access to schooling or even a presence in public spaces, which were deemed male domains. After independence from colonial rule in the 1950s and 1960s, few women were available for paid work in the growing modern sector. Muslim family laws reflected and reinforced women's family attachment and their subordination to male guardianship.

During the oil boom in the Middle East and North Africa, state expansion and public education created a population of educated women willing to enter the workforce. The family unit also changed with male migration to oil-rich countries. Although in most cases male kin tended to oversee the moral and financial well-being of the women and children, in some cases men migrating to the Gulf or to Europe effectively abandoned their families or started new ones. After the oil boom, unemployment, inflation, and poverty broke down extended family units and forced increasing numbers of women to take up jobs outside their homes. Conflict in Israel, Palestine, Lebanon, Afghanistan, Iraq, and Sudan, as well as the effects of revolution and repression in Iran in the early to mid-twentieth century, also led to family disruption through violent deaths and forced migration. The movement in almost all Muslim-majority countries from rural to urban predominance further challenged the customary ties of family life. It has become increasingly difficult for the traditional patriarchal family model—father as provider, mother as childbearer and rearer of children in the home—to be maintained. The dual adult-worker pattern has not yet established itself as the norm, but there are signs that this change may be occurring in varying degrees across the Muslim world. What is more, the traditionally very high fertility rates of Muslim-majority countries have been declining. In Iran, Lebanon, Turkey, and Tunisia, the number of children per woman has fallen from six to two in just a few decades. Among the urban middle class in particular family size is smaller, and the age at first marriage has risen to the mid- to late-twenties.

Recent Changes and Challenges. The ongoing debate throughout the Islamic world on Sharīʿah-based family law is a crucial one, for it involves not only the suggestion that family responsibilities be passed from the family unit and religious authorities to the state, but it also has implications for the definition of basic individual rights of women, men, and children. The status of women is not an isolated issue but lies at the core of the whole debate, for the woman has always been seen as the center of the family unit.

Discussions of Muslim family law reflect these concerns, as Qurʾānic family law defines relations between men and women through legislation on marriage, divorce, child custody, inheritance, and polygyny. Islamic family law currently operates in most Muslim-majority countries, with the exception of Turkey and Tunisia. In the 1980s a number of countries moved to stiffen the application of Sharīʿah family law, including Saudi Arabia, Pakistan, Iran, Egypt, Algeria, and Nigeria. In the 1990s this occurred in Afghanistan, Indonesia, and Malaysia, and in the second decade of the new century, in Mali, previously known for its very tolerant practice of Islam and strong musical culture. In all three periods it reflected the growing political and cultural influence of Islamist movements, which see the family as the rock on which indigenous religious socialization and culture stand. Islamist movements argue for greater family cohesion in what is perceived as a rapidly changing, unpredictable, and hostile world. In the Islamic Republic of Iran, for example, the family became the platform for the enunciation of the Islamic state's goals and ideals, and the subject of government legislation by the Shīʿī *ʿulamāʾ* in many areas of life other than family law—education, leisure activities, literature, and politics.

Since the early 1990s, however, women's groups have emerged throughout the Muslim world to call for changes in the status of women in the family and the society and for reform of family laws that place women in a subordinate position vis-à-vis husbands or male kin. They advocate for greater rights in marriage, divorce, child custody, and inheritance; an end to male guardianship and control over women's mobility; the right of mothers to pass on their nationality to the children (if the children are born of foreign fathers); the criminalization of "honor killings"; and greater economic and political participation. The 2003–2004 reform of the very patriarchal Mudawana, Morocco's family law, is an example of a successful campaign that was framed in terms of national development imperatives, children's well-being, women's rights, and an alternative vision of the family. Other groups and campaigns for equality and rights are Iran's One Million Signatures Campaign, Malaysia's Sisters in Islam, and Nigeria's BAOBAB for Women's Human Rights. But women's rights advocacy faces opposition from conservative civil-society groups and from governments. Thus the Islamic Republic of Iran continues to enforce restrictions on women's mobility, appearance, and equality within the family, and it has harassed, arrested, or forced into exile women's-rights activists. After the overthrow of Libyan leader Muʿammar al-Qadhdhāfī in 2011, the leader of the new Western-backed transitional government issued a statement that Sharīʿah law would be "the basic source of legislation, and so any law which contradicts Islamic principles is void." He specifically mentioned that polygamy would be legal. In August 2012 a controversy arose in the new, democratic Tunisia when the Ennahda-dominated constituent assembly sought to replace words referring to the "equality" of women and men with words connoting "complementarity" and "partnership." The offending article stipulates that the state guarantees "the protection of women's rights... under the principle of complementarity to man within the family and as an associate of man in the development of the country." Many Tunisian women feared a backsliding on women's rights norms and laws, and thousands protested in the capital city of Tunis. A petition addressed to the assembly, stating that "the state is about to vote on an article in the constitution that limits the citizenship rights of women, under the principle of their complementarity to men and not their equality," received more than eight thousand online signatures. In Turkey, where an Islamic party has ruled since 2001 and has been widely seen as democratic and moderate, secular and Islamic women alike took to the streets in early June 2012 to protest Prime Minister Recep Tayyip Erdoğan's remarks about banning abortion.

Modern Role of the Family. Increasing nuclearization, the changing status of women, the high cost of marriage (especially in Egypt), and the high rate of divorce (especially in Iran) has led to public debates, some protests, and many disappointed individuals. To some observers such developments suggest the disintegration of the Muslim family and Islamic culture. To others, the Muslim family is adjusting or reorganizing in response to contemporary needs or challenges. Yet others feel that the problems require appropriate public policies. Modern states have taken over some functions of the family, through programs and policies of social provisioning. Public schooling, health care, child care, government employment, family allowances, pensions, bank loans, and unemployment insurance are among the social services and social policies available to citizens. Nonetheless, especially in parts of the Muslim world devoid of a welfare or development state, the family is an essential focus of solidarity and support for its members, and affective ties remain strong.

In places where the family unit itself has been dispersed because of war, natural disaster, or economic need, the values and the functions of the family are resurfacing in different forms. Workers abroad group together on the basis of old family ties; young men entering the workforce find jobs in the same factories or businesses as their sisters, cousins, or uncles. For men of elite political groups, family ties continue to be important as political party bases shift. Newcomers to the city make connections through family members. Men on their own in a new place may turn to Islamic religious "brotherhoods," or groups where, as they themselves say, they "feel like one of the family." Women whose husbands are working abroad often form kin-like ties with neighbors. Women in the workforce continue to rely on family ties for support; and in this connection, some would point out that the growing trend of women's entrepreneurship calls for equal inheritance rights. Through its adaptations and evolution, the family unit in the Muslim world has proven to be an interdependent, dynamic, and flexible social institution. For many it remains the best way to provide for individual needs as well as group survival.

The British historian Lawrence Stone found the English family of past centuries to be a searching, acting, moving institution. The Muslim family, from its earliest foundations to its modern expression, might be viewed in the same way, as a structure flexible enough to deal with new pressures and strong enough in its religious and social manifestations to respond to and become part of changing conditions.

[*See also* Divorce; Family Law; Inheritance; Marriage; Polygyny; Women and Islam; *and* Women and Social Reform.]

BIBLIOGRAPHY

Barakat, Halim. "The Arab Family and the Challenge of Social Transformation." In *Women and the Family in the Middle East: New Voices of Change*, edited by Elizabeth Warnock Fernea, pp. 27–48. Austin: University of Texas Press, 1985.

Charrad, Mounira. *States and Women's Rights: The Making of Postcolonial Tunisia, Algeria, and Morocco*. Berkeley: University of California Press, 2001.
Esposito, John L., and Natana J. DeLong-Bas. *Women in Muslim Family Law*. 2d ed. Syracuse, N.Y.: Syracuse University Press, 2001.
Fernea, Elizabeth Warnock, ed. *Women and the Family in the Middle East: New Voices of Change*. Austin: University of Texas Press, 1985.
Haeri, Shahla. *Law of Desire: Temporary Marriage in Shi'i Iran*. Syracuse, N.Y.: Syracuse University Press, 1989.
Kian-Thiébaut, Azadeh. "From Motherhood to Equal Rights Advocates: The Weakening of Patriarchal Order." *Iranian Studies* 38, no. 1 (March 2005): 45–66.
Letsch, Constanze. "Turkish Women Join Pro-Choice Rally as Fears Grow of Abortion Ban. *The Guardian*, June 3, 2012. http://www.guardian.co.uk/world/2012/jun/03/turkish-women-rally-abortion-ban.
Levy, Reuben. *The Social Structure of Islam*. Cambridge, U.K.: Cambridge University Press, 1957.
Maudūdī, Abul Aʿlā. *Purdah and the Status of Woman in Islam*. Translated and edited by al-Ashʿari. Lahore, Pakistan: Islamic Publications, 1972.
Minault, Gail, ed. *The Extended Family: Women and Political Participation in India and Pakistan*. Columbia, Mo.: South Asia Books, 1981.
Moghadam, Valentine M. *Modernizing Women: Gender and Social Change in the Middle East*. 2d ed. Boulder, Colo.: Lynne Rienner, 2003. 3rd ed. 2013.
Moghadam, Valentine M., and Tabitha Decker. "Social Change in the Middle East." *The Middle East*, edited by Ellen Lust. 12th ed., pp. 65–98. Washington, D.C.: CQ Press/Sage, 2010.
Rugh, Andrea. *Family in Contemporary Egypt*. Syracuse, N.Y.: Syracuse University Press, 1984.
Stone, Lawrence. *The Family, Sex, and Marriage in England, 1500–1800*. London: Weidenfeld & Nicholson, 1977.
"Tunisia: Thousands Rally for Women's Rights." World News Australia, August 14, 2012. http://www.sbs.com.au/news/article/1682492/Tunisia-Thousands-rally-for-womens-rights.
Yount, Kathryn M., and Hoda Rashad, eds. *Family in the Middle East: Ideational Change in Egypt, Iran, and Tunisia*. London and New York: Routledge, 2008.

ELIZABETH J. FERNEA
Updated by VALENTINE M. MOGHADAM

FAMILY LAW. Issues of law affecting the family, known as family law, are central to the Sharīʿah. The Qurʾānic verses that concern themselves with issues of law deal to a great extent with matters affecting the family. Many of the *ḥadīth* concentrate on the same area, and it is therefore no surprise that the leading texts of classical Islamic jurists concentrate similarly on the subject of family law.

Premodern Doctrinal Discourses on Islamic Family Law. At the heart of family law in the Islamic legal tradition is the marriage contract. Classical jurists do not differ substantially about the particular attributes of family law, although there are, of course, many differences of detail. Modernists often see Islamic family law as patriarchal and insensitive to the position of the woman, who is not viewed as an equal partner in the relationship. Much Western criticism has concentrated on the right of polygyny, the power of the husband to terminate unilaterally the relationship, the lack of the wife's similar entitlement, and the rights the husband has over both his wife and as *walī* (guardian) of his children.

In broad outline, marriage (*nikāḥ*) is a contract into which the groom enters with the bride or the bride's legal guardian. The guardian can contract his minor daughter in marriage without her consent, although she does have a right, in certain situations, to rescind the contract when she reaches puberty. The contract is created by the two "pillars" of offer (*ījāb*) and acceptance (*qabūl*) in the presence of two Muslim male witnesses or one Muslim male and two Muslim female witnesses. The groom contracts to pay his wife a dower (*mahr*). Marriages can be considered void (*bāṭil*) or irregular (*fāsid*) under certain circumstances, such as marriages with *maḥārim*, or female ascendants and descendants or those related through affinity. In contrast, a *fāsid* marriage is irregular in that, after the required separation of the parties, the particular defect can be removed, at least in theory, and they can then remarry, such as if the marriage occurs when entered into in the absence of witnesses. In a *fāsid* relationship, if consummation has occurred, then a *mahr* must be paid to the wife, and any children who are born to the couple are deemed to be legitimate. As polygyny is permitted to the maximum of four wives, a fifth marriage would be *fāsid*.

Divorce by the husband is effected by a unilateral pronouncement known as the *ṭalāq*, which is a repudiation that cuts off the marital tie. The power to exercise *ṭalāq* belongs to the husband and does not depend on any judicial involvement or consent of the wife. There are a number of different forms of *ṭalāq*, some seen to be more meritorious than others. The most meritorious is the *ṭalāq aḥsan*. When the wife is free from her menstrual flow, the husband pronounces a *ṭalāq*; he must then refrain from any sexual intercourse for the duration of the *ʿiddah* period, which is a period of three menstrual cycles or three months in the case of women who no longer menstruate. At the end of this time, the marriage is terminated. The wife's right to bring a marriage to an end (*khulʿ*) is restricted; it involves consent of the husband and consideration paid by the wife. Mālikī law, in particular, gives prominence to the *qāḍī* (judge) who, in certain situations, can separate the parties.

During marriage, the wife is entitled to maintenance and support, which includes food, clothing, and accommodation. This entitlement, however, terminates after the *ʿiddah* period of a divorce, and there is no ongoing entitlement to financial assistance. The entitlement can also be suspended if she is "disobedient," for example, if she refuses to acquiesce in the husband's desire that she not leave the house. Legal adoption of children is not permissible in Islamic law. The mother initially has the entitlement to custody (*ḥaḍāna*) of a child, but the father acquires custody as soon as the child reaches a certain age. Although each school has different rules, the mother's custody of a child does not extend beyond the age of puberty, by which time, according to all schools, the father has acquired the residual custodial right over the child.

Modern Reforms. The absence of equality between husband and wife was seen as a handicap by those involved in the drive by some Muslim states toward a process of Westernization. Reforms in the family-law area were designed to solve particular perceived problems in an eclectic manner, formally following the jurisprudential principle of *taqlīd* (imitation) and based on the right of the ruler to define and confine the limits of judicial intervention (*al-siyāsah Sharīʿah*). Thus, differences of detail between the schools have enabled reformers in Ḥanafī countries to adopt the stance taken by jurists of schools other than their own in situations where a change has been seen as desirable. For instance, in 1915, Ottoman rulers enacted legislation by imperial edict designed to improve the legal status of Muslim wives and provide them with certain rights to petition for divorce. These rights, which were not available in the dominant Ḥanafī law of the Ottoman Empire, were based on Ḥanbalī and Mālikī law and the "weaker" minority Ḥanafī doctrine. Similarly, criminal law was used to introduce what were seen to be improvements to family law; for instance, in Egypt in 1923, it became a criminal offense for a registrar to register a marriage when the bride was under the age of sixteen and the bridegroom under the age of eighteen. Egypt used procedural devices to restrict further the solemnization of child marriages by precluding the court from hearing any claim arising out of a marriage if the husband had not attained the age of eighteen and the bride the age of sixteen at the time of the litigation, and the courts were barred from considering the question of a disputed marriage unless the marriage had been registered. These early reforms were followed by the adoption of a somewhat more unorthodox approach, namely, *talfiq* ("combining together" the doctrine of one school or jurist with another). This approach allowed reforms viewed as socially desirable to be introduced, while ensuring that there was no significant departure from the Sharīʿah.

After 1945 reforms tended to be based more on the alleged right of a Muslim state, through its rulers, to exercise *ijtihād* (independent deduction). Perhaps the most celebrated example of this approach is the abolition of the entitlement of polygyny by Article 18 of the Tunisian Code of Personal Status (1956), based on a reinterpretation of verse 4:3, which states, "Marry women of your choice, two or three or four; but if ye fear that ye shall not be able to deal justly [with them], then only one...." The Tunisians equate justice not merely with *nafaqah* (financial support) but also with love and affection. It is then argued that only the Prophet can treat two wives equally in this way; therefore, the irrefutable presumption is that a Muslim husband cannot fulfill the requirements laid down in the Qurʾān.

Reforms in other Muslim countries relating to polygynous marriages have not been so dramatic; most countries simply make second marriages dependent on the permission of a court (e.g., Syria in 1953 and Iraq in 1959) or an arbitration body (e.g., Pakistan and Bangladesh in 1961). Similarly, stipulations can be made in the marriage contract that the husband cannot have a co-wife. If he does take a second wife, then the first wife is entitled, for that reason alone, to seek dissolution of the marriage (as in Jordan, 1976, and Morocco, 1958). Indeed, even in the absence of such a stipulation, the Moroccan *qāḍī* may consider whether the second marriage has caused any injury to the first wife. The end result of all these developments has been the enactment of codes of family law in almost all Islamic countries.

Reappraisal of Reforms. Even such limited reforms have been subjected to critical reappraisal in the light of Islamic revivalism. One example of such a development in Egypt demonstrates this trend that now appears to be active throughout the Muslim world. In Egypt in 1979, Law 44 was issued by a presidential decree that amended the existing 1920 and 1929 laws. It required that a pronouncement of *ṭalāq* by the husband be registered, and that notification of the *ṭalāq* must be given to the wife. The divorce did not take effect if the notice failed to reach her. In the event of a judicial application by the wife for a divorce, which arbitrators dealt with, the court was empowered to dissolve the marriage, although the wife had to pay compensation. These reforms were far from radical, yet the 1979 law did not survive; in July 1985 the Constitutional Court judged it unconstitutional. A new law, Law 100 of 1985, was enacted, one that complies more closely with the perceived orthodoxy. For instance, Article 6A in the 1979 law gave a first wife the right to ask for a divorce solely on the basis of a second marriage by her husband. Article 11A of the replacement Law 100 of 1985 states that a first wife who finds herself in this position must petition a court for a divorce, alleging that she has suffered harm as a result of her husband's marriage to a second wife; the court must then try to reconcile the parties, and it can grant a divorce only after such endeavors have proved to be unsuccessful. Thus, the attempt in 1979 to introduce a substantial reform that would have given the first wife an automatic right to terminate the marriage under these circumstances was replaced by a more limited provision. Islamist tendencies were primarily responsible for the demise of this short-lived 1979 reform.

Contemporary Developments. It does not appear that the return to a form of Islamic orthodoxy is merely a passing phase in the Muslim world. It seems that the complete abandonment of Islamic family law in exchange for Western-inspired legal codes is an approach that no longer commands popular support. Many twentieth-century reforms, including those prohibiting child marriage, placing limitations on polygyny, or attempting to equalize property entitlements between spouses upon divorce are not likely to be repealed. However, early-twentieth-century approaches to achieving these reforms—often negatively viewed as secularist attempts to imitate Western norms and ignore Islamic legal processes for achieving change—no longer hold the degree of currency they once did.

In response to this trend, contemporary reform movements—particularly those inspired by local activists and women—are increasingly adopting the approach of advocating for change *through* Islamic legal processes. Instead of stepping outside of the boundaries of religious law to acquire desired reforms, activists now advocate for such reforms by demonstrating that these interpretations are possible from *within* the canon of Islamic law.

The Campaign for Monogamy launched in 2003 by the Malaysian organization Sisters in Islam is an example that demonstrates this trend. Under the Malaysian Islamic Family Law Act of 1984, the state permitted the practice of polygyny, but within new boundaries established by reformed codes. These laws outlined that a man could marry a second wife only by applying to the court. In doing so, the applicant had to demonstrate to the court that the additional marriage was necessary; that he was financially capable of supporting additional dependents; that he had the ability to treat his wives equally; and that the second marriage would not cause harm to the first wife, including a decrease in her living standards. Despite the passage of these laws intended to place limits on polygyny, state courts rarely, if ever, enforced them. Men would often engage in polygynous relationships in foreign countries or in regions with relaxed enforcement policies and then, after paying a small fine, proceed to register the second marriage after the fact. In addition to the lack of enforcement of these policies, women's groups pointed out that the initial reforms were inadequate, because they neither included a provision requiring the applicant to inform his first wife of his second marriage nor made legal allocations allowing the first wife easy access to divorce if she wished to exit the marriage.

In response to these issues, Sisters in Islam published a memorandum outlining their proposed reforms and, several years later, launched a publicity campaign aimed at educating the Malaysian populace with regard to their position. In their "Memorandum on Reform of the Islamic Family Laws on Polygamy," they explored the religious textual basis for polygyny, and ultimately argued that the Qurʾān recommends monogamous marriage. On the basis of these religious textual arguments, and in reference to recent judicial laxities with regard to enforcing current laws, the memorandum called for a renewed strict enforcement of past laws limiting polygyny; increases in penalties for men disobeying such laws; and the addition of provisions requiring the first wife's permission for a man's second marriage, as well as easy recourse to divorce if she wished to leave the marriage. In taking a religious textual approach to articulating their position, the Sisters in Islam were able to situate their proposed reforms within the framework of Islamic law, thereby establishing the legitimacy of their claims in anticipation of potential criticism from religious elites, state institutions, or the public.

The "woman's divorce" campaign in Egypt is another example of how contemporary activists are choosing to place arguments for reform within the Islamic legal tradition. Aiming to address the challenges faced by wives in obtaining a divorce when attempting to leave abusive marriages, activists focused on promoting *khulʿ*, a form of divorce in Islamic legal doctrine that permitted a wife, with or without cause, to obtain a divorce from her husband through the court. Egyptian legal reformers and activists worked for more than a decade to draft and pass a new *khulʿ* law through the Egyptian parliament—a goal that was finally achieved in January 2000. After the law was passed, however, opponents brought the law to the attention of the Egyptian Constitutional Court, arguing that the law was unconstitutional because it both eliminated the requirement for obtaining the husband's consent for divorce and curtailed his ability to appeal the divorce. Given that parties supporting the new law were able to demonstrate that *khulʿ* was doctrinally supported from within the Islamic legal tradition, however, the court ruled that the new law was constitutional and, therefore, legally active.

Neither the Malaysian and nor the Egyptian case has remained without challenges. As for the Malaysian case, although activists have been careful to articulate their calls for reform from within the religious tradition and have achieved a high degree of publicity in doing so, the state has yet to respond to their requests, let alone formalize their demands into law. In the Egyptian case, parliamentarians introduced and passed an amendment requiring spousal arbitration to be part of the *khulʿ* process. Along with creating a larger role for state actors and family members to play in divorce proceedings and thereby slowing the process, the required arbitration offered uncooperative husbands an opportunity to make the divorce process more difficult for the wife. Since their failure to attend arbitration sessions required the rescheduling of such meetings, displeased husbands could, in this manner, intentionally extend the timeline for divorce proceedings. This extended timeline, the inefficiencies within state institutions in collecting child support or other properties entitled to the wife, and general social disapproval of women seeking divorce are all factors that have resulted in a far lower percentage of women filing for divorce than legal reformers had initially anticipated upon passage of the *khulʿ* law.

Like other legal systems, Islamic legal practice has proven to be dynamic, changing, and fluid. Being the combined product of religious doctrine, jurists' law, and the everyday practices of laymen and women, Islamic family law was practiced in varying times and places in starkly different ways. While challenges certainly still exist for those disadvantaged by the law in contemporary times, an increasingly varied group of voices—among them women—are playing an important role in shaping legal reforms.

BIBLIOGRAPHY

Abou El Fadl, Khaled. *Speaking in God's Name: Islamic Law, Authority and Women*. Oxford: Oneworld, 2001.

El-Alami, Dawoud S. *The Marriage Contract in Islamic Law*. London and New York: Graham & Trotman, 1992.

Anderson, J. N. D. *Law Reform in the Muslim World*. London: Athlone, 1976.

An-Naʿim, Abdullahi A., ed. *Islamic Family Law in a Changing World: A Global Resource Book*. London: Zed Books, 2002.

Coulson, Noel J. *A History of Islamic Law*. New Brunswick, NJ: Aldine Transaction, 2011.

Dasuqi, Muhammad Ibn Ahmad. *Hashiyat al-Dasuqi ʿala al-Sharh al-Kabir*. 4 vols. Cairo: Dar Ihyaʾ al-Kutub al-ʿArabiyya, n.d.

Esposito, John L., with Natana J. DeLong-Bas. *Women in Muslim Family Law*. Rev. ed. Syracuse, NY: Syracuse University Press, 2001.

Hallaq, Wael B. *The Origins and Evolution of Islamic Law*. Cambridge, U.K.: Cambridge University Press, 2005.

al-Marghinani, Burhan al-Din ʿAli ibn Abi-Bakr. *Al-Hidaya: Sharh Bidayat al-Mubtadi*. 4 vols. Cairo: Dār al-Salām, 2000.

Pearl, David. *A Textbook on Muslim Personal Law*. 2d ed. London: Croom Helm, 1987.

Rapoport, Yossef. *Marriage, Money and Divorce in Medieval Islamic Society*. Cambridge, U.K: Cambridge University Press, 2005.

Shaham, Ron. *Family and the Courts in Modern Egypt: A Study Based on Decisions by the Shari'a Courts, 1900–1955*. Leiden, Netherlands: Brill, 1997.

Sonbol, Amira El-Azhary, ed. *Women, the Family and Divorce Laws in Islam*. Syracuse: Syracuse University Press, 1996.

Tucker, Judith E. *In the House of the Law: Gender and Islamic Law in Ottoman Syria and Palestine*. Berkeley: University of California Press, 1998.

Tucker, Judith E. *Women, Family, and Gender in Islamic Law*. Cambridge, U.K.: Cambridge University Press, 2008.

Welchman, Lynn, ed. *Women's Rights and Islamic Family Law: Perspectives on Reform*. London: Zed Books, 2004.

DAVID STEPHEN PEARL
Updated by SARAH ISLAM

FAMILY PLANNING. Concern with population growth rates, coupled with worries about economic and social development, have spurred Muslim debate on the use of family planning measures. In terms of popular usage, family planning—used to space, rather than prevent, births—has become increasingly accepted. The average number of children born to women in Muslim countries has decreased by around 60 percent since 1970. Despite this substantial drop, the Muslim population is expected to grow at around twice the rate of non-Muslims for the next twenty years if current trends continue. By 2030, Muslim populations are predicted to drop to around replacement rates (2.2 total fertility rate, or TFR, meaning the number of children born to a woman in her lifetime), while non-Muslim states' total fertility rates are projected to be well below that, 0.7 on average.

In the nineteenth and early twentieth centuries, populations in Muslim countries grew slowly, as high birth rates were offset by high mortality rates. Following World War II and continuing in the early twenty-first century, countries with a majority of Muslim citizens are, generally speaking, characterized by birth rates that have declined substantially and are coupled with a strong rise in life expectancy. Muslim countries of sub-Saharan Africa are a major exception, as their total fertility rates remain high. Various factors have combined to decrease the total fertility rate in many Muslim countries. They include availability of medical services, widespread community health and sanitation programs, greater literacy, the education and higher status of women, migration to urban areas, and employment availability. As a result, population growth has slowed considerably. These figures differ by region. Muslim minority, less-developed countries have fewer children (2.6 TFR, 2010–2015) than Muslim-majority countries (2.9 TFR, 2010–2015), and more developed non-Muslim majority countries still fewer (1.6 TFR, 2010–2015).

Although some Muslim countries have the resources to support a growing population, others with more limited resources fear the impact of population growth on their ability to provide services and generate employment for their citizens. National family-planning programs have been implemented successfully in a number of countries. Muslim countries in the Middle East, North Africa, and Asia, with a few exceptions, have slowed their rate of natural increase considerably; some, particularly in the Middle East, have accomplished this without a national program. In many countries, incorporating family planning into national maternal and child health programs helped increase its use. Progress in guaranteeing good health care for women, as well as raising women's status in general, has correlated strongly with increased contraceptive prevalence. Lower birth rates reflect not only family planning use, but also better women's health and higher women's literacy levels.

Since the beginning of Islam, the Muslim community has encouraged large families, to ensure a strong and vibrant Muslim population. However, religious scholars (ʿulamāʾ) assert the religious permissibility of family planning in the *fiqh* (jurisprudence) literature on marriage and family. The Qurʾān makes no mention of family planning measures, but a few *ḥadīth* texts mention *ʿazl* (*coitus interruptus*, or withdrawal) as a means of birth control. The *fiqh* discussion centers on the question of the permissibility of *ʿazl*, and schools differ in their response. *ʿAzl* used for no reason is judged to be *makrūh* (reprehensible), but major variables that determine its permissibility include the status of the woman involved (free or slave) and whether she gives her consent to its use. As *ʿazl* is considered to be detrimental to the woman, depriving her of her right to children, free women, but not slave women, had the right to consent to its use. Jurists noted that sexual intercourse was not only for the purpose of procreation; wives also had the right to sexual pleasure. The minority of ʿulamāʾ who opposed use of *ʿazl* interpreted its use as infanticide. Almost all major jurisprudence traditions, both Sunnī and Shīʿī, accorded women a say in the use of family planning and considered it a permissible practice.

As the jurists were male and *ʿazl* was controlled by the male partner, this was the only contraceptive method discussed in the *fiqh* literature. Medical texts, however, document that women have used various other means of contraception. These methods included infusions, suppositories, sexual techniques, and magic.

Contemporary ʿulamāʾ tend to resolve the religious permissibility of family planning along the same lines of reasoning as their medieval colleagues. The twentieth century introduced a variety of contraceptive methods whose use is controlled primarily by women. Accordingly, the majority of ʿulamāʾ rule that use of contraceptive methods is permissible for Muslims as long as the husband and the wife agree to it. This position follows the logic of the classical texts in that, although use of contraception may be injurious to the wishes of one spouse, if both agree, then the rights of both are guaranteed. The major stipulation is that family-planning methods must remain temporary and not permanently alter what God has created, and not destroy a living being. Methods such as sterilization of the husband by vasectomy or the wife by tubal ligation are forbidden as permanent alterations, although they are increasingly sought by women and men who have completed childbearing. If physicians assure that these methods are reversible, some consider the procedures religiously permissible. An exception is to guarantee health; a physician's verdict on the medical necessity of sterilization (as well as abortion) has priority and renders the procedure permissible. Islamically justified reasons for using family planning may include avoiding the economic hardships associated with a large family, and allowing for the education and good upbringing of one's children, as well as the mother's health. A famous reason given by classical jurists is to preserve the beauty and grace of the wife.

Less well-educated religious leaders in small towns and villages sometimes still hold that family planning is prohibited by Islam. Their reasoning follows a different line, which is argued on deterministic grounds. They base their premise on a *ḥadīth* that states, "Marry, have children and multiply that I will be proud of you on Judgment Day." They prohibit family planning on the basis that it opposes the supremacy of the will of God. Some countries have introduced educational programs to train these religious leaders in line with the positions of more educated religious leaders.

Some Muslim scholars, as well as economists and development experts, have challenged Islam's pronatalist policy by questioning whether the traditional way of defining the strength of Islam as proportional to the number of its adherents still applies. Maḥmūd Shaltūt, rector of al-Azhar University during the early part of the regime of Gamal Abdel Nasser, argued in a classic statement for both the permissibility of family planning and the role of the state in implementing family-planning programs. Although in early Islam strength was equated with a large population, Shaltūt maintained that in the twentieth century, large populations may weaken rather than strengthen communities. Factors such as poverty, malnutrition, and lessened public morality that are concomitant with large populations in developing areas all make the Muslim community vulnerable to enemies. Shaltūt stated that if family planning would contribute to alleviation of these social ills, it was permissible in Islam; he implied that the state was responsible for the facilitation of such programs.

Contemporary *ʿulamāʾ* and political leaders who oppose family planning generally cite reasons having as much to do with politics as religion. The terms used for contraception often indicate political stances. "Birth control" (*taḥdīd al-naṣl*) carries the negative sense of limiting or eliminating progeny; "family planning" (*al-takhṭīṭ al-ʿāʾilī* or *tanẓīm al-usrah*) has the more positive connotation of spacing births in the best interests of all family members. While most ʿulamāʾ hold that any family has the option privately to employ family planning measures, most also uphold the general principle of supporting strong families, and oppose government programs which set limiting birth as a national policy rather than a tool to strengthen families.

While many political Islamists espouse a moderate view on family planning, some inveigh against national programs and birth control. Abul Aʿla Maududi (d. 1979), the philosopher and political leader, stated that a movement designed to limit or stop reproduction is repugnant to Islam. Religiously based political parties in Pakistan and Bangladesh state that family planning is both unnecessary and counter to Islamic belief. Rather, Muslims should rely on God for sustenance and further Muslim inventiveness and dedication in the conquest of the desert and better use of resources. In surveys of unmet need for contraception, a small minority still cites religious reasons for not using family planning. Iran's national family-planning program was downsized when the Islamic Republic came to power. During the war with Iraq, Iranian patriotic needs called for manpower to strengthen its national defense and downsized the family-planning program to produce more soldiers. The resulting high population growth strained economic resources. A national program, implemented in 1986, has become one of the most effective in the region.

In vitro fertilization and sperm or egg donation are prohibited in conservative Muslim circles as a form of adultery, as they unify the products of two individuals who are not married. Traditionally, Sunnī and Shīʿī schools both took a hard line against the use of reproductive technologies. However, when Ayatollah Ali Hussein Khamanei, the Supreme Leader of Iran, issued a fatwa in 1999 that permitted reproductive technologies—specifically, donor sperm and eggs to be used under certain conditions—Shīʿī scholars became more open to reconfiguring the reasoning behind productive technology. While Sunnī scholars generally follow established precedents laid out in jurisprudence, Shīʿī scholars are more open to independently based religious reasoning, or *ijtihad*, which allows them room in ruling on contemporary issues.

The rising age of marriage, high youth unemployment, and high-priced housing are factors that combine to delay marriage, and thus sexual relations within marriage. Concern that the use of family planning contributes to greater immorality—in the form of premarital sexual activity, adultery, and abortion—is widespread. Negative positions on family planning may seek to limit unmarried women's sexual activity. A double standard on sexuality ensures that women's sexual activity outside of marriage is denounced, but not that of men. Groups that criticize family planning often also advocate restricting the extension of greater rights to women in personal status, education, or employment.

[*See also* Abortion *and* Surrogate Motherhood.]

BIBLIOGRAPHY

Ali, Kamran Asdar. *Planning the Family in Egypt: New Bodies, New Selves*. Cairo, Egypt: American University in Cairo Press, 2003. A case study of state-sponsored family planning and its impact on women in Egypt.

Bowen, Donna Lee. "Islamic Law and Family Planning." In *Islam and Social Policy*, edited by Stephen P. Heyneman, pp. 118–155. Nashville, Tenn.: Vanderbilt University Press, 2004. Survey of Muslim theological and popular opinions on family planning in medieval and contemporary times.

Bowen, Donna Lee. "Muslim Juridical Opinions Concerning the Status of Women as Demonstrated by the Case of Azl." *Journal of Near Eastern Studies* 40, no. 4 (1981): 323–328. Presentation of Muslim legal schools' positions on contraceptive use.

Himes, Norman Edward. *Medical History of Contraception*. New York: Schocken Books, 1970. Originally published in 1936. Chapter 6, "The Islamic World and Europe during the Middle Ages," details contraceptive methods used in that period.

Inhorn, Marcia C. "Making Muslim Babies: IVF and Gamete Donation in Sunnī versus Shīʿah Islam." *Culture, Medicine and Psychiatry* 30, no. 4 (December 2006): 427–450. http://www.ncbi.nlm.nih.gov/pmc/articles/PMC1705533/.

Maududi, Abul Aʿala. *Birth Control: Its Social, Political, Economic, Moral and Religious Aspects*. 3d ed. Translated and edited by Khurshid Ahmad and Misbahul Islam Faruqi. Lahore, Pakistan: Islamic Publications Limited, 1983.

Musallam, Basim F. *Sex and Society in Islam: Birth Control before the Nineteenth Century*. Cambridge: Cambridge University Press, 1983. Excellent study of family planning in theory and practice, and the demography of Muslim nations during the medieval and early modern periods.

Nazer, Isam R., ed. *Islam and Family Planning*. 2 vols. Beirut, Lebanon: International Planned Parenthood, 1974. Collection of articles by Muslim theologians (ʿulamāʾ) on all aspects of marriage, family, and family planning. First published in Arabic.

Omran, Abdel Rahim. *Family Planning in the Legacy of Islam*. London: Routledge, 1992. Comprehensive collection and discussion of Qurʾānic, *ḥadīth*, and jurisprudence references relating to marriage, the family, and family planning.

Pew Research Center Forum on Religion and Public Life. "The Future of the Global Muslim Population: Projections for 2010–2030." Washington DC, January 2011. http://www.pewforum.org/uploadedFiles/Topics/Religious_Affiliation/Muslim/FutureGlobalMuslimPopulation-WebPDF-Feb10.pdf. Report on Muslim populations worldwide. Roudi-Fahimi, Farzaneh, and Mary Mederios Kent. "Challenges and Opportunities–The Population of the Middle East and North Africa." Special issue, *Population Bulletin* 62.2 (June 2007): http://prb.org/pdf07/62.2MENA.pdf. Comprehensive survey of population and demographic issues and their implications for policy.

Shaltūt, Maḥmūd. "Tanẕīm al-Nasl." In *Al-islām: ʿAqīdah washarīʿah*. Cairo, Egypt: 1966. Controversial reading of Islamic social theory by the politically astute rector of al-Azhar.

DONNA LEE BOWEN

FATAYAT NAHDLATUL ʿULAMĀʾ. A young women's organization in Indonesia, Fatayat Nahdlatul ʿUlamāʾ is an integral part of Nahdlatul ʿUlamāʾ (NU), the largest Islamic organization in the country. NU has also established an organization for adult women called Muslimat NU, as well as one for female students called Female Students of the NU Association (IPPNU). In line with the vision of its founding, Fatayat NU seeks to strengthen the rights of women and make women's rights a strategic issue. Fatayat NU is pioneered by Murthosiyah, Khuzaimah Mansur, and Aminah Mansur, with support from Kyai Haji Dahlan, the chairperson of NU.

Since it was officially established in Surabaya on 24 April 1950, Fatayat Nahdlatul ʿUlamāʾ has focused on providing foreign-language training to women, as it recognizes the importance of language as a means of communicating with other people, and strengthening not only individual women's knowledge, but also the organization's network throughout the world. This informal educational training has proven to be particularly important to volunteers and Fatayat administrators who want to continue their education abroad. It has also served to strengthen the Islamic discourse among, and intellectual struggle of, women in the Muslim world.

Fatayat pilot activities appear to differ from those of other Indonesian Muslim women's organizations, which have tended to emphasize formal education and philanthropic efforts, such as maternity hospitals, and schools and kindergartens, including those established by Muslimat NU and Aisyiyah Muhammadiyah. Fatayat also differs from Nasyiatul Aisyiyah of Muhammadiyah and IPPNU, both of which emphasize programs and activities for students and scouts. Fatayat is also distinct from the Rahima Foundation in Jakarta, Kapal Perempuan in Jakarta, and Rifqa An-Nisa in Yogyakarta, all of which are non-governmental organizations (NGOs) without a central management board, which draw people together from similar cultural backgrounds. Fatayat NU has a solid base of young women, particularly from peasant and rural communities, as well as young urban women who follow NU's interpretation of Islamic tradition. Organizationally, Fatayat NU has rural, sub district, district, provincial and central boards. Membership currently numbers approximately 4 million.

Fatayat NU has a number of programs and divisions addressing different areas, including management, advocacy, politics, legal issues, the environment, health, research and development, and *daʿwah* (missionary work). Some of these programs have broad national and international relevance, such as reproductive health, gender awareness, and political education. These agendas are supported by international organizations such as the United Nations Children's Fund (UNICEF), Academic Education Development (AED), Helen Keller Indonesia (HKI), the Australian Government Overseas Aid Program (AUSAID), the Ford Foundation, the Asia Foundation, and the domestic institutions of some ministerial departments. Several international women activists and researchers also collaborate with Fatayat NU, including Asma Barlas, Margot Badran, Amina Rasul, Ziba Mir Hosseini, Vivien Wie, and Ahmed Ragaʾa Abdel Hamid Ragab, among others. In addition, Fatayat has contributed to Committee on the Elimination of Discrimination against Women's (CEDAW) monitoring and overseeing of the recognition of women's rights in Indonesia, particularly by working to raise awareness of women's rights in Indonesian society. It often finds that women are aware only of their duties, not their rights, particularly in the domestic arena.

Fatayat NU initiated a massive program addressing reproductive health called Bina Balita (Health Improvement in Under Five Years) in 1989. This program reached fifteen provinces and 308 districts in Indonesia. Another program, conducted in 1993, called Somavita (Marketing Vitamin A) promoted vitamin A intake specifically among women living in the slums of Jakarta—women who rarely receive attention from NGOs and other women's organizations. In running these programs, Fatayat cooperates with existing Islamic organizations and NGOs working on women's issues, such as Legal Assistance and Legal Campaign Advocacy Indonesian Women's Association for Justice (LBH APIK), Kalyanamitra, and Fiqhun NisaʿP3M (Center for Pesantren and Community Development) in Jakarta. Maternal-and child-health issues were also positively addressed by Fatayat NU in the provinces, such as Yogyakarta, through the Fatayat Welfare Foundation, from 1990 to 2003.

Along with the development of the women's movement, under the direction of Sri Mulyati Asror (1989–2000) Fatayat NU began to hold gender awareness training. The participants, in addition to administrators of Fatayat NU, were from pesantren of NU. The first venue was Maslakul Huda Boarding School in Pati, Central Java, and this first session was led by Kyai Haji Sahal Mahfudz. Fatayat NU also strengthens the rights of women through gender sensitivity training, as well as through the establishment, in 1998, of LKP2, a consulting agency specializing in women's empowerment. It has offices in twenty-six districts. As a consulting agency, LKP2 deals with women's issues, including reproductive health and domestic violence. LKP2 played a pivotal role in drafting the Domestic Violence Act, which became law in 2004. To support the programs of LKP2, Fatayat NU also established the Center for Reproduction of Health). Since 2006, in cooperation with the Ministry of Health, Fatayat has conducted reproductive health education for brides.

In 1997, the issue of gender equality was raised during the National Assembly of 'Ulamā', hosted by NU in Lombok NTB. With the encouragement of its members, NU had issued a *fatwa* No. 004/MN-NU/11/1997) on the position of women in Islam (*Makanatul mar' ah fi al-Islam*). This decision was a new milestone for NU, as it had previously been known as a conservative and male-dominated organization.

Under the leadership of Maria Ulfah Anshor (2000–2010), a program of gender mainstreaming in Fatayat NU was implemented with the intent of leading to gender equality. A re-interpretation of Islamic teaching was conducted, as in the case of abortion, resulting in the publication of a book on jurisprudence on abortion (*Fikih aborsi*). To gain legal legitimacy and wider moral appeal, Fatayat NU filed a draft on anti-human trafficking to the National Assembly of 'Ulamā' held in 2006. Believing that this effort must be sustainably implemented, Fatayat published a guideline book for migrant workers in 2009. The book was distributed throughout the Middle East, Hong Kong, Singapore, and Malaysia.

Fatayat has also engaged in political education and advocacy against discriminatory regulations, such as laws on pornography and health. Since 1999, political education has been conducted through the Voters Education Network for People, in collaboration with campus organizations, and interfaith and other youth NGOs. In 2010, Fatayat worked with the State Minister for Women Empowerment and the Gender-Islamic Studies of Indonesia University by managing a workshop for female leadership for women of pesantren, known as Nyai throughout Banten province.

All Fatayat NU programs are disseminated through its own media ventures, including books, the magazine *Suara Fatayat*, the official web site (http://fatayat.or.id), its mailing list, and newspapers, as well as through the active encouragement of dialogue and discussion.

BIBLIOGRAPHY

Arnez, Monika. "Empowering Women Through Islam: Fatayat NU Between Tradition and Change." *Journal of Islamic Studies* 21, no. 1 (2010): 59–88.

PBNU. *Hasil-Hasil Musyawarah Nasional Alim Ulama NU*. 2–5 Rajab 1427. 27–30 July 2006. Jakarta, Indonesia: PBNU, 2006.

Keputusan Musyawarah Nasional Alim Ulama tentang Kedudukan Wanita Dalam Islam, no. 004/MN-NU/11/1997. Jakarta, Indonesia: PBNU, 1997.

Affiah, Neng Dara, et. al. *Menapak Jejak Fatayat NU, Sejarah Gerakan, Pengalaman dan Pemikiran*. Jakarta, Indonesia: PP Fatayat NU, 2005.

Rofiah, Nur, and Ala' I Nadjib. *Mari Kenali Hak-Hak Buruh Migran Indonesia* (Let's Identify Migrant Workers). Jakarta, Indonesia: PP Fatayat NU, 2009.

PP Fatayat NU. *Panduan Singkat Melawan Perdagangan Manusia*. Jakarta, Indonesia, PP Fatayat NU, 2007.

PP Fatayat NU. *Sistem Pengkaderan Fatayat NU, Pengkaderan Untuk Pemberdayaan*. Jakarta, Indonesia: PP Fatayat NU, 2005.

PP Fatayat NU and Seri Buku Saku. *Pendidikan Kesehatan Reproduksi Bagi Calon Pengantin* (Reproductive Health Education for Brides). Jakarta, Indonesia, 2007.

Suara Fatayat 5 (May 2008).

Ulfah, Maria. "Penguatan Partisipasi Politik Perempuan Untuk Indonesia yang Lebih Baik." (Speech on the Fifty-Ninth Anniversary of Fatayat NU). Jakarta, Indonesia: PP Fatayat NU, 2009.

ALA' I NADJIB

FATIMA BINT MUBARAK, SHEIKHA.

(BCE 1940), mother of the United Arab Emirates.

Her Highness Sheikha Fatima bint Mubarak was born in Al Hayer, Al Ain. One of several wives to Sheikh bin Zāyid, Sulṭān al-Nahayān (d. 2004), they married in the 1960s. Sheikh bin Zāyid was the founder and first president of the United Arab Emirates (UAE) after its federation in 1971 and, previously, ruler of the Eastern Region of Abu Dhabi. Sheikha Fatima played a pivotal role in supporting her husband during unification and the establishment of basic infrastructure for the country. As first lady, she is referred to as the mother of the nation.

She has also played a pioneering role in women's development in the UAE. Since the establishment of the General Women's Union in 1975, Sheikha Fatima has chaired the umbrella women's organization. She is also chairperson of the Family Development Foundation. Her leadership role for women extends to the rest of the Arab world, heading the Cairo-based Arab Women's Organization (AWO). One of her greatest achievements has been in the area of literacy, for which she mounted numerous campaigns to eradicate the illiteracy that mostly affects women. By 2003, 80.7 percent of girls aged 11 and older were literate, with 99 percent of all girls 10 and younger attending school.

It is in the areas of women's and children's education that Sheikha's accomplishments have largely occurred. She has steered a number of programs adopted by women's organizations in all seven emirates. Some programs address skills development, such as those needed to achieve computer literacy. Other programs aim to enhance women's understanding of a number of subjects, such as those related to raising children, marriage, health, and beauty. Numerous courses are provided through women's societies to develop women's knowledge of religion and traditional handicrafts.

Sheikha Fatima has enabled women's empowerment through her support and funding of various endeavors and awards. The Sheikha Fatima bint Mubarak Award for Excellence is granted to one exceptional female student each year.

Sheikha Fatima holds the vision of women shouldering the development of the nation through their unique strengths. She encourages women to enter fields that have been occupied traditionally by men, such as politics and the media. Yet, she emphasizes women's participation as built on their feminine capacities, thus encouraging a unique approach to development in which women's feminine strengths are embraced.

She encourages women's participation through their capacities as mothers and nurturers and through their abilities acquired through higher education. By facilitating women's active role in the productive spheres, both private and public, Sheikha Fatima aims to achieve holistic development on the human, socioeconomic, and political levels for the UAE.

Sheikha Fatima has received numerous awards for her impact on women in the UAE and beyond. In 1997 alone, she received five United Nations awards: from the UN's Children's Fund (UNICEF), the World Health Organization (WHO), the UN's Population Fund (UNFPA), the UN's Volunteers (UNV) Programme, and the UN's Development Fund for Women (UNIFEM). She has received numerous other awards for her contributions to development and women's empowerment, including the International Family Organization Award in 1999, the UAE University Award in 2008, the Al Owais Cultural Foundation Cultural and Scientific Achievement Award in 2009, and the UNDP Memorial Shield of Honour in 2011.

BIBLIOGRAPHY

DeLong-Bas, Natana. *Notable Muslims: Muslim Builders of World Civilization and Culture*. London: Oneworld, 2006. See especially page 95.

Emirates Centre for Strategic Studies and Research. "Second AWO Conference and UAE Efforts in Support of Arab Women's Issues." http://www.ecssr.ac.ae/ECSSR/print/ft.jsp?lang=.%20Family%20Development%20Foundation.

"Sheikha Fatima Bint Mubarak: Mother of Nation." http://motherofnation.ae/.

Sultan Bin Ali Al Owais Cultural Foundation. "Sheikha Fatima Bint Mubarak." http://www.alowaisnet.org/en/winnersbio/abijgjfcfjedfhgejj.aspx.

Swaroop, Sangeetha. "Her Highness Sheikha Fatima bint Mubarak: National Heroine and International Champion of Women Rights." *Al Shindagah* 76 (June–July 2007).

WANDA KRAUSE

FĀṬIMAH. Fāṭimah, the youngest daughter of Muḥammad, is an important persona in Muslim salvation history, in which her status has been elevated through the centuries. She is mentioned rarely in the earliest sources, and even her date of birth is disputed. Her mother, Khadījah al-Kubrā (the Great), died shortly after her birth. As a young child, she accompanied her father during his Meccan mission and consoled him when he was mistreated. This role of caring for her father continued throughout her short life, earning her the title of *umm abīhā* (mother of her father). Fāṭimah was either nine or nineteen at the time of her marriage to ʿAlī, son of Muḥammad's supportive uncle Abū Ṭālib. Her health deteriorated because of the poverty and hardships of the early Medinan years, along with childbearing. She bore four children, al-Ḥasan, al-Ḥusayn, Zaynab, and Umm Kulthūm. She died in 632 CE, some months after her father Muḥammad.

The *ḥadīth* "Whatever hurts Fāṭimah hurts me" is cited by Sunnīs when referring to the Prophet's opposition to ʿAlī's intention to marry other women in addition to Fāṭimah. The Shīʿī use the same *ḥadīth* to argue that, because Fāṭimah was opposed to and did not ratify Abū Bakr's caliphate, it was not legitimate. The dispute regarding the Garden of Fadak, reportedly promised to Fāṭimah by Muḥammad but denied to her by Abū Bakr on the premise that prophets leave no inheritable estate, serves as a metaphor for the core Shīʿah and Sunnīs as to whether the Prophet's spiritual legacy is passed down through his bloodline or not.

Fāṭimah is revered by all Muslims, but her position is unique in Shīʿī theology and eschatology, where she is presented as the one who fought until the last for the true legacy of the Prophet and who will therefore be invited to judge on the Last Day. The Shīʿah understand the Qurʾānic term *kawthar* (overflowing abundance) in "Verily We granted you *al-kawthar*" (108:1) to refer to Fāṭimah, because she is the only child through whom Muḥammad and Khadījah's line continues, thus undermining the claims that without a son, Muḥammad's name and legacy would not survive beyond his life. She was the fruit of Muḥammad and Khadījah's strengths and, from the Shīʿī perspective, the female counterpart to the male Prophet. She also bears the titles of Zahrāʿ (the Radiant, referring to her spiritual power) and Batūl (the Virgin, referring to her chastity, piety, and independent status). As the link between the two agnate lines of Muḥammad, the last Prophet, and ʿAlī, the first Shīʿī imam, Fāṭimah is central to the (otherwise all male) holy family of five—which includes Muḥammad, ʿAlī, al-Ḥasan (the second Shīʿī imam), and al-Ḥusayn (the third Shīʿī imam)—represented symbolically by the Hand of Fāṭimah, often depicted on Shīʿī ritual objects.

A shrine containing a replica tomb, the *zareen* (*zarīn*) of Fāṭimah, makes up part of the South Asian Shīʿī imam *bargahs* (ritual centers) and is a place of pilgrimage. For many, Fāṭimah functions as a saint who comes to the aid of those calling upon her to alleviate their travails or to grant their requests.

[*See also* Khadīja bint Khuwaylid.]

BIBLIOGRAPHY

Lammens, Henri. "Fatima." In *The Quest for the Historical Muhammad*, edited by Ibn Warraq, pp. 218–336. Amherst, N.Y.: Prometheus Books, 2000. Despite the cynical and derogatory tone, it is one of the few historical critical studies on Fāṭimah.

Massignon, Louis. "Der gnostische Kult der Fatima in shiitischen Islam." In *Opera Minora*, edited by Y. Moubarac, vol. 1, pp. 514–522. Beirut, Lebanon: Dar Al-Maaref-Liban, 1963. This 1938 work contains a respectful account of Fāṭimah and a translation of an elegy by Ibrāhīm Ṭūsī (1350 CE). The elegy is an example of how the status of Fāṭimah in popular devotion was elevated through the centuries.

Sharīʿatī, ʿAlī. *Ali Shariati's Fatima Is Fatima*. Translated by Laleh Bakhtiar. Tehran, Iran: Shariati Foundation, 1981. See part 2, pp. 123–226. A lecture delivered by Sharīʿatī to young Iranian women for whom Fāṭimah and the details of her life are most familiar. Insightful, inspiring, and empowering for the intended audience. Although the translation is not the best, this text is a good example of the power that Fāṭimah holds for Shīʿah.

Spellberg, D. A. *Politics, Gender, and the Islamic Past: The Legacy of ʿAʾisha bint Abi Bakr*. New York, 1994. In her discussion of ʿĀʾisha, Spellberg compares her to Fāṭimah, as the opposing figure in both family and community politics.

GHAZALA ANWAR

FĀṬIMID DYNASTY.

The Fāṭimid dynasty was a major Ismāʿīlī Shīʿī dynasty that ruled over parts of North Africa and the Middle East from 909 until 1171 CE Ruled by the following fourteen caliphs, the Fāṭimids were also acknowledged as Ismāʿīlī imams:

1. al-Mahdī (909–934)
2. al-Qāʾim (934–946)
3. al-Manṣūr (946–953)
4. al-Muʿizz (953–975)
5. al-ʿAzīz (975–996)
6. al-Ḥākim (996–1021)
7. al-Ẓāhir (1021–1036)
8. al-Mustanṣir (1036–1094)
9. al-Mustaʿlī (1094–1101)
10. al-Āmir (1101–1130)
11. al-Ḥāfiẓ (as regent 1130–1132, then as caliph-imam 1132–1149)
12. al-Ẓāfir (1149–1154)
13. al-Fāʾiz (1154–1160)
14. al-ʿĀḍid (1160–1171)

Early Fāṭimids. By the mid-ninth century, the Ismāʿīlīs had organized a dynamic, revolutionary movement, generally designated as *al-daʿwah al-hādīyah* or the rightly guiding mission. The aim of this movement, led secretly from Salamīyah in Syria, was to install the Ismāʿīlī imam in a new Shīʿī caliphate, in rivalry with the Sunnī ʿAbbāsids. The Ismāʿīlī imams traced their ʿAlid ancestry to Ismāʿīl, the eponym of the Ismāʿīlīyah and the original heir designate of his father, the early Shīʿī imam Jaʿfar al-Ṣādiq (d. 765 CE). The early Ismāʿīlī *daʿwah*, propagated by a network of *dāʿīs*, or missionaries, throughout the Islamic world, achieved particular success in North Africa as a result of the efforts of Abū ʿAbd Allāh al-Shīʿī, who was active from 893 among the Kutāma Berbers of the Lesser Kabylia, in present-day eastern Algeria. By 903 Abū ʿAbd Allāh had commenced his conquest of Ifrīqiyah, covering modern Tunisia and eastern Algeria, ruled at the time by the Sunnī Aghlabids as vassals of the ʿAbbāsids. By 909 Abū ʿAbd Allāh entered Qayrawān, the Aghlabid capital, and ended their rule.

In 902 CE the Ismāʿīlī imam ʿAbd Allāh al-Mahdī (who had succeeded his ancestors in the leadership of the *daʿwah*) left Salamīyah to avoid capture by the ʿAbbāsids. After brief stays in Palestine and Egypt, he lived in Sijilmāsa, in southern Morocco, from 905; he continued to hide his identity while maintaining contact with the *dāʿī* Abū ʿAbd Allāh. In June 909 Abū ʿAbd Allāh set off at the head of his Kutāma army to Sijilmāsa, to hand the reins of power to the Ismāʿīlī imam. ʿAbd Allāh al-Mahdī entered Qayrawān on 4 January 910 and was immediately proclaimed caliph. The Ismāʿīlī *daʿwah* finally led to the establishment of a *dawlah*, or state, headed by the Ismāʿīlī imam. The Shīʿī caliphate of the Fāṭimids commenced in Ifrīqiyah and came to be known as the Fāṭimid dynasty or Fāṭimīyah, named for the Prophet's daughter and ʿAlī's wife, Fāṭimah, to whom al-Mahdī and his successors traced their ancestry.

Consolidation and Resistance. The first four Fāṭimid caliph-imams, ruling from Ifrīqiyah, encountered numerous difficulties while consolidating their power. In addition to the continued hostility of the ʿAbbāsids, the Umayyads of Spain, and the Byzantines, the early Fāṭimids devoted much energy to subduing the rebellious Khārijī Berbers belonging to the Zanātah confederation, especially the prolonged revolt of Abū Yazīd. They also confronted hostile Sunnī Arab inhabitants of Qayrawān and other cities of Ifrīqiyah, led by their Mālikī jurists. The Fāṭimids were city builders and founded al-Mahdīyah and al-Manṣūrīyah (the precursor of Cairo); these served as their new capitals in Ifrīqiyah.

In line with their universal claims, the Fāṭimids continued their *daʿwah* activities after they assumed power. The *daʿwah* was reinvigorated from the time of al-Muʿizz, who firmly established Fāṭimid rule in North Africa and successfully pursued policies of war and diplomacy, resulting in territorial expansion. Al-Muʿizz also made detailed plans for the conquest of Egypt, a perennial objective of the Fāṭimids in their eastern strategy of expansion. Jawhar, a commander of long service to the dynasty, led the Fāṭimid expedition to Egypt in 969 CE A new residential and administrative complex was founded north of Fusṭāt and rapidly developed into a city, al-Qāhirah (Cairo). Al-Muʿizz arrived in his new capital city in 973, marking the end of the North African phase of the Fāṭimid caliphate.

Fāṭimid Empire and Contributions. Naval and military power, the splendor of the court, Egypt's artistic productions, and burgeoning international trade helped to project the Fāṭimid regime as an equal of the Byzantine and ʿAbbāsid empires. Politically and militarily, however, its efforts to advance through Syria were checked in the second half of the tenth century CE by a resurgence of Byzantine power and armies of the Qarmaṭīs of Baḥrayn, and later by the incursions of the Turkish Seljuks. Despite these setbacks, by the end of al-ʿAzīz's reign, the Fāṭimid empire had attained its greatest extent, at least nominally, with Fāṭimid sovereignty recognized from the Maghrib to the Red Sea, Syria, and Palestine.

At the same time, Ismāʿīlī *dāʿīs*, acting as secret agents of the Fāṭimid state, continued their activities both within and outside Fāṭimid dominions, with Cairo serving as the headquarters of the Ismāʿīlī *daʿwah*. But within the Fāṭimid state, the Ismāʿīlī doctrines made little headway among the population at large. In Fāṭimid Egypt, the population remained predominantly Sunnī with an important community of Coptic Christians. Indeed, the Ismāʿīlī *daʿwah* had its greatest lasting success outside of Fāṭimid dominions, especially in Yemen, Iraq, Iran, and Central Asia.

The Fāṭimids established many institutions of learning in Cairo, including al-Azhar, originally a mosque but converted to a university, and the Dār al-ʿIlm, or "House of Knowledge," established in 1005 CE by al-Ḥākim. During al-Ḥākim's reign, certain *dāʿīs* preached extremist ideas that culminated in the proclamation of this controversial caliph-imam's divinity and the formation of the Druze movement, which was opposed by the Fāṭimid regime.

Women's Role and Contributions. The Fāṭimid caliph-imams, as noted, traced their ʿAlid ancestry to the Prophet Muḥammad's daughter Fāṭimah, the foremost female figure in the annals of the Ismāʿīlīs and other Shīʿī communities. Fāṭimah's birthday was celebrated under the Fāṭimids, who also named her in the Friday *khuṭbah*s as well as on their coins.

The Fāṭimids generally esteemed the status of women, especially those affiliated in some way with their court. Compared to almost all other medieval Muslim dynasties, the Fāṭimids were particularly concerned with learning and teaching, including the religious education of the Ismāʿīlīs, both men and women. They elaborated distinctive traditions of learning and instituted a variety of lectures or teaching sessions for furthering the education of Ismāʿīlī converts. Generally designated as *majālis* (sing. *majlis*), the sessions related to *ḥikmah*, as esoteric Ismāʿīlī doctrine was known, were designated as *majālis al-ḥikmah* or "sessions of wisdom." These sessions had been initiated already in North Africa during the time of Abū ʿAbd Allāh al-Shīʿī, who lectured to the Kutāma Berbers on the virtues of the Prophet's family (*ahl al-bayt*) and the ʿAlid imams acknowledged by the Ismāʿīlīs, with separate sessions for Berber women. Subsequently, these lectures, normally delivered by the chief *dāʿī* (*dāʿī al-duʿāt*), developed with increasing formalization into an elaborate program of instruction, especially after the Fāṭimids established themselves in Cairo. By the rule of al-Ḥākim, different types of sessions were organized for different audiences. A separate session was held for the Ismāʿīlī women at al-Azhar Mosque, while the royal and noble women received their religious instruction at the Fāṭimid palace. The Ismāʿīlī *dāʿīs* operating within the Fāṭimid state, and at least the major *dāʿīs* active outside Fāṭimid dominions, held similar sessions for the exclusive benefit of their male and female converts.

Under the Fāṭimids, numerous royal ladies attained positions of prominence, with substantial wealth and prestige, as mothers, wives, or daughters of the caliph-imams. The original base of these women's prominence was, of course, the Fāṭimid court. Among such women, several also wielded political influence and enjoyed power as regents, with significant impacts on the events of the Fāṭimid state and the course of the dynasty's history. In the latter category, the two foremost figures were al-Ḥakim's half-sister Sitt al-Mulk and al-Mustanṣir's mother Raṣad.

Sitt al-Mulk, a daughter of al-ʿAzīz, is in fact one of the most famous women of Islamic history and, like many other daughters of the Fāṭimid caliph-imams, she never married for dynastic reasons. This influential and shrewd Fāṭimid princess, with a large retinue and impressive land holdings, seems to have exercised some influence on her much younger half-brother al-Ḥākim, who succeeded their father al-ʿAzīz to the Fāṭimid throne in 996 CE at the age of eleven. However, in the final years of al-Ḥākim's rule, relations deteriorated between the caliph and Sitt al-Mulk, who gave protection in her own palace to al-Ḥākim's sole son, ʿAlī. The latter had been bypassed as heir designate by al-Ḥākim, who had named a cousin, ʿAbd al-Raḥīm ibn Ilyās, to that position. ʿAlī, the future Fāṭimid caliph-imam al-Ẓāhir, was, in fact, brought up under Sitt al-Mulk's close tutelage. On al-Ḥākim's mysterious disappearance in 1021, Sitt al-Mulk used all her power and influence to eliminate ʿAbd al-Raḥīm and declare her sixteen-year-old nephew as caliph-imam, but she retained the reign of government in her own hands as regent. Until her death in 1023, Sitt al-Mulk, who is given various honorifics such as *al-sayyidah al-ʿammah* in the literature, ruled efficiently, restoring order to the affairs of the Fāṭimid state and also confronting certain religious and social issues that had earlier caused serious grievances.

By contrast to Sitt al-Mulk, who was a member of the Fāṭimid household, Raṣad was originally a Sudanese or Nubian slave purchased by the caliph al-Ẓāhir from a Jewish merchant named Abū Saʿd al-Tustarī. Raṣad bore the next Fāṭimid caliph, al-Mustanṣir, who succeeded to the throne at the age of seven, in 1036 CE, while Raṣad acted as regent for him and exercised considerable influence with the support of the black regiment of the Fāṭimid armies. By 1045 Raṣad, who initially shared power with Abū Saʿd al-Tustarī, seized all power and maintained it for a long period. The arrival of Badr al-Jamālī in Cairo in 1074 effectively ended Raṣad's supremacy within the Fāṭimid establishment, though she continued to exercise some influence as the queen mother. Indeed, for almost four decades, Raṣad assumed a key role in the court politics and affairs of the Fāṭimid state, appointing viziers and extending the all-important court patronage to various other individuals. Subsequently, when viziers, rather than caliphs, held effective power in the Fāṭimid state, several daughters of Fāṭimid viziers played crucial roles in the affairs of state, especially when they were also married to Fāṭimid caliphs. In addition, some of these women acted as patrons of the arts and mosques.

Women also played active roles in the Ismāʿīlī *daʿwah* activities in Fāṭimid times. In this context, the most eminent figure was the Ṣulayḥid queen of Yemen, Sayyidah Arwā, who bore the epithet of Ḥurra. The Ṣulayḥids ruled over parts of Yemen from 1047 to 1138 CE, recognizing the suzerainty of the Fāṭimids. Married to the second Ṣulayḥid ruler, al-Mukarram Aḥmad, Arwā was the co-ruler of Yemen with her husband from 1074 and the sole effective ruler from 1084. Queen Arwā maintained close relations with al-Mustanṣir and his two successors in the Fāṭimid dynasty. She was, in fact, formally entrusted by al-Mustanṣir with the leadership of the Ismāʿīlī *daʿwah* in Yemen as the *ḥujjah* of Yemen, a rank higher than *dāʿī* and the highest rank in the *daʿwah* organization of any region, on the death of her husband in 1084. A few years later, she was also given responsibility for the *daʿwah* activities in India. Queen Arwā thus exercised both political and religious authority in Yemen on behalf of the Fāṭimid caliph-imams. By the time of her death, in 1138, she had already founded the independent Ṭayyibī *daʿwah*, ensuring the survival of the only form of the Mustaʿlian *daʿwah* after the downfall of the Fāṭimid dynasty.

Decline and Dissent. Fueled by factional rivalries within the Fāṭimid armies and economic troubles exacerbated by famines, plagues and insufficient Nile floods, the Fāṭimid caliphate began its decline during the long reign of al-Mustanṣir, who was eventually obliged to call on the Armenian commander Badr al-Jamālī for help. In 1074 CE Badr arrived in Cairo with his Armenian troops and speedily restored relative peace and stability to the Fāṭimid state. Badr became the "commander of the armies" (*amīr al-juyūsh*) and the first of the "viziers of the sword," in addition to attaining the highest positions of the Fāṭimid state. Henceforth, military men, frequently appointed as viziers, rather than caliphs themselves, exercised effective power in the Fāṭimid state. Badr (d. 1094) also ensured that his son al-Afḍal would succeed him as the real master of the Fāṭimid state.

On the death of al-Mustanṣir in 1094 CE, the Ismāʿīlīs split into the Nizārī and Mustaʿlian factions, named after al-Mustanṣir's sons, who claimed his heritage. From this point forward, these two branches of the Ismāʿīlīyah recognized different lines of imams. The cause of Nizār (d. 1095), the designated successor of al-Mustanṣir who was ousted by al-Afḍal, was taken up in Iran by Ḥasan-i Ṣabbāḥ (d. 1124), who founded the independent Nizārī *daʿwah* and state. The Mustaʿlian Ismāʿīlīs of Fāṭimid Egypt and elsewhere acknowledged al-Mustaʿlī, who was installed as the Fāṭimid caliph by al-Afḍal, also as their imam. By 1132, in the aftermath of al-Āmir's assassination and the irregular succession of his cousin al-Ḥāfiẓ, the Mustaʿlian Ismāʿīlīs themselves split into the Ḥāfiẓī and Ṭayyibī branches. Only the Ḥāfiẓīs, concentrated mainly in Egypt, recognized al-Ḥāfiẓ and the later Fāṭimids as their imams.

The final decades of the Fāṭimid caliphate were extremely turbulent. Reduced to Egypt proper, the Fāṭimid state was now continuously beset by political and economic crises, worsened by disorder within the Fāṭimid armies, the arrival of the Crusaders, and the invasions of the Zangids of Syria. Ṣalāḥ al-Dīn (Saladin), initially a lieutenant of the Zangids and the last of the Fāṭimid viziers, ended Fāṭimid rule in 1171 CE and ordered the *khuṭbah* (Friday sermon) read in Cairo in the name of the ʿAbbāsid caliph.

BIBLIOGRAPHY

Cortese, Delia, and Simonetta Calderini. *Women and the Fatimids in the World of Islam*. Edinburgh: Edinburgh University Press, 2006.

Daftary, Farhad. *The Ismāʿīlīs: Their History and Doctrines*. 2d ed. Cambridge, U.K.: Cambridge University Press, 2007.

Daftary, Farhad. "Sayyida Ḥurra: The Ismāʿīlī Ṣulayḥid Queen of Yemen." In *Women in the Medieval Islamic World*, edited by Gavin R. G. Hambly, pp. 117–130. New York: St. Martin's Press, 1998.

Halm, Heinz. *The Empire of the Mahdi: The Rise of the Fatimids*. Translated from the German by M. Bonner. Leiden, Netherlands: E. J. Brill, 1996.

Halm, Heinz. *Die Kalifen von Kairo: Die Fatimiden in Agypten 973–1074*. Munich: Beck, 2003.

Lev, Yaacov. "The Fāṭimid Princess Sitt al-Mulk." *Journal of Semitic Studies* 32 (1987): 319–328.

Maqrīzī, Taqī al-Dīn Aḥmad al-. *Ittiʿāẓ al-ḥunafāʾ*. Edited by J. al-Shayyāl and M. Ḥ. M. Aḥmad. 3 vols. Cairo, Egypt: Lajnat iʾyāʾ al-turāth al-Islāmī, 1967–1973.

Nuʿmān ibn Muḥammad, al-Qāḍī Abū Ḥanīfa al-. *Iftitāḥ al-daʿwah*. Edited by W. al-Qāḍī. Beirut, Lebanon: Dār al-Thaqāfah, 1970. See also English translation, H. Haji, *Founding the Fatimid State: The Rise of an Early Islamic Empire* (London: I. B. Tauris, 2006).

Walker, Paul E. *Exploring an Islamic Empire: Fatimid History and Its Sources*. London: I. B. Tauris, 2002.

FARHAD DAFTARY *and* D. S. RICHARDS
Updated by FARHAD DAFTARY

FATWĀ. A *fatwā* (pl. *fatāwā*) is a religious opinion on a matter of Sharīʿah that is issued by a *muftīyah* (f.) or a *muftī* (m.), a jurisprudent qualified in the vocation of *iftāʾ*. The term *fatwā* is derived from the root *fata*, which includes in its semantic field the meanings "clarification" and "explanation." In the Qurʾān, the term is used in two verbal forms meaning "asking for a definitive answer" and "giving a definitive answer" (4:127, 176). Varying widely in form and scope, *fatwās* have ranged from single-word responses ("yes," "no," "permitted," etc.) to book-length treatises on a vast array of topics. Collected volumes of *fatwās*, written by a particular authority or related to a certain topic, are also popular. For instance, various *fatwā* collections on women's affairs appear under the title *Fatāwā al-nisāʾ* (women's *fatwās*), including topics ranging from ritual and hygiene to family law.

In general, *fatwās* bear resemblance to the opinions of Roman jurisconsults or the responsa of Jewish scholars. *Fatwās* are often simple clarifications of rules regarding routine matters, such as prayer and fasting; however, *fatwās* also contribute to the continuing dynamism of religious thought and practice, particularly when inquiries pertain to the religious implications of cultural, political, intellectual, or scientific developments in society. As such, *fatwās* provide a rich source of information about the social and economic affairs of Muslim societies and are a key historical resource in discerning nuances of gender relations, particularly with regard to issues of marriage and divorce in different societies.

Questioners have included women and men of every socioeconomic status, from the ordinary populace to members of the elite. *Muftīs* have included local-level scholars who occasionally and informally reply to queries, as well as, at the other extreme, the greatest legal minds of an era or powerful state officials at the apex of *fatwā*-issuing bureaucracies. While throughout history women have been recognized as *muftīyahs*, and while some contemporary efforts have been made to increase the numbers of women in the profession, the office remains dominated by men. This is particularly true when it comes to state-sponsored positions. In some Muslim societies, women are effectively limited to issuing *fatwās* informally or only with regard to designated "female issues." Nonetheless, this is not part of formative or classical doctrines and stems from other structural barriers to women's religious authority. There are a handful of highly distinguished contemporary *muftīyahs*, however, including the Iranian Ayatollah Zohreh Ṣefātī and the Egyptian Dr. Su'ad Saleh.

Fatwās are delivered through a variety of mediums, both formal and informal, and *muftīs* may work individually or collectively, in private practice or in public offices. A formal *fatwā* may serve as a technical tool in the proceedings of a court, or as a scholarly endeavor through which a legal doctrine is expanded or modified. Alternatively, a *fatwā* may be issued on a scholar's own initiative, in the form of a treatise or lecture. Radio, television, and the Internet have also provided new mediums for the issuing of *fatwās*, and in this more global, public domain, the nature of the *fatwā* audience and reception has also undergone noteworthy developments.

Process and Function. *Fatwās* have taken many regional forms depending on local legal cultures and their role in governance. Consequently, a rich interpretive legacy has produced contradictory *fatwās* as well as *fatwās* that reached the same ends by different reasoning. This plurality of interpretation was celebrated as evidence of the broad applicability and inherent flexibility of Islamic law.

Fatwās are sometimes categorized as being either minor or major. A minor *fatwā* usually involves one or more of the following: an explanation of the law in complicated cases or to people who have no direct access to its technical formulations; instructions on correct social behavior or lawful religious beliefs and practices; or suggestions for settling disputes without further recourse to courts. Such *fatwās* contribute to social stability by providing formal administrative organization and informal networks for conducting affairs. A major *fatwā*, by contrast, either involves a significant statement on public policy or requires a jurist to perform *ijtihād* (independent reasoning) in order to derive a legal ruling on an unprecedented and difficult issue. Such *fatwās* by noted *muftīs* are apt to be collected, circulated, and widely cited. Responses issued for a general audience are likely to be nontechnical, whereas those issued for a scholarly audience would contain precise citations of sources and indicate the methods of reasoning employed.

Compared with court judgments of Muslim *qāḍīs* (judges), *fatwās* have a distinct role and authority. Court judgments are binding and enforceable, whereas the opinions of *muftīs* are generally only advisory, although, in some jurisdictions, individuals who are qualified to issue *fatwās* also preside over religious courts and, in such capacity, have the authority to issue binding rulings. Especially before the rise of the modern nation-state, the work of *muftīs* complemented that of the court judges, and, in many instances, *fatwās* served as the link between legal scholars and the courts. Yet unlike court judges, who were investigators of evidential facts, *muftīs* took the configurations of fact presented in questions as given. Hence, a judge's interpretive work is directed more at understanding evidence contained in testimony and oath, while that of the *muftī* focuses more specifically on indications in the textual sources of the law. Whereas judges are permitted to act on the basis of their own knowledge about cases, *muftīs* are not, unless this information is provided in questions. For these reasons, the opinion contained in a *fatwā* is constrained at the outset by the formulation of the question, which should, at least in theory, pertain to actual—not hypothetical—events. The jurisdiction of *fatwās* is also wider than that of court rulings and extends to matters such as *ʿibādāt* (religious duties or obligations), which are excluded from the power of courts. *Fatwās* could also present both a more lenient view (*rukhṣah*) and a more stern (*ʿazīmah*) view on a certain religious matter, or the *fatwā* could resort to legal devices (*ḥillah*) to circumvent an otherwise undesirable application of the law.

Fatwās from different regions and epochs vary widely in language, conventional formulas, and rhetorical style. Theoretical treatises suggest the proper wording for openings and closings and special terms of address and other related expressions, such as "Allāhu yaʿlam," (God knows best), which appears at the end of most *fatwās*. The treatises also consider the physical organization of *fatwā* texts and recommend against such practices as leaving blank spaces or using more than one sheet of paper, so as to guard against additions or alterations. Unlike the question, which could be written in the hand of the questioner or a secretary, before typescript, the *fatwā* itself generally had to be written in the authoritative script of the *muftī*. Among written *fatwās*, many—perhaps the great majority—were considered routine and, as a consequence, were delivered directly to questioners, in some cases without leaving a bureaucratic trace. However, for some societies, massive collections of such *fatwās* exist in archives.

Levels of competence among *muftīs* were specified in treatises concerned with the practice of issuing *fatwās* (the *adab al-muftī* literature). The highest rank was the "absolute" or "independent" interpreter, a jurist who is highly qualified to engage in independent legal reasoning (*ijtihād*). As a matter of principle, when issuing *fatwās*, such *muftīs* did not follow the opinions of other jurists or the positions of the established schools of legal thought but interpreted the law directly through their personal analyses of its basic sources, the Qurʾān and the sunnah (traditions of the Prophet). Within certain trends of Shīʿi thought, Muslims are obliged to select and follow a living *mujtahidah* (f.) or *mujtahid* (m.), who engages in *ijtihād*. *Fatwās* issued by that jurist would be binding on the individual. Below this highest category were "non-independent" or "affiliated" *muftīs* of several levels, all classified as *muqallids*, followers, to some degree, of established doctrine.

Although the *muftī* of a given locale was typically a well-known figure, some questioners had to make inquiries or travel to find a suitable scholar to issue a *fatwā*. Or, opponents in a dispute, such as a wife and husband, would approach different *muftīs* to obtain competing *fatwās* to buttress their respective positions. Beyond their responses in matters covered by the Sharīʿah, *muftīs* also addressed issues well beyond strictly legal topics, although some early theorists argued that *muftīs* should not respond to questions in certain fields, such as Qurʾānic exegesis or theology.

Although theoretically *fatwās* should be delivered free, gifts and various forms of pious support were common. Official *muftīs*, however, were salaried or received set fees from their questioners, and many grew wealthy in their positions. In historical contexts in which there were formal requirements to obtain *fatwās* as part of the litigation process, *muftīs* issued opinions that had direct bearing on court outcomes; in other contexts, approaching a *muftī* amounted to a cheaper, less confrontational, and more efficient alternative means of dispute resolution. If the response of a private *muftī* proved undesirable, the questioner was free to consult a different *muftī* for another opinion. Otherwise, a believer who sought clarification through a *fatwā* could presume that his or her confusion would dissipate, even in those instances in which public interest (*maṣlaḥah al-murāsalah*), necessity, or custom determined the remedy.

Historical Trends. Before the rise of modern school curricula, knowledge of Sharīʿah was the centerpiece of higher education in societies characterized by restricted literacy. As a consequence, a limited group of scholarly interpreters controlled a body of cultural capital, which included not only ritual provisions, but also the precise rules of a variety of contracts, transactions, and dispositions that structured legal-economic relations. In such social settings, it was considered incumbent on those who had acquired knowledge to communicate such, either through teaching or issuing *fatwās*. Reciprocally, it was incumbent on individuals to seek out this knowledge whenever the need to clarify a principle of Sharīʿah arose. Until about the eleventh century BCE, a *muftī* was simply someone who issued *fatwās*; knowledge and scholarly recognition were the only prerequisites. After this period, a public office of *muftī* was created in many jurisdictions and functioned as part of the governing bureaucracy.

The modern period witnessed significant changes both in the content of *fatwās* and the practices of issuing them, in part as a result of the major transformations that engulfed the Muslim world during the nineteenth and twentieth centuries. The increase in European domination over Muslim territory changed the sociopolitical significance of the institution of *iftāʿ*. The pertinence of *fatwās* diminished somewhat as colonial powers assumed control; at the same time, *fatwās* also became tools for mobilizing the population in anticolonial resistance and in struggles for national independence.

Simultaneously, the print media in the nineteenth and twentieth centuries also reinforced the role and impact of *fatwās*, which were needed to address new day-to-day challenges in economic, political, scientific, and technological fields. Not only did the scope of *fatwās* widen, but their language, presentation, and style also adapted. In addition, most Muslim nation-states established national institutions or committees devoted to issuing collective *fatwās*. For example, the Egyptian Dār al-Iftāʿ, founded in 1895, has since served to articulate and defend an official national understanding of Islam through *fatwās* issued in response to government queries on state policy or to the concerns of individual citizens. In such a context, *fatwās* aim to clarify unusual or subtle points of law not covered by existing provisions of modern civil law, or aim to modify existing law or widespread cultural practices. For instance, in some countries, such as Egypt, where female genital cutting is prevalent, jurists have teamed with government representatives and public health experts to discourage the practice and disavow it as having any religious significance.

An estimated one-third of the world's Muslims now live in non-Muslim-majority countries. In this context, the demand for *fatwā*s on such issues as the French ban on headscarves in public schools has given currency to *fiqh al-aqallīyāt*, or the jurisprudence of (Muslim) minorities. Organizations such as the Fiqh Council of North America, established in 1986, and the European Council for Fatwa and Research (ECFR), founded in 1997, have sought to provide authoritative rulings that address the concerns of minority Muslims, facilitate their adherence to Islamic law, and stress the compatibility of Islam with life in diverse modern contexts. For example, an ECFR ruling issued in 2001 allowed a female convert to Islam to remain married to her non-Muslim husband of several decades, even though a female convert's marriage to a non-Muslim is automatically rendered null and void according to a strict application of normative Islamic law. Although this type of ruling has been widely welcomed, it has also been criticized as a divisive system of exceptions.

Far less formal than the deliberations of such councils are the *fatwā*s issued online by "cyber-muftis." Websites such as Islam Online (http://www.islamonline.net) and Fatwa-Online (http://www.fatwa-online.com) are among a large number of sites offering instant *fatwā*s to readers from all over the world. These sites, along with radio shows and satellite television programs offering call-in *fatwā*s, have contributed to the changing, and thriving, nature of contemporary *iftāʿ*. Muslims may now consult any number of *muftīyah*s and *muftī*s worldwide: anonymously, instantly, and from the comfort of their home or local Internet café. The instantaneous and global nature of this new medium for issuing *fatwā*s allows for more opinions to circulate simultaneously and cross-culturally. While such online environments have allowed for diversification in perspective and representation, making it easier, for example, for women's interpretations to be expressed and heard, ultra-conservative and fanatical interpretations have also consequently developed global reach. It is perhaps too early to tell what the long-term impact of this trend will be on either women as legal authorities or on religious issues of specific relevance to women.

[*See also* Law, *subentry* Women's Legal Thought and Jurisprudence; Muftīyah; Religious Authority of Women; Saleh, Suʿad; Ṣefātī, Zohreh; *and* Sharīʿa, Fiqh, Philosophy, and Reason (Theoretical Overview).]

BIBLIOGRAPHY

Art, Gö. "Women and Sexuality in the Fatwas of the Sheikhulislam in Seventeenth Century Ottoman Empire." In *Women and Sexuality in Muslim Societies*, edited by Pınar Ilkkaracan, 81–90. Istanbul, Turkey: Women for Women's Human Rights, 2000.

Baljon, J. M. S. "The Status of Women in Muslim Family Life on the Indo-Pakistan Subcontinent as Reflected in 20th-Century Fatwas." *Sharqiyyât* 4, no. 3 (1992): 185–198.

Bunt, Gary R. *Islam in the Digital Age: E-Jihad, Online Fatwas, and Cyber Islamic Environments*. London: Pluto Press, 2003.

Calder, Norman. *Islamic Jurisprudence in the Classical Era*. Edited by Colin Imber. New York: Cambridge University Press, 2010. Discusses the social function of *fatwās* and relationship between scholars, *muftīs*, judges, and rulers. With an introduction and afterword by Robert Gleave.

Masud, Muhammad Khalid, Brinkley Messick, and David S. Powers, eds. *Islamic Legal Interpretation: Muftis and Their Fatwas*. Cambridge, Mass.: Harvard University Press, 1996. Includes twenty-five case studies covering the early modern and modern periods and a broad range of Muslim and non-Muslim countries.

Nasir, Jamal J. *The Status of Women Under Islamic Law and Modern Islamic Legislation*. 3rd ed. Leiden, Netherlands, and Boston: E. J. Brill, 2009. Concise introduction to normative rules concerning women in Islamic legal theory with some discussion of modern legal developments.

Ragab, Ahmed. "Epistemic Authority of Women in the Medieval Middle East." *Journal of Women of the Middle East and the Islamic World* 8, no. 2 (2010): 181–216.

Spectorsky, Susan A. *Women in Classical Islamic Law: A Survey of the Sources*. Leiden, Netherlands, and Boston: E. J. Brill, 2010. Provides an accessible overview of relevant Sunnī *fiqh* from the formative and classical periods, with a focus on the history and development of the laws of marriage, divorce, and related subjects.

Stowasser, Barbara Freyer, and Zeinab Abul-Magd. "Legal Codes and Contemporary Fatawa: Muslim Women and Contesting Paradigms." *Hawwa: Journal of Women of the Middle East and the Islamic World* 6, no. 1 (2008): 32–51.

Tucker, Judith E. "'And God Knows Best': The Fatwa as a Source for the History of Gender in the Arab World." In *Beyond the Exotic: Women's Histories in Islamic Societies*, edited by Amira El Azhary Sonbol, 168–179. Syracuse, N.Y.: Syracuse University Press, 2005.

MUHAMMAD KHALID MASUD, BRINKLEY MESSICK, *and* AHMAD S. DALLAL
Updated by JOSEPH A. KÉCHICHIAN *and* JOCELYN HENDRICKSON
Updated by CELENE AYAT LIZZIO

FEMALE GENITAL CUTTING. Female genital cutting (FGC) refers to cutting part or all of the female genitalia and/or its alteration. There are four types of female genital cutting: circumcision, excision, infibulation, and introcision. Circumcision refers to the cutting of the tip of the clitoris with or without the partial or complete removal of the clitoris. Excision includes the removal of the clitoris and part or all of the labia minora. Infibulation refers to the total removal of the clitoris and labia minora and the sewing of the labia majora, with a small opening for the urine and menstrual blood to flow. Introcision is the process of pricking, incising, and even burning all or part of the vagina. Genital cutting affects approximately 130 million girls and women worldwide. An estimated two to three million experience genital cutting every year (Seager, 2008, p. 54), mostly in Africa. In the 1990s, more than 50 percent of girls and women in Egypt, Eritrea, Mali, Chad, Ethiopia, Somalia, Sudan, and Burkina-Faso went through the ritual of genital cutting. FGC is a cross-cultural practice observed by diverse religious communities and cultures. In Egypt, Eritrea, Mali, and Sudan, FGC is performed on a large percentage of Muslims and Christians. In Kenya, Christians have a higher percentage of genital cutting than Muslims (38 percent compared to 28 percent) (Seager, 2008, p. 54). FGC continues to be practiced in these regions and among immigrants to the West coming from places where genital circumcision is prevalent.

Despite the fact that the original practice of FGC predates Islam, it is perceived as an emblem of Islam in regions where it is practiced. Circumcision, whether for males or females, is not mentioned in the Qurʾān, but in traditional literature (*ḥadīth*), Muḥammad mentions circumcision (*khitān*) as obligatory for men for hygienic reasons, and optional for the Medinan women who had undergone it (*ḥifẓ*, protection) (Ibn al-Jawzī, 1996, pp. 28–29). He warns, however, that female circumcision should not harm women. Although circumcision is not religiously based, in the world where women's bodies and sexuality represent men's honor and ownership, FGC is used to boost the marketability of women for marriages, to increase the sexual gratification and pleasure of men, and to discourage premarital or extramarital sex (Anwar, 2006, p. 113). Women's conformity to patriarchal values confers the virtue of obedience and respect at the individual, familial, and societal levels as well. As a violation of women's reproductive rights, FGC has a damaging impact on women's physical and mental health. The genital cutting is often performed rigorously and violently—to the extent that the female sexual organ may fail to function for sexual purposes. Mentally, the circumcised girls and women endure the memory of the pain and violence carried out on their sexual organs as a reminder of being female in a patriarchal world. Nevertheless, efforts to eradicate FGC have met with resistance. Most governments are reluctant to intervene because FGC has structural bases in the society, such as the concept of tribal honor. Still, feminists, human rights activists, and non-governmental agencies continue their mission to eradicate FGC through parental and community education.

[*See also* Clitoridectomy.]

BIBLIOGRAPHY

Anees, M. Ahmad. *Islam and Biological Futures: Ethics, Gender, and Technology*. London and New York: Mansell, 1989.

Anwar, Etin. *Gender and Self in Islam*. London: Routledge, 2006.

Dorkenoo, Efua. *Cutting the Rose, Female Genital Mutilation: The Practice and Its Prevention*. London: Minority Rights Publication, 1995.

Ibn al-Jawzī, Jamāl al-Dīn. *Kitāb aḥkām al-nisāʿ*. Beirut: Dār al-Fikr, 1996.

Jawad, Haifaa A. *The Rights of Women in Islam*. New York: St. Martin's Press, 1998.

Seager, Joni. *The Penguin Atlas of Women in the World*. 4th ed. New York: Penguin, 2008.

Etin Anwar

Female Qur'ānic Figures. The Qur'ān mentions female figures in multiple roles. As Arabic is gender specific, only those references to females or which use of the pronoun "she" are discussed.

There are four chapters in the Qur'ān with titles referring to females: chapter 4: "The Women"; chapter 19: "Mary"; chapter 58: "She Who Disputes"; and chapter 60: "She Who is Put to a Test." While chapter 4 does include gender issues such as marriage and divorce, the only female referred to by name, and as a sign of God (23:50) in the Qur'ān, is Mary, the mother of Jesus. Mary characterizes the Qur'ānic view of females because "she was purified," "morally obligated to God" (66:12), and "a just person" (5:75). Mary was commanded in the Qur'ān to pray with others. A modern Qur'ān commentator has said that Mary was able to participate in a mixed-gender prayer based on 3:43, where Mary is told "to bow down with those [males] who bow down," because God saw her "as a man." Although some have posited that this suggests the possibility of opening the ranks of religious leadership to women, the majority opinion remains that it does not.

"She Who Disputes" refers to Khawlah bint Thalabah, who complained to the Prophet about her husband who had divorced her using a pre-Islamic phrase: "Be as the back of my mother!" (33:4, 58:2). The Prophet forbade the practice based on the verse, wives "are not your mothers" (58:2).

"She Who is Put to a Test" speaks of females who emigrated from Mecca to Medina. Once they became tested and proven believers, Muḥammad was told not to return them to their non-Muslim spouses in Mecca. Instead their dowry was to be returned to the husbands and then they were permitted to remarry. When these females gave their allegiance, they pledged they would not: ascribe partners with God, steal, commit adultery, kill their children, make false charges to harm another's reputation, or rebel against anything honorable (60:13).

Verses that speak to or about females refer to women in their natural roles as mothers, wives, sisters, daughters, and as individual females who may be single, married, divorced or widowed.

Mothers are to be respected and appreciated for what they have endured as children are born from their wombs (16:78). Mothers are described as those who "carried [them] in feebleness"

(31:14), "painfully" (53:32), and "gave birth to them" (58:2). Moses's mother (28:7), and all mothers, are told to breastfeed (2:233).

In addition to the mention of Mary as mother, the Qur'ān refers indirectly to mothers of some of the other prophets/messengers. These include the mothers of Cain and Abel, Ismā'īl, Isaac, Moses, and Yahyā (John the Baptist), meaning "he who lives," because he breathed life into his barren mother's womb. Other mothers referred to are the mother of Mary and the wives of Muḥammad, "his spouses are their mothers" (33:6). Men are forbidden to marry their mothers as well as their foster mother, "those who breastfeed" (4:23).

Praiseworthy wives include the wives of some of the prophets/messengers such as the spouse of Adam (both she and Adam are blamed for the fall from Eden and "from whom disseminated many men and women" [4:1]); the wives of Abraham: Hagar, his second wife, who was the founder of the city of Mecca (*umm al-qurā*, or the Mother of the Towns, 6:92, 42:7) and is said to be buried in the semicircular area of the Ka'bah; and Sarah, who could not believe she would have a child because of her age; the wife of Job, found in the commentaries on 38:44; the wife of 'Imrān who "dedicated" what was in her womb to the temple (3:35); the barren wife of Zechariah (19:8) who competes "with [Zechariah] in good deeds" (21:90); and the spouses of Muḥammad.

Other praiseworthy wives include Āsiya, the wife of the pharaoh, who prayed for God "to build for [her] a house near to [God] in the Garden" (66:11); the spouses of the Prophet "who draw closer their outer garments over themselves" (33:59); the "companion wife" (70:12, 80:36) who is forgotten on the Day of Judgment; and temporary wives, whether they be from *mut'a* or *misyar* marriage. Mention is made of wives a man is forbidden to marry, of widows and divorcees, the latter often referred to as women who have been "set free" (2:227, 2:231, 33:38, 33:49).

Blameworthy wives include those of some prophets/messengers, such as the wives of Noah (66:10) and Lot (7:83, 15:59–60, 66:10), as well as others, such as the wife of the Aziz of Egypt (Zulaykha [12:25–33]); the wife of Abū Lahab (111:4–5), and "those [wives] who show resistance (*nushuz*) to their husbands" (4:34).

Sisters are mentioned briefly and include the sister of Moses (28:11–12); the share of sisters in inheritance (4:12, 4:176); and those sisters whom it is forbidden to marry (4:23, 24:31, 33:50, 33:55).

Praiseworthy daughters are the daughters of Lot (11:78–79, 15:71); Mary, the daughter of 'Imrān; the infant daughter who is buried alive (81:8); and the daughters of Midian (28:27) and those of Muḥammad, who "draw closer their outer garments over themselves" (33:59).

Blameworthy daughters are idols that pre-Islamic Arabs "assigned as daughters of God" (6:100), while the Qur'ān makes clear that God did not have any daughters (or sons) (16:57, 43:16, 52:39).

Females as individuals may be believing females "who show not their adornments"...and draw their head coverings over their bosoms" (24:31); "good females" (24:26); and females who submit, remain steadfast, fast, guard their private parts, remember God frequently, and are sincere, humble, and charitable (33:35); and who repent and worship (66:5).

Other references include free, chaste females (4:25, 5:5, 24:4, 24:23); female virgins (55:36, 66:5); females who give their allegiance, becoming "ones who submit," such as "the woman controlling the people of Saba" (27:22–44) (described by commentators as the Queen of Sheba); females among the people of the book (5:5, 5:57); post-menopausal females beyond childbearing age (24:60, 65:4); females who emigrate (60:10–13); females invited to Muḥammad's disputation with the Christians (3:61); females who shepherd their sheep (28:25–34); female witnesses (2:282); females who have a share of what they deserve or earn (4:32); female prisoners of war, "bond servants" and "right-hand possessed" (4:3, 4:24, 4:25, 4:36, 16:71, 23:6, 24:31, 24:33, 24:58, 30:28, 33:50, 33:52, 33:55, 70:38), as well as females whose right hand possesses (24:31, 33:55); "the ladies who cut their hands" (12:30, 12:50); lovely, large-eyed females; and females who are in their waiting periods after divorce.

Females with whom there is displeasure include female polytheists (2:221, 4:3), thieves (5:39), and hypocrites (9:68, 33:60, 48:6). In addition, there are "bad females" (24:26); "adulteresses" (24:2–3); "those who commit indecency" (4:15–16); females "who deride one another" (49:11); and those who: "abort their children" (6:140), "take lovers to themselves" (5:5), or are "licentious" (5:5). Specific female wrongdoers include the woman "who breaks what she spun after firming its fibers," which is compared to giving deceitful oaths (16:92); the wife of Abū Lahab "around whose neck is a rope of palm fibers" (111:4–5); the "cunning" of Zulaykha, which is described as female cunning (12:28); and "the women who practice magic, blowing on knots" (113:4).

Males are warned about their treatment of females: A mother "is not to be pressed for her child" (2:233) nor should men "marry females their fathers had married" (4:22) nor "two sisters" (4:23). They are: not "to inherit women against their will" (4:19–22), specifically done in pre-Islamic times to avoid paying a woman her dowry; "to deal with wives justly," and, because this is not possible, husbands are admonished to take "just one wife" (4:129); not to have intercourse with their wives during their menstruation (2:222) or when they are fasting (2:187); and not to divorce them by saying, "Be as my the back of my mother" (33:4, 58:2). They are clearly told that a wife has a right to defend herself against any accusation by a husband who is the only witness and that a wife is allowed to dispute her husband's treatment of her (24:6–9).

There is renewed controversy in the contemporary period in regard to husbands purportedly having the right to beat their wives whose resistance (*nushuz*) they fear (4:34), after two stages of disciplinary measures, especially when husbands are not allowed to harm wives they are divorcing (2:231). Some commentators state that this "privilege" of disciplining a wife is given only to husbands who support their wives financially. Traditional commentators continue to hold that the verse says, "beat them," while recent translations make the verse say "go away from them," which was the sunnah of the Prophet.

Men are told: "not to appoint with [women] secretly" (2:235); not to approach men with lust instead of women (7:81, 27:55) nor to cherish women for lust (3:14); not to separate out from the bellies of their flocks for themselves while if the animal be born dead it would be for females (6:139); not to slander (24:10–16), wrongly accuse (24:23–24), malign (33:58), or persecute believing women (85:10); and not to force female prisoners of war into prostitution when the female slave "wants chastity" (24:33).

The Qur'ānic view of females therefore provides examples of both praiseworthy and unworthy mothers, sisters, daughters, and wives, but the greatest emphasis is upon females as individuals who are free to make their own choices.

BIBLIOGRAPHY

Abdel Haleem, M. A. S. *The Qur'an*. London: Oxford University Press, 2004.

Abu Sulayman, Abdul Hamid. *Marital Discord: Recapturing Human Dignity through the Higher Objectives of Islamic Law*. Herndon, Va.: IIIT, 2008.

Bakhtiar, Laleh. *The Concordance of the Sublime Quran*. Chicago: Kazi Publications, 2011.

Bakhtiar, Laleh, trans. *The Sublime Quran: Original Arabic and English*. Chicago: Kazi Publications, 2007.

Bakhtiar, Laleh. "The Sublime Quran: The Misinterpretation of Chapter 4 Verse 34." *European Journal of Women's Studies Special Issue: Living in Translation: Voicing and Inscribing Women's Lives and Practices* 18, no. 4 (2011): 431–439.

Encyclopedia of Islam. 2d ed. 11 vols. Leiden, Netherlands: Brill Academic Publishers, 1986–1999.

Ibn Kathīr, Ismāʿīl ibn ʿUmar. *Qiṣaṣ al-anbiyāʾ*. 2 vols. Edited by Mustafā ʿAbd al-Wāhid. Cairo: Dār al-Kutub al-Ḥadītah, 1968.

Mahallī, Jalāl al-Dīn Muhammad ibn Ahmad. *Tafisr al-Jalalayn*. Great Commentaries of the Holy Quran. Translated by Feras Hamza. Louisville, Ky.: Fons Vitae, 2008.

Makaram-Shirazi, Grand Ayatullah Naser. Persian translation of the Qur'ān. http://www.parsquran.com.

McAuliffe, Jane Dammen, gen. ed. *Encyclopaedia of the Qur'ān*. 6 vols. Leiden: Brill Academic Publishers, 2001–2006.

Mousavi Lari, Hujjat al-Islam. "*Chastising Husbands Who Beat Their Wives*" (Persian text). Not published.

Murata, Sachiko. *Temporary Marriage in Islamic Law* (Persian text). Tehran: Hamdami, 1979.

Qutb, Sayyid. *In the Shade of the Quran*. Translated and edited by M. A. Salahi and A. A. Shamis. 18 vols. to date, vol. 3, pp. 111–140. Leicester, U.K.: The Islamic Foundation, 1999–.

Sharīʿati, ʿAlī. *Hajj: Reflections on its Rituals*. Translated by Laleh Bakhtiar. Chicago: Kazi Publications, 1992.

Smith, Jane, and Yvonne Haddad. "The Virgin Mary in Islamic Tradition and Commentary." *The Muslim World* 79, no. 3–4 (October 1989): 161–187.

Tabatabaie, Ayatullah. *al-Mizan*. Vol. 8, pp. 199–222. Tehran: World Organization for Islamic Services, 1992.

LALEH BAKHTIAR

FEMINISM. [*This entry has three subentries:*

Concept and Debates
Nature of Islamic Feminism *and*
Sources.]

CONCEPT AND DEBATES

Despite the tenacity of the belief that feminism is a Western concept, it is incontrovertibly not a Western invention: feminism/s have been developed by women within diverse cultures, religions, and societies around the globe on their own terms. Both Muslim and non-Muslim women in both East and West, beginning in the nineteenth century and continuing through the present, have created, interpreted, and reinterpreted feminism as an expression of awareness that women have been subordinated and often oppressed and deprived of their rights in the family and society, as women, thus leading women to seek to change this. Muslim women have created two sorts of feminisms—secular and Islamic. Muslim women created secular feminism/s in parts of the East (Africa and Asia) in the late nineteenth and early twentieth centuries. In the late twentieth century, women in both the East and West produced Islamic feminism. In Muslim societies secular feminism/s and Islamic feminism now exist side by side and are reenforcing each other and are increasingly merging.

Muslim women have historically articulated their feminisms, both secular and Islamic, from within Islam, critiquing the patriarchal versions of their religion and moving beyond constraints imposed upon them. Muslim women as secular and Islamic feminists in Africa and Asia have struggled in their own nations and cultures to redress the inequities of patriarchal domination and the deprivation of their rights. Muslim women as Islamic feminists in their new communities in the West confront patriarchal practices imported from their countries of origin and perpetuated as Islamic while at the same time they navigate the terrain of Western secular societies trying to secure rights important to them as Muslim women. Muslim women have sometimes participated in general feminist movements in the Western countries in which they live.

Muslim women as feminists in countries of the East, while operating within their own religious and cultural contexts, have often simultaneously embraced the universal ideals of human rights, citizens' rights, and nations' rights as compatible with and supportive of their feminisms. Contrary to what is sometimes suggested, Muslim women have not been forced to choose between their liberation and rights as women, on the one hand, and their religion and cultures on the other. This is not to suggest that they have not often been pressured to accept a patriarchal version of Islam and society—in some places such pressures have been impossible for women to resist without being ostracized—nor that women were not made to feel treasonous for proceeding along their own more egalitarian path within Islam. Rather, it is to emphasize that there has been space for Muslim women—which they have used often against all odds and at great risk—to combat gender inequities in their societies.

Secular Feminisms in Muslim Societies in Africa and Asia ("The East"). The feminisms that Muslim women, along with women compatriots of other religions, created in various parts of Africa and Asia in the late nineteenth and first half of the twentieth century were nation-based. "Secular feminism" has been used to signify the feminisms developed by Muslims as citizens within in the context of nation-states rather than as Muslims solely within the framework of their religious community (*ummah*). (The term "secular feminism" mirrored the term "secular nationalism," which included all citizens irrespective of religion in a polity not framed by religion but guaranteeing the freedom of religion.) Although there have been striking similarities in the contours of Muslim women's secular feminism/s in various nations, the plural is used in recognition of the distinctiveness of multiple nation-based feminist movements that have characterized Muslim women's secular feminist experience.

In the course of modernization in the late nineteenth and early twentieth centuries, Muslim women, with female compatriots of other religions, became aware that they—specifically, women of the middle and upper classes—were restricted in their movements and deprived of opportunities as women. This became evident to them when they compared themselves with men of the same class and circumstances. Some men also questioned these practices, including, most famously, the Egyptian lawyer Qāsim Amīn, whose works *The Liberation of Women* (*Tahrīr al-mar'ah*, 1899) and *The New Woman* (*al-Mar'ah al-jadīdah*, 1900), sparked heated public debates about the issues, albeit according to a Western model of development. Drawing upon this awareness and Islamic modernist thinking then current, women began to understand that many imposed practices such as domestic seclusion, gender segregation, and face veiling (the form of veiling at the time) were not religious requirements as they had been made to believe, but rather were simply social customs. Women in Muslim societies in Africa and Asia reveal in their memoirs, essays, and stories that they were reacting against such practices, which they saw as restricting the opportunities for advancement that modernization offered. This would later be referred to as a rising "feminist consciousness."

Women's involvement in national independence movements to free their countries from Western colonial rule, or in pushing for national reform in Turkey and Iran in the early twentieth century, first catapulted Muslim women into the public arena alongside women compatriots of other religions. Many more women appeared on the scene as feminist activists during processes of early postcolonial nation-building. Muslim women's secular feminisms emerged as organized social and political movements (unlike the future Islamic feminism, which arose as a new global discourse).

The discourse that Muslim women elaborated in the course of their feminist militancy served the goals of their collective agenda. Their secular feminist discourse was a composite of gender-sensitive articulations of Islamic modernist, secular nationalist, and humanitarian discourse. The central tropes of Muslim women's emergent secular feminisms were liberation and rights: liberation from patriarchal domination and winning the practice of their intrinsic rights. (Liberation and rights were the parallel concerns of Muslim nations suffering colonial domination and deprivation of their sovereign rights.)

Secular feminism focused primarily on the public sphere, or society, which its protagonists saw as "the secular sphere" (or sphere of the nation) wherein they claimed gender equality. First-wave feminists understood the private or family sphere as "the religious sphere" and accepted the prevailing patriarchal family structure within which women and men had separate but unequal roles that were held to be religiously ordained. (In countries where Muslims and Christians together pioneered as feminists, both accepted the framework of the patriarchal family of their respective religions, but it was only Muslims who campaigned for family reform.) Secular feminists acknowledged a public/private split and, while working to effect change on the public and private fronts simultaneously, accorded priority to the public or societal sphere as a strategic choice. Later Muslim women, as second-wave secular feminists, would challenge the notion of the patriarchal family as "Islamic."

Muslim women's feminisms were launched from the starting point of their own lives as women. Their secular feminisms began as gendered Islamic reform projects that disentangled religious prescription from social custom to clear the way for change. Muslim women's move into the "secular" public space of the nation was supported by religious arguments. The Islamic scrutiny to which Muslim women, as incipient feminists, subjected practices said to be so ordained, such as female domestic seclusion and face veiling, and their moves to reject practices they discovered not to be ordained by religion, would be a hallmark of Muslims' secular feminisms. The future feminist Hudā Sha'rāwī recounted in her memoirs that a group of women (of whom she was the youngest member) meeting in a weekly women's salon in the 1890s in Cairo discussed how face veiling was not a religious requirement, as they had been made to believe. Later the Lebanese scholar of religion Naẓīrah Zayn al-Dīn—tutored at home by her father, also a religious scholar—exposed face veiling as un-Islamic in her book *Sufūr wa-al-Hijāb* (Unveiling and Veiling), published in 1928 and aimed at a wider audience.

As a pioneer of women's independent, organized feminist activism, the feminist movement in Egypt was in many ways prototypical of secular feminist activism elsewhere in the Muslim world in the first half of the twentieth century. Women also experimented in public activism in Turkey and Iran, but in these countries the state largely co-opted women's independent feminist struggle. In Egypt the first set of feminist demands were presented by the teacher and writer Malak Ḥifnī Nāṣif (known by the pen name Bāḥithat al-Bādiyah) to the Muslim Nationalist Congress in Cairo in 1911, at the height of the national independence struggle. Delivered in absentia because women were not then permitted to appear in public before men, the demands included women's freedom to attend congregational prayer in the mosque and their access to all areas of education and work they might choose. In 1923 Muslim and Christian women under the leadership of Hudā Sha'rāwī formed the first explicitly feminist organization, the Egyptian Feminist Union, through which they agitated for education, work, and political rights for women, campaigned for reform of the Muslim Personal Status Code, and fought to end legalized prostitution (with support from the Islamic establishment at al-Azhar University). They also provided health services to poor women and trained them in income-generating work, believing health and economic well-being to be a prerequisite to women's advancement. In 1948 Durrīyah Shafīq founded the Bint al-Nīl (Daughter of the Nile) Union, reaching women more broadly throughout Egypt, especially through literacy programs. In 1945 women established the Arab Feminist Union in Cairo as a regional organization through which Muslims and Christians could jointly further their demands.

From the final third of the twentieth century into the twenty-first century, rising second-wave feminists in the Muslim world turned their attention to issues of the woman's body, sexuality, and violence against women. In Egypt in 1972 Nawāl al-Saʿdāwī, a feminist physician, writer, and founder of the Arab Women's Solidarity Association (1984), published a book in *al-Mar'a wa-al-jins* (Woman and Sex), attacking various forms of violence against women, including obsessive concern with women's virginity, which often lead to psychological trauma, domestic bodily abuse of women, and the sexual exploitation of women for commercial purposes. The Moroccan feminist sociologist Fatima Mernissi, in *Beyond the Veil* (1975), drew attention to the oppressive consequences for women of the common belief that women were omnisexual beings who produced *fitnah* (chaos).

An intensifying focus of feminist attention was wife-beating and the bodily harassment of women. In Turkey in the late 1980s activists struck back at the habitual public molestation of women in the Purple Needle campaign. They marched to protest wife battery, which was seen by many as condoned by Islam and in 1990 opened the Purple Roof Shelter for Women for victims of abuse. Young women in eastern Turkey embarked on a campaign against wife-beating through the organization VACAD they created in 2004, with branches throughout the area to combat domestic violence. Other countries, ranging from Lebanon to Saudi Arabia, have since founded shelters for victims of domestic violence and in some cases have begun national awareness campaigns designed to raise public attention and discussion of the issue.

Honor killing is a brutal cultural practice that feminist activists have been fighting as a heinous injustice from Mediterranean countries to Pakistan and among some Muslim immigrant communities in Western countries, using the language of human rights. When honor killing was transported to Muslim communities in the West, it was claimed by perpetrators—and readily believed by non-Muslim Western observers—to be Islamic. However, although honor killings do occur in some Muslim countries, it is a tribal and cultural, rather than "Islamic," practice limited to certain countries, some of which have begun to address the issue seriously. In eastern Turkey, for example, VACAD and Ka-Mer (established in 1996) have fought against honor killings. In Jordan the journalist Rana Husseini first drew attention to the issues surrounding honor killings in 1994, particularly what she perceived to be lack of institutional seriousness about the problem. Her coverage of the problem led not only to a campaign to change the laws allowing lighter sentences for those convicted of honor killings, rather than prosecuting them as murder, but also resulted in a landmark address to parliament by King Hussein in 1997, emphasizing women's rights.

In the 1970s and 1980s Muslim and Christian women in Egypt and Sudan fought for the eradication of female genital mutilation (FGM). Although this is a cultural phenomenon found mainly in countries along the Nile, it has been commonly seen as Islamic, and activists accordingly mobilized both religious and human rights arguments to combat it. In the 1990s the practice, which Islamists were then proclaiming to be religious, was on the upsurge and also appeared in immigrant communities in the West. Although it has therefore been important to fight the practice through religious argumentation, secular feminists have also employed medical and psychological argumentation against the practice, noting its detrimental effect on women's health and well-being, as well as highlighting the complications it can produce in childbearing.

To confront the urgent matters of the body and sexuality, Muslim women and men from the Middle East, South Asia, and Southeast Asia formed the Coalition for Sexual and Bodily Rights in Muslim Societies, as a transnational solidarity network of activists and academics. The coalition was cofounded by Women for Women's Human Rights, which was established by the Turkish therapist and feminist activist Pinar İlkkaracan in 1993 and was at the forefront of issues of sexuality. The coalition confronts the full range of these issues around sexuality, drawing on multiple discourses to combat deeply entrenched regressive thinking and related discrimination and violence.

In the 1980s and 1990s secular feminists focused renewed attention on the reform of Muslim family laws, agitating for gender equality, as opposed to the proposed "Islamic" alternative of gender inequality typically referred to as "complementarity." Under the leadership of Marieme Helie Lucas, they organized the transnational network called Women Living Under Muslim Laws (WLUML) in 1984. Along with engaging in solidarity actions and advocacy campaigns, WLUML undertook extensive research of laws—statutory, customary, and Islamic—in some twenty Muslim countries in Africa and Asia from 1991 to 2001 and published a handbook called *Knowing Our Rights*. Among the organizations that have been part of WLUML are Shirkat Gah, which Farida Shaheed helped found in 1975, Ain o Salish Kendra in Bangladesh, founded by the lawyer Salma Sobhan in 1986, and Baobab for Women's Human Rights in Nigeria, created in 1996 and led by Ayesha Imam.

Shirkat Gah and the Women's Action Forum, founded in 1981, fought against injustices to women arising from the institution of the Hudood Ordinances, criminal and penal law based on Sharīʿah in Pakistan, by employing Islamic and human rights arguments. Later (after the rise of Islamic feminism), secular feminists and Islamic feminists would join forces in the battle against the iniquities of *ḥudūd*.

From the late 1970s the gains Muslim women as feminists had made during the first two-thirds of the century were threatened by the spread of conservative political Islam in the Muslim world following the rise to power of an Islamist state in Iran and Islamist movements in other countries which set out to reimpose many patriarchal practices that had all but disappeared. Calls were made for women to retreat from the public sphere and return to their "proper place"—in the home. Secular feminists, who had historically placed their feminism in the framework of an enlightened Islam, did not wish to be drawn into argumentation structured by those who deployed a patriarchal interpretation of Islam to control women. Eventually it would be necessary to combat Islamist patriarchal encroachments, an, to do this effectively, a new feminist language was required. With the spread of Islamism, feminists were buffeted between autocratic secular states and increasingly radicalized Islamist movements, finding themselves stranded between secular and "Islamic" patriarchies.

[*See also* Family Law; Mernissi, Fatima; Nāṣif, Malak Ḥifnī; Shafīq, Durrīyah; Shaʿrāwī, Hudā; Women and Islam, *subentry on* Role and Status of Women; Women and Social Reform, *subentry on* An Overview; Women's Action Forum; *and* Women's Movements.]

BIBLIOGRAPHY

Abu-Lughod, Lila, ed. *Remaking Women: Feminism and Modernity in the Middle East*. Princeton, N.J.: Princeton University Press, 1998.

Ahmed, Leila. *Women and Gender in Islam: Historical Roots of a Modern Debate*. New Haven, Conn.: Yale University Press, 1992.

Badran, Margot. *Feminism in Islam: Secular and Religious Convergences*. Oxford: Oneworld, 2009.

Badran, Margot. *Feminists, Islam, and Nation: Gender and the Making of Modern Egypt*. Princeton, N.J.: Princeton University Press, 1995.

cooke, miriam. *Nazira Zeineddine: A Pioneer of Islamic Feminism*. Oxford: Oneworld, 2010.

Hibri, Azizah Y. al-. "Redefining Muslim Women's Roles in the Next Century." In *Democracy and the Rule of Law*, edited by Norman Dorsen and Prosser Gifford. Washington, D.C.: CQ Press, 2001.

İlkkaracan, Pınar., ed. *Women and Sexuality in Muslim Societies*. Istanbul: Women for Women's Human Rights, 2000.

Karam, Azza M. *Women, Islamisms, and the State: Contemporary Feminisms in Egypt*. New York: St. Martin's Press, 1998.

Mernissi, Fatima. *Beyond the Veil: Male-Female Dynamics in Modern Muslim Society*. Rev. ed. Bloomington: Indiana University Press, 1987.

Mernissi, Fatima. *Women and Islam: An Historical and Theological Enquiry*. Translated by Mary Jo Lakeland. Oxford: Basil Blackwell, 1991.

Moghadam, Valentine M., ed. *Identity Politics and Women: Cultural Reassertions and Feminisms in International Perspective*. Boulder, Colo.: Westview Press, 1994.

Moghadam, Valentine M. "Islamic Feminism and Its Discontents: Toward a Resolution of the Debate." *Signs* 27, no. 4 (2002): 1135–1171.

Najmabadi, Afsaneh. "Feminism in an Islamic Republic: 'Years of Hardship, Years of Growth.'" In *Islam, Gender, and Social Change*, edited by Yvonne Yazbeck Haddad and John L. Esposito, pp. 59–84. New York: Oxford University Press, 1998.

Qāsim Amīn. *The Liberation of Women; and, The New Woman: Two Documents in the History of Egyptian Feminism*. Translated by Samiha Sidhom. Cairo: The American University in Cairo Press, 1992.

Sa'dāwī, Nawāl al-. *The Hidden Face of Eve: Women in the Arab World*. London: Zed Press, 1979.

Women Living Under Muslim Laws. *Knowing Our Rights: Women, Family, Laws and Customs in the Muslim World*. 3d ed. London, no publisher, 2006.

Yamani, Mai, ed. *Feminism and Islam: Legal and Literary Perspectives*. New York: New York University Press, 1996.

MARGOT BADRAN
Updated by NATANA J. DELONG-BAS

NATURE OF ISLAMIC FEMINISM

Islamic feminism first surfaced as new discourse (not as a social movement) simultaneously in the East and West near the end of the twentieth century. Beginning necessarily within the framework of Islam, Islamic feminists have critiqued the patriarchal versions of their religion, which are often claimed by authorities to be "Islamic," along with their concomitant constraints imposed upon women, in favor of trying to secure the rights that are important to them as Muslim women and which they see as inherent in their understanding and practice of their faith. This has been true in both Muslim-majority countries and Western countries where Muslim women live as minorities.

This new Islamic feminism has transcended national boundaries, making it a global feminism for a new age. Islamic feminism started as a new interpretative effort by women scholars and intellectuals, and some men, who had embarked on woman-sensitive rereading of the Qur'ān and other religious sources. Their recovery of the gender-egalitarian voice of scripture spread instantaneously around the world via the Internet.

Women—and a few men—in the Islamic Republic of Iran were among the pioneers of Islamic feminist discourse; they circulated their ideas of a gender-just Islam in a journal called *Zanān*, founded by Shahla Sherkat in 1992 and one of the first in which the term "Islamic feminism" was used. Other early sites of nascent

Islamic feminism included Turkey, where some disaffected Islamist women were moving away from the constraints of patriarchal political Islam; Egypt, where some religiously identified women sought to ground a discourse of women's liberation (they were uncomfortable with the term "feminism") firmly in the Qurʾān; Malaysia, where professional and activist women challenged gender injustice in the name of religion; and South Africa, where antiapartheid activists were turning their attention from the newly won liberation of their country to the liberation of their Muslim community, particularly questioning the full meaning of "social justice" and insisting that gender justice must necessarily be a part of it. Meanwhile in the West, specifically in the United States, Muslim scholars elaborated what others came to call Islamic feminism, which was circulated widely through the Internet by Muslim women's and progressive Muslim groups.

Islamic feminism seeks rights and justice for women and men in all aspects of their lives. It is based on a rereading of the Qurʾān and sunnah (the sayings and deeds of Prophet Muḥammad preserved in the *ḥadīth)* and revisiting *fiqh* (Islamic jurisprudence). *Ijtihād* (independent intellectual investigation of religious sources) is the methodology of Islamic feminism, and, more specifically, *tafsīr* (interpretation of the Qurʾān) which has taken two forms: a close reading of the scripture as text, and a dynamic dialogue with the scripture, such as Amina Wadud, Asma Barlas, Nimat Hafez al-Barazangi, Riffat Hassan, and Nasr Abū-Zayd have undertaken.

Islamic feminism articulates the principles of gender equality and social justice, shifting from an earlier primary focus on rights and liberation, as found in the Qurʾān. It is more radical than secular feminisms in enunciating full gender equality across the public/private spectrum in keeping with its understanding of a holistic Islam. It does not accept, as secular feminisms had done until more recently, the patriarchal model of the family in which complementary but unequal gender roles are understood to be religiously ordained, but rather it promotes an egalitarian model of the family. Islamic feminism, moreover, demands gender equality not only in the secular part of the public sphere but in the public religious domain, insisting on women's Islamically licit access to the religious professions and ability to publicly perform religious rituals. Islamic feminism conceptualizes a public sphere inclusive of the religious and the secular, rather than equating the public sphere solely with the secular. Islamic feminism disrupts the binary oppositions of East/West, secular/religious, and public/private, and it supports the separation of religion and state.

Two seminal treatises considered to be foundational texts of Islamic feminism are *Qurʾān and Woman: Rereading the Sacred Text from a Woman's Perspective*, in which the African-American theologian Amina Wadud laid the groundwork for a Qurʾānic exposition of gender equality and social justice, and *"Believing Women" in Islam: Unreading Patriarchal Interpretations of the Qurʾān*, in which the Pakistani-American scholar Asma Barlas deconstructed the patriarchal takeover of Qurʾānic egalitarianism.

In Islamic jurisprudence, the legal anthropologist Ziba Mir-Hosseini and the lawyer and legal scholar Azizah al-Hibri have produced compelling critiques of *fiqh*. Importantly they have made clear that Sharīʿah, commonly translated as "Islamic law" and thought to be sacred and immutable, is simply the product of human thought and consequently subject to change. Focusing attention on *ḥadīth*, Fatima Mernissi and, later, the Turkish religious-studies scholar Hidayet Tuksal have used traditional Islamic methodology to expose widespread misogynist *ḥadīth* as spurious.

The theoretical basis of Islamic feminism is the gender-sensitive analysis of religious sources which the creators of these analytical works place in the framework of the intellectual endeavor of religious reinterpretation. Muslim women as secular feminists recognized this as a feminist endeavor and called it "Islamic feminism." Those who wrote the path-breaking texts of Islamic feminism did not identify themselves as feminists (except for Mernissi), but as scholar-activists. Eventually, however, many came to accept, though not to prefer, the designation of their work as "feminist" and themselves as feminists. The issue of identity and the term "Islamic feminism" have been hotly debated. Given the volatile environments in which Muslim women now find themselves, most women who think and act as feminists tend, for political and pragmatic reasons, not to use feminist terminology, or to employ it guardedly.

A pioneering organization that exemplifies the combined intellectual and activist work of Islamic feminism is Sisters Islam (SIS), founded by professional women in Malaysia in the 1980s, supporting the rights of Muslim women within an egalitarian framework of Islam. SIS reached out to the broader Muslim community by disseminating booklets on subjects such as the equality of women and men and the Islamic view opposing wife-beating. SIS also connected with the broader transnational community of Muslim women, a practice that was to be a hallmark of Islamic feminism. In 2009 SIS launched a global movement for equality and justice for women living in Muslim contexts, Musawah, which hosts training sessions for women leaders from around the world, led by progressive interpreters of the Qurʾān and *ḥadīth*, with the goal of challenging the use of religion to justify discrimination against women.

Islamic feminism in Indonesia from the start reached out to rural areas through organizations such as the Center for Pesantren and Democracy Studies, founded by the activist Lily Munir, and the NGO Rahima, spearheaded by Kyai Muhammad Hussein. These organizations promote egalitarian Islam through curriculum revision in the grassroots Islamic boarding schools (*pesantrens*) found throughout the country.

Muslim activists employing Islamic arguments, as Pakistani feminists had done earlier, continue to fight injustices arising from *ḥudūd* laws. A landmark victory was achieved in Nigeria where *ḥudūd* laws had been recently instituted in several northern states. Two secular women's organizations, Baobab and the Women's Rights and Protection Association (est. 1999), supported two women condemned to death for *zinah* (adultery) in lower Sharīʿah courts by providing them with legal support to appeal the cases in the higher Sharīʿah courts; after studious examination of *fiqh*, these appeals led to acquittals.

Jurisprudential arguments were also used successfully in Morocco. Feminist activists from many associations, such as the Democratic Association of Moroccan Women (est. 1985), the Union of Feminine Action (est. 1987), and the Democratic League for Women's Rights, in long years of struggle, employed democracy and human-rights arguments and, in the final round, stepped up Islamic feminist arguments. Relentless campaigning by the activist women, particularly through the One Million Signatures Campaign, played an important role in achieving the overhaul of the Mudawana, or Family Law, in 2004, which is now the most egalitarian Sharīʿah-based family law in the Muslim world and the only explicitly Islamic law that provides for dual headship of the family, by wife and husband. The success of Morocco's activists inspired Iranian women to launch their own One Million Signatures Campaign to educate the Iranian public about discriminatory laws against women and their impact on women's daily lives, and to seek reforms to them. A victory of another sort was won in Yemen in 1997, when women activists across the ideological spectrum banded together, mobilizing the discourses of secular feminism and Islamic feminism to stave off the enactment of a new Family Law.

Muslims in the West as immigrants, new citizens, and converts are employing Islamic feminist discourse as they move forward with their new lives in the communities they are building and in society at large. Women need advice on a wide range of legal matters. In the United States, Karamah: Muslim Women Lawyers for Human Rights was created in the late 1990s by Azizah al-Hibri to provide such advice and to develop woman-sensitive Islamic jurisprudence. The Canadian Council of Muslim Women (CCMW, est. 1982), which is concerned with issues of gender and the interface between their Muslim and Canadian identities, fought a proposed change in the Arbitration Act in Ontario that would have made legally binding outcomes of family disputes that were mediated in a religious community. They argued that the existing Canadian Charter of Rights and Freedoms protected the equality of citizens and that that equality would be jeopardized by the legalized use of any religion (which could be defined in a patriarchal way) in mediating family disputes. The CCMW asserted that Canadian laws were compatible with the egalitarian principles of Islam and succeeded in defeating the bill that could have been detrimental to all women.

The problem of wife-beating that was a concern of secular feminists continues to be tackled by Islamic feminists. In Spain, when an imam published a book declaring that beating one's wife is sanctioned by scripture, Muslim women's organizations, comprising immigrants and converts, including the Asociación An-Nisa, Asociación Cultural Inshal-lah, and Asociación Baraka protested and successfully sued the imam, who was convicted for incitement of gender violence, which is prohibited by the Spanish constitution. It was ruled that his personal interpretation did not constitute the only possible reading of the Qurʾān.

Muslim women also face problems relating to the importation of brutal practices, such as honor killing, into their new communities in the West. These practices are understood in their countries of origin to be simply the products of custom but are passed off in the West, by their perpetrators, as Islamic. Accordingly Muslim women in the West use Islamic feminist discourse against honor killings. L'Associazione delle Donne Marocchine, under the direction of its founder Souad Sbai and in collaboration with others opposed to the practice, took the lead in fighting honor killing in Italy.

The mosque and other forms of sacred space are central in feminist efforts to realize an egalitarian Islam. Issues manifested mainly in the West, but which also appeared in South Africa, concern women sharing main mosque space with men and giving *khuṭbahs* (sermons), and, more specifically to North America, women acting as imams leading mixed congregations in prayer. The theologian Amina Wadud led the way in South Africa by pioneering what was called the "pre-*khuṭbah*" talk in a mosque in Cape Town in 1994, which occasioned women entering the main mosque space for the first time. A decade later Wadud acted as imam, leading a congregation in New York in prayer and delivering the *khuṭbah*. This activist move provoked a debate on the lawfulness of a woman acting as imam before a mixed congregation of women and men, in which readings of the *ḥadīth* and jurisprudence texts in favor of the practice were widely circulated. In Saudi Arabia, where feminist debate goes on behind the scenes, women were catapulted into public protest when they were told that women would be removed from the broader area around the Kaʿbah, called the *maṭāf*. Their protest in the press, in which they quoted from the Qurʾān to support their determination not to be shunted away, was echoed by an outcry from women in other parts of the Muslim world. The matter was resolved when it was officially announced that the removal would not take place.

In the contemporary global *ummah*, the distinction between secular feminism and Islamic feminism today is increasingly blended in concepts and actions. This was perhaps seen most visibly in the strong presence and leadership of women from all backgrounds during the Arab Spring and in some of the nonviolent civil protests that occurred in the years before it. In some cases, direct reference to Islam was made to support the quest for gender equality in issues ranging from access to stadiums to watch live soccer games (Iran) to demanding changes in the government (Kefaya, the "Enough" movement, in Egypt). Muslims as feminists who accept gender equality and social justice as core principles of Islam and seek to implement them include those who announce their feminism publicly and many more who think and act as feminists but without declaring their attitude openly.

BIBLIOGRAPHY

Abu-Lugod, Lila, ed. *Remaking Women: Feminism and Modernity in the Middle East*. Princeton, N.J.: Princeton University Press, 1998.

Abū Zayd, Nasr. *Rethinking the Qur'ān: Towards a Humanistic Hermeneutics*. Amsterdam: SWP Publishing, 2004.

Ali, Kecia. *Sexual Ethics and Islam: Feminist Reflections on Qur'an, Hadith, and Jurisprudence*. Oxford: Oneworld, 2006.

Badran, Margot. *Feminism Beyond East and West: New Gender Talk and Practice in Global Islam*. New Delhi: Global Media Publications, 2007.

Badran, Margot. *Feminism in Islam: Secular and Religious Convergences*. Oxford: Oneworld, 2009.

Badran, Margot. *Gender and Islam in Africa: Rights, Sexuality and Law*. Stanford, Calif.: Stanford University Press, 2011.

Barazangi, Nimat Hafez. *Woman's Identity and the Qur'an: A New Reading*. Gainesville: University Press of Florida, 2004.

Barlas, Asma. *"Believing Women" in Islam: Unreading Patriarchal Interpretations of the Qur'ān*. Austin: University of Texas Press, 2002.

Coleman, Isobel. *Paradise Beneath Her Feet: How Women Are Transforming the Middle East*. New York: Random House, 2010.

cooke, miriam. *Women Claim Islam: Creating Islamic Feminism Through Literature*. London: Routledge, 2001.

Esack, Farid. *On Being a Muslim: Finding a Religious Path in the World Today*. Oxford: Oneworld, 1999.

Hafez, Sherine. *An Islam of Her Own: Reconsidering Religion and Secularism in Women's Islamic Movements*. New York: New York University Press, 2011.

Hassan, Riffat. "Equal before Allah? Woman-Man Equality in the Islamic Tradition." *Harvard Divinity Bulletin*, January–May 1987, pp. 2–4.

Karam, Azza M. *Women, Islamisms, and the State: Contemporary Feminisms in Egypt*. New York: St. Martin's Press, 1998.

Mernissi, Fatima. *Beyond the Veil: Male-Female Dynamics in Modern Muslim Society*. Rev. ed. Bloomington: Indiana University Press, 1987.

Mir-Hosseini, Ziba. *Islam and Gender: The Religious Debate in Contemporary Iran*. Princeton, N.J.: Princeton University Press, 1999.

Mir-Hosseini, Ziba. "Muslim Women's Quest for Equality: Between Islamic Law and Feminism." *Critical Inquiry* 32 (Summer 2006): 629–645.

Mirza, Qudsia, ed. *Islamic Feminism and the Law*. London: Routledge, 2011.

Moghadam, Valentine M., ed. *From Patriarchy to Empowerment: Women's Participation, Movements, and Rights in the Middle East, North Africa, and South Asia*. Syracuse, N.Y.: Syracuse University Press, 2007.

Salime, Zakia. *Between Feminism and Islam: Human Rights and Sharia Law in Morocco*. Minneapolis: University of Minnesota Press, 2011.

Stephan, Maria J., ed. *Civilian Jihad: Nonviolent Struggle, Democratization, and Governance in the Middle East*. New York: Palgrave Macmillan, 2009.

Wadud, Amina. *Inside the Gender Jihad: Women's Reform in Islam*. Oxford: Oneworld, 2006.

Wadud, Amina. *Qur'an and Woman: Rereading the Sacred Text from a Woman's Perspective*. 2d ed. New York: Oxford University Press, 1999.

MARGOT BADRAN
Updated by NATANA J. DELONG-BAS

SOURCES

Islam and feminism are generally presented as diametrically opposed and incompatible. The agonizing relationship between feminism and religion is manifest in discussions about Islam. Until now people of faith have not occupied a comfortable position in feminist circles, as they follow ideals that are located in a tradition that historically assigns to women a subordinate status. Yet, there are among Muslim women and feminists ideas about Islamic feminisms.

A brief discussion about feminism in relation to Islam is inevitably restricted to a few broad subjects. The present outline does not imply a depreciation of all local manifestations and evolutions of feminism and Islamic feminism in the various Muslim countries. The premise is that, notwithstanding the internal contradictions and differences in realizations, successes, and methods in each country, there seems to be a certain unity and solidarity between the women's movements. From this point of view, this article summarizes the origins of feminism in Muslim societies, its impact, and the emergence of a religious, that is, Islamic, feminism.

The rise of women's movements in the Middle East can be described in several phases. First comes a phase of awakening: the status of women becomes an issue, existing social habits are questioned, and women's organizations are created. In the second phase the fledgling women's activism is inserted into the nationalist struggle. The third phase takes place in the new states: women assist in and/or collide with the reconstruction of states. Generally speaking this gave rise to the creation of two feminist movements in the Arab world: a first stream is Western-oriented and secular. This movement attracted mainly women from the upper and middle classes. In the first years of the independent states, this was the dominant movement. Not infrequently this silted into a form of state feminism. The second movement is anti-Western, in which one tries to frame the feminist goals within one's own Islamic framework. This movement has become increasingly popular since the revival of Islam. This format is, of course, also a gross generalization. These phases did not necessarily happen successfully, but often simultaneously. Moreover, not all phases occurred in all cases.

A First Feminist Flow in Muslim Societies: Western-Oriented and Secular. The first steps of women's activism coincided with the development of various reform movements, either secular or within Islam, which arose in the nineteenth century. The first feminist Middle East text is attributed to Qāsim Amīn (1863–1908). In 1899 he wrote *The Liberation of Women*, in which he stresses that the degradation of women in Islamic countries, which had increased over the course of centuries, did not have its origin in Islam but had been adapted from the views and customs of people who had subsequently become Muslims. Feminist historians today find his ideas on women already in *Women of Islam* (1896) written by the Turkish feminist Fatma Āliye Hanim (1864–1936). It is, however, the work of Amīn that led to the beginning of the feminist debate in the area. His writings found their way to other countries of the Middle East and fueled the discussion there, too. Although the discussion about women was initiated by men, controversies in the Egyptian press between women can be found as well (e.g., in 1892 about women's suffrage).

In the early twentieth century, among intellectuals in Iran, Egypt, Turkey, and Syria, the status of women was connected with the idea of modernity. The status of women was seen as a barometer for the modernity of the state. Reformers argued in favor of education for women and attacked traditional social practices such as arranged marriages, polygamy, and concubinage. Critical voices resounded from both secular and

Islamic angles. The call for more women's rights was part of a larger societal change, due to the influence of and contacts with the West, the transition from a rural to an urban society, industrialization, and commercialization. The masculine calls for reform to modern states were not always so woman-friendly. They wanted skilled and educated women in order to educate their children and to acquire social recognition. According to these reformers the role of women was acted out mostly in the home, which explains why the concern of men for the development and education of women was attacked by some women. Others used this discourse to their own advantage and took it up to a certain extent. However, regardless of the motivation, the debate created new openings and opportunities for women. The controversy about motives facilitated, for example, the emergence of a separate women's press throughout the Middle East, including women's magazines and newspapers of different type, with a feminist content and scope. The growth of the women's press was an important step in the dissemination and communication of ideas, although this important step was limited to a relatively small audience of literate women from highly urbanized areas.

The first women's organizations in the late nineteenth and early twentieth centuries were essentially charitable organizations. They focused on improving the health of women, religion, and literacy. Their activism has played an important role, as many of the later feminist pioneers took their first steps in such charitable organizations. They gave women experience and political visibility. As a result of colonialism and imperialism, a strong nationalist movement emerged in the Middle East and triggered organization and activism. The women's organizations in the Middle East saw their efforts in the light of defending and strengthening national culture and family values. Unlike Western feminism, there is a strong link with the national struggle. Nationalist activism offered women an opportunity to act outside the closed world of women, under the flag of patriotism. Women's activism was in itself a feminist act. Yet the idea within the women's movements in those days was to realize women's rights as a natural part of general civil rights. Only in a second phase did they try to add explicit feminist demands to the agenda. Nationalism was a double-edged sword for women: on the one hand it liberated and emancipated women, but on the other hand, it limited them. Feminist demands were always subordinated to nationalist requirements. The role of women remained neatly enclosed within the boundaries of national ideology.

Although women had contributed to the fight for sovereignty, this was not rewarded when the state was created. The creation of a new state was often based on the idea of the citizen as a man or a woman, which made the explication of women's rights, in theory, obsolete. Independent women's movements were silenced. Only the state-controlled organizations survived. This was a pernicious development for the evolution of feminism. In Turkey, for example, obtaining certain women's rights from the state weakened the independent women's movement. Feminism was synonymous with state feminism, and independent grassroots movements were discouraged. There was no broad-based growth of feminism that took into account the requirements of different women. Women from lower classes or from rural areas were easily overlooked. The only ones who benefited from state-imposed women's rights were a small elite of highly educated, wealthy women who were not representative of the whole female population. This gave feminism a negative connotation as an elitist, distant, and inauthentic movement. Feminism seemed to be imported from the West, it had grown from a Western ideology, and it had little relevance to women from the Middle East. And instead of being considered a result of modernization, an emancipated woman was considered to be a "Westernized" woman.

The Second Feminist Flow: A Religious Feminism for the Liberation of Muslim Women? Since the 1970s there has appeared the idea of Islam as a medium for change in the Middle East. As an alternative to the difficult relationship with modernity, Muslims propose an Islamic modernism that makes a distinction between modernization and Westernization. Modernization is associated with technology, science, and a higher standard of living. This aspect is usually desired and welcomed with open arms. Westernization, on the other hand, is usually rejected, because it is connected to the problems of Western culture, such as promiscuity, erosion of family and community, and drug and alcohol abuse. The alternative offered by Islamic modernism considers Islam as a dynamic and progressive religion that allows reinterpretations and adjustments to the modern age. The image of women under Islamic modernism proposes an ideal Muslim woman as devout, virtuous, and kept apart. This idealized image serves as a symbol of the difference from the Western woman. The symbolic utility of women has political and religious leaders mobilizing women for their movements. Women are taught Islam, used as propaganda, mobilized in street actions, and encouraged to wear Islamic dress. Muslim modernists pay great attention to women and to how women should behave in order to function properly.

However, modernization has changed women's lives during the years of Western authority and in the contacts with Western society. Many women enjoyed teaching, having a career, traveling, and coming into contact with Western feminist ideas. This interaction with a much more diverse group of individuals than just the family group has led to a growing resistance to the prevailing ideal woman. Women are strengthened by modernization and education. Education has induced them to question Islamic interpretations. Today, women in the Middle East challenge the public view of the position of women in Islam. Their attitudes toward Islam are diverging: from turning their backs to Islam and religion in general, to accepting Islam while rejecting some aspects of the organized religion and the religious leaders' authority, or even to openly discussing Islamic sources and interpretations. The latter ones seek their own interpretations of Islam that better reflect women's rights, and they refer to male dominance in history and Qurʾānic interpretation.

Access to holy books and religious sources of their respective traditions—due, inter alia, to better and higher education for women—induces Muslim women to understand better the broader historical context of some texts that have reinforced gender inequality. A growing number of Muslim women understand they are excluded from total participation in society, not because this is prescribed by Islam but because Islam appeared in a strongly patriarchal social context. In line with this, feminists consider interactions between men and women as being imposed not by religion but by social praxis often legitimized by religion. Gradually a gender discourse has arisen which is "feminist" in its aspiration and demands, yet "Islamic" in its language and sources of legitimacy, meaning that women have acquired the words and the method—that is, the intellectual weapons—needed to criticize those who speak in the name of Islam. Doing so they achieve new frames of reference to reformulate Islamic concepts and laws.

This new discourse has been labelled Islamic feminism, a term that continues to be contested and is considered controversial. Questions such as, "Can we put the emerging feminist voices in Islam into categories?" and "Can we generate a definition that reflects all the differing positions and approaches of so-called Islamic Feminists?" show up in reflections on what "Islamic feminism" is. Examining the dynamics of Islamic feminism and the discourse about how opponents depict them might help us to understand. What is clear is that, as with other feminists, their positions are local, diverse, multiple, and evolving.

In its attempts to make a "change," feminism unavoidably confronts the established patriarchal power. Since the beginning of Islam, women's roles in religion have been circumscribed by the power and control of men, the *ʿulamāʾ*, as guardians of religion, formulators and interpreters of laws, and judges. The "new" feminism—which is called "Islamic feminism"—has focused on the field of Qurʾānic interpretation (*tafsīr*) and has successfully uncovered the Qurʾānic egalitarian message. Scholars such as Azizah al-Hibri (1997) and Afsaneh Najmabadi (1998) emphasize in their arguments the gender-inclusive language of the Qurʾān (which has disappeared in the corpus of *tafsīr* that clearly defends male superiority and patriarchal culture). Amina Wadud (1992) and Leila Ahmed (1992) relate, in their reasoning, more on Islamic virtuous women as examples for humanity. With access to holy scripts and religious sources of their respective traditions, women acquire insights into the broader historical context of certain texts that work to the disadvantage of gender equality.

In order to be part of a pluralistic women's movement, Muslim feminism seems to emphasize the notion of empowerment and to use a rights discourse. Sherin Saadallah (2004) considers this a tactical change within the feminist movement, which allows it to incorporate Muslim feminism into a feminist project. Metaphorically, feminism can be compared to a plant that is trying to find, in every society and in every community, fertile soil without sealing itself off hermetically. Currently, several scholars agree on the plurality of feminism. And, in particular, since it has become visible that women's movements worldwide are concerned about the same themes, the will to gain independence and to empower women is at the heart of every Muslim feminist project. Finally, in this line the usefulness of the acquired knowledge must be taken into account. The rereading of the Qurʾān and its reinterpretations are based on the reformist model. According to critics this does not lead to reinterpretations at the level of social sciences. This is much larger and is about paying attention to the jurisprudential texts in which the rules of the Qurʾān and the sunnah—and thus, also regarding the oppression of women—are elaborated. The daily bodily harm or psychological assaults are prescribed in texts that function as Qurʾānic explanations. Most of the feminists, however, do not pay attention to those *fiqh* books, which are full of realities constructed by males and which overleap "real" life. Pieternella van Doorn-Harder (2006) disapproves, therefore, of the use of bombastic language about all the freedoms that the Qurʾān is supposed to promise women, especially when those same women are living in daily oppression and mistreatment. Relevant Qurʾān interpretations and interpretations that wish to stand in the middle of women's lives should therefore pay attention to the jurisprudential books. Only those interpretations that are rooted in both the Qurʾān and jurisprudence and that take as a starting point women's daily experiences might be able to bridge the gap between ideals and realities.

BIBLIOGRAPHY

Abu-Lughod, Lila. *Remaking Women. Feminism and Modernity in the Middle East*. Princeton, N.J.: Princeton University Press, 1998.

Ahmed, Leila. *Women and Gender in Islam: Historical Roots of a Modern Debate*. New Haven, Conn.: Yale University Press, 1992.

Badran, Margot. "Islamic Feminism: What's in a Name?" *Al-Ahram Weekly Online* 569 (January 2002): 17–23.
Doorn-Harder, Pieternella, van. *Women Shaping Islam: Indonesian Women Reading the Qur'an.* Urbana: University of Illinois Press, 2006.
Hibri, Azizah Y. al- "Islam, Law and Custom: Redefining Muslim Women's Rights." *American University Journal of International Law and Policy* 12 (1997): 1–44.
Mahmood, Saba. *Politics of Piety: The Islamic Revival and the Feminist Subject.* 2d ed. Princeton, N.J.: Princeton University Press, 2012.
Mir-Hosseini, Ziba. "The Quest for Gender Justice: Emerging Feminist Voices in Islam." *Islam21: A Global Network for Muslim Intellectuals & Activists* 36 (2004): 6–8. http://www.islam21.net.
Najmabadi, Afsaneh. "Feminism in the Islamic Republic: Years of Hardship, Years of Growth." In *Islam, Gender, and Social Change*, edited by Yvonne Yazbeck Haddad and John L. Esposito, pp. 59–84. Oxford and New York: University Press, 1998.
Saadallah, Sherin. "Muslim Feminism in the Third Wave: A Reflective Inquiry." In *Third Wave Feminism: A Critical Exploration*, edited by Stacy Gillis, Gillian Howie, and Rebecca Munford, pp. 216–226. Houndsmills, Basingstoke, U.K., and New York: Palgrave Macmillan, 2004.
Tohidi, Nayereh. "The Issues at Hand." In *Women in Muslim Societies: Diversity within Unity*, edited by Herbert L. Bodman and Nayereh Tohidi, pp. 277–294. Boulder, Colo.: Lynne Rienner Publishers, 1998.
Wadud, Amina. *Qur'an and Woman: Rereading the Sacred Text from a Woman's Perspective.* 2d ed. New York: Oxford University Press, 1999.

ELS VANDERWAEREN

FERTILITY AND INFERTILITY TREATMENTS. The ability to produce offspring—that is, fertility and reproductive potential—is a subject of enormous social concern in Muslim societies and occupies a central place in religious discourses and the construction of social roles.

Reproductive capacity was a significant factor in the construction of the female identity in medieval Islam. It was not through gender, but rather through social roles, that legal rights were allocated. Thus, for the female, her social role as "mother"—that is, producer of offspring—garnered her greatest allocation of legal rights within the family framework and potential for honor and respect.

Fertility and Infertility Treatments in Medieval Muslim Societies. Given the importance of producing offspring, medieval Muslim physicians prescribed numerous remedies for infertility and miscarriage. Medieval medical encyclopedias, such as those written by ʿAlī ibn al-ʿAbbās al-Majūsī, Abū al-Qāsim al-Zahrāwī, and Ibn Sīnā regularly contained chapters dealing with illnesses related to the female reproductive organs and complications in pregnancy and childbirth. Scholars of medicine also wrote entire treatises on infertility and its possible remedies.

The treatment of disease in medieval Muslim societies stemmed from various medical traditions. On the one hand, the pervasive belief in divine will gave rise to the belief that illness, death, and infertility ultimately rested in the hands of God; on the other hand, the Hippocratic and Galenic theories, based on the idea that human physical health was dependent on maintaining a bodily balance of the "four humours," informed much of the edifice of Greco-Islamic medical treatment. In the case of women's health, Hippocratic theories described the womb as an independent creature inside the female body, which, when not affixed by pregnancy, would move toward other bodily organs such as the liver, heart, or brain to increase its access to moisture. This, along with any imbalances in blood represented by menstrual blood, led to diseases of the reproductive organs, many of which caused infertility. People also resorted to many other treatments based on home remedies and local curing traditions. A significant alternative was prophetic medicine (*al-ṭibb al-nabawī*), which was developed by scholars of the religious sciences and was based on passages from the Qurʾān and prophetic traditions deemed to offer insight with regard to human biology and effective treatment of illness.

The combination of these influences led to the prescription and practice of a wide array of treatments for infertility. These included prescribing specific drugs to restore the balance of the humors; weight loss; eating specific foods prescribed or proscribed by prophetic traditions; increasing sexual intercourse and/or stimulation of the reproductive organs; herbal remedies; practices warding away the unseen effects of black magic and the evil eye; and, finally, increased spiritual devotion by way of individual worship or visitations to Ṣūfī masters and their shrines as attempts to beseech God to lift the given ailment and/or cause of infertility.

The need for appropriate medical care for expectant mothers resulted both in the entry of women into the medical sciences as trained physicians and in the development of midwifery as a profession and recognized social role. Though elite medical training remained dominated by male practitioners, female doctors have been mentioned in numerous historical sources.

Midwifery and wet nursing not only were dominated by women, but their social significance in promoting fertility, reproductive capacity, and women's health also expanded to such a degree such that they became permanent fixtures in families—often managing the care of a woman beginning with her own birth, through her marriage, and on to her own pregnancy and care of her children.

Medieval religious scholars wrote treatises advising couples to exercise patience and perseverance in asking God to grant them progeny, but Islamic law recognized infertility on the part of the husband or the wife to be a just cause for divorce by either party. This legal framework recognized that the inability to conceive a child was not always due to a wife's physiology, but could, in fact, be due to the husband's; this was an idea that has largely been absent in other medieval cultural traditions, which often viewed infertility as strictly a female issue. The outcome of such circumstances varied according to regional and temporal contexts, social status, and personal circumstance. Theoretically speaking, however, in general, if the wife was infertile, the husband could remain with her monogamously, divorce her, marry an additional wife, or attempt to conceive with a slave woman under his ownership. As for a husband's infertility, the wife could choose to remain with him; however, she also had just cause to request a divorce and potentially remarry if she desired.

Contemporary Developments and Discourses on Infertility in the Muslim World. Infertility, contraception, and abortion have remained issues of central concern in the Muslim world in modern times. The Middle East hosts one of the highest per capita concentrations of in vitro fertilization (IVF) clinics in the world. The cultural and economic significance of producing offspring, along with the relative permissibility of pursuing certain infertility treatments from a religious perspective are two factors among others that have contributed to and shaped the growth of this industry in that region.

The *fatwā* issued on March 23, 1980, by the Grand Shaykh of al-Azhar University in Egypt regarding the permissibility of IVF was one of the earliest and most influential issued in the Sunnī world on the topic of reproductive technology. According to this *fatwā*, IVF is permitted so long as the procedure involves transfer of gametes between spouses. In other words, surrogacy and the usage of third-party donor gametes were prohibited.

In the late 1990s, the Grand Ayatollah of Iran, Ali Hussein Khamenei, issued a *fatwā* permitting donor gametes to be used under certain conditions. Viewing the donation of gametes as equivalent to adopting a child, Khamenei asserted that, although the infertile couple would carry parental rights as adoptive parents, the child could legally inherit only from his or her biological donor parents. His position on the permissibility of sperm donation was revised in 2003 by the Iranian parliament, however, because sperm donation came to be viewed by some as a form of polyandry. However, embryo donation was still permitted so long as the donor couple and the receiving couple were married, thus maintaining the parallel to religious laws on adoption. Egg donation was also permitted, so long as the receiving husband contracted a temporary *mutʿah* marriage—a practice permitted only in Shīʿī Islam—with the egg donor to ensure that all involved parties were legally married. Surrogacy also remained licit, although jurists have held differing positions with regard to the details of this procedure.

The introduction of new technologies has enabled termination of marriages to be avoided in many cases, allowing many individuals to avoid the bleak socioeconomic consequences of divorce which, statistically speaking, have a greater negative impact on women than on men. The usage of third-party gametes—a procedure that is legally practiced in the Shīʿī world and illegally practiced in some parts of the Sunnī world—has also led to similar outcomes. On the other hand, intracytoplasmic sperm injection (ICSI), a procedure introduced in Belgium in 1992 that involves injecting the weak sperm of an infertile male into fertile ova, has had the opposite effect. Although this procedure has led to positive outcomes for many couples, it has left many older women who have remained in life-long marriages with their infertile husbands at risk for divorce. Because older women are often beyond the age of producing viable eggs, their infertile husbands, eager to pursue the new possibility of producing children, have sometimes opted to divorce the current spouse or to marry an additional, younger wife to pursue this medical procedure.

Due to the significance of kinship, lineage, and familial ties in Muslim societies, issues related to infertility, contraception, and abortion have always been of central concern, historically and in modern times. This has brought contemporary scientific developments in those areas into religious juridical discourse, and it has made those juridical discourses an important venue in which contemporary social and political battles have been fought. Reproductive capacity has always been a significant factor affecting conceptions of gender in all societies. Understanding how the debates on reproduction are changing offers insight into how the place of women in Muslim (and other) societies has changed and will continue to change.

BIBLIOGRAPHY

Duben, A., and C. Behar. *Istanbul Households. Marriage, Family, and Fertility 1880–1940*. Cambridge, U.K.: Cambridge University Press, 1991.

Fahmy, K.. "Women, Medicine, and Power in Nineteenth Century Egypt." In *Remaking Women. Feminism and Modernity in the Middle East*, edited by L. Abu-Lughod, pp. 35–72. Princeton, N.J.: Princeton University Press, 1998.

Hoodfar, H. "Devices and Desires: Population Policy and Gender Roles in the Islamic Republic." *Middle East Report* 24 (1994): 11–17.

Inhorn, M. C. *Quest for Conception: Gender, Infertility, and Egyptian Medical Traditions*. Philadelphia: University of Pennsylvania Press, 1994.

Inhorn, M. C. *Infertility and Patriarchy: The Cultural Politics of Gender and Family Life in Egypt*. Philadelphia: University of Pennsylvania Press, 1996.

Inhorn, M. C. *Local Babies, Global Science: Gender, Religion, and In Vitro Fertilization in Egypt*. New York: Routledge, 2003.

Inhorn, M. C. "Middle Eastern Masculinities in the Age of New Reproductive Technologies. Male Infertility and Stigma in Egypt and Lebanon." *Medical Anthropology Quarterly* 18 (2004): 34–54.

Inhorn, M. C., and F. van Balend, eds. *Infertility around the Globe: New Thinking on Childlessness, Gender, and Reproductive Technologies*. Berkeley: University of California Press, 2002.

Musallam, B. F. *Sex and Society in Islam*. Cambridge, U.K.: Cambridge University Press, 1983.

Musallam, B. F. "Crafting an Educated Housewife in Iran." In *Remaking Women: Feminism and Modernity in the Middle East*, edited by L. Abu-Lughod, pp. 91–125. Princeton, N.J.: Princeton University Press, 1998.

Omran, A. *Family Planning in the Legacy of Islam*. London: Routledge, 1992.

Omran, A., and F. Roudi, "The Middle East Population Puzzle." *Population Bulletin* 48 (1993): 1–40.

Paidar, P. *Women and the Political Process in Twentieth-Century Iran*. Cambridge, U.K.: Cambridge University Press, 1995.

Schleifer, A. *Motherhood in Islam*. Cambridge, U.K.: Fons Vitae, 1986.

Serour, G., ed. *Proceedings of the First International Conference on Bioethics in Human Reproduction Research in the Muslim World*. International Islamic Center for Population Studies and Research, al-Azhar University, 10–13 December 1991. Cairo, Egypt: IICPSR 1992.

Serour, G., ed. "Medically Assisted Conception. Dilemma of Practice and Research: Islamic Views." In *Proceedings of the First International Conference on Bioethics in Human Reproduction Research in the Muslim World*, pp. 234–242. International Islamic Center for Population Studies and Research, al-Azhar University, 10–13 December 1991. Cairo, Egypt,: IICPSR 1992.

Serour, G., ed. "Bioethics in Reproductive Health: A Muslim's Perspective." *Middle East Fertility Society Journal* 1 (1996): 30–35.

Serour, G., ed. M. Aboulghar, and R. Mansour. "Bioethics in Medically Assisted Conception in the Muslim World." *Journal of Assisted Reproduction and Genetics* 12 (1995): 559–565.

Serour, G., ed. M. El Ghar, and R. Mansour. "Infertility: A Health Problem in the Muslim World." *Population Sciences* 10 (1991): 41–58.

Sonbol, A. E. *The Creation of a Medical Profession in Egypt, 1800–1922*. Syracuse, N.Y.: Syracuse University Press, 1991.

Sonbol, A. E. "Adoption in Islamic Society: A Historical Survey." In *Children in the Muslim Middle East*, edited by E. W. Fernea, pp. 45–67. Austin: University of Texas Press, 1995.

SARAH ISLAM

FINANCIAL INSTITUTIONS. The last two centuries have seen the emergence of modern government in the Islamic world. An important part of this process has involved the creation of institutions for macroeconomic management. The role of the state in the economy has been formalized with the introduction of ministries of finance, planning, industry, agriculture, and commerce. At the same time, central banks have been created, and a large number of organizations that play some role in the regulation of economic activity, from chambers of commerce to worker's syndicates and trade unions, have emerged. Some of these are mere agents of government, but others enjoy considerable autonomy.

There has always been a tendency to see economics and economic principles as gender-neutral, with gender being a passive, rather than active, presence in economic relations. Yet, in both traditional and contemporary Islamic institutions, Islamic law in all its genres and interpretations has, in many ways, worked in favor of gender difference rather than against it. The notion of economic rights for men and women with respect to money and property has remained a constant in economic and legal transactions. Where equal rights for women are/were vague, women have taken the opportunity to subvert the social and political spaces to which they might be confined and to turn them to their advantage. As women in the Muslim world increasingly dominate the labor force, carve out careers, and actively engage in the business world as entrepreneurs, financial institutions have increasingly accommodated them as important clients and members.

Western economics is, for the most part, believed to be universally applicable, reflecting the assumed value-free and culturally independent nature of its methodology. At the policy level, however, experience from many parts of the world indicates that such assumptions are simplistic, if not completely misleading. Yet, the universality of economic epistemology is seldom questioned in the West, but it is in the Islamic world, where the subject has its own axioms. The school of Western thought known as institutional economics has perhaps a more relevant approach for dealing with Islamic societies. Institutionalists believe that the political and social structures of a country influence how its economy works and that other disciplines, including law, sociology, and anthropology, are relevant to economic problems. A neoclassical approach that tries to isolate supply and demand from the market environment in which they operate is not very instructive in Islamic societies. The institutions involved in economic policy formation or execution are staffed by people with beliefs and values and nowhere more so than in an Islamic society. Simplistic economic models that assume so-called rational maximizing behavior fail to explain much of what is actually taking place in particular economies, where, after all, it is social beings who are the economic agents, not impersonal mechanistic forces. Models within which men and women often negotiate different terms of engagement are shaped and inculcated by the specificity of existing cultural mores in every Muslim society.

Islamic Financial Institutions. Institutions concerned with the collection of taxes and the disbursement of the proceeds have existed since the time of the Prophet. The Bayt al-Māl (house for money) is traditionally responsible for taxation. It is usually a public institution that is responsible for the expenditure of public income and welfare provision. Thus, Bayt al-Māl "acts as a treasury complemented with the task of planning and distributing society's wealth in the whole socio-economic and political set-up of the nation" (Namazi, 2010, p. 75).

The finances of citizens of the Islamic state were administered separately from those of the royal household through the Bayt al-Māl al-Muslimīn. Responsibilities were wide-ranging, from public works, such as the construction and maintenance of roads and bridges, to social expenditures, which were designed to help the poor and needy. The latter was financed with revenue from the *zakāt* (Islamic tax on wealth). The *zakāt al-fiṭr* (alms on feast), one of the five pillars of Islam, is an obligation by all Muslims, both men and women, who have the capacity to do so, to pay alms annually during the month of Ramadan. In the past, this was paid, either directly or via appointed *zakāt* collectors, to the Bayt al-Māl al-Muslimīn, which would administer one of the remits of its public duty—to achieve socioeconomic justice through the alleviation of poverty and disadvantage in society. *Zakāt* is the Muslim equivalent of Western charity, although it is an embedded and fundamental principle of Islam and has a much longer history (see Lubis et al., 2011; Toor and Nasar, 2003).

Zakāt collection in the contemporary period varies from a centralized, obligatory payment system through state institutions, as in Saudi Arabia or Pakistan; "voluntary" collections by the government, as in Bangladesh; or decentralized and undertaken locally through *zakāt* committees. The idea of *zakāt* being voluntary is questionable, because all Muslims have a socio-religious obligation to pay *zakāt al-fiṭr* as the act of cleansing one's "wealth" and purifying the soul, bringing the devout Muslim closer to God.

Zakāt does not refer simply to money, but can include gold, silver, shares, merchandise, or livestock. Women, for example, who may have no liquid assets but a significant quantity of gold jewelry would be required to pay *zakāt al fiṭr* because the jewelry is seen as an investment. In Saudi Arabia, a separate department exists in the Ministry of Finance and National Economy, tasked with collecting and distributing *zakāt*, while in other Muslim countries this process has been privatized, as in Malaysia, or decentralized, as in Pakistan. Most governments now operate e-portals so individuals can pay their *zakāt* either online or via their cell phones. This has been especially important to women in countries in which strict purdah cultural norms are imposed through gender segregation in public, and cyberspace offers a gender-free zone within which to pay accounts and manage their affairs. Distribution can be more complex especially in provinces or towns, where local decision making is placed in the hands of *zakāt* committees. In Pakistan, for example, women are members of the *zakāt* committees, along with *ummahs* and the judiciary, that assess the question of need, identify projects, and investigate potential social investment. The role of Muslim women in the family and the community and their responsibility for the well-being of the community, as expressed through a duty of care and charitable work, are highly valued and recognized in their appointment to the *zakāt* committees.

Shared Productive Resources—*waqf* and *waqifs*. Islam recognizes the private ownership of property; indeed, there are well-defined laws governing the inheritance of property in the Qurʾān itself. However, there has always been provision for the voluntary transfer of land, property, and other income-producing assets to a *waqf* (charitable trust), and such transfers have been actively encouraged throughout Islamic history. This constitutes a charitable endowment to God from which all or part of the revenue can be used in service of the community as a whole residing in a particular area or state and is administered by the *waqf*. Accompanying this endowment is the inviolable right over *waqf* property that protects it from confiscations, disbursement, or repossession. Individuals or families (*waqifs*) that establish *waqfs* are able to protect their assets by handing them over as a public trust, while maintaining the right to appoint the administrators or employees, which would naturally include family members. A *waqf* could be one in which the founder stipulates whether all rights and assets remain exclusively for philanthropic purposes for its beneficent community or whether specific family members might receive a proportion of the resources/benefits from the endowment. Most effectively, it enables families to protect inheritable private property from one generation to the next.

In the past, men would frequently establish *waqfs* in the names of their wives and daughters, usually for gender-specific purposes, for example, supporting lower-class women who were widowed or divorced, the education of young girls, or shelters for women. Ahmed (1992), in her historical study of women and Islam, found that more than 30 percent of the *waqfs* in Egypt are named after upper-class women. Then, as now, wealthy women set up charitable foundations of their own supporting causes for which they have a passion, such as women-led development projects, skills projects, and women and the creative arts.

Family *waqfs* are also a means of securing private property and its endowment within the family and remain a legitimate means by which wealthy families can guarantee the inheritance of family property across generations. They are thus able to avoid the strictures of Islamic inheritance law whereby, for example, women have the right to receive an inheritance, but only half that of a man. A family *waqf* permits the *waqif* to endow an equal and viable property share to children, and this frequently benefits women. Moreover, it is not unusual for women to establish a *waqf* to protect their assets and property, no matter how much or how little, and to endow it in a way that suits them. For women who are divorced or widowed, establishing a family *waqf* ensures that their property will be inherited by their children and not by a new husband or stepchildren. Up until the early twentieth century, *waqfs* bestowed both rights and status on women that might not be extended to them under *ʿādah* (customary law) or Sharīʾah law and, in this way, were a means to circumvent existing sociocultural mores.

Engendering Economic Institutions. As European influences and global trade permeated the Muslim world, financial institutions in both legal and operational terms took on a Western hue. Along with economic development, the expansion of large corporations, and the pressures of global trade, even the most devout and conservative Muslims of the Middle East have been obliged, for overseas business purposes at least, to engage with contemporary conventional banking institutions. The successor to Bayt al-Māl al-Muslimīn was a central Islamic commerce and finance bank operating on the principle of profit-and-loss sharing. The first such bank, the National Commercial Bank, was established in 1953 in Saudi Arabia and is now one of the largest financial institutions in the Arab world.

From the 1970s onward, the entry of Muslim countries into the international economy coincided with the implementation of five-year development plans in which women's employment was encouraged and facilitated and universal women's education was underwritten by the public sector. Moreover, the private finance sector also responded to the rising profile of women in economic development, from the establishment of women-only banking and savings-and-loan cooperatives in South Asia to the expansion of Islamic banking facilities for women in the Muslim world. Under Sharīʾah law, women had gained the guaranteed right to own property almost a century and a half before Western women, and many women thus required appropriate and unfettered access to all banking facilities. Moreover, by 2003 almost 70 percent of women in Asia participated in the labor market and, even in the Arab world, which had the lowest rates of participation, the number of women entering the labor market had increased by 50 percent. This trend was followed by a commensurate expansion of Islamic banks of one form or another, as women, faced with discrimination within conventional banking, deliberately sought out establishments that adhered to the principles of Sharīʾah and within which women's rights over their finances and accounts were respected and recognized.

From the late 1990s, Islamic banks began to target and expand their female customer base. In countries where gender segregation in public was de jure, separate branches or banking facilities were extended to women and, even where it was not, Islamic banks began to offer separate facilities. In the Middle East, this financial drive was almost palpable as, by 2009, it was estimated that women held $500 billion in assets, which constituted 22 percent of the total managed funds in the region. In Saudi Arabia, where separate banking has existed for decades, it is estimated that women own $11 billion in cash deposits alone, whereas in 2006 the National Commercial Bank revealed that women owned 40 percent of real estate assets, 20 percent of the stock, and 18 percent of the current accounts in the Kingdom. Of little surprise, therefore, is the National Commercial Bank's long-standing commitment to women-only branches, of which it has established forty-six, with other banks in the region following suit. Moreover, since 2000 there has been an upsurge in financial institutions offering specialist gender-specific finance products that conform to the principles of Sharīʾah, most especially with respect to investment funds. These, however, sometimes have involved strategies from gimmickry to establishing "offshore" accounts. For example, in Malaysia, the Eoncap Islamic Bank offers a savings product for women called An-Nisa ("lady" in Arabic), which also provides medical benefits, such as mammograms, while in the Middle East one financial service company launched its Ladies Wealth Management Division in 2010 in Saudi Arabia, and in 2009 a Cayman Islands–based wealth management company launched the Ameerah fund across the Middle East, which offers women advice on Sharīʿah-compliant investing.

It is important to note, however, that Sharīʿah-compliant banking practices are not simply geared to the wealthy female client. In the Middle East, where the number of working women has increased exponentially, and in Southeast Asia, where approximately 70 percent of women participate in the labor market, offering services to this client base is fundamental. Islamic banking offers women respect and privacy, with Arab banks, for example, targeting working women who are offered credit cards and loans in their own right. Moreover, women are keen to maintain control of their own financial affairs through the modern-day version of the family *waqf*—the trust fund, investment portfolio, and the designated savings account. While wealthy women establish trust funds and investment portfolios for their children, working women with a small disposable income set up special savings accounts in the name of their daughters as an investment in their future. Like their mothers and grandmothers before them, they are paving the way for their children through the principle of self-help and good financial management.

The adoption of Islamic banking principles has not been confined to formal financial institutions. The Grameen Bank, established by Professor Muhammad Yunus in the mid-1970s, operates from a set of Islamic principles based on self-help, profit sharing, and group saving. The experiment was first carried out in Bangladesh, taking banking directly to the rural poor and placing women in the position of principal borrowers. Initially envisaged as a loan scheme to finance entrepreneurial incentives and income-generating activities, Grameen Bank, which is based on a system of graduated loans, has been used by women to fund other objectives. For example, the bank did not encourage giving loans to buy land, on the grounds that this would contribute to landlessness. Yet, rural women would often pool their loans and form agricultural cooperatives whereby they could significantly increase their income and acquire land in a context within which women's access to land was restricted. In Bangladesh, the increase in male migration to the Middle East for higher-paid employment led to a new phenomenon by which women would take out loans for their daughter's dowry. This money was sometimes invested in the daughter's future husband, with the mother paying for visa papers, visas, and travel documents and expenses. While male migration may mean long periods of separation, it is viewed as a pathway to upward mobility, with wives micromanaging the remittances from overseas to accrue capital to invest in a house and property. Thus, working under the Grameen model, women's use of funding has extended beyond the original remit to making clear investments in not only their own future, but also that of their children.

Irrespective of the genre of the economic institution, women have played a fundamental role in the expansion of Islamic banking, both as clients and as banking personnel within the system itself. In the Middle East, where public gender segregation drove the push for separate banking facilities, the once niche market in Saudi Arabia spread across the Arab world and beyond in the process of the globalization of Islamic banking. This development has led to a commensurate expansion of female employment in all Islamic financial institutions, in both the Middle East and Asia, in the belief that female financial personnel would attract women's banking and investment to the banking establishment. Asia is also leading the way in gender-inclusive Islamic banking practices recruiting tertiary-educated female Islamic scholars as Sharīʾah advisors to financial institutions. Malaysia's Sharīʾah Advisory Council has two female scholars on its eleven-member board, while Indonesia includes six women on its thirty-five-member National Sharīʾah Council. Furthermore, since the 1990s, the profile of Muslim women as role models in the Islamic finance industry has led to a sharp increase in the numbers of women undertaking tertiary studies in this area. One academic interviewed by Power (2008) stated that, at the American University of Beirut, over half of the finance students were female. In view of the fact that the world of banking and finance is actively recruiting women and, in the principal Muslim Asian and Arab states, over 50 percent of the tertiary student population is female, the indications are that women's status and profile in financial institutions are on the rise.

Moreover, the spectacular rising profile of Southeast Asian and Arab women in national and global economic decision making is a clear indication of how far women have come in entering the highly patriarchal world of banking and finance. Leading the way is Malaysia with two women CEOs of national banks, one of whom, Fozia Amanulla, was the first female CEO of any Islamic bank in Malaysia. Zeti Akhtar Aziz, who is the central bank governor in Malaysia, is recognized as the major transformational force in making Kuala Lumpur the hub of Islamic banking in Asia. Indonesia also stands out as a country in which women have made their mark in business and finance. Sri Mulyani Indrawati, considered to be one of the most powerful women in Asia, was voted best finance minister in Asia, a post she held from 2007 until she stepped down in 2010 to take up her appointment as managing director of the World Bank.

In the Middle East and Central Asia, eight women have been appointed minister of finance since 2001: Turkmenistan, United Arab Emirates, Kuwait, Jordan, Kazakhstan, Kyrgyzstan, Lebanon, and Syria. One of *Forbes Magazine*'s "world's 100 most powerful women" and at the top of *CEO Middle East* magazine's "100 most powerful Arab women" 2012 list is Sheikha Lubna al-Qasimi of the United Arab Emirates (U.A.E.), the first woman ever to hold a cabinet position in that nation. In 2004 she was appointed minister of finance, and in 2008 she became minister for trade. Al-Qasimi is also a passionate advocate for women's rights in the U.A.E. Among her peers as powerful Arab women are, from Saudi Arabia, Lubna Olayan, the CEO of the Olayan Financing group and the first-ever female keynote speaker at the Jeddah Economic Forum, and, from Kuwait, Shaikha Al-Bahar, who is CEO of the National Bank of Kuwait, one of the highest-rated banks in the Middle East. All these women are recognized as outstanding role models in the Muslim world, being some of the first women to break into the higher echelons of national and international financial institutions. As the demand for female specialists in finance and Islamic banking practice increases, women such as these will no longer be the exception that proves the rule.

BIBLIOGRAPHY

Ahmed, Leila. *Women and Gender in Islam: Historical Roots of a Modern Debate*. Yale University Press: New Haven, Conn. 1992.

Bloomberg—Kuala Lumpur. "Islamic Banking Attracts More Female Executives." *Al Arabiya News*, January 2, 2011. http://english.alarabiya.net/articles/2011/01/02/131901.html.

Cons, Jason, and Kasia Paprocki. "Contested Credit Landscapes: Microcredit, Self-Help and Self-

Determination in Rural Bangladesh." *Third World Quarterly* 31, no. 4 (2010): 637–654.
Doumani, Beshara. "Endowing Family: Waqf, Property Devolution, and Gender in Greater Syria, 1800 to 1860." *Comparative Studies in Society and History* 40, no. 1 (1998): 3–41.
Gooch, Liz. "A Path to Financial Equality in Malaysia." *The New York Times*, 26 September 2010. http://www.nytimes.com/2010/09/27/business/.
Hasan, Samuil. "Tradition and Modernity in Islam: A Reading through Power, Property and Philanthropy." *Intellectual Discourse* 19 (2011): 161–174.
Humaidan, Iman Mohammad al-. *Women and Waqf.* Kuwait: Awqaf Public Foundation, 2007.
Kuran, Timur. *Islam and Mammon: The Economic Predicaments of Islamism*. Princeton, N.J.: Princeton University Press, 2004.
Lubis, Muharman, Nurul Ibtisam Yaacob, Yusoff Omar, and Abdurrahman Dahlan. "Enhancement of Zakat Distribution Management System: Case Study in Malaysia." Kuala Lumpur: Kulliyyah of Information and Communication Technology (ICT), International Islamic University Malaysia, 2011. http://www.irep.iium.edu.my/4261/.
Namazi, Mahmood. "Bayt al-Mal and the Distribution of Zakat." *Message of Thaqalayn* 11, no. 2 (2010): 75–84.
Naqvi, Syed Mawab Haider. *Perspectives on Morality and Human Well-Being: A Contribution to Islamic Economics*. Leicester, U.K.: Islamic Foundation, 2003.
Power, Carla. "Middle East: Women's Money talks." *TIME Magazine*, July 30, 2008, http://www.time.com/time/magazine/article/0,9171,1827866,00.html.
Reuters-Dubai. "Growth in Mideast Women-Only Bank Branches & Funds." *Al Arabiya News*, October 24, 2010. http://www.alarabiya.net/articles/2010/10/27/123873.html.
Shane, Daniel. "Revealed: 100 Most Powerful Arab Women 2012." http://www.arabianbusiness.com/revealed-100-most-powerful-arab-women-2012-448409.html.
Sheikh, Bisma. "Islamic Economics, Development and International Relations: What Is the Effect of the Waqf System on the Development of Economies in the Middle East and Their Relations with the West?" December 14, 2011. http://aladinrc.wrlc.org/handle/1961/10693.
Stibbard, Paul, David Russell, and Blake Bromley. "Understanding the Waqf in the World of Trust." *Trust and Trustees* 18, no. 8 (2012): 785–810.
Toor, Imran Ashraf, and Abu Nasar. *Zakat as a Social Safety Net: Exploring the Impact*. Research Report 53. Karachi, Pakistan: Social Policy and Development Center, 2003.
Warde, Ibrahim. *Islamic Finance in the Global Economy*. Edinburgh: Edinburgh University Press, 2000.
"Women Ministers of Finance and Economy from 2000." Worldwide Guide to Women in Leadership. http://www.guide2womenleaders.com/finance_ministers2000.htm.

YVONNE CORCORAN-NANTES

FITNAH. The Arabic root *f-t-n* means "burn." It is used also for the purpose of testing or refining a metal, such as gold, *fitnah* is usually understood as a "temptation" or "trial." The term appears over thirty times in the Qurʾān, most frequently referring to trials faced by people. God tested Moses (20:40), David (38:24), and every soul with good and evil as an ordeal (21:35), according to the Qurʾān. The Qurʾānic use of the term focuses upon external struggles, as opposed to internal struggles of faith or commitment. The major *ḥadīth* collections, such as those of al-Bukhārī and Muslim, have sections on *fitan*, trials of the community.

The term is used for trials and temptations to which the Muslim community is exposed. The upheaval following the murder of the caliph ʿUthmān in 656 and lasting through the battle of the Camel, the schisms that led to the formation of the Khawārij and the Shīʿī, and the seizure of power by Muʿāwiyah, founder of the Umayyad dynasty in 661, is referred to as the first *fitnah*, or the "Great Fitnah." *Fitnah* can thus mean "civil strife, war, division" and situations that tempt Muslims to depart from the path of unity. It was also applied to religious disturbances, such as the riots between the

Ashʿarīs and the Ḥanbalīs in Baghdad in the tenth century. The disorders that brought the collapse of the Umayyad caliphate in Andalusia and the rise of the factional kings in the early eleventh century were also called the *fitnah*. Hence *fitnah* carries a great deal of negative connotation, with lexicographers defining it as "sedition, insurrection, riot, war, anarchy, crime, sin, and error," among other terms.

In the context of women in Islam, the term is often translated as "sexual temptation or enticement, discord, and seduction." Some traditions (*aḥādīth*) speak directly on the correlation of women and *fitnah* including a narration from *Ṣaḥīh al-Bukhārī* stating, "The Prophet said, 'After me I have not left any affliction (*fitnah*) more harmful to men than women,'" though the veracity of such traditions is dubious. Modern scholars attribute to this *ḥadīth* and other traditions the restrictive mandates formulated by some Muslim jurists (*fuqahā'*). Women have been severely constrained by certain Muslim schools of thought and in countries where these stricter interpretations of *fitnah* dominate society. Women who visit a graveyard or a mosque, drive a car or travel an extended distance without an escort (*maḥram*), speak too loudly during prayer, and participate in society, in general, can be sources of *fitnah*, according to some Muslim jurists. Some Muslim scholars strongly implicate women as the inherent source of this *fitnah*, while others readily claim that *fitnah* is not caused by women but by men and their lack of self-control. The doctrine of *fitnah* is also a crucial facet in debates concerning the veil (hijab), though some modern scholars are critical of this connection, because only scant proof of the application of the doctrine of *fitnah* in early juristic discussion of the veil can be found. Furthermore, scholars question the belief that *fitnah* will be the inevitable result of a woman's participation in society, based on countless *aḥādīth* sanctioning women's involvement in public and spiritual life.

BIBLIOGRAPHY

Abou El Fadl, Khaled. *Speaking in God's Name: Islamic Law, Authority and Women*. Oxford: Oneworld, 2001.

DeLong-Bas, Natana J. *Wahhabi Islam: From Revival and Reform to Global Jihad*. Oxford and New York: Oxford University Press, 2004.

Meisami, Julie Scott. "Writing Medieval Women: Representations and Misrepresentations." In *Writing and Representation in Medieval Islam: Muslim Horizons*, edited by Julia Bray, pp. 47–88. London: Routledge, 2006.

Mernissi, Fatima. *Beyond the Veil: Male-Female Dynamics in Modern Muslim Society*. Bloomington: Indiana University Press, 1987.

Kruk, Remke. "The Bold and the Beautiful: Women and '*fitna*' in the 'Sīrat Dhāt al-Himma': The story of Nūrā." In *Women in the Medieval Islamic World: Power, Patronage and Piety*, edited by Gavin G. R. Hambly, pp. 99–116. New York: St. Martin's Press, 1998.

Roald, Anne Sofie. *Women in Islam: The Western Experience*. London and New York: Routledge, 2001.

JOHN ALDEN WILLIAMS
Updated by MATTHEW LONG

FIVE PILLARS OF ISLAM. The five ritual practices in Islam include declaration of Islamic faith (*shahādah*), prayer (*ṣalāt*), almsgiving (*zakāt*), fasting (*ṣawm*), and pilgrimage (*ḥajj*). In Islamic sources, a variety of terms are used to describe these practices: *arkān* (sing. *rukn*) (pillars), *daʿāim* (sing. *diʿāma*) (pillars), *ʿibādāt* (sing. ʿibāda) (acts of worship), *qawāʿid* (sing. *qāʿida*) (principles), and *farāiḍ al-Islām* (sing. *farīḍa*) (Islamic obligations). These practices are required of all Muslim men and women, although they sometimes take different forms, depending on gender.

Origin. The Qur'ān does not present all five acts together; rather, it treats each separately—with the exception of prayer and almsgiving, which are mentioned together in many Qur'ānic verses. Leaving the *shahādah* aside, the obligatory status of the other four observations is clearly understood from the Qur'ānic exposition.

The five pillars are isolated as the essential foundation of Islam in the *ḥadīth* literature. The prophetic traditions that bring the pillars together can be divided into three categories: (1) The variants of the famous *ḥadīth* that declares, "Islam is built upon five (principles)," and then enumerates them. Major *ḥadīth* collections contain different versions of the tradition transmitted by 'Abdullāh ibn. 'Umar, the prominent companion of Muḥammad and the son of 'Umar, the second caliph. All these variants are in consensus regarding the last four principles, but they differ in their understanding of the first pillar, the *shahādah*. The canonical Shī'ī collections also report similar traditions of enumeration with the addition of "devotion to the *imām*" (*walāyah*) to the pillars. (2) According to some traditions, the Prophet introduces converts to some or all the pillars as the required practices of Islam. In some reports, the proclamation of the *shahādah* by the converts draws attention. (3) According to the famous tradition known as the *ḥadīth* of Gabriel (Jibrīl), the angel visits the Prophet in human form in the presence of a group of companions and asks him about Islam, faith (*īmān*), goodness (*iḥsān*), and the end of the world. In his reply, the Prophet explains both the pillars of Islam and Islamic faith.

The existence of the traditions about the pillars in the sources as early as the *Sīra* of Ibn Isḥāq (d. 768) and the wide dispersion of such traditions in the *ḥadīth* collections suggest that these practices had gained recognition as the fundamental identifiers of Islam early in the Muslim community. Singling out *ṣalāt*, *zakāt*, *ṣawm*, and *ḥajj* as religious duties, al-Shāfi'ī (d. 820) considered every Muslim responsible for the knowledge of these observances because they were so obviously obligatory. Consequently, the pillars became a framework for the *ḥadīth* collections, which had been arranged by subjects (*muṣannaf*), such as the early works entitled *al-Muwaṭṭa'* of Mālik b. Anas (d. 795) and *al-Muṣannaf* of al-Ṣan'ānī (d. 827) and the later canonical collections including the *Saḥīḥ*s of al-Bukhārī (d. 870) and Muslim (d. 875). The pillars have also become the standard division of the books of jurisprudence (*fiqh*).

Pillars. ***Shahādah.*** Literally meaning "witnessing," it is the utterance of the following statement with a sincere intention: "I bear witness that there is no god but God and I bear witness that Muḥammad is His messenger." These are perhaps the words that Muslims repeat most in their lives. They are even spoken into the ears of a newborn and are the final rites given on one's deathbed. Recitation of the *shahādah* is also required at the end of every two units of the ritual prayers (*tashahhud*), in the call to prayer (*adhān*), and in the second call to prayer (*iqāma*). The two components of the *shahādah*, "*Lā ilāha illā Allāh*" and "*Muḥammad rasūl Allāh*" (There is no god but God; Muḥammad is his messenger) are found separately in the Qur'ān (37:35; 47:19; 48:29). However, their utterance is not precisely identified in the Qur'ān as a ritual observation, unlike the other pillars.

There are ambiguities in the *ḥadīth* literature regarding the inclusion of the *shahādah* among the five pillars. Although it is completely absent from the pillars in a version of the tradition transmitted by Ibn'Umar (al-Ṣan'ānī, 1970, 3:126), in other versions of the same tradition, it is replaced by other acts such as "belief" (*īmān*) (al-Bukhārī, *īmān*, 2) or "service ('*ibādah*) to God and denial of other than Him" (Muslim, *īmān*, 20).

However, the profession of "God's unity and Muḥammad's messengership" has gained a general acceptance as the first pillar, probably because it sounded more meaningful than an act of belief or a concept that is not completely distinguishable from the other four pillars. This preference may be interpreted as an indication of the stage that Muslim orthodoxy reached after the early theological disputes over the difference between faith and action that occupied the first century of Islam. Thus, the first pillar seems to have evolved to something compatible with 49:14 and the prophetic traditions, most noticeably the *ḥadīth* of Gabriel, that make a distinction between belief and actions. Furthermore, the Qur'ān repeatedly designates "testifying faith" as an important act for believers. The profession of faith also stands out as the salient feature of the conversion scenes depicted in the *sīrah* and *ḥadīth* literatures. This recurrence in the Qur'ān and the prophetic traditions might urge Muslims to accept the *shahādah* among the pillars of Islam. As a result, the *shahādah* has been regarded as an utterance necessary for any man or woman who wishes to formally embrace Islam and be known as a Muslim, accepted as a member of the community and given Islamic rights and responsibilities. This is why the jurisprudential texts contain discussions of the external aspect of the *shahādah* and attempt to determine whether it has been properly performed.

Ṣalāt. This word refers to the ritual prayer with all its prerequisites and special body movements. The *ṣalāt* is prescribed in the Qur'ān (2:238; 4:103), but when and how it should be performed are only generally indicated. Elaborate details are provided in the *ḥadīth* literature.

According to the prophetic traditions, the *ṣalāt* was made into a duty to be performed five times a day (before sunrise, at noon, in the mid-afternoon, after sunset, and after dark) during the heavenly journey of the Prophet (*mi'rāj*) that is reported to have occurred in the Meccan period.

The prayer must be preceded by ritual purity. Major purity, which is necessary after sexual activity, is secured by washing the whole body (*ghusl*). Minor purity is attained by washing the hands, the face (with the mouth, the nose, and the ears), the arms, and the feet and by wetting the hair and the neck (*wuḍū'*). If water is not found, major and minor purities are performed by wiping the arms and the face with the hands that have touched the clean earth (*tayammum*). Standing, bowing, prostrating, and sitting on the knees are the major movements of a *ṣalāt*. All of these are performed in the direction of Mecca and accompanied by Qur'ānic and non-Qur'ānic recitations in Arabic. Muslims can pray everywhere and alone, but prayer within a congregation led by an *imām* is considered to be more meritorious for males than prayer performed alone.

Muslim women cover their whole bodies while praying, except for their faces, hands, and feet. They are exempted from praying while they menstruate (*ḥayḍ*) and after childbirth until their bleeding stops (*nifās*). They are not required to make up (*qaḍā'*) what they miss during these periods. *Ḥayḍ* and *nifās* are regarded as major impurities; therefore, women must bathe after them in order to be able to perform ritual prayers and touch and recite the Qur'ān.

It is traditionally considered to be better for female worshippers to pray at home, unlike males. Women joining the congregational prayers are generally placed in a separate section within the mosque. Most of the legal schools (*madhāhib*) approve of a female prayer leader leading a gathering of women. However, according to the traditional view, a woman cannot lead men or a mixed-gender congregation. The nontraditional participation of women in the congregation has produced some controversies in recent years. For instance, Amina Wadud's leading of a mixed congregation in Friday prayers in 2005 triggered debates throughout the Muslim world.

Zakāt. An obligatory charity incumbent upon those who hold a certain amount of wealth (*niṣāb*) as long as one year, *zakāt* consists of the annual payment of a certain percentage of wealth to one of the eight categories listed in the Qur'ān (9:60), which include the poor, the needy, the officials who collect the *zakāt*, those whose hearts are to be reconciled to Islam, the captives, the debtors, for the cause of God and the wayfarer. The types of property that are subject to *zakāt* include money, gold, silver, livestock, crops, and other sources of income, such as merchandise. The obligatory percentage varies according to the type of property possessed; for money, gold, silver and merchandise, the charity due is one fortieth of the total amount.

In the early Islamic centuries, the *zakāt* was collected by state authorities. But after some time, governmental collection ceased, and it was largely left to individuals to donate the required amount, although some local rulers occasionally attempted to revive the *zakāt* collection. Today, some Muslim countries, such as Sudan and Pakistan, apply *zakāt* and have been working on developing the system.

Muslim women, married or single, are obliged to give *zakāt* from their wealth. Some legal schools exempt women from the *zakāt* for the gold that they wear as jewelry, just as men are exempted for the silver that they wear.

Ṣawm (or Ṣiyām). The fast during the month of Ramadan. Unlike a Jewish or Christian fast, a Muslim fast involves complete abstinence from eating, drinking, smoking, and engaging in sexual relations from dawn until sunset and is practiced for an entire month. Ramadan is given prominence, for it was the month when the Qur'ān was revealed (2:185). During this month, Muslims take pains to recite the Qur'ān as often as they can and they perform special supererogatory night prayer (*tarāwīḥ*) that is marked by long Qur'ānic recitations. At the end of Ramadan, they celebrate one of the two Islamic festivals, the festival of fast-breaking (*'Īd al-fiṭr*). On this day, the alms of fast-breaking (*zakāt al-fiṭr*) are given to the poor as a sign of gratitude to God.

The sick, the elderly, travelers, and pregnant or breast-feeding women do not have to fast. If they are able, they make up the missed fast days later. Otherwise, they feed a needy person for each day they have missed. Women in menstruation or postpartum bleeding do not fast. But they should make up the number of days that they miss.

The convivial atmosphere characteristic of the month of Ramadan makes it special for women all over the Islamic world. Preparation of the fast-breaking meal (*ifṭār*) and the night meal (*saḥūr*) for their families and guests gives them both responsibility and pleasure. After the *ifṭār* meal, many women join the *tarāwīḥ* prayer.

Ḥajj. The pilgrimage to Mecca. Every physically and economically capable Muslim adult is required to perform this pilgrimage at least once in his or her lifetime. The *ḥajj* takes place in the month of *Dhū al-ḥijjah* in the Islamic calendar and includes a series of rituals that are said to have been converted from the pre-Islamic Arabian practices, purified from polytheist references, and given their final shape by the Prophet at the end of his life. Some important rites of the *ḥajj* make symbolic reference to the striking events from the lives of Abraham, his wife Hagar, and his son Ishmael.

Male pilgrims should wrap a two-piece seamless garment (*iḥrām*) around themselves at certain checkpoints (*mīqāt*) when they are on their journey to the *ḥajj*. Female pilgrims are free to use their daily clothes during the *ḥajj*. When they arrive in Mecca, they circumambulate the Ka'ba seven times (*ṭawāf*) and run forth and back between the two hills, Ṣafā and Marwa, seven times (*sa'y*). On the ninth day of the month *Dhū al-ḥijjah*, the pilgrims must be at the plain of 'Arafāt, just outside Mecca, from noon to sunset. During the following days, which are the days of the festival of sacrifice (*'Īd al-aḍḥā*), they perform the ritual of stoning at Mina, offer an animal sacrifice and circumambulate the Ka'ba again to complete their *ḥajj*.

About two million people visit Mecca for pilgrimage each year. The proportion of female pilgrims has grown in the last decades, and now nearly one-half of the pilgrims are women. Legal schools have discussed the religious validity of a woman traveling for the *ḥajj* alone without her husband or any close male relative (*maḥram*). Most scholars allow such a woman to travel for the obligatory *ḥajj* with a group of trustworthy pilgrims who would protect her. Saudi Arabia does not issue *ḥajj* visas for women who are unaccompanied by a *maḥram* and would like to travel with a group unless they are older than the age of forty-five. Women who are menstruating during the *ḥajj* can perform all of the observations except the *ṭawāf*. They should postpone the *ṭawāf*, one of the major obligations of the *ḥajj*, until the end of their menstruation. If their travel schedule does not allow them to wait that long, they take a bath and perform the *ṭawāf* while they are still in menstruation. In this case, some scholars suggest they should offer an animal sacrifice, but this is not required in Ibn Taymiyyah's (d. 1328) opinion.

Knowledge of the Pillars. The Prophet Muḥammad is reported to have said, "The search for knowledge (*al-'ilm*) is incumbent upon all Muslims" (Ibn Mājah, *Muqaddima*, 20). Muslim scholars have generally understood the *'ilm* here to mean the knowledge of religious duties applicable to all (*farḍ 'ayn*), and some of them even identified it with the knowledge of the five pillars. Probably motivated by the tradition, the concise manuals that focus on only the pillars (*fiqh al-'ibādāt*) have been produced along with the comprehensive jurisprudence books that elaborate acts of worship (*'ibādāt*), as well as human interrelations (*mu'āmalāt*). Recently, we have been observing the publication of such manuals in different languages written exclusively for women.

BIBLIOGRAPHY

Primary Works

Ibn Bābawayh al-Qummī, Abū Ja'far al-Ṣadūq Muḥammad b. 'Alī. *Man lā yaḥḍuruhu al-faqīh* (One for Whom the Jurisprudent Is Not Present). 4 vols. Edited by Muḥammad Jawād al-Faqīh. Beirut, Lebanon: Dār al-Aḍwā', 1992.

Bukhārī, Muḥammad b. Ismā'īl, al-. *Ṣaḥīḥ al-Bukhārī*. al-Riyāḍ: Bayt al-Afkār al-Dawlīyah lil-Nashr, 1998. Translation of the *Ṣaḥīḥ* by Muhammad Muhsin Khan. Riyadh, Saudi Arabia: Maktaba Dār al-Salām, 1994.

Ibn Hishām, 'Abd al-Malik. *The Life of Muhammad: A Translation of Isḥāq's Sīrat rasūl Allāh*. Translated with introduction and notes by A. Guillaume. London: Oxford University Press, 1955.

Ibn Isḥāq, Muḥammad. *Sīrat Ibn Isḥāq al-musammāh bi-kitāb al-mubtada' wa-al-mab'ath wa-al-maghāzī* (The Prophet's Biography by Ibn Isḥāq Named as the Book of Beginning, Mission, and Expeditions [of Muhammad]), edited by Muḥammad Ḥamīd Allāh. Rabat: Ma'had al-Dirāsāt wa-al-Abḥāth lil-Ta'rīb, 1976.

Kulaynī, Muḥammad b. Ya'qūb b. Isḥāq. *Al-Kāfī* (What Is Sufficient). 8 vols. Tehran, Iran: Dār al-Kutub al-Islāmīyah, 1957–1961.

Ibn Mājah, Muḥammad Muṣṭafā al-A'ẓamī. Riyadh, Saudi Arabia: M.M. al-A'ẓamī, 1983.

Makkī, Abū Ṭālib Muḥammad b. 'Alī. *Qūt al-qulūb fī mu'āmalat al-maḥbūb wa-waṣf ṭarīq al-murīd ilā maqām al-tawḥīd* (The Nourishment of the Hearts in the Relationship with the Beloved and the Description of the Path of the Wayfarer to the Station of Unity). 2 vols. Beirut, Lebanon: Dār al-Kutub al-'Ilmīyah, 2009.

Mālik b. Anas. *Al-Muwaṭṭa'*. 2 vols. Edited by Muḥammad 'Abd al-Bāqī. Cairo, Egypt: Dār Iḥyā' al-Kutub al-'Arabīyah, 'Īsā al-Bābī al-Ḥalabī, 198–.

Muslim b. Ḥajjāj al-Qushayrī al-Naysābūrī. *Ṣaḥīḥ Muslim.* 5 vols. Edited by Muḥammad Fu'ād 'Abd al-Bāqī. Beirut, Lebanon: Dār Iḥyā' al-Turāth, 1956–1972. Translation by Nasiruddin al-Khattab: Riyāḍ, Saudi Arabia: Dār al-Salām, 2007.

Ṣan'ānī, 'Abd al-Razzāq b. Hammām. *al-Muṣannaf.* 11 vols. Edited by Ḥabīb al-Raḥmān al-'Aẓamī. Beirut, Lebanon: al-Maktab al-Islāmī, 1970–1972.

Shāfi'ī, Muḥammad b. Idrīs. *Islamic Jurisprudence: Shāfi'ī's Risāla.* Translated, with an introduction, notes, and appendices, by Majid Kahadduri. Baltimore: Johns Hopkins University Press, 1961.

Ibn Taymiyyah, Aḥmad b. 'Abd al-Ḥalīm. *Majmū' fatāwā Shaykh al-Islām Aḥmad ibn Taymiyyah* (Compilation of Shaykh al-Islām Aḥmad Ibn Taymiyyah's Fatwās).37 vols. Edited by 'Abd al-Raḥmān ibn Muḥammad al-Ḥanbalī. Riyadh, Saudi Arabia: Maṭābi' al-Riyāḍ, 1961 or 1962–1966 or 1967.

Secondary Works

Ayoub, Mahmoud M. "Pillars of Islam." In *The Oxford Encyclopedia of the Islamic World.* 6 vols. Edited by John L. Esposito. New York: Oxford University Press, 2009.

Bianchi, Robert. "Ḥajj". In *The Oxford Encyclopedia of the Islamic World.* 6 vols. Edited by John L. Esposito. New York: Oxford University Press, 2009.

Denny, Frederick Mathewson. *An Introduction to Islam.* 3d ed. Upper Saddle River, N.J.: Pearson Prentice Hall, 2006.

Jazīrī, 'Abd al-Raḥmān, al-. *Kitāb al-Fiqh 'alā al-madhāhib al-arba'a.* 4 vols. Cairo, Egypt: al-Maktabah al-Tijārīyah al-Kubrā, 1964–1969.

Kamal, Ahmad. *The Sacred Journey: Being Pilgrimage to Makkah.* New York: Duell, Sloan and Pearce, 1961. Brief guide to the *ḥajj* published in Arabic and English together.

Ministry of Hajj, Kingdom of Saudi Arabia. http://www.hajinformation.com/main/p10.htm.

Qaradāwī, Yusuf, al-. *Fiqh al-zakāt.* 2 vols. Beirut, Lebanon: Mu'assasat al-Risālah, 1977.

Sayyādī, Abū al-Hudā Muḥammad b. Ḥasan, al-. *Ḍaw' al-shams fī qawlihī ṣallā Allāh 'alayhi wa-sallam "Buniya al-Islām 'alā khams."* 2 vols. Maṭba'at Maḥram Afandī al-Būsnawī, 1974.

al-Shiekh, Abdallah, and Stewart, Devin J. "Zakāt." In *The Oxford Encyclopedia of the Islamic World.* 6 vols. Edited by John L. Esposito. New York: Oxford University Press, 2009.

Wensinck, A. J. *The Muslim Creed: Its Genesis and Historical Development.* New York: Barnes and Noble, 1965.

Wizārāt al-Awqāf wa al-Shu'ūn al-Islāmiyya bi al-Kuwayt. *Al-Mawsū'a al-Fiqhiyya al-Kuwaytiyya.* 45 vols. Kuwait: Wizarat al-Awqaf al-Kuwaytiyya, 1983–2006.

Zysow, A. "Zakāt". In *Encyclopaedia of Islam.* 2d ed. Brill Online. [http://www.brillonline.com/].

Halim Calis

Friday Prayer. Muslims are obliged to pray at five prescribed times each day, preferably in congregation. However, the midday Friday prayer is to be carried out in congregation only in a mosque. Exceptionally, regular prayer can be offered individually at home or in a workplace. Friday is mentioned in the Qur'an as *Yawm al-jumu'ah*, the day of congregational prayer, and the mosque where regular *jumu'ah* is held, is called *masjid al-jami'*.

According to tradition, shortly before the Hijrah (emigration from Mecca to Medina in 622 CE), the Prophet Muḥammad sent instructions to his representative in Medina, Mus'ab ibn 'Umayr, to establish the Friday prayer (*ṣalāt-al jumu'ah*). Thus, the first such congregational prayer was observed by Mus'ab with twelve companions before the Prophet's Hijrah. According to another tradition, As'ad ibn Zurarah established congregational prayer in Bayadah with forty persons, even before the revelation of chapter 62 of the Qur'ān, entitled *al-Jumu'ah*.

Friday prayer is obligatory according to the Qur'ān, and, based on *ḥadīth*, several jurists describe it as an obligation (*fard, wājib*) on all adult, free, male Muslims. Attendance in *jumu'ah* congregation is not obligatory on women, though they are welcome. A remarkably large number of women join, separately, in five-times-daily as well as Friday prayers in the two major mosques in Mecca and in Medina. Many large mosques, such as the Faisal Mosque in Islamabad, have separate space for women, as do most of the mosques and Islamic centers in the United States, Canada, and Europe.

There is no evidence in the Islamic sources for holding a women-only Friday congregational prayer led by a woman, although women can offer their five daily prayers in a congregation of their own. The reasons for not allowing a female imam to lead a regular male congregational prayer or five daily prayers in the mosque or the Friday congregational prayer is functional, rather than gender-based. First, this was not the general practice (sunnah) of the Prophet; second *imāmah* (leading prayers) in the mosque is a full time responsibility and does not allow regular periodic absence of the imam for personal reasons; and third, the imam is responsible for private, one-on-one counseling of members of the community. In principle, private meetings between a woman and a stranger are prohibited by the Prophet.

While one-on-one meeting is not allowed, two or more women can seek counseling from a scholar or use electronic means of communication such as e-mail, fax, Facebook, or websites available for this purpose.

There is no evidence on attending *salāt al-jumuʿah* by the *sahabiyat*, although the wife of the second rightly guided caliph ʿUmar used to attend early morning and before regular night prayers in the Prophet's mosque, where separate space and a separate entrance was made for women. The Prophet neither directed nor forbade women to come for *jumuʿah* or for daily prayers in the *masjid*, but he desired their presence in the *ʿīd* congregation. A separate tent was erected for them, and the Prophet used to go to them and give them a sermon separately (Muslim).

According to Prophetic sunnah, *salāt al-jumuʿah* is not an obligation on believing women; therefore, many scholars do not consider it a matter of right. Their prayers in their homes, according to the Prophet, carries the same reward as praying in the *masjid* has for men. However, a growing number of Muslim women in North America, Europe, and Australia have a tendency to attend *salāt al-jumuʿah* because of its educational and inspirational value. An analogy (*qiyās*) can be made on the basis of the Prophet's desire that women attend *salāt al-ʿīd* in order to learn their *dīn*. On the analogy of *salāt al-ʿīd*, a separate arrangement for them with a separate entrance, as in the Mosque of the Prophet in Medina, is typically made. There is *salāt al-jumuʿah* consensus among most Muslim scholars that it will be against the Prophetic sunnah for a mixed congregation to be led by a woman.

The Friday prayer consists of two *rakaʿāt*, or units of afternoon prayer, rather than the usual four, and is preceded by a *khuṭbah*, or sermon for educating the community. After the *adhān* (call to prayer), the imam (prayer leader) delivers the *khuṭbah* in two parts, starting with praise for God and salutations to the Prophet Muḥammad and Ibrāhīm (Abraham). The imam then offers comments on social, political, economic, cultural, or behavioral issues in light of the Qurʾān and the sunnah. The imam also seeks God's forgiveness for all Muslims, and his guidance in daily life. The entire *khuṭbah* normally takes a maximum of fifteen minutes. When it ends, *iqāmah*, or the call for forming rows, is made, and the imam leads the two *rakaʿāt* (units) of prayers in a loud voice, in contrast to the regular afternoon prayer, which is offered silently.

Culturally, Friday is observed in most of the Muslim world as a holiday. The Qurʾān, however, instructs Muslims to cease work only when the call for prayer is made and until the prayer is over. Thus, *jumuʿah* is not considered a day of rest. Some scholars hold that this day brings extra blessings in trade and business if traders strictly follow the Qurʾānic command to stop trade at the time of congregation and restart business when the congregation is over.

The unique educational aspects of this weekly congregation are the creation of cohesion in the community, political orientation through selection of knowledgeable leadership, and creation of a global ethical community (*ummah*) of the believers.

BIBLIOGRAPHY

Alūsī al-Baghdādī, al-. *Rūḥ al-maʿānī fī tafsīr al-Qurʾān al-ʿaẓīm wa-l-sabʿ al-mathānī*. Beirut: Muʾassasat al-Risālah, 2010. Beirut. Vol. 27.

Brown, Alan, ed. *Festivals in World Religions*. London and New York: Longman, 1986.

Bukhārī, Muḥammad ibn Ismāʿīl, al-. *Al-Jāmiʿ al-ṣaḥīḥ*. Ankara: Hilal Yayınları, 2d print., 1976, 9 volumes.

Ibn al-Qudamah. *Al-Mughnī*. Cairo: Dar Hajar, 1986.

Ibn Kathīr, Ismāʿīl ibnʿUmar. *Tafsīr al-Qurʾān al-ʿazīm*. 5th ed. Beirut, 1996. Vol. 4.

Ibn Mājah, Muḥammad ibn Yazīd. *Sunan*. Riyadh: al-Mamlakah al-ʿArabīyah al-Saʿūdīyah, 1999.

Jazīrī, ʻAbd al-Raḥmān. *Kitāb al-fiqh ʿalā al-madhāhib al-arbaʿah*. Lahore, 1971. Vol. 1.

Jeffery, Arthur, ed. *Islam: Muhammad and His Religion*. New York: Liberal Arts, 1958.

Mawdūdī, *Sayyid* Abū al-Aʿlā. *Tafhīm al-Qurʾān*. Lahore, 1947. Vol. 1.

Mawdūdī, *Al-Jāmiʿ al-ṣaḥīḥ*. Abū al-Aʿlā. *Towards Understanding the Qurʾān*. Translated and edited by Zafar Ansari. Leicester, U.K.: Islamic Foundation, 1988–2009.

Mazharī, Muḥammad Thanāʾ Allāh al-ʿUthmānī. *Tafsīr al-Mazharī*. Quetta, 1983. Vol. 9.

Ibn al-Hajjaj, Muslim, *Al-Jāmiʿ al-ṣaḥīḥ*. English translation by Abdul Hamid Siddiqi, Lahore, 1976, vol. 2, pp. 416–417, *ḥadīth* nos. 1923, 1924, 1925.

Sayeed, Asma, "Early Sunni Discourse on Women's Mosque Attendance." *ISIM Newsletter*, July 2001, p. 10.

Nuʿmānī, Shiblī. *Sīrat al-nabī*. *Azamgarh*: Maʿarif, 1947. Vol. 1.

ANIS AHMAD

G

GAMES AND SPORTS. Islamic tradition recognizes that human beings need to eat, drink, relax, and enjoy themselves. Hanzalah, a companion of the Prophet, said, "There is a time for this and a time for that." The mind gets tired and so does the body, so there is no harm in relaxing the mind and refreshing the body with permissible (according to religious obligations) sport or play. The prophet Mohammad is reported to have said that all persons have a duty to keep their body healthy.

Prayer is one of the five pillars of Islam. It includes body movements that manifest worshipping God in both one's soul and one's body. There are many kinds of games and sports that the Prophet recommended to Muslims. The *ḥadīth* instruct, "Teach your children the art of archery, swimming, and horse riding." Further support for participation in games and sport is found in the example of Muhammad racing with his wife ʿĀʾishah.

The legal category designated by the term *ḥalāl*, which means "acceptable," "allowed," or "permitted," provides a moral standard for Muslims. The Qurʾān is a guide for living, and offers basic guidelines for determining if an aspect or type of play, games, leisure, recreation, or sport is *ḥalāl* or *ḥarām* ("forbidden"). Most of the physical activities recommended by *ḥadīth* relate to preparations for military defense against enemies, but some recreational activities, which have no obvious benefit and may interfere with important works, are known as *lahw* and *laʿib*; participation in them is not recommended. According to some interpretations and *ḥadīth*, dice, games of chance, and card games are prohibited, and fall into the category of *lahw* and *laʿib*.

Sports in Modern Islamic Culture. In many Islamic countries in the early twenty-first century, broad and varied programs of physical education and sports are replacing the more limited programs of decades past. Modern sports are more recreational, compared to the ancient sports, which involved training for warfare and combat, or grew out of religious or political traditions. The eighteenth and nineteenth centuries saw the emergence of new sports. Many sports originated in England, the U.S., and Europe and spread through the world because of the political predominance of these countries and their dominant media, with television and the Internet transmitting professional sports to all parts of the globe almost instantly.

Islamic law sets behavioral boundaries and standards of modesty that impact Muslim athletes. Men are not allowed to expose their body between the belly button and knee, and Muslim girls are often required to be in sexually segregated spaces or to cover all of their bodies except their hands and face, according to some passages in the Qur'ān that are traditionally interpreted to require the veiling of women (24:30–31, 33:59). In observing these behavioral and social prescriptions, many Muslim women cannot participate in international competitions or be spectators at some male competitions.

Not many women have participated in Olympic competition, because of Muslim dress code restrictions. However, women athletes from Algeria, Libya, and Syria participated in the 1980 Olympic Games and, in 1984, Egypt sent its first six female athletes to the Olympics. The first two Muslim women Olympic gold medalists were Nawal El Moutawakel of Morocco (1984, 400-meter hurdles) and Hassiba Boulmerka from Algeria (1992, track and field, 1500 meters). Boulmerka had to leave Algeria to train because of threats made against her by people who thought her running outfit revealed too much of her body. In the summer Olympic Games in Athens, Greece in 2004, the first woman ever to represent Afghanistan, Robina Muqimyar, ran in the women's 100-meter dash and Susi Susanti, who played badminton for Indonesia, won a gold medal. Iranian women participated in the Olympics for the first time in 1964 in Tokyo to compete in two disciplines, gymnastics and track and field. Syrian women have participated in numerous Olympic games. In addition, Muslim women from different countries have engaged in team sports since 2000, with the greatest number of participants taking part in the Olympic Games in Beijing in 2008. It is clear, then, that there is diversity in Muslim women's participation in sports in different countries, and that the overall trend in participation in international sports events is progressive.

At the same time, Muslim women's athletic participation domestically varies from country to country. Mountain climbing and hiking are popular recreational activities in Iran and, in 2005, two Iranian women were the first Muslim women to climb Mount Everest in a mixed expedition of climbers. In Germany, with a Muslim minority population of 3.5 to 4 million Muslims among its 82 million people, only about 5 percent of sports club members are Muslim women. In Saudi Arabia, physical education remains banned for girls in public schools due to concerns about a potential negative impact on virginity, although there are rising public calls for girls' access to physical activity due to concerns about the dual crises of obesity and type-two diabetes. There are also a rising number of private athletic clubs for women.

Some Olympic sports, such as swimming, remain out of reach for many Muslim women due to Islamic dress requirements. Because Muslim women are not able to participate in many international athletic activities, Islamic feminists have tried to increase opportunities for Muslim women's participation in sports in different ways. In the Islamic Republic of Iran, a cultural movement emerged to develop sports of a kind that would be considered suitable for Muslim women and in keeping with Islamic mores. For Muslim women's participation in international competitions, wherever possible, special clothes have been designed. From 1993, Muslim and later non-Muslim women competed together every four years in a competitive event that enjoyed an Islamic ambience, with the aim of setting standards for cultural and athletic competitions for Muslim women. The women competed by wearing the usual athletic attire, but they were not exposed to the gaze of men. The female judges, journalists, doctors, and coaches hold the events successfully in stadiums, gyms, or swimming pools. These competitions are organized by the Islamic Federation of Women's Sport (IFWS), which was founded in 1991, and supported by international organizations such as the International Olympic Committee (IOC), the Olympic Council of Asia (OAC), and with cooperation from the Muslim Countries Federation.

In 1997, the Second Muslim Women's Games were hosted by Pakistan. Pakistanis, however, encountered strong opposition to the competition, and to women's participation in sports in general. Thus, the Islamic Countries' Women's Sports Solidarity Council (ICWSSC) decided to organize the second Islamic Countries' Women's Sport Solidarity in Tehran. In 2001 and 2005, Iran hosted the Women's Sport Solidarity games. Support from some clergy members and politicians was critical to holding the games and gaining international women's participation.

Muslim-majority countries also have different regulations regarding the permissibility of women as spectators at sports events. In April 2005, the first Islamic solidarity games for males were held in Saudi Arabia and women of different nationalities attended as spectators. Yet, in Iran, women are banned as spectators at some male sport events, such as wrestling, swimming, and soccer, because of concerns about a conflict of dress code with Islamic requirements, or their not being a suitable situation due to morality and safety necessities for women in attendance. Women are allowed to attend certain other sports as spectators, such as basketball.

In May 2007, the Islamic Circle of North America (ICNA) presented the Annual Islamic Games at Crossroads South, South Brunswick, Canada. The purpose of the Islamic Games was to promote athletic skill and participation in sports among Muslim athletes and to allow Muslim schools to participate and compete with each other. More than six hundred Muslim athletes, both male and female of all ages, participated in basketball, cricket, soccer, track and field, and volleyball.

Women and Sports in Islamic Culture. According to many researchers and scholars, Islam supports the participation of Muslim women in physical activity (Pfister, 2003). After studying Islamic sources and authorities, one may arrive at the conclusion that sports ought to be obligatory for women on health grounds. Walseth and Fasting (2003) found that many women strongly emphasized that participating in athletics was a fulfillment of Islamic requirements.

Although in some countries, such as Iran, Muslim women cannot watch some male competitions, including soccer and wrestling in stadiums (because of the clothing worn by the male athletes, or perceived morally improper situations for women), they can watch sports on television in the privacy of their own homes. The changes in the status of Muslim women owe to the growth of the feminist movement, the spread of education, and the increased participation of women in the labor force. These changes will result in more participation of women in sports at the local level, and perhaps even at the regional or national level for the skilled individual. The reasons women have not been active athletes in the past are tradition, culture, education, limited facilities, and restrictions owing to religious practices. In recent years, women have had more opportunities to participate in leisure and recreational activities through the educational system, and in private sports clubs as facilities become increasingly available to them. As the understanding of the benefits of a healthier lifestyle become increasingly widespread, more women will participate in physical activities. However, there are differences in women's athletic participation from country to country, and in rural areas as compared to urban areas, because of differences in educational systems, the structure of individual sports, and available facilities—and of course, tradition.

Global sporting goods industries are starting to design clothing for all levels of competition. Aheda Zanetti of Sidney, Australia, has designed a two-piece, head-to-toe bathing suit. It consists of a long-sleeve top, close-fitted hood, and long pants made of a stretchy, lightweight fabric. Nike and Speedo have also entered the Muslim women's market. Nike sponsored a runner from Bahrain who won a gold medal in the 200-meter race at the Asian Games in Qatar. Nike and the United Nations, through a partnership, have designed a volleyball uniform that permits Muslim women to participate in the sport without violating modesty requirements. Although some international sport federations have permitted specialized uniforms conforming with Islamic dress codes, there are other federations which have not accepted modified uniforms, such as when the Iranian women's soccer team was barred from the 2012 Olympic qualifying games because of a disagreement over the wearing of headscarves.

In February 2008, a great step was taken toward showing respect for Muslim women's dress code requirements in sports by a group hosted by the Sultan Qaboos University in Oman, and supported and managed by the International Association of Physical Education and Sport for Girls and Women. A declaration titled "Accept and Respect," agreed upon by sixteen scholars from European, Middle Eastern, and Far Eastern countries, supports Islamic recommendations for women's participation in sports and respect for Muslim dress codes by international sport federations and national governments.

BIBLIOGRAPHY

Alsinani, Yousra, and Benn, Tansin. "The Sultanate of Oman and the Position of Girls and Women in Physical Education and Sport." In *Muslim Women and Sport*, edited by Tansin Benn, Gertrud Pfister, and Haifaa Jawad, pp. 125–137. New York: Routledge, 2010.

DeLong-Bas, Natana J. *Notable Muslims: Muslim Builders of World Civilization and Culture*. Oxford: Oneworld, 2006.

International Association of Physical Education and Sport for Girls and Women. http:// www.IAPESGW .org.

Karfoul, Nour El-Houda. "Women and Sport in Syria." In *Muslim Women and Sport*, edited by Tansin Benn, Gertrud Pfister, and Haifaa Jawad, pp. 138–153. New York: Routledge, 2010.

Kleindienst-Cachay, Christa. " 'Balancing Between the Cultures ...' Sports and Physical Activities of Muslim Girls and Women in Germany." In *Muslim Women and Sport*, edited by Tansin Benn, Gertrud Pfister, and Haifaa Jawad, pp. 92–108. New York: Routledge, 2010.

Koushkie Jahromi, Maryam. "Physical Activities and Sport for Women in Iran." In *Muslim Women and Sport*, edited by Tansin Benn, Gertrud Pfister, and Haifaa Jawad, pp. 109–124. New York: Routledge, 2010.

Pfister, Gertrud. "Women and Sport in Iran: Keeping Goal in Hijab." In *Sport and Women: Social Issues in International Perspectives*, edited by Ilse Hartmann-Tewe and Gertrud Pfister, pp. 207–223. London: Routledge, 2003.

Al-Ansari, Mona. "Women in Sports Leadership in Bahrain." In *Muslim Women and Sport*, edited by Tansin Benn, Gertrud Pfister, and Haifaa Jawad, pp. 79–91. New York: Routledge, 2010.

Al-Qaradawi, Yusuf. *The Lawful and the Prohibited in Islam*. Translated by Kamal El-Helbawy et al. Washington, D.C.: American Trust Publications, 1960.

Theodoulou, Michael. "First Muslim Women conquer Mount Everest." *The Christian Science Monitor*. June 1, 2005, http://www.csmonitor.com/2005/0601/p07s01-wosc.htm.

Walseth, Kristin, and Kari Fasting. "Islam's View on Physical Activity and Sport." *International Review For The Sociology Of Sport* 38, no. 1 (2003): 45–60.

EARLEEN HELGELIEN HANAFY
Updated by MARYAM KOUSHKIE JAHROMI

GEBALY, TAHANY EL. (b. 1950). Egyptian lawyer, women's and human rights activist, and Supreme Constitutional Court judge. Justice

Tahany el Gebaly received her law degree from Cairo University in 1973; she later studied public law, constitutional law, and the Islamic sharīʿah at the graduate level. Entering private practice, el Gebaly took a wide variety of criminal and personal status cases, as is common for Egyptian lawyers. She was involved in some prominent political cases, such as that of an Egyptian soldier charged with shooting Israelis. El Gebaly was also active in the legal profession and was the first woman elected to the Egyptian National Bar Association since the organization's founding in 1912. She also served on the Permanent Bureau of the Arab Lawyers' Union, an organization for all of the bar associations in the Arab world.

Before ascending to the bench, el Gebaly was active in the women's rights, human rights, and political fields. With regard to women's rights, she served with several local and global nongovernmental organizations as well as providing advice to some international organizations, such as UNICEF and the United Nations Development Program. She participated in efforts to reform women's legal status, including an amendment to the personal status law that gave women greater rights to seek a court-ordered divorce. Politically, el Gebaly was a member of the Nasserist Party, though she left that organization several years before becoming a judge.

In 2003 Chief Justice Fathi Neguib, who had come to be acquainted with el Gebaly's legal work on behalf of women's rights, spearheaded her nomination to the country's Supreme Constitutional Court (SCC). The Court has jurisdiction over constitutional disputes as well as some ancillary judicial responsibilities. The appointment was unprecedented for the Court itself—no woman had ever served on the SCC before—and was virtually unprecedented for judicial work in Egypt. While no statute barred women's appointment, very strong social conservatism as well as some religious objections had blocked women from serving on the bench (in the rare instances in which they had previously served in judicial positions, they were only allowed roles that did not involve sitting in judgment in cases).

Justice el Gebaly broke traditions in some other ways as well. Egyptian judges are barred from engaging in partisan activities, and by tradition they take a very circumspect role in public debates. Judicial decisions are issued by majorities, with no dissenting views published. As a result, most judges have a very limited public persona, though some do speak generally about issues, particularly those that affect the judiciary and legal institutions. El Gebaly froze her organizational commitments, but she has been outspoken on a series of public issues and regularly delivers lectures, participates in public discussions, and takes policy positions especially on matters with a legal, constitutional, or women's rights dimension. Her role became particularly prominent after the Egyptian revolution of 2011 when issues of political reform and constitutional design took center stage in political debates. For instance, in March 2011 she recommended that voters reject a set of constitutional amendments submitted to them in a referendum by the country's interim ruling military council. She not only served as a prominent participant in public debates over how to draft a new constitution after the 2011 revolution but also worked with other public figures to develop a set of consensual principles that should guide the content of the document. Her views are generally liberal and nationalist and strongly supportive of women's legal rights and a strong role for women in the public sphere. She is critical of authoritarian aspects of the Egyptian system as well as of the social and religious conservatism of Islamist groups.

[*See also* Egypt *and* Law, *subentry* Courts.]

BIBLIOGRAPHY

Abbas, Shorouk. "A Bird's Eye View on Current Events." *Cairo West*, August 2011.

DeLong-Bas, Natana J. "Tahany el Gebaly." In *Notable Muslims: Muslim Builders of World Civilization and Culture*. Oxford: OneWorld, 2006.

Elbendary, Amina. "A Question of Judgment." *Al-Ahram Weekly*, no. 625 (13–19 February 2003).

Shihata, Samia Farid. "A Woman Justice." *Al-Ahram Weekly*, no. 835 (8–14 March 2007).

NATHAN J. BROWN

GENDER ADVISORY BOARD, UNITED NATIONS COMMISSION ON SCIENCE AND TECHNOLOGY FOR DEVELOPMENT.

The Gender Advisory Board (GAB) advises on and monitors the implementation of recommendations on mainstreaming gender into science and technology in development policy. GAB acts as the primary advisory body to the United Nations Commission on Science and Technology for Development (UNCSTD), a subsidiary commission of the United Nations Economic and Social Council (ECOSOC).

The creation of the GAB was recommended by the Gender Working Group (GWG) of the United Nations, which published a report in 1993 titled *Science and Technology for Sustainable Human Development: The Gender Dimension* (later changed to Gender Equity in Science and Technology for Development) that explored, across multiple sectors, how science and technology affects the lives of both men and women throughout the world. In that report, the GWG discussed the three overlapping realms of science and technology, sustainable human development, and gender and identified seven key transformative action areas, including, among others, gender equity in science and technology education and relating better with local knowledge systems. The establishment of an advisory board was to help ensure the report's implementation throughout the United Nations system.

ESOSOC ratified the GWG's recommendations and the GAB was formally established in 1995. From its initiation, the GAB consisted of members from seven countries, including such members as Farkhonda Hassan, Shirley Malcolm, and Syeda *Tanveer Kausar Naim*. In addition, the GAB established regional secretariats in Kampala, Uganda; Jakarta, Indonesia; Montevideo, Uruguay; and Toronto, Canada. The board continued to develop and assist over eight national committees dedicated to science and technology work, as well as collaborated with governments and additional United Nations agencies.

Then co-chair, Farkhonda Hassan, lamented the lack of scientific production throughout the Muslim world. Hassan decried the fact that scientists in Muslim countries publish at a fraction of a percent compared to their colleagues in the United States and Europe. However, despite an increase in funding for science and technology research in the Muslim world, Hassan warned that social barriers and gender discrimination, not the teachings of Islam, reflect biases that encourage girls to focus their studies away from science (Hassan, 2000).

In addition to organizing various international conferences and workshops, GAB helped coordinate Gender in Science, Innovation, Technology, and Engineering (GenderInSITE), an international network of key decision-makers in science and technology that campaigned to effectively develop policy and programs that considered the concerns and knowledge of both men and women.

Funding from the Government of the Netherlands sustained the Gender Advisory Board's work from 1996 to 2006, when funding was not renewed and the regional secretariats were forced to close. ECOSOC expanded the mandate of GAP-UNCSTD for three years as of January 2012 to complete its programmatic activities.

BIBLIOGRAPHY

Gender Working Group. *Science and Technology for Sustainable Human Development: The Gender Dimension*. New York: United Nations, 1993.

Hassan, Farkhonda. "Islamic Women in Science." *Science* 290, no. 5489 (2000): 55–56.

DOMINIC T. BOCCI

GENDER CONSTRUCTION.

[*This entry includes three subentries,*

Early Islam
Historical *and*
Contemporary Practices.]

EARLY ISLAM

Images of women and gender roles in early Islam were based on the Qurʾān, *ḥadīth*, and traditions and legal literature (*fiqh*), which tended to construct ideal images of, a protective stance toward, and acceptable (*halal*) and unacceptable (*haram*) activities for women. The most prominent examples of individual females were the Prophet's wives and family members, including daughters and granddaughters, although other women are also present in the historical record in roles such as warriors, businesswomen, and slaves. Muḥammad's wives, in particular, as the "Mothers of the Believers," were considered the exemplars for proper behavior for Muslim women, albeit with an emphasis on particular aspects of their conduct as determined by the male recorders of *ḥadīth* and male elaborators of jurisprudence. These writings tend to be prescriptive, rather than descriptive, reflecting an idealized vision, rather than lived reality. Walther (1995) has observed that one of the challenges this approach presents to gender construction is that it creates the illusion of the exclusion of women from initiating or contributing to decision-making processes in early Islam, resulting in the misleading impression that they played no important role in society and did not make important contributions.

Muslims generally assert that the Qurʾān improved the status of women by guaranteeing their right to life through the prohibition of female infanticide, affirming women's right to own and control property, assigning women inheritance rights, and limiting the number of wives a man could have. However, scholars, such as Leila Ahmed, have noted a concomitant limitation on female empowerment and sexual autonomy, particularly with respect to agency in marriage and divorce and assertion of a single type of legally acceptable marriage—patrilineal, patriarchal—in contrast to the prior surrounding environment of a diversity of marriage practices. Because such concern was placed on controlling women's sexuality, women's public activities, including participation and leadership in warfare, business, and religion, also came to be curtailed. The examples of Khadījah (Muḥammad's first wife) and ʿĀʾishah (Muḥammad's favorite and highly influential wife) become particularly instructive in this regard, with Khadījah representing pre-Islamic society through her economic independence as a businesswoman and marriage proposal to Muḥammad, and ʿĀʾishah representing Islam through her seclusion, veiling, and more limited public life.

Veiling and seclusion were commanded for Muḥammad's wives in the Qurʾān as a sign of his status, and to emphasize that they were set apart from the rest of society. Yet, there were preceding pressures on Muḥammad that led him to insist that his wives veil and seclude themselves, most notably from ʿUmar ibn al-Khaṭṭāb, who thought it unseemly for Muḥammad's wives to appear in public. Additionally, veiling in surrounding societies served as a symbol of elitism and male power and prerogative. Veiling nevertheless had an impact on non-elite women as well, as veiling was reserved for free women. Slave women had to remain unveiled as a public symbol of their status.

Ali (2010) points to the ongoing institution of slavery as critical to the development of gender roles, as elaborated in the law during the early centuries of Islam, drawing a parallel between enslavement and femaleness as legal disabilities and slave ownership and marriage as legal institutions. She posits that the analogy between marriage and slavery is key to understanding Muslim marriage law, as the strict gender differentiation of marital rights, the importance of women's sexual exclusivity, and the imposition of rules about unilateral divorce were all derived from the central idea that licit sex requires male control or dominion. The sexual commodification of women in general thus became a matter of cultural production in which the status of wives and slaves, as well as husbands and masters, upheld perceptions of the religious necessity of male agency and female passivity in matters of marriage and sexuality. In Ali's analysis, a woman is rendered perpetually like a slave in certain matters in the eyes of the law, because she cannot contract marriage for herself or others, her sexuality is only licit when it is under the exclusive dominion of a particular man, and her movements and visitors can be restricted by her husband, even if this interferes with her God-given rights and prerogatives, such as managing her own property, although women always have recourse to the courts, at least in theory.

The most prominent practices that became obligatory for Muslim women, based on the example of the Prophet's wives, relegated women to the private space of the home. Although this was ostensibly done to offer women protection, it nevertheless served to cement the powerful role of the patriarchal male in controlling women. The main role assigned to the "Mothers of the Believers" came to be that of impeccable morality and manners: segregation, quiet domesticity, modest comportment, public invisibility via veiling, ascetic frugality, and devout obedience to God and the Prophet, including in his role as a husband—examples that all Muslim women thereafter were expected to strive to follow. Assigning roles centered on the provision of domestic comfort and privacy to the first female elite of Islam meant that domesticity came to define the core of female social righteousness and became the critical criterion of the Muslim woman's true citizenship in the community of faith. In the process, other roles played by Muḥammad's wives—such as being his helpmates, supporters in his mission, and, in the cases of ʿĀʾishah and Umm Salama, people with whom he enjoyed an intellectual relationship—are often overlooked or downplayed.

Yet, even the Prophet's wives are not always portrayed as perfect exemplars in the *ḥadīth* and *fiqh*; in some instances, they act as embodiments of female emotionalism, irrationality, greed, and rebelliousness. The purpose of these portrayals was often to place limitations on female roles in religion and society by asserting scripturalist proof of "women's nature." They were also sometimes used to enhance or disparage particular tribes or families by praising or denouncing a particular female's behavior, which was understood to reflect the family's honor or lack thereof. Thus, the application of Qurʾānic revelations of restriction that were originally directed at Muḥammad's wives to all women came to symbolize all that early Islamic society asserted was "wrong" with the female sex, including tendencies toward petty jealousies, envy, and domestic squabbles.

Furthermore, these idealized or demonized representations do not present a complete picture of women's roles and agency, particularly during the Prophet's lifetime. Women of the Prophet's generation, especially ʿĀʾishah, played important roles as transmitters of *ḥadīth*.

The first convert to Islam was a woman—Khadījah. The text of the Qurʾān was placed into the safekeeping of a woman, Hafsa bint Umar. Muḥammad himself appointed a woman, Umm Waraqa, as imam for her entire household. After Muḥammad's death, his wives ʿĀʾishah and Umm Salama, acted as imams for other women. Women during the Prophet's lifetime often converted to Islam without the approval of their families and husbands, or even with their direct disapproval, including, most famously, Umm Habiba, the daughter of Muḥammad's fiercest enemy, Abū Sufyān. Women emigrated to both Abyssinia and Medina. Women also actively participated in warfare, such as in the Battle of Uhud, fighting, carrying water, nursing the injured, and removing the dead and wounded from the battlefield. Women even dared to question Muḥammad, such as in the famous case of Hind bint Utayba, Abū Sufyān's wife, after a loss in battle, when she and other women were called to take an oath of allegiance to Muḥammad, showing that the women of the Qurashī aristocracy were considered highly enough esteemed not only to take the oath, but also to participate in the negotiations with the new military leader. There is nothing in early Islamic literature to suggest that any of these activities were considered inappropriate or wrong, thus opening the door to using these early Islamic examples to reconstruct gender roles in ways that encourage women's access to public space and participation in decision-making processes.

Additionally, scholars have challenged certain practices affiliated with these constructed gender roles, such as veiling and seclusion, as overemphasizing legalistic practices at the expense of the spiritual equality proclaimed by the Qurʾān and demonstrated by Muḥammad's example. Ahmed (1992), for example, observes the presence of two messages in the Qurʾān that have come to be contradictory in practice: one that portrays an ethical-moral vision in which men and women are each other's equals, and another that focuses on the regulation of society, in which men seem to enjoy a superior status to women. Historically, more attention has been given to the latter than the former, even though the regulatory approach is clearly tied to a particular context, while the ethical-moral vision is more universal in nature. Wadud (1992) argues that these differences are due to the time periods in which they were revealed: the universal, generic message for humanity appears in the Makkan verses, while particular social reforms appropriate to a given context were outlined in the Medinan verses. Stowasser (1994) also observes that all of the Qurʾānic legislation related to the Prophet's wives dates to the last six or seven years of his life, when he served as head of state in Medina, suggesting that these regulations had more to do with the establishment of a state hierarchy and elite status than with spirituality per se. Although the result was increasing levels of restraints on women, male interpreters posited this as symbolic of the "perfecting" of Islamic society.

Many Qurʾānic passages address equality and reciprocity between husbands and wives, such as 2:229, which asserts that husbands and wives have equal rights over each other, and assures the right of women to economic independence. Passage 33:35 further establishes the absolute moral and spiritual equality of men and women, and their equal responsibilities, with respect to matters of faith and ethics. Wadud (1992) notes that the Qurʾān teaches that women and men are both given spiritual potential and free will, and that both women and men are held responsible for surrendering themselves to God, for believing in God and Revelation, and for fulfilling the requirements of worship and observing modesty. Thus, in Wadud's analysis, the purpose of the Qurʾān is not to permanently or universally assign gender roles (which she argues are culturally specific, rather than religiously mandated), but to be descriptive of conceptual ideas, which both women and men are then responsible for implementing in society. Wadud posits that, rather than projecting women as "inherently" evil, the Qur'ān posits woman as possessing "inherent good," as a potential child-bearer and primary nurturer and as one who is placed on an "absolute par" with man in terms of spiritual potential and the potential to reach Paradise.

Stowasser (1994) has further observed that the Qur'ān's message about female characters is not necessarily monolithic. Some—such as Pharaoh's wife and Mary, the mother of Jesus—serve as examples to emulate, given their embodiment of the virtues of obedience to God, purity, modesty, and motherly love. Others, such as Zulaykha and the wives of Lot and Noah, exemplify rebellion against God, unbelief, disobedience toward a righteous husband, sexual misconduct, cunning, aggression, and, ultimately, a threat to social stability. What these examples therefore make most clear, according to Stowasser, is that a woman's faith and righteousness—or lack thereof—depend on her own will and actions, rather than on a relationship with a man, whether righteous or sinful. What should matter is the woman's commitment to God (Stowasser, 21).

Despite such powerful support from scripture and from Muḥammad's own example, the reality of non-Arab men interpreting and developing Islamic law after the first century of Islam meant the adoption of older cultural systems in which women's roles were limited to the domestic sphere, and emphasis was placed on the promotion of a patrilineal, patriarchal order, rather than on the egalitarian vision of the Qur'ān. Walther (1995) notes an increasing tendency toward strict prescriptions and punishments with respect to veiling and adultery, respectively, by the ninth-century writings of Al-Shafi'i (d. 824), and a tendency to cite *ḥadīth* of less certain chains of transmission that emphasized men's superiority. Mernissi (1991) has also commented on the manipulation of sacred texts as a "structural characteristic of the practice of power in Muslim societies" (p. 9), seeing, on the one hand, the desire of male politicians to manipulate the sacred, and, on the other, the fierce determination of scholars to oppose them through the elaboration of *fiqh* with its concepts and methods of verification and counter-verification. Perhaps nowhere are the battles of *ḥadīth* transmissions with respect to gender roles more prevalent than in the cases of *ḥadīth* transmitted on the authority of 'Umar ibn al-Khaṭṭāb and Abu Hurayra versus those transmitted by 'Ā'ishah. Mernissi has noted the tendency historically to give more weight to the former, despite their misogynist tendencies and the fact that 'Ā'ishah arguably would have known more about how the Prophet treated women.

Indeed, many major Islamic institutions, including those restricting women, came into existence only after Muḥammad's death, during the reign of the second caliph, 'Umar ibn al-Khaṭṭāb, who was known for his harsh treatment of women in both private and public life. The historical record mentions him being ill-tempered with his wives and physically assaulting them, as well as recording that Muḥammad rebuked him for this behavior. It was 'Umar ibn al-Khaṭṭāb who tried to confine women to their homes and prevent them from attending prayers at the mosque. When this was unsuccessful, he instituted segregation during prayers and appointed a separate imam for each sex, albeit always a male imam, even though this departed from Prophetic precedent. 'Umar ibn al-Khaṭṭāb further forbade the Prophet's wives from going on pilgrimage—a ban that remained in place until the last year of his reign. Ahmed notes that the historical record does not mention any protest by Muḥammad's wives about these restrictions, but attributes this to the "guardians of Islam" erasing female rebellion from history as a matter of duty in presenting a particular image of the Islamic past. The only recorded rebellion was that of ʿĀʾishah in opposition to ʿAlī's succession to the caliphate—a rebellion that culminated in the Battle of the Camel, in which ʿĀʾishah's forces lost decisively to ʿAlī's. This incident became a paradigm in legal and theological literature for keeping women out of politics and for vindicating the seclusion of women.

The early history of the construction of gender roles in Islamic societies has become an important topic of research today with respect to women's rights and status, because of their proximity to the primary sources of Islam and their potential implications for reinterpretation and reconstruction of both values and roles.

Bibliography

Ahmed, Leila. *Women and Gender in Islam: Historical Roots of a Modern Debate*. New Haven, Conn.: Yale University Press, 1992.

Ali, Kecia. *Marriage and Slavery in Early Islam*. Cambridge, Mass.: Harvard University Press, 2010.

Esposito, John L., and Natana J. DeLong-Bas. *Women in Muslim Family Law*. 2d ed. Syracuse, N.Y.: Syracuse University Press, 2001.

Mernissi, Fatima. *The Veil and the Male Elite: A Feminist Interpretation of Women's Rights in Islam*. Translated by Mary Jo Lakeland. Reading, Mass.: Addison-Wesley Publishing Company, 1991.

Stowasser, Barbara Freyer. *Women in the Qurʾān, Traditions, and Interpretation*. New York: Oxford University Press, 1994.

Wadud, Amina. *Qurʾān and Woman: Rereading the Sacred Text from a Woman's Perspective*. New York: Oxford University Press, 1999.

Walther, Wiebke. *Women in Islam: From Medieval to Modern Times*. 2d ed. Princeton, N.J.: Markus Wiener Publishers, 1995.

Natana J. DeLong-Bas

Historical

Anthropological studies have shown that the nature of gender—that is, the meaning of being men and women and the content of relations between them in society—is grounded in underlying cultural models that guide the institutionalization of traditions and generate social constructions of reality. In the Arab and Islamic East, centuries of the Islamic tradition accommodating diverse historical practices have woven a construction of gender that is identifiably, often uniquely, Islamic.

This construction begins with the Islamic imagery of the primordial beginnings of humankind, which tells the story of gender against a conceptual tapestry weaving dress, morality, and kinship with notions of space, privacy, and temporal rhythm into one meaningful cultural whole. (For a full discussion of the innovative idea of rhythm for the study of Islam, see El Guindi, 2008.) This sacred Islamic imagination of human beginnings does not associate shame with sexuality, link religiousness with asexuality, or confine sin to a single gender. Nor does it situate gender primacy in the creation process. This establishes an ideational foundation about gender and sexuality. Gender is formulated in terms of a complementarity of male and female, and sexuality is considered a normal aspect of the human character that is not in conflict with gender, religion, or religiousness. The imagery of Prophet Muḥammad, founder and messenger of Islam, is of a man candid about sexual matters in the emerging seventh-century community, the *ummah*. This finds support in the most sacred, divinely revealed source in Islam, the Qurʾān. The following citations concern gendered beginnings, and explicitly express these premises: verse 51:49 states: "All things we created in zawjayn [pairs]"; verse 49:13 states: "we have created you a thakarun [male] and untha [female]"; and verse 2:187, using the metaphor of dress, states: "They [feminine gender] are *libas* [dress] to you [masculine plural] and you [masculine plural] are *libas* [dress] to them [feminine gender]." This expression of a simultaneous creation of two gendered humans is also an ideational basis for the construction of gender complementarity. This premise finds characteristic correlates in the various cultural traditions of the Arab and Islamic region of the Middle East to this day.

The Islamic model of the social world (mostly compatible with Arab culture) translates socially as two dominant worlds: a dual-gendered world and a world of kinship. This model interweaves the two worlds to shape a general vision about gender, while also scripting the identity of individual men and women. Experientially, a person is born into a separate men's or a women's world and, at the same time, into a world of kinfolk that brings the sexes together. At the level of traditional manifestations of culture, this can be seen empirically through exploring cultural practices—especially birth ceremonies that mark the beginning point in individual life cycles, such as the Egyptian one El Sebou' (a birth ceremony held on the seventh day after the biological birth of individuals of either sex). The Islamic birth ceremony, also celebrated on the seventh day after birth, is called al-ʿAqiqa. The two sociocultural worlds of gender and kin determine and, in many ways, control the identity and the behavior of Muslim men and women.

The World of Kinfolk. A Muslim woman's birth as a kinswoman assures her entry into a world of kinsfolk related to her in one or all three interrelated categories of kin relations: consanguinity (perceived biological relatives); affinity (marital relatives); and suckling (relations developed through suckling by non-procreative mothers). The latter exists in the Arabo-Islamic region and has been recently empirically studied in Qatar (El Guindi, 2010; 2011; April 2012; July 2012). This circle of relatives is socially and legally bound to meet obligations toward a woman throughout her lifetime, after marriage, at death, and continuing after her death. It is bound to provide financial, social, moral, and behavioral support, protection, and security. Both sexes are bound by such obligations, which are enforced socially by the constraints of family reputation and by law. Focusing on the study of women only diminishes understanding and is conceptually flawed, as the classic study on veiling has clearly shown (El Guindi, 1999).

Kin bonding is reflected in naming rules and patterns, which apply to both sexes, and is particularly vivid in the Arabian and Gulf region of the Arab world, where family names are preceded by *al* (pertaining to family of), *ibn* (son of), *bin* (children of), *bint* (daughter of), *bani* (sons of), or *awlad* (descendants of). These and other variants represent singular, plural, and gendered forms meaning "offspring of." Arabians in particular see their social worlds as ascending upwards from remote kin roots traceable in the form of genealogical trees (El Guindi, 2012). Both sexes are bound in terms of identity, responsibility, obligation, and reputation by these kin roots and extended family relations. Kinship is interconnected with gender construction.

A World of Women, A World of Men. In the Arab-Islamic tradition, gender is constructed in terms of two unambiguous sexes: male and female. Other forms, such as *khanith* (cross-gendered individuals) in Oman, are accepted within this dual model without transforming it. There is a strong separateness between the two, even without enforced physical separation, expressed symbolically, ritually, and behaviorally. In some cases, such as in Arabian and Gulf societies, partial or total sexual segregation exists in physical space, evident in architecture, and in institutions of learning and places of employment. But even with little or no public physical separation, an autonomous gender identity (especially economic) is pervasive. At Qatar University, for example, in which students are segregated on campus and in the classroom, a distinct difference exists (recognized by Qataris themselves) between the two sexes, to the extent that one can argue they constitute two strongly different cultural sub-traditions, which, in some respects, are as different in attitudes, behaviors, responses, and outlooks as a Qatari person from a Jordanian, for example. Publicly, women feel and behave as though they are entitled to gender privacy, and vigorously protect their sexual space from male intrusion. Gender and family privacy constitute a quality supported by the culture and by men in the society. As a result, women's attitudes and expectations of entitlement extend to acting privileged, which is often unsustainable both socially and economically. But, at the same time, this builds a strong self-image among women. The comfortable environment of same-sex interactions also builds strong self-images and self-assurance, particularly among the women. Underlying the conceptual division between the two sexes is Islam's acceptance of sexuality as human, while nevertheless recognizing its potential disruptive nature to society, which drives a need for regulations and controls for cross-sex public behavior. It is postulated that Islam's acceptance of the reality of the strong nature of human sexuality underlies public measures of control between the sexes. Significantly, a conceptual gender complementarity brings together gendered autonomous selves through mechanisms of kinship relations.

Bibliography

El Guindi, Fadwa. *By Noon Prayer: The Rhythm of Islam*. Oxford: Berg Publishers, 2008.

El Guindi, Fadwa. "The Cognitive Path through Kinship." *Journal of Behavior and Brain Sciences* 33 (2010): 384–385.

El Guindi, Fadwa. *El Sebou': Egyptian Birth Ritual*. Watertown, MA: Documentary Educational Resources, 1986. Film.

El Guindi, Fadwa. "Kinship by Suckling: Extending Limits on Alliance." *Anthropologicheskii Forum (Forum for Anthropology and Culture)*, Peter the Great Museum of Anthropology and Ethnography (Kunstkamera), Russian Academy of Sciences, Special Forum on Kinship, Forum 15 (2011): 381–384.

El Guindi, Fadwa. "Milk and Blood: Kinship among Muslim Arabs in Qatar." *Anthropos* 107 (July 2012): 545–555.

El Guindi, Fadwa. "Suckling as Kinship." *Anthropology Newsletter* 53, no. 1 (April 2012):. http://www.anthropology-news.org/index.php/2012/04/02/suckling-as-kinship/.

El Guindi, Fadwa. *Veil: Modesty, Privacy and Resistance*. Oxford U.K.: Berg Publishers, 1999.

Fadwa El Guindi

Contemporary Practices

Contemporary gender construction practices among Muslims are diverse and are, in many ways, both a continuation of and a departure from those of the past. This entry discusses how one contemporary community of interpretation, here termed Progressive Muslims (PM), constructs the concept of a religiously ideal Muslim woman by examining their views of a) the nature of female and male sexuality; b) the role and function of women (and, by implication, men) in broader society and the public sphere, especially the purpose and function of seclusion and veiling for women; and c) gender roles in the context of marriage.

First and foremost, Progressive Muslim thought rejects a number of presuppositions that underpin premodern (embedded) Muslim thought on gender that have been described variously in the literature as the gender dualism or the gender complementarity thesis. This theory is premised on supra-cultural generalizations regarding the biological and mental functions and capacities that differentiate the sexes. In a nutshell, the gender dualism thesis presupposes that men are rationally superior to women, who, in turn, are highly emotional beings with weak or deficient rational faculties—a thesis that Progressive Muslim thought rejects. Progressive Muslims also do not subscribe to another aspect of the gender dualism thesis, which is premised on the assumption of the artificial separation between body and mind, sexuality and spirituality, and which identifies women with the "irreligious" realm of sexual passion and as repositories of all "lower" aspects of human nature, and thus as the very antithesis of the "illuminated" sphere of male (religious) knowledge, so that males are the sole sources of religious authority. Furthermore, Progressive Muslim thought considers that the premodern Muslim scholars' frequent conceptual linking of women with the notion of socio-moral chaos (*fitnah*) is based on flawed assumptions concerning the nature of women and, by implication, female sexuality.

Progressive Muslims reject the active concept of female sexuality to which traditional Muslim thought subscribes, according to which the nature of woman's aggression is sexual in nature, and men are irresistibly attracted to it. This view of female and male sexuality constructs women as a threat to a healthy social order, which in turn, is constructed as entirely belonging to males. Progressive Muslim thought does not consider the female (or male) body to be sexually corrupting or pudendal *per se*, as does traditional Muslim thought, but as erotic. It also disagrees with another element of the gender dualism thesis, which is premised on the idea that the male sexual nature is pervasive and aberrant and is aroused beyond control by the mere sight, smell, or voice of a woman.

Some *ḥadīth* reflect a misogynist vision of women, and thus they have been used historically to construct this premodern (embedded) view of female and male sexuality, particularly those transmitted by Abu Hurayra (although by no means do all *ḥadīth* fall into this category). Progressive Muslims tend to dismiss this select group of *ḥadīth* as remnants of the patriarchal nature of the traditional, male-dominated interpretative communities of the past.

Asma Barlas (2002) provides a detailed and systematic discussion of the issue of the nature of female sexuality and gender from the Progressive Muslim perspective. Employing the full array of Progressive Muslim methodological tools—such as comprehensive contextualization, thematic and holistic approach to interpretation, and the notion of an ethico-religious values-based approach to interpretation of the Qurʾān and *sunnah* as the most hermeneutically powerful tool—Barlas argues that the Qurʾān does not fix the nature of either gender, but it considers males and females to have essentially the same sexual natures. Barlas emphasizes the Qurʾān's and *sunnah's* principle of the ethico-moral equality of the sexes before God to argue that the normative sources of Islam do not distinguish between the moral and social praxis of men and women; that they do not ascribe a particular type of sexual identity for certain types of behaviors to either sex; and that they do not advocate that sex or sexual differences are a determinant of moral personality, gender roles, or inequality.

Progressive Muslims consider that the theory of gender dualism and the above described natures of male and female sexualities serve as an ideational foundation to justify a particular construction of a religiously "normative" male and female gender. In premodern Muslim (embedded) thought, they are embodied in a number of practices that are employed to regulate female and male sexual instincts, including the veiling of women, female seclusion, surveillance, and gender segregation. Progressive Muslim thought interprets the Qurʾān- and *ḥadīth*-based evidence regarding these practices quite differently on the basis of the comprehensively contextual, holistic, and aims-based methodology and, on this basis, do not consider the character of all of these practices as being religiously normative.

Progressive Muslims also reject a number of conceptual assumptions that inform premodern Muslim thought concerning marriage, which is based on the construction of a highly interdependent and gender-based nature of the rights and responsibilities for husbands and wives. For example, the Progressive Muslims disagree with premodern Muslim law's conceptualization and rationale behind the marriage contract, which was likened to that of a slave contract or an exchange (*bay'*) according to which, in essence, a woman's sexual and reproductive rights are exchanged for her entitlement to be materially/financially maintained. Progressive Muslim thought furthermore emphasizes that this understanding of the purpose of the marriage contract fundamentally shaped questions pertaining to the wife's rights to her reproductive organs (and, therefore, sexual gratification), mobility, custody rights, and divorce, rendering them under the complete authority (*'iṣmah*) of her husband.

Based on the approach outlined above, Progressive Muslims argue that the Qur'ān merely reflects, rather than advocates, the patriarchal values and gender constructs prevalent among its direct recipients. Progressive Muslims consider that the Qur'ān's approach to issues of women's rights, when interpreted from a holistic, historical, and comprehensively contextual vantage point, permits (if not demands) mitigation of the entrenched patriarchal practices, and that its ultimate goal (*maqāṣid*) is a completely gender-egalitarian society, the laws of which do not discriminate on the basis of gender.

As far as the relation of the patriarchal and misogynist *ḥadīth*-based evidence to the above-mentioned gender construction criteria is concerned, one methodological tool that is used by Progressive Muslim theoreticians to dismiss their *sunnah* compliance is the fact that Progressive Muslims consider *sunnah* and *ḥadīth* not to be conceptually and epistemologically identical bodies of knowledge. They argue that the *'ibādah/'amal* elements of *sunnah* were, in the early period of Islamic thought, ultimately derived from a particular Qur'ān-*sunnah* hermeneutic, rather than the later developed *ulum al-ḥadīth* sciences. According to this view, the *sunnah* compliance of a particular *ḥadīth* is not merely established on the basis of epistemological and methodological constraints and weaknesses inherent in the classical *ulum al-ḥadīth*, but on overall considerations stemming primarily from the *uṣūl al-fiqh* sciences and overall teachings, as evident in and intellectualized by the Ṣūfī version of Islamic ethics.

In summary, Progressive Muslim thought constructs the normative male and female gender concepts by subscribing to the view that females are fully autonomous human beings inherently equal to men, and that women's religious identity is solely based upon their level of *taqwā* (reverence of God), and no other considerations.

BIBLIOGRAPHY

Barlas, Asma. *"Believing Women" in Islam: Unreading Patriarchal Interpretations of the Qur'ān*. Austin: University of Texas Press, 2004.

Duderija, Adis. *Constructing A Religiously Ideal "Believer" and "Woman" in Islam: Neo-Traditional Salafī and Progressive Muslims' Methods of Interpretation*. New York: Palgrave Macmillan, 2011.

Hidayatullah, Aysha. "Women Trustees of Allah: Methods, Limits, and Possibilities of 'Feminist Theology' in Islam." PhD diss., University of California–Santa Barbara, 2009.

Shaikh, Sadiyya. "Knowledge, Women and Gender in the *ḥadīth*: A Feminist Interpretation." *Islam and Christian-Muslim Relations* 15, no. 1 (2004): 99–108.

ADIS DUDERIJA

GENDER EQUALITY. Gender equality has been one of the most central issues in contemporary debates about Islam, both within Muslim communities and externally. Especially in the United States and Europe, the status of women and issues such as the hijab, polygamy, and male guardianship have become proxies for larger normative debates about the nature of Islam. However, the relationship between Islam and gender equality is difficult to generalize, given enormous historical, geographical, and sectarian variations. Even in a single community, an individual woman's life opportunities and status are not solely a function of her religion, but also are influenced by other factors, including her socioeconomic status, family, and ethnicity. Additionally, it can be at times impossible to isolate the effect of Islam on women's status from local customs or state laws. Furthermore, the bulk of scholarly and public attention has concentrated on the lives of Middle Eastern women, both within their countries of origin and as migrants.

This entry provides an overview of the historical and contemporary debates concerning gender equality and Islam. First, it describes the role of women in the Qur'ān, sunna, and Islamic law. Then it provides a brief historical overview of gender equality in the Muslim world. Finally, it examines several contemporary issues: veiling, family law reforms, and women's political participation.

I. Gender Equality in the Qurʾān, Sunna, and Islamic Law. Both supporters and critics of Islam turn to the Qur'ān, sunna, and Islamic law to justify their claims about Islam's stance towards women. For more than a millennium, differing interpretive traditions have employed these sources to address and settle disagreements over issues.

As with Judaism and Christianity, gender is an inherent aspect of God's plan for humanity from the first humans. However, unlike her Judeo-Christian counterpart, the Qur'ānic Eve (unnamed in the Qur'ān, but identified as Ḥawwaʿ in later sources) is not responsible for tempting Adam into eating the forbidden fruit, which results in their expulsion; they are equally responsible. Furthermore, Islam does not have a doctrine of original sin; Adam and Eve's punishment does not extend to future generations, nor is Eve's role explicitly linked to future women—though medieval scholars, such as al-Ṭabarī, have argued that Eve was solely culpable and that her role reveals women's deficiencies (Stowasser, 1994).

The Qur'ān explicitly states that men and women have equal religious responsibility before God and that male and female believers will be rewarded equally (33:35, 40:8). However, in other realms they have differentiated roles and rights. In some cases women have lesser positions than men. For example, two women's testimonies are equivalent to that of a single man (2:282), men have authority over their wives and may discipline them in the case of disobedience (*nushuz*, 4:34), women typically inherit less than male relatives (4:7–20), and polygamy is permitted under certain circumstances (4:3). However, the Qur'ān provides some protections explicitly for women. For example, a bride directly receives the dower (*mahr*, 4:4), husbands are required to provide maintenance (*nafaqa*) for their wives (2:233), and husbands should treat their wives kindly (4:19).

Contemporary feminist scholars, particularly Fatima Mernissi (1991), have been critical of the treatment of women in the ḥadīth literature, especially when stripped of its historical context. Mernissi argues that much of the ḥadīth literature stands in contrast to the equality of the Qur'ān and the experience of Muḥammad's wives, and therefore the authenticity and chains of transmission of certain *aḥādīth*, such as the hijab and injunctions against women's political leadership, must be re-examined. Leila Ahmed (1992) undertakes such an explanation, contextualizing the relation between religion and gender in space and across time.

The interpretation and application of the Qurʾān and sunna in legal matters is dependent upon a variety of factors, including the legal school, particulars of a given case, and the socio-historical context. While there is a measure of consensus between the four major Sunni schools of jurisprudence, they vary on particulars ranging from a wife's potential recourses if her husband is unable to provide her maintenance to what constitutes equitable treatment in a polygamous marriage. An important distinction between the Sunni schools of jurisprudence and Ithnā ʿAsharī (Twelver) Shiism is the former's explicit rejection of temporary marriage (*mutʿah*). In analyzing whether women are disadvantaged in comparison to men in Islamic law, Judith Tucker (2008) concludes that women's status varies substantially between issues. While women have less freedom than men to independently initiate marriage or divorce, Islamic law largely guarantees the property rights of both married and unmarried women and imposes safeguards in the case of divorce.

A key issue in Islamic exegesis is how much of Qurʾānic and ḥadīth material relates specifically to Muḥammad's wives (Mothers of the Believers, *Ummahāt al-Muʾminūn*) and how much can be generalized as normative practice for all Muslim women. For example, the Qurʾān indicates the special status of Muḥammad's wives (33:32), and they were under certain restrictions such as not remarrying after Muḥammad's death (33:52), stipulations that were not obviously applicable to other Muslim women. Another issue revolves around veiling, concerning the exact manner in which women should dress and whether veiling was a requirement of all Muslim women or merely Muḥammad's wives.

II. Gender Debates: From the Hijrah to the Twenty-first Century The Early Muslim Community. The introduction of Islam is often characterized as improving the rights of women in the Arabian peninsula by ending female infanticide and providing women's legal rights with respect to marriage, divorce, and inheritance. Leila Ahmed (1992), however, argues the contrary, that Islam was a step back compared to rights that women previously held by comparing the roles of the Prophet's wives Khadījah and ʿĀʾishah as exemplars of the pre-Islamic and Islamic traditions. She contrasts Khadījah—an independent, older, wealthy widow who proposed marriage to Muḥammad and supported his ministry during their nearly twenty-five years of monogamous marriage—to ʿĀʾishah—Mu⊠ammad's child bride, given into a polygamous marriage by her father, who was subject to evolving Muslim practices of female seclusion and restrictions. Ahmed characterizes ʿĀʾishah's political and religious leadership after her husband's death as anomalies resulting from her living in a transitional period, thereby ensuing from pre-Islamic (*jāhilīyah*) rather than Islamic influence (43).

However, many of Muḥammad's wives and other early converts offer an active role model for women in the early Muslim community. Khadījah provided financial support for Muḥammad in the early years of his ministry. Umm Waraqa served as a prayer leader for a mixed community and transmitted the Qurʾān before it was codified in writing. ʿĀʾishah played an active, though controversial, role in the political struggles of the early Muslim community after Muḥammad's death. ʿĀʾishah, Umm ʿUmmra, and other women rode into battle alongside their male relatives. Additionally, Muḥammad's wives served as important sources of the sunna.

The Medieval and Early Modern Eras. Less is known about the lives of women in the medieval era, particularly women who were not members of the social and political elite. However, while far less common than their male counterparts, a number of women held important public roles. More than eight thousand women, by

Mohammad Akram Nadwi's count (2007), served as Islamic scholars, particularly in the study of ḥadīth. Among the better known were Zaynab bint Sulaymān, Fāṭimah bint Muḥammad, Sitt al-Wuzara, and Zaynab bint Aḥmad. Rābiʿah al-ʿAdawīyah played a significant role in the Sufi tradition. Additionally, a number of women ruled countries in their own name from India to Yemen to North Africa.

Ahmed (1991) argues that the rise of the Abbasid dynasty, influenced by Persian and Byzantine practices, represented a decisive turning point for gender equality in public life. Among elite families, the seclusion of women and concubinage became increasingly common. However, during the Ottoman Empire, Muslim and non-Muslim women frequently benefited from the expansive religious court system, especially in relation to property rights. An increasing number of women were landholders, merchants, and supporters of religious endowments (Peirce 1993; Zilfi 1995; Faroqhi 2002).

Islamic Modernism. In the nineteenth century, as a result of changing sociopolitical structures and the increased heterogeneity of public discourse, Islamic modernists became champions of religious reform in response to European critiques of Muslim society, particularly in Egypt and India (Moaddel, 1998). While these reformers—including Ahmed Khan, Chiragh Ali, Mumtaz Ali, Rifāʿah Rāfiʿ al-Ṭahṭāwī, Muḥammad ʿAbduh, and Qāsim Amīn—diverged on a number of issues, they nearly uniformly advocated for increased gender equality, especially with respect to polygamy, education, veiling, and seclusion. In addition to highlighting the general religious and intellectual equality between the sexes, they also frequently emphasized the gap between current practices and authentic Islamic doctrines.

One point often stressed by reformers was the importance of understanding Islam in its historical context, a point exemplified in their treatment of polygamy. Chiragh Ali and Muḥammad Abduh, for example, both emphasized that particular historical and social conditions resulted in polygamy in the earliest Muslim community. In reality, polygamy was prohibited since the Qurʾān only permitted it contingent on a husband's equal treatment of all his wives (4:3, 3:4), a situation that Abduh and Ali argued was impossible.

Influenced by his extended travels in France, Rifāʿah Rāfiʿ al-Ṭahṭāwī became a passionate advocate for girls' education, including coeducation. He argued that women were intellectually capable, and also that increased women's education was in keeping with Islamic tradition. Not only would education improve family life and public morality, but universal primary education was a necessity for Egypt's political and economic development. Qāsim Amīn, writing nearly half a century later, echoed al-Ṭahṭāwī's call for women's basic education on the basis of its societal benefit. Additionally, in *The Liberation of Women*, he argued that seclusion and the veiling of the face had no basis in the Qurʾān or Sharīʿah.

Islamic Fundamentalism. In contrast to Islamic modernism, Islamic fundamentalism has provided very different solutions to Western and secular encroachment, particularly with respect to gender equality. Lamia Rustum Shehadeh's study of the role of women in fundamentalist Islam concludes that "despite the vast differences in [prominent thinkers'] religio-political and economic ideologies," they share three elements: the primacy of women's domestic role; essential gender differences that necessitate different roles for men and women; and "the element of danger inherent in women's nature," which views sexuality outside of marriage as a danger for the entire Muslim community (2003: 219).

Islamic Feminism. With its roots in late nineteenth- and early twentieth-century Islamic modernism and secular feminism, Islamic feminism grounds its justifications for gender equality in the reinterpretation of the Qurʾān. Islamic feminism has gained momentum in the last twenty years due to a number of factors: the expansion of the middle class; concern over Islamist and conservative interpretations of gender roles; increased women's participation in economic and political life; and the expansion of women's religious education, enabling them to closely engage religious texts (Badran, 2009). Scholars such as Amina Wadud (1999) and Fatima Mernissi (1991), as described above, have argued that the Qurʾān presents justification for the equality of the sexes, one that has been lost in the intervening centuries. Islamic feminist interpretations have helped lead to more gender-equitable revisions of the Moroccan and Indonesian family laws.

III. Contemporary Issues Veiling. Since Hudā Shaʿrāwī and Saiza Nabarawi famously removed the veils covering their faces in 1923 in a Cairo train station, the veil has become the most visible and symbolic battleground in the debate over gender equality in Islam, both in predominantly Muslim and non-Muslim countries. The veil has been the subject of court cases and political debate in a number of European countries, most notably France, which in 2010 adopted a law that banned the *niqāb* in public because it was viewed as contrary to the country's egalitarian principles. This is in addition to a 2004 law that banned girls from wearing the hijab in public schools. However, legal bans are not limited to countries with Muslim minorities; Syria, Turkey, and Tunisia have all implemented laws banning certain types of veils in public buildings as being in conflict with the secular traditions of the state.

Family Law Reform. Alongside the veil, the reforms in family laws and personal status codes have been decisive in articulating the role of Islam within the modern state. Morocco's recent reforms to its family law, the Mudawana, have been some of the furthest reaching. Following the 1997 elections, the Moroccan government, in partnership with the king, began pushing for serious reforms to Morocco's personal status laws with the goal of increasing women's rights. The reforms proposed to increase the minimum marriage age from fifteen to eighteen, augment women's rights in divorces, restrict polygamy, and expand women's legal rights. While proponents argued that the reforms increased gender equality within an Islamic framework, critics claimed that certain changes to the law, especially with respect to the minimum marriage age, ran contrary to established legal principles and were promulgated in capitulation to Western feminism. The Islamist Justice and Development Party (al- ʿAdl wa-al-Iḥsān, PJD) initially opposed the reform, staging mass protests in the streets of Casablanca in 2000. PJD leader Abdelkrim Khatib went so far as to compare the reforms to a war on believers. However, by 2004, the PJD had acquiesced, in part due to fear of a potential backlash from the 2003 Casablanca bombings, and declared its support for the law.

Women's Political Participation. Across the world, women in predominantly Muslim countries are allowed to vote and hold public office, with the exception of Saudi Arabia, which will enact women's suffrage in 2015. Sheikh Hasina Wazed and Khaleda Zia (Bangladesh), Megawati Sukarnoputri (Indonesia), Atifete Jahjaga (Kosovo), Benazir Bhutto (Pakistan), Mame Madior Boye (Senegal), and Tansu Çiller (Turkey) have all served as head of state or government in countries with significant Muslim populations. Afghanistan, Bangladesh, Bosnia and Herzegovina, Djibouti, Indonesia, Jordan, Morocco, Niger, Pakistan, Senegal, Somalia, Sudan, Tanzania, and Tunisia all have quotas for women, either in a number of seats reserved for female candidates at the national level or quotas for the percentage of parliamentary candidates that must be women. While most Islamist parties have fielded successful female candidates, there remains debate on whether a woman may become a country's elected head. For example, the Egyptian Muslim Brotherhood has issued statements that women may run for any public office, except the presidency. Despite women being barred by the Iranian constitution from running for president, parliamentarian Azam Taleghani and other women have made multiple bids for the office, all disqualified by the Guardian Council, in order to draw attention to gender discrimination in Iran and to encourage the amendment of the constitution to enable women to be elected president.

BIBLIOGRAPHY

Ahmed, Leila. *Women and Gender in Islam.* New Haven, Conn.: Yale University Press, 1992.

Badran, Margot. *Feminism in Islam: Secular and Religious Convergences.* Oxford, U.K.: Oneworld, 2009.

Faroqhi, Suraiya. *Stories of Ottoman Men and Women: Establishing Status, Establishing Control.* Istanbul: Eren, 2002.

Mahmood, Saba. *Politics of Piety: The Islamic Revival and the Feminist Subject.* Princeton, N.J.: Princeton University Press, 2005.

Mernissi, Fatima. *The Veil and the Male Elite: A Feminist Interpretation of Women's Rights in Islam.* Translated by Mary Jo Lakeland. Reading, Mass.: Addison-Wesley Publishing Company, 1991.

Moaddel, Mansoor. "Religion and Women: Islamic Modernism versus Fundamentalism." *Journal for the Scientific Study of Religion* 73, no. 1 (1998): 108–130.

Nadwi, Mohammad Akram. *Al-Muḥaddithāt: The Women Scholars in Islam.* Oxford: Interface Publications, 2007.

Peirce, Leslie. *The Imperial Harem: Women and Sovereignty in the Ottoman Empire.* New York: Oxford University Press, 1993.

Shehadeh, Lamia Rustum. *The Idea of Women in Fundamentalist Islam.* Gainesville: University Press of Florida, 2003.

Stowasser, Barbara Freyer. *Women in the Qur'ān, Traditions, and Interpretation.* Oxford: Oxford University Press, 1994.

Tucker, Judith E. *Women, Family, and Gender in Islamic Law.* Themes in Islamic Law, vol. 3. Cambridge: Cambridge University Press, 2008.

Wadud, Amina. *Qur'an and Woman: Rereading the Sacred Text from a Woman's Perspective.* Oxford: Oxford University Press, 1999.

Walther, Wiebke. *Women in Islam.* Princeton, N.J.: Markus Wiener, 1993.

Zilfi, Madeline, ed. *Women in the Ottoman Empire: Middle Eastern Women in the Early Modern Era.* Leiden: Brill, 1997.

ELIZABETH L. YOUNG
and FATMA MÜGE GÖÇEK

GENDER STUDIES AND WOMEN. [*This entry contains two subentries,*

History of the Field *and*
Methodologies.]

HISTORY OF THE FIELD

Gender Studies and Women examines the impact on women of living in "Islamic" societies, how women have participated in these societies and at what levels, and how gender roles have been defined and constructed in the past and are being redefined and reconstructed in the present. As a field of research and intellectual study, women and gender studies related to Muslim women and the Muslim world dates to the second half of the twentieth century. Although, prior to this time, there were a few studies touching on the status and role of women in Muslim societies, notably W. Robertson Smith's *Kinship and Marriage in Early Arabia*, Gertrude Stern's *Marriage in Early Islam*, and Margaret Smith's biography of Rabi'a the Mystic, little systematic scholarship on Muslim women was undertaken prior to this time. This early scholarship assumed that "Islam is responsible for the degradation of Muslim women," positing as evidence examples from pre-Islamic and early Islamic times, as well as contemporary examples of women's suffering in "more orthodox Muslim lands" (Smith, 2001, p. 156). Much of the work is descriptive and accepts the texts at face value as historical evidence. In addition, this earlier scholarship tended to view Muslim women strictly through the lens of their relationships with men or as extraordinary figures who were considered noteworthy precisely because they were unusual and, therefore, not "representative" of Muslim women. This was due, in part, to the reality that historical sources were largely written by men and tended to focus on male figures, activities, roles, and interactions with power, although perceptions of women as marginal people who were largely outside of the roles of power and decision making and, thus, importance, also played a role.

The second wave of feminism in the Western world during the 1960s and 1970s was accompanied by a growing interest in social history and certain purportedly "universal" paradigms that were not believed to be culturally or religiously specific. Marxism and modernization and development, for example, were expected to produce certain results (respectively rising class consciousness or increased Westernization and secularization), particularly in Middle East/North Africa (MENA) countries. As a result, interest grew in the study of previously understudied or marginalized populations, including the peasantry, immigrant populations, and women. This shift in focus also brought attention to the use of different types of research materials. In the past, attention had largely been given to the Qur'ān, ḥadīth, and legal literature, which were assumed to describe what Islamic societies were and how they functioned. However, archival research, particularly into court records, found that reality was often very different from the theoretical presentations offered in these texts. Consequently, more complex and multilayered methods of analysis were developed in order to capture nuances and to recognize that there was not one single model for "Muslim women." Rather than a monolithic category, "Muslim women" came to be understood to include a multiplicity of backgrounds, heritages, socioeconomic classes, and geographic locations, thus necessitating multiple methods and languages of research.

The major spark that ignited serious academic interest in women and gender studies in Islam was Edward Said's pivotal book, *Orientalism*, which pushed for reconsideration of the "Orient" in general outside of visions of exoticism, harems, difference from the West, and the oppression/repression/suppression of women. Initial research projects began with the explicit goal of restoring women to history, as most histories up until this point ignored the status, role, and contributions of women as "outside of history," presuming them to be unimportant. One example of such a restorative project from a descriptive, rather than analytical or prescriptive, approach was Wiebke Walther's *Women in Islam/From Medieval to Modern Times*. This work restored individual Muslim women to the record in fields including history, culture, religion, society, and literature. Other studies examining particular countries and time periods also began to emerge, including Judith Tucker's *Women in Nineteenth Century Egypt*, which moved away from standard focus on elites to interrogating historical resources for evidence of non-elite women's activities, looking for change over time and challenging assumptions that Westernization and development necessarily benefited women by showing that, in fact, in many cases, rather than liberating women, state policies reduced women's status to little better than slaves.

One of the earliest collections that attempted to bridge all of Islamic history was Nikki Keddie and Beth Baron's *Women in Middle Eastern History*. Covering the early Islamic era, the

Mamluks, modern Turkey, and Iran, and the modern Arab world, this collection of essays examined the relative freedom and agency experienced and expressed by Muslim women across time and space, in part to place the contemporary era into perspective. The findings indicated that gender boundaries in the Middle East have not been fixed since time immemorial, but, rather have changed in conjunction with changes in family patterns, socioeconomic necessity, the public role of religion, and women's activities and access to public space.

One of most pivotal works of the early 1990s that looked holistically at Islamic societies across time and space was Leila Ahmed's *Women and Gender in Islam*. This work was one of the first to examine the historical origins and developments in Islamic discourses about women and gender, showing it to be a lived and contested reality filled with nuance and variations. Although the work was initially undertaken with the intention of presenting a synopsis of recent findings on the material conditions of Muslim women, Ahmed quickly changed her focus to discourses about women and gender to investigate how gender was articulated socially, institutionally, and verbally in various Muslim societies. At the time of her writing, little to nothing was known about women's history prior to the nineteenth century. Thus, part of her goal was to make women's history visible again. She also decided to include discourses from surrounding societies and civilizations that had an impact on the foundations and developments in Islamic discourses to show that "Islamic societies" did not exist in a vacuum, but engaged in cross-pollination of ideas with other societies, ultimately finding that Islam effected a transformation that brought the Arabian socioreligious vision and gender organization in line with the rest of the Middle East and Mediterranean regions.

Ahmed's work was soon followed by more in-depth studies of the past, one of the most important of which was Gavin Hambly's edited collection, *Women in the Medieval Islamic World*, which solidly restored medieval Muslim women to history in a variety of capacities—as rulers, noblewomen, power brokers, warriors, patrons, artists, poetesses, heroines, agents of marriage and divorce, travelers, and builders. These findings called for a new vision of women's agency across history.

During this time, some Muslim women also began to publish critiques of the treatment of women in their societies, such as Dr. Nawāl al-Saʿadāwī, whose academic and literary contributions challenged issues ranging from female genital cutting and its physical and psychological impact on young girls to the construction of gender roles in Egypt that devalued women and resulted in social phenomena ranging from domestic violence to denial of women's voice and agency, even in decisions related to her person. Research about pivotal female figures in Western-oriented feminist movements also began to be undertaken, focusing on early twentieth century Egypt, Turkey under the rule of Kemal Ataturk, and the Shah's Iran of the 1930s as exemplars of women's rights activism. Women and gender studies of Islamic societies thus tended to focus initially on these areas, although later expansions into Levant studies and North Africa also began to emerge, particularly as interest in female leadership and activism in independence movements came to be of interest. Studies of women's history in the Gulf states remain in their infancy.

With the expansion of geographic locations and time periods came attention to increasing areas of specialization and the incorporation of theories and methodologies from other disciplines into women and gender studies, as well as greater contextualization of women in "Islamic" societies. Having debunked the idea of a monolithic category of "Muslim women," women and gender studies began to examine women's activities and roles in a variety of fields and from different perspectives, including sex and sexuality, country studies, historical periods, human rights issues, and Islamic law, particularly family law and personal status law. Attention was particularly given to socioeconomic history, legal studies, postcolonial theory, and challenging patriarchy because women's status and bodies have continued to be looked upon as a lens onto broader trends, such as tendencies toward authoritarianism in which the state takes control over the bodies of its subjects.

A pivotal example of this type of scholarship was Margot Badran's *Feminists, Islam, and Nation*, which retold the history of the development of Egyptian nationalism through the lens of the Egyptian feminist movement, reexamining a known historical phenomenon in a new way by seeing it through women's eyes. In the process, she uncovered the beginnings of analysis and critiques of patriarchy, which was deemed responsible for many of the ills facing Egyptian society, which was based on maleness and privilege, particularly with respect to hierarchies designed to keep certain portions of the population submissive and subordinate. Thus, women's status became a reflection of class differences enforced by the state, suggesting that liberation of the people necessitated liberation of women, as well. Another study of this type was Leslie Peirce's *The Imperial Harem*, which examined an old topic—elite women—in a new way. Rather than portraying harem women as passive victims of male whimsy or as scheming connivers of harem politics, Peirce shows the myriad of ways in which harem women were active agents of their own careers, using the tools available to them to gain influence, power, and status.

In another example, issues of state control and regulation of the population are examined through portrayals of sex and sexuality. Afsaneh Najmabadi's *Women with Mustaches, Men without Beards*, uses Qajar images of beauty—or lack thereof—to explore themes related to gender and sexuality, as well as images of the state in which the masculinity of the nation is compared to the femininity of the homeland. Najmabadi contends that we do not need historical, literary, or artistic sources that refer to women in order to study women's history. By looking gender-analytically at sources about men, it is possible to discover certain things about women. She further argues that the push in Iran for hetero-normalization was a reflection of the Iranian national program of Westernization, in which same sex practice and homoeroticism, which had long been part of Iranian culture, came to be set aside as "backwards" and antimodern. This imagery of defined male and female categories, including with respect to the nation and homeland, also created the vision of a homeland and its honor in need of protection, just as women and their honor were purportedly in need of protection.

Islamic law was one of the first fields to be addressed in-depth with respect to women because of its impact on their lives at a very personal level, particularly as it pertains to marriage, divorce, child custody, and inheritance rights. As new historical information came to light, greater contextualization of contemporary practices, as well as use of historical precedents to press for contemporary reforms, became possible. For example, Esposito with DeLong-Bas's *Women in Muslim Family Law* provided an analysis of the development of Islamic family law over time and space, giving particular attention to contemporary reforms and examining court cases that have led to these changes. In addition, this analysis was one of the first to include portions of the Islamic world that were not Arab, suggesting a breaking away from the paradigm that equates "Muslim" with "Arab" and offering insights from other countries, including Pakistan, India, and Malaysia.

A different approach to legal questions examined the terminology used to discuss certain issues pertaining to women, looking for parallels in language and linguistic structures. For example, Kecia Ali's *Marriage and Slavery in Early Islam* examined the language used to describe marriage and slave relations, finding that the terminology is essentially the same, rendering women as objects of marriage and slavery, rather than as independent agents. Placing Islamic texts within the broader framework of legal texts from surrounding societies, she examined definitions of licit sexuality as a means of constructing masculinity and femininity in the early Islamic era.

Legal studies were further bolstered by research into court records and archival resources, particularly as spearheaded by Amira Sonbol's edited collection, *Women, the Family, and Divorce Laws in Islamic History*, which brought attention to lived realities, rather than the idealized visions described in jurisprudential literature. These articles brought to light court records that demonstrated that, far from being passive victims of male power, Muslim women of the past knew their rights, particularly where property and divorce were concerned, and were not afraid to assert them in court.

Perhaps one of the most important, and certainly the most contested, developments in women and gender studies addressing Islamic societies has been the attention given to the question of "Islam." Analysis of Islamic literature and Islamically oriented political movements, ranging from the *Wahhābī* movement of Saudi Arabia and Usuman dan Fodio's Sokoto caliphate to the Muslim Brotherhood and the Jamaat-i Islami, were undertaken with the goals of understanding women's roles within them and their portrayals of the "ideal" woman: how she was expected to behave, her role in the family and society, and the rules and regulations women were expected to follow. Political ideologies, such as Islamism, Salafism, and secular feminism, were also researched in an attempt to understand how gender is constructed and by whom. Attention has been given not only to descriptions of women and their roles and functions, but also to the prescription of "how things should be" in the twenty-first century, in particular, as critiques of patriarchy have been applied to religious texts by women in order to bring about readings and interpretations more favorable to women, especially by calling for equality between women and men.

The challenge to male-dominated religious interpretation was first issued by Fatima Mernissi's path-breaking *The Veil and the Male Elite: A Feminist Interpretation of Women's Rights in Islam*, which sought to shatter the power of the selective use of scripture in assigning gender roles to women by challenging the authenticity of certain ḥadīth used to assign women lesser status, while leaving out those calling for a more egalitarian vision. This work sparked other studies raising similar questions about selective use of Qurʾān verses and legal manuals. Mernissi accused religious scholars of misusing sacred texts as political weapons to create false images of women as submissive, passive, and voiceless, and called instead for a re-reading of these same texts that recognizes women's agency and strength (which was apparently what made them so threatening to the men of their time periods). Her purpose in doing so was to create new models of Muslim women to be imitated.

Mernissi's work was complemented by a later work by Barbara Stowasser, *Women in the Qur'an, Traditions, and Interpretation*, which showed the historical trajectory of male interpretations of female characters in the Qurʾān and of the Prophet's wives, looking at how they have been interpreted in the past up until today to justify certain models of gender relations. Stowasser found that medieval interpretations came to dominate socio-moral paradigms of ideal Muslim womanhood—interpretations that continue to play a role into the present, although some scholars are calling for more contemporary interpretations reflecting contemporary conditions and circumstances.

Exposure of these male-created visions of the ideal female led to calls for a direct return to scripture to determine the divine intent for women. No work of this type has been more influential than Amina Wadud's *Qur'an and Woman*, which asserted a methodology of reading Qur'ān verses in relation to each other, rather than in isolation, and with the goal of reading equality back into the text. Setting aside the old standard of defining and measuring women only in comparison to men, Wadud called for challenging gender biases from a pro-faith perspective. In the process, she inserted her voice into the previously largely male realm of Qur'ānic exegesis. A later work, *Inside the Gender Jihad*, is her personal record of her quest for equality in Islam as she has lived and worked inside of it, struggling against patriarchy while seeking to pursue a moral life in submission to God.

A later work, inspired by Wadud's hermeneutical work, was Asma Barlas's *"Believing Women" in Islam: Unreading Patriarchal Interpretations of the Qur'an*, which asserts that the teachings of the Qur'ān are radically egalitarian, rather than patriarchal. Barlas argues that patriarchal interpretations, inequality, and oppression have been read into the tradition from the outside, but are not inherent to the text itself. Calling for a methodology of textual polysemy, in which texts can be read in multiple modes, Barlas rejects interpretations based on interpretive reductionism or essentialism in favor of privileging an interpretation of the text that is faithful to God's justice and egalitarianism.

Other works approached the question of scripture and scriptural authority from the perspective of the authors, rather than the texts themselves. For example, Denise Spellberg's *Politics, Gender, and the Islamic Past: The Legacy of 'A'isha bint Abi Bakr* looked not so much at the relative "truth" of a given historical text as it did how 'A'isha was portrayed in those texts in order to examine how gender roles were constructed and by whom. This enabled a more comprehensive examination of how one woman's life story was used, rewritten, and reinterpreted in order to fulfill various agendas to the point of being presented in multiple and even conflicting images, none of which were determined by her, demonstrating the "power of interpretation in the formation of historical meaning" (Spellberg, 1).

Similarly, Ziba Mir-Hosseini's *Islam and Gender: The Religious Debate in Contemporary Iran* set the stage for recognition of variations within "Islamic" discourses, even of the most purportedly conservative variety. Rather than lumping all government religious figures into a single category, she examined the nature of religious authority as expressed by three groups—traditionalists, neo-traditionalists, and modernists—noting that each group had a different interpretation of gender, respectively, inequality, balance, and equality. The study was pivotal because of the important role played by religion in the public sphere in Iran. Suggesting the potential for multiple interpretations within the unity of state-sponsored "Islam" allowed for nuance to enter into the debate. It also called for more careful scholarly attention to this reality.

Since then, other contemporary works on Iran and gender issues, such as Minoo Moallem's *Between Warrior Brother and Veiled Sister: Islamic Fundamentalism and the Politics of Patriarchy in Iran*, have challenged the politics of patriarchy that have led to a sacralization of politics at the same time that religion has been desacralized. Arguing that Iranian women, leading up to the 1979 Revolution, had deliberately rejected rules, laws, norms, and values in their rejection of the state and its oppressive authority, Moallem observed a need for similar action today, as the Islamic State has insisted upon a monolithic, masculinist narrative of an Islamic nation that not only marginalizes the voices of women, but attempts to obfuscate the reality of multiple and diverse discourses present today.

Studies of women's increasing forays into religious interpretation and claiming religious authority have also been undertaken, most notably in Masooda Bano and Hilary Kalmbach's edited collection, *Women, Leadership and Mosques: Changes in Contemporary Islamic Authority*. Ranging from the Middle East and Europe to China and Indonesia, the articles in this collection point to the myriad of ways in which women are exercising religious authority today, suggesting that the era of male dominance of the fields of religious interpretation and leadership is coming to an end.

In recent years, scholarship on women and gender has also begun to address previously socially taboo subjects, particularly sex and sexuality. Part of the impetus for exploring these topics came from the proliferation of gay and lesbian studies that began in the 1990s. Within this field came studies of sexual expression and identity—a topic that remains contested in many parts of the Islamic world today where homosexuality is understood to be a behavior, rather than an identity. Some studies have further focused on contemporary youth practices and the social schizophrenia introduced by norms of propriety in the public domain that do not permit mixing between unrelated men and women, particularly in self-identified Islamic states, and the realities of the private domain in which youth exploration of not only sexual activity, but often alcohol and drugs, also occurs.

Academic research has also branched beyond written texts to include visual and electronic sources. Film-making has become particularly important in addressing issues related to women and gender as women film directors shape, control, and redirect how we look at the issues. For example, Ziba Mir-Hosseini's "Divorce Iranian Style" takes viewers inside the courtroom and peoples' homes to look at how divorces are enacted and why, showing a disconnect between the legal and religious ideals of clerics and judges compared to the realities of peoples' lives. Likewise, Pervez Sharma's "A Jihad for Love" takes viewers inside the lives of gays and lesbians in the Middle East, showcasing the difficulties they face trying to live as whole persons in societies that do not accept same sex love, despite a lengthy historical literary tradition of the same.

Finally, greater attention is also being given today to women outside of the MENA region. Of particular importance are studies of Indonesia, the world's most populous Muslim country, where one of the most important developments has been the foundation of *pesantren* (religious schools) for girls by women. The importance of female study of the Qur'ānic text should not be underestimated, as study leads to interpretation and argumentation. Pieternella van Doorn-Harder's *Women Shaping Islam: Reading the Qur'an in Indonesia* particularly notes the capacity of Muslim women leaders to use Islam as a significant force for societal change and improving the economic, social, and psychological condition of Indonesian women.

Bibliography

Ahmed, Leila. *Women and Gender in Islam: Historical Roots of a Modern Debate*. New Haven, Conn.: Yale University Press, 1992.

Ali, Kecia. *Marriage and Slavery in Early Islam*. Cambridge, Mass.: Harvard University Press, 2010.

Badran, Margot. *Feminists, Islam, and Nation: Gender and the Making of Modern Egypt*. Princeton, N.J.: Princeton University Press, 1995.

Bano, Masooda, and Hilary Kalmbach, eds. *Women, Leadership and Mosques: Changes in Contemporary Islamic Authority*. Leiden, Netherlands: E.J. Brill, 2012.

Barlas, Asma. *'Believing Women' in Islam: Unreading Patriarchal Interpretations of the Qur'an*. Austin: University of Texas Press, 2002.

Boyd, Jean. *The Caliph's Sister*. London: Frank Cass, 1989.

DeLong-Bas, Natana J. *Wahhabi Islam: From Revival and Reform to Global Jihad*, rev. ed. New York: Oxford University Press, 2008.

Esposito, John L. with Natana J. DeLong-Bas. *Women in Muslim Family Law*. 2d ed. Syracuse, N.Y.: Syracuse University Press, 2001.

Hambly, Gavin R. G., ed. *Women in the Medieval Islamic World*. New York: St. Martin's Press, 1998.

Kandiyoti, Deniz. *Women, Islam and the State*. London: Macmillan, 1991.

Keddie, Nikki, and Beth Baron, eds. *Women in Middle Eastern History: Shifting Boundaries in Sex and Gender*. New Haven, Conn.: Yale University Press, 1991.

Mernissi, Fatima. *The Veil and the Male Elite: A Feminist Interpretation of Women's Rights in Islam*. Reading, Mass.: Addison-Wesley, 1991.

Mir-Hosseini, Ziba. *Islam and Gender: The Religious Debate in Contemporary Iran*. Princeton, N.J.: Princeton University Press, 1999.

Moallem, Minoo. *Between Warrior Brother and Veiled Sister: Islamic Fundamentalism and the Politics of Patriarchy in Iran*. Berkeley: University of California Press, 2005.

Najmabadi, Afsaneh. *Women with Mustaches and Men without Beards: Gender and Sexual Anxieties of Iranian Modernity*. Berkeley: University of California Press, 2005.

Nashat, Guity. *Restoring Women to History*. Bloomington, IN: Organization of American Historians, 1988.

Peirce, Leslie P. *The Imperial Harem: Women and Sovereignty in the Ottoman Empire*. New York: Oxford University Press, 1993.

Said, Edward W. *Orientalism*. New York: Pantheon Books, 1978.

Smith, Margaret. *Muslim Women Mystics: The Life and Work of Rabi'a and Other Women Mystics in Islam*. Oxford: Oneworld, 2001. (Originally published in 1928)

Smith, W. Robertson. *Kinship and Marriage in Early Arabia*. Boston: Beacon Press, 1903.

Sonbol, Amira El Azhary, ed. *Women, the Family, and Divorce Laws in Islamic History*. Syracuse, N.Y.: Syracuse University Press, 1996.

Spellberg, D. A. *Politics, Gender, and the Islamic Past: The Legacy of 'A'isha bint Abi Bakr*. New York: Columbia University Press, 1994.

Stern, Gertrude. *Marriage in Early Islam*. London: Routledge and Kegan Paul, 1939.

Stowasser, Barbara Freyer. *Women in the Qur'an, Traditions, and Interpretation*. New York: Oxford University Press, 1994.

van Doorn-Harder, Pieternella. *Women Shaping Islam: Reading the Qur'an in Indonesia*. Urbana: University of Illinois Press, 2006.

Wadud, Amina. *Inside the Gender Jihad: Women's Reform in Islam*. Oxford: Oneworld, 2006.

Wadud, Amina. *Qur'an and Woman: Rereading the Sacred Text from a Woman's Perspective*. New York: Oxford University Press, 1999.

Walther, Wiebke. *Women in Islam: From Medieval to Modern Times*. Princeton, N.J.: Markus Wiener Publishers, 1993.

Natana J. DeLong-Bas

Methodologies

Several approaches and theoretical constructs can be identified within the context of women and gender studies in Islam. This article identifies a list of key figures who have played a vital role in shaping the disposition of Muslim women along with uniting and strengthening their voices. This group is by no means inclusive but presents unique worldviews that provide readers with a wide array of data and work, outlining the struggles that women have faced and continue to face, and the constant debates involved. Issues discussed include women's voices in scriptural interpretation, feminism as essential in the development, and inclusion of Muslim women in the religious realm; the controversy over veiling, gender discrimination, and challenges facing the patriarchal norms suppressing women; contemporary Islamophobia; problems associated with the reconstruction of the Muslim '*ummah*;' and young Muslim women's piety. A discussion of the contemporary impact and influence across space and history in association with different cultural, religious, and intellectual frameworks is also provided.

Women's Voices in Scriptural Interpretation. A number of methodologies are used in interpreting the Qur'ān from a Muslim woman's perspective. Three major scholars who address Qur'ān hermeneutics are Amina Wadud, Asma Barlas, and Nimat Barazangi, all of whom address the lack of female interpretations, traditional patriarchal interpretations, whether interpretation is a stagnant versus an ongoing process, and the various theologies used to approach and analyze the Qur'ān, as well as the Qur'ān's content Amina Wadud's revolutionary work, *Qur'an and Women: Rereading the Sacred Text From a Woman's Perspective*, uses textual analysis to discuss three categories generally used to interpret women's rights in the Qur'ān: Traditional, Reactive, and Holistic. She argues that Traditional *tafsīr* or interpretation, provides interpretations of the entire Qur'ān, from classical or modern times, with specific objectives in mind: legal, historical, grammatical, rhetorical, or esoteric. However, while *tafsīr* may be different based on each of these objectives, all objectives share an atomistic methodology. This includes interpreting each verse of the Qur'ān separately, beginning with the first and ending with the last. What Wadud sees as problematic is that this method does not look at the Qur'ān thematically nor does it discuss in detail the relationship between these Qur'ānic verses. Because this *tafsīr* was written exclusively by male interpreters, only men's perspective and experiences were taken into consideration, excluding women's experiences and perspective. The lack of women's voice, in this context, is perceived as voicelessness reflected in the Qur'ānic text itself. Reactive interpretation is primarily expressed by some modern scholars, who may be opposed to Islam in general or the message of the Qur'ān in particular, using the poor status of women in some Muslim societies as justification for their negative reactions. Wadud maintains that Reactive interpretation fails to draw a distinction between text and interpretation. She further argues that, although some feminist ideals and rationale might contribute to this Reactive interpretation, this can be overcome by demonstrating the link between liberation and the primary source of Islamic theology. Finally, Holistic interpretation reconsiders the whole method of Qur'ānic exegesis with respect to different social, economic, moral, and political concerns, including the issue of women. It is on this category of interpretation, which is relatively modern, that Wadud grounds her book. Wadud's conclusion is that, "Qur'ānic guidance can be logically and equitably applied to the lives of humankind in whatever era, if the Qur'ānic interpretation continues to be rendered by each generation in a manner which reflects its whole intent. This method shows its adaptability to present and future realities" (Wadud, 1999, p. 104).

Asma Barlas argues against critics of Islam who reduce the Qur'ān to one specific reading/interpretation of the text (interpretive reductionism). She emphasizes that the Qur'ān is polysemic, and (like all texts) can be read in "multiple modes" (Barlas, 2001, p. 4). She further asserts that the Qur'ān's treatment of women and men is "not based in claims about either sexual difference or sameness" (Barlas, 2001, p. 6), noting that exegesis was not limited historically to religious and scholarly interests, but was performed for political gain. She further elucidates that conservative theories worked toward generalizing the particular; the idea that the Qur'ān is relevant to all times and places is accepted by Muslims, but is interpreted differently. Conservatives de-historicize and de-textualize the Qur'ān in order to protect their idea of its universality, while critical scholars argue that revelation occurs in historical time so that the Qur'ān's universality "lies in the ability of new generations of believers to derive new meaning" (Barlas, 2001, p. 60) so that interpretation is ongoing, rather than fixed. Barlas describes her book "as much a critique of sexual/textual oppression in Muslim societies as it is a concerted attempt to recover what Leila Ahmed calls the 'stubbornly egalitarian' voice of Islam" (Barlas, 2001, p. 2). She further notes that *tafsīr* has superseded the Qurʾānic text in most Muslim societies as a source of influence. She considers the failure to generate an antipatriarchal (or at least contextually legitimate) reading of the Qurʾān a theological problem in addition to a hermeneutical one. Epistemologically, Barlas draws guidance for her reading of the Qurʾān from the Qurʾān itself. She "ascribes intention/ality to the text" and in doing so recognizes the masculine references to God as a "bad linguistic convention" (Barlas, 2001, p. 22). In addressing Text and Textualities and the relationship between the Qurʾān on the one hand and *tafsīr* and *ḥadīth* narratives on the other, her first aim is "to identify the methodology Muslims have traditionally used to read the Qurʾān" (Barlas, 2001, p. 31); her second aim is "to examine two conceptualizations of the relationship between Divine Speech and time, the conservative and the critical, and their implications for Qur'anic exegesis" (Barlas, 2001, p. 31).

Finally, Nimat Barazangi uses an educational curriculum instruction methodology to approach the central question of why the authority to interpret "religious" texts has been exclusive to male religious elites. She believes that nothing will change the condition of Muslim women and Muslim society at large unless women are recognized as having the same authority to interpret the Qurʾān. Her strategy is reflected in her proposal of the curricular framework, "Self-Learning of Islam" (S-LI), as a means of self-realization and self-identity grounded in the Qurʾān to guard against misinterpretation of Islam against women's interests.

Feminism. Feminism is often seen as a Western concept with more secular intentions. However, Islamic feminism has been essential in the development and inclusion of Muslim women in the religious realm. Secular feminism is often perceived as clashing with Islamic feminism because of prejudices constantly perpetuated by certain Western perspectives. Scholars such as Margot Badran identify the historical events associated with activism and the prominent issues that need to be reevaluated.

Badran's work largely centers on gender activism and feminist movements in the Middle East. Primarily concerned with Egypt, Badran's works *Feminist, Islam and Nation* and *Feminism in Islam: Secular and Religious Convergences* follow the trajectory of the women's rights movement from the late nineteenth century to the present day. Through biographical sketches of key figures in the movement's history, such as Huda Shaʾrawi, Nabawiyya Musa, Zainab al-Ghazālī, and Nawāl al-Saʿdāwī, Badran delineates distinct periods of mobilization concomitant with various global trends in the rising feminist tide, the scope of women's movement into the public sphere, and the social and political climate of women's growing activism. She argues for the indigenous growth of a feminist consciousness in Egypt as well as demonstrates the highly active nature of women's organizing. Her work similarly traces the growth and impact of Islamic feminism in Turkey, Yemen, and Nigeria, and advocates for the need for a female-centered *ijtihād*. Badran contends that feminism grounded within an Islamic framework represents the best approach for effectively overcoming traditional patriarchal norms in Muslim majority countries. As Badran has been a leading figure in the scholarly discussion of Islamic feminism, her work has provided an important foundation upon which succeeding scholars have understood the complexities inherent within such approaches. Her discussions of the conceptual overlap between secular and Islamic feminisms, the different discourses inhered within those approaches (nationalist, Islamist, reformist, etc.), and the need to re-examine religious sources (the Qur'ān, *ḥadīth*, *fiqh*, etc.) have led to increased interest in an Islamic-based framework of women's rights. Her work is situated within a larger body of literature that, over the course of the last two decades, has similarly examined the nature of women's roles within Islam and in the modern state, following that of Leila Ahmed and Lila Abu Lughod. Such scholars as Elizabeth Fernea, Amina Wadud, Valentine Moghadam, Nimat Barazangi, and others have all been shaped by and continue to shape the discourse and intellectual framework set by the work of scholars such as Badran. Her work has received wide reaching attention, including acceptance of her work as halal by the then Sheikh al-Azhar, Muḥammad Tantawi. Through historical analysis of the writings of women's rights activists over the last century as well as interviews with contemporary activists, Badran has particularly traced the contours of women's struggle for equality in Egypt. Contrary to much theorizing about the lack of a true feminist movement in Egypt, her analysis demonstrates that Egypt has witnessed a long history of feminist activism that has attempted to articulate a new notion of womanhood, as women have vociferously challenged patriarchal norms that have restricted their roles to the private realm of the household.

Leila Ahmed also underscores various attempts by early feminists to promote gender changes, including Huda Sha'rawi's work with the Wafdist Women's Central Committee and Malak Hifni Nassef's role in articulating a feminist framework in Egypt. She notes the tensions that arose between those espousing a more secular (and therefore Western) approach versus those advocating for an Islamic-based system of rights and laws. Huda Sha'rawi initially founded "The Intellectual Association of Egyptian Women" in 1914, followed by the Egyptian Feminist Union (EFU) in 1923. As Ahmed noted, the organizational and political success of the EFU helped bring about significant gains for women in Egypt. The EFU's main aim was to raise women's intellectual and moral levels and to enable them to attain political, social, and legal equality. The most fundamental outcome of the Egyptian feminist movement was the establishment of The Arab Feminist Union (AFU) in Cairo in 1944 and its movement toward a broader concept of Pan-Arab feminism.

Saba Mahmood has also argued for a reevaluation of notions of agency, freedom, and resistance in her assessment of women's piousness associated with the mosque movement in Egypt. Secular-liberal politics, to which feminism has been intimately tied, has located women's agency in resistance and struggle against traditional religious structures that have oppressed them and denied them freedom of choice in making life decisions. She suggests thinking of agency, "not as a synonym for resistance to relations of domination, but as a capacity for action that historically specific relations of subordination enable and create" (Mahmood, 2001, p. 203). Mahmood provides a theoretical assessment of women's agency vis-à-vis their pious activities within the mosque movement in Egypt. She draws on ethnographic data collected on Muslim women to challenge normative feminist and liberal notions that conflate agency singularly with resistance to "tradition," and hence religion. The Islamic mosque movement in Egypt has involved the mobilization of women to educate themselves on religious scriptures, generating changes in a range of social behaviors, including manners of dress and speech, considerations of appropriate entertainment, investment patterns, caring for the poor, and the parameters for conducting public debate (Mahmood, 2001, p. 204). She highlights Muslim women's perspectives that modernity and secular politics have undermined religious approaches to daily life, though she notes the incongruency of an empowerment movement advocating subjugation of the individual will to God. Mahmood problematizes the notion that Muslim women are unwittingly brainwashed and reproduce the conditions of their own subjugation in advocating for a return to Islamic ways of being. Here she argues for a reassessment of the theoretical underpinnings of agency and resistance, noting that actively choosing to submit to the will of God and controlling desire is a demonstration of women's agency and freedom. As part of this critique, she refers to Judith Butler's notion of "subjectivation," which is the "reconceptualization of power as a set of relations that do not simply dominate the subject, but also, importantly, form the conditions of its possibility" (Mahmood, 2001, 210). Women's agency is conceived of as the ability to both resist and subordinate oneself. Within this context, submission to God involves certain techniques of self that include docility and shyness. Docility is defined as the quiet and willing adherence to instruction while shyness involves modesty and diffidence. Both are performed repeatedly and embodied over time with the goal of training "one's memory, desire and intellect to behave according to established standards and conduct" (Mahmood, 2001, p. 214).

Ziba Mir-Hosseini examines both the popular reform movement in Iran and emerging feminist Islamic discourses that argue for women's equality within the context of Sharīʿah. She briefly traces both the evolution of the Iranian family law code from its inception following the revolution to contemporary reform efforts to improve women's status within the code, as well as the history of Muslim women's activism. Mir-Hosseini offers a generalized historical analysis to answer the question of how Islamic discourses within a global framework are impacting the shape of women's rights, with a particular focus on Iran. She questions why Islamic juridical texts have subjugated women, concluding that patriarchal interpretations are to blame for leaving women vulnerable to male domination. She underscores contemporary inconsistencies with the way the West has viewed Muslim women, including the failure of the invasion of Afghanistan and the removal of the Taliban to lead women to remove their burqas. She similarly highlights the way in which the invasion of Iraq led to conservatism in ethical principles by radical Islamic groups and the overturning of the Baʿath regime's family code. Focusing on the reform movement in Iran, she notes that women's struggles have deep implications for Muslim women's rights in the global context. Here, Iran represents a case of a *Sharīʿah* state that is grappling with its democratic principles and, under reformist governments, has allowed for a freedom of dialogue that has engendered Islamic feminism. The Family Protection Law as established under the Pahlavi monarchy was overturned with the reinstitution of *Sharīʿah*-based personal status laws under Ayatollah Khomeini in 1979. Though touted as protecting women's rights and status within Islam, most women believed and felt differently about the new religiously based family code. Women were denied the right to divorce and pre-revolution restrictions on male-initiated divorce were eliminated, leading to an increase in divorces that no longer required female consent and generating a high degree of family discord. Massive dissatisfaction with the changes in this area of law led to the restoration of some Pahlavi-era reforms. Mir-Hosseini highlights how this change in thinking was tied to a reform movement known as the "New Religious Thinking," in which reformists argued for a more dynamic, plural, and open Islam that could engage with Western discourses. Islamic feminism, she argues, is a more contemporary construct, growing out of much earlier feminist activism but tied to a particular geopolitical climate that provides women increasing space to negotiate their rights and roles within Islam. She argues that Muslim women have always advocated for their rights, but, under colonial domination, nationalist demands superseded those of women, thus hindering true feminist activism. She claims that there can be no one definition of Islamic feminism as the needs and visions of Muslim women vary across location, culture, and ideological approaches. What many Muslim feminists have in common, however, is their attempt to reinterpret the religious canon, focusing on the equality inherent in the Qurʾān.

Veiling. The issue of the hijab has been covered by an array of scholars throughout history. The hijab itself has been quite a controversial symbol in both the Islamic and Western worlds and the created controversies around veiling or unveiling have been challenging to overcome and theorize. Some believe veiling is an oppressive act that disables women from seeking an active place in society. Others argue that veiling or unveiling can be the result of choice and religiosity. Major scholars addressing the challenges of hijab interpretation are Elizabeth Fernea, Leila Ahmed, Nadia Fadil, Haleh Afshar, and Saba Mahmoud.

Based on ethnographic research, Elizabeth Fernea has argued that the veil is a complex symbol that can have multiple implications and different impacts. Although it is perceived by most Muslims as a religious requirement, it can be a symbol of conservatism or a reaction against modernization. The veil is further seen by others as an Islamic approach to solving old and new problems. Thus, however it is used, the veil "means different things to Westerners than it does to Muslim Middle Easterners" (Fernea, 1993, p. 154).

In *Women and Gender in Islam*, Leila Ahmed discusses the history of the veil, as well as its contemporary practice, especially in Egypt. In *A Quiet Revolution*, she questions why the resurgence of the veil, from the Middle East to America, took root so swiftly and what this shift means for women, Islam, and the West. Ahmed examines the intertwining of nationalism, socialism, Islam, anti-imperialism, and the veil through the themes of politics, dress, and women's changing roles. The significance of Ahmed's book resides in its comprehensive discussion of the resurgence of the veil in both the Middle East and the United States.

Nadia Fadil asserts that much attention has been focused on hijab as either a political or pious act for Muslim women and that very little has been theorized about not veiling and the choices women make to either remove the veil or not wear it at all. She argues that not veiling is a technique of the self and, like veiling, it equally points toward women's piety and their understanding of their religious traditions as wearing the veil. Here, not-veiling serves as a technique through which Muslim women express an Islamic identity that is rooted in liberal ethics. Fadil provides a theoretical assessment of not-veiling among Muslim women and takes as its point of departure Saba Mahmood's *Politics of Piety*. She looks to the contemporary situation with the Muslim community in Belgium and the cultural, religious, and political tensions that drive women's choices about veiling or not veiling. Fadil argues that in the face of the continued Orientalist fascination with veiled Muslim women, there is a growing scholarly literature that seeks to understand the complex nature of veiling practices in the Muslim world. This literature has attempted to reintroduce agency in the decision-making practices of Muslim women and normalize the practice of veiling. However, Fadil contends that this singular focus on hijab has contributed to the continued isolation of Muslim women as an analytical construct. Furthermore, this myopic focus on veiled women fails to understand practices of not-veiling and the constructs of self in Muslim women's identity formation. She contends that not-veiling is a choice that Muslim women arrive at through active decision-making processes and represents a particular aesthetic of self. Fadil's research takes place within the sociopolitical landscape of contemporary Belgium, where debates about minority and national identities have raged, mirroring those in neighboring countries. Like their French neighbors, Belgium has a large minority population from French-speaking North African countries. Debates on the headscarf have been heavily influenced by those occurring in France. Unlike in France, however, religious institutions have played a more decisive role in Belgian society. "As of today, a large part of the Belgian civil society as much of civil society is organized along confessional lines, particularly Catholicism" (Fadil, 2011, p. 87). Nevertheless, hijab has not been legally banned in schools as is the case in France. Fadil argues that not-veiled women have been viewed with less anxiety than their veiled sisters. These women are seen as conforming to the norms of their host communities and assimilating into the secular, ideological landscape. She argues that this misses the complexities of women's religious beliefs. Moreover, she states that the contemporary ban on hijab represents "a body politics of secular governmentality that seeks to regulate Muslim female conduct according to specific notions of nationhood" (Fadil, 2011, p. 89) and is an extension of colonial era regulations that forced women to unveil in certain parts of the east. Hijab is equated with conservative, traditional practice while not-veiling is tied to secular normativity. The motivations behind not-veiling, however, go unexplored and are assumed to be a natural state, inhering women with passivity in accepting liberal culture. However, Fadil asserts that not-veiling is "tied to a certain ethical labour power upon the self" (Fadil, 2011, p. 95), rendering it an active process of self-fashioning as a liberal ethical subject. This liberal, ethical, nonveiled self does not deny the existence of an existential, divine being and cannot be conflated with the secular. However, the choice to not-veil, like the choice to veil and the choice to be obedient to a transcendental power, is equally an expression of women's rational agency.

Haleh Afshar contends that *mohajebeh* (veiled) women are singled out as objects of both pity and fear, viewed at once as passive victims compelled by cultural imperative, and, in some cases, law, to wear hijab, but also potentially dangerous in that they would choose to veil, self-identify as Muslim and accept their own subjugation. Afshar (2008) notes that there is a "gendered perception of Islam and the umma" (p. 419) and that Muslim women specifically have become objects of discrimination and hatred as well as pity and misguided activism. *Mohajebeh* women are deemed ignorant and subject to the will of their families and husbands. Western governments and activists seek to improve Muslim women's lives by liberating them from the misogyny of the hijab, which they view as everything that is wrong with Islam. Afshar counters, however, that wearing hijab is most often the choice of Muslim women, for religious, political, and personal reasons, making it a mark of deliberate self-identification as part of the Islamic community. Educated *mohajebeh* women are seeking to redress the real inequalities within the Islamic community by focusing not on hijab but on looking to reinterpret the sacred texts and reexamine women's historical roles within Islam. Muslim women argue that "Islam requires submission only to God" (Afshar, 2008, p. 423) and that the Qurʾān grants them wide ranging rights. Afshar claims that the hijab is not a marker against which the West can determine women's status in the Islamic world. In another article, Afshar et al. found that young Muslim women of immigrant backgrounds in Britain may have more in common with white, convert Muslim women as opposed to young, religious Muslim men and those of their parents' generation. Moreover, they contend that young Muslim women have donned the hijab as a political act, visibly marking themselves as Muslim in the contentious post-9/11 world, highlighting the complex, multifaceted and situated nature of their identities, which are rooted as much in faith as in their British nationality. Veiled Muslim women have been caught between their co-religionists, with separatist viewpoints, and their host communities, where much of the rhetoric is Islamophobic in nature. Afshar et al. argue that, in this climate, young Muslim women consciously wear the hijab as a political symbol of membership in the Muslim community. However, they also contend that, despite this, young veiled Muslim women refuse to retrench from their active lives in British society. For *mohejebeh* women, it is possible to be both Muslim and British and, in this regard, they share much in common with young British convert women who have donned the veil. Hijab is a signifier of their Islamic identity, but not one that necessarily precludes national identity.

Finally, Saba Mahmoud has found that hijab attempts to train and embody the sense of shyness. She notes that *ṣabr* (patience) and endurance are also expressions of pious behavior to which women aspire. She suggests that Muslim women are willingly veiling in order to preserve their faithfulness in God's eyes.

Gender Discrimination. Gender discrimination has been fostered through years of male-dominating societies. These societies have established the idea that women are inferior and must fit into a preconstructed role in society. Leila Ahmed challenges the patriarchal norms that suppress women from gaining equality throughout the Islamic world.

Ahmed's major book, *Women and Gender in Islam: Historical Roots of a Modern Debate*, is largely seen as "the authoritative text on the subject." Making use of historical data regarding the role of women in ancient and pre-Islamic society in Arabia, Ahmed argues that gender discrimination inherent in current Islamic practices have roots in the patriarchal norms of the societies to which Islam spread. Such local, cultural misogyny was absorbed into the ideological superstructure of Islamic societies, resulting in continued discrimination against women in the contemporary period. Ahmed explores the various discourses surrounding women (1) in the *jāhilīyah* (pre-Islamic era); (2) since the founding of Islam; and (3) in the colonial and postcolonial world. She contrasts a more egalitarian ancient past with that of medieval and modern Islamic society, noting that sexually based forms of discrimination and women's subjugation were a product of urbanism. Examples provided demonstrating the greater role of women in ancient society include the presence of female figurines and large burial mounds for women at the Neolithic site of Catal Huyuk in Turkey celebrating their importance, and texts from new Kingdom Egypt demonstrating the equality of women in the realms of marriage, inheritance, and property ownership. Her research also highlights discriminatory practices with regard to veiling, seclusion, divorce, and property rights in the various societies of Mesopotamia, which continued through the Hellenic and Byzantine periods of Middle Eastern history. Ahmed argues that these histories, peripheral to the birthplace of Islam as they may be, are of vital importance for understanding the development of Islamic discourses around women, given Islam's historical penchant for absorbing many of the local cultural habits of the places where it spread. According to Ahmed, pre-Islamic Arabia exhibited a range of forms of marriage and sexual practice, including matrilineality and polyandry, though neither necessarily implies that the *jāhilīyah* was more egalitarian than the Islamic period. This is shored up by the fact that female infanticide was also widely practiced in Arabia before the coming of Islam. Ahmed argues that Islam selectively sanctioned or prohibited various customs in Arabian tribal societies, particularly favoring patriarchy, as seen in emphasis on paternity and male proprietary rights to female sexuality. With the first community of believers, Ahmed concedes that Islam provided women with rights heretofore unseen among Arabs, including property ownership and public participation in society. With the passing of the Prophet Muḥammad, however, much of this changed as patriarchal practice was instantiated by the various caliphates that later arose. With the emergence of nineteenth-century Western, colonial influence in the region, both men and women became embroiled in larger discussions about women's place in modern (and Islamic) societies. However, "those proposing an improvement in the status of women from early on couched their advocacy in terms of the need to abandon the (implicitly) 'innately' and 'irreparably' misogynist practices of the native culture in favor of the customs and beliefs of another culture—the European" (Ahmed, 1992, p. 129). The role of women changed as they moved out of seclusion, into schools and then the public sphere.

Margot Badran and miriam cooke focus on Egypt's feminist and women's movements that emerged as part of the social differentiation that took place as an outcome of the nineteenth-century nationalist and intellectual *Nahḍah* (Renaissance) discourse. Muslim modernist Muḥammad Abduh (1849–1905) advocated for gender reform and the need to improve on female education. Women's voices became increasingly louder as they began to actively fight for reform in personal status laws detrimental to women's freedom and well-being. Egyptian feminism grew out of an expanded body of knowledge and the observations Arab women made about their own lives during times of great transformation. The Islamic Reform Movement and the *Nahḍah* discourse made women aware "that certain so-called Islamic practices, such as veiling, segregation, and seclusion imposed upon urban women, were not ordained by Islam as they had been led to believe" (Badran and Cooke, 1990, p. xxiv).

Islamophobia. Islamophobia is defined by Haleh Afshar as "unfounded hostility towards Islam, and the fear or dislike of all or most Muslims" (p. 413). Islamophobia is yet another process of othering Muslims, conceiving of Islam as a traditional, unbending religion that actively resists Western (global) efforts of modernizing, or "normalizing," Arab countries. Afshar emphasizes that Islamophobia's Orientalist origins make it possible for contemporary global society to continue to essentialize and mischaracterize Islam and the realities of Muslim women's lived experiences. She highlights a number of cross-cultural examples, including U.S. President George Bush's post-9/11 declaration of a clash of civilizations and U.K. opposition leader, David Cameron's, notion that Islamic terrorism has to be defeated. She also examines France's drive to illegalize Islamic veiling. Afshar concludes by noting that mutual respect among communities, including feminists, is imperative. Similarities and differences must be understood if Islamophobia is to be overcome. This includes a more nuanced understanding of Muslim women's active participation in their communities and religion.

Afshar argues that contemporary Islamophobia is rooted in Orientalist misunderstandings of Arab culture and practice, with a particular conception of Muslim women as oppressed, in need of saving, and subject to maintaining male honor. Afshar contends that Islamophobia creates a double burden—the demonization of hijab adds another layer of inequality Muslim women already face and blinds both Muslim and non-Muslim feminist actors to the importance of the "global sisterhood of women" (p. 411). Afshar takes a comparative theoretical approach, examining not only the concepts of Orientalism and Islamophobia in detail, but also the cross-cultural problematics *mohajebeh's* face in the United States, United Kingdom, and France. She also details the ways in which *mohajebehs* are actively combating real gender discrimination within the Muslim community. Afshar contends that contemporary Islamophobia is rooted in historical Orientalist constructs that posit the East in distinction to a modern Occident. Here, the countries of the Arab world are disparaged as uncivilized and backward. Similarly, Arab Muslim women who veil, or *mohajebehs*, have become the central focus of Western misunderstandings of cultural and religious practice. Western perceptions view *mohajebehs* as needing saving from the jealous ignorance of their husbands. "Over the decades scholars have considered the ways that this process of otherization has misrepresented and caricaturized the Oriental Other in terms of sex, gender, race, ethnicity and religion" (p. 413).

Afshar et al. conducted a generational study focusing on first-, second-, and third-generation immigrant South Asian Muslim women, as well as convert Muslim women and young, radicalized Muslim men. They made use of a snowball method to meet informants, conduct interviews, deploy structured questionnaires, and hold a number of focus groups in order to understand the way in which diasporic Muslims have self-identified in the post-9/11 context. They also drew from interview data generated by a Canadian research project to understand Muslims in the Diaspora. In the aftermath of 9/11, Muslims in the United Kingdom have been targeted in a discriminatory campaign that has branded them as radicals, fundamentalists, and a threat to Western ways of being. British media and politicians have decried that all Muslims have a similar political agenda, with terrorist, or jihadist, tendencies. Many Muslim groups, such as *Hizb el-Tahrir*, have announced the impossibility of maintaining both a Muslim and British identity. Their attempts to combat such Islamophobic viewpoints have been similarly inflammatory and have helped to fuel already existing tensions in their host communities.

The *Ummah*. The Qur'ān associates the term ummah with a number of possible meanings including a religious community, nation or group of people. Haleh Afshar synthesizes the problems associated with the reconstruction of the Muslim "umma," highlighting the positive impact an ummah can have, depending on how it is defined and by whom.

Afshar et al. (2005) contend that organizations such as *Hizb el-Tahrir* call for a more cohesive Islamic position vis-à-vis the Western national structures within which they live. They call for a return to the Muslim *ummah*, which transcends all borders and requires "the explicit and public support of its women who are expected to endorse the traditional gender hierarchies that many Muslim women no longer wish to accept" (p. 264). These organizations call for all Muslims, including the *mohajebeh* (veiled) woman, to renounce their European nationalities as there is no room within the *ummah* for Muslims to assume more than their Islamic identity. Many *mohajebeh* women, however, see the *ummah* far more expansively, believing that the *ummah* covers the many facets of their various identities. Similarly, Muslim women's ideas about their roles within the *ummah* differ markedly from the position espoused by *Hizb el-Tahrir* (the liberation party). Furthermore, the authors claim that this attempt to build the Muslim *ummah* has led to the ethnicization of political Islam. Here, Muslim organizations are creating specific boundaries between themselves and the West. Identity, they claim, is far too multifaceted and fluid for this approach to succeed. They further argue that Islam in the European context is represented by a wide range of differing ethnic groups, schools of thought, doctrinal tendencies, and linguistic traditions. For this reason, Islam has become *the* marker of identity for youth in Europe and provides an avenue through which they can transcend the multiple facets of identity to maintain social solidarity in the face of Western contempt. For the men of *Hizb el-Tahrir*, this is much more significant than for Muslim women, whose understandings of Islamic traditions differ from that of men. The authors argue that Muslim women find it much easier to negotiate the multiple layers of their identities and that they are capable of being both Muslim and British.

Majority vs. Minority. Minority Muslim women are often heavily misjudged and publicly scrutinized. Christine Jacobsen attempts to understand young Muslim women's piety in Norway and the way in which these women are engaging and deploying Islam.

Increasing support for Islamic movements by women has generated a great deal of tension between feminism and religion and has led to questions about Muslim women's ability to make free choices. She argues that women's agency is a reflection of their "techniques for self-construction that can be seen as the effects of particular forms of liberal governance" (Jacobsen, 2011, p. 67). Muslim women are actively involved in developing a sense of self in line with religious principles. She utilizes previous ethnographic interview data collected on Muslim youth in Norway to look at questions of women's piety and freedom within the context of the Islamic revival movement, reexamining secularist interpretations of the motivations driving Muslim youth in their participation in religious endeavors. Searching for women's agency in Islam, Jacobsen's article takes as its point of departure Saba Mahmood's *Politics of Piety*. She states that Mahmood's argument highlights the way in which liberal politics has marginalized religious perspectives as static, traditional, and backward, denying Muslim women any freedom of choice and failing to understand the complex nature of their piety. Moreover, she underscores Mahmood's contention that certain religious practices, such as praying and veiling, are a process of self-fashioning and reconfiguring "one's affects and interiority" and that Western notions of the self does not correspond to those of Muslims. Mahmood asserts that submission to God is a form of self-fulfillment espoused by Muslims, as opposed to autonomy advocated by the West. Given this perspective, Jacobsen argues that one facet of Muslim women's pious behavior is the control of *nafs*, or willful self, in order to maintain balance among all the desires of the self. Here, terminating desire helps to maintain humility and goodness. She draws on Janice Boddy's work (1989) that envisions three aspects of human metaphysics: *aql* (reason), *nafs* (life force), and *rūḥ* (soul), as well as Lise Lien's work on the moral soul as inauthentic, where desire is deemed natural and a truer self. Jacobsen argues that a moral ethic that poses submission to God represents the Muslim self. In the production of this self, Muslims work to suppress individual desire. "Disciplining nafs is not about being prevented from 'realizing one's true self', but about realizing a self that is truly Muslim" (Jacobsen, 2011, p. 74). Agency, therefore, can be seen in the active submission of the self to God.

Conclusion. Women and gender studies pertaining to Islam and Muslim women clearly include a variety of methodologies addressing impact and influence across space and history in association with different cultures, religious, and intellectual contexts. Although the diverse group of women discussed is not inclusive, it presents samples of worldviews that provide a wide range of perspectives for further studies.

SELECT BIBLIOGRAPHY

Afshar, Haleh. "Can I See your Hair? Choice, Agency and Attitudes: The Dilemma of Faith and Feminism for Muslim Women Who Cover." *Ethnic and Racial Studies* 31, no. 2 (2008): 411–427.

Afshar, Haleh, Rob Aitken, and Myfanwy Franks. "Feminisms, Islamophobia and Identities." *Political Studies* 53 (2005): 262–283.

Ahmed, Leila. *Women and Gender in Islam: Historical Roots of a Modern Debate*. New Haven, Conn.: Yale University Press, 1992.

Ahmed, Leila. *A Quiet Revolution: The Veil's Resurgence, from the Middle East to* America. New Haven, Conn.: Yale University Press, 2011.

Ali, Souad T. "Women in Islam and Civil Society: An Overview of the Disparity between Religion and Culture." In *A Lecture on Gender Issues*, pp. 107–121. Kosovo: Kosovar Gender Studies Centre (KGSC) 107–121, 2010.

Badran, Margot."Understanding Islam, Islamism and Islamic Fundamentalism." *Journal of Women's History* 13, no. 1 (2001): 47–52.

Badran, Margot. *Feminism in Islam: Secular and Religious Convergences*. London: Oneworld, 2009.

Badran, Margot, and miriam cooke. *Opening the Gates: A Century of Arab Feminist Writing*. Bloomington: Indiana University Press, 1990.

Barlas, Asma. *Believing Women in Islam: Unreading Patriarchal Interpretations of the Quran*. Austin: University of Texas Press, 2001.

Barazangi, Nimat. *Woman's Identity and the Qur'an: A New Reading*. Gainesville: University Press of Florida, 2004.

Boddy, Janice. *Wombs and Alien Spirits: Women, Men, and the Zar Cult in Northern Sudan*. Madison: University of Wisconsin Press, 1989.

Fadil, Nadia. "Not-/Unveiling as an Ethical Practice." *Feminist Review* 98 (2011): 83–109.

Fernea, Elizabeth W. "The Veiled Revolution." In *Everyday Life in the Muslim Middle East*, edited by Donna Lee Bowen and Evelyn Early. Bloomington: Indiana University Press, 1993.

Jacobsen, Christine M. "Troublesome Threesome: Feminism, Anthropology and Muslim Women's Piety." *Feminist Review* 98 (2011): 65–82.

Mahmood, Saba. "Feminist Theory, Embodiment, and the Docile Agent: Some Reflections on the Egyptian Islamic Revival." *Cultural Anthropology* 16, no. 2 (2001): 202–236.

Mahmood, Saba. *Politics of Piety: The Islamic Revival and the Feminist*. Princeton, N.J.: Princeton University Press, 2005.

Mir-Hosseini, Ziba. "Muslim Women's Quest for Equality: Between Islamic Law and Feminism." *Critical Inquiry* 32 (2006): 629–645.

Wadud, Amina. *Qur'an and Woman: Re-reading the Sacred Text from A Woman's Perspective*. Oxford: Oxford University Press, 1999.

SOUAD T. ALI

GENDER THEMES.

[*This entry contains three subentries,*

Shīʿī Devotional Literature
Ṣūfī Devotional Literature *and*
Sunnī Devotional Literature.]

SHĪʿĪ DEVOTIONAL LITERATURE

Shīʿī devotional literature encompasses a variety of genres, both prose and verse, is typically hagiographical and commemorative, and focuses on the family of the Prophet Muḥammad (*ahl al-bayt*). Hagiography and Karbala literature, the two genres of devotional writing that predominate in Shīʿism, both focus on the exemplary piety and charismatic personalities of Muḥammad's blood descendents, and the women of the *ahl al-bayt* figure prominently in this literature. The Prophet's daughter Fāṭimah al-Zahrāʾ, granddaughter Zaynab bint ʿAlī, and Fāṭimah Maʿsūmeh, the sister of the eighth Imam Reza, are the subjects of an extensive and vibrant hagiographical corpus written in various Islamic languages, including more recently English and French. Karbala devotional literature is written from the imagined perspective of the women of the *ahl al-bayt* who survived the battle and were taken prisoner to Damascus, where they spread the message of Imam Ḥusain's martyrdom in 680 CE

Gender themes permeate Shīʿī devotional literature. Poems and narratives about the *ahl al-bayt* present these individuals as ideal Muslims and social and ethical exemplars to be imitated. Through the socially engaged examples of the women and men of the *ahl al-bayt*, Shīʿī devotional literature conveys important religious lessons and messages. Family relationships and their attendant responsibilities, marriage, commitment to social justice, the proper observance of cultural rituals, and countless other mundane activities of daily life shape the gendered themes that permeate Shīʿī devotional literature.

Hagiographical Literature. Hagiography is a dynamic genre of religious writing that praises the piety and spiritual accomplishments of individuals socially recognized as worthy of veneration. There are three distinguishing characteristics of Shīʿī hagiography: First, it does not emphasize asceticism as a preliminary sign of spiritual attainment. Second, it is centered on networks of kinship, a direct blood relationship to the Prophet Muḥammad through Fāṭimah and/or ʿAlī being essential. Third, although hagiographical traditions tend to minimize women's capacity for spiritual attainment, the women of the Prophet's family constitute significant religious role models for both Shīʿī women *and* men. Clearly, this third characteristic is functionally dependent on the first two. What makes Shīʿī hagiography unique is its inclusion of women as full human beings whose spiritual attainments are expressed in gendered terms. The women of the *ahl al-bayt* are simultaneously portrayed as mothers, daughters, sisters, and wives; as learned in the religious sciences; and as brave heroines.

Fāṭimah al-Zahrāʾ in Shīʿī Hagiography. Beginning around the tenth century, hagiographical texts composed in Arabic, Persian, and in later centuries, Urdu, portray Fāṭimah al-Zahrāʾ as a transcendent figure whose generative light (*nūr*) was the source of prophecy that established her as the mother of the Imamate (*umm al-āʾimma*). Fāṭimah is extolled for her role as the witness to her family's suffering. Shīʿīs believe that she visits every assembly of mourning (*majlis-e ʿazā*) to gather the tears shed for Imam Husain and the heroes of Karbala. Hagiographical traditions on Fāṭimah accord her the ultimate authority for interceding on the Day of Judgment. She will intercede on behalf of those loyal to her family and condemn those who were not. Hagiographies of Fāṭimah portray her as a saint, venerated for her humanity, with attendant feelings, emotions, and desires. These hagiographical traditions also portray Fāṭimah in her very human roles of mother, daughter, and wife, and as a woman with material and emotional needs

Miracle stories (*muʿjizat kahānī*) are a distinctively South Asian genre of hagiographical literature typically recited in the home and reflecting women's everyday experience and concerns (Schubel, 1993, p. 37). One of the most popular of these miracle tales is Bībī Fāṭimah kī kahānī (The Story of Lady Fatimah), which narrates the story of Fāṭimah's invitation to a Jewish wedding in Medina. Fāṭimah is ashamed to attend the wedding because her clothing is in tatters and she knows that her family's poverty will be cruelly mocked. As she laments her misfortune, angels descend from heaven and adorn her in richly embroidered robes and sumptuous jewels. When Fāṭimah arrives at the wedding, the women lose consciousness, causing consternation for all. Fāṭimah exhorts the women to pray to God, for it is he who has the power to raise the dead back to life. Fāṭimah prays for the unconscious bride and brings her back to life. Awed by this miracle, the male and female wedding guests convert en masse to Islam.

This story is also popular in the Persian Shīʿī hagiographical tradition, where it is presented in the dramatic form of the *taʿziyeh* (passion play) popularly known as *ʿarūs-e Quraysh* (The Wedding of the Qurayshi Daughter). During the Qajar dynasty (1785–1925) in Iran, *taʿziyeh* reached its zenith as a hagiographical performance genre, and The Wedding of the Qurayshi Daughter was so popular that women traveled great distances to watch this account of Fāṭimah's piety and power (Mottahedeh, 2005, p. 81).

Karbala Devotional Literature. Karbala devotional literature was written in both prose and verse form and is a popular genre of Shīʿī literature, composed in Arabic and Islamic languages such as Persian, Turkish, Urdu, Bengali, and Swahili. The centrality of the feminine in the *marthiya* (elegy) finds its origins in pre-Islamic Arabia, where women spontaneously composed laments at the graveside of deceased male relatives. For pre-Islamic Arabian women, tribal notions of honor (*ʿizzat*) prohibited expressions of grief, except through the ritualized conventions of the *marthiya*, through which women were expected to weep as they extolled the merits (*rithāʾ*) of the deceased. The Arabic *marthiya* was a distinctly feminine genre of poetry. With the advent of Islam, and particularly following the battle of Karbala, this literature became associated with Imam Husain's martyrdom and the women of the *ahl al-bayt*. The conventionalized style that developed out of the pre-Islamic Arabic *marthiya* tradition and its status as a feminine poetic genre lent itself to Shīʿī Karbala devotional literature. The first *marthiya* lamenting the martyrdom of Imam Husain is attributed to his sister Zaynab. At the court of the Umayyad caliph Yazīd, following the battle of Karbala in 680 CE, Ḥusain's sister Zaynab was given the special role of the *dhākirah*, or rememberer (an orator of the heroic actions and suffering of the heroes of Karbala). Thus began the Shīʿī tradition of remembrance. Because women were the only survivors of the battle of Karbala (with the exception of Imam Husain's son ʿAlī Zayn al-ʿābidīn, who became the fourth Imam), Karbala devotional literature use the feminine voice and feminine emotions, and this usage established the ritual context in Karbala devotional literature in which the female relatives of Imam Ḥusain mourn the loss of the battle's heroes. Zaynab's voice is especially important in Karbala devotional literature, since Shīʿī believe that God bestowed on her the role of messenger of Imam Husain's martyrdom. Because Zaynab provided the first testimony of the events of Karbala and what had befallen the Prophet's family, all the rest of Shīʿī commemorative literature exists as a form of second memory. Following the battle of Karbala, literary forms such as the *marthiya* came to refer specifically to Imam Ḥusain's martyrdom. These forms of commemorative literature essentially remained a feminine genre even though male writers have typically composed Karbala commemorative literature by invoking the voices of the female survivors of the battle, and thus have engaged in a form of literary transvestitism. The memory of Karbala is refracted through a feminine idiom, and the emotional remembrance of that event is distinctly female-centered.

The Feminine Voice in Karbala Devotional Literature. The sixteenth-century Ṣafavid court poet Moḥtasham Kāshānī wrote a Persian-language *marthiya* known as the *Karbalā-nāmeh* (Karbala Narrative; also known as the Haft Band), in which he assumes Zaynab's voice and emotion as she delivers two apostrophic speeches to her grandfather Muḥammad and mother Fāṭimah al-Zahrāʾ, who lay buried in Medina. By using Zaynab's voice, Moḥtasham emotionally engages the listener with Zaynab's grief and exhortations for justice while also motivating men and women to follow her model of faith and bravery.

Zaynab is typically portrayed in Karbala devotional literature as a larger-than-life heroine endowed by God with the responsibility to spread the message of what has befallen her family. In the *Karbalā-nāmeh*, Zaynab's status as the messenger of martyrdom is affirmed through her apostrophic speeches to Muḥammad and Fāṭimah. Zaynab's speech to Muḥammad is so impassioned that it "sets the world aflame." She punctuates each statement of how the Imam has suffered with the declaration "This is your Ḥusain!" Following her speech to her grandfather, Zaynab addressed her mother in her grave with such powerful words that she "roasted the beasts of the earth and the birds of the air." This second speech is more political in tone: Zaynab calls upon her mother to bear witness to the bloodshed that has taken place and to enact justice for the iniquitous acts that have harmed the *ahl al-bayt*. Karbala devotional literature conventionalizes Zaynab as a fearless leader committed to justice and as the preserver of the Shīʿī community in the battle's aftermath. Zaynab's example guides Shīʿīs in how correctly to remember Karbala, and through her words and actions, she teaches men and women how to imitate Imam Husain and his family's model of faith and sacrifice.

Gender Themes. Other women of the *ahl al-bayt* also serve as imitable models for the Shīʿīs. Like Zaynab's, their representation is a combination of conventionalized characterizations found in Karbala devotional poetry throughout the Shīʿī world and their embodiment of localized cultural and gender ideals. After Zaynab, the second most popularly invoked female figure in Karbala devotional literature is Imam Husain's youngest daughter, Sakīnah (also known as Roqayya in the Perso-Arabic tradition). Just three or four years old, Sakīnah survived the battle of Karbala and was brought as a prisoner of war to Yazīd's court in Damascus. According to tradition, Sakīnah died from her grief while imprisoned. In Arabic, Persian, and Urdu Karbala devotional poetry, Sakīnah is portrayed as the beloved favorite of her father Ḥusain and her uncle ʿAbbās, who was martyred when he tried to fill waterskins at the bank of the Euphrates River in order to quench his niece's thirst. Touching domestic vignettes in Karbala devotional literature seek to intensify the grief that Shīʿīs devotees feel for these heroes, portrayed as gentle and caring family men.

One of the most popular events in South Asian Karbala literature is the battlefield wedding of Imam Ḥusain's daughter Fāṭimah Kubrā to her cousin Qāsem. According to a tradition first mentioned in Rowẓat al-Shohadāʾ (Garden of the Martyrs), Ḥusain Vāʿez Kāshefi's early sixteenth-century Persian hagiography of Fāṭimah and the Imams and a chronicle of the battle of Karbala, after their wedding, Qāsem went to the battlefield, where he fought valiantly and was killed before he could consummate his marriage to Fāṭimah Kubrā. By the seventeenth century, Rowẓat al-Shohadāʾ was introduced to the Shīʿī Qutb Shahi dynasty of Hyderabad, and it was quickly translated into the vernacular languages of Deccani-Urdu and Telugu. This vignette rapidly became popular, and translations of Kāshefi's text were embellished with South Asian Muslim marriage customs, transforming Fāṭimah Kubrā and Qāsem into an idealized Indian bride and groom. Sakīnah figures prominently in this Karbala literature about the seventh Muharram Mehndī (referring to a popular prenuptial ritual in which the groom's feet and hands are decorated with henna) as the idealized sister-in-law aggrieved by her inability to perform the customary prenuptial rituals required of a respectable Muslim family.

Shīʿī devotional literature is didactic as well as experiential. Through a variety of strategies of narrative engagement, the men and women of the *ahl al-bayt* are brought to life, presenting a variety of gendered selves and practices. Shīʿī devotional literature elevates the spiritual achievements of the *ahl al-bayt* while simultaneously presenting them as real men and women, yet it also transforms them into culturally and socially relevant gendered beings whose model can be imitated.

[*See also* Religious Biography and Hagiography.]

BIBLIOGRAPHY

Aghaie, Kamran Scot, ed. *The Women of Karbala: Ritual Performance and Symbolic Discourses in Modern Shiʿi Islam.* Austin: University of Texas Press, 2005. These essays explore the ways in which women participate in Muharram rituals and the role of feminine voices and emotions in Shīʿī devotional literature.

Clarke, Lynda. Some Examples of Elegy on the Imam Husayn. *Al-Serat* 12 (Spring and Autumn 1986): 13–28. Includes a useful analysis of the history and function of women's voices in Arabic *marthiya*.

Mottahedeh, Negar. "Karbala Drag Kings and Queens." *Drama Review* 49, no. 4 (Winter 2005): 73–85. Explores the female roles traditionally played by young men and boys in Qajar-era (eighteenth and nineteenth centuries) *taʿziyeh* and the element of transvestite performance.

Pinault, David. "Zaynab bint ʿAli and the Place of the Women of the Household of the First Imams in Shiʿite Devotional Literature." In *Women in the Medieval Islamic World: Power, Patronage, and Piety*, edited by Gavin R. G. Hambly, pp. 69–98. New York: Palgrave, 1998. In-depth assessment of the meaning and function of Zainab's voice and emotion in Shīʿī devotional literature.

Pinault, David. *Horse of Karbala: Muslim Devotional Life in India.* New York: Palgrave, 2001. Chapter 4 assesses women's roles in Shīʿī devotional literature in South Asia.

Ruffle, Karen G. *Gender, Sainthood, and Everyday Practice in South Asian Shiʿism.* Chapel Hill: University of North Carolina Press, 2011. An ethnographic and literary analysis of the use of gender themes in Karbala devotional literature and Shīʿī hagiography in Hyderabad, India.

Schubel, Vernon J. *Religious Performance in Contemporary Islam: Shiʿi Devotional Rituals in South Asia.* Columbia: University of South Carolina Press, 1993. Chapter 2 focuses on the role of miracle narratives in the household rituals of Shīʿī women in Karachi, Pakistan.

Sharīʿatī, ʿAlī. "Fatima Is Fatima." In *Shariati on Shariati and the Muslim Woman*, translated by Laleh Bakhtiar, pp. 75–214. Chicago: Kazi, 1996. Based on a series of lectures delivered in Tehran in 1971 in which Fatimah is portrayed as a revolutionary model for Iranian women and men.

Sharif, Tayba Hassan Al Khalifa. "Sacred Narratives Linking Iraqi Shiite Women across Time and Space." In *Muslim Networks: From Hajj to Hip Hop*, edited by miriam cooke and Bruce B. Lawrence, pp. 132–154. Chapel Hill: University of North Carolina Press, 2005. Focuses on Iraqi Shīʿī women refugees in the Netherlands and how they have used the religious narratives of Karbala to tell their own personal stories of exile and loss.

KAREN G. RUFFLE

ṢŪFĪ DEVOTIONAL LITERATURE

The poetic, biographic, and didactic compositions of Ṣūfī devotional literature from the ninth through twelfth centuries drew a strong connection between the earliest foundations of Islam, particularly the *sunnah* of the Prophet Muḥammad, and Ṣūfī belief and praxis. Perhaps because of this, the wives and daughters of the Prophet also served as models of faith and devotion for female Ṣūfī practitioners, particularly through the *ṭabaqāt* genre of sacred biography. The corpus of Ṣūfī devotional literature that emerged from the thirteenth to eighteenth centuries added philosophical, narrative poetry, epic, and metaphysical works that borrowed heavily from pre-Islamic Persian literary forms. Here, too, women are represented among the ranks of the Ṣūfīs, while the development of tropes of the feminine reached its zenith in this period. Since the explosion of print culture in the late nineteenth and early twentieth centuries, Ṣūfī devotional literature has adopted and adapted new media forms as these emerged in the public sphere, from chapbooks to the Internet and new social networking media. It has also continued to chronicle the lives of female Ṣūfī saints, although the devotional activities of ordinary women, particularly as these involve patronage of Ṣūfī shrines and *pīrs*, are sometimes condemned. Essential themes of devotion to God and his representatives on Earth, the spiritual development of the individual, and the importance of service to others have remained intact within this body of literature, but its audience has broadened. It comprises a broad collection of genres, including reprints of medieval books and treatises; hagiographies, including biographical collections; discourses, usually compiled and arranged by the disciple(s) of a renowned *shaykh*; letters, particularly correspondences between *shaykhs* and their disciples; *ta'wil*, or esoteric interpretations of the Qur'ān; collections of devotional poetry; popular literature on healing, magic, numerology, and similar topics; and a variety of didactic and ethico-moral writing.

Early Ṣūfī Devotional Literature: Ninth to Twelfth Centuries. There is little evidence of the poetry and metaphysical formulas penned by female Ṣūfīs before the ninth century; even the poetry and composed by the famous eighth/ninth century mystic woman of Baghdad, Rabi'a al-'Adawiyya (d. 801), survives only in the literature written by subsequent generations. The work of al-Jāḥiẓ (d. 868) contains the earliest known written accounts of Rābi'ah, including some of her poetry. Rābi'ah, rumored to have spent some time as a singer before embarking on the Ṣūfī path, elevated the secular love poetry associated with this class of women during the Umayyad and early Abbasid eras into esoteric teachings on the relationship between God and the mystic seeker. She is credited with bringing the theme of love as the ideal path to God into the world of Ṣūfīs, ushering it into a central place in Ṣūfī poetry and mystical practice. However, the development of love poetry, and love as the quintessential mystic path to God, had been unfolding even prior to Rābi'ah's time; elements of the pre-Islamic *qaṣīdah* (ode), *khamrīyah* (wine-poem), and Persian Sasanian courtly love poetry had been its primary sources.

The ninth to twelfth centuries saw the development of numerous additional forms of Ṣūfī devotional literature, among them "shath" (ecstatic sayings), biographies (especially the genres *ṭabaqāt* and *tadhkira*), treatises outlining different beliefs and methods of pursuing the spiritual life, and ethical literature combined with manuals of practice. None of these were intended for general public audiences, nor did they take the place of personal instruction under the tutelage of a spiritual master (*shaykh* or *pīr*). Instead, these various forms of devotional literature served to highlight particular developments in Ṣūfī metaphysical thought and defend viewpoints that were under attack. Besides the narratives of Rābi'ah's life and work, the few stories of women included in such works as al-Sarrāj's (d. 988) *Kitāb al-lum'a*; al-Kalābādhī's (d. 1000) *Kitāb al-ta'arruf li-madhhab ahl-al-tasawwuf* and *Ma'ani al-akhbār*, and al-Ghazālī's (d. 1111) *Ihya' ulūm al-dīn*, should be understood in this vein, rather than as a testament to these women's accomplishments alone. Among the numerous genres of Ṣūfī ethico-didactic literature, *futuwwa* (spiritual chivalry) manuals served to both highlight the importance of upholding certain moral precepts and to emphasize particular forms, or branches, of Ṣūfī praxis. In this regard, the work of Abu Abd al-Raḥmān al-Sulamī (d. 1021), author of *Kitāb al-futuwwa al-ṣufīyya* (Book of Ṣūfī Chivalry), is particularly important for outlining what Rkia Cornell has argued was a woman mystic's counterpart to this praxis.

Cornell's translation of al-Sulamī's *Dhikr al-niswa* understands al-Sulami's use of the term *niswan*, derived from *niswa* (a spiritual category of women), to mean "practitioners of female chivalry." If al-Sulami did intend to trace a quintessentially "women's" spiritual discipline, however, his effort stands out for its uniqueness. Many of the women whose stories are relayed in the sacred biographies of this time period remain unnamed, identified primarily by their actions or their encounters with notable male spiritual seekers. Some are identified by their first names, or by their family or geographic affiliations. By the end of this period, the inclusion of biographies of women, usually as an appendix to a major work on Ṣūfīs and other important figures from Islamic sacred history, had become an accepted literary convention, exemplified by such works as Ibn Sa'd's (d. 845) *Tabaqat al-Kubr* and Abu Nu`aym al-Isfahānī's (d. 1038) *Ḥilya al-Awliya*.

Medieval and Early Modern Ṣūfī Devotional Literature: Thirteenthth to Eighteenth Centuries. The thirteenth century marks the flowering of Ṣūfī devotional literature and its development as a popular idiom of poetic and narrative expression. With it began the age of Jalāl al-dīn Rūmī (d. 1273) and Ibn al-ʾArabī (d. 1240), whose poetry and narratives have remained a central influence on Ṣūfī thought and devotional life. The thirteenth century also witnessed the expansion of creeds and guidelines developed by earlier Ṣūfīs, reflecting an increased preoccupation with the "inner sciences" (metaphysical knowledge, gnosis), and with sacred history (including the history of Sufism). In this period too, idioms expressing the human–divine relationship became standard fare in Ṣūfī and Ṣūfī-themed writing. Depictions of women were, at best, ambivalent: although some authors praised the spiritual prowess of extraordinary women, most depicted women as morally deficient, imperfect in their faith, and obstacles on the (male) mystic's path to God. Poetic and narrative uses of the feminine principle, however, served as a mark of, and guide to, the ideal stance of the mystic. Ṣūfī literature drew liberally from the symbolism of womanhood, casting gender reversal—in which the male poet or mystic takes on the persona or qualities of a woman—as a means to overcoming the selfish ego (*nafs*), and as an exemplary way to reach the Divine. Notably, the elaboration of the trope of lover and Beloved, in which the mystic lover longs for a glimpse of the Divine Beloved, abasing himself and ultimately ceding his entire being to a vision of Divine Unity, became the quintessential model of mystic endeavor. Women, too, were also cast in this mold of spiritual seeker in Ṣūfī (and Ṣūfī-inspired) poetry and narratives.

In one form of expression, the trope of the mystic lover courting death to reach his or her Divine beloved was recast in the language of star-crossed lovers doomed to die and thus achieve union or *fana'*, the ultimate goal of the mystic in classical Ṣūfī formulations. This trope dominated Persian and Persianate Ṣūfī writing from the fourteenth century, as seen in depictions of the wandering, grief-stricken female soul, in the guise of legendary South Asian heroines such as Hīr and Sassī, who achieved final union with their beloved Ranjha and Punnu. The retelling of the Persian romance of Khusrau, Shīrīn, and Farhād, popularized by the poet Niẓāmī (d. 1209), was adapted and recast in musings on human–divine love by Ṣūfī mystics from Ḥāfiz (d. 1390) to Ḥaẓrat ʾInayat Khān (d. 1927). In the 26,000-verse *Mathnawi* of Jalāl al-dīn Rūmī (d. 1273), the mystic journey to God is expressed in feminine terms through short moralistic tales, while other Ṣūfī poets elaborated tales popular throughout the Muslim lands: Yusūf and Zulaykha, taken from the Biblical and Qurʾānic story of Joseph as a slave in the house of Potiphar; the Prophet Muḥammad's *mi'rāj*, or journey to Heaven; and Layla and Majnūn, an Arab legend in which the hero, deprived of his beloved flesh-and-blood Layla, loses his mind but gains a vision of the eternal Divine. Metaphysical–philosophical treatises also expounded the meanings of female and feminine as qualities of humanity and reflections of aspects of the Divine, as in the examples of Ibn al-ʾArabī's *al-Futūḥāt al-Makkiyya* and *Al-Insān al-kullī*.

Although mystic poetry and narrative didactic tales dominated the landscape of medieval Ṣūfī devotional literature, the production of biographical writing continued to expand. As the Ṣūfī orders proliferated, demand for knowledge about the founders—and representatives—of these mystic associations increased. The convention of appending the stories of women to large collections of sacred memorials continued, too. Ibn al-Jawzī (d. 1200) included 240 Ṣūfī women among his biographies of saints, but his successors were, comparatively, less attentive to including women among the ranks of the saints. Farīd al-Dīn' Attar's (d. 1220) *Tadhkirāt al-Awliya* contains the story of only one female saint, Rābi'a al-'Adawiyya. Jamī's (1492) work, *Nafaḥāt al-uns,* contains 570 biographies of Ṣūfī men and 34 biographies of Ṣūfī women. Maulana Fazlullāh Jamālī's (d. 1535 or 1536) *Siyar al-'Arifin* and Abdul Muḥaddith Dihlawī's (d. 1642) *Akhbār al-Akhyār* each incorporate the stories of only a handful of holy women. By the eighteenth century, *tadhkiras* had become a major source of information about saints whose fame was well known within and across the Muslim-majority lands.

Ṣūfī Devotional Literature from the Nineteenth Century: Beyond the Society of Mystics. The nineteenth century saw a renewed interest in the classical literature of Sufism; this was fueled in part by Muslims' encounters with European colonialism, and in part by the birth of what has been labeled "neo-Sufism," characterized by a spirit of renewal and reform (*tajdid wa-islah*), by the activism of its adherents, and by its attention to the foundational sources of Islam. Reform-minded Ṣūfīs were among the most prolific writers, producing didactic literature that defended their practice of Sufism as being in accordance with Islamic Sharī'ah, while the ideal Ṣūfī *shaykh* was regarded as much for his ability to serve as moral exemplar of Islam as for his ability to perform miracles. The biographical literature of this period emphasized the genealogy of the *shaykh* as part of the evidence for his moral character. This fueled popular demand for details about the spiritual accomplishments of his female relatives. In some cases, the life stories and work of women of saintly lineages served to highlight the prestige of an entire Ṣūfī order, as in the case of Nana Asma'u (d. 1864) poet, diplomat, educator, and daughter of *Shaykh* 'Uthmān dan Fodio, founder of the Sokoto Caliphate in today's Nigeria.

Since the early twentieth century, Ṣūfīs have addressed female audiences, penning didactic-etiquette literature, as in the case of Maulana Ashraf 'Ali Thanawī's *Bihishtī Zewar* (d. 1943). Works like these also contained the stories of saintly women of Islamic and Ṣūfī heritage. The twentieth-century Ṣūfī master both drew upon older trends and established new ones by writing biographies exclusively dedicated to female saints, as in the case of the Ni'matullāhī *shaykh*, Dr. Javad Nurbakhsh's (d. 2008) *Sufi Women*, published in 1983. By the close of the twentieth century, many Ṣūfī orders from Asia, Africa, and the Middle East had spread outward to Europe, Australia, and the Americas. A legacy as well as a sign of their widespread appeal has been the willingness of some orders to engage discussions of the increasing relevance—and visibility—of women in the orders. The proliferation of cheaply printed demotic literature (of various genres) since the late nineteenth century has reflected this relevance and visibility. In some cases, it has allowed women on the margins of formal membership in the Ṣūfī orders to develop their own healing practices, drawing upon information in books on "magic," and Qur'ānic prayer formulations to attract clients who are willing to pay them for remedies such as amulets. In other cases, it has been the women of Ṣūfī orders who have taken it upon themselves to highlight the accomplishments of women Ṣūfīs, thus underscoring the importance of women to the development of some of the central concepts, institutions, and practices of Sufism.

Bibliography

Elias, Jamal. "Female and Feminine in Islamic Mysticism." *Muslim World* 78, no. 3–4 (July–October 1988): 209–224.

Mojaddedi, Jawid. *The Biographical Tradition in Sufism: The tabaqat genre from al-Sulāmī to Jāmī.* Richmond, Surrey, U.K.: Curzon Press, 2001.
Murata, Sachiko. *The Tao of Islam.* Albany: State University of New York Press, 1992.
Nasr, Seyyed Hossein. "Persian Sufi Literature: Its Spiritual and Cultural Significance." In *The Legacy of Medieval Persian Sufism*, edited by Leonard Lewisohn, pp. 1–10. London: Khanaqahi Nimatullahi Publications, 1992.
Nurbakhsh, Javad. *Sufi Women.* New York: Khanaqahi Nimatullahi Publications, 1983.
Pemberton, Kelly. *Women Mystics and Sufi Shrines in India.* Columbia, S.C.: University of South Carolina Press, 2010.
Roded, Ruth. *Women in Islamic Biographical Collections: From Ibn Sa'd to Who's Who.* Boulder, Colo.: Lynne Rienner, 1994.
Schimmel, Annemarie. *My Soul Is a Woman: The Feminine in Islam.* New York: Continuum Books, 1997.
Smith, Margaret *Muslim Women Mystics: The Life and Work of Rabi'a and Other Women Mystics in Islam.* Oxford: Oneworld Books, 1994. Reprint, 2001.
Al-Sulami, Abu Abd al'Rahman. *Dhikr an-niswa al-muta'abbidat aṣ-sufiyyat.* Translated, with an introduction, by Rkia Cornell as *Early Sufi Women: Dhikr an-niswa al-muta'abbidat aṣ-sufiyyat.* Louisville, Ky.: Fons Vitae, 2005.

Kelly Pemberton

Sunnī Devotional Literature

Sunnī devotional literature is one of the most popular types of Islamic literature, written for the believers to develop or heighten feelings of devotion toward God, the prophets, and Muslim mystics. The purpose of devotional literature is to explain religion and give strength and comfort in affliction and spiritual uplifting. This kind of literature includes but is not limited to prayers, hymns, songs, autobiographical narratives about the prophets' and saints' lives, and guides to prayer and spiritual growth. Based on Qur'ānic teachings and the *sunnah* of the Prophet Muḥammad, its main concern is the exemplary Muslim life, emphasizing the relationship between the individual and the community and the individual and the divine. Despite the fact that gender themes occupy a significant portion of Sunnī devotional literature, creating a significant space for feminine sanctity, very little research has been done on the origins, influence, and significance of gender in Sunnī devotional literature.

The Qur'ān is the primary devotional literature for Sunnī women. In Sunnī tradition, women participate actively in devotional expression. The Qur'ān refers to several specific women who triumphed spiritually, despite worldly trials: Asiya, the wife of Pharaoh, who was thought to be the same woman who saved the life of the infant Moses; Mary, the virgin mother of Jesus (66:11–12); and the Queen of Sheba as a model of wisdom and leadership (27:23–44). Qur'ānic devotions on prayer are used for educating, equipping, and encouraging women to know, love, enjoy God, others, and themselves. For instance, Muslim women recite special devotional prayers from the Qur'ān from the time of conception through delivery, including prayers to help a woman conceive and others for having a healthy, beautiful, and God-fearing child. An example of such prayer is the prayer of the Prophet Zakariah in his old age for his barren wife: "O my Lord! Grant me from You, a good offspring. You are indeed the All-Hearer of invocation" (3:38). The ḥadīth literature calls the woman who dies during pregnancy and childbirth a martyr. Therefore, the Qur'ān encourages a prayer for parents: "My Lord! Forgive me and my parents. Bestow Your mercy on them as they took care of me when I was young" (17:24).

The second and most prominent gender theme in Sunnī devotional literature is related to the birth of the Prophet Muḥammad, known as *mawlid*. In Sunnī circles, the 12th of Rabi'al-Awwal is more famous than other months of the Muslim calendar. The *mawlid* was first celebrated by the Shīʿī Fatimid dynasty in Egypt between 969 and 1171 CE. Some prominent Sunnī leaders also started to observe it as a special celebration. The first *mawlid* text by a Sunnī scholar was written by Muḥammad ibn Salama al Quda'i (d. 1062 CE), who was a prominent Shāfiʿī judge and historian (Katz, 2007). The *mawlid* texts have historically been recited during the celebration of the Prophet's birth and include narratives about the Prophet's mother Amina. For instance, the *mawlud* in Turkish by Süleyman Çelebi in the fifteenth century describes the physical experience of Amina's delivery, when she was giving birth to the Prophet, and how a white bird came floating and stroked her back to relieve her pain. When this verse of the poem is recited, the women participants in the *mevlud* (Turkish spelling of *mawlid*) ceremony are sprinkled by the cantor with rosewater and stroke each other's backs.

The third type of Sunnī devotional literature in which women especially excelled is visionary or spiritual autobiography. Khadīja, ʿĀ'ishah, and Fāṭimah are the ultimate archetypes in Sunnī devotional literature, which presents their narratives as inspiring examples of the perfect women. The influence of this kind of literature is so profound that Fāṭimah became the most popular name throughout the Muslim world. The Sunnīs shared with Shīʿīs devotional literature celebrating Fāṭimah as a figure. Her other popular names are common between both Muslim communities, such as Batul owing to her modesty, al-Mubarakah (the blessed), al-Zakiyah (the virtuous), al-Siddiqah (the righteous), al-Radiyah (the satisfied), al-Muhaddithah (the eloquent), al-Zahra (the blossomed), and al-Tahirah (the pure). Moreover, she was often compared to the Virgin Mary, bringing the reader's attention to the similarities between these two blessed women. The mother of Fāṭimah is the pious Khadīja, who, like the Virgin Mary's mother St. Anne, herself became a mother of the sacrificial son, Ḥusayn. In some societies, such as Egypt, popular religious practices even overlap around the two figures in Muslim and Christian local religious folk celebrations. The devotional literature as well as the practice of women glorifies the female presence in the religious imaginary. Many Sunnī *mawlid* style works, such as Süleyman Çelebi's *Wasila al-Najat*, devote a special chapter to her "death," which is titled *The Death of Fatima al-Zahra*, or Fāṭimah's Features. This section of *Wasila al-Najat* describes the last days of the Prophet and how Fāṭimah welcomes Azrael (the Angel of Death), who came to take the Prophet's soul. After the death of Muḥammad, Fāṭimah expresses her deep sorrow and never ceases her mourning. Although Fuzuli, a famous medival Azerbaijani poet, was a Shīʿī, his *Hadiqat al-Saadah*, with a full chapter on Fāṭimah (Chapter Four), was used by Sunnī Turkish Muslims to learn about her life. Perhaps the most famous story about Fāṭimah in Sunnī devotional prayer is the following narration: One day Fāṭimah asked her father, Muḥammad, to provide her with a servant to help her in household chores. However, instead of giving her a servant, Muḥammad advised her to say *subhan-Allah, alhamdulillah*, and *Allahu-akbar* [Glory to God, All praise is due to God, and God is the Greatest] thirty-three times each when she went to bed, which would be better than having the servant that she had asked for.

Similar spiritual and devotional autobiographies were often written by both men and women. However, men were more active in producing devotional literature than women because of social and political circumstances. Nonetheless, vocal heritage is more influenced by women's religious narratives than the devotional written literature. Sufism also allows more contribution by women in formulating images, as men have more influence on devotional literature related to *fiqh*. For instance, in the Sunnī world, different narrations about the life of a famous mystic, Rābiʿa-ʿAdawīya al-Qaysiyya of Basra (d. 801), by three famous Sunnī Sufi writers, Abū Hamīd bin Abū Bakr Ibrāhīm (1145/1146–1221 CE), Farīd ud-Dīn, and ʿAttār, are well-known. The purpose of this book was to express the importance of this woman who established the Doctrine of Selfless Love, which is well expressed in her prayer: "O my Lord, if I worship Thee from fear of Hell, put me in hell, and if I worship Three in hope of Paradise, exclude me thence, but if I worship Thee for Thine own sake, then withhold not form me Thine Eternal Beauty" (Smith, 1994, p. 50). As a mystic, Rābiʿa's major contribution to ritual prayers was her emphasis on the centrality of the love of God in religious experience. She declared that her love for God allowed no room for love even of his prophet. Rābiʿa "gives a clear idea of a woman renouncing this world and its attractions and giving up her life to the service of God" (Smith, 1994, p. 9). In Sunnī communities, females, therefore, could play an important role as the spiritual leaders (shaykhas) for their students and disciples. For instance, one of the spiritual leaders of Muḥammad Ibn ʿAli Ibn ʿArabī's (b. 1165 CE) was Fāṭimah of Cordoba, who was in her nineties then.

In general, the early autobiographies of Fāṭimah, Khadīja, and other famous Muslim women are models for the Muslim life and guides to devotion. Similar autobiographies were often written in later centuries by Ṣūfī orders. However, there is a lack of research in the field of identifying and translating Sunnī women's devotional literature. There is a need to explore answers to many questions, including the oral and written methods of composition of these ritualistic prayers and stories, their audience, their awareness of a female visionary tradition, and so on. Nevertheless, the devotional literature for Sunnī women describes an area of female experience of mysticism, spirituality, and subjective experience of the divine, which was intended to nurture the devotional meditations. Women not only learned these meditations, but also contributed to its formation and richness and provided the structure and content of the devotional literature. Moreover, it proved that Muslim women could teach men what God or His prophet and Muslim saints had taught.

REFERENCES

Isgandarova, Nazila. "Islamic Spiritual Care in a Health Care Setting." In *Spirituality and Health: Multidisciplinary Explorations*, edited by A. Meier, T. O'Connor, and P. Van Katwyk. Waterloo, ON: WLU Press, 2005: 85–104.

Isgandarova, Nazila. "Muslim Spiritual Care and Counselling." In *The Spiritual Care Givers Guide to Identity, Practice and Relationships: Transforming the Honeymoon in Spiritual Care and Therapy*, edited by T. O'Connor, E. Meakes, and C. Lashmar. Waterloo, ON: WLU Press, 2008: 235–243.

Isgandarova, Nazila. "Mosques as Communities of Memories vis-à-vis Muslim Identity and Integration in the European Union." *European Journal of Economic and Political Studies* 2, no. 2 (2009): 61–70.

Isgandarova, Nazila. "The Compassionate Engagement in Islam." [*yjhm.yale.edu/essays/nisgandarova20100302.htm*] *Yale Journal for Humanities in Medicine*.

Isgandarova, Nazila. "The Contribution of Muslim Charities in the West to International Development." *OIDA International Journal of Sustainable Development* 1, no. 1 (2010): 39–44.

Isgandarova, Nazila. "The Concept of Effective Islamic Spiritual Care." *The Journal of Rotterdam Islamic and Social Sciences* 2, no. 1 (2011): 101–103.

Isgandarova, Nazila. "What the Spiritual Caregiver Should Know While Dealing with Survivors of Ethnic Violence." *Khazar Journal of Humanities and Social Sciences* 14, no. 3 (2011): 35–50.

Katz, M. H. *The Birth of the Prophet Muḥammad: Devotional Piety in Sunni Islam*. Abingdon, U.K.: Routledge, 2007.

Smith, M. (1994). *Rābiʿa: The Life and Works of Rābiʿa and Other Women Mystics in Islam*. Oxford: One world Publications, 1994.

NAZILA ISGANDAROVA

GHAMIDI, JAVED AHMAD. (b. 1951), Pakistani scholar of Islam. Ghamidi is known for a number of different views on religious law that differ from many other scholars, particularly on issues concerning women.

Ghamidi was born in a small village outside Lahore, Pakistan. He graduated from Islamia High School, Pakpattan, in 1967 and Government College, Lahore, with a bachelor's degree in English in 1972.

He was an early member of Pakistan's Jamāʿat-i Islāmī political party. In the 1970s Ghamidi's thought began to diverge from the modernist interpretations endorsed by the Jamāʿat, particular those of its founder, Abul Ala Maududi. He was subsequently expelled from the Jamāʿat in 1977 and began a sustained critique of Maududi's thought.

In his scholarship Ghamidi is a traditionalist: his views on contemporary issues are informed through reference to the Qurʾān and sunnah, or traditions of Muḥammad. His three major books include his annotated Qurʾān *al-Bayān*, his legal philosophical treatise, *Burhān*, and *Mīzān*. As Ghamidi's major exegetical work, *Mizān* is his application of Qurʾānic law to a gamut of social and political issues.

Ghamidi interprets the Qurʾān through a form of coherence theory. Unlike most traditionalist scholars, who interpret the Qurʾān primarily on the *āyāt* or verse level, he insists that the text should be interpreted primarily in terms of whole *suwar* or chapters. He argues that Muslims in the present day are not under obligation to wage military jihad to spread Islam, but only as a last resort to end oppression. He also argues that the stoning punishment for apostasy was specific to the Prophet's time.

Ghamidi is also notable for his views on women. He does not regard women's head covering as mandated under Islamic law, but rather a desirable Islamic custom. He has also asserted that a woman's testimony in court is equal to that of a man's. While he holds some exceptional views regarding women and religious law, much of his underlying perspective on gender roles follows traditionalist thought. He has written that men and women do have different capacities an, in the family specifically God has granted men a degree over women.

In 2006 Ghamidi's view on proposed women's rights legislation put him in the center of the political spotlight in Pakistan. At the time he was the head of the Council of Islamic Ideology, advising the government on proposed reforms to the *hudūd* laws, dealing with rape and other serious crimes. Ghamidi has long argued they are un-Islamic, and was a prominent voice pushing for reform.

After the 2011 assassination of Punjab's governor Salmaan Taseer during attempts to reform Pakistan's blasphemy laws, Ghamidi was one of a few public personalities who continued to speak out against the laws. The death threats that began against Ghamidi and his family in 2006 increased, and he chose to flee with his family to Malaysia, where he currently resides.

BIBLIOGRAPHY

Hassan, Riffat. "Islamic Modernist and Reformist Discourse in South Asia." In *Reformist Voices of Islam: Mediating Islam and Modernity*, edited by Shireen T. Hunter. Armonk, N.Y.: M.E. Sharpe, 2007.

Masud, M. K. "Rethinking Shari'a: Javed Ahmad Ghamidi on hudud." *Die Welt des Islams* 47, no. 3–4 (2007): 356–375.

ABBAS JAFFER

GHAZĀLĪ, ZAYNAB AL- (1917–2005). Born 2 January 1917 in Egypt, Zaynab al-Ghazālī al-Jabīlī (pronounced "Gabīlī") was a prominent writer and teacher of the Muslim Brotherhood and the founder of the Muslim Women's Association (1936–1964). The daughter of an al-Azhar University–educated independent religious teacher and cotton merchant, she was privately tutored in Islamic studies at home, in addition to attending public school through the secondary level. She obtained certificates in ḥadīth, preaching, and Qur'ānic exegesis. Her father encouraged her to become a Muslim leader, citing the example of Nusaybah bint Ka'b al-Māzinīyah, a woman who fought alongside the Prophet in the Battle of Uhud. Although for a short time she joined Hudā Sha'rāwī's Egyptian Feminist Union, she came to see this as a mistaken path for women, believing that women's rights were guaranteed in Islam.

At the age of eighteen, al-Ghazālī founded Jamā'at al-Sayyidāt al-Muslimāt (Muslim Women's Association), which, she claimed, had a membership of 3 million throughout the country by the time it was dissolved by government decree in 1964. Her weekly lectures to women at the Ibn Ṭulūn Mosque drew a crowd of three thousand, which grew to five thousand during the holy months of the year. Besides offering lessons for women, the association published a magazine, maintained an orphanage, offered assistance to poor families, and mediated family disputes. The association also took a political stance, demanding that Egypt be ruled by the Qur'ān.

The similarity of its goals to those of the Muslim Brotherhood was noted by the Brotherhood's founder, Ḥasan al-Bannā, who requested that al-Ghazālī's association merge with the Muslim Sisters, the women's branch of his organization. She refused until 1949, shortly before his assassination, when, sensing that it was critical for all Muslims to unite behind his leadership, she gave him her oath of allegiance and offered him her association. He accepted her oath and said that the Muslim Women's Association could remain independent. During the 1950s, the Muslim Women's Association cooperated with the Muslim Sisters to provide for families who had lost wealth and family members as a result of President Gamal Abdel Nasser's crackdown on the Muslim Brotherhood.

Al-Ghazālī was instrumental in regrouping the Muslim Brotherhood in the early 1960s. Imprisoned for her activities in 1965, she was sentenced to twenty-five years of hard labor but was released under Anwar el-Sadat's presidency in 1971. She describes her prison experiences, which included suffering many heinous forms of torture, in a book entitled *Ayyām min ḥayātī* (*Days from My Life*, 1978). She depicts herself as enduring torture with strength beyond that of most men, and she attests to both miracles and visions that strengthened her and enabled her to survive. She describes herself as the object of Nasser's personal hatred, for she and her colleague 'Abd al-Fattāḥ Ismā'īl "robbed" him of the generation that had been raised on his propaganda. She believed that the superpowers were involved in singling her out to Nasser as a threat, and indeed affirmed that Islam's mission means the annihilation of the power of the United States and the Soviet Union. Nonetheless she denied that the Muslim Brotherhood intended to assassinate Nasser, for "killing the unjust ruler does not do away with the problem" of a society that needs to be entirely reeducated in Islamic values (*Ayyām min ḥayātī*, 1978, p. 185). In her book she condemned tactics of murder, torture, and terrorism and denied that the Muslim Brotherhood wanted to usurp power. Later however she justified the threat of violence against unbelievers in order to bring them forcibly "from darkness to light," comparing such tactics to snatching poison from the hands of a child (interview with the author, June 1981). She defined the Muslim Brotherhood as the association of all Muslims and said that Muslims who did not belong to it were deficient, although she did not go so far as to call them unbelievers. At that time she supported the Iranian Revolution, but in a later interview (13 September 1988), she said that both the Shiism of the regime and the tactics of violence against its citizens had led her to conclude that it was not really an Islamic state.

The Muslim Women's Association was taken from al-Ghazālī's hands in 1965 and merged with a rival association of the same name founded by a former member of her group. The rival group was a religious voluntary association. Such associations, which number in the thousands, have played a major role in the religious life of women in Egypt since the twentieth century, offering lessons in the Qurʾān and Islamic law, classes in sewing and other crafts, and preschools for children, among other social services.

After her release from prison al-Ghazālī resumed teaching and writing, first for the revived Muslim Brotherhood's monthly magazine, *Al-Daʿwah*, banned by Sadat in September 1981, and then for another Islamist publication, *Liwāʾ al-Islām*, and also contributed articles to other Islamic journals. In addition to her articles and prison memoirs, al-Ghazālī published six other books, including a commentary on the first fourteen chapters of the Qurʾān, *Naẓarāt fī Kitāb Allah* (Reflections on the Book of God, 1944).

Al-Ghazālī described herself as a "mother" to the Muslim Sisters, as well as to the young men she helped organize in the early 1960s. She was editor of a women's and children's section in *Al-Daʿwah*, in which she encouraged women to become educated, but to be obedient to their husbands and stay at home while raising their children. She blamed many of the ills of society on the absence of mothers from the home. This conservative stance appears to be contradicted by the historical figures she used as models of womanhood in short vignettes in that same section, courageous women warriors from the early period of Islam, including members of the extremist Khārijī sect, which was virtually obliterated in warfare with the larger Muslim community.

Al-Ghazālī's own example as an activist in the public sphere who divorced her first husband for interfering with her Islamic activities and threatened her second husband with the same also appears to contradict her own advice, raising the question of the extent to which she can serve as a model for other women. When asked about this, she said that her case was special, because God had given her the "blessing"—although not viewed as such by most people—of not having conceived any children. This gave her a great deal of freedom. Her husband was also quite wealthy, so she had servants to do her housework. She further regarded it as a boon that her husband was a polygamist, for whenever he went to see one of his other wives, "it was like a vacation" for her. She insisted, nonetheless, that she remained obedient to her husband. She believed that Islam allows women to be active in all aspects of public life, as long as that does not interfere with their first and most sacred duty: to be a wife and mother. Her second husband died while she was in prison (having divorced her under threat of imprisonment himself). Having fulfilled her duty of marriage, she felt free to devote all of her energies to the Islamic cause.

Academics have debated the discrepancy between al-Ghazālī's prescriptions for women's social roles and her own activism, some seeing her as hypocritically arrogating special privileges to herself that she would deny to other women, while others described her as an "Islamic feminist." Al-Ghazālī herself saw feminism as a Western conspiracy to undermine Islam and rob women of their humanity, although she also claimed that Islam makes men and women equal. In her later writings she affirmed women's independent personality and right to balance public activism with domestic duties.

Although the Islamic movement throughout the Muslim world today has attracted large numbers of young women, especially since the 1970s, Zaynab al-Ghazālī and Nadia Yassine of Morocco stand out thus far as the only women to distinguish themselves as major Islamist leaders.

[*See also* Egypt; Shaʿrāwī, Hudā; *and* Women's Movements.]

BIBLIOGRAPHY

Primary Works

Al-Dāʿiyya Zaynab al-Ghazālī: Masīrat jihād wa-hadīth min al-dhikriyāt min khilāl kitābātihā [The Activist Zaynab al-Ghazālī: A Journey of Struggle and a Narration of Memories through Her Writings]. Edited by Ibn al-Hāshimī Cairo: Dār al- Iʿtiṣām, 1989.

Ayyām min ḥayātī [Days from My Life]. Cairo and Beirut: Dar al-Shuruq, 1978. English translation: *Return of the Pharaoh: Memoir in Nasir's Prison.* Translated by Mokrane Guezzou. Leicester, U.K.: Islamic Foundation, 1994.

Humūm al-marʾah al-muslimah wa-al-dāʿiyah Zaynab al-Ghazālī [Concerns of the Muslim Woman and the Activist Zaynab al-Ghazālī]. Edited by Ibn al-Hāshimī. Cairo: Dar al- Iʿtiṣām, 1990.

Ilā ibnatī [To My Daughter]. 2 vols in one. Cairo: Dār al-Tawzīʿ wa-l-Nashr al-Islāmiyya, 1994. A series of very brief pieces on social problems.

Malik wa-āmāl al-shaʿb [A King and the Hopes of the People]. Cairo: Dār al-Kitāb, 1954.

Min khawāṭir Zaynab al-Ghazālī fī shuʾūn al-dīn wa-al-ḥayāt [From the Reflections of Zaynab al-Ghazālī on Matters of Religion and Life]. Cairo: Dār al- Iʿtiṣām, 1996.

Mushkilāt al-shabāb wa-al-fatayāt fī marḥalat al-murāhiqa: Rudūd ʿalā al-rasāʾil [The Problems of Youths and Girls in Adolescence: Responses to Letters]. Cairo: Dār al-Tawzīʿ wa-l-Nashr al-Islamiyya, 1996.

Naḥwa baʿth jadīd [Toward a New Renaissance]. Cairo: Dār al-Shurūq, 1986.

Naẓarāt fī Kitāb Allāh [Reflections on the Book of God]. Edited by ʿAbd al-Ḥayy al-Faramāwī. Cairo: Dar al-Shurūq, 1994. A commentary on Suras 1–14.

Secondary Works

Ahmed, Leila. *Women and Gender in Islam: Historical Roots of a Modern Debate.* New Haven, Conn.: Yale University Press, 1992.

Badran, Margot. "Competing Agenda: Feminists, Islam and the State in Nineteenth- and Twentieth-Century Egypt." In *Women, Islam and the State*, edited by Deniz Kandiyoti, pp. 201–236. Philadelphia: Temple University Press, 1991.

cooke, miriam. *Women Claim Islam: Creating Islamic Feminism Through Literature.* London and New York: Routledge, 2001.

Hatem, Mervat. "Secularist and Islamist Discourses on Modernity in Egypt and the Evolution of the Postcolonial Nation-State." In *Islam, Gender and Social Change*, edited by Yvonne Yazbeck Haddad and John L. Esposito, pp. 85–99. New York and Oxford: Oxford University Press, 1998.

Hoffman, Valerie J. "An Islamic Activist: Zaynab al-Ghazâlî." In *Women and the Family in the Middle East: New Voices of Change*, edited by Elizabeth Warnock Fernea, pp. 233–254. Austin: University of Texas Press, 1985.

Hoffman, Valerie J. Interviews with Zaynab al-Ghazālī. June 1981 and September 13, 1988.

Hoffman, Valerie J. "Muslim Fundamentalists: Psychosocial Profiles." In *Fundamentalisms Comprehended*, edited by Martin E. Marty and R. Scott Appleby, pp. 199–230. Chicago: University of Chicago Press, 1995.

Karam, Azza. *Women, Islamisms, and the State.* New York: St. Martin's Press, 1998.

Mahmood, Saba. *Politics of Piety: The Islamic Revival and the Feminist Subject.* 2d ed. Princeton, N.J.: Princeton University Press, 2012.

Shehadeh, Lamia Rustum. *The Idea of Women in Fundamentalist Islam.* Gainesville: University Press of Florida, 2003.

Talhami, Ghada Hashem. *The Mobilization of Muslim Women in Egypt.* Gainesville: University Press of Florida, 1996.

Zuhur, Sherifa. *Revealing Reveiling: Islamist Gender Ideology in Contemporary Egypt.* Albany: State University Press of New York, 1992.

VALERIE J. HOFFMAN

GORANI, HALA. (b. 1970), American journalist. Hala Basha-Gorani is an anchor and correspondent for CNN International who has reported on the Middle East for many years. She was born on 1 March 1970 in Seattle, Washington. Her parents are from Aleppo, Syria. She grew up in Washington, D.C., and Paris. She holds a bachelor of science in economics from George Mason University and a graduate degree from the Institut d'études politiques.

As a teenager, Gorani had watched the film *The Killing Fields* (1984), which highlighted the important role of a journalist in war-torn Cambodia. This film sparked her interest in becoming a reporter. Her first work was published in her school magazine soon afterward.

While in France Gorani started work as a journalist for the newspaper, *La Voix du Nord*, and also started writing for Agence France-Presse. In 1994 she joined France 3, the second largest French public television channel. She next moved to London to work for Bloomberg Television. In 1998 she moved to Atlanta, Georgia, to work for CNN.

Fluent in English, French, and Arabic, Gorani has reported from every country in the Middle East. Fascinated by the variety of lifestyles there, she was based for a time in Dubai, which she described as "like a gem which is growing all the time." Her understanding of the region has seen her put together controversial pieces, including one on poverty in Bahrain and another on everyday security problems for Iraqis.

Gorani's career has intersected with many conflicts and controversial situations, including the 2006 Israeli bombings of southern Lebanon, for which she won an Edward R. Murrow Award. She also reported on the Arab Spring of 2011 from both Egypt and Jordan and won a George Foster Peabody Award in 2012 for "distinguished and meritorious public service by radio and television stations, networks, producing organizations and individuals." In June 2012 she was part of a small team of journalists permitted to enter Syria to cover the civil war raging there. Her special series on gay life in the Middle East was the first international television program to address the topic and earned her a nomination for the Gay and Lesbian Alliance Against Discrimination (GLAAD) Award.

As well as coverage of the Middle East, Gorani reported on the 2002 and 2007 French presidential elections, and the 2010 Haiti earthquake. She has interviewed many politicians, including Palestinian activist Saek Erekat, Lebanese prime minister Rafik Hariri, Egyptian foreign minister Amr Moussa, Iraqi prime minister Nouri al-Maliki, and Israeli leaders Ehub Barak and Shimon Peres, as well as the Dalai Lama, Jimmy Carter, Tony Blair, and Gerry Adams. Her success in breaking through the proverbial glass ceiling in the media has inspired other Muslim women to pursue media careers, particularly as reporters.

BIBLIOGRAPHY

Crane, Kelly. "The Other Side of CNN Anchor Hala Gorani." http://gulfnews.com/life-style/people/the-other-side-of-cnn-anchor-hala-gorani-1.103575.

Sakr, Naomi. *Arab Media and Political Renewal: Community, Legitimacy and Public Life*. London: I.B. Tauris, 2007.

JUSTIN J. CORFIELD
and NATANA J. DELONG-BAS

GUARDIANSHIP. The concept of male guardianship over women stems from Qur'ānic 4:34: "Men are the guardians (*qawwamūn*) of women, because God has given the one more (strength) than the other, and because they support them from their means." Classical and medieval exegetes interpreted this as men's moral responsibility to protect women, without indicating any specific legal implications. Abū Bakr al-Jaṣṣāṣ (d. 981), for example, interpreted male guardianship over females in terms of careful protection of their honor (*ta'dīb*), management of their affairs (*tadbīr*), and preservation and maintenance of their interests. Likewise, Ismā'īl Ibn Kathīr (d. 1373) interpreted the verse to indicate the role of men as leaders on whom women can rely to manage their affairs. Hence, in this verse, the idea of guardianship refers to men being responsible for providing protections for and maintaining the interests of women.

The guardians are naturally the women's *maḥram*—namely, men whom Muslim women are forbidden to marry. Aḥmad b. Lu'lu' Ibn al-Naqīb (d. 1368), in his legal manual *'Umdat al-Sālik wa 'Uddat al-Nāsik*, elaborated that *maḥram* develop through blood relationships with women (e.g., father, grandfather, son, grandson) and through marriage (e.g., husband or the husband's father, brothers, or sons). In addition, *maḥram* can be formed by fostering relationships through shared breastfeeding during infancy (*riḍā'*).

In male-dominated societies where the idea of personal security is not fully acknowledged and women are often exposed to economic hardship, the broad precept of guardianship has been articulated mostly in legal formulations rather than ethical dimensions. In this sense, men's economic protection is inevitably understood as the basis for a claim of guardianship, thereby resulting in the limitation of women's personal capacity, seclusion, and restriction of their movements. For example, a woman is not able to perform *ḥajj* unless a male guardian accompanies her. Nonetheless, medieval Muslim jurists were not necessarily strict in their legal articulation. Yaḥyā b. Sharaf al-Nawawī (d. 1278), in his widely cited *Minhāj al-Ṭālibīn*, stated that a woman could embark on long-distance travel to perform *ḥajj* without her *maḥram* if she did so with two or more reliable women.

Historical studies of women in different times and systems of male dominance reveal intriguing examples of flexibility and processes of negotiation in which women attempted to reduce men's guardianship authority. Jonathan Berkey (1991) observed that women during the Mamlūk periods who wished to attend lessons were allowed to leave home without their husbands' permission. Similarly, Ronald Jennings's analysis (1999) of the sixteenth-century legal practices of women in the Ottoman city of Kayseri and Leslie Peirce's (2003) study of law and gender at the Ottoman court of Aintab demonstrated that women were not required to be accompanied by their guardian when presenting their legal affairs in court. In general, however, women are not supposed to challenge the authority of their *maḥram* since such an act is deemed to be a grave mistake.

With the emergence of modern states in which the concept of guardianship is institutionalized as state policy, as in Saudi Arabia, male guardianship over women is perceived as a form of discrimination, which constrains women's legal capacity as fully functioning members of society. This perpetuates the historically rooted practice of guardianship as a manifestation of men's respect for and assurance of women's rights.

BIBLIOGRAPHY

Berkey, Jonathan P. "Women and Islamic Education in the Mamluk Period." In *Women in Middle Eastern History: Shifting Boundaries in Sex and Gender*, edited by Nikki R. Keddie and Beth Baron, pp. 143–157. New Haven, Conn., and London: Yale University Press, 1991.

Ibn al-Naqīb, Aḥmad b. Lu'lu'. *Reliance of the Traveller: A Classic Manual of Islamic Sacred Law*. Translated by Nuh Ha Mim Keller. Evanston, Ill.: Sunna Books, 1994. English translation of *'Umdat al-Sālik wa 'Uddat al-Nāsik*.

Ibn Kathīr, Ismā'īl b. *'Umar Tafsīr al-Qur'ān al-'Aẓīm*. Edited by Yūsuf 'Abd al-Raḥmān al-Mar'ashlī. 4 vols. Beirut: Dār al-Ma'rifah, 1987.

al-Jaṣṣāṣ, Abū Bakr Aḥmad b. 'Alī al-Rāzī. *Aḥkām Al-Qur'ān*. 3 vols. Beirut: Dār al-Kutūb al-'Arabī, 1971.

Jennings, Ronald C. "The Legal Position of Women in Kayseri, a Large Ottoman City, 15-90-1630. " In *Studies on Ottoman Social History in the Sixteenth and Seventeenth Centuries: Women, Zimmis and Sharia Courts in Kayseri, Cyprus and Trabzon*, by Ronald C. Jennings, pp. 115–141. Istanbul: ISIS Press, 1999.

al-Nawawī, Abū Zakarīyā Yaḥyā b. Sharaf. *Minhāj al-Ṭālibīn*. Edited by Aḥmad b. ʿAbd al-ʿAzīz al-Ḥaddād. 3 vols. Beirut: Dār al-Bashāʾir al-Islāmiyya, 2005.

Peirce, Leslie. *Morality Tales: Law and Gender in the Ottoman Court of Aintab*. Berkeley: University of California Press, 2003.

FACHRIZAL A. HALIM

GUILDS. Works by Bernard Lewis, Claude Cahen, Samuel Stern, André Raymond, and others demonstrate the existence of diverse scholarly approaches to the study of the origins of guilds in the Islamic world. One reason for these varying attitudes is the predominance of numerous terms the sources use—thus presenting a lack of uniformity—when referring to guilds, including *futūwah*. These sources consist of travelogues, manuals outlining ordinances pertaining to the regulation of urban life (*ḥisbah*), and collections of legal opinions (*fatāwā*). Nevertheless most scholars agree that guilds played important and multifaceted roles in cities and rural areas throughout the medieval Islamic world. Not only did guild authorities oversee the production of goods and regulate their quality as well as market prices, but these individuals also organized and managed the male working population on the basis of professional affiliations.

The internal organization of many guilds was hierarchical in arrangement and included roles such as apprentice (*mubtadiʾ*) and master (*muʿallim*). At the peak of this hierarchy was the leader, also known as the *ʿārif* or *shaykh*, who was usually chosen by guild members. Several sources describe the hierarchical organization of guilds, including manuals composed for guild members, and indicate that the guilds may have been social collectives colored with religious hues. For example, guild members were described in some of the manuals as connected, through their *shaykh*, to ʿAlī (d. 661 CE), Muḥammad (d. 632 CE), and Adam. Indeed the hierarchies of the professional guilds not only resounded with those of mystical orders, but guilds and mystical orders alike demanded participation in a variety of rituals by initiates and veterans alike.

Few sources indicate the nature of women's labor in the medieval Islamic world, let alone its organization, which Maya Shatzmiller's 1994 seminal study highlights. Women appear infrequently in sources discussing guilds, primarily because they often worked in private domains. Extant sources suggest women's labor in urban centers of the Islamic world was confined to textile and food production. Women taught one another skills associated with a particular trade, and male family members also educated women. While guilds handled the sale and distribution of goods produced by their members—and it is significant to note, as mentioned earlier, that these guilds organized the male rather than the female working population—intermediaries handled the organization of goods women produced. One exception to the absence of a discussion in the sources regarding women's labor and its organization in the Islamic world is a *ḥisbah* manual by a North African historian named al-ʿUqbānī suggesting women met regularly at a woman's home to spin flax and wool.

While the discussion above has focused on the medieval Islamic world, it is significant to note that the late eighteenth and nineteenth centuries were years of change for guilds due to economic transformations. Muḥammad ʿAlī's efforts to industrialize Egypt and the impact of colonization on the Middle East are two key nodes for further study. While many guilds suffered due to economic transformations, innovations were introduced to the guilds due to the proliferation of new professions, and these innovations helped some guilds survive. For example, in late nineteenth-century Port Saʿid, there were guilds for individuals working in new professions. Coal heavers, for example, were now organized into their own guild. While men comprised most of the guilds, individuals previously unattached to guilds, such as rural migrants and women, entered a number of these professional collectives. Over the course of the late twentieth century, guilds gradually fell apart; guilds that continue to exist to this day revolve around traditional crafts.

BIBLIOGRAPHY

Cahen, Claude. "Y a-t-il eu des corporations professionnelles dans le monde musulman classique?" In *The Islamic City: A Colloquium Held at All Souls' College, June 28–July 2, 1965*, edited by A. H. Hourani and S. M. Stern, pp. 51–63. Oxford, U.K.: Cassirer, and New York: University of Pennsylvania Press, 1970. This article contextualizes guilds in the context of medieval Islamic urban landscapes and responds to Lewis's articulation of Massignon's study of guilds.

Chalcraft, John. "The Coal Heavers of Port Saʿid: State-Making and Worker Protest, 1869–1914." *International Labor and Working-Class History* 60 (Fall 2001): 110–124. This article focuses on the coal heavers of Port Saʿid and revisits their protests in the late nineteenth century in Egypt based on two documents the coal heavers wrote. Those interested in the history of guilds ought to consult the article to understand the organizational nuances of a professional group from the nineteenth century.

Lewis, Bernard. "The Islamic Guilds." *Economic History Review* 8 (1937): 20–37. This is a classic articulation of the origins of guilds based on Massignon's explorations of the Ismāʿīlī roots of guilds.

Massignon, Louis. "Les corps de métier et la cité islamique." *Revue Internationale de Sociologie* 28 (1920): 473–489. This is one of the earliest scholarly studies on the origins of guilds in the Islamic world focusing on the Ismāʿīlī roots of guilds in the ninth century.

Raymond, André. *Artisans et commerçants au Caire au XVIIIe siècle*. 2 vols. Damascus: Institut Français de Damas, 1973–1974. Raymond examines guilds in relation to their social and economic context in this key scholarly work. He also demonstrates the relevance of a variety of written historical sources to the study of guilds, including travelogues and court records.

Shatzmiller, Maya. *Labour in the Medieval Islamic World*. Leiden, Netherlands, and New York: E. J. Brill, 1994. Chapter seven of this book is particularly important for understanding women's labor and its organization in the medieval Islamic world.

Stern, Samuel M. "The Constitution of the Islamic City." In *The Islamic City: A Colloquium Held at Old Souls' College, June 28–July 2, 1965*, edited by A. H. Hourani and S. M. Stern, pp. 25–50. Oxford, Cassirer, and Philadelphia: University of Pennsylvania Press, 1970. This article, like Cahen's above, contextualizes guilds in medieval Islamic urban landscapes and responds to Lewis's articulation of Massignon's approach to guilds.

SABAHAT F. ADIL

GUMAA, ALI. (b. 1952), Grand Mufti of Egypt. Assigned to this post in 2003, Ali Gumaa (Ar., ʿAlī Jumʿah) was the first scholar not from the traditional religious schooling system to assume it. Gumaa obtained his bachelor's degree in commerce from Ain Shams University in Cairo in 1973. He then joined the faculty of Arabic and Islamic Studies at al-Azhar University as an undergraduate student. He excelled in his studies, having already studied informally with prominent scholars in various Islamic disciplines. He became part of the teaching staff at al-Azhar University upon graduation and continued his graduate studies there, obtaining a PhD in the theory of Islamic jurisprudence in 1988.

In addition to teaching at the university, Gumaa conducted daily "study circles" at al-Azhar mosque, attracting hundreds of scholars and "knowledge-seeking" young women. He also won the trust of the former Shaykh of al-Azhar, Jād al-Ḥaqq, who dispatched Gumaa to several important international conferences on his behalf, giving him exposure to complex issues and problems facing the Muslim world, as well as an awareness of interfaith and intercultural discourses.

The focus of Gumaa's writings is the universal, as well as contemporary, relevance of Islam to current issues, and the humane face of Islam. His Path to Our Heritage provides a classification of the Islamic sciences and theoretical and analytical tools to approach them. He focuses on connecting the classical Islamic sciences with modern social sciences. Since 2003 Gumaa has attempted to reform and elevate the profile of Dār al-Iftāʿ, the official Egyptian religious institution responsible for issuing authoritative opinions (*fatāwā*). He has founded an official website at which users can browse through thousands of *fatwā*s in several languages: Arabic, English, German, and French. He has plans to introduce pages in Turkish, Farsi, Malay, and Urdu as well.

Two main issues regarding women's rights became controversial in the public debate in Egypt after 2000: female genital mutilation (FGM) and the covering of a woman's face, or wearing of the *niqāb*, as did the religious stance on both. The first had been the subject of debate for many decades and became a sensitive issue after the law effectively criminalized it, although Islamic movements and parties continued to view FGM as a permissible practice. The second issue came to the surface when some universities banned women students from wearing the *niqāb* during exams, to verify their identity. On both issues, Gomaa took a mainstream moderate position, denying that FGM is an Islamic practice and declaring it a cultural one instead, and stating that *niqāb* is not a religious obligation.

Gumaa's religious opinions also side with women on other issues and support their equality within the framework of Islamic principles and values. They have resulted in severe attacks against him in Salafī media, which accuse him of supporting secular views and adhering to Ṣūfī ideas.

To address the public, Gumaa writes a weekly article in *al-Ahrām* (the Pyramids), the largest Egyptian newspaper. He has also founded Welfare of Egypt, a nongovernmental organization to address issues of sustainable development, including poverty and unemployment, and the need to provide greater opportunities for underprivileged children to attain a primary education. The organization has launched a program for supporting research in the social sciences, including women's studies.

BIBLIOGRAPHY

Gomaa, Ali. *The Good Words: Contemporary Fatwas.* Cairo: Dar al-Salam, 2005.

Gomaa, Ali. *Women in Islamic Civilization Between Religious Texts, Legal Tradition, and the World in Which We Live.* Cairo: Dar al-Salam, 2006.

Gomaa, Ali. *Women's Issues in Islamic Jurisprudence.* Cairo: Nahdet Misr, 2008.

HEBA RAOUF EZZAT

H

Ḥadīth. [*This entry contains two subentries,*
Transmission *and*
Women and Gender in the.]

Transmission

One of the most important arenas of Muslim women's religious education across much of Islamic history is the transmission of reports ascribed to Prophet Muḥammad (*ḥadīth*). Women's activities in this field fluctuated over time in response to currents in social, political, and intellectual history, and this history is fertile ground for exploring key issues, such as the development of law and *ḥadīth* as distinct fields of religious learning, methods of *ḥadīth* education, and the history of the *ʿulamāʾ* as a social class. This article provides a historical overview and discusses some of the salient characteristics of women's *ḥadīth* transmission. The focus here is on Sunnī women's involvement, which is better documented and more widespread than in Shīʿī communities.

Historical Overview. The trajectory of women's participation as *ḥadīth* transmitters over the course of Islamic history is a striking one with dramatic fluctuations. Female Companions (those belonging to the first generation of Muslims) set an important precedent, signaling the acceptability of this type of public role for Muslim women. Depending on the sources consulted, approximately 12 percent to 20 percent of female Companions are credited with narrating reports on the authority of Prophet Muḥammad. While most of these women are known for narrating only a handful of reports, some were prolific transmitters. Additionally a few female Companions are said to have exercised influence not just in the narration of reports, but also in the derivation of law. ʿĀʾisha bint Abī Bakr (d. 678), the youngest of Muḥammad's nine wives, who was also reputed to be his favorite one, is among the most prolific of all Companion-Narrators. Ibn Ḥanbal (d. 855) lists close to 2,400 reports on her authority. Umm Salamah (d. ca. 679), another of Muḥammad's wives, is credited with close to 375 reports. In addition to the well-known legal discernment and rulings of ʿĀʾishah, historical records attest to the contributions of women such as Fāṭima bint Qays, known for asserting her own precedent to influence the outcome of debates about the rights of divorced women.

Following the Companion generation, women's involvement as transmitters declined dramatically, staying low or nonexistent for nearly two and a half centuries in the generations immediately after the Companions. However, their participation was welcome anew beginning around the mid-tenth century. The Ayyūbid and Mamlūk eras (c. tenth to sixteenth centuries) witnessed high levels of women's active engagement as students and acclaimed teachers of compilations of *ḥadīth* in a range of subjects, including law, history, and asceticism. Though women's presence in this arena declined again during the Ottoman period and thereafter, this decline was less severe, and *ḥadīth* learning persists as an important field for women's religious learning up to the modern era.

Contrary to popular understanding, Islamic law does not proscribe women's religious learning. On the contrary the pursuit of religious knowledge is strongly encouraged for both sexes. In this respect Muslim women, particularly of early and classical Islam, appear to have been better positioned than women of other major religious traditions, such as Hinduism, Judaism, and Christianity, each of which restricted women's access to religious learning. Islamic law, on the other hand, does regulate areas that influence women's mobility and public participation such as male-female interactions and women's travel when unaccompanied by male guardians. While these prescriptions may negatively influence women's access to education, the correlation is not constant or predictable. The widespread involvement of women as students and teachers of *ḥadīth* during the classical eras belies the notion that Islamic legal norms concerning travel and interaction between the genders unilaterally hampered women's access to education. Women's successful engagement in this arena, as well as their marginalization during some eras of Islamic history, has various causes. For example, the professionalization of *ḥadīth* learning, beginning around the eighth century, led to a contraction in opportunities for women. In the classical era the popularization of *ḥadīth* learning, particularly after collections such as the *Ṣaḥīḥ*s of al-Bukhārī and Muslim received recognition and widespread authority, created new opportunities for women to learn and teach *ḥadīth*. These historical developments are examined in greater detail in some of the works cited in the bibliography below.

Methods and Curriculum of *Ḥadīth* Study. *Ḥadīth* transmission prevailed as an accommodating area for women's religious learning due to its flexible and less formalized methodologies of learning and teaching and also due to the fact that, unlike fields such as law and theology, it did not require long periods of tutelage between teachers and students. Memorization and the faithful reproduction of individual reports or compilations were the primary skills required of most *ḥadīth* transmitters. Knowledge of Arabic, its morphology, syntax, and grammar, were desirable but not absolute prerequisites. Indeed, for the generation of female Companions, they only needed to have met the Prophet and have relayed information about their interaction to knowledge-seekers eager to model their behavior according to the Prophet's practices. While women of subsequent generations were likely literate, especially since they tended to belong to families of the scholarly elite, they would not all have received advanced training in areas such as law, exegesis, or theology. In this regard it is important to note that women excelled primarily in the reproduction or faithful transmission of texts, but were not similarly recognized in the commentarial tradition of *ḥadīth* scholarship. This area required a more complex understanding not just of Arabic, but also of history, law, Qurʾānic exegesis, and theology. While women of the educated elite were exposed to these areas of education, they were nonetheless not known for authoring works that required them to creatively draw on their knowledge to produce authoritative interpretations.

The pedagogy of *ḥadīth* learning varied considerably depending on the age of the student and his/her historical contexts. Historical records indicate that girls and women either studied texts in domestic settings with their relatives (often their male guardians) or attended assemblies for learning *ḥadīth*. These assemblies were at times coeducational and were held in a variety of locations including *madāris*, mosques, mausoleums, and private homes. In the classical era very young girls (some of them infants) were brought into the presence of learned aged *shaykhs* and *shaykhas* to receive certification (*ijāzas*) to transmit traditions on their authority. These children would be expected to learn and master the works later on in life and transmit them accurately. The practice of granting *al-ijāzah* to youth (both male and female) by elderly teachers was one means of assuring shorter chains of transmission back to Muḥammad or to the compiler of a given work. This custom appears to have proliferated in the Mamlūk period and was particular to *ḥadīth* learning among both men and women. Another feature of *ḥadīth* learning which rendered it more amenable to women's participation was that there does not appear to have been a set curriculum or course of study that needed to be mastered in order for a woman to excel in this arena. As mentioned earlier, advanced knowledge of Arabic was likely particularly for acclaimed female transmitters of the classical eras. However, women could attain enviable reputations in this arena on the basis of their transmission of a limited number of works, particularly if those works were major collections, such as the *Ṣaḥīḥs* of al-Bukhārī or Muslim.

The practice of *ḥadīth* transmission has evolved considerably in the modern period. The oral rendition of texts is no longer the primary means for guaranteeing their authenticity and accurate transmission particularly as printing methods have evolved to minimize errors in reproduction of these texts. Nevertheless the oral performance and memorization of *ḥadīth* collections, especially the *Ṣaḥīḥ* compilations, persists as a means of accruing spiritual blessings (*barakāt*). In this vein Muslim women continue to devote themselves to the study and teaching of *ḥadīth* and its auxiliary sciences. The Madrasat al-Ḥadīth al-Nuriyya in Damascus attests the persistent importance of this area of learning. Devoted to teaching women the sciences of *ḥadīth*, law, and Qur'ān, the school was established in the early twenty-first century, and fulfills the needs of scores of both full-time and part-time matriculants. Moreover, as in the early and classical periods, women thrive outside of institutional frameworks and continue to avail themselves of informal networks of learning throughout the Muslim world in order to acquire mastery as *ḥadīth* scholars.

BIBLIOGRAPHY

Abou-Bakr, Omaima. "Teaching the Words of the Prophet: Women Instructors of the *Ḥadīth* (Fourteenth and Fifteenth Centuries)." *Hawwa* 1, no. 3 (2003): 306–328.

Berkey, Jonathan. *The Transmission of Knowledge in Medieval Cairo: A Social History of Islamic Education*. Princeton, N.J.: Princeton University Press, 1992.

Chamberlain, Michael. *Knowledge and Social Practice in Medieval Damascus, 1190–1350*. Cambridge, U.K., and New York: Cambridge University Press, 1994.

Nadwi, Mohammad Akram. *al-Muhaddithāt: The Women Scholars in Islam*. London: Interface, 2007.

Sayeed, Asma. *Women and the Transmission of Religious Knowledge in Islam*. New York: Cambridge University Press, 2013.

ASMA SAYEED

WOMEN AND GENDER IN THE

"*Ḥadīth* (pl. *aḥādīth*)" refers to the collected reports of the Prophet Muḥammad's words and deeds as recounted by his wives and Companions. The *ḥadīth* are in the form of stories, reports, or traditions, and serve a variety of functions in Islamicate culture and Islamic jurisprudence: some lend context to broad Qurʾānic mandates, or provide commentary on the specific doctrines revealed in the Qurʾān, while others deal with the mundane aspects of everyday life and conduct, providing a window into the normative practices of the Prophet and his Companions. The collection and transmission of *ḥadīth* in this way has assisted Muslims in modeling their own lives after the example, or *sunnah,* set by the Prophet during his lifetime. *Ḥadīth* are therefore an important basis for Islamic law and jurisprudence, second only to the Qurʾān.

Aḥādīth were primarily preserved orally until the systematic, written compilation of *aḥādīth* began in earnest in the ninth and tenth centuries. These written collections, which Orientalists often refer to as the Prophetic "Traditions," were recorded in six canonical compendia, all of which were compiled by men. Even so, nearly 15 percent of all *aḥādīth* in these official volumes can be sourced to the Prophet's wife, ʿĀʾishah (612–678), whose contribution to *ḥadīth* collections outweighs even that of that of ʿAlī, the Fourth Caliph and the first male convert to Islam. As the Qurʾān and the *sunnah* form the two principle sources of Islamic law, Islam is one of very few living religions to include women's voices in canonical texts, in legal source material, and among the voices of "official" history.

In spite of the inclusion of female transmitters, the *ḥadīth* include a spectrum of attitudes about gender and women, some of which are problematic from a contemporary perspective. The traditions include a report of the Prophet characterizing women as the most harmful temptation left to the Muslim community. In another *ḥadīth,* angels are said to weep when a woman leaves her husband sexually frustrated. Other *aḥādīth* assert that women are morally or religiously defective, sources of *fitnah,* unclean, bound to obey their husbands unquestioningly, and intellectually unfit for political rule.

These misogynist *aḥādīth,* however, make up a very small portion of the seventy thousand total. Many of them further conflict with dozens of *aḥādīth* that clearly bestow full humanity upon women, urge husbands to deal with their wives with gentleness, affirm that the Prophet accepted the testimony of a woman as equal to that of a man, elevate mothers above fathers, indicate that many Muslim women went unveiled during the Prophet's lifetime, and make it clear that the Prophet himself often answered to and asked counsel of his wives.

As Fatima Mernissi and Khaled Abou El Fadl have also noted, many of the most problematic *aḥādīth* for women are sourced to Abū Hurayrah (603–681), a convert to Islam who became a Muslim three years before the death of the Prophet. In spite of his late conversion, Abu Hurayrah is responsible for transmitting more of the Prophet's traditions than most of the companions, including those who had lived with or known the Prophet for decades. Abū Hurayrah appeared to be a controversial figure even when he was alive, and other Companions would frequently correct him or note that he was contradicting himself. According to one report, the Prophet's wife ʿĀʾishah summoned him to come and see her, and she told him, "Abū Hurayrah! What are these reports from the Prophet that we keep hearing that you transmit to the people! Tell me, did you hear anything other than what we heard, or see anything other than what we observed?" He is reported to have responded, "O mother, you were busy with your kohl and with beautifying yourself for the Prophet, but I—nothing kept me from away from him." (Abou El Fadl, 2001, p. 216). These and other issues initially led jurists to regard Abū Hurayrah as an unreliable source. Subsequently, however, political issues factored into classical Sunnī jurists' categorization of Abū Hurayrah as reliable.

Women factor into *ḥadīth* literature as historical figures in addition to being transmitters. Although the Prophet's wives never achieved the status of the Prophet himself, they eventually attained a lofty status in the annals of "official" Islamic history as "Mothers of the Believers." Classical hagiographers, however, frequently presented the Prophet's wives as petty, jealous, or irrational creatures on the one hand and examples of ideal womanhood on the other. The Prophet's wives were thus positioned as archetypal figures who glorified domesticity at best, and legitimated the continued subjugation of all women at worst.

In the late nineteenth and early twentieth centuries, social reformers such as Zaynab al-Ghazālī (1917–2005), Moḥammad Ḥusayn Haykal (1888–1956), and Bint al-Shati (1913–1998) reframed *ḥadīth* literature, presenting the Prophet's wives as models for the modern Muslim woman to emulate. Other reformers, the most notable of whom may be Shaykh Muḥammad ʿAbduh (1849–1905), further suggested that all Muslims were implicitly authorized to rely on their own intellectual faculties when engaging in textual interpretation, initiating a wave of scholarship that revisited the *ḥadīth* as a source of women's liberation rather than a justification for their subjugation and relegation to the domestic sphere.

Decades later contemporary intellectuals and academics have continued this tradition of self-authorized epistemology, turning to Qurʾān and *ḥadīth* literature to advocate for women's rights within an Islamic framework. Scholars such as Asma Barlas (2002) and Barbara Stowasser (1994) have argued that these misogynist *aḥādīth*, rather than the Qurʾān, are responsible for introducing misogyny into the normative practices of Islam, as well as into the epistemological assumptions grounding Islamic jurisprudence. Wiebke Walther (1981) further points out that some of the objectionable *aḥādīth* include anecdotes about towns that had not even been founded during Muḥammad's lifetime, suggesting that *ḥadīth* literature captured various attitudes in opinions within the broader Muslim community, in addition to recording the *sunnah* of the Prophet.

At present *ḥadīth* are still considered an important source of revelation, and Sunnī compendia continue to regard Abū Hurayrah—and his gendered *aḥādīth*—as reliable.

[*See also* ʿĀʾishah; Ghazālī, Zaynab al-; *and* Mernissi, Fatima.]

BIBLIOGRAPHY

Abou El Fadl, Khaled. *Speaking in God's Name: Islamic Law, Authority and Women*. Oxford: Oneworld, 2001 A thorough review of the Islamic legal system and its ethical, methodological, and historical foundations, which suggests among other things that an authoritarian reading of the sources has had problematic consequences for Muslim society in general, and Muslim women in particular.

Barlas, Asma. *"Believing Women" in Islam: Unreading Patriarchal Interpretations of the Qurʾān*. Austin: University of Texas Press, 2002. An investigation of the Qurʾān, the *ḥadīth*, and Muslims' reading thereof to justify the existence of patriarchy and sexual oppression.

Badran, Margot. *Feminism in Islam: Secular and Religious Convergences*. Oxford: Oneworld, 2009. An overview of Muslim feminist activism in Egypt from the late nineteenth century to the present day.

Stowasser, Barbara Freyer. *Women in the Qur'an, Traditions, and Interpretation*. Oxford: Oxford University Press, 1994. A discussion of women and female figures as they have occurred in the Qurʾān and *ḥadīth*, as well as in classical and modern interpretations thereof.

Walther, Wiebke. *Women in Islam: From Medieval to Modern Times*. Translated by C. S. V. Salt. Princeton, N.J.: Marcus Weiner Publishing, 1993. An examination of women as they have been presented throughout the ages in Islamic texts, law, society, and culture.

Kristina Benson

HAGARISM. Michael Cook and Patricia Crone wrote *Hagarism: The Making of the Islamic World* from which the eponymous term Hagarism is drawn. Hagarism was the name applied to the religious movement emerging from Arabia that would eventually become Islam. In their book, the authors present a radical reinterpretation—sometimes called revisionist—of the early history of Islam that has greatly affected the field in numerous arenas since its publication in 1977. Appraisals of their thesis and conclusions have been mixed, more often negative, but their inventive approach and extensive research have fixed this study among the most important works in the field.

Part of their radical reimagining of early Islam arises from Crone and Cook's method. In the fashion of other skeptical Western scholarship, Crone and Cook view the early Islamic sources—purporting to accurately construct the history of the community—with a great deal of dubiousness, because the early histories of Islam were composed well after Islam had developed and spread. Crone and Cook include the Qurʾān as one of the anachronistic texts, postulating that its composition occurred well after the eighth century. Crone and Cook, therefore, utilize a number of Near Eastern reports and letters, composed in Syriac, Hebrew, Armenian, and other languages, to recast the establishment of the movement that came to be known as Islam.

In their view, Hagarism originated from the Arabs—seen as descendants of Hagar and Ishmael—who were the driving force of this movement that stormed out of Arabia into Palestine. Crone and Cook theorized that the movement was a type of Jewish-Messianism in its embryonic stages. As time progressed, the Arabs, or Hagarenes, needed a way to discard the movement's Judaic identity. Thus, they adopted Christian and Samaritan concepts into their developing system, particularly the latter. This amalgamation of traditions is what Crone and Cook called Hagarism. As the seat of Arab power shifted from Palestine to Iraq in the eighth century, so did external influences on Hagarism, for it reverted back to Judaic influence, but this time stemming from Rabbinic Judaism. This would be the final phase of transition before Hagarism was obscured in favor of Islam.

Hagarism's impact on the study of Islam has been deep and protracted. Scholars have predominately rejected their work, with some railing against it as "disastrous" and "a travesty." Others simply felt as if the argument was lacking. Critics faulted their method on the grounds that many of the outside sources utilized were themselves of suspect authority. Cook and Crone have never mounted a defense of their work and have, separately, stated that their book was an attempt to rethink and challenge the conventional narrative of Islam. Despite the many negative adjudications, some scholars highlight the benefits derived from the study, such as the importance of non-Islamic sources, particularly Syriac, on the study of Islam. Since its publication, both Crone and Cook have attained positions of prominence at highly regarded institutions and published numerous books and articles. Some of their publications continue to hold fast to theories laid down in *Hagarism*, but most all of their works continue to demonstrate the revisionist philosophy they came to be known for in *Hagarism*.

BIBLIOGRAPHY

Binder, Leonard. *Islamic Liberalism: A Critique of Development Ideologies*. Chicago: University of Chicago Press, 1988.

Bonner, Michael D. *Jihad in Islamic History: Doctrines and Practice*. Princeton, N.J.: Princeton University Press, 2006.

Crone, Patricia, and M. A. Cook. *Hagarism: The Making of the Islamic World*. Cambridge, U.K.: Cambridge University Press, 1977.

Grabar, Oleg. "Review of *Hagarism: the Making of the Islamic World*," by Patricia Crone and Michael Cook,

Speculum: a Journal of Mediaeval Studies 53:4 (1978): 795–799.

Lassner, Jacob. *Jews, Christians, and the Abode of Islam: Modern Scholarship, Medieval Realities.* Chicago: University of Chicago Press, 2012.

Manheimer, Eric I. "Review of *Hagarism: the Making of the Islamic World,*" by Patricia Crone and Michael Cook, *The American Historical Review* 83:1 (1978): 240–241.

Morony, Michael G. "Review of *Hagarism: the Making of the Islamic World,*" by Patricia Crone and Michael Cook, *Journal of Near Eastern Studies.* 41:2 (1982): 157–159.

Nemoy, Leon. "Crone-Cook's 'Hagarism'," *The Jewish Quarterly Review.* 68:3 (1978): 179–181.

Serjeant, R B. "Review of *Hagarism: the Making of the Islamic World,*" by Patricia Crone and Michael Cook, *Journal of the Royal Asiatic Society of Great Britain & Ireland* 110:1 (1978): 76–78.

Shoemaker, Stephen J. *The Death of a Prophet: The End of Muhammad's Life and the Beginnings of Islam.* Philadelphia: University of Pennsylvania Press, 2012.

Wansbrough, J. "Review of *Hagarism: the Making of the Islamic World,*" by Patricia Crone and Michael Cook, *Bulletin of the School of Oriental and African Studies, University of London.* 41:1 (1978): 155–156.

Matthew Long

Ḥajj, Women's Patronage of.

[*This entry includes two subentries:*

Historical Practice, *and*
Contemporary Practice.]

Historical Practice

While pilgrimage to Mecca is one of the obligatory duties required of Muslims, *ḥajj* patronage and the creation of pious establishments supporting it fall under the category of voluntary Muslim "good works" *(khayrāt)*. Muslim women's patronage history has been mostly explored in such areas as charity and pious endowments (*waqf*), and is especially well documented for the Ottoman period. Wealthy commoners, as well as the ruling class, could and did provide support for the poor, orphans, and widows, or financed religious activities and education. Religious charitable works were the dominant form of women's philanthropy. However, major projects, such as institutions and buildings in prestigious locations, entailed outcomes that were too significant, lasting, and visible to be allowed, except to the members of ruling households or court and military elites. A certain hierarchy of piety prevailed within the ruling family as well: for example, in the Ottoman dynasty the right to build mosques in major cities was reserved for sultans and certain female family members (mothers, favorite concubines, sometimes sisters and daughters), but denied to princes.

Patronage of the *ḥajj* and beneficence to the holy cities of Mecca and Medina, especially, were a matter of state interest and promoted the ruler's legitimacy in the eyes of subjects from the time of the caliphate and for Muslim pilgrims from all corners of the Islamic world after its decentralization. Queens and princesses played an important role in demonstrating both piety and charity by their participation in the pilgrimage, lavish distribution of gifts and alms en route and during the pilgrimage, and sponsorship of charitable establishments in the holy cities of Mecca and Medina. Jerusalem, as the third-most-sacred city in Islam, was also patronized by rulers and royal women; less is known about building projects and pious endowments in lesser cities along the pilgrim routes. The vast majority of extant sources provide information about Sunnī elite patronage. We know much less about Shīʿī women's sponsorship of the *ḥajj* and their support of Shīʿī pilgrim destinations, such as Karbala and Najaf in Iraq. Extant records were created by men; premodern Muslim women themselves did not record their charitable deeds except through *waqf* documents (*waqfiyyas*).

It is difficult to separate activities like elite women's participation in the annual pilgrimage, which was aimed at multiple pious, political, and social goals, from the patronage extended from the capitals to the holy cities, and *sharīfs* of Mecca and other dignitaries through distributions of revenue from charitable foundations. Royal ladies traveled to the Hejaz in splendidly equipped caravans, carrying lavish gifts to sanctuaries and officials, as well as supplies for the travelers and local poor, escorted by armed guards to protect against Bedouin plunder or kidnapping. Funding came from both private and state treasuries. Construction and maintenance of buildings and infrastructure, as well as major charity projects, were regulated and supervised by central and local authorities. Endowed land included that for building on and estates located outside Arabia, the income from which supported the foundation's activities. Female patrons acted through their agents (*wakil*), and court eunuchs. The mother of the Fāṭimid caliph al-Mustanir (1036–1094), Lady Rasad, had a Jewish agent. In the Ottoman period, the chief black eunuch of the sultan's harem became the exclusive supervisor of royal women's charitable foundations and projects. From 1691 on, this official often "retired" to the post of the supervisor of the eunuch guard of the tomb of the Prophet Muḥammad in Medina.

Arabic historical records about *ḥajj* patronage name some early Abbasid queens; in the later Abbasid period, sources describe some Saljuk Turkish benefactresses of Hejaz institutions, while in Egypt only sparse Fāṭimid and Ayyubid data is available. Material is considerably more ample for the Mamluk period (1250–1517). From the Fāṭimids on, the Hejaz was controlled, supplied, and patronized by the powers controlling Egypt. After 1500, the geopolitical situation around Arabia, and therefore the *ḥajj*, changed dramatically. The appearance of the Portuguese in the Indian Ocean signaled the beginning of Christian-Muslim naval warfare, resulting in competition for carriage and piracy, including attacks on pilgrim ships. The rise of the Ṣafavid state in Iran created a new source of Shīʿī-Sunnī tensions, and often interrupted overland pilgrim traffic from the east. The Mughal expansion led to the renewed Islamization of India, which sent more pilgrims to Mecca and spurred royal patronage of the Hejaz sanctuaries. The Ottoman conquest of Arab countries put an end to the Mamluk state and made the sultan the "Servant of the Two Sanctuaries" (*khadim al-haramayn*). His legitimacy needed to be asserted and demonstrated to the Ottoman subjects, to the *sharīf* descendants of the Prophet Muḥammad, and to Muslims elsewhere. Since no Ottoman sultan ever performed the *ḥajj*, representation of the state was delegated to their mothers, wives, and adult daughters.

Charity and patronage associated with the *ḥajj* are grander in scale and expected to bring higher spiritual rewards than those supporting the construction and restoration of local shrines and visits to them (*ziyāras*). Labor costs were also higher in Arabia. Significant philanthropic activities by women date back to the early Abbasid queens Khayzuran (d. 789 CE) and Zubayda (d. 831). The former made her first pilgrimage to Mecca in 776 as a slave-consort of the Abbasid caliph, al-Mahdi; in 788 she returned as queen-mother of the caliph Harun al-Rashid (r. 786–809). To celebrate her triumph, she purchased the former home of the prophet Muḥammad in Mecca and converted it into a mosque. Harun's wife Zubayda was a pious woman who had one hundred female slaves recite the Qurʾān in unison; she performed several pilgrimages. During the one in 805, she witnessed the effects of a recent drought and determined to have an aqueduct constructed, which carried to Mecca the water of the Spring of Hunain some twelve miles away. She also had wells, reservoirs, and caravanserais built along the nine-hundred-mile-long road from Mecca to Kufa, which was named in her honor *Darb Zubayda*. Endowments established by Zubayda paid for maintenance of the hostels and fortifications along the Kufa road and for the restoration of monuments in Medina, as well as other places. Shaghab, the mother of the caliph al-Muqtadir (r. 908–932), not only created many endowments in Mecca and Medina, but donated one million dinars from her estates each year in support of pilgrimage.

Not all public displays of charity were equally welcome. After Zubayda's husband died and her son, al-Amin (r. 809–813), was killed in the war against his half-brother al-Ma'mun (r. 813–833), the latter apparently prevented Zubayda from going on pilgrimage again, until he was asked on her behalf by his bride Buran at their wedding in 825. Perhaps he did not wish to stir up political opposition in places where Zubayda's past philanthropy was still evident.

We know of Seljukid ladies of Damascus, Abbasid slave girls, and Fāṭimid and Ayyubid princesses and queen-mothers who gained reputations for piety, charity, personal religious learning, and generosity toward Mecca and Medina as well as their own local capitals (Damascus, Cairo, and pre-Mongol Baghdad were important points of departure for pilgrimage caravans). In 1098–1099 the former stewardess (*qahramana*) of the Abbasid caliph al-Muqtadi (1075–1094) built a *ribat* (hospice) for widows who chose to lead a life of seclusion in Mecca. Ibn Jubayr (1183–1184) reports Turkish princesses ransoming pilgrim prisoners, especially strangers whom no one else would ransom. Because pilgrims did not carry weapons, they were particularly vulnerable to raiding by the Bedouin and, during the Crusades, to Christian-Muslim warfare. In 1187 the ruler of Egypt, Ṣalāḥ al-Dīn (Saladin) sent troops to protect a caravan in which his sister Sitt al-Sham (d. 1220) was returning from a pilgrimage to Mecca. Ibn Battutah was granted accommodation by several female patrons. Leaving Mecca after one of his several pilgrimages, he was given protection by Sitt Zahida (d. ca. 1326), a pious and learned woman who traveled despite her blindness, protected and served by a troop of pious brethren.

While the lavishness certainly served political and public relations ends, it was also part of a devotional demonstration. In Egypt, Baraka Khatun (d. 1372), the mother of the Mamluk sultan al-Ashraf Sha'ban II (r. 1363–1376), was presented with a magnificent pilgrimage procession in 1368, called in her honor "the Year of the Sultan's Mother." On the other hand, many charitable acts lacked drama and overt advertising. Among these were provision of spare camels for the sick and foot pilgrims, distribution of water on the march, and supply of medical remedies and services. On such occasions, the benefactresses were not always present. Such services, while impersonal, benefited concrete individuals and helped spread the good name of the patrons and their dynasties. That the individual and the devotional were never far from the social aspects of philanthropy is confirmed by the wording of Zubayda's inscription at a reservoir in Mecca, articulating her spiritual intent:

> Umm Ja'far, the daughter of Abu al-Fadl Ja'far the son of the Commander of the believers Mansur—may Allah be pleased with the Commander of the Believers—ordered the construction of these springs in order to provide water for the pilgrims to the House of Allah and to the people in this sanctuary, praying thereby for Allah's reward and seeking to draw nigh unto him

Zubayda's charitable water projects survived until modern times; during the reign of the Ottoman sultan Süleyman the Magnificent (r. 1520–1566) they were restored and the water supply improved, probably at the expense of his favorite wife, Hürrem, or her only daughter Mihrimah.

Foundations established in Hürrem's name supported hospitals, hostels, and almshouses in Mecca, Medina, and Jerusalem, although some of them were built only after her death (they were funded by Egyptian tax revenues). Hürrem Sultan was commemorated in a Meccan inscription as "the Zubayda of her time and age" (in Jerusalem, she was compared to Emperor Constantine's mother, St. Helena). The mother of the conqueror of Syria and Egypt, Sultan Selim I (r. 1512–1520), ordered the annual distribution of one thousand golden *ashrafiyya* coins to the poor of Medina (funded by revenues from a public bath in Istanbul). An Ottoman princess gave one hundred black slave women to be employed as cleaners in Mecca; the forty-two who remained in 1573 were freed.

The practice of sacred charity by elite Ottoman women continued on a large scale through the seventeenth century. As *haseki sultan* (favorite), at the very end of Ahmed I's reign (1603–1617), Kősem Sultan (1623–1651) established a set of pious charitable services, including the furnishing of water to pilgrims making their way to the holy cities (a service that employed thirty camels, six camel drivers, and six water carriers); the annual distribution of shirts, woolen cloaks, shoes, and turban materials to the poor of the two cities and the poor among the pilgrims; and the recitation of the Qur'ān in the sanctuaries of Jerusalem, Mecca, and Medina. As *valide sultan* (Queen Mother) from 1623 to 1651, when her sons Murad IV and Ibrahim I and her grandson Mehmed IV reigned, she continued to undertake personal charities. Her daughter-in-law Turhan Sultan, a favorite concubine of Sultan Ibrahim I (r. 1640–1648) and the mother of his successor, Mehmed IV (r. 1648–1687), sponsored the provision of water for pilgrims to Mecca and Medina, employing sixty-five camels in the undertaking. She also created endowments for the recitation of the Qur'ān in several places, including by 130 individuals in each of the sanctuaries of Mecca and Medina. In 1678, Rabia Gülnush Emetullah, a favorite concubine of Sultan Mehmet IV (r. 1648–1687) and mother of Sultan Ahmet III (r. 1703–1730), founded an enormous pious endowment for Mecca, funded by revenues from four carefully selected villages in Egypt, as well as from Cairo's Nile port of Bulaq. The endowment deed specifies as superintendent the then-chief eunuch Yusuf Agha (tenure 1671–1687), who was the first Ottoman chief harem eunuch to be assigned to Medina (after exile in Cairo). The tradition of ladies from the imperial harem seeing off the pilgrimage caravan on the day of departure and hanging embroidered silk fabrics over the *mahmal* (litter carried by a camel) continued until the twentieth century. However, support of travel to and sojourn at the two holy cities was a drain on the private resources of individuals and government services. In 1572–1573 the Ottoman dynasty appeared in the Hejaz in the person of Princess Shah Sultan, whose safe conduct specified that she wished to visit Jerusalem before proceeding to Mecca and Medina. For the trip to Jerusalem, the governor of Damascus was to provide special escort; the central authorities expected her to receive all necessary supplies there. (From 1708, the governor of Damascus began to serve as commander of the Damascus pilgrimage caravan.)

Acts of charity performed by important foreign visitors carried particular significance and could be intended or perceived as challenging local authorities. After sending a particularly lavish caravan with several princesses in 1507, the Mamluk sultan Qansuh al-Ghawri (r. 1501–1517) refused to permit one of them to return from the Hejaz because she had become politically dangerous to him; she had to remain in Mecca, where she eventually died. Matters became delicate when Shah Tahmasp of Iran (r. 1524–1576) sent to the Hejaz his consort, the mother of Prince

Isma'il. Shī'ī pilgrims from Iran often combined their journey to Mecca with a visit to the Iraqi pilgrimage centers of al-Najaf and Karbala, in Ottoman hands since 1534. The mother of Shah Isma'il visited there in 1563–1564. The shah's representative was not allowed to establish soup kitchens there, even if they served only Iranians. In 1573–1574 Shah Tahmasp's sister Perikhan had asked for permission to have the two Iraqi sanctuaries covered with carpets from Persia; the request was denied, although the gifts were later received and stored away.

During the reign of the Mughal emperor Humayun (1530–1556), political exiles settling in the holy cities included his brother Kamran and his wife Mah Chichek Begam. The emperor Akbar (r. 1556–1605) was represented by one of his wives, Salima, and his aunt, the court historian Gulbadan Begam. When the two queens, accompanied by other senior ladies of his harem, extended their stay in Mecca over several years (1575–1582), the Ottoman administration grew somewhat alarmed by their ostentatious distributions of alms. Indian Timurid women supported pilgrims with donations that sometimes exceeded the emperors' contributions. The daughter of Emperor Awrangzeb (r. 1658–1707), Zib al-Nisa', provided 7,000 rupees to Mulla Safi al-Din Qazini, who wrote a narrative of his *ḥajj* experience. Sailing from India to Arabia and back, even in imperial ships, was dangerous. Emperor Akbar had to delay the journey of his wife and sister until he was able to secure the necessary Portuguese safe conduct. Ships returning from the Red Sea or the Persian Gulf were particularly attractive targets to Indian Ocean pirates (initially Portuguese, later Dutch and English) because they were more likely to carry silver and gold. From the late eighteenth century, most Indian voyagers used English vessels. When Asaf al-Dawla, the *nawab-wazir* of Awadh (Oudh), died in 1797, his widow Bahu Begam took all moveable property from Lucknow to Faizabad against the wishes of the East India company; her will specified a large gift to the holy shrine at Karbala.

By 1850, 80 percent of Muslims lived outside the Arab Near East. Most pilgrims came from India, and India produced the largest financial contributions to the *ḥajj*. Nawab Sikandar Begum of Bhopal reached Jidda in January 1864 with a shipload of gifts destined for the Holy Cities. In 1894, Faizunnesa Choudhurani (1834–1903) performed *ḥajj* and founded a religious college (*madrasah*) and an inn (*musafirkhana*) at Mecca. This advocate of female education, who maintained strict *purdah*, was awarded the title of *nawab* by Queen Victoria in 1889, making her the first woman in Bengal to receive this title.

In the twentieth century, the patronage of the *ḥajj* and maintenance of Hejaz sanctuaries were assumed by the Saudi state, although many institutions dating from the medieval and early-modern charitable endowments were still known to function in the 1940s and 1950s.

BIBLIOGRAPHY

Abbott, Nabia. *Two Queens of Baghdad: Mother and Wife of Hārūn al-Rashīd*. Chicago: University of Chicago Press, 1946.

Faroqhi, Suraiya. *Pilgrims and Sultans: The Ḥajj under the Ottomans 1517–1683*. London: Tauris, 1994.

Hathaway, Jane. *Beshir Agha: Chief Eunuch of the Ottoman Imperial Harem*. London: Oneworld Publications, 2005.

Johnson, Kathryn. "Royal Pilgrims: Mamluk Accounts of the Pilgrimage to Mecca of the Khawand al-Kubra (Senior Wife of the Sultan)." *Studia Islamica* 91 (2000): 107–131.

Lambert-Hurley, Siobhan, ed. *A Princess's Pilgrimage: Nawab Sikandar Begum's A Pilgrimage to Mecca*. Bloomington: Indiana University Press, 2008.

Lev, Yaacov. *Charity, Endowments, and Charitable Institutions in Medieval Islam*. Gainesville: University Press of Florida, 2005.

"Patronage by Women in Islamic Art." Special issue, *Asian Art* 6.2 (1993).

Peters, Francis E. *The Ḥajj: The Muslim Pilgrimage to Mecca and the Holy Places.* Princeton, NJ: Princeton University Press, 1994.

Peirce, Leslie P. *The Imperial Harem: Women and Sovereignty in the Ottoman Empire.* New York: Oxford University Press, 1993.

Tolmacheva, Marina. "Female Piety and Patronage in the Medieval Ḥajj." In *Women in the Medieval Islamic World: Power, Patronage, and Piety*, edited by Gavin Hambly, pp. 161–178. New York: St. Martin's Press, 1998–.

Marina Tolmacheva

Contemporary Practice

Women's participation in the *ḥajj* has risen dramatically since the 1960s, particularly among younger, better educated, and more urbanized groups. The trend is remarkably uniform at the global level and across virtually every region and nation. Between 1968 and 1993, the proportion of women among all overseas pilgrims increased from about 34 percent to 43 percent. In several countries—Indonesia, Singapore, Lebanon, and Palestine—women were the majority of *ḥajj* participants year after year.

Nonetheless, large disparities remain in female *ḥajj* rates, not only between countries, but within them. Variations in women's pilgrimage are closely related to differences in education, income, and culture. Female education is a strong predictor of women's pilgrimage. Even primary school education—in either secular or Islamic institutions—expands young women's horizons and opportunities sufficiently to encourage high levels of pilgrimage. Income also promotes pilgrimage for women as for men, but women's rates are especially high in communities with strong traditions of female land ownership, and with local commercial networks that are dominated by women merchants.

Patriarchal cultures continue to suppress women's pilgrimage, but patriarchy's effects vary enormously in different cultural and economic environments. The greatest contrasts appear between cosmopolitan maritime zones, inland agricultural economies, and isolated mountain regions. *Ḥājjah* (female pilgrims to Mecca) are most common in coastal regions with strong traditions of maritime commerce. Lower pilgrimage rates prevail in inland agricultural regions, with provincial capitals and villages often sending more women than richer metropolitan centers. Women are least likely to make the *ḥajj* if they live in nomadic or mountainous regions, particularly if they belong to minority ethnic and tribal communities.

In Turkey, women regularly make up the majority of *ḥajj* pilgrims in the western coastal regions around the Sea of Marmara and along the shores of the Aegean Sea. These areas have the highest incomes, the greatest levels of female literacy, and the largest numbers of European immigrants. In Central Anatolia, female pilgrims are most common along the Mediterranean coast and least common near the more mountainous and isolated districts of the Black Sea. Eastern Turkey has by far the lowest percentage of *ḥājjah*, particularly the Kurdish provinces in the southeast where poverty, illiteracy, and ethnic segregation combine to severely limit women's abilities to engage in any type of travel, except for permanent migration to big cities and foreign countries where job prospects are more promising.

In Pakistan, ethnic and economic differences create contrasting environments for women who want to make the *ḥajj*. In the booming towns and villages of Punjab in northeast Pakistan, most pilgrims are women, particularly where Islamic primary and secondary schools for girls are widespread. Female pilgrimage is also common in the southern cities of Karachi and Hyderabad, where educated northern Indian migrants are most concentrated. The lowest levels of female pilgrimage appear among the tribal societies of the Pashtuns in the northwest and the Balouchis in the southwest along the mountainous borders with Afghanistan and Iran. Pilgrimage is least popular for both men and women in the rural districts of Sindh, where feudalism, tribalism, and poverty are the most intense.

In Indonesia, *ḥājjah* frequently make up the majority nationwide, with particularly high rates in the capital city, Jakarta, and in the maritime trading centers of the Outer Islands. Female pilgrimage closely follows historical routes of international commerce: along the Makassar Straits in western and southern Sulawesi and eastern Kalimantan, near the Straits of Malacca in eastern and central Sumatra, and in the smaller islands of Nusa Tenggara to the east of Java. *Ḥājjah* are also dominant in Western Sumatra, where the Minangkabau community retains long traditions of matrilineal inheritance, including land ownership.

Nigerian women have vastly different opportunities to make the *ḥajj* depending on their ethnic background. Women are the majority of *ḥajj* pilgrims among the Yoruba of southwestern Nigeria, especially in central Lagos and Ibadan, where female business networks control much of the retail trade. Yoruba men frequently delay their own pilgrimages until they have first saved enough money to send their mothers to Mecca; only then do they make the journey themselves, and whenever possible, they also take their wives and daughters. In contrast, the Hausa regions of northern Nigeria have consistently lower levels of female pilgrimage, even in the wealthier cities. In central Nigeria—also known as the Middle Belt—where Christians and Muslims live side by side in relatively equal numbers, there are competing pilgrimage campaigns to Jerusalem and Mecca, which boost female *ḥajj* participation as well. This is the center of Nigeria's most violent and tenacious religious conflicts, and the pattern of dueling pilgrimages merely aggravates the problem.

Many aspects of the *ḥajj* help to break down gender biases by strengthening the equality of the sexes and highlighting women's contributions to the development of Islam. Women are explicitly prohibited from veiling or covering their faces during the pilgrimage. They usually wear normal loose-fitting dress, rather than the distinctive white towels that men don for the major rituals. At night, women sleep in rooms with their families or with other women, but throughout the day they are in close and casual contact with strangers from every corner of the world—both men and women—in ways that would be discouraged in daily life back home.

One of the most emotional and symbolically charged rites of the pilgrimage is the *al-saʿy*, in which *ḥajj* pilgrims reenact the drama of Hagar, the wife of Ibrāhīm and the mother of Ismāʿīl. Imitating Hagar's desperation after being left alone in the desert with her infant son, pilgrims run back and forth between two hills searching for water. Afterwards, like Hagar, they drink from the blessed well of Zamzam, which the angel Gabriel revealed to her just as she was tempted to abandon hope of survival. The famous Iranian writer, Ali Shariʿati, portrays Hagar as the central heroine not only of the *ḥajj* but of monotheism in general. For Shariʿati, Hagar is an icon of struggle, faith, and liberation that every pilgrim should emulate during the *ḥajj* and in their own communities, where they should continue her fight for equality and justice.

Finally, as was true historically, women continue to play an active role in providing financial support to pilgrims seeking to make the *ḥajj* irrespective of the gender of the donors or recipients. This remains true even in the midst of the flurry of government-supported *ḥajj* programs, which, despite strong marketing and controls, have not supplanted the previous networks of private, informal, and illegal support for pilgrims who want to avoid state controls. Malaysia and Turkey are excellent examples of countries with a flourishing traffic in fugitive pilgrims, including women, who are tolerated because the costs of strict enforcement are prohibitive.

BIBLIOGRAPHY

Bianchi, Robert R. *Guests of God: Pilgrimage and Politics in the Islamic World*. New York: Oxford University Press, 2004.

"The Chinese Ḥajj," *National Geographic Channel*, February 8, 2012.

"From Xian to Mecca—The Road to Ḥajj," al-Jazeera, November 8 and 11, 2010.

Robert R. Bianchi

Ḥammām.

The ḥammām, the public bath, served the spiritual, physical, and social wellness of the Muslim community. Women entered and bathed separately from men to safeguard and protect modesty. Larger ḥammām had duplicate women's and men's areas; smaller Ḥammāms scheduled different times for women and men. Before the proliferation of private baths in houses and apartment buildings, most villages had at least one communal bath. Towns and cities had small bathhouses in each residential quarter, and one or more larger baths. Ḥammāms were often conspicuous charitable projects funded by a wealthy or politically well-connected woman to project her legitimacy, assert her status, and secure the affection of the community. In the last century, as private residences were plumbed to provide private bathing, many Ḥammāms fell into disuse. Those still in operation today serve people who enjoy the camaraderie of traditional social bathing, as well as tourists who have been persuaded through romantic literature, Orientalist paintings, and tourist guides that a visit to the ḥammām is an "authentic experience" of Muslim culture.

Islam associates the clean, pure body with strength and spiritual favor, and the dirty, defiled body with weakness and separation from the divine. An impure person should not enter the mosque or touch the Qurʾān; the prayers of a person whose body is unclean go unheard. The devotions of Islam require that observant people regularly perform ablution to cleanse their bodies of blood, excrement, and accumulated debris to restore ritual purity (*ṭahārah*).

Women have additional requirements for bathing, because women's reproductive blood is considered to be especially contaminating. Fluids from sexual activity and blood from menstruation or childbirth must be cleansed by full-body ablution (*ghusl*) before a woman may pray or fast, and before she can resume sexual intimacy with her husband. A woman's visit to the Ḥammām was a legitimate reason to go outside of her home and catch up on the local news and gossip. At the bath, she might spend most of the day massaging, scrubbing, bathing, steaming, applying henna, and talking with her friends. A visit often preceded festive occasions: the preparation for a wedding, the fortieth day after a child's birth, recovery from an illness, and the presentation of new clothing. As a woman returned home from the ḥammām, her henna and cleanliness announced her piety, purity, and worthiness.

At a public bath, a woman experiences her body in the context of a cooperative female bathing group. A woman cannot complete full ablution by herself as effectively as can women assisting each other. Thorough scrubbing of the back side, pubic depilation, hennaing hands and feet, and hairdressing require more reach and leverage than a woman can easily manage alone. Awkwardness was often eased by traditional phatic responses; a woman would apologize as she asked another's assistance in scrubbing her back side. The scrubber would respond, "A flower is beautiful from all sides."

In the Ḥammām, a woman is among other women, interacting with the array of bodies, infant to elder, each aware of each other's states of reproduction and wellness: a fleshly companionable reality, rather than one imagined through clothing.

BIBLIOGRAPHY

Aksit, Elif Ekin. "The Women's Quarters in the Historical Hammam." *Gender, Place and Culture: A Journal of Feminist Geography* 18, no. 2 (2011): 277–293. *Academic Search Complete*, EBSCO*host* (accessed February 17, 2012).

Cichocki, Nina. "Continuity and Change in Turkish Bathing Culture in Istanbul: The Life Story of the Çemberlitaş Hamam." *Turkish Studies* 6, no. 1 (2005): 93–112. *Academic Search Complete*, EBSCO*host* (accessed February 20, 2012).

Courtauld, Pari. *A Persian Childhood*. London: Rubicon, 1990.

Guppy, Shusha. *The Blindfold Horse: Memories of a Persian Childhood*. London: William Heineman, 1988.

Scarce, Jennifer. *Domestic Culture in the Middle East: An Exploration of the Household Interior*. Edinburgh: National Museums of Scotland, 1996.

Catherine Cartwright-Jones

Harem. Though many societies maintain formally or informally gendered spaces, the word "harem" is applied to Muslim domestic household spaces where the women's areas are separated from men's areas. The word "harem" means "forbidden" and is the women's space forbidden to outsiders. This private interior domestic space is created to house a man's wife, or wives and concubines, his pre-pubescent children, unmarried daughters, and female domestic workers. This space is established and maintained for the modesty, privilege, and protection of the women, so they may tend their household duties and raise their children without unnecessary disruption. Female relatives and trusted female friends may visit a harem. In previous centuries eunuchs guarded the harem and were permitted inside. A husband may be expected to give notice before he enters the women's space, by clearing his throat or making some other noise. The husband and male family members occupy the exterior household spaces. The male spaces are accessible to male kin, male friends, and associates, to whom the interior harem is forbidden.

Men who can provision and seclude the female members of a family tend to be well-to-do; establishing and maintaining the physical space of the harem and its inhabitants is expensive. Large harems and strict seclusion are rare: a claim to, and privilege of, the powerful and wealthy. In rural areas, or in households with limited resources, it is difficult or impractical to maintain strictly gendered spaces. In a nomadic tent or a household with a single room, a curtain may define women's space, though less securely than a wall.

There is no single model of a harem. The structure and extent of monogamy or polygyny in a harem is based on the family's personalities, resources, local norms, and placement in the community. Historical documentation of women's lives within harems is scarce, and colonial western writings about life in a harem tend to be limited or conjectural, through a visitor's or outsider's view. Though there were probably more harems maintained in the past than the present, the spatial seclusion of women is still practiced in many culturally Muslim regions. Where strict seclusion is neither norm nor law, there remain gradients of women's spaces, behaviors in private and public, blurring the original definition of harem.

Women share household duties and companionship in a polygynous harem. They also share the affections of the husband. Ideally the husband dispenses resources and affection equally among all wives, though wives frequently perceive and contest inequalities. Women in a polygynous harem may compete with each other to secure favors and benefits for their children and extended families. A woman secluded in a monogamous harem may be isolated and bear all household responsibilities, but will have the exclusive attention of her husband, and exclusive access to his resources. Some men and women maintain monogamous partnerships by choice. Men with limited means usually cannot afford to support more than one wife.

The gendered space of the harem in Islam is theorized as preserving social purity and honor, though the acquisition of wives and concubines has also been a strategy to accumulate political power through connections among powerful families. Some claim that gender separation is divinely ordained; others argue that gender separation and seclusion of women was a traditional practice in the region and was a cultural habit adapted into Islamic religious doctrine. Women secluded within a harem are protected from harassment by outsiders, but are also prevented from making acquaintance with outsiders. Seclusion insures the fidelity of a woman and paternity of her children. Women in public spaces may be harassed by those believe that outside of the harem a woman's honor is compromised and her social position is inferior.

When a woman goes outside of the harem, she may continue to seclude herself from the gaze of outsiders. A woman may extend the seclusion of the harem into public spaces by covering, concealing, walking, and gesturing modestly, and averting eye contact. Greater personal concealment may be used to claim greater virtue for the woman and for her family, as a conspicuously guarded gate signifies greater honor of the harem within.

The great tragic romances of Muslim literature, stories of forbidden, platonic, and courtly love, made dramatic use of the tensions caused by gendered spaces and the boundary disruptions of the harem. The western Orientalist imagining of a harem as a private brothel where dozens of women lounged in perpetual competitive lust for one man's affections was popular trope for paintings, operas, and stories, but is entirely false.

BIBLIOGRAPHY

Loosley, Emma. "Ladies Who Lounge: Class, Religion and Social Interaction in Seventeenth-Century Isfahan." *Gender and History* 23, no. 3 (2011): 615–629.

El Cheikh, Nadia Maria. "Revisiting the Abbasid Harems." *Journal of Middle East Women's Studies* 1, no. 3 (2005): 1–19.

CATHERINE CARTWRIGHT-JONES

HASHMI, FARHAT. (b. 1957), a Pakistani scholar of Islam and educator. Born in the town of Sargodha in Punjab, Pakistan, Farhat Hashmi received her initial religious education from her father, Abdur Rehman Hashmi, who was an active member of the religio-political organization the Jamaʿat-i-Islami (Islamic Party). She herself was active in the student wing of the Jamaʿat while pursuing her bachelor's degree from Sargodha Degree College and her master's in Arabic from Punjab University in Lahore. Hashmi spent a number of years teaching at the International Islamic University in Islamabad, after which she and her husband, Idrees Zubair, left for Glasgow, Scotland, where they both earned their PhD degrees in Islamic studies, with a specialization in *Ḥadīth* sciences, *ḥadīth* being the sayings of the Prophet Muhammad (Al-Huda International Welfare Foundation). On her return to Pakistan, she rejoined the International Islamic University, but soon left it and, in 1994, established Al-Huda International, an Islamic institute of learning for women that primarily offers one-to-two-year courses of study for a diploma.

Al-Huda is the primary ground for Hashmi's recognition. Its uniqueness lies in the fact that it has been able to make inroads into the middle and upper classes of the urban areas of

Pakistan—a feat that other religious groups had historically been unsuccessful at accomplishing. Hashmi's pedagogy has been influenced by the teaching tools used by the Jamaʿat-i-Islami in its religious-learning circles and the exposure that she received while studying and traveling in the United Kingdom and Muslim-majority countries like Saudi Arabia in the Middle East. Her students highlight her educational qualifications, charismatic personality, and the manner in which she relies on logic and science to help them understand the relevance of the Qurʿān to their daily lives as playing a key role in their rediscovering themselves as Muslims and understanding what it means to live a Muslim life (Ahmad, 2009).

Hashmi's success is visible in her school's national and international expansion; in how her students, numbering in the thousands, have transformed their ideology, behavior, and lifestyles to accord with the religious discourse that they internalize while at this school; and in the enthusiasm with which they work toward spreading its ideology in mainstream society through systematic religious outreach, which includes setting up branches of the school all around the country and in various parts of the world, such as the United States, Canada, Britain, and Dubai. This is significant since they are internalizing and spreading a specific understanding of Islam (Ahmad, 2008).

Although Hashmi does not claim any doctrinal affiliation, her Qurʾānic exegesis and teachings are similar to the Ahl-e-Hadith school of thought in South Asia. Like its proponents, she draws upon a literal interpretation of the Qurʾān, relies heavily on the Sunnah, is critical of the idea of having intermediaries between oneself and God, and desires to remove cultural accretions and societal traditions. Her doctrinal positioning has resulted in her being critiqued by those Muslims, such as the Bareilvi and Shīʿah, who practice their faith differently. Some Pakistanis also criticize her on specific injunctions, such as her prescription of veiling for women, her stance on music as being un-Islamic, and her rejection of a number of customary rituals, like those that take place at events like weddings, and so forth.

Hashmi and her husband have three daughters and a son. The entire family is actively involved in transforming society from the bottom up and creating, through their religious teachings, a particular kind of culture that is informed by their understanding of what true Islam is.

BIBLIOGRAPHY

Ahmad, Sadaf. "Identity Matters, Culture Wars: An Account of Al-Huda (Re)-defining Identity and Reconfiguring Culture in Pakistan." *Culture and Religion* 9, no. 1 (2008): 63–80.

Ahmad, Sadaf. *Transforming Faith: A Story of Al-Huda and Islamic Revivalism among Urban Pakistani Women*. Syracuse, N.Y.: Syracuse University Press, 2009.

Al-Huda International Welfare Foundation. http://wp.farhathashmi.com/.

SADAF AHMAD

HAYʾAT. Originally an Arabic word meaning "form," "quality," "group," and "organization," inter alia, the Persianized form *hayʾat* is used in the context of contemporary Iranian Shiism to denote an organized social group of Shīʿah performing a religious rite (e.g., celebrating the birth of the imams or commemorating their martyrdom). In its more specific and prevalent usage, however, *hayʾat* refers to a collection of people, usually exclusively male, who would gather together in localities, cities, or villages for the purpose of mourning and commemorating the martyrdom of Imam Ḥusayn at Karbalā in Muḥarram in 680 CE, especially during ʿĀshūrā, the tenth day of the month. Associated activities take place in assemblies held in buildings erected especially for the mourning of martyred imams, known either as *ḥusaynīyah* or *takīyah*, as well as in mosques and private homes. Women are just observers of general *hay'at* activities, while exclusively female religious gatherings (*sufrahs*) are usually formed in private homes (see Maẓāhirī, 2008, pp. 294–295, 312). Participation in *hay'at* is voluntary and based on inner conviction.

There is usually a dual structure to the *hay'at* gatherings: a sermon by a speaker, followed by the eulogy, or remembrance of the martyrs. The latter is called *rawẓah-khvānī* and is the recitation of *Rawẓat al-shuhadā'* by Ḥusayn Vā'iẓ Kāshifī (d. c. 1504), or similar works on the martyrdom of the imams. During the mourning ceremonies of Muḥarram, professional reciters and preachers would recount the story of the martyrs, arousing the emotions of attendees who respond by *sīnah-zanī* (beating the chest) and singing dirges at appropriate intervals in the narrative. Other expressions of grief during the mourning processions (*dasta-gardānī*) include *zanjīr-zanī* (beating oneself with chains), *tīgh-zanī* or *qamah-zanī* (mortifying oneself with swords or knives), and theatrical representations of the Karbalā tragedy called *shabīh-khvānī* or *ta'zīah*.

The application of the term *hay'at* to these religious groups dates back less than a century, even though the actual formation of mourning *dastahs* (groups) and assemblies can be traced further back in time. After their emergence during the early history of Islam, they absorbed new, foreign (mostly Christian) elements under the Ṣafavids (1502–1722), flourished during the Qājār era (1785–1925) when the phenomenon we now know as *hay'at* first emerged, and continued, despite some turbulence, under the Pahlavis (1925–1979). Under the Islamic Republic (1979–the present), a new chapter has been opened in the organization of *hay'at*. They are now formed throughout the year, not only in Muḥarram, and their function now goes far beyond mere mourning rites to include educational, recreational, and cultural activities mostly aimed at preventing the cultural "invasion" (*taḥājum*) of the West. As a whole, *hay'at* practices have become more specialized, age-specific, and in some cases, state-sanctioned. It could be argued that they now function largely as state-sponsored organs and pressure groups. In more recent years, new trends have appeared in the works of some *hay'at* eulogists (*maddāḥīn*) who implement unusual lyrics or melodies that contravene established norms.

BIBLIOGRAPHY

Calmard, J. "'AZĀDĀRĪ." *Encyclopaedia Iranica*, December 15, 1987, http://www.iranicaonline.org/articles/azadari. In this *Encyclopaedia Iranica* entry on mourning, Calmard provides a succinct and precise description of the rites of Muḥarram that are particularly relevant to the topic of *hay'at*.

Maẓāhirī, Muḥsin Ḥisām. *Rasānah-yi Shī'a: jāmi'ashināsī-i ā'īnhā-yi sūgvārī va hay'at ha-yi maẕhabī dar Iran.* 2d ed. Tehran, Iran: Sāzimān-i Tablīghāt-i Islāmī, Shirkat-i Chap va Nashr-i Bayn al-milal, 2008. An extended and revised version of an earlier monograph, this is a comprehensive study of Iranian Shī'ī mourning rites and religious *hay'at* practices from a sociological perspective. As both a compendium of the author's observational sampling and a study of relevant primary sources and secondary literature, the work provides an informed insider's view on the topic.

MINA YAZDANI

HEALTH CARE. The health care accorded to Muslim women refers in its broadest sense to a wide range of public institutions, social organizations, and professionals committed to women's general well-being and development from birth to death. For some researchers it refers specifically to processes by professional health caregivers that address both the physical and mental dimensions of health, implying that such aspects as the meaning and interpretations of illness and disease, their impact on individual women and the treatment proposed for them derives from a modern understanding of health care. There are limitations to this understanding, for it is evident that the well-being of women is registered in the fundamental source of Islamic consciousness, the Qurʾān.

Over its long history Islamic interpreters have focused on the importance of community well-being, emphasizing the obligation of the *ummah* to care for all of its members and giving special attention to the least-advantaged, particularly widows and orphans. This suggests a framework for public discussion of the priorities of health care investment in order to assure that no one group within the *ummah* is privileged or left behind in favor of another. This is as true of gender as it is of other groupings. By this logic the health care of females can be said to be basic to Islamic public policy; it is not restricted to professional caregivers or their construction of health care. Indeed in the Muslim world today there are prolonged and intensive debates about gender, gender roles, and sexuality, and their implications for Islamic health care.

Health Care Systems and Muslim Women's Health Care. Given that Muslim women are found in most countries of the world, and that Islamic society has embraced many different cultural forms, it would seem a hazardous business to depict commonalities across this diverse landscape. Nevertheless there are some health specificities that we can address; how women as *women* have vied for resources to maintain well-being is one.

Care for women after the initial expansion of Islam was left, for the most part, to women, whether as midwives, women assistants, or ordinary family members. As traditional Islamic society evolved, the public, political, and social spheres were dominated by men, while domestic development and maintenance were the responsibilities of women. This structure of society dovetailed well with Islam's legal view of the complementarity of men and women. The net result, however, was that women's health was assigned as the responsibility of the family, while men's health was a matter of concern for the state, since healthy males were needed to serve the public good. Women's health thus remained in the private sphere but men's assumed a public dimension. Furthermore women's rights to well-being derived fundamentally from their reproductive capacity, for their "purpose" was to produce the heirs and leaders of the next generation of Muslims. Even current evidence suggests that male-female preferences in children continues to play a role in family development: for example, Sulayman al-Qudsi found in his study of four Arab countries that the number of male/female surviving children impacted on expected fertility levels. Anecdotal evidence suggests that the permanency of marriages was sometimes predicated on the basis of whether the female could produce male children; however, the evidence demonstrates only the social-cultural preference for sons among Middle Eastern Arabs/Muslims.

The growth of Muslim medical professionals in the Middle Ages, largely under the influence of ancient Greek medicine, appears to have been dominated by males, for the major figures of the Golden Age such as the classical Muslim physicians al-Razi and Ibn Sīnā were overwhelmingly male, and their research and studies (which subsequently influenced the West) were performed on male subjects. In medieval Europe male dominance even encompassed what was previously women's medicine—gynecology—as Monica Green shows. The counterpart trend in Islamic civilization may well have been with the growing male *ʿulamāʾ* class supported by Islamic cultural influences around the central role of *kalām* and Sharīʿah. Although these medical sources—written exclusively by men—offer few examples of women, it would be hard to believe that women made no impact whatsoever on this important developing field. Some sources indicate that women served as nurses in Islamic institutions before the practice was adopted in other parts of the world and two female surgeons were known in the twelfth century, under the Almohads. In fact peripheral mentions in other historical records suggest that women's impact on and participation in health care occurred in informal, rather than formal, settings; perhaps scholars need to look beyond theoretical or practical manuals written in formal settings and include analysis of other types of records to establish the actual contributions of women.

The influence of modernity on the Islamic world disrupted the public/private model at several levels. First, the growth of modern states, evolving out of the breakdown of Muslim empires and the colonial incursions of the West, required a more sophisticated role for both men and women, although it tended to leave accepted gender norms intact. This played out in the field of health care, as well as in the political realm. To take one example, Egypt's male physicians reacted to colonialism by linking Muslim women's role to the creation of a modern state. Thus Hibba Abugideiri's analysis, following Lisa Pollard, shows that Egypt's medical establishment affirmed that women "nurtured the nation," as a way of reasserting the religious characterization of women's maternal, domestic nature in the now secular institution of medicine. This demonstrated a shift from religious to secular authority, while leaving the gender roles intact. A moment's reflection will raise the question about whether health care systems throughout Muslim countries may have responded to colonialism by adopting "modern" medicine as the frontispiece for proposed reforms as a way of deflecting criticism; advocating medicine for women may have been a way of appearing to be "modern" without changing the traditional gendered cultural space.

Second, as Western critiques of Islam grew more petulant, women's health and women's position became a source of contention and adaptation. In Egypt, for example, the British, led by Evelyn, 1st Earl Cromer in 1883–1907, decried that Islam could not be modernized, as was evidenced by its women; his views were countered by writers such as Qāsim Amīn (1863–1908), who focused his reformist agenda around women, counter-arguing that once liberated, Egypt's women would change both Egypt and Islam. For him the role and scope of women's influence in society challenged the Islamic gendered status quo, resulting in the rise of an Islamic feminist consciousness with the attendant desire to throw off those cultural restrictions that hampered women's equality. In this way women's health and women's bodies became the field of international debate on whether Islam could be modernized. Brilliant Muslim writers like Huda Shaʿarawi (1882–1947) determined to give a refined response to the negative Western perspectives on women, while women leaders like Qut al-Qulub (1899–1968) glorified the traditional role of the Qurʾān in women's formation and their place in contemporary pious society as the normative basis of their place in society. Other women contemporaries, such as Malak Hifni Nasif (1886–1918) contended for deepening women's involvement in traditional Islamic scholarship. By this time it would appear that the shift toward reading Islamic social potential through women and their health was firmly established and critics who worried about the "modernizing" influence of these medical forces on women had already lost the field.

Third, the educated class within Islamic societies accepted the Western position that women could be educated as much as men and consequently their position in society should be commensurate with their abilities. Rural women from economically strong families, encouraged by the growth of local educational opportunities, began to embrace higher education. The result was that they flooded into major universities in the Muslim world to develop their skills and prepare themselves for a leading intellectual role in the expanding economies. Among the elite Muslim families a similar pattern emerged; the difference was that they migrated to Western institutions to study because of the lack of sophisticated opportunities at home. They often returned with Western ideas about women's roles that broke the stereotypes of sex and gender at home. As women studied to be doctors and psychologists, among other medical professions, and were thus capable of dealing with illness and disease in both men and women, traditional roles were slowly being eroded. While these women continued to raise families while they worked, they nevertheless broke the rigid perception that only males could function as leading professionals. Their work was also an implicit criticism of an inherent paternalism within the medical profession and highlighted the resistance that women had toward it. When they returned home from studying abroad, they brought a fresh standard of evaluation: they often found women's health care in abysmal condition, especially in rural areas. Many further pointed out the human and social costs of such neglect and fingered these as reasons for high infant mortality and mother morbidity rates. They brought a new sensitivity to the health of women and voiced concerns for future generations when mothers were in such poor condition. This in turn moved reformers to focus on women's health as a powerful political fulcrum.

The post–World War II period has seen further evolution of Muslim women's health care. A global awareness of the comparatively negative position of women's health around the world took the public stage; the plight of developing countries, many of them Muslim, in obtaining proper maternity care consistently was a theme in international studies. Cognizant of these challenges, many Muslim women who studied in Western countries, especially in the United States and Canada, joined organizations dedicated exclusively to women's health, such as the women's health movement. They worked vigorously toward continuous and exclusive focus on women's health as the means for lifting the well-being of women and improving health outcomes for all societies. The advent of feminism in the West turned the academic acumen of women professionals to the continuing recalcitrance of health care systems in addressing the inequities in conceptualization, research, delivery, and care of women's health. Feminists argued that the conventional system was flawed in its bias toward male well-being with little consideration for the distinctive health care requirements for women. Arguments were made, as in Indonesia, that, since women provided a significant amount of the workforce, they should have commensurate health and other services. The upshot was that health care systems in some Islamic countries came under increasing scrutiny for their inequities.

Contemporary migration patterns have brought new strains to health care, as Muslim women immigrants are often left outside of health care systems in their new host countries, despite the best of intentions, sometimes due to cultural norms surrounding the privacy of women's bodies. It is evident that, in some countries, Muslim women will not speak about the breast in public, will seldom seek help when they notice changes in their breasts, and place a low priority on their own health. Physicians complain that such antipathy to testing means they do not see these women until their cancers are too far gone for adequate treatment. Generally the risk of morbidity is high among these women. In the

United States, for example, studies highlight Muslim women's resistance to cervical cancer screening; and in the Netherlands gender differences are noted in the utilization of health care. Some of these cultural norms constrain women in their home countries as well. In Iran, for example, physicians have reported encountering barriers to mammography testing, highlighting ongoing challenges in the delivery of health care initiatives and the need for cultural consideration and deliberate construction of more appropriate health care delivery. Still these concerns are not just cases of women from developing countries being unfamiliar with medical protocols—similar reluctances can be seen in Canada, especially among older women immigrants, who do not want to "be a burden." Clearly, social status, education, and poverty are critical factors in health care access for some of these people. Cultural and religious elements may only be a lesser contributing element.

Requirement Differences in Muslim Women's Health Care. Women all over the world are living longer than men, with the age gap at death around six years, and tend to use health care services more than their male counterparts. Yet there are major noteworthy differences in the gender dimensions of health that go beyond the scope of reproductive capacities. For example, in the United States more women than men die of heart attacks; heart disease is a major threat, targeting women ten years older than men; women suffer from depression on a magnitude of three to four times that of men; American women have adverse experiences with drugs more commonly than men; autoimmune diseases like multiple sclerosis and rheumatoid arthritis occur in American women three times more frequently than in men; four out of five sufferers of bone loss and osteoporosis are women; and women are twice as likely to be infected by sexually transmitted diseases in the U.S. These examples are sufficient to indicate that Muslim women in the U.S., and probably around the world, have health care risks that cannot be confronted with the current systems of care, at least not without major disruption to family welfare. The social position of women means that they struggle more with health care costs, especially in poorer countries, and even in the United States, where millions have no health care coverage at all. Immigrant women are most often exposed to this jeopardy, making them reluctant to see a physician for fear of the cost to the family or to their meager income.

Muslim cultural preferences with respect to the privacy of the female body also impact women's health. Where an Australian or Swedish woman may only prefer to have a female physician attend her delivery, or may indeed consult a male gynecologist because of his expertise or reputation, Muslim values of preventing unrelated males access to the female body sometimes present difficulties in contemporary hospital settings, as physicians who serve conservative Muslim populations in Canada will attest. However, this social preference acts as a constraint, not as a deterrent to health, for most women, even rural traditional believers, will opt for male physicians when necessary. They often find that strict adherence to gender-specific care can be a barrier to immediate health care. For example, insisting on female gynecologists for delivery may be quite impossible for many mothers simply because their doctor may not be available when they must go to the hospital. They will then have to accept the male physician on duty at that time. Such gender concerns also impact physicians' careers. In Iran men are restricted from specializing in gynecology, and women are barred from urology. Cultural values can also have a direct impact on health care preferences: 96.3 percent of Emirate women wanted a female doctor for gynecological examinations, and 94.5 percent preferred a female doctor for the stomach.

Modern staffing provisions may make these preferences impossible.

By contrast when governments invest in women's health, significant changes can be made. For example, in Bahrain, free public health care, both at the primary and maternity level, are available. It is not surprising that the maternal mortality dropped dramatically—to 0.22 per 1,000 live births, compared to the 2000 world average of 0.44 per 1,000. Information on maternity and other women's health concerns are freely available to women as is family planning assistance. While this data refers to maternity issues, there are studies that confirm this in other areas of treatment.

Reproductive Health Care. Traditionally having a successful pregnancy and delivery was the hallmark of a Muslim woman's life course, making fertility a primary expected characteristic in a wife. Any difficulties arising in getting pregnant were quite likely to be laid on the woman, rendering infertility a cause for anxiety for women due to fear of divorce. Islamic law appeared to offer some hope of not being divorced if a wife could not conceive since Muslim men were legally allowed to marry up to four wives. However, while we know now that about one third of infertility issues lie with men, even in some countries to this day, failure to produce a child may be grounds for divorce or the taking of a second wife. Thus fear of infertility on either spouse's part remains a major concern for many Muslim women.

In some cases technology can be called in for help with conception. Where some illness or genetic impediments do not allow pregnancy, Islamic attitudes to in vitro fertilization and surrogate mothering appear to be fairly firm: it is allowed if the male's sperm is utilized because this maintains paternity while allowing another woman to fulfill the symbolic role of "additional wife." Where the strength of male sperm is deemed unable to penetrate the egg, the physician may recommend applying to a sperm bank. Most Muslim males refuse this option, however, and most religious scholars have forbidden it because of the change in paternity. Hence modern technologies cannot solve some of the continuing problems surrounding reproduction and health.

If birthing and childbearing were traditionally viewed as "women's work" with little or no input from Muslim men, the slow growth of science around reproduction moved women's bodies into the arena of evidence-based medicine, and hence into a sphere where males have come to have control. Concomitantly the medicalization and hospitalization of the maternity experience has wrought major changes for women. For one thing, where the midwife or woman relative may have helped the pregnant woman in the mother's own home, surrounded by female friends and relatives and perhaps other children, during childbirth, hospital births have increasingly exercised active control over the social dimension of birth. The experience of childbirth has been altered by these protocols, for the expectation in the labor room in a hospital is quite different than that of the home. The hospital environment alone produces some fear. Moreover medical procedures, such as epidural anesthesia or cesarean delivery, have changed the birthing process, and in some countries their numbers have increased dramatically. Hassan Ba'aqeel found a stunning 80.2 percent increase among women in Saudi Arabia in only ten years. Controversies swirl around these procedures, especially the latter, where the accusation is made that male doctors prefer controlled hospital procedures to waiting for nature to take its course. Some Muslim women, who value the social interaction with friends and relatives in an important experience of their lives, may be increasingly wary of this medicalization of the birthing experience.

The binary sexual notion continues to hold sway over Muslim women's lives—specifically with regard to childcare and the health of children. It is generally held to be a Muslim cultural concept, rooted in long-held beliefs in the woman's roles as nurturer and homemaker. Sharing child-rearing responsibilities is a fairly contemporary concept around the world and is applied only among more educated Muslim families. Muslim mothers are expected to forgo career and personal achievement while the children are small, except among the wealthy elite classes, whose children are cared for by employees. In Pakistan, where women's equality rights under Islam are regarded as "Western," women often must continue to care for children even if they work full-time. But there are striking changes afoot. With personal and cultural expectations so high, Muslim women have begun to limit childbearing, and the figures are stark: in Morocco, Syria, and Saudi Arabia, for instance, birth rates have declined by 60 percent. Iran now has a birth rate equal to the least reproductive region in the United States, New England. Such figures, should they remain consistent, signal a dramatic change in Muslim family values around the world with evident implications for health care: where states have invested heavily in reproductive health and child care facilities that are no longer needed, considerable reorientation in health care organization will be necessary—finances might be better invested in senior women's health given the rise of that cohort.

Health Care Differences Among Muslim Women. Another feature of health care for women relates to differences in health needs. It is obvious that post-menopausal women will have different health needs than a twenty-year-old woman pregnant for the first time. Accidents claim more youth than do cancers, while cancers claim more women over thirty. Many studies have documented that women in general, and Muslim women in particular, have poor health outcomes; they restrict medical visits until absolutely necessary, and they are reluctant to utilize family resources for health care professionals. Furthermore there are major impediments to access by rural Muslims. Modern technology may aid in overcoming some of these barriers, as has occurred when Canadian health care workers provided cell phones to community health workers in Bangladesh so they could continuously check on breast cancer victims' progress; this circumvented the need for expensive and debilitating travel.

Disparities are reflected, too, in illness patterns, with major lifestyle diseases like diabetes and obesity now dominant in Arab populations and Southeast Asia, in contrast to South Africa where HIV/AIDS predominates. Saudi Arabia has elevated breast cancer numbers (30 percent of breast cancer cases are in women under the age of forty, compared with only five percent in the United States), suggesting that major awareness campaigns need to be launched. Saudi women created the largest human awareness ribbon to date when four thousand of them turned out in Riyadh in support of breast cancer research. Since the country now has the largest female university in the world, perhaps greater resources will be allocated to address some of these glaring female health care problems. It is also significant that this was organized by women themselves, demonstrating the principle that Muslim women play a much greater role through informal organizations than formal.

Jordan has attractive health care awareness organizations, including the well-known Royal Health Awareness Society under Queen Rania; in partnership with WHO and the Jordanian Ministry of Health, it promotes national standards for healthy schools. Campaigns for maternity and breast cancer have also been promoted. Such state-sponsored groups may slowly shift public opinion about women's health care from being the personal problem for the individual woman to a public-supported, civic responsibility. Perhaps then other Muslim countries, like Afghanistan, will then follow suit.

Health care for Muslim women would appear to be a major arena for development in all countries of the world. The history of it, the access to it, and the nuanced Muslim attitudes to it all are loci of research and development today. These are necessary if Muslim women are to be properly served. This might be seen as a basic matter of justice for a sizable portion of the world's population.

BIBLIOGRAPHY

Abugideiri, Hibba. *Gender and the Making of Modern Medicine in Colonial Egypt*. Farnham, Surrey, U.K.: Ashgate Publishing Ltd., 2010.

Ahmadian, Maryam, et al. "Barriers to Mammography Among Women Attending Gynecologic Outpatient Clinics in Tehran, Iran." *Scientific Research and Essays* 6, no. 27 (2011): 5803–5811.

Al-Qudsi, Sulayman. *Labor Participation of Arab Women: Estimates of the Fertility to Labor Supply Link*. Cairo: Economic Research Forum for the Arab Countries, Iran, and Turkey, 1996. http://idl-bnc.idrc.ca/dspace/bitstream/10625/34535/1/126385.pdf.

Ba'aqeel, Hassan S. "Cesarean Delivery Rates in Saudi Arabia: A Ten-year Review.' *Annuals of Saudi Medicine* 29, no. 3 (May–June 2009): 179–183.

Barazangi, Nimat Hafez. *Woman's Identity and the Qur'an: A New Reading*. Gainesville: University Press of Florida, 2004.

Brockopp, Jonathan E., and Thomas Eich. "Muslim Medical Ethics: From Theory to Practice. Columbia: University of South Carolina Press, 2008.

DeLong-Bas, Natana J. "Women, Islam, and the Twenty-first Century." *Oxford Islamic Studies Online*, 2008. http://www.oxfordislamicstudies.com/Public/focus/essay1107_women.html/.

Dhami, Sangeeta, and Aziz Sheikh. "The Muslim Family: Predicament and Promise." *Western Journal of Medicine* 173, no. 5 (November 2010): 352–356.

Eberstadt, Nicholas. "The Islamic World's Quiet Revolution." *Foreign Policy* March 9, 2012. http://www.foreignpolicy.com/articles/2012/03/09/the_islamic_worlds_quiet_revolution/.

Gerritsen, Annette A. M, and Walter L. Deville. "Gender Differences in Health and Health Care Utilisation in Various Ethnic Groups in the Netherlands: A Cross-sectional Study." *BMC Public Health* 9 (April 2009): 109ff. http://www.biomedcentral.com/1471-2458/9/109/.

Ginsburg, Ophira. "Mobile Health Solutions for Breast Cancer Case-Finding, Referral, and Navigation in Rural Bangladesh. Vimeo. http://vimeo.com/35889318/.

Green, Monica H. *Making Women's Medicine Masculine: The Rise of Male Authority in Pre-Modern Gynaecology*. New York: Oxford University Press, 2008.

Manca, Donna. Family doctor who delivers babies in an East Asian community hospital in Edmonton, Alberta, Canada. Personal communication with the author, 2012.

Matin, Mina, and Samuel LeBaron. "Attitudes Toward Cervical Cancer Screening among Muslim Women: A Pilot Study." *Women and Health* 39, no. 3 (2004): 63–77.

McLean M., et al. "Muslim Women's Physician Preference: Beyond Obstetrics and Gynecology." *Health Care Women International* 33, no. 9 (September 2012): 849–876.

Moghadam, Valentine M. *Modernizing Women: Gender and Social Change in the Middle East*. 2d ed. Boulder, Colo: Lynne Rienner Publishers, 2003.

Musaiger, Abdulrahman Obaid. "Socio-cultural and Economic Factors Affecting Food Consumption Patterns in the Arab Countries." *Journal of the Royal Society for the Promotion of Health* 113, no. 2 (1993): 68–74.

Pollard, Lisa. *Nurturing the Nation: The Family Politics of Modernizing, Colonizing and Liberating Egypt (1805–1923)*. Berkeley: University of California Press, 2005.

Prasad, Amrit, and Fazana Saleem-Ismail. "Health Inequities: Country and Regional Experiences." *The Social Determinants of Health: Assessing Theory, Policy and Practice*. Papers presented at an International Conference held at London, 26–28 November 2008, edited by Sanjoy Bhattacharya, Sharon Messenger, and Caroline Overy. New Delhi: Orient Blackswan, 2010.

Qāsim Amīn *The Liberation of Woman*; and *The New Woman: Two Documents in the History of Egyptian*

Feminism. Translated by Samiha Sidhom Peterson. Cairo: American University of Cairo Press, 2000.
Robinson, Kathryn, and Sharon Bessell, eds. *Women in Indonesia: Gender, Equity, and Development*. Singapore: Institute of Southeast Asian Studies, 2002.
Ruzek, Sheryl. *The Women's Health Movement: Feminist Alternatives to Medical Control*. New York: Praeger Publishers, 1978.
Shaheed, F. "The Cultural Articulation of Patriarchy: Legal Systems, Islam and Women. South Asia Bulletin 6, no. 1 (Spring 1986): 38–44.
Society for Women's Health Research (SWHR). http://www.womenshealthresearch.org/.
Waugh, Earle. *Visionairies of Silence: The Reformist Sufi Order of the Demirdashiya al-Khalwatiya in Cairo*. Cairo: American University in Cairo Press, 2008.
World Health Organization. *The World Health Report 2004*. Geneva, Switzerland: WHO, 2004.

EARLE WAUGH

HEALTH ISSUES. Health issues often relate directly to state policy and priorities, and connecting them to a sociocultural system is extremely difficult. Furthermore, because Muslim women live in diverse communities throughout the world, including minority situations, their health issues differ widely. Since health more broadly includes mental or physical health, as well as social well-being and cultural safety, the topic may reach beyond what many conventional writings on women's health may report. Thus, issues relating to state control of health resources, Muslim legal traditions, and reformist activities all impact on issues that Muslim women face with their health.

At the same time, Muslim women's agency in their own health can be an issue. Many studies imply that Muslim women rarely undertake initiative about their own health. The fact is, however, that most studies focus almost exclusively on formal and official health institutions for their analysis. This skews clear understanding away from care they may undertake in nonformal settings, such as, for example. through midwives, local "healers," or family emphases on health and proper diet. Against the general trend, Bucar (2010) has argued that, within certain boundaries, women do exercise effective agency regarding their health. Hence, a very prevalent issue is evaluating the evidence from research, much of it guided by biomedical models, which may provide only one aspect of Muslim women's agency. Other studies with a different perspective have affirmed women's independence in some health areas (Keefe, 2006). Hence there appears to be no unanimity in the research on just what constitutes Muslim women's health issues.

In most studies, health issues encompass an array of topics; only a small number will be addressed here. We will pay particular attention to those that may be linked, more or less, with some confidence to a significant Islamic sociocultural milieu—that is, Muslim women accept them as having some connection with their religious beliefs. However, it must be remembered that health issues reflect deep cultural linkages to other social, economic, and political systems, making the drawing of specific conclusions linking women, Islamic beliefs, and health care difficult. This entry will look at seven critical areas in attempting to spell out how Islamic influences impact on female believers' health: the global contexts of health issues; the issues that foreground the notion of a universal Islam; issues around the female body; age-related issues; sexual and reproductive issues; mental health issues and social issues. Obviously these are not exhaustive, but they do touch on some of the most important discussions taking place today.

The Global Contexts of Health Issues. Global health analyses stress that health issues cannot be easily disentangled from other crucial aspects of women's lives. This is certainly true of Muslim women. Women who come from developed countries have consistently better access to health care than others; women who belong to the elite or wealthier classes have better care than others. Like class, ethnicity also plays a role in health, sometimes determining who will receive care and who will not. It is a given in the literature that education impacts positively and directly on health; however, Muslim women around the world often have limited educational opportunities. Furthermore, all sources point out that the place of residence determines health outcomes to a great extent, since availability of health resources, and publicity about them, influences women's utilization. These social determinants are the subject of widespread discussion among public health theorists, and Muslim women are sometimes points of concern in those discussions. A good example of the impact of such social determinants is Hussain's 2009 study of literacy rates in West Bengal; Muslim literacy rates have declined in the state, and now stand 11.7 percent below the average across all other religious communities. Bengali Muslims appear to have retreated from education. Where newer technologies can provide better service, literacy would seem to be critical for access, so women's health may well be jeopardized by this decline. By extrapolation, we might surmise that one global issue is the health education provided to Muslim women across many different social and political environments.

Another global issue relates to life expectancy. Worldwide, women live longer than men. This implies that there are more aged Muslim women than men. Increasingly, one of the issues that predominates discussions about Muslim women is the reality of an aging cohort of women who may live without the support of a male partner and/or a community network. This feature can be linked to poverty, too. Women in all cultures are poorer than their male counterparts for a variety of reasons; in Muslim communities, patriarchal social norms, among other variables, restrict women's access to careers outside the home, which, in turn, means lower income. Expectedly, one way to see poverty impact on Muslim women's health is in life expectancy: an average woman's life expectancy in Saudi Arabia is now seventy-six, while an average Somali women only lives to be around fifty-two. Thus longevity is a global issue among Muslim women that various states must soon address.

Issues in Foregrounding A "Universal Islam." Ideologically, many claim that Islam expresses the same kind of doctrine and takes the same legal stance about equality wherever it has taken root. The reality may be quite different. In Islamic societies, the allocation of resources for women's health may be contested, especially where the allocation is for a female-only health initiative. At issue is the equitable use of resources for men and women, an argument deriving from the affirmation of equality of both sexes in the Qurʾān itself (49:13). Debates about systemic inequality within cultures and the role of religion in maintaining it have been the hallmark of health discussions for several centuries, and Islamic domains are no different than others. Thus, generalizations about health issues related to Muslim women must be contextualized within their own particular jurisdictions, since there is no universal Islamic definition of equity that can be applied across all societies.

Ethnicity can also sometimes be a detrimental factor in Muslim women's health. In some states, inter-ethnic identity determines who will have access to care and who will not. A recent example of this is a study of Arab-Israeli women. Even though the health care system was altered to address Arab women's health issues, their use of that system was far less than it should have been. The result is that their health status lagged behind that of Jewish women (Elnekave and Gross, 2003). This is also true in Europe (Netuveli et al., 2005).

A quantifiable sense of inequity appears as the result of the growth of wealth in some Muslim countries—poorer states cannot afford the costs of contemporary health demands. In that case, the wealthy state can raise the resources for women at the same time as men, while poorer states can only afford to provide a minimal amount for both. The result is that women in a poor state have far fewer resources than their counterparts in a wealthier Muslim state. One might then argue that there is inequity between Muslim states on resources allocated to women (Razzak et al., 2011). The point is that what equity in health allocations means varies from state to state in the Muslim world, and it varies across borders.

The Female Body Issue. Throughout the world, there are some aspects of Muslim women's health that reflect the influence of distinctive Islamic sociocultural perceptions. One issue relates to the social-cultural perceptions of the female body, how it should be understood, and who should control it. For example, biomedicine builds upon Western cultural norms that hold that, where major access to the body is necessary for testing, diagnosis, and treatment by health care professionals, then the gender of the professional is irrelevant to those activities. The primacy of "evidence" in these situations and the means to obtain it largely trump the individual's sense of privacy.

In most traditional Islamic societies, the view is that all social contacts with the opposite sex have a gendered dimension, including those with health professionals—there are few "neutral" environments. It is an operative norm. Restrictions to the male "gaze" are part of the gift of protection that Islamic values afford Muslim women. This norm circumscribes not only interaction with health care professionals, but also applies to non-family members. It also influences social and cultural areas, as for example, in dress codes and in the separation of males and females during rituals such as prayers. The norm also impacts on such things as birthing protocols, business meetings, seating arrangements in public places, and eye contact. The freedom to be a woman who controls all gendered evaluations is a perspective that Muslim women value deeply within their religious tradition. Obviously it is a norm that comes into play in situations related to health.

In the contemporary Muslim world, the norm is challenged by several factors. Educated Muslim women, for example, may choose a male gynecologist because of his superior reputation, while others might prefer the counsel of the best female gynecologist in order to remain connected to the traditional gendered norm. Moreover, it is evident that even in places like Saudi Arabia, with its emphasis on traditional norms, a male specialist might be required for some procedures, such as Caesarean sections (Ba'aqeel, 2009). The growth of modern biomedical services in Muslim women's lives has also impacted on the norm: even rural women recognize the successes of the professionalization of medicine and they seek out the best authority for their health condition, even if the gendered norm cannot be maintained.

Gendered social situations also dictate access to health in some countries. In rural areas of poorer countries such as Afghanistan, male physicians must evaluate female patients through a partition which allows limited access. Furthermore, being the primary person responsible for family health often means that children or husbands are the first to be supplied with professional care, while women find other ways of caring for themselves. It also means that Muslim women may defer to husbands or fathers in the use of household resources for health purposes or in determining when professional public access to the female's body is warranted. Some Western scholars now refer to this distinctive sense of a Muslim female person as the "Islamic body" (Sargent and Larchanche, 2007), suggesting that Muslim social norms are operative. While biomedical manuals may not contain such concepts, it does provide a convenient reference for the Muslim woman's experience, encapsulating personal comfort, ease of discussion, and acceptable health treatment for themselves in the light of gender norms. Clearly these societal norms are likewise subject to evolution and contextualization in the contemporary world.

Age-Related Issues. Health risks exist at all age levels for Muslim women. Whereas in North America girls and women up to age thirty-five overwhelmingly die from accidents, globally a much more diversified picture emerges. Country-dependent malnutrition and youth diseases predominate, and risks associated with birth and poor maternity care are much more evident. If Muslim women live in the developing world, the statistics tell us that 99 of 100 cases of death from childbirth and pregnancy occur there (Centers for Disease Control and Prevention, 2006). Studies indicate that Muslim women in underdeveloped countries die from childbirth issues that could have been avoided—hemorrhage or obstructed delivery, for example. Some, especially in places like the Sudan, do not receive proper nutritional care or effective delivery services. Some of these women are very young, and they have neither the experience nor the understanding of the medical processes involved in birth.

Worldwide, from ages thirty-five to forty-four, chronic diseases, such as cancer and heart diseases, move to the top of the list. In that, women in the rest of the world mirror their Western sisters. At the same time, menopausal Muslim women all over the world have an increased life expectancy, with the result that many outlive their partners and live well into their senior years. Official patterns for these senior women do not vary much as a collective group from their sisters elsewhere in the world, but other problems arise for them, including osteoporosis, loneliness after the loss of a spouse, and depression. Their health problems reflect the same patterns found in women from other cultures, and the increasing number of senior women means chronic and sometimes multiple health issues. Muslim seniors are likewise affected by Alzheimer's and other debilitating dementias. In effect, then, Muslim women's life-courses can be quite different than their spouse's, depending on a variety of factors, including age.

In fact, it appears that many Muslim societies have not yet grappled with a large cohort of senior widowed citizens who have little in the way of economic support and whose ability to live socially productive lives is restricted by age-related diseases. Close relatives must now designate caregivers and must dedicate resources for these seniors' well-being at a time when families are struggling with rising financial demands, or when whole families have to be wage-earners. Furthermore, Muslim states have few institutional options to offer, because traditionally families have always cared for the elderly, which is understood to be an important Islamic requirement. Serious social dislocation may well be the outcome.

Sexual and Reproductive Issues. In Islam, sexuality is subject to cultural and religious norms. Muslim women expect that they will marry and have a family. This is the pattern portrayed in Divine Writ and established in social mores for both sexes. It follows, then, that personal valuation is dependent upon the fulfillment of these norms. For example, great controversy surrounds the use of clitoridectomy (female circumcision). While this practice is not explicitly sanctioned in the Qur'ān, and indeed has been viewed as un-Islamic, it has become a women's health issue in the modern Muslim world. Depending upon the severity of the modifications, sexual intercourse can be very painful, childbirth can be hazardous, and psychological impacts can be significant.

Restrictions on girls begin at the onset of the menarche, and it is sometimes combined with hijab-wearing and increased gender segregation. In the past, in many Muslim environments, a first marriage was more or less arranged by parents. The pattern could be altered, of course, if the young person was no longer at home, or if the parents were ill or unable to initiate negotiations. The norm is that sexual relations for Muslim women should be totally curtailed until after marriage. Consequently, female movement at puberty may be restricted based on notions of family honor and personal protection. Many traditional Muslim women throughout the world regard sexual behavior in marriage as fundamentally dependent on the husband, who dictates whether contraceptives will be used, and what type and when. A wide disparity exists among Muslim women on the number of children they bear, depending upon their social, political, and economic situations. In modern settings, women appear to be making family-planning decisions more than their mothers, with the result that birth rates have declined precipitously in some Muslim countries. For example, Iranian birthrates have declined by 70 percent. Factors such as education, career development, economic realities, and altered family structures are some of the more important variables influencing this change.

Sexuality and family relationships also play a role in medical screening for female problems so that tests such as cervical screening, mammograms, and pap smears often require approval from husbands and families. Public information campaigns to increase women's awareness of the value of such screenings appear to have limited impact on women's participation, because some issues related to the female body are not considered appropriate to discuss in public. In several countries with majority Muslim populations, projects aimed at providing information about breast cancer, diabetes, and even obesity have played only minimal roles in public campaigns because of this factor. Yet these diseases are nearing epidemic proportions; six of the ten top countries in the world for diabetes are in the Middle East. Because Islam has been criticized for its treatment of women since the onset of European imperialism, it is virtually impossible to have an impartial discussion on Muslim women's sexuality or the female body in the West. Stereotypes are still difficult to identify and defuse in the charged atmosphere of international cultural studies, but it is safe to say that Muslim societies are in the throes of dynamic change and women are at the forefront of that change. Culturally, then, female sexuality is one such issue that is particularly intractable.

Mental Health Issues. Historically, Islamic health assumptions placed little emphasis on distinctions between the mind and the body. Unlike biomedical culture, with its ancient Greek divisions between the physical and the mental, Islamic medicine argued for a more diversified model of the human composition, including such aspects as the soul provided by God early in conception. Because there was a cultural antipathy to mental illness, Islamic societies have built up a resistance to according mental health issues much legitimacy. Indeed, researchers noted a worldwide stigma attached to mental illness (Kessler and Ustun, 2008). Where there is widespread antipathy toward mental illness, those cultures unfamiliar with contemporary diseases of the mind and those exhibiting these behavioral issues can suffer from strong social disapproval and ostracism. Families with a history of mental problems may find it more difficult to find mates for their relatives, with a resulting disruption of the normal pattern of mate-seeking.

In fact, illnesses related to the mind and the psyche constitute a risk in the modern world, and Muslim women must wrestle with them. According to the U.S. Mental Health Report, half of all Americans have sought help for mental health issues. While it could be that that statistic is country-specific, it is clearly a problem around the world. Based on extrapolated figures, around 7 percent of Muslim women throughout the Muslim world must deal with depression and dysthymia. Some political and cultural issues (such as war and/or civil strife in the Middle East) may be critical in helping to create these mental health issues. Researchers note that it would not be unusual for Muslim women to deal with several of the following problem areas: family disagreements over educational goals, differences of opinion over potential spouses, conflicts over lifestyle, anti-dress stances of governments, balancing full-time employment and homecare tasks, inability to produce a male child, racial or religious stereotyping, Islamophobia, insecure marriages and fear of divorce, chronically ill spouse or children, a lack of proper nutrition or financial support for their families, and changing family dynamics, to mention only a few. The trauma of September 11, 2001, has had a dramatic impact on many Muslim women who are the more publicly visible members of the Muslim community; antagonistic neighbors may make their lives miserable. Muslim women have also been at the forefront of violence, either from wars fought in their home countries, or from local strife and anti-Muslim agitation. Post-traumatic stress disorder takes an immense toll on people in these situations, as we know from studies on Palestinians (Qouta and El-Sarraj, 2004). Mental illness takes a sizable toll on families and friends, as well as on the productivity of a significant cohort of workers in developing societies. Because of the stigma, fewer resources are allocated for their treatment, with the result that numbers of cases go untreated or are hidden from the public. Women may constitute a large number of these hidden cases.

Social Health Issues. A very real issue for some Muslim women relates to social diseases. Despite Islam's strong stance against extramarital sex, Muslim women have not been untouched by the AIDS/HIV epidemic. Especially in African countries, STDs have had a major impact on women's health, and AIDS has destroyed some Muslim women's lives. Where some would argue this derives from premarital sex, the fact is that Muslim women often contract HIV from their husbands, so they must bear the humiliation of the disease in a community antagonistic to it, even though they themselves are not responsible for it. Furthermore, they must deal with Muslim family law. In some places, like some countries in Africa, *Sharīʿah* is utilized to require women to accept their husband's sexual demands, so that, even if he is HIV-positive, the law is applied as a coercive to the point of providing justification for her infection. The epidemic is made worse when women become pregnant and give birth to HIV-infected children.

Another social issue is smoking. Cigarettes have been widely adopted by women, particularly in the privacy of their own homes. The results include complications for their babies and cancer. While Islam takes a strong stand against drugs and alcohol, in some locations, the use of these habit-forming drugs has had detrimental effects on individuals and families. Addictive behavior is to be found in all cultures, but the issue is largely hidden in predominantly Muslim societies because of the social opprobrium surrounding the use of narcotics. Similarly, other illnesses related to modern lifestyle are growing: in Muslim countries that are in transition to wealthy modern states, such as the United Arab Emirates, the evolution toward a contemporary cosmopolitan society has major implications for women's health. Among these contemporary issues the following are on the rise: stress levels, hypertension, a variety of infections because of global contacts and moving outside the home, physical and psychological role shifts, inequitable allocation of resources, lack of women-specific care, lack of preventive medicine, pressures of international feminism and family violence. While none of these directly relate to the Islamic nature of their home societies, the fact is that these issues reflect that Islamic societies must now face some of the same issues that women face in the developed world.

Conclusion. The issues selected here represent only partially the dynamic and vigorous situation that Muslim women around the world encounter. These issues cut across national and state boundaries, are reflected in both countries of Muslim minorities and majorities, and reflect the rapid change underway in most jurisdictions where Muslim women live. This survey demonstrates that Muslim women are not immune to the influences we perceive in cosmopolitan societies around the world, even when they live in remote areas of the world. As a consequence, health issues for Muslim women will likely continue to evolve with the growing interdependence of societies.

[*See also* Female Genital Cutting *and* Motherhood.]

Bibliography

"Afghanistan Unveiled." http://www.pbs.org/independentlens/afghanistanunveiled/.

Alexander, Linda Lewis, Judith H. LaRosa, et al. *New Dimensions in Women's Health*. 5th ed. Sudbury, Mass.: Jones and Bartlett Publishers, 2010.

Alvi, Hayat. "Women in Afghanistan: A Human Rights Tragedy Ten Years after 9/11." *Human Rights & Human Welfare Working Papers*. (November 8, 20110): http://www.du.edu/korbel/hrhw/workingpapers/2011/66-alvi-2011.pdf.

Ba'aqeel, Hassan S. "Cesarean Delivery Rates in Saudi Arabia: A Ten-Year Review." *Annuals of Saudi Medicine* 29.3 (May-June 2009): 179–183.

Bartlett, Linda, Sara Whitehead, Chadd Crouse, and Sonya Bowens. "Maternal Mortality in Afghanistan: Magnitude, Causes, Risk Factors and Preventability." US Centers for Disease Control and Prevention (November 6, 2002): http://www.afghana.com/Articles/maternalmortalityafghanistan.doc.

Bucar, E. M. "Dianomy: Understanding Religious Women's Moral Agency as Creative Conformity." *Journal of the American Academy of Religion* 78.3 (2010): 662–686.

Centers for Disease Control and Prevention."Assisted Reproductive Technology Success Rates: National Summary And Fertility Clinic Reports." (2006): http://www.cdc.gov/ART/.

Eberstadt, N. "The Islamic World's Quiet Revolution." http://www.foreignpolicy.com/articles/2012/03/09/the_islamic_worlds_quiet_revolution.

Elnekave, Eldad, and Revital Gross."The Healthcare Experiences of Arab Israeli Women in a Reformed Healthcare System." *Health Policy* 69 (2003): 101–116.

International Diabetes Foundation. "IDF Diabetes Atlas: Regional Overviews." http://www.idf.org/diabetesatlas/5e/regional-overviews.

Keefe, S. Krehbiel. "'Women Do What They Want': Islam and Permanent Contraception in Northern Tanzania." *Social Science and Medicine* 63 (2006): 418–429.

Kessler, Ronald C. and T. Bedirhan Ustun, eds. *The WHO World Mental Health Survey: Global Perspectives on the Epidemiology of Mental Disorders*. New York: Cambridge University Press, 2008. "Health Statistics: Life Expectancy at Birth: Female (Most Recent) by Country." NationMaster.com. http://www.NationMaster.com/graph/hea_lif_exp_at_bir_fem-health-life-expectancy-birth-female.

Mahid, Hauwa. "The *Hijab* in Nigeria, the Woman's Body and the Feminist Private/Public Discourse." Institute for the Study of Islamic Thought in Africa (ISITA) Working Paper Series. (March 2009): http://www.bcics.northwestern.edu/documents/workingpapers/ISITA_09-003_Mahdi.pdf.

Matin, Mina, and Samuel LeBaron. "Attitudes towards Cervical Cancer Screening among Muslim Women: A Pilot Study." *Women and Health* 39 (2004): 63–77.

Netuveli, Gopalakrishnan, Brian Hurwitz, Mark Levy, Monica Fletcher, Greta Barnes, Stephen R. Durham, and Aziz Sheikh. "Ethnic Variations in UK Asthma Frequency, Morbidity, and Health-Service Use: A Systematic Review and Meta-analysis." *The Lancet* 365 (2005): 312–317.

Qouta, Samir, and Eyad El Sarraj. "Prevalence of PTSD among Palestinian Children in Gaza Strip." *ArabPsy-Net Journal* 2 (April-May-June 2004): http://www.arabpsynet.com/archives/op/OPj2.Qouta.PTSD.pdf.

Rahimi, Wali M. "Status of Women: Afghanistan." UNESCO Principal Regional Office for Asia and the Pacific. (1991): http://unesdoc.unesco.org/images/0009/000916/091693eo.pdf.

Sargent, C., and S. Larchanche. "The Muslim Body and the Politics of Immigration in France: Popular and Biomedical Representations of Malian Migrant Women." *Body and Society* 13, no. 3 (2007): 79–102.

United States Public Health Service Office of the Surgeon General. "Mental Health: A Report of the Surgeon General." (1999): http: //www.surgeongeneral.gov/library/mentalhealth/home.html.

EARLE WAUGH

HIBRI, AZIZAH AL-. (b. 1943), American feminist lawyer, philosopher, scholar, and activist. Al-Hibri was born in Lebanon into a family of prominent personalities in Islamic scholarship and leadership as well as in other fields. She obtained her BA in philosophy at the American University of Beirut in 1966 before she moved to the United States for further education. She earned a PhD in philosophy in 1975 and a JD in law in 1985, both from the University of Pennsylvania.

Al-Hibri held a position as professor of philosophy at Texas A&M University until she embarked in 1983 on her law studies. After obtaining her JD, she practiced corporate law on Wall Street for several years. In 1992 she was appointed professor at the T. C. Williams School of Law at the University of Richmond, where she currently teaches. She has received numerous academic honors and awards, including the Virginia First Freedom Award (2007) and the Dr. Betty Shabazz Recognition Award (2006).

Al-Hibri started her academic career in philosophy as a Marxist feminist. During this period she cofounded and edited *Hypatia: A Journal of Feminist Philosophy*. She eventually found that the possibilities of influencing and changing society from the position of a philosopher were intolerably slow, and for this reason turned to law. Her identity as a Muslim has informed much of her academic work within law, and in addition to being a scholar of American law, she is also an expert on Islamic jurisprudence. She has written extensively on topics like Muslim women's rights, Islam and democracy, and human rights in Islam, including recent titles like *Divine Justice and the Human Order: An Islamic Perspective* (2006) and *The Nature of the Islamic Marriage: Sacramental, Covenantal, or Contractual* (2005). She also participates actively in more general feminist debates, for instance, through her contributions to *Shattering the Stereotypes* (2005) and *Is Multiculturalism Bad for Women?* (1999). She travels extensively in connection with her academic work and has lectured over large parts of the Muslim World, as well as in Europe.

Al-Hibri has devoted a significant part of her life to supporting Muslim women's emancipatory struggles and promoting interfaith understanding within and beyond academia. In 1993 she cofounded the organization KARAMAH, Muslim Women Lawyers for Human Rights, to give an authentic voice to Muslim women in the international arena. She has advised governmental and nongovernmental forums and organizations on issues related to law, women's and human rights, and interfaith understanding in a range of Muslim countries and in Europe. She is also prominently active as an advisor and expert in the United States and is or has recently been on a number of advisory boards, including the PEW Forum on Religion in Public Life, the Pluralism Project (Harvard University), and *Religion and Ethics Newsweekly* (PBS). Her expertise on interfaith issues has been sought by the U.S. administration on a number of occasions, and in June 2011 she was appointed by President Barack Obama to serve as a commissioner on the U.S. Commission on International Religious Freedom.

[*See also* KARAMAH (Muslim Women Lawyers for Human Rights).]

BIBLIOGRAPHY

Al-Hibri, Azizah. "The Burden on U.S. Muslims." In *Shattering the Stereotypes: Muslim Women Speak Out*, edited by Fawzia Afzal-Khan. Northampton, Mass.: Olive Branch Press, 2005.

Al-Hibri, Azizah Y. "Is Western Patriarchal Feminism Good for Third World Minority Women?" In *Is Multiculturalism Bad for Women?* edited by Susan Moller Okin. Princeton, N.J.: Princeton University Press, 1999.

Al-Hibri, Azizah. "Muslim Women's Rights in the Global Village: Challenges and Opportunities." In *Shattering the Stereotypes: Muslim Women Speak Out*, edited by Fawzia Afzal-Khan. Northampton, Mass.: Olive Branch Press, 2005.

Londin, Jesse. "Dr. Azizah al-Hibri, KARAMAH." An interview with al-Hibri on the Lawcrossing website http://www.lawcrossing.com/article/336/Dr-Azizah-al-Hibri-KARAMAH/.

University of Richmond. School of Law. "Azizah Y. al-Hibri." http://law.richmond.edu/people/faculty/aal-hibri/. University of Richmond profile.

MARIT TJOMSLAND

HIJAB. The word *hijab* is used in the contemporary Islamic world both in reference to a head-covering and to a particular style of dress considered modest and Islamic. This style of dress can be distinguished from various rural dress traditions, and it has become much more popular in Muslim communities since the 1970s.

The English term "veil" is commonly used to refer to Middle Eastern women's traditional head, face, or body covers. However, in Arabic, different terms refer to diverse articles of women's clothing that vary according to region and era. Some of these Arabic terms are *burquʿ* (burqa), *ʿabāyah*, *ṭarḥah*, *burnus*, *jilbāb*, and *milāyah*. Overgarments such as the *ʿabāyah* of Arabia and Iraq and the *burnus* of the Maghrib tend to be very similar for both sexes. The word *niqāb* refers to a face veil, which in its contemporary form covers the nose and lower face, but not the eyes.

Origins. The veiling and seclusion of women did not arise with the advent of Islam, nor are these institutions indigenous to Arabs. Strict seclusion and the veiling of matrons were in place in Roman and Byzantine society. Some evidence indicates that in the southwestern Arab region, only two clans (the Banū Ismāʿīl and Banū Qaḥṭān) may have practiced some form of female veiling in pre-Islamic times. No seclusion or veiling existed in ancient Egypt either, although some women may have used a head veil in public in the later period, during the reign of Ramses III (twentieth dynasty).

Long before Islam, veiling and seclusion were practiced in Mesopotamian cultures and among the Sassanians of Persia. In ancient Mesopotamia, the veil for women was regarded as a sign of respectability and high status; decent married women wore it to distinguish themselves from women slaves and unchaste women—indeed, the latter were forbidden to cover their head or hair. In Assyrian law, harlots and slaves were forbidden to veil, and those caught illegally veiling were liable to severe penalties. Thus veiling was not simply to mark aristocracy but to distinguish "respectable" women from disreputable ones.

Successive invasions led to some synthesis in the cultural practices of Greek, Persian, and Mesopotamian empires and the Semitic peoples of the regions. Veiling and seclusion of women appear subsequently to have become established in Judaic and Christian systems. Gradually these spread to Arabs of the urban upper classes and eventually to the general urban public. Covering of the head (but not the face) was also widespread in rural areas.

At the inception of Christianity, Jewish women were veiling the head and face. Biblical evidence of veiling can be found in Genesis 24:65, "And Rebekah lifted up her eyes and when she saw Isaac...she took her veil and covered herself"; in Isaiah 3:23, "In that day the Lord will take away the finery of the anklets...the headdresses...and the veils"; and in 1 Corinthians 11:3–7, "Any woman who prays with her head unveiled dishonors her head—it is the same as if her head were shaven. For if a woman will not veil herself, then she should cut off her hair, but if it is disgraceful for a woman to be shorn or shaven, let her wear a veil. For a man ought not to cover his head, since he is the image and glory of God; but woman is the glory of man."

In medieval Egypt, public segregation of the sexes existed among Jewish Egyptians; women and men entered their temples from separate doors. Evidence suggests also that Jewish women of that period veiled their faces, as did Muslim women, who were urged in prescriptive literature to behave more modestly.

Veiling of Arab Muslim urban women became more pervasive under Ottoman rule as a marker of rank and exclusive lifestyle, and the geographic and occupational coding of dress was noted in seventeenth-century Istanbul. By the nineteenth century, upper-class urban Muslim and Christian women in Egypt wore the *ḥabarah*, which consisted of a long skirt, a head cover, and a *burqa*, a long rectangular cloth of white transparent muslin placed below the eyes, covering the lower nose and the mouth and falling to the chest. In mourning, a black muslin veil known as the *bisha* was substituted. Perhaps related to the origins of the practice among Jews and Christians, the word *ḥabarah* itself derives from early Christian and Judaic religious vocabulary.

Hijab is not a recent term, but it was revived in the 1970s. It had been part of the Arabian Arabic vocabulary of early Islam. *Ḍarb* (adopting) *al-hijab* was the phrase used in Arabia in discourse about the seclusion of the wives of the Prophet. When the veil became a focus of feminist and nationalist discourse in Egypt during the British colonial occupation, *hijab* was the term used. The phrase used for the removal of urban women's face or head covering was *rafʿ* (lifting) *al-hijab* (not *al-ḥabarah*), which was, at that time, also a reference to modernization and enlightenment.

Qurʾānic References. The Qurʾān has a number of references to "hijab", none of which concerns women's clothing, but rather a spatial partition or curtain. At the time of its founding, as Islam gradually established itself in the Medina community, "seclusion" for Muḥammad's wives was introduced in a Qurʾānic verse: "O ye who believe, enter not the dwellings of the Prophet, unless invited...And when you ask of his wives anything, ask from behind *hijab*. That is purer for your hearts and for their hearts" (33:53).

Other references further stress the separating aspect of hijab. For example, *al-hijab* is mentioned in nongendered contexts separating deity from mortals (42:51), wrongdoers from the righteous (7:46, 41:5), believers from unbelievers (17:45), and light from darkness and day from night (38:32). With regard to the sexes, one verse tells men and women to be modest, and women to cover their bosoms and hide their ornaments: "Tell the believing men to lower their gaze and be modest. That is purer for them. And tell the believing women to lower their gaze and be modest, and display of their adornment only that which is apparent, and to draw their *khimār* over their bosoms, and not to reveal their adornment save to their own husbands" (24:30–31).

Another verse states, "O Prophet, tell thy wives and thy daughters, and the women of the believers to draw their *jilbāb* close round them...so that they may be recognized and not molested" (33:59).

These verses refer not to *hijab* but to *khimār* (head cover) and *jilbāb* (a dress or cloak), and the focus of both verses is modesty and special status. The desirability of modesty is further stressed by referring to the contrasting concept of *tabarruj* (illicit display): "O ye wives of the Prophet! Ye are not like any other women. If ye keep your duty, then be not soft of speech, lest he in whose heart is a disease aspire, but utter customary speech. And stay in your houses. Bedizen not yourselves with the bedizenment of the Time of Ignorance" (33:32–33).

In none of these verses is the word *hijab* used. The terms *khimār*, *jilbāb*, and *tabarruj* were used in reference to the Prophet's wives, who held a special status as the "mothers of the believers." *Al-tabbaruj* (immodest display of a woman's body combined with flirtatious mannerisms) was used to describe women's public manners in the pre-Islamic "days of ignorance." The phrase stands in contrast with *al-tahhajub* (modesty in dress and manners), a term that derives from the same root as *hijab*. In the Islamic revival in Egypt, an influential pamphlet critiquing *tabbaruj* and calling for Islamic dress was widely distributed.

Meaning. *Hijab* is derived from the root *h-j-b*; its verbal form *ḥajaba* translates as "to veil, to seclude, to screen, to conceal, to form a separation, to mask." *Hijab* translates as "cover, wrap, curtain, veil, screen, partition." The same word refers to amulets carried on one's person (particularly as a child) to protect against harm. Another derivative, *ḥājib*, means eyebrow (protector of the eye) and is also the name used during the caliphate periods for the official who screened applicants who wished audience with the caliph.

Evidence from its usage in the Qur'ān and from early Islamic feminist discourse could support the notion of *hijab* in Islam as referring to a sacred divide or separation between two worlds or two spaces: deity and mortals, men and women, good and evil, light and dark, believers and nonbelievers, or aristocracy and commoners. The phrase *min warā' al-hijab* (from behind the *hijab*) emphasizes the element of separation or partition.

The connection among clothing, modesty, and morality in Islam can be found in the Qur'ānic imagery of creation. Here clothing acquires meaning beyond the familiar: "Satan tempted them, so that he might reveal to them their private parts that had been hidden from each other" (7:20); "We have sent down to you clothing in order to cover the private parts of your body and serve as protection and decoration; and the best of all garments is the garment of piety" (7:26). In another context—"[women] are a garment to you and you are a garment to them" (2:187)—the interdependence and complementarity of the sexes is expressed. By using the imagery of clothing, Islamic creation focuses on gender relations rather than on irreversible sin and conceptually links clothing with morality, privacy, sexuality, and modesty.

The English term "veil" (and its correlate "seclusion"), therefore, fails to capture these nuances and oversimplifies a complex phenomenon. Furthermore, the "veil" as commonly used made the act of concealing exotic, rather than ordinary, and mysterious rather than virtuous. The word implied a single referent and condition, whereas it ambiguously refers at various times to various objects of dress with distinct social meanings, as in a transparent or heavily ornamented female face cover, a transparent head covering, or an elaborate headdress. Limiting its reference obscures historical developments; differentiations of social context, class, group, or special rank; and sociopolitical articulations. In Western feminist discourse "veil" is politically charged with connotations of the inferior "other," implying and assuming a subordination and inferiority of the Muslim woman, whereas the historic use of the veil to distinguish women of high status is forgotten. Moreover, it was in the Hellenic, Judaic, and Christian systems to which the West traces its roots that veiling was associated with seclusion in the sense of the subordination of women.

Contemporary Issues. The Qurʾānic terms *hijab*, *khimār*, *jilbāb*, and *tabbaruj* reappeared in the mid-1970s as part of an emergent Islamic consciousness and movement and heightened religiosity that spread all over the Islamic East. It was distinguished at first by the voluntary and active participation of young Muslim college women and men. Women's visible presence became marked when they began to don a distinctive but uniform dress, unavailable commercially, which they called *al-zīyy al-Islāmī* (Islamic dress).

A *muḥajjabah* (woman wearing hijab) wore *al-jilbāb*—an unfitted, long-sleeved, ankle-length gown in austere solid colors and thick opaque fabric—and *al-khimār*, a head cover resembling a nun's wimple that covers the hair low to the forehead, comes under the chin to conceal the neck, and falls down over the chest and back. Whereas the nun's wimple is an aspect of her seclusion and a sign of her state of celibacy and asexuality, the Muslim woman wears *al-khimār* in order to desexualize public social space when she is part of it. Modesty extends beyond her clothing to her subdued, serious behavior and austere manner, and is an ideal applied to both sexes. A *munaqqabah* (woman wearing the *niqāb*, or face veil) more conservatively adds *al-niqāb*, which covers the entire face except for eye slits; at the most extreme, she would also wear gloves and socks to cover her hands and feet.

This Islamic dress was eventually adopted by many other urban women outside of college campuses, and then by those of provincial towns and rural areas. By dressing this way in public, women translated their vision of Islamic ideas into their own behavior. Some women also signaled their support for Islamist groups where these became popular, or they were able to distinguish themselves from women identifying with other political groups or who were non-Muslims, for instance in Syria, Lebanon, and Palestine. The new dress style affirmed the wearer's Islamic identity and morality and, to some degree, rejected Western materialism, commercialism, and values. The vision and gender conceptualization expressed in *hijab* derives from these women's understanding of early Islam and the Qurʾān. Controversy arose in Arab countries (other than Saudi Arabia) as to whether its increasing use was due to imposition by religious institutions or leaders or whether it was a form of peer emulation; the enforced veiling in Iran after the Islamic revolution and in Sudan under the Bashīr-Turābī regime raised such questions. The opponents of hijab-wearing accused Islamist movements of supporting its use or even paying women to adopt it.

The Islamic movement, known as the awakening, or *ṣaḥwah*, involved far more than a new dress code, which also applied to men. The movement aimed to empower the Muslim community and orient it away from neo-imperialism, while also opposing *al-tabarruj* and supporting modesty in behavior, voice, and body movement, as well as the enactment of Islamic values. Gradually, the movement shifted from establishing or reestablishing an Islamic identity and morality to asserting Islamic nationalism, engaging in participatory politics, and resisting authoritarian regimes and Western dominance. Embedded in today's hijab is imagery that combines notions of modesty, morality, identity, and resistance. Opposed to the hijab are women (and men) who decry the absence of choice, or who have wanted to see more positive gender relations established by opening, rather than restricting, women's share of public space. Resistance through *al-hijab* or against it, whether it means attire or behavior, has generated dynamic discourse around gender, Islamic ideals, women's status, and the propriety of reforming Islamic laws and customs.

Debate over the hijab continued in certain Muslim-majority countries where it was outlawed in public-sector jobs, as in Tunisia and in Turkey, and continued globally, especially after September 11, 2001. In Turkey, where Kemalists decried Islamic dress, women pursued lawsuits for the right to wear Islamic dress, and Prime Minister Recep Tayyip Erdoğan declared that he would not bring his wife, who wears Islamic dress, to public functions, so as not to break the law. In France, where about 5 million Muslims live, a ban on religious symbols and apparel in public schools went into effect in September 2004, sparking protests by Muslims, and four German states have banned the wearing of headscarves. In Italy, an older law was revived in 2004, as well as a newer one to restrict the wearing of *niqāb* or burqa; a similar law was enacted in Maaseik, Belgium. In the United Kingdom, schools may uphold their uniform codes, thereby disallowing *niqāb*, which was criticized publicly by the former foreign secretary, Jack Straw. Meanwhile, in Iraq, far more women have adopted Islamic dress in areas controlled by militias, due to attacks on the unveiled as well as, in some cases, women who were driving. In contrast, Somali security forces in Mogadishu were stripping veils from women and even burning them in the spring of 2007, following the overthrow of Islamist leaders in January of that year.

[*See also* Dress, *subentries on* Contemporary *and* Historical; Modesty; Seclusion; Taliban; Veiling, *subentries on* Historical Discourse *and* Contemporary Discourse; *and* Women and Islam, *subentries on* Role and Status of Women *and* Women's Religious Observances.]

BIBLIOGRAPHY

Ahmed, Leila. *Women and Gender in Islam: Historical Roots of a Modern Debate* (New Haven, Conn.: Yale University Press, 1992). Good overview of literature on gender in the Middle East from ancient to modern times, drawing on archaeological findings, anthropological insights, and historical documentation on gender. The textual survey is framed from the perspective of feminist gender studies (misogyny, patriarchy, androcentrism), but is itself a critique of Western feminism.

Amīn, Qāsim. *al-Aʿmāl al-kāmilah li-Qāsim Amīn*, edited by Muḥammad ʿImārah (Beirut, Lebanon, 1976). This book is divided into two parts; the first is the author's analysis and commentary on Amīn's reformist thought on women's issues, with a focus on the hijab. The second part is a reprint of Amīn's two original books on women's issues, *Taḥrir al-marʿah* (1899) and *al-Marʿah al-jadīdah* (1900), considered among the first classic Arab feminist works.

El Guindi, Fadwa. *Veil: Modesty, Privacy, and Resistance* (Oxford, U.K., and New York: Berg, 1999). An anthropological analysis that considers the issue from a structuralist, historical, and psychological perspective, based primarily on the author's fieldwork in Egypt in the late 1970s. Also includes a chapter on male veiling.

Hammami, Rema. "From Immodesty to Collaboration: Hamas, the Women's Movement, and National Identity in the Intifada." In *Political Islam: Essays from* Middle East Report, edited by Joel Benin and Joe Stork, pp. 194–210. Berkeley: University of California Press, 1996.

Heath, Jennifer, ed. *The Veil: Women Writers on Its History, Lore, and Politics*. Berkeley: University of California Press, 2008. Twenty-one essays that discuss the significance of veiling, past and present, in various countries, religions, and cultures.

Luṭfī, Hūdā. "Al-Ṣakhawī's Kitāb al-nisāʾ." *Muslim World* 71.2 (1981): 104–124. Informative discussion of al-Ṣakhawī's volume on women and a good source for the social and economic history of fifteenth-century Muslim women.

Mawdūdī, Sayyid Abū al-Aʿlā. *Purdah and the Status of Woman in Islam*. Translated and edited by al-Ashʿari (Lahore, Pakistan, 1972). Widely read source on the subject for believers in the Islamic movement, providing a nonorthodox interpretation of the Qurʾān on gender issues.

Zuhur, Sherifa. *Revealing Reveiling: Islamist Gender Ideology in Contemporary Egypt* (Albany: State University of New York Press, 1992). Field study of Egyptian Muslim women and ideologues in the contemporary Islamic movement, the origins of their gender ideology, and women's differing views about contemporary and political trends. Examines the historical basis of Muslim ideas about gender, gender relations, Islamism, and modesty and their expression in contemporary Egypt, along with a history of the women's movement in Egypt.

FADWA ELGUINDI
Updated by SHERIFA ZUHUR

HONOR. The notion of honor figures prominently in ideas about respect and social status. As a comparative sociological concept, it denotes enhanced status and capacity for social relations. In more narrowly cultural terms, honor is a composite aspect of persons, social conduct, morality, and social metaphysics.

The grounds for and expressions of honor are many and vary with what is important and problematic in personal interaction. Honor first appeared in tribal "codes" idealizing bravery, independence, generosity, self-control, and abilities to control interactions with others. Common grounds and symbolic vehicles of honor in these milieus are ownership (in some sense of controlling the use) of land and other productive resources, the independence and generosity this facilitates along with family and kinship solidarities, the control of women's fertility, and personal characteristics of courage, wisdom, honesty, and self-possession. Although honor is sometimes represented as complementary to religion in tribal settings, piety is an essential part of honor in all its forms. For tribesmen there is no honor apart from identity as a Muslim: the generous host, provident husband, and deferential wife and offspring are justified as God's pleasure.

Islamic piety looms larger as a source of honor for others. For descendants of the Prophet, Ṣūfī *pīr*s, and recognized "holy" families, honor may inhere primarily in religious identity. A composed demeanor, disinclination to conflict, and avoidance of degradation of others is the presumed style of religious people and sets a standard that others emulate.

Widespread distinctions between "face" or "point of honor" that can be manipulated in interaction, in contrast to honor as all that is sacred (*sharaf, ḥarām*), have been productively united in two ways. One is by looking beyond talk about honor to the art of talking well and the way in which verbal performances demonstrate cultural mastery, particularly in poetic constructions. This more nuanced understanding of honor as expression has also opened up the realms of women's claims to honor and expressions of it through verbal performances.

Often honor is seen to reside in the female members of a group, so that the group's honor is dependent upon the ability of the group to protect and preserve female chastity. In such cases maintaining the group's honor may be manifested by controlling female members' mobility and access to public spaces and limiting female interactions with unrelated (non-*maḥram*) males to Islamically legitimated circumstances, such as business transactions or medical treatment. In such cases honor is often perceived as something that can be easily lost, rather than as something that can be gained or earned. Loss of honor by the group is considered shameful and can be subject to punishment, including the most severe—"honor killings" in which suspected "illicit" sexual activity, whether through intercourse or a suspected telephone relationship, is punishable by death. The death of the individual accused of causing the dishonor is presumed to restore the honor of the group as a whole. Although "illicit" relationships require two parties, usually only the woman in question is punished.

The rise of new technologies, such as cell phones, e-mail, and the Internet, has expanded women's access to public space through communications technology without necessarily changing physical limitations. This raises the question of whether honor can be maintained or lost in virtual reality.

Another new perspective has come with uncovering the ways in which concepts of honor and shame are related to metaphysical notions of persons and behavior as balances of socialized reason (*ʿaql*) and animal appetites (*nafs*). Honor tips this balance in favor of reason-governed behavior, and shame toward behaviors denominated by emotion and appetites. These concepts are generalized from Islamic contexts as a sort of "folk" or ethnopsychology. For instance hospitality (and material generosity generally) is ideally extended with humility and deference to show that egoism and ambition are subordinated to God's pleasure. The host and the parent become symbolic intermediaries or conduits in their realms, much like *pīr*s and religious teachers in theirs, each with particular and situationally appropriate honor. Thus, honor also takes on associations with the "greater" (personal) and "lesser" (communal) jihad or struggle for religion.

[*See also* Shame.]

BIBLIOGRAPHY

Abu-Lughod, Lila. *Veiled Sentiments: Honor and Poetry in a Bedouin Society*. Berkeley: University of California Press, 1986.

Baker, William Gary. *The Cultural Heritage of Arabs, Islam, and the Middle East*. Dallas, Tex.: Brown Books, 2003.

Caton, Steven. "The Poetic Construction of Self." *Anthropological Quarterly* 58 (1985): 141–151.

Gilsenan, Michael. *Recognizing Islam: Religion and Society in the Modern Middle East*. Rev. ed. London: I.B. Tauris, 2000.

Grima, Benedicte. *The Performance of Emotion among Paxtun Women: "The Misfortunes which Have Befallen Me."* Austin: University of Texas Press, 1992.

Jamous, Raymond. *Honneur et baraka: Les structures sociales traditionnelles dans le Rif*. Cambridge, U.K.: Cambridge University Press, 1981.

Meeker, Michael E. *Literature and Violence in North Arabia*. Cambridge, U.K.: Cambridge University Press, 1979.

Nydell, Margaret K. *Understanding Arabs: A Guide for Modern Times*. 4th ed. Yarmouth, Me.: Intercultural Press, 2006.

Péristiany, J. G., ed. *Honour and Shame: The Values of Mediterranean Society*. Chicago: University of Chicago Press, 1966. See the essays by Pierre Bourdieu, "The Sentiment of Honour in Kabyle Society," and Ahmed Abou-Zeid, "Honour and Shame among the Bedouins of Egypt."

JON W. ANDERSON
Updated by NATANA J. DELONG-BAS

HONOR KILLINGS. So-called honor murders are a worldwide phenomenon, one not restricted to any religion, country, or social class. These murders occur when the family of the victim, usually a woman, decides to murder her because she is regarded as having tarnished the family's image and reputation. The loss of image or reputation could result from an "illegitimate affair" with a man who is not an immediate relative; marriage to a man from a different faith; pregnancy out of wedlock; falling victim to rumor, suspicion, incest, or rape; loss of virginity; choosing a certain dress code or lifestyle that is against the family's beliefs and traditions; or going missing from the home for a period. Sometimes women are killed for financial or inheritance reasons and families hide behind honor to escape legal punishment. These are some examples of why these murders happen and why they specifically target women.

According to United Nations and World Health Organization figures released in 2000, around 5,000 women are murdered annually in so-called honor killings in countries including Bangladesh, Brazil, Ecuador, Egypt, Great Britain, India, Israel, Italy, Jordan, Morocco, Pakistan, Palestine, Sweden, Turkey, Yemen, and Uganda. The origins of honor-based violence against women and issues such as female chastity and virginity are not exclusive to any ethnicity, religion, or geography. Starting with those ancient civilizations that have left us a record of their laws and social customs, there is a consistent pattern of "blame" in cases of sexual misdeed, adultery, and betrayal—and this blame rests with the woman. Rome, Assyria, India, and the ancient American cultures consistently depicted women as the original source of wrongdoing and even evil.

Religious beliefs are not the motive behind the majority of these murders. Rather, it is "wrongful cultural beliefs and traditions" that motivate certain individuals or family members to take the law into their own hands and kill a female relative to cleanse the honor of their family. These murders are reported to have taken place in communities of various religions, such as Islam, Christianity, Hinduism, Yazidism, and Sikhism.

To illustrate some religious teachings regarding adultery, in the Islamic religion, laws are very clear against relying on hearsay "evidence" and are also very strict about proving adultery. (Because it is nearly impossible to prove adultery in Islam, adultery is considered a private and personal issue.) Islam further speaks against the murder of civilians; Muslims believe the soul is God's property and humans cannot take it away. Meanwhile, in the Old Testament book of Leviticus, the death penalty was imposed on a man who committed adultery with a married woman. The issue of virginity is stressed in Deuteronomy (22:13–21), where the text suggests that, in the event the husband of a bride claims that his wife was not a virgin on their marriage day, the bride's parents would be summoned by a judge to show that the linen from the marriage bed was stained with blood to prove their daughter was a virgin. The punishment for a non-virgin woman while still single in her father's home is stoning to death (Deuteronomy 22:13–21). Also according to Deuteronomy (22:28–29), a raped virgin woman must marry her attacker, regardless of her feelings toward him.

Historians and researchers have documented that forms of abuse of women have precedents in all societies in different times, in both the West and the East. Even the majority of penal codes in ancient civilizations always referred to the culprits as women adulterers and their partners, a clear indication that women were considered the source of all evil. Men, on the other hand, enjoyed the right to multiple sexual partners and even to publicly keep mistresses. For example, throughout the duration of the Roman Empire, the status of women depended mostly on male relatives. Fathers enjoyed the power of life and death over their daughters. Once a woman married, her father's authority was transferred to her husband. Roman law stipulated that if a husband surprised his wife in a compromising position, he had a legal right to kill her without fear of prosecution or punishment. But if a husband violated the marriage trust, his wife had not even the right to touch him with the tip of her fingers.

In India, ancient Hindu law was very harsh on women. Women were seen as a necessary evil; they were needed to produce children, but at the same time they were believed to be a never-ending source of shame and disgrace and were always considered the root of marital discord.

In Europe, in the fourteenth century, "wise and smart women" were considered sorceresses by the Church, often for using herbs to cure illnesses. They were killed, burned, or locked in hospitals for the mentally ill, in the name of religion, as well as to preserve the values of the society. In Renaissance Italy, women were executed for adultery. In her book *The Second Sex* (1989), French philosopher, novelist, and essayist Simone De Beauvoir described many plays and operas written during the 1880s in Europe that portrayed women as sinners and evil creatures. In these plays, it was clear that punishing "evil women" was not left to the husband; it was the responsibility of the community because the woman's misbehavior offended the whole of society.

Consequently, although honor crimes are often associated by the media and in popular culture with "Islam," the reality is that honor crimes are a global phenomenon that can occur in a variety of contexts. Activists have found that increasing awareness and opening public conversations about honor killings are critical to ending this practice. Activists around the world, such as Asma Jahangir, Hina Jilani, Aruna Papp, Asma Khader, and Dianna Nammi, have taken it upon themselves to expose the murder of and defend women who are killed for reasons related to family honor. In conclusion, so-called honor crimes stem from a long and complicated socio-political and religious history, stretching back to ancient civilizations.

BIBLIOGRAPHY

Burckhardt, Jacob. *The Civilisation of the Renaissance in Italy*. London: Folio, 2004.

De Beauvoir, Simone. *The Second Sex*. Translated and edited by H. M. Parshley. New York: Vintage Books, 1989.

Frischauer, Paul. *Sex in the Ancient World*. Translated into Arabic by Faeq Dahdouh. Ninaoi Press, 1999.

Goldstein, Matthew A. "The Biological Roots of Heat of Passion Crimes and Honour Killings." *Politics and the Life Sciences* 21, no. 2 (September 2002): 28–37.

Pantel, Pauline Schmiitt, ed. *A History of Women in the West*. Vol. 1: *From Ancient Goddess to Christian Saints*. Georges Duby and Michelle Perrot, gen. eds. Cambridge, MA: Belknap Press of Harvard University Press, 2002.

Saadawi, Nawal. *Woman Is the Origin: Studies on Women and Men in Arab Society*. 2d ed. Beirut: Arab Institute for Research and Publishing, 1990.

RANA HUSSEINI

HOSPITALITY. Across Muslim societies hospitality stands out as an important social practice associated with traditional values of generosity, honor, and shame. At its most basic level, hospitality is a form of reciprocity where exchanges between hosts and guests occur according to social conventions that influence the transaction. In this exchange people expect to receive and give hospitality without tabulating with whom they have interacted or the amount exchanged. According to some, hospitality rites emerged in Arabia out of necessity in order to shield nomads from the harshness of desert life and enable them to depend on more than the good will of strangers. Others attribute it to Qurʾānic codes that outline how human beings should treat each other at both the individual and community levels. Regardless of its source the social obligation to provide and receive is not taken lightly as reputations and relationships are at stake. Although friends exchange hospitality, it does not occur in the exclusive domain of friendship. Rather hospitality emerges as a critical element in establishing, maintaining, and obligating social relations within a community and between strangers.

Examples of hospitality vary, but commonalities exist as social customs govern the form of the exchange as well as the roles and behaviors for the participants. Both men and women can serve as hosts with women typically hosting other women. In some places, such as in early twentieth-century Arabia, as noted by Christian missionaries, women were responsible for welcoming male guests when their husbands were absent, although this tended to be the exception, rather than the rule. Hosts are responsible not only for providing refreshments, food, and, at times, lodging for their guests, but also guaranteeing the safety of those under their invitation. Hosts may additionally offer perfume or incense at the entry of the home. Hosting should never be rushed and guests should not be impatient, as sincerity and loyalty in both offering and receiving hospitality is a matter of personal honor. Gifts may also be offered by either the host or the guest, reflecting additional generosity.

Hosting can occur in one's house or in a public venue, such as a restaurant. In the case of the latter, the host pays for the guest, seeing to his/her needs as if they were in the host's home. Guests may insist on contributing—at a restaurant for example, paying part of the bill. However it is commonly understood that such resistances or offerings on the part of the guest are rhetorical strategies to acknowledge the host's generosity. Among Bedouin nomads more extensive gifts of hospitality are possible with a host providing shelter, food, and security to even a stranger for three days. During that period no questions are asked and afterward the guest will leave, expecting nothing further.

Regardless of what is provided, the host should always give generously, making sure that the guest is not wanting. So there is no mistaking the bounteousness of the host's provisions, food and drink are often given in excess. Hospitality might appear altruistic, but a person's generosity can influence his/her honor and standing in the community. Guests are expected to acknowledge the host's generosity, showing ample appreciation by effusively giving thanks. If a guest enjoyed himself, he will speak highly of the host; gossiping or negative talk is an act of ingratitude that reflects poorly on both host and guest. There are a number of other rules for guests that are culture specific: do not use one's left hand, do not show the soles of the feet, do not act rudely, do not act greedily (but wait to be offered), do not discuss business issues until social conventions have been completed, and do not linger once the meal has ended.

The development of the tourism industry, Westernized lifestyles, and state development (as opposed to village or tribal governance) has transformed hospitality rites. Now visitors can partake in "traditional" hospitality at restaurants, hotels, touristic heritage sites, and coffeehouses where Bedouins serve coffee and extend custom into commercial environments. Additionally, as patronage systems often link up with hospitality and honor systems, important individuals might host events and invite visitors as a way to develop prestige and create political indebtedness.

[*See also* Honor.]

BIBLIOGRAPHY

Abu-Lughod, Lila. *Veiled Sentiments: Honor and Poetry in a Bedouin Society*. Updated ed. Berkeley: University of California Press, 1999.

Fernea, Elizabeth Warnock. *Guests of the Sheikh: An Ethnography of an Iraqi Village*. Garden City, N.Y.: Doubleday, 1965.

Long David E. *Culture and Customs of Saudi Arabia*. Westport, Conn.: Greenwood Press, 2005.

Shryock, Andrew. "The New Jordanian Hospitality: House, Host, and Guest in the Culture of Public Display." *Comparative Studies in Society and History* 46 (2004): 35–62.

Unit 5: Hospitality and Friendship. http://www.globalsecurity.org/military/library/report/1997/arab_culture/f8hospit.pdf.

Elizabeth Faier

Houris. The English version of the word comes from the Persian *ḥūrī*, a singular noun formed from the Arabic plural *ḥūr*. A recent attempt to derive the Arabic word from Syriac (meaning "white grapes") has been widely publicized, but it is mistaken, as there is good evidence for the use of *ḥūr* in pre-Islamic poetry. The pre-Islamic examples, which include a line by the Christian ʿAdī ibn Zayd, refer to women. The meaning is arguable, but the term most probably means "dark-eyed," making a comparison with the eyes of gazelles and oryx, or "fair-skinned," which is common in early poetry. There are four references to *ḥūr* in the Qurʾān, with the usage shifted to the next world, as is not infrequently the case: *al-jannah* ("the garden"—heaven), *al-nār* ("the fire"— hell), *niʿmah* ("well-being"—heavenly bliss). All the passages are Meccan and quite early. Three (44:54, 52:20, and 56:22) have *ḥūr* followed by another adjective, *ʿīn*. This may be translated as "maidens with dark, lustrous eyes." There is a more complex passage in 55:70–76:

> In which are good and beautiful women,
> With lustrous eyes, confined in tents,
> Untouched before by either men or *Jinn*,
> Who recline on green cushions and fine carpets.

Three other Meccan passages (78:33, 37:48, and 38:52) obviously refer to the same beings without using the word *ḥūr*, and in addition there are three Medinan passages (2:25, 3:15, and 4:57) that refer to "pure spouses" (*azwājun muṭahharah*). Muslim commentators have reasonably taken these Medinan passages to be later references to the *ḥūr*. There are a few lines in Umayyad poetry that have variations on the phrase *ḥūr ʿīn* and that seem to be based on the Qurʾān rather than on earlier poetry, but that is the end of the primary evidence.

The main sources for later Muslim ideas about *ḥūr* lie in *ḥadīth* and *tafsīr*. Most of this material is the speculation of a male-dominated society, which dwells in a very literal fashion on the sexual delights that the *ḥūr*, whose virginity is perpetually renewed, will give their husbands, God's elect, in Paradise. Thus the modern *jihadī* view that their martyrs will each have seventy-two (sometimes seventy) *ḥūr* in Paradise is based on a *ḥadīth* of highly doubtful authenticity first recorded in the *Jāmiʿ* in Abū ʿĪsā al-Tirmidhī (d. 892), which was later taken up in *tafsīr* of Ibn Kathīr (d. 1373). The commentators hold that married, virtuous, believing women will meet their husbands in Paradise and again become their legal wives. This raises the question of the relationship between these believing women and the *ḥūr*. Discussion is not very thorough, but the believing women are thought to be greatly superior. More austere views about the *ḥūr* are also to be found, though they are much less prominent. The commentator ʿAbd Allāh al-Bayḍāwī (d. c. 1286) was among those who held that there was no substantial identity between the women, food, and other delights of Paradise and their earthly equivalents, and some more modern commentators also try to confer a spiritual character on the promised delights.

[*See also* Martyrdom.]

BIBLIOGRAPHY

Wensinck, A. J.-[C. H. Pellat]. "Hūr." In *Encyclopaedia of Islam*. 2d ed., edited by H. A. R. Gibb, B. Lewis, C. H. Pellat,, et al., vol. 3, pp. 581–582. Leiden, Netherlands: E.J. Brill, 1954–2005.

ALAN JONES

HOUSEHOLDS. An administrative household may be defined as a conglomeration of kinship and patron-client ties in which governmental and often military functions are concentrated. In most pre-modern societies, women could fulfill virtually any non-military role in such a household.

Arguably, the administrative household dates to the beginning of human civilization inasmuch as the ruler's residence, family, and entourage served in most early civilizations as the locus of government. Early Islamic empires adopted the household-based administrative culture of ancient Near Eastern regimes as channeled through the Sasanian and Byzantine Empires, which ruled most of the region before the Muslim conquests of the seventh century. The ʿAbbāsid caliphate (750–1258 CE) offers the first well-documented example of an Islamic household-based administration. Founded in 762, the ʿAbbāsid capital

Baghdad reproduced the caliphal household hierarchy, for the caliph's palace stood at its center, ringed by the residences of his sons, his African eunuchs, and the officials of his government. Women of the caliphal family occupied the palace's harem, a section that, corresponding to the literal meaning of the word, was taboo in the sense of being off-limits to all but immediate family members and a sizable staff of female servants and eunuchs. The ʿAbbāsid harem was the site of dynastic reproduction, and ʿAbbāsid narrative sources document a handful of influential caliphs' mothers, notably Zubayda, consort of Hārūn al-Rashīd (r. 786–809) and mother of al-Amīn (r. 809–813), whose charitable foundations for the holy cities of Mecca and Medina established a tradition followed by royal women through the end of the Ottoman Empire. Parallel cases existed in the rival Shīʿah Fāṭimid caliphate, which ruled Egypt, Syria, and the western Arabian peninsula from 969 to 1171.

In the ninth century, the ʿAbbāsids began systematically to import elite military slaves, or *mamlūks*, from among the Turkic peoples of Central Asia; lacking ties to the local population, they were supposedly loyal only to the caliph. The caliphs even married them to women imported from their homelands, who must have acquired considerable influence in the caliphs' household and those of *mamlūk* officers, although ʿAbbāsid sources preserve little trace of their influence. Autonomous Turkic and Iranian powers within the ʿAbbāsid domains, whose rulers modeled their households on the ʿAbbāsid prototype, likewise employed *mamlūks*, although the extent to which they imported "female *mamlūks*" is unclear. The Mamlūk sultanate, which ruled the former Fāṭimid territories from 1250 until its defeat by the Ottomans in 1516–1517, unquestionably imported slave girls from Central Asia and, later, Circassia to serve as wives and concubines to the sultan and his *mamlūk* officials. Little is known about these women, however, apart from the famous Shajar al-Durr, a "*mamlūka*" who ruled in her own right for two years (1249–1250) at the beginning of the sultanate.

As the most recent empire to dominate the Islamic heartland, the Ottomans have left the most extensive record of women's role in a regime based on administrative households. A watershed in imperial household culture occurred shortly after the Ottoman conquest of Constantinople in 1453, when Sultan Meḥmed II (r. 1451–1481) moved with his male pages to the newly-built Topkapı Palace, leaving the female members of his household in the Old Palace, located on the current site of Istanbul University. This remained the residence of Ottoman imperial women until c. 1530, when Ḥurrem, wife of Süleymān I (r. 1520–1566), relocated to Topkapı, accompanied by a large staff of eunuchs and female servants. Until the mid-nineteenth century, the sultan's wives and/or concubines, mother, and unmarried daughters and sisters resided in the Topkapı harem; when the sultan died or was deposed, they returned to the Old Palace.

The Ottoman imperial household was transformed by the global crisis of the seventeenth century, which included a dynastic component: the dearth of candidates for the throne following the death of Meḥmed III (r. 1595–1603), apart from underage or mentally challenged princes. Fearing for the dynasty's survival, the court abandoned the practice of sending princes to learn statecraft by governing Anatolian provinces, along with the tradition whereby a newly enthroned sultan executed his brothers. Princes were now raised in the harem, where their mothers, along with the chief harem eunuch, shaped their education and outlook. These powerful women were integral to the empire's adaptation to the crisis since they provided political stability during brief, tumultuous reigns, and shaped policy by building alliances with grand viziers and other officials. During much of the seventeenth century, the sultan's mother was the de facto head of the imperial household.

By this time, the imperial household stood at the top of an empire-wide household hierarchy that extended through the households of government ministers, provincial governors, and provincial notables. These lower-ranking households were often headquartered in palatial mansions and featured large numbers of clients, including *mamlūks* and eunuchs. In the eighteenth century, the life-tenure tax farm (*mālikāne*) gave provincial notables, or *aʿyān*—subdistrict governors, regimental officers, and even long-distance merchants and Muslim scholar-officials, or *ʿulamāʾ*—an unassailable economic base that enabled them to dominate provincial administration. In an *aʿyān* household, the wives, daughters, and sisters of the household head helped to generate and preserve household wealth since, under Islamic law, a woman retained her property after marriage and could acquire more in her own right.

The westernizing Tanẓimat reforms (1839–1876) aimed in part to curb the influence of *aʿyān* households. Nonetheless, the dynasties that replaced these notables in several Ottoman provinces, notably Egypt and Tunisia, adopted this household culture themselves. The women of these regimes fulfilled much the same function as women in the Ottoman palace, although princesses could also cement marriage alliances between dynasties, as when the granddaughter of the Ottoman sultan Abdül Ḥamid II (r. 1876–1909) married the son of Egypt's khedive ʿAbbās II Ḥilmī (r. 1892–1914).

With the fall of monarchies in many predominantly Muslim countries after World War II, the administrative household lost its centrality as a template for political organization. Its traces remain, however, within the monarchies of the Persian Gulf and Jordan and, to some extent, in powerful non-royal families in the region.

[*See also* Harem *and* Property.]

BIBLIOGRAPHY

Abbott, Nabia. *Two Queens of Baghdad: Mother and Wife of Hārūn al-Rashīd*. Chicago: University of Chicago Press, 1946. Republished with a foreword by Sarah Graham-Brown, London: Al Saqi Books, 1986.

Hathaway, Jane. *The Politics of Households in Ottoman Egypt: The Rise of the Qazdağlıs*. Cambridge, U.K.: Cambridge University Press, 1997.

Mernissi, Fatima. *The Forgotten Queens of Islam*. Translated by Mary Jo Lakeland. Minneapolis: University of Minnesota Press, 1993.

Peirce, Leslie. *The Imperial Harem: Women and Sovereignty in the Ottoman Empire*. New York and Oxford: Oxford University Press, 1993.

JANE HATHAWAY

ḤUDŪD. *Ḥudūd* (sing. Ḥadd) are fixed and mandatory punishments for certain offenses mentioned in the Qurʾān and Sunnah. These offenses are theft, robbery, unlawful sexual intercourse, unfounded allegation of unlawful sexual intercourse, drinking alcohol, and apostasy. The penalties are specific numbers of lashes, amputation of the right hand or of the right hand and left foot, and capital punishment, in some cases by stoning to death.

Jurists have made it very difficult to obtain convictions for *Ḥadd* offenses. This is achieved by the use of strict definitions of the offense, high standards of evidence, and the doctrine of uncertainty (*shubhah*). Strict definitions of the punishable behavior exclude many acts that are similar but fall outside the definition. Proof of a *Ḥadd* offense is either a confession or the concurring testimonies of two Muslim male eyewitnesses of good reputation. For the offense of unlawful intercourse, four such witnesses are required

(Qur'ān 24:4). Circumstantial or hearsay evidence is not admitted. Only the Mālikīs accept the pregnancy of an unmarried woman as evidence for unlawful intercourse. Finally, there is the doctrine of uncertainty. The *sharīʿah* (Islamic law) lists situations in which it is assumed that the perpetrator might have been unaware or uncertain of the unlawful nature of his behavior. A *Ḥadd* penalty cannot be applied in such cases. This is true, for instance, if a father steals from his son, if a woman is raped, or if a man sleeps with a woman believing her to be his wife even though the marriage contract is null and void.

Because of these restrictions, the severe punishments for *Ḥadd* offenses were seldom applied, but even if no *Ḥadd* sentence could be pronounced, people who had stolen or robbed were not automatically acquitted. They could still be punished for such acts because judges and high officials had the discretionary power to impose punishments (*taʿzīr, siyāsah*) for acts that were sinful under the *sharīʿah* or that threatened the security of the state.

During the nineteenth century, with the advent of colonialism and Western expansion, Islamic criminal law was replaced by Western-style law codes nearly everywhere in the Muslim world. However, in the second half of the twentieth century, some countries have reintroduced Islamic criminal law. This happened in Libya (1972–1974), Pakistan (1979), Iran (1979), Sudan (1983), and northern Nigeria (2000).

The rules concerning the *Ḥadd* offenses are gender-neutral, men and women being treated equally. In practice, however, women are at a disadvantage, especially with regard to charges of unlawful intercourse. According to the Mālikī legal school, pregnancy of an unmarried woman is full evidence for a conviction. Moreover, in some countries where Islamic criminal law is applied, a woman's report of having been raped is legally taken as a confession of unlawful intercourse unless she can prove that she was coerced. In addition, if she identifies her attacker, she is liable for a conviction of unfounded allegation of unlawful sexual intercourse, which would entail flogging.

[*See also* Human Rights; *and* Law, *subentry on* Women's Legal Thought and Jurisprudence.]

BIBLIOGRAPHY

Peters, Rudolph. *Crime and Punishment in Islamic Law: Theory and Practice from the Sixteenth to the Twenty-First Century*. Cambridge, U.K.: Cambridge University Press, 2005.

Peters, Rudolph. "The Re-Islamization of Criminal Law in Northern Nigeria: The Safiyyatu Hussaini Case." In *Dispensing Justice in Islam: Qadis and Their Judgments*, edited by Muhammad Khalid Masud, Rudolph Peters, and David S. Powers, pp. 219–243. Leiden, Netherlands: Brill, 2006.

Quraishi, Asifa. "Her Honor: An Islamic Critique of the Rape Provisions in Pakistan's Ordinance on Zina." *Islamic Studies* 38, no. 3 (1999): 403–441.

Serrano, Delfina. "Rape in Maliki Legal Doctrine and Practice (8th–15th Centuries C.E.)." *Hawwa* 5, nos. 2–3 (2007): 166–207.

RUDOLPH PETERS

HUMAN RIGHTS.

The term "human rights," or *ḥuqūq al-insān* in Arabic, has only recently come into common use, as have the analogous terms *ḥuqūq-i insān* in Persian, *insan haklari* in Turkish, and *hak asasi anusia* in Bahasa Indonesian.

Early Reception. Concepts analogous to human rights have certain precursors in the Islamic heritage of philosophy and theology, but human rights lack precise equivalents in medieval *fiqh* (jurisprudence). In *fiqh* the category *ḥaqq al-ʿabd*, the right of the individual Muslim, was used to distinguish cases in which legal action against a wrongdoer was left to the discretion of the injured party from cases belonging to the category of the right of God, *ḥaqq Allah*, in which prosecution was mandatory and to be undertaken by the state. One non-controversial *fiqh* principle corresponding to a modern human right was the right of the owners of property to seek legal relief against interference with their property.

Rather than constructing doctrines or proposing institutions designed to curb the powers of a ruler or to protect the individual from a ruler's oppression, Islamic legal thought long concentrated on defining the theoretical duties of believers, including rulers, vis-à-vis God. According to the prevailing perspective, rulers had the obligation to rule according to Sharīʿah; their subjects were to obey them unless the order constituted a sin. The development of institutions that could place real curbs on political despotism or make them accountable to those they ruled was neglected; rebellion was commonly proposed as the remedy for tyranny.

To deal with the practical problems of protecting rights and freedoms, Muslim intellectuals and statesmen began to adopt the principles of European constitutionalism in the nineteenth century. In the latter half of the twentieth century, after the common acceptance of the principles of constitutionalism, the related question of the compatibility of international human rights principles with Islamic doctrine was raised. But it is important to note that this debate was highly politicized due to the legacy of colonialism and imperialism. During the latter half of the twentieth century, Western support for Israel and many authoritarian Arab/Muslim regimes brought charges of double standards and hypocrisy to the human rights debate.

Constitutionalism and Rights. In the nineteenth century, early clashes between inherited Islamic doctrines and emerging human rights norms revolved around the question of the equality of Muslims and non-Muslims before the law. The issue was complicated as European powers pressed for the elimination of discriminatory laws against non-Muslims. This was to foreshadow future debates about the status of women in Muslim societies.

A fundamental pact announced in Tunisia in 1857 under European pressure guaranteed equality for all before the law and in taxation, as well as complete security for all inhabitants irrespective of religion, nationality, or race. Tunisia was the first Muslim country to promulgate a constitution, doing so in 1861 and affirming the rights established in the pact; however, the constitution was suspended by the French Protectorate (1881–1956). In Tunisia, as in many other Muslim countries, the independence struggle against European domination accentuated people's consciousness of the importance of rights and democratic freedoms. After independence, the 1956 Tunisian Constitution stated that the republican form of government was the best guarantee of "human rights."

The most important early reforms in the direction of modern human rights were undertaken in the Ottoman Empire, which had many non-Muslim subjects and which, owing to its military and economic vulnerability, was also exposed to pressures from European powers. The *hatt-i şerif* of 1839, reinforced by the *hatt-i hümayun* of 1856, was part of a series of modernizing reforms in the Tanzimat period that aimed to establish the security of life, honor, and property, fair and public trials, and equality before the law for all Ottoman subjects irrespective of religion. The principle of nondiscrimination based on language and race was added by the *hatt-i hümayun*. In 1840 the new penal code affirmed the equality of all Ottoman subjects before the law.

By mid-century reformist pressures prompted the adoption of the 1876 Ottoman Constitution, which contained a section on *hukuk-i umumiye*, or public liberties, of Ottoman subjects, providing for equality regardless of religion, free exercise of religions other than Islam and freedom of worship, inviolability of personal freedom, and guarantees against arbitrary intrusions, extortion, arrest, or other unlawful violations of person, residence, or property. There were also provisions for freedom of the press, association, and education. This constitution was suspended in practice and not revived until after the Young Turk Revolution in 1908. The Young Turks' reforms expanded constitutional rights or protections, prohibited arrests and searches except by established legal procedures, abolished special or extraordinary courts, and guaranteed press freedom. Turkey's second republic saw in 1961 the promulgation of a constitution that undertook in its preamble to ensure and guarantee "human rights and liberties" and made men and women equal (Article 12). In the area of free exercise of religion, conditions were imposed to safeguard the policy of secularism adopted by Mustafa Kemal Atatürk (1881–1938), the first president of the Turkish Republic. Article 2 of the 1982 Turkish Constitution proclaimed Turkey to be a state governed by the rule of law that respects human rights.

Elsewhere in the Islamic world, popular agitation against the despotism of the Qājār dynasty culminated in Iran's first constitution in 1906. Iran's Shīʿī clerics were divided about the religious legitimacy of constitutionalism and its attendant rights provisions. One group of pro-constitutionalist clerics, whose most articulate champion was Ayatollah Muḥammad Ḥusayn Nāʾīnī (1860–1936), argued that a democratic constitution was compatible with the core values of Islam and should be supported because it placed limits on monarchial tyranny. Another group led by Ayatollah Faẓlullāh Nūrī (1842–1909) opposed the constitution, citing opposition to the equality in law between Muslims and non-Muslims, freedom of the press and speech, and the supremacy of human-made law over divine law.

After the 1979 Islamic Revolution in Iran, official spokesmen invoked Islam as the reason for the clerical regime's hostility to international human rights, which they often dismissed as products of an alien, Western cultural tradition. Iran, however, did not repudiate its ratification of the International Covenant on Civil and Political Rights. The 1979 Iranian Constitution in Article 20 states that all citizens shall be protected by the law and enjoy "human, political, economic, social, and cultural rights" but then qualifies them by stating they must be "in conformity with Islamic criteria." Other articles in the constitution (Articles 21–42) that refer to basic rights and freedoms are similarly qualified by reference to religion and, in case there is any doubt, Article 4 states that Islamic principles shall prevail over the entire constitution and that Islamic jurists of the nonelected Guardian Council are the interpreters of what constitutes Islamic criteria.

By the end of the twentieth century, all Muslim countries had adopted constitutions containing some or all of the rights or principles set forth in international human rights law. The 1989 Algerian Constitution was noteworthy for its guarantee of equality before the law regardless of gender (Article 28), fundamental liberties and human rights (Article 31), and human rights advocacy (Article 32). Like most Muslim countries, however, Algeria retained Islamic personal-status rules and constitutional provisions that accorded Islam a privileged status, perpetuating the ambiguous relationship between religious and constitutional norms.

Fiqh survived longest as the official law of the land in Saudi Arabia. However, changes inaugurated in 1992 suggested that the country might be moving gradually toward a governmental system that would accord at least limited recognition to rights and constitutionalism—albeit subject to Islamic criteria. The principle that Islam entails limits on human rights was adopted in the 1992 Saudi Basic Law of Government; Article 26 provided that "the state protects human rights in accordance with the Islamic Sharīʿah." What the Sharīʿah limits on rights would entail was not defined. The basic law provided for many citizen entitlements in the area of social welfare, but only a few rights in the political or civil area were recognized. These included the provision that no one should be arrested, imprisoned, or have his or her actions restricted except as provided by law (Article 36); that homes should not be entered or searched save in cases specified by statutes (Article 37); that communications should not be confiscated, delayed, read, or listened to except in cases defined by statutes (Article 40); and that private property must be protected and could only be taken for the public interest and with fair compensation (Article 17).

Muslim States and International Human Rights Law. It was in the aftermath of World War II that the modern international formulations of human rights were established, setting standards that became incorporated in international law. Muslim states were among the founding members of the United Nations, whose 1945 Charter called for respect for human rights and fundamental freedoms; all Muslim countries eventually joined the UN.

Recent scholarship has shown that Muslim countries and their representatives actively participated in the formulation and negotiation of the Universal Declaration of Human Rights and two legally binding covenants (International Covenant on Civil and Political Rights/ICCPR and International Covenant on Economic, Social and Cultural Rights/ICESCR). Some were supportive and others were not. There was no voice of Muslim unanimity, but instead a diversity of opinions reflecting national and individual interests.

Aspects of the Universal Declaration of Human Rights passed by the General Assembly in 1948 provoked criticism from representatives of Muslim countries, although in the end only Saudi Arabia failed to support its passage. Muslim nations differed greatly in their willingness to ratify the human rights conventions subsequently drafted under UN auspices. Muslims sometimes charged that international rights norms had a Western or Judeo-Christian bias that precluded their acceptance in Muslim milieus. In terms of the compatibility of international rights norms and Islamic law, the alleged conflicts centered on civil and political rights; problems related to the compatibility of Islam with economic, social, and cultural rights were rarely raised. The principles of freedom of religion—notably the right to convert from Islam to another faith—and the full equality of persons, regardless of sex or religion, seemed to pose particular problems.

The Charter of the Organization of the Islamic Cooperation (OIC), an international organization founded in 1969 to which all Muslim countries belong, indicated in its preamble that members were "reaffirming their commitment to the UN Charter and fundamental human rights." The OIC Charter came into force in 1973. In 1990, however, the OIC issued the Cairo Declaration on Human Rights in Islam, which diverged significantly from international human rights standards; it was not made clear how this declaration was to be reconciled with the conflicting obligations undertaken by OIC members in ratifying international human rights covenants or in their individual constitutional rights provisions, which, in many cases, corresponded to the international norms.

Like the many other self-proclaimed "Islamic" human rights schemes that proliferated from the 1960s onward, the OIC Declaration extensively borrowed terms and concepts from the International Bill of Human Rights, presenting a hybrid mixture of elements taken from Islamic and international law. The OIC Declaration asserted that "fundamental rights and universal freedoms in Islam are an integral part of the Islamic religion," but then proceeded to insert "Islamic" qualifications and conditions on the rights and freedoms guaranteed under international law—in conflict with international human rights theory, which does not permit religious criteria to override rights. Representative provisions included the rule in Article 24 that all the rights and freedoms stipulated in the Declaration were subject to the Sharīʿah, without defining what limits this would entail.

There was no provision for equal rights for all persons regardless of sex or religion. Instead, Article 1 stated that "all human beings are equal in terms of basic human dignity and basic obligations and responsibilities [not "rights"], without any discrimination on the grounds of race, color, language, sex, religious belief, political affiliation, social status or other considerations." Article 6 further provided that "woman is equal to man in human dignity" [not "rights"], but it imposed on the husband the responsibility for the support and welfare of the family. In contrast, Article 13 provided that men and women were entitled to fair wages "without discrimination." Article 5 provided that, on the right to marry, there should be "no restrictions stemming from race, color or nationality," but did not prohibit restrictions based on religion.

The provisions regarding religion did not aim for neutrality: Article 10 stated that Islam was the religion of unspoiled nature and prohibited "any form of compulsion on man or to exploit his poverty or ignorance in order to convert him to another religion or to atheism." Article 9 called for the state to ensure the means to acquire education "so as to enable man to be acquainted with the religion of Islam." The favored treatment of Islam carried over to freedom of speech, with Article 22(a) stating that expressing opinion freely was allowed "in such manner as would not be contrary to the principles of the Sharīʿah." Article 22(c) barred the exploitation or misuse of information "in such a way as may violate sanctities and the dignity of Prophets, undermine moral and ethical values or disintegrate, corrupt or harm society or weaken its faith." Article 18 stipulated a right to privacy in the conduct of private affairs, in the home, in the family, and regarding property and relationships. Article 15 set forth "rights of ownership" to "property acquired in a legitimate way, barring expropriation except for the public interest and upon payment of immediate and fair compensation."

Noteworthy by their absence were provisions calling for the observance of democratic principles in political systems and guarantees of freedom of religion, freedom of association, freedom of the press, and equality and equal protection of the law. Although torture was prohibited in Article 20, there were no provisions explicitly endorsing international rights norms in the area of criminal procedure—only the vague assurance in Article 19 that the defendant would be entitled to "a fair trial in which he shall be given all the guarantees of defense." Since Article 25 stated that the Sharīʿah "is the only source of reference or the explanation or clarification of any of the articles of this Declaration," the possibility was left open that a trial would be deemed "fair" as long as it was conducted in conformity with Sharīʿah norms, which were historically underdeveloped in the area of criminal procedure. There was no principle of legality per se; the provision in Article 19 that there should be no crime or punishment except as provided for in the Sharīʿah seemed to open the door to the application of *taʿzīr* (discretionary) penalties, as well as rules regarding *ḥadd* crimes. Article 2 prohibited taking life except for a reason prescribed by the Sharīʿah. Reflecting the third-world setting in which Muslim nations elaborate their positions on rights, Article 11 prohibited colonialism and stated that "peoples suffering from colonialism have the full right to freedom and self-determination." In sum, the OIC

Declaration suggested that the official approach of Muslim countries to civil and political rights was distinguishable from that of non-Muslim countries by reason of their reliance on Sharīʿah rules.

In the early twenty-first century, due in part to the legacy of colonialism and the failures of the postcolonial state, "secular" discourses in the Muslim world are widely discredited and viewed as inauthentic. Thus, contemporary Muslim human rights scholars have attempted to anchor human rights discourses within an Islamic paradigm; that is, the universal is particularized within the dominant idiom of Muslim societies.

The most visible proponent of such an approach is the human rights activist Shirin Ebadi, who won the 2003 Nobel Peace Prize on behalf of her struggle for the rights of children and women in her native Iran. Other intellectual voices include Khaled Abou El Fadl and Abdullahi An-Naʿim. El Fadl has offered critiques of modern-day fundamentalists and articulated a reading that emphasizes a rights-based discourse that is premised on Islamic values and the legal debates of Islamic jurists from the medieval era. An-Naʿim has argued that Islamic law and understandings of Sharīʿah must be contested and not treated as incapable of reinterpretation—that is, Sharīʿah is not divine writ itself, but rather is based on inherently fallible human interpretation and subject to change. He also believes that the state should not enforce Sharīʿah on society.

In a post–September 11, 2001, world, the ubiquitous authoritarian state is the most significant human rights abuser in the Muslim world where torture, illegal detention, and the absence of judicial process are common. As well, human rights abuses at Abu Ghraib prison in Iraq and the Guantānamo Bay detention camp have tarnished the reputation of the West as the standard bearer of universal human rights.

Governments, organizations, and individuals throughout the Muslim world continue to take a variety of opposing positions on human rights. There is a divide between those using "Islamic" discourses to legitimate human rights and those who interpret sacred text to obtain the opposite meaning. It remains unclear as to which forces are ascendant, though polling data firmly and consistently reveal that Muslims do admire and support human rights and democracy. With respect to gender equality, constitutional debates in the Arab World after the Arab Spring have revolved around the Islamist suggestion that women are "complementary" to men. Secular and liberal groups have protested this language, arguing that this erodes full equality for women and have demanded language that is more strict and avoids any ambiguity.

[*See also* International Laws and Treaties on Women's Status; Law; *and* Women and Social Reform.]

BIBLIOGRAPHY

Abou El Fadl, Khaled. *The Great Theft: Wrestling Islam from the Extremists.* New York: HarperCollins, 2005.

Abou El Fadl, Khaled. "The Human Rights Commitment in Modern Islam." In *Human Rights and Responsibilities in the World Religions*, edited by Joseph Runzo, Nancy M. Martin, and Arvind Sharma, pp. 301–364. Oxford: Oneworld, 2003.

Abou El Fadl, Khaled. *Islam and the Challenge of Democracy.* Edited by Joshua Cohen and Deborah Chasman. Princeton, NJ: Princeton University Press, 2004.

Abou El Fadl, Khaled. *Speaking in God's Name: Islamic Law, Authority and Women.* Oxford: Oneworld, 2001.

Akbarzadeh, Shahram, and Benjamin MacQueen. *Islam and Human Rights in Practice: Perspectives Across the Ummah.* New York: Routledge, 2008.

An-Naʿim, Abdullahi Ahmed. *Islam and the Secular State: Negotiating the Future of Sharia.* Cambridge, MA: Harvard University Press, 2007.

An-Naʿim, Abdullahi Ahmed. *Muslims and Global Justice.* Philadelphia: University of Pennsylvania Press, 2011.

An-Na'im, Abdullahi Ahmed. "Why Should Muslims Abandon Jihad? Human Rights, and the Future of International Law." *Third World Quarterly* 27, no. 5 (2006): 785–797.

An-Na'im, Abdullahi Ahmed. *Toward an Islamic Reformation: Civil Liberties, Human Rights, and International Law*. Syracuse, NY: Syracuse University Press, 1990.

Baderin, Mashood A. *International Human Rights and Islamic Law*. Oxford: Oxford University Press, 2002.

Baderin, Mashood A. "Islam and the Realization of Human Rights in the Muslim World: A Reflection on Two Essential Approaches and Two Divergent Perspectives." *Muslim World Journal of Human Rights* 4, no. 1 (2007): Article 5.

Badran, Margot. *Feminism beyond East and West: New Gender Talk and Practice in Global Islam*. New Delhi: Global Media, 2007.

Chase, Anthony. *Human Rights, Revolution, and Reform in the Muslim World*. Boulder, CO: Lynne Rienner, 2012.

Chase, Anthony. "Liberal Islam and 'Islam and Human Rights': A Skeptic's View." *Religion and Human Rights* 1, no. 2 (2006): 145–163.

Coulson, Noel J. "The State and the Individual in Islamic Law." *International and Comparative Law Quarterly* 6 (1957): 49–60.

Dalacoura, Katerina. *Islam, Liberalism, & Human Rights: Implications for International Relations*. 3d ed. New York: I.B. Tauris, 2007.

Ebadi, Shirin with Azadeh Moaveni. *Iran Awakening: One Woman's Journey to Reclaim Her Life and Her Country*. New York: Random House, 2007.

Johansen, Baber. "The Relationship between the Constitution, the *Shari'a* and the *Fiqh*: The Jurisprudence of Egypt's Supreme Constitutional Court." *Zeitschrift für ausländisches öffentliches Recht und Völkerrecht (Heidelberg Journal of International Law)* 64, no. 4 (2004): 881–896.

Keddie, Nikki. *Women in the Middle East: Past and Present*. Princeton, NJ: Princeton University Press, 2006.

Kurzman, Charles, ed. *Liberal Islam: A Sourcebook*. Oxford: Oxford University Press, 1998.

Mayer, Ann Elizabeth. *Islam and Human Rights: Tradition and Politics*. 5th ed. Boulder, CO: Westview Press, 2013.

Monshipouri, Mahmood. *Human Rights in the Middle East: Frameworks, Goals, and Strategies*. New York: Palgrave Macmillan, 2011.

Moosa, Ebrahim. "The Dilemma of Islamic Rights Schemes." *Journal of Law and Religion* 15, no. 1/2 (2000–2001): 185–215.

Moustafa, Yousry. "The Islamisation of Human Rights: Implications for Gender and Politics in the Middle East." *IDS Bulletin* 42, no. 1 (2011): 21–25.

Reinbold, Jenna. "Radical Islam and Human Rights Values: A 'Religious-Minded' Critique of Secular Liberty, Equality, and Brotherhood." *Journal of the American Academy of Religion* 78, no. 2 (2010): 449–476.

Saeed, Abdullah, and Hassan Saeed. *Freedom of Religion, Apostasy and Islam*. Aldershot, UK: Ashgate, 2004.

Şentürk, Recep. "Sociology of Rights: 'I am Therefore I Have Rights': Human Rights in Islam between Universalistic and Communalistic Perspectives." *Muslim World Journal of Human Rights* 2, no. 1 (2005).

Wadud, Amina. *Qur'an and Woman: Rereading the Sacred Text from a Woman's Perspective*. Oxford: Oxford University Press, 1999.

Waltz, Susan. "Universal Human Rights: The Contribution of Muslim States." *Human Rights Quarterly* 26, no. 4 (2004): 799–844.

NADER HASHEMI
and EMRAN QURESHI

HYGIENE. Hygiene in Islam is dictated by the scriptures of the Qurʾān and Sunnah, as recorded largely in the ḥadīth. Issues related to hygiene are determined by God and were presented by the example of the Prophet Muḥammad. Attention has been given to this topic both historically and in the contemporary era, with remarkable continuity in attention to Muḥammad's personal example, not only in matters of worship, but also in his relations with other people.

Cleanliness is the aspect of hygiene most explicitly discussed in the Qurʾān (4:43, 5:7). Cleanliness is equated with spirituality: cleansing of the body not only cleans the body of impurity, but is also intended to lead to a cleansing of the mind from impure thoughts. According to a famous ḥadīth, "The key to Paradise is prayer and the key to prayer is being purified."

The Qur'ān addresses two areas in which hygiene is important—*'ibādāt* (worship) and *mu'āmalāt* (relations between human beings). With respect to *'ibādāt*, men and women were seen as equal. For example, both are required to perform ablutions before prayers (5:6) as a means of both physically and mentally preparing themselves for worship. Legal schools (*madhāhib*) vary as to whether ablutions are required before reading the Qur'ān or going on pilgrimage. Major ablutions (*ghusl*) are required after activities involving emissions of bodily fluids, such as sexual intercourse, while minor ablutions (*wuḍū'*) are required prior to prayer, provided that *ghusl* has previously been performed when necessary. *Ghusl* is recommended before the Friday congregational prayer (*jum'ah*). Women are required to perform *ghusl* after menstruation and childbirth as a reflection of this concern with bodily cleanliness after the emission of body fluids, rather than necessarily as a gender construct, although some legal scholars have expounded on this requirement in ways that emphasize regularity in women's ritual uncleanliness that some scholars argued resulted in mental deficiencies. Nevertheless, Muḥammad's example reflects a less legalistic and negative approach to menstruation, as he considered menstruation a biological fact, rather than a deficiency, and he continued to spend time with and enjoy the company of his menstruating wives, refraining only from vaginal intercourse during this time. In the contemporary era, some jurists have issued *fatāwā* making it clear that menstruating women may still study the Qur'ān.

Hygiene with respect to interpersonal relationships comes into play with respect to practices such as grooming (trimming of fingernails and toenails, removal of body hair, and making certain that the beard is free of food or debris, for example), tooth cleansing (the Prophet was known to clean his teeth with *siwak* after eating), breath freshening, and the use of perfume (the Prophet emphasized the importance of presenting oneself in a pleasant manner so as not to offend others with body or mouth odor). The connection of hygiene to both worship and relationships between human beings suggests the importance of the discipline of both body and mind in righteous living.

Changes to the study and practice of medicine from the nineteenth through the early twenty-first century have resulted in greater attention being given to hygiene in medical circles. In an Islamic context, care is often taken to link medical advances and recommendations with scriptural sources, emphasizing the importance of caring for the body God has provided. Thus, germs and disease are to be prevented from entering the body through the engagement of proper hygiene.

The connection between health and hygiene is promoted by many health organizations, both nationally and internationally, in contemporary Muslim societies.

[*See also* Ablutions *and* Menstruation].

BIBLIOGRAPHY

Badawi, Jamal A. al-Tahara. *Purity and State of Undefilement*. Indianapolis: Islamic Teaching Center, 1979.

Katz, Marion H. "The Study of Islamic Ritual and the Meaning of *wudu*." *Der Islam* 82, no. 1 (2005): 106–145.

al-Kaysi, Marwan Ibrahim. *Morals and Manners in Islam: A Guide to Islamic Ādāb*. Leicester, U.K.: Islamic Foundation, 1986.

Kuskular, Remzi. *Cleanliness in Islam: A Comprehensive Guide to Tahara*. Somerset, N.J.: The Light, 2007.

NATANA J. DELONG-BAS

I

ʿIBĀDAH. *ʿIbādah* (pl. *ʿibādāt*) refers to service, servitude, and, by extension, the very essence of religious worship in the Islamic tradition. The concept of *ʿibādah* lies at the very heart of the expression of the relationship between humanity and God in the Qurʾān and its subsequent elaborations in Islamic law and religious practice. The Qurʾān uses the verbal form *yaʿbudūn* (to worship) to illustrate the creation of human beings as linked to the notion of a primacy placed on the worship of God: "I did not create the jinn and human beings but to worship me (*illā li-yaʿbudūnī*)" (1:56). This concept of servitude is extended to all of creation in a number of Qurʾānic passages, including, "None is in the heavens and the earth but comes before the All-Merciful as a servant" (19:93). Thus, the demonstration of service or worship by the servants of God (*ʿibād Allāh*) is ultimately the prescribed goal of all existence. Although Qurʾānic discourses recognize that there are distinctions between women and men, these distinctions do not operate at the level of the essential nature of human beings, nor do they prescribe a gendered hierarchy in the Divine recognition and acceptance of the *ʿibādah* undertaken by women and men.

The performance of ritual acts of worship has been the subject of considerable Qurʾānic and legal discourse. Works of *fiqh* (jurisprudence) commonly treat acts of religious worship (*ʿibādāt*) in contrast to religious transactions involving individuals (*muʿāmalāt*). The distinction between religious worship and transactions is a theoretical distinction, rather than one that corresponds to the multivalent expressions of religious worship in social practice. While both Shīʿī and Sunnī works on law tend to treat *ʿibādāt*, preceded by issues of ritual purity (*ṭahārah*), in a manner based on the exposition of the ritual acts of worship among the "five pillars of Islam," the relationship between *ʿibādāt* and *muʿāmalāt* is not unambiguous. For instance, the connection between the performance of ritual acts of worship and *muʿāmalāt* can be seen in the prescriptions related to a range of religious obligations that extend beyond the five pillars of Islam, such as the provisions relating to marriage, the hunting and slaughter of animals, the taking of oaths, the expiation of sin, circumambulation of the Kaʿbah during pilgrimage, and even the degree to which transactional matters are to include praise, glorification, and remembrance of God. In terms of the distinction between *ʿibādāt* and *muʿāmalāt*, there are few, if any, distinctions related to *ʿibādāt* or ritual acts of worship and the obligation to perform them that are gender-specific.

ʿIbādah in Islamic discourses cannot be seen as solely resulting from the accumulated weight of textual stipulations, but rather should be viewed as the product of cumulative interpretive enterprises forged by Muslim communities over time. Thus, the range of acts of worship considered a reflection of *ʿibādah* have been historically determined with reference to the Qurʾān, *sunnah*, and social practice. For example, the Qurʾān was revealed in seventh-century Arabia when its first audience of Arab reciters or "readers" held certain culturally embedded and socially inscribed ideas about women. Thus, specific injunctions were addressed to that culture. Some prevailing practices were prohibited explicitly: infanticide, sexual abuse of female slaves, denial of inheritance to women, and the denial of conjugal rights to women, and prohibiting women from remarriage. Other practices were modified in accordance with new patterns of worship and their corresponding forms of social regulation: polygamy, the oath of divorce, sexual violence and spousal abuse, and concubinage.

The Qurʾān rarely addresses the details of specific forms of religious worship and their relationship to gender. Instead, the text alludes to a number of dimensions of religious worship and social practices that are assumed to be known elements of religious life while remaining neutral concerning their practical manifestations, such as patriarchy, economic hierarchy, the division of labor between men and women within a particular family, and the role of women in the economic sphere.

BIBLIOGRAPHY

Ibn al-Muṭahhar al-Ḥillī, al-Ḥasan ibn Yūsuf. *Qawāʿid al-aḥkām fī maʿrifat al-ḥalāl wa al-ḥarām*. 3 vols. Qom, Iran: Muʿassasat al-Nashr al-Islāmī al-Tābiʿah li-Jamāʿt al-Mudarrasīn bi-Qom, 1992.

Modarressi, Hossein. *An Introduction to Shīʿī Law: A Bibliographical Study*. London: Ithaca Press, 1984.

Murata, Sachiko, and William C. Chittick. *The Vision of Islam*. New York: Paragon House, 1994.

Padwick, C. E. *Muslim Devotions: A Study of Prayer Manuals in Common Use*. London: Oxford, 1961.

Wadud, Amina. *Qurʾan and Woman: Rereading the Sacred Text from a Woman's Perspective*. New York: Oxford University Press, 1999.

TARIQ AL-JAMIL

ICONOGRAPHY. As figurative arts were an integral part of Islamic visual culture, images of women made a certain contribution to the formation of iconographic traditions in the Muslim world. While the iconography of Muslim women can be observed from various angles, this differs from time to time and varies from region to region.

Iconographic sources for Muslim women during early Islamic times remain relatively limited, compared with female icons that developed under other religious traditions, such as Christianity, Buddhism, and Hinduism. This is mainly due to the general aversion to the public presence of women in Muslim society, especially those who were of high social rank. This tendency, together with the theoretical prohibition of figural art in religious contexts, hindered the development of sculptural and pictorial representations of female figures. Two of the powerful female members of the family of the Prophet Muḥammad—his first wife Khadīja (d. c. 619) and their daughter Fātimah (d. 633)—were thus never venerated as idolized images in the two- or three-dimensional form.

In contrast to such a conservative idea of female icons, women played an important iconographic role in the secular sphere. Besides their ultimate symbol of fertility, the beauty of female characters was often celebrated by poets during medieval times. This was particularly the case with the literary traditions in the Islamic East, and, thanks to the tenacity of pre-Islamic pictorial legacy, many female characters depicted in Persian literary works acquired distinctive iconographic features. In book painting, the main female characters were often depicted with the emphasis on their physiological peculiarities. East Asian or Turkic Central Asian features, for example, their round faces with long, narrow eyes, were linked to a particular aesthetic view to the so-called moon-faced Buddha (*bot-i mahruy*), an idea that had permeated the Iranian world in the course of the spread of Buddhism before Islam. Women were also used as figurative motifs in the objects of the medieval Islamic world, although some of the motifs appear to have functioned as mere decorative devices rather than pictorial idioms of iconographical significance.

Among the genres of Islamic architecture, the enclosed quarters for female family members, called "harem" in Turkish (the term derived from "haram" [forbidden place] in Arabic), stands out for its unequivocal association with Muslim women. While this was a custom rather than a sensation in Muslim cultural contexts, the idea of female seclusion in Islamic society, especially under the Ottomans, generated a romantic, if not distorted, fascination among Europeans. Muslim women in the harem thus became visual icons of the declining and decadent Orient during the nineteenth century, and this developed into an established genre of the Orientalist paintings of the time.

Apart from the harem, other building types of Islamic architecture convey masculine connotations, despite the fact that many female patrons were associated with the construction of religious and secular buildings during medieval and early modern times. Although they were not patrons themselves, the wives of powerful rulers were often behind the construction of architectural marvels, such as the Taj Mahal in Agra, the tomb complex of the wife of the Mughal emperor Shah Jahan, and the Bibi Hamum Mosque in Samarqand, which was built to commemorate the wife of Timur. These could have been viewed as the visual incarnation of the perfect beauty.

While the symbols of sovereign and authority, such as the crown and the turban, were predominantly used among the members of the male ruling class in the pre-modern Islamic world, the female head covering (hijab) became one of the most powerful symbolic devices that have been entrusted to define the images of Muslim women. Despite a popular notion toward the Islamic doctrine, the hijab is not worn because of the dress code stipulated by the Qurʾān. The image of veiling Muslim women is more likely to have evolved as an iconographic symbol of modesty and morality during modern times. As Islamic revival grew, the veil became a spatial curtain that metaphorically segregated men and women in public space.

In recent years, Muslim women are, as victims of conservatism or pioneers of modernism, given full attention in every aspect of the socio-political discussion inside and outside the world of Islam. Iconographically and symbolically, stereotypes of Muslim women, mostly veiled, are often featured in the contemporary arts from the Islamic world. All in all, this mode of neo-Orientalism will serve to create new visual icons of Muslim women.

[*See also* Veiling; Harem; *and* Art, *subentry on* Women in Islamic Art]

BIBLIOGRAPHY

Baer, Eva. *The Human Figure in Islamic Art: Inheritances and Islamic Transformations*. Costa Mesa, Calif.: Mazda, 2004.

Malik, Amna. "Dialogues between 'Orientalism' and Modernism in Shirin Neshat's 'Women of Allah.'" In

Global and Local Art Histories, edited by Gregory Minnesale and Celina Jeffery, Newcastle-upon-Tyne: Cambridge Scholars Publishing, 2007, pp. 145–169.

Melikian-Chirvani, Assadullah Souren "The Buddhist Heritage in the Art of Iran." in *Mahayanist Art after AD 900*, edited by William Watson, Colloquies on Art and Archaeology in Asia 2, London: Percival David Foundation of Chinese Art, 1972, pp. 56–65.

Roberts, Mary. *Intimate Outsiders: The Harem in Ottoman and Orientalist Art and Travel Literature.* Durham, N.C.: Duke University Press, 2007.

Shirazi, Faegheh. *The Veil Unveiled: The Hijab in Modern Culture.* Gainesville: University of Florida Press, 2001.

YUKA KADOI

ʿIDDAH. *ʿIddah* can be defined as the waiting period that the woman should respect when her marriage is dissolved by divorce or the husband's death. It is addressed in a number of Qurʾānic verses, such as 2:228, prescribing that "Divorced women shall wait concerning themselves for three monthly periods [*qarʿ*, pl. *qurūʾ*]." Other verses pertaining to the *ʿiddah* are 2:234, 33:49, and 65:4. This article describes the norms pertaining to *ʿiddah,* both in classical Islamic legal doctrine and present-day personal status codes. It will also address how these formal norms are applied in practice, as several studies show that often the "law in action" differs from the "law on the books."

Islamic Norms. During the waiting period, whether upon the husband's death or a divorce, the woman is not allowed to remarry—it is thus a temporal marriage impediment for women. Among other functions the *ʿiddah* serves to preclude any confusion about the paternity of children born after the dissolution of her marriage. As the wife remains in the marital home during the *ʿiddah,* and as her freedom of movement is severely restricted (in Ḥanafī doctrine, she cannot even leave the house), the *ʿiddah* safeguards the woman's honor and protects her against false accusations. Besides, in case of the husband's death, the *ʿiddah* is inspired by respect for the deceased.

The waiting period following divorce has another remarkable consequence, namely that the husband may revoke the divorce; it thus permits the husband the opportunity to contemplate his decision. However this is not true for all types of divorce: Islamic law distinguishes between revocable, minor irrevocable (*baʾin baynuna sughra*) and major irrevocable (*baʾin baynuna kubra*) divorce. That the husband's right to revoke the divorce is delimited to a fixed period of time is one of the main reforms brought about by Islamic law: in pre-Islamic times men could divorce their wives and take them back indefinitely, whereas the *ʿiddah* secures that, after a specific period, the woman is entirely released from the control of her former husband.

A divorce is revocable in the event of *ṭalāq,* and judicial divorce on the grounds of nonpayment of maintenance (this can be revoked by the payment of the due sum). The husband can take his wife back by revoking the divorce through word or through deed, such as resuming sexual life with her. He does not need his wife's consent to revoke the divorce. During the waiting period, the wife continues to live in the marital home and receives maintenance.

Divorce through *khulʿ*, as well as other types of judicial divorce, are irrevocable; if the man wants the woman back, he needs to remarry her. Some divorces are irrevocable in a way that cannot be remedied by remarriage: if the husband has pronounced the *ṭalāq* more than two times, the divorce becomes irrevocable and the couple can only remarry after an intermediate marriage of the woman. After an oath of denial of paternity (*liʿan*) the couple can never again remarry.

In the event of an irrevocable divorce the wife lives in the marital home, but there is difference of opinion on the issue of maintenance: according to the Mālikī and Shāfiʿī schools, the irrevocably divorced wife will only receive maintenance if she is pregnant, while the Ḥanafī doctrine also grants maintenance to the wife when she is not pregnant.

The length of the *ʿiddah* varies. The waiting period for a divorcee is three menstrual periods (in Shīʿī law, the *ʿiddah* after a temporary marriage is two menstrual periods). There is some controversy between the schools on the length of the *ʿiddha*, which has its origins in the difference of interpretation of *qarʿ* used in 2:228: according to the Ḥanafī doctrine, it means the period of menstruation, whereas the other schools interpret it as the period between menstruations. Therefore the *ʿiddah* expires under Ḥanafī law with the end of the third menstrual period after the divorce, whereas, according to the other schools, it ends at the beginning of the third menstrual period. If the marriage has not been consummated the wife is not obliged to observe the *ʿiddah* period, unless dissolution was the result of her husband's death. If a woman is past menopause, she must wait three months; the general term for the *ʿiddah* of a widow is four months and ten days. If a woman is pregnant she cannot remarry until she has given birth. Islamic law recognizes that pregnancy, because of "sleeping" of the fetus, may last much longer than nine months; Mālikī law even admits pregnancies of four or five years.

Practice. Defining the length of the *ʿiddah* in menstrual periods is a weapon in the hands of women, as the woman is the only one who knows when she has had her three menstruations. This means that if she wants to remarry quickly, she can claim to have a short menstrual cycle, whereas if she wishes to stretch her waiting period for whatever reason, she can claim to have a long or irregular one. An important reason for a woman to stretch her cycle may be to continue to receive maintenance and boarding. But another reason may be related to paternity: as Islamic law prohibits sex outside of marriage, a child born out of wedlock has no rights vis-à-vis its biological father. However, if the woman claims that she got pregnant before the dissolution of her marriage, the former husband is considered the father. Given that the schools recognize that an embryo can fall asleep in the womb, such claim is accepted when a woman gives birth years after her divorce or the death of her husband.

Modern Codifications. Upon codification and reform of divorce law in many Muslim majority countries, the concept of the waiting period was upheld, even in countries such as Tunisia, where the Personal Status Code of 1956 differed significantly from Sharīʿah. This means that the woman cannot marry during the *ʿiddah* and that the husband should provide for housing and maybe maintenance during this period. Nevertheless the norms were generally slightly altered. For example, the possibility of revocation of a *ṭalāq* has been silently abolished in many countries, as their legislation provides that not the husband, but the court, pronounce the divorce, and logically a judicial divorce cannot be revoked by the husband. This is, for example, true in Morocco, where *ṭalāq* became a judicial decision in 2004.

But legislation also introduced other alterations to the classical norms of *ʿiddah*. In much legislation the *ʿiddah* is counted in months instead of menstruations, and the maximum period of pregnancy has generally been limited to one year.

Practice. Legal reforms may jeopardize the opportunities provided by classical rules pertaining to maintenance and paternity, as the wife can no longer stretch her *ʿiddah* as before. But besides legislation other actors may play a role. For example, the Tunisian legislation, granting men and women equal divorce rights, offers women the right to maintenance during the waiting period upon divorce. In practice, however, judges deny maintenance to women who, in one way or another, have caused the divorce or agreed with it. Another example comes from the former People's Democratic Republic of Yemen, where the *ʿiddah* was used as a device to circumvent the prohibition of polygamy that was introduced by legislation: in practice, a husband could repudiate his wife, marry another during the waiting period, and then revoke the repudiation.

The Nigerian case of Safiyyatu Husseini, on the other hand, testifies to how the waiting period and the notion of the sleeping embryo can save lives in a state where Islamic capital punishments have been reintroduced. Safiyyatu, a divorced woman, was prosecuted for the Islamic crime of fornication on the grounds that she was pregnant while unmarried; she thus risked being stoned to death, in accordance with the fixed Islamic legal penalty for proven *zinah*. Safiyyatu, however, claimed that she had not had sex outside marriage: she argued that the child had been conceived before her divorce, even if this had taken place long before. The court released her, on the grounds of the concept of the sleeping embryo. This famous case demonstrates that, until this day, the *ʿiddah* is used to soften the sharp edges of some legal norms.

BIBLIOGRAPHY

Ali, Kecia. *Marriage and Slavery in Early Islam*. Cambridge, Mass: Harvard University Press, 2010.

Clarke, L. "*ʿIddah*." In *The Oxford Encyclopaedia of the Muslim World*, edited by John L. Esposito, pp. 510–511. Oxford: Oxford University Press, 2009.

Grand'Henry, Jacques. "*Qur*', 'menstruation, pureté,' un cas d'ambivalence sémantique en arabe." *Anthropos* (1975): 270–275.

Hawting, G. R. "The Role of *Qur'an* and *hadith* in the Legal Controversy about the Rights of a Divorced Woman during Her "Waiting Period (*idda*)." *Bulletin of the School of Oriental and African Studies* 52, no. 3 (1989): 430–445.

Jamil, Javed. "Extra-ordinary Importance of *ʿiddah* in family health." *Islam and the Modern Age* 31, no. 3 (2000): 117–124.

Jansen, Willy. "Mythe of macht? Langdurige zwangerschappen in Noord Afrika." *Tijdschrift voor vrouwenstudies* 10, 3, no. 2 (1984): 158–179.

Kruk, Remke. "Pregnancy and Its Social Consequences in Medieval and Traditional Arab Society." *Quaderni degli studi arabi* 5–6 (1987–1988) : 418–430.

Layish, Aharon. "The Prohibition of Reinstating a Divorced Wife in the Druze Family." *Bulletin of the School of Oriental and African Studies* 41, no. 2 (1978): 258–271.

Linant de Bellefonds, Yvon. *Traité de droit musulman comparé*. 3 vols. Paris: Mouton, 1965–1973.

Moulyneux, Maxine. "Women's Rights and Political Contingency: The Case of Yemen, 1990–1994." *Middle East Journal* 49, no. 3 (1995): 418–431.

Moustafa, Ahmed Helmy. *Al-nafaqa al-zawjiya, wa ma fi hukumha: fi daw' al-madahib al-fiqhiya wa-al-qawanin al-ʿarabiya*. Cairo, 2008.

Nasir, Jamal J. *The Islamic Law of Personal Status*. 2d ed. London and Boston: Graham and Trotman, 1990.

Nik Badli Shah, Nik Noriani. "The Islamic Marriage Contract in Malaysia." In *The Islamic Marriage Contract: Case Studies in Islamic Family Law*, edited by Asfa Quraishi and Frank E. Vogel, pp. 183–199. Cambridge, Mass.: Harvard University Press, 2008.

Peters, Ruud. "The Re-Islamization of Criminal Law in Northern Nigeria and the Judiciary: The Safiyyatu Husseini Case." In *Dispensing Justice in Islam: Qadis and Their Judgments*, edited by Muhammad Khalid Masud, Rudolph Peters, and David S. Powers, pp. 219–244. Leiden, Netherlands: Brill, 2006.

Peters, Ruud. *A Survey of Islamic Law*, 2006 (unpublished).

Robana, Zakia. *The Traditional Women of the Mediterranean Island of Djerba (North Africa), A Narrative Anthropology*. Lewiston, N.J.: Edwin Mellen Press, 2010.

Schacht, Joseph. *The Origins of Muhammadan Jurisprudence*. Oxford: Clarendon Press, 1967.

Smith, M. G. "Secondary Marriage in Northern Nigeria." *Africa* 23 (1953): 298–323.

Stiles, Erin. "Broken *Edda* and Marital Mistakes: Two Recent Disputes from an Islamic Court in Zanzibar." In *Dispensing Justice in Islam: Qadis and Their Judgments*, edited by Muhammad Khalid Masud, Rudolph Peters, and David S. Powers, pp. 95–116. Leiden, Netherlands: Brill, 2006.

Voorhoeve, Maaike. *Gender and Divorce in North Africa: Sharia, Custom and the Personal Status Code in Tunisia*. London: I. B. Tauris, 2013.

Zawba'i, Laila Hasan Muhammad. *Ahkām al-ʿidda fī al-sharīʿah al-Islāmīyah*. Amman, Jordan: Mu'assasat al-warraq lil-nashr wa-al-tawzi', 2007.

L. Clarke
Updated by Maaike Voorhoeve

Immigration and Minorities (Theoretical Overview). The contemporary global and transnational context in which human migration has reached unprecedented levels is one in which questions about authenticity and identity often take center stage, requiring new approaches to self-understanding at both the individual and communal levels. This is particularly true for immigrant and minority communities seeking to claim an authentic identity in a new home country or in a surrounding context of difference from mainstream culture and/or society.

Our goal in dedicating a theme to these issues was twofold: First, we felt it was important to address the growing realities of immigration and the resulting diaspora communities where Muslims live as minorities in non-Muslim majority contexts, such as in the cases of the United States and Europe; and, second, we wanted to highlight and address the often unacknowledged reality of Muslims living as minorities within a Muslim-majority context, such as in the cases of Shīʿī populations in Sunnī-majority Saudi Arabia, the Hazāra of Afghanistan, the ethnic Chinese in Indonesia, and even Western converts to Islam as a minority within their home societies as they practice and express their faith within larger faith communities of those born and raised Muslim, often with particular accompanying cultural practices and interpretations. By raising questions about what constitutes a minority and who has the right to define it, we hope to draw attention to the complexity of constructing minority identities and the impact of the label of "minority" when assigned by an outside majority versus being the choice of the minority group itself. We also hope to expand academic conversation about immigration by acknowledging that there are multiple types of immigration and, thus, diaspora communities today, as immigration is not only a phenomenon that occurs between countries, but also within countries, such as from the countryside to cities, or refugees escaping from armed conflicts, sometimes by migrating within the country and sometimes outside of it. The result is a variety of types of diaspora communities that often take on new identities tied to their reasons for migration. How, where, and to what degree such populations are to be integrated and who is to guide that integration remain open questions.

The articles contained within this theme examine not only the challenges of both constructing and maintaining an authentic identity when living in a minority context, but also the various venues in which authenticity and identity are constructed and expressed and by whom. Also addressed is the question of what constitutes appropriate minority leadership and what the goal of the leadership should be: Should the leadership keep the minority community tied to its context in its home of origin, thus maintaining a particular cultural interpretation of Islam, or should new leadership be developed within the new minority context in order to adapt the interpretation of Islam and what it means to live as a faithful Muslim in this new culture and society? At the heart of the matter is the question of whether "Islam" must be immutable or whether it is designed and intended to adapt to new circumstances and contexts. This has an impact on both religious and legal interpretations, as questions about the degree to which one should participate in the new host society as citizens or remain separate from it become central to definitions of being "Muslim."

This brings us to the challenge of religious freedom and the degree to which religious freedom can and should be exercised in cases where there is a religion or ideology of state, such as in the case of non-Muslims living in Muslim-majority contexts in which a relationship to Islam is central to the state's claim to legitimacy, and in the case of, for example, a Shīʿī minority living within a Sunnī-majority state, as in Saudi Arabia, or a Sunnī minority living within a Shīʿī state, as in Iran. Is the state's main obligation to protect the majority interpretation of Islam, or is the state's main obligation to act as a state that protects all of its citizens equally? If there is a religion of state, should adherence to that religion be a requirement of citizenship? If so, what status should non-adherents to that religion hold within the state? Is it appropriate, for example, to reinstitute the status of people of the book or *dhimmī*, or is a new solution needed in the contemporary context? Ultimately, which is to be primary—religious identity or national identity—and who decides?

To take the issue a step further, what happens when Sharīʿah is identified as the law of the country? If it is a religious law, should nonmembers of that religion be bound by it? If they are free to follow their own law as an alternative, what implication does that have for their relative inclusion as citizens of the state or for the relative coherence of the state? Conversely, if one lives in a context in which Sharīʿah is not part of the legal system, how and to what degree does one follow it? These central questions are at the heart of many debates throughout the Muslim world today, particularly in countries impacted by the Arab Spring. Although some have posited international standards for religious freedom as a guideline, critics have noted that these standards, as well as other international standards, such as those addressing women's rights, are typically constructed according to secular, Western definitions of rights, raising the specter of what they perceive to be another neo-imperialist Western agenda. Thus, the need for an "authentic" Islamic solution to the problem is clear, returning us to the issues raised at the beginning of this article.

Finally, we address the question of women's status and leadership in immigrant and minority contexts, demonstrating that, within these contexts, gender constructs become a mix of importations, indigenous creations, and redefinitions. By showcasing a variety of roles and approaches within the North American context, we hope to challenge the notion of a monolithic "Islam" in the West, highlighting the diversity of expressions and interpretations represented by a multitude of ethnic and geographic backgrounds, particularly where women's leadership is concerned.

NATANA J. DELONG-BAS

INDIA. Women's issues such as treatment of widows, education, child marriage, polygyny, and gender segregation (purdah) formed an important strand of socio-religious reform movements among Hindus and Muslims in South Asia during the colonial period. Within the Muslim community, mostly male reformers, enabled by the dynamic medium of print, emerged in the nineteenth century and turned the attention of the reading public toward the problem of the lack of education among Muslim women.

In South Asian historiography, Gail Minault has examined the works of Nazir Ahmed, Altaf Husain Hali, and Syed Mumtāz ʾAlī in the late nineteenth century to argue that their proposal for women's education was instrumental in structuring a new model of *sharafat* or "respectability": one not based on birthright or wealth but good character, where cultivation of individual piety, domestic efficiency, frugality, and restraint were to renew the Muslim community. From the twentieth century onward, Minault demonstrates how major women's journals such as *Tahzib-i Niswan*, *Khatoon*, and *Ismat* played a leading role in providing a forum for Muslim women's voices and in generating connections among its female readers. Syed Mumtāz ʾAlī started *Tahzib-i Niswan* in 1898 in Lahore and was assisted in its editorial work by his wife Muhammadi Begum. Shaikh Abdullah and his wife Wahid Jahan Begum founded *Khatoon* in Aligarh in 1904, and Rashidul Khairi started *Ismat* in 1908 in Delhi. While most of Syed Mumtāz ʾAlī's efforts in social reform concentrated on activism through journalism, Shaikh Abdullah and Wahid Jahan Begum opened a school for girls in Aligarh in 1906, and Rashidul Khairi ran his own press, Ismat Book Depot, which regularly published writings advocating women's education (Minault, pp. 31–55, 110–155). Urdu women's journals not only provided greater journalistic and literary opportunity for women, but also empowered them to raise funds for myriad causes, to organize political activities, to form groups and associations clustered around readership, and to publicize marriages of couples who lived up to reformist ideals. Women were encouraged to donate in order to participate in the social and political affairs of the community, and journals routinely published details of donations at the end pages of their issues.

Muslim colonial social reforms in India, much like other communities, were contingent upon local politics and regional culture. In the princely state of Bhopal, women had been rulers for four generations beginning in 1819 with Qudsia Begum, followed by Sikandar Begum, Shah Jahan Begum, and Nawab Sultan Jahan Begum. While each of these rulers consolidated women's political influence in the region, Nawab Sultan Jahan Begum, after acceding in 1901, took an active role in social reform, especially in the spread of women's education and access to medical care (Lambert-Hurley, pp. 81–89, 125–136). While Urdu remained the language of reform among *sharīf* Muslims of north India, in Bengal the middle class Muslims often referred to themselves as *bhadralok*, a term usually used for Bengali Hindus. Their pioneering advocates for female education, Nawab Faiz-unnisa Chaudhurani and Rokeya Sakhwat Hossein, wrote in Bengali and developed a unique Bengali identity distinct from Urdu-speaking Muslims (Amin, pp. 107–148).

One of the outcomes of the educational debates of late nineteenth century and the journalistic networks of the early twentieth century was the formation of women's organizations or *anjumans* (associations) aimed at the spread of feminist consciousness in general and women's education in particular. In 1914, Anjuman-i Khawatin-i Islam held its first conference in Aligarh on the inauguration of a residence hall at Aligarh Girls School; it was presided over by Sultan Jahan Begum of Bhopal, who emphasized the urgency of education among Muslim women. Beginning in Aligarh, Anjuman-i Khawatin-i Islam held its conference annually and passed resolutions on matters of urgent concern. Various other organizations that channeled their energies into social and educational reform included Anjuman-i Himayat-i Islam of Lahore, Anjuman-i Islam of Bombay, and the All-India Muhammadan Educational Conference based in Aligarh (Minault, pp. 158–204). Women's journals carried reports of these conferences regularly and also formed their own *anjumans* for further discussion. Groups of *Tahzib-i Niswan* readers organized their own clubs in several cities to converse on issues of social reform and the journal published their reports in separate columns titled "Anjuman-i Tahzib."

By the early twentieth century, a greater number of female voices were added to Urdu print culture to raise new issues and generate feminist consciousness about gender relations in society. The contours of the reformist debate gradually expanded beyond the issue of education and introduced fragile issues of family dynamics involving arrangement of marriages, polygyny, and marital dissolution into the discussion of gender equality. These issues were addressed not only in journals but also in novels authored increasingly by women. The first novel to effect change authored by a woman in Urdu was *Islah unnissa* (Reform of Women) published in 1881. Written by Rashid-unnissa hailing from the state of Bihar in North India, it was a critique primarily directed at folk and ritualistic practices of local Islam, especially the performance of festivities during marriages. Novels eventually became the primary vehicle for women to express their concerns and several women employed the genre of novel to elaborate issues of purdah, polygyny, education, and the rights of women in greater detail. Among them, Sughra Humayun Mirza, Nazr Sajjad Hyder, Abbasi Begum, Akbari Begum, Tayyaba Begum, Khatoon Akram, Zafar Jahan Begum, and Jameela Begum wrote in the early decades of the twentieth century and became well known to the Urdu reading public. Most of these writers focused on concerns of incompatible marriages and polygyny to document the harmful impact on women of discord and conflict within marital relationships.

Compatibility and consent in marriages also turned practices of purdah and veiling into a contested terrain where women reformers raised the prospect of men and women meeting each other before their marriage and further emphasized unveiling. In 1939, the Dissolution of Muslim Marriages Act was ratified, which allowed Muslim judges to dissolve a marriage on the initiative of women in certain circumstances. While agendas of social reform continued to recast the family in a new image, the question of women's work also started to preoccupy women writers from the 1930s on and an increasing number of them argued that financial independence and self-sovereignty should be the aim of education. As women gained greater entry into schools and universities, acquiring degrees and more social mobility, the discourse of *sharafat* or "respectability" among Muslim elites that had informed the origins of the reform movement transformed the ideal of woman from an efficient homemaker to a worker balancing family and employment. Bolstered by greater visibility and participation in public affairs, women like Shaista Suhrawardy Ikramullah, Jahan Ara Shahnawaz, and Begum Aziz Rasul saw burgeoning careers in politics after independence.

As in India, the experience of colonialism throughout the Muslim world emphasized a discourse of "modernity," which placed women's emancipation at the heart of reformist projects involving education, unveiling, familial reform, and public participation of women. In her investigation of Egyptian feminism, Margot Badran has demonstrated that women sought to critique patriarchy through multiple models including Islamic feminism, secular feminism, and nationalism in which all have existed side by side and have been mutually interactive (Badran, pp. 1–10). Outside Egypt, Parvin Paidar has examined a similar role of women and the feminist movement in twentieth-century Iran. Looking closely at the discourses of "modernity" in the early twentieth century and of "revolution" in the later period, Paidar demonstrates how the feminist movement constructed new categories of "woman," "family," "Islam," and the "nation" (Paidar, pp. 118–140, 267–300). Like their Egyptian and Iranian counterparts, Indian Muslim women too maintained their relationship to several discursive practices simultaneously including Islam, liberalism, and nationalism; and Islamic modernism in South Asia was a polyphonic space characterized by plurality of opinions and views.

The departure of the British produced violent social upheaval and Partition effected disillusionment among the Muslim elite, especially the groups who had fought for social reform, leaving several displaced and on a different side of the border than their previous homes. In the post colonial period, discussion about Muslim women in India has become reduced to heated debates about "Muslim personal law," informed by the rise of Hindutva and allegations of appeasement of Muslims marginalizing the voices and experiences of Muslim women. In a nation wide survey of Muslim women, Zoya Hasan and Ritu Menon found that, compared to Hindus, Muslims were generally poor, particularly in the northern parts of the country, and that this adversely affected their prospects for education and standard of living. Moreover, most were not working and, if employed, were engaged in home-based labor or self-employment. Hasan and Menon argue that the unequal status of Muslim women—characterized by poverty, low educational opportunities, and financial dependence, especially in the North, combined with communal politics and biased personal laws—is perpetuating their structured disempowerment (Hasan and Menon, pp. 232–244).

The story of Muslim women's activism in India is a checkered trajectory characterized by the dynamism of upper and middle class groups calling for "*sharif*" social reform during the phase of colonialism, followed by the painful disarray of agendas and ideologies brought upon by the division of the subcontinent into India and Pakistan. In recent decades, feminist struggles of Muslim women have targeted two enemies: the male patriarchal elite within the community and Hindutva ideologues without. It is hoped that these struggles will reap their rewards and that Muslim women will come to enjoy equality of status and opportunity in contemporary India.

[*See also* Pakistan.]

BIBLIOGRAPHY

Amin, Sonia N. "The Early Muslim *Bhadramahila*: The Growth of Learning and Creativity, 1876 to 1939." In Bharati Ray, ed., *From the Seams of History: Essays on Indian Women*. Delhi: Oxford University Press, 1995.

Badran, Margot. *Feminism in Islam: Secular and Religious Convergences*. Oxford: Oneworld Publications, 2009.

Hasan, Zoya, and Ritu Menon. *Unequal Citizens: A Study of Muslim Women in India*. Delhi: Oxford University Press, 2004.

Lambert Hurley, Siobhan. *Muslim Women, Reform and Princely Patronage: Nawab Sultan Jahan Begum of Bhopal*. London: Routledge, 2007.

Minault, Gail. *Secluded Scholars: Women's Education and Muslim Social Reform in India*. Delhi: Oxford University Press, 1998.

Paidar, Parvin. *Women and the Political Process in Twentieth Century Iran*. Cambridge: Cambridge University Press, 1995.

ASIYA ALAM

INDONESIA. Indonesia is a remarkably diverse archipelagic nation composed of twelve thousand islands and encompassing some three hundred ethnic groups. With a population of 246 million, 87 percent of which is Muslim, Indonesia is the largest Muslim country in the world. Despite this fact, until recently Indonesian women were excluded from most published academic collections on women and Islam. This was the case for several reasons, including Indonesia's marginal location relative to the Muslim world's historic heartlands and a tendency on the part of earlier generations of Western observers to see Indonesian Islam as a "veneer" under which lay a syncretic mixture of Ṣūfii mysticism, animism, and Hinduism. As is the case elsewhere in the Muslim world, however, Indonesian Islam has undergone multiple waves of reform. The most recent followed in the wake of the Iranian Revolution in 1979. The past several decades in particular have witnessed a visible shift toward more normative varieties of Islam, with an important focus on gender roles and the status of women.

Complementarity or Hierarchy? Early visitors to the archipelago were impressed by the apparently high status of women, their relative autonomy, their high degree of public visibility, and their involvement in petty marketing and family finances. In a cultural paradigm widespread across Muslim and Buddhist Southeast Asia, men's and women's roles were viewed not as equal, but as complementary. Yet despite this idealized emphasis on complementarity, the status of Indonesian women has long been in tension with more patriarchal aristocratic and normative religious models, as well as the gender ideals of the colonial and postcolonial state.

Among the culturally and politically dominant Javanese (at 40 percent of the population, Indonesia's largest ethnic group), the complementary gender pattern is historically associated with *abangan* Javanese of nominal or syncretic Muslim persuasion. The pattern contrasts with both that of the *santri* (Indonesian, an observant Muslim, literally a student of an Islamic boarding school) and of the aristocratic *priyayi* (the traditional bureaucratic elite). Contrary to the stipulations of Shāfiʿī jurisprudence (the Sunnī legal school historically dominant in observant Muslim circles in Indonesia), in the complementary pattern, daughters inherit shares of family property equal to or sometimes even greater than those of their brothers upon the death of their parents or prior to death, according to need. In this model husbands and wives work cooperatively in the fields and in family-based business enterprises according to their talents and capacities. While it is the wife who oversees the household, the husband helps out by performing the heavier chores. Moreover he assists his wife with childcare and is especially attentive and affectionate when his children are young.

Among the aristocratic *priyayi*, by contrast, family relations are hierarchically ranked and the father is recognized as the undisputed head of the household. His superior position and status are expressed and reinforced by those ranked beneath him through appropriately deferential speech and behavior. He ideally spends little time involved in day to day household activities and in interactions with his children that could possibly diminish his dignity. Informed by a highly idealized model of feminine devotion, the wife's role in this model is to serve her husband selflessly and to sacrifice her own desires for the well-being of her family.

Women and Colonialism. Rather than exercising a liberalizing influence, the Dutch rulers in colonial Indonesia reinforced the *priyayi* conception of gender roles and implemented a strict division between public and domestic spheres. On the model of the middle-class Victorian family, Dutch officials identified the husband as family patriarch and breadwinner and the wife as homemaker and mother. This emphasis was particularly strong during the period of the Ethical Policy, put into place in the early twentieth century when large numbers of men were recruited to work for the Dutch as clerks and petty administrators. One effect of this division of public and domestic domains was *priyayi* women's greater dependence on their husband's salaries and a corresponding diminution in their autonomy.

The hierarchical model of gender relations as developed under Dutch colonialism was vividly described in the published letters of the great Javanese *priyayi* writer Kartini, who later became a national heroine and model of Indonesian femininity. In her letters to Dutch friends, Kartini lamented the fact that young *priyayi* women were not allowed to continue their educations but were secluded (*dipunpingit*) within the household by age ten or twelve and could not go out unless accompanied by an appropriate chaperone and only with permission. During their time in seclusion, they learned to be modest young ladies and proper wives. They were taught to always be in control of their behavior: to walk slowly, to speak softly, and to avoid opening their mouths too widely when laughing or eating.

Notwithstanding ethnographic depictions of *priyayi* as nominal Muslims, many of the more patriarchal aspects of *priyayi* gender conceptions are consonant with, and have been informed by, *santri* interpretations of Islamic law. *Priyayi* drew heavily, for example, on the Muslim concept of *kodrat* (Indonesian) to legitimate the "naturalness" of the hierarchical gender order and women's inferior position relative to men. The term *kodrat* connotes "God's will" or "God's omnipotence." It is related to the Arabic *qadr/qadar/qudara-t*, which means similarly "(God's) will or power" and has connotations of "fate" or "ability." In its Indonesian usage *kodrat* provides a normative—and in particular, patriarchal—reference point for what are considered to be basic social and biological differences between the genders. According to his *kodrat*, the husband leads as well as provides for and protects his wife and children, reflecting the Islamic ideal of *nafkah*. By contrast, *priyayi* women conformed to their *kodrat* by providing sexual service to their husbands, giving birth to and raising children, and assuming primary responsibility for household chores and organization.

Women and Nationalism. As Indonesia's first president, Sukarno (r. 1945–1966) instituted a form of neo-*priyayi* tradition as the dominant culture of the new republic. "Familism" was enshrined in the 1945 constitution and further elaborated during the Guided Democracy period (1957–1965) when the president abolished the elected parliament and instituted a centralized, executive-driven government. In this model, the *bapak* or "father" was the ultimate governmental authority, just as he was within the family. Conversely "the *priyayi* ideals of women as dedicated housewives became the ideal type for Indonesian women as a whole" (Dzuhayatin, 2001, p. 258). The irony, as Dzuhayatin points out, is that this tradition of women as middle-class housewives and no more was an ideal originally introduced to the archipelago only in the nineteenth century by the Dutch.

In fact Indonesian women had been active participants in the early twentieth-century struggle for national independence and had remained politically active in the early years of the republic. As Japanese control was lifted at the end of World War II, several large and active women's organizations emerged. Among these groups were the non-religious Union of the Women of the Indonesian Republic (Perwari); the nationalist-oriented federation of women's organizations, the Indonesian Women's Congress (Kowani); and the Indonesian Women's Movement (Gerwani), which was associated with the Indonesian Communist Party or PKI. In the early years of Sukarno's presidency, Perwari, Kowani, and Gerwani actively debated issues of women's education, marriage reform, and polygyny, with their Muslim membership often taking a more conservative position. The situation for women changed considerably, however, during the period of Guided Democracy, when Sukarno's agenda focused on nationalism and anti-imperialism and his presidency became increasingly authoritarian. Even the communist-linked Gerwani, the most vocal of women's organizations, had to subordinate its agenda to Sukarno's nationalist and anti-imperialist project.

In the aftermath of an attempted left wing military officers' coup on 1 October 1965, the Communist Party was blamed for the attempt and targeted for destruction. Over the months that followed, several hundred thousand communist supporters were rounded up and executed. Gerwani was vilified and attacked as well. In her analysis of the Indonesian women's movement, *Sexual Politics in Indonesia*, the feminist scholar Saskia Weiringa argues that the young General

Suharto, who took up the reins of government during the chaos following the failed coup, used a campaign of sexual slander against Gerwani to justify his takeover of the presidency from Sukarno. In the process he succeeded in linking the idea of women's political activity with sexual and moral depravity. Weiringa views this moment as essentially ending the women's movement in Indonesia. In describing gender roles under the New Order (the regime that succeeded the Sukarno government in a prolonged transition from 1965 to 1967), Weiringa writes, "the gendered nature of this state is best described by the forcible return of women to an Indonesian model of meek womanhood contained within a hierarchical male order" (Weiringa, 2002, p. 5).

Women and the New Order State. Suharto's New Order reinstated the "family principle" or *azas keluarga,* the ideology that affirmed the family as the foundation of state and society. Although in practice there was a measure of contextual flexibility to the system, the formal model was one in which Indonesian women were unambiguously subordinate to men within the family, public life, and political affairs. In official pronouncements the New Order presented a highly conservative gender ideology through its own neo-*priyayi* elaboration of *kodrat wanita*. In this ideology women were positioned in the role of the middle-class housewife selflessly serving her husband, family, and the nation. Men, conversely, were identified as natural actors and leaders in the public sphere as well as in the home.

Two state-sponsored women's organizations played a central role in the propagation and acceptance of the government's gender ideology: the Pembinaan Kesejahteraan Keluarga (PKK) or the Family Welfare Movement and the Dharma Wanita or Women's Good Work. Established in 1974 for non-elite women, the PKK had a pervasive presence across all of Indonesia, from the most remote mountain villages to big cities. The organization had multiple functions. The first and most important was to promote *pembangunan* development, an integral component of which was the state's conservative gender ideology. This ideology emphasized above all, women's "responsibilities as custodians of the household and for bearing and nurturing the next generation of Indonesians" (Robinson, 1999, p. 248). The PKK actively and enthusiastically promoted the five duties of the Indonesian woman (the *panca dharma wanita*) as: producer of the nation's future generations, wife and faithful companion to her husband, mother and educator of her children, manager of the household, and citizen.

The organization also implemented the Family Welfare Program and its many related projects in neighborhoods and villages, including important programs for maternal and child health, many of which brought significant social benefits. The PKK was especially active in promoting the state's family planning program, which proved to be one of the more successful implemented in a Muslim country.

The elite women's organization Dharma Wanita was founded originally under Sukarno (with precursors under the Japanese) but took on an expanded role during the New Order when membership became compulsory for all women civil servants and civil servants' wives. The organization's objectives in this case were to encourage women's civil service and participation in national development in accordance with their "natural" roles as wives and mothers. For the good of national development, women were expected to subordinate their own interests and careers to the careers of their husbands. In both the PKK and Dharma Wanita, the woman's position within the organization reflected her husband's rank and position within the government bureaucracy, not her own.

Women, Islam, and Modernity. Despite these conservative gender projects, important legislation and social programs were put into place during the New Order, which dramatically improved the status of women. Women benefited from the 1974 marriage law, which set the minimum age of marriage at sixteen for females and enshrined the right to self-choice of marital partner. The law made divorce more difficult for Muslim men, requiring the involvement of a religious court. The law also declared that a man must obtain the permission of the court before taking an additional wife and provide a letter of consent from his current wife or wives indicating their agreement. Women also benefited from the educational policies of the New Order government, which succeeded in achieving near-universal primary education and dramatically increasing women's participation in secondary and tertiary education. As important, these educational developments have been accompanied by the substantial movement of women into the expanded civil service and professions.

Although the New Order generally kept a tight rein on political Islam, educational expansion as well as improvements in transportation and communications laid the foundation for the Islamic resurgence that began in the late 1970s and increased in momentum through the 1980s, culminating with the fall of the Suharto regime in the spring of 1998. This period saw a proliferation of mosque building, increased numbers of men attending Friday services, a rise in the popularity of religious study groups (*pengajian*), and a visible increase in the numbers of women in Muslim dress and headscarves. The period also witnessed a proliferation of Islamist groups, many but not all of which were conservative on gender matters. Groups like the Laskar Jihad, the Indonesian Mujahidin Council (MMI), the Indonesian Liberation Party (HTI), and the Islamic Defenders Front (FPI) espouse strict-constructionist interpretations of the Qurʾān and sunnah; most also seek to establish an Islamic state based on Sharīʿah law. They resist the active participation of women in public life and seek to limit women's interactions with unrelated (non-*maḥram*) men. Their rhetoric emphasizes the religious obligations of women rather than their rights, and extols the evils of globalization and the threat of western cultural decadence and consumerism.

The same social and educational developments achieved during the New Order era, however, have also supported the rebirth of an Indonesian women's movement and the rapid expansion of NGOs and other institutions dedicated to advocacy and research on gender issues. Some of these organizations work within a secular paradigm and some are associated with the young women's wings of the long-established moderate Muslim mass organizations, Nahdlatul Ulama (NU) and Muhammadiyah. NU's Fatayat NU and Muhamadiayah's Nasyiatul Aisyiyah are both actively working to further a rights-based agenda. They seek to change attitudes by challenging traditional Islamic teachings on gender and offering contextualized interpretations of key religious texts. Muslim gender activists place a lesser emphasis on matters of individual autonomy and choice than their secular counterparts in Indonesia. But they have otherwise joined with the secularists in promoting improvements in the situation of Indonesian women.

BIBLIOGRAPHY

Blackburn, Susan. *Women and the State in Modern Indonesia*. Cambridge, U.K., and New York: Cambridge University Press, 2009. Traces women's activism and the policies of the Indonesian state in the twentieth century.

Brenner, Suzanne A. "Islam and Gender Politics in Late New Order Indonesia." In *Spirited Politics: Religion and Public Life in Contemporary Southeast Asia*, edited by Andrew C. Willford and Kenneth M.

George, pp. 93–118. Ithaca, N.Y.: Cornell University Southeast Asian Program.

Dzuhayatin, Siti Ruhaini. "Gender and Pluralism in Indonesia" In *The Politics of Multiculturalism: Pluralism and Citizenship in Malaysia, Singapore and Indonesia*, edited by Robert W. Hefner, pp. 253–267. Honolulu: University of Hawaii Press, 2001.

Geertz, Clifford. *Religion of Java*. Glencoe, Ill.: Free Press, 1960. The foundational work on Javanese social categories and varieties of religion.

Geertz, Hildred. *The Javanese Family: A Study of Kinship and Socialization*. New York: Free Press of Glencoe, 1961.

Hefner, Robert W. *Civil Islam: Muslims and Democratization in Indonesia*. Princeton, N.J.: Princeton University Press, 2000. Traces the history of Islam and democracy in Indonesia with an emphasis on the Suharto regime and its aftermath.

Kartini, Raden Adjeng. *On Feminism and Nationalism: Kartini's Letters to Stella Zeehandelaar, 1899–1903*. Translated with an introduction by Joost Coté. Monash, Australia: Monash Asia Institute, 2005.

Reid, Anthony. *Southeast Asia in the Age of Commerce, 1450–1680*. 2 vols. Vol. 1: *The Lands Below the Winds*. New Haven, Conn.: Yale University Press, 1988. A history of life in Southeast Asia on the eve of western imperialism and colonialism.

Robinson, Kathryn. "Women: Difference versus Diversity." In *Indonesia Beyond Suharto: Polity, Economy, Society, Transition*, edited by Donald K. Emmerson, pp. 237–261. Armonk, N.Y.: M. E. Sharpe, 1999.

Sen, Krishna. "Indonesian Women at Work: Reframing the Subject." In *Gender and Power in Affluent Asia*, edited by Krishna Sen and Maila Stivens, pp. 35–62. London and New York: Routledge, 2002.

White, Sally, and Maria Ulfah Anshor. "Islam and Gender in Contemporary Indonesia: Public Discourses on Duties, Rights and Morality." In *Expressing Islam: Religious Life and Politics in Indonesia*, edited by Greg Fealy and Sally White, pp. 137–158. Singapore: Institute of Southeast Asian Studies, 2008.

Wieringa, Saskia. *Sexual Politics in Indonesia*. New York: Palgrave Macmillan, 2002. Analyzes the interaction between nationalism, feminism, and socialism in Indonesia beginning in the twentieth century with a focus on the communist women's organization Gerwani.

NANCY J. SMITH-HEFNER

INFERTILITY, TREATMENT OF. *See* Fertility and Infertility Treatments.

INHERITANCE. The Islamic law of inheritance, *mīrāth*, is a distinctive and complex area of the Sharīʿah. Divine revelation specifies extensive and elaborate rules for devolving an individual's property upon death, whether immovable or movable assets. The fourth *sūrah* (chapter) of the Qurʾān lays out a mandatory, in principle immutable and unequivocal, scheme of intestate succession with fixed shares for specified heirs. Given these Qurʾānic prescriptions, adherence to inheritance rules is a grave religious matter. Legal reforms across the Muslim world at varied times and in diverse political contexts, with the objective of codifying, harmonizing, or modernizing personal status and family law have not sought to touch the Islamic law of inheritance. Inheritance is a fundamental source of wealth for Muslims, both men and women, rooted in rights rather than individual caprice, so the inheritance principles are of profound social importance. However there are varied customary or sociocultural influences and practices, as well as legal strategies for estate planning, which interplay, and even interfere, with the transfer of property through inheritance, and are often to the detriment of women.

While the primary source of the Islamic law of inheritance is integrally the Qurʾān, where there is no direct instruction, there are marked disparities in the Sunnī and Shīʿī legal frameworks, specifically differences with respect to categories of heirs. In the societies of pre-Islamic Western Arabia, the *ʿasaba*, or male relatives connected to the deceased through male ties, inherited. Instead of extended tribalism, the Sharīʿah restricted heirs to immediate and near relatives, for the first time allowing women to inherit, whether as sisters, daughters, mothers, grandmothers, or widows, although in most instances stipulating their fractional shares to be half those of a male inheriting in the same capacity. However the Sunnī inheritance scheme, based on the premise that the Qur'ānic verses on inheritance came to reform the pre-Islamic customary system of inheritance, reconciles the fixed portions allotted to the Qur'ānic sharers, the *dhaw-al farā'id*, with the claims of the *'asaba*, who are treated as residuary heirs. This has led to the development of detailed guidance and divergences between jurists, with estates distributed across a range of immediate, near, and distant relatives. The Shī'ī, in contrast, hold that the Qur'ānic system of inheritance was meant to supplant altogether the *'asaba*-based scheme, in practice keeping more of the inheritance within the nuclear family and sometimes placing the daughter(s) of the deceased in a more favorable position than under Sunnī law.

Due to the religious quality and validity of the norms on compulsory fractional shares, including lesser shares for women, calls for reform and equal inheritance rights, from within the *ummah* (universal Muslim community) are rare and generally met with resistance and rejection. Some Muslim feminists explain the apparent inequality between men and women, in terms of inheritance shares, within a wider Islamic legal framework. Wives are entitled to maintenance from their husbands, including shelter, food, and clothing, and the payment of *mahr* (dower) in consequence of a marriage, but a wife has no corresponding obligations to her spouse.

Islamic law does not differentiate between testate and intestate succession. However the Qur'ān expressly provides for testamentary bequests (2:179), without specifying their permitted scale. By reference to the *sunnah*, it is established that a will (*wasaya*) is restricted to one-third of the net assets of the deceased. The will enables gifts to charity, but where such bequests are for noncharitable purposes, in Sunnī law they are confined to those who are not benefiting under the scheme of intestacy. In Shī'ī law bequests to those entitled to fixed shares in an estate are permitted in some circumstances. Islamic wills have a significant role in providing for vulnerable children, such as orphaned grandchildren, who would not, as a rule, receive a fractional share of an estate. Bequests to such children may be explained by the verse of bequest (2:179) and modest legal reforms inspired by the Egyptian Will Act 1946 have provided for mandatory bequests to orphaned grandchildren in a range of countries.

Islamic inheritance law typically involves a number of Qur'ānic heirs leading to fragmentation of property, such as land, into shares that may be of little social or economic use. A variety of legal strategies can be deployed to avoid fragmentation, which have potential to both benefit or disadvantage women and interact with local customs. One device is the *waqf* (endowment) by which the owner (*waqif*) permanently ties up property to the use of beneficiaries for specific purposes, particularly the *waqf ahli* or *waqf dhurri*, the endowment of family for the benefit of the *waqif*'s descendants and relatives until their extinction whereupon it devolves to charitable purposes. Traditionally the *waqf* was a foundation for financial power of women, but in many Muslim countries the *waqf ahli* has been abolished, limited, and/or taken over by modern states.

Another mechanism is the simple lifetime gift (*hibah*), which is permitted even to someone who would upon the donor's death be among the Qur'ānic heirs, although disposal of property close to the time of death during *marad al-mawt* (death sickness) is limited. Some Sunnī schools of law allow the donor to retain use of the property which is the subject matter of the gift (Malikī) or stipulate that the recipient should maintain the donor during his or her lifetime (Ḥanafī). It is a widespread practice in Indonesia that women and girls receive such gifts as a customarily implemented compensation for the perceived disadvantages of the compulsory inheritance norms. In other, particularly rural or agricultural, contexts lifetime gifts are used to concentrate land within the hands of the most active farming son or sons of the donor.

Consolidation of property may be also a post-inheritance adjustment, with complex sales and exchanges among Qurʾānic heirs to reduce fragmentation. Typically a woman may relinquish a share in land to a brother in return for cash compensation. However renunciation of all or part of her inheritance rights (*tanazul*), without a compensatory exchange of property is not uncommon across a range of Muslim countries, thereby altering the impact of inheritance rights. Complex, yet compelling sociocultural pressures and familial demands may induce a woman to claim a property share to which she is legally entitled, to sell a share to a relative (for cash or symbolically), or to renounce a share. Renunciation may indicate the vulnerability or powerlessness of women, but that is not necessarily or always the case. However the Qurʾānic inheritance framework does not conceive of beneficiaries rejecting their shares, although over time renunciation was incorporated within formal processes under the Sharīʿah. Widespread renunciation by women, therefore, may be an area where advocacy and education on the compulsory rules could lead to their empowerment.

BIBLIOGRAPHY

Al-Faruqi, M. "Women's Self-identity in the *Qur'an* and Islamic Law." In *Windows of Faith: Muslim Women Scholar-Activists in North America*, edited by Gisela Webb. Syracuse, N.Y.: Syracuse University Press, 2000. An analysis of inheritance principles within a wider Islamic legal framework is presented in this chapter from a Muslim feminist perspective.

Bowen, John Richard. *Islam, Law and Equality in Indonesia: An Anthropology of Public Reasoning*. Cambridge, U.K., and New York: Cambridge University Press, 2003. This book illustrates the interaction between inheritance principles and local customary practices within the Indonesian context.

Esposito, John L., and Natana DeLong-Bas. *Women in Muslim Family Law*. 2d ed. Syracuse, N.Y.: Syracuse University Press, 2002. This book provides an accessible guide to the key principles governing inheritance and also explains the institution of the *waqf*.

Moors, Annelies. *Women, Property and Islam: Palestinian Experiences, 1920–1990*. Cambridge, U.K., and New York: Cambridge University Press, 1995. A detailed analysis of the interplay between kinship, property, inheritance principles, and sociocultural influences, within a specific context, is presented in this book.

Sait, Siraj, and Hilary Lim. *Land, Law, and Islam: Property and Human Rights in the Muslim World*. London and New York: Zed Books, 2006. This book, specifically chapters 5, 6, and 7, provides a general overview on inheritance principles and estate planning techniques, considering, with examples, how customary practices interact with inheritance rights to affect the position of women.

ANN ELIZABETH MAYER
Updated by HILARY LIM

INTERFAITH DIALOGUE. Moved by Islamic principles and values, Muslim women are increasingly contributing to interfaith dialogue initiatives. Interfaith dialogue is now recognized as a critical tool for peace building and conflict transformation. Interfaith dialogue assumes that misunderstanding and lack of accurate knowledge about faith traditions of others contribute significantly to negative hostile images and stereotyping, which become a pretext during violent ethnoreligious conflicts. Dialogue—defined as a safe process of verbal and non-verbal interaction to exchange ideas, thoughts and information between people from different religious backgrounds—aims to clarify misunderstandings and increase accurate knowledge of others' perspectives, belief structures, and traditions. More specifically, interfaith dialogue aims to gain a better understanding of religiocultural traditions of others and to explore similarities and differences between them without making any judgments.

Interfaith dialogue is based on the idea that religious traditions can bring moral, social, and spiritual resources for social change and that religious texts and prophetic stories can provide examples of peacemaking, forgiveness, and compassion, which can lead to a change of attitudes and behaviors and encourage interacting or even making peace with the "other." Interfaith dialgoue differs from debate, as it does not aim to eliminate differences between religions or opinions. It does not look for winners or losers. Neither does it aim to undermine any religious tradition nor create a unified religious system. Interfaith dialogue aims to contribute to establishing tolerant and respectful relationships, social, political, and economic institutions and structures through actively and constructively engaging the "other." It emphasizes candid discussion of religious traditions and belief systems and exposes stereotypes in a mutually respectful way. Listening empathetically and actively is key in this process.

Theological Roots of Interfaith Dialogue in Islam. Although there has been an increase in the number of interfaith dialogues that include Muslims since 11 Septmeber 2001, interfaith dialogues are not new in the Muslim world. Islamic history is rich with examples according to which Muslims have sought constructive and respectful relations with non-Muslims. Dialogue between different religious communities is encouraged by foundational Islamic texts, such as the Qurʾān and the ḥadīth. Muslims are commanded to respect other religions and their followers. Qurʾānic verses such as "Had God so willed, He could have made you one community. But that He may try you by that which He has given you [He has made you as diverse as you are]. So vie with one another in good works. To God you will all return, and He will then inform you of that wherein you differ" (5:48) urge Muslims to go beyond mere coexistence and to actively seek mutual understanding and cooperative relationships because, according to Islam, different ethnic and religious communities are a Divine Plan and therefore must be celebrated not eliminated. Other verses of the Qurʾān also support this view (e.g., 49:13). These verses and others make it clear that religious diversity is a blessing. Therefore Muslims are asked to respect other traditions and to invite them to a dialogue as the verse (3:64) indicates: "Say: O People of the Book: Come to an agreement between us and you, that we worship none but God, and that we shall ascribe no partners to Him, and that none of us shall take others for lords beside God. And if they decline [your invitation for dialogue], then say: Bear witness that we shall [continue to] submit to God in Islam."

The Prophet's tradition also supports this view. One of the first recorded Muslim-Christian dialogues took place during the time of the Prophet in 615 CE in Abyssinia between Muslim emigrants and Ethiopian Christians. Efforts to establish constructive relations with non-Muslims continued throughout the Prophet's life by signing treaties with other religious communities to live in peace with them, displaying great respect for their religious beliefs and practices, and encouraging constructive relations with them in every aspect of daily life. The Prophet himself encouraged listening to and understanding of people from different religious backgrounds, displayed respect and tolerance in his personal interactions with them, and said: "Souls are like recruited troops. Those who get to know one another will develop mutual understanding, those who are strangers to each other are more likely to dispute" (Shafiq and Abu-Nimer, 2007, p. 1).

Other Historical Precedents. The Prophet's approach to dialogue and reconciliation was continued by his followers after his death. For instance, the caliph ʿUmar proactively renegotiated an agreement with the Christian Patriarch of Jerusalem in order to bring the Jewish community, which was expelled during the Christian era, back to Jerusalem. He also invited seventy Jewish families to join Muslims in cleaning the sacred sites in Jerusalem and employed twenty Jews for the protection and maintenance of the Holy Sites. The dialogue between Saint Francis of Assisi and Sultan Malik al-Kamil of Egypt (1223 and 1225) is another quite well-known example. This tolerant and respectful attitude contributed to the peaceful coexistence between Muslims and non-Muslims during the Andalusian and Ottoman eras.

Despite historical precedent, not all Muslims support interfaith dialogue. Various Muslim groups and leaders see interfaith dialogue as *bidʿah* (innovation) aimed at creating one single religious tradition and, therefore, oppose it. Others fear that recognizing other religions will dilute and undermine one's own faith, rendering it *ḥarām* (forbidden), while others confuse interfaith dialogue with ecumenism, which is seen as a Christian tradition. These groups often refer to Qurʾānic verses to support their points of view. Supporters of interfaith dialogue work on intrafaith dialogue and education to clarify what interfaith dialogue is, to explain the context and clarify Qurʾānic verses that are used to oppose interfaith dialogue, and document the Prophet's example and other precedents that encourage it.

Interfaith Dialogue and Muslim Women. Interfaith dialogue initiatives involving Muslims gained new impetus after the 11 September attacks in 2001. They included visits and talks at religious sites, conferences, publications, and media campaigns, as well as structured meetings under the supervision of experienced facilitators. Muslim women, like women of other faiths, have initiated and participated in various interfaith activities, either through faith-based institutions or outside of them. In fact, similar to women in other faith traditions, Muslim women's involvement in peacemaking often gravitates toward interfaith or cross-border dialogues.

Generally interfaith dialogues focus on traditional clergy. Traditional clergy in the Muslim world is exclusively male, although there are many influential Muslim women religious and spiritual leaders, religious scholars, and woman-led organizations. Many of these women religious leaders play informal roles in their communities and have recognized authority. Focusing only on formal leaders leads to marginalization of women or excludes them altogether. Women are rarely invited to participate in official interfaith delegations or negotations. Various programs (e.g., Harvard University's Pluralism Project and United States Institute of Peace Program on Religion and Peacebuilding, and Berkeley Center for Religion, Peace and World Affairs) have tried to give voice to the critical perspectives of women of faith by including Muslim, Buddhist, Christian, Jewish, and Sikh women. Still women's interfaith initiatives have been mostly ad hoc and have taken place mainly at the grass-roots level through informal channels and processes often linking interfaith dialogue, advocacy, development, and education, such as the Muslim Women's Peace Advocacy Movement in Mindanao, Philippines.

Because Muslim women's work has been mostly informal and at the community level, their contributions have been largely unrecognized or neglected. Their absence and invisibility have limited their influence in official negotiations and decision-making processess and ability to impact the agendas. Peace treaties and outcomes of dialogue processes fail to include women's perspectives or concerns. Women do not benefit from training opportunities in negotiation, mediation, or interfaith dialogue nor do they have access to resources or funds available to men. This in turn deprives young Muslims of inspirational role models.

Their invisibility does not mean that Muslim women have been ineffective. On the contrary, Muslim women have been quite successful in shaping religious motivations, interpretation, and behaviors by putting pressure on religious leaders, and educating and influencing their families and communities. Women have a significant impact on their children's education and development of their worldview. Consequently women, as mothers, have a greater influence than clerical leaders in the development of their children's perception of other faiths.

Additionally their unoffical capacity has, at times, provided them with unique opportunities to make positive contributions. Because they do not represent a particular faction or group, they are not perceived as a threat. This allows them to work under the radar, gives them flexibility to work with groups that official religious leaders may not be able to work with, and gives them mobility to go to areas official representatives may not be able to go to. They are not restricted by political constraints or discourses, which allows them more flexibility in working on relationship-building in creative ways.

Increasingly, Muslim women are engaging Islamic texts, values, and principles to create space for themselves in public areas and are becoming more active in civil society. Inspired by Islamic precepts of peace and dialogue, they take proactive roles in society and engage with women from other faith communities. Islam plays a central role in their efforts, and Qur'ānic verses and Islamic dress give them legitimacy and access to influential religious institutions that are not available to other secular/feminist women. For instance the Women's Islamic Initiative in Spirituality and Equality (WISE) of New York focuses on strengthening an authentic expression of Islam through interfaith collaboration, youth and women's empowerment, and arts and cultural exchange. Islamic values and principles of peace, nonviolence, and dialogue play a key role in their work. WISE established a Shūrā Council consisting of only women, which has become a legitimate and respected institution.

Different formats of interfaith dialogue are preferred by different groups. Some Muslim women's interfaith initiatives involve only women, while others include both men and women. Many women who feel marginalized or silenced by the presence of men prefer women-only initiatives. For instance Alif-Aleph, an interfaith organization in the U.K., is committed to developing positive relations between British Muslims and British Jews by creating a safe environment for Muslim and Jewish women, who may feel marginalized or uncomfortable in a mixed setting. Others, such as Ibtisam Mahameed, founder of Women's Interfaith Encounters (WIE) of Northern Israel, see women and men's roles as complementary and states that if men and women unify to achieve their aims, it will be better than working separately.

A majority of the interfaith dialogues involving Muslim women focus on relationship building and bringing parties together. It is likely that social construction of gendered roles for women among many of the faith communities as nurturers, caregivers, and centers of the family endow them with skills central to interfaith dialogue, such as sociability, hospitability, empathy, good listening, sensitivity, non-adversarial attitude, and ability to create a cooperative atmosphere. Ibtisam Mahameed, supports this view when she notes that coexistence and dialogue are areas where women have been particularly masterful due to their sociocultural context. She states: "There is no solution [to extremism] other than spreading the culture of coexistence and dialogue, skills that women master and possess" and adds, "women are able to see many things at the same time and have a vision of future based on mutual understanding" (Mahameed). In her work she puts these skills into use and aims to promote mutual respect and understanding by encouraging each community to learn about one another's religion and culture. By focusing on the principles and values of peace building and nonviolence in each religious tradition, WIE brings people together to change stereotypes and create conditions for peaceful relations between different faith groups in the region.

Soraya Jamjuree, the founder of Friends of Victimized Families and a lecturer at Prince Songklah University in Pattani Province of South Thailand, focuses on reconciliation between Muslims and Buddhists. Inspired by a strong sense of responsibility derived from Islamic principles of vicegerency and justice, she aims to build a healthy relationship and bond between Muslims and Buddhists and to improve coping skills and reduce pain. She also works to promote understanding between different ethnic, religious, and linguistic communities through her community radio program. Similarly the Federation of Muslim Women Association of Nigeria aims to respond to conflict in their community through interfaith activism.

Others have combined interfaith work with empowerment of women within their Islamic context. For instance the Islamic Foundation in the U.K. ran a six-week course titled Women in Faith to assist women who want to get involved in interfaith work or to enhance the capacity of those who are already working in this area. Some of the interfaith organizations, such as The Mindanao Commission on Women (MCW) established in 2001 by Muslim, Christian, and indigenous women leaders of Mindanao, Philippines, attempts to influence public policy and public opinion about peace and development and to become a significant voice in articulating a Mindanao peace and development agenda from a women's perspective by focusing on mobilization, education, persuasion, and lobbying.

On the other hand, Tayyibah Taylor, the founding editor in chief and publisher of *Azizah* magazine in the U.S., has sought to serve as a vehicle for Muslim women's voice and empowerment and focused on interfaith initiatives with various groups of Buddhists, Jews, Christians, and Muslims. In spring 2010 she was one of eight Muslims to meet His Holiness the Dalai Lama in an Islam-Buddhism Common Ground event.

In conclusion Muslim women continue to contribute to interfaith dialogue as committed, creative, and brave partners. Despite many challenges, such as lack of opportunities for engaging in official interfaith dialogues and lack of funding, these Muslim women assume their power and carve for themselves space to build bridges with women across faith traditions. Their contributions and success stories are gradually redefining what it means to be a religious leader and expanding our understanding of the role of informal as well as formal dialogue processes in building peace and resolving conflicts.

BIBLIOGRAPHY

Abu-Nimer, Mohammed, Amal I. Khoury, and Emily Welty. *Unity in Diversity: Interfaith Dialogue in the Middle East.* Washington D.C.: United States Institute of Peace, 2007.

Baylon, Gloria J. "Mulsim Women 'Largely Excluded' from Formal Mindanao Peace Talks—Rasul." *Zambo Times*, February 8, 2011. http://www.zambotimes.com/archives/27878-Muslim-women-largely-excluded-from-formal-Mindanao-peace-talks-Rasul.html/.

Berkeley Center for Religion, Peace, and World Affairs, Georgetown University. "Women, Religion, and Peace Interview Series." February 29, 2012. http://berkleycenter.georgetown.edu/wfdd/publications/women-religion-and-peace-interview-series/.

Kadayifci-Orellana, S. Ayse, and Meena Sharify-Funk. "Muslim Women Peacemakers as Agents of Change." In *Crescent and Dove: Peace and Conflict Resolution in Islam*, edited by Qamar-ul Huda. Washington, D.C.: United States Institute of Peace, 2010, pp. 179–204.

Mahameed, Ibtisam. Complete interview transcript. http://dotsub.com/view/a8a58e63-1e1c-48f9-bf16-b928d6c130d8/viewTranscript/eng/.

Morgan, Robin. "Women of the Arab Spring." *Ms.*, Spring 2011. http://www.msmagazine.com/spring2011/womenofthearabspring.asp/.

Mubarak, Fatheena. "Women's Interfaith Initiative in the UK: A Survey." Interfaith Network for the U.K., 2006. http://www.interfaith.org.uk/publications/womenssurvey06.pdf.

Rood, Steven. "Forging Sustainable Peace in Mindenao: The Role of Civil Society. East-West Center, Washington, D.C., Policy Studies 17, 2005. http://scholarspace.manoa.hawaii.edu/handle/10125/3491.

Shafiq, Mohammed, and Mohammed Abu-Nimer. *Interfaith Dialogue: A Guide to Muslims*. Herndon, Va.: International Institute of Islamic Thought, 2007.

S. AYSE KADAYIFCI-ORELLANA

INTERNATIONAL LAWS AND TREATIES ON WOMEN'S STATUS. The principle of nondiscrimination on the basis of sex and gender are enshrined in modern international law in the form of specific provisions or entire treaties.

The philosophical underpinning of these treaties and provisions can be traced back to various religious and philosophical origins and, in modern history, to early women's rights movements, such as the Seneca Falls Convention of 1848, which led to the Declaration of Sentiments and Resolutions. The declaration, modeled on the U.S. Declaration of Independence (1776), moved beyond its predecessor in demanding equal rights for women and men.

Women's participation in the 1919 Paris Peace Conference is an important point in the history of international women's movements and the development of international law. The conference, which led to the establishment of the League of Nations (1920–1946), included women in some provisions and decisions. Consequently some aspects of women's rights were enshrined in the Covenant of the League of Nations. For example, Article 23, paragraph (a) of the Covenant asks the member states "to secure and maintain fair and humane conditions of labour for men, women, and children." Paragraph (c) of the same article requires the member states to "entrust the League with the general supervision over the execution of agreements with regard to the traffic in women and children." Also Article 7 maintains that "all positions under or in connection with the League, including the Secretariat, shall be open equally to men and women."

Also noteworthy is the Latin American women's movement, which led to the founding of the Inter-American Commission of Women (IACW) in 1928. The establishment of IACW was followed in 1933 by the adoption of the Montevideo Convention on the Nationality of Married Women, article 1 of which states "There shall be no distinction based on sex as regards nationality, in their legislation or in their practice." IACW is also credited with the drafting of the 1938 Declaration of Lima in Favor of Women's Rights during the Eighth International Conference of American States. The declaration lists equal civil and political rights with men, as well as fair and protective labor conditions.

Following these relative successes of the international women's movement, in 1937 the League of Nations created the Committee of Experts on the Legal Status of Women, the predecessor to the Commission on the Status of Women (CSW), which was established in 1946 by the United Nations. The founding conference of the UN in 1945 also witnessed important participation of women. Several government delegations included women, four of whom were among the 160 signatories of the UN Charter, namely Minerva Bernardino (Dominican Republic), Bertha Lutz (Brazil), Wu Yi-Fang (China), and Virginia Gildersleeve (U.S.).

These women delegates, particularly those who were also members of the Inter-American

Commission on Women, were instrumental in the inclusion of the principles of equality and nondiscrimination on the basis of sex in the United Nations Charter. As a result the preamble to the charter reaffirms "faith in fundamental human rights, in the dignity and worth of the human person, in the equal rights of men and women and of nations large and small." The principle of nondiscrimination on the basis of sex is also enshrined in articles 1(3), 55, 68, and 76, which affirm that human rights and fundamental freedoms belong to all "without distinction as to race, sex, language or religion." Article 8 further calls for equal opportunity of employment in the United Nations for eligible men and women.

A year after the UN charter came into force, at the inaugural session of the UN General Assembly (GA) in London on 12 February 1946, "An Open Letter to the Women of the World" initiated by Marie-Hélène Lefaucheaux of the French delegation and signed by sixteen women delegates was delivered to the GA by Eleanor Roosevelt, one of the U.S. delegates. Roosevelt urged governments to take the letter home and encouraged women everywhere to come forward and "share in the work of peace and reconstruction as they did in war and resistance" (Pietilä, 2007, p. 12).

Soon after the official inception of the UN, the Commission on the Status of Women (CSW) was set up in accordance with article 68 of the charter, initially in 1946 as a sub-commission of the Commission on Human Rights, and soon after, due to pressure from the members, as an autonomous body from 21 June 1946. Two of the fifteen original members of CSW were representatives of Muslim majority countries, namely Alice Kandalft Cosma of Syria and Mihri Pektas of Turkey.

Women played a decisive role in the drafting of the Universal Declaration of Human Rights (UDHR) (1946–1948). The drafting committee was chaired by Eleanor Roosevelt. The attempt to exclude any sexist phrases from the text and insert gender sensitive language is particularly noteworthy. The Muslim delegate, Shiasta Ikramullah of Pakistan, had a major impact on the drafting of UDHR. She, along with other CSW members backed by the Soviet delegates, "effectively challenged conservative Christian governments and NGOs to secure the unprecedented recognition in international law of women's 'equal rights as to marriage, during marriage and at its dissolution'" (Reilly, 2000, p. 51).

Consequently the principles of nondiscrimination on the basis of sex, as well as other provisions of great importance to women, found their way to the two covenants: the International Covenant on Economic, Social and Cultural Rights and the International Covenant on Civil and Political Rights, both of which were approved by the UN GA but entered into force only in 1976.

The involvement of some individuals representing Muslim majority countries in constructing the human rights standards enshrined in the two covenants is notable. They include Halima Embarek Warzazi of Morocco, who chaired the UN GA's Third Committee, which approved the final draft version of the two covenants. Charles Malik and Karim Arkoul of Lebanon, Jamil Baroody of Saudi Arabia, Begum Aziz Ahmed of Pakistan, and Bedia Afnan of Iraq were also significant participants in this regard.

Apart from the international bill of rights, other international conventions and declarations of significance to the rights of women with specific equality and nondiscrimination provisions include: International Labour Organization (ILO) Maternity Protection Convention (1919); ILO Convention concerning Employment of Women during Night (1919); ILO Convention concerning Employment of Women on Underground Work in Mines (1935); Convention for the Suppression of Traffic in Persons and the Exploitation of the Prostitution of Others (1949); ILO Convention

Concerning Equal Remuneration for Men and Women Workers for Work of Equal Value (1951); Convention on the Political Rights of Women (1952); Convention on the Nationality of Married Women (1957); UNESCO International Convention Against Discrimination in Education (1960); Convention on Consent to Marriage, Minimum Age of Marriage, and Registration of Marriages (1962); and Declaration on the Protection of Women and Children in Emergency Armed Conflict and Convention on the Rights of Migrant Workers and Members of their families (1974).

The above-mentioned conventions all reflect in their own capacity international consensus on specific issues pertaining to women's rights. However, as Shaheen Sardar Ali asserts, these instruments have "restricted scope and lack enforcement provisions" and therefore have "had very little impact on the condition of women worldwide. Neither did they succeed in integrating women's human rights into the mainstream human rights framework" (Ali, 2000, p. 203).

In addition to international treaties, it is important to note a number of international conferences, which marked a wave of progress in regard to international law and women's rights in the 1960s and 1970s.

The first international conference on human rights was held in Tehran in 1968, where "a resolution was adopted recommending guidelines for a long term United Nations programme for the advancement of women" (Rehof, 1993, p. 7). The 1968 Tehran Declaration recognized for the first time the right to family planning as a human right. This was opposed by the Holy See and some Muslim-majority countries.

UN Resolution 3010 (XXVII) of 18 December 1972 proclaimed 1975 as International Women's Year. In 1974 the United Nations Economic and Social Counsel (ECOSOC) resolutions 1849 (LVI) and 1851 (LVI) called for an international conference as a focal point of the International Women's Year. Consequently the first UN World Conference on Women was held in Mexico City in 1975. The conference adopted the World Plan of Action for the Implementation of the Objectives of International Women's Year, which promoted gender equality and the principle of nondiscrimination on the basis of gender. It also sought to integrate women in development and peace-building processes. The Plan of Action also led to the creation of the International Research and Training Institute for the Advancement of Women (INSTRAW) and the United Nations Development Fund for Women (UNIFEM). UNIFEM and INSTRAW, along with the Division for the Advancement of Women (DAW) and Office of the Special Adviser on Gender Issues and Advancement of Women (OSAGI) were merged into a new organization in 2010 called UN Women as part of the UN reform agenda.

Subsequent to the Mexico conference, the GA proclaimed the years 1976–1985 as the UN Decade for Women. In 1980 the second UN Conference on Women was held in Copenhagen "to review the implementation of the World Plan of Action and develop it further for the second half of the Decade" (Ali, 2000, p. 208). The midpoint of the decade also marked the coming into force of the Convention on the Elimination of All Forms of Discrimination against Women (CEDAW). CEDAW was adopted by the UN GAW in 1979 and came into force in 1981 after its twentieth ratification. The CEDAW committee was subsequently established under Article 17 of the Convention with the main task being the examination of the reports submitted by state parties in accordance with Article 18 of the Convention. As of October 2011, 187 countries have ratified CEDAW. To date all Muslim-majority countries (referring here to members of the Organization of Islamic Cooperation [OIC]) with the exceptions of Iran, Sudan, and Somalia, have ratified CEDAW. A major critique of CEDAW is the sheer number of reservations entered on ratification, in particular those entered by Muslim-majority countries.

The midpoint of the decade was also marked by the second World Conference on Women in Copenhagen in 1980, and less significantly by the Universal Islamic Declaration of Human Rights (UIDHR) in 1981 (UIDHR, 19 September 1981). Although there are a number of equality provisions in this document (Article 3, for example), nevertheless women's rights are largely denied in the name of Islamic principles.

The third UN Conference for Women held in Nairobi marked the end of the decade in 1985.

Another great step forward during the UN Decade for Women was that the very concept of "development" came under scrutiny from the point of view of women. Before the Nairobi conference, two comprehensive surveys on development had been produced. The GA requested in 1980 that an interdisciplinary and multi-sectoral world survey should be prepared by the secretary-general in collaboration with other UN agencies and organizations on the role of women in development (UN resolution 35/78 5 December 1981).

The Cairo Declaration on Human Rights in Islam, another alternative to the UN human rights treaties, was adopted by the OIC on 5 August 1990. The Cairo Declaration, like the UN treaties, enshrines the principles of equality and nondiscrimination (e.g., 1 and 6). However these equality provisions, much like the UIDHR, are in line with the traditional understanding of the roles and duties of men and women within the family.

Another significant step forward in the call for elimination of gender bias in international law was the 1993 UN World Conference on Human Rights held in Vienna. It was at this conference that the human rights of women and the girl child were declared as "an inalienable, integral and indivisible part of the universal human rights" (Vienna Declaration and Programme of Action, Part I, Paragraph 8). In 1993 the UN General Assembly also adopted the Declaration on the Elimination of Violence Against Women after a long and thorough preparation process directed by CSW.

The International Conference on Population and Development in Cairo 1994 (ICPD) raised "sensitive and crucial issues relating to reproductive rights of women and men's shared responsibility, including family planning, child rearing and housework." (Sardar Ali, 2000, p. 210). The Inter-American Convention on Violence Against Women (Convention of Belem do Para) was adopted in 1994.

Prior to the Fourth World Conference on Women in Beijing in 1995, two noteworthy documents were drafted in regard to the rights of Muslim women: the Tehran Declaration on the Role of Women in Development of Islamic Society and the Islamabad Declaration on the Role of Muslim Women Parliamentarians in the Promotion of Peace, Progress and Development of Islamic Societies. These documents are important to note as not only were they created by Muslim women for Muslim women, but they also went well beyond both UIDHR and the Cairo Declaration in addressing women's rights. The Tehran Declaration, for example, not only asks all OIC members to adhere to the UN charter, but also takes a rights-based approach in recognizing the interdependence and indivisibly of rights. The Islamabad Declaration goes further by asking adherence of OIC member states to international conventions on the rights of women and recognizes Muslim women's right to participate in public and political life.

The very important Beijing conference was held the same year at which the Beijing Declaration and Platform for Action for Equality, Development and Peace was adopted. The declaration not only includes the international norm of nondiscrimination on the basis of sex and highlights the fact that women's rights are human rights (Sardar Ali, 211), but also has a strong emphasis on the empowerment of women and gender mainstreaming.

The year 2000 was marked by the global summit held at the United Nations in New York, which launched the Millennium campaign for the realization of the Millennium Development Goals (MDGs). Among the goals, the third and fifth goals are directly related to women's rights by promoting gender equality and empowerment of women and improving maternal health.

Another crucial international law document produced in 2000 was the Security Council's Resolution 1325 on Women, Peace and Security which "calls for integration of women in all conflict resolution processes as well as actions for resettlement, rehabilitation and post-conflict reconstruction. It also recommends special training for all peace keeping personnel on the protection, special needs and human rights of women and children in conflict situations (S/RES/1325)" (Pietilä, 2000, p. 34).

Beijing + 10 took place in 2005 during the twenty-third special session of the GA and Beijing + 15 was held at the fifty-fourth session of CSW in 2010. The first was a ten-year review and the second the fifteen-year review of the Beijing Declaration and the PFA.

The UN reforms of 2006 led to the creation of the UN Human Rights Council, which replaced the Human Rights Commission (1946–2006). A special Rapporteur on violence against women was appointed by the United Nations Commission on Human Rights (resolution 1994/45). However since the UN reforms, the special rapporteur reports to the Human Rights Council. Rashida Manjoo of South Africa has been since 2009 the special rapporteur on violence against women.

Bibliography

Ali, Shaheen Sardar. *Gender and Human Rights in Islam and International Law: Equal before Allah, Unequal before Man?* The Hague and Boston: Kluwer Law International, 2000.

McMillen, Sally. *Seneca Falls and the Origins of the Women's Rights Movement*, Oxford and New York: Oxford University Press, 2008.

Pietilä, Hilkka. *The Unfinished Story of Women and the United Nations*. New York and Geneva, Switzerland: United Nations, UN Non-Governmental Liaison Office, 2007.

Rehof, Lars Adam. *Guide to the travaux préparatories of the United Nations Convention on the Elimination of All Forms of Discrimination against Women*. Dordrecht, Netherlands, and Boston: Martinus Nijhoff Publishers, 1993.

Reilly, Niamh. *Women's Human Rights: Seeking Gender Justice in a Globalizing Age*. Cambridge, U.K.: Polity Press, 2000.

http://www.un.org/womenwatch/daw/CSW60YRS/CSWbriefhistory.pdf. This background note is based on the United Nations Blue Book Series on *The United Nations and the Advancement of Women, 1945–1996* and the United Nations CD-ROM *Women Go Global*, 2000.

Stamatopulou, Elissavet. "Women's Rights and the United Nations." In *Women's Rights, Human Rights: International Feminist perspectives*, edited by Julie Peters and Andrea Wolper, pp. 18–36. London and New York: Routledge, 1995.

Waltz, Susan. "Universal Human Rights: The Contribution of Muslim States." *Human Rights Quarterly* 26 (2004): 799–844.

International Treaties and Declarations

Convention on the Elimination of All Forms of Discrimination against Women, G.A. res. 34/180, 34 U.N. GAOR Supp. (No. 46) at 193, U.N. Doc. A/34/46, entered into force Sept. 3, 1981 (CEDAW). http://www.ohchr.org/EN/ProfessionalInterest/Pages/CEDAW.aspx.

Effective Mobilization and Integration of Women in Development, UN resolution 35/78 5 December 1980. http://www.un.org/documents/ga/res/35/a35r78e.pdf.

Final Act of the International Conference on Human Rights, Teheran, 22 April to 13 May 1968. http://untreaty.un.org/cod/avl/pdf/ha/fatchr/Final_Act_of_TehranConf.pdf.

United Nations, Charter of the United Nations and Statute of the International Court of Justice, 24 October 1945, 1 UNTS XVI. http://treaties.un.org/doc/Publication/CTC/uncharter.pdf.

Vienna Declaration and Programme of Action, G.A., A/CONF.157/23, 12 July 1993. http://www.unhchr.ch/huridocda/huridoca.nsf/(symbol)/a.conf.157.23.en/.
For a list of member states' ratification of CEDAW see http://treaties.un.org/Pages/ViewDetails.aspx?src=TREATY&mtdsg_no=IV-8&chapter=4&lang=en.

Roja Fazaeli

International League of Muslim Women. Founded in Syracuse, New York, in 1981 by seven Muslim women to meet the needs of both local and international communities, the International League of Muslim Women is a nonprofit organization dedicated to the service of those in need, whether Muslim or non-Muslim, based on the League's understanding of Islamic tenets. The organization has nearly thirty chapters in the United States, as well as several abroad, including in Ghana and Senegal. Most of the League's members identify themselves as followers of the late Imam Warith Deen Muhammad, head of the Nation of Islam, rendering the organization a lens onto African American Muslim life and community service.

The League's mission statement identifies its members as Muslim women with a desire to provide service to the needy and promote a spirit of unity, collective work, responsibility, self-determination, creativity, and faith. It does this by working with both individuals and families through activities ranging from provision of guidance, counseling, and mentoring, particularly for parents and children, to addressing peoples' physical needs, such as food and clothing. The League is also active in interorganizational community development and interfaith activities, using its spiritual foundation as a means of responding to the needs of members of local and international communities. Chapters remain independent in determining their specific activities and in building local alliances and partnerships while remaining tied to the central principles and objectives of the organization. The organization holds a national conference annually to allow women from different chapters to come together to discuss their local initiatives, build networks, and determine common goals.

The original Syracuse, New York, chapter began with a series of initiatives designed to address a variety of needs within the local African American Muslim community that resonated with populations elsewhere. Funds were initially raised to provide food, clothing, shelter, and money for needy individuals, families, and groups. Activities then expanded to the establishment and maintenance of the Muslim Pioneer House (a home for senior citizens), a nonprofit resale shop (which solicits and accepts donations of gently used items for resale at discounted prices), and the An-Nisa House (a shelter for battered women). The League also established a Junior League of Muslim Women to encourage activism among female Muslim students. In all of these activities the overriding purpose was to promote unity among Muslim women and to inspire a sense of community and security among them, while connecting them to a healthy and progressive vision of community life.

Other chapters have developed their own methods of addressing similar issues of concern—domestic violence, drug use and abuse, and poverty—such as exemplified by the Florida chapter's annual fund-raiser Shop 'Til You Drop Day, which raises money to provide personal items for women living in homeless shelters, seeking refuge in battered women's shelters, or recovering from addiction in drug abuse shelters. The Florida chapter also hosts an annual interfaith picnic and participates in a variety of local interfaith activities. Other chapter activities include hosting annual Grandmother-Mother-Daughter Luncheons that also honor pioneering women and outstanding students. The Baltimore chapter focuses on feeding the homeless, creating baskets for seniors, sponsoring senior movie nights, visiting the sick, and sponsoring an annual coat drive.

All of these grassroots initiatives demonstrate the League's participation in the fabric of American community life. They also show African American Muslim women's agency and initiative in identifying issues of community concern and developing their own methods of addressing them.

BIBLIOGRAPHY

Ali, Asia. Keeping It Moving at All Ages." The International League of Muslim Women—Baltimore Chapter. *Muslim Journal Online*, July 23, 2012. http://www.muslimjournal.net/?p=745.

http://www.sfltimes.com/index.php?option=com_content&task=view&id=11927&Itemid=144.

NATANA J. DELONG-BAS

INTERNET, BLOGS, AND SOCIAL NETWORKING. Information and communication technology (ICT) user number growth in the Middle East is one of the fastest in the world. Increasing competition among ICT providers leads to lower costs, which are welcomed by the generally young populations in the Middle East. For example, in the period from 2000 to 2011, the penetration of ICT in Bahrain has increased from 6.3 percent of the total population to 57.1 percent; in Iran from 0.38 percent to 46.9 percent; in Qatar from 4 percent to 82 percent; in the Palestinian West Bank from 1.7 percent to 58.9 percent; in Saudi Arabia, from 8.2 percent to 43.6 percent. Penetration of ICT in the Middle East is slightly higher than the world average (35.6 percent compared to 32.6 percent). By comparison, in the same period, the percentage of ICT users in Afghanistan grew from less than 0.001 percent to 4.2 percent, in Bangladesh from less than 0.01 percent to 3.5 percent, in Indonesia from 1 percent to 22.4 percent, in Egypt from 0.6 to 26.4 percent, and in Morocco from 0.3 percent to 49 percent.

Unfortunately, global ICT user statistics disaggregated by gender continue to be very fragmentary, and therefore it is impossible to provide a comprehensive and accurate picture of ICT use among Muslim women. For example, the United Nations (UN) database on gender statistics, "Gender Info 2010," does not provide any information on the "gender digital divide," and the UN report, "World's Women 2010," concluded that "inequalities in the access to ICT are further marginalizing women," devoting only two pages to dicusssion of this issue. However, available data from 2008 to 2010 suggest that, in Muslim majority countries, the female-male ICT use ratio varies considerably. For example, in Iran, 9.5 percent of women, compared to 12.5 percent of men, use the Internet; for Egypt these figures are 19.4 percent and 23.7 percent respectively; for Turkey, 29.9 percent and 50 percent; for Morocco, 49.2 percent and 74.4 percent; and for Qatar, 77.8 percent and 83 percent. Bahrain is an exception to the trend in terms of the gender digital divide, as 60.3 percent of women use the Internet in that country, compared to only 47.6 percent of men.

The use of social media, such as Facebook and Twitter, has increased sharply since the so-called Arab Spring uprisings in the MENA (Middle East and North Africa) region. In January 2011, 13 percent of MENA-based Internet users had Facebook accounts; by November 2011, this number had increased to 22 percent. Twitter was used by about 9 percent of MENA Internet users. While there is a gender divide in the use of social media in MENA—for example, two-thirds of Facebook users in the region are men—women tend to be more open to communication with the rest of the world, being more likely to use English and share information about the uprisings outside of their own countries.

Data on Muslim female ICT users in Muslim-minority countries is even more incomplete.

While reports on the use of ICT acknowledge the importance of gender as a factor affecting ICT use among ethnic migrants, there is very little data demonstrating its impact quantitatively. In all European countries, the gap between the numbers of ethnic minority (including Muslim) male and female ICT users continues to exist; however, it is gradually decreasing, partly due to a large number of ICT training programs in Europe targeting women. For example, in 2005, 42 percent of Dutch Moroccan female migrants used the Internet at least weekly, while 52 percent of male migrants did. There was a more pronounced gap between female and male Dutch Turkish ICT use, at 38 and 55 percent, respectively. ICT usage among German Turkish female and male migrants was at 25 and 46 percent, respectively.

The level of IT literacy goes hand in hand with the level of education, and the ability to speak English, the lingua franca of the Internet. The countries where female education indicators are high are also the countries where the digital gender gap is not as severe. One example is Bahrain, where the literacy rate among women in 2009 was 98 percent of the male rate (with the total adult literacy rate at 91 percent). Both access to the Internet and knowledge of English at a communicative level are tied to socioeconomic status; only those able to afford a computer and an Internet connection are able to participate in global debates in a relatively unconstrained manner. However, those not possessing a connected PC or knowledge of English are not entirely excluded, as Internet cafes are common and relatively cheap across the Middle East. ASCII-ized Arabic (Arabic written using Latin characters), as well as Standard Arabic, are common languages used online as identified in a study of female university students in the United Arab Emirates (Palfreyman and Al-Khalil, 2003).

Studies on Muslim women's activity online tend to be qualitative and demonstrate that, although a numerical minority as ICT users, they are able to use the Internet, blogs, and social networks to their benefit individually and in organizations. Users' Muslim identity may overlap with other relevant identities, be they ethnic, gender, sexual, racial, or linguistic. Thus it is difficult to talk about a homogenous "Islamic online community."

Women's Political Cyberactivism. ***Afghanistan.*** The Internet mobilization by Muslim women for political purposes dates as far back as 1997, when the official Web site of the Revolutionary Association of the Women of Afghanistan (RAWA) was founded. Since then, the organization (itself existing since 1977) has been able to communicate its goals ("Afghan women's freedom from the clutch of fundamentalism, occupation and patriarchy"; increasing the involvement of women in political and social activities in an attempt to restore human rights to women; and creation of an independent, democratic Afghani government) on a global scale. RAWA's activism has provided a critical voice throughout all the recent dramatic periods of Afghanistan's history, including the Soviet occupation, the Taliban regime, and the U.S.-instigated occupation that removed the regime, but has not restored peace and democracy. The RAWA Web site enables interaction on the guest-book page, and this is where two dominant discourses compete to undermine the narratives produced by the RAWA women. The first one is a specific form of neo-Orientalism, a confrontational ideology that draws from anti-Islamic sentiment and presents Islam as inherently conflicted with modernity and democracy. Guestbook entries representing a neo-Orientalist approach suggest that, for example, Afghan women should "get off their buts [*sic*] and do something," "stop wearing the burqua [*sic*]," and "stop blaming the US" (Bickel, 2003). The second discourse, produced by quasi-religious extremists, accuses the RAWA women of betraying Islam in favor of Western values, and has strong misogynist undertones. Individuals posting on the guest book in this spirit threaten to bring women "under control" through "purification" and "female circumsison [*sic*]" (Bickel, 2003). These entries contain very strong, offensive language that suggests aggression and brutal power. Both of these discourses expect Afghan women to side with them in the perceived combat between Western and Islamic values, as well as in the real military conflict between the allied forces and the Taliban.

However, the RAWA women create discourses that simultaneously challenge both positions. They refuse to take sides in the conflict; rather, they take the side of all women by stating that the United States presence in Afghanistan is an unlawful occupation that can in no way result in the establishment of a democratic state, and the Taliban, allegedly in the name of Islam, have brought oppression, torment, and poverty; and they accuse the national and international nongovernmental organizations of corruption. Through these statements, they criticize the attempts of all these agents to control and interfere with women's lives. The women of RAWA advocate an alternative third way, which would entail establishing a secular democratic state with the aid of the freedom- and independence-loving people of Afghanistan. However, they embrace Islam as their religion, which they see as appropriated and abused by quasi-religious extremists who use it as an excuse to control women. Their slogan is "Neither the US nor Jehadies and Taliban, Long Live the Struggle of Independent and Democratic Forces of Afghanistan!" The Internet enables Afghan women to engage on a political level, maintain a defined, powerful political identity, and publicize their viewpoint on the current socio-political situation.

Iran. Using the Internet for political purposes is dangerous for activists in some countries. For example, in Iran, women have employed ICT—in particular, blogs—for activism and resistance since the early 2000s. They have critiqued both the Iranian regime and conservatism in relation to social issues prevalent in some sections of Iranian society. In 2004, Nasrin Alavi published a book titled *We Are Iran: The Persian Blogs*, which provided a comprehensive picture of Iranian bloggers' political dissent. During political events such as presidential elections, female bloggers are particularly active and are the target of repressions that sometimes continue for long periods. For example, in 2009, Somayeh Tohidlou, a female supporter of Mir Hussein Mosavi active in the Iranian blogosphere, was jailed for seventy days and was subjected to seventy lashes. Her ordeal was highly publicized on Facebook, where other users expressed support for her in large numbers. Another female blogger, a recipient of the "Reporters Without Borders" award, was imprisoned for one year and received a thirty-year "professional ban" in 2010 for spreading "propaganda" against the leaders of the Islamic republic.

Recognition by Western media can have dangerous consequences for Iranian bloggers, who are often accused of collaboration with the West to the detriment of the Iranian state. Social issues are also the focus of Iranian female bloggers' attention; in particular, they discuss challenges faced by Iranian women who, while technically having access to the same resources and services in the gender-segregated society, encounter barriers in accessing high-profile professions, such as judges, and are often limited by conservative attitudes toward gender roles and sexuality. Many blogs published by Iranian women broach the questions of sexual practices, premarital relationships, and affairs. This has marked their first opportunity to conduct such discussions in the public sphere, facilitated by the anonymity uniquely available online. However, as pointed out by Akhavan (2011), the overwhelming attention that Western media direct to sexuality-oriented blogs contributes to, and reproduces, the neo-Orientalist discourse that fetishizes Muslim women by picturing them as possessing a repressed but rampant sexuality. She also criticizes the way in which news reports on Iranian women's blogs present their capabilities as limited exclusively to the cybersphere and impose the narratives of liberation without investigating the bloggers' own views regarding their political aims. One group of Iranian female bloggers who are overlooked by the Western news are religious women who use blogs to communicate their views and participate in networks. Another group (not synonymous with the religious women) are the supporters of the government who also inhabit a section of the Iranian blogosphere; in that sense, being a blogger does not necessarily mean being secular and/or oppositional.

Arab Countries. The role of social media has been emphasized in analyses of the role of women in the series of revolutions known as the Arab Spring. It is an uncontested fact that women from all backgrounds came out in force to protest against oppressive regimes in Tunisia, Egypt, Yemen, Libya, Bahrain, and Syria. Muslim women in the Middle East have gained unprecedented visibility due to global media coverage showing them at protests and demonstrations along with men. Social media have enabled many women to document and discuss their civic engagement. For example, the beginnings of the Egyptian uprising are traced by some to Asma Mahfouz, a blogger who posted a video on Facebook calling on people to come to Tahrir Square. The first Bahraini woman arrested for incitement and insulting the royal family by publicly reciting her poems critical of the monarchy gained international fame as videos of her performance went viral on YouTube. Manal al-Sharif from Saudi Arabia used Twitter and Facebook to draw international media attention to her campaign demanding that women be allowed to drive cars; she argues that the refusal of the state to grant women the right to drive stems from tradition, not Islamic teaching.

However, it is unclear how this mass participation of women is going to translate into securing gender equality measures in the Middle East. On the one hand, some authors argue that women, through online and offline participation and activism, have managed to carve out a larger space for debate, both in the private and the public spheres, about important social issues such as sexual harassment and sexual identity (Radsch, 2012). Others warn that women are far from having secured their role in the post-authoritarian regimes. Women Spring, an umbrella movement for women's organizations from across the Middle East, points out that women often fight in revolutions alongside men, only to be deprived rights and freedoms once the common enemy, such as a colonial power, is overcome. It also points to countries such as Egypt and Tunisia where the process of sidelining women in the political sphere and limiting human rights has already begun. Arab bloggers and activists argue that political revolutions cannot succeed without simultaneous revolutions of thought that would secure women's freedom.

Online Negotiations of Identity. Muslim women's presence is significant in both mainstream and Islamic Internet spheres. Their ability to tailor and adjust their usage of the latest social media like Facebook, Twitter, or Flickr means that they are able to focus on just those audiences, functions, or elements of these services that are of interest to them, and ignore others, such as those considered *ḥarām* ("forbidden"). In a study of Qatari girls' use of Facebook, Leage and Chalmers (2010) observed that participants were very discerning in revealing personal information; they claimed to use Facebook for communicative purposes rather than identity expression, but displayed high levels of creativity in the presentation of their personas on Facebook both visually and textually; finally, they used Facebook in creative and socially intelligent ways that did not collide with cultural and community norms, family expectations, or religion.

However, in some *loci*, the Internet has the potential to reposition and shift, sometimes very subtly, some established cultural patterns. For example, Muslim women increasingly use online Islamic matchmaking services, such as www.singlemuslim.com or www.muslima.com. This is common especially among Muslim women in the diaspora (in particular, second- and third-generation) and converts living in the West. Such groups may not have access to, or choose to, utilize kinship networks when looking for a spouse. Unlike in traditional matchmaking, here women seek out partners independently. The process on such Web sites remains entirely *ḥalāl*, as the objective is to find a spouse, not a boyfriend or a casual sexual contact. However, constructions of femininity are varied and include both traditional ideas about the role of woman as well as self-representations of professional and independent women who refuse to accept traditional women's roles and interests (for example, they may engage in extreme sports or martial arts) and, more importantly, see their husband as a partner and companion in their spiritual Islamic journey. Thus, while being faithful to Islamic rules, these women challenge such concepts as arranged marriage and male leadership of the household. In a scoping study by Piela (2011a), such women constituted the majority of the sample.

Social media affords the important ability to publish one's work. While Muslim women's blogs attract a lot of attention, especially in the context of the Arab uprisings or the Iranian elections, there is also a large amount of visual material produced by female Muslims. The publication of such visual self-representations, facilitated by sites such as YouTube and Flickr, has the potential to challenge the neo-Orientalist media discourse about Muslim women. Visual dominant representations usually focus on the *niqāb* (which is worn by a minority of Muslim women), which ignites the most controversy, or, alternatively, place Muslim women in the visual context of extreme poverty, natural disasters, terrorist attacks, and military conflict, thus creating associations that become automatic and largely unquestioned. In contrast, self-portraits of Muslim female photographers are overwhelmingly ordinary and "everyday." Their religious identity is often conveyed through a range of signifiers, not only by the otherwise ubiquitous hijab; for example, the commitment to fasting during Ramadan may be expressed by a face turned away from food (Piela, 2010a). Although these expressions are much less pervasive than the dominant discourse, they undermine its legitimacy by demonstrating diversity, intimacy, and ordinariness.

One such activity that could be classified as "everyday" is setting up and managing an Internet business, and many Muslim women engage in online entrepreneurship with success. Female Muslim designers and entrepreneurs have led the way in carving out their market niche, which enables them to sell and advertise worldwide a range of items: most commonly, modest clothing, from wedding dresses to swimwear, as well as Islamic educational toys and books. Online fashion spaces provide an abundance of choices for women committed to modest clothing, including those who choose to wear a headscarf and those who do not, thereby widening the understanding of what modest clothing may comprise. Web sites where such items may be purchased often include links to the business's Facebook and Twitter accounts and blogs, which are useful marketing tools and allow advertising promotions and new products. They also enable the followers to discuss the products and leave reviews.

Women's Critical Voices in the Virtual World. Muslim women are aware of the problematic ways in which they are represented and the need to challenge those representations. An international collective of women have created the Web site "Muslima Media Watch," which is a Muslim feminist forum for locating and critiquing "one-dimensional and misleading" portrayals of female believers. Contributors tease out and discuss assumptions, stereotypes, and common tropes in news and media stories about Muslims and Islam, citing "burka ban controversies" as one of the most frequent and persistent discourses; they also publish book reviews and provide a commentary on global issues. As the site is technically a blog, powered by a blog service provider, readers may comment on the articles and share or "like" them on social media, such as Facebook or Twitter, thus increasing their impact. The site is quite outstanding in that it brings together efforts of geographically dispersed women who insist on the need for fair and balanced reporting, as well as coverage of non-sensationalist and positive news stories about Muslims.

The Internet encourages Muslim women to speak globally and act as critical, global citizens. It facilitates mobilization around a cause, and a trigger for such mobilization may come from a country other than one's own. An example of a global event in which Muslim women spoke out was a YouTube debate focusing on the controversial video titled *Fitna*, released by Geert Wilders, a far-right politician in the Netherlands. The video presented Islam as a dangerous and oppressive religion, recycling the age-old Orientalist narratives, spiced up with Wilders's own Islamophobic agenda. In their study of the debate that ensued following the premiere of *Fitna*, Van Zoonen, Vis, and Minhelj (2010) identified multiple, varied responses from Muslim women who spoke out to challenge the *Fitna* narrative. For instance, they discuss extraordinary videos produced by young women from Egypt that deconstruct *Fitna* and demonstrate how it manipulates the verses of the Qurʾān. They creatively cut and mix images, sound, and text, or make testimonials by directly speaking to the camera. It is an outstanding example of how the Internet encourages women's engagement with Islamic texts and provides a platform from which they are able to communicate their own understandings of these texts to global, Muslim and non-Muslim, mixed-gender audiences. This is, as the authors noted, a highly unique intervention, as it is highly contested whether women are allowed to read out and interpret Islamic texts to mixed-gender audiences.

Women's Online Religious Activity. This contestation notwithstanding, interpretation of Islamic texts by women in online spaces is happening on a wide scale, both in women-only and mixed-gender groups. In contrast to religious academics or scholars who have more resources, including publishing power, and who engage in such activities as part of their professional career, online groups are populated by women who could be defined as ordinary, "grassroots" Muslims who feel that, in order to apply Islamic laws to their lives correctly, they need to be able to understand the hermeneutic principles that guide the process of interpretation. The online groups, however, are very eclectic, in terms of both their membership and purpose, and women who join them represent a whole spectrum of political and religious views. One characteristic that they share is that they define themselves as active Muslims, regardless of the variety of Islam that they embrace. They rarely define this affiliation, preferring to outline their views, which helps them avoid being labelled with a fixed and not-so-useful tag of "reformist," "progressive," "moderate," "liberal," "conservative," "radical," or "revivalist." Two exceptions to this rule are women who describe themselves as *salafiyah*, indicating a connection to the Saudi-originating sect, or "just Muslim," rejecting any label except the primary one.

Moreover, women's views and positions often shift; depending on the context, they may express views that, in traditional attitude research, would be classified diametrically differently. This lived reality of female believers, as reflected by their online communication and affinities, reflects the often contradictory nature of human identity, which may be fed into by contrasting, rather than consistent, views. The novel feature of these groups is the potential to bring together women representing varied religious and political attitudes in the ambitious project of learning about Islam and, sometimes, learning to interpret Islam; the outcome of these debates may be either consensus or disagreement, but Islam-based arguments produced by women to support their points of view are definitely creative and constructive, thus fulfilling the objective of committing to Islamic education.

Muslim female converts are finding the Internet a particularly useful tool. In particular, those living away from larger concentrations of other Muslims are able to participate in various activities together with other Muslims. The Internet serves two primary roles for both converts and those considering or preparing for a conversion to Islam. First, it constitutes a mine of information for those unable to access Islamic libraries or schools. It is possible to find information of varying degrees of complexity, from the basic tenets of Islam to theological discussions and justifications of *fatwās*. Secondly, the Internet fulfils a social function, in that geographically dispersed converts may be able to overcome isolation by interacting with other Muslims online. Converts are also a pronounced group of women seeking spouses on Islamic matchmaking sites. Van Nieuwkerk (2006) has described a case whereby a woman converted to Islam by pronouncing the *shahādah* in English in the virtual "presence" of two other women who were talking to her in a chat room at that moment. Those for whom a conversion to Islam is the outcome of a previous interaction with Muslims may be embracing not only Islam, but also one of its schools or groups of followers, and thus may enter an online community built around its teachings, traditions, or scholars and imams. Such communities are diverse and plentiful on the Internet, providing space to learn about Islam and socialize. Female converts often describe their journey to Islam upon joining such a community; such narratives may include reasons why they felt attracted to the faith, how their family and friends reacted to the conversion, how they were received by the wider society, and, finally, descriptions of their increased spiritual peace and contentment.

Assessment. It has been noted that access to and use of the Internet does not constitute empowerment per se. As many examples provided here demonstrate, using the Internet, especially blogs and social networks, for political purposes carries a tangible danger for critics of politically and socially oppressive regimes. Women are in a particularly risky position, as their attempts to defy existing power structures pose a double challenge: as political critics and activists, they enter an area traditionally dominated by men, thereby risking both state and cultural sanctions. However, the increased visibility of Muslim women's activities resulting from their expert use of technology is definitely a breakthrough in terms of the symbolic control of the "Women in Islam" discourse. As a result of women's self-expression and public renegotiation of identities and subject positions, traditional understanding of gender roles is gradually evolving.

On the one hand, Muslim women challenge neo-Orientalist notions of a submissive, silent Muslim woman unable to voice her own agenda, and, on the other, they often openly critique misogynist prejudices present in traditional understandings of their religion and provide alternative, gender-justice oriented readings. It is vital that all countries begin to systematically document the fluctuations of women's access to digital technologies so that initiatives to close the gender digital gap can be more targeted and effective, and women can have the opportunity to access the space in which, increasingly, global citizenship is performed.

BIBLIOGRAPHY

"Africa," Internet World Stats, 2012, http://www.internetworldstats.com/stats1.htm.

Akhavan, Niki. "Exclusionary Cartographies: Gender Liberation and the Contemporary Blogosphere." In *Gender in Contemporary Iran: Pushing the Boundaries*, edited by Roksana Bahramitash and Eric Hooglund, pp. 62–82. Abingdon, Oxon, U.K.: Routledge, 2011.

Alavi, Nasrin. *We Are Iran*. London: Portobello Books, 2006.

"Bahrain: Statistics 2010," UNICEF, 2011, http://www.unicef.org/infobycountry/bahrain_statistics.html.

Bickel, Beverly. "Weapons of Magic: Afghan Women Asserting Voice via the Net." *Journal of Computer Mediated Communication* 8.2 (2003). http://jcmc.indiana.edu/vol8/issue2/bickel.html.

Bridge–IT Network. "Migrants, Ethnic Minorities and ICT: Inventory of Good Practices in Europe," 2010, http://www.lmi.ub.es/bridgeit/documents/Bridge_IT_Good_Practices_final.pdf.

Eltahawy, Mona. "Why Do They Hate Us? The Real War on Women Is in the Middle East." *Foreign Policy* (May/June 2012): http://www.foreignpolicy.com/articles/2012/04/23/why_do_they_hate_us?.

Hafkin, Nancy, and Sophia Huyer. "Women and Gender in ICT Statistics and Indicators for Development." *Information Technologies and International Development* 4.2 (2008): 25–41.

"ICT Statistics by Gender 2010," International Telecommunication Union, 2010, http://www.itu.int/ITU-D/ict/statistics/Gender/index.html.

Leage, Rodda, and Ivana Chalmers. "Degrees of Caution: Arab Girls Unveil on Facebook." In *Girl Wide Web 2.0: Revisiting Girls, the Internet, and the Negotiation of Identity*, edited by Sharon R. Mazzarella, pp. 27–44. New York: Peter Lang, 2010.

Lewis, Reina, Emma Tarlo, and Jessica Cameron. "Modest Dressing: Faith-based Fashion and Internet Retail." London: University of the Arts, 2010. http://ualresearchonline.arts.ac.uk/4911/1/LCF_MODEST_FASHION_ONLINE.pdf.

"Middle East," Internet World Stats, 2012, http://www.internetworldstats.com/middle.htm.

Muslimah Media Watch, http://www.patheos.com/blogs/mmw/.

Niva, Steve. "Between Clash and Co-optation: US Foreign Policy and the Specter of Islam." *Middle East Report* 208 (1998): 26–29.

Palfreymann, David, and Muhamed Al Khalil. "A Funky Language for Teenzz to Use: Representing Gulf Arabic in Instant Messaging." *Journal of Computer Mediated Communication* 9.1 (2003): http://jcmc.indiana.edu/vol9/issue1/palfreyman.html.

Pascall, Nancy. "Women and ICT Status Report 2009," European Commission: Information, Media and Society, 2009, http://ec.europa.eu/information_society/activities/itgirls/doc/women_ict_report.pdf.

Piela, Anna. "Beyond the Traditional-Modern Binary: Faith and identity in Muslim Women's Online Matchmaking Profiles." *CyberOrient*. 5.1 (2011a).

Piela, Anna. "Challenging Stereotypes: Muslim Women's Photographic Self-Representations on the Internet." *Online: Heidelberg Journal of Religions on the Internet* 4.1 (2010a): 87–110.

Piela, Anna. *Muslim Women Online: Faith and Identity in Virtual Space*. New York: Routledge, 2012.

Piela, Anna. "Muslim Women's Online Discussions of Gender Relations in Islam." *Journal of Muslim Minority Affairs* 30.3 (2010b): 425–435.

Piela, Anna. "Piety as a Concept Underpinning Muslim Women's Online Discussions of Marriage and Professional Career." *Contemporary Islam* 5.3 (2011b): 249–265. http://www.cyberorient.net/article.do?articleId=6219.

"Qatar's Digital Media Landscape," Supreme Council of Information and Communication Technology, 2012, http://www.ictqatar.qa/en/documents/document/qatar-digital-media-report-2011.

Radsch, Courtney. "Unveiling the Revolutionaries: Cyberactivism and the Role of Women in the Arab Uprisings." Houston, TX: James A. Baker III Institute for Public Policy, 2012.

Revolutionary Association of the Women of Afghanistan (RAWA), htpp://www.rawa.org.

United Nations. "Gender Equality and Empowerment of Women through ICT." New York: United Nations Department of Economic and Social Affairs, 2005. http://www.un.org/womenwatch/daw/public/w2000-09.05-ict-e.pdf.

United Nations. "Gender Info 2007." New York: United Nations Statistics Division, 2007. http://unstats.un.org/unsd/demographic/products/genderinfo/default.htm.

United Nations. "The World's Women 2010: Trends and Statistics." New York: United Nations Department of Economic and Social Affairs, 2010. http://unstats.un.org/unsd/demographic/products/Worldswomen/WW_full percent20report_BW.pdf.

Van Nieuwkerk, Karin, ed. *Women Embracing Islam: Gender and Conversion in the West*. Houston: University of Texas Press, 2006.

van Zoonen, Liesbet, Farida Vis, and Sabina Minhelj. "Performing Citizenship on YouTube: Activism, Satire and Online Debate around the Anti-Islam Video Fitna." *Critical Discourse Studies* 7.4 (2010): 249–262.

"Women and the Arab Spring: Taking their Place?" Arab Women Spring, 2012, http://arabwomenspring.fidh.net/index.php?title=Foreword.

"Young Political Activist Receives 50 Lashes for Blogging," International Campaign for Human Rights in Iran, 2011, http://www.iranhumanrights.org/2011/09/somayeh-tohidlou/.

ANNA PIELA

INVESTMENT AND COMMERCE, WOMEN'S: HISTORICAL PRACTICES.

Muslim women have a long and varied history of investment of different types and participation in commerce, traceable back to the lifetime of the Prophet Muḥammad. Muḥammad's first wife, Khadīja bint Khuwaylid, was a successful businesswoman, active in the caravan trade. Khadīja's example sets the historical, religious, and, therefore, legal precedent for the permissibility of Muslim women's involvement in investment and commercial activity.

In many pre-modern societies, women did not have extensive property rights and often lost whatever property they owned upon marriage or to pressure from male relatives. In patriarchal tribal societies, women's right to property was rarely recognized. Thus, Islamic law's recognition of women's inalienable right to own and manage property and to receive inheritance was an important change for women. Because these rights were protected by Islamic law, women were often able to successfully defend those rights in the courts, as evidenced in, for example, the Ottoman archives. Court records show that Muslim women were aware of their rights and often fought for them in the courts, even against relatives and husbands, who sometimes pressured them to either give up their property or sell it, making themselves the beneficiaries. There are numerous records of women in sixteenth- and seventeenth- century urban Turkey, eighteenth-century Aleppo, and nineteenth-century Cairo who went to court to protest unjust exclusion from inheritance. So beneficial were the Islamic courts with respect to protecting women's rights that many Christian, Armenian, Greek, and Jewish women also sought the safeguard of the Sharīʿah courts and registered both their inheritances and property transactions there.

Historically, women's capacity to invest or engage in commerce was typically the result of either receipt of *mahr* (dower) upon marriage or inheritance. *Mahr* constituted Muslim women's major claim to assets as *mahr* permitted the transfer of property and wealth from either one household to another or from one generation to another. Dowers could consist of cash or gold, but also often included jewelry, clothing, furniture, household goods, and/or real estate. This property, at least in theory, was the woman's to do with as she pleased, including selling it and investing the proceeds.

In terms of investment, historical records, such as those from the Ottoman Empire, show that women were allowed to borrow money from money lenders (often at a time of crisis, such as upon the death of a husband or divorce), own shares in residential and commercial units and either rent them out or sell them, and set up charitable family foundations and shops in the markets. Middle-class women were particularly likely to own property and engage in business activities, including selling and buying real estate, lending money at interest, and renting out shops. (Women shopkeepers were rare, but women landlords of shops were not.)

Women's most prominent economic activity lay in the real estate sector. For example, in eighteenth-century Aleppo and seventeenth-century Kayseri, Turkey, women accounted for 40 percent of all property transfers. Furthermore, in Aleppo, women represented one-third of those dealing in commercial property and one-third of buyers. Women in these places also sold two to three times more than they bought, likely evidencing their inheritance of shares in properties, which they then sold, possibly due to a need for cash. Although such high rates of women's participation in the real estate sector may seem surprising, it is important to contextualize this participation by recognizing that most people could afford to buy houses or shares of houses in medieval Cairo and eighteenth-century Aleppo, meaning that one did not need to command large resources in order to deal in property. Although, overall, women owned less real estate than men, women tended to concentrate their assets in the solid investment of real estate, whereas men tended to diversify their investments. Women further inherited smaller portions than men, rendering women's property holdings relatively modest.

In terms of investment patterns, middle-class women were most likely to invest heavily in real estate, while wealthy women were more likely to engage in commerce, particularly the slave and spice trades, and as silent partners in commercial ventures. Many women also ventured into making loans at interest, sometimes to other women, but often to family members, including husbands. Many women secured these loans through the courts so as to be able to reclaim them, if necessary. Court records document numerous cases of this sort, with women representing themselves, demonstrating that Muslim women historically had material resources and legal rights and knew how to assert them. That said, it also must be acknowledged that, historically, the women who wielded sufficient wealth to be independent of male relatives were very small in number.

The largest number of women engaged in commerce and investment would have done so on a small scale, with local client bases and product lines that could be managed by individuals. Thus, most women engaged in small-scale business were active in the traditionally female fields of sewing, embroidery, and textile production, particularly the production of silk, cotton, and linen. Here, women operated as individual agents, either purchasing the raw materials on their own, processing them, and then selling them at the market or participating in the "putting out" system whereby a trader provided the raw materials and took the processed product to sell to weavers, paying the female processers by the piece. These patterns of production have been documented in seventeenth-century Bursa, eighteenth-century Aleppo, and early-nineteenth-century Cairo. Income from these ventures was modest, so some women took the ventures to the next level, either by adding value by using the produced cloth to make jackets or clothing items that they further embroidered, or by teaching their skills to young girls or hiring young girls as apprentices in order to increase total production.

Although "investment" is typically defined in financial terms as referring to the generation of material wealth, Muslim women also have a long history of investing in their communities through charity work and establishment of *awqāf* (charitable endowments). Scholars speculate that at least part of the impetus for doing so may have been to protect their property from male relatives and to retain control over it. Nevertheless, it must be recognized that Muslim women were strong providers of community resources, such as hospitals, caravanserais, fountains, mosques, and even libraries. For example, in the Ayyūbid principalities of Syria, women of the ruling households held villages and agricultural land in what appears to have been full private ownership. These assets were often used for charitable works. In Ayyūbid Damascus (1174–1260), the women of the ruling elite established twenty-six religious institutions. In Cairo, female members of the Ayyūbid household established two *madrasahs*, as well as other religious buildings. Thus, analysis of Muslim women's investment must include not only their input into various endeavors, but also the desired outcome.

In the contemporary era, many past patterns of wealth, investment, particularly in real estate, and engaging in small-scale commercial ventures may still be observed, although often with a new twist. As in the past, much of Muslim women's wealth, particularly in the Gulf Cooperation Council (GCC), remains inherited or obtained through marriage, rather than being self-made. Particularly where the wealthiest Muslim women are concerned, participation in commerce and investment is based on their status as being already among the economic elites of society. In most of these cases, business investments and positions within corporations have been transferred to these women by male family members, such as through the death of a husband or, more frequently, a father. In some instances, the choice to leave the business to a daughter, rather than a son, has been deliberately made based on the merit and business acumen of the daughter. One example is Lubna al-Olayan of Saudi Arabia who inherited her father's business, Olayan Financing Group, as the preferred heir over her brothers.

Although these observations are important with respect to large quantities of wealth, care should be taken not to overlook instances in which Muslim women generate smaller quantities of wealth for themselves based on entrepreneurship and creativity, such as in the case of "cottage industries" that poorer women run from their own homes or small businesses with a localized clientele. In other words, commerce and investment must be considered on both the small and large scales in order to fully encompass Muslim women's activities. There are far more Muslim women operating small businesses and generating small portions of wealth than there are wealthy magnates.

As was also often the case in the past, in the early twenty-first century, many of the businesses and wealth generated by Muslim women are female-oriented, meaning that women provide services or goods to other women, particularly when launching a new business. For example, there is currently an expanding trend in the fashion and beauty sector of establishing spa chains, making jewelry, and fashion design for everything from clothing to custom-made computer covers and mobile phone sheaths, all of which target female clients. In other cases, women look at the reality of other women's lives, particularly the increasing number who are struggling to juggle careers and families in the absence of quality day-care centers and at a time when women are still expected to carry the full burden of household chores. Creating services, such as cooked meals or running errands like grocery shopping, has proven to be an effective means of building a small, localized business for many entrepreneurial women who start by providing these services on their own and often branch into hiring other women to help carry out the tasks when the client base expands. In some cases, advertising is done by word of mouth, although more women are turning to the Internet to advertise—and search for—services and products. Services for women by women are boosted by the underlying assumption that women best know what other women need and are interested in. In some places, such as Bangladesh, women are more likely to trust other women as moneylenders on this basis.

Also similar to the past is the idea that "investment" encompasses more than just financial gains. At this time, many Muslim women, particularly those of lower-income brackets, enter into commercial ventures with the intent of investing in their families, particularly the futures of their children, typically in terms of material possessions, nutrition, and education. This has been shown, for example, in Bangladesh through contemporary case studies of Grameen Bank loans to poor rural women.

There have also been some major changes and developments with respect to encouraging women to participate in investment and commerce in more diversified ways, largely because they, particularly in the GCC, wield considerable financial resources, despite the fact that their participation at the board and executive team level within financial services companies is low, as are the number of women entrepreneurs. Of the estimated $500 billion in wealth held by women in the Middle East and North Africa as of 2012, $385 billion is held by women in the GCC and largely derives from family assets. This wealth is mostly invested in safe asset classes, such as cash/bank deposits and bonds. Financial institutions have attempted to put this money to better use by providing ladies-only bank branches and establishing targeted funds such as TNI Dana Women Fund, to encourage stronger levels of investment, rather than simply holding assets. This has proven successful in the UAE, where large numbers of women are diversifying their holdings, with more than ten thousand businesswomen investing in fields ranging from trade, industry finance, and real estate to tourism, fairs and exhibitions, and construction and services. Another initiative from the UAE intended to encourage businesswomen to expand their horizons through networking and knowledge-building is being carried out under the umbrella of the Emirates Business Women Council (EBWC), as initiated by Invest A.D. and the UAE Chambers of Commerce and Industry. The purpose is to create a platform for Emirati businesswomen to network, collaborate, and exchange ideas in the area of finance and investment.

Similarly, in Saudi Arabia, concerted efforts are being made to expand the low participation rate of women in the economy. As of 2011, women constituted only 16.5 percent of the labor force in general and only about 10.4 percent of the private sector labor force. Yet, Saudi women were reported in 2006 to own $11 billion in cash deposits alone, as well as ownership of 40 percent of real estate, 20 percent of the stocks, and 18 percent of current accounts in the Kingdom. Endeavors have thus been undertaken by banks, particularly the National Commercial Bank, which has established forty-six women-only banks throughout the Kingdom, to create services and investment portfolios tailored to the interests and needs of women investors.

It is expected that the women of the GCC will continue to move beyond the traditional confines of the home and family as they continue to make their mark at work, in education, and in socioeconomic development. There are some examples of GCC women moving into leadership positions in the political, social, and economic spheres, such as the appointment in 2004 of Sheikha Lubna al-Qasimi to the post of minister of finance and then, in 2008, as minister of trade; the appointment of Shaikha al-Bahar as CEO of the National Bank of Kuwait; and the election of women to various boards of chambers of commerce and industry in Saudi Arabia—all of which are expected to continue to change the business culture by encouraging stronger women's presence in investment and commerce.

BIBLIOGRAPHY

Abd ar-Raziq, Ahmad. *La Femme au temps des Mamlouks en Egypte*. 2 vols. Cairo: Institut Français d'Archeologie Orientale du Caire, 1973.

Ahmed, Leila. *Women and Gender in Islam*. New Haven, Conn.: Yale University Press, 1992.

Doumani, Beshara. "Endowing Family Waqf, Property Devolution, and Gender in Greater Syria, 1800 to 1860." *Comparative Studies in Society and History* 40, no. 1 (1998): 3–41.

Gerber, Haim. "Social and Economic Position of Women in an Ottoman City: Bursa, 1600–1700." *International Journal of Middle East Studies* 12, no. 3 (1980): 231–244.

Goitein, Shelomoh Dov. *A Mediterranean Society: The Jewish Communities of the Arab World as Portrayed in the Documents of the Cairo Geniza*. 5 vols. Berkeley: University of California Press, 1967.

Hasan, Samuil. "Tradition and Modernity in Islam: A Reading through Power, Property and Philanthropy." *Intellectual Discourse* 19 (2011): 161–174.

Jennings, Ronald C. "Women in the Early Seventeenth-Century Ottoman Judicial Records—The Sharia Court of Anatolian Kayseri." *Journal of the Economic and Social History of the Orient* 18, Part 1 (1975).

Lutfi, Huda. "Al-Sakhawi's Kitab al-Nisa' as a Source for the Social and Economic History of Muslim Women during the Fifteenth Century A.D." *Muslim World* 71, no. 2 (1981): 104–124.

Marcus, Abraham. "Men, Women and Property: Dealers in Real Estate in Eighteenth-Century Aleppo." *Journal of the Economic and Social History of the Orient* 26, Part 2 (1983).

Rapoport, Yossef. *Marriage, Money and Divorce in Medieval Islamic Society*. New York and Cambridge, U.K.: Cambridge University Press, 2005. See especially pp. 12–30.

Reuters-Dubai. "Growth in Mideast Women-only Bank Branches and Funds." *Al-Arabiya News*, Oct. 24, 2010.

Roded, Ruth, ed. "An Early Legal Compendium: Purity, Legal Competence and Property Ownership." In *Women in Islam and the Middle East: A Reader* London: I. B. Tauris: 1999, 95–102.

Shane, Daniel. "Revealed: 100 Most Powerful Arab Women 2012." http://www.arabianbusiness.com/revelead-100-most-powerful-arab-women-2012-448409.html.

Tucker, Judith. *Women in Nineteenth Century Egypt*. Cambridge, U.K.: Cambridge University Press, 1985.

Zahrinebaf, Fariba. "From *Mahalle* (Neighborhood) to the Market and the Courts: Women, Credit, and Property in Eighteenth-Century Istanbul." In *Across the Religious Divide: Women, Property, and Law in the Wider Mediterranean (ca. 1300–1800)*, edited by Jutta G. Sperling and Shona K. Wray, pp. 224–237. New York and London: Routledge, 2010.

NATANA J. DELONG-BAS
and SARA BAZOOBANDI

IRAN. Commonly held views on Iranian women tend to regard the situation of Muslim-Iranian woman as one of categorical victimhood. However, a close examination of their situation in the past century shows a far more nuanced picture of Iranian women, conveying that they can be seen as agents of social change. Although it is true that there are areas where the situation of women, especially vis-à-vis their legal rights, is discriminatory, in many other spheres, women have taken major strides. Evidence of women being influential in the Iranian political arena can be found in the eighteenth and nineteenth centuries. Aristocratic Qajar women were instrumental in the assignment of governorships and granting foreign development concessions during the reigns of Fath' Ali Shah (r. 1797–1835) and Nasir al-Din Shah (r. 1848–1896). In 1852, the Queen Mother, Malak Jahan Khanom, acted as a reactionary force and contributed to the downfall of Amir Kabir, who was making strides toward modernization of the court. Her actions have been criticized as a mechanism of corruption and ineffectiveness of the court at that time. These women were not the norm of the Qajar dynasty, but notable exceptions.

Shireen Mahdavi writes that travelers' journals describe women as veiled and secluded from the public during the Qajar dynasty, a continuance from the Safavid dynasty, which declared Shiism the official religion of state. Mahdavi also noted that the Qajars strengthened the legacy that the Safavids instituted in secluding and veiling women. However, she also commented that the seclusion of women was largely an urban, upper-class phenomenon. Missionary accounts document that upper-class, urban women spent their time engaged in domestic activities such as sewing, embroidery, pickling, and jam making. Rural and lower-class women were documented as being engaged in agricultural production and therefore not secluded.

The Safavids developed what was then a cottage industry of Persian rugs into a national industry, with rugs handmade by tribal women and children. The first large-scale carpet factory was built by Shah Abbas (1588–1629) in Isfahan (Savory).

Madhavi further observes that placing women in seclusion also contributed to the further urbanization of Iranian cities. Private homes with gates became common, as did gardens, which separated the men's areas of the house from the women's. When women went outside the home, they wore a *chador*, a long, fully covering cloak with latticed fabric around the eyes. Inside the home, women wore skirts if they were not expected to perform chores. This was the clothing of high-class, urban women.

In the nineteenth century, Fatemeh "Tahereh" Zarrin-Taj Baraghani, who was raised in a family of famous Shīʿī scholars, shocked everyone by denouncing the religion and publicly removing her veil. This action has been interpreted in a variety of ways, either as a signal of her involvement in the Babi movement, a commitment to Sufism, or a proto-feminist demonstration.

A cursory review of major political events of the twentieth century illustrates the role women have played as a major social and political force in several historical events. Starting with the late nineteenth century, women protested against a semicolonial treaty, which gave the British a monopoly over the production, sale, and export of tobacco, known as the Tobacco Régime, for fifty years. Iranian women embarked on a major protest against the British and announced that, because their religious leaders had banned this concession through a *fatwā*, breaking the *fatwā* for tobacco use meant that their authority would not be respected. Furthermore, if the authority of the religious leaders was to be disrespected, then marriages performed by them did not carry religious sanction and were annulled; therefore, women refused to allow their men to enter into their bedrooms unless they stopped supporting the British monopoly over tobacco. Others took leading roles in the anticolonial effort and, as Sahimi argues, Zainab Baji or Deh-Bashi Zainab invited men to join in the direct fight against foreign oppression, announcing to a group of men, "If you men do not have the courage to punish the oppressors, wear our veil and go home. Do not claim to be men; we will fight instead of you" (Sahimi, 2010). The battle over the British tobacco monopoly was won.

Later on, with the advent of the constitutional revolution (1905–1911), many women fought in the armed struggle against the monarchy and against the bombarding of the parliament by the falling Qajar dynasty. In the aftermath of the First World War, and with the establishment of the Pahlavi dynasty and a constitutional monarchy, a policy of modernization/westernization was adopted by Reza Shah (1925–1941), who aimed to bring women into both the public sphere and the formal labor force. Similar to Mustafa Kemal Atatürk, Reza Shah encouraged the Western secular model for women and imposed a forced deveiling policy, which many women of especially religious background protested against.

Reza Shah was ousted from power by the British for declaring Iran an independent zone. Once the war ended, however, Mohammad Reza Pahlavi (Reza Shah's son) was brought into power by the Allied forces. He continued his father's effort for modernization/Westernization along with secularization. He also took further steps toward modernizing the situation of women and bringing them into the formal labor force by advocating for formal education and opening many schools for girls, as well as opening doors for women to enter colleagues and universities. His policies by and large benefited women of secular middle-class background. To the extent that veiled women were banned from holding formal employment in the growing public sector, these policies also prevented women from traditional backgrounds and lower income households from having access to education and many jobs in the formal and public sector.

The Shah, who started his rule after World War II, was initially open to opposition, including allowing independent women's organizations. However, he soon changed his more democratic attitude for a repressive one. This was to some extent related to the fact that, in the early 1950s, a popular prime minister, Mohammad Mossadegh, campaigned on nationalization of the oil industry and mobilized people to rally behind him. The effort faced fierce resistance by the British who were the main beneficiaries of Iran's oil industry. An uprising to support the popular prime minister was crushed by a military coup backed by the CIA in 1953, and the Shah (who had been forced to leave office in 1951) was brought back into power. This incident changed the post-World War II political atmosphere, in which the Shah had allowed political freedom. After the coup, the Shah became repressive toward all opposition and extremely intolerant of other political groups, including independent women's organizations that had previously flourished impressively.

By the mid-twentieth century and toward the 1960s and the 1970s, masses of middle-class secular women had been part of the growing labor force in different parts of the economy, outside of their traditional role in the agricultural sector, and as part of the rising manufacturing sector (mainly in the carpet industry) and the growing service sector. However, perhaps the most significant breakthrough was entering into the public sector. Moreover, the Shah mobilized a large number of middle-class educated young women to take part in his modernization of the rural area, bringing basic health care and education to rural women. This initiative was part and parcel of the White Revolution of 1963, which was aimed at facilitating Iran's modernization and transition into the twentieth-century global market. The White Revolution further gave women the right to vote. The development of a new economy provoked the Bazaar and religious forces to the point that the Shah's major effort toward modernization/Westernization led to the formation of the religious opposition headed by Ayatollah Khomeini.

What should not be overlooked is the fact that women throughout the history of modern Iran have formed several women's groups aimed at improving the status of women. After the 1953 clampdown on all civil and grass roots organizations, independent women's right activism was limited, if not eliminated, as women's efforts became co-opted by the state under the nationwide Women's Organization, which nonetheless managed to lobby for the Family Protection Law, passed in 1967 and amended in 1975, to change family laws in favor of women.

During the Shah's era, although major strides were made in the areas of education, labor force participation, health, and political participation, a growing number of women were forced to leave the declining rural economy. The women, who were mostly from traditional religious backgrounds and increasingly urban middle class yet also including the Bazaaris and massive migrants, subsequently became marginalized. Large cities, such as the capital, were flooded by rural peasants. Concurrently, there was a growing dissatisfaction, even among the secular and religious middle-class population, over the lack of freedom of expression due to the Shah's rising authoritarianism. Increased political repression and dictatorial rule, as well as the Shah's imposition of secularization, led to rising dissatisfaction with the Shah, which mobilized millions of Iranians against his rule toward the end of the 1970s.

Although there were many different groups of political forces mobilized against the Shah, the mosques were the only organizations that had remained and retained their structure. Thus, they became an important venue for political mobilization. With the revolution of 1979, the most organized opposition group was the religious authorities, headed by Ayatollah Khomeini. In the late 1970s, the Ayatollah changed his earlier views (published during the 1960s) regarding women's participation and their public role and called upon women for their mass support. In fact, many pious women who wore the veil were at the forefront of street demonstrations, making it hard, if not impossible, for regime officers and police soldiers, who saw their sisters and mothers marching, unarmed, to fire. This pacified the revolution and made it one of the least bloody uprisings/revolutions of the twentieth century. As the events leading to the revolution unfolded, an increasing number of women not only were at the forefront of the street marches, but they also carried flowers, putting them in soldiers' gun barrels to win their hearts.

Women's massive role in the revolution became a key to the Ayatollah's success. Yet, the Ayatollah, once in power, quickly changed some of the earlier legal reforms made to end discriminatory practices in family law in particular. Then, Iran was invaded by Saddam Hussein, who enjoyed the political and military support of the Americans. Ironically, the war against Iraq brought a new opportunity for women. As is common with many wars and similar to what happened during two world wars in Europe and North America, women's work became essential. The Ayatollah called upon women to enter into the public sphere as volunteers. He formed the army of 20 million to fight against the enemy as well as build the country by working as volunteers in mosques to give basic education and deliver health and educational services to those in poor neighborhoods and rural areas.

Unlike the Shah, who had sought secular middle-class young women to work for development projects, the Ayatollah called upon religious women. One of his successful programs was a mass-based literacy campaign. The success was due, on the one hand, to the fact that it was delivered in the mosque, where men were not able to prevent their wives from attending—not to mention the fact that the Ayatollah made a jihad against illiteracy a religious duty; on the other hand, the type of education delivered was considered Islamic and, therefore, not a threat to the traditional values of the institution of family, which, in the context of a rapidly rising urban society, suffered major disruption.

While men were at war, a shortage of labor to assist social programs promised by the social justice claim of the Ayatollah during the revolution occurred and volunteers were needed. For this reason, women became part of the social landscape, paving the way for the massive presence of women in the public sphere, this time not just from the secular middle class, but also from the religious segments and low-income households. Ironically, mass participation of women took place while legal changes undermining women's rights were being adopted, which slowly mobilized women against it, interestingly bringing religious as well as secular women together.

It has been argued that basic literacy is the engine of development and improvement of women's status. There is certainly evidence for this in Iran where, after two decades of the revolution, women's entry into primary and secondary schools and their percentage in the educational system increased. This stands in marked contrast to situations, such as in Afghanistan, where women were sent back home and schools were closed, reflecting a drastic drop in women's status. Today, in Iran, there are more women studying at the university level than men (more than 60 percent), and many of them are in scientific departments, such as engineering.

In addition, the opening of Azad University (Open University) transformed the dynamics of women's presence in small cities, as well as large ones. When Open University opened several branches in small cities, many young women from large cities left their families to live alone in smaller cities and vice versa. This meant that a large number of young women left their families and lived alone for a long time. As a result, they gained independence and became empowered enough to make their own life decisions, particularly with respect to marriage. To illustrate an example, the age of marriage rose from 19 years in the mid-1960s to 23.2 in 2006 in urban areas. The corresponding figures for rural areas are from 14 to 23.4 years.

Another interesting facet of women's volunteer work after the revolution was improvement of some of the basic health indicators. Under the Shah, family planning had started in Iran but, similar to that in other countries in the Third World, had failed. In the aftermath of the revolution, particularly when the religious authorities endorsed family planning, the dynamics changed since those who tended to have large families were the poor and religious individuals. In urban areas, millions of women became aware of preventive methods of contraception. In the case of rural areas, many young women received basic health care skills and were trained to become health care workers (*Behvarz*). They were paid a salary by the ministry of health and the campaign was highly effective in bringing down the fertility rate. The birth rate dropped as a result from 6.56 in 1970 to 2.07 in 2000. Moreover, infant mortality declined from 122 per 1,000 births in 1970 to 34 in 2002 and life expectancy increased from 54 in 1970 to 72.8 in 2002 for women and from 52.2 to 69.6 for men.

Other than health and education indicators, there has been an increase in formal employment from 13.2 in 1966 to 15.5 percent in 2006. These figures, however, tend to be lower than women's real participation since, as Jennifer Olmsted and Valentine Moghadam have argued, the female participation rate during the Shah's regime was over reported while, in the aftermath of the revolution, there was a tendency to underreport the real participation rate. It is worth realizing that millions of women are in the informal sector and own micro-enterprises, which have a high tendency to fall outside of official statistics. Fieldwork indicates that many women do not even consider their contribution to the family income as "work" (something that only a time use survey can prove.) Therefore, official data on real employment figures can underestimate and undermine the reality of women's work and, for this reason, the International Labour Office struggles with indicators to report female work.

What is alarming, however, is the growing unemployment rate, which is up to 28.3 percent, although, ironically, this itself is an indication that, increasingly, women seek employment and do not rely on their husbands' incomes, not to mention the fact that two-income families are becoming a norm in large cities because it is harder for lower and low-income households to survive on only one income.

Moreover, in addition to health, education, and employment, women have taken large strides in political participation. This was highly evident in the countdown to the election of the reformist president Mohammed Khatami in 1997. Khatami's main campaign targets were youth and women and he enjoyed massive support from both. This in turn led to his government being more responsive toward women's demands, which shifted toward more equality and reform in the legal system, especially family law.

The reform era also witnessed a rise in the number of nongovernmental organizations (NGOs), many of them headed or highly supported by women, and other organizations and campaigns, which targeted women's social, economic, and political status. In the parliament, a women's faction was formed that pressed for the adoption of the UN Convention on the Elimination of All Forms of Discrimination against Women (CEDAW). This attempt, however, was ultimately blocked by the Guardian Council.

With the election of Mahmood Ahmadinejad in 2005, some have argued that a turning point took place against improvement of women's status. Twenty-first century women in Iran are adamant to show that their rights are not to be taken back. Even something as negative as high unemployment is an indication of the fact that a large number of women no longer define their role as housewives and are seeking jobs. Moreover, high divorce rates, especially in large urban areas, show that women are standing up against repressive marital arrangements. Finally, it is important to mention the high participation of women in political rallies during the 2009 election.

A recent and forthcoming survey conducted for the World Bank reveals a picture of a rising number of female entrepreneurs showing that women continue to resist and press for change and are seeking economic empowerment by venturing into the entrepreneurial world. Although their success in bringing legal changes has been limited, education, health, employment, and political participation remain spheres in which women show their constant and strong presence.

Since the 2009 election, many women have supported the Green Movement. Although it is evident that there is no turning back for women as far as their social, political, and economic situation is concerned, Iran's political instability and economic condition will continue to impact the fate of women. For instance, the World Bank survey on entrepreneurship illustrated that women disproportionately suffered from the impact of international economic sanctions. Moreover, the government continues to adopt policies that attempt to curtail women's public presence.

Iranian women are and will continue to be agents of their fate as well as the fate of their country and are determined to resist attempts to oppress and victimize them.

BIBLIOGRAPHY

Ansari, Sarah, and Vanessa Martin, eds. *Women, Religion and Culture in Iran*. Richmond, Surrey, U.K.: Curzon Press, 2001.

Bahramitash, R. "Family Planning, Islam and Women's Human Rights in Iran." *International Development Studies Journal* 4.1 (2007a): 33–50.

Bahramitash, R. "Female Employment and Globalization during Iran's Reform Era (1997–2005). *Journal of Middle East Women's Studies* 3.2 (2007b): 86–109.

Bahramitash, R. "Islamic Fundamentalism and Women's Employment in Iran." *International Journal of Politics, Culture, and Society* 16.4(2003): 551–568.

Bahramitash, R., and H. S. Esfahani. *Veiled Employment: Islamism and the Political Economy of Women's Employment in Iran*. Syracuse, N.Y.: Syracuse University Press, 2011.

Bahramitash, R., H. S. Esfhani and J. Olmstead *A Quantitative Analysis of Women's Entrepreneurship in MENA: Similarities and Differences with other Regions*. Forthcoming.

Bamdad, B. a.-M. *Iranian Women from the Constitutional Revolution to the White Revolution (zan-e irani az engelaah-e mashrootivat taa engelaab-e sefid)*. Tehran: Ibn Sinaa Publications, 1968.

Bayat-Phillip, M., ed. *Women and Revolution in Iran, 1905–1911*. Cambridge, Mass.: Harvard University Press, 1978.

Floro, M., and J. M. Wolf. "The Economic and Social Impacts of Girls' Primary Education in Developing Countries." In *Advancing Basic and Literacty (ABEL) Project*. Washington, D.C.: U.S. Agency for International Development. Office of Education and Women in Development, 1990.

Kian, A. "Gendered Occupation and Women's Status in Post-revolutionary Iran." *Middle Eastern Studies* 31.3 (July 1995): 407–421.

Mahdavi, Shireen. "Women, Shi'ism and Cuisine in Iran." In *Women, Religion and Culture in Iran*, edited by Sarah Ansari and Vanessa Martin. Richmond, Surrey, U.K.: Curzon Press, 2001.

Moghadam, V. "Women, Work, and Ideology in the Islamic Republic." *International Journal of Middle East Studies* 20.2 (1988): 221–243.

Olmsted, J. "Gender and Globalization: The Iranian Experience." In *Veiled Employment*, edited by R. Bahramitash and E. Hooglund. New York: Routledge, 2011.

Paidar, P. *Women and the Political Process in Twentieth-century Iran*. Cambridge, U.K.: Cambridge University Press, 1995.

Rostami-Povey, E. "Feminist Contestations of Institutional Domains in Iran." *Feminist Review* 69.1 (2001): 44–72.

Sahimi, M. "Iranian Women and the Struggle for Democracy." http://www.pbs.org/wgbh/pages/frontline/tehranbureau/2010/04/iranian-women-and-the-struggle-for-democracy-in-the-pre-revolution-era.html. In *Tehran Bureau*.

Sanasarian, E. *The Women's Rights Movement in Iran: Mutiny, Appeasement, and Repression from 1900 to Khomeini*. New York: Praeger, 1982.

Savory, Roger. *Iran under the Safavids*. Cambridge, U.K.: Cambridge University Press, 1980.

ROKSANA BAHRAMITASH

IRAQ. The modern state of Iraq has its origin in part of the ancient kingdoms of Sumeria and Mesopotamia and embraced a polytheistic system of belief that mirrored the Roman calendar and the seasons. Of the many deities in the Sumerian hierarchy was the goddess of sex, fertility, and war: Inana. Inana's temple, situated between the Tigris and Euphrates Rivers, was a site of ritual prostitution, indulgence, and a much-adorned polytheism. In the seventh century, Inana's legacy was replaced by the introduction of the monotheism of Islam. Islam came to Iraq through the conquest of tribal regions surrounding the Arabian Peninsula after Muḥammad's death in 632 CE The majority of Iraqis are Shīʿī, owing their allegiance, both spiritually and genealogically, to the Prophet Muḥammad's grandsons, Hassan and Hussein. The city of Karbala, just south of Baghdad, where Hussein was martyred by his rival Yazid Ibn Muawiyya in 680, remains an important site of pilgrimage for women, who go to honor their foremother, the Prophet's daughter, Fatimah, and to mourn the loss of her son.

Islam in Iraq, as in other Levantine countries, ebbed and flowed with the rise and fall of dynasties, such as the Abbasids, whose dynastic seat was Baghdad from 750 until the Mongols invaded in 1258. During the Abbasid period, women's participation in society was curtailed, as the practice of seclusion became more prevalent. Women, once active in political life and culture, were relegated to the domestic sphere. However, women were still able to influence society, especially noblewomen at court. One of these women, al-Khayzuran bint Atta, was particularly influential, convincing her aging husband to appoint her sons as his heirs and retaining influence over her more famous son, the caliph Harun al-Rashid. Such were her influence and antics at the Abbasid court, that Al-Khayzuran's life at the Abbasid court may have inspired the character of Scheherazade, the narrator of the *1001 Arabian Nights*.

The centuries following the Abbasids brought more dynastic rule, with varying degrees of Islamicization of Iraq: the Mamluks; Ottomans; and, eventually, a secular, British, rule. The establishment of modern European and American styles of education occurred through British influence and the establishment, briefly, of a Hashemite monarchy in Iraq. Beginning in the 1920s, women began to be university educated. The overthrow of the British-supported Hashemite royal family in Iraq in 1958 and the installation of the Baʿath Party as leaders of the new Republic of Iraq ushered in decades of a precarious balance between secular and religious. Between 1970 and 1980 until the start of the war with Iran, education in Iraq was among the best in the Middle East, with almost gender parity and a literacy rate of 90 percent for Iraqis between the ages of fifteen and forty-five. Outside the realm of education, Personal Status Laws in Iraq were separated from Sharīʿah and secularized, granting women unprecedented access to divorce, inheritance, and disallowing polygamy except in exceptional circumstances. The Baʿath Party also established the General Federation of Iraqi Women (GFIW), which, although mostly for propaganda purposes within a frame of state feminism, offered women at the local level access to vocational and educational training.

The outbreak of war with Iran in 1980 signaled the decline of education as well as an increasing Islamic conservatism, which negatively impacted Iraqi women. As an Islamic state, like its enemy Iran, the war effort emphasized martyrdom. Then-president of Iraq Saddam Hussein promised widows a tract of land and financial compensation for the loss of their primary breadwinner. Many women, even those who were university educated, were unable to find employment to support their families. The condition of Iraqi women continued to decline through the 1990s as Saddam Hussein, in an effort to reinforce his own legitimacy, began to court powerful Sunnī leaders and tribal elders. The effect of this liaison was a gradual repeal of secular laws that benefited women, including the most progressive personal status laws in the region, in favor of Sharīʿah. During this period, single-sex education was reintroduced at the high school level and the sentence for an honor killing was reduced to a maximum of eight years.

More than two decades after the war, Iraqi widows still struggled, especially with the introduction of sanctions against the country following the invasion of Kuwait in 1990. The international community, in an effort to punish Saddam Hussein's aggression, enforced strict economic sanctions that inevitably left Iraqis, especially women, languishing in an even more precarious economic and social position. The Oil-for-Food program, introduced in 1997, was now the main source of sustenance for 80 percent of Iraqis. In 2003, with the U.S.-led invasion of Iraq and the overthrow of the Baʿathist regime, Shīʿī authorities such as Muqtada Sadr replaced the Sunnī authorities of the Baʿath Party, and the once-progressive personal status laws in Iraq were replaced wholesale with Sharīʿah Law. Postinvasion Iraq ushered in a period of terroristic policing of women and sectarian competition between groups such as al-Qaida in Mesopotamia and Shīʿī militia groups. Young women, especially, not used to the new rigid limitations on movement and unofficial dress code, were terrorized by religious vigilantes. Further violence against women was manifest in the actions of groups claiming affiliation with anticoalition groups initiating a campaign to actively involve women by recruiting them as suicide bombers.

The new constitution of Iraq guarantees that 75 seats in parliament must be given to women and that, as an Islamic state, no law can be enacted that contradicts the Sharīʿah. Further, the controversial Article 41 guarantees that the state will not intervene in personal status affairs and that those are to be governed by the religion of those affected. Critics of Article 41 argue that it undermines moderate Islam and enables conservatives. In postinvasion Iraq, women are being forced to rely heavily upon religious leaders and institutions for support that was once provided by the state, creating an uneasy tension between sectarian groups, moderates, and conservatives.

Bibliography

Aghaie, Kamran Scot, ed. *The Women of Karbala*. Austin: University of Texas Press, 2005.

Ahmed, Leila. *Women and Gender in Islam*. New Haven, Conn.: Yale University Press, 1993.

Al-Ali, Nadje. *Iraqi Women*. London: Zed Books, 2007.

Esposito, *The Oxford History of Islam*. New York: Oxford University Press, 1999.

Lasky, Marjorie P. "Iraqi Women under Siege." Washington, D.C.: Code Pink, 2007.

Mernissi, Fatema. *Scheherazade Goes West*. New York: Washington Square Press, 2001.

Susman, Tina. "Iraqis Divided by Treatment of Women in Constitutions." *The Los Angeles Times*. 9 October 1997. http://articles.latimes.com/2007/oct/09/world/fg-constitution9.

UNESCO. "Situation Analysis of Education in Iraq." Paris: UNESCO, 2003.

Alexandra M. Jerome

Islam and Patriarchy. Patriarchy is by no means exclusive to Muslim societies, but nonetheless it is prevalent in much of the Muslim world. Patriarchal elements and principles can be found in the public rituals, practices, mores, and customs of Islam, as well as of most other religious traditions (especially Judaism and Christianity). Within the Islamic tradition, patriarchy is more highly pronounced in the context of the Sharīʿah (Islamic law). According to the verdicts of the Sharīʿah, women receive less inheritance than male family members, their testimony counts as half of a man's testimony, and men have more power in the case of divorce. Custody of children (after a certain age) is automatically given to the father or the father's father. These decrees can be counted as unmistakable characteristics of a patriarchal system that gives a disproportionate share of power and control to men. Yet many Muslims and scholars of Islam argue that the presence of patriarchy in Muslim rituals, cultures, norms, and laws are not an accurate reflection of the Qurʾān, the divine word, and the tradition of the Prophet (ḥadīth and sunnah). In other words, Islam is not inherently patriarchal, but is shaped and formulated in societies with a predominantly patriarchal framework, and hence is bound by it. This view contends that the Prophet did not make patriarchy his way of life. It further posits that the Qurʾān does not prescribe patriarchy as the norm, nor does it stipulate a gendered division of labor.

A cursory word search in the Qurʾān reveals that the word *ab* (father) is used 111 times, and various plural forms of it, *āba* (fathers), are used 63 times. The word *umm* (mother) is repeated 37 times, and *ummahat* (mothers) 16 times. This disproportion in the usage of terms notwithstanding, the content of the verses not only fails to substantiate patriarchy, but can be interpreted as implying that patriarchy is a kind of *shirk* (idolatry). For instance, some of the verses suggest that the fathers had no sense at all (2:170), knew nothing (5:104, 18:5, 6:19, 14:10, 11:87, 11:62), were engaged in indecency (7:28), associated others with Allah (7:173, 9:23), were in manifest error (21:54), or followed the way of Satan (31:21). These references principally denigrate *shirk* and call one to *tawhid* (unity of the divine). Patriarchy as implicated in *shirk* can be seen in the following verses of the

Qur'ān: "Do not take your fathers and your brothers for allies if the denial of the truth is dearer to them than faith" (9:23). The Qur'ān calls for the unity of the divine as well as the unity of humanity (39:6), commands respect for parents regardless of gender (17:24), and specifically emphasizes the work and sacrifice of the mother in bearing and nursing the child (46:15, 31:14).

A much-debated statement of the Qur'ān, often translated as "Men are maintainers of women" (2:228), is central in discussions about patriarchy and Islam. The error of patriarchy is its imposition of sexism. The question is, Do the above statement and related Qur'ānic verses support and strengthen patriarchal constructs and their sexist implications? Can there be a soft, nonsexist patriarchy? Is the answer to the search for a just Islamic society an Islamic matriarchate—or as some prefer to call it, a gynocentric society—that does not mirror patriarchal male domination of women by imposing matriarchal female domination of men?

Most interpretations of the statement "*Ar-rijal qawwamun ala-nisa'*" (Men are maintainers of women) fall into the two categories of ambivalent sexism—benevolent or hostile—or lie somewhere in between. While hostile sexism may imply that women are incapable of their own maintenance and therefore are in need of a male guardian for their protection, benevolent sexism often suggests that women are given a high status and therefore must be cherished and served by men. It is in connection with these latter interpretations of the verse that women are perceived as the honor (which is the correct and original meaning of *harem;* place of *hurma*; respect) of the man. Recent studies of the psychology of women by Glick and Fiske have shown that benevolent sexism is as detrimental, if not more so, to women's cognitive performances as hostile sexism. Ironically, this interpretation (benevolent sexism) is popular in Muslim women's circles as a means of prevailing over oppressive gendered hierarchies. Such women suggest that the term *qawwamun* (sing. *qawwam*), often translated as "maintainers and protectors," refers to the male responsibility to provide and to be in the service of the women of their household, rather than maintaining and controlling them. They do not share the view that this notion amounts to women's gendered self-stereotyping.

Needless to say, neither Islam nor Muslim societies are monolithic. Islam from the very beginnings of its spread to various parts of the world lent itself to cultural adaptations and simultaneous development with a multiplicity of cultures. The Near East and the Arab world maintained its pre-Islamic patriarchal culture and wedded it to Islamic law in the realm of jurisprudence through the process of *ijtihad* (deriving the law from the sources, mainly the Qur'ān and ḥadīth). East Asia, Southeast Asia, and parts of Africa shaped their own varieties of Islamic culture. In Southeast Asia, for example, there are communities of Muslims for whom matriarchy and a matrilineal or matrifocal system is the way of life. The largest and most stable surviving matriarchy, the Minangkabau, live in the largest Muslim country, Indonesia. They reside in villages around Mount Merapi in Sumatra, where land is owned by women and is passed down from mothers to daughters. A man is a guest at his wife's house and must leave when she so desires. The Minangkabau find no contradictions in their culture, which consists of three equally important and interwoven strands: ancient customs and beliefs (*adat*), Islam, and the state.

Yet there are states that use Islam to justify and institutionalize patriarchy, especially when the age-old customs of the land support it. These efforts, however, have not been able to silence the voices of women (and men) who challenge patriarchal oppression in both the state and the family unit. Formulation of the Sharī'ah in a patriarchal context has given it a patriarchal color, but Islam is a message of unity and justice that neither promotes gender duality nor justifies gender hierarchy.

BIBLIOGRAPHY

Davary, Bahar. *Women and the Qur'an: A Study in Islamic Hermeneutics*. New York: Edwin Mellen Press, 2009.

Glick, Peter, and Susan T. Fiske. "Ambivalent Sexism Revisited." *Psychology of Women Quarterly* 35, no. 3 (2011): 530–535.

Kandiyoti, Deniz. *Women, Islam, and the State*. Philadelphia: Temple University Press, 1991.

Sanday, Peggy Reeves. *Women at the Center: Life in a Modern Matriarchy*. Ithaca, N.Y.: Cornell University Press, 2002.

Wadud, Amina. *Qur'an and Woman: Rereading the Sacred Text from a Woman's Perspective*. New York: Oxford University Press, 1999.

BAHAR DAVARY

ISLAM AND PEACEBUILDING.

Muslim women have played significant roles in response to communal conflicts and unjust socio-political systems since the early history of Islam. Empowered by Islamic values and principles of peace, they have participated in social, political, economic, and intellectual life, as poets, scholars of Islam, spiritual teachers, warriors, heads of state, and businesswomen. They have stood up against oppressive regimes and military commanders, organized nonviolent protests, reached out to other communities to rebuild relationships and heal wounds in their societies, responded to the specific needs of widows, orphans, and other victims of war, and provided education for women and girls in various fields including, but not limited to, conflict resolution and peacebuilding in Islam. On occasion, Muslim women have also taken active roles in supporting or even leading armies, such as ʿĀʾishah, Muḥammad's wife, Nusaibah bint Ka'b al-Ansariya, who fought during the Uhud war, and Hassiba Ben Bouali of Algeria, who fought during the Battle of Algiers in 1956–1957.

Historical Precedents. Although the public sphere in the Muslim world traditionally has been male-dominated, Muslim women have assumed diverse roles in their societies. To expand the role of Muslim women in peacebuilding, it is helpful to appreciate the diversity of the experiences of Muslim women throughout the centuries. Famous female companions of the Prophet, such as his wives Khadīja, ʿĀʾishah, and Umm Salama, his daughter Fāṭimah, and the first Muslim martyr Sumayya, who refused to recant under torture and abuse, continue to inform and inspire many Muslim women today. Some women, such as Umm Waraqa, became preachers. Others, such as Ash-Shifa bint Abdullah and Samra bint Nuhayk al Asadiyya, served as public administrators and were granted public responsibilities, such as overseeing public health and safety. Al Udar al-Karimah Shihaab ad-Din Salaah (d. 1360), the vicegerent Queen of Yemen, has been recognized as a champion of the poor and is still remembered for her contributions to public security, administrative order, social justice, and the construction of schools and mosques.

Muslim women have long been prominent in peacemaking. Islamic history offers numerous examples of courageous Muslim women who have stood up to the commanders of invading armies, mediated conflicts, and reconciled opponents. For example, in 1375 the famous scholar of Islam, Ibn Qunfudh of Morocco, recorded the nonviolent resistance of Lalla Aziza from Seksawa, Morocco, who resolved a conflict between two rival groups based on Islamic principles of justice and protection of God's creation. Relating the encounter between Aziza and al-Hintati, the governor of Marrakesh and a powerful general who was attempting to conquer south Morocco,

Ibn Qunfudh describes how Lalla Aziza met the general alone and confronted him with his own faith—Islam—and spoke of God's demands for justice, and the wrong of harming God's creation. It is recorded that, as a result of this encounter, the general left the people of Seksawa unharmed. Lalla Aziza's tomb is considered a sanctuary and it is still used as a space for mediating conflicts. Even during the independence war with France, her tomb was a safe haven where many people would seek peace and calm in the midst of the conflict.

Another woman known for her unique gift of resolving conflicts is Ghazal Ahmad ʿAlwan al-Magdashiyya of Yemen (b. 1860). Although she did not receive any formal education and was illiterate, Ghazal Ahmad was recognized as a versatile poet and mediator, and as one of the region's powerful political voices. She is on record as having successfully resolved a number of conflicts through *zamil*, a particular kind of poetry that has been an important component of Yemeni conflict resolution tradition for centuries. Her poetry reflected her mastery of tribal and regional laws, as well as her capacity to resolve conflicts in her community.

Contemporary Era. The modern era brought new challenges for the Muslim world in general and Muslim women in particular. For instance, a perceived threat from globalization—often associated with Westernization—at times has led to reactionary attitudes toward Western influences. Reactions to the process of globalization cannot be understood without understanding the traumatizing and disempowering impact of colonization. Associated with control and exploitation by foreign powers, the experience of colonization and subjugation has also been interpreted in the historical context of hostile Muslim-European relations during the Crusades. Colonialism was facilitated through the Orientalist process of abstraction and essentialization of the "Muslim other." Orientalist discourse associated Islam with ignorance and backwardness and argued that Muslim women were oppressed as a result of Islam. Therefore, in order to "rescue" Muslim women, the Muslim world must be modernized by reforming Islam or secularizing the Muslim world.

Within this context, women's status has become a deeply contested issue. Many of the first feminist approaches in the Muslim world reflected this Orientalist and colonial attitude and mainly depicted Muslim women as victims of an oppressive religion who needed to be saved from it. The subtext of many women's organizations that came to operate in the Muslim world was that Islam as a religion was fundamentally oppressive and Muslim women could only be saved by either conversion or secularization. This attitude created a conflict with conservative male leaders in Muslim society and disempowered many Muslim women. Western peacebuilding interventions, as well as attempts to encourage women's rights and empowerment, were considered as Western cultural encroachments that must be prevented. Additionally, such an attitude was quite offensive to many Muslim women, who found Islamic values and traditions to be quite liberating and a safeguard against patriarchal and tribal social structures. In their view, authentic and genuine Islamic teachings are not the source of discrimination and injustice against women. On the contrary, many Muslim women argue that Islam was in fact a revolutionary movement that aimed to emancipate women from oppressive practices, such as infanticide of newborn girls, and gave them the rights to inherit, divorce, and work, among others.

This environment contributed to the rise of more conservative interpretations of religious texts and made it harder for women to challenge the patriarchal structures. Increasingly, women's participation in public decision-making has been curbed, and women's peacebuilding initiatives have been limited to the private realm. Therefore, a majority of the peacebuilding initiatives has continued to be ad hoc, through informal channels and processes. Still, Muslim women assertively played and continue to play significant roles in addressing social issues and in working for peace.

Theological Roots for Peacebuilding in Islam. In this challenging context, basing their efforts and peacebuilding initiatives on Islamic sources such as the Qur'ān, ḥadīth, and sunnah, which are rich in values and practices that promote reconciliation and peace among Muslims and between Muslims and non-Muslims, has inspired and empowered women and provided them with legitimacy. Building their initiatives on holy texts and historical precedent has also created a sense of ownership and given women the tools they need to persuade religious and community leaders.

Various values and principles of Islam inspire Muslim women to work for peace. Peace in Islam begins with God, since "al-Salam" (peace) is one of the "Most Beautiful Ninety-Nine Names of God" in the Islamic tradition. References to peace in the Qur'ān indicate that peace is a positive state of safety or security, which includes being at peace with oneself well as with fellow human beings, nature, and God. While war is permitted under very strict rules to defend a community or to correct an injustice, verses in the Qur'ān and other Islamic sources give preference to values such as forgiveness, patience, justice, compassion, mercy, social responsibility, unity, forgiveness, and love, among others.

Tawḥīd, the "principle of unity of God and all being," for example, urges Muslims to recognize the connectedness of all beings, and particularly all human communities, and calls them to work toward establishing peace and harmony among them. *Khilafah* (stewardship or vicegerency) is closely tied to the Islamic understanding of social responsibility and reminds Muslims, irrespective of their gender, ethnicity, and race, that they are responsible for order on earth, because they are God's representatives. Therefore, Muslims, as God's vicegerents, should contribute to bringing all creatures under the sway of equilibrium and harmony and living in peace with creation. *Fitrah*, or the original constitution of human beings, recognizes that each individual, irrespective of his or her gender, is furnished with reason and has the potential to be good and choose to work for the establishment of harmony. Moreover, this principle recognizes the goodness that inheres in each and every human being at birth, regardless of different religious, ethnic, racial, or gender backgrounds. As Tawakkul Karman, Nobel Peace Prize Laureate for 2011, noted in her acceptance speech, the Qur'ān urges "O you who believe, enter into peace, one and all," and includes the warning, "Whosoever kills a human being for other than manslaughter or corruption in the earth, it shall be as if he had killed all of humanity."

'Adl, or justice, on the other hand, is the key to establishing harmony and sustainable peace among God's creation, as the Qur'ānic conception of peace cannot be attained unless a just order is first established. The concepts of *rahmah* (compassion) and *rahim* (mercy) remind Muslims that actions must be dedicated to God, who is Himself merciful and compassionate, thus implying that a true Muslim cannot be insensitive to the suffering of other beings (physical, economic, psychological, or emotional), nor can a true Muslim be cruel to any creature. Thus, justice must be accompanied by compassion and mercy, while torture, inflicting suffering, or willfully hurting another human being or another creature is unacceptable according to Islamic tradition. *Afu*, or forgiveness, which is repeatedly emphasized in the Qur'ān, urges Muslims to

reconcile. The Qur'ān stresses that forgiveness is of higher value than maintaining hatred, as the believers are urged to forgive when they are angry. Love is another key Islamic value for building peace because love (*hubb*), according to Islam, is the source and cause of all creation. The source for human beings to love one another and all creation is rooted in the loving nature of God Himself. Love comes from God and is often associated with peace, mercy, and forgiveness and is a sign to be reflected upon. Transforming enmity into love is a sign of the mercy of God and emphasizes the importance of transforming hostile relations into love and friendship. As Cemalnur Sargut, a renowned Muslim sheikha from Turkey, asks her followers: "Let us unite and let us be the one committed to spread the message of Allah: of his love, compassion, peace and tranquility to humanity at large which is now reeling under hatred, violence, wickedness."

Legacy of Muslim Women Peacebuilders. Although a majority of the peacebuilding work of Muslim women has been ad hoc and informal, Muslim women's determination and scholarship have helped them to create space in official peace negotiations as well. For example, Asha Hagi Elmi of Somalia, the founder and chairwoman of Save Somali Women and Children, as well as the founder of the Sixth Clan Movement during the Arta Peace Talks, is the first woman to be represented in a peace process in Somalia, where obstacles to women's political participation stems from the traditional religious and cultural interpretations of the jurists, which excluded women from economic, social, and political power structures and limited their role mostly to the private realm. Somali women like Asha Hagi developed an effective strategy that was built on an Islamic perspective. Women involved in the movement also had very high levels of Islamic education and knew Sharīʿah well. Consequently, they were able to bring women to the negotiation table with their own identities, and as equal partners in decision making.

Despite significant challenges and social inequalities, countless Muslim women in countries as diverse as Somalia, Egypt, Pakistan, Palestinian Territories, Syria, Afghanistan, Iraq, Libya, Kenya, Sudan, and Thailand, among others, are working tirelessly to address conflicts and build peace. Their efforts are inspired by and derived from their faith, history, culture, and intellectual heritage, all of which Muslim women have adapted to the cultural and traditional sensitivities of their unique communities. Although their contexts differ significantly and they have employed different approaches, they all base their efforts in Islam as a resource that empowers them.

Women in the Muslim world who have contributed to building sustainable peace and establishing just systems in their communities have been recognized internationally as well. Shirin Ebadi, a lawyer and activist from Iran who fought for democracy and human rights in her country, is the first Muslim woman to receive the Nobel Peace Prize, which she was awarded in 2003. She was followed by Tawakkul Karman of Sanaa, Yemen, mentioned earlier, who is called "the Mother of the Yemeni Revolution" and "the Queen of Peace" for her inspirational efforts to stand up against the regime of Ali Abdullah Saleh. She was the second Muslim woman and the first Arab Muslim woman to be granted this prestigious award, in 2011. In order to defend freedom of information and journalists, Karman had previously founded Women Journalists Without Borders and published the *Semi-Annual Press Freedom Report* on violence against Yemeni journalists; she also organized weekly sit-ins and led rallies protesting unjust policies of the government.

Both Karman and Ebadi are courageous and strong women who have defied intimidation and pressure and have stood up against injustice, but they are not alone. The vigorous roles of women in the 2011 uprisings in the Arab world (the "Arab Spring") have focused the limelight on Muslim women, revealing how women are defining and reframing the issues that impact their lives. Women like Asmaa Mahfouz and Israa Abdel Fettah of Egypt, Lina Ben Mhenni or Radhia Nasraoui of Tunisia, or Najla Elmangoush and Amina Megheirbi of Libya or Razan Zaituouneh of Syria, among many others, who have played leading roles in the Arab uprisings of 2011, are leading these movements and transforming their societies.

Peacebuilding activities of Muslim women reflect both unity and diversity. Derived from these core Islamic principles and values, peacebuilding efforts undertaken by Muslim women take different forms, including advocacy, mediation, observation, education, transnational justice, and interfaith/intrafaith dialogue. As advocates, they attempt to empower the weaker party(ies) in a conflict situation, restructure relationships, and transform unjust social structures. These activities often aim at strengthening the representativeness and inclusiveness of governance. For example, Razan Zaitouneh of Syria and Asmaa Mahfouz of Egypt, like Tawakkul Karman, and Shirin Ebadi, advocate for peace, justice and equality in their societies. The Sudanese Women's Civil Society Network for Peace is another organization advocating for women's issues and women's agendas in peace processes and bringing together women from conflict areas, such as Nuba Mountains, Darfur, Beja, and Blue Nile. As intermediaries, they aim to bring the parties together to resolve their conflict and establish peace. Their activities include fact-finding, good offices, peace-process advocacy, facilitation, conciliation, and mediation. Wajir Peace and Development Committee (WPDC), of Kenya, led by the late Dekha Ibrahim (1964–2011), was founded by a group of women to restore peace by involving all stakeholders, especially women and youth. They successfully brought parties together and contributed to the reduction of violence in their communities. Also, Amina Rasul-Bernardo, of the Philippine Council for Islam and Democracy (PCID), was recognized as "Mindanao Peace Champion" by the United Nations-sponsored Action for Conflict Transformation (ACT) for Peace Program in 2011 for her efforts to promote peace in her community.

As observers, Muslim women actors often serve as watchful eyes to discourage violence, corruption, human rights violations, or other behavior deemed threatening and undesirable. As observers, they may actively monitor and verify the legitimacy of elections, or may form "peace teams" or "living walls" between sides active in conflict situations. For example, Kisima Peace and Development Organization of Somalia aims to establish sustainable peace through human rights and development. They also take on activities including mediation, advocacy, and education among Muslims in Somalia. Kisima also monitors human rights violations and advocates human rights through raising awareness, lobbying, human rights education, and mainstreaming of gender and human rights into the programs. Kisima is part of the Somali human rights defenders' organizations that issued the Declaration of Somali Human Rights Defenders. One of the critical projects Kisima worked on is systematic human rights investigations, documentation, monitoring, and advocacy (IDMA), together with nine other Somali human rights organizations.

As educators, Muslim women actors aim to sensitize society to inequities inherent in the cluture; to foster an understanding of and build the skills of advocacy, conflict resolution, pluralism and democracy; and to promote healing and reconciliation. For example, the Afghan Institute for Learning (AIL), founded by Sakena Yacoobi, is recognized as an exemplary organization in this area. Established in Peshawar in 1995, AIL developed programs focusing mainly on the health and education of Afghan women and children. By teaching women to read the Qur'ān, Yacoobi equipped her students with knowledge of the Qur'ānic principles of equality of men and women and their rights derived from Islam. In addition to teaching women their rights, her programs included training on how to negotiate on the basis of shared values, such as diversity, equality, fairness, and justice, among others. Initially, AIL supported eighty underground home schools for 3,000 girls in Afghanistan after the Taliban closed girls' schools in the 1990s. In 2010 AIL was serving over 350,000 women and children each year through its educational learning centers, schools, and clinics, in both Afghanistan and Pakistan.

As agents of transnational justice, Muslim women actors seek accountability for atrocities and human rights abuses during war times via local and international tribunals or truth commissions. For example, the Women's Rights Movement in Morocco has called for establishing mechanisms to investigate human rights abuses in the country and bring to trial those responsible. Women of the movement proactively made suggestions, for example, regarding the Personal Status Code, and introduced materials into the Family Law. A key element conducive to their success was their efforts to develop sociological, legal, and religious arguments to convince the decision makers of the legitimacy of their demands. The women's movement also became actively involved in calling for the investigation of human rights violations and disappearances that took place during the 1980s and 1990s (the era is called the Years of Lead or Sanawat ar-Rusas). The influential work of the Moroccan anthropologist Nadia Guessous—a collection of the life stories of women who suffered at the hands of the state during the Years of Lead—also strengthened the calls for transitional justice and led to various reforms in the national laws regarding violence against women, as well as inclusion of female victims of human rights abuse into the Equity and Reconciliation Commission, established in 2004; this was one of the first attempts made in the Arab world to address human rights violations perpetrated in the post-independence period.

Muslim women also encourage intrafaith and interfaith dialogue in order to contribute to the peace process. Interfaith activities aim to bring different religious parties together to develop better understanding of each other's religious tradition and clarify misunderstandings. Palestinian peace-worker Ibtisam Mahameed, founder of Women's Interfaith Encounters (WIE) and a member of Jerusalem Peacemakers, for example, has been bringing together Muslim, Jewish, Christian, and Druze women and religious leaders. WIE focuses on the values of peacemaking and nonviolence and promotes interfaith respect and understanding by encouraging each community to learn about each other's religion. Friends of Victimized Families in South Thailand, founded by Soraya Jamjuree, also focuses on reconciliation between Muslims and Buddhists and addresses the needs of widows and orphans. Jamjuree's contributions to peace in the region, as well as her group's enhancement of women's rights, were recognized with an award by the National Human Rights Commission of Thailand on March 8—Women's Day—in 2006.

In conclusion, Muslim women are finding in Islam a set of values and norms that affirm and encourage their own efforts to resolve conflict and build social peace. They are engaging in a process of rediscovering and finding new ways of valorizing historical, or archetypal, Muslim women figures whose stories inspire courage in modern-day peacemakers. Rather than accepting the role of a passive victim or a person who must be defended or emancipated, they are demonstrating that Muslim women can be active agents of change and peacebuilding. By invoking Islam as a mandate for gender equality and peacemaking, they are stepping beyond more discreet ways of influence behind the scenes, such as using informal networks to relay information or attempting to persuade male members of the household to support and join peacemaking efforts. In the process, they are drawing upon and extending the range of resources within Islam for peacemaking, and adding new examples of empowered women to those provided in Muslim history. Their experiences move us away from essentialized and stereotypical images of Muslim women and instead help us to understand the diverse roles they play and the contributions they make in peacebuilding and reconciliation in their communities.

BIBLIOGRAPHY

Abdullahi, Abdurrahman M. "Women and Constitutional Debate in Somalia: Legal Reforms During Reconciliation Conferences (2000–2003)." http://www.scribd.com/doc/15421298/Women-and-Constitutional-Debate-in-Somalia.

Abu-Nimer, Mohammed, and S. Ayse Kadayifci-Orellana. "Muslim Peace Building Actors in Africa and the Balkans." *Peace and Change* 33. 4 (October 2008).

Abu-Nimer, Mohammed, Amal Khoury, and Emily Welty. *Unity in Diversity: Interfaith Dialogue in the Middle East.* Washington, D.C.: United States Institute of Peace Press, 2007.

Combs-Schilling, Elaine M. "Etching Patriarchal Rule: Ritual Dye, Erotic Potency, and the Morrocan Monarchy." *Journal of the History of Sexuality* 14 (April 1991): 658–681.

Kadayifci-Orellana, Ayse, and Meena Sharify-Funk. "Muslim Women Peacemakers as Agents of Change." In *Crescent and Dove: Peace and Conflict Resolution in Islam*, edited by Qamar ul Huda, pp. 179–204. Washington, D.C.: United States Institute of Peace, 2010.

Miller, W. Flagg. "Public Words and Body Politics: Reflections on the Strategies of Women Poets in Rural Yemen." *Journal of Women's History* 14.1 (Spring 2002): 94–122.

Timmons, Debra M., and Mary E. King. "The Sixth Clan—Women Organize for Peace in Somalia: A Review of Published Literature," University for Peace, 2004, http://www.upeace.org/library/documents/somalia_the_sixth_clan.pdf.

S. AYSE KADAYIFCI-ORELLANA

ISLAM AND WOMEN

[*This entry contains three subentries,*

An Overview
Contemporary Discourses *and*
Eighteenth-Century to Early Twentieth-Century Debates.]

AN OVERVIEW

Women at the Rise of Islam. Women played a critical role in the early history of Islam. The Prophet Muḥammad was born in the city of Mecca in approximately 570 CE and began receiving revelations at the age of forty, in 610 CE. He was extremely distressed by his first revelatory experience and feared he was going insane. In confusion and distress, he turned to his wife Khadīja. *Ṣaḥīḥ al-Bukhārī*, second in authority only to the Qur'ān for the majority of Muslims, contains the description of how Khadīja comforted and counseled Muḥammad, eventually convincing him that his was a true calling from God. In doing so, she became the first person to accept the revelations received by Muḥammad and the first follower of Islam. Interestingly, the story itself is told on the authority of another important woman in early Islam—Muḥammad's second wife, ʿĀʾishah. Through the revelation of the Qur'ān, Muḥammad instituted revolutionary changes affecting the status of women, prohibiting the common practices of female infanticide (16:58–59, 17:3) and unlawful inheriting of women (4:19), guaranteeing women a share of inheritance (4:7) and the right to their own earnings (4:32).

Khadīja, ʿĀʾishah, and Muḥammad's other wives and female companions provide role models for Muslim women, and Muḥammad's relationships with the women of his household and community serve as an ideal for Muslims. The picture painted by *aḥādīth* and biographical literature is one of dynamic, outspoken women who actively participated in the life of the community in Medina. Many of them transmitted the stories that still serve as the primary source of information on Muḥammad and the earliest community of Muslims.

After the death of Muḥammad, the Muslims rapidly defeated both the Persian and Byzantine Empires, conquering vast amounts of territory encompassing peoples of many different cultures. Over time, people from the conquered territories converted to Islam, bringing their existing understandings, assumptions, social customs, and traditions to emerging interpretations and institutions of the new faith. Social and cultural norms have had an impact on religious ideas and practices throughout Muslim history to the current day. This is why the status and situation of Muslim women varies from time to time and place to place.

Popular Images and Stereotypes of Muslim Women. The non-Muslim world has long been fascinated with the status and role of women in Islam. Popular views in the imagination of many non-Muslims in Europe and North America have been bifurcated between the romanticized view of a decadent and indolent life in the mysterious "harem" and veiled, secluded, and silenced women, under the oppressive control of the men in their lives. Writing for a popular literary magazine, in 1902, columnist Mary Mills Patrick describes life in "the Harem" for a "domestic Turkish woman" as one of indolence and luxury.

"Who in America," the author asks, "can enjoy the luxury of a bath that lasts all day, undisturbed by hurry or anxiety, or any thought of neglected duties?" (Patrick, 1902, p. 341).

Writing just a few years earlier, Stanley Lane-Poole paints a similar picture of the life of Egyptian women in his 1898 work, *Cairo: Sketches of Its History, Monuments, and Social Life*. In addition to food, gossip, and visits to the public bath, Lane-Poole adds stimulation "of their husbands' affections" to the list of "simple pleasures" enjoyed by women living in "the harim." These types of portrayals of Muslim women became fodder for Hollywood, which wove these images into the fabric of the popular imagination throughout the twentieth century, from silent films to *Harum Scarum* and *I Dream of Jeannie* to Princess Jasmine in Disney's *Aladdin*. In the twentieth and early twenty-first century, the image of Islam has been forever altered by the Iranian revolution, the issue of veiling in Europe, and the tragic events of September 11, 2001. The image of the Muslim woman has borne the brunt of that change, perhaps because the veil is the most visible sign of Islam in the public sphere. Now, instead of the chiffon pantaloons and velvet bras of the harem, Muslim women are depicted swathed in all-enveloping black shrouds, faceless and voiceless creatures oppressed by their "evil" and "violent" religion. All of these stereotypes arise in the imaginations of outsiders looking at Muslim women from across a chasm of ignorance. The stereotypes thrive because most non-Muslims in Europe and North America lack the knowledge necessary to overcome them.

Islam's Sacred Sources. There are two main textual authorities in Islam. The first is the Qurʾān (literally "reading" or "recitation"), which in the original Arabic, according to Muslims, contains the literal and direct words of God dictated by the angel Gabriel to the Prophet Muḥammad a few verses at a time over a period of 23 years, from 610 CE until shortly before Muḥammad's death in 632 CE The verses were written by Muḥammad's followers as they were revealed, and they were compiled into a single text shortly after his death. Muslims believe that the Arabic Qurʾān in its present arrangement dates from the time of the Caliph Uthman ibn Affan, who reigned from 644 CE to 656 CE. The second textual source is the Prophetic Traditions, narratives by or stories about the Prophet's behavior and attitude in the early Muslim community, known as *aḥādīth.*

The word ḥadīth in Arabic literally means a story or narrative. Ḥadīth as a technical term in Islam means a story about the Prophet Muḥammad. Such stories contain the sunnah (lit. practice) of the Prophet, detailing his words and actions, or those things of which he tacitly approved (things that he witnessed others doing or saying and did not correct or criticize). The stories were passed on orally for generations before being collected and written down. The collections of *aḥādīth* used today by Muslims were compiled in the second half of the ninth century CE, approximately two and one half centuries after Muḥammad. Of the more than half a dozen ḥadīth popular collections used by Muslims, the most well-known and respected are *Ṣaḥīḥ al-Bukhārī* and *Ṣaḥīḥ Muslim.* While the Qurʾān lays out general principles, the Prophet and the early community serve as practical examples of how to incorporate and implement those principles in the daily lives of individuals and societies. Both the Qurʾān and the Prophetic Traditions inform Muslim belief and practice related to women.

The Qurʾān and Women.

> The submitting men and the submitting women, the believing men and the believing women, the obedient men and the obedient women, the truthful men and the truthful women, the patient men and the patient women, the reverent men and the reverent women, the charitable men and the charitable women, the fasting men and the fasting women, the chaste men and the chaste women, and the men and women who remember God frequently—God has prepared for them forgiveness and a great reward. (Qurʾān 33:35).

The above verse provides the framework in which Muslims see the status of women in Islam. Both men and women are responsible for performing the same religious duties, and both can expect to reap the same spiritual rewards. Both are thus equal in the sight of God. Likewise, 3:195 echoes the notion of male and female spiritual equality:

> And their Lord has accepted of them, and answered them: "Never will I suffer to be lost the work of any of you, *be he male or female*: You are members, one of another: Those who have left their homes, or been driven out therefrom, or suffered harm in My Cause, or fought or been slain,- verily, I will blot out from them their iniquities, and admit them into Gardens with rivers flowing beneath;- A reward from the presence of God, and from His presence is the best of rewards.

Both man and woman were created from "a single soul," according to the Qurʾān (4:1), and thus share the same essence. The sense of spiritual equality is augmented by recognition of Adam and Eve's mutual responsibility in disobeying God by eating the forbidden fruit: "And they both ate from it. They became conscious of their nakedness and began to cover themselves with leaves from the garden" (20:121).

Stories of Women in the Qurʾān. The status of women is further highlighted by the stories of women that are told in the Qurʾān. Mary, the mother of Jesus, is honored with her own chapter. Chapter 19 of the Qurʾān is titled "Mary," in which the story of the annunciation and birth of Jesus is told. Jesus is identified throughout the Qurʾān as "the Messiah, son of Mary." Mary's name appears thirty times in the Qurʾān. Other women whose stories appear in the Qurʾān are the mother and sister of Moses; the wives of

Adam, Abraham, Noah, Lot and Pharaoh; and the Queen of Sheba. Each of these women plays a key role in the Qur'ānic accounts of sacred history. Of these, only the wives of Noah and Lot are held up by the Qur'ān as examples of disbelieving women. The rest are cited as examples of believing women.

The stories of the wives of Pharaoh, Noah, and Lot demonstrate the moral and spiritual independence of women. Pharaoh is one of the most egregious disbelievers described in the Qur'ān. His wife, however, is cited as an example of a believer who is destined for paradise (66:11). The wives of Noah and Lot are cited as examples of disbelievers who are destined for hell in spite of being married to two of God's messengers (66:10). The spiritual fate of the women is based solely on their own beliefs and actions. The men in their lives have no responsibility for their final destiny. This Qur'ānic framework of spiritual equality is widely accepted by Muslims, but other verses have traditionally served as the basis on which a temporal hierarchy has been established.

Chapter 4 of the Qur'ān is titled "The Women" (*al-Nisa'a*). It is in this chapter that many of the injunctions dealing with family matters such as marriage and inheritance are found. The rights granted to women in the Qur'ān are seen by Muslims as a revolutionary departure from the customs of pre-Islamic Arabia, where female infanticide was common and women were not guaranteed a share of inheritance and could, themselves, be inherited as property. The Qur'ān outlaws female infanticide (16:58–59, 17:33) and inheriting women (4:19) and guarantees women a share of inheritance (4:7).

Family Relations: Marriage, Divorce, Inheritance. The Qur'ān encourages marriages (24:32) and provides specific instructions on the requirements and etiquette of marriage. The spousal relationship is described eloquently in the Qur'ān: "And among His Signs is this, that He created for you mates from among yourselves, that ye may dwell in tranquility with them, and He has put love and mercy between your (hearts): verily in that are Signs for those who reflect" (30:21). Husbands and wives are also described as each other's garments (2:187). The Qur'ān portrays marriage as a warm and loving relationship, while also dealing with practical matters. A written contract and a dower (*mahr*) are required for a valid marriage (4:24–25). Unlike the Western concept of dowry, which is paid by the bride or her family to the groom, it is the Muslim groom who must pay the bride. The amount of the dower is agreed on by the couple and becomes the wife's property, to do with as she pleases (4:4, 24). The terms of the marriage contract are also mutually agreed on by the couple and binding on both. Either party may stipulate any condition that does not violate the teachings of the Qur'ān.

The Qur'ān deals with marriage in detail, and it deals with divorce in even greater detail. Although a man may unilaterally declare a divorce without judicial process, the Qur'ān places conditions and restrictions on divorce that protect the interests of women and children. Among these conditions is arbitration that includes representatives of both the husband and the wife (4:35). Men are prohibited from taking back the dower and from treating their wives harshly (4:19–25). Another safeguard for women is the mandatory waiting period of three menstrual cycles before a divorce is final. In case of pregnancy, the divorce is not final until the woman gives birth. During the waiting period, the husband must provide support and lodging for the wife (65:2). After a divorce, a father is required to support his children, even if they live with the mother, and if the mother is nursing his child, the father must continue to support her as well (2:233). Along with these distinctly woman-friendly ideas and ordinances, the Qur'ān also contains verses that have been used to establish and maintain a gender hierarchy in Muslim societies. Most notable among the verses used to establish a gender hierarchy in which the man is the head of the household is 4:34. Differences in translations reveal important differences in the interpretation of this verse. One of the most popular English translations of the Qur'ān is that of Yusuf Ali. The Yusuf Ali translation of Qur'ān 4:34 reads:

> Men are the protectors and maintainers of women, because Allah has given the one more (strength) than the other, and because they support them from their means. Therefore the righteous women are devoutly obedient, and guard in (the husband's) absence what Allah would have them guard. As to those women on whose part ye fear disloyalty and ill-conduct, admonish them (first), (Next), refuse to share their beds, (And last) beat them (lightly); but if they return to obedience, seek not against them Means (of annoyance): For Allah is Most High, great (above you all).

There are a number of aspects of this verse on which various interpreters disagree. The first relates to the term that Yusuf Ali translates as "protectors and maintainers" (*qawwamun'ala*), which is understood to define the male–female dynamic. Yusuf Ali's translation captures a general concept on which Muslims tend to agree—that men bear primary responsibility for the physical protection and financial support of women. Where interpretations differ on this part of the verse is the degree and nature of authority granted to men over women. Muhammad Pickthall's translation of *qawwamun'ala* is "in charge of." Where Yusuf Ali's translation highlights men's responsibility toward women, Pickthall's highlights men's authority over women. Both responsibility and authority are facets of the man's position as head of the family. Patriarchal interpretations emphasize male authority, while feminist interpretations emphasize male responsibility and even make authority contingent on responsibility.

Perhaps the most controversial portion of 4:34 occurs near the end, where men are advised on how to deal with, according to Yusuf Ali, "those women on whose part ye fear disloyalty and ill-conduct," or according to Pickthall, "those from whom ye fear rebellion." It is in this context that the issue of corporal punishment arises. Yusuf Ali translates the Qur'ān's advice this way: "admonish them (first), (Next), refuse to share their beds, (And last) beat them (lightly)." Pickthall renders the sentence as "admonish them and banish them to beds apart, and scourge them." Although most translators and interpreters understand this verse to allow husbands to engage in some type of corporal punishment, a few contemporary translators offer an entirely different understanding. For example, the Progressive Muslims and the authors of the Reformist Translation, such as Laleh Bakhtiar and Amina Wadud, render this segment as: "advise them, and abandon them in the bedchamber, and separate from them," applying the metaphorical interpretation, "separate from them," to the Arabic phrase *idribuhunna*, which more traditional translators render as "beat/scourge them." The metaphorical reinterpretation of the verse may be said to reflect contemporary disapproval of corporal punishment. However, even among those who understand the verse to allow corporal punishment there is general agreement that any such punishment must be minimal and noninjurious, which led Yusuf Ali to insert the adverb "lightly" in parentheses. Strict limitation on the severity of any corporal punishment is seen throughout the history of Muslim interpretation, appearing as a Prophetic admonition in the ḥadīth collections and scholarly commentary found in Qur'ānic commentaries.

Another area of dispute is what is meant by the term *nushūz*, which Yusuf Ali translates as "disloyalty and ill-conduct" and Pickthall translates as *rebellion.* Immediately preceding this mention of fear of *disloyalty and ill-conduct* or *rebellion,* the verse describes righteous women being *devoutly obedient* and guarding what *Allāh would have them guard,* as Yusuf Ali translates it. Elsewhere in the Qurʾān, believers are said to *guard their chastity* (23:5), so at a minimum, this is understood to refer to the wife's sexual fidelity. However, it is also extended to include protection of the husband's wealth, property, and other vital interests in his absence. Once again, the emphasis in Yusuf Ali's translation is on responsibility, which is now reciprocal. The husband is responsible for the protection and maintenance of his wife and the wife is responsible for safeguarding her husband's interests in his absence. Pickthall's translation again emphasizes male authority and the fear of female *rebellion* against that authority. In common usage, the term *nushūz* has been linked only to women in the context of marital discord. However, it is important to note that the Qurʾān applies the term equally to men in the same context (4:128). Muslim scholar Heba Raouf Ezzat, described by wamda.com as one of "the 100 most influential Arabs on Twitter," highlights this neglected dimension of family politics, showing that, while the Qurʾān orders men to keep domestic conflicts private, women may seek help from their extended family and community, which provides greater privacy for women in domestic conflicts.

Qurʾān 4:34 is not the only verse that is seen as establishing a gender hierarchy in Islam. In the discourse on divorce, the Qurʾān says: "women shall have rights similar to the rights against them, according to what is equitable; but men have a degree (of advantage) over them" (2:228). Within the specific context of divorce, this is understood to refer to the fact a man can unilaterally declare his wife divorced, whereas a woman who wishes to divorce her husband must seek a divorce from a Muslim judge. However, some scholars understand the degree that men have over women in a more general sense. Here, as in the case of 4:34, the emphasis may be on male authority or on male responsibility.

The Qurʾānic ruling on inheritance assigns the son a share equal to that of two daughters (4:11). Read alone, this may appear to privilege sons. However, because men are understood to bear complete financial responsibility for the women in their families, on the basis of 4:34, the distribution of inheritance outlined in 4:11 is seen as fair and equitable. A woman, at least ideally, is not financially responsible for anyone, including herself, whereas a man is responsible for not only his wives and children, but also for his widowed mother and his unmarried sisters.

The division of inheritance in 4:11, together with 2:282, which calls for financial contracts to be attested by "two witnesses, out of your own men, and if there are not two men, then a man and two women," has led some to argue that a woman is equal to half a man. Others argue that this understanding is the product of an overtly patriarchal society that did not consider women eligible to engage in legal and commercial transactions in the first place.

Crime and Punishment. In issues of crime and punishment, the Qurʾān also demonstrates a mix of equality and disparity. In the case of theft, the text says: "As to the thief, male or female, cut off his or her hands: a punishment by way of example, from God, for their crime" (5:38). Just as good actions are given equal rewards for both men and women, the evil act of theft incurs the same punishment. This is also the case with adultery, according to 24:2, which states that men and women guilty of adultery are both subject to one hundred lashes. Where the disparity seems to appear is in 4:15, in which women found guilty of "lewdness" are ordered to be confined to their homes until death or until God "ordains another way" for them. On the basis of ḥadīth, most scholars hold that the punishment given in 24:2 is the other way ordained by God and the latter verse abrogates the former, solving the apparent disparity. Yusuf Ali disagrees with this interpretation and understands "lewdness" in 4:15–16 to refer to homosexuality, specifically to female homosexuality in 4:15 and male homosexuality in 4:16. Understanding "lewdness" as homosexuality in 4:15–16 solves the apparent discrepancy between these verses and 24:2, but it raises a serious discrepancy between 4:15 and 4:16. In the first, women guilty of homosexuality are punished by life imprisonment, whereas men receive no specific punishment and may be left alone. Yusuf Ali appears to be unique in understanding these verses to be addressing homosexuality, but his thinking deserves scrutiny because his translation remains one of the most popular English translations of the Qur'ān.

***Aḥādīth* and Women.** As previously noted, the Qur'ān is not the only source to which Muslims turn for information on women. The Prophetic Traditions contain not only direct commands of the Prophet to and about women; they are also a rich source of detailed information on the women in the Prophet's life and his relationships with those women. According to *aḥādīth*, the first person to believe in the Prophet's message was his wife Khadīja. It was she who offered him comfort and support in the traumatic aftermath of his first revelatory experience, when he thought himself to be going mad. On hearing of his experience, she took him to her cousin, a Christian monk with knowledge of Hebrew Scriptures, who confirmed for Muḥammad the validity of his experience. Her support continued to sustain Muḥammad during the first difficult years of his mission. The Prophet's later wives are among the most important transmitters of *aḥādīth*. These stories portray the Prophet as a loving husband and father who delighted in the company of his wives and daughters. The Prophet advised his companions that the best of them were those who treated their wives best. Like the Qur'ān, *aḥādīth* affirm both the spiritual equality of men and women and the traditionally accepted gender hierarchy, as the Prophet is reported to have said, "women are the twin halves of men," (*Sunan al-Tirmidhi*, Book 1, *ḥadīth* 113) and also, "if I were to command anyone to prostrate before another, I would command women to prostrate themselves before their husbands, because of the special right over them given to husbands by God" (*Sunan Abu Dawud*, Book 11, *ḥadīth* 2135). There are thousands of *aḥādīth* in the canonized collections, and here, too, patriarchal interpretation has dominated Muslim understanding and use of the texts. As in the case of the Qur'ān, the contemporary period has witnessed scholarly challenges to patriarchal interpretations of the *aḥādīth*.

Sexual Modesty and Veiling. Perhaps no topic has dominated public discourse on women in Islam in the twenty-first century as the veil, whether it is the headscarf (hijab) or face veil (*niqāb*). A number of countries have discussed banning or restricting head and/or face covering. The French law popularly known as the Burqa ban, which went into effect in April 2011, received tremendous international attention. Under the law, women can be fined for covering their faces in public. Earlier, in 2004, France outlawed the wearing of "conspicuous religious symbols," which includes Muslim headscarves, in public schools. Although the earlier law also restricts the wearing of other religious attire, it was popularly called the "Hijab ban" because Muslims were widely perceived as the primary target of the legislation. Turkey, a secular Muslim country, prohibits wearing headscarves in government buildings, including schools and libraries. Over the years, a number of attempts have been made by Egyptian authorities to prevent women from wearing face veils in public schools. Women who wear the *niqāb* have challenged these efforts in the Egyptian courts with mixed results.

The legal discourse on veiling and efforts to ban or restrict it have made it a political issue, a question of personal religious liberty, rather than a religious question of proper attire. What is lost in that discourse is the fact that Muslims disagree on whether covering the head and/or face is a religious obligation. Here too, interpretations of the Qurʾān and *aḥādīth* vary. Muslims do agree that the Qurʾān requires sexual modesty of both men and women. Both are told to lower their gaze and guard their modesty/chastity (24:30–31). Women are further admonished to cover their cleavage/bosoms with their coverings and conceal their beauty from men outside their familes, except "what is ordinarily apparent of it" (24:31). This is where interpretation comes into play. As Fatima Mernissi points out, the Arabic word "hijab" is never used in the Qurʾān to refer to women's clothing, nor is there any command to cover the head. Others argue on the basis of *aḥādīth* that "what ordinarily appears" of a woman's beauty is the hands and face and that everything else must be covered. This is the most common understanding, which is why so many Muslims and non-Muslims alike believe that head covering is mandatory for Muslim women. The word *niqāb* is also taken from the *aḥādīth*. Though it appears in the context of being prohibited on the pilgrimage, those who argue for covering the face see this as evidence the Prophet's wives covered their faces and believe that following their example is the ideal.

There is a growing resurgence of veiling among Muslim women throughout the world. Women who choose to wear either a head scarf or face veil do so out of a sense of piety and pride in their identity as Muslims. Women who choose not to wear either a head scarf or face veil are equally committed to their faith and their identity as Muslims.

The Qurʾān presents men and women as spiritual equals who are individually responsible for their beliefs and actions in this world and the next, and women are clearly granted particular rights and protections by text. At the same time, however, there are verses of the Qurʾān that serve as the basis for a gendered hierarchy within the family and society, and these have been and are used to privilege men over women. The responsibility for and authority over women granted to men within that gendered hierarchy are sometimes offered as reasons for restricting women in order to protect them.

Conclusion. There are more than a billion Muslims in the world, at least half of whom are women. The experiences of Muslim women are as varied as the women themselves. Some cover their heads, some do not, and some veil completely. They are daughters, sisters, wives, mothers, grandmothers, and aunts. Many are oppressed, and many are not. Many who are oppressed fight that oppression through their commitment to their faith, a faith with ongoing interpretive traditions in which Muslim women are actively involved. The gender hierarchy discussed in this article is seen by a number of contemporary Muslim scholars as the result of patriarchal interpretations, interpretations that are not in keeping with the Qurʾānic emphasis on the spiritual and religious equality of men and women discussed herein. These scholars, such as Amina Wadud in *Qurʾān and Woman: Rereading the Sacred Text from a Woman's Perspective* and Asma Barlas in *"Believing Women" in Islam: Unreading Patriarchal Interpretations of the Qurʾān*, call for a new approach to the texts. Fatima Mernissi, in her seminal work, *The Veil and the Male Elite: A Feminist Interpretation of Women's Rights in Islam*, addresses misogynistic uses of *aḥādīth* and to challenge the centrality of the veil as a symbol of female piety. The works of these and other Muslim women scholars and activists underscore the gap between how Muslim women see their rights and the struggle for them and how they are seen by secularists and non-Muslims. Such scholars and activists play a crucial role in the ongoing reinterpretation of their religion and in changing the images of Muslims around the globe.

BIBLIOGRAPHY

El Ahmad, Khaled. "The 100 Most Influential Arabs on Twitter." [Wamda.com].

Ahmed, Leila. *A Quiet Revolution: The Veil's Resurgence, from the Middle East to America*. New Haven, Conn.: Yale University Press, 2011.

Ahmed, Leila. *Women and Gender in Islam: Historical Roots of a Modern Debate*. New Haven, Conn.: Yale University Press, 1992.

Badran, Margot. *Feminism in Islam: Secular and Religious Convergences*. Oxford: Oneworld, 2009.

Barlas, Asma. *"Believing Women" in Islam: Unreading Patriarchal Interpretations of the Qur'ān*. 1st ed. Austin: University of Texas Press, 2002.

Al-Bukhari, Muhammad ibn Isma'il. *Sahih al-Bukhari*. http://www.sahih-bukhari.com/.

Ezzat, Heba Rauf. *Women and Political Agency in Islam*. Herndon, VA: International Institute of Islamic Thought, 1995. [English translation of Arabic title].

Lane-Poole, Stanley. *Cairo; Sketches of Its History, Monuments, and Social Life*, first published in 1898. The Middle East Collection. New York: Arno Press, 1973.

Mernissi, Fatima. *The Veil and the Male Elite: A Feminist Interpretation of Women's Rights in Islam*. Reading, Mass.: Addison-Wesley, 1991.

Mernissi, Fatima. *Women and Islam: An Historical and Theological Inquiry*. New Delhi: Kali for Women, 1993.

Nouraie-Simone, Fereshteh. *On Shifting Ground: Muslim Women in the Global Era*. New York: Feminist Press at the City University of New York, 2005.

Patrick, Mary Mills. "Life in the Harem" in the column "The World Over: *Pen Pictures of Travel*." *Current Opinion* 32, January–June 1902: 341–343.

Sachedina, Abdulaziz. "Woman, Half-the-Man? The Crisis of Male Jurisprudence." In *Intellectual Traditions in Islam*, edited by Farhad Daftary, pp. 160–178. London: I. B. Tauris, in association with the Institute of Ismaili Studies, 2000.

Wadud, Amina. *Qur'ān and Woman: Rereading the Sacred Text from a Woman's Perspective*. 2d ed. New York: Oxford University Press, 1999.

Aisha Musa

Contemporary Discourses

Socioreligious discourses such as discourses on Islam and women do not occur in a vacuum. Rather, they may usefully be understood as responses to social and political developments in the societies in which they arise. Discourses on Islam and women since 2000 have occurred in the context of three significant sociopolitical situations: Muslim American women's reinterpretations of religion after 9/11, the politico-religious discourses of Iranian women's organizations after the rise to power of radical Islamists in Iran in 2005, and emerging discourses on women and Islam in Tunisia after the 2011 Arab Spring revolution.

The American Discourse. The attack on the Twin Towers in New York on September 11, 2001, created a strong negative sentiment toward Islam in the American public, and women's subordinated position in Islam soon became a main focal point of this resentment. While the position of women in Islam was a burden for all American Muslims, it hit conservative religious elements particularly hard, as the climate for their version of the religion got very hostile. Moderate interpretations of Islam became correspondingly popular, both among Muslims who wished to distance themselves from the terrorists and among Americans more generally. This created a new space for American Muslim women scholars and activists within conservative, liberal, and radical religious environments. They represent a new generation of American Muslims seeking to redefine women's role in Islam from their point of view as American women and to distance themselves from the patriarchal values of the societies in which Islam is traditionally practiced.

Liberal and radical scholars and activists within this trend challenge the very fundamentals of the gendered order in conventional understandings of Islam by contesting classical interpretations of Qurʾānic verses and dogmas such as women's obligation to veil, the requirement of gender-segregated, male-led prayers, and the unacceptability of homosexuality. While more conservative members of the trend generally are less direct in their challenges to patriarchal hegemony in Islam, they do join the demands for gender justice and equal rights. These demands have produced results. The dominant American Muslim organization, the Islamic Society for North America, in 2001 elected its first woman president, Dr. Ingrid Mattson, who substantially reoriented the organization's profile in the direction of increased freedom of thought and interpretative pluralism. For instance, in 2007 the female Islamic scholar and interpreter Laleh Bakhtiar, in an English interpretation of the Qurʾān, changed the meaning of the verse normally used to justify a husband's right to beat a quarrelsome wife to his right to divorce her, arguing that both grammatically and contextually this was a more adequate interpretation. While some men in the Islamic Society for North America wished to ban this interpretation of the Qurʾān within the organization, President Mattson prevented this, pointing to the society's aim to represent the diversity of Islam in North America and to the equal legitimacy of various schools and interpretations within Islam. Other American Islamic organizations have since elected female leaders. Several of these leaders are American-born and have further contributed to the ongoing reinterpretation of Islam in America—a reinterpretation that seeks to harmonize Islam with American society.

The Iranian Discourse. In Iran, because of a general prohibition of non-Islamic political parties and organizations, most discourses on women's issues take place within a religious framework. There are women's political organizations subscribing to radical Islamist ideologies and to reformist ideologies. Such Islamic women's organizations have become increasingly successful in influencing the political discourse in Iran in the direction of a greater focus on women's rights—a topic that most political parties otherwise have given little attention to. Case-by-case cooperation across organizational and ideological divisions has enabled the women's movement to promote women's issues in the political sphere. Women's issues hence play a significant role in contemporary Iranian politics, owing to the combined efforts of women's organizations to put them on the agenda. Although the profiles of the different women's organizations vary, they share a demand for gender justice and an interpretation of Islam as sanctioning gender equality. They consider the patriarchal nature of Iranian society, not Islam, to be at the root of the gender injustices that they currently live under. Among the most central shared demands of these organizations are demands for women's rights, gender-neutral legislation, institutionalization of gender-sensitive planning, and increased female representation in national politics. Female candidates for political offices are repeatedly presented by several women's organizations, although in the great majority of cases, they are turned down by the clearing bodies for religious candidates. Women such as Azam Taleghani have presented themselves even as candidates for the presidency, arguing that Sharīʿah does not prohibit a woman from leading an Islamic state. Demands for legal equity are most often voiced in relation to personal status and family law. Polygamy, divorce regulations, inheritance, and child custody are areas of current Iranian jurisprudence that are particularly challenged by the women's movement. In the discursive climate of increasing hostility to political dissent in general and expressions of feminism in particular since the 2005 elections, the women's movement has kept alive the public discourse on women's rights. Together with the democratic movement, to which it is closely related, it has also developed a broader discourse on basic civil, political, and individual rights. Since the controversial 2009 elections, the two movements have been central in the Green Movement in the first popular uprising since the revolution in 1979. Islamic women's organizations in Iran have thus been rather successful since 2005 in influencing public discourse and political agendas toward gender justice and recognition of rights. However, the national political structures that they work within have so far prevented them from achieving significant lasting changes in political institutions.

The Tunisian Discourse. Tunisia is the Arab country that has most radically broken with its Islamic judicial past since independence, as a consequence of the postcolonial regime's modernization (in the sense of Westernization) of Tunisian society. Consequently, women in Tunisia for decades have enjoyed unprecedented freedoms in relation to movement, education, career, and family life. But modernization never included democracy and human rights—a fact that the revolution in January 2011 set out to rectify. Women's rights and gender equality were put on the agenda only after the revolution, and then primarily by political forces that, for religious reasons, wanted to regulate rather than expand them. However, since freedom for Tunisian women enjoys considerable support in the population, post-revolutionary discourse on women and Islam has been ambivalent. The largest Islamist party, Ennahda, which also won the October 2011 constitutional-assembly elections, is in this context a particularly interesting discursive arena. Though it clearly aims to represent an alternative to the secular hegemony on women's rights, during the election campaign it claimed that it does not intend to change the personal law in which Tunisian women's freedoms are embedded, and that it supports total individual freedom in lifestyle choices like dress and diet. Souad Abderrahim, an unveiled member of the constitutional assembly for Ennahda since October 2011, became an icon of this moderate Islamist discourse on women and Islam during the election campaign.

In contrast, since the revolution Islamists outside Ennahda's constituency have been vocal in demanding a return to Sharīʿah. The legalization of polygamy in particular has become a symbolic demand for these more radical forces. Schools and universities constitute a central discursive arena for the radical Islamists. Students have on several occasions initiated strikes demanding gender segregated classes and veiled female teaching staff. In November 2011 a major incident of this kind drew much attention: two female students dressed in *niqāb* appeared at Manouba University in Tunis demanding to follow courses despite a ban on the full-face veil in Tunisian institutions of education. In response to the university leadership's refusal of the girls' demand, a group of radical Islamists occupied the university for weeks. In this situation, Ennahda expressed support for the radicals rather than for the university's enforcement of national law. In the same vein, Souad Abderrahim soon after the October 2011 election took a radical turn when she declared that unwed mothers are a moral disgrace for Tunisia and do not deserve any legal support or protection. These are some of several incidents after the election that suggest that the party's discourse on Islam and women may be less uniformly moderate than it appeared during the election campaign.

The three contemporary discourses on Islam and women explored here were all initiated by

Muslims and discussed in religious terms. They clearly can influence broader political discourses and situations in quite different directions. While the American and Iranian discourses share a willingness to challenge patriarchal hegemony in Islam in a quest for greater gender justice and more women's rights, they still differ in several respects, the American discourse being an attempt to create a genuinely American Islam in an overwhelmingly Christian society and the Iranian discourse being an attempt to carve out more female space in a solidly Islamic state. The Tunisian discourse seeks quite opposite results. Based on a moderate but conventional, patriarchal interpretation of Islam, it represents an attempt to regulate, rather than promote, Tunisian women's freedom. This illustrates the multifaceted nature of contemporary Islam and the broad range of discursive possibilities that currently are being explored by believers.

Bibliography

Afzal-Khan, Fawzai, ed. *Shattering the Stereotypes: Muslim Women Speak Out*. Northampton, Mass.: Olive Branch Press, 2005.

Ahmed, Leila. *A Quiet Revolution*. New Haven, Conn.: Yale University Press, 2011.

Barrouhi, Abdelaziz. "Le mysterieux monsieur Ghannouchi." *Jeune Afrique* 51, no. 46 (2011): 44–48.

Dahmani, Frida. "Souad Abderrahim, le pasionaria d'Ennahdha se dévoile." http://www.jeuneafrique.com/Article/ARTJAWEB20111110160949/JeuneAfriqueJeuneAfrique.html.

Hoodfar, Homa, and Shadi Sadr. "Can Women Act as Agents of Democratization of Theocracy in Iran?" Geneva: United Nations Research Institute for Social Development, 2009.

Tahmasebi-Birgani, Victoria. "Green Women of Iran: The Role of the Women's Movement during and after Iran's Presidential Election of 2009." *Constellations* 17, no. 1 (2010): 78–86.

Marit Tjomsland

Eighteenth-Century to Early Twentieth-Century Debates

Historical debates regarding Muslim women have tended to address their role in the family, education, veiling, and seclusion as both social and religious affairs. Based on the Qurʾān, *aḥādīth*, and legal literature, these debates have, in some cases, resulted in reforms regarding marriage, inheritance, and divorce, securing women's legal and financial rights.

Debates about a reformed status for women began in earnest in the eighteenth century and were not necessarily Western-inspired or driven but had indigenous roots. Shah Walī Allāh, a Muslim scholar in India, began efforts to reform Muslim society by removing social inequalities and establishing concepts of basic social justice. To achieve this aim, he called for interpreting the Qurʾān and *aḥādīth* within the context of changing times. He studied the views of different schools of Islamic jurisprudence, including Ḥanafī, Mālikī, Shāfiʿī, and Ḥanbalī, and adopted a balanced and logical approach, formulating a systematic approach to thought and beliefs, geared toward the creation of consensus. His movement provided bases for the future work of Sir Syed Ahmed Khan and Qāsim Nanotavi. Similarly, in Arabia, Muḥammad Ibn ʿAbd Al-Wahhab began a revival (*tajdīd*) and reform (*iṣlāḥ*) movement to "purify" Islam, returning to strict adherence to monotheism (*tawḥīd*) and rejecting associationism (*shirk*). He also referred to many law schools in his writings, both Sunnī and Shīʿī, although he did not rely exclusively on any of them, teaching instead that only those interpretations consistent with the teachings and values of the Qurʾān and *sunnah* could be considered. His teachings on *tawḥīd* and *shirk* spread as far as Indonesia, India, and West Africa, among other places. Finally, in what is today Nigeria, Usuman dan Fodio led a reformation movement, rejecting any rulings in *fiqh* that contradict the Qurʾān, sunnah, and *ijmāʿ* (consensus of legal scholars). These eighteenth-century movements established the necessary religious and legal foundations for nineteenth-century movements faced with colonial empires and pressures for modernization.

In the nineteenth century, calls for reform occurred within the context of modernization, as exemplified by the works of the scholar and activist Jamāl al-Dīn al- Afghānī, and published in the journal *al-Urwa al-Wuthqa*. The main center of reform, however, was early twentieth-century Egypt, where Muḥammad ʿAbduh and Rashīd Riḍā expanded on al-Afghānī's ideas, calling for modernization, expanded education, and emancipation, largely through Riḍā's journal, *Al-Manār*. Although a movement for reform had been founded earlier in Algeria by Amīr ʿAbd al-Qādir and supported in succession by ʿAbd al-Halim Ibn Simayah and Muḥammad Ibn al-Khudījah, major concentrated efforts toward reform began only after a 1903 visit by Muḥammad ʿAbduh. After formulation of the Association of Algerian Ulama in 1931, highly organized efforts of Islamic reformism were started. These efforts seemed to be compatible with those of earlier reformists, including Ibn ʿAbd al Wahhāb, al-Afghānī, Abduh, and Indian scholar, Muḥammad Iqbal. All of these reformists taught that the reason for the social degeneration of Muslims was related to ignoring the teachings of the Qurʾān. They particularly gave attention to the status of women, arguing for implementation of the rights guaranteed by the Qurʾān.

Education. Education for both women and men was one of the hallmarks of the eighteenth-century revival and reform movements. Dan Fodio specifically criticized the *ulamāʾ* for ignoring women's issues and focused his efforts on women's education. His educated daughters and sons carried on his mission. One of his daughters, Nana Asmaʾu, was a particularly renowned scholar and writer, who also translated her father's writings into local languages. She played a pivotal role in spreading the reform movement not only through her own teachings and writings, but also through her educational efforts among women, known as ʿYan Taru. Ibn ʿAbd al-Wahhāb preached a gender-balanced vision of society in which both women and men were to be educated as a matter of religious obligation. The donation of books as *awqāf* (charitable endowments) to schools to create libraries was a hallmark of eighteenth- and nineteenth-century Saudi women's support for education and literacy.

In the beginning of the nineteenth century, Muḥammad ʿAlī in Egypt introduced new employment and educational opportunities for women. By the end of the nineteenth century, upper-class Egyptian women had started organizing themselves into debate groups, discussing issues ranging from education to female seclusion, polygyny, veiling, and family law. They were supported, and sometimes inspired, by male reformers, including al-Afghānī, ʿAbduh, and, most importantly, Qāsim Amīn in Egypt. Amin denounced polygamy, called for women's emancipation, and emphasized the need for women's mental growth and intellectual enlightenment through education.

In India, Muslim reformers of the nineteenth century started efforts to introduce female education, restrict polygyny, and ensure women's rights under Islamic law. To promote modern education for Muslims, Sir Syed Ahmad Khan convened the Mohammedan Educational Conference in the 1870s. The majority of male participants were proponents of education and called for improved social status for women. However, progress in women's literacy was slow. By 1921, only four out of every one thousand Muslim women were literate. In 1937, the Muslim Personal Law restored inheritance of property rights.

The role and position of women in Ottoman society during this time served as a point of conflict between progressive and conservative parties. Between 1839 and 1876, major reforms took place in the fields of administration, legislation, and education. Although criticism of veiling, segregation, and polygyny had previously been deemed a violation of Islamic teachings, a more moderate approach gradually came into being. Emine Sniye and Fatma Aliye, the main supporters of this moderate view, contended in 1910 that reformation would be possible only through the education of women. After the collapse of the Ottoman Empire and the foundation of the modern secular state of Turkey by Mustafa Kemal Ataturk, coeducation became permitted in 1921. Rezā Shāh of Iran implemented the same measure.

In Afghanistan, under the rule of King Ammānullāh, employment and education were modernized. He proclaimed that modern education does not conflict with Islamic teachings and opened schools and introduced a study-abroad program for girls. His wife, Queen Soraya, encouraged women to contribute to nation-building and established the first women's hospital and school for girls in Afghanistan. As minister of education, she also arranged to send young women to Turkey for higher education in 1928. These initiatives were carried to the next step in 1965 with the formation of the Democratic Organization of Afghan Women, which focused on fighting against illiteracy, forced marriages, and the bride price.

Nevertheless, throughout the twentieth century, some leaders remained opposed to more public roles for women, considering their place to be in the home.

Family. During the eighteenth century, some reforms in the application of family law were supported by leaders of revival and reform movements. Although Shah Walī Allāh was in favor of polygyny, he nevertheless inclined more toward monogamy so as to protect women's rights. He further advocated that husbands should treat their wives with kindness and that dowers should be given to wives without any delay on marriage, as well as cheerfully. Ibn ʿAbd al-Wahhāb called for agency for both women and men in marriage and divorce, asserting that the Qurʾān teaches a balanced vision of rights between women and men—a vision that he recognized did not always exist in practice. He particularly supported the right of a woman to a voice in her marriage, the woman's right to stipulate conditions favorable to her in her marriage contract, and the woman's right to initiate divorce based on her recognition of her inability to continue in the marriage. Dan Fodio discouraged the practice of female circumcision, which was prevalent in the Sudan, Somalia, and his own country, declaring that this practice is neither necessary nor a part of Islam.

In 1880, in Afghanistan, ʿAbd al-Raḥmān Khān modified laws and gave the right of repudiation of marriage to girls by allowing the option of puberty (the option for a girl to accept or reject the marriage when she reaches puberty) in cases in which girls were married as minors. He also allowed women to initiate divorce based on nonpayment of maintenance or unkind behavior.

With regard to the unilateral male right to repudiation of marriage via *ṭalāq*, Indian courts initially considered it an unconditional right, although, over time, some limitations were introduced, based on the Qurʾān, uncodified Muslim legal traditions, and colonial precedent. During the colonial period, unilateral male repudiation was considered irrevocable. However, in 1905, the judgment in *Sarabai v. Rabiabai* 1905 declared that the irrevocability of the triple *ṭalāq* was "good in law, though bad in theology." The availability of unilateral male repudiation was criticized by some judges, although they continued to accept the practice because they believed that the Islamic tradition did not provide an alternative. The majority of Indian Muslims followed the Ḥanafī law school, so judges decided such cases according to rules of the Ḥanafī school, rather than using the method of *talfīq* , which permits borrowing from other schools of Islamic jurisprudence. Nevertheless, to frame reformist legislations in the Dissolution of Marriages Act of 1939, *talfīq* was used to adopt certain opinions from the Mālikī law school that granted women more rights.

In the Middle East, the codification of Muslim family law originated with the promulgation of the Ottoman Law of Family Rights (OLFR) 1917, accompanied by standardized procedures for the *Sharīʿah* Courts. Prior to this, issues related to Muslim Family Law were addressed by the predominant beliefs of the Islamic law school of the particular *qāḍī* (judge), which granted the judge great discretion in rulings. Some scholars have argued that the OLFR was precipitated by the difficulty women faced under the Ottoman-preferred Ḥanafī school in obtaining judicial divorce. The new Turkish state abandoned the Ottoman law in 1926 and adopted the Swiss civil code to administer family matters. The OLFR was applicable in Ottoman successor states that were founded at the end of World War I. Although the Egyptian government had not adopted OLFR, legislation issued in the 1920s and 1940s regarding family laws were similar to the laws adopted by other nations in that region. In the 1950s, codifications in Family Laws were published in Jordan, Syria, Tunisia, Morocco, and Iraq, sometimes introducing reforms. For example, the Syrian code introduced the provision of financial compensation for a wife who is divorced in distressing circumstances, thereby increasing the cost for a husband inclined to abuse his power of *ṭalāq*. Iraq amended its 1959 law in 1978, prohibiting forced marriage and adding penalties for anyone forcing someone into marriage.

With respect to polygyny, although the right of a man to have up to four wives is technically permitted by the Qurʾān, Islamic modernists noted that the Qurʾān also requires the man to treat all of those wives equally—something that the Qurʾān later asserts is not possible. Some reformists also noted a trend in the Qurʾān toward limiting polygyny, which suggested to some that the Qurʾānic intent was toward monogamy. In 1956, citing these grounds, Tunisia prohibited polygyny, granted the wife the option of filing for divorce on "reasonable grounds," and discouraged the practice of *ṭalāq* (divorce) without arbitration, as well as the *ʿiddah* (waiting period) that follows divorce. Tunisia further required that every divorce occur through a court, as well as revising custody laws.

Hijab and Seclusion. In the eighteenth century, during Dan Fodio's movement, two extremes could be found: women were either seen roaming in a waist cloth, or secluded in their houses. Dan Fodio worked to improve women's position and dignity in society and arranged regular lectures in various cities, with women and men in a separate seating arraignment. The main focus of his reforms was training of women. In India, Shah Walī Allāh, in his book *Hujjatullah e Al Baligha*, discussed various women's issues. He was in favor of veiling and female seclusion, although he did allow the outside activity of women in dire situations, provided they observed his understanding of the Islamic dress code. In Arabia, Ibn ʿAbd al-Wahhāb asserted the right of women to have access to the public sphere—for education, fulfillment of religious obligations, medical treatment, and engaging in business and commercial transactions, even in cases in which this would involve interaction with a non-*maḥram* (unrelated) male. With respect to prospective marriage partners, he recommended that the potential spouses be permitted to meet, albeit with a chaperone in place, to determine whether they were compatible, suggesting that absolute gender segregation was not inherent to the movement.

Overall, the veil became a political flashpoint because of its multiple symbols—representing oppression to some and liberation to others. Many upper- and middle-class women in Egypt, for example, had given up the veil as a sign of oppression during the colonial era, although some, such as Zaynab al-Ghazali, continued to call for the veil as an expression of modesty, piety, and loyalty to home and family. In Turkey, the veil was banned to highlight the new republic's commitment to secularism. In Iran, Rezā Shāh granted women the right to higher education abroad in 1925 and forbade veiling in 1936. Various Muslim women writers, women's organizations, and women's magazines addressed the question of the veil, along with other issues related to women's status and rights, particularly the harem and purdah. In Afghanistan, King Ammānullāh, under the influence of Maḥmūd Tarzi, abolished polygyny and veiling.

In Egypt, the issue of unveiling was dealt with gradually and was a focal point for feminist movements in the middle of the twentieth century. The change in attitudes toward working women could be noticed in the Constitution of 1956 and the Charter of 1962. The Constitution granted women the right to vote and hold elective political office. The charter provided for the women's participation in social and political affairs.

BIBLIOGRAPHY

Altwaijiri, Othman, Abdulaziz. "Islam Today: Women in Islam and Their Status in the Islamic Society." *Journal of the Islamic Educational, Scientific and Cultural Organization* 11.1 (1992): 15–24.

An-Naim, Abdullahi. "The Dichotomy between Religious and Secular Discourse in Islamic Societies." In *Faith and Freedom: Women's Human rights in the Muslim World,* edited by Mahnaz Afkhami, pp. 51–60. New York and London: I. B. Tauris, 1995.

Azim Abdul Islahi. "Shehu Uthman Dan Fodio and His Economic Ideas." http://mpra.ub.uni-muenchen.de/40916/. MPRA Paper No. 40916. Islamic Economics Institute, King Abdulaziz University, Jeddah, 2008.

Baden, Sally. "The Position of Women in Islamic Countries: Possibilities, Constraints, and Strategies for Change." Report prepared for the Special Programme WID, Netherlands Ministry of Foreign Affairs (DGIS), pp. 1–42. Brighton, U.K.: BRIDGE Institute of Development Studies, University of Sussex,September 1992.

Bridging World History. http://www.learner.org/courses/worldhistory/unit_video_17-3.html.

Dehalvi Wali Ullah Shah. *Hujjatullahe Al Baligha,* "Keeping Good Relation and Rights of Spouses" pp. 411–586. Translated by Maulana Abdur Rahim. Lahore, Punjab, Pakistan: Qaumi Kutub Khana, 1983.

DeLong-Bas, Natana J. *Wahhabi Islam: From Revival and Reform to Global Jihad.* New York: Oxford University Press, 2004.

Ehsan, Sara. *Role of Female in Society.* Rawalpindi, Punjab, Pakistan: Riphah Academy of Research and Education, 2010.

Encyclopedia of Islamic Civilization and Religion. Abingdon, U.K.: Routledge, 2008.

Esposito, John L. "Changing Role of Muslim Women, The." *Islam and the Modern Age* 7.1 (February 1976): 29–55.

Esposito, John L. "Women's Movements." In *The Oxford Encyclopedia of the Modern Islamic World.* New York: Oxford University Press, 1995: vol. 4, pp. 348–351.

Esposito, John L, with Natana J. DeLong-Bas. *Women in Muslim Family Law.* Syracuse, N.Y.: Syracuse University Press, 2001.

El Fadl Abou Khaled., "Islam and the Theology of Power." MER221 http://www.merip.org/author/khaled-abou-el-fadl.

Al-Faruqi, Lamya. "Women in a Qura'nic Society." *Islamic Order* 8.2 (1986): 73–84.

Al-Faruqi, Lamya. "Women's Rights and the Muslim Women." *Islam and the Modern Age* 3.2 (May 1997): 76–97.

Fatima, Dr. Samar. "Nature and Effects of the Islamic Attitude to Women." *Islamic Studies* 21.1 (1982): 105–121.

Ghadbian, Najib. "Islamists and Women in the Arab World: From Reaction To?" *The American Journal of Islamic Social Sciences* 12.1 (1995): 19–35.

Janawardena, Kumari. *Feminism and Nationalism in the Third World.* London: Zed Books, 1986.

Kandiyoti, Deniz. "Reflection on the Politics of Gender in Muslim Societies: From Nairobi to Beijing." In

Faith and Freedom: Women's Human Rights in the Muslim World, edited by Mahnaz Afkhami, pp. 19–31. New York and London: I. B. Tauris, 1995.

"Leading Ladies: Soraya Tarzi: The Afghan Queen." http://dawn.com/2012/01/29/leading-ladies-soraya-tarzi-the-afghan-queen/.

Masaud, F. Samar. "The Development of Women's Movements in the Muslim World." *Quarterly Journal of the Hamdard Islamicus* 8.1 (Spring 1985): 81–86.

Maumoon, Dunya. "Islamism and Gender Activism: Muslim Women's Quest for Autonomy." *Journal of Muslim Minority Affairs* 19.2. (1999): 269–284.

Mayer, Elizabeth, Ann. "Rhetorical Strategies and Official Policies on Women's Rights: The Merits and Drawbacks of the New World Hypocrisy." In *Faith and Freedom: Women's Human rights in the Muslim World*, edited by Mahnaz Afkhami, pp. 105–132. New York and London: I. B. Tauris, 1995.

Mernissi, Fatima. "Arab Women's Rights and the Muslim State in the Twenty-first Century: Reflection on Islam as Religion and State." In *Faith and Freedom: Women's Human Rights in the Muslim World*, edited by Mahnaz Afkhami, pp. 31–50. New York and London: I. B. Tauris, 1995.

Moghandam, M. Valentine. "Islamization, Women, and Cultural Relativism." In *Gender and National Identity: Women and Politics in Muslim Societies*, edited by M. Valentine Moghandam, pp. 90–191. Karachi: Oxford University Press, 1994.

Molyneux, Maxine. "Women's Right and Political Contingency: The Case of Yemen, 1990–1994." *The Middle East Journal* 49.3 (Summer 1995): 418–431.

"Shah Wali Ullah's Reform Movement." http://storyofpakistan.com/shah-wali-ullahs-reform-movement/.

Shah Waliullah Dehlavi. *Encyclopedia of World Biography*. http://www.encyclopedia.com/doc/1G2-2506300051.html.

"Shehu Usman dan Fodio (1754–1817) Islamic Reformer." http://www.turntoislam.com/forum/showthread.php?t=4022.

Sirman Nüket. *Turkish Feminism: A Short History*. http://www.wluml.org/node/260.

"The Status of Women and the Women's Movement." http://www.mongabay.com/history/pakistan/pakistan-the_status_of_women_and_the_women's_movement.html.

Subramanian, Narendra. "Legal Change and Gender Inequality: Changes in Muslim Family Lawin India." *Law & Social Inquiry* 33.3 (Summer 2008): 631–672.

El Tayeb Eldin Elzein Salah. "The Ulma and Islamic Renaissance in Algeria."*American Journal of Islamic Social Sciences* 6.2 (1989): 257, 288.

Tuppurainen, Johanna Anne. "Challenges Faced by Muslim Women: An Evaluation of the writings of Leila Ahmed, Elizabeth Fernea, Fatima Mernissi and Amina Wadud," P. 82. Ph.D. diss., University of South Africa, 2010.

Welchman Lynn. *Women and Muslim Family Laws in Arab States: A Comparative Overview of Textual Development and Advocacy*. Amsterdam: Amsterdam University Press, 2007. https://openaccess.leidenuniv.nl/bitstream/handle/1887/13374/Women%20and%20Muslim%20Family%20Laws%20in%20Arab%20States.pdf?sequence=1.

FARKHANDA ZIA MANSOOR
and NATANA J. DELONG-BAS

ISLAMIC BIOGRAPHICAL COLLECTIONS, WOMEN IN. Biographical collections of prominent Muslims, comprising entries for anywhere from seventy to twelve thousand individuals, are a unique Islamic literary genre. Hundreds, if not thousands, of works of this type were compiled from the ninth century CE to this day. The proportion of women included in the biographical collections, all of which were composed by learned Muslim men, ranges from less than 1 percent to 23 percent from the advent of Islam to the fifteenth century, and drops drastically in the subsequent centuries. The result is the concentration of information about thousands of Muslim women in certain key collections.

Prominent male scholars composed all of the Islamic biographical collections up to the late nineteenth century, so they provide us with an indication of which women and what qualities were deemed to be important. Where women's voices do appear, they are mediated by men. Women are not infrequently narrators of stories, beginning with episodes from the life of the Prophet Muḥammad and through other important events in Islamic history and culture. Women's voices are also heard through sacred and profane verse of their own composition.

The criteria for inclusion of women in Islamic biographical collections are varied. The female Companions of the Prophet Muḥammad—the women of his family, but also early female converts and other women who came into direct contact with him—are typically included, as are the next generation known as the female Successors—those who did not meet the Prophet himself, but one of his Companions. Although the number and proportion of women of this second generation is far lower than those of the female Companions, they include an interesting variety of sacred and profane roles. Most were transmitters of ḥadīth traditions from the Prophet, but some were legists in their own right, or ascetics, such as Hafsa bint Sirin. Others of the second generation were worldly and even notorious—royal women and slave singers. Through the centuries the most prominent women in the biographical collections were transmitters of knowledge, learned women, and scholars. These women studied with and taught men who were not their kin, raising challenging historical questions about the rules and customs of modesty and seclusion. Devout women represent a very large proportion of biographical dictionaries of Sufis. They not only mingled with men who were not family members, but were often actually aggressive in their spiritual superiority. The renowned Rābiʿah al-ʿAdawīyah admonished leading Ṣūfī masters, and the almost anonymous Bint Umm Hassan al-Asadiyya belittled the knowledge of another. Other roles of women in Islamic history deemed worthy of being memorialized by male Muslim scholars, albeit to a lesser extent, were women of the ruling elite, particularly those with political influence, philanthropists, poets, and singers.

The attitude toward women that emerges from these collections is multifaceted. The fact that leading male Muslim scholars memorialized women in their works—even if far below their proportion in the population—indicates that they did not view Islamic eminence as exclusively male. Moreover they recorded the achievements of women without undue gender-based comment. Thus the essential contributions of women to Islamic civilization were recognized. Nevertheless Muslim women's accomplishments appear to have been acknowledged generally when men of equal quality were not available. Also the standard of excellence was clearly male, and women may be referred to as "as good as men," or even "better than men," particularly in the spiritual sphere. In relating genealogy and kinship bonds, semi-matrilineal lineage may be cited in addition to patrilineal lines, indicating that ascriptive qualities may be transmitted through women as well as men. When strong, outspoken women are described, the portrayal may be interpreted in positive terms, but also as a warning to men of the danger they represent.

The impact of these works was to maintain the legitimacy of Muslim women engaging in approved endeavors and to warn of the dire consequences of women who overstepped the bounds of legitimacy, particularly in the realm of politics. Prominent women of the early Islamic centuries were archetypes, serving as role models for future generations. The men who collected information on large numbers of female transmitters of knowledge, learned women, and devout women probably did so for scholastic reasons, but they also documented a society in which women's contributions to crucial Islamic learning was valued and their spiritual achievements appreciated. The handful of biographies of Muslim women who attained roles normally regarded as male—warrior for Islam, expert in Islamic law, jurisconsult (mufti), de jure ruler—served as precedents for feminists to argue that there was no barrier to preclude women from these positions. Nusaybah bint Kaʿb fought to protect the Prophet, and Shajar al-Durr was sovereign of Egypt in the Middle Ages.

Beginning in the latter part of the nineteenth century a number of women began composing biographical collections of prominent women, most notably the Lebanese Zaynab Fawwāz and the Egyptian Qadriyya Husayn. Some of the titles of their works indicate a tie to existing Islamic biographical collections, but they seem to have been inspired by the female worthies genre, popular in the West as well. The earliest biographical collection of this type in Arabic was actually composed by a Christian woman of Syrian origin. But some female Muslim authors expanded the Islamic genre to include the lives of famous non-Muslim and even Western women. Collections of famous women of the Islamic world continue however to be popular to this day.

Bibliography

Booth, Marilyn. *May Her Likes Be Multiplied: Biography and Gender Politics in Egypt*. Berkeley: University of California Press, 2001. A study of women's biographies in late nineteenth- and early twentieth-century Egypt in biographical collections and in the press.

Ibn Saʿd, Muhammad. *Kitāb al-tabaqāt al-kubra* [Book of Generations]. Edited by Ihsan al-ʿAbbas. 9 vols. Beirut, 1960–1968. The earliest extant Islamic biographical dictionary contains a section devoted to women.

Roded, Ruth. *Women in Islamic Biographical Collections: From Ibn Saʿd to Who's Who*. Boulder, Colo., and London: Lynne Reinner, 1994.

Sulamī, Muhammad ibn al-Husayn. *Early Sufi Women: Dhikr an-niswa al-mutaʿabbidat as-Sūfiyyat by Abū ʿAbd ar-Rahman as-Sulamī*. Edited and translated by Rkia Elaroui Cornell. Louisville, Ky.: Fons Vitae, 1999. The section on women from the earliest extant dictionary of Sufis compiled in the eleventh century.

Ruth Roded

Islamic Literature.

[*This entry contains two subentries,*

Contemporary *and*

Historical.]

Contemporary

Islam and literature have been in conjunction with each other since the time of the Prophet Muḥammad. The term "Islamic literature," or "*adab Islami*," to use its Arabic appellation, however, involves a specific kind of relationship between Islam and literature in contemporary times. It refers to a specific body of literature that emerged synchronously with the rise of contemporary Islamic movements in the 1970s and 1980s. It is, as noted by Malti-Douglas, part of "a parallel Islamic literary body that encompasses all genres hitherto promulgated by more secularly-minded intellectuals: plays, novels, short story and poetry. As such, it sits alongside the more canonical secular literary tradition and functions in a dialectic way with it" (Malti-Douglas, 2001, pp. 5–6). What is distinctive about contemporary cultural production labeled Islamic literature, in other words, is that it differentiates itself from secular literature with its clear Islamic stance. Its defenders consider Islamic literature a new form of committed literature with the aim of propagating an Islamic vision of the world.

Islamic writers in the Turkish context identify Islamic literature as a literature deriving from Muslim imagery. The post-revolutionary government in Iran considers literature not as "a mere source of aesthetic enjoyment... but as an effective means of politicizing, educating and inspiring" (Milani, 1992, p. 232). The Islamic Writers Alliance, a professional Muslim organization based in the United States, on the other hand, while defining Islamic fiction produced in English, underlines its committed stance as such: Islamic fiction refers to "creative, imaginative and non-preachy fiction books written by Muslims and marketed primarily to Muslims.... Islamic fiction authors intend for readers to learn something positive about Islam when they read Islamic fiction stories" (Islamic Fiction Books). These somewhat similar responses deriving from various contexts indicate that Islamic literary products can be apprehended in the context of contemporary transnational Islamic revivalism in Muslim and Western contexts.

Contemporary Islamism, as a social movement, refers to a new awareness positing that Islam is not a mere theological phenomenon, but a political ideology that imposes rules and regulations for all spheres of life including artistic and literary fields. What characterizes this new awareness is its critical stance toward what Islamic authors call the secular Western modernity and its search for creating an alternative frame of reference. Such a search led Islamic writers not only to employ classical forms like poetry, but also to adopt modern literary genres, such as the novel, to narrate Islam to the masses. It should be noted that the novel has traditionally been perceived in a negative way in Islamic circles. It has long been construed as having a destructive impact on communitarian morality since it exposed individual private lives and immoral scenes. However, in the context of Islamic revitalization, the novel was appropriated as a genre to convey Islamic messages and imagine an Islamic order. As a result a specific kind of Islamic literary narrative fictionalizing an ideal Islamic order emerged in various Muslim contexts ranging from Egypt to Turkey. Some intellectual and literary figures, such as Najib al-Kilani in Egypt, published introductory works on the concept of Islamic literature, whose translation to other languages provided a ground for developing cultural products under the label "*adab Islami*." Through literary journals and almanacs Islamic authors attempted to form connections with literary works from other Muslim contexts in accordance with the bounded universalism of Islamic discourse.

It should be noted that the dominant voices in early periods of Islamic movements were male actors of Islamism. In the Turkish context, for instance, the intellectual sphere was dominated by male actors who gave lectures, published books, and discussed religious issues in the public sphere in the 1980s. The emergence of the Islamic literary sphere, however, seems to have opened a channel for women to express their views. All of the few outstanding female Islamists, such as Emine Şenlikoğlu and Sevim Asımgil, were active in the literary field as novelists or short story writers. Women reflected upon social and political matters and transmitted their messages through literary narratives, rather than "intellectual" books in the 1980s. This is also true for the Iranian context where the post-revolutionary period witnessed an incredible increase in women's fiction writing.

Islamic literary fiction published by women can be categorized into two groups. The early period, mostly the 1980s and 1990s, was dominated with narratives conveying similar Islamic messages to people. The period beginning with the-mid 1990s, however, witnessed the publication of self-critical narratives in which women authors take a critical stance toward their own Islamic communities and practices. The novels written by Islamic women in the early period, indeed, do not differ from, but rather share a common discourse with, those of males since Islamic groups in those years voiced a collectivist discourse that placed an emphasis on collective harmony. Islamic cultural products did not portray conflicting representations between genders. These narratives published by both male and female writers, in the Turkish context, were categorized under the title of "salvation novels," a self-description emerging from Islamic circles.

Salvation novels formed a coherent genre with identical narrative structures. And with their easily read popular forms, many became best sellers in Islamic circles in the 1980s and 1990s.

Salvation novels are characterized by their message-bearing narratives in which Islam is presented as the only solution to the problems of the modern world. These novels' central plots are based on the struggle between Islamic and secular (or Western, sometimes Christian) worldviews. The Islamic stance is mostly represented by "stable" male characters. Typically, "degenerate westernized" characters, on the other hand, usually appear as female figures. The representation of female figures holds a central position in these novels and serves several functions for novelists. Through the encounter of these depressed female protagonists with Islamic male figures, novelists convey their messages on the role of women in Islam and their criticisms toward modernity and secular order. The portrayal of women, at the beginning of the narrative, as depressed or wretched characters allows novelists to criticize the modern secular order via women. These women are depressed since, as a novelist writes, they live according to the "necessities of modernity" represented as drinking, flirting, dancing, and enjoying "immoral" love affairs. In the course of the narrative, female characters are made to encounter and fall in love with Islamic male protagonists. This encounter and love affair marks a turning point for female characters who begin to question their lifestyles and to learn more about the Islamic way of life. In the course of the narrative all the female characters are led to salvation, represented by their adoption of a headscarf. They are then turned into Islamic activists seeking collective salvation. All novels end up with a "happy ending" represented by the salvation (Islamization) of all characters.

The female characters' adoption of Islamic identity and veiling not only signifies the individual stories of transformation, but also women's dress code, as novelists commonly portray, is framed in terms of the morality of general society. Women in the Islamic vision of the world express both what an ideal Islamic society fears (i.e., disorder, *fitnah*) and needs (order). Women are usually perceived as the source of *fitnah* with their unveiled outlook and potential to seduce men. Hence, veiling of female characters is represented as a major moral remedy to *fitnah* and degeneracy brought about by modern secularism for Islamic writers. Islamic salvation novels, in this regard, function as educational material as much as artistic products. Research shows that these novels are widely read among girls who are students in Qur'ān courses, *imam hatip* schools (religious high schools), and university youth. Students note that these novels were given to them by their fathers and brothers. Fatma Karabıyık Barbarosoğlu, a novelist in Islamic circles, points out that Islamic novels present those girls living an enclosed circles with an important "public sphere experience." This suggests that young readers come across characters that they would never be in contact with otherwise and internalize the answers developed by Islamist protagonists on controversial issues such as polygamy in Islam and the position of women in modern times.

To develop their Islamic position, novelists engage in a discursive struggle with different ideologies and religions ranging from socialism, liberalism, secularism, and feminism to Christianity. Salvation novelists in the Turkish context, for instance, have a homogenous perception of feminists. They attribute several qualities to feminists such as "being slaves of fashion" or turning into a commodity in the name of modernity. *Musluman Kadının Adı Var* (The Muslim Woman Has a Name) by the 1980s female-salvation novelist, Şerife Katırcı Turhal, is indicative of Islamic novelists' desire to respond to feminists and develop an Islamic vision. This book signifies a reply to the well-known Turkish liberal feminist Duygu Asena's book *Kadının Adı Yok* (The Woman Has No Name) in which she takes a critical stance toward the unequal position of women in modern society. Turhal, on the other hand, through the mouth of her pious female character, argues that women have a strong status in Islam and shares a complementary and harmonious position with men: "Those who say that 'the woman has no name' refer only to the woman who is annihilated in the world in which they have produced.... Muslim women have always been there.... They have always stood shoulder to shoulder with men" (Turhal, 1999, pp. 157–160).

This collectivist Islamic discourse and the harmonious narratives of salvation novels have begun to be challenged, however, by a young generation of Muslim writers of the mid-1990s. While the writers of salvation novels were born in the 1940s and were members of newly urbanized classes, this younger generation of Islamic writers was born in the 1960s and has acquired university education and modern professions. The novels published by these women can be categorized under the title of self-exposing and self-critical novels. Narratives of these new novels sharply differ from salvation novels. While salvation novels depict Muslims as a homogeneous collectivity and narrate the struggle and victory of Muslim agents against a "decadent" secular order, the new novels portray Muslims with internal conflicts and contrasting desires, torn between their religious ideals and more worldly concerns in the face of modern urban relations. In other words, they make the inner conflicts of Islamic identities and conflict within the group visible. In terms of sheer numbers, self-critical novels are difficult to compare to the salvation novels of the 1980s. Yet these novels seem to be based on a common narrative with their Muslim protagonists who are portrayed as squeezed between their Islamist ideals of the 1980s and their new life experiences in the context of the 2000s.

The period beginning with the mid-1990s in the Turkish context has witnessed the success of Islamic groups in the economy and politics. Islamic groups have benefited from liberalizing policies and begun to form their own middle classes. In brief, status and settings of Islamic actors were transformed in the new period. It is in such a context that new professions, market forces, and desires led to the emergence of new narratives. The collective harmony of salvation novels was mostly challenged by disappointed Muslim female actors. New self-critical narratives voiced the frustrations of head-covered women who had modern professions but had little input in public life. Several female novelists created characters that are educated but frustrated head-scarved housewives, directing their criticisms toward male actors and Islamic groups who become insensitive to their situation. These new female protagonists are critical of secularists who discriminate against Muslim women because of their headscarves. They also take a critical stance toward the roles that collective Islamism attributes to women. The female protagonist of Halime Toros's *Halkaların Ezgisi* (The Melody of the Circles), Nisa, for instance, resists the framing of women in Islamist politics that posits that women need to be modest since otherwise they contribute to disorder (*fitnah*). She critically notes that such an Islamic understanding grants "rights to men" and "responsibilities for women." These new novels do not signify a resignation from Muslim identity, but, rather, a search for developing an Islamic self. In the context of changing conditions, Islamic characters are no longer so sure of the virtues of the collective Islamic identity to which they were once committed. The narrative form of the novel allows them to revise life histories and develop a coherent self in the face of changing social relations.

BIBLIOGRAPHY

Aktaş, Cihan. *Üç İhtilal Çocuğu*. İstanbul: Nehir, 1991.
Çayır, Kenan. *Islamic Literature in Contemporary Turkey: From Epic to Novel*. New York: Palgrave Macmillan, 2007.
Göle, Nilüfer. *The Forbidden Modern: Civilization and Veiling*. Ann Arbor: University of Michigan Press, 1996.
Islamic Fiction Books. http://www.islamicfictionbooks.com/index.html.
Malti-Douglas, Fedwa. *Medicines of the Soul: Female Bodies and Sacred Geographies in a Transnational Islam*. Berkeley: University of California Press, 2001.
Milani, Farzaneh. *Veils and Words: Emerging Voices of Iranian Women Writers*. Syracuse, N.Y.: Syracuse University Press, 1992.
Şişman, Nazife. *Kamusal Alanda Başörtülüler: Fatma Karabıyık Barbarosoğlu ile söyleşi*. İstanbul: İz Yayincilik, 2001.
Szyka, Christian. "On Utopian Writing in Nasserist Prison and Laicist Turkey." *Die Welt des Islams* 35, no. 1 (1995): 95–125.
Toros, Halime. *Halkaların Ezgisi*. İstanbul: Kırkambar yayınları, 1997.
Turhal, Şerife Katırcı. *Müslüman Kadının Adı Var*. İstanbul: Adese, 1999.

KENAN ÇAYIR

HISTORICAL

Islamic literature may be defined as written works that were initiated by or uniquely connected to the religion and civilization of Islam. Foremost among these are the Qurʾān, compilations of words and deeds of the Prophet (ḥadīth), biographies of the Prophet Muḥammad (*sīrah*), biographical collections of great Muslims, historical chronicles, Qurʾānic exegesis (*tafsīr*), and others.

The vast majority of these works were composed by men, although women were frequently cited as sources. This gendered bias as well as the overall purpose of these works determined the quantity and quality of references to women and the attitude toward them in each genre. In referring to women, male Muslim writers reflected the patriarchal societies in which they lived, much like the men who dominated other literary traditions. Women's voices do appear to some extent in Islamic literature, albeit mediated by men, as narrators of stories and historical and cultural events. Women's voices are also heard in sacred and profane verse of their own composition interposed in these works.

The attitude toward women in Islamic literature has generally been as spiritual and legal persons, but socially subaltern and dependent. Women are often regarded as needing protection from men. Strong women may be portrayed as a danger to men and broader society. Moreover "woman" is often a metaphor for weakness. Nevertheless minority voices that differed from the mainstream view of women were also preserved.

Over the centuries canonical works were learned by heart, expanded, and amplified. Women appear to have had a minor role in the historical development of Islamic literature, and even today, after more than a century of feminism in the Muslim world, male literati still dominate. Nevertheless from the nineteenth through the twentieth centuries, women, feminists, and gender activists have had a growing involvement in Islamic literature.

The Qurʾān. The Qurʾān is regarded by Muslims as divine, eternal, and universal. The meaning of the Qurʾān however has been interpreted largely by men functioning in patriarchal societies. In the Qurʾān only one woman is actually named (Maryam), although a large number of verses refer to women. Numerous verses are gender-related, including exhortations addressed to the believing men and the believing women, revelations specific to women or to relations between men and women, and laws pertinent to marriage, illicit sexual relations, divorce, and inheritance.

Spiritually women and men are regarded in the Qurʾān for the most part as equal in the eyes of God, and they have similar religious duties (33:35). Symbolically woman is often interpreted as weak, flawed, or passive. Socially women's position is depicted overall ambivalently. Preference for the birth of a son over that of a daughter is a sin (16:58–59), and the burying alive of a girl-child is specifically mentioned as evil (81:8–9), but women have less power in such social matters as marriage and acting as a witness and receive a smaller portion of inheritance than men. Some contemporary scholars have challenged these presentations as being linked to a specific patriarchal context, rather than necessarily implying permanent divine intent. Similarly, although a Qurʾānic phrase has been widely quoted throughout the centuries to support the superiority of men over women (4:34), the interpretation of this verse is the matter of much debate today.

The impact of the Qurʾān on women's lives has been manifest in family and criminal laws, in gender roles depicted in Qurʾānic stories, and in gender norms. For these reasons Muslim liberals, women, and feminists have engaged in reinterpreting and translating the sacred text with an eye to eliciting more equitable gender messages.

Biographies of the Prophet Muḥammad. The earliest extant biography (*sīrah*) of the Prophet Muḥammad was produced by Ibn Isḥāq two centuries after Muḥammad's death, in Baghdad, the imperial and cultural capital of a patriarchal society. It has come down to us in the version of Ibn Hishām. This classical genre comprised relatively little on women compared to other Islamic sources on the Prophet because its focus was on battles led by Muhammad, rather than his legal judgments or normative behavior.

The impact of the dramatic biographies of the Prophet on women lies primarily in the virtuous or evil female role models they project. Women feature prominently only in the battle of Uḥud, where Muslim and pagan women play a variety of auxiliary roles similar to those described in tales of pre-Islamic tribal warfare, generally appearing as daughters, wives, sisters, and mothers of the combatants. Although they very rarely engaged in combat, the "woman warrior" was nevertheless present, portrayed positively in cases where she fought to defend the faith or Muslim community, such as Nusaybah bint Kaʿb, who served as a human shield, protecting the Prophet during the Battle of Uḥud, and negatively in cases where she opposed the Muslims or sought to defile them after death, such as in the case of Hind bint Utbah, who exalted in the defeat of the Muslims at Uḥud and bit the liver of Muḥammad's uncle Ḥamzah, who had been killed in battle.

Over the centuries numerous biographies of the Prophet have been produced by Muslim and non-Muslim men, encompassing materials on Muḥammad's life story beyond the military. The first woman to write about the Prophet's life was the Orientalist Nabia Abbott (1942). The first Muslim woman was ʿAʾisha ʿAbd al-Raḥmān (1959). The feminist Assia Djebar wrote a novel about this period (1991), and the Islamist Nadia Yassine posted vignettes from the life of Muḥammad on her website (2010).

Compilations of Words and Deeds of the Prophet (ḥadīth). The words and deeds of the Prophet were rigorously critiqued and compiled by male scholars at the height of the Abbasid Empire centered in Baghdad, at the time of the coalescence of Islamic culture. Women played a quantitatively and qualitatively significant role as primary transmitters of these Prophetic traditions. ʿĀʾishah, Muhammad's favorite wife, related 1,210 ḥadīths, and some 1,000 other female Companions of the Prophet composed 17 percent of the trustworthy transmitters of the first generation. From the second generation the number and proportion of women transmitters dropped sharply, although they did not disappear completely. Moreover when compilations were transmitted, women were not excluded from this scholarly endeavor.

Ḥadīth compilations contain much information relevant to women. Of special interest for gender issues are the books of prayer and *ḥajj* pilgrimage—related to the purity of men and women—as well as the books of marriage, divorce, and other family matters. But ḥadīth with implications for women may be found throughout these rich compilations.

Although there are sayings attributed to the Prophet with positive attitudes toward women, there are also some extremely misogynist ḥadīths, particularly those narrated by Abū Hurayrah. Overall the gender messages seem varied. Because the ḥadīth have such a tremendous impact on women's lives as a source of law and normative practices, the reliability of certain canonical Muslim ḥadīth scholars has been challenged by some Islamic feminists in recent years, beginning with Fatima Mernissi.

Biographical Collections of Great Muslims. Islamic biographical collections were compiled from the ninth century CE to this day by scholarly Muslim men in various patriarchal societies. The proportion of women included in the biographical collections ranges from less than 1 percent to 23 percent from the advent of Islam to the fifteenth century and then drops drastically. Thus information about hundreds and thousands of Muslim women is conveniently concentrated in biographical entries. Women's voices do appear in the biographical entries—albeit mediated by men—in narratives of historical events, as well as sacred and profane verse.

The women included in the Islamic biographical collections were first and foremost the female Companions of the Prophet Muḥammad, the second generation of female Successors who were engaged in both sanctified and irreverent endeavors, and transmitters of ḥadīth and other knowledge. Others were learned women and scholars, Ṣūfīs, women of the ruling elite, philanthropists, poets, and singers.

The essential contributions of women to Islamic civilization were recognized in these collections, although Muslim women's accomplishments appear to have been acknowledged only when men of equal quality were not available. Descriptions of strong, outspoken women may be interpreted positively, but also as a warning to men of the danger they represent.

These works sustained the legitimacy of Muslim women engaging in Islamically approved endeavors, and provided female role models for future generations. They documented a society in which women's contributions to crucial Islamic learning was valued and their spiritual achievements appreciated. The handful of biographies of Muslim women who attained "men's" roles—warrior for Islam, expert in Islamic law, jurisconsult (*mufti*), de jure ruler—served as precedents for feminists.

From the latter part of the nineteenth century, a number of women in Egypt began composing biographical collections of prominent women. They expanded the Islamic genre to include the lives of famous non-Muslim and even Western women, such as Cleopatra and Joan of Arc. Collections of famous women of the Islamic world continue to be popular to this day.

Historical Chronicles. The historical chronicle appeared in the Islamic world in the ninth century CE, encompassing events from ancient times to the lifetime of the author. Compilation of historical material on the classical periods of Islam reached its culmination in al-Ṭabarī's *History of Prophets and Kings*. Subsequent Muslim historians continued his annalistic descriptions of events to their time. Historical chronicles contain short, infrequent, and scattered references to women, but place women's activities in the context of political, social, and religious history deemed important by the great Muslim chroniclers.

The royal women who appear in the chronicles are generally mothers, concubines, and wives who were said to have great influence over the ruler. The power of these women was described as a function of the weakness of the ruler and was usually depicted as being used for corrupt purposes. These women often became infamous in the context of the selection of an heir to the ruler, particularly after his death. At the same time royal women were also recognized for their major charitable works and majestic celebrations of life-cycle events.

On the one hand, tales of evil, corrupt royal women were regarded as evidence of the harm that befalls polity and society when the natural patriarchal state of affairs is upset. On the other hand, charitable acts of female relatives of the ruler served as models for future generations of Muslim women. From the late nineteenth century Muslim feminists have reclaimed some of these powerful women documented in the historical chronicles.

Exegesis of the Qur'ān (*tafsīr*). Classical interpretation of the Qur'ān is dated to the ninth century CE when Islamic urban culture reached a high point. The men who composed *tafsīr* were undoubtedly influenced by this patriarchal society. The genre matured in an abundance of works composed by men up to the fifteenth century. Although the life experience and gender norms of these men clearly influenced their understanding of women in the Qur'ān, their work has not yet been systematically studied from this perspective. The quantity and organization of references to women in Qur'ānic exegesis to some extent follow traditionally accepted gender messages in the sacred text.

Women are referred to in the *tafsīr* in elaboration of tales about pre-Islamic female heroes. Muslim women appear in narratives describing the circumstance of revelation of verses aimed to explicate their meaning. The ramifications of Qur'ānic gender laws and customs are often explained by interpretation.

The attitude toward women in Qur'ānic exegesis often seems to be rather negative. Pre-Islamic female heroes are portrayed as worse than their image in the Qur'ān. Narratives about women in Muḥammad's life depict them as childish, petty, and jealous, in contrast to the stark text of the Qur'ān. Legal and customary material is explicated and expanded, often restricting women more than is justified by the original text.

The impact of Qur'ānic exegesis on the lives of women may be even greater than that of the Qur'ān itself, since most Muslims understand the sacred book through its interpretation. The first woman to undertake *tafsīr* of the Qur'ān, ʿA'isha ʿAbd al-Raḥmān, avoided verses with social implications, although more contemporary Islamic feminists have reinterpreted the Qur'ānic text with an eye to unearth its egalitarian message.

Fundamentals, Norms, and Models. The literary works described above are fundamental sources of Islamic religion, history and culture, and Muslims return to them to this day. Some other types of Islamic literature are: tales of the pre-Islamic prophets, a large variety of legal works, and Ṣūfī prose and poetry. This Islamic literature documents the gender norms of previous centuries and provides role models for Muslim women. It served as the underpinning of Islamic patriarchy, but it also contains material that is being reclaimed by Islamic feminists.

BIBLIOGRAPHY

Primary Works

Al Tafsir. http://www.altafsir.com/.

Bukhari, Muhammad ibn Isma'il. *The Translation of the Meanings of Sahih al-Bukhari: Arabic-English.*

Translated by M. Muhsin Khan. 9 vols. Medina: Islamic University, 1973–1976. http://www.searchtruth.com/hadith_books.php.
Ibn Hishām, ʿAbd al-Malik. *Al-Sira al-nabawiyya li-Ibn Hisham*. Edited by M. al-Saqaʾ et al. Beirut: Dar al-Khayr, 1990.
Ibn Hishām, ʿAbd al-Malik. *The Life of Muhammad: A Translation of Ishāq's Sīrat rasūl Allah*. Translated by A. Guillaume. Oxford: Oxford University Press, 1955.
Ibn Saʿd, Muhammad. *Kitāb al-tabaqāt al-kubra* [The Book of Generations]. Edited by Ihsan al-ʿAbbas. 9 vols. Beirut: Dâr Sâdir, 1960–1968.
Qurʾān. http://quran.com/.
Tabari, Muhammad Ibn Jarir. *The History of al-Tabari*. Various translators. Albany: State University of New York Press, 1989–.

Secondary Works

Merguerian, Gayane Karen, and Najmabadi, Afsaneh. "Zulaykha and Yusuf: Whose 'Best Story'?" *International Journal of Middle East Studies* 29 (1997): 485–508.
Mernissi, Fatima. *The Veil and the Male Elite: A Feminist Interpretation of Women's Rights in Islam*. Translated by Mary Jo Lakeland. Reading, Mass.: Addison-Wesley Publishing Company, 1991.
Peirce, Leslie P. *The Imperial Harem: Women and Sovereignty in the Ottoman Empire*. New York: Oxford University Press, 1993.
Smith, Jane I., and Yvonne Yazbeck Haddad. "Eve: Islamic Image of Woman." *Women's Studies International Forum* 5 (1982): 135–144.
Stowasser, Barbara Freyer. *Women in the Qur'an, Traditions, and Interpretation*. Oxford University Press, 1994.

RUTH RODED

ISLAMIC SOCIETY OF NORTH AMERICA.

Women's involvement in the Islamic Society of North America (ISNA) is one of working behind the scenes and gradually acquiring public visibility. Although all office holders were men for more than thirty years, women were deeply involved in founding and maintaining ISNA from the beginning. Women's contributions were generally not recorded in official documents, so women rarely received public recognition for their contributions, particularly as volunteers.

ISNA's story begins with the founding of the Muslim Student Association of the U.S. and Canada (MSA) in 1963, which brought the few and scattered Muslim student campus groups together into a single umbrella organization, better to serve their needs. The MSA grew quickly, especially after the U.S. and Canada relaxed their racist immigration laws, resulting in Muslim immigration from all over the world. The MSA began as an organization focused on the needs of students, finding prayer space, worrying about halal food, and addressing other spiritual needs related to living as a tiny minority in a non-Muslim country. Many of these students ended up staying in their new countries, marrying, and having children. After graduation they realized the MSA could no longer meet all their needs. In 1983 a new umbrella group—the Islamic Society of North America—was created and placed in a "parent" position to the original MSA. Under the first president, Ilyas Ba-Yunus, most of the resources and activism were transferred to ISNA. The MSA was later reinvigorated under the leadership of Ghulam Nabi Fai in 1985.

While men were elected to official positions, women attended meetings as secretaries. These women were most often wives of the students, although there were a few women students. While the men were busy with their studies, the women did the important yet mundane work required for an organization to exist and grow: writing and answering letters; filling envelopes; taking minutes; and preparing meals. The now enormous bazaar attached to the annual ISNA conference was initiated in 1968 by MSA women, Zeba Siddiqui, Nishat Balbale, and others, to raise funds. They made and sold clothing and other handicrafts, as well as hosting a garage sale with used items donated from members.

Like their Western counterparts of the 1960s and 1970s, Muslim women realized that serving as auxiliaries in organizations committed to social justice and equality was not enough to address issues they considered important, so they slowly asserted themselves and moved into positions of leadership. Frustrated with the lack of women's representation at the highest levels, Shareefa Alkhateeb and other women founded the Muslim Women's Auxiliary Committee in 1968. Along with Ilham Altalib, Freda Shamma, Khadija Haffajee, and others, they pressed for more inclusion of women as conference speakers and executive members. They also organized women's events at MSA/ISNA conferences, as well as meetings, seminars, lectures, weekend schools, and children's camps.

Although in the early years of the MSA custom and religious interpretation barred women from holding leadership positions, the pressure of some women, the support of some men, such as Sheikh Abdalla Idris Ali (president, 1992–1997), Jamal Badawi (board member), and Sheikh Muhammed Nur Abdullah (president, 2001–2005), and their understanding that Islam allowed women's leadership, brought change. Khadija Haffajee, the first woman elected to the ISNA executive board in 1997, both reflected this now dominant understanding and paved the way for women's representation on the executive board by socializing her male colleagues into accepting a more visible public presence for women. In 2006 Ingrid Mattson, a Canadian convert, was elected by ISNA's general membership as ISNA's first female president. She had been elected the first female vice president in 2001. Although Salafī organizations criticized this as "un-Islamic," Mattson was reelected for a second term.

BIBLIOGRAPHY

Abdullah, Omer Bin. "Building a Community: A Student Action." *Islamic Horizons*, July–August 2003, pp. 42–53.

Ali, S. "Building a Women's Movement." *Islamic Horizons*, May–June 2003, pp. 16–24.

Ba-Yunus, Ilyas. "An American Journey: Graduating from MSA to ISNA." *Islamic Horizons*, September–October 2003, pp. 40–49.

Enayatulla, Sabrina. "The New MSA: Empowered to Serve Students." *Islamic Horizons*, November–December 2003, pp. 38–45.

Haffajee, Khadija. Interview with author, May 10, 2012.

Haffajee, Khadija. "Rawahil." In *Muslim Women Activists in North America: Speaking for Ourselves*, edited by Katherine Bullock, pp. 79–88. Austin: University of Texas Press, 2005.

Idris Ali, Abdalla. Interview with author, May 8 and 28, 2012.

Shamma, Freda. "Muslim Activist: Mother and Educator." In *Muslim Women Activists in North America: Speaking for Ourselves*, edited by Katherine Bullock, pp. 165–175. Austin: University of Texas Press, 2005.

Katherine Bullock

Israel. Located on the southeastern coast of the Mediterranean, the State of Israel was established in 1948 and is bordered by Lebanon to the north, Syria to the northeast, Jordan to the east, and Egypt to the southwest. The Palestinian territories of Gaza and the West Bank lie to the south-west and east, respectively. East Jerusalem and the Old City, within whose walls lie religious sites of great significance to the world's Jewish, Christian, and Muslim communities, have been under Israel's control since 1967, though not without controversy. The status of the Arab population in Israel is a fiercely debated one, such that even the nomenclature used to describe it is contested between greater emphases on the Israeli or Palestinian dimensions of identity (ICG, 2012). Arabs, divided between the majority Muslim and smaller Christian and Druze communities, are estimated to make up just over 20 percent of the country's total population of nearly 8 million. Figures issued by Israel's Central Bureau of Statistics in 2012 put the total Muslim population in the country at 1.354 million, the majority based in the north of the country and one-fifth of whom are concentrated in the city of Jerusalem. Seventy percent describe themselves as either religious or very religious, but among women this rate rises to 80 percent. Muslims are generally exempt from military conscription, though some, particularly from the Bedouin community, do enlist and serve in the Israel Defense Forces (IDF).

The data underscore some of the gaps facing Muslim women, not only relative to the Jewish population but also in comparison to the Christian and Druze communities. For example, the employment rate of 18.9 percent among Muslim women in 2011 is one-third that of Jewish women (58.9 percent), less than half that of Christian women (47.4 percent), and trails Druze women (23 percent). Among Muslim men, the rate is just over 60 percent. In the sphere of higher education, Muslims composed 7.7 percent of all students, within which women represented a majority in bachelor's and master's degrees, but just under 38 percent of doctoral students (CBS data). The first Muslim woman in the 120-seat Israeli parliament (Knesset) was Hussniya Jabara, elected in 1999 as a candidate for the Meretz Party. In the Eighteenth Knesset term, there was a sole Arab, Hanin Zoabi of the National Democratic Assembly (Balad), among the twenty-three female Knesset members who, in turn, make up less than a fifth of all parliamentarians.

The challenges faced by Muslim women in Israel has been described as one of "compound discrimination"—as women, as Arabs, and as Muslims. At one level, the Arab population as a whole faces significant political and economic inequalities that some consider to represent a form of "second-class citizenship." The U.S. State Department's Country Reports on Human Rights Practices (2012), for example, notes that "Arab citizens of the country faced institutional and societal discrimination." The 2003 report of Israel's Orr Commission, which found that "government handling of the Arab sector has been primarily neglectful and discriminatory," called for steps toward remedying the gaps. Particularly difficult is the situation of the Bedouin population, found mainly in the south of the country, where indicators on issues such as unemployment, education, health, and services are especially poor. The state has announced a number of initiatives in recent years aimed at investment and development in spheres such as education, though the extent to which such programmes are successful in addressing concerns remains to be seen.

In addition to these broader inequalities, there are the specific community-based challenges for Arab and Muslim women arising from issues such as patriarchy. For example, "The Future Vision of the Palestinian Arabs in Israel," a report published in 2006 by the National Committee for the Heads of Arab Local Authorities in Israel with the input of dozens of leading Arab activists and scholars, noted that "patriarchy is still the dominant quality in the Palestinian Arab family, even within families with two educated parents. The inferiority of women is the outcome of the patriarchal society." This in turn highlights debates about the relationship between customs and norms within the Muslim community and the state. In other words, although some argue that the rights and opportunities available to Muslim women in Israel is higher relative to other countries, not least in comparison to states within the Middle East, others contend that the state's policies vis-a-vis the Arab population, and, by extension, the female Muslim population, do not sufficiently address, and may even compound, existing problems. Although there has been a decline in birth rates among Muslim women in recent years, from 4.7 in 2000 to 3.5 in 2011, this remains higher than other religious communities, both Arab (2.0 among Christians and 2.3 among Druze) and

Jewish (3.0). At the legal level, Israel's judicial system has secular as well as religious courts, with the latter including Muslim *Sharīʿah* courts. The *Sharīʿah* courts deal with personal status issues, such as marriage, though they have been critiqued by feminist organizations. Polygamy is banned in Israel; however, within the Bedouin community, in particular, it is estimated that between one in five and one in three marriages is polygamous.

Both locally and through broader international networks and agencies, there are a growing number of civil society organizations in Israel that are active on the issue of women's rights in general, as well as those of Arab and Muslim women in particular. Their activities include raising awareness, legal assistance, and health services. Fourteen of the nongovernmental organizations (NGOs), including Adalah—The Legal Center for Arab Minority Rights in Israel, Kayan-Feminist Organization, and the Mossawa Center for the Rights of Arab Citizens of Israel, have contributed to the Working Group on the Status of Palestinian Women Citizens of Israel.

Bibliography

"The Future Vision of the Palestinian Arabs in Israel," National Committee for the Heads of Arab Local Authorities, Israel, 2006.

"The Moslem Population of Israel." http://www1.cbs.gov.il/reader/newhodaot/hodaa_template.html?hodaa=201211289. The Central Bureau of Statistics.

"The Status of Palestinian Women Citizens of Israel." http://www2.ohchr.org/english/bodies/cedaw/docs/ngos/WomenCitizens_of_Israel_for_the_session_Israel_CEDAW48.pdf. Submission to the Committee on the Elimination of Discrimination against Women (CEDAW) by The Working Group on the Status of Palestinian Women Citizens of Israel.

Naysan Rafati

J

JAMEELAH, MARYAM. (1934–2012), revivalist ideologue. Maryam Jameelah was born Margaret Marcus to a Jewish family in New Rochelle, New York. While a student at New York University, she developed a keen interest in religion and began to explore other faiths. She became acquainted with Islam around 1954, having read Marmaduke Pickthall's *The Meaning of the Glorious Koran* (1930) and the works of Muhammad Asad, himself a convert from Judaism to Islam. Jameelah cited Asad's *The Road to Mecca* (1954) and *Islam at the Crossroads* (1947) as critical influences on her decision to become a Muslim. Having found personal meaning, direction, purpose, and comfort in Islam, she converted in 1961.

Jameelah quickly became a public spokesperson for Islam, defending Muslim beliefs against Western criticism and championing Muslim causes, such as that of the Palestinians. Shortly after her conversion, she began to write for the *Muslim Digest* of Durban, South Africa. Her articles outlined a pristine view of Islam and sought to establish the truth of the religion through debates with its critics. Through her work with this journal, she became acquainted with the works of another contributor—Mawlānā Sayyid Abū al-Aʿlā Mawdūdī (d. 1979), the founder and leader of the Jamāʿat-i Islāmī (Islamic Party) of Pakistan. Jameelah began a correspondence with Mawdūdī, which was later published. The letters discussed a variety of issues, ranging from the discourse between Islam and the West to Jameelah's personal spiritual concerns. Jameelah also conveyed the difficulties her conversion had created for her in her family and community. Mawdūdī responded by advising her to move to Pakistan to live among Muslims. Jameelah traveled to Pakistan in 1962 and joined Mawdūdī's household in Lahore. She soon married a member of the Jamāʿat-i Islāmī, Muhammad Yusuf Khan, as his second wife. They had five children together, one of whom died in infancy. Jameelah considered these early years in Pakistan (1962–1964) as formative in her maturation as a Muslim and defender of a conservative interpretation of Islam, although she also later expressed her perception of a disconnect between her ideal vision of Islam and its lived reality in Pakistan.

Jameelah dedicated much of her time to writing books outlining a systematic explanation of the Jamāʿat-i Islāmī's ideology. Although she never formally joined the party, she became one of its chief ideologues. She authored over thirty books dedicated to the defense of conservative Islamic values and culture, and was particularly concerned with the debate between Islam and the West, an important, although not central, aspect of Mawdūdī's thought. She sharpened the focus of Muslim polemic against the West and laid out the revivalist critique of Christianity, Judaism, and secular Western thought in methodical fashion. Her works often fell into the trap of citing the worst moral and ethical transgressions of the West—usually isolated incidents—to condemn the West in its entirety. She was particularly critical of Western materialism, secularism, and modernization, which she believed threatened traditional Islamic values, and supported polygyny, veiling, and gender segregation as ordained by the Qurʾān and ḥadīth, based on a more literal, rather than contextual, interpretation of these textual sources.

Jameelah's significance lies not in the force of her observations, but in the manner in which she articulated an internally consistent paradigm for revivalism's rejection of the West. In this regard, her influence far exceeds the boundaries of Jamāʿat-i Islāmī and has been important in the development of revivalist thought across the Muslim world. Her works have been translated into many languages, including Urdu, Persian, Bahasa Indonesia, Turkish, and Bengali.

By the early 1990s, the logic of her discursive approach led Jameelah away from revivalism and the Jamāʿat-i Islāmī. Increasingly aware of revivalism's own borrowing from the West, she distanced herself from revivalist exegesis and even criticized her mentor, Mawdūdī, for his assimilation of modern concepts into the Jamāʿat-i Islāmī's ideology. Her writings from this time and afterward embodied this change in orientation and revealed the influence of traditional Islam.

BIBLIOGRAPHY

Esposito, John L., and John O. Voll. *Makers of Contemporary Islam.* New York: Oxford University Press, 2001. Contains a biography of Maryam Jameelah.

Haddad, Yvonne Yazbeck, Jane Bandy Smith, and Kathleen Dean Moore. *Muslim Women in America: The Challenge of Islamic Identity Today.* Oxford: Oxford University Press, 2006.

Jameelah, Maryam. "An Appraisal of Some Aspects of Maulana Sayyid Ala Maudoodi's Life and Thought." *Islamic Quarterly* 31, no. 2 (1987): 116–130. Maryam Jameelah's critique of Mawdūdī.

Jameelah, Maryam. *At Home in Pakistan (1962–1989): The Tale of an American Expatriate in Her Adopted Country.* Lahore, Pakistan: Muhammad Yusuf Khan & Sons, 1990.

Jameelah, Maryam. *Is Western Civilization Universal?* Lahore, Pakistan: Mohammad Yusaf Khan, 1973. Critique of modernism and its impact on Islamic societies.

Jameelah, Maryam. *Islam and Modernism.* Lahore, Pakistan: Mohammad Yusaf Khan, 1968. Representative of Maryam Jameelah's polemic against the West.

Jameelah, Maryam. *Islam and the Muslim Woman Today: The Muslim Woman and her Role in Society, Duties of the Muslim Mother.* Lahore, Pakistan: Mohammad Yusaf Khan, 1976.

Jameelah, Maryam. *Islam and Orientalism.* Rev. ed. Lahore, Pakistan: Muhammad Yusuf Khan & Sons, 1981. Critique of Western conceptions of Islam.

Jameelah, Maryam. *Islam in Theory and Practice.* Lahore, Pakistan: Mohammad Yusaf Khan, 1967. Maryam Jameelah's account of the ideology and operations of Jamāʿat-i Islāmī.

Jameelah, Maryam. *Islam versus the West.* Lahore, Pakistan: Muhammad Ashraf, 1962. One of Maryam Jameelah's most celebrated works denouncing the West.

Jameelah, Maryam. *A Manifesto of the Islamic Movement.* Lahore, Pakistan: Mohammad Yusaf Khan, 1969. One of Maryam Jameelah's most lucid articulations of the objective of Islamic revivalism.

Jameelah, Maryam. *Memories of Childhood and Youth in America (1945–1962): The Story of One Western Convert's Quest for Truth.* Lahore, Pakistan: Muhammad Yusuf Khan & Sons 1989.

Jameelah, Maryam, and Maulana Maudoodi. *Correspondence between Maulana Maudoodi and Maryam Jameelah.* 4th ed. Lahore, Pakistan: Mohammad Yusuf Khan, 1986. Outlines Maryam Jameelah's first contacts with Jamā'at-i Islāmī.

Rozehnal, Robert. "Debating Orthodoxy, Contesting Tradition: Ismal in Contemporary South Asia." In *Islam in World Cultures: Comparative Perspectives,* edited by R. Michael, Feener, pp. 103–132. Santa Barbara, Calif: ABC-CLIO, 2004.

Seyyed Vali Reza Nasr
Updated by Natana J. DeLong-Bas

Jewelry and Gems. The theological aversion to luxury and ostentation in the Islamic world did not restrain the upper classes from making lavish use of gold, silver, and precious stones for personal adornment at secular levels. While very little Islamic jewelry has been discovered in burial contexts, surviving pieces of jeweled ornamentation testify to their essential integration into the socio-economical nexus of Islamic society throughout the ages. Such objects were mostly made by Jewish goldsmiths, since the handling of gold was considered immoral according to the Islamic doctrine.

Although it remains difficult to define the date and provenance of Islamic jewelry with precision due to the lack of archaeological evidence, its stylistic and technical details offer some clues for the understanding of the chronological development and geographical diversity. It appears that the model for jewelry during the early Islamic period was derived from the modes of Late Antique, Byzantine, and Sasanian body ornaments, judging by those represented in the context of architectural decoration. Some literary records of this time refer to gemstones—such as rubies, emeralds, and pearls—and such precious material is often discussed as a subject of gift exchange as well as of mineralogical investigation. These sources also reveal some aspects of the fashion for jewelry among women, since female figures, most probably slave attendants, are depicted or described as being adorned by jeweled objects.

Many of the earlier extant examples of Islamic jewelry are considered to have come from the early medieval periods (10th–13th centuries), particularly those ascribed to Fātimid and Seljūk territories. The examples include several forms of body accessories, including bracelets, necklaces, amulets, pendants, earring, rings, hair ornaments, and belt fittings. Although there is little information as to the exact ownership for this kind of small object, some types of jewelry are likely to have been possessed by both men and women; others were probably of more feminine preference. More information for the jewelry in vogue among Muslim women is available from the early modern period onward, including a large number of surviving examples and pictorial sources of jewelry from Islamic India, especially those associated with the Mughals.

Most surviving pieces of pre-modern Islamic jewelry are made of gold and silver. The design is predominantly geometric and non-figurative, apart from the occasional use of shapes and motifs derived from animals. The pieces are mainly worked in precious metal, and the techniques range from granulation, filigree, to repoussé. The use of gemstones, including diamonds, is a prominent decorative feature in extant examples ascribed to later periods, particularly those produced in the Indian Subcontinent under Muslim rule. Such a diverse tradition of jewelry making indicates not only a fashion consciousness of the time but also its versatile role in Muslim culture. For instance, amulets are still popularly worn by both Muslim men and women as an apostrophic symbol to protect against evil spirits—mirroring the superstitions of the Middle Ages. For women, jewelry must have formed part of the dowry of a young bride and was probably considered as an indication of family wealth and tribal affiliation.

As in any cultures, it may have been passed on from generation to generation.

While many regional features of handcrafted jewelry have gradually been merged into an anonymous, machine-made style due to commercialization and mass-production in modern and contemporary times, some body ornaments by degrees acquired new cultural, even political implications. Jewelry remains an integral part of feminine identity among Muslim women, especially for those who could show limited areas of the body in the public space under conservative environments. In political contexts, jewelry became an important symbol of social status, pride, and beauty among the consorts of a powerful ruler. This is particularly the case with the employment of the crown in the coronation ceremony—the crown worn by Pahlavī Queen Faraḥ in 1967 is perhaps the most lavish presentation of jewelry among Muslim women in recent history.

The tradition of jewelry making is at best preserved in tribal costumes in the contemporary Islamic world, and in some regions it is well incorporated into urban fashion styles. Besides famous Turkmen jewelry, a distinctive feature evolved in the mode of jewelry in North Mesopotamia (Kurdistan), the Arabian Peninsula (particularly Yemen and Oman), and the Berber cultural sphere in North Africa. Compared with the metropolitan style of jewelry art, the body ornament of ethnographical quality, mostly made of silver, is characterized by massiveness, intricately executed ornamental details, and harmony of colors, and it is often magnificently worn by tribal women.

At popular levels, the art of body painting called henna remains ubiquitous among young Muslim women. Often used for weddings and holiday celebrations, it developed initially as a symbol of blessings (*barakah*) and eventually as an important form of self-expression among women in the Islamic world, though reserved for limited occasions. Although it is not jewelry *per se*, its stylistic complexity evokes the glitter of precious metal as well as the shine of gemstones. Another popular adornment bearing, to some extent, the feminine character is a type of amulet in the form of the spread-hand, known as the *khamsah* ("five") or Hand of Fatima. While it remains unclear as to its exact origins, it is one of the most widespread talismans in the western parts of the Islamic world and is generally thought to commemorate Fāṭimah Zahrā', the daughter of the Prophet Muḥammad.

[*See also* Cosmetics.]

BIBLIOGRAPHY

Al-Bīrūnī. *Kitāb al-Jamāhir fī Ma'rifat al-Jawāhir* (Book on Precious Stones). Islamabad, 1989.

Carvalho, P. *Gems and Jewels of Mughal India: Jewelled and Enamelled Objects from the 16th to 20th Century, The Nasser D. Khalili Collection of Islamic Art, No. 18.* London, 2010.

Content, D. *Islamic Rings and Gems: The Benjamin Zucker Collection.* London, 1987.

Diba, L. S. *Turkmen Jewelry: Silver Ornaments from the Marshall and Marilyn R. Wolf Collection.* New Haven, 2011.

von Gladiss, A. *Schmuck im Museum für Islamische Kunst.* Berlin, 1998.

Hasson, R. *Early Islamic Jewellery.* Jerusalem, 1987.

Hasson, R. *Later Islamic Jewellery.* Jerusalem, 1987.

Jenkins, M. and M. Keene. *Islamic Jewelry in the Metropolitan Museum of Art.* New York, 1982.

Jenkins, M. and M. Keene. "Djawhar (ii) jewel, jewelry", in the *Encyclopaedia of Islam*, New Edition, Supplement, 12 (2004), pp. 250–62.

Keene, M. *Treasury of the World: Jewelled Arts of India in the Age of the Mughals.* London, 2001.

Rajab, J. S. *Silver Jewelry of Oman.* London, 1997.

Wenzel, M. *Ornament and Amulet: Rings of the Islamic Lands, The Nasser D. Khalili Collection of Islamic Art, No. 16.* London, 1993.

Al-Qāḍī al-Rashīd b. al-Zubayr. *Kitāb al-Dhakhā'ir wa 'l-tuḥaf.* (Book of Treasures and Gifts), edited by M. Hamidullah. Kuwait, 1959.

"Islamic art: jewellery" in the *Dictionary of Art*, vol. 16 (London, 1996), pp. 529–33.

YUKA KADOI

JIHAD. Connoting an endeavor toward a praiseworthy aim, the word "jihad" bears many shades of meaning in the Islamic context. It may express a struggle against one's evil inclinations or an exertion for the sake of Islam and the *ummah* (Islamic community), for example, in trying to convert unbelievers or working for the moral betterment of Islamic society ("jihad of the tongue" and "jihad of the pen"). In books on Islamic law and commonly in the Qurʾān, the word means an armed struggle against the unbelievers. Sometimes the "jihad of the sword" is called "the lesser jihad," in opposition to the peaceful forms named "the greater jihad." Often used today without religious connotation, its meaning is roughly equivalent to the English word "crusade" ("a crusade against drugs"). Either "Islamic" or "holy" is currently added to the word when it is used in a religious context (*al-jihād al-Islāmī* or *al-jihād al-muqaddas*).

The concept of military jihad goes back to the wars fought by Prophet Muḥammad and their written reflection in the Qurʾān. The concept was influenced by the ideas on war prevailing among the pre-Islamic tribes of northern Arabia, among whom war was the normal state, unless a truce had been concluded. War between tribes was regarded as lawful, especially if the war was a response to aggression. Ideas of chivalry forbade warriors from killing noncombatants, especially children, women, and old people. These rules were incorporated into the doctrine of jihad in the latter half of the ninth century CE.

The Qurʾān frequently mentions jihad and fighting (*qitāl*) against unbelievers. Verse 22:40 ("Leave is given to those who fight because they were wronged—surely God is able to help them—who were expelled from their habitations without right, except that they say 'Our Lord is God.' "), revealed not long after the Hijrah, is traditionally considered to be the first verse dealing with the fighting of unbelievers. Many verses exhort the believers to take part in the fighting "with their goods and lives" (*bi-amwālihim wa-anfusihim*), promise reward to those who are killed in jihad (3:157–158, 169–172), and threaten with severe punishments in the hereafter those who do not fight (9:81–82, 48:16). Other verses deal with practical matters such as exemption from military service (9:91, 48:17), fighting during the holy months (2:217) and in the holy territory of Mecca (2:191), the fate of prisoners of war (47:4), safe conduct (9:6), and truce (8:61).

Muslim exegetes have not agreed among themselves whether the Qurʾān allows fighting the unbelievers only as a defense against aggression or under all circumstances. In support of the first view, a number of verses can be quoted that expressly justify fighting on the strength of aggression or perfidy on the part of the unbelievers: "And fight in the way of God with those who fight you, but aggress not: God loves not the aggressors" (2:190); and "But if they break their oaths after their covenant and thrust at your religion, then fight the leaders of unbelief" (9:13). In those verses that seem to order the Muslims to fight the unbelievers unconditionally, the general condition that fighting is only allowed in defense could be said to be understood: "Then, when the sacred months are drawn away, slay the idolaters wherever you find them, and take them, and confine them, and lie in wait for them at every place of ambush" (9:5); and "Fight those who believe not in God and the Last Day and do not forbid what God and His Messenger have forbidden—such men as practice not the religion of truth, being of those who have been given the Book—until they pay the tribute out of hand and have been humbled" (9:29). The bulk of classical

Qur'ān interpretation, however, did not go in this direction. It regarded the Sword Verses, with the unconditional command to fight the unbelievers, as having abrogated all previous verses concerning the intercourse with non-Muslims. This idea is no doubt connected with the pre-Islamic concept that war between tribes was allowed, unless there existed a truce between them, the Islamic *ummah* taking the place of a tribe.

Classical Doctrine. The doctrine of jihad was written in the works on Islamic law developed from Qur'ānic prescriptions and the example of the Prophet and the first caliphs, as laid down in the ḥadīth (traditions). The crux of the doctrine is the existence of a unified Islamic state, ruling the entire *ummah*. It is the duty of the *ummah* to expand the territory of this state in order to bring as many people as possible under its rule. The ultimate aim is to bring the whole earth under the sway of Islam and to extirpate unbelief: "Fight them until there is no persecution [or "seduction"] and the religion is God's entirely" (2:192 and 8:39). Expansionist jihad is a collective duty (*farḍ kifāyah*), which is fulfilled if a sufficient number of people take part in it. If this is not the case, the whole *ummah* is sinning. Expansionist jihad presupposes the presence of a legitimate caliph to organize the struggle. After the conquests had ended, the legal specialists ruled that the caliph must raid enemy territory at least once a year in order to keep alive the idea of jihad.

Sometimes jihad becomes an individual duty (*farḍ 'ayn*), as when the caliph appoints certain persons to participate in a raiding expedition (*ghazāh*) or when someone takes an oath to fight the unbelievers. Moreover jihad becomes obligatory for all free men capable of fighting in a certain region if this region is attacked by the enemy; in this case jihad is defensive.

The aims of fighting unbelievers are conversion or submission. In the latter case the enemies are entitled to keep their religion and practice it, against payment of a poll tax (*jizyah*) (see 9:29 quoted above). Although the Qur'ān limits this option to the people of the book, that is, Christians and Jews, it was in practice extended to other religions, such as the Zoroastrians (al-Majūs).

Whenever the caliph deems it in the interest of the *ummah*, he may conclude a truce with the enemy, as the Prophet did with the Meccans at al-Ḥudaybīyah. According to some schools of law, a truce must be concluded for a specified period of time, no longer than ten years. Others hold that this is not necessary if the caliph stipulates that he may resume war whenever he wishes. The underlying idea is that the notion of jihad, aiming at the domination of Islam and the expansion of its territory, must not fall into oblivion.

Although the legal doctrine had not yet been fixed in all its details, it is commonly assumed that the notion of jihad played a crucial role as a motivating force during the wars of conquest in the first century of Islam. It provided a unifying ideology that transcended tribal factionalism. After the conquests the idea of jihad was kept alive by raiding enemy territory, but this did not result in substantial territorial gains. The main purpose of jihad was the defense of Muslim lands. This became especially important during the Crusades (eleventh to thirteenth centuries CE), when many works were written exhorting the Muslims to take up jihad against the "Franks" and extolling sacred Jerusalem. From the fourteenth century the Ottoman sultans expanded their territory in northwestern Anatolia at the expense of the Byzantine Empire, which lost its capital, Constantinople, in 1453. Some Western historians have argued that the Ottoman state owed its existence to the struggle against the unbelievers. Although this is now disputed, the importance of jihad in Ottoman history is beyond doubt. Ottoman sultans meticulously observed the rules of jihad in their foreign policies. The last instance was the call for jihad issued by the Ottoman government when it entered World War I in 1914.

Contemporary thinking about jihad however offers a wider spectrum of views. On the one hand there is the now widespread notion that jihad is defensive warfare, similar to the *justum bellum* in international law. But on the other hand there are the ideologues of the radical Islamic opposition who call for jihad as a means to spread their brand of Islam. Some of these radical groups call for the use of violence to defeat established governments. In order to justify their armed struggle against Muslim authorities, they declare them to be apostates for not ruling according to the Sharīʿah (*takfīr*).

Jihad and Women. Contemporary Muslim authors writing on jihad often include chapters on women and jihad, containing reports on women participating in the military campaigns during the lifetime of the Prophet Muḥammad. Although not expressly mentioned, it seems that these authors want to illustrate the courage of the earliest Muslim women and their ardor for the cause of Islam. These reports show that the women would nurse the wounded, prepare food, distribute water, and encourage the warriors. Only rarely did they participate in fighting. It seems that the Prophet Muḥammad only allowed them to accompany the troops if they were really needed. If the Muslim army was sufficiently strong, Muḥammad is said not to have permitted women to join the fighters, preferring to protect women against the terrors of warfare and encouraging them to devote themselves to the affairs of the family. The following ḥadīth substantiates this: "It has been reported from ʿĀʾishah that she said: 'I said: " 'Oh Messenger of God, is some form of *jihād* obligatory for women?' He said: 'Yes, a form of *jihād* without fighting, namely the *ḥajj* and the *ʿumrah*' " (Al-ʿAsqalānī, *Bulūgh al-Marām*, edited by R. M. Raḍwān [Cairo: Dār al-Kitāb al-ʾArabī, n.d.] no. 1081 on the authority of Bukhārī, Ibn Mājah).

The Sharīʿah rules of jihad address men, instructing them concerning their obligations to take part in armed struggle and explaining to them how to behave during warfare. Women only play a marginal role in the doctrine. Only in situations of emergency are they allowed and, indeed, obliged to participate in fighting. This is the case when the enemy attacks Muslim territory and cannot be repelled without the help of women. Furthermore they are presented as the essential noncombatant. This is also the case for the enemy, as expounded by hadīths, such as:

> Once when Rabāḥ ibn Rabīʾ rode out with the Messenger of God, he and the companions of the Messenger of God passed by a woman who had been slain. The Messenger of God halted and said: "She was not one who would have fought." Then he looked at the faces of the men and said to one of them: "Catch up with Khālid ibn al-Walīd and tell him that he must not slay children, serfs and women" (Aḥmad b. Ḥanbal, al-Nasāʾī).

As a consequence, if a Muslim army conquered land and the inhabitants had not formally surrendered and not been granted safe conduct, women, on the strength of this ḥadīth, might not be killed. However they could be enslaved and in that case they became part of the war booty (*ghanaʾīm*) to be distributed among the military.

BIBLIOGRAPHY

Arberry, Arthur J., trans. *The Koran Interpreted.* London and New York: Macmillan, 1955. All Qurʾānic quotations herein follow this standard English translation.

Bonner, Michael. *Jihad in Islamic History: Doctrines and Practices.* Princeton, N.J.: Princeton University Press, 2006. Traces how the notion of jihad was used and changed throughout the history of Islam.

Bonney, Richard. *Jihād from Qurʾān to Bin Laden.* Basingstoke, U.K.: Palgrave Macmillan, 2004. A complete survey of jihad doctrine and jihad struggles throughout Islamic history.

Hamidullah, Muhammad. *Muslim Conduct of State: Being a Treatise of Muslim Public International Law Consisting of the Laws of Peace, War and Neutrality, Together with Precedents from Orthodox Practice.* 6th ed. Lahore: Sh. M. Asraf, 1973. Survey of classical jihad doctrine based on an extensive reading of classical sources, but somewhat marred by the author's apologetic approach.

Hūfi, Aḥmad Muḥammad. *Al-jihād*, pp. 25–31. Cairo: al-Qāhirah, 1970. Contains a short chapter on jihad and women.

Khadduri, Majid. *War and Peace in the Law of Islam.* Baltimore: Johns Hopkins University Press, 1955. Reliable survey of the classical doctrine of jihad.

Peters, Rudolph. *Islam and Colonialism: The Doctrine of Jihad in Modern History.* The Hague and New York: Mouton, 1979. Deals with jihad as a means of mobilization in anticolonial struggles and with new interpretations of jihad doctrine.

Peters, Rudolph. *Jihad in Classical and Modern Islam: A Reader.* 2d ed. Princeton, N.J.: Markus Wiener Publishers, 2005. A collection of texts dealing with the jihad doctrine. The last chapter discusses the use of the jihad doctrine in the twenty-first century.

Shaybānī, Muḥammad ibn al-Ḥasan. *The Islamic Law of Nations: Shaybānī's Siyar.* Translated by Majid Khadduri. Baltimore: Johns Hopkins University Press, 1966. Translation of one of the earliest works on jihad.

RUDOLPH PETERS

JORDAN. Since its independence from Britain in 1946, Jordan has compensated for its lack of natural resources by emphasizing human development, which has been to the benefit of women as well as men. Women's participation in the public sphere has been a development priority since the 1970s, and women are increasingly well represented in education, the labor force, and politics, including in Islamic parties. Royal family members Princess Basma; Queen Noor; and Queen Rania, wife of the current King Abdullah II, all publicly promote female empowerment through their respective foundations.

Most public resistance to women's participation in Jordanian society comes from tribal and religious actors defending a restricted, conservative role for women in the name of traditional patriarchal values. The Parliament, in particular the House of Representatives, is one forum for debates on this topic, which have the potential to affect law and policy. The monarchy has the last word in the political sphere, but there are communities in Jordan, particularly in rural areas, where conservative views are dominant, and these ideas are not easily changed by legal reforms or policy.

In the most simplistic rendering, the monarchy is a guardian of women's rights, and works in partnership with women's organizations and advocates to reform religious or cultural customs standing in the way of gender equality. In reality, the lines cannot be so easily drawn. The laws as they are written still include provisions that discriminate against women, and, although the monarchy has demonstrated a commitment to women's advancement through policies and the Queens' public advocacy, obstacles to women's legal parity with men remain. Religious organizations are also not uniformly opposed to women's rights. The Islamic Action Front and other religious groups offer alternative platforms for promoting women's education and empowerment; some women choose to pursue leadership roles through Islamic channels. Jordan's active public sphere includes a number of female voices who engage with ongoing debates on the balance between liberal feminism in the Western model and an approach to gender parity based on Jordanian and Islamic customs.

Jordan's government is a constitutional monarchy, with an elected 120-member House of Representatives (*majlis al-nawwāb*) and a 60-member Senate (*majlis al-ʿayyan*), whose membership is by royal appointment. The reigning Hashemite monarchy claim descent from the Prophet

Muḥammad, and Islam is the religion of the state according to the constitution. The 1976 Personal Status Law, based on the Ḥanafī school of Islamic law, governs family relations such as marriage, divorce, and custody, and includes several provisions significant for women. The Cabinet passed a list of amendments to the law in 2012 that, among other things, made it easier for women to initiate divorce and more difficult for men to marry girls between the ages of fifteen and eighteen. Under the original law, marriages to girls between fifteen and eighteen were illegal, but could be authorized by a judge given certain conditions. The Jordanian National Commission for Women submitted formal recommendations for the amendments, which were written by the Chief Islamic Justice Department.

Article 9 of the Nationality Law, which forbids Jordanian women married to foreign spouses from passing Jordanian citizenship to their children, has been a longtime target for women's activism. In 2012, a group of women staged protests in front of the Prime Ministry, demanding the right to pass on their citizenship, but the law remains in effect. Activists have been calling on the government to repeal Article 9 as part of its obligations under the Convention on the Elimination of All Forms of Discrimination Against Women (CEDAW), which Jordan has ratified, since 2001.

Honor crimes do occur in Jordan, and four were reported in 2011. The Jordanian Penal Code permits reduced sentences for perpetrators of honor crimes, under a policy that has its basis in the Napoleonic and Ottoman Penal Codes. Sentences have been reduced for men charged with honor crimes in 50 different cases between 2000 and 2011 in Jordan. Jordanian women have spoken out against honor crimes by forming organizations denouncing the practice, and government and civil society organizations operate shelters for victims of domestic violence throughout the country.

Though they remain a minority in government and in the workforce, Jordanian women of all different demographics are leading progressive trends within the country. The high proportion of educated women, including at the university level, has translated into a greater role for women in the workforce. Nearly 40 percent of Jordanian university students are female, and female illiteracy in the country is at 9.9 percent, compared to 3.6 percent for males. In 2010 women made up 16.4 percent of the workforce.

Educational opportunities for women have accompanied greater female participation in politics, though women still occupy only a small proportion of government posts. A quota allocates 20 percent of Municipal Council seats for women, and 12 of 120 seats in the House of Representatives are reserved for female candidates. The Islamic Action Front, one of Jordan's oldest political parties, permits women to join its governing board (*majlis al-shūrā*) and operates women's committees in each of its divisions. As more Jordanian women opt to participate in public life through employment, politics, or volunteerism, the avenues available for them to do so are increasingly diverse.

Charities and nongovernmental organizations (NGOs), including Queen Noor's Noor al-Hussein Foundation and Queen Rania's Jordan River Foundation, often operate in lower-income communities where conservative tribal and Islamic attitudes are dominant. Service organizations adapt their programs to accommodate the prevailing cultural mores in these contexts, which emphasize women's roles within the family. Jordan is a developing country in which the gap between elites and others can appear quite dramatic, and women have a wide range of perspectives on the proper nature of their participation in society. Perhaps the greatest accomplishment of Jordanian women is the diversity of viewpoints they have brought to public conversation on the issue.

BIBLIOGRAPHY

Ababneh, Sara. "Islamic Political Activism as a Means of Women's Empowerment? The Case of the Female Islamic Action Front Activists." *Studies in Ethnicity and Nationalism* 9, no. (2009): 1–24.

Bint Talal, Basma. *Rethinking an NGO: Development, Donors, and Civil Society in Jordan*. London: I.B. Tauris. 2004.

"Country summary: Jordan." http://www.hrw.org/sites/default/files/related_material/jordan_2012.pdf. Human Rights Watch. 2012.

Husseini, Rana. "Debate Continues over Personal Status Law." http://jordantimes.com/debate-continues-over-personal-status-law. *Jordan Times*. February 14, 2012.

Husseini, Rana. "JNCW to Lobby Parliament to Endorse Personal Status Law." http://jordantimes.com/jncw-to-lobby-parliament-to-endorse-personal-status-law. *Jordan Times*. February 14, 2012.

Husseini, Rana. "Jordanian Women's Rights Activists Protest for Citizenship Rights." http://www.albawaba.com/editorchoice/jordanian-womens-rights-activists-protest-citizenship-rights-414643. *Jordan Times*. February 27, 2012.

"Jordan Human Development Report 2011: Small Businesses and Human Development." Jordan Ministry of Planning and United Nations Development Programme, 2011.

"The Jordanian Labour Market in Numbers: 2010." http://www.mol.gov.jo/LinkClick.aspx?fileticket=itpOLbpsI9k%3d&tabid=356. Ministry of Labour, Jordan.

"Jordan Slashes Illiteracy Rate Tenfold over 50 Years." http://jordantimes.com/jordan-slashes-illiteracy-rate-tenfold-over-50-years. *Jordan Times*. September 8, 2012.

"National Situation Analysis Report: Women's Human Rights and Gender Equality, Jordan." www.euromedgenderequality.org. Euromed Gender Equality Programme. 2009–2010.

SUSAN MACDOUGALL

JOSEPH, SARAH. (b. 1970), CEO and Editor of *emel*, a British Muslim lifestyle magazine. She was born Sarah Askew in 1970, in London, to Joe Askew, an engineer with the Royal Air Force, and his wife, Valerie, who established Askew's Modeling Agency. Sarah attended St. George's School, and then St. Thomas More School, both in London. She went on to study in the Department of Theology and Religious Studies at King's College, London, where she earned a BA with honors; she then did postgraduate work, producing a thesis on Britons Embracing Islam. She was the first British woman to win the King Faisal Foundation-Prince of Wales Chevining Scholarship in 1999–2000.

Raised with a mixed Jewish and Roman Catholic heritage, Joseph embraced Islam when she was sixteen, finding in Islam a religion and way of life that she believed promoted women and their participation in society. She married Mahmud al-Rashid, a human-rights lawyer and a founder of the Association of Muslim Lawyers, in 1992. They have three children.

Joseph has long been a commentator in London on Muslim life and practices. In the 1990s, she started working at the magazine *Trends*, and appeared regularly on the television programs *Panorama* and *Dimbleby*. In 2003, she and her husband founded *emel*, which remains the only Muslim lifestyle magazine published in Britain. Politically unaligned, the magazine posits that Islam informs all aspects of life—not only politics, but also consumerism and fashion. Its aim is to show a positive image of the Muslim community in Britain. Initially the magazine was available only in Muslim bookshops or by subscription, but it currently enjoys readership in over thirty countries. The magazine has also entered into a partnership with the bank Lloyds TSB in the creation and promotion of a user-generated, content-driven community Web site designed to promote Sharīʿah-friendly banking services. In 2004, Joseph was awarded the Order of the British Empire (OBE) for her services to "interfaith dialogue and the promotion of women's rights." After the London terrorist bombings of 7 July 2005, she was appointed as a member of the delegation to Downing Street to meet the British Prime Minister, and was then appointed a member of the Home Office Task Force to combat extremism.

Because of her political influence, Joseph has been listed by both the Prince Al-Waleed Bin Talal Center for Muslim-Christian Understanding of Georgetown University and the Royal Islamic Strategic Studies Centre of Jordan as one of the world's 500 most influential Muslims. She also made the list of Britain's 100 most powerful Muslims in the Muslim Power 100 drawn up by Carter Anderson. Her radio work has won a Sony Gold Award for Best Speech Programme for *Beyond Belief* with Ernie Rae, and a Sandford St. Martin Trust Merit Award for *All Things Considered* with Roy Jenkins.

BIBLIOGRAPHY

Byrne, Clair. "Muslim Lifestyle Magazine Goes Mainstream," *The Independent*, September 29, 2005.

Lewis, Raina. "Marketing Muslim Lifestyle: A New Media Genre." *Journal of Middle Eastern Women's Studies* 6, no. 3 (Fall 2010): 58–90.

Rigoni, Isabelle. "Media and Muslims in Europe." In *Yearbook of Muslims in Europe Vol. 1*, edited by Jorgen S. Nielsen, Samim Akgönül, Ahmet Alibasic, Brigitte Maréchal, and Christian More, pp. 475–506. Leiden, Netherlands: Brill, 2009.

"Sarah Joseph CEO at Emel Magazine." http://www.youtube.com/watch?v=lK-fmRddt10.

JUSTIN CORFIELD *and* NATANA J. DELONG-BAS

JUDGMENT, FINAL.

In the Islamic worldview, death is not the end of life, but only the end of the appointed period during which a human being is tested. It is a transitional phase during which the *ruh* (spirit) is separated from the body. To signify this transition from a physical to spiritual form of life, the Qur'ān describes the dead being received and interrogated by angels (4:97).

Having tested human beings on earth, God's justice dictates that He hold them accountable for their deeds, highlighting that judgment is based solely on the actions of the individual. There is no doctrine of original sin in Islam. *Qiyāmah* (resurrection) is an integral part of the Qur'ānic ethos and intrinsically linked to creation. According to the Qur'ān, eschatological judgment is inevitable (3:9), for God is swift in dealing with the reckoning (*ḥisāb*) of the soul. Belief in the last judgment—along with a concomitant belief in paradise (*jannah*) as the ultimate home of those who perform good deeds and in the banishment to hell (*jahannam*) of those who do not believe in God and do evil—is one of the pillars of faith. It is important to remember that God's judgment and reward or punishment is equally applicable to both genders. Hence, contrary to some reports in later ḥadīth literature, women are as likely to enter heaven as men, for God's judgment is predicated on action and piety, not gender.

The rendering of accounts—required of all people—is to be given to God alone (13:40; 26:113). God is "prompt in demanding an account" (2:202, 3:19, and 199) of each person's actions, which will have been inscribed on a "scroll." The day of judgment is described as the day when the world will be rolled up like a scroll; an atom's weight of good will be manifest and so will an atom's weight of evil.

Time of the Last Judgment. The Qur'ān has a variety of allusions to the time of the day of judgment: nobody, including the Prophet, can anticipate when it is expected to happen, because only God knows its exact date (7:187; 31:34; 33:63; 41:47; 43:85; 79:42–4); or, "the hour" *(al-sa'a)* may be very close (33:63; 42:17; 54:1; 70:6–7; it is "as a twinkling of the eye or even nearer," 16:77; 54:50); or, it will occur suddenly (*baghtatan*; 7:187; 12:107; 22:55; 43:66; 47:18).

A number of preliminary "signs of the hour" are enumerated in the Qurʾān. Most of these signs are natural catastrophes and some of them appear collectively. In 81:1–14, it is related that the sun will be darkened, the stars will be thrown off their course, the mountains will be set moving, the pregnant camels will be neglected, the savage beasts will be herded together, the seas will be set boiling (or will overflow), the souls will be joined (with their bodies), the buried female infant will be asked for what sin she was slain, the scrolls will be unrolled, heaven will be stripped away, hell will be set blazing, and paradise will be brought near. The mountains (will fly) like "tufts of carded wool" (101:5) and graves will be overturned.

Later ḥadīth literature added other signs of the impending Day of Judgment, including the rising of the sun in the West, the appearance of the Antichrist (*al-dajjal*), and the descent from heaven of the Messiah Isa (Jesus), son of Mary, who will fight the Antichrist, and break the crosses. Verses 39:67–75 contain a detailed description of the events of the resurrection. The entire earth will be grasped by God's hand and the heavens will be rolled up in his right hand. The trumpet shall be blown and all creatures will die, except those whom God wills. Then, it will be blown again and they will be resurrected to await judgment. Every soul shall be paid in full for what it has earned. Some reports suggest that everyone will have to cross a narrow bridge to get to paradise. Those whose deeds are evenly matched will be in the "Heights"(al-aʾraf).

After the accounting is done, the disbelievers shall be taken to hell until, "when they have come forth, and its gates will be opened... It shall be said, Enter the gates of hell, do dwell therein forever!" (39:72; 40:76) "Then those that feared their lord shall be driven into paradise, until, when they have come forth, and its gates are opened, and its keepers will say to them: '... enter in, to dwell" (39:73).

BIBLIOGRAPHY

Smith, Jane. "Eschatology." In *Encyclopedia of the Qurʾān*, edited by Jane Dammen McAuliffe, pp. 44–53. Leiden, Netherlands: Brill, 2004.

Hasson, Isaac. "Last Judgment." In *Encyclopedia of the Qurʾān*, edited by Jane Dammen McAuliffe, pp. 136–144. Leiden, Netherlands: Brill, 2004.

Rahman, Fazlur. *Major Themes of the Qurʾān*. Minneapolis, Minn.: Bibliotheca Islamica, 1980.

Smith, Jane Idleman, and Yvonne Yazbeck Haddad, eds. *The Islamic Understanding of Death and Resurrection*. New York: Oxford University Press, 2002.

Liyakat Takim

Justice, Social. Social justice is a relative term that is dynamic and dependent on the community in question. The community thus defines what is just and equitable in a given society. Social justice as a principle is gender neutral and inclusive because of its stress on the word "social." In principle social justice assumes equality between genders. The question of egalitarianism in the Muslim world has been a controversial issue in the contemporary era, especially given the Western experience of women. (For the purposes of this article, it is assumed that Western women and Muslim women are not homogenous; however the totality referred to here is the general women's experience in Western liberal democracies and the Muslim world respectively.) The argument in Islamic cultures is that men and women are in a non-conflictual partnership that delegates certain responsibilities and rights to each gender. This argument is poised in opposition to the leftist origins of Western feminist argument that assumes that the relationship is conflictual.

The assumption that men and women are not in an inherently conflictual relationship could be a valid argument in theory; however, the second part of the argument—that each gender has different responsibilities and rights—allows for abuse in practice because there is no delegating authority that specifies those rights and duties. This license is therefore at the heart of cultural and traditional misgivings that women across the Muslim world experience. It is therefore necessary to call on the main sources of Islamic law—the Qurʾān and *Sunnah*—to examine women's position according to the texts, and also to pay attention to the jurisprudential principle of "public welfare" (*maṣlaḥah*) and the "goals of Islamic law" (*maqāṣid*) in order to begin to define women's position in Islam.

The Qurʾān repeatedly talks about men and women throughout the text by clearly addressing the two genders as the faithful (men and women), the just (men and women), etc. The Qurʾān also repeatedly mentions that God makes no distinction between people, except based on their faith (*taqwā*) and actions, which is inclusive of men and women, rich and poor, white and colored, etc. This is not to negate the fact that there are some verses that draw controversy, but it is important to note that these controversial verses are not repetitive, which delegates them to contextualization. That is to say, repetitive verses are more general and indicate the spirit of Islamic law, as opposed to singular verses that need contextualization in order to assure proper understanding of the circumstances in response to which they were revealed.

The second textual source, the ḥadīth, also is quite egalitarian, especially when it addresses motherhood. The ḥadīth record, for example, the Prophet Muḥammad's statement that "Paradise is at the mother's feet." Another well-known ḥadīth tells the story of a man who came to the Prophet and asked, "O Messenger of God, who among the people is the most worthy of my good companionship?" Muḥammad responded: "Your mother." The man asked: "Then who?"

Muḥammad said: "Your mother." The man asked again: "Then who?" to which Muḥammad responded: "Your mother." The man asked a fourth time: "Then who?" and Muḥammad responded: "Your father." These ḥadīth clearly emphasize the importance of mothers and how their children should respect and treat them.

The third source in Islamic law is analytic and depends on human reason (*ijtihād*) for development, particularly through elaboration of the principle of public welfare (*maṣlaḥah*) and the goals of Islamic law (*maqāṣid*). The principle of public welfare stresses the importance of developing Islamic law based on the idea that good is lawful and that what is lawful must therefore be good with respect to society. It basically extends Islamic law to adapt and change according to the time and place in which it exists. Public welfare also integrates the use of human reasoning (*ijtihād*) in the application of Islamic law (without crossing the realm of *Qatiyat* (Absolutes) that are clearly stated in the textual sources).

Thus the principle connotes issues such as egalitarianism, creating a civil society, and governance according to Islamic law and Islamic mores. By implication public welfare and preserving the mind, religion, self, posterity, and wealth are the essence of the ideal Islamic state. There are also egalitarian principles that safeguard women's rights under Islamic law. The words of Abū Isḥāq al-Shāṭibī (d. 1388), a jurist who wrote extensively on public welfare and the goals of Islamic law, are particularly instructive in this regard.

People went to al-Shāṭibī, asking him about his legal opinion of a Bedouin woman who was teaching the Qurʾān to other women and girls. Al-Shāṭibī responded that, if the woman knows how to read it without making any mistakes and if she does not sing the Qurʾān instead of just reciting it, then her teaching is valuable. Al-Shāṭibī added, however, that what is common to a lot of women, as well as men, is that they do not read the Qur'ān accurately. This approach makes it clear that al-Shāṭibī appreciated the Bedouin woman's efforts (given that she sticks to the rules of recitation) and he also equated men and women in their failure to know how to read the Qur'ān accurately. In other words he did not partake in blaming the Bedouin woman on the basis of her gender.

Thus, according to textual sources and, more specifically, the goals of Islamic law, justice for Muslim women necessitates not only egalitarianism and respect for constituting a family, but also guarantees the application of the jurisprudential principles mentioned above that entail the preservation of faith, the mind, posterity, the self, and wealth.

Bibliography

Abdelkader, Deina. *Social Justice in Islam*. London and Herndon, Va.: International Institute of Islamic Thought Press, 2000.

Abou al-Ajfan. *Al-Shatibi's Fatawa (al-Fatawa li'l-Imam Abi Ishaq al-Shatibi)*. Tunisia: Kwakib Press, 1984.

Raysunim, Ahmed al-. *The Theory of Maqasid According to Al-Shatibi (Nazariyat al Maqasid 'Ind al-Imam al-Shatibi)*. Herndon, Va.: International Institute of Islamic Thought, 1991.

Deina Abdelkader

K

Kadeer, Rabiya. (b. 1946), Uighur human rights activist. Born into poverty in Xinjiang Province in northwest China, Rabiya Kadeer, through extraordinary determination, was able to rise to a position of both economic and political prominence. However, her decision in 1997 to use her position to publicly criticize the government's actions against her fellow Uighurs (one of China's ten officially recognized Muslim minority groups) resulted in a swift and tumultuous descent, eventually leading to an eight-year prison term, solitary confinement, and exile to the United States.

Living through periods of famine in her youth, Kadeer showed an entrepreneurial drive that led to government sanctions against her during the notorious Cultural Revolution (1966–1976) initiated by Mao Zedong. However, once China decided to carry out major economic reforms that encouraged both domestic businesses as well as international trade, Kadeer's business instincts were allowed to flourish. She soon developed trade relationships with neighboring countries Russia and Kazakhstan, built a seven-story department store in the provincial capital, Ürümqi, and established several nongovernmental organizations (NGOs) to support Uighur women, students, and orphans. One of her most important projects was the Thousand Mothers Movement. As the mother of eleven children, living in one of the least developed regions of China, she was aware of the importance of women being able to receive job training and assistance in starting their own small businesses.

Kadeer's success as a businesswoman and her efforts to improve the lives of her people won her the respect of the central government. In 1994, she was appointed to China's national advisory group, the Chinese People's Political Consultative Conference (CPPCC), and the following year she was sent to Beijing as an official representative to the UN Fourth World Conference for Women. At the height of her economic success, she was said to be the seventh wealthiest person in China.

In 1997, in the aftermath of a violent government suppression of a demonstration by Uighur activists in the city of Gulja, Kadeer decided to speak out against the state's policies regarding the treatment of Uighurs in Xinjiang. Her fall from grace was precipitous. Her businesses and NGOs suffered immediately, and, in August 1999, on her way to meet with a US Congressional delegation, she was arrested and charged with sharing state secrets. Sentenced to eight years in prison, she ended up serving six, two in solitary confinement. In 2004, while in prison, she was awarded the Rafto Human Rights Award (Norway's annual humanitarian award), and she was nominated for the Nobel Peace Prize in 2005 and 2006.

After much pressure from the United States and other foreign governments, as well as major international human rights organizations, she was released in March 2005, a few days before a state visit to China by then–US Secretary of State Condoleezza Rice.

Released into US custody, Kadeer settled in Washington, D.C., where even in exile she has maintained a very active role in Uighur political rights organizations. Soon after her arrival in the United States, she was elected head of the Uighur American Association, and the following year was made president of the World Uighur Congress. She is often compared to the Dalai Lama by international human rights organizations, which laud her efforts to bring the world's attention to the conditions placed on the political and religious lives of the Uighur population in China. From the Chinese government's perspective, she is like the Dalai Lama in that she is also a fomenter of ethnic separatism, unrest, and even violence.

In 2009, after a documentary about her life, *The Ten Conditions of Love*, was released, she was invited to speak at several international film festivals, although, in some cases, after protests from the Chinese government, she was denied a visa. Despite China's ongoing campaign to discredit her, Kadeer continues to be an influential spokesperson for the Uighur community in China.

Bibliography

Daniels, Jeff. director. *The Ten Conditions of Love*. 2009. Common Room Productions. Film.

Eckholm, Eric. "Exile in U.S. Becomes Face of Uighurs," *New York Times*, July 8, 2009.

Kadeer, Rabiya. "Fighting for Uyghur Rights." *The American Journal of Islamic Social Sciences* 23, no. 3 (2006): 144–148.

Kadeer, Rabiya, and Alexandra Cavelius. *Dragon Fighter: One Woman's Epic Struggle for Peace With China*. Carlsbad, Calif.: Kales Press, 2009.

Jacqueline Armijo

Kahlawy, Abla al-. (b. 1948), Egyptian Islamic scholar and preacher. Daughter of the famous Egyptian artist Mohamed al-Kahlawy, she was trained as an Azhari Islamic scholar and is among the most famous female ʿulamā (Islamic scholars) in the Arab World.

Al-Kahlawy was able to gain access to prestigious career paths and religious spaces that have long been dominated by male scholars in Muslim communities. Upon receiving her doctorate in comparative jurisprudence from al-Azhar University in Egypt in 1978, al-Kahlawy assumed key positions in several Islamic academic institutions. In 1979, she served as president of the Sharīʿah department in the Faculty of Education, Women's College in Mecca, Saudi Arabia. Subsequently, she held the position of dean of Islamic and Arabic Studies at the Women's College of al-Azhar University in Egypt. She has also authored several renowned books on Islamic jurisprudence, the most important of which are: *Faʿlyat al-Zakāt fi Himayat al-Iqtisad wa al-Tanmiya* (The Importance of Alms in Securing Economy and Development, 1996), *Al-Marā bayn Tahārat al- Bātin wa al- Zāhir* (Women: The Inside and Outside Sanctity, 1997), and *Qadāy al- Marʾa fi al-Ḥajj wa-al-ʿUmrā* (Women's Issues in the Hajj and ʿUmrah, 2005).

Al-Kahlawy earned religious influence and respect for her thorough knowledge of the Qurʾān and *Sunnah*. Her teachings critique the misogynistic interpretation of Islamic texts and attempt to curtail tendencies toward extremism.

The true values of Islam, she stresses, encourage tolerance, moderation, compassion, and peace. On gender issues, her view emphasizes Islam's core idea of gender equality, which she believes is part and parcel of the Qur'ānic notion of the equality of all human beings. She is also a strong advocate for women's equal access to divorce under Islam through *khulʿ*. Her religious instructions and spiritual guidance target both men and women in Muslim communities. According to al-Kahlawy, a pious society can only be achieved through the everyday actions—such as honesty, humbleness, and tolerance—of its individual members.

Al-Kahlawy's traditional Islamic version of women's rights and the good society contributed to expanding her public role and legitimacy. While in Mecca, she held daily religious lessons for women at the al-Masjid al-Ḥarām (Sacred Mosque) in the center of Mecca. Her lessons in Mecca gained international esteem, because the pilgrimage to Mecca attracts millions of Muslims from all over the world. Upon returning to Egypt, al-Kahlawy continued preaching. Her lectures at al-Azhar, al- Kaḥlāwá, al- Hamd, and al-Hossari, all time-honored mosques, draw hundreds of women. In addition to the traditional medium of preaching at mosques, al-Kahlawy also lectures on several religious satellite television programs. In her programs, she passes on religious knowledge and deals with daily issues that concern women specifically, and Muslims broadly, from an Islamic perspective.

Abla al-Kahlawy embodies a marriage between traditional religious learning and a charismatic ability to connect with audience. She has the depth of knowledge of an *ʿālima* (Islamic scholar), yet she is noted for her understandable everyday language and compassion. Many in her audience call her "Mama Abla." In addition to her educational accomplishments and career achievements, al-Kahlawy is also famous for her commitment to charitable causes. In 2010, she established Al Bākyāt al-Sālihat (Enduring Good Deeds), a charitable nongovernmental organization, which provides a wide variety of services for the sick, the poor, orphans, and the elderly.

Notwithstanding her religious upbringing, al-Kahlawy finds no contradiction or tension between the arts and religion. She writes poems and is the author of a number of short stories, including "Musafir bi-la Tariq" (A Traveler Without a Way) and "ʿAmant bi-Allah" (I Believe in God).

BIBLIOGRAPHY

Al-Kahlawy, Abla. *Fa'lyat al-zakāt fi Himayat al-Iqtisad and al-Tanmya*. Cairo, Egypt: Kaḥlāwá, 1996.

Al-Kahlawy, Abla. *al-Khulʿ : Dawā' Mā Lā Dawā' La-hu : Dirāsah Fiqhīyah Muqāranah)*. Cairo, Egypt: Dār al-Rashād, 2000.

Al-Kahlawy, Abla. *Al-Marā beyn Tahārat al- Bāten wa al- Zāher (Women: The External and Internal Sanctity)*. Cairo, Egypt: Al-Hay'a al-Masrya al-ʿama lel-Ketab, 1997.

Al-Kahlawy, Abla. Personal interview, September 29, 2012.

Al-Kahlawy, Abla. *Qadḥāyā al-mar'ah fī al-Ḥajj wa-al-ʿUmrah*. Beirut, Lebanon: Dār al-Maʿrifah, 2005.

Bano, Masooda, and Hilary Kalmbach. *Women, Leadership, and Mosques*. Boston: Brill, 2011.

Esposito, John L., and İbrahim Kalın. *The 500 Most Influential Muslims in the World: 2009*. Amann, Jordan: Royal Islamic Strategic Studies Centre, 2009.

Ismail, Bakr. *Al- Ustāzā al- Doctora Abla al Kahlawy: Hāyātha and Fekraha*. Cairo, Egypt: Dār al- Kotb wa al-wath'k, 2003.

NERMIN ALLAM

KAR, MEHRANGIZ. (b. 1944), Iranian lawyer, writer, and human rights activist born in Ahwaz, Iran. She was admitted to Tehran University in 1963, where she attained her BA in law and political science. Upon graduating she worked for Sazman Ta'min Ejtemai (Organization of Social Security), a semi-governmental organization in Iran (1967–1977). In 1969 she married the journalist Siamak Pourzand. Pourzand died while under house arrest in Iran on 29 April 2011. Kar and Pourzand had two daughters, Leily and Azadeh.

Before the 1979 Islamic Revolution, Kar was known for her writings in publications such as *Ferdawsi*, *Keyhan*, and *Rastakhiz*, which focused on social issues in Iran and international politics. Three months after the Islamic Revolution, Kar received her license to practice law. She worked as a human rights lawyer until 2000. She also continued writing and contributed to numerous reformist newspapers and magazines such as *Zanan*. She is the author of more than a dozen books in Persian, including *Raf-e Tabiz az Zanan, Moghayeseye Convension Raf-e Tabiz az Zanan ba Ghavanin Dakheli Iran* (2000), and *Khoshonat Aleih Zanan dar Iran* (2001), which are considered seminal works in the academic study of women's rights in Iran. Kar has also published her autobiography in English: *Crossing the Red Line, the Struggle for Human Rights in Iran* (2007).

In 2000 Kar was one of the seven individuals who were arrested and imprisoned on their return to Iran from Germany after attending the symposium, Iran after the Elections, held by the Heinrich Böll Institute in Berlin. All seven "were accused of acting against the national security of the Islamic Republic and of 'desecrating Islamic sanctities' by taking part in the conference. The Revolutionary Court issued a statement declaring that during the conference 'the sacred Islamic regime of Iran and its principles were insulted' " (Dabashi and Mack, 2000). Due to these accusations and the paper Kar had presented on constitutional reform, she spent two months in solitary confinement in Tehran's Evin Prison and on 13 January 2001, was convicted and sentenced to four years imprisonment for acting against national security, spreading propaganda against the regime of the Islamic Republic, violating the Islamic dress code at the Berlin Conference, denying the commands of Sharīʿah, and disseminating propaganda against the Islamic regime. Kar was subsequently diagnosed with breast cancer and given permission to undergo medical treatment in the United States, where she has remained.

Kar has been awarded numerous prizes for her writing and activism, including: the Ludovic Trarieux Prize (2002), the Democracy Award of the National Endowment for Democracy USA (2002), the Hellman/Hammett Grant from Human Rights Watch (2002), and a Human Rights First Award (2004).

Kar has served as a fellow at the National Endowment for Democracy, the Woodrow Wilson Center, American University, the University of Virginia, and Columbia University. She has also been a Radcliffe Fellow at Harvard, and in 2005–2006 was based at the Carr Center for Human Rights Policy at Harvard's John F. Kennedy School of Government. At Harvard Kar was also a resident fellow with the Dubai Initiative (DI) of the Belfer Center for Science and International Affairs at the Kennedy School. Kar has been recognized as a Scholar at Risk through an international network of universities and colleges working to promote academic freedom. She is currently a visiting Researcher at Brown University's Pembroke Center.

BIBLIOGRAPHY

Primary Works

Crossing the Red Line: The Struggle for Human Rights in Iran. Costa Mesa, Calif.: Blind Owl Press, 2007.

Khoshonat Aleih Zanan dar Iran [Violence against Women in Iran]. Tehran: Entesharat Roshangaran, 2001.

Raf-e Tabiz az Zanan, Moghayeseye Convension Raf-e Tabiz az Zanan ba Ghavanin Dakheli Iran [Elimination of Discrimination against Women, Comparison of the Convention on Elimination of All Forms of Discrimination Against Women and the Iranian National Laws]. 3rd ed. Tehran: Nashr Qatre, 2000.

Secondary Works

Dabashi, Hamid, and Arien Mack. "Arrested in Iran." *The New York Review of Books*, June 15, 2000. http://www.nybooks.com/articles/archives/2000/jun/15/arrested-in-iran/.

Kar, Mehrangiz, "Biography." http://www.mehrangiz-kar.net/english/biography.php.

Pembroke Centre for Teaching and research on Women. "Mehrangiz Kar Appointed Visiting Professor at Pembroke Center." http://pembrokecenter.org/research/documents/FINAL_2011_Pembroke-Research_Newsletter_000.pdf.

Roja Fazaeli

KARAMAH (Muslim Women Lawyers for Human Rights). KARAMAH: Muslim Women Lawyers for Human Rights is a US-based nonprofit organization that derives its name from the term *karamah* ("dignity"), which is found in the Qur'ānic verse, "We have given dignity to the children of Adam" (17:70). The organization KARAMAH thus envisions a world in which all human beings, regardless of gender or any other markers of difference, enjoy their God-given right of dignity. The organization seeks to achieve this goal through education, community outreach, and scholarship on Islamic law, which, taken together, can empower women to transform religious and cultural institutions for the betterment of themselves and their communities.

The organization was founded in 1993 at the University of Richmond by Dr. Azizah al-Hibri, Esq., Professor Emerita of Law, Commissioner on the US Commission on International Religious Freedom, and pioneer in scholarship on democracy, human rights, and women's rights in Islam. In reaction to discourses within the feminist movement that considered women's rights and religion to be antithetical, al-Hibri sought to find ways to reconcile the two. Through the founding of KARAMAH, she sought to advance her conviction that Islamic religious values and human rights were not mutually exclusive. She also aimed to create an organization to support the rights of Muslim women worldwide. KARAMAH became this platform, starting with scholarship and branching out to educational programs, lectures, advocacy, legal outreach, and the development of a global network of Muslim jurists and leaders.

Al-Hibri and KARAMAH are part of a global movement of Muslim women scholars who are interpreting the Qur'ān through a reading that privileges *tawhīd*, or the Oneness of God. According to al-Hibri, this principle provides the basis for the metaphysical equality of all humans as creatures of God, thus challenging the patriarchal lens through which the Qur'ān has been read, as well as the misogynistic interpretations of the text that have been portrayed and accepted as the objective norm by previous interpreters. Such a reading also allows for a reexamining of classical Islamic jurisprudence, as jurists' rulings, too, were a product of their patriarchal societies. It is through a reformulation of Islamic law that KARAMAH effects long-term change, pushing the boundaries of women's rights through a holistic reading of the Qur'ān and the traditions of the Prophet Muḥammad that challenges a hierarchical worldview, replacing it with the Qur'ānic principle of human equality.

As a cornerstone of its educational programming, KARAMAH also holds an annual Law and Leadership Summer Program that brings together Muslim women from across the globe to develop their understandings of Islamic jurisprudence, leadership, and conflict resolution, training and empowering them to effect nonconfrontational, sustained change for women's rights in their respective societies. Over the past few years, KARAMAH has also spearheaded several initiatives for Muslim-American civil rights, as well as a domestic violence program that, in collaboration with other Washington, D.C.–based nonprofit organizations, seeks to combat domestic violence and its detrimental effects in the Muslim community. Through such educational programs, advocacy, and scholarship, KARAMAH continues to build a positive reputation and strong, effective outreach programs.

BIBLIOGRAPHY

Al-Hibri, Azizah Y. "An Introduction to Muslim Women's Rights." In *Windows of Faith: Muslim Women Scholar-Activists in North America*, edited by Gisela Webb, pp. 51–71. Syracuse, N.Y.: Syracuse University Press, 2000.

"Vision & Mission." KARAMAH: Muslim Women Lawyers for Human Rights. http://karamah.org/about/vision-and-mission.

Ailya Vajid

Karman, Tawakul. (b. 1979), Yemeni journalist and activst. Tawakul Karman was born to a family of ten children in the Mekhlaf district of Taiz in Yemen. She earned an undergraduate degree in commerce from the University of Science and Technology, Sanaa, and a graduate degree in political science from the University of Sanaa. Her father, Abdel Salam Karman, served as Justice Minister in President Ali Abdullah Saleh's government. Her brother, Tariq Karman, is a poet, and her sister, Safa Karman, works for the Al Jazeera news network.

Karman's activism began in 2004, when she removed her *niqāb* (total face veil) at a human rights conference and called for other women to do so as well. She then started working as a journalist. In 2005, she and seven other female journalists founded Women Journalists Without Chains (WJWC) to promote human rights, particularly freedom of opinion and expression. At that time, she was affiliated with the newspaper *Al-Thawrah* (The Revolution). In 2007, WJWC released a semiannual report about abuses of press freedom by the Yemeni government since 2005. In 2009, WJWC targeted the Ministry of Information for organizing trials against journalists. Karman's activism for press freedom coincided with her joining the Islamist opposition party, Islah; the party's platform advocated gender equality and expanded roles for women in the public sphere, while opposing the regime of President Saleh. In 2010, thirteen of Islah's parliament members were women, one of whom was Karman.

Karman had begun campaigning for political reform in 2007, leading demonstrations in Tahrir Square in Sanaa every Thursday to protest government abuses of press freedom. After the Egyptian uprising in January 2011, she and some fifty others began staging protests against the Saleh regime, which was ultimately ousted in February 2012. She was briefly arrested in January 2011, but was quickly released when the protest movement expanded rapidly in response. Karman became one of the leading figures in the protest movement, speaking publicly and posting her speeches on YouTube, denouncing the Saleh government, and demanding democratic rule. Her cell phone was systematically tapped, she received death threats, and her family was harassed. Despite meeting legal requirements, she was denied a newspaper license.

Karman's larger significance lies in her representation of a new breed of female social activists born in the Arab Spring. These women have participated first, simply as women, not primarily as mothers, sisters, or wives; second, as citizens and political activists aiming to mobilize both women and men and surmount the restrictions imposed on their gender, while pushing men and women alike to shake off the yoke of repressive government; and third, sometimes as leaders of the opposition. These women have consistently demonstrated strong leadership qualities and are distinguished by the fact that men are willing to follow them in societies still characterized by male superiority. Though their actions have not dismantled all the obstacles standing in the way of women's equality with men, these women activists have greatly contributed to a new type of gender relationship by proving that women can be leaders, even in conservative societies like Yemen, where tribal ties and state nepotism are paramount.

For her nonviolent activism and leadership, Karman came to be known as the "Iron Woman" and "Mother of the Revolution" in Yemen. She was awarded the Nobel Peace Prize in 2011 with two other women.

BIBLIOGRAPHY

Baker, Aryn, and Erik Stier. "The Woman at the Head of Yemen's Protest Movement," *Time* magazine, February 16, 2012.

Finn, Tom. "Middle East/Yemen: Undaunted by Death Threats: The Thorn in Saleh's Side," *The Guardian*, March 26, 2011.

Holmes, Oliver. "Just off Freedom Square in Yemen," *Press Freedom Online: Committee to Protect Journalists*, October 27, 2009. http://cpj.org/blog/2009/10/just-off-freedom-square-in-yemen.php.

Karman, Tawakul. "Our Revolution's Doing What Saleh can't: Uniting Yemen," *The Guardian*, April 9, 2011.

Karman, Tawakul. "Nobel Lecture," *Nobelprize.org*, December 10, 2011. http://www.nobelprize.org/nobel_prizes/peace/laureates/2011/karman-lecture_en.html.

Karman, Tawakul. "The World Must Not Forsake Yemen's Struggle for Freedom," *The Guardian*, November 1, 2011.

Karman, Tawakul. "Yemen's Unfinished Revolution," *New York Times*, June 18, 2011.

Khosrokhavar, Farhad. *The New Arab Revolutions that Shook the World*. Boulder, Colo.: Paradigm Publishers, 2012.

Mekay, Emad. "Arab Women Lead the Charge." Inter Press Service, February 11, 2011. http://www.ipsnews.net/2011/02/arab-women-lead-the-charge/.

"Tawakul Karman." Women's Islamic Initiative in Spirituality and Equality. http://www.wisemuslimwomen.org/muslimwomen/bio/tawakul_karman/.

FARHAD KHOSROKHAVAR

KASHMIR. Kashmiri women have expressed their political agency throughout major historical events: the nationalist awakening in the 1930s; the Quit Kashmir movement in the 1940s; the invasion by raiders from the North West Frontier Province of Pakistan in 1947; the period preceding and succeeding the accession of the former princely state of Jammu and Kashmir to the Indian dominion when, on 26 October 1947, the monarch of the state, Maharaja Hari Singh, signed the "Instrument of Accession" to India, officially ceding to the government of India jurisdiction over defense, foreign affairs, and communications; the onset of the militant movement in the late 1980s; and the era of gross human rights violations by the Indian army, paramilitary forces, Pakistani-trained militants, mercenaries, and state-sponsored organizations in the 1990s and 2000s. How did these women navigate the undulating, often impenetrable terrain of formal spaces of political power?

Cultural Syncretism in Kashmir: Challenging a Patriarchal Society. Kashmiris have long taken pride in inhabiting a cultural space between Vedic Hinduism and Ṣūfī Islam. Lalla-Ded (fourteenth century), revered by both the Pandits and Muslims of Kashmir, is the finest symbol of their essentially syncretic culture. A woman ascetic, she pursued the goal of self-knowledge and then disseminated the esoteric Shaiva doctrine, which until then was only available in Sanskrit, among the populace in their own language. The renowned Kashmiri scholar Prem Nath Bazaz assesses the "splendid" role that Kashmiri women of ancient times played in the social and cultural life of Kashmir, but these women were affiliated with the royalty in a monarchical regime, free from economic constraints and societal limitations that tormented women of other classes.

Lalla-Ded, on the other hand, intervened in patriarchal national history by speaking from her location outside privilege. Professor Neerja Mattoo, author of several publications on Kashmiri literature, astutely draws a comparison between Lalla-Ded and medieval Christian women mystics: "For them [medieval Christian women mystics], too, the only way to validate their words and to get out of the all-pervasive, constricting presence of male authority was this claim of a personal relationship with God." Lalla-Ded was greatly influenced by discourses on mysticism and the different schools of Ṣūfī thought given by Mir Sayyid ʿAlī Hamadānī, Shah Hamadan, a regal Central Asian Islamic scholar and mystic who disseminated and perpetuated Islamic teachings in predominantly Brahmanical fourteenth- and fifteenth-century Kashmir. Among later women mystics influenced by Lalla-Ded was the seventeenth-century mystic poet Roph Bhavani, the content of whose *vaakhs* (verses) is also the theory and practice of Shaivism. These women mystics have since achieved an iconic goddess-mother persona.

Reminiscences about Women's Agential Roles or Lack Thereof, 1947 and 1989. In terms of a substantive indigenous or modern feminist movement in Kashmir, one example is the institute Markaz Behbudi Khawateen, established by Begum Akbar Jehan. Jehan represented the Srinagar and Anantnag constituencies of Jammu and Kashmir in the Indian parliament from 1977 to 1979 and 1984 to 1989, respectively, and was the first president of the Jammu and Kashmir Red Cross Society, from 1947 to 1951 The institute imparts literacy, training in arts and crafts, health care, and social security as tools of empowerment.

Another example of a powerful agential role played by Kashmiri women is the Women's Self-Defense Corps (WSDC), formed in 1947. Krishna Misri writes about the formation of the National Militia and Women's Defense Corps—volunteer forces of men and women organized under the leadership of the first Muslim prime minister of Jammu and Kashmir, Sheikh Mohammad Abdullah—to ward off the hordes of tribesmen from the North West Frontier Province, backed by the Pakistani army, when they crossed the border of the princely state of Jammu and Kashmir on 22 October 1947, in order to coercively annex the region. Women's empowerment was further bolstered in 1950 when the government of Jammu and Kashmir developed educational institutions for women on a large scale, including the first university, and a college for women, which provided an emancipatory forum for the women of Kashmir, broadening their horizons and opportunities. The educational methods employed in these institutions were revisionist in nature, not revolutionary.

In the second half of the twentieth century, Kashmiri women like Begum Akbar Jehan, Mehmooda Ahmad Ali Shah, Sajjida Zameer, and Krishna Misri made a smooth transition from keepers of home and hearth to people engaged in sociopolitical activism within the confines of nationalist discourse. Sajjida was in the forefront of the cultural movement, designed to awaken and hone a political consciousness through mass media:

> The women's militia played a substantive role in repulsing the raiders. Zoon Gujjari of Nawakadal, Srinagar, Jana Begum of Amrikadal, Srinagar, and Mohuan Kaur, a refugee from Baramullah, Kashmir, were active participants in the women's movement. Kashmiris from all walks of life, irrespective of religion or race, actively participated in the various activities of the Cultural Front of the militia. (e-mail from Sajjida Zameer to author, 1 April 2008)

Ironically, today, asymmetrical gender hierarchies legitimized by the forceful dissemination of fundamentalist and militarized discourses portend the debasement and prostration of women.

The militant separatist movement in Jammu and Kashmir in 1989 scorched the landscape, blighting educational and economic opportunities. Despite their active role in the political mobilization of 1931, the Quit Kashmir movement (anti-monarchical movement) of 1946, and the fierce nationalism of 1947, terror made women revert from the public to the private realm. But there are a few exceptions.

Parveena Ahangar, after her son was said to have been arrested and killed in the custody of the security forces, instead of lamenting voicelessly, formed an organization called the Association of Parents of Disappeared Persons (APDP), comprising other bereaved mothers like her. The APDP relies on the cultural and moral authority of the mother, sanctioned by religion, and mobilizes women to courageously challenge the apathy and complacency of the political and bureaucratic machinery.

On the other hand, the Dukhtaran-e-Milat (DM), instead of pressing for women's political empowerment, claims that the image of woman as a burqa-clad, faceless and voiceless cultural icon, devoid of agency, is sanctioned by the interpretations of religious scriptures that this vigilante group subscribes to, ignoring their diverse interpretations and the rich heterogeneity of cultural traditions and the paradoxes within them.

The retrieval of the conviction of the women volunteers of Women's Self-Defense Corps, and of the vision of women activists who were harbingers of change in the sociopolitical and cultural realms, would facilitate the recomposition of women's roles in the significant process of nation building.

[*See also* India *and* Pakistan.]

BIBLIOGRAPHY

Bazaz, Prem Nath. *Kashmir in Crucible.* New Delhi: Pamposh Publications, 1967. Reprint, Srinagar: Gulshan Books, 2005.

Khan, Nyla Ali. *Islam, Women, and Violence in Kashmir: Between India and Pakistan.* New York: Palgrave Macmillan, 2010.

Lok Sabha. "Obituary References." 2000. http://parliamentofindia.nic.in/lsdeb/ls13/ses4/24072.htm.

Mattoo, Neerja. "Lalla-Ded as the Voice of the Marginalized." Paper presented at the Series on Mystic Masters, India International Centre, New Delhi, March 2007.

Misri, Krishna. "Kashmiri Women Down the Ages: A Gender Perspective." *Himalayan and Central Asian Studies* 6, no. 3–4 (2002): 3–27.

Zameer, Sajjida. Member of the 1947 Women's Militia organized by the National Conference, and former director of the Education Department, J & K. April 2008.

NYLA ALI KHAN

KHADĪJA BINT KHUWAYLID. First wife of the Prophet Muḥammad, Khadīja bint Khuwaylid was also the first convert to Islam. Born in Mecca around the year 555 CE, she had already been once divorced and once widowed before she met Muḥammad. She was an independent businesswoman, much admired and quite wealthy. Many historians believe her to be representative of the opportunities for women extant in pre-Islamic Arabia. She hired Muḥammad to work in her trading company because of his reputation as a trustworthy young man. He supervised her caravans on their way to Syria. According to the earliest biography of Muḥammad, it was on his journey to Syria that he first was recognized by a Christian monk as a future prophet. When he returned, successful in his trade mission, Khadīja proposed marriage, a practice which would not be allowed women after the advent of Islam.

Muḥammad was twenty-five at the time of his marriage and she was, according to most sources, forty, although one early text records her age as twenty-eight. The marriage raised the economic status of Muḥammad and allowed him to meditate on spiritual matters. Khadīja became the mother of all the Prophet's surviving children. Four girls, Zaynab, Umm Kulthūm, Ruqayyah, and Fāṭima, outlived their mother, but her sons died in infancy. Early Islamic historians disagree on whether there were two sons, ʿAbd Allāh and al-Qāsim, or three or even four. The other names mentioned are al-Ṭayyib and al-Ṭāḥir, but these may be just additional names for ʿAbd Allāh. Among the girls, Fāṭima (d. 633 CE) became the most famous and important. Without male heirs, Fāṭima's marriage to the Prophet's first cousin, ʿAlī ibn Abī Ṭālib (d. 661 CE), made her the mother of Muḥammad's most direct male descendants.

At the age of forty, according to Islamic tradition, Muḥammad received his first revelation from the angel Gabriel during the month of Ramadan. He returned to Khadīja deeply shaken by the experience; he was unsure of the source of his vision. His wife comforted him, believed in his divine mission, and became the first convert to Islam.

Their marriage was, by all accounts, a happy and devoted one. Only with Khadīja did he remain in a monogamous union. Her death in 619 CE caused Muḥammad much grief. Years afterward in Medina, he often referred to his love for Khadīja. This prompted jealousy from his youngest wife, ʿĀʾishah (d. 678 CE), who wished to be his favorite. When she remarked that God had replaced Khadīja with a better wife, meaning herself, Muḥammad rebuked her sharply, defending his first wife's pivotal supportive role in his life. Both Sunnī and Shīʿī Muslims acknowledge that Khadīja was the Prophet's favorite wife, but after her death, only Sunnīs admit this status for ʿĀʾisha. Along with her daughter, Fāṭima, Khadīja was compared to the two ideal women of the Qurʾān: Mary, the mother of the prophet Jesus, and Asiya, the wife of pharaoh. Sunnī sources describe Khadīja and her daughter, Fāṭima, as the only two perfect women in history.

BIBLIOGRAPHY

Ibn Hisham. *The Life of Muhammad: A Translation of Ibn Ishaq's Sirat Rasul Allah*, translated by A. Guillaume. New York: Oxford University Press, 1955; reprinted, 1967.

DENISE A. SPELLBERG

KHALED, AMR. (b. 1967). Born in Alexandria, Egypt, and currently residing in London, Amr Khaled is a Muslim preacher and televangelist. Selected by *Time* magazine as one of the top one hundred most influential people who shape our world, Khaled is one of the key figures of the contemporary Islamic revivalist movement in the Arab world, although his "rock-star" popularity extends into the United States, as well. His Website received 26 million hits in 2006 (more than Oprah's), and has 923,277 registered members. Accessible in eighteen languages, including English, French, Dutch, and Hebrew, it is the third most popular Arabic website in the world, behind Al-Jazeera and an e-mail portal. His Facebook page has more than 3.5 million "likes." Khaled's message of self-empowerment and emphasis on values and the spiritual dimensions of Islam have resonated with youth across the Muslim world, who have identified him as their "top contemporary role model" (Ahmad, 2007, p. 276).

A significant segment of Khaled's following is Muslim women. Many female fans say they feel as though he is speaking to them personally. It is not unusual for Khaled to personally respond to both female and male fans when they contact him via text messages, e-mails, or even phone calls. He also makes himself accessible to his audience, often sharing glimpses of his personal life with them. On his official Web site he regularly updates his fans on his life journey through messages and videos. In response to critics of his openness and willingness to speak to women, Khaled explains that he talks to them because he respects them and their central role in Muslim society. He often cites stories from prophetic history (*sīrah*) that illustrate women's competence and ability to change the course of their societies' future. Despite criticism by some Khaled has also encouraged women to cover their hair. According to media reports thousands of women across the Middle East began to don the headscarf after listening to Khaled, although Khaled works with women of all backgrounds.

Khaled is neither a traditional cleric nor a scholar. He did not receive religious credentials from al-Azhar University, although he holds a diploma from an Islamic studies institute in Egypt and a PhD in Islamic studies from the University of Wales. He began his career as an accountant in Cairo before he became one of the world's most popular Islamic televangelists. In the eyes of his followers Khaled's nonconventional educational background is his strength. It allows him to present himself as someone who, like his viewers, has struggled with religious issues and wants to share his insight from his own spiritual journey and development. Further his sermons, which are delivered in colloquial Egyptian, are peppered with cultural idioms and "allusions to pop culture and contemporary issues among youth" (Moll, 2010). Part of his attraction also lies in his reflection of popular fatigue with political Islam, particularly among women.

While Amr Khaled's popularity reflects an interest in personal piety among educated, upwardly women, it also reflects changing societal norms related to gender. Many attracted to his message are educated working women. It is not clear whether his ideas have influenced these women to change their behavior or if his ideas are attractive to them because they are perceived to support the choices they have already made. Nevertheless, it is clear that Khaled's message and the visual presentation of his satellite television shows, particularly *Life Makers*, provide a new model for women—one that encourages them to participate in the public realm and play an active role in their respective societies while simultaneously fulfilling the obligations of their faith.

BIBLIOGRAPHY

Ahmed, Akbar S. *Journey into Islam: The Crisis of Globalization*. Washington, D.C.: Brookings Institution Press, 2007.

Amr Khaled official website. http://www.amrkhaled.net/.

Aslan, Reza. "The War for Islam." *The Boston Globe*, September 10, 2006. http://www.boston.com/news/globe/ideas/articles/2006/09/10/the_war_for_islam/?page=3.

Atia, Tarek. "Amr Khaled: A Preacher's Puzzle." *Al-Ahram Weekly*, October 20–26, 2005.

Moll, Yasmin. "Islamic Televangelism: Religion, Media and Visuality in Contemporary Egypt." *Arab Media and Society* 10 (Spring 2010). http://www.arabmediasociety.com/?article=732/.

Pandya, Sophia. "Religious Change Among Yemeni Women: The New Popularity of 'Amr Khaled." *The Journal of Middle East Women's Studies* 5, no. 1 (Winter 2009).

Shapiro, Samantha. "Ministering to the Upwardly Mobile Muslim." *The New York Times Magazine*, April30,2006.http://www.nytimes.com/2006/04/30/magazine/30televangelist.html?pagewanted=1&ei=5090&en=4c56a0ffa67fa4ca&ex=1304049600&partner=rssuserland&emc=rss.

White, Lesley. "The Antidote to Terror." *Sunday Times* (London), May 14, 2007. http://www.timesonline.co.uk/tol/news/uk/article1667358.ece.

Wright, Robin. "Islam's Up-to-Date Televangelist; Amr Khaled Has Bridged the Religious and Secular With His Feel-Good Message." *Washington Post*, September 11, 2007.

HADIA MUBARAK

KHAN, DAISY. (b. 1958), Muslim women's rights activist. Daisy Khan was born in 1958 in Kashmir into a Muslim family that recognized the importance of education for boys and girls alike. She moved to the United States when she was fifteen years old. Close to her grandmother, a practicing mystic, Khan grew up learning to value tolerance, harmony, and the unity of religious experience, regardless of one's professed faith. Her family's emphasis upon Muslim women's education eventually led Khan to become an activist for Muslim women's rights.

She began her activist career when she founded the American Society for Muslim Advancement (ASMA) with her husband, Imam Faisal Abdul Rauf. Within that organization, she began two movements known as the Women's Islamic Initiative in Spirituality and Equality (WISE) and the International Shura Council of Muslim Women, the latter a global movement to empower Muslim women on the basis of their Islamic rights. While both movements have already made significant impacts, it is perhaps her work with the Shura Council that will have the greatest impact on Muslim women's rights and Khan's own legacy.

Khan's extensive experience as an activist led her to structure the Shura Council as a diverse group of women scholars, activists, and specialists who are able, ideally, to connect Islamic principles to pressing social issues. The group's goal is to arrive at holistic strategies that can be implemented by Muslim populations throughout the world.

One of the most important opinion papers issued under Khan's guidance is titled "Jihad Against Violence" (2009). Her guiding principles are clearly illustrated in this work. She bases her emphasis on jihad on a Qur'ānic verse: "O those who believe! Be Godfearing of God and look for an approach to Him and struggle (jihad) in His way so that perhaps you will prosper" (5:35). Her goal is to combat all forms of violence committed in the name of Islam—from violent extremism to domestic violence:

> We must announce our commitment to resisting injustice generally and violence specifically through peaceful means and from the unique perspective of women. We must speak comprehensively and holistically to a diversity of discourses to effectively oppose violence. We must act upon our positions by preventing our children and members of our communities from subscribing to a deviant understanding of our faith and by creating institutions, mechanisms, and systems able to successfully combat violence. Already, thousands of organizations led by Muslim women courageously and effectively tackle violence on a daily basis. We must support these efforts, unifying our individual efforts to 'command the good and forbid the evil,' as decreed in the Qur'ān. Most importantly, we must affirm peace. We must think, speak, and act, both wisely and courageously, overflowing with a powerful spirit of mercy, justice, and peace. This is our Jihad Against Violence. (p. 6)

Khan's activism, and her influence on Islam as a lived religion, led to her being named one of the top 140 Twitter feeds of 2012 by *TIME* magazine, and one of the top seven women to follow on Twitter that same year by *Glamour* magazine. Khan regularly writes for the "On Faith" column in the *Washington Post* and for the *Huffington Post.*

BIBLIOGRAPHY

Asma (American Society for Muslim Advancement). Home Page. http://www.asmasociety.org/.

"Daisy Khan: Executive Director and Co-Founder, American Society For Muslim Advancement." American Society for Muslim Advancement. http://www.asmasociety.org/about/b_dkhan.html.

Khan, Daisy. "Islamophobia is America's real enemy." *The Guardian*, February 9, 2012, http://www.guardian.co.uk/commentisfree/2012/feb/09/islamophobes-us-muslims-enemy.

"Jihad Against Violence: Muslim Women's Struggle for Peace," WISE (Women's Islamic Initiative in Spirituality and Equality, July, 2009.
Women's Islamic Initiative in Spirituality and Equality. http://www.wisemuslimwomen.org/.

LALEH BAKHTIAR

KHAWĀRIJ. The Khawārij (singular form, "Khariji") were literally "the exiters," or "those who withdrew," making them the third major sectarian group in early Islam. Neither Sunnī nor Shīʿī, they came into existence as a result of "the great *fitnah*" (strife) between 656 and 661 CE, under the rule of the fourth caliph and first imam, ʿAlī.

ʿAlī was challenged by Muʿāwiyah for leadership of the *ummah*. When ʿAlī agreed to submit his quarrel with Muʾawiyah to arbitration at the battle of Siffīn, a number of his followers, mainly from the tribe of Tamīm, accused him of rejecting Qurʾānic verse 49:9: "If two parties of the faithful fight each other, then conciliate them. Yet if one is rebellious to the other, then fight the insolent one until it returns to God's command." These followers believed that ʿAlī was the legitimate caliph and that Muʾawiyah was a rebellious aggressor who was not entitled to arbitration. By agreeing to arbitration, ʿAlī had committed the grave sin of rejecting God's *āyāt* (signs; verses of the Qurʾān), and had thus excluded himself from the true community of the faithful. They believed he should have obeyed 8:39–40: "Fight them until there is no *fitnah* (temptation), and religion is wholly unto God," as a matter of following God's *ḥukm* (ruling). "Lā ḥukma illā lillāh" (no ruling but for God) became their watchword.

As a result, the dissenters left ʿAlī's camp in Kufa. Although they were persuaded by ʿAlī to return, the attempted arbitration there failed, and they left the city with many sympathizers. It was at this point that they were labeled Khawārij, or "exiters," for having made a deliberate break with the collective *ummah*, and began raiding ʿAlī's territories. When attempts at conciliation failed again, ʿAlī was forced to fight them; he ordered that those who escaped should be captured, to prevent them from spreading their new beliefs in nearby cities. The bloodshed during this conflict caused them to swear vengeance, and, on a Friday in January 661, ʿAlī was murdered at the mosque in Kufa by a Khariji, Ibn Muljam al-Murādī.

From 690 until 730, the Khawārij gained much support in southern Mesopotamia, and Basra (in present-day Iraq) soon became their intellectual center. They also had adherents in South Arabia and upper Mesopotamia. Arab armies carried the doctrine to North Africa, where it soon became the dominant form of Islam among the Berbers.

Although the Khawārij have been portrayed in Islamic history as the original extremists and apostates who committed the grave sin of creating *fitnah* within the *ummah*, they nevertheless upheld some of the most central values of the Qurʾān's teachings. For example, they always insisted on the absolute equality of all races, with all Muslims treated equally, regardless of tribe or race ("there is no *nasab* [inherited honor] in Islam"). "Even a black slave" might be the first in the community if he had enough support. This meant that they were successful in recruiting non-Arabs for their cause, although many early Khawārij came from the Bedouins, as well as from South Arabian tribesmen opposed to the hegemony of the northern Arabs and to their ban on agriculture. They also took very seriously—at a time when few did—the obligations of Muslims toward *dhimmī*, or protected non-Muslims.

The Khawārij also upheld the equality of women as full members of the Muslim community; women had the right to serve as imams, and both concubinage and the marriage of girls aged nine years and under were prohibitied. They permitted women to participate in jihad, when it was undertaken as military action, as a matter of religious duty, grounding this belief in Muḥammad's own insistence that women were permitted to accompany military expeditions and fight in battle. Those who were killed in battle were exposed, naked, by the enemy as a matter of disgrace and a rejection of their taking on such masculine roles. Over time, as more non-Arab tribes assimilated into the movement, these public roles for women were suppressed.

The Khawārij are noted for their steadfastness and unwillingness to compromise, which are especially well illustrated by their introduction of *takfīrī* ideology (the practice of declaring anyone who disagreed with them not only unbelievers (*kuffār*), but also subject to jihad as holy war). Heresiographers mention more than twenty Khawārij sects, each of which tended to elect its own imam and to regard itself as the one true Muslim community. The Khawārij's basic tenets affirmed that a Muslim who commits a major sin (*kabīrah*) is an apostate from Islam and outside the protection of its laws. Also, if the imam has sinned or lost his sense of social justice (*ʿadālah*), he might be deposed. Non-Khārijī Muslims were deemed to be either polytheists or infidels, but people of the scriptures (*ahl al-kitab*) who sought Khārijī protection were to be treated generously. One Khawārij sect, the Ṣufrīyah, believed that, although non-Khārijī Muslims were polytheists, it was nevertheless permissible to dwell in truce with them as long as they did not attack.

The most well-known sects of Khawārij were the Azāriqah, the Ṣufrīyah, and the Ibādīyah. The Azāriqah excluded from Islam all Muslims who would not make common cause with them, and they practiced *istiʿrāḍ* (review of the beliefs of their opponents). Those who failed to pass were killed, including women and children, since the children of polytheists were to be damned along with their parents. They left the other Khawārij of Basra in 684 to fight in southern Iraq and Iran, and all of them were killed in wars. The Ṣufrīyah concentrated on North Africa and established an imamate around 770 at Sijilmāsah in southern Morocco, where they were active traders. The Ibādīyah have survived to the present. They produced some of the earliest *mutakallimūn* (theologians) in Islam and were willing to live peaceably with other Muslims who did not harass them. From their Basra headquarters, they sent out teams of teachers to spread their doctrine and, where possible, set up imams in the provinces. They built a great following among Berber tribes from Tripolitania to Morocco and were recognized as far away as Oman, where they are still today the majority population; the ruling family are Ibādīyah. They are also found in the oases of the Mzāb and Wargla in Algeria, on the island of Jerba off Tunisia, in Jabal Nafūsa and Zuwāghah in Libya, and in Zanzibar and some ports in East Africa. Numbering less than one million, they emphasize their sympathy with other Muslims (with whom they will pray and cooperate socially and politically, although they rarely intermarry), and prefer to be called Sunnī, never Shīʿī.

BIBLIOGRAPHY

Ahmed, Leila. *Women and Gender in Islam: Historical Roots of a Modern Debate*. New Haven, Conn.: Yale University Press, 1992.

Baghdādī, ʿAbd al-Qāhir al-. *Moslem Schisms and Sects (Al-Farq bayna al-Firaq), Being the History of the Various Philosophic Systems Developed in Islam*. Translated by Kate Chambers Seelye. New York: AMS Press, 1966.

Levi della Vida, Giorgio. "Khāridjites." In *Encyclopaedia of Islam*, new ed., vol. 4, edited by P. J. Bearman, Th. Bianquis, C. E. Bosworth, E. van Donzel, and W. P. Heinrichs, pp. 1074–1077. Leiden, Netherlands: Brill, 2005.

Lewicki, T. "Ibāḍiyya." In *Encyclopaedia of Islam*, new ed., vol. 3, edited by P. J. Bearman, Th. Bianquis, C. E. Bosworth, E. van Donzel, and W. P. Heinrichs, pp. 648–660. Leiden, Netherlands: Brill, 2005.

Rubinacci, R. "Azāriḳa." In *Encyclopaedia of Islam*, new ed., vol. 1, edited by P. J. Bearman, Th. Bianquis, C. E. Bosworth, E. van Donzel, and W. P. Heinrichs, pp. 810–811. Leiden, Netherlands: Brill, 2005.

Salem, Elie Adib. *Political Theory and Institutions of the Khawārij*. Baltimore: Johns Hopkins University Press, 1956.

Shahrastānī. "Kitāb al-Milal waʾl Niḥal (The Khārijites and the Murjiʿites)." *Abr-Nahrain* 10 (1970–1971): 49–75. Like Baghdādī, this Sunnī author offers a hostile but nevertheless useful description.

Vaglieri, L. Veccia. "Ḥarūrā." In *Encyclopaedia of Islam*, new ed., vol. 3, edited by P. J. Bearman, Th. Bianquis, C. E. Bosworth, E. van Donzel, and W. P. Heinrichs, pp. 235–236. Leiden, Netherlands: Brill, 2005.

Williams, John Alden. *The Word of Islam*. Austin: University of Texas Press, 1993. See chapter 6 for a translation of the *Muqaddimat al-Tawḥīd*, an extensive Ibāḍī statement of doctrine, with commentaries, dating perhaps to the tenth century, which is still highly regarded by Ibāḍī scholars today.

JOHN ALDEN WILLIAMS
Updated by JUSTIN CORFIELD *and* NATANA J. DELONG-BAS

KHAYR AL-NISĀʾ BEGAM. Often referred to as Mahd-i ʿUlyā (The Highest Cradle), Khayr al-Nisāʾ Begam was the de facto ruler of the Ṣafavid state in the name of her husband from February 1578 until her own death in July 1579 in Qazvīn.

Khayr al-Nisāʾ was a daughter of the local ruler of Māzandarān, Mīr ʿAbd Allāh Khān ibn Mir Maḥmūd (d. 1561/1562 CE) of the Marʿashī Sayyid dynasty, and of Fakhr al-Nisāʾ Begam (d. 1579). After the death of her father in the course of internal fights for power, she, her mother, and two brothers, along with a small group of supporters, found refuge at the Ṣafavid court. In 1565/1566 she was given in marriage to a royal prince (*mīrzā*) Muḥammad ibn Shāh Ṭahmāsp, the then governor of Herat, who was to rule the Ṣafavid state under the name of Muḥammad Khudābanda (r. 1577–1587). Five children are known: four sons Sulṭān Ḥamza Mīrzā (b. c. 1566/1567, Herat), ʿAbbās Mīrzā (b. 27 January 1571, Herat)—the future Shāh ʿAbbās I, Abū Ṭālib Mīrzā (b. 1574/1575, Shiraz), and Ṭahmāsp Mīrzā (b. after 14 May 1576, Shiraz), as well as one daughter, Shāh Begam (b. May/June 1578, Qazvīn).

With her infant son Ḥamza Mīrzā, she followed her husband from Herat to Shiraz when he was appointed governor by Shāh Ṭahmāsp in 1573/1574 CE. Her second son, ʿAbbās Mīrzā, stayed behind with a guardian as nominal governor of Herat. The Ṣafavid chronicles mention that her political entourage in Shiraz was composed of some Qizilbāsh *amīrs* and Māzandarānī supporters of old. After the death of Shāh Ismāʿīl II ibn Shāh Ṭahmāsp (r. 1576–1577) in Qazvīn, one of the political factions at the court succeeded in bringing Muḥammad Khudābanda to the throne. Once there, Khayr al-Nisāʾ was instrumental in eliminating the rival faction led by Parī Khān Khānum, a daughter of Shāh Ṭahmāsp.

Taking advantage of the fact that Muḥammad Khudābanda was disabled by a serious eye illness, she openly took control of the affairs of state in his name and, later, in the name of her eldest son Ḥamza Mīrzā. She exercised power with the support of the grand vizier Mīrzā Salmān and a party formed of her own Māzandarānī family and followers, set against the political and economic interests of the Qizilbāsh tribes. She gained full control over central and provincial administration as well as—to some degree—military affairs. Contemporaneous sources, both internal to the Ṣafavid state and external ones, point to the extent of her political power (see Qumī, 1980, pp. 658, 662; "No affair was conducted without her advice"). Not only did she approve decrees and nominations, but she also participated in military expeditions, such as the campaign against the Ottomans (conducted during the winter of 1578–1579) where she officially represented the twelve-year old Ḥamza Mīrzā (the nominal commander in chief) but became the de facto leader of the army, actively participating in debates at war councils alongside *amīrs*.

Her aggressive pro-Māzandarānī and anti-Qizilbāsh stance, including the transfer of much tribal land so that it became possessions of the Crown, finally met with organized opposition from the military elite defending their economic and political positions. A plot was hatched in Qazvīn, in which even the grand vizier Mīrzā Salmān finally joined. The coup spread from the court circles down to military quarters where soldiers were encouraged to sound off that the shah should not "delegate his power to a woman" (Qumi, 1980, pp. 695–696), while the Qizilbāsh *amīrs* called for her execution. The rebel *amīrs* entered the private royal quarters of the residence in Qazvīn on 25/26 July 1579 and strangled Khayr al-Nisāʾ Begam and her mother that same night.

Khayr al-Nisāʾ appears to be a rare example of an influential female political figure in the early modern history of Iran. She certainly was an exceptionally strong personality who was able to impose herself in sociocultural circumstances generally resistant to the presence of women in the public and decision-making spheres. The combination of her high birth status (as a Sayyid) and high acquired status (as a ruler's spouse) was certainly decisive in this respect, while her husband's physical disability opened a range of possibilities that she used to her advantage. Her activities seem to have been supported by her family circle, including her mother, and might have been modeled on other female political figures of Māzandarān in the sixteenth century, such as Bībī Zuhrā or Tītī Begam (otherwise little known). All in all, Khayr al-Nisāʾ's participation in the exercise of power, although truly rare in its extent and depth, was not exceptional in and of itself in the Turko-Iranian milieu of the period. Role models existed beyond the Ṣafavid dynasty (for example, the Timurids and the Mughals), but also within the Ṣafavid sphere, both at court (for example, Parī Khān Khānum II, Shāhzāda Sulṭānum, and Zaynab Begam) and in the provinces.

BIBLIOGRAPHY

Primary Works

Iskandar Beg, Munshī. *Tārīkh-i ʿālam-ārā-ye ʿAbbāsī* (The World-Adorning History of ʿAbbās). Edited by Īraj Afshār. Tehran: Amīr Kabīr, 1955. A major official chronicle of the Ṣafavid dynasty.

Navīdī, ʿAbdī Beg Shīrāzī. *Takmilat al-akhbār* (The Perfection of Chronicles). Edited by ʿAbd al-Ḥusayn Navāʾī. Tehran: Nay, 1990. The author's patron was Parī Khān Khānum II, daughter of Shāh Ṭahmāsp, who was a sister-in-law of Khayr al-Nisāʾ Begam and the leader of a rival political faction.

Qumī, Qāżī Aḥmad. *Khulāṣat al-tavārīkh* (The Essence of Histories). 2 vols. Edited by Iḥsan Ishrāqī. Tehran: Dānishkada-i Tehrān, 1980 (Vol. 1) and 1984 (Vol. 2).

Secondary Works

Hinz, Walter. "Schah Ismaʿil II: Ein Beitrag zur Geschichte der Safaviden." *Mitteilungen des Seminars für Orientalische Sprachen an der Friedrich-Wilhelms-Universität zu Berlin* 36, no. 2 (1933): 19–99. On the political crisis and the difficult circumstances surrounding the accession of Shāh Muḥammad Khudābanda after the death of Shāh Ismaʿīl II.

Savory, Roger M. "The Significance of the Political Murder of Mirzā Salmān." In *Studies on the History of Safavid Iran*, by Roger M. Savory. London: Variorum, 1987. Originally published in *Islamic Studies: Journal of the Central Institute of Islamic Research* 3 (1965): 181–191.

Szuppe, Maria. "La Participation des femmes de la famille royale à l'exercice du pouvoir en Iran safavide au XVIe siècle." Part 1: *Studia Iranica* 23, no. 2 (1994): 211–258; Part 2: *Studia Iranica* 24, no. 1 (1995): 61–122. Detailed study of the women of the Ṣafavid dynasty and their participation in public sphere.

Szuppe, Maria. "Status, Knowledge, and Politics: Women in Sixteenth-Century Safavid Iran." In *Women in Iran from the Rise of Islam to 1800*, edited by Guity Nashat and Lois Beck, pp. 140–169. Urbana and Chicago: University of Illinois Press, 2003.

MARIA SZUPPE

KHUṬBAH. *Khutbah*, (root word *kha ta ba*) simply means a sermon, an address, a discourse, or a lecture with an ethical, religious, social, or political message. In its various derivations, the terminology carries a variety of meanings. While expanding on the qualities of the true servants of God (*ʿibād*), the Qurʾān mentions: "The true servants of the Merciful One are those who walk on the earth gently and when the foolish *address* them (*khatabahum*), they simply say: Peace to you" (25:63). Elsewhere it is used in the sense of a matter, an issue, or a business. During a discourse with his guests, Abraham asks: "What then is the business (*khatbukum*) of which you (have come), O Messengers (of God)" (15:57). In pre-Islamic Arabia, a *khaṭīb* (orator, speaker) enjoyed high status in society. Such persons (pl. *khutab*) were instrumental in motivating people to wage war; they were also sent as emissaries to neighboring tribes or states to negotiate and plead their case. Their majesty of words, flow of ideas and emotions, and power of oration was highly valued in pre-Islamic Arabia.

The Qurʾān called itself *kalām* (speech), *dhikr* (remembrance), *dhikra* (reminder), *mawʿizah hasanah* (beautiful advice), *bayān* (elaborate discourse), *al-furqān* (the benchmark for truth), and so on, but does not use the term *khuṭbah* for itself. Nevertheless it had an impact on the substance as well as on the style of *khuṭbah*, as manifested in the *khutab* of Prophet Muḥammad. The *khutab* (pl. of *khuṭbah*) delivered by him were neither verbose nor long or extended. "Make your prayer longer and shorten your *khuṭbah*" is the Prophetic instruction [Muslim, *Kitab al-Jumuʿah*, *ḥadīth* 47]. His shortest possible discourses were with heavy ethical and edifying content. The most famous and often quoted is his final *khuṭbah*, addressed to the whole of humanity, which was delivered during his first and last *ḥajj* (pilgrimage), on the tenth of *Dhū al-Ḥijjah*, 632 CE:

> O Men, your lives and your property shall be inviolable until you meet your Lord...Remember that you will indeed meet your Lord and that He will indeed reckon your deeds... whoever of you is keeping a trust of someone else shall return that trust to its rightful owner... O Men, to you a right belongs with respect to your women and your women, a right with respect to you...Do treat your women well and be kind to them, for they are your partners and committed helpers...Learn that every Muslim is a brother of every Muslim and that the Muslims constitute one brotherhood...Nothing shall be legitimate to a Muslim unless it was given freely and willingly. Do not therefore do injustice to your own selves. O Allah, have I conveyed Your message? (Haykel, 1976).

This is perhaps his longest *khuṭbah.*

Muḥammad transformed the context and style of the pre-Islamic *khuṭbah*, which was often delivered to rouse the emotions of people and incite them to go to war. He made the *khuṭbah* brief, simple, issue-oriented, and instructional. Prophetic *sunnah* (practice) made *khuṭbah* an integral part of public devotion. Every Friday, wherever a Muslim community exists in the world, a congregational weekly afternoon prayer (*ṣalāt al-jumuʿah*) is offered preceded by a *khuṭbah* in two segments. The first *khuṭbah* consists of praise to God, salutation to Muḥammad, recitation of some part of the Qurʾān, and a Prophetic ḥadīth, followed by a brief comment on a current social, economic, moral, or political issue. It may not take more than five to ten minutes. This concludes with invocation seeking God's protection. The imam or the leader of prayers sits down for a few seconds, then stands up again and starts the second segment of the *khuṭbah.* This again begins with praise of God, seeking His help and guidance and seeking His forgiveness for Muslims all over the world. It also reminds them of their social obligation to help the needy and deserving and to act fairly and equitably, and to observe peace and justice. The *khuṭbah* is followed immediately by two *rakaʿāt* (units) of prayer. In view of the educational role of the *khuṭbah*, Muslim jurists consider it part of devotion (*ʿibādah*). It is perhaps due to this aspect that the two *rakaʿāt* of *ṣalāt al-jumuʿah* replace the normal four *rakaʿāt* of *zuhr*, the daily afternoon prayer.

The *khuṭbah* is also a major part of the yearly congregations held globally in the Muslim community (*ummah*), irrespective of a majority or minority context. In the case of *ʿĪd al-Fiṭr*, celebrated after the completion of the one-month-long fasting in Ramadan, as well as during *ʿĪd al-Aḍḥā* celebrated at the conclusion of the *ḥajj* or pilgrimage on the tenth of *Dhū al-Ḥijjah*, the *khuṭbah* is delivered after the two *rakaʿāt* of thanksgiving prayer are over, unlike the *jumuʿah* sermon. The purpose, again, is to educate the community on social, economic, political, legal, and ethical issues.

Due to the high educational value of the *khuṭbah*, Muḥammad asked women to come to the *ʿĪd* congregation, even when not in a state of ritual purity, which is required as a precondition for making *ṣalāh*, or prayer. He would himself walk to their separate enclosure and deliver the *khuṭbah* to them. Most of the jurists therefore regard *khuṭbah* as a part of *ʿibādah*, to be listened to quietly, without resorting to talking or even physical gestures.

In general during the second part of the *khuṭbah*, the imam typically implores the help of God and requests Him to forgive the shortcomings of Muslims. A request is also made to have special blessings conferred upon the four rightly guided caliphs as well as those who followed the *sunnah* of Muḥammad and his successors. Supplication is also made for the Muslim *ummah* and those who govern the affairs of Muslims. This also symbolizes the legitimacy of the Muslim ruler and the unity of the Muslim *ummah*. Historically the name of the Ottoman *sulṭān* was mentioned in the *khuṭbah* until the abolition of the caliphate in 1924, even in places like the Indo-Pakistan subcontinent, which at that time was ruled by the British colonialists.

There are other important occasions when the *khuṭbah* is delivered as part of a religious ceremony, such as officiating at a marriage (*nikāh*). The *nikāh khuṭbah* provides counsel to the couple who enter married life in order to complete their faith (*īmān*) and follow the Prophetic *sunnah*. It also reminds the couple to observe their rights and responsibilities toward each other, their in-laws, and other members of the extended family.

When Muḥammad passed away, the Muslim community in Medina encountered a severe psychological shock. ʿUmar ibn ʿAbd al-Khaṭṭāb, for example, found it difficult to accept the fact and refused to believe that the Prophet had passed away. Abū Bakr gave a short sermon as follows: "O Men, if you have been worshipping Muhammad, then know that Muhammad is dead. But if you have been worshipping God, then know that Allah is living and never dies." He also quoted the Qurʾān: "Muhammad is but a messenger, there have been messengers before him. So, if he dies or is killed, would you turn back on your heels? Whoever turns back on his heels can never harm God in the least. God shall soon reward the grateful" (3:144).

Historically, women have not been permitted to deliver the *khuṭbah* to a mixed gender setting, based on traditions from the times of the caliphs and throughout history, although they were permitted to serve in this capacity if the congregation consisted only of other women. Nevertheless there were examples of women serving as imams of their households during Muḥammad's own lifetime, an example that female scholars and activists are looking to today in their quest for greater inclusion in leadership within the Muslim community. The debate about whether a woman can deliver the *jumuʿah khuṭbah* came to the forefront in August 1994 in South Africa, when a female scholar was invited to deliver a pre-*jumuʿah* talk. Traditionally the *khuṭbah* is supposed to be delivered by the same person who leads the prayer, the established norm (*sunnah*) from the time of the Prophet being that the ruler himself or his governor or chief justice or a scholar (*ʿālim*) is assigned to lead the congregation. Delivering the *khuṭbah* and leading prayers is subject to certain criteria which are not met by all men, including regularity and availability to lead the five daily prayers plus the Friday service and *ʿĪd* congregations; ritual purity (which can be challenging for women to meet at all times due to menstruation); knowledge of the Qurʾān and its proper recitation; and seniority in age. Some have also claimed that it is easier to maintain concentration with a male imam presiding, although this is a matter of preference and custom, rather than a matter of Sharīʿah. Today's challenges by women for the right to deliver the *khuṭbah* highlight their increasingly important roles in other aspects of society, particularly due to rising education levels, arguing that being barred from serving as imams and delivering the *khuṭbah* simply on the basis of sex fails to take into consideration their other capabilities.

To conclude *khuṭbah* is a means of instructing and enlightening the community of believers. In most of the religious schools, *khuṭbah* is part of academic training. Some outstanding contemporary *khutabah* include Mufti Muhammad ʿAbduh (d. 1905), Jamāl al-Dīn al-Afghānī (d. 1897), and Hassan al-Banna (d. 1949). Some *khutab* (discourses) are known for their high academic and intellectual impact on mainstream Muslim thought. These include *The Reconstruction of Religious Thought in Islam* by Allama Muhammad Iqbal (d. 1938); *The Life of the Prophet in the Light of the Qur'an* by Mawlana Abdul Majid Daryabadi (d. 1977); *The Cultural Side of Islam: Islamic Culture* by Muhammad Marmaduke William Pickthall (d. 1936); *Khutbat-i-Madras* (Eng. trans. *Muhammad, the Ideal Prophet*) by Sayyid Sulaiman Nadvi (d. 1952), and *khutbat* (Eng. trans. *Let Us be Muslims*) by Mawlana Sayyed Abul ʿAla Mawdudi (d. 1979).

The *khutab* of the four Rightly Guided caliphs, particularly of Abū Bakr, ʿUmar ibn ʿAbd al-Khaṭṭāb, and ʿAlī ibn Abī Ṭālib, are regarded as models of public policy statements. ʿAlī's *Nahj al-Balagha* (tr. S. M. Askari Jaʿfari, 1960), is considered a compendium of wisdom by both Shīʿī and Sunnī Muslims.

The weekly Friday sermon particularly is a highly effective means of communicating to the members of Muslim community the essence of Islamic teachings and Islamic perspectives on current social, political, economic, security, and cultural issues. It educates the Muslim *ummah* on how to respond collectively to emerging global issues.

BIBLIOGRAPHY

Fatāwā al-ʿĀlamgīrīyah. Quetta, Pakistan: Balouchistan Book Depot, 1985.

Hanifi, Zainuddin ibn Najim, al-. *Al Bahr al-Ra'iq sharh kanz addaqaiq* (*al-juz al-thani*), Beirut: Dar al-Maʿrifa, n.d.

Haykal, Muhammad Hussain. *Hayat-i-Muhammad, The Life of Muhammad*. Translated by Ismaʿil Raqi al-Faruqi. Indianapolis, Ind.: American Trust Publications, 1976.

Ibn ʿĀbidin. *Radd al-Muhtar ʿala Durr al-Mukhtar*. Quetta, Pakistan: Maktaba Rashidiyah, 1399 AH.

Jazīrī, ʿAbd al-Raḥmān. *Kitāb al fiqh ʿala al-madhāhib al-arbaʿah*. Vol. 1: *Qism al-ʿibada*, pp. 389–400. Beirut: Dar Ibn Hazm, n.d.

Marghīnānī, ʿAlī ibn Abī Bahr, al-. *al-Hidayah*. English tr. Charles Hamilton, Lahore, Premier Book House, n.d. Muslim, Abul Hussain 'Asakar ud Din, Sahih Muslim, tr. Abdul Hamid Siddiqui, Lahore, Shaikh M. Ashraf 1972.

Sābiq, al-Sayyid. *Fiqh al-sunnah*.Translated by Muhammad Saʿeed Dabas and Jamal al-Din M. Zarabozo. Indianapolis, Ind.: American Trust Publications, 1985–1992.

Wadud, Amina. *Inside the Gender Jihad: Women's Reform in Islam*. Oxford: OneWorld Publications, 2006.

ANIS AHMAD

KUWAIT. Kuwait was settled early in the eighteenth century, probably by water-seeking nomads from the interior of the Arabian Peninsula; its first government was formed in the 1750s. Meager freshwater supplies and access to the sea made fishing, pearling, and long-distance trade main sources of family income. Wives of sailors and pearl fishers headed their families during the men's long absences. Given the minimal wages earned by their husbands, women who could do so also worked for money as petty traders, teachers, and household help.

Wealthy families sequestered their women in fortress-like houses with solid external walls and enclosed courtyards. Outsiders could not see in or even hear the voices of the household's women. Regardless of their social class, women venturing outside their houses had to cover their faces and bodies so that unrelated men could not see them.

Education for Kuwaitis of both sexes was limited until the 1930s, when a school for boys and then one for girls were established in the municipality. Oil was discovered in 1938 and exports began after World War II, bringing the state unprecedented income. Under Amir Abdullah al-Salim (r. 1950–1965), along with the provision of other services, public education for girls and boys was made mandatory.

As oil income and the resident foreigners generating and helping to spend it increased, Kuwaiti society became more cosmopolitan. Leading merchants sent their sons and even a few daughters abroad to be educated. Adela al-Sayer, who later became a leader of one of Kuwait's first women's organizations, was among the first Kuwaiti women to drive, taking the family car for a jaunt during one of her school vacations to the applause of men along the way.

Male graduates returning to Kuwait saw women as integral to their hopes for modernization. Young graduates encouraged their sisters and made spaces for them in the burgeoning Kuwaiti print media. "Woman's Corner" columns in Kuwaiti magazines carried their articles on values, especially the concepts of honor and modesty, sparking debate about women's roles in building a new Kuwait.

Kuwait's constitution was adopted in 1962. It promised equal rights to all Kuwaiti citizens but made the family the basic unit of Kuwaiti society. The constitution incorporated a wide array of civil rights and liberties, and provided for an elected representative assembly with real legislative authority. Women's political access was limited by the 1959 election law. Only men could vote and run for office, but women did benefit from other state policies. Family allowances, health care, and subsidies for basic foods improved Kuwaiti life chances greatly, and compulsory education gave girls both skills and ambitions to use them, at home and in the larger society.

As ambitious women found jobs in government and the economy, divisions among Kuwaitis regarding women's proper "place" became more prominent. Urban Kuwaitis, who saw themselves as autonomous citizens, tended to have inclusive attitudes towards women's rights to participate in society and politics. Rural Kuwaitis, concentrated in the new suburbs, were closer to tribal culture, which obligates the amir as tribal leader to provide for them. They preferred that women defer to men.

Women themselves are divided over the issue of women's rights. The most interesting divisions are among Islamist women. Like male Shīʿī Islamists, Shīʿī Islamist women tend to favor a limited range of women's rights, such as voting rights for women but not the right to run for office. Sunnī Islamists are more likely than Shīʿa to oppose women's rights, and there are differences among Sunnīs, too. Sunnī women are split by their location in Islamist families, with women from Salafī families (the Salafīn resemble Wahhābīs from Saudi Arabia in their religious beliefs) arguing against even voting rights, while many women in the Muslim Brotherhood (Ikhwān) participated alongside liberal women in the successful May 2005 achievement of full political rights for Kuwaiti women.

Kuwaiti women are involved in public life. In addition to holding jobs, most in the public sector, activists participate in associational life and have been politically engaged for decades, even before they had obtained full rights. At first they were concentrated in same-sex organizations like the mostly upper-class Women's Cultural and Social Society and the middle-class Arab Women's Development Society, both founded in 1963 and each devoting some of their efforts to women's rights issues. As their public roles grew in prominence, women moved into political and professional organizations with mixed-sex membership. Rola Dashti, an economist, was the first woman to be elected head of the Economists' Society, and she was one of the four "first" women elected to the parliament in 2009. The others are Massouma al-Mubarak, who had held two cabinet portfolios prior to her election, Aseel al-Awadhi, a philosopher, and education professor Salwa al-Jassar.

Kuwaiti female activists come from many backgrounds, and not only from the ruling family. Psychologist Buthaina al-Muqhawe and attorney Badria al-Awadhi led efforts to reform laws that discriminate against women. Sara Akbar, Kuwait's first female petroleum engineer, now heads a private international oil company and was the only woman to serve among those extinguishing the oil-well fires that choked Kuwait after liberation. During the occupation, women worked in the Resistance. Some, like Asrar al-Qabandy, were brutally tortured and murdered for their efforts.

Young women continue to move into public life. In 2008, then-education minister Nouria al-Subeih agreed under Islamist pressure to enforce the 1996 gender-segregation law more rigorously. Private university students who had not yet felt the full force of the law, and recent graduates from several institutions, organized to roll this decision back. Led by Hussa al-Humaidhi, Voice of Kuwait (Sawt al-Kuwait) embarked on a campaign to teach Kuwaitis about their rights. In addition to annual events highlighting the constitution, Sawt gathers information about laws that restrict civil liberties and publishes it alongside the names and photographs of MPs and how they voted on the bills.

Kuwaiti women have enviable academic and professional records and continue to make their way in the private and public sectors. Although their paths are sometimes obstructed by class conflict and male backlash, they have shown their ability to achieve professionally without losing their cultural and religious roots.

[*See also* Dashti, Rola, *and* Mubarak, Massouma al-.]

BIBLIOGRAPHY

Al-Mughni, Haya. Women in Kuwait: The Politics of Gender. 2nd ed. London: Saqi Books, 2001.

Rizzo, Helen Mary. Islam, Democracy, and the Status of Women: The Case of Kuwait. New York: Routledge, 2005.

Tétreault, Mary Ann. "Women's Rights and the Meaning of Citizenship in Kuwait." Middle East Reports Online, 10 February 2005, at http://www.merip.org/mero/mero021005.html.

Tétreault, Mary Ann, Katherine Meyer, and Helen Rizzo. "Women's Rights in the Middle East: A Longitudinal Study of Kuwait." International Political Sociology 3 (2009): 218–237.

MARY ANN TÉTREAULT

L

LAND TENURE. Land tenure in the Islamic world is heavily affected by political factors. The three main influences on land tenure are the rules and choices imposed by political elites, Islamic law, and customary provisions, including pre-Islamic systems and adaptations to specific environments. Land tenure includes formal rules of ownership, rules guiding access to land for non-owners, and the distribution of landholdings according to these rules.

The liberalization of land tenure in the nineteenth century allowed individual property holdings in land. It was followed, beginning in the 1950s, by a wave of land reforms intended to equalize access to land. Land tenure in the Middle East is now moving again toward more private land ownership. In some places, such as the Gulf countries, women are increasingly investing in land ownership.

Regardless of the tenure type, the production unit in agriculture has been the family. While the male head of household was typically the one holding the rights to the land, some women might also be so recognized as landowners. Some might also be managers, if not rights holders, although anecdotal evidence suggests that women were rarely directly involved in land management. Everywhere, women were involved in production if not always in the fields. Inheritance laws and male relatives often disenfranchised women de facto, but, especially in the upper classes, there were exceptions. Women could have access to income from farming through wage labor.

Islamic Land Law. In many traditional Islamic systems the state (or the ruler), as the representative of the Islamic community, was the ultimate owner of the land. While the state or the ruler held residual ownership, the actual farmers held usufruct rights. This allowed actual practices of access to land to be governed by non-Islamic rules, since property rights were not involved. Many traditional practices governing access to land were based on use by a community rather than by an individual. Collective landholding could result from the institution of *waqf* (land entailed so not subject to further transfer), or it could reflect an undivided inheritance. Only a small portion of the agricultural land in the Islamic world was owned outright, giving the owner rights against the state. However, the practical difference between freehold and usufructuary tenure was small, and either could be combined with sharecropping.

Early Modern Political Changes. The contemporary growth of individual property holdings in land can be traced back to the land laws of the mid-nineteenth century, which stipulated the registration of land in the name of an individual, usually male. In Palestine and elsewhere, social forces prevented many actual farmers from registering their land. In some places, women were also frequently pressured to give over their rights to land to a male relative.

Over time, this evolution created a class of large and often absentee landholders. These large landholders also introduced mechanization, switched from sharecropping to wage labor as a means for organizing cultivation of the land, and financed agriculture through bank credit rather than moneylenders. They also fostered changes in the irrigation system where that was appropriate. The end result was a highly unequal pattern of distribution of rights over land.

Socialism and Land Reform. Land reform began in Egypt after the Revolution of 1952. It was initially motivated by the desire to dispossess the old ruling class. Everywhere, land reform was the outcome of the deliberations of urban intellectuals and politicians; small farmers were an afterthought. In Egypt, the first wave of agrarian reform divided the estates among their former workers. These smallholders were then organized into agrarian reform cooperatives. The second wave, after 1961, continued this process, but especially consolidated the relationship between owners and renters and required all farmers to join a government cooperative. Women rights holders were often represented by a male family member. Perhaps a third of the farmland was initially affected by the regulations on rentals, and all land was brought under the supervision of the cooperatives after 1961. The reforms (land tenure rules, cooperatives, subsidies on inputs, and marketing quotas) had the effect of making the government into the partner of each farmer and structured Egyptian agriculture for a generation after the 1952 reform.

Agrarian reforms of various types, often modeled on the Egyptian experience, were enacted in Iraq, Syria, Tunisia, Algeria, Iran, Pakistan, and elsewhere. In Algeria, the one-quarter of the land that had been held by colonial farmers largely passed into the "self-management" sector after independence in 1962. Workers on the estates took over management responsibility, within the framework of a government bureaucracy. The agrarian reform law of 1971 organized the larger Algerian-owned farms into cooperatives, covering 22 percent of the land. In a similar process in Tunisia, women were often excluded from cooperative membership, but were hired as workers. In the late 1980s and early 1990s, Algeria passed a number of laws that restored to individuals the right to own land and to dispose of it fully. Rights based on work gave way to rights based on property ownership.

Liberalization. Recent changes in Egypt have modified the strong pattern of government involvement in agriculture. The system of enforced crop rotation, subsidized inputs, and marketing quotas has been dismantled, and the village cooperatives have lost much of their role. The agrarian reform cooperatives have survived, although they too are weaker. A land law implemented in 1997 restricted the rights of tenants in favor of owners, thus changing the status of the roughly one-quarter of the land that was under tenancy.

Various factors enter into the debates about land law. In the name of equity, some argue that land tenure systems should permit maximum access to the land by farmers and farm workers. Others argue that the inviolability of private property is grounded in Islamic law, and that accumulation is no sin. At all times, rulers and the state have manipulated land law. Little thought has been given to devising a land tenure system that will foster development, or allow some voice to the small farmers. The relative uncertainty of land ownership is likely to continue into the near future, and this will shape the development patterns of the Islamic countries.

BIBLIOGRAPHY

Batatu, Hanna. *The Old Social Classes and the Revolutionary Movements of Iraq: A Study of Iraq's Old Landed and Commercial Classes and of its Communists, Baʿthists, and Free Officers*. Princeton, N.J.: Princeton University Press, 1978. Thoroughly documented account of social change in Iraq in the twentieth century, with many specific references to land tenure and land distribution.

Hooglund, Eric J., ed. *Twenty Years of Islamic Revolution: Political and Social Transition in Iran since 1979*. Syracuse, N.Y.: Syracuse University Press, 2002.

Hopkins, Nicholas S. *Agrarian Transformation in Egypt*. Boulder, Colo.: Westview Press, 1987. Analysis of land tenure, land use patterns, and irrigation in an Upper Egyptian village.

Metral, Françoise. 'State and Peasants in Syria: A Local View of a Government Irrigation Project.' *Peasant Studies* 11, no. 2 (1984): 69–90. Account of how land tenure and irrigation in the Ghab project were transformed by resettled peasants.

Meyer, Ann Elizabeth, ed. *Property, Social Structure, and Law in the Modern Middle East*. Albany, N.Y.: State University of New York Press, 1985. Collection of papers, including some on irrigation and land law; note papers by Attia, Leveau, and Hammoudi.

Radwān, Samīr M. *Agrarian Reform and Rural Poverty: Egypt, 1952–1975*. Geneva, Switzerland: International Labour Office, 1977. Probably the best summary of the effects of agrarian reform in Egypt.

NICHOLAS S. HOPKINS

LAW. [*This entry contains two subentries,*

Courts *and*
Women's Legal Thought and Jurisprudence.]

COURTS

Women were among the first Muslims to resort to the informal courts of the new Muslim community, as they brought their disputes to the Prophet (d. 632 CE) for resolution—a customary practice that was acknowledged in the Qurʾān. Ḥadīth and historical literature contain anecdotes about women who asked the Prophet and early caliphs to resolve marital disputes and contractual disagreements, as well as to handle criminal matters. Muslim women were recognized as full legal persons by early Muslim legal actors.

Late Antiquity. As Muslim societies expanded beyond Arabia, caliphs appointed judges for garrison towns and, gradually, for conquered territories. Although homes, mosques, and the marketplace all served as courts, eventually, under the Umayyads (661–750 CE), courts convened primarily in mosques. Available historical evidence suggests that women—and their legal representatives—accessed these courts as both petitioners and witnesses. Because women were able to acquire and to independently control wealth through inheritance, gifts, dowries, salaries, trade, and investment revenues, they had corresponding legal rights that they pursued in courts.

Medieval Proliferation of Courts. As the ʿAbbāsids (750–1258 CE) elaborated an increasingly technical bureaucracy, jurists transformed Islamic law to meet the new and changing sociopolitical demands. As a result, courts proliferated throughout Southwest Asia. Petitioners, including women, approached the court directly in the first few centuries of Islamic history. (Although with time, petitioners were increasingly represented by experts, such as a *wakīl*.) Although lower-class women frequented ʿAbbāsid courts, which also employed some women as court auxiliaries, elite ʿAbbāsid women were discouraged from appearing (directly) before ʿAbbāsid judges because of their social status. Historical evidence indicates that women solicited courts to deal with a variety of legal needs, including custody issues, alimony, and divorce. Yet women prominently appear to have solicited courts to manage their property holdings, as attested by Egyptian papyri of the ninth and tenth centuries. Under the Fāṭimids (909–1171 CE), elite women appear to have been specifically involved in charitable activities—such as financially sponsoring educational institutions and establishing charitable trusts—that necessitated court involvement.

In the Mamlūk era (1250–1517 CE), the financial autonomy of women was manifest in their solicitation of courts to buy, sell, or rent property that they had inherited or received as matrimonial gifts. In fifteenth-century Granada courts, women challenged their fathers for control over their marital property gifts and negotiated with their husbands to relinquish marital property rights in exchange for a divorce. Granadian women also acted as executors for the property of minors and court records document their property transactions, loans, and investments.

In Mughal India (1526–1857 CE), women imposed marriage contract stipulations that were the subject of court claims. Stipulations included preventing a husband from marrying a second wife, from having a concubine, or from leaving his wife for longer than a specified period; breaches of these contract stipulations were grounds for divorce, which women exercised in court. Mughal women, like Ottoman women, exercised their control over property—that they inherited, sold, purchased, rented, and received as marital gifts—in court.

Ottoman Courts. Recent scholarship based on Ottoman (1299–1923 CE) court archives has established that women experienced plurality, flexibility, and a high degree of accessibility in Ottoman courts. Ottoman court records indicate that women sought court intervention in both rural and urban areas, for commercial and domestic legal needs, and Ottoman judges did not require or enforce seclusion of women. Ottoman women were particularly involved in the administration of trusts (*awqāf*), which were recorded in Ottoman court records as part of the court's notarial services. Women requested legal opinions from Ottoman jurisconsults for primarily economic questions and marginally for domestic issues in the seventeenth century.

Ottoman jurists were flexible in their application of custody laws and assessment of alimony, in ways that were often favorable to women. In eighteenth-century Aleppo, mothers and matrilineal female relatives were awarded custody of children in more than 50 percent of surviving cases—despite the availability of patrilineal guardians. As in other times and places, Ottoman women included stipulations in their marriage contracts to prevent husbands from marrying additional wives or keeping concubines. Ottoman court records from the eighteenth and nineteenth centuries indicate that non-Muslim women frequented Ottoman courts for a variety of matters, including marriage, divorce, commercial, and criminal cases.

Colonialism and Reform. As European imperialism expanded throughout the Muslim world, women's access to courts and their treatment under Islamic legal systems became an ideological battlefield. During the era of European colonialism and reformist movements, secular and Islamic courts were identified as distinct domains. For instance, in Egypt, family law issues were relegated to Islamic courts in 1883 and court registration of inheritance, marriage, and divorce became obligatory in 1897. It is not entirely clear how this broad transformation in the courts—particularly the procedural requirements—affected women. In response to colonial pressures, Muslim societies debated the legal and social status of women. These broad sociopolitical dynamics generated various reform movements that primarily enacted substantive legal changes. For example, in the 1930s, Reza Shah of Iran required all marriages to be registered in court and, in 1924, Turkey made all divorces subject to court rulings. Some judicial processes, particularly divorce proceedings, appear to have become slower and less effective for women as the state's expanding bureaucratic apparatus complicated judicial procedures.

Modern Courts. In the post colonial era, throughout North Africa, Southwest Asia, and Southeast Asia, modern nation-states emerged, enacting legal codes and further bureaucratizing courts. Most modern legal systems in Muslim-majority states are mixed civil and Islamic legal systems, although Islamic law is primarily applied in family law matters. Recent studies suggest that women are the majority of plaintiffs in family law cases. In some contemporary Muslim-majority states, women serve as judges in civil courts, although they represent a minority of the judiciary. After Iran's 1979 Revolution, female judges were limited to acting as court advisors. As evident throughout the world, women's access to contemporary courts is dependent on economic and social factors, including the availability and skill of lawyers. Indeed, women sometimes neglect pursuing their legal rights in court because of cultural and familial limitations.

Throughout Islamic history, women have had varied access to and treatment in courts, depending on socioeconomic class, local culture, and internal court dynamics.

[*See also* Divorce; Family Law; Fāṭimid Dynasty; Inheritance; Mahr; Mughal Empire; Ottoman Empire, *subentry on* Women's Socioeconomic Role; Property; Qāḍī; *and* Waqf, Women's Constructions of.]

Bibliography

Primary Works

al-Ḥimyari al-Ṣanʿānī, ʿAbd al-Razzaq ibn Hammam (744–827). *Muṣannaf fī al-ḥadīth*. Edited by Maʿmar ibn Rāshid and Ayman Naṣr Azharī. 12 vols. Beirut: Manshurat Muḥammad ʿAli Bayḍūn, Dar al-Kutub al-ʿIlmīyah, 2000.

Ibn Abī Shaybah, ʿAbd Allāh ibn Muḥammad (775/6–849). *Muṣannaf fī al-aḥādīth wa-al-āthār*. Edited by Saʿid Laḥḥam. al-Ṭabʿah 1 ed. 9 vols. Beirut: Dar al-Fikr, 1989.

Ibn Anas, Mālik (d. 795). *al-Muwaṭṭaʾ [English and Arabic]*. Translated by Jīhān Abd al-Raʾūf Hibah. 1st ed. 2 vols. Beirut: Dār al-Kutub al-ʿIlmīyah, 2007.

Ibn Saʿd, Muḥammad (c. 784–845). *The Women of Madina*. Translated by Aisha Bewley. London: Ta-Ha Publishers, 1995.

Secondary Works

Cortese, Delia, and Simonetta Calderini. *Women and the Fatimids in the World of Islam*. Edinburgh: Edinburgh University Press, 2006.

Hallaq, Wael. *The Origins and Evolution of Islamic Law*. Cambridge, U.K. and New York: Cambridge University Press, 2005.

Jackson, Sherman. *Islamic Law and the State: The Constitutional Jurisprudence of Shihāb al-Dīn al-Qarāfī*. Leiden, Netherlands: E.J. Brill, 1996.

Jennings, R. "Women in Early Seventeenth-century Ottoman Judicial Records: The Sharia Court of Anatolian Kayseri." *Journal of the Economic and Social History of the Orient* 18 (1975): 53–114.

Meriwether, Margaret L. *The Kin Who Count: Family and Society in Ottoman Aleppo, 1770–1840*. Austin: University of Texas Press, 1999.

Rapoport, Yossef. *Marriage, Money, and Divorce in Medieval Islamic Society*. Cambridge, U.K.: Cambridge University Press, 2005.

Shatzmiller, Maya. *Her Day in Court: Women's Property Rights in Fifteenth-century Granada*. Cambridge, Mass.: Islamic Legal Studies Program, Harvard Law School; distributed by Harvard University Press, 2007.

Tillier, Mathieu. "Women before the Qāḍī under the Abbasids." *Islamic Law and Society* 16, no. 3–4 (2009): 280–301.

Zilfi, Madeline C., ed. *Women in the Ottoman Empire: Middle Eastern Women in the Early Modern Era*. Leiden, Netherlands: Brill, 1997.

Lena Salaymeh

Women's Legal Thought and Jurisprudence

Muslim women's legal thought and jurisprudence has a history as long and diverse as Islam itself.

What unites Muslim women across five continents, more than fourteen centuries of history, and innumerable ethnicities and cultures is their devotion to Islam as the most legitimate source for a good and just society. According to Islamic doctrine, the foundation of a just society is Sharīʿah, roughly translated as Islamic law. More correctly, Sharīʿah is God's divine will and guidance insofar as one can know it. It is the ideal to which every jurisprudent, or *faqīh*, has aspired. Since Islam's inception in the seventh century, Muslim women have played an essential role in defining Sharīʿah. As inspirational and iconic examples for future generations of Muslim women, as jurisprudents participating in the academic discipline by which scholars define Sharīʿah (*fiqh*), as transmitters of the traditions (ḥadīth) of the Prophet, his family (*ahl al-bayt*), and Companions, as teachers, and as warriors, Muslim women have actively engaged in Islamic legal thought and jurisprudence. Their methodologies, philosophies, effectiveness, and visibility have all been impacted by the cultures and societies in which they lived and the historical context of their time.

The Prophetic Period (610–632 CE). Examples of women's legal thought first appear in biographies of the Prophet (*sīrah*) and ḥadīth literature. Possibly the earliest example records Khadījah reassuring her husband, Muḥammad, of his prophethood after he received his first revelation through the angel Gabriel in 610 CE. Khadījah immediately sought counsel with her Christian cousin, Waraqah, who recognized and confirmed Muḥammad's revelation as divine in origin. This tradition not only establishes Khadījah's preeminent position as the first person to enter Islam, but also positions her as the affirmer of the first revelation, beginning a long tradition of Muslim women's essential participation in the development of Sharīʿah. *Sīrah* and ḥadīth literature are replete with influential women who were active and visible in the public sphere when the Prophet was alive, and who helped define the structure of the first Muslim community and society (*ummah*), which has served as the definitive example for Muslim communities and societies ever since. These women include Fāṭimah bint Muḥammad, ʿĀʾishah bint Abū Bakr, Hafsa bint ʿUmar ibn al-Khaṭṭāb, Zaynab bint Ḥusayn ibn ʿAlī, Umm ʿAtiyya, and Umm Salamah.

The Formative Period (Seventh to Tenth Centuries). During this time, the first Qurʾān was compiled; diacritical markings came to be included; the first compilations of ḥadīth, namely al-Bukhārī and Muslim, were completed; the first biographies of the Prophet, among them Ibn Isḥāq, Ibn Waqidi, and Ṭabarī, were written; the foundations of the four Sunnī law schools were established, and the genesis of the *ithna ʿAshari* community began after the Greater Occultation of the Twelfth Imam. The vast production of Islamic jurisprudence was made possible by a Muslim society that placed a significant and pronounced emphasis on intellectualism, resulting in a rapidly expanding scholarly class whose work defined Sharīʿah. Women such as Salama al-Fazariyya and Umm ʿAtiyya, who were companions of the Prophet, and Karima bint Ahmad of Marv, an authoritative source for al-Bukhārī, as well as other teachers, jurists, and warriors (Khārijī women), were essential to the formation of Sharīʿah during this early medieval era of Islamic empires. Many women who were subjects of ḥadīth and *sīrah* also became transmitters of these traditions and memorizers and interpreters of the Qurʾān, while continuing to expound upon the meaning of Islam following the Prophet's death. These women included female companions of the Prophet and, over time, expanded to include later related generations and also geographically and ethnically removed generations. Muslim women were visible, vocal, and active in the public sphere at the start of this formative period; however, during the ʿAbbāsid period (750–1258 CE), and following rapid expansion into the neighboring Byzantine and Sassanian empires, the visibility of elite and educated women in the public sphere declined dramatically. With that came the reduction and restriction of women's voices in jurisprudence. Historians such as Leila Ahmed have posited that the rapidly expanding Islamic empire assimilated cultural mores from the conquered territories that were largely androcentric, and that assimilation and adaptation essentially overrode Islam's emphasis on spiritual egalitarianism. The new Islamic empire, wherein Muslims were the ruling minority of most regions, lent itself to the silencing of women's voices in the face of military, economic, and other administrative expediencies requiring men's leadership in the public sphere.

The Late Medieval and Early Modern Periods (Eleventh to Eighteenth Centuries). During the late medieval and early modern eras, elite women, despite their segregation and seclusion (or possibly because of it), became politically significant and influenced Islamic thought through their patronage—building schools, mosques, and hospitals. This period, therefore, is witness to a dramatic decline in women's direct participation in jurisprudence. The few who were educated did so through the consent and encouragement of their male guardians, who were typically of the clerical classes. Examples of elite women patrons are Sayyida Hurra, the Ismāʿīlī Ṣulayḥid queen of Yemen (1047–1138); Shajar al-Dur, who helped retain Ayyūbid control of Egypt after the death of her husband, Ṣalāḥ al-Dīn al-Ayyūbī (r. 1240–1249); and any number of the powerful women of the Ilkhanid era and the Mamlūk Empire.

The Modern and Contemporary Periods. A slow revival of women's legal thought and jurisprudence began to take shape in the nineteenth century. This revival coincided with the decline of the Ottoman Empire, the rise of European and American imperialisms, and the rise of various intellectual and nationalistic movements, including Islamic nationalism and modernism, and Arab and Turkish nationalisms. The first generation of Islamic modernists, including Jamāl al-Dīn al-Afghānī, Muḥammad ʿAbduh, and Rashīd Riḍā, maintained that Islam was compatible with reason and science and sought to reorganize Muslim society in order to bring Islam into the modern world. At the heart of their reform efforts was a general call to revive the classical jurisprudential method of *ijtihād*, or independent jurisprudential reasoning. It was in this environment of renewal, revival, and reform that Muslim women began to reinterpret Islamic traditions and revive classical and early medieval Muslim women's voices.

The reinvigoration of *ijtihād*, together with a concerted effort to modernize Islamic society, boded well for women at the turn of the twentieth century. Modern Muslim women scholars echoed the call for a reopening of *ijtihād*, specifically to revive and reinstate the voices of women in Islamic legal thought and to revive the long-dormant value of gender justice in Islam. They drew inspiration and authority from classical iconic female figures such as ʿĀʾishah bint Abū Bakr and Zaynab bint ʿAlī (the Prophet's granddaughter and sister to the third Shīʿī imam Ḥusayn). They also used the jurisprudential method of *ijtihād* to interpret the Qurʾān and ḥadīth. The iconic women of Islamic history were revived and presented as heroines of women's empowerment and enfranchisement. Wardah al-Yāzijī (d. 1924), Malak Ḥifnī Nāṣif (d. 1918), and Naẓīrah Zayn al-Dīn are among the most prominent women of their time.

Since the advent of nation-states in the postcolonial era following World War I, women's legal thought has increasingly centered on the needs of

Muslim women in emerging Muslim-majority nations as well as the needs of Muslim women as minorities in developed nations, such as the United States and the European Union. Contemporary Muslim women's jurisprudence has focused on subjects directly affecting them, including laws pertaining to polygamy, child marriages, women's rights in marriage and divorce, women's right to inheritance, and honor killings. In all cases, Muslim women negotiate a difficult space in which they are both the subject and interpreter of the law, and a reciprocal space in which perceptions of gender roles inform the law, as the law also defines gender roles. Women's scholarly output depends largely on their access to education and employment, economic and social class, rural or urban status, and various internal and external challenges—their responses to which define their religious philosophy and methodology.

Following the monumental Fourth World Conference on Women held in Beijing in 1995, Muslim women's legal thought and jurisprudence has increased exponentially. In the United States, Professor Amina Wadud has popularized contemporary Muslim women's legal thought as a "Gender Jihad" because of its emphasis on gender equality and justice. Kecia Ali, Azizah al-Hibri, Nimat Hafez Barazangi, Aminah McCloud, Mohja Kahf, and Riffat Hassan are just a few examples of American Muslim women scholar-activists who are challenging the stereotype of Muslim women as only subjects of Sharīʿah and not its legislators.

Examples of women's legal thought and jurisprudence outside of Europe and America include Fatima Mernissi, Morrocco; Dr. Haifa Jamal al-Lail, Dean of Effat University in Saudi Arabia; Ayatollah Zohreh Ṣefātī in Qom; Nasrin Mosaffa, Professor of International Relations and International Human Rights at Tehran University, Iran; parliament member Shukria Barakzai in Afghanistan; and Hanan al-Lahham, religious instructor in Damascus. Several women's organizations have also formed. Sisters in Islam, founded in 1988 by Zainah Anwar and based in Malaysia, is a non-governmental organization with global and local objectives. Globally, its members work with other women's organizations and through universities to promote and teach an egalitarian and just Islam. In 2009 they launched Musawah (Equality), a global initiative that promotes gender equality in the family. Locally, they work with lawmakers, human rights organizations, and educational institutions to advance gender equality in Malaysia's family law. Karamah (Dignity) is a non-governmental organization of Muslim women lawyers based in Washington, D.C., and founded by Azizah al-Hibri in 1993. The organization's mission is to educate Muslims and non-Muslims concerning gender equality and justice in Islam. Working with institutional, educational, and human rights organizations, Karamah hosts several leadership workshops, summer programs, and lecture series on various aspects of Islamic law dealing with human rights, gender equality, and ethics.

Understanding contemporary women's jurisprudence requires a multifaceted approach. First is the issue of sources. Though all Muslim jurists agree on the immutability of the Qurʾān, there is a wide divergence of opinion regarding the use of ḥadīth and *sunnah*. This necessarily leads to the second issue, which is that of methodology. Although many Muslim women, more Shīʿī than Sunnī, work within the boundaries of one of the four Sunnī schools of law or the Shīʿī Jaʿfarī school of law, most in fact devise their own methodology, citing a need to reinvigorate the practice of *ijtihād*. Third is the issue of context, which can be broken down further into historical periods, geographies, education, and culture. Context indeed informs the methodologies that are utilized and the way in which sources are interpreted. Many contemporary Muslim women scholars implement the philosophies of Muḥammad ʿAbduh and Fazlur Rahman, who maintained that the vast majority of Islamic law is open to reform and reinterpretation and indeed should be reinterpreted to keep Islam relevant in every time and place. The peculiar predicament facing Muslim women today is that they find themselves caught between hostile and conservative Islamists on the one hand, and severe bias and bigotry from anti-Islam pro-democracy advocates and Islamophobes in the West on the other hand, which, ironically, legitimize the most conservative and essentialist interpretations of Islam.

[*See also* Ahmed, Leila; ʿĀʾishah; Anwar, Zainah; Barazangi, Nimat Hafez; Fāṭimah; Ḥadīth, *subentry on* Transmission; Hibri, Azizah al-; KARAMA (Muslim Women Lawyers for Human Rights); Khadīja bint Khuwaylid; Mernissi, Fatima; Musawah; Nāṣif, Malak Ḥifnī; Ṣefātī, Zohreh; Shajar al-Durr; Sharīʿah, Fiqh, Philosophy, and Reason (Theoretical Overview); Sisters in Islam; Wadud, Amina; Warriors, *subentry on* Women; *and* Zaynab bint ʿAlī.]

BIBLIOGRAPHY

Abdi, Zahara. "Exemplary Shia Women: Madam Zohreh Sefati." *Islamic Insights*, March 9, 2008. http://islamicinsights.com/religion/religion/exemplary-shia-women-madam-zohreh-sefati.html.

Afkhami, Mahnaz, ed. *Faith and Freedom: Women's Human Rights in the Muslim World.* Syracuse, N.Y.: Syracuse University Press, 1995.

Ahmed, Leila. *Women and Gender in Islam: Historical Roots of a Modern Debate.* New Haven, Conn.: Yale University Press, 1992.

Awde, Nicholas, trans. and ed. *Women in Islam: An Anthology from the Qur'an and Hadiths.* New York: Hippocrene Books, 2005.

Bani-Etemad, Rakhshan, director. "We Are Half of Iran's Population." *Link TV*. http://www.linktv.org/bridgetoiran/we-are-half-of-irans-population.

Coleman, Isobel. *Paradise Beneath Her Feet: How Women are Transforming the Middle East.* New York: Random House, 2010.

Goldziher, Ignaz. *Muslim Studies.* Translated by C. R. Barber and S. M. Stern. Edison, N.J.: Aldine Transaction, 2006.

Hambly, Gavin R. G., ed. *Women in the Medieval Islamic World: Power, Patronage, and Piety.* 6th ed. New York: St. Martin's Press, 1999.

Roded, Ruth. *Women in Islamic Biographical Collections: From Ibn Saʿd to Who's Who.* Boulder, Colo.: Lynn Rienner Publishers, 1994.

Tucker, Judith. *Women, Family, and Gender in Islamic Law.* Cambridge, U.K.: Cambridge University Press, 2008.

Wadud, Amina. *Inside the Gender Jihad: Women's Reform in Islam.* Oxford, U.K.: Oneworld Publication, 2006.

Wadud, Amina. *Qur'an and Woman: Rereading the Sacred Text from a Woman's Perspective.* 2nd ed. New York: Oxford University Press, 1999.

Webb, Gisela, ed. *Windows of Faith: Muslim Women Scholar-Activists in North America.* Syracuse, N.Y.: Syracuse University Press, 2000.

Yamani, Mai, ed. *Feminism and Islam: Legal and Literary Perspectives.* New York: New York University Press, 1996.

SORAYA SAATCHI

LEBANON. Assessing women's status is not an easy proposition in a complex country like Lebanon. It is

- at the crossroad of various civilizations and cultures that enriched it, but were also a source of internal upheaval;
- close to a democracy, and yet a country where political power is often inherited;
- the only Arab country where Islam is not the religion of the state and yet one where the various religious sects have their own personal status laws.

In this intricate setup, the Lebanese woman has tried to carve a place for herself in the public sphere. On the political scene, more than one outstanding woman emerged as far back as the sixteenth century. Among the most prominent ones, one could mention Princess Nasab of Tanukh,

Princess Hubus Arslan, and Naifeh Jumblatt (El-Khatib, 1998). These women and a few others belonged to the privileged families who ruled the country at the time. It is only with "Al-Nahdah," a period of enlightenment that began in Egypt in the mid-nineteenth century, and with the support women received from enlightened men pioneers, like Butrus al-Bustānī, Aḥmad Fāris al-Shidyāq, and Qāsim Amīn, that their status started improving.

The Lebanese women's movement emerged in this conducive atmosphere. It started toward the end of the nineteenth century, when prominent Lebanese women moved with their families to Egypt, running away from Ottoman oppression. There they started voicing their demands for women's rights to education and work, through articles they published in magazines they owned. Freedom of choice regarding veiling was also at the forefront of their requests.

The early decades of the twentieth century witnessed a significant upsurge in women's activities through philanthropic institutions and participation in political life. Women fought hard for their civil and political rights and played a very active role in securing Lebanon's independence. Among them were Ibtihaj Kaddoura, Laure Tabet, Najla Saab, Anna Tabet, and Nazek Beyhum.

Following the liberation of their country from the French Mandate in 1943 and the end of the sectarian discord that had split the women's movement, the Lebanese Women's Council was established in 1953. That same year Lebanese women were granted their full political rights. This was not, however, translated into women's political participation. Between 1953 and 1975, nine women ran for parliamentary seats, but only one of them, Myrna Boustani, was elected—in 1963, to complete her father's term after his tragic death, because he had no male heir.

No major change was witnessed during the fifteen years of civil strife (1975–1990). Women did not, however, remain inactive. Although few of them were fighters, they joined political parties and militias. Women's associations focused their interests on relief work, relegating for later any steps to secure their rights.

It took almost thirty years to have another woman join the Parliament, with Nayla Mouawad—the widow of the assassinated President René Mouawad—being appointed in 1991. It is significant that when she ran for election a year later in 1992, she secured the highest number of electoral votes countrywide. The legislative elections that followed marked each time the election of a minimum of three and a maximum of six women. In almost all cases, the successful women candidates were relatives of prominent male politicians belonging to feudal political families.

At the governmental level, the National Commission for Lebanese Women (NCLW) was established in 1998, to develop strategies for women's empowerment and implement the Beijing Platform for Action and the CEDAW resolutions ratified by Lebanon in 1997.

At the executive level, in 2004, two women (Wafa Dika Hamzah and Leila el-Solh Hamadeh) were appointed ministers for the first time. This new trend was not, however, followed systematically and the new Council of Ministers formed in 2011 did not include any woman minister. The situation is not any better at the local council's level where women represent less than 3 percent.

Obviously, the Lebanese woman has not succeeded in securing her share on the political scene. Among the reasons one could mention are the prevailing patriarchal system, the hegemony of the feudal families over political life, the sectarian distribution of political representation, and the reluctance of most religious denominations to be represented by a woman. More specifically, one could note women's absence from decision-making positions in political parties and their limited financial means in comparison to their male competitors (Helou, 1998).

A close look at the economic sector reflects the same situation. Although legally women have the right to own and administer property and to use their incomes and assets at their discretion, the centrality of the family along with the prevailing patriarchal system and the ensuing distribution of gender roles within the household prevent them from doing so.

It should be noted, though, that the number of enterprises owned by women—although not always managed by them—has increased, as well as the proportion of women in the labor force. This increase could be attributed to the high level of education of Lebanese women who represent more than half of university graduates and to the harsh economic conditions due to civil strife.

Lebanese women have not, however, succeeded in breaking the glass ceiling and few of them have reached decision-making positions, whether in the public or private sector. The female labor force participation remains low also. Although no accurate reliable figure related to the latter is available, it stood at 27 percent in 2007 according to the World Bank (2009).

In addition, working women suffer from wage discrimination. The ratio of estimated female to male earned income is 0.31, according to the 2004 national household survey (Ministry of Social Affairs, 2006). Furthermore, the National Social Security Fund Law discriminates against women with regard to social and health benefits.

Efforts have been undertaken to correct the prevailing situation by non-governmental organizations (NGOs). The Working Women's League has been lobbying to remove legal discriminatory provisions related to work and to ensure the implementation of laws that assert gender equality.

Presently, civil society is also pushing very hard to amend the nationality law, which does not allow Lebanese women to pass their nationality to their foreign husbands and children. A campaign for this purpose was launched in 2002 by the Collective for Research and Training on Development-Action (CRTD-A) and is still being pursued.

Perhaps the most significant progress has been made in respect to honor crimes. Article 562 of the Penal Code had originally acquitted men who killed female relatives engaged in illegal sexual intercourse. Laure Moghaizel led lobbying against this law, resulting in a 1999 amendment assigning men reduced sentences, rather than acquittal. In 2011, the whole article was repealed from the Penal Code.

Major problems arise also from the personal status laws that regulate matters related to birth, marriage, divorce, child custody, and inheritance by each of the eighteen religious sects recognized in Lebanon. This diversity in legislation violates the principle of equality of all citizens before the law and is incompatible with the Universal Declaration of Human Rights, to which Lebanon is committed. Several unsuccessful attempts have been undertaken since 1974 to adopt a unified civil personal status law, be it at the governmental or civil society level. The optional civil law, proposed in 1998 by President Elias Haraoui and approved by the Cabinet, was blocked by the Parliament, following the strong opposition of all religious leaders who saw it as trespassing over their prerogatives.

In 2007, "All for Civil Marriage in Lebanon," a group of young professionals and students, launched a campaign in favor of civil marriage and by 2009 completed a new draft for an optional civil law. However, the likelihood of its adoption in the near future seems to be remote. To circumvent this situation, many Lebanese of various religious sects resort to civil marriage abroad, marriage that is legally recognized and registered in Lebanon.

Lebanese women are not only subject to discriminatory laws but suffer also from the absence of laws in certain domains, like domestic violence. Draft legislation was submitted in 2009 by KAFA, the Lebanese Council to Resist Violence Against Women, and other non-governmental organizations to the Council of Ministers, but was referred to a ministerial committee for further examination. The draft law presently (2012) being discussed by a Parliamentary Commission has been rejected by Dar el-Fatwa, the highest authority of the Sunnī community, because it is in conformity with Western rather than Lebanese values and allows police intervention in family affairs. This has not stopped concerned non-governmental organizations from pursuing their efforts through the creation of 24-hour hotlines, providing free legal advice and shelter as well as launching campaigns to raise awareness about the plight of the victims.

Despite all these efforts and sporadic government interest in reform, there is still a lot to be done, if Article 7 of the Constitution, which stipulates equality in the rights and duties of all citizens, is to be implemented. It requires changing the prevailing patriarchal system and the stereotyped gender distribution of roles, in addition to reducing the hegemony of the various religious sects through the enactment of an optional civil personal status law.

Lebanese youth, both young women and men, are working relentlessly to introduce changes, calling for the implementation of existing laws that promote equality, amendment of discriminatory laws, and adoption of new laws that reinforce equality.

BIBLIOGRAPHY

El-Khatib, H. *Noushou' el-haraka annisa 'iya el-lubnaniya wa 'aliyataha 'ala el-moujtam' fi marahel tatwiriha* [The Lebanese women's movement and its impact on society at its different stages of development]. Beirut: Dar-el-Hadassah, 1998.

Ellis, K. C. *Lebanon's Second Republic: Prospects for the Twenty-first Century.* Gainesville: University Press of Florida, 2002.

Helou, M. Deputies and candidates in the legislative elections of 1992 and 1994. Bahithat, 4, 170–202. Beirut: Lebanese Association of Women Researchers, 1998.

Khalaf, M. Lebanon. In *Women's Rights in the Middle East and North Africa, Progress amid Resistance,* edited by S. Kelly and J. Breslin, pp. 249–281. New York: Freedom House, 2010.

Lebanese NGO Forum. "A Brief Review of the Current State of Violations of Women's Rights in Lebanon." Retrieved from http://www.lnf.org.lb/windex/violation.html.

Living Conditions of Households: The National Survey of Household Living Conditions: 2004. Beirut: Lebanese Republic, Ministry of Social Affairs; Central Administration for Statistics, United Nations Development Program.

Traboulsi, F. "An Intelligent Man's Guide to Modern Arab Feminism." Al-Raida (centenary issue), xx, no. 100 (2003): 15–19.

United Nations Development Program (UNDP). *Lebanon National Human Development Report: Towards a Citizen's State.* Beirut: UNDP, 2009.

World Bank. (2009). Gender stats—create your own table. Retrieved from http://go.worldbank.org/MRER20PME0. (February 12, 2012).

MONA CHEMALI KHALAF

LIBYA. The history of Libyan women prior to the twentieth century remains largely unwritten owing to a number of factors, most notably a dearth of sources that deal with women and their lives, with the important exception of the Sharīʿah court records (*sijillat*), some of which date as far back as the early seventeenth century. Over the course of the nineteenth and twentieth centuries, a number of regional and transnational events significantly altered Libyan society and impacted the lives of women. Among these were state modernization efforts carried out during the second Ottoman period (roughly 1835–1911) as well as the effects of Italian colonialism in Libya (1911–1943), both of which impacted the social structures and political economies of the Libyan territories.

The emergence of Libya's oil economy in the 1950s and 1960s under the monarchy of King Idris al-Sanusi (r. 1951–1969) and the autocratic regime of Colonel Muʿammar al-Qadhdhāfī (r. 1969–2011) precipitated the mass migration of rural Libyans to coastal cities, and resulted in the large-scale urbanization of the population, as well as the incorporation of growing numbers of women into the urban workforce, most notably in the spheres of education, health care, and administration. Also facilitating the entry of women into the workforce was growing access to primary, secondary, and higher education for all Libyans, particularly in the post-independence period, resulting in a concomitant increase in literacy among both men and women. In 2009, the literacy rate for adult males and females in Libya was estimated at 95 percent for males and 82 percent for females. However, the gap in literacy between men and women, as well as overall literacy rates among both groups, essentially closed among young people in the latter decades of the twentieth century due to the increasing availability of education. Some 2009 estimates placed literacy rates for Libyans aged fifteen to twenty-four as high as 100 percent for both females and males (World Bank, 2009). Enrollment of women in both secondary and higher education in Libya eclipsed enrollment of men, despite a slightly higher overall male population, including among school-aged youth and adults (World Bank, 2003, 2006, 2009).

Despite growing educational and employment opportunities for women, the family unit (which for most Libyans still includes the extended family) has remained the key determinant of most aspects of Libyan women's lives. In general, Libyan families are patriarchal and patrilineal, although within a family, the matriarch often wields significant influence. In most cases, it is the family that determines the nature and degree of a woman's participation outside of the home, whether educationally, professionally, or socially. Such considerations are typically mediated by prevailing social norms as influenced by local religion and custom. Regional, ethnic, religious, and cultural variations, as well as the relative degree of importance of tribal or extended kinship structures, have also impacted the social, economic, and political lives of Libyan women, as has their location within urban or rural settings. Sunnī Islam is the predominant religion of Libyan society, and as in most of North Africa, the Maliki school of jurisprudence has historically dominated. There also exists a small Ibadi community among the country's Amazigh (Berber) population, the largest numbers of which are concentrated in the western Jabal Nafusa mountains, the western coastal city of Zuwara, and the southwestern desert. Arabic is spoken as a first language by the majority of Libyans today, with roughly 5 percent speaking Berber dialects (usually in addition to Arabic). Additional linguistic groups within Libya include the Tebu speaking people of southern Libya, and the Touareg, Tamasheq Berber speaking nomads concentrated mainly in the southwestern part of the country. Touareg are distinct among other groups in Libya in that their society is matrilineal; moreover, Touareg men, rather than women, veil, and women have historically been the bearers of literacy in Touareg society. Until the twentieth century, Jewish communities dating from antiquity represented a sizable minority in the country, though most Jews emigrated from Libya in the twentieth century, particularly during the Italian Fascist period in Libya, after the establishment of the state of Israel in 1948, and following the 1967 Arab–Israeli war. Libya's Christian population is generally limited to small, expatriate communities, including Greek, Italian, and Maltese. However, the majority of expatriate and migrant workers hail from neighboring African and Arab states, with smaller groups coming from South and Southeast Asia. Women constituted a significant minority of Libya's foreign-born labor force; however, the Libyan uprising of 2011 precipitated a mass exodus of expatriate communities and migrant workers, including women.

Law and Sharīʿah. Within the cities and towns of the Ottoman provinces of Tripolitania and Cyrenaica, Sharīʿah courts exercised jurisdiction, including personal status issues (*al-ahwal al-shakhsiyya*) that subsumed marriage, divorce, inheritance, and child custody law, and, frequently, business contracts; minority religious groups established their own religious courts. In the nineteenth century, however, civil courts were established as part of Ottoman legal reforms to handle nonpersonal status cases. Among many of the rural tribes, however, customary law continued to play an important role.

Although most historical sources prior to the twentieth century are virtually silent about women and the issues that affected them, extant court records from a number of Libyan towns and cities provide rare insight into some of the most significant and private aspects of women's lives and represent a potentially fruitful source for the partial recovery of women's social history. During the Ottoman and colonial periods, particularly in cities and towns, women approached the courts to secure rights guaranteed by the Sharīʿah, though the extent to which women chose to utilize the courts remains unclear. The dual system of Sharīʿah and civil courts persisted with only minor interruption through the Italian colonial and monarchical periods until the government of Colonel Qadhdhāfī dissolved the separate religious courts, and declared that Sharīʿah would henceforth constitute the principal source of all legislation. Codified personal status law continued to reflect a selective interpretation of Sharīʿah; the implementation of Islamic law across the legal spectrum, however, remained limited. *Ḥadd* penalties were rarely, if ever, carried out in practice.

Generally speaking, Libyan laws under the monarchical and Jamāhīrīyah governments have rarely restricted women's mobility, employment, dress, or participation in "public" life (in a strictly nonpolitical sense); rather, families and social mores have tended to regulate these areas. Politically, however, both women and men have experienced repression and disenfranchisement under Libya's twentieth-century regimes. Though women were employed in a number of professions, they were rarely appointed to key government positions. First ladies, such as Queen Fatima al-Sanusi and Safiyya al-Qadhdhāfī, as well as other female relatives of Libya's rulers, generally kept low public profiles compared to their male counterparts.

Notable Libyan Women. In the twentieth century, Libyan women made increasing contributions to education and the arts, including literature, poetry, and music. Khadija al-Jahmi (1921–1996) was a notable radio broadcaster, author, activist, and advocate for women's rights, and one of the most prominent female public figures in twentieth century Libya. Zaʾima al-Baruni (1910–1976), daughter of a former Ottoman parliamentarian and leading figure in the Tripolitanian anticolonial resistance, was a writer, historian, educator, social activist, and founding member of the Libyan Women's Renaissance Association (*Jamʿiyyat al-Nahda al-Nisaʾiyya*), established in Tripoli in1958. More recent figures include Umm al-ʾIzz al-Farisi, a poet, academic, and advocate for women's rights, and the literary critic and poet, Dr. Fawzia Bariun. It is important to note, however, that the Qadhdhāfī regime actively pursued a policy of suppressing the emergence of public figures in Libya, both male and female.

During the 2011 Libyan uprising, women actively participated in demonstrations on both sides of the conflict. Following the collapse of the regime, discussions emerged within Libya concerning the role of women in government, with many women's groups and activists calling for greater representation of women in politics and government. In 2011, Libya's National Transitional Council (NTC) appointed Dr. Salwa al-Daghili, a constitutional lawyer and academic, to head the NTC's legal advisory committee. In addition, Dr. Fatima Hamroush was appointed Minister of Health. Despite the appointment of women to a small number of high-level positions in the interim government, the extent to which women will be included in any future government remains to be seen.

BIBLIOGRAPHY

Ahmida, Ali Abdullatif. *The Making of Modern Libya: State Formation, Colonization, and Resistance*. 2d ed. Albany: State University of New York Press, 2009.

Anderson, Lisa. *The State and Social Transformation in Tunisia and Libya, 1830–1980*. Princeton, N.J.: Princeton University Press, 1986.

Baldinetti, Anna. *The Origins of the Libyan Nation: Colonial Legacy, Exile and the Emergence of a New Nation-State*. London: Routledge, 2010.

Dajani, Ahmad Sidqi. *Al-Harakah Al-Sanusiyah: Nasha'atuha wa-namu'uha fi al-qarn al-tasi'ashar*. [The Sanusiyya Movement: its Emergence and Development in the 19th Century]. Beirut: Dar Lubnan, 1967.

Dajani, Ahmad Sidqi, and 'Abd al-Salam Ad'ham, eds. *Watha'iq tarikh Libiya Al-hadith: Al-watha'iq Al-'Uthmaniyah* [Documents from Modern Libyan history: Ottoman Documents], *1881–1911*. Benghazi: University of Benghazi, 1974.

Evans-Pritchard, E. E. *The Sanusi of Cyrenaica*. Oxford, U.K.: Clarendon Press, 1963.

Layish, Aharon. *Divorce in the Libyan Family: A Study Based on the Sijills of the Shari'a Courts of Ajdabiyya and Kufra*. New York: New York University Press, 1991.

Library of Congress. *Libya Country Study*: http://lcweb2.loc.gov/frd/cs/lytoc.html.

Marwan, Muhammad 'Umar. *Sijillat Mahkamat Tarabulus Al-Shar'iyah*, (Sijillat from the Shari'a courts of Tripoli) 1174–1271 H/1760–1854 M. 880–03. Vol 1. Ed. al-Jamahiriyah al-'Arabiyah al-Libiyah al-Sha'biyah al-Ishtirakiyah al-'Uzma: Markaz Jihad al-Libiyin lil-Dirasat al-Tarikhiyah, 2003.

Poddar, Prem, Rajeev S. Patke, and Lars Jensen. *A Historical Companion to Postcolonial Literatures: Continental Europe and Its Empires*. Edinburgh: Edinburgh University Press, 2008.

Rossi, Ettore. *Storia Di Tripoli e Della Tripolitania. Dalla Conquista Araba Al 1911* (Story of Tripoli and Tripolitania. From the Arab Conquest to 1911). Rome: Ist. Per l'Oriente, 1968.

Vandewalle, Dirk J. *A History of Modern Libya*. Cambridge, U.K.: Cambridge University Press, 2006.

World Bank. *World Development Indicators*. "Libya." http://data.worldbank.org/country/libya.

Najla Naeem Abdurrahman

Literary Salons. People have been gathering nightly to hear and recite verbal art in the Middle East since the emergence of language in *homo sapiens*, perhaps 200,000 years ago. The reasons are prosaic, but important: humans bond over literature, relieving isolation, trauma, and grief; literature transmits culture to the young and the alien in face-to-face performance across space and time, like verbal DNA; and, when humans perform verbal art, the experience provides them with an opportunity to compete and cooperate in a ritual game, thus gaining or losing status and forming alliances that translate into cultural capital in other realms of life.

The first evidence of salon-like gatherings in the Middle East comes from the Sumerians and dates before 3000 BCE. While the evidence pertains to the royals and the elites, serving to sanctify kingship, other strata of society have left us little or no traces of their gatherings, which must have existed. This era witnessed the earliest invention of metal tools and the stable production of the raw materials to make beer and wine, which were indispensible for socializing in salons. This period also evinces the rise of the first cities as well as the specialization of professions and division of labor; it is little wonder that the first organized religions concurrently emerged to help redress the frustrations and injustices of social hierarchies, class struggle, and professional rivalries. Drinking salons likely gave small groups of friends an opportunity to escape and vent in venues that ranged in degrees of warmth, competitiveness, and bacchanalia.

The textual and archeological evidence of early Islam speaks of salons among royalty, with little or no mention of salons at lower strata of society. Royal salons (the *majlis*) seemed to have been hierarchical, with a caliph or other patron at the head of the room, with others attending at and for the pleasure of the patron, sometimes despite their own personal preference or discomfort. However, in ninth-century Iraq, we begin to see in sources the parallel burgeoning of salons outside the courts by an emerging, new-money sub-nobility, often dubbed *aḥsāb* or *dhul ṭarīf* (self-made or new money), in competitive emulation of royalty. The sub-nobility in the ninth century comprised chancery workers, qadis, military generals, physicians, and, in the tenth century, merchants, who mingled outside the strictures of their jobs as Muslims, Christians, Jews, and Zoroastrians in gardens, orchards, mosques, monasteries, reception halls, or loggias of homes, and even the waiting rooms of certain physicians. These gatherings were typically at night and, if outdoors, under the moonlight. However, rather than simply ape the stiff hierarchies of the royal salons, the sub-nobility adapted a more intimate, more egalitarian salon (*mujālasah*) that featured friends and colleagues taking turns in speaking and hosting, invitation by guest (in addition to host), mutual requests for passing of food or drink, and hosts aiming to impress their guests with wine, food, flowers, fine textiles, sprigs of fresh basil, and perfumed oils. Not only were the salons more egalitarian than before, but the literature recited in them promoted those very ideals. One work in particular on salon-crashers, *K. al-Taṭfīl* (The Book of Party Crashing), not only elicited peals of laughter from untold generations of audiences, but promoted a more liberal ethos of inclusion and a capacious definition for the emerging bourgeoisie, including bazaari and long-distance merchants, engravers, coppersmiths, and cobblers, as well as barley-, linen-, and cotton-mongers. In Egypt, Syria, and Iraq, we have no indications of mixed-gender salons, and ample evidence that men preferred a homosocial/homoerotic salon to themselves; however, home layouts suggest sub-nobility women held their own homosocial/homoerotic salons in homes and other venues, enabling them to gain prestige for their knowledge and performance of literatures, build networks, and gain social capital. In Andalusia, the *Romance of Bayad and Riyad* presumes that women commonly hosted single-sex or mixed-gender salons, sometimes behind the backs of fathers and other patriarchs.

The salons of the sub-nobility restructured political culture from the ninth century onward. They enabled like-minded, newly moneyed individuals to come together as a nās (a people or public) and share common concerns about society and its leadership. Ibn Qutaybah (d. 889), in his *Maʿārif* (Types of Knowledge), gives them politico-cultural purpose: "gatherings organized *for* the commonweal, established *for* guidance, or pursued *for* the sake of cultivating manliness." Literature that idealized the rulers and societies of yore implicitly posed a critique of contemporary rulers and society by comparison. A ruler could hardly pass a week without wondering how his reputation would withstand the test of time in salons.

Al-Tanūkhī (d. 994), for example, tells a salon-type story about an Egyptian woman as part of a long line of literature (*adab*) about women who check patriarchy, despite the burden of misogyny.

(Implicitly, such narratives inscribe great rhetoric as a necessary counterbalance to state power, even if a woman is speaking.) It was said that the Caliph al-Ma'mun was passing by an Egyptian village, when the owner of that estate, Maria the Copt, invited him to stay for the night and honor the estate with his presence. Barely containing his contempt and sense of privilege, he obliged while still dismissing her capacity to host generously and properly. Maria offered grand shows of country hospitality that night, but at daybreak, the Caliph hurried to depart along with his entourage without seeing her, depriving her of the honor of displaying further hospitality that morning. The woman intercepted him with *her* entourage of ten servants, and yet the Caliph still said mockingly to his people, "Here comes the Coptic lady, bringing you gifts of the countryside: vinegar-sauce, salt fish and bitter aloes." The gifts instead turned out to be nuggets of pure gold befitting prophets and kings, and God's deputy was forced to acknowledge their beauty before the assembly. Speechless, he asked her to take them back; they were too much. With righteous indignation, Maria refused, "No!" she said, "I swear to God, I won't!" In contrast to the Caliph's ungenerous attitude of privilege, she proceeded to dramatize a more generous angle on privilege—this black fertile land that turns to gold day after day compels her to display her munificence as any man would. Shaming the Caliph, she said, "O Commander of the Faithful, do not break our hearts, nor deride us." Humbled finally, the Caliph departed "amazed at the magnitude of her manliness [*murū'a*: pun on her name], and the extent of her wealth." Stories such as this illustrate the capacity of women to gain rhetorical skills, but they also demonstrate the interest male littérateurs showed in tales of women parrying power with their skills, which evoke the example of Laylā al-Akhyālīyah of the Umayyad period, among others.

Beyond fulfilling a role in social functions, it deserves to be mentioned that salons fulfilled a deeply emotional purpose for both men and women. They helped quiet the most perennial fears that humans have about irrelevance in life, mortality, and legacy in death. In short, salons enabled people to freely and voluntarily form "communities of love" that allay those fears by asserting life against the odds of time. The poet al-Buḥturī (d. 897) composed an elegy for a friend upon his death and said, "May showers bless our salons that you made joyful, / Alas to our salons that you left bereft. / You made our salons by your memory lively; / You now attend hereafter another forever. / Your memory is a friend to us present, / Though you yield your body to others. / Our day will relish the taste of your memory; / So, those with whom you gathered will enjoy your company still." In a similar vein, the physician Ibn Buṭlān (d. 1068), having neither wife nor children, put his hopes in his salon community: "If I die, no one will weep my death / except my salon for medicine and books; they will weep."

In the nineteenth and twentieth centuries, salons served as an important venue for creatively responding to the challenges of modernity, colonialism, and European supremacy. Most visibly, the Cairo-based salon of the Mayy Ziyādah flourished and brought together the luminaries of the Arabic Renaissance (*nahḍah*) and introduced Egypt to the work of New York-based Kahlil Gibran. Currently, television and academic institutions have largely fulfilled the entertainment and educational functions of the salons, but the need to socialize and form alliances still continues to propel salons under the name *dīwān* or *dīwānīyah* in Kuwait and other Gulf States.

Bibliography

Ali, Samer M. *Arabic Literary Salons in the Islamic Middle Ages: Poetry, Public performance, and the presentation of the past*. Notre Dame, Ind.: University of Notre Dame Press, 2010.

Bencheikh, Jamel-Eddine. *Poétique arabe: essai sur les voies d'une creation*. Paris: Éditions Anthropos, 1975.

Ibn Qutaybah, Abū Muḥammad ʿAbdullāh b. Muslim. *Al-Maʿārif* Edited by Tharwat ʿAkkāshah. Cairo, Egypt: Dār al-Maʿārif, 1992.

Khaldi, Boutheina. "Arab Women Going Public: Mayy Ziyadah and her Literary Salon in a Comparative Context." PhD thesis, Indiana University, 2008.

Al-Khaṭīb al-Baghdādī, Abū Bakr Aḥmad b. ʿAlī. *Al-Taṭfīl wa ḥikayāt al-ṭufayliyīn wa ākhbārihim wa nawādirihim wa ashʿārihim*. Edited by Bassām ʿAbd al-Wahhāb al-Jābī. Beirut, Lebanon: Dār Ibn Ḥazm, 1999.

Schoeler, Gregor. *The Oral and the Written in Early Islam*. Translated by Uwe Vagelpohl, edited by James Montgomery. London: Routledge, 2006.

Al-Tanūkhī, al-Muḥassin b. ʿAlī. *Al-mustajād min fiʿlāt al-ajwād*. Edited by Yūsuf al-Bustānī. Cairo, Egypt: Dār al-ʿArab, 1985.

SAMER M. ALI

M

Madrasah. *Madrasah* (*madāris*, pl.) is an Arabic word frequently translated into English as "school." In Arabic-speaking countries, it refers to both religious and secular schools and to schools that combine secular and religious curricula. In most non–Arabic-speaking countries in Asia and Europe, *madrasahs* are formal or informal Islamic schools that teach Qurʾānic recitation, Islamic values, jurisprudence, and Arabic grammar (among other subjects) to schoolchildren and tertiary-level students. A distinction must be made here between "modern" *madrasahs* that function like a regular school, with the use of classrooms, tables, and chairs, and "traditional" *madrasahs* that require students to sit on the floor during class and promote an ascetic life by boarding in school dormitories. In the Malay cultures of Southeast Asia, the latter are also known as *pondok* or *pesantren.*

Across cultures, *madrasahs* differ in design, teaching material, gender ideology, politics, and the extent to which they integrate into wider society. Traditionally, *madrasahs* are patriarchal institutions; the central components include the mosque, the male religious teacher, and the texts he uses to teach. However, because *madrasahs* are not homogeneous, the extent of male domination and gender bias varies cross-culturally. Relations in *madrasahs* function according to pan-Islamic gender and sexual scripts that implement gender segregation, strict dress codes, and the domestication and docility of girls, devaluing female leadership and autonomy. The gendered roles taught in a *madrasah* depend on the processes of ethnicization that the *madrasah* undergoes in its gendered cultural context. Depending on the background of the male or female teacher, Islamic gender ideologies and instructions for girls will vary by *madrasah.*

Historically, *madrasahs* catered to boys from lower socioeconomic groups, while patriarchal gender ideologies of purdah confined girls' education to the home. However, women scholars of Arab history have shown that, in the medieval Arab world, women were Islamic authorities and teachers, indicating that women's participation and role in Islamic education were contextual and diverse. In most Islamic countries in the early twenty-first century, girls have opportunities to study Islam in both informal and formal *madrasahs*; female religious teachers are required to teach female students in coeducational or female-only *madrasahs.* Traditional *madrasahs*, such as *pondoks pesantrens* in Indonesia, offer gender-segregated residential quarters for students. The male religious teacher in charge of the school entrusts his wife (or wives) and daughters with caretaking roles, including enforcing Sharīʿah-based surveillance of female sexuality. Scholars have noted that same-sex experimentation in dormitories is not uncommon.

In the gender cultures of Southeast Asia, young women's *madrasahs* lifestyles integrate with the globalizing forces of regular society, posing challenges for the maintenance of male-defined piety in *madrasahs*. Women's rights activists use *madrasahs* and *pondok/pesantrens* as platforms for gender mainstreaming in Muslim communities. It is not uncommon for influential male Muslim scholars from *madrasah* backgrounds to be active in the Muslim feminist movement in Indonesia. Female students thus have opportunities to become Islamic specialists in *madrasahs* and may become respected leaders among women, or, in some cases, heads of *madrasahs* or *pondok/pesantrens*.

The Ṣūfī orders often attached to *madrasah* are popular among women who, either through acquired or ascribed power, may become *murshidāt* (spiritual leaders). The latter possibility is usually kinship-based, and, if not the daughter or wife of the founder of the school, then his son-in-law or a loyal disciple usually inherits the leadership, maintaining the patriarchal design of the institution. It must be noted however, that women were instrumental in the formation of Sufism. The first Arab Ṣūfī female mystic, Rābiʿah al-ʿAdawīyah, is just one example of an unmarried woman whose spiritual power and knowledge enabled her legal autonomy free from male authority. She continues to be exalted by Ṣūfī men and women in Muslim cultures around the world. Ṣūfī women leaders can be found in most Muslim cultures today in the varieties of *madrasahs* and Ṣūfī orders.

[*See also* Pesantren *and* Sufism and Women, *subentries* Historical Overview *and* Contemporary Thought and Practice.]

BIBLIOGRAPHY

Noor, Farish, Yoginder Sikand, and Martin van Bruinessen, eds. *The Madrasa in Asia: Political Activism and Transnational Linkages*. Amsterdam: Amsterdam University Press, 2008. Comprehensive coverage on *madrasahs*, including chapters on women.

Schimmel, Annmarie. *My Soul Is a Woman: The Feminine in Islam*. New York: Continuum, 2003.

Smith, Bianca J., and Mark Woodward, eds. *Gender and Power in Indonesian Islam: Leaders, Feminists, Sufis and Pesantren Selves*. London and New York: Routledge, forthcoming. This volume challenges Arab-centric gender ideologies and practices associated with Islam by re-orienting understandings through cultural examinations of varieties of Islam in Indonesia, the world's largest Muslim-majority nation. It focuses exclusively on Muslim women's roles in *pesantrens* (*madrasahs*) and Ṣūfī orders to reveal varieties of female leadership, authority, spiritual power, and feminism.

Smith, Margaret. *Rabi'a the Mystic and Her Fellow-Saints in Islam*. Amsterdam: Philo Press, 1978.

Winkelmann, Mareike Jule. *From Behind the Curtain: A Study of a Girls' Madrasa in India*. Amsterdam: Amsterdam University Press, 2005.

BIANCA J. SMITH

MAHR. *Mahr* is a nuptial gift that the man makes to the woman at the time of marriage and that, upon receipt, becomes her sole property with complete freedom of use and disposal. Without *mahr* the *nikāḥ* (marriage contract) is not valid. *Mahr* attempts to bring some equity to a marriage that structurally favors the man. The term *mahr* itself is not used in the Qurʾān, which instead has the terms *ṣadaqah* (gift; "and give to the women their gifts willingly," 4:4), *ajar* (reward or recompense; "so marry them with the permission of their families and give them their rewards,"

4:25), and *farīḍah* (appointed portion; "and if you divorce them before you have touched them, then give them half of the appointed portion," 2:237).

The amount and time of payment of the *mahr* may be specified or remain unspecified at the time of *nikāḥ*. There is no set amount for *mahr*, and it can be paid in cash, kind, or service, as long as the latter two can be translated into a monetary value against which a purchase can be made. The *ḥadīth* literature suggests the amount of gold equivalent in weight to a date stone as a minimum amount. Generally the amount of the *mahr* reflects the qualities and the socioeconomic (family) status of the woman. Classical jurists differed as to whether *mahr* is like a payment made to buy and secure exclusive right of access to the woman's body and reproductive functions (*bāy*ʿ), or whether it is an act of worship (ʿ*ibādāh*); there is also disagreement as to whether it came due at the time of the marriage (*mahr mu*ʾ*ajjal*), or whether its payment could be deferred to a later point in time. Those who considered *mahr* similar to sale or an act of worship were against the postponement of its payment until separation or death. Others considered the deferred *mahr* permissible, as long as the payment was not deferred for an indefinite period, as a concession to those who would otherwise not be able to marry.

In practice, many Muslim women do not receive their *mahr*, which is either given to the father for the wedding trousseau or deferred for other reasons. A high deferred *mahr*, stipulated in the *nikāḥ* contract by the woman's family, continues to be used as a deterrent to the husband's exercise of his right to *ṭalāq* (unilateral extrajudicial divorce) or mistreatment of the wife (or marrying another woman), since the *mahr* becomes payable at the time of divorce. Indefinitely deferred *mahr* acts as alimony in case of divorce, if it is stipulated in terms of a material (like gold) whose value does not depreciate over time. The wife is expected to forgive the deferred *mahr* at the time of her or her husband's death.

Some Muslim scholars see *mahr* as a token of the man's willingness and ability to bear the expenses of the woman's material needs, since she bears all the responsibility in the reproductive cycle. This role of the provider in the family, symbolized in the *mahr*, is also seen as justifying the husband's authority over his wife.

[*See also* Divorce; Marriage; *and* Polygyny.]

BIBLIOGRAPHY

Averroës. *The Distinguished Jurist's Primer: A Translation of* Bidāyat al-mujtahid. Translated by Imran Ahsan Khan Nyazee. Reading, U.K.: Garnet, 1994. A twelfth-century CE classic of Islamic jurisprudence; summarizes the philosophical positions undergirding different classical legal opinions. Discusses *mahr* in the Book of Marriage (*Kitāb al-nikāḥ*).

Esposito, John L., and Natana J. DeLong-Bas. *Women in Muslim Family Law*. 2nd ed. Syracuse, N.Y.: Syracuse University Press, 2001. Includes an introductory summary (pp. 24–26).

Khan, Maulana Wahiduddin. *Women in Islamic Shari*ʿ*ah*. Translated by Farida Khanam. Lahore, Pakistan, 2000. Somewhat apologetic, meant as a practical guide for lay South Asian Muslims. See ch. 9, pp. 125–137.

Mir-Hosseini, Ziba. *Marriage on Trial: A Study of Islamic Family Law: Iran and Morocco Compared*. Rev. ed. New York and London: I. B. Tauris, 2000. A feminist perspective on the social practice and legal application of family law in two very different Muslim countries.

Qaisi, Ghada G. "A Student Note: Religious Marriage Contracts: Judicial Enforcement of 'Mahr' Agreements in American Courts." *Journal of Law and Religion* 15, nos. 1/2 (2000–2001): 67–81. An interesting note on the intersection of American law and Muslim family law. Discusses how the contractual freedom to determine aspects of the marriage contract under American law affords Muslim couples the possibility of taking disputes related to *mahr* to American courts.

GHAZALA ANWAR

MALAY AND INDONESIAN LITERATURE. The literatures of modern Malaysia and Indonesia have a common heritage in classical Malay literature, the earliest forms of which comprised oral genres including myths, legends, folk tales, romances, epics, poetry, proverbs, origin stories, and histories. Early Malay literature was influenced by Indian epics such as the Mahābhārata and the Rāmāyana.

By the fourteenth century Islam had become established in the Malay peninsula and Jawi (an Arabic-based script) was adopted for writing the Malay language. The earliest writings produced in Malay/Jawi were religious books called *kitab* or *risalah*, containing the basic teachings of Islam such as *syahadat* (Malay, the Muslim confession of faith) and the pilgrimage to Mecca.

By the nineteenth century oral literature had been largely superseded by written literature, which included writings by Muslim scholars on Islamic law, the Qur'ān, ḥadīth (traditions relating to the deeds and sayings of the Prophet Muḥammad), theology, Sufism, and tales of Islamic prophets. There were a number of popular styles, notably the *hikayat* (an Arabic word meaning "story") and *syair* (verse), both of which incorporated Islamic motifs and themes. For example, the 1840 *Syair Siti Zubaidah* depicts cultural and religious interaction between the Malay-Muslim world and China. The heroine of the tale, Siti Zubaidah, rescues her husband, Sultan Zainal Abidin, from exile, only to have him take on a second wife after his rescue.

With the postwar independence of the nation-states of Indonesia and Malaysia, the Malay language developed into two related but separate modern languages—Bahasa Indonesia in Indonesia and Bahasa Malaysia in Malaysia. Because most Malaysians are conversant in English, there is also a body of literary work written in that language.

With the largest population of Muslims in the world (almost 90 percent of its 240 million people identify as Muslims), Indonesia is a secular state, albeit with a constitution based on the principle that its citizens must follow a formal religion. Although Malaysia's constitution names Islam as the official religion of the country, there is still debate as to whether the country, with 60 percent of its population identifying as Muslim, is an Islamic state.

The two countries share commonalities in their historical and contemporary engagement with Islam. Muslim women in Malaysia and Indonesia have long enjoyed freedoms and rights that are sometimes denied to Muslim women in other parts of the world. Women have always owned property and worked outside the home, and wearing the headscarf was not part of Malay Muslim culture. Men and women have always been able to mix freely in public spaces.

Since the 1970s the *dakwah* (proselytizing of Islam) movement has led to a revival of Islamic awareness in the region, although, until the fall of Indonesia's President Suharto in 1998, this was more marked in Malaysia than in Indonesia, where the movement kept a low profile. A heightened awareness of Islam is now felt in almost every sphere of society. *Dakwah* has given rise to a very popular genre of literature known as *sastera Islam* (Islamic literature), which promotes Islamic beliefs and doctrine, praises key Islamic figures, and criticizes practices and views that do not accord with the values of Islam, in line with the goals of the International League for Islamic Literature.

A very popular example of this genre of writing is the 2004 Indonesian novel, *Ayat Ayat Cinta* (*Verses of Love*). Written by Habiburrahman El Shirazy, and subsequently made into a highly successful film, the novel relates the tale of the young Muslim Indonesian Fahri who, while studying in Cairo, becomes the love interest of four young women. While many readers and viewers admired Fahri's adherence to the teachings of Islam, others, in particular women's activist groups, criticized it as encouraging polygamy, a practice that has not been widespread in Indonesia but which is on the rise in recent years.

Polygamy is also the theme of the 2002 short story "Mariah" by the Malaysian writer Che Husna Azhari. The village imam (Islamic religious leader), despite having been married to Cik Yam for fifteen years, takes the widow Mariah as his second wife. Cik Yam not only agrees to his plan, she even arranges the wedding for her husband. It is expected that Muslim men who wish to practice polygamy would choose widows or orphans—women who need protection. The imam, in marrying Mariah, is thus complying with this expectation. Furthermore, even after fifteen years of marriage, the imam and Cik Yam have not been able to have children, a further vindication of his taking a second wife. However, this story can also be read as a critique of the imam, who uses his position as a pious man to justify his actions and uses religion to satisfy his desires.

A more personalized account of living as a Muslim is Dina Zaman's 2007 *I Am Muslim*, in which the author provides anecdotes on the complex world of ordinary Malaysian Muslims. Dina's critique of some aspects of contemporary Islam incurred the wrath of some of her readers.

Two important contemporary female Muslim writers in Indonesia are Abidah El Khalieqy and Helvy Tiana Rosa, both of whom are committed to the idea of a worldwide Muslim community and whose devotion to Islam is complete. Helvy Tiana Rosa is the co-founder of Forum Lingkar Pena (Pen Circle Forum), an Islamic literary movement and community that produces *dakwah* literature. Set in Aceh her 1999 story "*Jaring-jaring merah*" ("The Red Net") sends a clear message that the role of Islam is to oppose injustice and to protect victims of violence. The character of Cut Dini in this story is emblematic of the role Helvy ascribes to Muslim women: personifications of spiritual strength.

In her questioning of Islamic restrictions on women's social and sexual behavior, her critique of male power, and her reference to taboo topics such as domestic violence and marital rape, Abidah's stance is somewhat more critical than Helvy's. Tineke Hellwig argues that Abidah's three novels *Perempuan berkalung sorban* ("Woman with a Turban around Her Neck," 2001), *Atas singgasana* ("On the Throne," 2003), and *Geni Jora* ("Jora's Fire," 2004) "present the quest for a modern Muslim female identity."

BIBLIOGRAPHY

Arimbi, Diah Ariani. *Reading Contemporary Indonesian Muslim Women Writers: Representation, Identity and Religion of Muslim Women in Indonesian Fiction*. Amsterdam: Amsterdam University Press, 2009. A comprehensive account.

Hellwig, Tineke. "Abidah El Khalieqy's Novels: Challenging Patriarchal Islam." *Bijdragen tot de Taal-, Land- en Volkenkunde* 167, no. 1 (2011): 16–30. The only extended analysis of Abidah El Khalieqy's work.

Ruzy Suliza Hashim, et al. "Literary Realities of Malaysian Women: Views from Malaysian Women Short Story Writers Writing in English." International Proceedings of Economics Development and Research 5 (2011): 392–396. A recent contribution to English-language writing in Malaysia.

Washima Che Dan. "Politically Incorrect Literature? A Feminist Critique of the Sexual Discourse of the Modern Malay Novel." *Sari* (2006): 91–105. Focuses on the work of Shahnon Ahmad but includes useful analysis of the trends in Islamic content and interpretation of modern Malay literature.

Pamela Allen

Malaysia. Malaysia is a multiethnic, multilingual, and multireligious society, in which ethnicity and religious affiliation are central elements in the constitution of social identity. Malays form, with a slight majority, the dominant ethnic group in the country, followed in number by ethnic Chinese, ethnic Indians and "aboriginals" (*orang asli* in Malay). The vast majority of Muslims in Malaysia are ethnically Malay and belong to the Sunnī branch of Islam and follow the Shāfiʿī school of Islamic law. Islam started to spread to the local poplulation of Peninsular Malaysia in the fifteenth century, and Islam became, at independence from British colonial rule in 1957, the official religion of Malaysia. Constitutionally, a Malay is defined as a person who speaks Malay, who follows the Malay *adat* (tradition, custom), and who adheres to the Muslim faith. Among the non-Malay population, there is a relatively looser relationship between religion and ethnicity. Although ethnic Indians are predominantly Hindu and ethnic Chinese are mainly Buddist/Thaotist, there is a minority of Muslims or Christians who are ethnic Indians or Chinese. This entry focuses on the Malay Muslim community.

Gender Relations in the Malay Context. Early ethnographic work on Malay gender relations has described the relationship between Malay men and women as relatively equal, giving room for a considerable degree of autonomy for Malay women in social and economic life (Firth, 1966). The relatively equal Malay gender relations are often explained with reference to the bilateral norms of Malay *adat* (local tradition and customary law), which downplays gender hierarchy in relation to other forms of hierarchies, such as age and class. For example, Malay *adat* includes two kinship systems: the bilateral form of organization (*adat temenggong*), which dominates the Malay Peninsula, and the matrilineal one (*adat perpatih*). Although the matrilineal system has weakened over time, the bilateral norm has existed parallel to and interwined with the Islamic system of ideas and laws and was never displaced completely by the patrilineal kinship system that Islam brought to the region. The relationsip between Malay *adat* and Islam is characterized by flexibilty, as it has made it possible for women to exploit the cultural system to their advantage and to transmit cultural componenets that significantly support their own power and automony (Wazir, 1992). *Adat* can thus be seen as a moderating force on Malay gender relations in regard to processes of Islamization and strengthening of male authority at the same time as patriarchal aspects of *adat* have been reinforced by the Islamization process. *Adat* and Islam have continued to develop in relation to each other and have become so intertwined with one another that it is very difficult to make a clear distinction between the two.

The 1970s and 80s were decades of dramatic economic and social change for Malaysia. In 1971, the government launced the New Economic Policy (NEP) as a means to reduce poverty in general and economic imbalances between the ethnic groups in particular. Important strategies were industrialization in the form of Free Trade Zones, financial support for Malay entrepreneurs, and state-funded higher-education programs at both local and foreign universities, all of which meant a considerable degree of Malay migration from rural to urban areas in a relatively short period of time. The many multinational manufacturing industries in the Free Trade Zones attracted huge numbers of young, unmarried Malay women, whereas Malay men were the main targets for the educational and entrepreneurial strategies. Aiwha Ong (1995) has argued that the NEP caused significant transformation of Malay gender relations, as female labor migration meant that unmarried women, for the first time in Malay history, were living and working away from their parents and kin, taking on roles that gave them a certain economic, social, and moral independence in relation to their families. Many of the growth-development policies came to rely on this female labour force. The newly achieved independence of Malay daughters was seen as a challenge to male authority as head of the household and a threat to the boundaries between the private and the public, along with a threat to traditional notions of female morality. Many of these women negotiated their new role within the family and society by assuming a more Islamic way of dressing, including veiling, which had previously not been a common practice in Malay culture.

The *Dakwah* Movement: A Modern Islamic Reform Movement. The 1970s was also the decade when the modern Islamic reform movement, locally and popularly called "the *dakwah* movement," was born. As an intellectual movement, developing parallel to processes of industrialization and modernization, it focused on improving the quality of the Muslim faith among Malays and strengthening the identity of the Muslim community, the *ummah*. The female body was very quickly turned into a key symbol in the politics of identity and modernity by both the religious reform movement and the government, which soon developled its own state-led *dakwah*. Women were explicitly urged to veil and to guard their modesty, and the Malay government stressed women's domestic and maternal roles.

Most of the Islamic groups that were formed in the 1970s and 1980s were found in urban areas and led by young and well-educated Malay men, but women from the same social environment were also actively recruited, and their participation and active engagement in the movement gave it the broad base of participants necessary for achieving some of the Islamization goals. Maznah Mohamad (2004) has described the situation that women *dakwah* activists found themselves in as paradoxical, because they were assured upward economic mobility (through higher education) at the same time as they were given a domesticated and secondary role to that of male participants. Veiling was, for these women, not in conflict with their participation in economic life and their contribution to building the new nation. Women's participation in the Islamic reform movement also gave women the opportunity to engage in the study of Islam, which has opened up spaces of religious agency for them. The Islamic University of Malaysia was a hub for combining the visions of modernization and Islamization of knowledge.

As Islamization in Malaysia has turned into an everyday practice, women have, for example, successfully appropriated traditionally male spaces—physical religious spaces, such as the mosque, as well as intellectual arenas, such as learned theological debates—that were earlier inaccessible to them. Religious studies in various forms have had a broad attraction for Malay women in the urban area of Kuala Lumpur since the early 1990s. Women engage in the study of the scriptural sources of Islam; they learn to recite, read, and understand the Qur'ān. They engage in interpretation of the Qur'ān and *ḥadīth* and discuss the texts in relation to contemporary life. Islamization as a wider social process has thus opened up possibilities for women to enter into religious debate and education, through which women have been able to assume active positions as critical mediators and interpreters of Islam in everyday life.

Female Collective Rituals. The acquisition of religious knowledge by women has further provided them with necessary conditions for assuming the authoritiative roles needed for the performance of certain collective rituals, *majlis doaa*, independently from men. The *majlis doaa*, as it is performed in the modern and urban context, has emerged out of the broader category of Malay rituals known as *kenduri*, central to Malay social and ritual life. The *kenduri* can be described as a feast, or a communal rice meal, in connection with a ceremonial event, often, but not always, including an element of prayer. In the literature on Malay social and cultural life, one finds four main categories of occasions that call for a *kenduri* to be held: religious celebrations, life-cycle crises, happy events, and the fulfilment of wishes. The initiative for a *kenduri* is usually taken by a particular person or an individual family. It can also be a collective enterprise; such a *kenduri* is arranged in the mosque (when the purpose is explicitly religious) or as a village well-being party. The *kenduri* requires communal cooperation in work and defraying expenses and, for Malays in general, hosting *kenduris* in connection to life-crisis events is an important means of acquiring social status and prestige. A detailed ethnography of *kenduri* in the province of Kelantan shows a gendered division of labor, in which the practical arrangement of cooking is mostly the women's responsibility and men perform the religious element of the ritual, the prayer, which is concluded by the sharing of the rice meal (Rudie, 1994).

With urbanization and modernization, the *kenduri* has gone through a process of transformation opening up a new category of collective ritual that is distincly religious and female in performance. In the contemporary, urban context, women are organizing collective rituals in their homes that show much similarity to the *kenduri* although framed in a more specifically religious context and given an originally Arabic religious term, *majlis doaa*. The basic structure of the event consists of an element of prayer, reading of the Qur'ān, and the repetition of God's name (*tahlil*). The gatherings last for about two hours and are always concluded by sharing a meal consisting of rice, side dishes, drinks, and sweets. The *majlis doaa* is held by women, independently of men, with women being responsible both for both the practical organization of the event and for the religious elements included in it. This has created a demand for female religious experts in the urban areas.

The Women's Rights Movement. The women's rights movement in Malaysia reflects the postcolonial, multiethnic, and multireligious situtation of the country and includes a variety of aspects, ranging from ethnicity-based female nationalism to globalized feminism within the context of identity politics (Ng, Mohamad, and Tan, 2006). The first wave of women's political activism was built up in the context of the anticolonial struggle against the Japanese occupation during World War II, when many ethnically defined associations were formed. Malay women were drawn into the ethno-nationalist independence movement and organized themselves in separate women's wings of the Malay-defined political parties, such as the Kaum Ibu wing of the United Malays National Organisation (UMNO). After independence in 1957, a number of multiethnic and nongovernmental women's organizations were formed around issues of, for example, equal pay for men and women that linked the international women's movements agenda to local processes of industrialization and emergence of a female labor force. In the late 1980s, the issue of domestic violence and violence against women emerged as the most central topic for the modern women's movement. In the public debates about the New Domestic Violence Act, enacted in 1995, Muslim women were effectively marginalized by conservative Muslim activists who placed the issue of domestic violence in the domain of Islamic law. The weakness of a multiethnic and religious struggle for women's rights in the face of conservative Islamic groups is one of the things that pushed Malay women to choose to organize themselves in exclusively Malay-Muslim women's groups (Spiegel, 2009).

One of the most well-known and important groups, for both the local and global Muslim feminist movement, that was formed in this context is Sisters-in-Islam (SIS), a group of professional, intellectual women based in Kuala Lumpur who propagate women's rights through feminist reinterpretation of Islamic texts. SIS takes on issues of restrictions on women's participation in social and political life brought about by the increasingly patriarchal interpretations of Islam made by actors in the Islamic beaurucracy, as well as gender inequalities in the practices of Sharīʿah legislation in Malaysia. SIS, along with other Muslim women's groups, struggles for changes in legislation of Muslim family law by entering into public debates and giving legal assisance to women who are the victims of injustices in the Sharīʿah courts. One of the issues of importance for the future in Malaysia which is high on the SIS agenda is allowing female judges in the Sharīʿah courts.

Malay Muslim feminist scholars and activists have argued that both the state and *dakwah* organizations are responsible for actively introducing aspects of patriarchal Muslim Arab or Middle Eastern gender and family relations, thereby intensifying Malay gender difference, segregation, and inequalities (see, e.g., Othman, 2006). A concrete example of the idea of women as subordinated and morally weak and in need of men's protection and support is promoted are the premarital courses offered by both state and nonstate religious authorities. These courses teach men and women their responsibiltites as husbands and wives and underline women's roles as nurturers and caregivers, in contrast to men's roles as head of family and breadwinner.

In the context of the Malaysian Sharīʿah law, one can also see transformations and tendencies toward an increased gender bias based on the idea of more male-centered family formations. The enactment of new Islamic marriage laws since 2000 strengthens the picture of a continued reinforcement of binary assymetry in gender and the enhancement of male privileges through increasing male entitlements (Maznah Mohamad, 2011). Although still uncommon, polygamy is increasing in Malaysia, and amendments to the family law have made it easier for men to contract polygamous marriages. Amendments have also been made that make it easier for men to divorce without having to take on financial responsibiltities toward women.

The reshaping of Islam, as it is practiced in Malaysia, is gendered. The interconnected processes of globalization and Islamization, in the form of the economic, social, and religious transformations that Malaysia has gone through since the early 1970s, have opened up new spaces and arenas for Malay women. They have gained access to education, economic independence, and religious knowledge and spheres, as well as to political voices. At the same time, moral and gender boundaries have been redrawn, and the modern, Malay, female, Muslim subject is constantly negotiated. In the religious field, women emerge as religious propagators and authorities of informal character at the same time as the male dominated sphere of religious bureaucracy and formal religious authority is strengthened. Although women may not challenge the gendered character of formal religious positions of authority, they have, through religious education, acquired tools for entering into debate about interpretations of Islam.

BIBLIOGRAPHY

Firth, Rosemary. *Housekeeping among Malay Peasants*. London: Athlone, 1966.

Frisk, Sylva. *Submitting to God: Women's Islamization in Urban Malaysia*. Copenhagen: University of Washington Press and NIAS Press, 2009.

Mohamad, Mazhah. "Women's Engagement with Political Islam in Malaysia." *Global Change, Peace & Security* 16, no. 2 (June 2004): 133–149.

Mohamad, Mazhah. "Malaysian Sharia Reforms in Flux: The Changeable National Character of Islamic Marriages." *International Journal of Law, Policy and the Family* 25, no. 1 (2011): 46–70.

Ng, Cecilia, Maznah Mohamad, and Beng Hui Tan. *Feminism and the Women's Movement in Malaysia: An Unsung (R)evolution.* New York: Routledge, 2006.

Ong, Aihwa. "State versus Islam: Malay Families, Women's Bodies and the Body Politic in Malaysia." In *Bewitching Women, Pious Men: Gender and Body Politics in Southeast Asia*, edited by Aihwa Ong and Michael G. Peletz, pp. 170–192. Berkeley: University of California Press, 1995.

Othman, Norani. "Muslim Women and the Challenge of Islamic Fundamentalism/Extremism: An Overview of Southeast Asian Muslim Women's Struggle for Human Rights and Gender Equality." *Women's Studies International Forum* 29 (July 2006): 339–353.

Rudie, Ingrid. *Visible Women in East Coast Malay Society: On the Reproduction of Gender in Ceremonial, School and Market.* Oslo, Norway: Scandinavian University Press, 1994.

Spiegel, Anna. *Contested Public Spaces: Female Activism and Identity Politics in Malaysia.* Heidelberg, Germany: VS Verlag für Sozialwissenschaften/Springer Fachmedien Wiesbaden, 2010.

Wazir, Jahan Karim. 1992. *Women and Culture: Between Malay Adat and Islam.* Boulder, Colo.: Westview Press.

Sylva Frisk

Mamlūk Dynasty. The Mamlūks were a horse-riding elite of manumitted slaves, who ruled over Egypt and Syria from 1250 to 1517. The distinctive trait of the dynasty was the continued reliance on purchase and training of Turkic or Circassian military slaves who formed a non-hereditary elite. The Mamlūks ruled some of the largest metropolises in the medieval world, most notably the capital, Cairo, which may have had up to a quarter million inhabitants. They were assisted by an indigenous Arabic-speaking scholarly elite, who filled the ranks of the state bureaucracy and judiciary.

The lives of Muslim women in the cities of the Mamlūk period are better documented than those in any other medieval period, and, in fact, shape much of what we know about women in medieval Islamic societies. This is primarily because the authors of the period produced hundreds of historical works, including chronicles, biographical dictionaries, and memoirs. Although all these works were written by men, the authors are increasingly open about their family life, in a manner unprecedented under previous dynasties. Any reticence about exposing details about the women of one's own household completely disappears from the late fifteenth-century works of al-Biqāʿī (d. 1480), al-Sakhāwī (d. 1497) and Ibn Ṭawq (d. 1509). The Mamlūk period is also the first period for which we have an extensive corpus of *fatwās* by jurists, much of it dealing with questions of personal law cases. Moralistic literature, such the *Madkhal* of the Cairene Mālikī jurist Ibn al-Ḥājj (d. 1336–7), is obsessed with women's non-normative behavior. Moreover, the documentary evidence for the Mamlūk dynasty is also richer than in earlier centuries, although not as rich as the Ottoman. It includes the Ḥaram collection, a small archive from the Mamlūk court in Jerusalem; endowment deeds, mainly from late fifteenth century Cairo, which are very useful in illustrating the economic participation of elite women in the economy; and about a dozen Muslim marriage contracts from the Mamlūk period found in the Egyptian countryside.

Slavery. While the distinctive character of the Mamlūk dynasty was its constant recruitment of military slaves, the recruitment of female slaves was equally integral to the working of the Mamlūk military elite. According to reports in chronicles, the number of female slaves in military households was higher than the number of male slaves. They included a select group of courtesans, who were trained in singing and music and enlisted in the musical bands (*jūka*) kept by all leading amirs. Many other slave-girls served as concubines, and some Mamlūk officers kept scores of them; Sunqur al-Nūrī (d. 1335), a governor in several towns in northern Syria, had as many as sixty, and there are many other examples of large harems.

In the Mamlūk system, slave girls in elite military households had almost as many opportunities as their male counterparts. Whereas a male slave could hope to become sultan, a female slave of humble origins could hope to become a sultan's consort, or, as in the case of Shajar al-Durr, even assume the reins of power herself. Shajar al-Durr, a former concubine of the Ayyūbid sultan of Egypt al-Ṣāliḥ Ayyūb, was the first ruler of the Mamlūk dynasty, as well as the only female ruler in Egypt's medieval history. She assumed power in the aftermath of the Crusader attack on Egypt in 1249, forming an alliance with the Turkish slave regiment of her former husband. Her short rule signals the emergence of the household slaves as the dominant force in the politics of the Near East in the late medieval period.

By the fifteenth century, the number of concubines in military households steadily decreased. It seems that the supply of slave-girls was severely affected by the recurrences of the Black Death from the middle of the fourteenth century onwards, and prices for slaves in general, and for Turkish slave-girls in particular, more than doubled. In a parallel development, the fifteenth century appears to signal a decline in the closely associated practice of polygamous marriages. One of the most striking developments in the second half of the fifteenth century was the transformation of the royal household from a polygamous to a monogamous institution, based on long-lasting marriages to only one wife or concubine at any given time.

It should be noted that female slavery was not restricted to the military elite, and not all slave-girls were concubines. Scholars bought and used concubines too, if they were able to afford them. Moreover, the majority of slave girls sold on the markets of Cairo and Damascus were not purchased as sexual consorts. Many served as personal attendants to female mistresses. Others were employed as domestics. Al-Sakhāwī devoted a short biographical entry to Abrak al-Sinīn, his domestic servant from her purchase in 1467–8 until her death in 1488. While most concubines were of Turkish origin, it is almost certain that most slave girls in the period were black Africans.

Economy. The Mamlūk military elite were supported by the allocation of rights to taxes from agricultural revenue on state-owned lands. The early Mamlūk sultans systematically confiscated privately owned land in order to distribute its revenues for Mamlūk soldiers and officers. This assignment of non-hereditary revenue rights, known as *iqtāʿ*, in return for military service, ensured the continuity of the Mamlūk system of one-generation aristocracy. But a side effect was the exclusion of elite women from access to this type of revenue, in contrast to the preceding Ayyūbid regime in Syria, where elite women often appear as landowners. As a form of compensation, elite women in the Mamlūk period were usually entitled to a substantive share in the family's patrimony, mainly in the form of trousseaux, "personal items," or heirlooms, which they received at the time of their first marriage.

From the second half of the fourteenth century, however, the *iqtāʿ* system began to break up, and the link between military service and access to revenue from land loosened. More and more land was alienated to support endowments (*waqf*, pl. *awqāf*) that were, for the most part, private or familial, although charitable in appearance. The rapid growth of family endowments at the expense of *iqtāʿ* allowed elite women greater access to landed revenue; they could become beneficiaries, administrators, and founders of endowments. In the abundant records of endowment deeds from fifteenth-century Cairo, women represent one-fifth of the total number of known administrators and founders. The prime example of this new wealth is the economic career of the lifelong wife of Sultan Qāʾitbāy, Fāṭima bint ʿAlī Ibn Khāṣṣbak (d. 1504), who, over the course of thirty years and even after the death of her husband, bought urban and rural real estate estimated to be worth several tens of thousands of gold dinars.

Away from the court of the sultan and lower on the social ladder, the vast majority of women made their living from the production of textiles, especially spinning and embroidery. Women would buy raw material, spin it at home, and then sell the finished product at the cotton- and flax-traders' shops. Other women made their living by providing typically female services, as midwives, hairdressers, washers of the dead, and attendants in baths and hospitals. There were also a large number of prostitutes in Cairo, described vividly in Ibn Daniyāl's shadow plays. All in all, Mamlūk sources reveal widespread participation of women in the labor force and a normative attitude towards women who work for wages.

Marriage. Muslim marriages in the Mamlūk period were subject to the overall framework of Islamic law yet show significant variability. By law, grooms were required to pledge a marriage gift (*mahr* or *ṣadāq*), but it was, for the most part, deferred to the time of the termination of the marriage and was commonly used as a security for divorcees and widows. The dowry, or trousseau, brought by the bride and donated by her family was often far more substantial than the groom's gifts, especially in elite families.

The other financial obligation of husbands was marital support. Up to the end of the thirteenth century, husbands supported their wives by buying food in the market and, literally putting bread on the table. By the fifteenth century, however, marital support came to consist of a variety of cash payments. Formal settlements with regard to payments in lieu of clothing were registered before a *qāḍī* and were effectively an integral part of the marriage contract. The spread of cash payments and allowances in the fifteenth century amounted to a significant monetization and formalization of marriage.

Divorce was a common occurrence in the Mamlūk period. In al-Sakhāwī's biographical dictionary of fifteenth-century women, three out of ten marriages ended with divorce (out of a sample of 171 marriages), and it is probable that the actual rate of divorce among the general population of Cairo was higher. The legal form of the majority of actual divorces in Mamlūk society was consensual separation (*khulʿ*), although the formalities of divorce deeds concealed the interplay of various legal and extralegal forces. Consensual separations meant that the wife gave up her financial rights, in particular, her claim to the late marriage gift, in return for a release from marriage. Most divorce negotiations were informal, and the role of the courts was mainly confined to putting an official stamp on the settlements brought before them. Judicial divorce (*faskh*), the most drastic sanction a wife could hope for from the courts, was generally reserved for grass widows (abandoned or deserted wives).

Arbitrary unilateral repudiations by husbands were not as common as one might expect, as most husbands were deterred, first and foremost, by the financial costs of divorce. Rather, repudiation was more often used as a threat against a disobedient wife. Sunnī law accords special status to threats of repudiation, which are usually called divorce oaths, or oaths on pain of divorce. In the Mamlūk period, divorce oaths were often used as pledges for commitments that went far beyond the domestic sphere and had nothing to do with the wife's behavior. Most notably, divorce oaths were incorporated into the oath of allegiance (*bayʿa*) sworn at the inauguration of Mamlūk sultans and used as a form of judicial oath.

Religion. Because practically all the religious texts that have survived were written by men, it is easy to imagine Mamlūk Islam as an exclusively male enterprise, but there is now sufficient evidence to show that, outside the formal and all-male *madrasah* system, women played a far from marginal role in religious life. The main venue for religious activity among the literate women of the traditionalist, and especially Ḥanbalī, elite was transmission of ḥadīth. This was not a marginal phenomenon; hundreds of female ḥadīth transmitters are mentioned in the biographical dictionaries, and women were major authorities for some of the most famous scholars of the Mamlūk period, such as Ibn Ḥajar al-ʿAsqalānī (d. 1449), al-Dhahabī, and al-Suyuṭī?.

Outside of the traditionalist Ḥanbalī circles of Damascus, women expressed their religiosity largely through mystical institutions. Women are often mentioned in connection with the visitation of graves, especially by the moralists who wanted them to abstain from wailing, dressing immodestly, or mixing with men. In spite of the objections of the moralists, it is likely that visitation represented a real spiritual undertaking for many women. The visitation of tombs was incorporated into poor women's weekly schedules, alongside their domestic chores and textile production. Mysticism offered women unique avenues of religious expression. In fact, the only female author of the Mamlūk period for whom we have a significant corpus is the Syrian mystic ʿĀʾisha al-Bāʿūnīyah (d. 1516).

The most distinctive expression of the mystical activities and aspirations of women in the Mamlūk period was the exclusively female mystical house, usually known as *ribāṭ*. The growth of the mystical Ṣūfī orders in the thirteenth century saw the rise not only of *zāwiyas* for men, but also of *ribāṭs* for women, who were as actively engaged in the spiritual quest that characterized the religious life of the period. The Ribāṭ al-Baghdādīyah, established in Cairo in 1285 in support of the mystic Zaynab al-Baghdādīyah and her followers, was the most famous female institution of this kind, but there were dozens of them in all major cities. Besides their spiritual functions, the female *ribāṭs* catered for the needs of poor single women who were excluded from other Ṣūfī foundations. The prominence of the all-women *ribāṭ* was a uniquely Mamlūk phenomenon; while Ṣūfī institutions for men survived well beyond the beginning of the sixteenth century, virtually none of their sister institutions survived into the Ottoman period.

[*See also* Egypt *and* Slavery.]

BIBLIOGRAPHY

ʿAbd al-Rāziq, Aḥmad, *La femme au temps des Mamlouks en Égypte*. Cairo: Institut français d'archéologie orientale, 1973. A general survey, comprehensive but outdated.

Berkey, Jonathan. "Women and Islamic Education in the Mamluk Period." In *Women in Middle Eastern History: Shifting Boundaries in Sex and Gender*, edited by N. Keddie and B. Baron, pp. 143–157. New Haven, Conn.: Yale University Press, 1992.

Duncan, David J. "Scholarly Views of Shajarat al-Durr: A Need for Consensus." *Arab Studies Quarterly* 22 (2000): 51–69. A survey of feminist and traditional historiography on Shajar al-Durr.

Guo, Li. "Tales of a Medieval Cairene Harem: Domestic Life in al-Biqāʿī's Autobiographical Chronicle." *Mamlūk Studies Review* 9, no. 1 (2005): 101–121. A rich account of the complexities of a polygamous household in Cairo, based on a late fifteenth-century diary.

Lutfi, Huda. "Manners and Customs of Fourteenth-Century Cairene Women: Female Anarchy versus Male Sharʿī Order in Muslim Prescriptive Treatises." In *Women in Middle Eastern History*, pp. 99–121. New Haven, Conn.: Yale University Press, 1992. On the portrayal of women in the prescriptive treatise of Ibn al-Ḥājj.

Petry, Carl. "The Estate of al-Khuwand Fāṭima al-Khāṣṣbakiyya: Royal Spouse, Autonomous Investor." In *The Mamluks in Egyptian and Syrian Politics and*

History, edited by A. Levanoni and M. Winter, pp. 277–294. Leiden: Brill, 2004.

Rapoport, Yossef. *Marriage, Money and Divorce in Medieval Islamic Society*. Cambridge, U.K.: Cambridge University Press, 2005. On the financial aspects of marriage in Mamlūk society, with particular focus on divorce.

Rapoport, Yossef. "Women and Gender in Mamluk Society: An overview." *Mamlūk Studies Review* 11, no. 2 (2007): 1–47.

Sayeed, Asma. "Women and Hadith Transmission: Two Case Studies from Mamluk Damascus." *Studia Islamica* 95 (2004): 71–94.

YOSSEF RAPOPORT

MARRIAGE.

[*This entry contains three subentries,*

Historical Practice
Modern Practice *and*
Legal Foundations.]

HISTORICAL PRACTICE

Societies in the past accommodated various kinds of conjugal relationships and recognized "wives" of differing status. Men in medieval Europe and pre-modern Africa, South Asia, and East Asia acquired a "legitimate," "principal," or "major" wife through a formal marriage involving some combination of prenuptial negotiation between their families, a public ceremony, a contract, and a dower or dowry, all of which entailed significant expense for both families. Formal marriage did political work, cementing ruling- and upper-class alliances. "Minor" or "secondary" wives, concubines, and slave wives were acquired with fewer or no formalities, or by purchase. Women in the latter type of union had less standing and fewer rights than principal wives, but their offspring were often counted as legitimate, thus insuring the continuity of the patrilineage. Muslim societies fit that pattern by recognizing marriage, a contractual relationship; temporary marriage (*mutʿah*, among the Twelver Shīʿī), which accorded the wife fewer rights; and concubinage between a man and a slave woman he owned. Family endogamy and the joint family household were cultural ideals attained most often by the wealthy due to financial and demographic constraints.

European expansion exposed these societies to northwestern European family practices that were deemed both a cause and effect of modern civilization, the attainment of which was understood to be the source of Europe's wealth and strength. In the nineteenth and twentieth centuries Muslim and other non-Western reformist intellectuals reconceptualized "the family" as consisting of the conjugal pair and their children, and as the basic unit in society. To foster sound family life, and hence to strengthen the nation, they advocated a cluster of practices including women's education, monogamy, and the restriction of divorce. The adoption of European-style political systems reduced the role of marriage in politics. The adoption of European-style legal systems preserved the rule of religious law in family affairs, but, unlike in the past, that law was usually codified and applied within a modern civil-law or common-law framework. Marital expectations and practices have been influenced further in the past century by urbanization, the spread of education, and global capitalist development.

Marriage in Pre-modern Muslim Societies. Before the late twentieth century, marriage was nearly universal and relatively early in the Muslim societies for which we have evidence (in contrast to northwestern Europe, where marriage was relatively late and nonuniversal). Arranged marriages were the norm. The wealthy tended to form joint households, in which a patriarch resided with his married sons, or married brothers and even cousins lived in the same house or compound. There was a cultural preference for endogamy, including cousin marriage. But mortality limited the pool of marriageable relations and, similarly, the number of men who married while their fathers were still living. Wealthy families married their sons off at a younger age, since they could afford to maintain them and their brides within a joint family household.

Rules of marriage: legal doctrines and actual practices. The various schools of Muslim law agreed on ruling out marriage between the closest blood, marital, or foster relations. Women were restricted to marrying men deemed suitable (*kufʾ*), that is, free Muslims of equal or superior status. But men could marry their social inferiors, including non-Muslims, so long as they were monotheists. Men's privilege of plural marriage was based on the Qurʾānic verse 4:3:

> If you fear that you will not act justly towards the orphans, marry such women as seem good to you, two, three, four; but if you fear you will not be equitable, then only one, or what your right hands own; so it is likelier you will not be partial (all translations are from Arberry).

The historical interpretation of this verse permitted men to have as many as four wives simultaneously, and sexual access to any number of women they owned as slaves.

Qurʾān 4:3 stipulated that plural wives be treated equally, and, as interpreted, that applied to maintenance, gifts, and spending the night with them. A man was not expected to feel equal affection for his wives nor have the same sexual relationship with each of them. Verse 4:129 advised:

> You will not be able to be equitable between your wives, be you ever so eager; yet do not be altogether partial so that you leave her as it were suspended. If you set things right, and are godfearing, God is All-forgiving, All-compassionate.

It was not unusual for a wealthy man in his later years to marry a woman much younger than his first wife or wives, or to acquire a young concubine. But he would fulfill his religious duty by continuing to maintain his first wife or wives equitably and by providing her or them with companionship, according to the jurists' interpretation of that verse.

The incidence of polygyny in Muslim history is mostly a matter of guesswork. Edward Lane estimated that 5% percent of married Muslim men in early nineteenth-century Cairo were polygynous. The Egyptian census of 1907 indicated a rate closer to 6% percent, and the Algerian census of 1906 a little over 7% percent. In Indonesia in the 1930s, in various regions, some 2% to 9% percent of married Muslim men were polygynous. Rates of polygynous marriage (as opposed to polygyny indicated in a census) are higher, since, if men are able to do so, they will often marry a second wife before divorcing the first, or else their polygyny triggers a divorce suit by the first wife.

Slave concubinage, still legal in the nineteenth century, is usually left out of accounts of polygyny, though it was a form of conjugality. A slave woman who gave birth to her master's child (*umm walad* or *mustawlada*) was not to be sold and would be freed upon her master's death, and indeed some concubines were freed and married by their masters. Their children were legitimate heirs. These rules may have been observed more faithfully in the upper and ruling classes, where harem slavery was the norm. The rights of a *mustawlada* were contingent on her master acknowledging paternity, which opened the door to abuses. Slave women were also acquired by the middling strata. In mid-nineteenth-century Cairo some men, including Europeans, preferred "slave wives" to formal marriage.

Women especially disliked polygyny, including concubinage, and had recourse to a variety of legal devices to protect themselves from it. The

Ḥanbalī school of law permitted the insertion of stipulations in a marriage contract, the most common of which required a man to secure the permission of his wife to marry an additional wife or acquire a concubine. Such a stipulation did not prohibit him from practicing polygyny, but it deterred him by enabling his wife to annul their marriage if he violated the stipulation. Mālikī jurists accepted post-nuptial agreements restricting a husband's right to plural marriage as enforceable in judicial practice (*ʿamal*). These agreements gave a woman the option of declaring herself divorced if her husband violated their terms. The Ḥanafī school recognized delegated divorce (*ṭalāq al-tafwid*), in one form of which a man gave his wife the option of declaring herself divorced at a time and for a cause of her choosing. Middle Eastern and North African women made use of all of these devices, and in India, where the Ḥanafī school predominated, women obtained delegated divorces. In Indonesia, where the Shāfiʿī school predominated, a bride could accomplish the same end by recourse to conditional divorce (*taʿliq al-ṭalāq*), in which a man declared his wife would be divorced if he violated his promise of monogamy, financial support, or some other commitment to her. The same legal devices were also used by women to guarantee they would not be moved from their home town, or away from their parents or children by a previous marriage, and that they might nurse an infant from a previous marriage.

The basic elements of contractual marriage consisted of a properly worded offer, acceptance, and contract, and a bridal gift or dower (*mahr* or *ṣadāq*) paid by the groom to the bride. The amount of the dower should reflect the "going rate" within the social stratum of the couple. Payment of it or an advance portion (*muqaddam* or *muʿajjal*) of it was a necessary condition for the groom to assume full marital authority, including his right to his wife's obedience and to sexual relations with her. The delayed portion (*muʾakhkhar* or *muʾajjal*) was due upon dissolution of the marriage by divorce or the husband's death—in the latter case, it became a debt against his estate. A contractually married woman was not required to join her husband until the dower was paid. To judge from the limited data available, most women married for the first time in their mid- to late teens, while men did so roughly ten years later. There was no minimum marriage age—that is, for the writing of a contract—but a young girl was not expected to join her husband and to consummate the marriage until she was judged physically capable of sexual intercourse.

The schools of law differed somewhat on the role and authority of guardians in arranging and contracting marriages, and on the extent to which brides and grooms had a say in the process. The preferred marriage guardian (*walī*) was a bride's or groom's father, and after him the paternal grandfather, and then the agnates in the order of priority they would have in inheritance. The guardian's authority was greater over minors and women than adults and men. Minors, defined as those who had not yet attained puberty or reached the age of fifteen, lacked full legal capacity. The father or paternal grandfather of a virgin minor was able to marry him or her off by compulsion (*jabr*). Decisions by other guardians required their charge's assent, though some schools accepted a minor girl's silence as assent. The marriage of non-virgin and adult women required their expressed assent to be valid; silence would not do. The Ḥanafīs allowed adult women to arrange and contract marriages on their own, provided that the groom and dower were suitable, and most Shīʿī jurists permitted non-virgin adult women to do so as well.

Here, too, the rules were more flexible than a reading of the formal doctrine of any school of law would suggest. Legal pluralism prevailed where the population adhered to more than one school of law, enabling women to venue shop—that is, to take advantage of the more favorable rules of the different schools of law while avoiding the less favorable rules. For example, the Shāfiʿī and Mālikī schools permitted married women to petition a judge for an annulment (*faskh*) on the ground of a husband's abuse, desertion, or nonsupport, or in the event of his going missing for a number of years, while the Ḥanafī school allowed annulment only for his impotence. The Palestinian mufti Khayr al-Dīn al-Ramlī (d. 1671) heard the case of a woman whose husband deserted her without support and who received an annulment from a Shāfiʿī judge. After the waiting period she wanted to marry herself without a guardian, according to Ḥanafī doctrine, and al-Ramli allowed it. Venue shopping of this sort was practiced in the Ottoman domains, India, Indonesia, Malaya, Yemen, East Africa, and West Africa in the precolonial and colonial eras.

By most accounts divorce and remarriage were more common among the middle and lower economic strata. Women who married themselves without a guardian may have been in many cases on their own and/or lacking close male kin, since to do so otherwise would risk a breach with their natal family. Polygyny was practiced by all classes, but it was associated more with the middle and upper strata. It was in that milieu, where divorce was less common, that women were more likely to seek legal guarantees to restrict their husbands to monogamy and to insure continued access to their parents and children by previous marriages. Upper class families enhanced their reputations by secluding women to a far greater extent than the majority, and they had the means to do so. Thus it was the women of that class who were the most concerned to guarantee their social autonomy with additional contractual stipulations of such things as their right to visit the public bath and to receive visitors regularly.

Ideals and realities. Abū Ḥāmid al-Ghazālī's (1058–1111) discussion of marriage acknowledged a plurality of opinions on different points, but it may be taken as representing a mainstream male perspective, since he addressed his points to men, not to men and women equally. In his view the benefits of marriage included children, the satisfaction of sexual cravings (while avoiding sin), the enjoyment of companionship with one's wife, freedom from domestic chores, and the merit earned through custodianship and guardianship of dependents. A man should not marry if he cannot support a family with a legitimate income, if he cannot treat a wife justly and give her what she is due, or if marital life would distract him from God. Later jurists often listed only two reasons for marriage: producing children and having a legitimate outlet for carnal desire.

In the legal treatises, a husband's obligations toward his wife (her *ḥuqūq*, or what she was due from him) always began with maintenance, which included the provision of food or money for food (*nafaqah*), clothing or an allowance for clothing (*kiswah*), and appropriate lodging (*maskan sharʿī*). The monetary value of the maintenance was contingent on the economic standing of the couple, though the lodging should be separate from the husband's family, and in a safe and respectable place. Al-Ghazālī's discussion of proper marital conduct began instead with the husband's obligation to treat his wife well, including his forbearance if she annoyed him, "out of compassion for [her] intellectual limitations" (al-Ghazālī, 1998, p. 60). More than that, he should spend time with her in pleasant companionship, though not in a way that would diminish his authority.

A woman's obligations in marriage began with obedience to her husband, including making herself available to him for lawful sexual intercourse (that is, except when she was menstruating or in childbed, and certain forbidden sexual acts). Similar to Euro-American law before the late twentieth century, Islamic jurisprudence lacked a concept of marital rape. Additionally a married woman was obligated to remain in the conjugal home and not go out without her husband's permission, with certain exceptions, such as to visit her parents. She was to guard her modesty and look after her husband's possessions. Unlike al-Ghazālī many jurists excluded housework from a wife's duties. The Qur'ānic verse 4:34 advised men to respond to a wife's disobedience, including her failure to fulfill her obligations, first, with words, and second, by shunning her, and finally by striking her, though the jurists insisted the blow not be harsh.

These discussions of marital relations were prescriptive, not descriptive. If the middle and upper classes aspired to and may have achieved something like this ideal of domesticity, it was out of the reach of the majority of Muslims—the peasants and the urban working classes. This was to some extent reflected in juridical discussions, which, for example, took account of women who left home daily to work without the permission of their husbands—they forfeited the maintenance they were due. But since these women contributed to the income of their households, it is doubtful that they and their husbands bothered with such calculations. The jurists' class bias also figured in their exemption of married women from the duty of housework, something that presumed the presence of slaves and servants.

The ruling class. Family and household did political work in all pre-modern societies, and the Muslim world was no exception. The large ruling-class harems that fascinated Westerners and fed stereotypes of Muslim sexual licentiousness were integral to ruling-class politics. The early Mughals made alliances by marriage with the women of subordinate ruling families, which led to the assembling of huge harems. The grand harems guaranteed the emperor an heir, made a display of his grandeur and virility, and symbolically embodied his claim to be the protector of the world. Similarly, the founder of the Qājār dynasty, Fatḥ ʿAlī Shāh (r. 1797–1834), married no fewer than 160 women in consolidating his rule over the Iranian plateau. In contrast the Ottoman imperial harem consisted of slave women who were trained to become the consorts of allies and subordinate men. In both models, the gifting of the daughters of subordinates to the ruler and the gifting of women from his harem to subordinates, the point was to establish a tie between the ruler and the subordinate.

Marriage and Modernity. Marriage and marital relations were among a cluster of issues raised by advocates of family reform and women's rights in the colonial and postcolonial eras. Modernist (male) reformers in Egypt, Ottoman Turkey, and India promoted the notion of the conjugal family as the basic unit in society and its important role in childrearing. The ideal conjugal family was stable, monogamous, and companionate. Thus women should receive at least an elementary education to enable them to be good mothers and companions for their husbands, and polygyny and divorce should be restricted. The reformers were in dialog with European family ideals and acutely aware of European criticisms of Muslim family life, but they insisted that Islam, if correctly understood, offered guidelines for a modern family life. Similarly, early feminists in Egypt, Turkey, and Iran, and women's periodicals in Turkish, Arabic, Persian, and Urdu advocated monogamy and companionate marriage, campaigned against child marriage, and spoke out for women's access to education and their right to pursue a career and to participate in politics.

Muḥammad Abduh (1849–1905) famously reinterpreted the Qur'ānic verses 4:3 and 4:129 to restrict polygyny by expanding the meaning of "equitable treatment" to include affection, a component of companionate marriage. To promote affection, modernists also recommended that the groom meet his prospective bride, unveiled, in advance of the wedding. In defense of stable marriage, the Prophet's reported dislike of divorce was emphasized.

The reorganization of the legal systems in colonized and defensively modernizing states introduced French civil law or English common law structures and procedures. Even though family life continued to be governed by religious doctrines, as personal status law (a modern coinage), there was now greater state supervision and uniformity in the application of law. The regulation of family life by the modern states offered opportunities to modernists and conservatives alike to implement their ideal visions.

Codification. The Young Turk regime issued the first family law code, the Ottoman Law of Family Rights (OLFR) of 1917. Short-lived in Turkey, its influence was longer lasting in the Levantine states, including Israel, as a source of Muslim family law. In place of pluralism, the OLFR incorporated elements of Shāfiʿī jurisprudence in a largely Ḥanafī code, using the method of *takhayyur*, or choosing among the doctrines of the legal schools to achieve the desired result. *Takhayyur* subsequently became the preferred method of codification, due to the flexibility it allowed. Nevertheless codification was a contentious and uneven process that produced different "national" Muslim family laws by the early twenty-first century. Egypt codified family law piecemeal before adopting a comprehensive law in 1979 (since revised in 1985 and 2000), and Algeria waited until 1984 to approve its Family Code. The Algerian law was influenced by colonial-era jurisprudence, or *droit musulman algérien*. Another colonial hybrid, Anglo-Muhammadan law, became the basis of Muslim family law in Pakistan, India, and Bangladesh. Tunisia (1956) and Morocco (1958) enacted family laws soon after independence, the Moroccan Mudawwanah undergoing revisions in 1993 and 2004. Although Reza Shah forced Iranian women to unveil in 1936, their rights in marriage were not addressed in legislation until 1967 and 1975, acts that were rescinded under the Islamic Republic (1979–). Indonesia passed a Marriage Act in 1974, and several states in neighboring Malaysia have passed laws. Still other states apply an as yet uncodified law, most notably Saudi Arabia, where judges apply Ḥanbalī jurisprudence. In postcolonial states with Muslim minorities, such as Israel, India, Thailand, and several African states, Muslim family affairs are governed by Muslim personal laws. In 1926 Turkey became the only Muslim majority state to abandon Muslim family law, by adopting the Swiss civil code.

Issues. Around the turn of the twentieth century there was a transnational campaign against child marriage spurred by notorious cases such as (the Hindu) Rukhmabai. The OLFR established minimum marriage ages, and most modern Muslim family laws set the minimum age for women and men at fifteen to eighteen and sixteen to twenty, respectively. The Islamic Republic of Iran set the legal age at puberty. In every code, marriage at an earlier age requires judicial permission. But in most countries nowadays women and men delay marriage well beyond the minimum age, because more women are completing secondary and university educations, as well as the rising cost of marriage. Working- and middle-class couples may become engaged or contractually marry in their early twenties, while putting off marital life for years to build up their savings.

Most states now require civil registration of marriages and divorces. Nonregistration deprives the couple, and especially the bride, of state recognition of their marital rights. Women who enter into clandestine *ʿurfī* ("traditional") or "Islamic" marriages are especially vulnerable, and the Egyptian PSL of 2000 addressed their situation by permitting them to divorce.

A nearly universal trend has been the enlargement of young women's and men's autonomy in choosing a spouse. Most family codes require the permission of a guardian only when minors marry, and the consent of brides, including minors, in marriage. Some codes expressly forbid forced marriage. Modern urban youth have more opportunities to meet prospective spouses on their own than in the past, at school, in the workplace, and in social activities. But parents continue to play a large role in prenuptial negotiations. Uncoerced arranged marriages are common in the Middle East and South Asia, where they are also the norm among Hindus.

Plural marriage has not been recognized in the Turkish civil law since 1926. Tunisia was unique in criminalizing polygyny in its 1957 family law. Most other family codes restricted polygyny by requiring judicial permission. Measures intended to discourage it include allowing and even encouraging brides to insert a stipulation of monogamy in the marriage contract, requiring a man to notify his first wife of an additional marriage, and recognizing polygyny as a basis for divorce or legal separation with continued maintenance. Modern Indonesian law recognizes the use of conditional divorce as a deterrent. In most countries nowadays polygyny is socially disapproved and is practiced by a small minority of men. The exceptions are Saudi Arabia and the Arab states of the Persian Gulf, where it is associated with the ruling class, and parts of Africa, where it is practiced by Muslims and non-Muslims alike.

Feminists advocating reforms in Muslim family law in recent decades have tended to stay within an Islamic frame of reference, and have achieved some gains with the support of religious scholars. In the 2000s, for example, the Egyptian marriage contract form was revised to include a choice of stipulations to ensure the husband's monogamy, the wife's right to complete her education, her right to have a career, and so on. This approach accepts the notion of complementary gender roles within the family and posits that there are solutions to be found in the Sharīʿah for the marital difficulties faced by women. It cannot be predicted whether post-2011 Islamist dominated parliaments will attempt to revise the existing laws governing marriage. However, Islamist ideals of marriage incorporate certain modern notions of marriage, in particular that it should be stable and emotionally fulfilling.

[*See also* Concubinage; Divorce, *subentries on* Historical Practice *and* Legal Foundations; Mutʿah; Polygyny; *and* Slavery.]

BIBLIOGRAPHY

Afary, Janet. *Sexual Politics in Modern Iran*. Cambridge, U.K., and New York: Cambridge University Press, 2009. Addresses the history of sexuality as well as marital relations in Iran.

An-Naʿim, Abdullahi A., ed. *Islamic Family Law in a Changing World: A Global Resource Book*. London and New York: Zed Books, 2002. A thorough account of contemporary Muslim family laws in all regions.

Arberry, A.J. *The Koran Interpreted*. New York: Macmillan, 1955. There is no definitive translation but this is one of the more highly regarded ones.

Blackburn, Susan. *Women and the State in Modern Indonesia*. Cambridge, U.K., and New York: Cambridge University Press, 2004. Several chapters concern marriage.

Charrad, Mounira M. *States and Women's Rights: The Making of Postcolonial Tunisia, Algeria, and Morocco*. Berkeley: University of California Press, 2001. An effort to explain the contrasting family law codes adopted in postcolonial Tunisia, Algeria, and Morocco. Compare with McLarney.

Dayrabī, Ahmad ibn ʿUmar al-. *Kitāb ghāyat al-maqsūd li-man yataʿata al-ʿuqūd ala madhāhib al-aʾimmah al-arbaʿah* [The Intended Aim for Whoever is Concerned with Marriage Contracts According to the Schools of the Four Imams]. Beirut: Dar al-Jil, 1989. A work of comparative Sunnī jurisprudence on marriage written in the seventeenth century.

Doumani, Beshara, ed. *Family History in the Middle East: Household, Property, and Gender*. Albany: State University of New York Press, 2003.

Duben, Alan, and Cem Behar. *Istanbul Households: Marriage, Family, and Fertility, 1880–1940*. Cambridge, U.K., and New York: Cambridge University Press, 1991.

Esposito, John L., and Natana J. DeLong-Bas. *Women in Muslim Family Law*. 2d ed. Syracuse, N.Y.: Syracuse University Press, 2001. A basic introduction.

Fyzee, Asaf A. A. *Outlines of Muhammadan Law*. 3d ed. London: Oxford University Press, 1964. Discusses Muslim family law in India.

Ghazālī, Abū Ḥāmid al-. *The Proper Conduct of Marriage in Islam [Adab an-Nikah]; Book Twelve of Ihya Ulum ad-Din*. Translated by Muhtar Holland. Hollywood, Fla.: Al-Baz Publishing, 1998. Al-Ghazālī (d. 1111) was one of the preeminent scholars of his era. This chapter of "The Revival of the Religious Sciences" deals with marital ethics as well as law.

Hopkins, Nicholas S., ed. *The New Arab Family*. Cairo Papers in Social Science, vol. 24, nos. 1–2. Cairo and New York: American University Press, 2003. A collection of articles discussing recent trends in marriage and family relations in several Arab countries.

Islamic Family Law. http://www.law.emory.edu/ifl/. A global comparative survey of contemporary law by the Law and Religion Program of Emory University.

Lal, Ruby. *Domesticity and Power in the Early Mughal World*. Cambridge, U.K., and New York: Cambridge University Press, 2005. Discusses family and politics in Mughal India.

Locher-Scholten, Elsbeth. *Women and the Colonial State: Essays on Gender and Modernity in the Netherlands Indies, 1900–1942*. Amsterdam: Amsterdam University Press, 2000.

Mayer, Ann Elizabeth. "Reform of Personal Status Laws in North Africa: A Problem of Islamic or Mediterranean Laws?" *Middle East Journal* 49, no. 3 (1995): 432–446. Shows the distinctly modern nature of postcolonial Muslim family law.

McLarney, Ellen. "The Algerian Personal Statute: A French Legacy." *The Islamic Quarterly* 41, no. 3 (1997): 187–217. Describes how colonial jurisprudence influenced the development of postcolonial Algerian family law. Compare with Charrad.

Minault, Gail. "Sayyid Mumtaz Ali and 'Huquq un-Niswan': An Advocate of Women's Rights in Islam in the Late Nineteenth Century." *Modern Asian Studies* 24, no.1 (1990): 147–172. A good introduction to reformist thought in South Asia.

Peirce, Leslie. *The Imperial Harem: Women and Sovereignty in the Ottoman Empire*. New York: Oxford University Press, 1993.

Ramlī, Khayr al-Dīn ibn Aḥmad, al-. *Al-fatawa al-Khayriyya li-naf' al-barriyya* [The Legal Rulings of Khayr al-Din for the Benefit of Creation]. 2d ed. 2 vols. Beirut: Dar al-Maʿrifa li-l-Tibaʿa wa al-Nashr, 1974. An important source of Ḥanafī jurisprudence in the late Ottoman period.

Rapoport, Yossef. *Marriage, Money and Divorce in Medieval Islamic Society*. Cambridge, U.K., and New York: Cambridge University Press, 2005.

Sonbol, Amira El Azhary, ed. *Women, the Family, and Divorce Laws in Islamic History*. Syracuse, N.Y.: Syracuse University Press, 1995.

Tucker, Judith E. *Women, Family, and Gender in Islamic Law*. Cambridge, U.K., and New York: Cambridge University Press, 2008. A discussion that takes account of the diverse schools of pre-modern Islamic jurisprudence.

Women Living Under Muslim Laws. http://www.wluml.org/. An excellent source for information and engaged analyses of contemporary issues in Muslim family law worldwide.

Yount, Kathryn M., and Hoda Rashad, eds. *Family in the Middle East: Ideational Change in Egypt, Iran, and Tunisia*. London and New York: Routledge, 2008.

Kenneth M. Cuno

Modern Practice

Marriage (*nikāḥ*) is intended to be a transformational and revolutionary stage in a Muslim individual's life cycle. By marriage, individuals pass from solitude to community life, from chaos to order, and from sinful conditions to worship.

In Islam, marriage is a contract between a man and a woman that renders them permissible to each other. The concept of marriage is cited twenty-three times in the Qur'ān, and the terms of wife, husband, and spouse are cited eighty-one times. 30:21 states: "And among His Signs is this, that He created for you mates from among yourselves, that you may dwell in tranquility with them, and He has ordained love and mercy between your hearts." Thus, family is the cornerstone of Muslim society, and the family institution is intended to protect young generations from the outer world's risks and prepare them for future responsibilities.

According to Islam, the first marriage and family was established between Adam and Eve. Qur'ānic verse 4:1 states: "O humankind! Be dutiful to your Lord, Who created you from a single soul, and from it He created its mate, and from them both He created many men and women." Because the first marriage took place in Paradise, marriages on earth are believed to be a sampling of life in Paradise.

Because marriage changes the social status of women and men, it is expected that the couple will design their new lifestyle together. It is generally recommended that women and men should be taught and educated about the responsibilities of the marriage contract prior to the marriage itself. A man is expected to become a healthy adult and have enough income to look after a family before marrying, while women must have reached puberty and are expected to be trained in caring for the household, suggesting that marriage is a social role that must be earned.

The Qur'ān states that women and men are equal in terms of rights and responsibilities. Chapter 26 groups men and women according to their character, with good men being reserved for good women and vice versa. It is recommended that women and men be able to evaluate their compatibility before marriage, such as in matters of physical appearance, attitudes, habits, inclinations, and aspirations. According to *Ṣaḥīḥ al-Bukhārī*, Prophet Muḥammad cited four qualities to be sought in a marriage prospect—wealth, nobility, beauty, and faith—with faith being the most important. Today it is also recommended by some to find a spouse who complements one's own nature, intellectual interests, and philosophy, as well as being of comparable age.

Practically speaking, finding and evaluating a potential spouse can be difficult if one comes from a traditional community where unmarried people of the opposite sex are not able to meet and discuss marriage plans, even if they are engaged. For example, in rural eastern and central Anatolian villages in Turkey and countries of the Arabian Peninsula today, unmarried women and men have relatively limited access to each other. Consequently they have turned to technology, namely the Internet and mobile communications, to get to know each other, while still technically respecting the parameters of the custom of not being alone together. This also helps to explain why online dating services and matchmaking sites have become popular, as they can facilitate this type of assessment while abiding by cultural standards.

According to the Qur'ān, both men and women have rights on each other during marriage (2: 28). Men are to show mercy and love to the women they marry, as well as provide them with food, clothing, and shelter. They are to be tolerant of their wives, abstain from criticizing them, praise their outlook, and not say harsh words toward them. Men are also to protect their bodies and minds from *ḥarām* (unlawful) acts, such as adultery. Traditionally, men serve as the protectors of the family and head of household, although they are to follow the guidelines given by the Qur'ān and Sunnah, rather than their own wills. Traditionally, women are expected to care for the home and family and to be sexually available to their husbands.

Ideally, the purpose of marriage is to form the family, creating an atmosphere in which a couple finds comfort, tranquility, and contentment with each other and raises children. Muḥammad encouraged the Muslim community to marry and have children, so that the Muslim family constitutes the strongest component of Muslim society. Members of the family are expected to be productive and constructive and to encourage one another to be good and righteous. The righteous woman is often described as the cornerstone and most important ingredient of the Muslim family. According to Muhammad, marrying a righteous woman is one of the joys of life: "The best comfort in this world is a righteous woman" (Nawawi, 1981). Because marriage was encouraged and practiced by Muḥammad, centuries after his death Muslims try to follow his methods and recommendations regarding issues related to marriage, including spousal responsibilities.

In the contemporary world, the concept of family in Muslim societies, as elsewhere, has changed from that of earlier periods. Interpretations of family dynamics and the structure of the family have evolved as Muslim communities have spread throughout the world, adapting to different sociological facts, geographical factors, and political and cultural environments. When Islam was a local religion around the Arabian Peninsula, family concepts were directly taken from the model of Prophet Muḥammad. With the expansion of Islam, new ethnic groups and countries maintained some portions of their cultural heritage after conversion to Islam. Consequently, there are many customs and traditions surrounding marriage, depending on the context.

In some Muslim societies, attention is given to the future marriage of the newborn baby right after birth. For instance, in rural zones of Turkey, where educational levels are lower than in urban settlements, there used to be the tradition of "notching the nacelle," in which two families who get along well and have babies of the opposite sex agree to marry their children in the future.

Traditionally girls were raised to fulfill two basic roles: wife and mother. In the past, families with many children considered girls (especially those who did not work or earn an income) as an extra cost element to the family. When the girl marries her husband, he becomes responsible for taking care of her. Consequently some families would marry off young girls because of financial concerns. In rural zones today, however, there is greater resistance to marriage of young girls because of social and cultural changes, as well as the rise of mass communications and transportation, which have led to changes in expectation levels, particularly where younger generations are concerned.

Immigration of young Turkish men to West Germany during the 1960s created another challenge for families in Turkey, as the values of the urbanized population and Turkish workers in Europe have clashed with traditional family dynamics. In Germany, houses are not detached, with a garden uniting two or three generations under the same roof. Additionally, cinema and TV presented new lifestyles with modern families composed of only the father, mother, and children living in flats. Furthermore, the Internet and new media and communications methods are reshaping marriage concepts, resulting in each generation creating its own definition of the "ideal spouse." Thus, in general, parents and children today have different expectations about marriage. In the past, marriage was taken seriously and was intended to last for a lifetime. Individual interests or desires were subordinated to the overall interests of the family and society. Today the tendency is more toward individual happiness and fulfillment, which is often reflected in rising rates of divorce.

Many scholars point to the liberation of women as the turning point that changed the status of women at home and at work. Before the urbanization process, an ideal wife was expected to be skilled at housework (cleaning, cooking, being a good mother to the children, and keeping the husband's secrets). As women entered the labor market, those with high income and education were able to finance their absence from home by paying for daycare, preschools, babysitters, housemaids, etc. On the other side, women with low incomes have suffered most from the duality of working outside the home while still dealing with housework and family obligations. These women generally depend on the support of their husbands and parents.

A woman's ability to generate income has become a factor in contemporary marriage negotiations. A working woman becomes an ideal prospect if she has a stable job, such as civil servant, nurse, or teacher in Turkey. This economic myopia creates many unhappy marriages in modern Muslim families. When parents do not approve the son-in-law or daughter-in-law, they can dispute heavily with their own children. In some cases youngsters are threatened economically. Nevertheless, in general, tolerance for the children's agency to choose their own marriage partners is on the rise in Turkey, although the level of tolerance depends on the openness of the community. In metropolitan areas and cosmopolitan cities where students, tourists, traders, and other visitors circulate frequently, the level of tolerance seems greater. In less mobile and visited rural areas of Turkey, there is more opposition to young persons choosing their own spouses. Furthermore marriage can be postponed for bachelor men if they have financial problems and are unable to provide for a family.

For some women, marriage can serve as an escape from their own problematic family relations. In Turkey there used to be frequent stories in the news regarding the trauma of child marriages. In some cases, both the bride and the groom marry young, but more often girls marry younger, either with their own consent or by family decision. One disappearing tradition is the runaway girl who leaves home as soon as she becomes a legal adult at eighteen years of age. In the past, young girls who did not receive an education after primary school used to stay at home and help with family affairs and housework. In small rural settlements girls remain strictly controlled by brothers, family members, and even by the neighborhood due to concerns about family honor. Honor killings, which are now a rarity in eastern Turkey, are the remnants of that old traditional rural lifestyle.

In Turkey two trends deeply changed the dynamics of contemporary marriages. First, the urban population surpassed the rural population during the 1990s, affecting perceptions about marriage. Second the rising level of education of both sexes, but particularly girls, has changed marriage practices. In 1997 it became compulsory for both girls and boys to remain in school until they are fourteen years old. This was revised to eighteen years in 2012, making it practically impossible for marriage to occur, whether by force or parental will, prior to that time Furthermore, in the Turkish legal system, girls and boys younger than eighteen can marry only by court decisions.

Changes have also occurred with respect to *mahr* (dower), which is supposed to be paid to the bride under Islamic law. In practice in many places, such as Saudi Arabia and southeast Turkey, it has become customary for a girl to "gift" her *mahr* to her father, making marriage of a daughter a profitable prospect for the father. This means that the *mahr* does not fulfill the purpose for which it was intended—providing the bride with a source of financial security in the event of divorce or death of the husband. Indeed, some fathers today are proving to be very greedy with respect to the *mahr*, setting it so high that no groom can meet it and thereby preventing their daughters from marrying. In some cases it appears that this is done deliberately so that the father can maintain control over the daughter's income if she is employed, even though, under Islamic law, a woman's income is her personal property. In South Asia there is the additional practice of *jahāz,* which are possessions given by the families of the bride and groom to the new couple. Although this is not an Islamic institution, it is a common practice among Muslim communities—in India and Pakistan, in particular—raising the cost of marriage for both families.

Under Islamic law, women are supposed to have a voice in their marriages. Underage girls are supposed to have the approval of their male guardian for marriage, although the guardian, in theory, should not be able to force them into marriage, while, according to some law schools, including the Ḥanbaī i, a woman who has been previously married (whether divorced or widowed) is supposed to be able to make her own choice about remarriage. In the contemporary era, the role of guardian is sometimes abused. In some cases guardians do not allow the girl any agency in choosing her husband. This practice is observed in less developed, undereducated, rural zones of Muslim countries such as Turkey or some Middle Eastern and North African (MENA) countries. In addition, there are cases today of girls secretly marrying as soon as they reach adulthood. This happens especially in families where poor communication or other problems are prevalent.

Contemporary practice of marriage is changing throughout the Muslim world, in some cases because of increased levels of education, employment, mobility, and consequently independence, among women, and in others because of financial pressures that have resulted in the approval of alternative forms of marriage that do not place full financial responsibilities upon the husband, and in still others a proliferation of oil wealth that enables men to have multiple wives. This is particularly the case in the oil-rich countries of the Persian Gulf, where new forms of marriage, such as *misyār* and *misfar* have been sanctioned and put into practice.

Misyār marriage can be observed in regions such as the Persian Gulf, Saudi Arabia, and Egypt. This is a new form of marriage that was developed during the second half of the twentieth century, first appearing in the Al-Qassim region of Saudi Arabia during the oil boom, suggesting to some that increased levels of wealth purchased new forms of marriages. Muslim scholars are divided on the topic of *misyār,* with some saying that this marriage is not legitimate and others accepting it as a necessity of modern life conditions.

Misyār marriage is different from regular marriage (*nikāḥ*) because both spouses willingly give up certain rights, such as the husband's right of housekeeping, the wife's right of living together, equal division of nights between wives in case of polygyny, and the husband's provision of housing and maintenance for the wife (*nafaqah*). In practice, the couple lives separately and meets when they please. Some rules of marriage in Sunnī law apply, such as agreement of the parties, two legal witnesses, payment of agreed *mahr* to the bride, and absence of a fixed time period for the marriage.

Major Saudi scholars, such as Muhammad Nāsiruddin al-Albāni and Muḥammad ibn al-ʿUthaymin, opposed *misyār* because they found it immoral and against the Islamic spirit of marriage. Concerns have also been raised about the social problems created by *misyār* marriages, such as absence of the father while raising the children and divorce that leaves women without protection. In many cases *misyār* is used as a second or third marriage by men. Women generally suffer negative outcomes, especially when they seek to end a marriage they entered into secretly or if the husband divorces them without notifying them of the same. Concerns have been raised about the ability of women to use *misyār* as a way of extracting money from the husband, or commercializing sex, provoking accusations that *misyār* is simply thinly disguised prostitution. Furthermore, many women are apparently unaware of their rights in *misyār* marriage, leading to abuses.

Misfār marriage, which has developed in countries such as Egypt and Saudi Arabia, occurs in the context of travel—a man decides to marry a woman for the course of his travel and end the marriage when they return to their country of origin. Like *misyār*, *misfar* marriage has been criticized by Muslim scholars, including the Saudi Grand Mufti, who declared it unlawful in 2010, based on concerns that it was thinly disguised *mutʿah* (temporary marriage), which is practiced by Shīʿīs but condemned by Suniis. The Mufti stated that marriage with the intent of divorce is *ḥarām* (impermissible), given that the purpose of marriage in Islam is supposed to be the creation of a stable and loving home where both spouses can find trust and peace of mind—a purpose clearly unfulfilled by *misfar*. Ironically many Saudi female university students have been left with no recourse but *misfar* if they wish to study abroad, as Saudi law still requires a male guardian (*maḥram*) to accompany them. Many Saudi women have protested this requirement, as their purpose in going abroad is to obtain an education, not find a husband.

In some countries today, such as Turkey and Tunisia, marriages are organized by secular laws, rather than Sharīʿah. In secular countries such as Turkey, mosques and imams cannot issue family certificates or other legal documents related to marriage. Only a municipal officer or village headman has the official authority to marry couples with their legal registration procedures. Consequently, in secular countries where Sharīʿah rules are not applied, the nature of the *nikāḥ* became dual, so that the religious ritual is a social announcement consisting of promises without official documentation, while the secular and legally valid procedure is realized by state officers. This means that religious *nikāḥ*, also known as *ʿurfī nikāḥ*, has become secondary. Obedience to the rules of *ʿurfī nikāḥ* is a matter of personal choice, which can lead to disadvantageous situations for women if they do not complete official *nikāḥ* procedures after the *ʿurfī nikāḥ*, particularly in the event of divorce, as their rights will not be guaranteed. In such cases it is recommended that Muslim women make dual contracts: one for the state-recognized official marriage, and the other for the religious ceremony. Like *misyār* and *misfar*, *ʿurfī nikāḥ* has come under fire by some religious scholars as being a cover for premarital sex and even prostitution.

Mutʿah is a temporary marriage arrangement typically associated with Shīʿī. During the time of the Prophet, *mutʿah* was practiced for a short periods under certain circumstances. The difference between *mutʿah* and *ʿurfī nikāḥ* is that the contract for *mutʿah* is made for a specific and limited time. Today it is practiced mostly in Iran, where Shīʿī belief is common. Sunnīs historically have rejected *mutʿah* as forbidden because of its focus on sexual pleasure, rather than on creating a family unit. Many today consider it a form of prostitution, because marriages for very short times (i.e., one hour) became common. In Tunisia, a recent increase seems to have occurred in temporary marriages because of difficulties related with state marriages and general economic and political turmoil.

Historically, marriages would take place within a local geographic area, where cultural codes are similar and residents had knowledge about other families. Media and transportation facilities today have changed the scene. Consequently intercity, interregional, interracial, international, and even interreligious marriages are becoming common. For example, after the tourism industry's rapid development in Turkey after the mid-1980s, thousands of marriages took place between Turkish, European, and Asian people.

Sociodemographic and cultural shifts in Muslim societies have also redefined and challenged the status quo, particularly the growth of urban populations with an increased level of income, education, and mobility. For instance, in Turkey there has been a rapid cultural and economic change since the 1980s, which has changed national, class, religious, gender, and sexual identities. The conversion from a state-controlled economy to a market-driven, liberalized, and privatized economy; combined with the European integration process, Islamic revival, and globalization, have altogether redefined identities. Yet, despite these changes, certain traditional attitudes toward women persist. According to one study of young female Turkish university students, parents insist that their daughters attain the highest levels of education possible while still remaining virgins. Transgression of gender rules is still associated with transgression against Islam.

Studies of marriage patterns in Turkey also reflect some changes. According to a study of more than twelve thousand households conducted by the Turkish Ministry of Family and Social Policies between 2006 and 2010 and published in 2012, the age at first marriage for both men and women has been increasing steadily since the 1950s. While 35 percent of men under eighteen years old were married in the 1950s, by 2010 only 0.02 percent married under eighteen years old. Similarly, whereas 65 percent of women married under the age of eighteen during the 1950s, this percentage had decreased to 9 percent by 2010. In 2010 only around 3 percent of marriages are decided by couples without the consent of their guardians. Only 0.05 percent of marriages are negotiated through *berdel*, that is, the exchange of brides between two families for a common family interest, such as ending a long conflict. Just over 4 percent of marriages today involve runaway brides, either by consent or by force. Nine percent of married couples said they were not given the chance to marry the person they preferred and that their marriage had been arranged. This was down from nearly 30 percent during the 1950s. The overwhelming majority of couples—over 93 percent—marry with both religious (*ʿurfī*) *nikāḥ* and official *nikāḥ* at once. Those marrying with only official *nikāḥ* have decreased from 9.7 percent in 2006 to 3.4 percent in 2010. Those marrying with only religious (*ʿurfī*) *nikāḥ* remained stable at around 3 percent. Between 17 and 20 percent of marriages are made with relatives, 55 percent of which are with cousins.

When surveyed about the ideal qualities for a husband, women responded that marrying for the first time was the most important quality (85 percent), followed by having similar family structures and values (76 percent), being pious (75 percent), belonging to the same school of Islamic law (59 percent), having a job (54 percent), sharing the same ethnic origin (51 percent), having a job that requires shorter working hours or timetable (47 percent), living in or coming from the same city (38 percent), and having a high income level (30 percent). Men said that they preferred to marry employed women (91 percent) and well-educated women (66 percent), with other responses being close matches to those described by women. Women seem to give greater attention to family issues and personality matches, while men seem more concerned with financial conditions. Ninety-five percent of married persons in Turkey had only one marriage, 86 percent of couples are in first marriages, 9 percent are widowed, 4 percent are divorced, and 0.06 percent live separately. Only 5 percent of first marriages end in divorce, although 88 percent of women stated that even a single incident of adultery would be enough to divorce. Perceptions of happiness differed according to location, socioeconomic status, and gender of respondents. Rural families were happier than urban ones, higher socioeconomic status owners were happier than lower ones, and men were happier than women in general terms in Turkish families.

In conclusion, contemporary practice of marriage takes on multiple forms and is carried out through different means. Although most religious parameters continue to be followed, greater distinction is being made between religion and culture or custom, the result being greater autonomy for the potential spouses in selecting marriage partners, at the same time that marriages are taking place later in life in favor of pursuing education and employment, particularly on the part of women.

BIBLIOGRAPHY

Ahmad, Syed Neaz. "A Proposal Saudis Can't Refuse." *The Guardian*, August 16, 2009. http://www.guardian.co.uk/commentisfree/belief/2009/aug/16/saudi-arabia-marriage/.

Al-Jassem, Diana. "Saudi Women in Misyar Unions Become Losers Due to Lack of Rights Awareness." *Arab News*, March 24, 2012.

Bajubair, Abdullah. "Local Press: Misyar Marriage Is Necessary, but…" *Arab News*, April 13, 2010. http://www.arabnews.com/node/342149.

Bensaied, Imed. "'Temporary Marriage' on the Rise in Post-revolutionary Tunisia." *France24*, January 1, 2012. http://www.france24.com/en/20120131-urfi-marriage-trend-seen-among-tunisian-university-students.

Dani, Abdullah al-. "Misfar Marriage is Unlawful, Says Grand Mufti." *Saudi Gazette*, March 4, 2010.

Elbani, Nasruddin. *Hadis-i şeriflere göre evlenme adabı* [Marriage Etiquette Based on *ḥadīth*]. Istanbul: Arslan Yayinlari, 2012.

Erol, S. Muhammed Saki. *Aile saadeti* [Family Happiness]. Istanbul: Semerkand, 2011.

Gressgard, Randi. "The Veiled Muslim, the Anorexic, and the Transsexual: What Do They Have in Common?" *European Journal of Women's Studies* 13, no. 4 (2006): 325–341.

Güzel, Hasan Celal. "Türk kadını modernleşmenin sembolü" [Turkish Woman: Symbol of Modernization]. *Vatan*, February 17, 2011.

Hāshimī, Muḥammad ʿAlī al-. *The Ideal Muslimah: The True Islamic Personality*. Translated by Nasiruddin al-Khattab. Riyadh, Saudi Arabia: International Islamic Publishing House, 1998.

ʿIbn Ābidin, Rad al-muḥtār. Beirut: Dar al-Kutub al-ilmiyyah, 1994.

Kalkan, Ahmed. "Müslümanın evliliği ve aile hayatı" [Marriage and Family Life of the Muslim]. Istanbul: Rağbet Yayınları, 2005.

Kavramlar Ansiklopedisi [Encyclopedia of Islamic Concepts]. Istanbul: Darulkitap, 2012.

Kose, Saffet. "Misyar Marriage—an Approach to Model of Family in the View of al-Qur'an and al-Sunnah." *İslam Hukuku Araştirmalari Dergisi* [Journal of Islamic Jurisprudence Research] 13 (2009): 13–34.

Lukic, Jasmina. "Editorial: Who are I? Women, Identity and Identification." *The European Journal of Women's Studies* 10 (2003): 371.

Mangera, Abdurrahman Ibn Yusuf. "Marriage: How to Perform the Nikah According to the Sunna in the Hanafi School?" 2008. http://spa.qibla.com/issue_view.asp?HD=12&ID=2123&CATE=167.

Maqsood, Ruqaiyyah Waris. "Payments to and from the Bride in Islamic Law and Tradition: A Practical Guide." http://www.zawaj.com/category/islamic-marriage-articles/mahr-islamic-marriage-articles/.

Mufti, Maha N. "Parallel Relationships." *Arab News*, May 17, 2012. http://arabnews.com/parallel-relationships.

Nawawi, Imam. 1401/1981. Sahih Muslim bi Sharh al-Nawawi, Beirut: Dar al-Fikr. 18 vol's in 9.

Ozyegin, Gul. "Virginal Facades: Sexual Freedom and Guilt among Young Turkish Women." *European Journal of Women's Studies* 16, no. 2 (2009): 103–123.

Qaradawi, Yusuf al-. "Temporary Marriage (Mutʿah)." In his *The Lawful and the Prohibited in Islam*, translated by Kamal El-Helbawy, M. Moinuddin Siddiqui, and Syed Shukry. Indianapolis, Ind.: American Trust Publications, 1999. Online at http://www.zawaj.com/articles/mutah.html.o.

Sahih Al-Bukhari (Book of Marriage). http://www.sahih-bukhari.com/Pages/Bukhari_7_62.php.

Selvi, Dilaver. *Delil ve örnekleriyle kadin ve aile ilmihali kitabi* [Catechism of Women and Family with Evidence and Examples]. Istanbul: Semerkand, 2011.

"Türkiye'de aile yapisi araştirmasi" [The Most Important Reason Divorce is Disinterest]. *Hurriyet Daily*, 2012. http://www.hurriyet.com.tr/saglik/20417671.asp/.

ZAFER ÖTER

Legal Foundations

The Qur'an describes marriage (*zawaj* or *nikāḥ*) as "a most solemn pledge" (4:19). The female and male were created from "one soul," the Qur'ān explains, in order for you to "find solace" together. The Qur'ān also proclaims: "They are as a garment to you, and you are as a garment to them." (2:187). Each other's garment suggests the marital union symbolically is a return to the original "one soul." The intimate marital relationship thus becomes a divine "wonder" in which "love and mercy" is instilled in the hearts of the couple bringing them tranquil "comfort" (30:21).

Islam recognized the practical and pragmatic objectives of marriage as well. As a socio-moral-legal institution, marriage is the only vehicle to produce legitimate heirs to sustain one's lineage and pass on family property.

Islam views adultery and/or fornication as the prime source of social ill and discord, the results of which lead to the breakdown of the fabric of society. Not surprisingly, therefore, such behavior must be avoided at all cost, hence restricting sexual fulfillment—for both men and women—to within the confines of marriage.

With sexual fulfillment primarily through marriage combined with the financial and nonfinancial obligations to each other and to their children, marriage facilitated social compliance with the moral dictates of Islam. According to the *ḥadīth*, marriage fulfills half of one's religion. Marriage, then, was the building block that sustained the moral Muslim societies. According to the jurists, unregulated sexual conduct would wreak havoc and discord upon society. Regulating sexual conduct, on the other hand, maintains social harmony. It is not surprising, then, that Muslim jurists held that marriage is obligatory for those with a high sex drive; for those with average sex drive, on the other hand, marriage is recommended; and for those with no sex drive—whether due to a medical condition or simple disinclination—marriage was deemed reprehensible. The law of marriage even addressed reasonable sexual access for each spouse. The jurists unequivocally held that mutual sexual enjoyment and access were mandatory for both husband and wife. Both are entitled to sexual access to each other, but the husband was entitled to more sexual access than the wife.

Marriage as a Civil Contract. Unlike the sacramental view of marriage in Christianity and Hinduism, marriage, in addition to its moral and social underpinnings, is considered a civil contract. The Arabic word for marriage is *nikāḥ* or *zawaj*. A marriage contract in Arabic is *aqd zawaj* or *aqd nikāh*.

A valid Muslim marriage contract requires an offer of marriage and an acceptance. Sunnī schools of law require that the offer and acceptance take place in the presence of two Muslim witnesses, but the Shīʿī Jaʿfarī school does not require witnesses.

The bride and groom must be of consensual age and sound mind; in addition, their relationship must not implicate any of the forbidden degrees of marriage. While a marriage contract can either be in writing or oral, starting sometime in the tenth or eleventh century, written contracts became the prevalent norm with oral contracts strongly discouraged to avoid deferred *mahr* disputes.

Unlike Sunnī law, Shīʿī law permits a temporary marriage contract called *zawaj al-mutʿah*. Such a marriage contract must include a specific reference to the contract's time duration. The contract terminates automatically at the end of the duration unless extended by consent. All other requirements for a valid marriage contract apply.

Guardianship. The consent of the bride and groom are required for the validity of the contract. Some scholars considered the bride's silence as apparent consent. The minority of scholars held that a young virgin bride may be married without her consent by her guardian. In this case, the bride would have the option to annul her marriage at reaching the age of majority.

The majority of marriages during the pre-modern period in the various Muslim societies were arranged marriages. Be that as it may, generally the bride was represented by her male guardian (*walī*), normally her father. This was a requirement for the validity of the marriage contract. In the pre-modern period women married between the ages of twelve and sixteen. The Ḥanafī and Jaʿfarī schools required a guardian only for young virgin brides and permitted a woman with sound discretion who had reached the majority age to marry without a guardian. The guardian, however, had a right to object to the marriage on the grounds that the groom was not of suitable social-moral-economic status and/or that the *mahr* was insufficient. The other schools of law required a guardian for the validity of the marriage.

The Islamic law of marriage evolved organically from the objective social and economic context of pre-modern Muslim society. The mode of production, division of labor, and economic system of today are drastically different from pre-modern times. The extended family provided the social welfare, safety, and stability for the entire community. The modern nuclear family is a product or a consequence of modernity. Marriage today in the West and in many modern majority Muslim countries does not have the same social-economic-moral implications as a marriage in pre-modern Muslim society.

Marriage in pre-modern Muslim societies was a union of families, not of individuals. Are the families of the bride and groom compatible socially, religiously, and economically? Are they suitable for each other? In fact, some jurists took the position that a marriage to someone not of her suitable social and economic status entitled the wife to invalidate the marriage.

The groom or the bride or both could be represented by an agent, the *wakīl* (distinct from the guardian, *walī*). The agent can conclude the marriage contract with or without the presence of either or both parties. This is also called a proxy marriage, in which a bride or groom appoints someone in his or her place to conclude the marriage contract.

The requirement of the male guardian strictly construed within patriarchy does support a reading of female minority or dependence. But such reading only tells part of the story. The requirement of a male guardian did play an important practical and socio-economic role. "[R]epresent[ing] the interests of the family as a social collectivity," the male guardian's "priorities were dictated by an acute sense of social status and honor," Wael Hallaq, a prominent Columbia University Islamic law historian, insightfully observed.

And the historical evidence confirms that women enjoyed rights equal to men in all aspects of life, from commercial trade, partnerships, investing in real estate, managing real estate, establishing and managing endowments, receiving and bequeathing property, and access to courts, to being qualified as religious scholars.

Viewed as a legal representative for the young bride in the marriage-contract negotiations, including conducting a socioeconomic-moral due diligence about the prospective groom, the male guardian becomes a voice of competent counsel. While a guardian could be disqualified in court because he was not always competent and effective counsel, that nevertheless did not negate his important role.

Voidable and Void Marriages. A Muslim marriage contract could be valid (*ṣaḥīḥ*), void (*bāṭil*), or irregular/voidable (*fasid*).

A valid marriage creates all of the marital rights arising out of the marriage: the husband's responsibility to maintain his wife during marriage (food, shelter, clothing, and domestic help) and in the event of divorce to pay the *mahr* (dower), waiting-period alimony (*ʿiddah*), and any jointly titled property division.

A *bāṭil* marriage creates no rights, as the marriage is void from inception. An example of a *bāṭil* marriage would be a prohibited family-degree marriage (prohibited affinity and consanguinity marriages specifically enumerated in Qurʾān 4:23), marriage of the insane, or a Muslim female marrying a non-Muslim male. Islamic law permitted a Muslim male to marry a woman of the Book (Jewish or Christian), but not vice versa, the traditional explanation for which is that the children of the marriage follow the religion of their father.

Other examples of void marriages are: a woman not properly divorced from her first husband when she married a new husband, a women remarrying her husband after they were irrevocably divorced for the third time, or a reconciliation of a married couple after the expiration of the waiting period for reconciliation.

A marriage contract is *fasid* if it lacks an element required for contract formation, that is, it is defective in some way. A *fasid* (voidable/irregular) marriage has different effects depending on whether the marriage was consummated. Once a marriage is consummated, certain marital rights arise and continue in effect until the marriage is legally dissolved, for example, where only one person witnessed the marriage or where the bride was underage. Pre-modern Islamic jurists held that the age of consent for females is puberty—as low as ten and as high as fourteen; for males reaching puberty—as low as thirteen and as high as seventeen. If either party is underage, the marriage would be voidable (*fasid*). The minor who reached the legal age had the option to seek to annul the marriage contract. If the underage party does not seek the annulment, the underage defect would be cured upon reaching legal age, thus validating the marriage. Nevertheless a voidable marriage would continue in effect as a valid marriage until it had been dissolved. The children of a voidable marriage are legitimate, the *mahr* (dower) is enforceable, and the wife is entitled to *ʿiddah* support (three-month-waiting-period alimony). Other examples of a voidable marriage contract would be a marriage with one witness instead of two or a non-Muslim witness to the marriage or a fifth marriage before a husband had divorced one of his wives. As long as the defect could be cured, the marriage is validated *nunc pro tunc* (retroactively) otherwise it is dissolved.

Financial Aspect of Marriage. As a civil contract the parties negotiate the terms of their marriage contract, including the financial and nonfinancial terms. The dower (*mahr or ṣadāq*) amount paid by the husband to the wife is a significant feature of Muslim marriages. The dower can be money or property. Originally, the agreed upon *mahr* was due upon the conclusion of the marriage contract and before consummation. A bride could refuse to consummate the marriage until her dower is paid. But, over time, custom divided the *mahr* amount into two portions: the immediate portion and the deferred portion.

The immediate portion is paid prior to consummation. The *mahr* received by the wife was considered her separate independent property. The husband has no legal or equitable claim to her *mahr*. The wife is not required to utilize the *mahr* for her support or the support of her children. The husband, as part of his implied contractual obligations, is required to provide the wife with food, shelter, clothing, and domestic help consistent with the lifestyle appropriate to the social status of the wife. The wife has no responsibility to contribute to her own support. In return, the wife provides sexual access and companionship for the husband.

Unless otherwise agreed upon in the contract, the deferred portion of the *mahr* is due upon the dissolution of the marriage or the death of the husband. The *mahr* is considered a first priority to be paid from the estate of the husband. In other words, the wife would receive her *mahr* from the estate, plus her inheritance. The deferred *mahr* acted as a deterrent to the husband's repudiation of the marriage and as a marital settlement to assist the wife financially after the divorce.

Generally, the failure of the marriage contract to include a *mahr* amount does not invalidate the marriage contract as the majority of the schools of law, including the Jaʿfarī school, do not consider the *mahr* to be an essential element of the contract. The *mahr* is a consequence of the consummation of the marriage contract, that is, the *mahr* is implied by law. If the amount was not agreed upon, then the imputed *mahr* (*mahr al-mithāl*), the appropriate *mahr* for a wife of the same socioeconomic status would be imputed by law. In fact some scholars have held that if the agreed upon *mahr* was lower than the imputed *mahr*, the wife is entitled to reform the marriage contract to increase the *mahr*.

Unlike in pre-modern Europe, where the property of the wife merged with the property of the husband, Muslim women maintained a separate, independent legal status. With this independent legal status, all the property acquired by the wife during the marriage continued to be her separate property with no legal or equitable claim by the husband. Similarly, all property acquired by the husband during the marriage was his separate property, although the wife had a legal and equitable claim to his property for purposes of support during the marriage and for support after the marriage—short term alimony, child support, and *mahr*. The modern marital regime in Western countries is either community property or equitable distribution. With marriage considered a civil contract enjoining economic partnership, the majority of Western regimes consider all assets acquired during the marriage by either wife or husband marital and subject to distribution between them at the dissolution of marriage. While pre-modern Islamic law does not support such regime, there is sufficient basis to establish a marital asset regime consistent with Islamic law in light of the political-social-economic transformations in modern nation-states, such as ongoing developments in India, Tunisia, and Morocco.

With the negotiations of the marriage contract open, many women made many demands other than the *mahr*. The Ḥanbalī school and the Jaʿfarī school permitted brides to include stipulations in their contracts such as restrictions on moving from the agreed upon marital domicile, restrictions on polygamy, permission to regularly visit family, permission to provide financial support to parents, and titling property in joint names. As long as the stipulation did not violate Sharīʿah, it was valid and enforceable. For example, stipulating that the wife will not inherit, will not take a dower, or will be entitled to sexual intercourse no more than once a year are invalid stipulations. A wife's remedy for a breach was annulment (*faskh*) of her marriage contract, according to the Ḥanbalī school. The Jaʿfarī school considered the husband's breach a sin but did not provide for an immediate *faskh*. The other schools, including the Ḥanafī school, did not recognize such stipulations, holding that only stipulations that are required under the Sharīʿah—such as maintenance and *mahr*—would be valid.

Polygamy. Although valid, contested interpretations existed regarding the permissibility of polygamy and some jurists interpreted monogamy in the Qurʾān, most pre-modern jurists permitted polygamy but concluded that monogamy was preferable nonetheless. A Muslim man could marry up to four wives. The husband had the obligation to treat his wives equitably—

financially and emotionally. Polygamy, while legal, constituted a small percentage of marriages in pre-modern Muslim societies, never reaching more than a few percent. In these few polygamous marriages, polygamy did serve a social and economic role in pre-modern Muslim societies, as men almost exclusively provided financial support to women. There were more women than men in pre-modern societies, due to disease, travel/work related deaths, life expectancy, and war. These, coupled with the need of male protection in a traditional tribal and/or urban patriarchal society, led to polygamy playing a practical social and economic role. Even from a simple sexual-fulfillment perspective, a pious Muslim widow, divorcée, or unmarried older women would not engage in a sexual relationship outside of marriage. As discussed above, adultery and fornication are capital sins and considered in the Muslim moral framework as a cause of social disharmony. Thus, polygamous marriage also satisfies the sexual needs of women, not only of men.

Modern Legal Foundation of the Islamic Law of Marriage. Sharīʿah (Islamic law) is more than simply law in the prescriptive sense. It is also a methodology—a process to engage the divine foundational texts to ascertain divine will or meaning. With no ecclesiastical hierarchy or central authority with a monopoly on interpretation of divine will, Sharīʿah evolved as a communitarian and pluralistic jurisprudential tradition. With such unique characteristics, strictly speaking, Sharīʿah cannot be codified. Codification by definition adopts a specific interpretation of divine will, which is not possible under the classical interpretive methodology. The Islamic law governing marriage in the pre-modern Muslim society, therefore, was not codified. The diversity of interpretations and various schools of law provided much local flexibility and context for the just resolution of family disputes. A major hallmark of the modern nation-state is the centralization of the law to accommodate certainty and efficiency—from domestic relations to corporate law.

By and large, Muslim majority countries were subject to a period of colonialism and occupation. After the colonial period Muslim majority countries modeled their new countries on the Western modern nation-state model, adopting statutory codes in place of the traditional non-codified Sharīʿah.

The survival of the classical interpretive methodology of the Sharīʿah disappeared, for all intents and purposes, with the emergence of the nation-state (technically, Sharīʿah was not a nation-state or emperor law but an independent jurist-made law), this notwithstanding the fact that modern manifestations of Sharīʿah are either a source of legislation or actual nation-state law in many Muslim countries (more than forty countries with an estimated 1.2 billion adherents). For example, Sharīʿah is the supreme law of the land in Saudi Arabia. Islamic law is a primary source of the family law codes in the majority of Muslim majority countries.

The pre-modern Sharīʿah governing marriage, therefore, continues to be relevant in the evolving laws governing marriage in Muslim majority countries.

BIBLIOGRAPHY

Averroës. *The Distinguished Jurist's Primer: A Translation of Bidāyat al-Mujtahid.* Translated by Imran Khan Nyazee. Reading, U.K.: Garnet, 1999.

Browning, Don S., M. Christian Green, and John Witte, Jr., eds. *Sex, Marriage, and Family in World Religions.* New York: Columbia University Press, 2006. The Islamic section is coedited by Azizah al-Hibri.

Esposito, John L., and Natana J. Delong-Bas. *Women in Muslim Family Law.* Syracuse, N.Y.: Syracuse University Press, 2001.

Hallaq, Wael B. *Sharīʿa: Theory, Practice, Transformations.* Cambridge, U.K., and New York: Cambridge University Press, 2009.

Hibri, Azizah Y. al-. "Muslim Women's Rights in the Global Village: Opportunities and Challenges." *The Journal of Law and Religion* 15 (Fall 2001): 29–81.

Hibri, Azizah Y. al-. "The Nature of the Islamic Marriage: Sacramental, Covenantal, or Contractual?" In *Covenant Marriage in Comparative Perspective*, edited by John Witte, Jr. and Eliza Ellison. Grand Rapids, Mich.: W. B. Eerdmans, 2005.

Jennings, Ronald. "Divorce in the Ottoman Sharia Court of Cyprus, 1580–1640." *Studia Islamica* 78 (1993): 155–167.

Jennings, Ronald. "Kadi, Court and Legal Procedure in 17th C. Ottoman Kayseri: The Kadi and the Legal System." *Studia Islamica* 48 (1978): 133–172.

Jennings, Ronald. "Women in Early 17th Century Ottoman Judicial Records: The Sharia Court of Anatolian Kayseri." *Journal of the Economic and Social History of the Orient* 18 (1975): 53–114.

Maghniyah, Muhammad Jawad. *Al-Fiqh ala al-madhahib al-khamsah: al-Jafari, al-Hanafi, al-Maliki, al-Shafii, al-Hanbali*. Bayrut: Darl al-Jawad, 1982.

Maghniyah, Muhammad Jawad. *Fiqh al-Imām Ja'far al-Sādiq*. 6 vols. Beirut: Dar al-Jawad, 1984.

Marcus, Abraham. "Men, Women and Property: Dealers in Real Estate in Eighteenth Century Aleppo." *Journal of the Economic and Social History of the Orient* 26 (1983): 137–163.

Moors, Annelies. "Debating Islamic Family Law: Legal Texts and Social Practices." In *Social History of Women and Gender in the Modern Middle East*, edited by Margaret L. Meriwether and Judith E. Tucker, pp. 141–175. Boulder, Colo.: Westview Press, 1999.

Nasir, Jamal J. *The Islamic Law of Personal Status*. The Hague and New York: Kluwer Law International, 2002.

The Qur'an: A New Translation. Translated by Tarif Khalidi. London and New York: Penguin Classics, 2008.

Rapoport, Yossef. *Marriage, Money and Divorce in Medieval Islamic Society*. Cambridge, U.K., and New York: Cambridge University Press, 2005.

Sakhawi, Muhammad ibn Abd al-Rahman al-. *Al-Daw al-lami li-ahl al-qarn al-tasi*. Dar Maktabat al-Hayah, 1427. Al-Sikhawi devotes an entire volume to women. In this volume you find many biographies of women jurists, businesswomen, and philanthropists, etc.

Sonbol, Amira. "Women in Shari'ah Courts: A Historical and Methodological Discussion." *Fordham International Law Journal* 27, no. 1 (2003).

Welchman, Lynn. *Women and Muslim Family Laws in Arab States*. Leiden, Netherlands: Amsterdam University Press, 2007.

Zaidan, Abdul Hakim. *Al-mufassal fī ahkām al-Mar'ah wa-al-bayt al-Muslim* [Detailed Account of Rules Relating to Women and the Muslim Household]. 2d ed. 10 vols. Beirut: Mu'assasat al-Risalāh, 1993.

Zarinebaf-Shahr, Fariba. "Women, Law and Imperial Justice in Ottoman Istanbul in the Late Seventheenth Century." In *Women, the Family, and Divorce Laws in Islamic History*, edited by Amira el-Azhary Sonbol, pp. 81–96. Syracuse, N.Y.: Syracuse University Press, 1996.

ABED AWAD

MARTYRDOM.

The Arabic word *shahīd* (pl. *shuhadā'*) translates to both "witness" and "martyr." In the Qur'ān, the word *shuhadā'* and other derivatives of *shahīd* mainly refer to "bearing witness" rather than "dying in the path of God" (Qur'ān 28:28; 65:2; 4:6; 4:15; and 24:4). More specifically, the word *shuhadā'* connotes the idea of bearing witness in its legal understanding; in other words, it mostly refers to witnesses present during the signing or dissolving of contracts.

But, in some verses, the use of the term differs from the legal meaning mentioned above (Qur'ān 22:78; 2:143; 48:28). In these verses, "Muslims should be living testimony towards the rest of humanity," so that the word *shahīd* refers to God's witness (Cook, 2007, p. 16). In other verses, the word *shahīd/shuhadā'* could be understood as referring to "martyr" on the basis of the "occasions of revelation" literature. For instance, in 3:138–42, dated to the battle of Uḥud (625 CE), in which the early Muslim community lost a number of prominent members, including Muḥammad's uncle Ḥamzah, this meaning could be considered contextually sound. According to scholars such as al-Ṭabarī, Muqātil b. Sulaymān, al-Marwadi, Ibn Kathīr, al-Rāzī, and al-Ṭūsī, this is a point where a semantic transition from "witness" to "martyr" occurs (Cook, 2007, pp. 16–17).

However, this ready equation made by certain exegetes between the Qurʾānic *shahīd* and "martyr" is questionable, because such a meaning is read back into the verses containing this term (including its plural) on the basis of later interpretation and not on account of its explicit Qurʾānic meaning. Finally, there are verses in the Qurʾān, such as 3:169–170, where no derivatives of the word *shahīd* are used, but the sense of martyrdom is implied: "Think not of those who are slain in Allah's way as dead. Nay, they live, finding their sustenance in the presence of their Lord; They rejoice in the bounty provided by Allah: And with regard to those left behind, who have not yet joined them (in their bliss), the (Martyrs) glory in the fact that on them is no fear, nor have they (cause to) grieve." However, it should be noted that particularly early *ḥadīth* literature, such as Mālik's *al-Muwaṭṭaʾ*, glosses "those who are slain in God's way" as those who die from painful illnesses and/or under painful circumstances, such as during labor for women, in addition to dying on the battlefield (Afsaruddin, 2008, pp. 121–123). Farhad Khosrokhavar (2002) suggests that the word *shahīd* came to mean "martyr" only after the conquest of Palestine by the Muslims in the seventh century CE, and Christian influence may be suspected here.

In its modern connotation, the word "martyrdom" implies a conscious or intentional act of sacrificing one's life by embracing death for one's faith or political cause. A prophetic *ḥadīth* describes a martyr as "he who is killed in defense of his belongings, or in self-defense, or for his religion" (Haghighat, 2009, p. 213). Although a small number of *aḥādīth* name other categories of martyrs (*Ḥadith* 82, *al-Bukhari*, vol. 4, Book 52), martyrdom in the cause of God is the most often cited.

The large body of literature that describes martyrdom in Islamic contexts refers to the martyr in exclusively masculine terms: "All his sins will be forgiven; he will be protected from the torments of the grave; a crown of glory will be placed on his head; he will be married to seventy-two *houris* and his intercession will be accepted for up to seventy of his relations" (Kohlberg, 2012). This masculinization of martyrdom belies the fact that Sumayya bint Khayyat (d. 615 CE) was the first Muslim martyr who actually died in the cause of faith. However, her martyrdom somehow never found its way into common remembrance within the Muslim tradition.

In Shīʿī Islam, no other martyrdom event is more celebrated, studied, or revered than the martyrdom of the third Imam, Ḥusayn ibn ʿAlī in Karbala during ʿĀshūrāʾ, the 10th of Muḥarram (October 10, 680). The martyrdom of Ḥusayn has become "a defining symbol for Shii Muslims of the profound injustice of the world" (Esposito, 2003, p. 33). It is understood as a model for imitation by all martyrdom seekers. Manochehr Dorraj consequently declared that "martyrdom in the struggle against social injustice and oppression is said to be the noblest of all causes. A Muslim's sincerity and devotion to the faith are measured by his/her readiness to sacrifice his/her life" (1997, p. 491).

The role of women in relation to martyrdom in Shīʿī Islam is intrinsically linked to the events of Karbala. The story of Karbala is one dominated by male martyrs. Ḥusayn is often called *sayyid al-shuhadāʾ* (lord of martyrs). While the women at Karbala, in particular, Ḥusayn's sister Zaynab, are, on the one hand, regarded as weak and in need of protection, on the other hand, they are revered as strong and able to cope with the loss of their men. In a sermon on June 5, 1989, Ayatollah Ruhollah Khomeini talked of Zaynab as a symbol of those sacrificing women who give everything in the way of God:

> We have repeatedly seen great Zaynab-like women cry out that they have lost their children and sacrificed everything they have in the way of God the Exalted and beloved Islam, and are proud to have done so. They realize that what they have achieved instead is higher even than the gardens of paradise, let alone the unimportant chattels of this world. (2001, p. 46)

Women have more often been regarded as the proud, self-sacrificing mothers of martyrs. During the Iran-Iraq war, Iranian mothers became symbols of a nation at war. A mother sacrificed her son for her homeland and her faith. An often cited *ḥadīth* during the eight-year war was *behesht zir-e paye madarn ast* ("Paradise is underneath the feet of the mothers"). Mateo Mohammad Farzaneh writes, "Women were accordingly encouraged to send their sons along the path of martyrdom just as Zeynab, Hussein's sister had done" (2007, p. 91). The mother of Hussein Fahmideh, a thirteen-year-old child-soldier who became known as a heroic martyr during the Iran-Iraq war and whose life and sacrifice Iranian schoolchildren studied in government-issued textbooks, spoke of her pride in having offered her son to the path of God. She stated, "I am proud of being the mother of a martyr and of a child such as Hussein who I offered as a present in the path of God, Islam and my faith" (Sheikhani, 2008). This notion of a sacrificing and sacrificial mother also reverberates in Palestinian narratives. As Laleh Khalili writes, "An important iconic figure in commemorations of martyrs is the martyr's mother, an older Palestinian woman who encouraged her son to fight at any cost, and who rejoices rather than mourns his death" (2007, p. 127).

In the past decade, as more and more women in the Middle East have signed up for so-called martyrdom operations (*esteshhadi*), this image of women as being protected by, enabling, or remembering Muslim martyrs has shifted, and a new, troubling, feminization of martyrdom has ensued.

BIBLIOGRAPHY

Afsaruddin, Asma. *The First Muslims: History and Memory*. Oxford: Oneworld, 2008.

Cook, David. *Martyrdom in Islam*. Cambridge, U.K.: Cambridge University Press, 2007.

Dorraj, Manochehr. "Symbolic and Utilitarian Political Value of a Tradition: Martyrdom in the Iranian Political Culture." *Review of Politics* 59, no. 3 (Summer 1997): 489–522.

Esposito, John L. *Unholy War: Terror in the Name of Islam*. New York and Oxford: Oxford University Press, 2003.

Farzaneh, Mateo Mohammad. "Shi'i Ideology, Iranian Secular Nationalism and the Iran-Iraq War (1980–1988)." *Studies in Ethnicity and Nationalism* 7, no. 1 (2007): 86–103.

Sheikhani, Leila. Goftegoo ba Madar Shahidan Fahmideh (Interview with the Mother of Martyrs Fahmideh), 7 November 2008: http://www.sajed.ir/new/index.php?option=com_content&view=article&id=11277&catid=274:barrators&Itemid=184.

Haghighat, Seyed Sadegh. "In the Name of Allah: Jihad from a Shi'a Hermeneutic Perspective." In *Hermeneutics, Scriptural Politics, and Human Rights: Between Text and Context*, edited by Bas de Gaay Fortman, Kurt Martens, and M. A. Mohamed Salih, pp. 205–218. New York: Palgrave Macmillan, 2009.

Ibrahim, Fouad. "Al-Shahada: A Centre of the Shiite System of Belief." In *Dying for Faith: Religiously Motivated Violence in the Contemporary World*, edited by Madawi al-Rasheed and Marat Shterin, pp. 111–123. New York and London: I. B. Tauris, 2009.

Khalili, Laleh. *Heroes and Martyrs of Palestine: The Politics of National Commemorations*. Cambridge, U.K.: Cambridge University Press, 2007.

Khomeini, Ruhollah. *The Position of Women from the Viewpoint of Imam Khomeini*. Tehran: Institute for Compilation and Publication of Imam Khomeini's Work, 2001.

Khosrokhavar, Farhad. *Suicide Bombers: Allah's New Martyrs*. Translated by David Macey. London: Pluto Press, 2002.

Kohlberg, E. "Shahīd." In *Encyclopedia of Islam Online*, 2nd ed., edited by P. Bearman, et al. Leiden, Netherlands: Brill, 2012.

Ṣaḥīḥ al-Bukhārī. Vol. 4, Book 52.

ROJA FAZAELI

MARY. Mary (Ar., Maryam), the mother of Jesus (Ar., ʿĪsā), ranks among the most revered women in Islam, along with Khadījah, the first wife of Muḥammad, and Fāṭimah, his youngest daughter. Through the Qurʾān, its exegesis, *ḥadīth*, and hagiography, Mary emerges as a model of feminine piety, motherhood, and unquestioning submission to God's will. This overview of Mary's significance for Muslims focuses on the Qurʾānic accounts of her life and summarizes major issues that have occupied exegetes and other scholars.

Mary is the only woman mentioned by name in the Qurʾān; an entire chapter (Sūrat Maryam) of the Qurʾān bears her name and elaborates on her piety and significance for Muslims. Seventy verses of the Qurʾān refer to her, and her name is mentioned specifically in thirty-four of these. The references depict an ascetic, exceedingly pious woman whose life manifested God's mercy and omnipotence.

According to the Qurʾānic account, the wife of ʿImrān, who is named Hannah in the exegetical literature, prayed for a child. On discovering that she would miraculously be blessed with one in her old age, she consecrated her unborn child to God. When Hannah gave birth to a daughter (who according to ancient Jewish tradition could not serve in the same manner as male children), she nevertheless surrendered this child, Mary, to a life of piety and service in the temple. God accepted the offering, and appointed Zechariah (Ar., Zakarīyā) as her caretaker (3:35–37). Among the early miracles associated with Mary is the divine provision of her food. She is said to have worshiped in a secluded area (*miḥrāb*) of the temple to which only Zechariah had access. Whenever he visited her, he found that she had food, which she asserted was provided to her by God (3:37).

Mary's chosen status is reaffirmed through the visitation of the Archangel Gabriel (Ar., Jibrīl), who appears to her in the form of a man and announces that she is to give birth to a son, though she herself has never had sexual contact with a man (19:17–19). The child, who will be named Jesus, would also exhibit divine favor through miracles, among them the ability to speak soon after birth (3:45–49). The Qurʾān is uncharacteristically detailed in its description of such incidents in Mary's life, matching the detailed accounts of few other prophets, such as Abraham and Moses.

Nevertheless, several matters are not clarified in the Qurʾān. The following four salient issues emerge from the exegetical and hagiographical literature.

1. God's choice of Mary and her purification: Verse 3:42 states "God has chosen you and purified you, and chosen you above the women of the world." Scholars have pondered the precise meaning of God's "choosing" Mary and the reason for the repetition of the word in the verse. A number of exegetes concur that the first choice of God refers to his acceptance of Mary for service in the temple, and the second refers to his blessing her with Jesus through a miraculous conception. There is also discussion of whether Mary's purification refers to a spiritual cleansing or an actual physical one wherein she was freed from feminine ritual impurities such as menstrual cycles and bleeding after childbirth. Within this context, exegetes also speculate on the specific processes by which the archangel Gabriel was a vehicle for the conception of Jesus, especially given that she did not have the requisite sexual contact.
2. Mary's chosen status with respect to other women: The Qurʾānic reference above that designates Mary as "the chosen over all the women of the world" has generated discussion about the relative status of other Muslim women such as Khadījah and ʿĀʾishah, the favored wives of Muḥammad, and Fāṭimah, his youngest daughter and the one through whom the Shīʿī imams trace

their descent from Muḥammad. Whereas some scholars have viewed the designation as absolute, thereby ranking Mary as superior to all other women in history, others have interpreted the verse as more limited. According to the latter perspective, Mary is the preferred woman of her time, and on equal footing with other pious female exemplars, such as Khadījah and Fāṭimah.

3. Mary's response to the annunciation and birth pangs: A third salient issue concerns Mary's incredulous reaction to the annunciation and her wish for death just before she gave birth (19:20, 19:23). Both reactions occasioned commentary about how these moments may be reconciled with Mary's absolute and unquestioning submission to divine will. As for the annunciation, some exegetes suggest that she was not questioning divine will, but rather asking how she could be pregnant when she had never had sexual contact with a man. Exegetes also grapple with her stated desire for death when she was about to give birth, given the idea that believers ought not wish for death as an escape from God's will and command for death (even in response to labor pains). In light of this, some scholars have speculated that Mary was reacting to the shame that the birth of a child out of wedlock would bring upon her family and their honor. According to such interpretations, death would be a lesser evil than the possibility of dishonoring herself and her family.
4. Prophecy: A final issue concerns whether or not Mary can be considered a prophet. Here, there is a consensus in the Sunnī and Shīʿī traditions that, though Mary experienced miracles and though God communicated with her through Gabriel (which are ordinarily two of the criteria of prophecy), her gender prevents her from being categorized as a prophet. Among the dissenters was the Andalusian Ẓāhirī jurist, Ibn Ḥazm (d. 1064), who forcefully asserted that Mary as well as other women who received such inspiration, such as the mother of Moses, and Āsiyah, the wife of the Pharoah, are all to be considered prophets.

Scholarly and popular discourse on the significance of Mary as it engages with a variety of issues, among them the four outlined above, has evolved throughout Muslim history. As such, it is a fascinating avenue for examining not only the image of Mary in Muslim thought, but also the ways conceptions of feminine piety have evolved in different periods throughout the Muslim world.

[*See also* Prophets.]

BIBLIOGRAPHY

Asad, Muḥammad. *Message of the Qurʾān* (Markfield, U.K.: Book Foundation, 2003). Asad's translation and exegesis of the Qurʾān not only provides his own translations and interpretations of the verses related to Mary but also incorporates perspectives from classical Arabic exegesis.

Fierro, Maribel. "Women as Prophets in Islam." In *Writing the Feminine: Women in Arab Sources*, edited by Randi Deguilhem. London: I. B. Tauris, 2002.

McAuliffe, Jane D. "Chosen of All Women: Mary and Fāṭimah in Qurʾānic Exegesis." *Islamochristiana* 7 (1981): 19–28. An analysis of Muslim literature and thought on the significance and relative ranking of Mary and Fāṭimah as exemplary women.

Stowasser, Barbara. *Women in the Qurʾān, Traditions, and Interpretations* (New York: Oxford University Press, 1994). Stowasser's chapter on Mary provides an insightful analysis of the development of her legacy from Qurʾānic references to exegesis and tradition literature that refers to her. Her work also permits a comparison of Mary's representation with that of other women in these sources.

ASMA SAYEED

MATTSON, INGRID. (b. 1963). The Canadian-born Mattson is the first woman and the first convert to Islam to head the Islamic Society of

North America (ISNA) (August 2006). She had served as vice president of the organization for five years before being elected president. She considers her election evidence that being female is not a barrier to leadership but a sign that the Muslim community respects scholarship and education above gender considerations.

Mattson has been described as a soft-spoken woman who wears a *hijab* yet is unafraid to challenge long-held assumptions among believers. A forceful advocate for women's rights, she wields a powerful administrative role in establishing American Muslim institutions.

Mattson did her undergraduate work at the University of Waterloo, Ontario, where she studied philosophy. Although raised Roman Catholic, during her senior year in Paris she became friends with some Muslims from Senegal. Their way of life and hospitality so impressed her that she converted to Islam.

After her graduation she traveled to Pakistan where she worked with Afghan refugee women. She then pursued her PhD in Islamic Studies at the University of Chicago, completing her degree in 1999. She is seen as a role model by many young Muslim men and women. Not only is she regarded as a scholar who emphasizes Islamic teachings on ethics and morality, but, more importantly, she is seen as an activist who carries out that responsibility and obligation. Mattson has described her approach to religion as a matter of personal spiritual connection, rather than attention to dogma. After her graduate work she was actively involved in the life of Canadian Muslims, helping them to become more active in Canadian society.

As the director of the Duncan Black Macdonald Center for the Study of Islam and Christian-Muslim Relations at Hartford Seminary, Mattson founded the Islamic Chaplaincy program there. This would have important consequences for mosques, colleges, prisons, hospitals, and the military in America, as the chaplain-imams would be American trained, dealing with American Muslims.

Mattson stresses Muslim piety and has asserted that one should fear God alone. With this firm belief, she has been able to stand up to discrimination among Muslims themselves. In what could be considered to be a historic document, as president of ISNA, she issued a public statement against someone in her own organization who banned the first translation of the Qur'ān into English by an American Muslim woman. Mattson approached the issue from an ethical and moral perspective, highlighting her support for diversity of thought and opinion within the Muslim community: "We do not recognize any particular scholar, school of thought or institution as necessarily authoritative for all Muslims. Further, we support the right of scholarly inquiry and intellectual discussion on issues related to Islam" (Mattson, 2007).

BIBLIOGRAPHY

Kuruvila, Matthai Chakko. "Woman Leads a Wave of Change for U.S. Muslims." *San Francisco Chronicle*, November 24, 2006. http://www.sfgate.com/news/article/woman-leads-a-wave-of-change-for-U-S-Muslims-2466249.php/.

Mattson, Ingrid. "Statements Made by ISNA Canada Secretary General Regarding Dr. Laleh Bakhtiar's Qur'an Question." October 24, 2007. http://www.isna.net/articles/Press-Releases/PUBLIC-STATEMENT.aspx.

Muhammad: Legacy of a Prophet. PBS documentary, 2002.

Laleh Bakhtiar

Medical Profession, Women in the. Women have always been involved in health services in all societies and civilizations. The Muslim world is no exception. We have ample evidence dating back to pre-Islamic Arabia, for instance, that acknowledges female circumcisers in early seventh-century Mecca prior to its Muslim conquest in 630. We also know of female *ṣaḥābah*—that is, companions of Muḥammad—who joined the early Muslim armies with their husbands, sons, fathers, and brothers and provided care (and maybe also cure) to the wounded men. The figure of Salmā Umm Rāfiʿ, Muḥammad's freedwoman (*mawlā*), was instrumental in legitimizing this practice among Muslim women. Salmā was also the midwife who assisted both Khadījah and Māriyah al-Qibtiyya when they gave birth to Muḥammad's children.

From early Muslim Arabia to the present, there are recurring references to female healers as integral members of Muslim societies. Indeed, evidence reveals that women healers enjoyed diverse professional training, qualifications, and expertise and dealt with male and female patients and colleagues alike.

References to Muslim female healers appear in a variety of Muslim sources, ranging from literature and legal writing to archival documents. Useful genres of sources are the *sīrah* (Muḥammad's biography); *ṭabaqāt* (literally, "generations"), which are biographical dictionaries that organize their subject matter into groups and place them in chronological order; chronicles; general histories; *ḥisbah* manuals regulating the markets; minutes (*sijill*) of the Muslim court; and state archival documents.

Premodern Muslim Medicine. Premodern Muslim medical systems were pluralistic and hence very complex. They were composed of several sub-systems, each promoting a unique etiology and practice and enjoying a different type of legitimacy. Today, in retrospect, we tend to think of three different etiological and therapeutic traditions: a Galenic-humoral tradition, inherited from antiquity; traditional folk medicine, based on customs and oral traditions; and religious medicine, called "Prophetic medicine," which relied on the sayings of Muḥammad. Each medical tradition constituted its own complex world of ideas and techniques. They competed with each other, each trying to present its competitors as mere "alternatives" or even charlatans.

One characteristic of the pluralistic medical system was the blurring of a clear or formal division of labor among healers. Theoretically, such a division did exist, based on medical discipline and gender. The humoral tradition, which played the role of learned medicine in premodern Muslim medical systems, sought to distinguish between physicians (*ḥakīm*s or *ṭabīb*s) on the one hand and surgeons (*jarrāḥ*s) and ophthalmologists (*kaḥḥāl*s) on the other. This professional differentiation was promoted by male physicians engaged in written literary discussions, which referred only to male practitioners. Female healers were not regarded as physicians and were therefore excluded from the professional hierarchy. According to humoral theory, women were relegated to being midwives (*dāya*s) and wet nurses (*qābila*s). Thus, medical professionalization was based on hierarchical differentiation.

Another characteristic of the premodern Muslim medical system was the impact of gender on medical ethics and clinical realities, both across gender lines and within one's gender group. Gender could potentially aggravate already emotionally charged medical situations.

Gender-related tensions could arise in two different yet intertwined spheres of medical practice. Tensions could emerge between male and female practitioners over livelihood, professional recognition, and status. Bitter rivals resorted to ethical arguments about competence and charlatanry, when, in fact, economic interests, authority, and legitimacy were at stake. Tensions concerning medical encounters could also arise over the correct code of healer–patient relations. The accepted behavioral code recommended physical and social separation between men and women who were not related to one another by marriage or blood ties. Gender alone, however, is not sufficient for explaining the accepted norms and patterns of physician and patient behavior. Gender segregation did not result in absolute separation but rather in a complex and overlapping set of interactions.

In practice, female healers carried out their medical craft alongside male colleagues in all branches of the medical art, transcending simple gendered divisions. For example, women's health was certainly not only women's business. Men, too, were important providers of women's healthcare. Even gynecological and obstetrical care, "naturally" a female field, was not the exclusive domain of female practitioners. Female healers, for their part, took on male patients who were more than willing to have a female healer. The sources do not bring up the claim that a woman treating a man (or vice versa) is something inherently wrong, even in cases that involved intimate body parts. The social convention seems to have allowed for a broad range of possibilities.

Much like their male counterparts, many female healers were professionals, specializing in all disciplines and medical conditions. They acquired their craft in a variety of ways and through various training routes, as apprentices or with a private tutor who may have been a relative. Many other female healers, however, did not hold any formal professional title. Women played a substantial role in health and healing in the domestic space and provided a broad range of indispensable care services. In some cases, the female healers acted as the required link between the female patients and male doctors. A female healer could, for example, bring a urine sample for the doctor to examine (uroscopy was a common and highly respected diagnostic method in humoralism). Male physicians may have referred to these healers as "old women" with an air of condescension. They could associate them with popular, folkloristic, or magical medicine, rather than "scientific" medicine, but female healers were respected professionals in their own field of medical expertise.

Formalization of Medical Training. During the nineteenth century, the Muslim world underwent profound changes related largely to European imperialism and, subsequently, decolonization and independence. With the new type of states and governments also came European medicine. Medical texts were translated, new medical schools were founded, hospitals of a new type were opened, and new public health measures, such as vaccinations, quarantines, and forensic medicine, were implemented. Female practitioners were part of these reforms. They assumed new responsibilities and occupied a more central role in the medical establishment.

Egypt, on which much research regarding women, medicine, and health has been carried out in comparison to other areas within the Middle East–North Africa region, witnessed the first school of midwives in 1832 in Cairo. The school offered a six-year curriculum, which focused on obstetrics and pre- and postnatal care—all relevant to midwifery—but also trained the girls in the preparation of common medicines, the dressing of wounds, and vaccination. To highlight the connection with modern medicine, the graduates were granted the professional title of *ḥakīma*, "female physician" (used officially for the first time). They were thus differentiated from the *dāya*, the traditional midwife. Interestingly, the curriculum combined aspects of modern medicine with traditional types of medicine: the students were instructed also in the art of cupping and the application of leeches, both so popular in indigenous traditional medicines.

The school was initiated by the state and was part of its much wider reforms in the realms of health, the military, and state formation. The students were lodged and fed for free throughout their studies. They also received a monthly stipend. Upon graduation, they were automatically appointed to a health clinic in Cairo or in the provinces and received a monthly salary and a military rank. The school graduates carried out duties that situated them between state and society. In addition to general health practice, they assisted at and reported births, certified traditional midwives, and carried out postmortems to verify cause of death. They were summoned to court as expert witnesses. They also were called by families and the police alike to inspect young runaways and abducted women and vouch for their virginity or defloration. In other words, the *ḥakīmas* were part of the mechanism of policing the population morally and criminally. At the same time, the *ḥakīmas* were highly controlled themselves by the (male) hierarchical medical establishment. The paternalism manifested itself, for example, in marrying off the female students to male doctors, without which no graduate could leave the school and start her "independent" career.

A similar process that connected female practice of medicine with modern hygiene and health, state control, and social engineering occurred in the core area of the Ottoman Empire of the nineteenth century and continued into republican Turkey. Fear of depopulation in the main Ottoman lands was connected with concerns regarding crucial economic and human resources—these were preconditions to military and political power in the national and international arenas. Health measures were targeted at women as the reproductive agents in society, and were administered to a large extent by women. In this context, medicine and health were transformed from a personal and individual experience into a political issue.

Parallel to the medicalization and politicization of health in the Middle East during the nineteenth century was the entrance of male doctors into traditional domains of female practice (although these domains never reached a hegemonic level). The Imperial Medical School (Mekteb-i Ṭıbbiye), an exclusively male institution, included in the advanced years of instruction a course on obstetrics and another on midwifery. However, the male establishment did not replace female practice, and, in 1842, a midwifery school was opened in Istanbul. The school offered more of a vocational course running for several months than a thorough medical education. The state wished to enforce the practice of licensed midwives with formal education, but many years would pass before the state could come even close to this aim, let alone really implement it. There were not enough male and female graduates to replace the traditional female healers, who were quite resilient in the face of state pressure: local communities continued to use the services of traditional female healers and did not necessarily adapt fully to the state criteria for quality.

One reason for the difficulties of the state in enforcing from above its image of female medical practice was the growing spread of foreign-educated female healers in the late Ottoman period and Mandate years. Like their male counterparts, they were Christian missionaries or medical staff associated with the foreign consulates. In the specific case of Palestine, there were also Jewish Zionist nurses and female physicians from Europe and the United States. The impact of female practitioners educated outside the Middle East became a major factor in health services. In Ottoman times, they resisted Ottoman regulations. They regarded themselves as experienced professionals and were not ready to comply with an Ottoman licensing test. Even if they were not licensed by the Ottoman state, the presence of foreign female doctors, nurses, and midwives, who were educated elsewhere, helped to establish the connection between female practitioners and a formal medical education in the Middle East.

Twentieth-Century Developments. During the twentieth century, female medical practitioners became an inseparable part of the medical establishment all over the Muslim world. The opening of the al-Azhar Medical School for Girls during the 1960s epitomized the process. The school's mission equates medical education for women with science, research, progress, and service to the community. The institution thus offers top medical training to those who wish to obtain it in a gendered Muslim framework.

The al-Azhar Medical School for Girls is part of an ongoing initiative in many Muslim communities across the Muslim world and the West to encourage women to be part of health services. Community leaders hope that with more female Muslim doctors available, sensitive to the cultural and religious needs of their patients, healthcare will become more easily accessible to more women. Shortage in female practitioners undermines awareness and timely treatment, particularly with respect to issues such as fertility problems, breast cancer, and maternity mortality, with deadly consequences. As a result, many Muslim-majority countries have encouraged girls in the study and practice of medicine through both educational programs and financial support.

[*See also* Education and Women, *subentries on* Historical Discourse, Contemporary Discourse, *and* Educational Reform; Health Care; Health Issues; Midwifery; Pregnancy and Childbirth; Science, Medicine and Education (Theoretical Overview); *and* Wet Nurses.]

BIBLIOGRAPHY

Abū Bakr, Umaymah, and Hudā al-Saʿdī. *Al-Nisāʾ wa-mihnat al-ṭibb fī al-mujtamaʿāt al-Islāmīya (qarn 7h–qarn 17h)*. Cairo: Muʾassasa al-Marʾa wa-al-Dhākira, 2004.

Abugideiri, Hibba. *Gender and the Making of Modern Medicine in Colonial Egypt*. Farnham, Surrey, U.K. and Burlington, Vt.: Ashgate, 2010.

Balsoy, Gülhan. *The Politics of Reproduction in Ottoman Society, 1838–1900*. London: Pickering & Chatto, in June 2013.

Demirci, Tuba, and Selçuk Akşın Somel. "Women's Bodies, Demography, and Public Health: Abortion Policy and Perspectives in the Ottoman Empire of the Nineteenth Century." *Journal of the History of Sexuality* 17 (2008): 377–420.

Fahmi, Khaled. "Women, Medicine, and Power in Nineteenth-century Egypt." In *Remaking Women: Feminism and Modernity in the Middle East*, edited by Lila Abu-Lughod, pp. 35–72. Princeton, N.J.: Princeton University Press, 1998.

Hatem, Mervat. "The Professionalization of Health and the Control of Women's Bodies as Modern Governmentalities in Nineteenth-century Egypt." In *Women in the Ottoman Empire: Middle Eastern Women in the Early Modern Era*, edited by Madeline C. Zilfi, pp. 66–80. Leiden: Brill, 1997.

Kozma, Liat. *Policing Egyptian Women: Sex, Law, and Medicine in Khedival Egypt*. Syracuse, N.Y.: Syracuse University Press, 2011.

Pormann, Peter E., and Emilie Savage-Smith. "Physicians and Society." In *Medieval Islamic Medicine*, pp. 103–108. The New Edinburgh Islamic Surveys. Edinburgh: Edinburgh University Press, 2007.

Shefer-Mossensohn, Miri. "To Be a Sick Sultana in the Ottoman Imperial Palace: Male Doctors, Female Healers, and Female Patients." *HAWWA: Journal of Women of the Middle East and the Islamic World* 9, no. 3 (2011): 281–312.

Sonbol, Amira. "Doctors and Midwives: Women and Medicine at the Turn of the Century." In *La France et l'Egypte à l'époque des vice-rois 1805–1882*, edited by Daniel Panzac and André Raymond, pp. 135–148. Cahier des Annales islamologiques 22. Cairo: Institut français d'archéologie orientale, 2002.

MIRI SHEFER-MOSSENSOHN

MEDICINE. [*This entry contains two subentries,*

Traditional Practice *and*
Contemporary Practice.]

Traditional Practice

The Arabic word *ṭibb* came to designate "medicine," meaning the preservation of present, and restoration of absent, health. In pre-Islamic times, the root *ṭ-b-b* also had magical overtones, as the passive participle *maṭbūb* could mean "enchanted." The pursuit of health is one of the fundamental shared human experiences, as physical well-being is of paramount importance to most people. Medicine evolved into a highly complex and variegated discipline from the seventh to the twenty-first centuries in the various lands of Islam, as evidenced by, for example, the tenth-century empires of the ʿAbbasīds and al-Andalus. Medicine transcended the confines of country and creed, as physicians from diverse religious, linguistic, and ethnic backgrounds shared in its scientific discourses. Islamic medicine also had a profound impact on surrounding cultures, notably the European university medicine as it developed from the twelfth century onward. It survives today, in modified form, in many Muslim countries and among Muslim communities across the world.

It is impossible to do justice to such a complex phenomenon as traditional medicine in Muslim societies in the narrow confines of a lexicon article. Therefore the present discussion focuses on the origins of Islamic medicine, and then addresses three thematic complexes: 1) popular medicine; 2) the Greek humoral tradition; and 3) the medicine of the Prophet. Where sources exist, women as either practitioners or objects of scientific or medical inquiry figure as important agents in the evolving sophistication of Islamic medicine.

Substrate of Popular Medicine. All societies possess a body of medical lore that makes sense to the members of that society and is considered efficacious by them but that is legitimated, not by formal structures of legal, scientific, or religious sanction, but rather by established custom. Throughout the Islamic world, this "popular" medicine has roots in the usage and tradition of remotest antiquity, and certain customs still encountered today find their counterparts in, for example, ancient Babylonia or Egypt. This medical folklore is not specific to certain groups; it crosses religious and ethnic lines with little modification and may be encountered as fully among Christians as among Muslims, in settled as well as nomadic populations, and among Turks or Persians as well as Arabs.

Popular medicine in Muslim societies has always had both practical and magical dimensions. Cupping, venesection, and cautery were common procedures believed to be useful treatments for a wide range of disorders. For example, in many parts of the Gulf, such as Kuwait and Saudi Arabia, midwives earned great reputations for treating all sorts of sickness, especially through the common practice of cautery. Midwifery was only one of several medical functions that women local healers performed within their profession. In fact, the traditional medical system of most tribal societies in Arabia was based on gender-segregated treatment by local healers who practiced popular medicine: male local healers dominated certain fields, such as bone-setting, male circumcision, and bleeding (practiced more commonly among Bedouin healers), and generally did not treat women patients. Women healers, by contrast, were proficient in midwifery, as well as treating common ailments that afflicted their female, and, in some cases, male patients.

Furthermore drug therapy consisted of an array of broths, elixirs, liniments, salves, and errhines (nasal powders), mostly prepared from herbal and other natural ingredients. Inorganic medicaments (such as minerals) are seldom encountered, but a wide range of animal products was used, including meat, gall, milk, and urine. Many external and internal disorders were treated using these remedies, but little could be done in the case of serious physical injury. Broken bones, for example, were massaged, rubbed with salves, and kept immobile to heal. Surgery was limited to simple procedures such as lancing boils, and any injury involving significant penetration of the body cavity was likely to be fatal.

Accompanying these measures was a broad range of animistic practices based on a belief—ubiquitous in pre-modern times—in the influence on personal health wielded by supernatural forces, especially the evil eye and spirit beings known as the *jinn*. To combat these powers, a vast array of charms, amulets, and talismans was used. Stones, animal parts, or magical sayings were carried personally or kept in the home, and various charms and other magical procedures were used to seek protection, especially from epidemic disease, with which spirits were most closely associated.

In the pre-Islamic period this medical lore could be found in all the various pagan and monotheistic communities, and we hear of both male and female practitioners. Beginning probably in the eighth century, emerging circles of Muslim scholarship began to argue against some aspects of it in the form of traditions (*aḥādīth*) ascribed to the Prophet Muḥammad, but, in the main, the lore is still widely encountered in Muslim societies. Epidemic disease, for example, is still considered by many to be the work of the *jinn*; recourse to amulets and charms for medical purposes is widespread; and manuals on how to deal with supernatural afflictions are frequently published and widely distributed.

Greek Humoral Tradition. Greek medicine is prominently linked with the name of Hippocrates of Cos, a physician of the fifth century BCE (who may not have written any of the many works later ascribed to him) and reached its high point with the work of Galen (d. c. 216 CE). This medical tradition viewed health as a state of balance among four "humors"—blood, phlegm, yellow bile, and black bile—embodying various combinations of four primary qualities: warmth, cold, heat, and dryness (yellow bile, for example, was characterized as dry and hot). All diseases and health problems, including psychological disorders, were explained in terms of excesses or imbalance in the interplay among these humors and qualities, and remedies were sought in treatments believed to have a contrary effect, which, by restoring balance, would also restore health. For an illness considered to represent imbalance toward the cold and moist, for example, drugs believed to have warming and drying properties would be used. Such factors as sleep, emotional states, exercise, eating and drinking habits, evacuation and retention, and environmental conditions were also recognized as influential, and all were integrated into the humoral system.

It is useful to consider a concrete example of how these different factors come together in causing a disease. Melancholy is, as its name suggests, a disease caused by black bile. This sounds easy: black bile causes melancholy; melancholy is cured by the removal of black bile. Yet this example illustrates that the medical theory was far more complex than this facile equation suggests, for melancholy can be innate and acquired. Some people have a natural mixture that predisposes them to melancholy. The excess of black bile in them, however, does not always lead to an acute illness; only when the black bile in the blood is stirred (e.g., in the spring) does melancholy ensue. People with this natural predisposition have a whole host of physical features (e.g., being hairy, having dark skin, lisping, having protruding lips and eyes). Melancholy is acquired in a variety of ways: the wrong food can lead to melancholy, but also the wrong lifestyle, and even mental activities, such as excessive thinking. Moreover three types of melancholy existed: hypochondriac, encephalic, and general. The therapeutic measures to counter the disease ranged from simple and compound drugs, to music, wine, and sexual intercourse. Melancholy was only one of many mental disorders for which physicians in the Islamic world developed sophisticated categories and therapies. Moreover music and hospitals played a particular role in the care of those suffering from mental diseases.

Galen's works and ideas came to dominate the medical discourse in the late antique world in both Greek and Syriac. This Galenism, especially as taught and interpreted in the amphitheaters of sixth- and seventh-century Alexandria, had a decisive influence on the learned medical tradition in the medieval Islamic world. During the great Greco-Arabic translation movement of the late eighth to the early tenth centuries, most Greek medical literature that had circulated in Alexandria became available in Arabic in Baghdad and thence other parts of the Arabic-speaking world. The translators, many of whom were Christians, also created a mode of discourse, complete with its own technical terminology, for the pursuit of original medical research in Arabic.

One area in which physicians in the medieval Islamic world went beyond their forebears is semiotics. In order to treat a disease, it was first necessary to diagnose it by recognizing its "signs." The complexion, urine, and pulse, for instance, could offer indications allowing the physician to deduce from what specific disease the patient suffered. Taking the patient's history obviously occupied a prominent place here, and a number of treatises on medical ethics give clear instructions on how the physician should proceed. In this area, too, Greek texts such as the Hippocratic *On Prognosis* (Arabic title: *Fī taqdimat al-maʿrifa*), and Galen's commentary on this work as well as his own *On Prognosis* (*Nawādir taqdimat al-maʿrifa*) offered important guidance. Two famous examples can illustrate that the physicians writing in Arabic were also capable of innovation, going beyond the Greek model.

The two diseases smallpox and measles have similar symptoms, such as high fever and rashes or pustules on the skin. The clinician Muḥammad ibn Zakarīyā al-Rāzī (d. c. 932) wrote a major and highly influential treatise on *Smallpox and Measles* (*Fī al-judarī wa-al-ḥaṣba*), in which he distinguishes between the two conditions and offers tools for differential diagnosis. This treatise continued to be highly influential, not only in the East but also in Europe, with Latin, English, and French translations appearing in the eighteenth and nineteenth centuries. In the field of ophthalmology, too, new diseases were discovered and distinguished from previously known ailments, as the example of *sabal* (pannus) shows. This disease, in which blood vessels from the limbus invade the cornea, does not appear in the classical Greek medical works. Yuḥannā ibn Miskawayh and his pupil Ḥunayn ibn Isḥāq, however, included it in their ophthalmological works, and advise on its treatment.

Such research, already under way among translators such as Yuḥannā and Ḥunayn, produced a vast array of specialized monographs, comprehensive medical encyclopedias, teaching texts, commentaries, and popular self-help manuals through the medieval period. This scholarship was Galenic in inspiration and content, but the contribution of Islamic culture was nonetheless considerable. Apart from the topics already discussed (nosology and ophthalmology), major advances were made in pharmacology and surgery, and certain ideas neglected by the Greeks (e.g., contagion) were raised to prominence only in Islamic times. Further, it was under Islamic auspices, and most particularly in the *Canon of Medicine* of Ibn Sīnā (known in the West as Avicenna, d. 1037), that the ideas of Galen, scattered through his many practical and theoretical works, were drawn together into a unified system. Latin translations of the *Canon* were the basis of the medieval European Galenism for the next six hundred years.

Many humoral medical authors and practitioners were Christians and Jews, but, just as peoples of different religious persuasions adhered to essentially the same tradition of popular medicine, humoral writers and physicians all pursued the same Galenic tradition and produced works that were not specifically Muslim, Christian, or Jewish in orientation. Insofar as they had a religious agenda, it was usually of a general monotheistic character, and it is often impossible to determine the religious identity of a medical author from his works. This reflects a broader cosmopolitan outlook in Islamic society, at least where medicine was concerned: individuals sought out medical help, teachers, students, and books with little if any attention to religious affinities.

Although religion did not play a major role in determining who was a legitimate physician, many doctors belonging to the medical elite tried to differentiate themselves from the medical other, the charlatan. Women in particular attracted the wrath of male physicians, and yet much of the standard medical care, the "bodywork," was probably carried out by them. Whether as mothers, sisters, aunts, grandmothers, wise women, nurses, or female physicians, women played a significant role in the medical marketplace. Nor should one imagine that women did not have access to male doctors; on the contrary, even in cases where women had to expose their private parts, they could they seek male medical advice.

A prominent topic in recent scholarship is Islamic hospitals: five factors came together that render them unique and that, together, mark a significant departure from previous institutions. They are briefly: 1) legal and financial security through the status of pious foundation (*waqf*) in Islamic law; 2) the "secular" character of the medical therapy; 3) the presence of elite practitioners; 4) medical research; and 5) medical teaching. The combination of these factors certainly constitutes innovation. Moreover only the institutional setting made it possible for physicians like Muḥammad ibn Zakarīyā al-Rāzī to carry out large-scale research or to encounter rare diseases.

This humoral medicine continues to be practiced, although in modified form. New medical ideas—whether those of Paracelsus in the sixteenth and seventeenth centuries, or those of French physicians in the nineteenth century—entered the Arabic medical texts. But many of the herbal remedies of humoral medicine are still prepared today as alternatives to modern Western biomedicine. And in India and Pakistan, where humoral medicine from the sixteenth century onward was associated with various saintly families and figures, it managed to survive under the rubric of *ṭibb* or *yūnānī ṭibb* ("Greek medicine"). It is still extensively studied and taught in this part of the Islamic world, and its remedies are manufactured on a large scale and widely promoted and consumed there.

Medicine of the Prophet. Prophetic medicine (*ṭibb al-nabī*), also known as "medicine of the Prophet" (*al-ṭibb al-nabawī*), a genre of medical (or rather, legal-medical) literature, developed from the tenth century onward. Legal scholars drew on collections of *ḥadīth* and sunnah to establish a religiously sound medical tradition. This genre gained greater prominence from the thirteenth century onward. People sometimes think that the authors of the manuals on Prophetic medicine wanted to counter the Greek influence. However, many such manuals incorporated, rather than rejected, humoral pathology. The works by Shams al-Dīn al-Dhahabī, as well as his contemporary Ibn al-Qayyim al-Jawzīyah (d. 1350), include numerous references to the Greek authorities. The literature on Prophetic medicine therefore shows how profound the impact of humoral pathology was, affecting not only elite medical ideas but also religious concepts.

In modern times, the medicine of the Prophet has enjoyed great popularity; and, as it is legitimated by direct appeal to the sanction of Muḥammad himself, its social role is closely linked to the strength of prevailing religious sentiments. A recent edition of Ibn al-Qayyim al-Jawzīyah's work is a bestseller in Arab countries, and a recent survey shows that, among Muslims in general, there is both awareness of the specific contents of the tradition and willingness to use it. Even medical journals and scientific publications in the Islamic world, though patterned after Western biomedical models, take up topics relating to medical utterances of the Prophet and his medicine. Similar discussions are regularly laid before the general public in the press, which publishes fatwas on issues related to medical ethics, including birth control, artificial insemination, autopsy, organ transplants, cosmetic surgery, euthanasia, and medical aspects of Islamic worship (e.g., whether one's fast is broken by taking essential medication). Justifying precedents are almost always drawn from medieval Islamic legal texts. Finally, there is also a large market for what one could call "fusion medicine," syncretic collections of Greek humoral pathology and modern (Western) medicine that are commercially highly successful. Therefore, in many ways, the medical tradition that developed in the medieval Islamic world continues to thrive and grow in many different ways.

Bibliography

Abugideiri, Hibba. "A Labor of Love: Making Space for Midwives in Gulf History." In *Gulf Women*, edited by Amira El-Azhary Sonbol. New York: Bloomsbury USA, 2012.

Álvarez-Millán, Cristina. "The Case History in Medieval Islamic Medical Literature: *Tajārib* and *Mujarrabāt* as Source." *Medical History* 54, no. 2 (2010): 195–214. Interesting, if controversial, exploration of the case history genre.

Brockopp, Jonathan E., and Thomas Eich, eds. *Muslim Medical Ethics: From Theory to Practice*. Columbia: University of South Carolina Press, 2008. Good introduction to the issues of modern medical practice in the Islamic world and its relation to the past.

Bray, Julia. "The Physical World and the Writer's Eye: al-Tānūkhī and Medicine." In *Writing and Representation in Medieval Islam: Muslim Horizons*, edited by Julia Bray, pp. 215–249. London and New York: Routledge, 2006. Shows what literary sources have to offer about the social aspects of medical practice.

Conrad, Lawrence I. "Arab-Islamic Medicine." In *Companion Encyclopedia of the History of Medicine*, edited by W. F. Bynum and Roy Porter, 2 vols., vol. 1, pp. 676–727. London and New York: Routledge, 1993. Best illustrates Conrad's view on how medicine developed in the Islamic world, with special emphasis on popular and religious practice.

Dols, Michael W. *Majnūn: The Madman in Medieval Islamic Society*. Oxford: Clarendon Press, 1992. Magisterial study of madness, with relevance to many other issues.

Gutas, Dimitri. *Greek Thought, Arabic Culture: The Graeco-Arabic Translation Movement in Baghdad and Early ʿAbbāsid Society (2nd–4th/8th–10th Centuries)*. London: Routledge, 1998. A treatment of the translation movement and the historical and social forces behind it.

Giladi, Avner. *Infants, Parents and Wet Nurses: Medieval Islamic Views on Breastfeeding and Their Social Implications*. Leiden, Netherlands, and Boston: Brill, 1999. Shows that although theoretical manuals on breastfeeding were mostly written by men, women still provided most of the medical and paramedical cases in this area.

Horden, Peregrine. *Hospitals and Healing from Antiquity to the Later Middle Ages*. Collected Studies 881. Aldershot, U.K.: Ashgate Variorum, 2008. Important collection on the history of the hospital, with much relevant material on Islamic hospitals.

Ebrahimnejad, Hormoz, ed. *The Development of Modern Medicine in Non-Western Countries: Historical Perspectives*. London: Routledge, 2009.

Interesting exploration of medicine with special focus on Persia.

Joosse, N. Peter, and Peter E. Pormann. "Decline and Decadence in Iraq and Syria after the Age of Avicenna? ʿAbd al-Laṭīf al-Baghdādī (1162–1231) between Myth and History." *Bulletin of the History of Medicine* 84, no.2 (May 2010). Recent challenge to the myth of "decline" in the so-called "post-classical" age.

Musallam, Basim F. *Sex and Society in Islam: Birth Control before the Nineteenth Century*. Cambridge, U.K., and New York: Cambridge University Press, 1983. Explores the issue of sexual intercourse and contraception, with an interesting chapter on medical authors such as al-Rāzī.

Perho, Irmel. *The Prophet's Medicine: A Creation of the Muslim Traditionalist Scholars*. Studia Orientalia 74. Helsinki: Finnish Oriental Society, 1995. Shows that prophetic medicine only emerged relatively late and did not rival the humoral tradition based on Greek models.

Pormann, Peter E. "Al-Rāzī (d. 925) on the Benefits of Sex: A Clinician Caught between Philosophy and Medicine." In *O Ye Gentlemen: Arabic Studies on Science and Literary Culture, in Honour of Remke Kruk*, edited by Arnoud Vrolijk and Jan P. Hogendijk, pp. 115–127. Leiden, Netherlands: Brill, 2007. Explores writings on medical intercourse, a genre that enjoyed much popularity in the medieval Islamic world.

Pormann, Peter E. "Female Patients and Practitioners in Medieval Islam." *The Lancet* 373 (2009): 1598–1599. Sheds light on the neglected question of women in Islamic medicine.

Pormann, Peter E. "The Formation of the Arabic Pharmacology: Between Tradition and Innovation." *Annals of Science* 68 (2011): 493–515. Highlights the innovative character of Arabic pharmacopoeias.

Pormann, Peter E., ed. *Islamic Medical and Scientific Tradition*. Critical Concepts in Islamic Studies. 4 vols. London: Routledge, 2010. Collection of articles that offers excellent access to the topic; the first two volumes deal with medicine.

Pormann, Peter. E. "Medical Methodology and Hospital Practice: The Case of Tenth-century Baghdad." In *In the Age of al-Farabi: Arabic Philosophy in the 4th/10th Century*, edited by Peter Adamson, pp. 95–118. Warburg Institute Colloquia 12. London: Warburg Institute, 2008. Novel argument for Islamic hospitals departing radically from their Byzantine antecedents.

Pormann, Peter E. "The Physician and the Other: Images of the Charlatan in Medieval Islam." *Bulletin of the History of Medicine* 79, no.2 (Summer 2005): 189–227. Good introduction to the topic of medical ethics and elite physicians' (often unsuccessful) endeavors to control medical practice.

Pormann, Peter E., and Emilie Savage-Smith. *Medieval Islamic Medicine*. New Edinburgh Islamic Surveys. Edinburgh: Edinburgh University Press, 2007. Now the standard introduction to the topic.

Rosenthal, Franz. *Science and Medicine in Islam: A Collection of Essays*. Aldershot, U.K.: Gower, 1990. Collected studies by a leading historian of Islamic society, culture, and science.

Savage-Smith, Emilie. "Attitudes Toward Dissection in Medieval Islam." *Journal of the History of Medicine and Allied Sciences* 50 (1995): 68–111. Dispels the myth that no dissection took place owing to an Islamic taboo.

Savage-Smith, Emilie. "Drug Therapy of Eye Diseases in Seventeenth-Century Islamic Medicine: The Influence of the 'New Chemistry' of the Paracelsians." *Pharmacy in History* 29 (1987): 3–28. Shows that contact with Western medical ideas continues in the early modern period.

Savage-Smith, Emilie, ed. *Magic and Divination in Early Islam*. The Formation of the Classical Islamic World 42. London: Ashgate, 2004. Masterly collection on magic in the Islamic world, with medical aspects occupying a prominent place.

Savage-Smith, Emilie. "The Practice of Surgery in Islamic Lands: Myth and Reality." In *The Year 1000: Medical Practice at the End of the First Millennium*, edited by Peregrine Horden and Emilie Savage-Smith, pp. 307–321. Social History of Medicine 13, no. 2. Oxford: Oxford University Press, 2000. Dispels the myth that invasive surgery (e.g., cesareans) were routinely performed in the Islamic world.

Shefer-Mossensohn, Miri. *Ottoman Medicine*. Albany: State University of New York Press, 2009. Novel approach to medicine in the early modern period in the Ottoman Empire.

Siraisi, Nancy G. *Avicenna in Renaissance Italy: The Canon and the Medical Teaching in Italian Universities after 1500*. Princeton, N.J.: Princeton University Press, 1987. Demonstrates that much of European

university medicine is based on "Arabic" authors in Latin translation, especially Avicenna (Ibn Sīnā).
Tibi, Selma. *The Medicinal Use of Opium in Ninth-century Baghdad*. Sir Henry Wellcome Asian Series 5. Leiden, Netherlands, and Boston: Brill, 2006. Fascinating case study of medicinal opium use.
Ullmann, Manfred. *Die Medizin im Islam*. Handbuch der Orientalistik 1, no. 1. Leiden, Netherlands: Brill, 1970. Standard reference book which remains the starting point for most in-depth studies of the topic.

Peter Pormann

Contemporary Practice

Medicine in modern Islamic societies must be understood in the context of Western political, economic, and scientific dominance. In the nineteenth century many Muslim rulers, convinced of European military and scientific superiority and anxious to defend and strengthen themselves and their societies, began to establish Western-style medical facilities. In 1822, for instance, Muḥammad ʿAlī, the ruler of Egypt, invited Antoine-Barthelemy Clot, a French physician, to organize his medical services. In 1827 Clot founded a hospital and medical school in Cairo where European medicine was taught. In 1839 the Ottoman Sultan, Mahmud II, opened a Western-style medical school in Istanbul. Muslim rulers from Morocco to Indonesia recruited European physicians to serve them and often to organize their health services. Contrary to what is commonly thought, modernization in medical practice in Islamic countries was intended not to displace the Sharīʿah but to support it.

The Introduction of Modern Medicine. In the era of direct colonial rule, beginning, for example, in Algeria in 1830 and in Egypt in 1882, the French and British authorities administered medical services and usually placed their nationals in the highest positions. Medicine was not a priority for colonial administrators, who generally established modern hospitals and public health facilities only in the European quarters of larger cities. In Algeria and Egypt medical facilities came to reflect the class structure of the colonial societies, with the best hospitals for the French or British, second-class hospitals for Jewish or Italian communities, and third-class hospitals for the Muslims. Over time a gradual process occurred in which first the urban areas and then the rural ones came to use Western medicine. Throughout the nineteenth century, Western medicine did not replace but was added to the wide array of traditional healers: herbalists, bonesetters, barbers, midwives, spiritual healers, and the like. The case of midwives is especially instructive in reflecting the change in the medical services and the population's use thereof. In Egypt and the main Ottoman centers, certified midwives were appointed by the state to deal with more than assisting births. They were a means of spreading health and regulating order, as envisioned by the state. Some of these new midwives were educated in the new midwifery schools, but others were, in fact, traditional midwives who applied for a license; yet others continued to practice traditional midwifery for their numerous customers in a formal or even non-formal way, under the state radar. Eventually, around the turn of the twentieth century, it becomes evident that Western medicine marginalized traditional practices and healers, although they never disappeared.

After political independence was won in the first part of the twentieth century, most Muslim governments began to require physicians to be trained and certified by Western-style medical schools, although some gave traditional practitioners a second-class medical status. Nationalist governments frequently made the extension of medical services an important political platform, and medical schools, hospitals, and other medical facilities and public health systems were expanded throughout the Muslim world. In Egypt, for example, the Department of Public

Health was made into the Ministry of Health in 1936, and in the 1940s resources were increased in response to the recurrence of deadly epidemics. A system of rural and urban health units instituted in the 1940s was enlarged under the regime of President Gamal Abdel Nasser, and Egypt today has a vast network of medical services.

Nevertheless inequities and organizational difficulties have resulted in widespread deficiencies. Oil-rich nations such as Saudi Arabia have spent billions on importing ultramodern medical facilities. Poorer nations like Pakistan, which spends less than 1 percent of its gross national product on health, have inadequate medical facilities. In many regions, medical schools have produced more specialists than needed while the basic needs of the rural and urban populace go unmet. Programs to train physicians, public health nurses, and other personnel to practice preventive medicine in rural and urban health centers are, however, becoming more common. In the second half of the twentieth century, various Muslim countries tried to encourage medical doctors, especially female doctors, to choose general practice outside the main urban centers. In many cases, this was part of a far-reaching demographical policy to stop population growth. In Iran, for example, first under the shah, and then in the Islamic Republic, there were effective family-planning programs (in 2012 a reversal to pro-natality seems to have occurred). In these policies, public-health officials, especially female practitioners who can approach women discreetly, play a central role.

As elsewhere in the world, modern medical technologies have created mixed results. Because of improved public health and medical services and the increased production of foodstuffs, populations have soared, outstripping resources. In some regions modern irrigation techniques now allow for the cultivation of two or three crops per year, but waterborne bilharzia (schistosomiasis) has spread into previously uninfected regions. Automobile and industrial pollution now chokes major cities of the Muslim world, resulting in a widespread deterioration of public health. The medical inequities of the preindependence era have continued and even become worse in many regions.

Medicine and Islamic Values. At the turn of the twentieth century, however, many Islamic reformers became disillusioned with modern medicine, claiming that its tendency to treat the patient symptom by symptom rather than as a whole person, is inherently dehumanizing and medically unsound. Modern medicine, they argue, has become overly materialistic and technocratic, addressing the financial interests of the medical industry, rather than the unique needs of the patient. They have called for a return to Islamic values to make modern medicine more humane and moral, based on preventive rather than curative medicine and addressed to the needs of the individual and his or her community. Medical reformers are trying to reinforce the concept of caring for the whole person rather than treating one organ or an isolated ailment, and for using natural remedies, nutritional regimens, and spiritual healing before more radical treatments and surgical intervention.

In 1982 the second International Conference on Islamic Medicine, held in Kuwait, addressed many of these questions. Specialists in Islamic medicine from many parts of the world called for integrating Islamic medical ethics derived from the Qurʾān and sunnah with modern medicine. Some called for Muslim medical students to learn the medical ethics of Islam by studying the Sharīʿah and *ḥadīth* and biographies of noted Muslim physicians. Others called for research programs to study the efficacy of the diverse traditional medicines of Islamic societies. The conference ended with recommendations to launch the World Islamic Medicine Organization, established after the first conference, to publish Kuwait's Islamic Code of Medical Ethics, and to further study the role of Islam in medical education. The conference participants repeatedly expressed their discomfort with aspects of modern medicine and a nationalistic pride in the medical achievements of earlier centuries.

In addition to such academic specialists in Islamic medicine, many Islamic religious authorities, commentators, and philosophers have attempted to bring modern medicine into the framework of Islamic ethics. They generally argue that, in Muslim societies, no activity of life, including the practice of modern medicine, should be secular. The Muslim scholars have responded to many medical issues, including euthanasia, human cloning, test-tube babies, organ transplantation, and the use of non-*ḥalāl* medicine in treatment. Religious scholars (*ʿulamāʾ*), Muslim academics, and practicing physicians and scientists, cooperate in a series of pan-Muslim conferences and inter-Muslim organizations to work toward a consensus in bioethical issues. They come from new Muslim communities in the West, the Middle East, Africa, and Southeast Asia.

In many cases the solution is to find sanctions for or prohibitions of modern medical practices within the Qurʾān or *ḥadīth*. For example, in Riyadh, Saudi Arabia, the religious authorities were asked to rule on the legality of organ transplants. In 1982, the senior *ʿulamāʾ* issued Decree Number 99, stating that organ donation and transplantation both during and after life are legal, provided that written consent is available from the donor or the next of kin. In Egypt, Shaykh Muḥammad Mutawallī al-Shaʿrāwī, the prominent Islamic commentator, has given his views on the ethics of cosmetic surgery. He has reasoned that if it leads to modifications in God's creation it should be viewed negatively, adding that beauty is a gift of God that is beyond human understanding and should not be measured by humankind. On the other hand, he suggests, if such surgical intervention relieves suffering, including psychological suffering, it would be acceptable under Islamic ethics. The consensus tries to strike a balance between accepting and respecting God's original creation, including the blemishes, while reflecting on the need to accommodate mental stress. Some scholars, for example, accept a request of a young woman to allow orthodontics in order to improve her marriage chances. Other scholars, however, will reject a request to allow the plucking of eyebrows. Diet simply for losing weight may be criticized, while dieting that also has also medical purpose will be legitimized.

The late Fazlur Rahman, a noted Pakistani philosopher and Islamic reformer, argued that, in the Qurʾān and *ḥadīth*, the needs of the living are more important than those of the dead, and therefore both dissection and organ transplants are legal. Regarding genetic engineering, he reasoned that, although tampering with the will of God was not acceptable, the genetic improvement of plants and animals had been accepted since the beginning of history, and so should the genetic improvement of human beings, as long as it involved no loss of human life or dignity. He argued that the technology involved in producing test-tube babies helped a husband and wife have children and so should be sanctioned. If, however, the reproductive cells were from donors rather than from the husband and wife, the procedure should be illegal, because, under Islamic law, adultery means not only extramarital relations but also confusing the genetic heritage of the child. Finally, regarding prolongation of life by artificial means, he reasoned that it was not acceptable, because the Qurʾān emphasizes the quality of life over the quantity of life. If the quality of life was also improved, it was acceptable, but this meant that the environment and food resources must be improved at the same time.

Like many, but not all, Islamic authorities, he argued that family planning is acceptable in Islamic ethics, as is abortion within the first four months of pregnancy. He observed that even when the *ʿulamāʾ* have objected to medical advances, Muslim communities have often accepted them, providing an additional argument for them on the basis of community consensus.

Because of differences in the Sharīʿah legal schools and the formal legislation in different Muslim states, the phenomenon of medical tourism is gaining momentum. Lebanon, for example, is sometimes the secret haven for Arab Sunnī Muslim infertile couples. Lebanon, with its big Shīʿī community, offers top fertility clinics that abide by Shīʿī rulings, which are currently more lenient toward gamete donation than the Sunnī consensus. As Marcia Inhorn has shown in numerous studies, it is important for many Muslim couples to have legitimate Muslim babies and look for possibilities also outside their homeland.

Modern Muslim scholars do consider certain types of artificial insemination to be permitted. However, the means of insemination are restricted. The only permitted means is the artificial transference of the husband's sperm to his wife while they are cohabiting. The use of reproductive faculties (sperm or womb) of third parties and the use of the procedure by an unmarried couple are not allowed by many Sunnī scholars and are considered by some jurists to be close to *zinah* (fornication). Professor Mustafa Shalabi, for example, does not allow the wife to use the sperm of her deceased husband or her ex-husband as this causes problems with the child's *nasab* (genealogy) and the distribution of the deceased's inheritance.

In addition medical practice in Islamic countries has also had to face controversial issues such as female circumcision. Modern medicine, however, has brought new dimensions to this traditional practice by, for example, reducing the side effects of circumcision, especially to young girls. Modern midwives, such as the Wolff sisters in Sudan, have taught local midwives to perform more hygienic female circumcision and to provide good aftercare to patients. Shaykh Maḥmūd Shaltūt, however, objects to female circumcision, arguing that no legal text supports it. Only male circumcision is *wājib* (obligatory), according to most jurists. Some Muslim scholars also argue against certain types of female circumcision, acknowledging the fact that excision and infibulation, for example, cause health problems including physical damage, primarily hemorrhage and injury to the urinary system. For this reason, many Muslim doctors refuse to perform circumcision on girls.

One of the most intractable issues for contemporary medical practice is the worldwide spread of AIDS. Because of the officially prescribed ideals of Muslim sexual behavior, a number of Muslim governments have been reluctant to disseminate information or even to collect statistics on the epidemic, preferring to view it as a foreign danger to be stopped at the borders. Muslim clerics often resist any open discussion of the issue, whether it concerns preventing the spread of HIV/AIDS or the use of methods to contain it (through, for example, the distribution of condoms). This attitude stems from the view that the HIV/AIDS epidemic results from human acts and is, therefore, a punishment from God. No effort on the part of Muslims, so it is argued, can ever surpass God's will. The stigma of HIV/AIDS infection further has deep roots within the Muslim community. Muslim physicians and social critics, such as Munawar A. Anees, however, have argued convincingly that there is a gulf between ideals and realities, that the community is responsible for the welfare of all of its members, and that this "denial syndrome" must stop. This is particularly true in cases, such as in South Africa, where HIV/AIDS infection is not always necessarily the result of illicit sexual behavior on the part of the infected person. There are many reported cases of women being infected while engaging in sexual relations with unfaithful husbands. Given that a woman who refuses sexual relations with her husband is considered "disobedient" and is shunned by the community, it is important to address this reality in all of its parameters.

In response to the many calls for the integration of modern medicine into an Islamic framework, Islamic hospitals have been established in many cities in the Muslim world. In Amman, Jordan, for example, the Islamic Hospital is large, active, and modern, resembling any Western hospital, except for the conservative Islamic dress worn by its employees, male and female physicians and staff members alike, and its insistence on conforming to Islamic values in its practices. Many of the Islamist (fundamentalist) movements have made medicine an important part of their social services, and their clinics and hospitals often dispense free medical and public health services.

Assessment. Many reformers have asked why Islamic civilization has not assimilated and advanced Western medicine as easily as it assimilated Greek, Persian, and Indian medicine in the early centuries of Islam. One common answer is that, in contrast to its relationship with the West, Islamic civilization was politically dominant over those more scientifically advanced civilizations, making it psychologically easier to incorporate new knowledge into the cultural framework. Another is that current medical research is far more complex and costly than in earlier centuries and thus more difficult to assimilate.

Whatever the answer to this question, implicit in it is another question: how can Muslim societies end their dependence on the West and advance on their own terms? Some believe that the Muslim world must return to its Islamic roots, for example by instituting the Qurʾānic *zakāt* tax (a tithe on income) to fund regional medical research centers where the wealth and talent of the region can be concentrated. Others argue with equal conviction that the solution lies in secular and democratic political, social, and economic reforms that would combine the wealth and talents of the region in a secular atmosphere. This conflict between Islamist and secularist views of medical, public health, and other social reforms is perhaps the most crucial of the early twenty-first century.

[*See also* Abortion; Family Planning; *and* Health Care.]

BIBLIOGRAPHY

Anees, Munawar A. "The Silent Killer: AIDS and the Muslim World." *The Minaret* (January–February 1994): 33–35.

Bell, Heather. "Midwifery Training and Female Circumcision in the Inter-War Anglo-Egyptian Sudan." *The Journal of African History* 39, no. 2 (1998): 293–312.

Brockopp, Jonathan E., ed. *Islamic Ethics of Life: Abortion, War, and Euthanasia*. Columbia: University of South Carolina Press, 2003.

Brockopp, Jonathan E., and Thomas Eich, eds. *Muslim Medical Ethics: From Theory to Practice*. Columbia: University of South Carolina Press, 2008.

Fahmy, Khaled. "The Anatomy of Justice, Forensic Medicine, and Criminal Law in Nineteenth-Century Egypt." *Islamic Law and Society* 6, no. 2 (1999): 224–271.

Faqih, S. R. al-. "The Influence of Islamic Views on Public Attitudes towards Kidney Transplant Donation in a Saudi Arabian Community." *Public Health* 105 (1991): 161–165.

Ghaly, Mohammed. *Islam and Disability: Perspectives in Theology and Jurisprudence*. London and New York: Routledge, 2009.

Gallagher, Eugene B., and C. Maureen Searle. "Health Services and the Political Culture of Saudi Arabia." *Social Science and Medicine* 21, no. 3 (1985): 251–262.

Gallagher, Nancy Elizabeth. *Egypt's Other Wars: Epidemics and the Politics of Public Health*. Syracuse, N.Y.: Syracuse University Press, 1990. Shows how malaria, relapsing fever, and cholera became major political issues in the post–World War II era.

Gallagher, Nancy Elizabeth. *Medicine and Power in Tunisia, 1780–1900*. Cambridge, U.K., and New York: Cambridge University Press, 1983. Discusses the transition from Galenic-Islamic to Western medicine in Tunisia in the context of European political and economic expansion.

Good, Byron. "The Transformation of Health Care in Modern Iranian History." In *Modern Iran: The Dialectics of Continuity and Change*, edited by Michael Bonine and Nikki R. Keddie, pp. 59–82. Albany: State University of New York Press, 1981.

Inhorn, Marcia C. *Local Babies, Global Science: Gender, Religion, and In Vitro Fertilization in Egypt*. New York: Routledge, 2003.

Inhorn, Marcia C. *The New Arab Men: Emergent Masculinities, Technologies, and Islam in the Middle East*. Princeton, N.J.: Princeton University Press, 2012. Inhorn has edited and co-edited numerous volumes that pertain to issues of health and technology across the Muslim world.

Inhorn, Marcia C. *Quest for Conception: Gender, Infertility, and Egyptian Medical Traditions*. Philadelphia: University of Pennsylvania Press, 1994.

Jundī, Aḥmad Rajā'ī, ed. *al-Abnāth wa-a'māl al-Mu'tamar al-'Ālamī al-Thānī'an al-Tibb al-Islāmī* [*Proceedings of the Second International Conference on Islamic Medicine*]. Kuwait: Munazzamat al-Tibb al-Islamic, 1982.

Khan, Muhammad Salim. *Islamic Medicine*. London: Routledge and K. Paul, 1986. Argues that the creative thought, balanced lifestyle, and healing forces known to the Islamic medical tradition can reform modern medicine.

Kuhnke, LaVerne. *Lives at Risk: Public Health in Nineteenth-Century Egypt*. Berkeley: University of California Press, 1990. Discusses epidemics of cholera, plague, and smallpox, as well as Western medical institutions introduced by Muḥammad 'Alī.

Morsy, Soheir A. "Towards a Political Economy of Health: A Critical Note on the Medical Anthropology of the Middle East." *Social Science and Medicine* 15B (1981): 159–163. Provides background to the study of traditional medicine.

Nanji, Azim A. "Medical Ethics and the Islamic Tradition." *Journal of Medicine and Philosophy* 13 (1988): 257–275.

Rahman, Fazlur. *Health and Medicine in the Islamic Tradition: Change and Identity*. New York: Crossroad, 1987. Indispensable study of Islamic ethics, medicine, and health, beginning with a comprehensive analysis of "Wellness and Illness in the Islamic World View."

Rispler-Chaim, Vardit. "Islamic Medical Ethics in the Twentieth Century." *Journal of Medical Ethics* 15 (1989): 203–208.

Rispler-Chaim, Vardit. *Islamic Medical Ethics in the Twentieth Century*. Leiden, Netherlands, and New York: Brill, 1993.

Rispler-Chaim, Vardit. *Disability in Islamic Law*. Dordrecht, Netherlands: Springer, 2006.

Rispler-Chaim, Vardit, ed. Special issue of *Medicine and Law* 21 (2002) dedicated to Muslim medical ethics and law.

Sonbol, Amira El Azhary. *The Creation of a Medical Profession in Egypt, 1800–1922*. Syracuse, N.Y.: Syracuse University Press, 1992. Surveys the introduction of Western medical institutions into Egypt.

Yacoub, Ahmed Abdel Aziz. *The Fiqh of Medicine: Responses in Islamic Jurisprudence to Advances in Medical Science*. London: Ta-Ha, 2001.

NANCY E. GALLAGHER
Updated by YASMIN SAFIAN, ROBERT GLEAVE, *and* MIRI SHEFER-MOSSENSOHN

MEDIEVAL COURT POETRY. The first hint of court poetry in the Arabo-Islamic cultural memory begins with the first courts in the pre-Islamic era, such as those of the Ghassānids (in present-day Syria) and Lakhmids (in present-day Iraq) in roughly the sixth century CE Those courts bequeathed the poetry of 'Alqamah ibn 'Abadah and al-Nābighah al-Dhubyānī. In terms of style, these early poets enshrined the ritual tripartite structure of the Arabic ode (*qaṣīdah*), and in terms of function they set models of poetry that function in society as ransom, gift exchange, oath, apology, and/or peace offering. Likewise, as the Prophet Muḥammad gained political and spiritual influence, Ḥassān ibn Thābit (d. 674) and Kaʿb ibn Zuhayr (d. 7th century) composed poetry projecting a wise-kingly reputation that served as an interface for those seeking the Prophet's favor. The Prophet's earthly need for poetry would enshrine many genres, such as praise (*madīḥ*) and even wine poetry (*khamrīyah*), despite the new-fangled Qurʾānic taboo, as insignias of authority that were particularly "Islamic." Court poetry flourished with the first empire builders of Islam, namely the Umayyads, from 661–750. The Umayyads looked to their Byzantine and Persian peers for insignias of power, such as coinage, monuments, and palaces, and, of course, viral poetry that was transmitted by public performance.

The Umayyad era was paradoxical, though: While the Umayyads enjoyed tremendous global reach, building a commonwealth from the Atlantic to the Indus Valley, they mismanaged two civil wars in their own backyard that traumatized the Muslim *ummah*, as believers witnessed the Prophet's kin and religion riven by war. Poets stepped in to guide and rehabilitate the Umayyads, while at the same time dressing the gaping wounds of the commonwealth with melodious, infectious poetry and song. Poets inherited a mythic role from the pre-Islamic era as oracle-rascal heroes, and they exercised that influence to reflect and shape an expanse of human needs and emotions, which forged a new universal imagined community: hopeful love poetry (*ghazal*), tragic love poetry (*ʿudhrī*), lampoon (*hijāʾ*), comic flytings (*naqāʾiḍ*), heroic praise of persons or places (*madīḥ*), heroic boast of self or people (*fakhr*), elegy of persons or places (*rithāʾ*), and those celebrating wine (*khamrīyah*) or comic bacchanalia (*mujūn*). Later, in the ʿAbbāsid era, these older genres morphed to meet emerging audience demands, and new genres developed, such as those romanticizing valor (*ḥamāsah*) and hunting (*ṭardīyāt*).

For the purpose of forging a new commonwealth, poets in particular deployed the female beloved for varied and diverging purposes as a metaphor. In praise poetry, the female beloved was often an avatar for the male patron, such as a caliph or governor, where the poet might protest his treatment at the hands of a cold beloved as a coded critique of political authority. In tragic love poetry, a series of couples emerged, such as Dhul Rummah–Mayyah and Majnūn-Laylī, where the poet projects the female beloved as indifferent and toying with his vulnerabilities, dramatizing a range of maddening discontents in an era of unprecedented trauma that sullied a putatively sacred *ummah*. Embodying the tragedy and ambivalence that many felt, Dhul Rummah says, "Mayyah is the disease; she is the cure." Conversely in romantic love poetry (*ghazal*), the figure of the female beloved was often deployed to connote hopeful attainment of an object desired.

It is assumed in today's scholarship that women contributed little to Islamic court poetry, but this is patently wrong. Poetesses like al-Khansāʾ (d. 7th century) and al-Ḥurqah (d. 7th century) composed lament (*marthīyah*) and incitement to fight (*taḥrīḍ*) and, most surprisingly, a warrior poetess dubbed al-Hujayjah, of the Banū Shaybān, raised armies and built military alliances to defend against an attack by the Sassanian emperor in the Battle of Dhū Qār, a monumental battle for early Islamic culture that dispelled the Sassanian's aura of invincibility. Later, at the Umayyad court, Laylā al-Akhyalīyah (d. c. 704) used her poetic skill to shame the court into making concessions, to lampoon a rival poet, al-Nābighah al-Jaʿdī (d. 684), and to immortalize her deceased lover, Tawbah. Lore about Layla trumpets her capacity to overwhelm with her sharp wit any man naive enough to confront her: When the Umayyad caliph ʿAbd al-Malik ibn asked her publicly, "What did Tawbah see in you that made him love you?" She parried, "What did people see in you that they made *you* caliph?"

In retrospect we can discern four overlapping persona types for poetesses in the Middle Ages: the grieving mother/sister/daughter (al-Khansāʾ, al-Khirniq bint Badr, and al-Fāriʿah bint Shaddād), the warrior-diplomat (al-Hujayjah), the princess (al-Ḥurqah, ʿUlayyah bint al-Mahdī, and Walladah bint al-Mustakfī), and the courtesan-ascetic (ʿArīb, Shāriyah, and Rābiʿah al-ʿAdawīyah). Rābiʿah's biography in particular projects a paradoxical persona that embodies the complimentary opposites of sexuality and saintliness. ʿAbd al-Amīr Muhannā, in his anthology, catalogs the work of more than four hundred poetesses across the centuries. The visibility and impact of these voices was likely unparalleled in any other medieval culture, though scholars have yet to examine the factors that supported that pattern.

In the ʿAbbāsid era, from 750 onward, court poetry increasingly appealed to a broader public that was ethnically more diverse and included men and women who rose to noble status, as well as an emerging sub-nobility, sometimes referred to as *aḥsāb*. This sub-nobility included chancery workers, judges, and a burgeoning class of merchants. By the tenth century it became conspicuous that court poetry was no longer primarily the plaything of the court. However, rather than aping courtly culture, the sub-nobility adapted it and to a large extent democratized the aesthetics and interests reflected in the literature. For example, salons spread like rhizomes in the ninth and tenth centuries among the sub-nobility in the cities; they became less hierarchical and more egalitarian; there was greater emphasis on turn taking, tolerance of foibles, and a warm sociability leavened by wine, flowers, fruits, and the occasional sprig of basil to awaken the senses. The story of Bayad and Riyad illustrates how, in Andalusia, female hosts, too, held single-sex and mixed salons, where men and women could declaim court poetry or sing it to the strum of a lute.

It is often assumed that court and folk poetry were antithetical, but recent research has shown that, despite the court's elitism, in practice there was a surprising degree of interplay. The elites often looked down upon the lower classes, but they also paradoxically romanticized the desert and the Bedouins. The ode (*qaṣīdah*) began as a Bedouin genre composed and performed in the hinterlands of Arabia and evoked desertscapes and culture. Long after Islamic culture became imperial and urban, poets continued to channel that romance particularly in the elegiac nostalgic first section of the ode, the *nasīb*, with wistful tropes such as the abandoned campground (*manzil*), desert abode (*dār*), campfire stones (*athāfī*), and traces in the sand (*rusūm*). This almost ritual practice in effect rendered nomadism the archetypal human condition.

BIBLIOGRAPHY

Abū al-Faraj al-Iṣfahānī. *Kitāb al-aghānī* [The Book of Songs]. Edited by al-Najdī Nāṣif, under Muḥammad Abū al-Faḍl Ibrāhīm. 24 vols. Cairo, Egypt: al-Hayʾa al-Maṣrīyah al-ʿĀmmah lil-Kitāb, 1992–1993.

Ali, Samer M. *Arabic Literary Salons in the Islamic Middle Ages: Poetry, Public Performance, and the Presentation of the Past*. Notre Dame, Ind.: University of Notre Dame Press, 2010.

Ali, Samir M. "The Rise of the Abbasid Public Sphere: The Case of al-Mutanabbi and Three Middle Ranking Patrons." *Al-Qantara: Revista de Estudios Árabes*, special issue on patronage in Islamic history, 29, no. 2 (2008): 467–494.

Hammond, Marlé. *Beyond Elegy: Classical Arabic Women's Poetry in Context*. Oxford and New York: Oxford University Press, 2010.

Meisami, Julie Scott. *Medieval Persian Court Poetry*. Princeton, N.J.: Princeton University Press, 1987.

Muhannā, ʿAbd al-Amīr ʿAlī. *Muʿjam al-nisāʾ al-shāʿirāt fī al-jāhilīyah wa-al-Islām: Khuṭwah naḥwah muʿjam mutakāmil*. Beirut, Lebanon: Dār al-Kutub al-ʿIlmīyah, 1990.

Stetkevych, Jaroslav. *The Zephyrs of Najd: The Poetics of Nostalgia in the Classical Arabic Nasīb*. Chicago: University of Chicago Press, 1993.

Stetkevych, Suzanne Pinckney. *The Mute Immortals Speak: Pre-Islamic Poetry and the Poetics of Ritual*. Ithaca, N.Y.: Cornell University Press, 1993.

Stetkevych, Suzanne Pinckney. *The Poetics of Islamic Legitimacy: Myth, Gender, and Ceremony in the Classical Arabic Ode*. Bloomington: Indiana University Press, 2002.

Samer M. Ali

MENSTRUATION. Like sexual emission, menstruation is a state necessitating full-bath lustration before the Muslim can obtain the ritual purity required for worship. The requisite elements are an intention to remove major impurity; washing the hands and then the genitals thoroughly; performing the ritual ablution (wuḍūʿ?); washing the entire body, beginning with the head (to the roots of the hair) and right side of the body, then continuing to the left.

Ḥadīth reports attributed to Muḥammad's wife ʿĀʾishah claim that women were "ordered" (*nuʿmar*) to make up fasts missed as a result of the exemption granted menstruants and not ordered to make up prayers missed for the same reason. In one ḥadīth, the Prophet explains that menstruation is "decreed" for the daughters of Adam, positioning it as "an integral part of God's plan . . . a biological fact" rather than a punishment (Katz, 198). The euphemism used repeatedly by the Prophet to refer to menstruation is *nafs* ("self" or "soul"), explained by Ibn Qutayba (d. 889CE) as the metaphor the Arabs used for blood, "due to blood's connectedness with or nearness to, or causality of life" (*Tafsīr Gharīb al-Qurʾān*, 25).

Although no *ḥadīth* suggests it, the schools of law (both Sunnī and Shīʿī) unanimously restrict menstruating women from touching the Qurʾān. It has become habitual throughout the Muslim world to link verse 56:79 ("No one may touch it but the pure") to the issue, despite its lack of any contextual bearing on the physical Qurʾān or the purity status of humans. Yet, some menstruants will only touch the pages of the Qurʾān via a medium or when wearing gloves. *Fatwās* have been issued, notably from Saudi Arabia, that menstruating female students may freely study Qurʾān during menstruation.

Ibn Kathīr's (d. 1373CE) exegesis details the Prophet's habits with his menstruating wives. He would eat with ʿĀʾishah and drink from the same vessel and recite Qurʾān while reclining in her lap. He gave license to all forms of spousal intimacy with the exception of vaginal intercourse; this is the meaning that many exegetes give to "keep away from women in the *maḥīḍ* (literally, place of menstruation)" (2:222). This verse also calls menstruation *"adhan"* (harm): some exegetes have historically and currently defined this as meaning menstruation is harmful to men. Others insist that it is harm to the woman, who "suffers" monthly. Many scholars (notably al-Sayyid Sābiq al-Qurṭubī) have included the infamous *ḥadīth* about "deficiencies of (woman's) mind and religion" in discussions on menstruation and purity. However, classical and post-classical jurists generally structured laws of purity in gender-neutral ways, even engaging in debates that challenged the notion that menstruation rendered a woman deficient in religion (Katz, 198–199).

Modern attitudes toward menstruation vary widely according to levels of education and entrenched cultural practices. In areas as diverse as Morocco, Syria, Egypt, and the United States, some pregnant women ignore the concession to leave off fasting, illustrating their belief that the menstruant's Ramadan fast is deficient. In Malay Muslim culture, euphemisms are generally negative, and women are restricted from touching the Qurʾān, entering graveyards, and engaging in sex. Perceived mental incompetence also colors social attitudes: it has been argued that women cannot be competent judges (Egypt) or discerning voters (Kuwait), on account of their menses. In many highly traditional enclaves, menarche is often the signal for young girls to be married off, often against their will. In certain areas of Pakistan, newly menstruating girls are forced into purdah, to don burkas, and to withdraw from school; in such situations, girls tend to have little or no factual information about menstruation, its hygiene, or its significance.

BIBLIOGRAPHY

Ibn Qutayba, *Tafsīr Gharīb al-Qurʾān*. 1958.

Katz, M. H. *Body of Text: The Emergence of the Sunni Law of Ritual Purity*. Albany, N.Y.: State University of New York Press, 2002.

CAROLYN BAUGH

MERNISSI, FATIMA. (b. 1940), Moroccan sociologist and writer. Born into a harem household in Fez to a middle-class family, Mernissi studied at the Mohammed V University in Rabat and later obtained a PhD in sociology from Brandeis University in the US. Returning to Morocco, she joined the sociology department at Mohammed V University. As one of the best-known Arab-Muslim feminists, Mernissi's influence extends beyond a narrow circle of intellectuals. Her major books, written in French, have been translated into several languages, including English, German, Dutch, and Japanese.

The main body of Mernissi's work explores the relationship between sexual ideology, gender identity, sociopolitical organization, and the status of women in Islam. Her special focus, however, is Moroccan society and culture. As a feminist, her work represents an attempt to undermine the ideological and political systems that silence and oppress Muslim women. She does this in two ways: first, by challenging the dominant Muslim male discourse concerning women and their sexuality; and, second, by providing the "silent" woman with a "voice" to tell her own story.

In her first book, *Beyond the Veil: Male-Female Dynamics in Modern Muslim Society* (1975), Mernissi has sought to reclaim the ideological discourse on women and sexuality from the stranglehold of patriarchy. She critically examines the classical corpus of religious-juristic texts, including the *ḥadīth*, and reinterprets them from a feminist perspective. In her view, the Muslim ideal of the "silent, passive, obedient woman" has no connection with the authentic message of Islam. Rather, it is a construction of the *ʿulamāʾ*, the male jurist-theologians who have manipulated and distorted religious texts in order to preserve the patriarchal system.

For Mernissi, Islamic sexual ideology is predicated on a belief that women's inherent sexual power, if left uncontrolled, would wreak havoc on the male-defined social order—hence the necessity to control women's sexuality and to safeguard Muslim society through veiling, segregation, and the legal subordination of women. Her book *The Veil and the Male Elite* (first published in French in 1987) critically examines the historical context of Muslim law and tradition and argues that the original message of the Prophet Muḥammad, which called for equality between the sexes, has been misrepresented by later political leaders and religious scholars. This argument is still vitally important today, particularly with the advent of the Arab Spring and its implications for gender relations.

Since the early twenty-first century, Mernissi has been conducting research on the social impact of the pan-Arab satellite television channels, culminating in her book *Journalistes Marocaines. Génération Dialogue* (2012). She believes that satellite channels have created a space where the free flow of information and debate are possible and that this has changed both communication behavior within families and, ultimately, the image of women. Mernissi further asserts that the satellite networks have played a large role in the Arab Spring.

Bibliography

Mernissi, Fatima. *Beyond the Veil: Male-Female Dynamics in Modern Muslim Society*. Rev. ed. Bloomington: University of Indiana Press, 1987.

Mernissi, Fatima, ed. *Doing Daily Battle: Interviews with Moroccan Women*. Translated by Mary Jo Lakeland. New Brunswick, N.J.: Rutgers University Press, 1989.

Mernissi, Fatima. *Dreams of Trespass: Tales of a Harem Girlhood*. Reading, Mass.: Addison-Wesley Publishing, 1994.

Mernissi, Fatima. *The Forgotten Queens of Islam*. Translated by Mary Jo Lakeland. Minneapolis: University of Minnesota Press, 1993.

Mernissi, Fatima. *Islam and Democracy: Fear of the Modern World*. Translated by Mary Jo Lakeland. Reading, Mass.: Addison-Wesley, 1992.

Mernissi, Fatima. *Journalistes Marocaines. Génération Dialogue*. Rabat, Morocco: Editions Marsam, 2012.

Mernissi, Fatima. *Scheherazade Goes West: Different Cultures, Different Harems*. New York: Washington Square Press, 2001.

Mernissi, Fatima. *The Veil and the Male Elite: A Feminist Interpretation of Women's Rights in Islam*. Translated by Mary Jo Lakeland. Reading, Mass.: Addison-Wesley Publishing, 1991.

Mernissi, Fatima. *Women and Islam: An Historical and Theological Enquiry*. Translated by Mary Jo Lakeland. Oxford: Basil Blackwell, 1991.

Mernissi, Fatima. *Women's Rebellion and Islamic Memory*. London: Zed, 1996.

Amal Rassam
Updated by Lisa Worthington

Mexico.

The principal mode through which women have come to know Islam in Mexico is via religious conversion. Although some accounts speculate that Muslims may have arrived in the country as early as the sixteenth century, migrants are known to have traveled to Mexico as of the late nineteenth century, during the rule of the Ottoman Empire. Most of these migrants were male, meaning that another mode through which Mexican women have encountered Islam is marriage. The 2010 census puts Mexico's Muslim population at 3,760 people, consisting of 1,392 women and 2,368 men, giving a ratio of 1.7 Mexican Muslim males to every female. Further research is required to examine the dependability of these figures however, as individuals may have reasons for hiding their Islamic identity, or census returns may have been completed by relatives. A number of converts to Islam are young adults who still live in their parental homes, where their new religious identity is not always accepted.

There are five Muslim groups of particular note. The most prominent of these is the Muslim Center de México, also known as the Centro Cultural Islámico de México. This group is headed by Omar (formerly Mark) Weston, a British-born entrepreneur who converted to Islam in Orlando, Florida and is perhaps Mexico's most active proponent of Islam. He has been responsible for a number of Islamic projects in Mexico, including a retreat in Tequesquitengo, Morelos, a *daʿwāh* (missionary) office in the Coyoacán district of Mexico City, a Yahoo! discussion group, and a Spanish-language magazine on Islam, *islamentuidioma* (Islam in your language). *Islamentuidioma* regularly features accounts of young women who have converted to Islam, telling the stories of how they came to belong to the tradition. Weston married a native Mexican master's-degree graduate, Vanessa, who exemplifies Islamic values in her commitment to her family and her faith. Their children bear Arabic forenames. The organization propagates the Muslim message and brings disparate Sunnī Muslims together from all over Mexico via the Internet, outreach work, and Islamic conferences. Omar was educated at the Medina in Saudi Arabia and followed the Wahhābī tradition until spending forty days with the Tablīghī Jamāʿat. He was a founding member of the Organización Islámica Para América Latina y el Caribe and his community collaborates closely with this organization.

The Muslim group in which women are the most prominent is the Nur Ashki Jerrahi Ṣūfī order in Colonia Roma, Mexico City, coordinated by Shaykha Amina Teslima al-Jerrahi, which meets every Thursday evening. This community practices a mixture of New Age mysticism and Western feminism. The Nur Askhi Jerrahi, a dervish order, was originally founded in New York by two female converts who received direct instruction from Sheikh Muzaffer Ozak al-Jerrahi of the Helveti-Jerrahi order, established in Istanbul, Turkey. Most women in attendance are described as being of Western appearance and from middle to upper socioeconomic backgrounds. The group has another center in Cuernavaca, Morelos. The dynamics to male-female relationships in Mexico often lead to a critique in such circles of Mexican men's treatment of women. This issue is manifest more broadly across the Mexican Muslim community, where veiling is often argued to avert unwanted male attention in addition to being a sign of personal devotion, and some female converts hold the view that Muslim immigrants will be more respectful towards women and therefore make better husbands and fathers.

The main competition to Omar Weston's Muslim Center de México is the Centro Educativo de la Communidad Musulmana, based in Polanco, Mexico City, which also draws people to the faith. This center runs, in coordination with Pakistani and Moroccan diplomats, the main prayer hall where the *jumʿah* (Friday prayer) is held for Muslims in Mexico City. Accordingly, it has attendees who come from divergent strands of Islam, including those appertaining to Weston's group. Gender segregation exists here, with the men joining the *jumʿah*, while the women congregate in the kitchen and meeting rooms below. Most of this community's female converts are professionals in their late twenties, who come from lower socio-economic family backgrounds.

Another key group is a Murabitun World Movement community, located in Chiapas in Mexico's south. In the journal of the Universidad Nacional Autonóma de México (UNAM), domestic anthropologist Gaspar Morquecho (2005) wrote of the traditional patriarchal structure found in Murabitun society, stressing particularly the social acceptability of punitive violence against women for breaches of the community's moral codes. His informant, Salija, was quick to clarify that any abuse of this chastisement would be reported to the group's leader and face investigation. Another community member, Aisha, emphasized the existence of equality between the genders, especially in terms of access to education and in having complementary, if not identical, roles in matters such as the raising of a family. The Murabitun World Movement has groups dispersed around the globe, each striving to set up self-contained Islamic communities that can sustain themselves with minimal engagement with non-Muslims, usually restricting such interactions to trade.

Many Shīʿī Muslims migrated to the Laguna region of Torreón from Syria and Lebanon during the early twentieth century and intermarried with Catholics from the local community. This has affected the transmission of religious knowledge from generation to generation; however, some descendants of the first generation are exploring their Islamic heritage.

A Salafi Muslim group, the Centro Salafi de México, exists in Colonia Lorenzo Botorini in

Mexico City, however its exact composition remains unknown at present, both in terms of gender mix and numbers. The community was founded by Muhammad Abdullah Ruiz, a former colleague of Omar Weston and erstwhile co-director of the Centro Cultural Islámico de México.

Women in Islam in Mexico have been making their mark. Verónica Lizbeth Márquez Villarreal, a former law student at UNAM, converted to Islam in her early twenties. She is now recognized for her commitment to her religion and her sport, taekwondo. The self-discipline and devotion that Lizbeth exhibited led to her representing her university in significant competitions. Marta Khadija Ramirez was an early convert, in 1983, who adopted the religion when it was broadly unheard of. In 1987 she became a citizen of the United States. By 2005 she was the president of the Los Angeles Latino Muslim Association, helping other Latin Americans connect with the Islamic faith. With conversion to Islam only really having gained momentum in Mexico since the mid-1990s, women are still in the process of developing their roles within this growing and diverse religious tradition.

[*See also* Canada *and* United States of America.]

BIBLIOGRAPHY

Alfaro-Velcamp, Theresa. "Mexican Muslims in the Twentieth Century: Challenging Stereotypes and Negotiating Space." In *Muslims in the West: From Sojourners to Citizens*, edited by Yvonne Y. Haddad, pp. 278–309. New York and Oxford: Oxford University Press, 2002.

Alfaro-Velcamp, Theresa. *So Far from Allah, So Close to Mexico: Middle Eastern Immigrants in Modern Mexico*. Austin: University of Texas Press, 2007.

Lindley-Highfield, Mark. "'Muslimization,' Mission and Modernity in Morelos: the Problem of a Combined Hotel and Prayer Hall for the Muslims of Mexico." *Tourism, Culture & Communication*, 8, no. 2 (2008): 85–96. http://www.ingentaconnect.com/content/cog/tcc/2008/00000008/00000002/art00004.

Morquecho, Gasper. "Chamulas islámicas: Igualdad genérica en el discurso, servidumbre tradicional en los hechos." In *La Jornada en línea*. Universidad Nacional Autonóma de México (UNAM), 2005. http://www.jornada.unam.mx/2005/07/04/informacion/83_chamulasislam.htm.

MARK LINDLEY-HIGHFIELD OF BALLUMBIE CASTLE

MICROFINANCE. Microfinance or microcredit refers to the granting of small loans to those who would not normally qualify for credit, lacking collateral or sufficent income. Pioneered by Muhammad Yunus (b. 1940), founder of Grameen Bank, microfinance has proven especially popular and successful with women. Yunus began his experiment in microfinance in 1976 while teaching economics at Chittagong University, Bangladesh. As an economist, Yunus found theorizing about poverty alleviation shallow if he could not accomplish something practical. Speaking with slum dwellers near campus, he identified a dichotomy: many had skills that could generate income, but lack of capital prevented this. When they could obtain credit, it was from unscrupulous moneylenders. Banks were not prepared to lend money to the poor. What began as an experiment supported by the government-run Janata Bank developed into an independent, not-for-profit financial institution in 1983. Grameen ("of the village") has now lent approximately $6 billion to the poor. Many organizations have adopted versions of its program and philosophy across the world, including for-profit companies and explicitly Islamic agencies. In 1997, the first Microcredit Summit was held in Washington, D.C., with 3,000 delegates from 137 countries. An Islamic Microfinance Network began in 2009.

Microfinance has a distinctive philosophy and modus operandi. Potential borrowers form solidarity or self-help groups consisting of five members. Borrowers own and run the bank. Staff travel to villages to meet borrowers and potential borrowers. After all five have undergone training and passed a test on Grameen's principles and values; two members receive small loans. There are four principles (discipline, unity, courage, and hard work) and sixteen affirmations, recited at every group meeting. Affirmations include commitments to education, the family, life-style, health, and social solidarity. Grameen thus aims to promote social as well as economic development, believing that poverty can become a museum relic (Yunus 2007a, p. 246). Once the first loans are repaid, the next two members become eligible, followed by the fifth. Each borrower is individually responsible for weekly repayments. However, because other members cannot borrow when any member defaults, "subtle-peer pressure" ensures timely repayments (Yunus 1999, p. 62). Loans are meant to finance cottage industries or small businesses such as handicrafts, poultry farming, or renting out a village's only cell phone. Groups are obligated to invest 5 percent of each loan into a fund, from which members can borrow interest-free loans. As loans are repaid, larger sums become available, culminating in a house-loan. When this loan has been repaid, borrowers are disqualified for loans and from running the Bank.

Grameen and other MFIs (micro finance institutions) provide training, marketing assistance, access to insurance and pension services. Grameen is committed to making information technology available to the poor. Microfinance advocates the concept of social businesses that prioritize promoting welfare as well as maximixing profit. The goal is to eventually change the nature of capitalism itself, so that values "other than money" dominate the world (Yunus 2007b, p. 216).

Women were among Grameen's first borrowers. Yunus soon realized that women were better than most men at repaying loans and tend to put money to use in a way that improves their own and their families' welfare. Meenai (2003) cites research showing that women also invest money in "male enterprises" (p. 191). Given that women form the majority of the poor, raising women out of poverty became a philosophical and operational priority. Ninety-seven percent of Grameen members are women. Yunus claims that 58 percent of borrowers have "crossed the poverty line" (2007a, p. 240). Grameen also gives loans to beggars, encouraging them to earn a living.

Targeting women has attracted criticism. Considerable research has focused on the degree to which microfinance has or has not empowered women. Meenai argues that even though women sometimes lose control of the money they borrow, their status within the family often improves because of their role in securing the loan (p. 190). Some studies suggest that homes marginally above the povety line benefit more from microfinance than those below (see Hulme and Mosely 1997). Rahman (1999) concluded that women borrowers do benefit from improved status within the family, becoming more self-confident and empowered. In Bangladesh, the number of women-led organizations has increased; more women have also entered politics. However, patriarchial attitudes in the wider society continue to limit opportunities for women to "create their own space in the prevailing power structures" (p. 150). Only a small number of Grameen staff are women, mainly due to difficulties involved in traveling through rural areas. Some point out that not everyone can launch a small business; thus, as a panacea to eliminate all poverty, microfinance falls short. It rarely results in creating large numbers of actual jobs.

Some opponents of the bank claim that it is part of a Christian conspiracy to undermine Islamic values and practices, including *purdah*. Critics say that it exploits women, because the type of work they do earns relatively little money. Some men tell women that, if they join the bank, they are "bad Muslims" (Yunus 1999, p. 107). Yunus and others defend microfinance against the criticism that it violates Islamic principles, pointing out that Grameen's aims of equity and social justice are profoundly Islamic. Providing people with work rather than giving hand-outs, too, builds on classical Muslim ideals. Interest is charged (20 percent), which for some contravenes Islamic principles (the prohibition of *ribā*). However, this is not exploitative (no collateral is required) and, because the borrowers own the bank, they pay interest "to themselves" (Yunus 1991, p. 110). Some Islamic MFIs do not charge interest but use alternatives such as a service charge or a profit-loss sharing system, which more recognizably fit an Islamic banking, or Sharīʿah-compliant model (Obaidullah, p. 418). Yunus cites an advisor to the president of Iran telling him that what he was doing contravened neither Sharīʿah nor the Qurʾān. Many Muslims appreciate microfinance because women who benefit usually work at home. In 2006, Yunus and Grameen received the Nobel Peace Prize. This recognized that poverty threatens peace and violates human rights.

BIBLIOGRAPHY

Hulme, D., and P. Mosely. "Finances for the Poor or Poorest? Financial Innovation, Poverty and Vulnerability." In *Who Needs Credit? Poverty and Finance in Bangladesh*, edited by G. Wood and I. A. Sharif, pp. 96–130. Dhaka: University Press, 1997.

Meenai, Zubair. *Empowering Rural Women: An Approach to Empowering Women through Credit-Based Self-Help Groups*. Delhi: Aakar Books, 2003.

Obaidullah, Mohammed. "Islamic Microfiance: The Way Forward." In *Islamic Capital Markets: Products and Strategies*, edited by Kabir Hassan and Michael Mahlknecht, pp. 415–428. Chichester, West Sussex, U.K.: Wiley, 2011.

Rahman, Aminur. *Women and Microcredit in Rural Bangladesh: Anthropological Study of the Rhetoric and Realities of Grameen Bank Lending*. Boulder, Colo.: Westview, 1999.

Yunus, Muhammad. *Banker to the Poor: Micro-Lending and the Battle Against World Poverty*. New York: Public Affairs, 1999.

Yunus, Muhammad. "Poverty is a Threat to Peace: The Nobel Prize Lecture." In *Creating a World Without Poverty* by Muhammad Yunis. New York: Public Affairs, 2007a

Yunus, Muhammad. *Creating a World Without Poverty: Social Business and the Future of Capitalism*. New York: Public Affairs, 2007b.

Internet

Islamic Microfinance Network, http://imfn.org/

Grameen Bank, http://www.grameen-info.org/

CLINTON BENNETT

MIDWIFERY. From the word "midwife" (Middle English: one who is with the wife), who is a person (usually a woman) trained to assist others in giving birth. The most common Arabic term to designate a midwife is *qābila* (she who receives [the newborn infant]), or *muwallida* (she who helps a woman give birth to a child [*walad*]). Another term still used in the Middle East today is the term used for a traditional midwife or *dāya*, a Persian word meaning "nurse" and "wet nurse." *Dāya* has served as a synonym for *qābila* since at least as early as the Mamlūk period. To indicate that a midwife was a professional or to distinguish her from nonprofessional yet experienced women who occasionally helped female family members and neighbors during and after childbirth, some additional Arabic titles were employed. Thus we find female doctors and professional midwives from the high Middle Ages on described as *imraʾa ʿārifa*, "a woman much acquainted with…, possessing knowledge of [bodily treatment]," a term similar to *sage-femme* in French, for instance.

There are indications in classical and medieval texts that midwifery in the big cities of the Middle

East and the Mediterranean—usually practiced by females, due to the modesty code—was a socially differentiated craft involving expertise in gynecology, obstetrics, and pediatrics and was occasionally highly appreciated by men: "[The craft of midwifery is] something necessary in civilization and a matter of general concern, because it assures, as a rule, the life of the new-born child" (Ibn Khaldūn, 2005, pp. 355–356). Professional midwifery entailed training through apprenticeship, typically by relatives, the application of particular birthing methods and the occasional use of certain instruments. They often worked for wages and were in competition with each other, so reputation afforded them important social capital.

It is reasonable to assume that such Muslim midwives had, through their involvement in the ritual aspects of birth and their occasional appearance in court as expert witnesses, a more public presence than volunteer helpers. This might be the result of urbanization and the rise of a qualified medical profession, processes that started in the Muslim Middle East, North Africa, and Spain as early as the eighth century, about three hundred years earlier than in Europe. However, nothing like the ecclesiastical and municipal laws regulating midwifery, the examination and supervision system, and the training schools for midwives in Europe from the fourteenth through the eighteenth centuries seem to have existed in these regions before the 1830s, and there is very little information about the frameworks for professional qualification.

Ibn Khaldūn acknowledged the expertise of urban midwives not only as obstetricians but also as pediatricians, thus echoing assertions by earlier scholars that they were widely regarded as professionals and trustworthy ("best informed of all people about the embryo; there is nothing in the womb they do not know" [Ibn Khaldūn, 2005, p. 330]). In the same period the Cairene Mālikī jurist Muḥammad ibn al-Ḥājj al-ʿAbdarī underscores in his *al-Madkhal* the midwives' shortcomings as craftswomen yet sees in midwifery a distinguishable occupation characterized by, among other things, wages.

Within the women's subculture, midwives made extensive use of ritual and magical devices to cope with the dangers involved in childbirth. They provided services associated with women other than birthing, whether female circumcision (a pre-Islamic rite adopted by some interpretations of Islamic law in a moderate, restricted version, and practiced, even today, among Muslims in a limited number of regions only, particularly Egypt and East Africa), or preparing deceased women for burial. Thus, they were central figures in birth, childhood, and adulthood rituals and ceremonies.

From historical and anthropological works on midwifery in the nineteenth and twentieth centuries, for instance in Iran, the Ottoman Empire, Egypt, the Sudan, and Morocco, it emerges that significant changes in the long tradition of midwifery, in either its popular or its more professional versions, occurred only in the last two hundred years or so, with the introduction of European medicine in the Middle East. The best examples of this development include the founding of Western-style midwifery schools and a system of regulating midwives. Yet remnants of the old traditional craft have, to a great extent, remained intact and can be traced today in vast areas of the Muslim worlds.

The foundation of the the School of Midwifery in Cairo, the first government institution for the medical education of women in the Middle East, was initiated by the French physician Antoine-Barthelemy Clot under the reign of Muḥammad ʿAlī, sometime between 1830 and 1832. Similar colleges were opened later in Istanbul and in Tehran. This took place more than two hundred years after the reconstruction of the maternity ward in the Hôtel Dieu in Paris (1618), where midwives were instructed. A new female profession—*ḥakīma,* a "doctoress"—came into being in Egypt, differing widely from the untrained folk midwives, the *dāya*s, due to their rational-empirical formation which—for better or worse—excluded the ritual-magical dimension of the profession.

Classical and medieval Arabic sources reflect an ambivalent attitude toward midwives on the part of Muslim male biographers, physicians, and jurists. Their writings reveal a mixture of a keen awareness of the midwife's essential role in society, on the one hand, with marginalization that sometimes results in the total absence of midwives in their texts, on the other. In the rich Arabic biographical literature, midwives, even those of the first generation of Muslims or the "professionals" of later periods, are almost totally absent. None of the women who served the Prophet's "holy family," for example, became mythological figures who could have raised the prestige of women practicing the profession.

Unlike the biographies and hagiographies dedicated to the life story of the Prophet, the idealized accounts of the lives of his relatives and companions and the members of the intellectual elites of the first generations of Muslims, biographical collections, particularly from the late Mamlūk period (e.g., by Muḥammad al-Sakhāwī, d. 1497) as well as personal diaries (e.g., by Ibrāhīm ibn ʿUmar al-Biqāʿī, d. 1480, and Aḥmad bin Muḥammad Ibn Ṭawq, d. 1509), often provide a vivid picture of everyday life at the time the authors lived. This picture concerns not only the public sphere but also the inner circle of family members, reflecting a wide range of professional activities of both men and women. Here too midwives, as well as female doctors, are underrepresented.

Since biographers of physicians in the medieval Muslim world were interested mainly in medicine as an intellectual domain and therefore tended to single out authors of medical compilations and treatises, as well as court physicians, one can hardly expect to find them allocating special entries to female medical practitioners, not to mention midwives. The latter were not only identified with a less prestigious medical practice in itself but were also associated with popular beliefs and superstitions. Biographical and medical texts from Muslim Spain seem to be the exception which proves the rule.

Most of the instructions in chapters and books on gynecology and obstetrics from the classical and medieval periods are addressed to male doctors who were supposed to supervise midwives, though not directly. This suggests that midwives were subordinate to the (male) physician's authority. According to medical texts, male physicians, as the representatives of learned medicine, were supposed to instruct midwives from outside the childbirth scene and to intervene in complex cases only. In the Ottoman world of the early modern period, for instance, female healers in general were excluded from the professional hierarchy of physicians. In reality, however, they extended medical care to males and females alike. Similar dynamics can be found in modern Egypt as well. In pre-modern Muslim countries childbirth took place in the family home; clinics and hospitals with obstetrical services were unknown before the nineteenth century.

Men's ambivalent attitudes toward birth and the mother-genitrix may well have contributed to the midwife's relative marginality in pre-modern Arabic-Islamic texts. Throughout history birth for them was wrapped in mystery, fears, and taboos. Midwives represent the epitome of the physical essence of femininity, with its periods of impurity during menstruation and childbirth and its creative power, which, combined, represented both mystery and threat to many. As such, midwives simultaneously invoked feelings of contempt and fear among men. These, in turn, made the midwife a likely target for misogynous sentiments, which were, on occasion, expressed (in the case of Ibn al-Ḥājj, for instance) or implicitly reflected in the way many of them ignored or were silent about the midwife's crucial role in society. On the other hand, as the future of a lineage was entrusted to her hands, it is hard to imagine men in patriarchal societies altogether ignoring the power of the midwife (in the case of Ibn Khaldūn, for example). Moreover medieval Muslim jurists from various regions and all schools of law recognized the importance of midwives as agents of the patriarchal system in their ongoing effort to control the female rites of passage through legal procedures. This explains why, despite their lowly image in Arabic-Islamic writings, midwives were granted, early in the development of Islamic law, exceptional legal status and consequently enjoyed a number of social privileges, the most significant of which was their role as expert witnesses in court.

When, in pre-modern Muslim societies, issues involving women's reproductive organs were brought before a Sharīʿah court, the *qāḍī* could authorize one or more midwives to conduct the necessary physical examinations and summon them to testify as experts. This was not necessarily a testimony based on direct observation but sometimes on circumstances; however, they were allowed to give testimony independently, that is to say, in the absence of male witnesses. Muslim jurists who accepted this rule, on occasion unwillingly, were nevertheless unanimous about relying on women's testimony on events that men were forbidden to watch (except when life was endangered, such as a complex delivery) due to Islamic codes of modesty. This principle, *infirād* (a testimony of women, or even a single woman, not validated by male witnesses), was an exception—justified by necessity—to the basic rule derived from Qur'ān 2:282, which implies that the testimony of a woman is less credible than that of a man.

In her capacity as the "overseer" in the birthplace, extending physical assistance, witnessing events involving women's bodies, and at the same time fulfilling prescribed ritual roles, the midwife in Muslim societies, whether as a "professional" or "folk midwife," found herself at the intersection of public and private spheres in a quasi-official yet still liminal status.

BIBLIOGRAPHY

Abugideiri, Hibba. "Off to Work at Home: Egyptian Midwives Blur Public-Private Boundaries." *Hawwa: Journal of Women of the Middle East and the Islamic World* 6 (2008): 254–283.

Bell, Heather. "Circumcision in the Inter-War Anglo-Egyptian Sudan." *The Journal of African History* 39 (1998): 293–312.

Cortese, Delia, and Simonetta Calderini. *Women and the Fatimids in the World of Islam*. Edinburgh: Edinburgh University Press, 2006.

Davis, Fanny. *The Ottoman Lady: A Social History from 1718 to 1918*. New York: Greenwood Press, 1986.

Demirici, Tuba, and Selçuk Akşin Somel. "Women's Bodies, Demography and Public Health: Abortion Policy and Perspectives in the Ottoman Empire of the Nineteenth Century." *Journal of the History of Sexuality* 17, no. 3 (2008): 377–420.

Fahmy, Khaled. "Women, Medicine, and Power in Nineteenth-Century Egypt." In *Remaking Women: Feminism and Modernity in the Middle East*, edited by Lila Abu-Lughod, pp. 35–72. Princeton, N.J.: Princeton University Press, 1998.

Gallagher, Nancy. "Writing Women Medical Practitioners into the History of Modern Egypt." In *Re-Envisioning Egypt 1919–1952*, edited by Arthur Goldschmidt, Amy J. Johnson, and Barak A. Schmidt, pp. 351–370. Cairo and New York: The American University in Cairo Press, 2005.

Giladi, Avner. "Liminal Craft, Exceptional Law: Preliminary Notes on Midwives in Medieval Islamic Writings." *International Journal of Middle East Studies* 42 (2010): 185–202.

Hatem, Mervat F. "The Professionalization of Health and the Control of Women's Bodies as Modern

Governmentalities in Nineteenth-Century Egypt." In *Women in the Ottoman Empire: Middle Eastern Women in the Early Modern Era*, edited by Madeline C. Zilf, pp. 66–80. Leiden, Netherlands, and New York: Brill, 1997.

Ibn al-Ḥājj al-ʿAbdarī. *Kitāb al-madkhal ilā tanmiyat al-aʿmāl bi-taḥsīn al-niyyāt wa-al-tanbīh ʿalā baʿḍ al-bidaʿ wa-al-ʿawaʾid allatī intaḥalat wa-bayān shanaʿātihā wa-qubḥihā*. Beirut: Dār al-Kitāb al-ʿArabī, 1972.

Ibn Ḥazm, ʿAlī ibn Aḥmad. *al-Muḥallā bi-al-āthār*, edited by ʿAbd al-Ghaffār Sulaymān al-Bindārī. Beirut: Dār al-Kutub al-ʿIlmiyya, 1988.

Ibn Khaldūn, ʿAbd al-Raḥmān. *al-Muqaddima*, edited by Etienne Quatremère. Paris: Bibliothèque Impériale, 1858; English translation: *The Muqaddima: An Introduction to History*. Translated with an introduction by Franz Rosenthal. Princeton, N.J.: Princeton University Press, 2005.

Kashani-Sabet, Firoozeh. *Conceiving Citizens: Women and the Politics of Motherhood in Iran*. Oxford and New York: Oxford University Press, 2011.

Kuhnke, LaVerne. *Lives at Risk: Public Health in Nineteenth-Century Egypt*. Berkeley: University of California Press, 1992.

Kuppinger, Petra. "Death of a Midwife." In *Situating Globalization: Views from Egypt*, edited by Cynthia Nelson and Shahnaz Rouse, pp. 255–282. London: Transactions Publishers, 2000.

Makhluf-Obermeyer, C. "Pluralism and Pragmatism: Knowledge and Practice of Birth in Morocco." *Medical Anthropology Quarterly* 14, no. 2 (2000): 180–201.

Pormann, Peter E., and Emilie Savage-Smith. *Medieval Islamic Medicine*. Edinburgh: Edinburgh University Press, 2007.

Shaham, Ron. *The Expert Witness in Islamic Courts: Medicine and Crafts in the Service of Law*. Chicago: University of Chicago Press, 2010.

Shefer-Mossensohn, Miri. "A Sick Sultana in the Ottoman Imperial Palace: Male Doctors, Female Healers and Female Patients in the Early Modern Period." *Hawwa: Journal of Women of the Middle East and the Islamic World* 9 (2011): 281–312.

Sonbol, Amira El Azhary. "Doctors and Midwives: Women and Medicine at the Turn of the Century." In *La France et l'Égypte à l'époque des vice-rois, 1805–1882*, edited by Daniel Panzac and André Raymond, pp. 135–148. Cahier des Anales Islamologiques 22. Cairo: Institut français d'archéologie orientale, 2002.

Sonbol, Amira El-Azhary. *The Creation of a Medical Profession in Egypt, 1800–1922*. Syracuse, N.Y.: Syracuse University Press, 1991.

AVNER GILADI

MINORITIES.

[*This entry contains two subentries,*

Minorities in Muslim Societies *and*
Muslim Minorities in Non-Muslim Countries.]

MINORITIES IN MUSLIM SOCIETIES

According to recent estimates, 250 million Muslim women live in minority situations in 142 countries around the world. The figure is staggering not just because of the numbers; it is also the presumption of differences among them, or even of attempting to delineate the Islam that they profess to adhere to, the cultural contexts in which they live, and the internal and external pressures brought to bear upon them. On the latter issue, they are somewhat spared having to justify the negative news reports about Muslim states continuously in the media, yet they have other, sometimes just as intractable, problems to handle because of their minority status. What follows is a snapshot sampling of how some of these women work out their identity.

There have always been Muslim women living in minority situations. Islam was a minority tradition even in the Hijaz for many years after the death of the Prophet. Moreover, there have probably been non-Muslim women living in Islamic societies right from the beginning, given Islam's acceptance of women from many religions marrying into Islam without conversion. The special concern of this article is Muslim minorities within Muslim societies, that is, small groups whose domicile could be anything from an Islamic nation-state (e.g., Shīʿīs in Saudi Arabia) to an identifiable cohesive Islamic group within a non-Muslim state (Islamists among the Uighur in China). A key element of these people is their diversity—encompassing their culture, their relationship to "formal" Islam, and their sense of Islamic identity.

For examples of diversity, we need look no further than the world's largest Muslim country, Indonesia. There, ethnic Chinese Muslim women must construct an identity within an environment that has been hostile to them in the past. Although the government has propounded Citizenship Bill 12/2006, hoping to devise an inclusive act that would lessen the internal tensions with groups such as the ethnic Chinese, Muslims of both genders still face discrimination. One way that this discrimination continues is the required purchase of an identity card. Chinese Muslims consider the requirement that they purchase such a card a way of signifying difference. They have responded positively to the situation. Lest there be additional practices that limit their community, they have responded by instituting cultural options—the use of mass media and popular preachers. Central to that programmatic initiative is a Chinese woman preacher, *ustadzah* Tan Mei Hwa, who takes to Surabaya's JTV in an Indonesian equivalent of an American televangelist. Unprecedented in its outreach, it is an extremely popular program. Begun during Ramadan, it has now gone to a weekly program in which she preaches and answers questions from viewers throughout Indonesia. Its success has broken barriers that government acts could not. This example is instructive, for it underlines that identity issues cannot always be manipulated by government actions; it also affirms the important positive role that Muslim women play in articulating their own identity.

A combination of religion and ethnicity sets Muslim women apart in other Muslims states as well. The Hazāra in Afghanistan exemplify this characteristic. Their identity has elements of language (Persian), ethnicity (Mongolian), religion (almost all Twelver Shīʿī and Ismāʿīlī), and distinctive cultural forms (dominant migratory history) all mixed together. Their independence from the Sunnī majority Pashtuns has meant that they have paid dearly for their individuality, and they are well known for their current obstinate resistance to the Taliban. Women have featured importantly in their history, for war erupted over a chief's wife who was raped by aggressive Pashtun soldiers in front of her husband, and a distinctive ethnicity was once again affirmed in the resulting carnage. Throughout history, it was women who often had to maintain traditions and re-create life after once again losing their men and homes to some combatant. These Muslim women reflect an inner strength that is manifested in the continuation of their communities, despite the constant movement, displacement, and military cultural history.

Scholars seldom probe converts for their faith experiences, perhaps concerned about authenticity, and Muslim women converts are studied even less. It is crucial, then, to signal that converts are an important part of minority Muslim women's lives, and they demonstrate interesting characteristics. The Irish women who converted and married Arab Salafī immigrants reflect an entirely different model—they live in a communal Muslim community in a sea of Irish Catholics. Although they do not fit the role of a minority within a Muslim society, it is instructive to see how these Salafī women converts have adapted to a new identity very different from their previous culture. (Parenthetically, it shows how little need Islamic converts have for an Islamic state.) Interestingly, they also reflect a theoretical divide between Olivier Roy, who argues that Salafīs are more like independent-minded Protestants than

Catholics, and Shanneik, whose exploration of the Irish converts sees them as more Catholic in their spiritual roots and behavior. The conversions took place before and during Ireland's economic boom between 1995 and 2007, commonly referred to as the "Celtic Tiger years."

The analysis of these minority Muslim women highlights that they had internalized a Catholic habitus—a stance toward religious truth and its embodiment in an ongoing restrictive theological society. Thus, when confronted with conversion into a strict Salafī tradition, they openly adapted the stance they had acquired while Catholics and applied it to their new-found religion. The result was that they transferred their identity easily to the religion of their husbands and did not find the conversion onerous. There was no need for them to adjudicate theological issues; they merely accepted one authoritative system in place of the other. Set apart almost hermetically by their conversion, they became founding members of a distinctive Muslim community. For example, they left debate on theology primarily to imams, even as they had done earlier with their priests. These Muslim minority women thus found no disconnect between the environment they had been raised in and the new tradition that they adopted at marriage and now used as the basis for a new Muslim community. Their experience is instructive as to how converts live simultaneously in two situations—in a culture that they now reject entirely and in a new religious culture that they are creating with their families and fellow converts. In short, minority Muslim women's identity is a very complicated issue and should not be subjected to simplistic analyses.

Finally, minority status and identity reflect strong community-based orientations; for example, in West Bengal, Hindus and Muslim make up a very diverse population. Since partition, West Bengal's Muslims have generally retreated into Muslim-centered social communities. Muslim girls, for example, are attending secular schools less and less, and illiteracy is a mounting concern: the 2001 census indicated that only 49.8 percent of the entire community was literate, with women much less likely to be literate than men. Muslims are split among several organizational groups, each with a distinctive vision of what the state should be: the Jamʿīyat al-ʿUlamāʾ-i Hind (JUH) argue for an India comprised of semi-autonomous, religiously led communities; the Ahl-i Ḥadīth Hind (AHA) resist any encroachment of secularism or modernism into religion—interestingly, both men and women are members and speak openly; Jamāʿat Islāmī Hind (JIH) was established by Muslim conservative reformer Abū al-ʿAlā al-Mawdūdī (d. 1979) and aims to establish a full-fledged Muslim state; and the Tablīghī Jamāʿat, a missionary enterprise that is modeled on Ṣūfī organizations but features both male and female missionaries—which is striking because women travel, with relatives, long distances from home to preach and instruct in mission practices—and even such things as tone of voice was indicated for women so they should not appear too authoritarian). These minority women, however, do not take the stance that a conservative view of their position hampers them. Rather, like JIH member Firoza Begum, they argue that women's empowerment really means total indoctrination into Islam, because only that kind of total commitment will bring about liberation. Almost all the women leaders among these groups see activism as a means of ingraining a proper community identity in the community's children, so most argue for internal Muslim training distinct from the secular education adopted by their Hindu neighbors.

BIBLIOGRAPHY

Aleaz, Bonita. "The State, the Community and Their Women: Vignettes of Islamic Groups in West

Bengal." *Journal of Muslim Minority Affairs* 29, no. 2 (2009): 261–276.
Monsutti, Alessandro. *War and Migration: Social Networks and Economic Strategies of the Hazaras of Afghanistan.* New York: Routledge, 2005.
Shanneik, Yafa. "Conversion and Religious *Habitus:* The Experience of Irish Women Converts to Islam in the Pre-Celtic Tiger Era." *Journal of Muslim Minority Affairs* 31, no. 4 (2011): 503–517.

Earle Waugh

Muslim Minorities in Non-Muslim Countries

About one- third of the global Muslim population of 1.4 billion lives outside Muslim majority countries. In some cases, Muslim minorities in non-Muslim countries outnumber the population of most Muslim countries. For example, the Muslim minority in India, with more than 177 million Muslims, is larger than any other Muslim community, after Indonesia and Pakistan. Muslim minorities today exist on all continents and carve their presence into the social, political, religious, and cultural lives of most countries in the world. According to Pew Research Center statistics, there were 2.6 million Muslims in the United States (0.8 percent of the overall population) in 2010, 44.1 million in Europe (6 percent), and 23.3 million in China (2 percent). India, China, Nigeria (75 million), and Ethiopia (28 million) are the only non-Muslim countries at present that have more than 20 million Muslims.

From one point of view, the emergence or existence of Muslim minorities in non-Muslim countries is inseparable from the historical facts of the expansion of Islam in the centuries after the death of Prophet Muḥammad and the following rise and decline of Islamic empires such as the Umayyad Caliphate in Andalusia and the Ottoman Empire in the Middle East and the Balkans, which left a permanent trace on the demographic and religious realities of Europe. Mongol invasions of parts of Europe in the thirteenth century also left behind Muslim populations in areas that had not witnessed their presence before. Thus, it is possible to conclude that the Islamic presence in Europe in the form of Muslim minorities has deep historical roots and authenticity.

However, Muslim minorities today in Europe, the United States, and Australia also originated from the large immigration movements that occurred in several phases during the colonialist enterprises, as well as after the demise of colonialism in Africa and Asia (colonialism being only one cause of the phenomenon). These large immigration movements were predominantly, but not exclusively, worker migrations. Muslim minorities today also consist of a considerable number of converts and their families in the West. In addition, the presence of Muslims in Europe and America steadily increased as a result of numerous wars fought in Muslim countries (or countries with significant Muslim populations, such as in the former Yugoslavia), which caused waves of refugee migrations toward the Western world.

The question of Muslim minorities in non-Muslim countries is of crucial importance in studying the issues of belonging, allegiance (to a state or a religion), and formation of identity in the modern world. These issues have been raised when it came to either autochthonous Muslim communities (in, e.g., China, India, Bulgaria, Russia, and Macedonia), or Muslim immigrant communities (as well as converts) in the West. The question has been solved in various ways in different countries and contexts; however, the crossroads before Muslim minorities in non-Muslim countries is limited to certain choices: isolation (and its extreme form, ghettoization), assimilation, or integration into the broader society of a non-Muslim state. Of these three, isolation and assimilation have been rejected by both the non-Muslim state and the Muslim minorities living in it, for various reasons, while integration has been hailed as the only entirely possible way to reconcile the allegiances of the community to both state and religion. During the process of negotiating the tension between the state and the religion, at the end of the twentieth and beginning of the twenty-first century, the focus of the media was on Islamic symbols that range from the minarets and mosques to what is perceived to be an Islamic code of dress. As was the case with the modernistic movements in many Muslim countries at the beginning of the twentieth century, the dress code for women became the subject of conflicts and debates that always circled back to the question of whether it is possible to have a fully integrated Muslim minority community in a non-Muslim state. The practice of wearing the *hijab* (covering the hair, considered by many Muslims to be a religious duty), *niqāb* (veiling of the face), and burqa (complete covering of female face and body) took center stage. The debates over veiling in some countries even resulted in banning (e.g., France banned *niqāb*s and burqas in 2010). The constant debates over what are perceived to be Islamic symbols are associated with the status of rapidly increasing Muslim minorities in Western countries and their visibility in the public life of these countries.

On the other hand, although the representatives of Muslim minority communities have struggled to get an equal share in the debate, their persistent problem is the weak organization and grouping of members of Muslim minorities solely according to ethnic criteria, which causes a lack of communication between diverse Muslim communities. Their ability to act in a unified and unifying way for their mutual interests is consequently lessened.

Another pressing issue is the relationship of countries with overwhelming Muslim populations to the Muslim minorities in non-Muslim countries. The Organization of Islamic Cooperation (OIC, previously known as the Organization of the Islamic Conference), is a body that acts as the collective voice of the Muslim world and protector of its interests. The role of the OIC has been extremely important in taking a stand on the relationship of some countries to their Muslim minorities (as in the cases of the Philippines, Thailand, and India). However, it has also been accused of polemics over the extent of OIC interference in the internal affairs of independent non-Muslim countries.

Depending on the region and country, Muslim minorities have started to organize themselves more effectively, thus asserting their presence in both the public and private spheres of life in non-Muslim countries. As a result of increased awareness of the importance of Muslim minorities today, several institutes and research institutions for the study of Muslim minorities have been established. For example, the Institute of Muslim Minority Affairs publishes the *Journal of Muslim Minority Affairs*, which is committed to detailed research on the state of Muslim minorities in the world.

Muslim minorities in non-Muslim countries present a litmus test not only for the democracy of Western countries but also for the Muslim world (*ummah*) in general, in the issues of religion, statehood, identity, mutual interests, allegiances, and belonging.

BIBLIOGRAPHY

"The Future of the Global Muslim Population: Projections for 2010–30." Pew Research Center. [http://www.pewforum.org/uploadedFiles/Topics/Religious_Affiliation/Muslim/FutureGlobalMuslimPopulation-WebPDF-Feb10.pdf].

Institute of Muslim Minority Affairs [http://www.imma.org.uk/].

Khan, Sa'ad S. "The Organization of the Islamic Conference (OIC) and Muslim Minorities." *Journal of Muslim Minority Affairs* 22, no. 2 (2002):2.

Maréchal, Brigitte, Stefano Allievi, Felice Dassetto, and Jørgen Nielsen, eds. *Muslims in the Enlarged Europe.* Leiden, Netherlands and Boston: Brill, 2003.

Organisation of Islamic Cooperation [http://www.oic-oci.org/].

DŽENITA KARIĆ

MIRACLES. Muslim understanding of the term "miracle" (*muʿjizah*) varies from theological and mystical contexts to popular Islamic contexts. The technical definition emphasizes an occurrence or event demonstrating the sincerity and authenticity of the prophets while refuting their opponents. However, the word "miracle" does not appear in the Qurʾān, which prefers to use the word "signs" (*āyāt*) to describe supernatural events or events that witness to God's work in the physical world. There is a third term, *karāmāt* (wonders, marvels), which refers to acts performed by mystical (Ṣūfī) saints, signifying their personal distinction as granted by God. However, these "wonders" are not to be equated with miracles or prophethood.

The Prophets and Tradition. Although the Qurʾān testifies to the performance of miracles by various prophets, such as Moses and Jesus, it denies that the Prophet Muḥammad performed any miracles, except for bringing forth the Qurʾān (29:50–51). When asked to work miracles, Muḥammad replied that he was only a messenger (17:88–95). Therefore, the Qurʾān became the miracle given to Muḥammad. The inimitability (*iʿjāz*) of the Qurʾān, or the inability of anyone to produce a book like the Qurʾān, is considered the sign of his being a prophet. However, there are verses in the Qurʾān that have led some Muslims to believe miracles occurred in relation to Muḥammad: these include the splitting of the moon (54:1–2); assistance given to Muslims at the Battle of Badr (3:122–124); and the Night Journey to Jerusalem (17:1).

As Islam developed and matured, the biographies of the prophet (*sīrah*) and the records of his deeds and sayings (*ḥadīth*) attributed various miracles to Muḥammad. These include feeding many people with just a few barley loaves, providing water at the Battle of al-Ḥudaybīyah in 628 CE, healing a broken leg by touch, making a wolf speak, and curing a mentally ill boy with the words "come out of him." Often these attributions parallel miracles given to other prophets, particularly Jesus. There is speculation that the presence of miracles in later Islamic traditions reflected a desire to counterbalance Christian claims that Jesus was superior to Muḥammad, based upon the miracles attributed to each.

Theological and Ṣūfī Opinions. Early theologians, philosophers, and other intellectuals wrestled not only with the miracles attributed to Muḥammad but also with the validity of the *karāmāt* (wonders). The ninth- and tenth-century Muʿtazilah school of rational thinkers limited miracles to prophets and accepted the miracle of the Qurʾān as a rational proof of Muḥammad's mission but denied the authenticity of *karāmāt.* The Ashʿarī school of theology and some philosophers, such as Avicenna (Ibn Sīnā, d. 1037 CE) considered *muʿjizah* as "miracles of prophets" and *karāmāt* as "wonders of the saints." Ṣūfī thinkers followed Ashʿarī thought on miracles and wonders and empathized that Ṣūfī saints keep their "wonders" quiet. However, in reality, saints became famous for their abilities and attracted numerous seekers and the curious among the populace. However, not all Ṣūfīs viewed such wonders positively; many cited them as distractions from the path toward God. The majority of modern Muslim thinkers accept miracles and their compatibility with science.

Miracles were defined as events that disrupt the habitual patterns of creation and are intended to authenticate the claims of a prophet. Miracles must come from God either directly or indirectly; they must disrupt the customs (*ʿādah*) of the people who receive the miracles; no one else should be able to perform the miracle in kind or quality; and miracles must be unique to the one who claims prophethood. Several criteria needed to be present for an event to be considered a miracle. Aside from being an act of God and thus contrary to the natural course of life, a miracle must be done by the one who claims to be a prophet, including an announcement (*daʿwah*) preceding the event, followed closely by the miracle itself.

Mary and Rābiʿa. Although not considered a prophet, Mary, the mother of Jesus, is associated with numerous miracles. Mary was revealed as a "sign" (*āyah*) (21:91; 23:50) and, according to tradition, was protected at birth from the "pricking of the devil" (meaning she was immune from sin and error), received miraculous food during her childhood (3:37), was the recipient of the miracle of pregnancy while remaining a virgin, and received miracles during childbirth, such as water from a brook, a palm tree bending toward her with dates, and the baby Jesus speaking from the cradle to defend her reputation (3:42–47; 19:16–35).

The most well-known female Ṣūfī mystic, Rābiʿa al-ʿAdawiyya of Baṣra (d. 801 CE), is considered to have performed *karāmāt* such as light emanating from around her, receiving sustenance for her and her guests, and, on pilgrimage, having her camel restored to life. However, as with other mystics, she disclaimed miraculous powers and did not encourage her reputation for performing miracles.

Popular Belief. Veneration of saints and pilgrimages to their tombs are two prominent displays of popular belief in and respect for miracles and wonders. Aside from a belief in the saints of the past, contemporary mystics are sought for their abilities to bless the seeker with various types of aid. Whether visiting tombs or living saints, some Muslim seekers hope to find cures for illnesses, answers to problems of everyday life, and, especially, miracles of fertility for those struggling to conceive.

Assessment. The movement from Qurʾānic denials of miracles given to Muḥammad (except for the miracle of the Qurʾān itself) to the attribution of such both to the Prophet and later to Ṣūfī saints is one of the most curious phenomena in the development of Islam. Orthodox theology in essence adapted to the needs of popular belief, reflecting the inherent desire for people to connect with God through either the Prophet himself or Ṣūfī saints, whether living or dead. The fact of miracles is commonly accepted among Muslims, and respect and honor are almost universally granted to Mary, although there is disagreement over the alleged miracles of the saints, such as Rābiʿa.

[*See also* Sainthood *and* Sufism and Women.]

BIBLIOGRAPHY

Horovitz, Josef. "The Growth of the Mohammed Legend." In *The Life of Muḥammad*, edited by Uri Rubin, pp. 269–278. Aldershot, U.K.: Ashgate, 1998. Includes a discussion about miracles in the traditions surrounding Muḥammad.

Schimmel, Annemarie. *Mystical Dimensions of Islam*. Chapel Hill: University of North Carolina Press, 1975. Provides a short explanation of Ṣūfis and miracles, see pp. 199–213.

al-Shaʿrāwī, Shaykh Muḥammad Mitwallī. *The Miracles of the Qurʾān*. London: Dar Al Taqwa, 1989. Detailed work defining miracles and explaining the different dimensions as to why the Qurʾān is considered a miracle.

Smith, Margaret. *Rabiʿa: The Life and Work of Rabiʿa and Other Women Mystics in Islam*. Oxford: Oneworld, 1994. Provides anecdotal evidence for the life and miracles of Rābiʿa.

Stowasswer, Barbara Freyer. *Women in the Qurʾan, Traditions, and Interpretation*. New York: Oxford University Press, 1994. Offers a concise study on the place of Mary in Muslim thought: see pp. 67–81.

CHARLES FLETCHER

Modernization and Development. Currently situated in larger discourses on postmodernity and globalization, modernization and development are two terms that fuel the contemporary global imperative to increase the economic, political, and social rights of an individual, striving to maximize human potential and economic capacity. On its own, the term "modernization" has many definitions but can generally be taken to assume a linear progression and evolution from the premodern to the modern. The term is often taken to characterize movement from some previously hindered beginning toward a realized potential. Frequently associated with urbanization and industrialization, modernization is achieved through various techniques of "development." Implying growth and advancement, development, whether economic (i.e., increased gross domestic product) or political (i.e., active participatory democracy), is achieved through a multiplicity of techniques and institutions used to facilitate social change and reform. Put simply, development is geared toward increasing an individual's choice and freedom in society, while modernity is a description of the future state seeking to be realized.

Historical Overview. Both terms are rooted in European Enlightenment logic and ideals—highlighting faith, tradition, and political authority as hindrances to progressive development towards modernity. For European philosophers, modernity was to be achieved through independent reasoning, science, and democratic participation. It was this emphasis on the individual that counters state abuses which act as impediments to societal potential.

Discourses of modernization often focus on the early modern period of Europe (1600–1800 CE). However, these analyses frequently overlook the immense international network of seafarers and global trade that controlled much of the world. At a time when European women were not allowed to control their property if they even had any at all, women throughout premodern Arabia and North Africa actively participated in commercial transactions and in public social, religious, and political life. Take, for example, Khadījah bint Khuwaylid (b. c. 555 1800 CE–d. c. 619 CE), the first wife of the Prophet Muḥammad, who was a wealthy business owner and merchant. In addition, Fatima al-Fihri (d. 880 CE) was said to have inherited her family's fortune, which she devoted to pious work, as well as erecting the Qarawīyīn Mosque in Morocco. The Islamic Golden Age (800–1400 CE) is replete with examples of Muslim women actively participating in thriving societies, as well as various examples of the Islamic charitable trust (*waqf*, pl. *awqāf*). These trusts, or religious endowments, devoted their profits or value to charity for the poor and other philanthropic endeavors, including the funding of schools and hospitals.

However, with the increased wealth of European colonial powers, land and economic resources were being claimed throughout Africa, Asia, and the Americas and and the profits sent to colonial metropoles. Extraction of immense wealth throughout colonial territories brought immense benefits to the imperial power, including a huge disparity of political and economic control. Captured most accurately, satirically or not, by Rudyard Kipling, growing Western powers suffered from "White Man's Burden," the belief by those in the West in the benefits and obligation to aide in the development and modernizing of the local populations throughout the colonial world. These modernization efforts started with the building of colonial administrative institutions, that is, courts, universities, hospitals. The salvation-oriented tones of development and modernization campaigns by colonial administrations were echoed in the missionary efforts of American and European Christian groups. Particularly in Africa, these missionary campaigns primarily provided medical and educational services to underserved communities throughout the developing world.

Postcolonial Identity and Arab Independence. With the slow European decolonization of Africa, Asia, and the Middle East, and the rise of international governance, development and modernization prerogatives became enshrined, on the one hand, in international human-rights documents and, on the other, in foreign policy–informed trade agreements facilitated by global powers.

Largely based on Enlightenment ideals, the concept of natural rights and political developments of the American and French Revolutions, the Universal Declaration of Human Rights was adopted by the United Nations General Assembly in 1948. Many have argued that human rights are an exclusively Western concept, but this overlooks many other cultural traditions' emphasis on personal dignity and the rights of others. Much of this discourse has focused on whether the teachings of Islam espouse similar rights.

Calls for modernization and development in the Muslim world continued to be adopted and discussed among Muslim intellectuals and leaders. With declared independence from colonial powers, Arab intellectuals actively discussed reform measures. Figures such as Jamāl al-Dīn al-Afghānī, Muḥammad ʿAbduh, and Rashīd Riḍā actively debated reform measures with Muslim intellectuals, many of whom believed that a return to the Islamic tradition was key to development toward modernity after colonial rule. It was Qāsim Amīn, who, in his work *The Liberation of Women*, advocated for legal reform of those laws affecting divorce, polygamy, and women's dress.

While government reform measures in the Muslim world have often been justified by religious texts, the Cairo Declaration on Human Rights in Islam (CDHRI) is often looked to as the Islamic perspective on human rights. Issued by the Organisation of the Islamic Conference (OIC), now the Organisation of Islamic Cooperation, in 1990, the declaration affirms human rights, starting by forbidding "discrimination on the basis of race, colour, language, belief, sex, religion, political affiliation, social status or other considerations," but only as prescribed by Sharīʿah. The CDHRI has been criticized for being subject to Sharīʿah, which many feel restricts the rights of religious minorities, women, and other vulnerable populations.

September 11th and the "Fight to Save Muslim Women." Despite this affirmation of human rights as central to Islam, governments citing Islam as a primary source of their laws, as well as Muslim communities throughout the world, are bad of major human-rights violations. Whether refusing to recognize the rights of the LGBT community, severely limiting freedom of speech through government censorship, or directly targeting ethnic and religious minority communities, Islam has been implicitly, if not explicitly, portrayed as one of the primary impediments to modernization in the Middle East, Africa, and Asia. This view that Islam is incompatible with modern capitalism and democratic governance has been a major assumption behind many perspectives influencing international foreign policy and economic trade.

This pervasive sentiment overlooks much of the nuance necessitated by state-specific human-rights violations. The term "Muslim world," referring to those countries that have a Muslim-majority population, applies to over fifty countries scattered throughout Asia, Africa, and the Middle East. However, categorizing these countries on the basis of faith traditions ignores vast disparities in economic resources, geopolitical realities, and local cultural customs; each of which inversely relate to the status of each state's development. For example, despite immense economic resources and modernization efforts, Saudi Arabia severely restricts women's mobility, and religious freedom is virtually non-existent. On the other hand, the international community expressed concern when Turkey, often deemed modern and praised for its secular politics, lifted the ban on headscarves in school.

However, despite poverty, illiteracy, famine, and disease, much of the discourse surrounding modernization and development throughout the Muslim world focuses on two overlapping and inextricable themes: the treatment of Muslim women and Muslim religious and political extremists.

Shortly after the United States' invasion of Iraq and Afghanistan, academics actively debated the delicate relationship between neo-imperialism, modernization, and Islam. In her now famous article "Do Muslim Women Really Need Saving?" Lila Abu-Lughod quotes former first lady Laura Bush, "Because of our recent military gains in much of Afghanistan, women are no longer imprisoned in their homes.... The fight against terrorism is also a fight for the rights of women" (2002). The events of September 11, 2001, exhumed many colonial arguments and impressions that the Muslim world is backwardly un-modern and in severe need of development.

Monitoring the status of modernization and development, the Arab Human Development Reports (AHDRs), independent reports published by the United Nations Development Programme, detail the economic and political weaknesses of much of the Muslim world. The first report was published in 2002 and provided an account of the major shortfalls in the area of human development, noting knowledge, women's empowerment, and freedom as the three main impediments to the region's progress. Published in 2006, the AHDR report titled *Towards the Rise of Women in the Arab World*, which was co-led by prominent Palestinian academic and feminist Islah Jad, recommends for the benefit of all of Arab society that countries fully ratify and implement the United Nations Convention on the Elimination of All Forms of Discrimination Against Women (CEDAW). In addition, the report recognizes the significant achievements in the advancement of women throughout the Arab world but notes that much remains to be accomplished in developing and utilizing their human capacities, as well as recognizing the human rights of women.

In addition to the active campaign to empower Muslim women, development professionals at the international level are actively promoting good governance in the Muslim world. As opposed to human-rights advocacy, which frequently roots its arguments in aspirations of social justice and those rights documented in international law, good-governance standards tend to focus on economic stability and political transparency. Frequently described as rule-of-law programs, these projects traditionally focus on institution- and capacity-building for high-level government figures. Much like the discussion of whether human rights are compatible within the Islamic legal tradition, scholars have vehemently upheld that the aspirations articulated by the rule of law are fully upheld by the Sharīʿah.

In conjunction with the Regional Bureau for Arab States (RBAS), which also facilitates publication of the AHDR, the UNDP Programme on Governance in the Arab Region (POGAR) actively seeks to increase citizen participation in government processes, while promoting the rule of law, government accountability, and transparency. It remains to be seen what role POGAR will play in the post–Arab Spring Middle East, particularly given that millions across the Muslim world continue to support some form of Islamic governance. To what extent the modern instantiation of the nation-state is compatible with contemporary Islamic notions of good governance remains to be seen.

BIBLIOGRAPHY

Abu-Lughod, Lila. "The Active Social Life of 'Muslim Women's Rights': A Plea for Ethnography, Not Polemic, with Cases from Egypt and Palestine." *Journal of Middle East Women's Studies* 6, no. 1 (Winter 2010): 1–45.

Abu-Lughod, Lila. "Do Muslim Women Really Need Saving? Anthropological Reflections on Cultural Relativism and Its Others." *American Anthropologist* n.s. 104, no. 3 (September 2002): 783–790.

Amīn, Qāsim. *The Liberation of Women and the New Woman: Two Documents in the History of Egyptian Feminism*. Cairo: American University in Cairo Press, 2000.

Kipling, Rudyard. "White Man's Burden: The United States and the Philippine Islands." *McClure's Magazine*, February 1899, p. 12.

Mattei, Ugo, and Laura Nader. *Plunder: When the Rule of Law Is Illegal*. London: Wiley-Blackwell, 2008.

Organization of Islamic Conference. "Cairo Declaration on Human Rights in Islam." http://www.oic-oci.org/english/article/human.htm.

Russell, Bertrand. *A History of Western Philosophy*. New York: Simon & Schuster/Touchstone, 1967.

United Nations Development Programme. *The Arab Human Development Report 2005: Towards the Rise of Women in the Arab World*. New York: Regional Bureau of Arab States, 2006.

DOMINIC T. BOCCI

MODESTY. Freedom from vanity (*al-tawāḍu'*) is a central concept in Islam, directly connected to the concept of *tawḥīd* (unity or divine oneness). According to the Qur'ān, Satan's fall from grace was a direct result of his vanity. Having been ordered by God to bow to Adam, all the angels complied except Satan. Satan explained his defiance as follows: "I am better than [Adam]; You created me from fire and created him from clay" (7:12).

Any Muslim who engages in vain and arrogant behavior, such as adopting an attitude of racial, gender, or class superiority, is embracing Satanic logic. The Qur'ān makes clear that, while God has bestowed on some humans more earthly gifts than he has on others, God created all humans from the same *nafs* (soul) and made them male and female, nations and tribes, so that they may come to know each other (49:13). Thus diversity was introduced into this world as a way of making the human experience more interesting and providing people with an incentive to communicate with one another. In the same passage, the Qur'ān also states that the most honored individuals in the eyes of God are the most pious.

The Qur'ān commends Christians and calls them "closest in friendship to Muslims" because "they do not act arrogantly" (5:82); the modesty of these believers evidences their faith in and submission to God. The Prophet said that a person with vanity in his heart, even if it weighs no more than a mustard seed, will not enter paradise. The Qur'ān is even clearer; it states that arrogant people are unjust, criminal, and nonbelievers (25:21, 45:31, 39:59), and that God will turn them away from divine revelation (or signs) and send them to hell eternally (7:146, 39:72).

Those who believe that they are more powerful than others install themselves as demigods on this earth, and their followers submit to them and not to God. This is *shirk*, believing in more than one god or in a god other than God. It negates *tawḥīd*. The Qur'ān is replete with examples of arrogant nonbelievers whom God disgraced, defeated, or destroyed, among them Pharaoh and his chiefs and the people of 'Ād and Madyan.

For these reasons, Muslim jurists discouraged all types of behavior that might constitute even early symptoms of arrogance. Muslims were enjoined not to strut vainly down the street, to raise their voices to imply superiority, or to indulge in excessive luxuries. The Prophet himself dressed and ate modestly; so did his Companions. He also mended his own garments, participated in housework and child care, and helped others, including widows and maids, in their tasks when they sought his assistance.

The emphasis on discouraging early symptoms of arrogance, combined with an increasingly entrenched patriarchal tradition in the Islamic world, has led some jurists to demand that Muslim women veil their faces and avoid public life. In fact, women during the life of the Prophet were not required to do either. Today, some jurists have found such excesses unjustifiable and have called for a return to moderation, which the Qurʾān describes as the defining characteristic of the Muslim *ummah* (2:143).

[*See also* Dress, *subentries* Contemporary *and* Historical; Hijab; Islam and Women, *subentries* An Overview, Contemporary Debates, *and* Eighteenth-Century to Early Twentieth-Century Debates; Seclusion; Shame; *and* Veiling, *subentries* Historical Discourse *and* Contemporary Discourse.]

BIBLIOGRAPHY

Abū Shuqqah, ʿAbd al-Ḥalīm Muḥammad. *Taḥrīr al-marʾah fī ʿaṣr al-risālah*. 5 vols. Kuwait: Dar al-Qalam, 1990–. Excellent and thorough discussion of women and Islam. See volumes 3 and 4 for a discussion of the veil.

Haddad, Yvonne Yazbeck, and John L. Esposito, eds. *Islam, Gender, and Social Change*. New York: Oxford University Press, 1998.

Azizah Y. al-Hibri

Mogahed, Dalia. (b. 1974), Egyptian-born American Muslim author, research analyst, and White House adviser to the president.

Dalia Mogahed emigrated from Egypt to the United States, eventually becoming a naturalized citizen. She earned an undergraduate degree in chemical engineering with a minor in Arabic from the University of Wisconsin and a master's degree in business administration (MBA) with an emphasis in strategy from the Joseph M. Katz Graduate School of Business at the University of Pittsburgh. After graduating, she worked as a marketing products researcher at Proctor & Gamble. She currently works as a research analyst for Gallup and is a member of the President's Advisory Council on Faith-Based and Neighborhood Partnerships. She lives in Washington, D.C., with her husband and two sons.

Mogahed serves as. the executive director and senior analyst for the Gallup Centre for Muslim Studies, a research organization examining what people worldwide think and feel as it pertains to any particular issue. She is known best for the book *Who Speaks for Islam?: What a Billion Muslims Really Think*, which she coauthored with John L. Esposito. The analysis from the book has been reported by *The Wall Street Journal*, the *Harvard International Review*, and the *Middle East Policy Journal*, in addition to other academic journals. The book is cited as the most comprehensive work of its kind, surveying approximately 90 percent of the world's Muslim population on topics such as free speech, perceptions of Western culture, and jobs and security. The results are strikingly similar to those found from American survey candidates on the same topics. The book also works to negate the extremist-Muslim stereotype and Islamophobia based on data.

In 2009 President Barack Obama appointed her to the President's Advisory Council on Faith-Based and Neighborhood Partnerships, making her the first hijab-wearing Muslim woman to hold a position in the White House. Her main responsibility is to relate to the president how government and faith-based organizations may work with each other in order to handle societal issues that arise through religion or other such issues. She works with and among other

American leaders from the government, military, and business sectors.

The main focus of Mogahed's work appears to be building understanding and relationships between Muslims and other groups and cultures. For example, for President Obama's 2009 trip to Cairo, Egypt, she presented a number of points to emphasize, including the necessity for mutual respect between governments and a cooperative approach to dealing with global issues.

For three consecutive years, *ArabianBusiness.com* has listed Mogahed on their annual Power 100 of the most influential Arab men and women who affect and develop ideas on a globally influential scale. She was ranked thirty-second in 2012, sixth in 2012, and third in 2010. She has also been on the 500 most influential list compiled by The Royal Islamic Strategic Studies Centre in 2009 and 2010. Also in 2010 she was named as the Arab World's Social Entrepreneur of the Year by Ashoka, a global organization that recognizes and empowers upcoming social entrepreneurs. Mogahed also received the Forward Under 40 award from the University of Wisconsin's alumni association for her continued work and contributions in her field.

Bibliography

"Dalia Mogahed." 2012. http://www.gallup.com/se/128111/Dalia-Mogahed.aspx/.

"Dalia Mogahed." 2012. http://www.goodreads.com/author/show/850812.Dalia_Mogahed/.

"Dalia Mogahed." 2012. http://www.huffingtonpost.com/dalia-mogahed/.

"Dalia Mogahed: First Muslim Woman Appointed to Advise President." http://factofarabs.net/era.aspx?id=357&tid=19.

Esposito, John L., and Dalia Mogahed. *Who Speaks for Islam? What a Billion Muslims Think*. Washington, D.C.: Gallup Press, 2008.

"100 Most powerful Arab Women in 2011." http://www.arabianbusiness.com/100-most-powerful-arab-women-2011-384182.html?view=profile&itemid=383762/.

"Power 100 2010: 3 Dalia Mogahed." http://www.arabianbusiness.com/power-100/list?view=profile&itemid=150716/.

"Revealed: 100 Most Powerful Arab Women 2012: 6 Dalia Mogahed." http://www.arabianbusiness.com/100-most-powerful-arab-women-2012-448295.html/.

Eren Tatari

Morocco.

Morocco. The roots of the Moroccan feminist movement go back to 1946, when the Sisters of Purity Association (the first feminist association in Morocco) publicly issued a set of demands including the abolition of polygamy, full and equal political rights, and increased visibility of women in the public sphere. These demands were taken up by female journalists, academics, and civil society in the decades after Morocco gained independence from France in 1956. Although on the eve of Independence, the state (i.e., male) feminism did not target the empowerment of women as individuals, middle- and upper-class women gained from it in two fields—education and job opportunities—granting them entry into the public sphere. It was the new post-independence bourgeois class that produced the first women pharmacists, jurists, medical doctors, and university professors. The general feminist trend of these women was liberal in the sense that they readily embraced "modern" ideas and practices without rejecting their local specificities, including being Muslim. This liberal trend was accompanied by changes in dress, as well as other social practices, such as the adoption of French ways of life. However, this style never succeeded in replacing traditional Moroccan practices and ways of life, including dress.

During this period, through journalistic and academic discourse, feminists started to question gender divisions, examine historical and ideological roots of gender inequality, and promote recognition of women's labor. They depicted women's condition not as a "natural state," but as a state that stems from historical practices, and women's work not as merely reproduction, but as production.

Legal Changes. Women in the movement were bitterly disappointed by the first Personal Status Code (Mudawwana), which relegated women to second-class citizenship in 1957. The fundamental principle of marriage required a wife's obedience to her husband in exchange for financial maintenance, and the husband retained the power to abandon his wife without a judge's authorization. Not surprisingly, the Moroccan feminist movement focused its efforts on the Mudawwana, which was seen as the prime locus of legal and civil discrimination against women.

The socialism and Arab nationalism of the sixties and seventies enhanced women's rights as a prerequisite for Morocco's overall development, invigorating the Moroccan feminist movement. Many women became active in leftist political parties, brandishing political engagement as a form of resistance against oppression.

Islamist Pressures. From the 1980s onward, the feminist movement also had to contend with growing support for Islamism, here defined as a social movement or organization based on the exploitation of Islam for political aims, or the exercise of political power in the name of religion only. Like any social movement, Islamism had its moderate (such as the recognized Justice and Development Party) and extreme (such as the unrecognized Justice and Charity Association) manifestations. In whatever shape, Islamism appealed particularly to young, unemployed males, who were easily led to believe that women working outside the home robbed them of opportunities. In response, feminists also began to push for women's rights from a religious perspective. They implemented new strategies, including a gradual downplaying of the "religious" role of the veil in their writings and practices; increased use of Arabic and references to the Qur'ān and *ḥadīth* (the sayings of Prophet Muḥammad); a gradual inclusion of children's rights within women's issues; and reinforcement of Islam as both culture and spirituality.

Feminist activists also endeavored to draw attention to the problems that women faced as a result of their lack of legal protection. They made excellent use of the media in depicting the victimization of women and children frequently accompanying divorce, thus reclaiming such social issues from the Islamists and reiterating the necessity of reforming the Personal Status Code. Nonetheless, a package of reforms proposed by the government in 1999, including the abolition of polygamy, ultimately failed in the face of Islamist and conservative opposition. Despite this setback, feminists continued their campaign, increasingly concentrating on the "goals of Sharīʿah" (*maqāṣid al-Sharīʿah*) instead of a rigid reading of Sharīʿah rules and traditions, which would return to the rationale of the text and which was supported by a school of Moroccan scholars. They also forged an alliance with King Muḥammed VI, who took the throne that year and did not welcome increased control by Islamists.

Types of Moroccan Feminism. From the 1990s onward, and under the influence of rising conservatism and Islamism in the region, two major types of female feminists stand out in Morocco: the secularists and the Islamists. Both types lead movements that are urban, middle-class, and centered on women's material (legal and social) rights. Both are also led by educated women and focus on gender representations and political strategies in order to affect state gender policies. Ideologically, the core difference between the two is not Islam, as neither group denies it, but the type and degree of Islamization involved. While Islamists take doctrinal or legal Islam as their reference, secularists opt, if at all, for a spiritual (universal) Islam. As for strategies, the secularists use academic scholarship, journalism, and activism, while the Islamists, being historically younger, use activism and journalism. Each type of feminism comprises, in turn, various nuances that depend on variables like location and political inclination. Since around 2000, the two types of feminism have started to interact and even converge, adding a considerable dose of Islamization to secularist thought and a considerable dose of secularization to the Islamists' camp. The change in both feminisms is a product of the overall local and regional political climate. The advent of the digital age and new media gave this interaction and convergence a new edge: the younger new media-savvy generation call themselves "democrats," focus on employment, and speak to both the secularists and the Islamists.

One thing that brings the two movements together is the reform of the Mudawwana. It is important to note that voices from inside the Islamist movement started to push for more reforms of the Mudawwana on the eve of the twenty-first century. Hence, strong Islamists like Nadia Yassine and Bassima Hakkaoui started to rally to demands initiated by Fatima Mernissi and others in the 1970s, again expanding the notion of feminism in Morocco.

Reform of the Mudawwana. In April 2001, the king formed a commission to study the possibility of revising the Mudawwana, but the final push for reform came after the May 2003 terrorist attacks in Casablanca, which stoked widespread antifundamentalist sentiment. The king announced a draft family law in parliament in October 2003. During the next few months, women's rights organizations, organized within the Spring of Equality network, (a network of the Moroccan women's associations that work on the reform of the Family Law) analyzed the details of the draft legislation and organized workshops, roundtables, and discussion groups to prepare for renewed lobbying efforts in parliament and to educate the public about the reforms. The final text was adopted in January 2004, securing several important rights for women, including the right to self-guardianship, the right to divorce, and the right to child custody. It also placed new restrictions on polygamy, raised the legal age of marriage from fifteen to eighteen, and made sexual harassment punishable by law. However, it did not completely abolish polygamy, unilateral repudiation of the wife by the husband, separation by compensation (*khulʿ*), or discrimination in inheritance rules. This was in part because such provisions are explicitly authorized by literal readings of the Qurʾān.

Whereas the 1998–2003 period was characterized by a flurry of ideological and political debates about women and their rights in Morocco, the period since 2004 has been characterized by calmer legal discussion about the gains and implementation of the new family law, the new labor code (promulgated in December 2003), and the revised nationality code (which took effect in April 2008).

Effects of the New Law. The implementation of the family law in particular varies from region to region, but it has generally been met with resistance. It is still very poorly understood in rural and sometimes even urban areas, and many male judges are reluctant to apply it. Moreover, the ongoing societal influences of patriarchy, tradition, illiteracy, and ignorance may prevent women from invoking their rights or reporting crimes such as rape, child abuse, sexual exploitation, and domestic violence. Existing efforts to overcome this societal resistance, such as education campaigns conducted in the mother tongues (Berber and Moroccan Arabic), have proven insufficient. Many feminists argue that the new family law can be adequately implemented only in a democratic context, while some advocate a purely secular government system. Another issue is that the law does not adequately address the problems of single women and the non-Moroccan wives of Moroccan men.

Nevertheless, Moroccan women have achieved considerable progress in consolidating legal equality and access to justice in recent years, and the autonomy, security, and personal freedom of women have also improved. Women now have more freedom to travel and to obtain employment and education, greater equality at home, and more leeway to negotiate their marriage rights. They are spearheading business ventures and advancing to higher levels of education. Important progress has also been made in protecting women from domestic violence, and support networks are getting stronger despite restrictive social norms. Women are increasingly taking up national and local political posts and becoming more involved with the judiciary. A 12 percent quota for women was applied to the June 2009 local elections, substantially increasing female political representation. The quota system in parliament brought new faces of Islamist women with strong demands in the 2007 and 2011 elections, facilitating awareness of women's issues.

Women's rights groups and individual activists have collaborated with the government to improve the rights of all women, but true equality remains a distant goal. Although the recent legal reforms have allowed the government to promote a modern and democratic image of Morocco at the international level, bringing certain benefits to society at large, more needs to be done to translate these changes into tangible gains for individual women in their daily lives.

[*See also* Family Law; Gender Equality; Guardianship; Mernissi, Fatima; Women's Rights; *and* Yassine, Nadia.]

Bibliography

Abouzeid, Leila. *Year of the Elephant*. Translated by Barbara Parmenter. Austin: University of Texas at Austin, 1989.

Aït Sabbah, Fatna. *La femme dans l'inconscient musulman*. Paris: Albin Michel, 1986.

Badran, M. "Feminisms: Secular and Religious Paradigms, a Selective Look at the Middle East." In *Feminist Movements: Origins and Orientations*, edited by Fatima Sadiqi, Farida Elkettani, Leila Baghdadi, Fatima Mouaid, and Souad Slaoui, pp. 73–88. Fez, Morocco: Faculty of Letters, 2000.

Barakat, Amina. "Renewed Efforts to End Violence Against Women." Inter Press Service, March 17, 2009. http://ipsnews.net/africa/nota.asp?idnews=46150.

Barkallil, N. "La naissance et le développement du prolétariat féminin urbain." PhD diss., University of Rabat, Morocco, 1990.

Belarbi, A. "Mouvements de femmes au Maroc." *Annuaire de l'Afrique du Nord* 28 (1989) pp 19–29.

Benjelloun, T. *Femme, culture, entreprise au Maroc*. Casablanca: Wallada, 1993.

Bennani, Farida, and Zineb Miadi. *Sélection des textes sacrés sur les droits humains de la femme en Islam*. Rabat, Morocco: Fondation Fridrich Ebert, 1995.

Ennaji, Moha. *Multilingualism, Cultural Identity, and Education in Morocco*. Boston: Springer, 2005.

Mernissi, F. *Beyond the Veil: Male–Female Dynamics in a Modern Muslim Society*. Bloomington: Indiana University Press, 1984.

Sadiqi, Fatima. "Female Perceptions of Islam in Today's Morocco." In *The New Voices of Muslim Women Theologians*, edited by Ednan Aslan, Marcia Hermansen, and Elif Medeni, vol. 2, Leiden: Brill, forthcoming.

Sadiqi, Fatima. *Women, Gender, and Language in Morocco*. Boston: Brill, 2003.

Tawfik, A. *Mudawwanat al-aḥwāl al-shakhṣīyah: maʿa ākhir al-taʿdīlāt dahīr 10–9–1993*. Casablanca: Dar al-Thaqafah, 1993.

Touahri, Sarah. "Morocco Retracts CEDAW Reservations." *Magharebia*, December 17, 2008. http://www.magharebia.com/cocoon/awi/xhtml1/en_GB/features/awi/features/2008/12/17/feature-02.

Fatima Sadiqi

Mosque, Women's Space and Use of.

This discussion outlines the problem of religious practice and the right of women to attend the mosque, the key feature of which is the identification of what is commonly referred to as the "women's area." According to the CAIR 2001 report, *The American Mosque: A National Portrait*, in nearly two-thirds of mosques, 66 percent of women make *ṣalāh* (prescribed prayer) behind a curtain or partition or in another room. One explanation of the common occurrence of this practice is the fact that the diaspora community in Europe and North America are inclined to subscribe to familiar cultural and social customs from their country of origin. Another explanation may be the usual influence of patriarchy; while the principle of gender equity is implicit in the text of the Qurʾān (the primary source of exegetical authority for Muslims), male commentators have long been accustomed to state that private worship for women is preferable. Such practices are not only ill-founded but draw upon extant popular ideas and obvious male prejudices. Most useful for comparison is the mention of the word *masjid* (mosque) in the Qurʾān, which does not attribute a hermeneutical status to male or female worshipper. In fact the Qurʾān makes no distinction between the sexes: "... I will not suffer the work of any worker among you to be lost, whether male or female" (3:194). The etymology of the word *masjid* can be traced to the Arabic verb *sajada*, to prostrate or bow down to God in worship (72:18; 24:36; 9:18). Within the framework of the Qurʾānic discourse, we find also the word *miḥrāb* in connection with the Virgin Mary (9:16–17 and al-Ṭabarī vol. 8:320). Al-Ṭabarī (vol. 3:246) describes the *miḥrāb* as a most honorable place; thus it may be true that, in reference to Mary, the word *miḥrāb* corresponds simply to a place of pious devotion. God commanded her to "bow down [in prayer] with those [the congregation] who bow down" (3:43).

The Prophet's Mosque. The archetypal mosque of the Prophet Muḥammad (*masjid al-Nabī*)—built in the year 622 at Medina—proved acceptable as an architectural precedent. According to ʿAlī ibn ʿAbd Allah Samhūdi (d. 1506), in *Wafāʾ al-wafā bi akhbār dār al-Mustafa*, the plan of the original edifice had two domestic chambers (later increased to nine) attached and a courtyard, with three doors: the door of mercy (*bāb ar-raḥmah*) to the west, the door of Gabriel (*bāb Jibrīl*), and the women's door (*bāb al-Nisaʾ*) to the east, and a shaded portico (*zullah)* to the north. Sixteen or seventeen months after the Prophet's migration to Medina, the axis of prayer (*qiblah*) was changed from Jerusalem to Mecca following a Qurʾānic revelation (2:137–147); this resulted in the alteration of the southern wall. This became the permanent sanctuary (*muṣallā*), three aisles deep parallel to the *qiblah* wall, where the *miḥrāb* is typically located, and where the imam stands to lead the faithful in the daily performance of the prayer, much like many mosques today.

The Legal Debate. Sayyid Mitawalli Darsh (the former imam of the London Central Mosque) offers a plausible explanation of the right of women to attend the mosque, which highlights the source of the ambiguities that remain today. Likewise, Asma Sayeed's critique, "Early Sunni Discourses on Women's Mosque Attendance," explores the theological and legal debates, which had been associated with the interpretation of the *ḥadīth* literature in the eighth and ninth centuries, about two hundred years after Muḥammad's death. Within the scope of a legal discussion, the jurists of the four Sunnī schools of law (Mālikī, Ḥanafī, Shāfiʿī, Ḥanbalī) have leaned heavily toward a probable inference in ʿĀʾishah's *ḥadīth*, "Had God's Apostle known what the women were doing, he would have forbidden them from going to the mosque" (al-Bukhārī, 12:828). Some jurists therefore take her opinion to support the claim that a woman's prayer in her domicile is preferable. Nevertheless, Ibn Qudāmah's (d. 1223) authoritative text, *al-Mughnī,* on Ḥanbalī jurisprudence also cites ʿAʾishah, who said that women used to offer their prayers with Muḥammad in congregation, and he explicitly said "do not stop the female servants of God from attending the mosque of God." Both *ḥadīth* have encouraged a vast collection of intractable legal opinion, see for instance Imam Muḥammad al-Shawkānī's (d. 1834) *Nayl al-awtār* (vol. 3, p. 150) "The Attendance of Women at the Mosques and the Preference of Offering their Prayers at Home." According to Ibn Ḥazm (d. 1064), the author of *al-Muḥallā* (see vol. 3, pp. 164–178), the idea of discouraging Muslim women from attending public worship in a mosque came from Abū Ḥanīfah (d. 767) and al-Malik (d. 795). Abū Ḥanīfah allowed elderly women special permission to attend the night (*ʿishāʾ*) prayer and the dawn (*fajr*) prayer, but he did not like them going out for the two feasts, that is, *ʿĪd al-Aḍḥā* and *ʿĪd al-Fiṭr*. Al-Malik appears to be more cautious, saying "We do not stop them going out to the mosques and allowing the elderly to attend the feast prayers and the prayer for rain." In fact, Imam al-Shāfiʿī (d. 820) and Ibn Ḥanbal (d. 855) supported that opinion as well. Ibn Ḥazm argued against it by stating that the merit of public worship includes women and it is derived from the *ḥadīth*: "the congregational prayer is twenty-seven times greater" [than that of the prayer offered alone] (al-Bukhārī 11:621).

The Inclusion of Female Congregants. In 1911 in Egypt, Malak Ḥifnī Nāṣif complained about the legal rights of women who had been denied the right to perform public worship and the right to enter the mosque by citing the Prophet's words, "Do not prohibit the female servants of God from entering God's mosques." Also in Egypt, in 1955, a zealous governor issued a proclamation making the congregational prayer compulsory for women at an earlier time on Friday and separate from men's prayer. Maḥmūd Shaltūt, the mufti (jurist-consult) of al-Azhar University, issued a *fatwā* (*responsa*) against this decree.

Today in the United States, France, and the United Kingdom, the number of female congregants is approaching that of the male congregants. In the Islamic Cultural Center of New York, the design rejects previous assumptions about a totally segregated women's area/room—the elevated balcony above the men suggests one example of the extent to which spatial stereotypes can be broken down, but some women reject the balcony concept pointing to its limitations. Indeed, in speaking for themselves, American Muslim women have staged pray-ins and sit-ins. One example is the Masjid Khadījah bint Khuwaylid mosque in Austin, Texas, where the women have on occasion staged pray-ins and sit-ins by sharing the same space with the men. In much the same way, contemporary scholars have studied and responded by way of a literary critique of patriarchal authority. An inspiring charter for women's mosques in China are the Hui Muslim or Huijiaotu, who have taken jurisdiction of religious practice and self-understanding mentored by a female teacher and religious leader (*nu ahong*). Although the practice of allowing women and men free public access to the mosque was established by explicit approval by the Prophet, it is important to realize that three descriptive markers—cultural/social norms, religious belief, and religious practice—further characterize the institution of congregational worship and in many crucial respects give reason to dispute the physical component of women's prayer space.

Bibliography

Darsh, S. M. *Islamic Essays*. London: Islamic Cultural Center, 1979.

Jaschok, Maria, and Shui Jingjun. *The History of Women's Mosques in Chinese Islam: A Mosque of Their Own*. Richmond, Surrey, U.K.: Curzon, 2000.

Kahera, Akel Ismail *Deconstructing the American Mosque: Space, Gender and Aesthetics*. Austin: University of Texas Press, 2002.

Sayeed, Asma. "Early Sunni Discourses on Women's Mosque Attendance." *International Institute for the*

Study of Islam in the Modern World News Letter 7, no. 1 (March 2001).
Stowasser, Barbara Freyer. *Women in the Qur'an, Traditions, and Interpretation*. New York: Oxford University Press, 1994.
Yildirim, Gulsah. "Woman Patrons of Ottoman Architectural Endowments in Kadinlar Saltanati Period (16th and 17th Centuries)." Master's thesis, University of Texas, Austin, 1999.

Akel Ismail Kahera

Motherhood. The state or condition of being a mother—a female parent. Arabic *umūma*, from *umm*, "mother." *Wālida*, she who has given birth to a child, *walad*, also designates a mother.

As with other cultures, Islam as orthopraxy considers the processes of life-giving, birth, lactation, and nurturance as the social concerns of society as a whole.

Although terms designating "father" (*ab*, *wālid*) appear in the Qur'ān about four times more frequently than those designating "mother," two verses (31:14; 46:15) that preach respect for both parents emphasize the special circumstances with which mothers cope during pregnancy, childbirth, breastfeeding, and weaning, thus implicitly encouraging believers to recognize the advantage the latter have over the fathers and to reciprocate accordingly. Maternal love finds expression also in Qur'ānic narrations such as the story of the infant Moses (28:7–12).

Unlike in the Qur'ān, in some post-Qur'ānic sources Adam's wife, Ḥawwā', is featured as responsible for the Fall. Ten punishments, among them menstruation, pregnancy, and suffering at childbirth, are supposed to remind the daughters of Eve of the fault of their first ancestress. These post-Qur'ānic developments clearly show the influence of biblical accounts. Women during parturition and menstruation are exempt from observing obligatory religious duties because of the presence of blood (which is equally defiling of men). However, unlike other cultural and legal systems prevalent among the Mae Enga, Jews, and Hindus, for example, Islamic law does not consider them to be in an ontological state of impurity during these phases, although popular social attitudes vary.

Ḥadīth reports attributed to the Prophet Muḥammad—for example, "The person who has the greatest right over the woman is her husband, and the person who has the greatest right over the man is his mother" (Ibn Abī al-Dunyā, 1997, p. 305), and "Paradise is under her [the mother's] foot" (Ibn Māja, 1988, p. 125, tradition 2241; Ibn al-Jawzī, 1993, p. 63—stress the childbearing role of women, valorizing the mother.

Sharīʿah rules from the classical period protect pregnant women and the strong ties they later establish with their small children. They inspire the observance of both the mother's and the child's rights to breastfeeding (*raḍāʿ*, *riḍāʿa*) for at least two full years and custody (*ḥiḍāna*, *ḥaḍāna*) for as long as the child is physically and psychologically dependent. During this period, "the physical mother-child relationship is transformed into an extended psycho-sociological unity" (Bouhdiba, 1985, pp. 214–215). This, in turn, guarantees the mother the long-term economic and social protection with which her children, particularly her sons, provide her as adults.

In a pro-natal spirit, the Sharīʿah offers concessions to help pregnant women observe the principle Islamic rituals in a state of physical weakness. *Ḥadīth* reports promise bereaved mothers the reward of being admitted into Paradise or being protected from the fires of Hell, thus encouraging them to fulfill their maternal destiny. Reflecting consciousness of the dangers involved in pregnancy and childbirth, they assure mothers that they will be granted the status of martyr (*shahīda*) in case of death.

Muslim scholars observe the importance of pregnancy and lactation, instructing men to choose fertile women of a good bodily and moral disposition to ensure the birth of many children of praiseworthy traits.

More explicit than the Qur'ān, *ḥadīth* literature underlines the mother's advantage over the father in terms of investment in children and of compensation in this world and the hereafter alike, both for herself and for those who pay tribute to her. Chapters dealing with "the priority one should give to his/her mother concerning filial piety" and "on the punishment of those who disobey their mothers" appear in treatises on the theme of appropriate behavior towards relatives.

Guidance as to the priority a Muslim should give to his mother is based on a comparison between the religious value of maternal piety and that of the fulfillment of some of the most central Islamic rituals. The obligation to respect one's mother crosses the lines of religious affiliation.

Unlike fathers, who are described in Islamic sources as possessing logic, mothers are marked by their love and compassion but also by their limited mental qualifications. The child is presented as strongly attached to his mother while regarding his father as an enemy.

In contrast with the positive image of the mother in Arabic-Islamic texts, we find also—albeit more rarely—narratives that reflect ambivalence concerning mother-child relationships: a mother who hits her little child, another who uses a tough device to wean him, or a reference to hostility between a mother and her (grown) son.

There are testimonies of the actual, mostly close, relations between mothers and their offspring in, for instance, biographical literature and letters from the Mamlūk period.

Contemporary literature continues to project motherhood as the norm for Muslim women, often highlighting the importance of education as a qualification for good mothering.

BIBLIOGRAPHY

Bouhdiba, Abdelwahab. *Sexuality in Islam*. Translated by Alan Sheridan. London: Routledge and Kegan Paul, 1985.

Ghazālī, Abū Ḥāmid Muḥammad al-. *Iḥyā' 'ulūm al-dīn*. 5 vols. Cairo: Mu'assasat al-Ḥalabī, 1967–1968.

Giladi, Avner. *Infants, Parents and Wet Nurses: Medieval Islamic Views on Breastfeeding and Their Social Implications*. Leiden, Netherlands, and Boston, Mass.: Brill, 1999.

Giladi, Avner. "Lactation." In *Encyclopaedia of the Qur'ān*, edited by Jane Dammen McAuliffe. 6 vols., vol. 3, pp. 106–107. Leiden, Netherlands: Brill, 2003.

Giladi, Avner. "Parents." In *Encyclopaedia of the Qur'ān*, edited by Jane Dammen McAuliff. 6 vols, vol. 4, pp. 19–22. Leiden, Netherlands: Brill, 2004.

Ibn Abī al-Dunyā, Abū Bakr. *Kitāb al-'Iyāl*. Al-Manṣūra, Egypt: Dār al-Wafā', 1997.

Ibn al-Jawzī, Abū al-Faraj 'Abd al-Raḥmān ibn 'Alī. *Kitāb al-birr wa-al-silah*. Edited by 'Ādil 'Abd al-Mawjūd and 'Alī Mu'awwaḍ. Beirut: Mu'assasat al-Kutub, 1993.

Ibn Mājah, Muḥammad ibn Yazīd. *Ṣaḥīḥ sunan Ibn Māja*. Riyadh, Saudi Arabia: Maktab al-Tarbiyya al-'Arabī li-Duwwal al-Khalīj, 1988.

Ibn Taymiyya, Aḥmad ibn 'Abd al-Ḥalīm. *Rasā'il min al-sijn*. 4th ed. Riyadh, Saudi Arabia: Dār Ṭayyiba, 1986.

Ibn Ẓafar, Muḥammad, *Anbā' nujabā' al-abnā'*. Edited by Ibrāhīm Yūnus. Cairo: Dār al- Ṣaḥwah, 1991.

Kueny, Kathryn. "The Birth of Cain: Reproduction, Maternal Responsibility, and Moral Character in Early Islamic Exegesis." *History of Religions* 48, no. 2 (2008): 110–129.

Moore, Henrietta L. *Feminism and Anthropology*. Cambridge, U.K.: Polity Press, and Minneapolis: University of Minnesota Press, 1988.

Qarāmī, Āmāl. *al-Ikhtilāf fī al-thaqāfa al-'arabiyya al-islāmiyya*. Beirut: Dār al-Madār al-Islāmī, 2007.

Reinhart, Kevin A. "Impurity/No Danger." *History of Religions* 30 (1990): 1–24.

Sakhāwī, Muḥammad ibn 'Abd al-Raḥmān al-. *al-Ḍaw' al-lāmi' li-ahl al-qarn al-tāsi'*. 12 vols. Cairo: Maktabat al-Quds, 1935–1936.

Schimmel, Annemarie. *My Soul Is a Woman: The Feminine in Islam*. Translated by Susan H. Ray. New York: Continuum, 1997. See chapter 6, "The Mothers," pp. 89–97.

Schleifer, Aliah. *Motherhood in Islam*. Cambridge, U.K.: The Islamic Academy, 1986.

Shawkat Salamah-Qudsi, Arin, "A Lightning Trigger or a Stumbling Block: Mother Images and Roles in Classical Sufism." *Oriens* 39 (2011): 199–226.

Spellberg, Denise A. "Writing the Unwritten Life of the Islamic Eve: Menstruation and the Demonization of Motherhood." *International Journal of Middle East Studies* 28 (1996): 305–324.

Stowasser, Barbara Freyer. *Women in the Qur'an, Traditions and Interpretation*. New York and Oxford: Oxford University Press, 1994.

Vajda, G., and J. Eisenberg. "Ḥawwāʾ." *The Encyclopaedia of Islam*. 3d ed. Leiden, Netherlands: E. J. Brill, 2007–.

AVNER GILADI

MOURNING. In most of the Sunnī legal schools, after a death, a three-day period of mourning is required, characterized by increased devotion and the receiving of visitors and the sympathy of others. While in mourning, clothing should be simple and elaborate decoration avoided. The Qurʾānic verse 2:234 has been interpreted as implying that widows should mourn (and not remarry) for four months and ten days (*ʿiddah*), ostensibly to determine any potential pregnancy and paternity questions. It is generally believed that mourning cannot affect the fate of the deceased in the afterlife, and some of the traditional sayings of the Prophet (*ḥadīth*) advise actions involving charity, prayer, and increasing knowledge during this period. In any case, death cannot be avoided and should not be treated as a tragedy, because "To God we belong and to him do we return" (2:156). This calm attitude precludes dramatic forms of mourning typically associated with women, such as wailing and prolonged weeping, slapping the face, and tearing clothes, as well as those considered to be more masculine expressions, such as slashing the body and face with swords and chains. There are several strong traditions that suggest the Prophet was critical of what he regarded as the extravagant mourning practices of the pre-Islamic period (*jāhilīyah*), particularly where women were concerned, based as they were on no powerful belief in an afterlife.

In Sunnī communities, women often lament more than men, especially in Bedouin society. The more restrained men or other women often attempt to calm them. The ways in which the community follows the deceased to the grave and the support that others give the immediate relatives are important social aspects of mourning, demonstrating that the mourner is not alone and that his or her loss is felt by many others. Prayers recited in the mosque and at the funeral are often restricted to men, leaving women outside of the formalities associated with death and implicitly leaving them to develop their own expressions for grief. There are *hadīth*s that suggest that ʿĀʾishah, one of the Prophet's wives, visited and prayed at her brother's grave. Furthermore, critical remarks made by the Prophet about women at the graveside have been interpreted as referring only to the loud wailing prevalent in the *jāhilīyah*. The implication is that there is no reason that well-behaved Muslim women should not visit graves and pray there as, indeed, Muslim women have throughout history, often as social outings in groups.

The practice of mourning in Sunnī communities is often distinct from the theory. Despite criticism from some religious authorities, various practices have grown up at gravesides, including the visiting of graves, the building of substantial structures over them, and the recital of prayers specifically for such visits (*ziyārah*). Although such practices are strictly forbidden by Ḥanbalī legal rulings, especially by the influential thinker Ibn Taymīyah (d. 1328), they are less rigorously treated in the other Sunnī legal schools (*madhāhib*, sing. *madhhab*), and many local customs and rituals have arisen concerning the treatment of the dead.

Shīʿah observe several events that involve elaborate mourning rituals, including ʿĀshūrāʾ.

The mourning is for the defeat and death of Imām al-Ḥusayn, the son of ʿAlī, by the forces of the caliph, a defeat that represented the victory of what came to be known as Sunnism over the idea that leadership should be restricted to the family of the Prophet. In 680 CE, the captive women were marched from Karbala to Damascus, and al-Ḥusayn's sister, Zaynab, initiated the mourning rituals by lamenting and describing the martyrdom story. These mourning practices have become a significant part of Shīʿī ritual and identity. They have been elaborated into passion plays, songs, hymns, ritual self-flagellation, processions, and the recounting of the martyrdom theme.

[*See also* Rites.]

BIBLIOGRAPHY

Abu-Lughod, Lila. "Honor and Sentiments of Loss in a Beduin Society." *American Ethnologist* 12, no. 2 (1985): 245–261.

Deeb, Lara. "Living Ashura in Lebanon: Mourning Transformed to Sacrifice." *Comparative Studies of South Asia, Africa, and the Middle East* 25, no. 1 (2005): 122–137.

Hegland, Mary Elaine. "The Power Paradox in Muslim Women's Majales: North-West Pakistani Mourning Rituals as Sites of Contestation Over Religious Politics, Ethnicity, and Gender." *Signs* 23, no. 2 (1998): 391–428.

Yasien-Esmael, Hend, and Simon Shimshon Rubin. "The Meaning Structures of Muslim Bereavements in Israel: Religious Traditions, Mourning Practices, and Human Experience." *Death Studies* 29, no. 6 (2005): 495–518.

Oliver Leaman
Updated by Natana J. DeLong-Bas

Mouza bint Nasser Al-Misnad, Sheikha.

Mouza bint Nasser Al-Misnad, Sheikha. (b. 1959), wife of the emir of Qatar and chairperson of the Qatar Foundation.

As Mouza was a daughter of Nasser bin Abdulla Al-Misnad—a key opponent to Qatar's ruling dynasty—her marriage to Ḥamad bin Khalīfa Āl-Thānī in 1977 was a key step in the consolidation of Āl-Thānī's power. Her wedding allowed for her father's return from exile in Egypt and helped to position Ḥamad—then crown prince of Qatar—as an important personal bridge between the emirate's various distaff tribes and clans.

Although her studies were interrupted for a time by her marriage, Mouza later resumed her education and completed a bachelor's degree in sociology at Qatar University in 1986. As one of the most educated members of the ruling family, she subsequently undertook many public educational and charitable roles. By the time of her husband's succession to the throne in 1995, Mouza was well positioned to serve as Qatar's de facto "first lady."

Unlike the wives of all other Gulf rulers, Mouza has been highly visible. She is often featured on television and in newspapers, and has taken on several leadership functions in the emirate. Crucially, she is often shown alongside her husband. This has undoubtedly helped to modernize the image of marriage in conservative Gulf societies.

Most notably, she is the founder and chairperson of the Qatar Foundation for Education, Science, and Community Development. Conceived as a vehicle to promote research and development in the emirate and bypass failing ministry-controlled universities and schools, the foundation has been tasked with massive multi-billion-dollar projects to set up branch campuses of high-profile international universities in Qatar, along with internationally recognized hospitals and think tanks, including Georgetown University, Cornell Medical School, and Carnegie Mellon, all of which fall under Mouza's direction.

Mouza has also been the driving force behind a number of other initiatives, including Silatech—an institute that focuses on implementing labor nationalization initiatives in Qatar—and the highly popular Al Jazeera Children's Channel. She has also been involved in the Qatar Ladies' Investment Company—a novel venture for the region, which has seen the Qatari National Bank join forces with Qatari women to provide investment training and advice by women to women.

Alongside these domestic commitments, Mouza has served as chairperson or spokesperson for a number of regional and international bodies, including the Arab Democracy Foundation—an appointment that has proved controversial, given the autocratic nature of her husband's government. In 2003 she served as UNESCO's special envoy for basic and higher education, and she has delivered keynote addresses at a number of UN-related conferences and workshops, most recently the UN Alliance of Civilizations Annual Conference in Rio de Janeiro in 2010.

Despite various headline accomplishments and the role model she provides for many young women across the Arab world, Mouza's critics nevertheless contend that she is little more than a figurehead for her husband's administration. In particular, it has been noted that her public role helps the emir to keep some distance from potentially controversial educational projects, while also winning Qatar favorable international headlines regarding women's rights. Criticism has also been directed at the vast spending of the Qatar Foundation and its perceived mismanagement of resources.

BIBLIOGRAPHY

DeLong-Bas, Natana. *Notable Muslims: Muslim Builders of World Civilization and Culture*. Oxford: Oneworld Press, 2006.

Fromherz, Allen. *Qatar: A Modern History*. London: I. B. Tauris, 2011.

Kamrava, Mehran. "Royal Factionalism and Political Liberalization in Qatar." *Middle East Journal* 63, no. 3 (2009): 401–420.

CHRISTOPHER M. DAVIDSON

MUʿĀMALĀH.

Muʿāmalāh (pl., *muʿāmalāt*) addresses the transactional interactions among humans and is contrasted to *ʿibadah*, interactions between God and the believer. Responsibilities of men and women are equal in *ʿibadah*, but there are differences tied to gender in *muʿāmalāh*. Although *muʿāmalāh* encompasses the social and economic aspects of life, Muslim legal sources rarely reflect lived experiences, emphasizing instead the prescriptions. Literature on the economic transactions and morality enforcement in Muslim societies, however, called *ḥisbah* literature, fills this gap by addressing *muʿāmalāt* practically.

The Qurʾān identifies believing women and men as those who "command right and forbid wrong," indicating that both genders are responsible for defending moral order. Academics have contended that women during the Prophet's lifetime actively participated in society alongside men, but their position as political and social agents has since been marginalized. In fact, the second caliph, ʿUmar, appointed a learned female Companion, Shifaʾ bint ʿAbd Allāh, as the *muḥtasib* (market inspector) in Medina. Despite the fact that historical notions of gender segregation have reserved this role for men only, there has been some resistance to such notions so as to allow women to reclaim these roles. For instance, in Nigeria, the *ḥisbah* (morality force) corps included no females between 1999 and 2003, but in July 2005, it recruited nine thousand guards, of whom nine hundred were women.

Muʿāmalāt are understood differently across the Muslim world, because they are time-specific and may be reinterpreted to suit practical changes, explaining why family laws in Muslim countries differ significantly. Marriage and *khulʿ* (divorce initiated by the wife) in early Islam were considered to be transactional activities: one party made the offer or request, and another declined or accepted. In marriage, the husband also offers his wife the dower, or *mahr*, in exchange for her *bud'* (vulva); she returns the *mahr* in the case of *khulʿ*. A woman's choice to marry and/or divorce, then, is also a case of *muʿāmalāt*, because it is a social transaction and because family laws, which include matters of marriage and divorce, are categorized as *muʿāmalāt*.

Muʿāmalāt also include financial and economic activities among Muslims. Under Islamic law, the husband is financially responsible for his wife and children, and women may retain the financial fruits of their labor. Muslim women have nonetheless historically relied on various means to support themselves and their families financially. Their professions and labors have ranged from owning businesses to prostitution. In many cases, although their labor was often limited to the domestic sphere, they have also been involved in agricultural tasks, primarily making cottage-industry products and often traveling to other cities and major markets to sell wool. In Ayyūbid and Mamlūk Egypt, the taxes that prostitutes were required to pay in order to keep their profession were collected by women. They have also held positions in administrative offices that afforded them jurisdiction over, at least, women's sections of the market, a feature of Muslim societies today as well. There is also ample evidence regarding women's real-estate activities, gleaned from documents and inscriptions such as the Geniza documents and *fatwās* (juridical decisions from religious authorities). Such transactions have continued until today. In Mauritania today, in fact, 80 percent of small businesses are controlled by women.

Although Islam grants women the right to inherit and own property, only 4.9 percent of the land in the United Arab Emirates is owned by women and 0.4 percent in Oman. In Tunisia, women who marry outside of their clans are denied rights to inherit land; in Pakistan, customary law prohibits women from inheriting land because of the understanding that the woman is passing her property on to her husband's family from her father's. In Southeast Asian Muslim regions, however, women are often guaranteed the right to own and inherit land and, when they are denied this, the Sharīʿah courts favor women and enforce this right.

[*See also* Divorce; Gender Equality; ʿIbādah; Inheritance; Mahr; Marriage; Women and Islam, *subentry on* Role and Status of Women; *and* Women's Entrepreneurship.]

BIBLIOGRAPHY

Ali, Kecia. *Marriage and Slavery in Early Islam*. Cambridge, Mass.: Harvard University Press, 2010.

Esposito, John L., and Natana J. DeLong-Bas. *Women in Muslim Family Law*. 2nd ed. Syracuse, N.Y.: Syracuse University Press, 2001.

Fullerton, E. "Women Gaining Stature in Business in Muslim Mauritania." *The Washington Post*, August 3, 1998.

Ghabin, Ahmad. *Ḥisba, Arts and Craft in Islam*. Wiesbaden: Harrassowitz, 2009.

Hussain, Jamila. *Islam: Its Law and Society*. Sydney: Federation Press, 2011.

Olaniyi, Rasheed. (2009) "*Hisba* and the *Sharia* Law Enforcement in Metropolitan Kano." IFRA Nigeria. http://www.ifra-nigeria.org/IMG/pdf/Rasheed_Olaniyi_-_Hisba_and_the_Sharia_Law_Enforcement_in_Metropolitan_Kano.pdf.

Sakai, M. "Environment." In *Encyclopedia of Women and Islamic Cultures*, edited by Suad Joseph, vol. 4, pp. 359–364. Boston: Brill, 2007.

Shatzmiller, Maya. *Labour in the Medieval Islamic World*. Leiden, Netherlands: Brill, 1994.

Stowasser, B. "The Women's *Bay'a* in Qur'an and *Sira*." *The Muslim World* 99, no. 1 (2009): 86–101.

Shehnaz Haqqani

Mubarak, Massouma al- (b. 1947). Kuwaiti women's rights activist, political scientist, first female cabinet minister, and former member of parliament. Dr. Massouma al-Mubarak obtained a bachelor's degree in political science from Kuwait University (KU) in 1971. She then earned a master's degree in the same field from the University of North Texas in 1976 and a master's and Ph.D. in international relations from the University of Denver in 1980 and 1983, respectively. While in the United States, she joined the feminist movement, which began her lifelong activism. Upon her return to Kuwait, she became a leading political pundit and women's-rights activist through her columns in various newspapers and membership in the following civil society organizations: the Kuwait University Faculty Association; the Kuwait Graduates Society; the Kuwait Economic Society; the Kuwait Journalists Association; the Women's Cultural and Social Society (WCSS), the oldest women's organization in Kuwait, which has been campaigning for women's rights since the 1960s; the Kuwait Human Rights Society; the Human Rights Committee; and the Women's Issues Committee, an alliance formed by the WCSS in 1995 with fourteen liberal associations that lobbied parliament for ten years for women to obtain political rights. Dr. al-Mubarak also held several faculty positions, including at Kuwait University from 1982 to 2005, with a term as head of the political science faculty from 2001 to 2002, and as a visiting professor at the University of Bahrain from 1990 to 1992 and at the University of Denver from 1986 to 1988. As a professor and feminist, she opposed in 2002 the enforcement of the controversial law banning the mixing of sexes at KU that had been passed in 1996 with the support of Islamist members of parliament. Even with their petition containing nine thousand signatures opposing the segregation, she and KU student activists failed to stop the law's implementation. However, one month after parliament passed the law ensuring women's right to vote and run for political office, Dr. al-Mubarak became the first and only woman to hold a cabinet post with fifteen men. On 20 June 2005 she was sworn in as the Minister of Planning and Administrative Development. According to the political science professor Abdullah Alshayeji, her appointment as a liberal Shīʿī woman served several purposes. First, it addressed one of the longstanding goals of the Kuwaiti women's movement. Second, it appeased the Shīʿī minority in Kuwait, who had lost the only Shīʿī cabinet minister through resignation in January 2005. Third, the government hoped that appointing a veiled woman to the cabinet would prevent criticism by Islamists who had insisted that the new law guaranteeing women's political rights include a statement requiring women politicians to abide by Islamic law. Finally, the government knew that the appointment would raise Kuwait's standing in the international community. In 2007 Dr. al-Mubarak was appointed a second time to the cabinet as Minister of Health. Unfortunately, she resigned her post in 2007 after a hospital fire resulted in the death of two patients, but in 2009 Dr. al-Mubarak succeeded in winning a seat in the National Assembly with three other women to become the first women to serve in the Kuwaiti parliament.

[*See also* Kuwait.]

BIBLIOGRAPHY

Alshayeji, Abdullah. "Beyond Women's Suffrage in Kuwait." Sada (20 July 2005) http://www.carnegieendowment.org/arb/?fa=show&article=21160. (Accessed 27 June 2011).

Mughni, Haya al-. *Women in Kuwait: The Politics of Gender*, 2d ed. London: Saqi Books, 2001.

Tétreault, Mary Ann, Helen Rizzo, and Doron Shultziner "Fashioning the Future: The Women's Movement in Kuwait." In *Mapping Arab Women's Movements*, edited by Nawar Al-Hassan Golley and Pernille Arenfeldt, pp. 254–278. Cairo, Egypt: The American University in Cairo Press, 2012.

Dina El Sharnouby and Helen Mary Rizzo

MUFTĪYAH. A mufti (feminine, *muftīyah*) is a person who issues a *fatwā*, that is, somone who gives an opinion on a point of law, in response to a query posed by a judge (*qāḍī*) or a private inquirer (*mustaftī*).

Most Sunnī and Shīʿī schools of jurisprudence recognize the eligibility of women to serve as muftis and do so not only on issues of particular relevance or interest to women but on any issue a believer might seek advice on.

To date, the literature on female muftis in the history of Islam is little explored, and the scope of women's role in the development of early Islamic jurisprudence has been the subject of very few studies. The crucial primary sources on this subject—that is, biographies, works on Islamic positive law, legal responsa, and court and administrative documents and records—have yet to be fully exploited to arrive at a more accurate and comprehensive picture of women's roles as legal scholars and muftis of their time. Biographical dictionaries point to hundreds of female jurists (*faqīhāt*), who are asserted to have attained a level of competence qualifying them to issue *fatāwā*. In the founding period of Islam, examples of *muftīyahs* include Hujayma bint Ḥuyay al-Awṭābiyya (d. 701) of Damascus, a foremost teacher of Islamic law (including to men), who, according to al-Ziriklī (1997, 8:77) regularly debated with the caliph ʿAbd al-Malik ibn Marwān (r. 685–705). Other examples are the Ḥanafī jurist Khadīja bint Muḥammad al-Jūzjānī (d. 983) and the Shāfiʿī jurist Amīnā bint al-Ḥusayn al-Maḥāmilī (d. 987) who was "particularly expert in the law of inheritance. Al-Barqani [*sic*] records that she used to give *fatwas* in the company of Abu Hurayrah" (Nadwi, 2007, p. 4).

Later figures include the Ḥanbalī jurist Khadīja bint al-Qayyim al-Baghdādiyya (d. 1299) and Amat al-Rahīm bint Muḥammad ibn Aḥmad al-Qasṭalānī (d. 1315). Ibn Rajab al-Ḥanbalī described Fāṭtimah bint ʿAbbās ibn Abī al-Fatḥ al-Baghdadīyah al-Ḥanbalīyah (d. 1333) as "the jurist, scholar, holder of higher *isnads*, the mufti, accurate, of great virtue, knowledgeable in different traditions, the unique one of her time, sought after from every corner" (Nadwi, 2007, p. 4). Other examples are the Shāfiʿī jurist Bāyy Khātūn bint Ibrāhīm al-Ḥalabiyya (d. 1535) and the Ḥanafī jurist Khadīja bint Muḥammad al-Bataylūni (d. 1523).

Although the functions of muftis and *qāḍīs* (judges) often coincided in one person in the Ottoman Empire, no example of a female *qāḍī* is known, despite the overwhelming evidence for the existence of female muftis. The only woman sometimes erroneously referred to as a female *qāḍī*, Thumal (d. 930), was an official of a *maẓālim*, not a religious court, and where her actions were relevant to religious matters, they needed to be confirmed by a (male) religious judge.

In the Shīʿī tradition, at the onset of the greater occultation in 941, the function of the mufti became subsumed in that of the *mujtahid*, a person who has acquired permission to engage in *ijtihād*. Women *mujtahids* are known in modern Iran at least since the seventeenth century, yet these *mujtahids* do not issue *fatāwā*, and no woman has ever attained the status of a *marjaʿ*, the highest source of emulation. Contemporary debates consider whether female *mujtahids* could, in theory, attain the *marjaʿīya*.

Current Initiatives. Despite the strong presence of female muftis in early and medieval Islam, *muftīyas* were virtually absent from the realm of Islamic authority in the nineteenth and twentieth centuries. Since the early 2000s a number of initiatives have emerged that either train women in *iftāʾ* or pave the way toward the appointment of female muftis. Cases in point are the *murshidāt* program in Morocco and the appointment of *vaizehs* in Turkey. Along similar lines, the grand muftis of Egypt, Syria, and Hyderabad, India, have appointed women to their *iftāʿ* councils.

In all cases, it must be underlined, the newly trained and appointed *muftīyahs* have only a limited mandate, in that they may give advice on women's issues only and/or may be overruled by the (male) grand mufti of their country. This limitation of the contemporary *muftīyahs*' authority is contrary to both their predecessors from the seventh to the sixteenth centuries and to the majority opinions in all four Sunnī schools of law according to which the authority of a *muftīyah* is fully equal to that of a mufti.

BIBLIOGRAPHY

Abou El Fadl, Khaled. *Speaking in God's Name: Islamic Law, Authority and Women*. Oxford: Oneworld, 2001.

Bauer, Karen. "Debates on Women's Status as Judges and Witnesses in Post-Formative Islamic Law." *Journal of the American Oriental Society* 130, no. 1 (2010): 8.

Kaḥḥālah, ʻUmar Riḍā. *Aʻlām al-nisāʼ fī ʻālamay al-ʻArab wa-al-Islām*. Beirut: Muʼassasat al-Risālah, 1977.

Nadwi, Mohammad Akram. *Al-Muhaddithāt: The Women Scholars in Islam*. Oxford: Interface Publications, 2007.

Ziriklī, Khayr al-Dīn. *al-Aʻlām: Qāmūs tarājim li-ashʻhar al-rijāl wa-al-nisāʼ min al-ʻArab wa-al-mustaʻribīn wa-al-mustashriqīn*. Beirut: Dār al-ʻIlm lil-Malāyīn, 1986.

MIRJAM KÜNKLER

MUGHAL EMPIRE. Women of the Mughal imperial elites of India played an important role in family and dynastic politics, as political advisers and mentors to their brothers, husbands, and fathers; diplomatic envoys; organizers of family rituals and ceremonies; and, at times, even co-rulers of one of the world's wealthiest empires. Their influence and power within the political structures of empire is considered by many scholars to be the result of the dynasty's Central Asian Turco-Mongol origins. As the descendants of Chinggis Khan (d. 1227) and Timur (Tamerlane, 1336–1405), the Mughal dynasty's allegiance to its inherited culture and values, including the rights and roles of women within the imperial household, remained central to its imperial institutions. As a natural requirement and result of their nomadic origins, the women of the Turco-Mongol cultural tradition led less circumscribed lives than their contemporaries in the Perso-Islamic world. Their public participation in important political and social institutions was not dramatically curtailed when the tribes converted to Islam, from about the thirteenth century. Even in the opening years of the fifteenth century, visitors to the royal court of Timur confirmed that elite women continued to participate in governing councils and act as regents for minor sons, hosted diplomatic festivities, and veiled only lightly.

The Timurids ruled the region of Mā Wārāʼ al-Nahr (Transoxiana) for one hundred years, in the latter decades as disunified and fractious rival princes. They were driven out in the final years of the fifteenth century by the invading Uzbek Mongol confederation. The refugees gathered in Kabul under the leadership of Muḥammad Ẓahīral-D Bābur (1483–1530), a descendant of both Timur and Chinggis Khan and the last independent Timurid prince. Anxious to expand out of his impoverished kingdom, Bābur led his armies south, managing to defeat the Afghan Lodhi sultans of northern India at the battle of Panipat in 1526, a victory that established the Timurids, later known as the Mughals (Persian: Mongol), in India.

Almost immediately an exodus began, as the Timurid elites made their way to the new imperial capital of Agra. Among the refugees was Bābur's daughter, Gulbadan Begum (1523–1603), who would later compose a memoir, the *Humāyūn-nāmah*, in which she described the transition from Kabul to her father's newest conquered territories. In her memoir she described the women who made the journey south: princesses of the Timurid and Chinggisid lineages, as well as tutors and serving maids, who had fled the Uzbek onslaught. Even Bābur's first wife emerged at the royal court in India, although she had divorced him thirty-two years earlier, in 1503. "In short, all the begims and khanims [ladies of the Timurid and Chinggisid royal lineages] went, a total of ninety-six persons, and all were appointed property and a home and furnishings and gifts to their hearts' content" (Gulbadan, 1972, pp. 13–14). As bearers of Central Asian imperial tradition, the refugees would have a profound influence on the development of the new royal court in India, articulating and reinforcing a particularly Timurid view of gender, power, and family.

Strategic Marriages and the Mughal Rajput Alliance. Over the next century, through a combination of military might and pragmatic alliance building with local elites, the Mughals would come to control most of the Indian subcontinent. By the mid-seventeenth century they ruled a population of one hundred million people and had become the second wealthiest empire of the period, after Ming China. At the heart of the imperial success was the effective partnership between the Muslim Mughal emperors and their nobility, a good number of whom were Hindu. Among the most critical foundations of these political alliances was the tradition of inter-dynastic marriage, instigated by Bābur's grandson, the emperor Akbar (1542–1605; r. 1556–1605).

Strategic political marriage had long been an established feature of the Timurid dynasty. Timur had married himself and his sons to women of the politically powerful Chinggisid lineage, taking the title *guregen*, son-in-law, in an ultimately successful effort to lay claim to Chinggisid ruling legitimacy. As carriers of political charisma, even after marriage, Timurid women maintained an identity independent of their husbands; their sons benefitted not only from matrilineal legitimacy, but maternal tribal support and loyalty, a fact that can only have enhanced the authority and power held by elite Timurid women. Furthermore Timurid custom allowed young and/or childless noblewomen to influence dynastic politics; it was often childless women who became the most powerful women of the Timurid period. Neither of Timur's Chinggisid wives, Saray Mulk Khanim or Tokel Khanim, had surviving children, yet foreign visitors at the royal court noted their power and influence. Among Timur's descendants in Mughal India, a woman's lineage and personal connections continued to be more important factors than maternity in establishing her power and influence, and her presence at the royal court enhanced the ruling charisma of the entire dynasty.

The emperor Akbar's marriage in 1562 to the daughter of Raja Bihari Mal of Amber, Hira Kunwar Sahiba Harkha Bhai (1542–1622), who was later given the name Maryam uz-Zamani, and his later marriages (both in 1570) into the Hindu ruling families of Bikaner and Jaisalmer, maintained the family tradition of politically strategic marital alliance. They were unique, however, in that the fathers and brothers of Akbar's Rajput brides were accepted into the upper echelons of the Mughal elite, while neither they nor the emperor's wives were required to convert to Islam. Inter-dynastic marriages remained a constant throughout Mughal history, not only resulting in a royal court culture that would become heavily influenced by Hindu ruling traditions but ensuring that many of the emperors themselves were born of Hindu Rajput mothers. Religion and ethnicity were not considered critical factors in the arrangement of marriages for Mughal men: Bābur and Humāyūn had married Shīʿī Muslims, Afghan, and Persian women, and, from the reign of Akbar and for the next two hundred years,

Rajput women regularly came into the dynasty as brides. It has been pointed out that the assignment of Islamicate royal titles to elite women of the dynasty not only affirmed and reinforced the significance of their role but also acted to minimize their multiethnic, multireligious ancestries, unifying them with the Mughal dynasty.

Matrilineal Political Legitimacy. In the peripatetic courts of the Timurid princes, women were valued companions and counselors. Bābur confirmed the continued dynastic importance of maternal lineage in his memoir, describing the much-admired ruler of Herat, Mīrzā Ḥusayn Bāyqarā (1438–1506), as "noble on both sides—he was a born king," because his mother, as well as father, was descended directly from Timur. Although this may suggest that he did not value his mother's imperial Chinggisid lineage, it was nevertheless his maternal relationship that allowed Bābur to seek refuge with his Mongol uncles and to call on the military assistance of Mongol warriors who owed allegiance to his royal mother.

When Babur's position as ruler of Ferghana was threatened shortly after his father's death, it was his grandmother, Esan Dawlat Khanim (d. 1505), who organized their response. He later praised her "strategy and tactics... she was very intelligent and a good planner. Most affairs were done by her council," he wrote (Bābur, 1995, p. 37). Captured by enemies in battle on four occasions, Esan Dawlat Khanim had already proven her fortitude and strength of character. Taken as spoils of war from her defeated husband, Bābur's grandfather Yūnus Khān (d. 1487), and given in marriage to a liegeman of the victorious Shaykh Jamal Khar, "her silence was taken for consent." On their only night together, however, the Khanim's attendants "seized him, brought him down with the Khanim's help, and killed him with knives, awls and spindles." When Esan Dawlat was brought before her captor she defended the murder, asserting, "I am the wife of Yunus Khan. Does Shaykh Jamal Khar give me to another? Is this allowable in Mohammedan law and the Muslim religion? He deserved killing." Not only did the murder go unpunished; Esan Dawlat Khanim was respectfully returned to her husband, unharmed and "with all honor" (Dughlat, p. 50).

Women, the *Ḥarīm*, and the Mughal "Golden Age." The lifetimes of Bābur and his son and successor Humāyūn (1508–1556; r. 1530–1540, 1555–1556) were marked by near-constant warfare and instability, in which Timurid-Mughal women and children were often caught up in the chaos and destruction of battle and conquest. It was not until the long and successful reign of Humāyūn's son, Jalāl al-Dīn Muḥammad Akbar (1542–1605; r. 1556–1605), who dramatically expanded the territories he had inherited, linking Mughal possessions in Afghanistan to Bengal, and south to the Godavari River in the Deccan, that the royal court stabilized and became increasingly institutionalized. As a statement of dynastic success and permanence, Akbar built a new imperial capital at Sikri, on a site that abutted the *dargah* of the Chishtī Shaykh, Salīm (1478–1572). Within the imperial complex at Fatehpur Sikri, a "large enclosure" was set aside for a *ḥarīm*, or *zanana*, a separate and distinct physical space within which to house the women of the royal family—five thousand of them, if we are to believe Akbar's memorialist Abū al-Faẓl (d. 1602). While this number included the emperor's wives and concubines, it also accounted for his children, unmarried or widowed sisters, aunts, and cousins, family retainers, and other dependents; its protected space also housed much of the dynasty's regalia and jewels, as well as the imperial seals. Abū al-Faẓl made note of the "sufficiently liberal" stipends and salaries of women at the Mughal court, from servants to highborn elites, described the "peculiar, imperial stamp" with which the *zanana* grants were marked, and the "sober and active" women who guarded the *zanana*, the most trustworthy of which guarded the apartments of the emperor himself.

There is no doubt that with stability came a greater degree of formality and ritual at the royal court. It is evident that the walls of the *ḥarīm* remained porous, and Mughal women retained a measure of their traditional political influence and agency. This is best illustrated by the example of the women's *ḥajj*, begun in November 1575. With the support of the emperor, Gulbadan Begum led an expedition of Mughal women on the pilgrimage to Mecca. The group included aunts, nieces, and wives of the emperor and they remained away from the royal court for a total of seven years, its members making the *ḥajj* four times. Upon their return to India the women were shipwrecked off the coast of Aden for a year, rescued by the serendipitous arrival of a Mughal ship. Yet they still insisted on making a pilgrimage to the Chishtī Ṣūfī shrine at Ajmer before returning to Akbar's capital of Fatehpur Sikri in March 1582.

One year before their return, in 1581, Akbar was faced with a rebellion by his half brother, Muḥammad Ḥakīm Mīrzā (1554–1585), who was serving as governor of the Mughal province of Kabul. When the emperor rushed north to deal with the insurgency, he chose to leave his mother, Hamida Banu Begum (1527–1604), in charge at the capital and appointed his half sister Bakht al-Nisa Begum (1550–1608) as the temporary governor of the critical Kabul province.

The most powerful women of the empire were sisters, aunts, and mothers of the emperors, such as Bābur's full sister, Khanzada Begum (1477–1545), who had been captured by the Uzbeks and briefly married to their leader, Muḥammad Shaybānī Khan (1451–1510), before Ismāʿīl (r. 1501–1526), shah of Ṣafavid Iran, defeated the Uzbeks at the battle of Merv in 1510 and sent the Timurid princess to her brother in Agra. Thereafter she was treated with great honor at the Mughal royal court, given the honorific title Sahib Begum (Great Lady) and served as a close adviser to her brother and an ambassador for her nephew, the emperor Humāyūn. It was very common for the elder women of the dynasty to participate in political decisions and intercede for the benefit of supplicants: Gulbadan Begum and Akbar's mother, Hamida Banu Begum, also known as Maryam Makani (d. 1604), regularly intervened in dynastic politics and one of Akbar's wives, Salima Sultan (1539–1611), once threatened the emperor Jahāngīr (r. 1605–1627) to bring the entire *ḥarīm* into the audience hall, should he refuse to go to them and listen to their advice.

Another powerful Mughal woman was the wife of the emperor Jahāngīr, who came to be known as Nūr Jahān (Light of the World; 1577–1645; m. 1611). She was born Mihr al-Nisa, the daughter of Persian immigrants Asmat Begum and Mirza Ghiyas Beg (d. 1622). Her father served at Akbar's court and become an important adviser to Jahāngīr, receiving the title Itimad al-Dawlah (Pillar of the State). When she married the emperor, Nūr Jahān was a thirty-five-year-old widow (of Sher Afghan Quli Khan, d. 1607) and the mother of a single child, her daughter Ladli Begum (b. 1594; she would later marry Jahāngīr's son Shahryar, 1605–1628). Observers of the royal court, particularly those writing in the period of Jahāngīr's successor, Shāh Jahān, described a "Nūr Jahān junta," made up of the queen, her father, and brother, ʿAbd al-Ḥasan Asaf Khan (d. 1641), all of whom exerted enormous influence and power in the court of Jahāngīr, although surely not without his approval.

They had no children together, but Jahāngīr never married again, and Nūr Jahān became his close adviser and supporter. He first offered her the honorific of Nūr Mahal (Light of the Palace), later amending it to Nūr Jahān. She was allowed to participate in council meetings and had drums beat at her advance, a prerogative of the Mughal kings. Nūr Jahān is said to have been a fine poet, writing under the pen name of Makhfi (the Veiled), a pen name shared by many Mughal women. She was a famous hunter as well; her marksmanship delighted her husband, the emperor, who showered her with golden ashrafis on the occasion of her killing four lions with six shots, from inside an elephant howdah.

Trade, Wealth, and Patronage. It had become common among elite women of the royal court to engage in trade; Maryam al-Zamani (1542–1622; m. 1562), the mother of Jahāngīr, owned ships that plied the Indian Ocean and Arabian Sea, carrying spices, opium, and textiles for export and returning with perfumes, brocade, amber, and ivory. The Portuguese capture of her ship, the *Rahimi*, led to the temporary collapse of Portuguese-Mughal relations. Nūr Jahān maintained a number of ships and dealt regularly with the English merchants rather than the Portuguese, with whom the Mughal court was often on bad terms, eventually becoming the official imperial protector of English goods.

Women of the royal household supported imperial and religious institutions with endowments (*awqāf*) and gifts of land (*madad-i maʿāsh*), assigned under their own seals. Like their contemporaries in the Ottoman and Ṣafavid empires, Mughal women used their wealth and influence to change the very face of the imperial landscape. In India their endowments funded the construction of schools and mosques, caravanserais, markets, mansions, and both pleasure and funerary gardens, containing imperial tombs. The first of these was the tomb of Humāyūn, built adjoining the Lodi gardens in Delhi, by the former emperor's widow, Hamida Banu Begim. Construction began in 1569. The architecture of Humāyūn's tomb has been described as an imperial manifesto, its classic dome and *chahar bagh* setting linking it to the Timurid Central Asian past, while its rooftop *chatris* and local red sandstone position it squarely in the Mughal future in Hindustan.

Additionally, Mughal women funded the regular charitable distribution of clothing and money—in particular contributing to the trousseaus of young women of limited means. Nūr Jahān is said to have supplied over five hundred girls with the money to marry respectably, while Jahāngīr allowed his father's foster sister, Hajji Koka, to recommend to him such deserving recipients of charity as the wives and daughters of deceased religious scholars. Shāh Jahān continued the tradition, allowing the female head of the *ḥarīm* bureaucracy, the *ṣadr-i anas*, to recommend deserving women.

Nūr Jahān's was clearly a family of powerful women—her brother's daughter, Arjumand Banu Begim (1592–1631), would marry Jahāngīr's son and successor, Shāh Jahān (1592–1666; r. 1628–1659). She bore all of his children, receiving the title Mumtaz Mahal, the Pearl of the Palace. On her death Shāh Jahān constructed the Taj Mahal to be their shared sepulcher. Management of the imperial household passed to her daughter Jahānārā (1613–1683), who was called by her father Sahibat al-Zamani (the Mistress of Her Age) or Padshah Begum (Lady King), and more generally as Begum Sahib (Great Lady). She controlled vast personal financial resources, part of which she had accumulated through her own trade relationship with Dutch merchants, but most of which, totaling cash and goods valued at over ten million rupees, had been left to her by her mother. She invested some of her wealth into construction projects in her father's new capital, Shahjahanabad. There she built a private mansion, a vast central marketplace of over fifteen hundred shops (the famed Chandni Chowk of Delhi), and a caravansary, the largest building in Shahjahanabad, apart from her father's enormous Jama Masjid, the Friday mosque.

Jahānārā was a recognized scholar who, at the instigation of her brother Dārā Shukūh (1615–1659), was indoctrinated into the Qādirīyah order of Ṣūfīs and composed the *Risālah-i Ṣaḥibīyah* as an exploration of her Ṣūfī leanings. She also authored a biography of the Ṣūfī Shaykh Muʿīnuddīn Chishtī, the *Mu'nis al-arwāḥ*, and a brief biography of the Ṣūfī Mullā Shāh, the *Ṣāḥibīyah*, with a dozen verses of her own poetry included in the volume. Under her beneficent patronage, a series of works on Sufism was produced that included commentaries on Rūmī's *Mathnavī*. A court poet of seventeenth-century Shahjahanabad, Mīr Muḥammad ʿAlī Māhir, composed his own *mathnavī* in praise of Jahānārā's patronage and generosity. She was buried, at her own request, having written her own epitaph, in an unmarked white marble sepulcher in the Delhi courtyard of the shrine of the famed Chishtī Ṣūfī shaykh Niẓam al-Dīn Awliyā', who had some years before been referred to by her brother Dārā Shukūh as "the patron saint of the House of Akbar."

Many Mughal women were noted scholars. Gulbadan Begum famously wrote a memoir, the *Humāyūn-nāma*, at the behest of her nephew Akbar, and is known to have owned a large and valuable library. The eldest daughter of the emperor Awrangzīb (1618–1707; r. 1659–1707), Zīb al-Nisā' Begum (1637–1702), was so accomplished a poet and scholar that her father sent for the famous Persian poet Mullā Muḥammad Saʿid Ashraf Māzandarāni (d. 1704) to mentor and tutor her and rewarded her with thirty thousand gold pieces for committing the entire Qur'ān to memory. She studied astronomy and mathematics, was a renowned calligrapher, arranged for the translation of many religious classics, and patronized many scholars and poets at her court.

Legacy and Continuity. The lives of generations of Timurid-Mughal women confirm a remarkable degree of cultural continuity. Benefiting from nomadic tribal tradition and as bearers of political charisma, elite Timurid women of Central Asia had led less circumscribed lives than many of their contemporaries in the Islamic world. Having fled the Uzbek advance and migrated into South Asia, the Timurid refugees remained loyal to their dynastic and ruling traditions. Even as their descendants found wealth and power in India, the development of a formal *zanana* did not entirely restrain or hamper the public activities of Mughal women, who continued to cross out of that space and into the public forum. Over the centuries of their rule in India, Mughal women retained social and political influence, as authors and artists, hunters, scholars, and travelers, merchants, and diplomats, counselors, and advisers to kings—active partners in the affairs of their dynasty.

Bibliography

Abū al-Fazl. *Ain-i Akbari*. Edited and translated by H. Blochmann. New Delhi: Munshiram Manoharlal, 1977.

Abū al-Fazl. *Akbarnama*. Edited and translated by H. Beveridge. 3 vols. Delhi: Manmohan Satish Kumar, 1972.

Bābur. *Baburnama*. Chaghatay Turkish text with Abdul-Rahim Khankhanan's Persian text; Turkish transcription, Persian edited and English translation by Wheeler M. Thackston. 3 vols. Cambridge, Mass.: Harvard University Press, 1993.

Bābur. *Bāburnāmah vaqāyi': Critical Edition Based on Four Chaghatay Texts*. Edited by Eiji Mano. Text in Chaghatai; introductory material in Japanese and English. 4 vols. Kyoto, Japan: Shukadu, 1995.

Balabanlilar, Lisa. "Begims of the Mystic Feast." *The Journal of Asian Studies* 69, no. 1 (February 2010): 123–147.

Balabanlilar, Lisa. *Imperial Identity in the Mughal Empire: Memory and Dynastic Politics in Early Modern South and Central Asia*. London and New York: I. B. Tauris, 2012.

Blake, Stephen. "Contributors to the Urban Landscape: Women Builders in Safavid Isfahan and Mughal Shahjahanabad." In *Women in the Medieval Islamic*

World, edited by Gavin R. G. Hambly, pp. 407–428. New York: St. Martin's Press, 1998.

Dale, Stephen Frederic. *The Garden of Eight Paradises.* Leiden, Netherlands, and New York: Brill, 2004.

Dale, Stephen Frederic. "The Legacy of the Timurids: The Timurid Renaissance." *Journal of the Royal Asiatic Society* 3d series, 8, no. 7 (1998): 43–58.

Gonzales de Clavijo, Ruy. *Embassy to Tamerlane, 1403–1406.* Translated by Guy Le Strange. New York: Harper & Brothers, 1928.

Gulbadan Begum. *The History of Humāyūn (Humāyūn-nāma).* Translated and edited by Annette S. Beveridge. Delhi: Idarah-i Adabiyāt-i Delli, 1972.

Hambly, Gavin R. G. "Armed Women Retainers in the Zenanas of Indo-Muslim Rulers: The Case of Bibi Fatima." In *Women in the Islamic World*, edited by Gavin R. G. Hambly, pp. 429–467. New York: St. Martin's Press, 1998.

Hambly, Gavin R. G. *Women in the Medieval Islamic World.* New York: St. Martin's Press, 1998.

Jahāngīr. *Jahāngīrnāma Tūzuk-i Jahāngīrī.* Tehran: Bunyad-i Farhang-i Iran, 1980.

Jahāngīr. *The Jahangirnama: Memoirs of Jahangir, Emperor of India.* Edited and translated by Wheeler M. Thackston. New York: Oxford University Press, 1999.

Kozlowski, Gregory C. "Private Lives and Public Piety: Women and the Practice of Islam in Mughal India." In *Women in the Islamic World*, edited by Gavin R. G. Hambly, pp. 469–488. New York: St. Martin's Press 1998.

Lal, Ruby. *Domesticity and Power in the Early Mughal World.* Cambridge, U.K., and New York: Cambridge University Press, 2005.

Manz, Beatrice. "Women in Timurid Dynastic Politics." In *Women in Iran from the Rise of Islam to 1800*, edited by Guity Nashat and Lois Beck, pp. 121–139. Urbana: University of Illinois Press, 2003.

Misra, Rehka. *Women in Mughal India, 1526–1748.* New Delhi: Munshiram Manoharlal, 1967.

Nashat, Guity, and Lois Beck, eds. *Women in Iran from the Rise of Islam to 1800.* Urbana: University of Illinois Press, 2003.

Soucek, Priscilla. "Timurid Women: A Cultural Perspective." In *Women in the Medieval Islamic World*, edited by Gavin R. G. Hambly, pp. 199–226. New York: St. Martin's Press, 1998.

Szuppe, Maria. "Women in Sixteenth Century Safavid Iran." In *Women in Iran from the Rise of Islam to 1800*, edited by Guity Nashat and Lois Beck, pp. 140–169. Urbana: University of Illinois Press, 2003.

Tirmizi, S. A. I. *Edicts from the Mughal Harem.* Delhi: Idarah-i Adabiyāt-i Delli, 1979.

LISA BALABANLILAR

MUHĀJIRŪN. The root word *hajara* means to emigrate, to separate, to desert, to leave or give up. *Hijrah* means departure, emigration, flight. *Muhājir* refers to the emigrant (pl. *al-muhājirūn*, also *al-muhajirin*). *Muhājirūn* are defined in a Medinan *sūrah* as "emigrants who have been driven out of their homes and their possessions, those who seek God's favor and good pleasure and help God and His Messenger" (*al-Hashr* 59:8). The Qurʾānic use of this terminology is not confined to this physical aspect of diaspora as a result of persecution, but it is in this sense that it is used for the first *hijrah* made by a group of twelve believing men and four women from Mecca to Habshah in 614-615 CE.

The Qurʾān also uses it in a sociological sense of returning, taking refuge in, and assuming fully the attitude of obedience to God: "Then did Lot believe him and Abraham said: I am emigrating unto my Lord (*inni muhājirūn ilā Rabbi*) (*al-ʿAnkabut* 29:26). The word *muhājir* (emigrant) is used here for a person who moves consciously toward the path of God. The Qurʾān also uses its feminine form *(muhājirat)* in *al-Mumtahinah* 60:10. However, the most common usage is *hajaru*, "As for those who migrated in the way of God" (*al-Hajj*22:58) or those who sacrifice their homes and belongings and struggle in the way of God, for example, *al-Baqarah* 2:218; *al-ʿImran* 3:195; *al-Anfal* 8:73; *al-Tawbah* 9:20; and *al-Nahl*16:41, 100.

In these verses, emigrants are defined as persons who were persecuted but did not surrender. On the contrary, they resolve to remove persecution, exploitation, injustice, and violence from society through systematic effort and struggle (*jihad*) against tyranny. In its various forms, the word is used in thirty-one places in the Qur'ān.

It is also used in the *aḥādīth* (sing. *ḥadīth*, the Prophet's statement, action, or endorsement). The famous (*mashhūr*) ḥadīth of 'Umar ibn al Khattāb on intention (*nīyya*) as the basis of every action states: "I heard God's Apostle saying, 'The reward of deeds is according to the intentions, and every person will get reward according to what he had intended, so whosoever emigrated for worldly benefits or for a woman to marry, his emigration was for what he emigrated.'" Here physical *hijrah* is gelled together with transition from one state of mind to another.

Historically, *muhājirūn* refers to those who migrated from Mecca to Medina in general, or who emigrated first to Ethiopia and from Ethiopia then came to Medina. When persecution of believers crossed all limits of tolerance in Mecca, the Prophet allowed the oppressed Muslims to migrate to Ethiopia, which was ruled by Najashi, a Christian king. The first group of *muhājirūn*, in 614-615 CE consisted of sixteen persons, including four *muhājirāt*. These were: Ruqīyah bint Muḥammad, wife of 'Uthmān bin 'Affān; Sahlah bint Suhayl, wife of Abū Ḥudhayfah bin 'Utbah; Umm Salamah, wife of Abū Salamah; and Laylah bint Abi Hashmah wife of 'Amīr bin Rabī'ah. The second group of emigrants to Ethiopia consisted of eighty-three men and nineteen women led by Ja'far bin Abī Ṭālib.

Umm Ḥabība Ramlah bint Abī Sufyān was among the later group of emigrants. She went through a traumatic period when her husband changed his faith to Christianity. After she lost her husband, in Ethiopia, the Prophet took her in marriage by proxy. Later on, most of those *muhājirūn* and *muhājirāt* who moved to secure places to save their faiths headed toward Medina (the town of the Prophet). Those who directly migrated from Mecca also faced hardships. For example, when Abū Salamah tried to leave Mecca for Medina, the tribe of his wife snatched his wife from him and his own tribe took away his children. He had to migrate alone, and only after one year were his wife and children allowed to emigrate and join him.

In its historic context, *hijrah* stands for the Prophet's emigration to Medina from Mecca on 24 September 622, which makes him a *muhājir*. The *muhājirūn* constituted one segment alongside the other important segment of the community (*ummah*), namely, the *ansār* or helpers (*al-Saff* 61:13). The *ansār* and the *muhājirūn* together constituted the community of believers or *mu'minūn* in Medina—a community not based on ethnicity, color, race, language, or geographical territory. The cohesive community of believers forged together in Medina offered the image of an ideal society to the later generations. This was taken as an example of brotherhood (*ukhuwwah*) between the *muhājirūn* and the *ansār*. Nevertheless, the sacrifices made by the muhājirūn were recognized by the state. Those who migrated before the conquest of Mecca enjoyed greater social respect. 'Umar, the second caliph, particularly, gave weight to sacrifices made by the *muhājirūn* when he fixed their stipends.

Initially used for those who, because of their persecution, made *hijrah* from their native land, the term is also applicable to Muslims in diaspora in the post-world-war period. A significant number of Muslims moved to Europe and North America to escape political victimization in their homelands, seek better economic prospects, acquire higher education, and avail themselves of better professional opportunities available in the West. It is estimated that over six million Muslim *muhājirūn* live in North America and another seven million in Europe. Many of these *muhājirūn* and *muhājirāt* have now their second and third generation living with them in the West. They encounter numerous personal, social, political and religious challenges. Their second and third generation, generally, do not see themselves as *muhājir*. However, born and raised in the West they go through an intellectual process of *hijrah* in an existential sense. Their search for identity persuades them to critically examine their relationship with the culture and values of country of their birth and the global Muslim *ummah*. In the North American context, other religious groups have faced similar challenges. As the second largest religious community in the United States and Canada, the Muslim community faces the challenge of developing a clear position on this and similar socio-economic and political issues.

The spread of Islam in South and South East Asia took place through *hijrah* of traders and professionals yet none of the Indonesian, Malay, or Pakistanis regard themselves as *muhājir*. Even a political group, founded on self-claimed *muhājir* identity in Pakistan, namely *muttaḥida muhājir* movement (*muhājir* alliance) evolved into *muttaḥida qawmī* movement (national alliance). In the North American and European context, those who at one time regarded themselves as *muhājir*, while proud of maintaining their cultural and religious identity, are going through a process of integration. Many of these Muslim women retain their practice of wearing head scarves, use of *ʿabāyah* (long shirt), or kaftans. Some cover part of their face as part of their religious identity.

Those who choose to accept Islam also make a *hijrah* from their previous life style to a conscious Islamic living. In this sense, *hijrah* is an on-going experience encountered by women and others who by choice enter into Islam.

[*See also* Minorities, *subentry on* Muslim Minorities in Non-Muslim Countries.]

BIBLIOGRAPHY

Abedin, Syed Z., and Z. Sardar, eds. *Muslim Minorities in the West*. London: Grey Seal, 1995.

Bashir, Zakaria. *Hijra, Story and Significance*. Leicester, U.K.: The Islamic Foundation, 1983.

Ba-Yunus, Ilyas, and Kassim Kosne. *Muslims in the United States*. Westport, Conn.: Greenwood, 2006.

Faruqi, Isma'il R. al- *The Hijrah: The Necessity of Its Iqamat or Vergegenwartigung*. Kuala Lumpur: ABIM, 1983.

Haddad, Yvonne. *Becoming American?: The Forging of Arab and Muslim Identity in Pluralist America*. Waco, Tex.: Baylor University Press, 2011.

Masud, Muhammad Khalid. "The Obligation to Migrate: The Doctrine of Hijra in Islamic Law." In *Muslim Travellers: Pilgrimage, Migration and the Religious Imagination*, edited by Dale F. Eickelman and James Piscatori, pp. 29–49. Berkeley, 1990.

Nu'mani, Shibli. *Sirah an Nabi, Nadwatul Ulama*. Lucknow, Vol. 1, 1946 (1918).

Ramadan, Tariq. *Muslims in France: The Way towards Coexistence*. Leicester, U.K.: The Islamic Foundation, 1999.

ANIS AHMAD

MUJTAHIDAH. A *mujtahidah* (pl. *mujtahidāt*) is a female jurist who has had extensive religious training and who employs *ijtihād* (independent reasoning) in her rulings. The terms *mujtahidah* and *mujtahid* are used mainly in Shīʿī *madhahib* (schools of law). Traditionally a *mujtahidah* is recognized as such by her peers on the basis of a major work of jurisprudence. This recognition usually takes the form of *ijazah* (permission) to engage in *ijtihād* and is usually appended to a book or other writing, certifying that the one who is granted the permission has studied the materials thoroughly, to the teacher's satisfaction, and is fit to interpret the sources.

There are many forms of female religious authority. For instance, historically women have been transmitters of *ḥadīth* (sayings of the Prophet). However, the number of women to attain the level of *mujtahidah* is unknown. At Jamiʿat al-Zahra, a women's *hawza* (Shīʿī seminary) in Iran, which is among the largest and most extensive institutions of religious training for women in the world, only twenty-seven women in 2009 studied the courses of *khārij-i fiqh* (highest level jurisprudence) and *uṣūl-i fiqh* (principles of jurisprudence) that could enable them to become *mujtahidah* in the more modern sense of the word. In the same year, Jamiʿat al-Zahra, according to its own reporting, had an estimated 12,000 students. Very few *mujtahidāt* have been the subjects of academic study. Two prominent exceptions are Noṣrat Amīn and Zohreh Ṣefātī. Amīn is revered as a religious authority by Iranian clerical circles and the Islamic Republic. Ṣefāti, although not as acclaimed as Amīn, has been given the honorific title of *ayatollah* (highest rank of Shīʿī clerics).

Hajiye Khanoom Noṣrat Amīn Beygom (1886–1983), known popularly as Noṣrat Amīn, was one of the most venerated *mujtahidāt* of the twentieth century. Born in Isfahan, Iran, Amīn began her religious education at an early age in a *maktab khānah* (Qurʾānic school). After marrying at the age of fifteen, Amīn continued her studies in the Islamic sciences of *fiqh* (jurisprudence), *uṣūl* (principles of jurisprudence), *ḥikmat* (metaphysics), and *falsafa* (philosophy), *tafsīr* (Qurʾānic exegesis), *ḥikmat* (traditions from the Prophet), *manṭiq* (logic), and *irfān* (mysticism). Her teachers included Ayatollah Mīr Sayyid ʿAlī Najafābādī (1986-1943) (Banooye Elm va Taghva ["The Lady of Knowledge and Piety"]). Amīn was also taught by ayatollahs Āqā Sayyid Abū al-Qāsim Dihkurdī (d. 1935) and Mīrzā ʿAlī Āqā Shīrāzī (d. 1956) amongt others. At the age of forty, Amīn received *ijazahs* of *ijtihād* from ayatollahs al-uʿẓmā Abdolkarim Haʾeri Yazdi (d. 1937) the founder of Ḥawza ʿIlmīya of Qom (The Centre of Shīʿī Religious Learning of Qom), Muḥammad Kāẓim Shīrāzī (d. 1948), Ibrāhīm Ḥusaynī Shīrāzī Iṣṭahbānātī (d. 1955/59), Ayatollah Mīr Sayyid ʿAlī Najafābādī, and Ayatollah Murtada Mazaheri Najafi Isfahani (known as Masjid Shāhī Iṣfahānī) (1870–1943). She also received an *ijazah* of *ravayat* (given to capable scholars who are deemed apt at transmitting a *ḥadīth* and, in the Shīʿī world, the *akhbār* (authoritative traditions narrated by the Shīʿī iimams), so as to ensure a reliable chain of transmission) from Ayatollah Mohammad Reza Najafi-Isfahani. These *ijazahs* demonstrate Amīn's recognition as a religious authority amongst her peers as a *mujtahidah*.

Noṣrat Amīn herself granted permissions of *ijtihād* and *ravayat* to both male and female *ʿulamāʾ* (religious scholars), including Ayatollah *al-ʿuẓmā* Sayyid Shahāb al-Dīn Ḥusaynī Marʿashī Najafī (1897–1990) and her student Zinat as-Sadat Homayouni (b. 1917). Amīn's books include *Sayr va Sulūk dar Ravish-i Awliȳ'-i Allāh* ("The Path of Religious Authorities and the Path toward God"), *Akhlagh va Rahi Saʿadat: Iqtibas va tarjameh az Taharat al-Iraqi Ibn Maskouyeh/ Miskawayh* ("Ethics and the Path to Happiness: Excerpting and Translating of 'Refinement of Characters' by Miskawayh"), and *Ravesh Khoshbakhti va Tausiya bi Khaharani Imani* ("The Path to Happiness and Advice to Faithful Sisters"). Amīn's principles of *tafsīr* (Qurʾānic interpretation), *Makhzan Al-Erfan dar Ulumi Qurʾān* ("The Treasure of Knowledge in the Interpretation of the Qurʾān"), was published in 1956 and was followed by fourteen additional volumes in the next fifteen years. In 1965, Amīn opened a secondary school for girls in Isfahan called Dabirestan-e Dokhtaraneh-e Amīn (Amīn's Girl's Secondary School). In the same year she also founded a pioneering introductory Islamic studies seminary exclusively for women, called Maktab-i Fatimah.

Zohreh Ṣefātī was born in the early 1950s in the city of Abadan in Iran. Like Amīn, Ṣefāti also attended a local *maktab khānah* for primary religious education. She was homeschooled for the duration of her secondary studies. Ṣefāti began her formal Islamic religious training at Abadan's

Markaz-i Ulum-i Islami (Women's Center for the Study of Islamic Sciences) in 1966. In 1970, she moved to attend the Qom Theological Seminary (Badiī). At the same time, Ṣefāti began holding lessons in her house. The number of students she attracted grew and, in 1974, she established Maktab-i Tawḥīd, the equivalent to Amīn's Maktab-i Fatimah. Following the 1979 Islamic revolution, Ayatollah Khomeini transformed Maktab-i Tawḥīd into Jami'at al-Zahra. Ṣefāti herself has taught *kharij-i fiqh* at Jami'at al-Zahra. –Ṣefāti, like Amīn, studied under high-ranking male clerics, namely, Ayatollah Meshkini (1922–2007), Ayatollah Shahidi, and Ayatollah Haqi. She received permissions of *ravāyat* from Ayatollahs Agha Asli Ali Yari Gharani Tabrizi and Mohammad Fazel Lankarani (1931–2007). According to Ṣefāti Ayatollah Lotfollah Safi Golpayegani (1919–2010) also granted her *ijazahs* of *ijtihād* and *ravāyat*. However, Ṣefāti has not attained authority comparable to that of Noṣrat Amīn. The latter was a scholar independent from political institutions. Ṣefāti has published less relative to Amīn. Her books include *Pajuheshi Fiqhi Piramun-e Senne Taklif* ("Jurisprudential Research Regarding the Age of Maturity"), *Noavarayhaye Fiqhi dar Ahkam-e Banovan* (New Jurisprudential Rulings on Women), and *Ziyarat dar Partoye Velayat (Sharhi bar Ziyarat-e Ashoura)* ("Pilgrimage under the Rays of Guardianship," a description of pilgrimage to Karbala). Ṣefāti is a member of the Islamic Republic's Women's Socio-Cultural Council.

BIBLIOGRAPHY

Abdus, Hamid. "Bānū Amīn, Ālgū-i Zan Musalmān (Lady Amīn, the Model of a Muslim Woman)." The Islamic Revolution Documentation Centre (Markaz-i Asnad-i Inghilāb-e Islamī). (June 13, 2007): http://www.aftabir.com/articles/view/religion/religion/c7c1182160677p1.php/

Abtahi, Seyed Morteza. "Be Monasebat-e Salgarde dar Gozasht-e Banoo Mujtahid-e Amin (On the Occasion of Annual Commemoration of Mutjahid Banoo Amin)." *Etemaad Meli* 926 (June 17, 2009):10, http://www.magiran.com/ppdf/nppdf/5061/p9780199764464.pdf.

Badiī, Muhammad. "Guftigu ba Faqih Pajuhandeh Bānū Zuhrah Ṣifātī (Interview with the Researcher Jurist, Lady Zuhrah Sifātī)." *Keyhan Farhangī* 199 (April 2003): http://www.noormags.com/view/fa/articlepage/19531?sta=%u0632%u0647%u0631%u0647+%u0635%u0641%u0627%u062a%u06cc.

"Banooye Elm va Taghva (The Lady of Knowledge and Piety)." *Payam-e Zan* 5 (July-August 1992): 34, http://www.hawzah.net/fa/magazine/magart/3992/4584/33228. http://www.hawzah.net/Hawzah/Magazines/MagArt.aspx?id=33228.

Fazaeli, Roja, and Mirjam Künkler. "Training Female 'Ulamā in Jama'at al-Zahra—New Opportunities for Old Role Models?" In *Knowledge and Authority within the Hawza*, edited by Robert Gleave, forthcoming.

Künkler, Mirjam, and Roja Fazaeli. "Women, Leadership and Mosques: Changes in Contemporary Islamic Authority." In *Women, Leadership and Mosques: Changes in Contemporary Islamic Identity*, edited by Masooda Bano, pp. 127–161. Leiden, Netherlands: Brill, 2011.

Makdisi, George. *The Rise of Colleges: Institutions of Learning in Islam and the West*, Edinburgh: Edinburgh University Press, 1981.

Nadwi, Muhammad Akram. *Al-Muhaddithat: The Women Scholars in Islam*. Oxford: Interface Publications, 2007.

Najafi, Hassan. "Ketab Shenasi Banoo Amin," *Etemaad Meli*, 946 (2009), http://www.magiran.com/npview.asp?ID=1882886.

Saiedzadeh, Mohsen. (written under the name of his wife Mina Yadegar Azadi). "Ejtehad va marjaiat Zanan (Ijtihādand Marjai'at of women)." *Zanan* 8 (1992).

Sakurai, Keiko. "Women's Empowerment and Iranian-Style Seminaries in Iran and Pakistan." In *The Moral Economy of the Madrasa: Islam and education today*, edited by Keiko Sakurai and Fariba Adelkhah, pp. 32–59. New York: Routledge, 2011.

Todeh Zare, Rasool. "Bānū Amīn: Her Life, On the Occasion of the Anniversary of the Death of Mujtahidah of the World of Islam, Haji-ye Lady Amīn Known as Bānū-i Īrānī." *Paygah-i itila risani-i Hawzah-yi Ilmīyah-yi Khaharān* (1999): http://www.

hawzah.net/hawzah/Magazines/MagArt.aspx?MagazineNumberID=4015&id=22611.
Va'īz-i Khiyabanī Tabrizī, and Haji Mulla 'Ali. *Ta'rīkh-i 'ulamā'-i mu'asirin*. Tabriz, Iran: Ketab Foroshi Elslami-e, 2003 (first published in 1947).

ROJA FAZAELI

MURSHIDAH. *Murshidah*, (pl., *murshidāt*), Arabic "(female) guide." This term nowadays primarily refers to women who fulfill much the same role as imams, except for leading Friday prayers. It came into widespread use in Morocco with the graduation of the first cohort of fifty *murshidāt* in May 2006. Their appointment occurred two years after Morocco's large-scale personal-status-code reform (Mudawwana) in 2004. King Muḥammad VI justified appointing women to roles of religious leadership as in keeping with "Morocco's moderate Islam." Appointing *murshidāt* can be seen as a symbol of modernity, something new in appearance if not substance. *Murshidāt* serve the political project of the palace rather than being vested with genuine religious authority. In this, they are no different from imams who serve under the direction of the Ministry of Islamic Affairs. Individual imams preach or carry out their duties as clergy in accordance with official guidelines. Imams in Morocco are civil servants, appointed by the ministry and in the service of the state.

Selection for the training program is competitive. Accepted applicants enroll alongside their male counterparts, for forty-five weeks of coursework in more than thirty subject areas, including religion, communications, history, geography, law, computer science, and psychology. Upon graduation, *murshidāt* are assigned to serve in one of Morocco's more than forty thousand official mosques. *Murshidāt* are most commonly assigned to the impoverished and marginalized urban areas. These are the same volatile parts of the country from which the terrorists who were involved in the deadly 2003 attacks in Casablanca hailed. Female religious leaders are primarily charged with providing counsel to women on issues such as family planning, domestic abuse, child rearing, and women's legal rights, in addition to tending to their spiritual needs. Assigning female religious leaders to otherwise underserved population groups can be seen as part of a larger plan to stem the tide of radical Islamists who recruit heavily among the poor and unemployed. The rationale is that potential terrorists have mothers, sisters, and wives who can exert influence on their male relatives if they themselves are properly guided. *Murshidāt*—in their function as civil servants—are also the monarch's eyes and ears in those parts of the country where the *Makhzan* (a term that refers to the governing elite connected to the royal palace) has no hold, areas where unemployment, poverty, crime, and lawlessness are rampant and illiteracy is high. According to Ahmed Taoufiq (b. 1943), appointed in 2002 as Minister of Habs and Islamic Affairs, the appointment of female religious leaders is intended to inspire women to become more involved in religious and public matters. This is an official call for moderate Muslim women to become more engaged in religious life beyond their home and not leave religious discourse mostly to Islamists.

In other parts of the Arab world, the term *murshidāt* is used to refer to women in the healing profession. In Yemen, female primary healthcare workers are called *murshidāt*.

BIBLIOGRAPHY

Gray, Doris H. *Beyond Feminism and Islamism: Gender and Equality in North Africa*. London: I. B. Tauris, 2012.

DORIS GRAY

MUSAWAH. Musawah (from Arabic musāwāh, "equality") is the global movement for equality and justice in the Muslim family. Initiated by Sisters in Islam, it was launched in Kuala Lumpur in February 2009, bringing together some 250 activists and scholars from 47 countries working on issues of equality and justice for women living in Muslim contexts.

What Musawah hopes to bring to the larger women's and human rights movement is:

- An assertion that Islam can be a source of empowerment, not one of oppression and discrimination;
- An effort to open new horizons for rethinking the relationship between human rights, equality and justice, and Islam;
- An opening of a new constructive dialogue in which religion is no longer an obstacle to equality for women but a source for liberation;
- A collective strength of conviction and courage to stop governments, patriarchal authorities, and ideological non-state actors from the convenient use of religion and the word of God to silence women's demands for equality; and
- A space where activists, scholars, and decision makers, working within the human-rights or Islamic framework, or both, can interact and mutually strengthen a common pursuit of equality and justice for Muslim women.

Musawah is responding to the urgent need expressed by many Muslim women activists to better understand Islam in order to engage in public discourse and to reshape the meaning and place of religion within their societies. To remain silent, they believe, is to cede the space and the discourse on Islam to those who believe that men and women are not equal, that Muslims must live in an Islamic state and be governed by a monolithic Islamic law, and that there can only be one truth and one interpretation of Islam that must be codified into law and any digression from it punished.

Increasingly in the early twenty-first century, Muslim women are claiming for themselves the right to shape the interpretations, norms, and laws that affect their lives. They are asserting that there cannot be justice in Islam without equality between men and women.

It is in this context that Musawah emerged to bring together activists and scholars to build a knowledge-based global movement. It continues to develop feminist knowledge in Islam. With knowledge comes the authority and courage to speak with conviction in the public space to promote and demand equality and justice in Islam and an end to the use of religion to justify discrimination against women.

Since its launch, Musawah has developed three key areas of work in knowledge-building, international advocacy, and outreach:

- To build and share knowledge that supports equality and justice in the Muslim family using a holistic approach that combines Islamic principles, international human-rights standards, national laws and constitutional guarantees of equality and non-discrimination, and the lived realities of women and men.
- To support of human-rights mechanisms, as well as groups and individuals working with these processes, at the international, regional, and national levels, to advance equality and justice in the Muslim family.
- To build a critical mass of organizations, groups, and individuals that support, use, and promote the Musawah Framework for Action and are empowered to engage in a constructive and informed public discourse on Islam and women's rights.

Musawah's work breaks the constructed dichotomies of religion versus secularism, Islam versus human rights, and religious feminists versus secular feminists. Its report *CEDAW and Muslim Family Laws: In Search of Common Ground* critiques the use of Islam and Shariʿah by key Organisation of Islamic Cooperation (OIC) governments to justify their reservations and resistance to demands for compliance with their international human-rights obligations. It offers the holistic approach of the Musawah Framework for Action as a means to engage in a more constructive dialogue toward the possibility and necessity for reform of discriminatory laws and practices adopted in the name of Islam. The CEDAW Committee and NGOs working on their shadow reports use the Musawah report as an important resource for their engagement with governments.

Musawah's Knowledge Building Initiative on *qiwamah* and *wilāyah*, commonly understood as mandating male authority over women in Islam, seeks to address the disconnect between the religious and legal notions of these twin concepts on the one hand, and the needs, aspirations, and lived experiences of real women and men on the other, in order to build a new Muslim legal framework on marriage as a partnership of equals. Activists and researchers from twelve countries are now engaged in a Global Life Stories project to document the lived realities of women as they confront and negotiate the myth of the male as provider and protector.

Musawah capacity-building training sessions for women leaders, "Understanding Islam from a Rights Perspective," are led by progressive Islamic scholars of the Qurʾān, *fiqh*, and *ḥadīth* and are much in demand. Participants find the training life-transforming, as they are exposed to concepts and tools that open the possibilities for reform and for equality and justice in their understanding of Islam. It gives participants the knowledge and courage to speak publicly on Islam and women's rights and to challenge the use of religion to justify discrimination against women. Musawah publications are today used by academics and activists in courses on law, gender, and social change, and in training, research, and advocacy for law reform.

BIBLIOGRAPHY

For general information, go to http://www.musawah.org and http://www.sistersinislam.org. For the Musawah Knowledge Building Initiative on *qiwamah* and *wilāyah*, see http://www.opendemocracy.net/5050/ziba-mir-hosseini-zainah-anwar/decoding-"dna-of-patriarchy"-in-muslim-family-laws.

CEDAW and Muslim Family Laws: In Search of Common Ground is available at http://www.musawah.org/cedaw-and-muslim-family-laws-search-common-ground, along with an Arabic translation.

Musawah Vision, a monthly newsletter, offers Muslim-family-law news and updates from the Musawah secretariat; http://www.musawah.org/resources/newsletters. Arabic and French translations are also available. Musawah's *Framework of Action*, translated into five languages, is at http://www.musawah.org/about-musawah/framework-action.

Wanted: Equality and Justice in the Muslim Family, which includes writings by scholars and activists on the possibility and necessity of equality and justice in Islam, http://www.musawah.org/wanted-equality-and-justice-muslim-family-english. Again, Arabic and French translations are available. For *Home Truths: A Global Report on Equality in the Muslim Family*, which contains summaries of reports from thirty countries on the status of their family laws and practices, the challenges faced and the possibilities for reform, see http://www.musawah.org/home-truths-global-report-equality-muslim-family-english. An Arabic translation is also available.

In addition, print editions of several of the online reports listed above, all published by Musawah in Kuala Lumpur, may be consulted: *Home Truths: A Global Report on Equality in the Muslim Family*, 2009; *Framework for Action*, 2009; *Wanted: Equality and Justice in the Muslim Family*, edited by Anwar Zainah, 2009; *CEDAW and Muslim Family Laws: In Search of Common Ground*, 2011.

ZAINAH ANWAR

Music. Music has long been a vital part of life in the Muslim world. Despite the controversy and suspicion aroused by some forms of music, women have regularly used music as a livelihood, a form of self-expression, and a means of articulating local, regional, and national cultural values. Women's participation is particularly valuable to trace, as it illustrates both general trends and gender-specific practices of music-making.

Elite Music. Music flourished for centuries under elite patronage. Women musicians gained renown, sustained musical practices, and created stylistic fusions as Islam spread to Syria, Mesopotamia, Persia, North Africa, and Spain. Women were singers, instrumental performers, teachers, composers, and holders and transmitters of vast repertories of complex music and improvisational practices. In the courts of the Umayyads, ʿAbbāsids, Fāṭimids, and Mamlūks, women singers and members of all-female orchestras entertained leaders, guests, and other women. *Qiyān,* the singing slave girls who had been the primary musical entertainers in the pre-Islamic era, played crucial roles in performing and preserving music of Muslim courts through the nineteenth century.

Women's early contributions to elite music are particularly well documented in sources such as Abū al-Faraj al-Iṣfahānī's *Kitāb al-aghānī,* which was completed in the ninth century. Elite women such as Sukayna bint al-Ḥussayn were important early patrons of music. Of the many *qiyān,* one of the most famous was Sallāma al-Qass (d. after 740), who played the *ʿūd,* sang laments, and recited the Qurʾān. In the Umayyad era (638–750) freewomen musicians joined the *qiyān* and included ʿAzza al-Maylāʾ (d. before 710), who sang and played the lute and lyre, and Jamīla (d. c. 715), who established her own singing school. In the ʿAbbāsid era (750–1258) music flourished under the patronage of caliphs such as Hārūn al-Rashīd (d. 809). Important women musicians included the composer and singer ʿUlayya bint al-Mahdī (d. 825), who was the half-sister of Hārūn al-Rashīd and Ibrāhīm ibn al-Mahdī (d. 839), and ʿĀtika bint Shuhda, a singer, professional mourner, *ʿūd* player, and the teacher of Isḥāq al-Mawṣilī. While women thrived as musicians in this period, the association of music, wine, and licentious activities in court and public taverns prompted conservative Muslim writers to attack musical performance and female performers.

Despite such criticism, women musicians continued to serve elites for centuries to come, particularly in Andalusia and the Ottoman court. Providing performances in the harem and palace for the sultan and seraglio, women musicians of the Ottoman court sang and played many instruments. These included *çeng* (harp), *kemançe* (spike fiddle), *ney* (flute), *tanbur* (long-necked lute), *kanun* (zither), *santur* (hammered dulcimer), violin, and frame drum. One of the earliest documented women composers in this tradition was Dilhayat Hanım (1710–1780), whose surviving compositions include the *fasıl,* one of several elaborate multi-movement suites cultivated in Muslim courts.

Folk Music. Throughout the centuries, folk music has played an important role in ordinary Muslims' lives as part of daily and life cycle rituals. The Arabian Peninsula illustrates a typical mixture of folk music genres performed in both extended family and tribal celebrations. Elaborate musical productions are central to weddings, particularly on *laylat al-ḥinnah* and *laylat al-zaffah,* and are often performed for single-gender groups of guests. Other folk genres include work songs used in farming, pearl diving, and home settings. While both mixed gender and women's folk ensembles are used in most of the peninsula, in Saudi Arabia, only women perform for women. Moreover, because women's performances are not broadcast there, women are important patrons of women's music-making and livelihoods.

Typical folk ensembles on the peninsula include a lead singer, chorus, and a variety of percussion instruments. Their performances use the Arabic *maqām* system of melodic modes but also incorporate African and Indian influences.

Folk music is used for similar occasions throughout the Muslim world, with local and regional variations, and women participate along with men or on their own. For example, in Morocco, the Berbers of the Atlas Mountain regions celebrate the *aḥwash* festival and use it to instill community values. Depending on local traditions, women either sing and dance with men of their village or perform in a separate phase of the ritual. Villagers adopt a circular or two-line formation and dance while singing pentatonic melodies and playing complex rhythms on percussion instruments. These joyful gatherings of song, dance, and poetry contests teach community members of both genders and all ages key values, including modesty, patience, and self-control.

Religious Music. Islamic religious music includes songs praising the Prophet Muḥammad, laments performed in Shīʿī rituals, and a variety of music used in Ṣūfī practices. Sung praises range from the *inshād dīnī* of Egypt to the *sholawat* of Indonesia. The *sholawat* genre encompasses both praises of the Prophet and narratives about his life. Women and men sing these texts to preexisting melodies of Arab, Indonesian, and mixed stylistic origins. Indonesian women have also cultivated their own genre called *qasida rebana*, which adds frame drums to the praises. Performed in an entertaining, upbeat fashion, these genres are used to strengthen the faith of listeners and attract new believers.

Shīʿī women perform music in mourning rituals during important periods like the month of Muḥarram. In countries such as Pakistan, Iraq, and Lebanon, women gather in public and private *majālis*, sessions commemorating the martyrdom of Imam al-Ḥusayn and the important roles played by women in his family, including his sister Zaynab and his mother, Fāṭimah al-Zahrāʾ. Dressed in black, women and girls chant, sing laments, rhythmically beat their chests, and ask for blessings and help. Their poignant lyrics may be performed in the voice of Sakīnah, Imam al-Ḥusayn's young daughter. The music-filled gatherings often emphasize Sayyidah Zaynab and help articulate her as a courageous, outspoken role model while simultaneously offering contemporary Shīʿī women a vehicle for expressing political resistance in the face of oppressive governments.

Music has also been central to many Ṣūfī rituals (*zikr/dhikr*), and women have synthesized and preserved elements of multiple Ṣūfī orders through their own practices. Around the southwest Indian Ocean, the women of Mayotte perform *debā*, a *zikr* that draws on practices of the Rifāʿī and Qādirī orders and features the singing of mystical texts in Arabic with drums and bells. In rural Uzbekistan, female spiritual leaders preserved Ṣūfī traditions through the Soviet era. Now, they chant Ṣūfī poems—including their own writings and those of other female poets—for women on religious holidays and in life cycle rituals. Often rocking back and forth in a seated position, they perform an ecstatic *zikr* based largely on Yassavi practices. Ṣūfī shrines are also important public centers of women's participation in Muslim life. In Pakistan and India, for example, women sing devotional songs at shrines in daily rituals and on saints' anniversaries.

Islamic beliefs are also incorporated into a women's ritual that, like Ṣūfī practices, uses music and dance to achieve ecstatic states. The *zār* ritual is performed to placate a type of *jinn* (spirit) possessing some women and helps them deal with the challenges of infertility, co-wifery, and expectations to bear male children. This counterhegemonic ritual combines drumming, chanting, dancing, incense, and animal sacrifice and is performed in northern Sudan, Egypt, Ethiopia, Somalia, Arabia, and southern Iran. Urban *zār* troupes, including female musicians and leaders, may take part in large public Ṣūfī performances.

Popular Music. Although popular music has not been well-documented or preserved through the centuries, it has been a continuous part of Muslim culture. For example, in the Mamlūk era (1250–1517), popular singers were regulated and taxed by the state. Performance in public has often been considered shameful, and as a result, women of the lower classes have been often responsible for performing popular music. The writings of European travelers and residents such as Edward Lane (1801–1876) attest to the prevalence and skill of female singers in cafés, streets, and homes in the nineteenth century.

In the twentieth century, popular female musicians in the Middle East and North Africa have achieved new levels of fame and success. Popular singers such as the Egyptian Umm Kulthūm (1904–1975), the Lebanese Fairouz (b. 1935), and the Algerian Cheikha Remitti (1923–2006) gained national, regional, and international recognition reaching well beyond the Muslim world. Singing both secular and sacred songs, and drawing elements from elite, folk, and popular traditions, such superstars used music as a creative means of self-expression, a resource for gaining personal independence, and a tool for articulating class and national identity. Cheikha Remitti, for example, and the *rai* singers who followed in her path, transformed an Algerian folk music tradition into a powerful vehicle for expressing social and political commentary and for articulating the national, ethnic, and class identity of Algerians and Algerian immigrants facing discrimination in Europe. Subsequent generations of popular musicians cultivated greater Western influence, as seen in the video clips of early twenty-first-century pop stars such as Ruby. Still subject to criticism for their provocative images, and still fusing elements from a wide range of musical traditions, this generation of popular female musicians illustrates the durability of key themes throughout centuries of music-making in the Muslim world.

[*See also* Umm Kulthūm.]

BIBLIOGRAPHY

Aghaie, Kamran Scot, ed. *The Women of Karbala: Ritual Performance and Symbolic Discourses in Modern Shiʿi Islam*. Austin: University of Texas Press, 2005. Several chapters address music.

Boddy, Janice Patricia. *Wombs and Alien Spirits: Women, Men, and the Zār Cult in Northern Sudan*. Madison: University of Wisconsin Press, 1989.

Danielson, Virginia. *The Voice of Egypt: Umm Kulthūm, Arabic Song, and Egyptian Society in the Twentieth Century*. Chicago: University of Chicago Press, 1997. Particularly thorough in its documentation of Umm Kulthūm's career up to 1964.

al-Iṣfahānī, Abū al-Faraj. *Kitāb al-aghānī* (Book of Songs). 25 vols. Bayrut: Dār al-Thaqāfah, 1955–1964. Most important historical account of music from the pre-Islamic era to the end of the ninth century. Contains song lyrics and biographical accounts of musicians.

Nettl, Bruno, and Ruth M. Stone, eds. *Garland Encyclopedia of World Music*. 10 vols. New York: Garland Publishing, 1998. Also available online through library subscription [http://glnd.alexanderstreet.com/].

Rasmussen, Anne K. *Women, the Recited Qur'an, and Islamic Music in Indonesia*. Berkeley: University of California Press, 2010.

Sultanova, Razia. *From Shamanism to Sufism: Women, Islam, and Culture in Central Asia*. London: I. B. Tauris, 2011. Several chapters address music.

Laura Lohman

Muslim Council of Britain. The Muslim Council of Britain (MCB) was founded in 1997. Its specific aims, as stated on its website, have been to promote a united forum on Muslim matters in Britain by working with a range of Muslim and non-Muslim individuals, groups, and organizations in an effort to encourage an enlightened awareness of Islam and Muslims in Britain, determining fair and equitable outcomes for Muslims in society, helping to remove patterns of disadvantage and discrimination, and improving cultural and intellectual relations between Muslims and non-Muslims for the betterment of society as a whole. It operates as an umbrella body, currently with around four hundred members, consisting largely of mosques and Islamic centers, but also including a range of voluntary, community, charitable, civic, student, and professional organizations and associations. The MCB aims to reflect the diversity of ethnicity, culture, and religiosity of Muslim communities in Britain today, although there continues to be criticism of its effectiveness

The first secretary general was Iqbal Sacranie, who remained in the post for two consecutive terms, stepping down in 2006, when Dr. Muhammad Abdul Bari was elected. Dr. Bari served two terms as secretary general of the MCB and remains chair of the East London Mosque Trust. Iqbal Sacranie was knighted in the 2005 Queen's Birthday Honours List for his services to the community and interfaith dialogue. The current chair is Farooq Murad, elected in 2010.

Although it has strong working links with the British government, the MCB's relationship with it has been tenuous at times, specifically in the aftermath of the "war on terror." After the 9/11 attacks, the MCB was originally encouraged to show support for the government in the war in Afghanistan, and it did. However, soon afterwards, the MCB publicly dissociated itself from the government's position. This led to a public distancing between the government and the MCB. Similarly, after the terror attacks in Madrid and Amsterdam in 2004, the government called on the MCB to help in its efforts to de-radicalize young British Muslim men increasingly regarded as a threat to British society. The leafleting of all the known mosques and Islamic centers in Britain was met with scepticism by many British Muslims, who regarded the actions of the MCB as "selling out." Furthermore, many public opinion surveys and much social commentary have argued that the MCB does not reflect the ethnicity or social standing of the majority of British Muslims, that it is not always focused upon domestic economic, political, and social concerns, and that it possesses strong politico-ideological influences, namely Jamāʿat-i Islāmī and Muslim Brotherhood leanings. The BBC's *Panorama* programme, presented by John Ware ("A Question of Leadership"), was broadcast on Sunday, August 21, 2005, one month after the July 7 bombings in the London transport system, now as "7/7." Although recorded before 7/7, the program explicitly set out to paint the senior hierarchy of the MCB as radically Islamist.

After 7/7, the government again sought to dissociate itself from the MCB and promote a "new" Muslim leadership in Britain, namely the British Muslim Forum and Sufi Council of Britain. Today, the MCB remains an organization that consists of volunteer officers, with an improved profile since the heady few years after the events of 7/7. The umbrella model of the MCB has now been replicated in other countries, notably France, Indonesia, and Australia.

The role of Muslim women in relation to the MCB has remained flimsy at best. There are few, if any, who work inside the organization, although it needs to be emphasized that all workers are volunteers, and this affects the role of women in more significant terms, given their domestic roles in addition to their professional roles. To date, the MCB has not made any significant advances on matters pertaining to Muslim women, in spite of wider social concerns that affect this group in British society. The MCB remains a male-dominated and thus arguably patriarchal organization that continues to try to improve the services it offers; however, there remain important disparities in relation to women.

Bibliography

Klausen, Jytte. *The Islamic Challenge: Politics and Religion in Western Europe*. New York: Oxford University Press, 2005.

McLoughlin, Sean. "The State, New Muslim Leaderships and Islam as a Resource for Public Engagement in Britain." In *European Muslims and the Secular State*, edited by Jocelyne Cesari and Seán McLoughlin, pp. 55–70. Aldershot, U.K.: Ashgate, 2005.

Tahir Abbas

Muslim Women's League. The Muslim Women's League (MWL) is a non-profit Muslim women's organization based in Los Angeles. The primary mission of the MWL is to set the agenda and develop a more positive discourse about Islam and Muslim women in North America. The organization aims to "reclaim the status of women as free, equal, and vital contributors to society" (Muslim Women's League). The mission statement of the organization reads "[T]he widespread lack of education about Islam and women's rights in Islam has led to many misconceptions about Muslims in the American society. In order to dispel these stereotypes, the MWL works to educate both Muslims and non-Muslims about Islam and women in Islam by participating in conferences, providing lectures, publications, media interviews, and ongoing classes on Quran" (Muslim Women's League). The organization's website, which contains articles on topics such as gender equality, violence against women, family law, sexuality, and reproductive health, serves as an invaluable resource for those seeking knowledge on Islam and Muslim women.

The Muslim Women's League was founded in 1992 in response to the atrocities committed against women in Bosnia-Herzegovina. As the Bosnian war was going on, women's organizations around the world organized to vocalize their concerns and to take action against the war and its negative impact on women in Bosnia. There was no Muslim women's group to coalesce around, and the MWL invented itself in that environment to be the platform for Muslim women to take action against the war. The organization first named itself the Muslim Women's Coalition Against Ethnic Cleansing. They sent two delegations to Bosnia to raise awareness about the war and women's problems and to raise money to send to women's groups in Bosnia. In 1995 Dr. Laila al-Marayati, the co-founder of the MWL, was asked to join the US delegation to the UN conference on Women in Beijing. This event was important for the organization as they had to officially develop an identity and present themselves as the certain voice of Muslim women.

The MWL has also been active in Palestine and Afghanistan, fund-raising, co-sponsoring, and participating in projects to empower the women and girls there through education. At the local level the organization received a grant to address reproductive health needs of Muslim women in southern California. They designed a health survey documenting the needs and attitudes of Muslim women toward reproductive health, and they are currently working on developing a sexual-education curriculum to be used in Muslim schools, grades five to eight. As part of this initiative, the MWL provides funds for free gynecological services to needy Muslim women at the UMMA Clinic in Los Angeles. The organization was also the first to host a seminar on domestic violence and Muslim women. In the past the MLW also sponsored summer sports camps for girls, held a luncheon to honor women in the media, organized a panel for Muslim lawyers and Islamic law scholars to speak about Muslim and American family law, and organized a symposium for journalists and politicians called Islam: Beyond the Stereotypes.

Despite its commitment to improving the status of Muslim women in the United States and around the world, ideological differences between traditional Muslim women, who view the MWL as being too radical or progressive, and the MWL create significant hurdles for the organization in reaching out to a wider audience and receiving more funding from the community. The cofounder of the organization, Laila Al-Marayati, attributes the lack of a strong national feminist Muslim women's organization and a social movement in North America to Muslim women's lack of commitment to progressive issues such as gender consciousness and equality.

The major challenge for the MWL—and Muslim women's organizations in the United States in general—is that only a few women actively participate in them. Outside of this small circle of activist volunteers, it is hard to promote interest among Muslim women toward these organizations and women's rights issues. Limitations in resources and funding, lack of human capital at their disposal, and ideological differences between them and their clients prevent Muslim women's organizations such as the MWL from achieving their goals, reaching out to more women, and taking on new and important projects.

BIBLIOGRAPHY

Al-Marayati, Laila. Interview with the author, 2008.

Ozyurt, Saba. "Ecological and Organizational Determinants of NGO Performance: A Comparative Analysis of Muslim Women's Organizations in the United States and the Netherlands." *Voluntas: International Journal of Voluntary and Nonprofit Organizations* (under review).

Rehman, Aamir. "The Human Capital Deficit in the Islamic Nonprofit Sector." Report Published by the *Institute for Social Policy and Understanding*, 2004. http://ispu.org/files/PDFs/human%20capital%20deficit.pdf/.

"The Muslim Women's League, Center Profile." The Pluralism Project, Harvard University. http://pluralism.org/profiles/view/74042/.

The Muslim Women's League. http://www.mwlusa.org/.

SABA SENSES OZYURT

MUTʿAH. A pre-Islamic tradition in both Iran and the Arabian Peninsula, *mutʿah* (temporary marriage) still has legal sanction among the Twelver Shīʿī, who reside predominantly in Iran. It is often a private and verbal contract between a man and an unmarried Muslim, Christian, Jewish, or Zoroastrian woman (virgin, divorced, or widowed). The length of the marriage contract (*ajal*) and the amount of consideration (*ajr*) given to the temporary wife must be specified; temporary marriage may be contracted for anywhere from one hour to ninety-nine years. A temporary marriage need not be registered or witnessed, although taking witnesses is recommended. In addition to the four wives legally allowed all Muslim men, a Shīʿī Muslim man is permitted to contract simultaneously as many temporary marriages as he desires, a practice disputed by Ayatollahs Ruhollah Khomeini and Murtaḍā (Murtazā) Muṭahharī. A Shīʿī Muslim woman is permitted only one temporary marriage at a time. The reciprocal obligations of temporary spouses are minimal. The man is not obliged to provide the daily maintenance (*nafaqah*) for his temporary wife, as he must in a permanent marriage. Correspondingly, the wife (*sīghah*) is under minimal legal obligation to obey her husband, except in sexual matters.

The man, but not the woman, has the right to end the contract at any time. If the *sīghah* would do so, she forfeits right to payment and owes the husband compensation. No divorce procedure exists in a temporary marriage, for the lapse of time specified in the contract automatically dissolves the temporary union. After the dissolution of each temporary union, no matter how short, the wife must undergo a period of sexual abstinence (*ʿiddah*); in case of pregnancy, *ʿiddah* serves to identify a child's legitimate father. Herein lies the legal uniqueness of temporary marriage, distinguishing it, in Shīʿī law, from prostitution, despite their striking resemblance. The objective of *mutʿah* is sexual enjoyment (*istimtāʿ*); that of permanent marriage (*nikāḥ*) is procreation (*tawlīd-i nasl*).

Mutʿah of women was banned in the seventh century by the second caliph, ʿUmar, who equated it with fornication (*zinah*). For Sunnī Muslims, therefore, temporary marriage is legally forbidden, although in practice some have resorted to it occasionally or have developed similar practical arrangements. The legitimacy of temporary marriage has continued to be a point of disagreement, passionate dispute, and, at times, animosity between Sunnī and Shīʿī (for a contemporary exposition of this ongoing dispute, see Kāshif al-Ghiṭāʿ, 1964; Shāfaʿī, 1973: Murata, trans., 1987, pp. 51–73; Ende 1980, 1990).

Mostly women of the lower class, often prostitutes, were available for a temporary marriage; they were mostly found at pilgrimage sites and trade centers to serve the needs of lonely male pilgrims and travelers. Respectable families would not give their daughters in temporary marriage, which, at least as of the sixteenth century, also occurred among Christians and Jews in Iran, often with expatriate Europeans. During the Pahlavi regime (1925–1979) the custom of temporary marriage, though not illegal, was perceived negatively and was something that was mainly associated with sites of pilgrimage (Mashhad, Qom, Karbala). Not only lonely men, but also unmarried women (widows, divorcees [*yaʿisah*]) sought/seek temporary marriage as a means to obtain sexual satisfaction.

There is also the option of a nonsexual relationship with a woman, known as *sīghah mahramīyat*, an arrangement made to allow women to be in an environment where they would come in regular and daily contact with one or more nonrelated men (e.g., a maid working in a house, women regularly receiving elegy recitation at home from a clergyman, women accompanied on pilgrimage. *Mutʿah* is at present a marginal urban phenomenon, popular primarily around pilgrimage centers in Iran. The Islamic regime (since 1979) has made a concerted effort to improve the social status of temporary marriage, but without much success. Its positive aspects were stressed (divine roots; moral and public health benefits; and at the time of war, social responsibility), in particular during the 1980s with the growing number of war widows owing to the high number of men killed. It was and is touted as the Islamic and morally superior answer to satisfying men's sexual needs in a socially responsible and healthy manner and thus preventing fornication. Despite the religious and legal rehabilitation of *mutʿah*, most urban, educated middle-class Iranians view it with some moral and emotional ambivalence. *Mutʿah* has never won the unequivocal approval accorded permanent marriage by the Iranians.

[*See also* Divorce, *subentry on* Modern Practice; Inheritance; Iran; Marriage; Women and Social Reform, *subentry on* Middle East.]

BIBLIOGRAPHY

Bāhunar, Muḥammad Jaʿfar, et al. *Taʿlīmāt-i dīnī* (Religious Education). Tehran, Iran 1981. A high school textbook, published after the revolution, in which the benefits of temporary marriage for youth was first discussed.

Benson, Linda. "Islamic Marriage and Divorce in Xinjiang: The Case of Kashgar and Khotan." *Association for the Advancement of Central Asian Research* 5, no. 2 (Fall 1992): 5–8. On the legitimacy of temporary marriage among Chinese Sunnīs.

Ende, Werner. "Ehe auf Zeit (*mutʿah*) in der innerislamischen Diskussion der Gegenwart." *Die Welt des Islams* 20 (1980): 1–43. On the Sunnī–Shīʿī debate the lawfulness of *mutʿah* and how Sunnīs have developed similar institutions.

Ende, Werner. "Sunnī Polemical Writings on the Shīʿī and the Iranian Revolution." In *The Iranian Revolution and the Muslim World*, edited by David Menashri, pp. 219–232. Boulder, Colo.: Westview Press, 1990. Analysis of the Sunnī views on Shīʿiism and the Iranian Revolution.

Gurjī, Abū al-Qāsim. *Temporary Marriage (Mutʿah) in Islamic Law*. Translated by Sachiko Murata, Qom, Iran: Ansariyan Publications, 1986. Summary of the major Shīʿī sources of jurisprudence on *mutʿah*.

Floor, Willem. *A Social History of Sexual Relations in Iran*. Washington, D.C.: Mage, 2008.

Haeri, Shahla. *Law of Desire: Temporary Marriage in Shīʿī Iran*. Syracuse, N.Y.: Syracuse University Press, 1989. First major ethnography on the institution of temporary marriage.

Ḥillī, Najm al-Dīn Abū al-Qāsim Jaʿfar. *Sahray ʿal-Islām* (Islamic Law). Vol. 2. Translated from Arabic into Persian by A. Aḥmad Yazdī and M. T. Dānishpazhūh. Tehran, Iran, 1968. Excellent compendium on Shīʿī marriage and divorce by the thirteenth-century Shīʿī scholar.

Kāshif al-Ghiṭāʿ, Muḥammad Ḥuṣayn. *Āʿīn-i mā* (Our Custom). Translated from Arabic into Persian by Nāṣir Makārim Shīrāzī. Qom, Iran, 1968. Contains a major chapter on temporary marriage, refuting some of the Sunnī allegations.

Khomeini, Ruhollah. "Non-Permanent Marriage." *Mahjuba* 2, no. 5 (1982): 38–40. English translation of his position on temporary marriage.

Khomeini, Ruhollah. *The Practical Laws of Islam*. 2d ed. N.p., 1985. Abridged version of his *Tawẓīḥ al-masāʿil* (Clarification of questions).

Muṭahharī. Murtaẓā. *Niẓām-i ḥuqūq-i zan dar Islām* (Legal Rights of Women in Islam). 8th ed. (Qom, Iran, 1974). Comprehensive treatment of the rights of women in (Shīʿī) Islam.

Shāfaʿī, Muḥsin. *Mutʿah va aṣar-i ḥuqūqī va ijtimāʿī-i an* (*Mutʿah* and Its Legal and Social Effects). 6th ed. Tehran, Iran, 1973. Extensive, if apologetic, treatment of *mutʿah*.

Ṭabāṭabāʿī, Muḥammad Ḥusayn. *Shiʿite Islam*. Translated by Seyyed Hossein Nasr (Albany, N.Y.: State University of New York Press, 1977). Major contribution to understanding Shīʿī theology and philosophy.

Ṭabāṭabāʿī, Muḥammad Ḥuṣayn, et al., eds. *Izdivāj-i muvaqqat dar islām* (Temporary Marriage in Islam). Qom, Iran, 1985.

Ṭūsī, Abū Jaʿfar Muḥammad. *Al-nihāyah*. Translated from the Arabic into Persian by M. T. Dānishpazhūh. Tehran, 1964. One of the four major sources of Shīʿī jurisprudence, compiled in the tenth century.

SHAHLA HAERI *and* WILLEM FLOOR